Microsoft® Access 2013: Essentials

Microsoft® Access 2013: Essentials

FLOYD JAY WINTERS & JULIE T. MANCHESTER
State College of Florida

Berkeley, CA

Microsoft Access 2013: Essentials

LABYRINTH
LEARNING™

Labyrinth Learning
2560 9th Street, Suite 320
Berkeley, California 94710
800.522.9746
On the web at lablearning.com

President:
Brian Favro

Product Development Manager:
Jason Favro

Managing Editor:
Laura Popelka

Production Editor:
Margaret Young

Production Manager:
Rad Proctor

eLearning Production Manager:
Arl S. Nadel

eLearning Development:
Judy Mardar and Andrew Vaughnley

Developmental Editors:
Trisha Conlon and Sandra Rittman

Indexing:
Joanne Sprott

Cover Design:
Mick Koller, SuperLab Design

Interior Design:
Mark Ong, Side-by-Side Studio

ITEM: 1-59136-485-X
ISBN-13: 978-1-59136-485-6

Manufactured in the United States of America.

GLOBUS 10 9 8 7 6 5 4 3 2 1

Contents in Brief

Table of Contents

ACCESS 2013 LESSON 4: QUERYING A DATABASE

ACCESS 2013 LESSON 5: USING REPORTS TO DISPLAY INFORMATION

ACCESS 2013 LESSON 6: REFINING TABLE DESIGN

ACCESS 2013 LESSON 7: CUSTOMIZING INPUT FORMS

ACCESS 2013 LESSON 8: CREATING COMPLEX QUERIES

ACCESS 2013 LESSON 9: CUSTOMIZING REPORTS

ACCESS 2013 LESSON 10: CUSTOMIZING THE DATABASE INTERFACE AND STARTUP OPTIONS

ACCESS 2013 LESSON 11: IMPORTING AND EXPORTING DATA USING WORD, EXCEL, AND HTML

ACCESS 2013 LESSON 12: MAINTAINING A DATABASE

Quick Reference Tables

GENERAL TASKS

CUSTOMIZATION TASKS

FORM TASKS

INTEGRATION TASKS

QUERY TASKS

REPORT TASKS

TABLE TASKS

Preface

In today's digital world, knowing how to use the most popular suite of desktop software applications is critical. Our goal is to teach new users how to take advantage of this technology and to help experienced users understand how the applications have changed from previous versions. We begin with fundamental concepts and take learners through a systematic progression of exercises, resulting in skill mastery.

An online student resource center accompanies this book. It contains Concepts Review quizzes, student exercise files, and other learning tools. The URL for the student resource center is printed on the inside front cover of this textbook.

Supplemental Options

Video Tutorials: Our easy-to-follow instructional design is complemented with hundreds of videos that demonstrate the concepts and skills covered in this textbook. All videos can be accessed online with a single license key. Videos are an option for all learners. Keys can be purchased at http://lablearning.com/Store/Shop-Videos.

eLab Course Management System: eLab is a web-based learning systems that integrates seamlessly with this textbook. eLab is an option for students enrolled in instructor-led courses that have adopted eLab as part of their course curriculum.

Visual Conventions

This book uses visual and typographic cues to guide students through the lessons. Some of these cues are described below.

`Type this text`	Text you type at the keyboard is printed in this typeface.
Action words	The important action words in exercise steps are presented in boldface.
Ribbon	Glossary terms are presented in black text with a blue background.
TIP	Tips, notes, and warnings are called out with special icons.
Command→Command→Command→Command	Commands to execute from the Ribbon are presented like this: Ribbon Tab→Command Group→Command→Subcommand.
FROM THE KEYBOARD Ctrl+S to save	These margin notes present shortcut keys for executing certain tasks.
FROM THE RIBBON File→Save	These margin notes show Ribbon paths for executing certain tasks.

It is recommended that students set their screen resolutions to 1024 x 768. This will help ensure that their screens most closely match the printed illustrations. Multiple factors, including screen resolution, DPI setting, monitor size, and window size, can affect the appearance of the Microsoft Ribbon. In this book, screen captures were taken with a screen resolution of 1024 x 768.

Acknowledgements

This textbook has benefited greatly from the reviews and suggestions of the following instructors.

Ann Blackman, *Parkland College*

Robert Caruso, *Santa Rosa Junior College*

Lori Collins, *Pike-Lincoln Technical Center*

Evangelina Gallegos-Garner, *South Texas Vocational Technical Institute*

Teresita Galvizo, *South East High School*

Margaret Gordon, *Manchester Community College*

Terri Holly, *Indian River State College*

Ray Janosko, *Community College of Allegheny County*

Joan Johnson, *Lake Sumter Community College*

Elaine Loughrey, *MiraCosta College*

John Mims, *Central New Mexico Community College Workforce Training Center*

Kay Nelson, *The Lifelong Learning Center, Missoula County Public Schools*

Mary Jo Slater, *Community College of Beaver County*

Microsoft® Access 2013: Essentials

Exploring Access 2013

LESSON OUTLINE

LEARNING OBJECTIVES

After studying this lesson, you will be able to:

- Start Access and identify elements of the application window
- Open and explore an existing database
- Identify database objects and explain how they are used
- Add data to an Access table
- Close a database and exit Access 2013

Have you ever wondered how sportscasters come up with fun and interesting facts about teams and players in a flash? Have you been taken by surprise when a customer service agent suddenly begins to recite your name, address, and a detailed purchase history? In most cases, these people have access to a powerful database from which they obtain the information.

In this lesson, you will explore the main elements of the Microsoft Access 2013 application window and its graphical user interface. You will discover how and when databases are used, learn about different kinds of databases, and explore database management software.

CASE STUDY

Updating Raritan Clinic East

Raritan Clinic East is an incorporated medical practice staffed by the finest clinical diagnosticians in the pediatric fields of neonatal care, general medicine, and emergency care. The practice serves a patient community ranging in ages from newborn to 18 years. Recently, the clinic moved to a brand new 21,000-square-foot state-of-the-art facility located in the center of a vast medical professional complex.

You work in the human resources department at the clinic and have been asked to review the records management system and develop a new database that will allow users to locate, retrieve, analyze, and report information more efficiently. You must determine how best to organize the data into a new database created with Access 2013.

In the old database file, the Employee Name field includes first name, last name, and specialty/position.

Employees

Employee Name	Address	Date Hired	Telephone
Judith Storm, Neonatal	234 McIntosh Dr., Sarasota, FL 34032	4/14/2010	(941)555-1235
John Ottome, GeneralMed	49 Osprey Ave., Sarasota, FL 34034	8/30/2010	(941) 555-8547
David Nealle, Emergency	100 Bee Ridge Rd., Sarasota, FL 34032	9/1/2010	(941)555-4327
Ruthann Good, GeneralMed	55 Lutz St., Tampa, FL 33172	9/11/2010	(941)555-4865
Mikayla Mansee-Emergency	19 Fruitville Rd., Sarasota FL 34201	9/14/2011	(941)555-9931
Anthony Adams, RN	53 Wildwood Terr., Bradenton, FL 34210	7/10/2011	(941)555-3648
Beverly Gauthier, RN	2552 Lime Ave., Sarasota, FL 34032	8/29/2010	(941)555-8162

Including several pieces of data in one field makes it difficult to find the right information quickly.

In the new database file, doctors' data is stored in one table and nurses' data is stored in another table.

The new database stores each category in a separate field.

Raritan Clinic East Doctors

DocID	Last Name	First Name	Street Address	City	ST	Zip	Telephone	Date Hired	Specialty
114	Storm	Judith	234 McIntosh Dr.	Sarasota	FL	34032	(941) 555-2309	4/14/2012	Neonatal
130	Ottome	John	49 Osprey Ave.	Sarasota	FL	34034	(941) 555-1304	8/30/2010	General Med
142	Nealle	David	100 Bee Ridge Rd.	Sarasota	FL	34032	(941) 555-1230	9/1/2010	Emergency
155	Good	Ruthann	55 Lutz St.	Tampa	FL	33172	(941) 555-2091	9/11/2010	General Med
20[illegible]	Lawrence	Robert	32 Magellan Dr.	Sarasota	FL	34033	(941) 555-5926	2/9/2011	General Med

Raritan Clinic East Nurses

Nurse ID	Last Name	First Name	Street Address	City	ST	Zip	Telephone	Date Hired	Position
108162	Gauthier	Beverly	2552 Lime Ave.	Sarasota	FL	34032	(941)555-8162	8/9/2010	RN
111098	Kennerly	John	333 Tuttle	Sarasota	FL	34022	(941)555-1098	2/13/2011	LPN
111763	Ramirez	Maria	680 Main St.	Sarasota	FL	34032	(941)555-1763	1/15/2011	LPN
112963	Kristoff	Michael	1001 Pineapple St.	Sarasota	FL	34042	(941)555-2963	10/8/2011	RN
113648	Adams	Anthony	53 Wildwood Terr.	Bradenton	FL	34210	(941)555-3648	3/20/2011	RN

Defining Access Databases

Video Library http://labyrinthelab.com/videos Video Number: AC13-V0101

If you have ever pulled a file from a file cabinet; used your phone to store friends' names, phone numbers, and addresses; or purchased an item from an online retailer, you have used a database. For most of recorded history, databases were paper based. Today, databases are often stored electronically, allowing users to retrieve detailed information with amazing speed and accuracy. However, in each case, these filing systems consist of individual pieces of related data that, when combined, make up a database.

What Is a Database?

A database is an organized collection of related data files or tables. For example, a medical clinic might have a filing system that includes doctors' files, nurses' files, and files containing the records for nurses aides. These files are related to the same business and may be linked to each other, and when taken together compose a database. Data are pieces of information such as names, numbers, dates, descriptions, and other information organized for reference or analysis. The data stored in the Raritan Clinic East database might be the names, addresses, salaries, and hire dates of the medical clinic employees.

Purpose of Databases

Databases are used for many reasons. Doctors use them to track patient visits, maladies, and medications. Teachers use them to track students' grades and attendance. Business owners use them to keep a record of inventory and sales, while analyzing expenses, calculating profits, and printing reports. And you may have a database on your cell phone or iPad to organize the music, photo, and video files that you own.

Database Management Software

Database management software allows users to store, manipulate, and retrieve database information. Command-line driven database management can be performed by Structured Query Language (SQL), which is a database management programming language used by MySQL, the most popular Open Source database management system. Other successful data management software systems include DB2, which is IBM's relational database management system, and Oracle, which supports some of the largest business enterprises in the world.

```
mysql> insert into employees (EmpID, Name, Hours, Rate) values (101, "Allen", 40, 10);
Query OK, 1 row affected (0.04 sec)

mysql> select * from employees;
+-------+-------+-------+------+
| EmpID | Name  | Hours | Rate |
+-------+-------+-------+------+
|   101 | Allen |    40 |   10 |
+-------+-------+-------+------+
1 row in set (0.00 sec)
```

The process of inserting a single record into a MySQL file using command line can be challenging.

Access 2013

Microsoft Access 2013 and FileMaker Pro are examples of graphical user interface (GUI) database applications used by small- to medium-sized businesses. The graphical interface provides convenient tools and actions that are available by clicking icons (images, representing commands), text boxes, checkboxes, and many other items, combined with easy-to-use menus. Microsoft Access is far more user friendly than the more challenging command-line code.

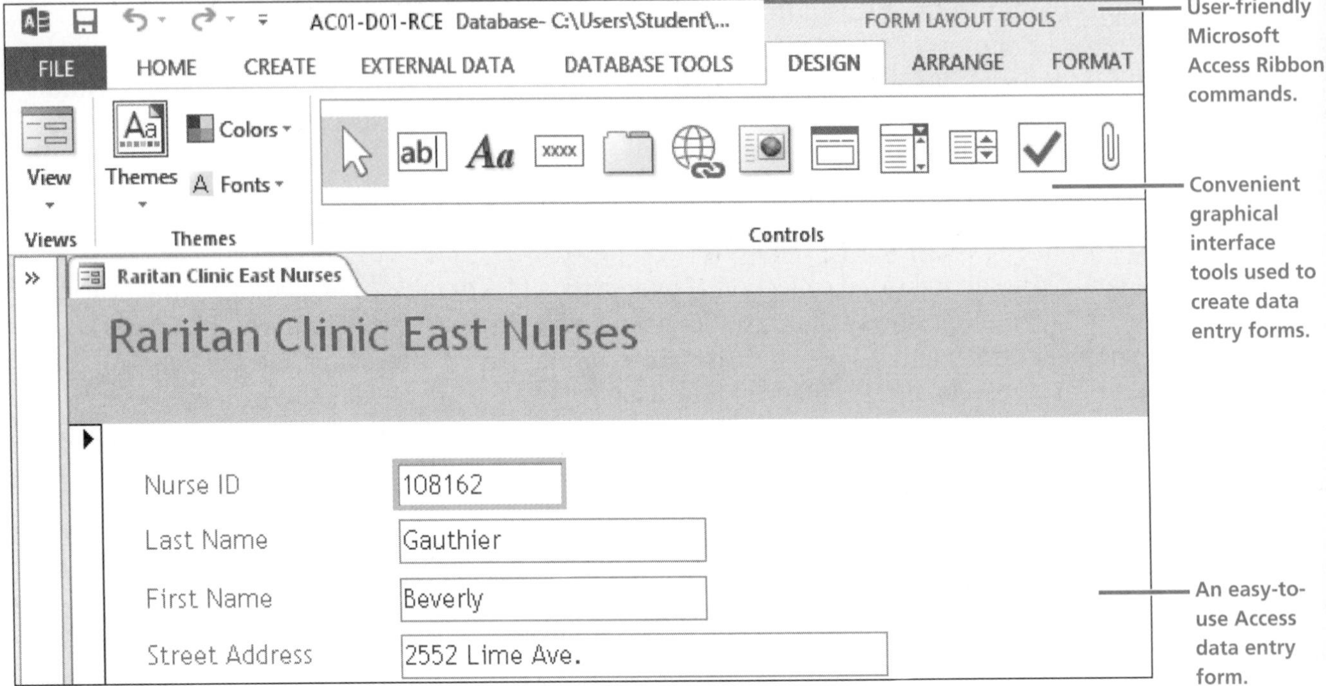

Exploring the Access Environment

Video Library http://labyrinthelab.com/videos Video Number: AC13-V0102

Each time you start Access 2013, it opens in *Backstage view*, which offers a variety of file options. From this view, you can open an existing file, create a new blank database, or select from a number of predesigned templates for various business and personal applications.

Starting Access

The process for starting Access 2013 is the same process used for starting other Microsoft Office applications. After you start Access, you are prompted to take action to create or open a database. Depending on the version of Windows installed on your computer, and whether Access has been used on the computer before, the starting procedures may vary.

DEVELOP YOUR SKILLS AC01-D01

Start Access 2013

In this exercise, you will launch Access 2013 from the Start screen (Windows 8) or Start menu (Windows 7).

Before You Begin: Navigate to the student resource center to download the student exercise files for this book.

Follow the step(s) for your version of Windows.

Windows 7

1. Follow these steps to start Access 2013:

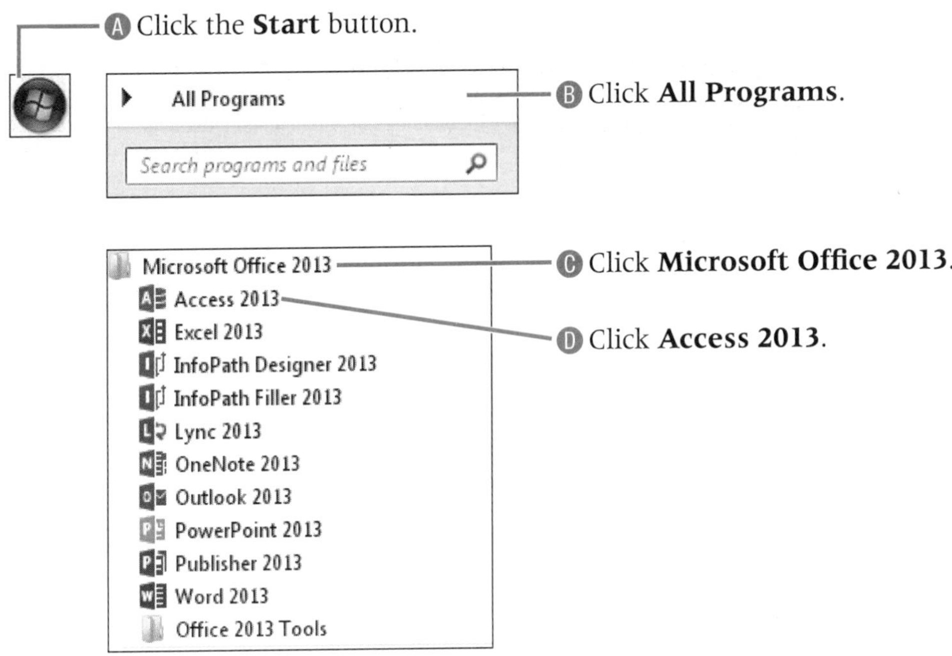

After you launch Access for the first time, the program may appear on the Start menu. You can launch Access directly from the Start menu or from the All Programs list.

Continue with step 2 below.

Windows 8

1. Locate and click the **Access 2013** tile.

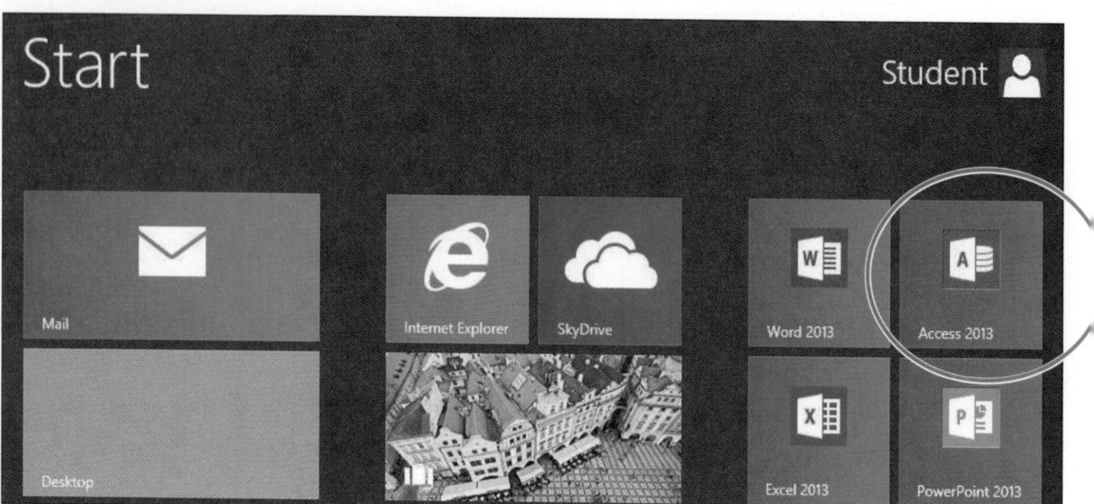

2. Leave **Access** open for the next exercise.
   Unless directed otherwise, keep Access and any databases being used open.

Opening an Existing Database

Video Library http://labyrinthelab.com/videos Video Number: AC13-V0103

There are several methods available to open an existing database. If you want to open a file you recently worked on, it will be shown in the Recent area in Backstage view. You can also click the Open Other Files link, which takes you to the Access Open window. From the Open window, you can retrieve a recent database file stored on your computer or on a network. You can also retrieve a database stored on Microsoft's SkyDrive, a cloud-based file hosting service that offers at least seven gigabytes of free storage over the Internet.

DEVELOP YOUR SKILLS AC01-D02

Open a Database and Save It with a New Name

In this exercise, you will open a database and save it to your file storage location with a different name. Access should be open in Backstage view.

1. Click **Open Other Files** to search for database files.

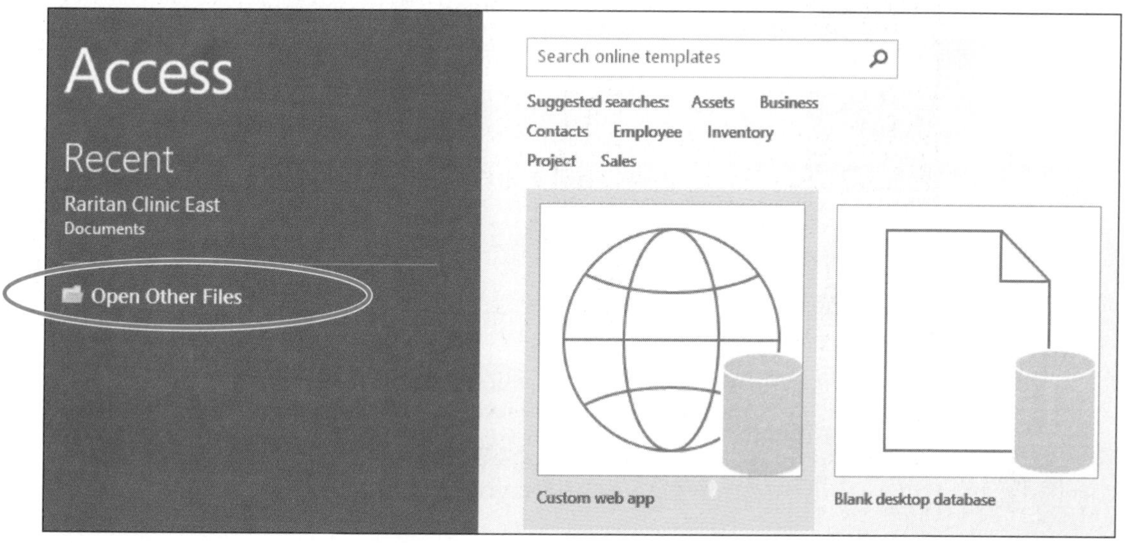

2. Follow these steps to open the Raritan Clinic East database file:

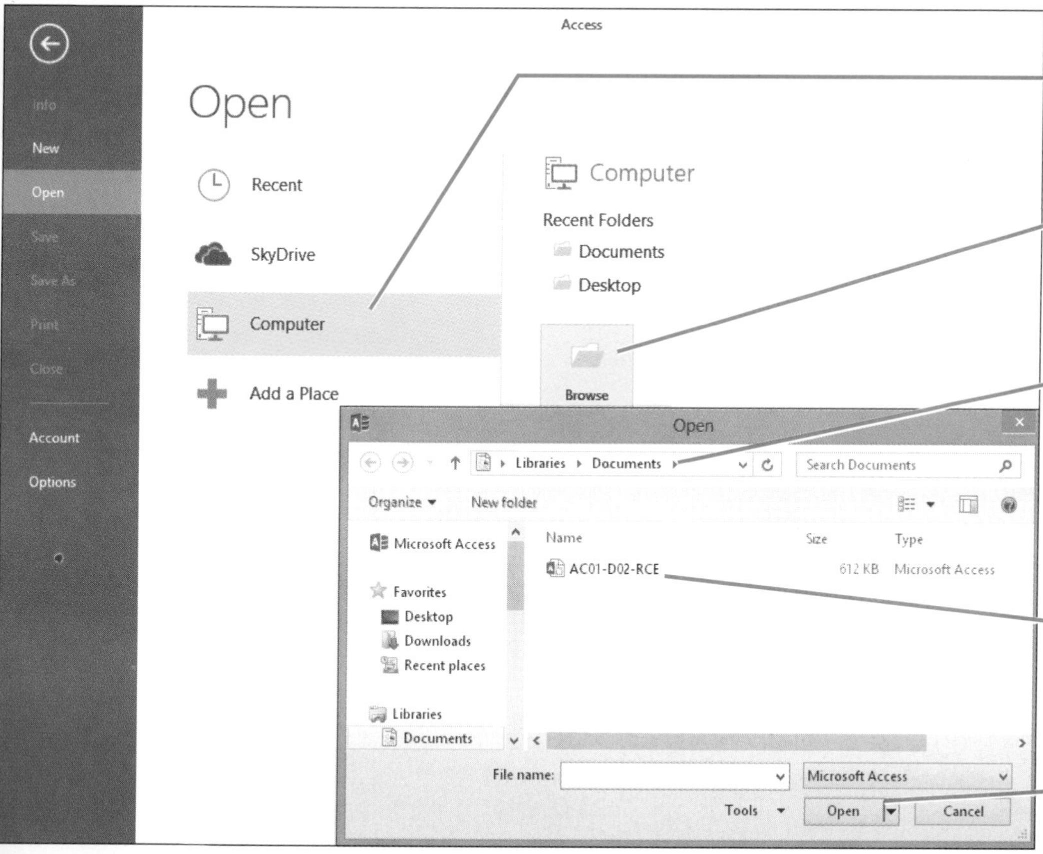

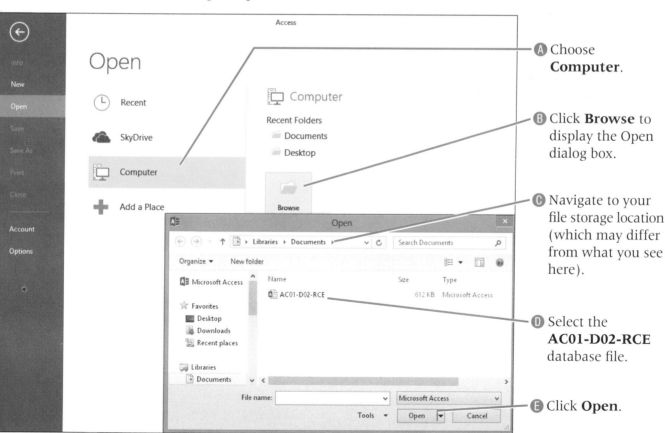

Ⓐ Choose **Computer**.

Ⓑ Click **Browse** to display the Open dialog box.

Ⓒ Navigate to your file storage location (which may differ from what you see here).

Ⓓ Select the **AC01-D02-RCE** database file.

Ⓔ Click **Open**.

Access opens the Raritan Clinic East database.

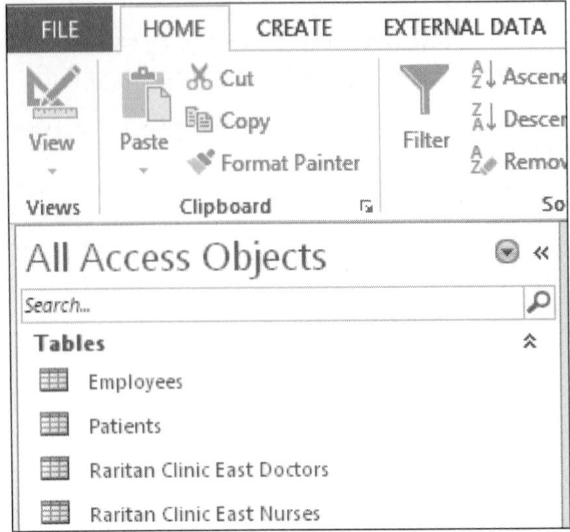

3. If a Security Warning bar displays, click **Enable Content**.
4. Click the **File** tab.
5. Follow these steps to rename and save the database:

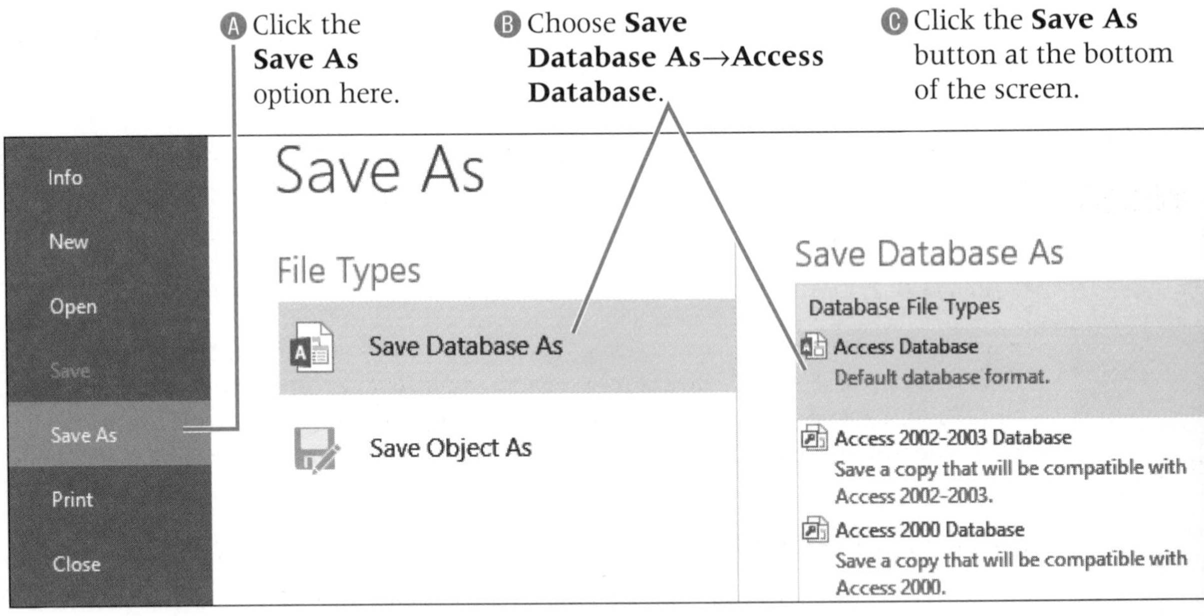

Access opens the Save As dialog box.

6. Navigate to your file storage location, type **AC01-D02-RCE-[FirstInitialLastName]** in the File Name box, and click **Save**.

   Replace the bracketed text with your first initial and last name. For example, if your name is Bethany Smith, your filename would look like this: AC01-D02-RCE-BSmith.

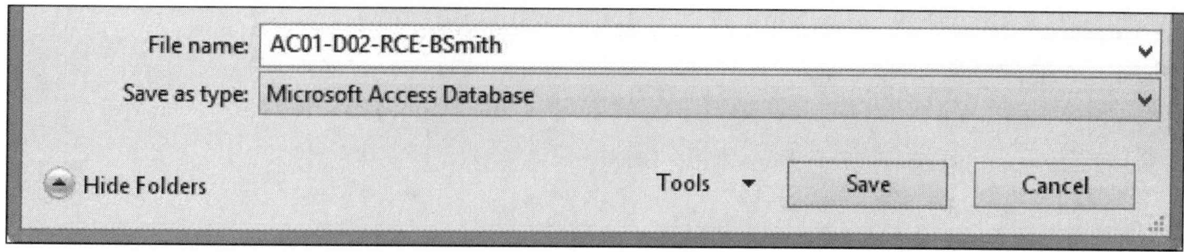

7. If a Security Warning bar displays, click **Enable Content**.

Identifying Features of the Database Window

Video Library http://labyrinthelab.com/videos Video Number: AC13-V0104

Now that you have opened the database file, explore the layout of the Database window. Compare the visual elements and features to those you have seen in other Microsoft Office applications. Access 2013 provides a Ribbon at the top of the window that contains tabs for groups of commands and toolbars, a Navigation Pane on the left side of the window that lists the objects in the database, and a Work Area for modifying database objects.

If you don't see the Ribbon, it might be unpinned. Just choose Home→Pin the Ribbon at the right end of the Ribbon. Or, press Ctrl+F1 to toggle the Ribbon.

Access 2013

The Work Area

The Work Area, or largest part of the screen, is where you work with your main database objects. This is where you design tables, queries, forms, and reports, and where you enter actual data into your tables and forms. If you have multiple objects open at once, Access places a tab for each at the top of the Work Area. You can switch between objects by clicking on the tabs.

The Navigation Pane

The Navigation Pane, or Objects Panel, lists existing database objects, specifically, tables, queries, forms and reports.

If you do not see the Navigation Pane, click the Shutter Bar Open/Close Button or press F11 to toggle the pane.

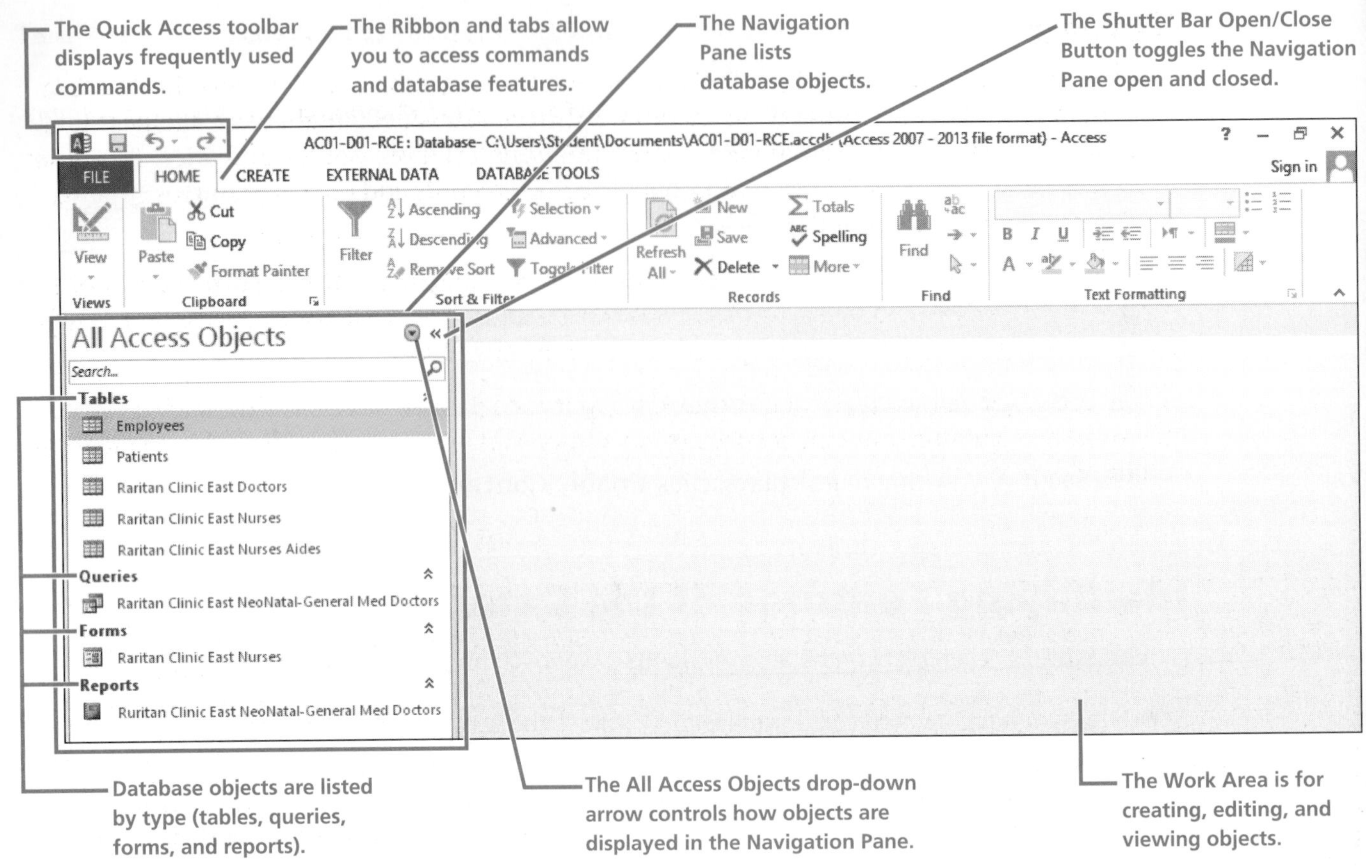

Introducing Access Objects

Video Library http://labyrinthelab.com/videos Video Number: AC13-V0105

A database object is a structure used to either store or reference data, such as a table, query, form or report.

ACCESS DATABASE OBJECT TYPES

Object	Description
Table	A file or collection of related records. Tables contain the data used in all other database objects. A table allows you to view many or all of the records in a file at the same time.
Form	A database screen used to enter, edit, or view the data for an individual record in a layout that is more convenient and attractive than a table layout. Because a form primarily displays only one record at a time it is a safer way to enter data.
Query	A database object or module used to request, search, select, and sort data contained in tables based on specific criteria and conditions.
Report	A database page that presents processed and summarized data from tables and queries as meaningful information in a format that is easy to read and designed to be printed.

Tables

A table contains the database data. Tables allow you to enter, edit, delete, or view the data in a row and column layout, similar to an Excel spreadsheet. A business might use a database table to list inventory items, such as an item's part number, description, vendor, and price. Two other examples of tables are the Raritan Clinic list of doctors' records and the list of nurses' records. A table stores multiple related records.

A record is a collection of details about an individual person, place or thing, such as a doctor's record or a nurse's record in the Raritan Clinic East database. In a Microsoft Access table, each record is displayed in a row. A record is made up of multiple fields.

A field is a single named piece of information about each person, place or thing, such as a doctor's ID, telephone number, or specialty. In a Microsoft Access table each field is displayed in a column.

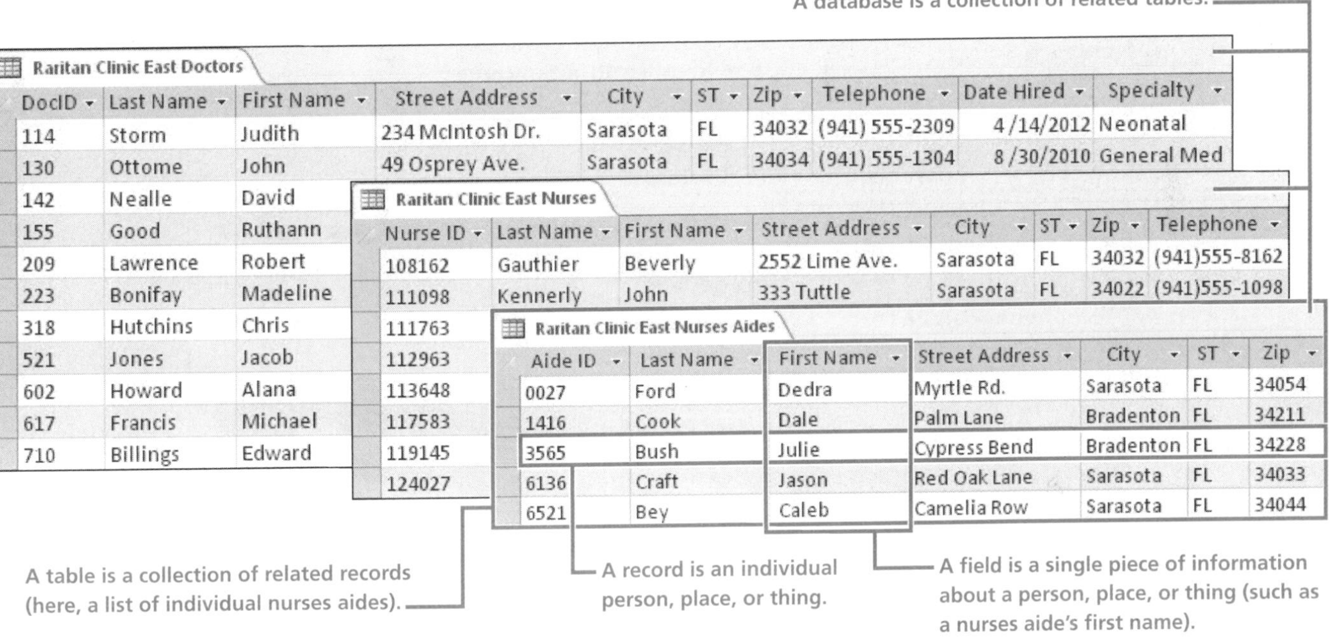

A database is a collection of related tables.
Raritan Clinic East Doctors
Raritan Clinic East Nurses
Raritan Clinic East Nurses Aides
A table is a collection of related records (here, a list of individual nurses aides).
A record is an individual person, place, or thing.
A field is a single piece of information about a person, place, or thing (such as a nurses aide's first name).

Tables can be opened in Design View, which shows the properties or descriptions of fields in the table, and Datasheet View, which displays actual data values.

QUICK REFERENCE	OPENING TABLES IN DATASHEET VIEW AND IN DESIGN VIEW
Task	**Procedure**
Open a table in Datasheet View	■ Double-click the table's name in the Navigation Pane. ■ Right-click the table and choose Open. ■ If the table is open in Design View, click the View menu ▼ and choose Datasheet View. ■ If the table is open in Design View, right-click the table's object tab in the Work Area and choose Datasheet View.
Open a table in Design View	■ Right-click the table's name and choose Design View. ■ If the table is open in Datasheet View, choose Home→Views→View menu ▼→ Design View. ■ If the table is open in Datasheet View, right-click the object tab in the Work Area and choose Design View.

Table Datasheet View and Design View are shown below.

The Object tab shows an identifying object icon and the name of the object.

Raritan Clinic East Nurses

Nurse ID	Last Name	First Name	Street Address	City	ST	Zip	Telephone	Date Hired	Position
108162	Gauthier	Beverly	2552 Lime Ave.	Sarasota	FL	34032	(941)555-8162	8/9/2010	RN
111098	Kennerly	John	333 Tuttle	Sarasota	FL	34022	(941)555-1098	2/13/2011	LPN
111763	Ramirez	Maria	680 Main St.	Sarasota	FL	34032	(941)555-1763	1/15/2011	LPN
112963	Kristoff	Michael	1001 Pineapple St.	Sarasota	FL	34042	(941)555-2963	10/8/2011	RN
113648	Adams	Anthony	53 Wildwood Terr.	Bradenton	FL	34210	(941)555-3648	3/20/2011	RN

Datasheet View displays actual data, or field values for records, and lets you add, delete, and edit records.

The Object tab shows an identifying object icon and the name of the object.

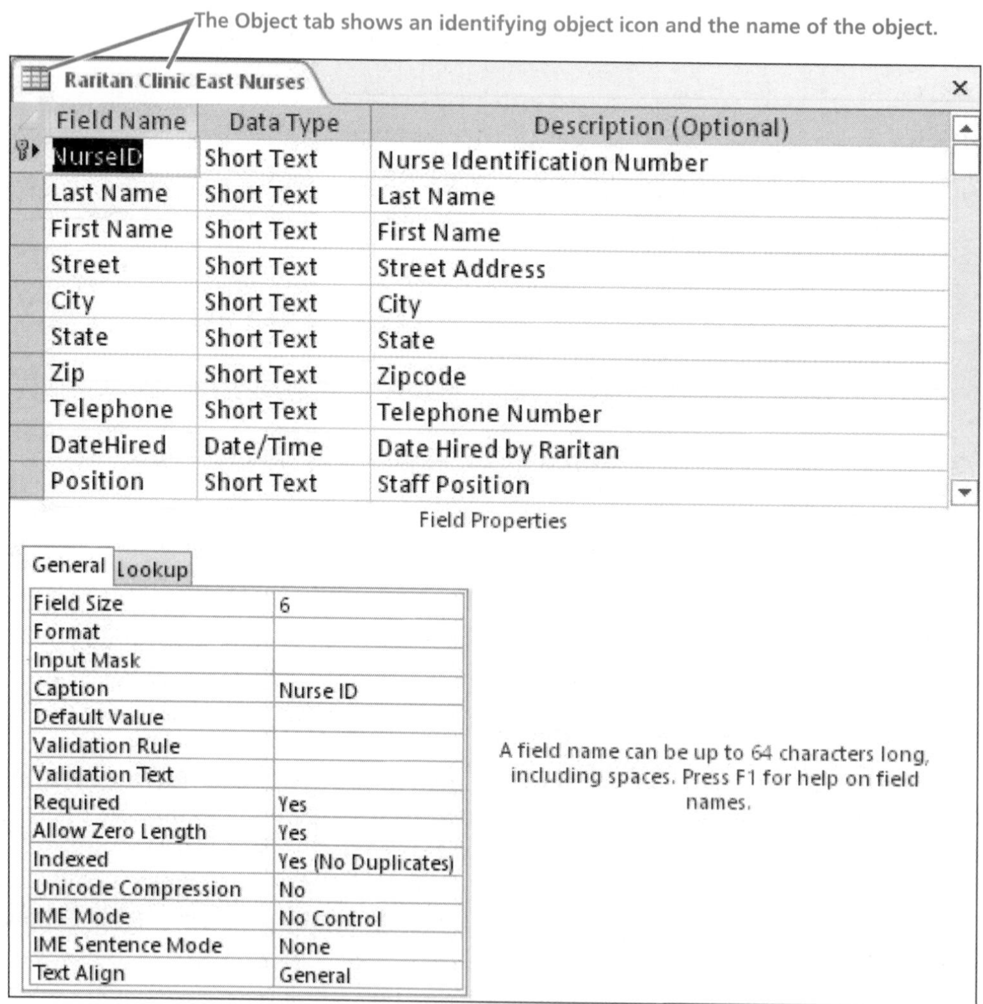

Raritan Clinic East Nurses

Field Name	Data Type	Description (Optional)
NurseID	Short Text	Nurse Identification Number
Last Name	Short Text	Last Name
First Name	Short Text	First Name
Street	Short Text	Street Address
City	Short Text	City
State	Short Text	State
Zip	Short Text	Zipcode
Telephone	Short Text	Telephone Number
DateHired	Date/Time	Date Hired by Raritan
Position	Short Text	Staff Position

Field Properties

General | Lookup

Field Size	6
Format	
Input Mask	
Caption	Nurse ID
Default Value	
Validation Rule	
Validation Text	
Required	Yes
Allow Zero Length	Yes
Indexed	Yes (No Duplicates)
Unicode Compression	No
IME Mode	No Control
IME Sentence Mode	None
Text Align	General

A field name can be up to 64 characters long, including spaces. Press F1 for help on field names.

Design View lets you create or edit a table, enter field names, and set field properties.

Navigating through Access tables and forms is very similar.

QUICK REFERENCE	NAVIGATING TABLES AND FORMS
Task	**Procedure**
Move to next field	■ Tap [Tab] or [Enter]; or click in the next field text box.
Move to previous field	■ Press [Shift]+[Tab]; or click in the previous text box.
Save entered data values	■ Tap [Tab] or [Enter]; or press [Shift]+[Tab]; or click in the next field text box.
Add new record	■ Click New (Blank) Record; or click Next Record until you reach an empty form.
Go to next record	■ Click Next Record; or click to move with mouse.
Go to previous record	■ Click Previous Record; or click to move with mouse.
Go to first record	■ Click First Record; or press [Ctrl]+[Home].
Go to last record	■ Click Last Record; or press [Ctrl]+[End].
Delete a record	■ Right-click record/row selector and select Delete Record or tap [Delete]. ■ Choose Yes to confirm.

DEVELOP YOUR SKILLS AC01-D03

Open a Table, Add a Record, and Edit a Record

In this exercise, you will explore a table in both Datasheet View and Design View. Then, you will add a new record and edit a field in another record.

1. Follow these steps to open a table in Datasheet View:

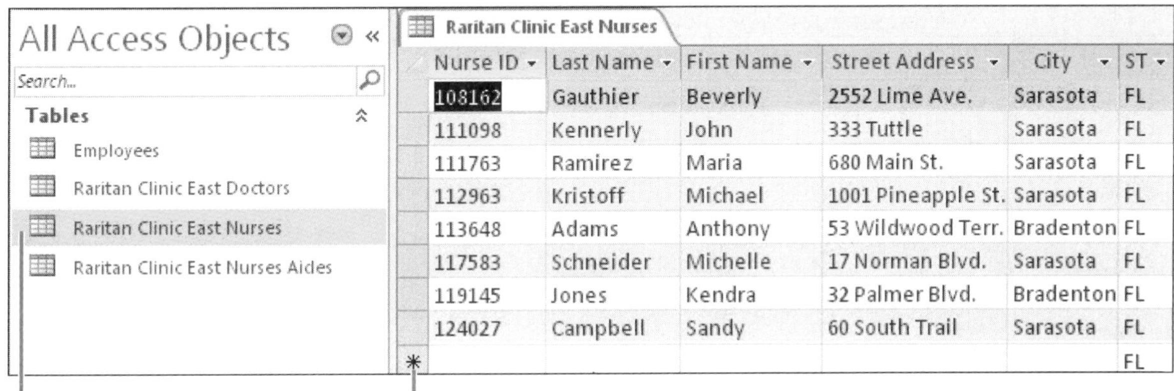

Ⓐ Double-click the **Raritan Clinic East Nurses** table in the Navigation Pane.

Ⓑ Notice the record status column displays an asterisk to indicate where a new record may be added.

If the table is not listed, click the All Access Objects drop-down arrow and select both Object Type and All Access Objects.

2. Follow these steps to add a new record and edit another record:

As you enter data, notice that you don't need to type the formatting characters in the Telephone, Date Hired, and Salary fields. Access automatically adds the formatting for you. Access will not allow you to move on to another record if the Nurse ID field is left blank.

Ⓐ Enter the new record for **Janice Lombardo**, tapping [Tab] after each new field.

Ⓑ Tap [Tab] after entering the salary to save the record.

Raritan Clinic East Nurses

Nurse ID	Last Name	First Name	Street Address	City	ST	Zip	Telephone	Date Hired	Position	Salary
108162	Gauthier	Beverly	2552 Lime Ave.	Sarasota	FL	34032	(941)555-8162	8/9/2010	RN	32,450.00
111098	Kennerly	John	333 Tuttle	Sarasota	FL	34022	(941)555-1098	2/13/2011	LPN	23,500.00
111763	Ramirez	Maria	680 Main St.	Sarasota	FL	34032	(941)555-1763	1/15/2011	LPN	25,750.00
112963	Kristoff	Michael	1001 Pineapple St.	Sarasota	FL	34042	(941)555-2963	10/8/2011	RN	30,250.00
113648	Adams	Anthony	53 Wildwood Terr.	Bradenton	FL	34210	(941)555-3648	3/20/2011	RN	28,000.00
117583	Schneider	Michelle	17 Norman Blvd.	Bradenton	FL	34212	(941)555-7583	2/24/2011	RN	31,700.00
119145	Jones	Kendra	32 Palmer Blvd.	Bradenton	FL	34212	(941)555-9145	11/7/2011	LPN	24,350.00
124027	Campbell	Sandy	60 South Trail	Sarasota	FL	34032	(941) 555-4027	2/15/2012	LPN	21,500.00
129022	Lombardo	Janice	5217 Palma Sola	Bradenton	FL	34209	(941) 555-9022	10/15/2012	RN	45,500.00
*					FL					0.00

Ⓒ Tap [↑] and [Tab] to navigate to the **City** field in **Michelle Schneider's** record. Change *Bradenton* to **Sarasota** and tap [Tab] to save.

Ⓓ Click the **Close** button when you are done.

If you make a mistake while entering data, tap [Esc] to back out of an unwanted entry, if you have not yet tapped [Tab] to move to the next field. Press [Esc] twice to back out of an unwanted record if you have not moved on to the next record.

3. Click the **Close** [×] button in the upper-right corner of the table.

Access saves your data whenever you press [Tab] or [Enter] in a table or a form. There is no need to save your data as long as you have entered a valid value for the ID field. If you modify the design of any table, query, form or report, Access will prompt you to save the changes made to any unsaved objects.

Forms

Video Library http://labyrinthelab.com/videos Video Number: AC13-V0106

Forms provide a quick, accurate, and user-friendly way to display individual records and enter data into tables. Forms may be opened in Design View, Layout View, and Form View.

In Design View, you can create a form, assign formatting to data fields, and edit the layout and content of the form. Layout View combines the editing ability of Design View with the layout look of Form View so you can better visualize and modify the form's appearance, but you cannot add, change, or delete records. Form View provides a user-friendly way to add, edit, and delete table records, but you cannot modify the form's layout.

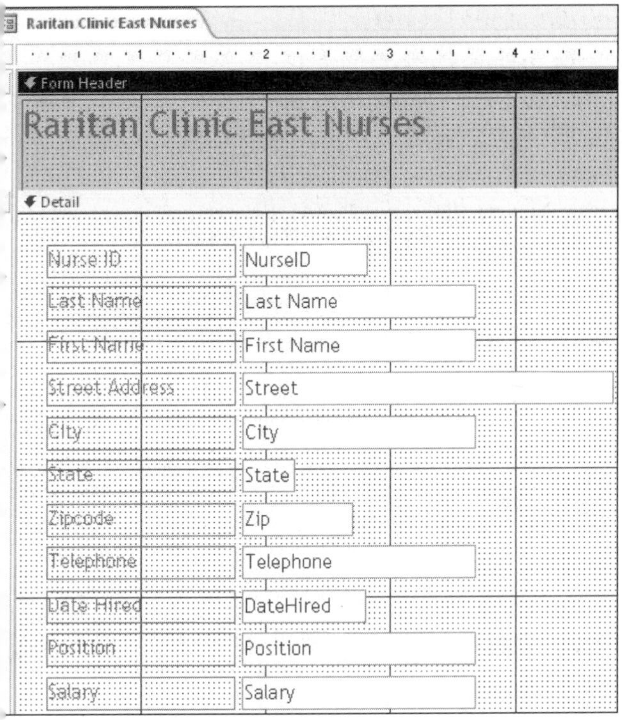

esign View enables you to create, customize, and modify a rm. Fields can be added, deleted, or repositioned; colors, nts, and sizes can be modified.

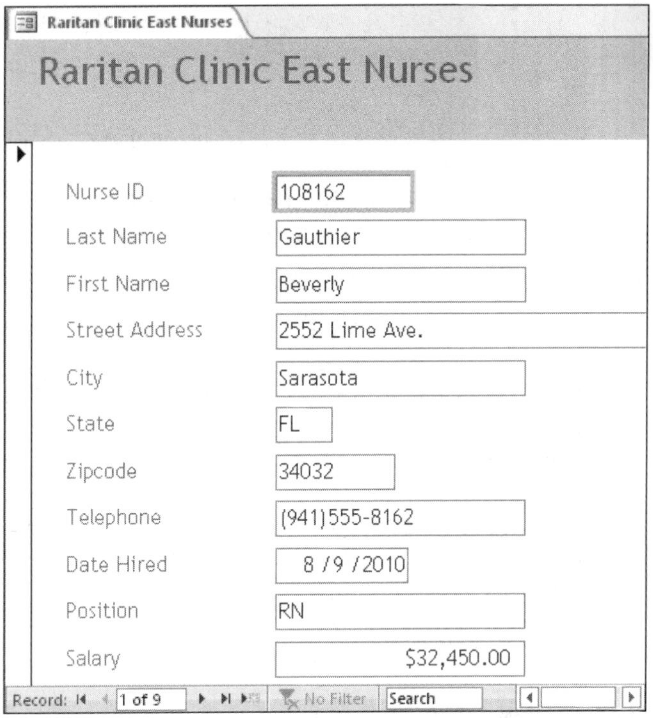

Layout View enables you to rearrange fields on the form while viewing actual data.

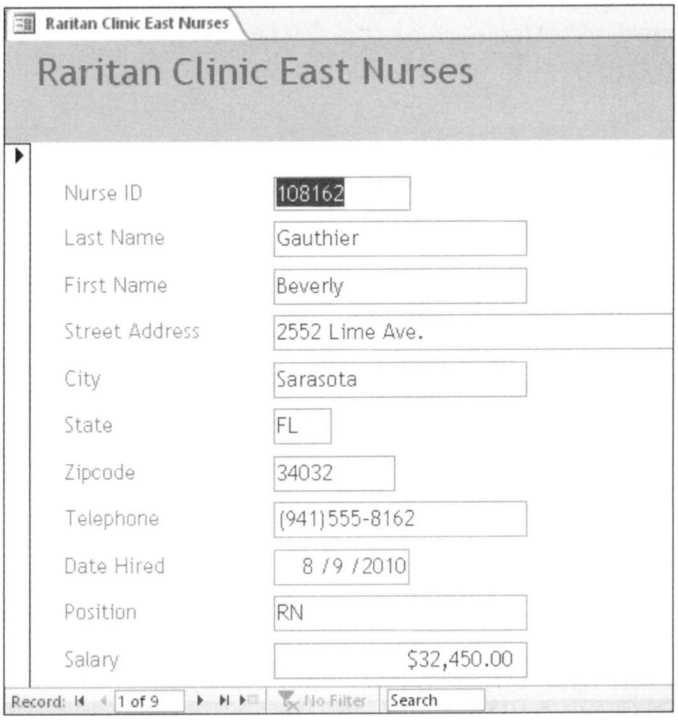

Form View enables you to enter new data and edit existing data.

The techniques for moving from field to field in Form View are the same as moving from field to field in a table in Datasheet View.

QUICK REFERENCE	OPENING FORMS IN DATASHEET, LAYOUT, AND DESIGN VIEWS
Task	**Procedure**
Open a form in Form View	■ Double-click the form name in the Navigation Pane. ■ Right-click the form and choose Open.
Open a form in Layout View	■ Right-click the form name in the Navigation Pane and choose Layout View. ■ If the form is open in Form View, click View menu ▼ and choose Layout View. ■ Right-click the object tab in the Work Area and choose Layout View.
Open a form in Design View	■ Right-click the form name in the Navigation Pane and choose Design View. ■ If the form is open in Form View, click View menu ▼ and choose Design View. ■ Right-click the object tab in the Work Area and choose Design View.

DEVELOP YOUR SKILLS AC01-D04

Add a Record Using an Existing Form

In this exercise, you will use an existing form to add a record to the table that you opened in the previous exercise.

1. Double-click the **Raritan Clinic East Nurses** form.
   Be sure to double-click the form, not the table.
2. Click the **Next Record** ▸ button a few times to page through the records.
3. Click the **Previous Record** ◂ button to go back to the first record.
4. Click the **New (Blank) Record** button.
5. Enter these data values, tapping Tab after entering a value in each field.

You do not have to enter the parenthesis or dash in the phone number, or enter the forward slashes between the numbers in dates. Access will add these for you.

You can use Shift + Tab *to move to a previous field. Note the pencil icon that appears on the left side of the form as you begin typing. It indicates that you are currently working in this record.*

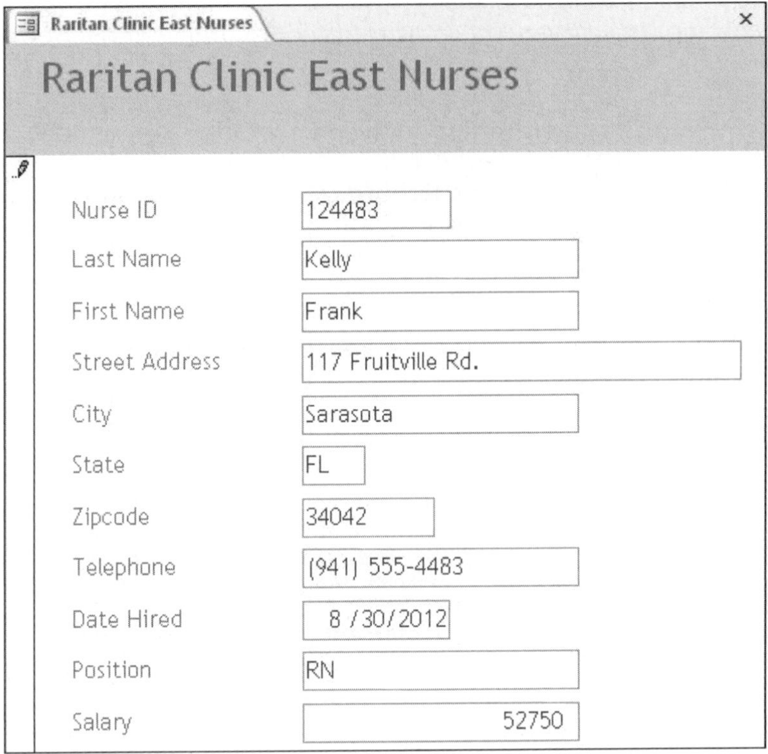
Raritan Clinic East Nurses

Nurse ID	124483
Last Name	Kelly
First Name	Frank
Street Address	117 Fruitville Rd.
City	Sarasota
State	FL
Zipcode	34042
Telephone	(941) 555-4483
Date Hired	8 /30/2012
Position	RN
Salary	52750

6. After entering the salary, tap Tab to save the record.

   When you tap Tab *after the last field in a form, Access will move to the next record or to a new blank record if you were working on the last record.*

Deleting Records Using a Form

Video Library http://labyrinthelab.com/videos Video Number: AC13-V0107

There will come a time when a record in a table is no longer needed or relevant. You can delete records using a table in Datasheet View, using a query, and using an open form. When you delete a record that has a record number, Access will not renumber the records. Consequently, if the last record number is 20, there may not be 20 records in the table since some records may have been deleted.

QUICK REFERENCE	DELETING RECORDS USING A FORM
Task	**Procedure**
Delete a record using a form	Choose Home→Records→Delete→Delete Record. Or, click the Record Selection bar and click Delete.

DEVELOP YOUR SKILLS AC01-D05

Delete a Record Using a Form

In this exercise, you will delete a table record using a form. The Raritan Clinic East Nurses form should be open.

1. Follow these steps to delete a record from the nurses table using a form:

Ⓐ If necessary, click the **Home** tab.

Ⓑ Click the **Previous Record** ◂ button to navigate to Michael Kristoff's record.

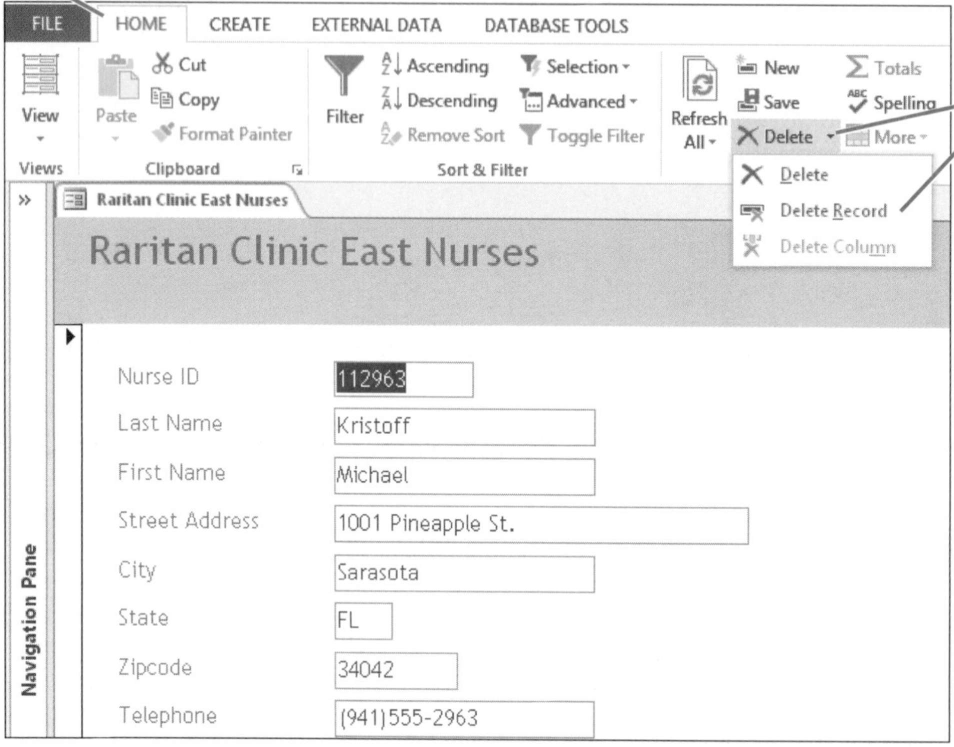

Ⓒ Click the **Delete menu ▾ button** and choose **Delete Record**.

FILE | HOME | CREATE | EXTERNAL DATA | DATABASE TOOLS

View | Paste | Cut | Copy | Format Painter | Filter | Ascending | Descending | Remove Sort | Selection | Advanced | Toggle Filter | Refresh All | New | Save | Delete | Totals | Spelling | More

Views | Clipboard | Sort & Filter

Delete | Delete Record | Delete Column

Navigation Pane

Raritan Clinic East Nurses

Raritan Clinic East Nurses

Nurse ID	112963
Last Name	Kristoff
First Name	Michael
Street Address	1001 Pineapple St.
City	Sarasota
State	FL
Zipcode	34042
Telephone	(941)555-2963

2. Click **Yes** in the Microsoft Access warning box.
3. Close the form.

Queries

Video Library http://labyrinthelab.com/videos Video Number: AC13-V0108

Queries allow you to extract data from database tables based on specific criteria and display those results in a row and column format. They allow you to find specific records, select specific fields, and sort, organize, and perform calculations on the table data. Queries can be created and modified in Design View or in the more advanced Structured Query Language (SQL) View.

QUICK REFERENCE	OPENING QUERIES IN DESIGN, SQL, AND DATASHEET/OPEN VIEWS
Task	**Procedure**
Open or run a query in Datasheet/Open View	■ Double-click the query name in the Navigation Pane. ■ Right-click the query and choose Open. ■ Open the query in Design View and choose Design→Results→Run.
Open a query in Design View	■ Right-click the query name and choose Design View. ■ If the query is open in Datasheet View, click View menu ▼ and choose Design View. ■ Right-click the object tab in the Work Area and choose Design View.
Open a query in SQL View	■ Open the query in Datasheet or Design View, click View menu ▼ and choose SQL View. ■ If the query is open in Design or Datasheet View, right-click the object tab in the Work Area and choose SQL View.

DEVELOP YOUR SKILLS AC01-D06

Open an Existing Simple Query

In this exercise, you will open a Select query in Design View, and then run it to select the doctors who specialize in Neonatal care or General Medicine.

1. Right-click the **Raritan Clinic East NeoNatal-General Med Doctors** query and choose **Design View**.

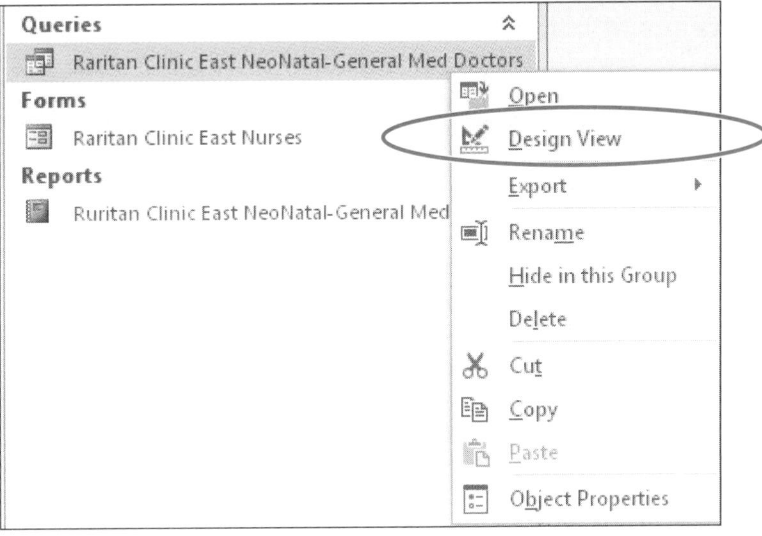

Access 2013

2. Follow these steps to run the query:

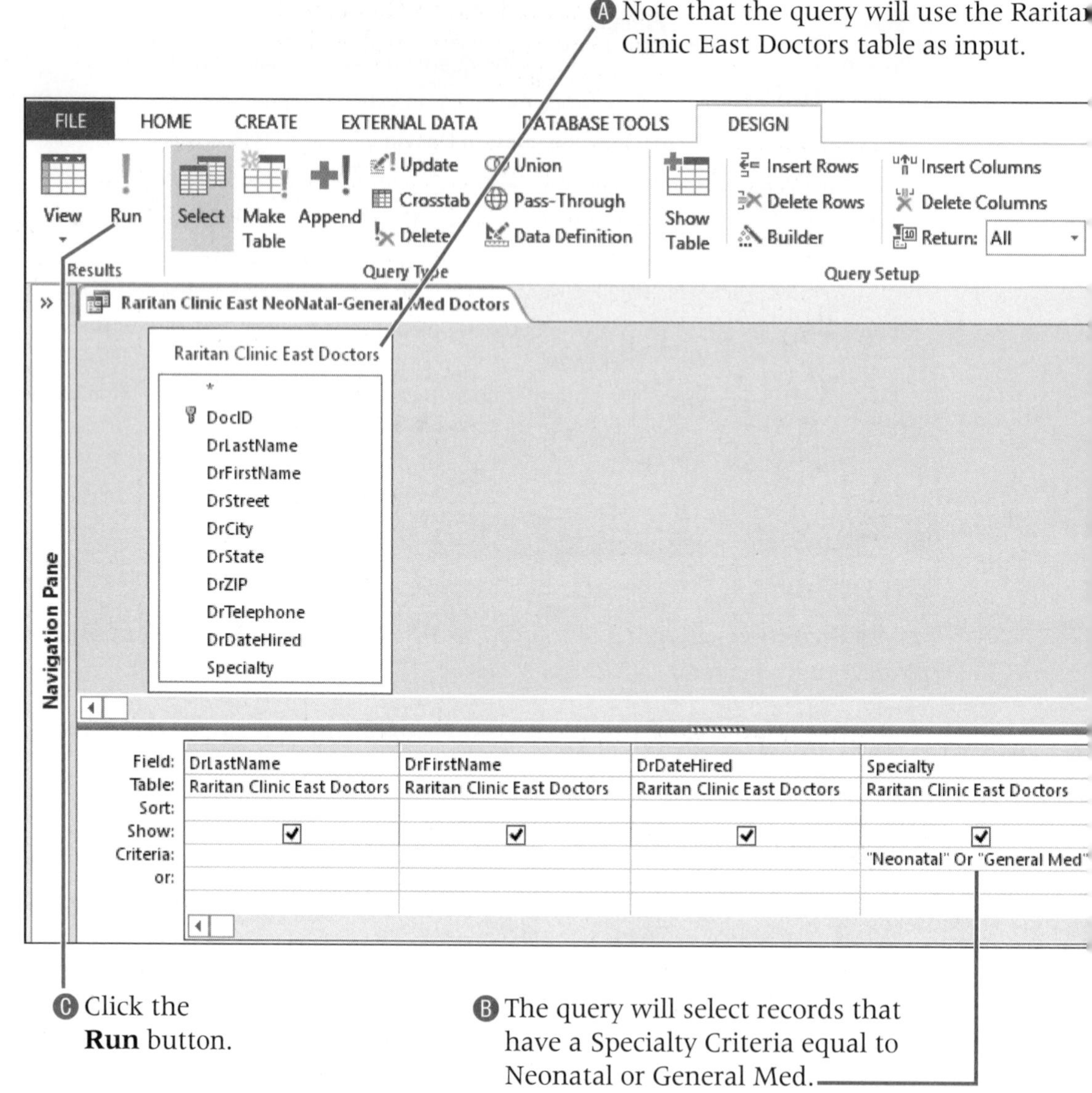

3. Follow these steps to analyze the query results:

Ⓐ The query returned results that contain the same fields that were displayed in Query Design View.

Raritan Clinic East NeoNatal-General Med Doctors

Last Name	First Name	Date Hired	Specialty
Storm	Judith	4/14/2012	Neonatal
Ottome	John	8/30/2010	General Med
Good	Ruthann	9/11/2010	General Med
Lawrence	Robert	2/9/2011	General Med
Bonifay	Madeline	12/3/2010	Neonatal
Hutchins	Chris	3/18/2012	General Med
Jones	Jacob	5/21/2012	General Med
Howard	Alana	6/2/2011	Neonatal
Billings	Edward	7/10/2011	Neonatal
Manford	Ryan	12/4/2011	General Med

Ⓑ The Specialty field identifies doctors who specialize in Neonatal care or General Med.

4. Click **Close** [×] at the top-right corner of the query window.

Reports

Video Library http://labyrinthelab.com/videos Video Number: AC13-V0109

Reports display information retrieved from a table or query in an organized and formatted layout, providing detailed or summary information that can be useful for documenting, reporting, and making decisions. Reports are designed to be printed. Reports can be opened in Design View, Layout View, Report View, and Print Preview.

QUICK REFERENCE	OPENING AND PRINTING REPORTS
Task	**Procedure**
Open a report in Report View	■ Double-click the report name in the Navigation Pane. ■ Right-click the report and choose Open.
Open a report in Print Preview	■ Right-click the report name and choose Print Preview. ■ If the report is open in Report, Design, or Layout View, click View menu ▼ and choose Print Preview. ■ Right-click the object tab in the Work Area and choose Print Preview.
Open a report in Layout View	■ Right-click the report name and choose Layout View. ■ If the report is open in Report View, click View menu ▼ and choose Layout View. ■ Right-click the object tab in the Work Area and choose Layout View.
Open a report in Design View	■ Right-click the report name and choose Design View. ■ If the report is open in Report View, click View menu ▼ and choose Design View. ■ Right-click the object tab in the Work Area and choose Design View.
Print a report	■ Right-click the report name and choose Print. ■ Open the report in Print Preview and click the Print button on the Ribbon.

DEVELOP YOUR SKILLS AC01-D07

View an Existing Database Report

In this exercise, you will view an existing report in Design View and Print Preview.

1. Follow these steps to open a report in Design View:

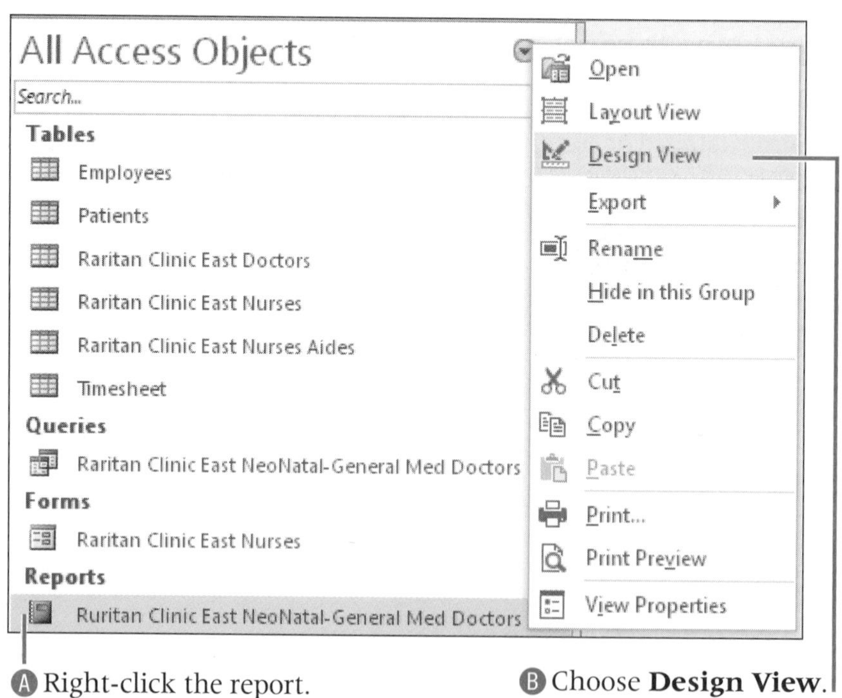

Ⓐ Right-click the report. Ⓑ Choose **Design View**.

The report opens in Design View. In Design View you can add, delete, and reposition fields, and change font sizes and colors.

2. Follow these steps to switch to Print Preview:

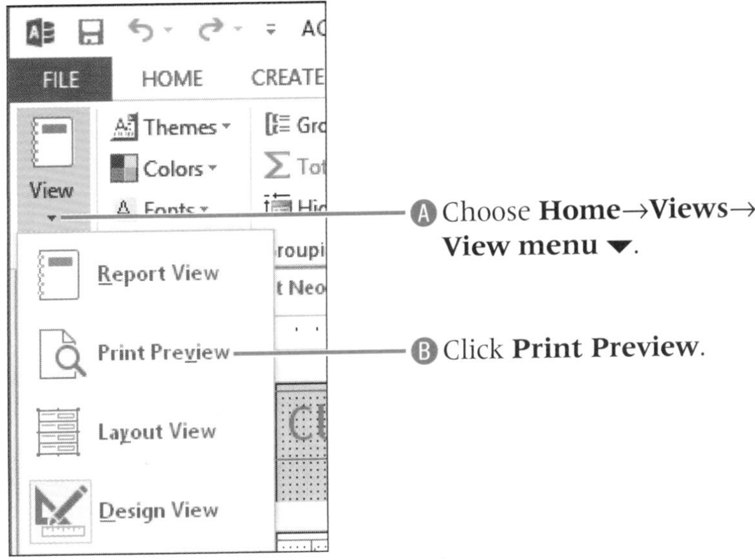

Raritan Clinic East NeoNatal-General Med Doctors

Specialty	Last Name	First Name	Date Hired	City	State	Zipcode	Telephone
General Med							
	Good	Ruthann	9/11/2010	Tampa	FL	33172	(941) 555-2091
	Hutchins	Chris	3/18/2012	Sarasota	FL	34042	(941) 555-3809
	Jones	Jacob	5/21/2012	Bradenton	FL	34212	(941) 555-4613
	Lawrence	Robert	2/9/2011	Sarasota	FL	34033	(941) 555-5926
	Manford	Ryan	12/4/2011	Bradenton	FL	34212	(941) 555-8422
	Ottome	John	8/30/2010	Sarasota	FL	34034	(941) 555-1304
Neonatal							
	Billings	Edward	7/10/2011	Bradenton	FL	34205	(941) 555-2237
	Bonifay	Madeline	12/3/2010	Bradenton	FL	34205	(941) 555-1902
	Howard	Alana	6/2/2011	Sarasota	FL	34032	(941) 555-9910
	Storm	Judith	4/14/2012	Sarasota	FL	34032	(941) 555-2309

A typical report might include a title, heading, detail lines showing individual records, and a footer that displays the date and page number.

3. Click the **Print** button to print the report based on the guidelines provided by your instructor.
4. Click the **Close Print Preview** button.
5. Click **Close** [×] to close the report.

Closing a Database and Exiting Access

Video Library http://labyrinthelab.com/videos Video Number: AC13-V0110

Remember that as long as a valid ID has been entered, Access automatically saves your data when you press [Tab] or [Enter] in a table or in a form. You don't have to repeatedly save your data.

If you modify the design of any table, query, form or report, Access will automatically prompt you to save any changes made to unsaved objects.

After all modified objects have been saved, you can close the database and exit Access. The procedures used to perform these tasks are the same as those used to close files and exit other Microsoft Office applications. Choose the File tab and select Close to close the database.

Because Access databases contain numerous objects, it is always a good idea to close each database object properly before exiting Access. This ensures that all objects in the database are put away carefully.

QUICK REFERENCE	CLOSING A DATABASE AND EXITING ACCESS
Task	**Procedure**
Close a database	Choose File→Close.
Exit Access	Click Close [×] in the upper-right corner of the Access window; or press [Alt]+[F4].

DEVELOP YOUR SKILLS AC01-D08

Close a Database and Exit Access

In this exercise, you will close the Raritan Clinic East database and exit Access.

1. Choose **File→Close** to close the database
2. Click the **Close** [×] button to exit **Access 2013**.

Concepts Review

To check your knowledge of the key concepts introduced in this lesson, complete the Concepts Review quiz by choosing the appropriate access option below.

If you are...	Then access the quiz by...
Using the Labyrinth Video Library	Going to http://labyrinthelab.com/videos
Using eLab	Logging in, choosing Content, and navigating to the Concepts Review quiz for this lesson
Not using the Labyrinth Video Library or eLab	Going to the student resource center for this book

Reinforce Your Skills

REINFORCE YOUR SKILLS AC01-R01

Add, Edit, and Delete Records

Kids for Change is a non-profit organization that helps young adults organize social/community service within the mindset of "think globally, act locally." In this exercise, you will explore the Access environment open the Kids for Change database, and add a record to a table. You will also edit a table and use a form to delete a record.

Explore the Access Environment

1. To start Access, follow the step for your version of Windows:
   - **Windows 7:** Choose **Start→All Programs→Microsoft Office 2013→Access 2013**.
   - **Windows 8:** Locate and click the **Access 2013 tile**.
2. Click the **Open Other Files** link in Backstage view, click **Computer**, and click **Browse**.
3. Navigate to your file storage location, choose **AC01-R01-K4C**, and click **Open**.
4. Use the **Save As** command and name the file `AC01-R01-K4C-[FirstInitialLastName]`.
5. Click the **Collapse** and **Expand** buttons in the Navigation Pane to show/hide the different database objects.
6. Click the **Create**, **External Data**, and **Database Tools** tabs to see the commands available in each one; then, return to the **Home** tab.

   At this point you are just exploring Access. Note that the Create tab has commands that allow you to create your own tables, queries, forms, and reports.

Add a Record and Edit Data Using a Table

7. Double-click the **Activities** table in the Navigation Pane/Objects Panel.

   Be sure to double-click the table, not the form.
8. Enter the data values for the record indicated, tapping Tab after each field.

Activities

Activity ID	Activity	Location	Day of Week	Meet Time
BCSat	Beach Cleanup	Coquina Beach	Saturday	9:00 AM
CCThu	Can Collection	Seabreeze School	Thursday	6:00 PM
ESSun	Eco-Bake Sale	Downtown Flea Market	Sunday	8:00 AM
GWWed	Garden Work	All Angels Church	Wednesday	5:00 PM
NCMon	Newspaper Collection	Seabreeze School	Monday	6:00 PM
RDTue	Recycling Drive	Seabreeze School	Tuesday	6:00 PM
SWFri	Sign Waving	Cortez Rd. & Tamiami Tr.	Friday	5:00 PM
PSSun	Petition Signing	Hernando Mall	Sunday	3:00 PM
*				

Be sure to tap Tab *after entering the Meet Time. Remember that you cannot save your data if you have not entered a valid value for the unique key field, or ID, for a record.*

9. Navigate to the **Location** field for **Newspaper Collection** and change the Location value from *Seabreeze School* to **`Bayshore School`**.

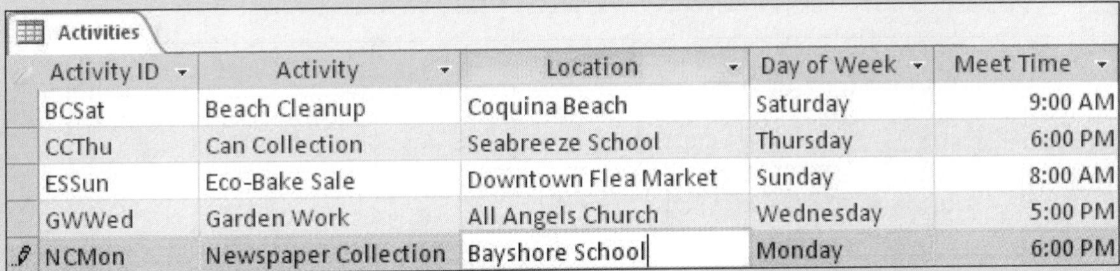

Activity ID	Activity	Location	Day of Week	Meet Time
BCSat	Beach Cleanup	Coquina Beach	Saturday	9:00 AM
CCThu	Can Collection	Seabreeze School	Thursday	6:00 PM
ESSun	Eco-Bake Sale	Downtown Flea Market	Sunday	8:00 AM
GWWed	Garden Work	All Angels Church	Wednesday	5:00 PM
NCMon	Newspaper Collection	Bayshore School	Monday	6:00 PM

Be sure to tap Tab *after entering the school name.*

10. **Close** × the Activities table.

Add a Record and Delete a Record Using a Form

11. Double-click the **Activities** form in the Navigation Pane/Objects Panel.

    Be sure to double-click the form, not the table.

12. Click the **New (Blank) Record** button then enter the data values shown.

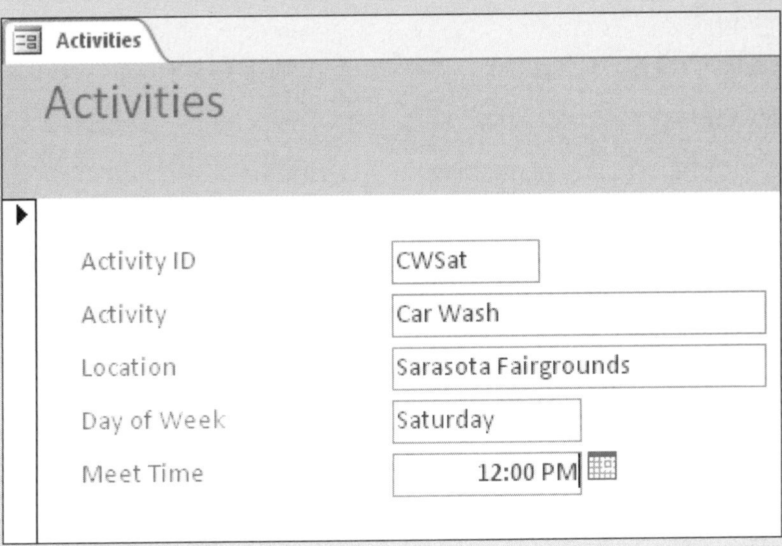

Activities

Activities

Activity ID	CWSat
Activity	Car Wash
Location	Sarasota Fairgrounds
Day of Week	Saturday
Meet Time	12:00 PM

13. Tap Tab or Enter after entering the Meet Time value to save your new record.

    You will not be able to move to a new record or save the data if you have not entered an ID.

14. Using the **Previous Record** ◂ and **Next Record** ▸ buttons at the bottom of the form, navigate to the **Garden Work** record.

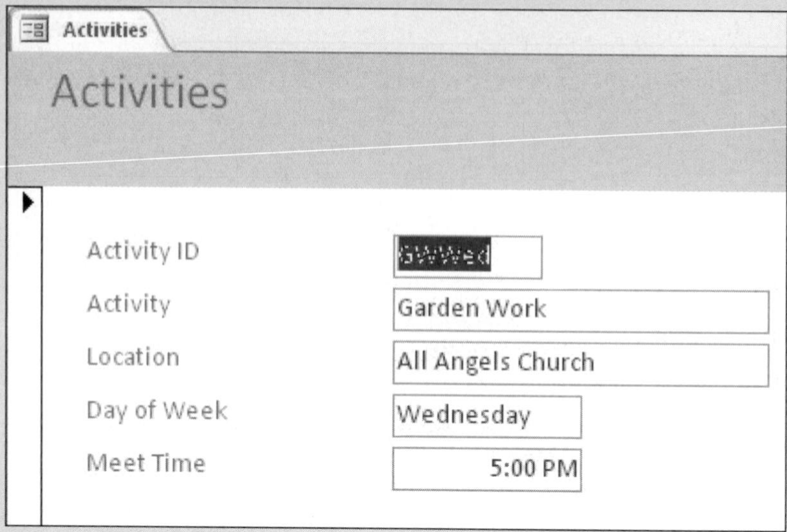

15. Click the **Record Selection** bar, then choose **Home→Records→Delete menu ▾→ Delete Record**.

    The record is removed from Form View and deleted from the underlying table.

16. Click **Yes** in the warning box.
17. Close the **Activities** form and display the Activities table in Datasheet View.

    The Garden Work record has been deleted and the new location for Newspaper Collection is Bayshore School.

18. Close the **Activities** table; exit **Access**.
19. Submit your final file based on the guidelines provided by your instructor.

    To view examples of how your file or files should look at the end of this exercise, go to the student resource center.

REINFORCE YOUR SKILLS AC01-R02

Run a Query and View a Report

In this exercise, you will run a query in the Kids for Change database to gather and display the activities scheduled from Monday through Friday. You will also run and print a report that lists staff members available on weekdays.

Run a Query

1. Start **Access**.
2. Click **Open Other Files** in Backstage view, click **Computer**, and click **Browse**.
3. Navigate to your file storage location, choose **AC01-R02-K4C**, and click **Open**.

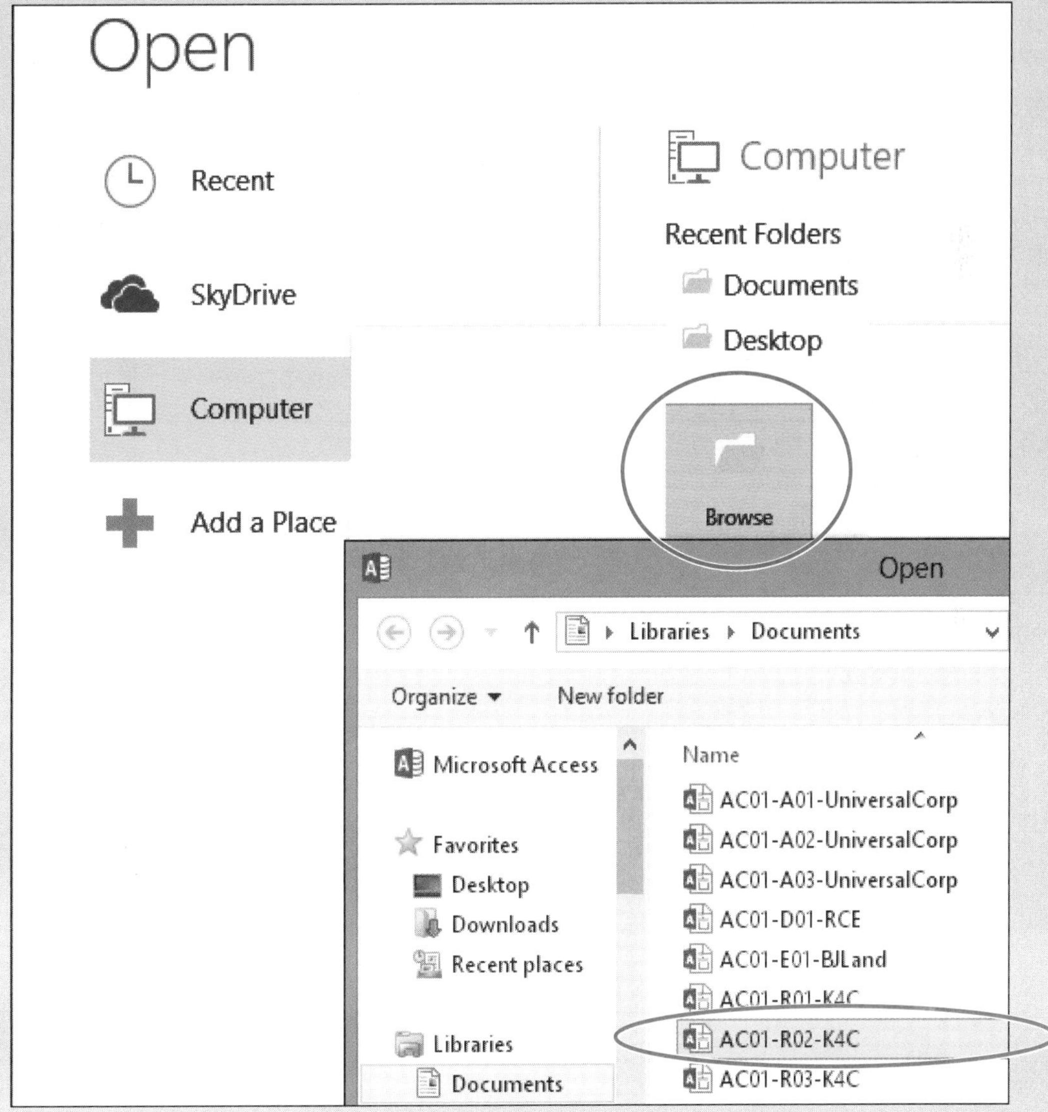

The database opens with the database objects displayed in the Navigation Pane.

4. Using the **Save As** command, name the file **`AC01-R02-K4C-[FirstInitialLastName]`**.

5. In the Navigation Pane, right-click **Weekday Activities Query** and choose **Design View**.
6. Hover the mouse pointer over the right edge of each grid column heading until the pointer becomes a resize pointer, then double-click to auto size each column.

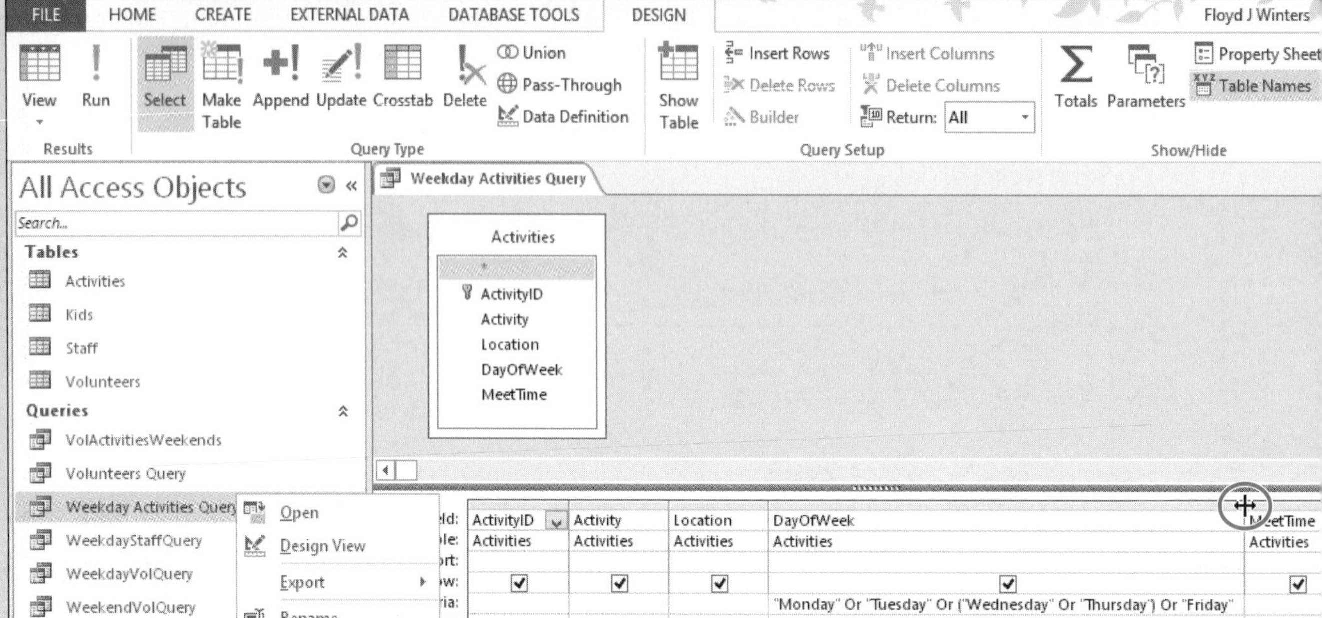

7. Choose **Design→Results→Run** to see the query results.

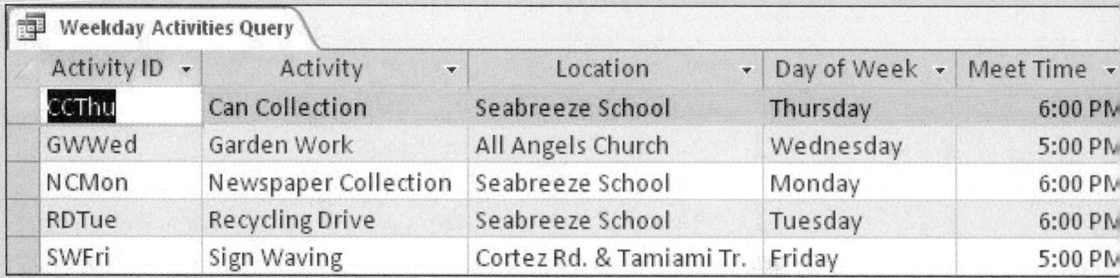

Weekday Activities Query

Activity ID	Activity	Location	Day of Week	Meet Time
CCThu	Can Collection	Seabreeze School	Thursday	6:00 PM
GWWed	Garden Work	All Angels Church	Wednesday	5:00 PM
NCMon	Newspaper Collection	Seabreeze School	Monday	6:00 PM
RDTue	Recycling Drive	Seabreeze School	Tuesday	6:00 PM
SWFri	Sign Waving	Cortez Rd. & Tamiami Tr.	Friday	5:00 PM

The query selects only the records in which DayOfWeek is a weekday (Monday through Friday).

8. **Close** [×] the Weekday Activities Query results.

View and Print a Report

9. Double-click **WeekdayStaffReport** to open it in Report View.
10. Click **View menu ▾** and choose **Print Preview**.

    Use the Print Preview Zoom tool to adjust the zoom level of the report.

Kids for Change

Weekday Staff Report

Day of Week	Activity	Location	Meet Time	Staff Last Name	Staff First Name	Staff Phone
Friday						
	Sign Waving	Cortez Rd. & Tami	5:00 PM	Kendall	Lonnie	941-555-2356
Monday						
	Newspaper Collection	Bayshore School	6:00 PM	Earle	Kevin	941-555-1368
Tuesday						
	Recycling Drive	Seabreeze School	6:00 PM	Jacoby	Jane	941-555-5050
Wednesday						
	Garden Work	All Angels Church	5:00 PM	Montagne	Francis	941-555-9032

11. Click the **Print** button.
12. Based on the guidelines provided by your instructor, send the **WeekdayStaffReport** to a printer, save it as a new database object, or publish it as a PDF or an XPS file.
13. Click the **Close Print Preview** button.
14. Close the **WeekdayStaffReport**, and any other open objects; exit **Access**.
15. Submit your final file based on the guidelines provided by your instructor.

    To view examples of how your file or files should look at the end of this exercise, go to the student resource center.

REINFORCE YOUR SKILLS AC01-R03

Add a Record, Run a Query, and Generate a Report

In this exercise, you will explore the Access environment, open the Kids for Change database, and change the scheduled day of an activity. You will use a form to delete a record and add a new record. Then, you will run a query that generates a list of staff members who are available on weekends. Finally, you open a report that displays a list of all Kids for Change volunteers.

Explore the Access Environment

1. Start **Access**.
2. Click the **Open Other Files** link in Backstage view, click **Computer**, and click **Browse**.

3. Navigate to your file storage location, choose **AC01-R03-K4C**, and click **Open**.

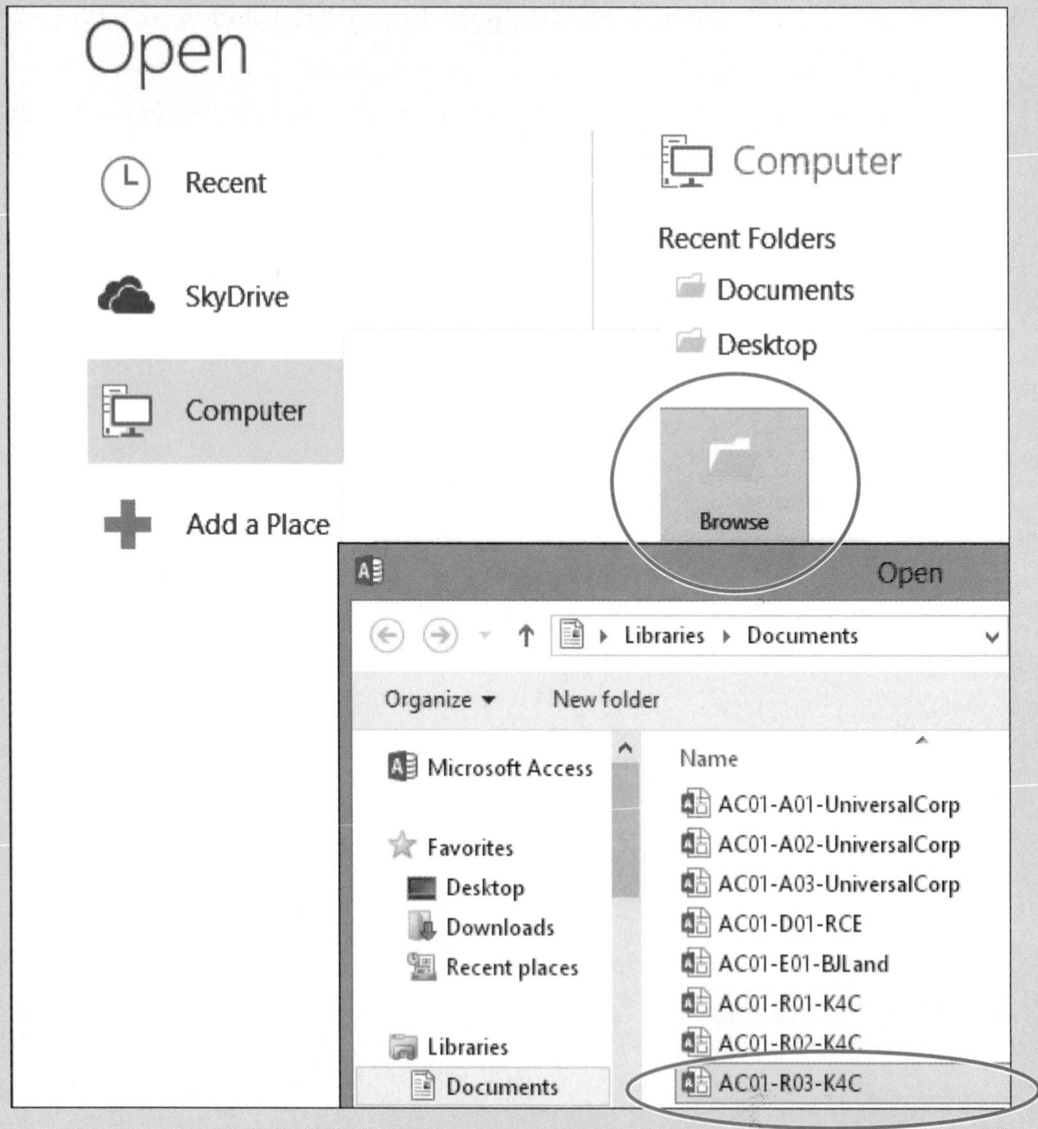

The database opens with the database objects displayed in the Navigation Pane.

4. Using the **Save As** command, name the file `AC01-R03-K4C-[FirstInitialLastName]`.

5. Click the **Collapse** and **Expand** buttons in the Navigation Pane to hide/show the different objects in the database.

6. Click the **Create**, **External Data**, and **Database Tools** tabs to see the commands available in each one; then, return to the **Home** tab.
   At this point you are just exploring Access. Note that the Create tab has commands that allow you to create your own tables, queries, forms, and reports.

Edit and Enter Data with a Table and a Form

7. In the **Kids for Change** database, double-click the **Activities** table in the Navigation Pane.
8. Using [↓] and [Tab], navigate to the **Day of Week** field for **Can Collection**.
9. Change the **Day of Week** value from *Thursday* to `Wednesday`.

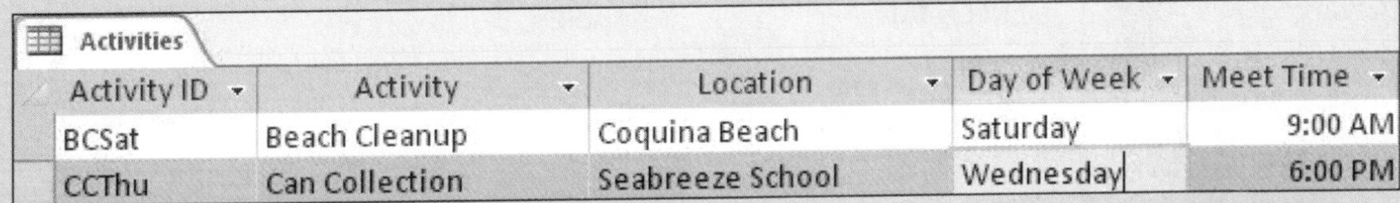

Activities

Activity ID	Activity	Location	Day of Week	Meet Time
BCSat	Beach Cleanup	Coquina Beach	Saturday	9:00 AM
CCThu	Can Collection	Seabreeze School	Wednesday	6:00 PM

10. **Close** [×] the Activities table.
    Remember that Access automatically saves your data once you tap [Tab] *as long as you have entered a valid ID for the record.*
11. Double-click **VolunteersForm**.
12. Using the **Previous Record** [◂] and **Next Record** [▸] buttons at the bottom of the form, navigate to the record for **Beverly Frith**.
13. Click the **Record Selection bar** and choose **Home→Records→Delete→Delete Record**.

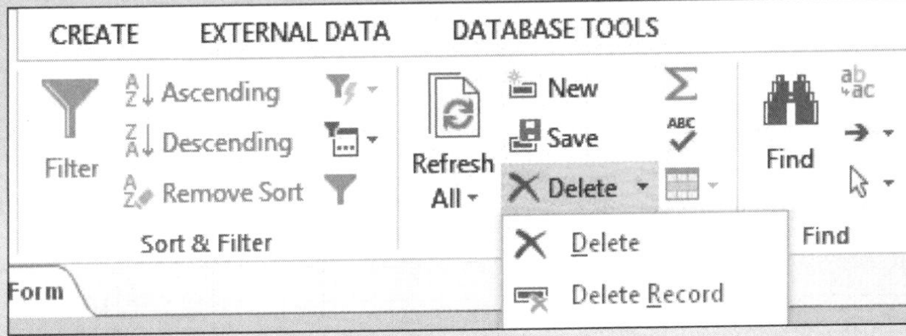

The record will be removed from Form View and deleted in the underlying table.

14. Click **Yes** in the Microsoft Access warning box.
15. Click the **New (blank) Record** [▸*] button at the bottom of the form, if necessary.

If you have just deleted the last record in the form, a new, blank record will already be displayed.

16. Tap [Tab] to move to the **Last Name** field. Type `Harris`.
    Because the Autonumber Data Type is selected for the ID for the Volunteers table, you cannot enter a value; Access automatically assigns consecutive numbers to the ID.

17. Add a new record using the data shown.

Volunteer ID	6
Last Name	Harris
First Name	Annie
Street Address	5140 Pine Ave.
City	Sarasota
State	FL
ZIP	34022
Telephone	941-555-5273
Available Day	Sunday

Tap [Tab] *after entering the Available Day field to save the new record. When you tap* [Tab] *after the last field in a form, Access will move to the next record or to a new blank record if you were working in the last record.*

18. Close the form.

Open and Run a Query

19. Right-click **WeekendVolQuery** and choose **Design View**.

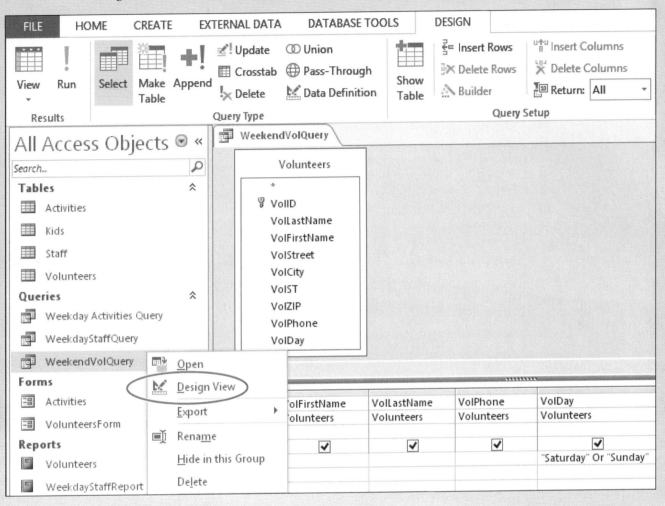

The query returns only the records in which DayOfWeek is a Saturday or Sunday.

20. Click the **Run** button on the Design tab to see the query results.

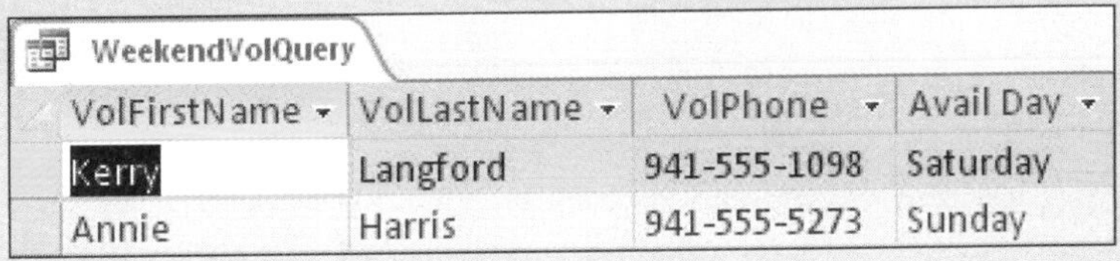

WeekendVolQuery

VolFirstName	VolLastName	VolPhone	Avail Day
Kerry	Langford	941-555-1098	Saturday
Annie	Harris	941-555-5273	Sunday

Only two volunteers are available on weekends.

21. **Close** [×] the WeekendVolQuery.

View and Print a Report

22. Double-click the **Volunteers** report to open it in Report View.
23. Click the **View ▾ menu** and choose **Print Preview**.

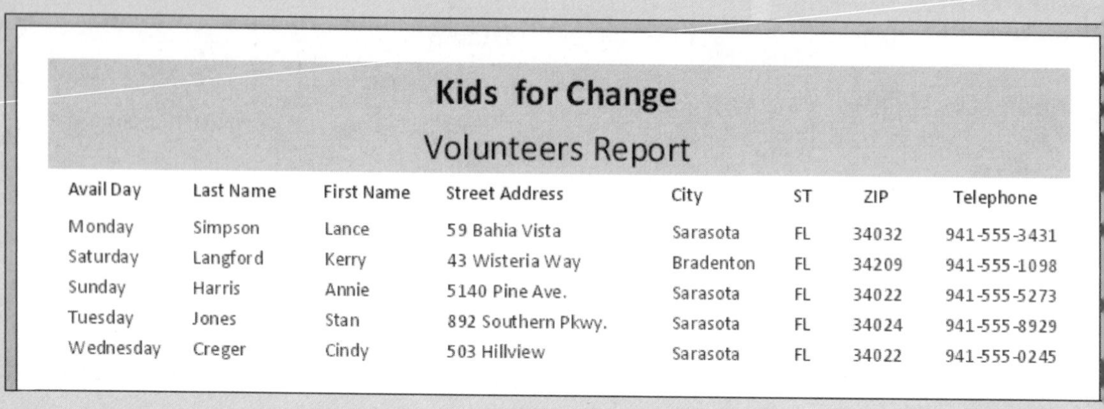

Kids for Change

Volunteers Report

Avail Day	Last Name	First Name	Street Address	City	ST	ZIP	Telephone
Monday	Simpson	Lance	59 Bahia Vista	Sarasota	FL	34032	941-555-3431
Saturday	Langford	Kerry	43 Wisteria Way	Bradenton	FL	34209	941-555-1098
Sunday	Harris	Annie	5140 Pine Ave.	Sarasota	FL	34022	941-555-5273
Tuesday	Jones	Stan	892 Southern Pkwy.	Sarasota	FL	34024	941-555-8929
Wednesday	Creger	Cindy	503 Hillview	Sarasota	FL	34022	941-555-0245

24. Click the **Print** button.
25. Based on the guidelines provided by your instructor, send the **Volunteers** report to a printer, save it as a new database object, or publish it as a PDF or an XPS file.
26. Click the **Close Print Preview** button.
27. Close the **Volunteers** report and any other open objects; exit **Access**.
28. Submit your final file based on the guidelines provided by your instructor.

Apply Your Skills

APPLY YOUR SKILLS AC01-A01

Add Data, Change Data Values, and Delete a Record

Universal Corporate Events is a meeting and event planning service. In this exercise, you will explore the Access environment, open the Universal Corporate Events database, open an existing form, and schedule a new event. Then, you will open a table, change a field, and delete a record.

Explore the Access Environment

1. Start **Access**. Open **AC01-A01-UniversalCorp** from the **AC2013 Lesson 01** folder in your file storage location and save it as **`AC01-A01-UniversalCorp-[FirstInitialLastName]`**.
2. Explore the Ribbon tabs to see the commands that are available in each one; then, return to the **Home** tab.

Work with Forms and Tables

3. Open the **Event Schedules** form in **Form View** and add this record.

Field Name	Data
Schedule ID	`BRDMiller`
Location	`Meadows Clubhouse`
Contact	`Gail Miller`
Event ID	`Holiday`
Menu Code	`DessSel`
Event Date	`7/2/2014`
Guests	`25`

In this case, you can enter the primary key (Schedule ID) value because it is the Short Text data type, not AutoNumber. Remember to tap [Tab] *or* [Enter] *after the Guests value to save the new record.*

4. Close the **Event Schedules** form.
5. Open the **Menus** table in **Datasheet View**.
6. Change the **Chg/PP** for the **Dinner-Buffet** (Menu Code = DinBuff) to **`23.00`**.
7. Delete the **Continental Breakfast** (Menu Code = ContBrk) record.

Menus

Menu Code	Menu Plan	Chg/PP
BoxLunch	Box Sandwich Lunch	10.00
BrkBuff	Buffet Breakfast	12.00
DessSel	Dessert Selections	7.50
DinBuff	Dinner-Buffet	23.00
DinSitDn	Dinner-Sit Down	35.00
HorsDvr	Hors d'oeuvre	8.00
LunchBuff	Buffet Luncheon	15.00
Thnksg	Thanksgiving Dinner	30.00

8. Close the table and the database; exit **Access**.
9. Submit your final file based on the guidelines provided by your instructor.
   To view examples of how your file or files should look at the end of this exercise, go to the student resource center.

APPLY YOUR SKILLS AC01-A02

Run a Query and View a Report

In this exercise, you will run a query to select events located at the Meadows Clubhouse. Then you will run a report that uses the results of the query as input for a printout of those events.

Explore and Run a Query

1. Start **Access**. Open **AC01-A02-UniversalCorp** from the **AC2013 Lesson 01** folder in your file storage location and save it as `AC01-A02-UniversalCorp-[FirstInitialLastName]`.
2. Run the **LocationSchedQuery** to select events by their location, in this case the **Meadows Clubhouse**.

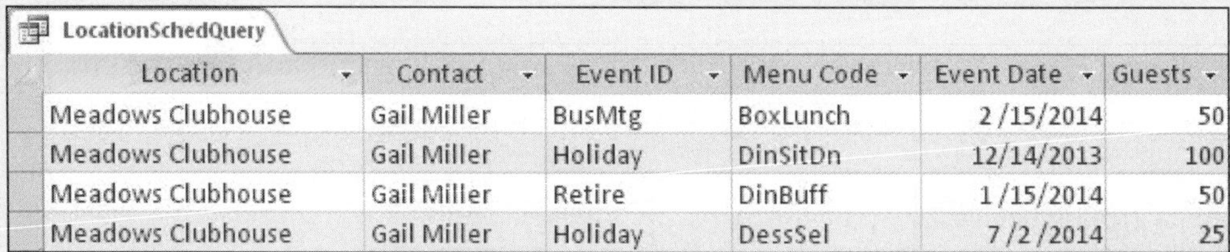

LocationSchedQuery

Location	Contact	Event ID	Menu Code	Event Date	Guests
Meadows Clubhouse	Gail Miller	BusMtg	BoxLunch	2 /15/2014	50
Meadows Clubhouse	Gail Miller	Holiday	DinSitDn	12/14/2013	100
Meadows Clubhouse	Gail Miller	Retire	DinBuff	1 /15/2014	50
Meadows Clubhouse	Gail Miller	Holiday	DessSel	7 /2 /2014	25

3. Close the query results.

View and Print a Report

4. Open the **Location Scheduling** report in **Print Preview**.

Universal Corporate Events

Location Scheduling

Event Name	Menu Plan	Guests	Location	Contact	Event Date	Attending
Business Meeting						
	Box Sandwich Lunch	50	Meadows Clubhouse	Gail Miller	2 /15/2014	50
Holiday Party						
	Dessert Selections	25	Meadows Clubhouse	Gail Miller	7 /2 /2014	25
	Dinner-Sit Down	100	Meadows Clubhouse	Gail Miller	12/14/2013	100
Retirement Party						
	Dinner-Buffet	50	Meadows Clubhouse	Gail Miller	1 /15/2014	50

5. Based on the guidelines provided by your instructor, send the **Location Scheduling** report to a printer, save it as a new database object, or publish it as a PDF or XPS file.

6. Close the report and the database. Exit **Access**.
7. Submit your final file based on the guidelines provided by your instructor.

   To view examples of how your file or files should look at the end of this exercise, go to the student resource center.

APPLY YOUR SKILLS AC01-A03

Add a Record, Run a Query, and Generate a Report

In this exercise, you will use a form to add a record to a table. You will then run a query to select the events that will use the Meadows Clubhouse as a venue. Finally, you will run a report using the query results and create a printout for the Meadows Clubhouse management so they can reserve the clubhouse for each event.

Explore the Access Environment

1. Start **Access**. Open **AC01-A03-UniversalCorp** from the **AC2013 Lesson 01** folder in your file storage location and save it as `AC01-A03-UniversalCorp-[FirstInitialLastName]`.
2. Explore the Ribbon tabs to see the commands that are available in each one; then, return to the **Home** tab.

Enter Data with a Form and Table

3. Open the **Event Schedules** form in the Navigation Pane.
4. Add this record.

Field Name	Data
Schedule ID	`BRDMiller`
Location	`Meadows Clubhouse`
Contact	`Gail Miller`
Event ID	`BusMtg`
Menu Code	`HorsDvr`
Event Date	`2/28/2014`
Guests	`35`

5. Close the form.

View Changes to a Query After Edits to a Table

6. Run the **EventsSchedQuery** to calculate the total cost of each event.

EventsSchedQuery

Event Name	Menu Plan	Chg/PP	Location	Contact	Event Date	Guests	Total Cost	Menu Code
Business Meeting	Box Sandwich Lunch	10.00	Meadows Clubhouse	Gail Miller	2/15/2014	50	$500.00	BoxLunch
Holiday Party	Hors d'oeuvre	8.00	Drake Country Club	Sue Croft	12/6/2013	150	$1,200.00	HorsDvr
Holiday Party	Dinner-Sit Down	35.00	Meadows Clubhouse	Gail Miller	12/14/2013	100	$3,500.00	DinSitDn
Retirement Party	Dinner-Buffet	23.00	Meadows Clubhouse	Gail Miller	1/15/2014	50	$1,150.00	DinBuff
Group Retreat	Dinner-Buffet	23.00	Brooksville Campgrounds	Lisa Luna	5/29/2014	80	$1,840.00	DinBuff

Note that the fourth event listed in the query, Retirement Party, currently has 50 guests expected and the Total Cost is $1,150.00.

7. Close the query.

8. Open the **Scheduling** table and increase the number of guests for the **Retirement Party** (Schedule ID = RTRMiller) to `60`.

9. Rerun the **EventsSchedQuery** to see the difference in Total Cost.

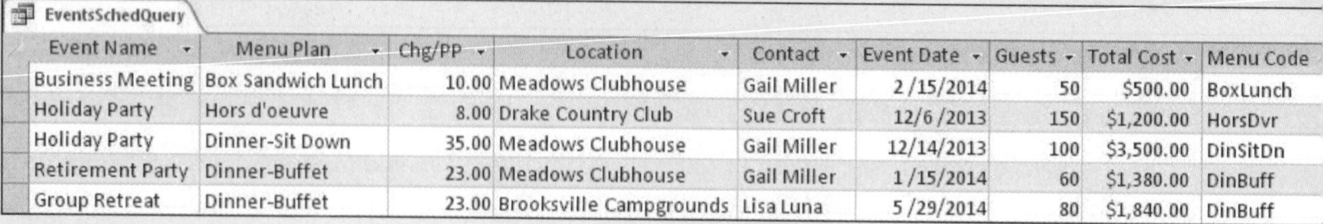

EventsSchedQuery

Event Name	Menu Plan	Chg/PP	Location	Contact	Event Date	Guests	Total Cost	Menu Code
Business Meeting	Box Sandwich Lunch	10.00	Meadows Clubhouse	Gail Miller	2/15/2014	50	$500.00	BoxLunch
Holiday Party	Hors d'oeuvre	8.00	Drake Country Club	Sue Croft	12/6/2013	150	$1,200.00	HorsDvr
Holiday Party	Dinner-Sit Down	35.00	Meadows Clubhouse	Gail Miller	12/14/2013	100	$3,500.00	DinSitDn
Retirement Party	Dinner-Buffet	23.00	Meadows Clubhouse	Gail Miller	1/15/2014	60	$1,380.00	DinBuff
Group Retreat	Dinner-Buffet	23.00	Brooksville Campgrounds	Lisa Luna	5/29/2014	80	$1,840.00	DinBuff

The Retirement Party now has a Total Cost of $1,380.00.

10. Close the **EventsSchedQuery** and the **Scheduling** table.

Produce and Print a Report

11. Open and preview the **Location Scheduling** report.

Universal Corporate Events

Location Scheduling

Event Name	Menu Plan	Guests	Location	Contact	Event Date	Attending
Business Meeting						
	Hors d'oeuvre	35	Meadows Clubhouse	Gail Miller	2/28/2014	35
	Box Sandwich Lunch	50	Meadows Clubhouse	Gail Miller	2/15/2014	50
Holiday Party						
	Dessert Selections	25	Meadows Clubhouse	Gail Miller	7/2/2014	25
	Dinner-Sit Down	100	Meadows Clubhouse	Gail Miller	12/14/2013	100
Retirement Party						
	Dinner-Buffet	60	Meadows Clubhouse	Gail Miller	1/15/2014	60

12. Based on the guidelines provided by your instructor, send the **Location Scheduling** report to a printer, save it as a new database object, or publish it as a PDF or XPS file.

13. Close the report and any other open objects; close the database. Exit **Access**.

14. Submit your final file based on the guidelines provided by your instructor.

Extend Your Skills

In the course of working through the Extend Your Skills exercises, you will think critically as you use the skills taught in the lesson to complete the assigned projects. To evaluate your mastery and completion of the exercises, your instructor may use a rubric, with which more points are allotted according to performance characteristics. (The more you do, the more you earn!) Ask your instructor how your work will be evaluated.

AC01-E01 That's the Way I See It

You will design and create a business database as you progress through the Access lessons. To begin, identify a business or a type of business for which you will create a database in the remaining lessons. Once you have identified your specific business or a business type, start Word and save a new document as **`AC01-E01-MyCompany-[FirstInitialLastName]`** in your **AC2013 Lesson 01** folder. Create a list of tables your database will need, as well as the fields that these tables will contain. Make sure your database design includes both text and numeric fields, which may be used for future calculations.

You will be evaluated based on the inclusion of all elements, your ability to follow directions, your ability to apply newly learned skills to a real-world situation, your creativity, and your accuracy in creating objects and/or entering data. Submit your final files based on the guidelines provided by your instructor.

AC01-E02 Be Your Own Boss

Your company, Blue Jean Landscaping, is a landscaping service that saves the customer money by employing the customer as a laborer. The company provides all plans and direction while the customer helps with the physical labor to cut costs and gain a sense of ownership of their new landscaping. In this exercise, you will take some time to analyze a business database and verify that the data is correct.

Open **AC01-E02-BJLand** from the **AC2013 Lesson 01** folder and save it as **`AC01-E02-BJLand-[FirstInitialLastName]`**.

- Ensure that the Large Equipment Query selects only equipment weighing more than 100 pounds.
- Using the Equipment Services Form, add **`Spreader`** to the Equip ID field for Pesticide Treatment.
- Add a new record for another landscape service and the corresponding tool/equipment of your choice.
- Remove Sprinkler Installation from the Services table.

You will be evaluated based on the inclusion of all elements, your ability to follow directions, your ability to apply newly learned skills to a real-world situation, your creativity, and your accuracy in creating objects and/or entering data. Submit your final files based on the guidelines provided by your instructor.

Transfer Your Skills

In the course of working through the Transfer Your Skills exercises, you will use critical-thinking and creativity skills to complete the assigned projects using skills taught in the lesson. To evaluate your mastery and completion of the exercises, your instructor may use a rubric, with which more points are allotted according to performance characteristics. (The more you do, the more you earn!) Ask your instructor how your work will be evaluated.

AC01-T01 Use the Web as a Learning Tool

Throughout this book, you will be provided with an opportunity to use the Internet as a learning tool by completing WebQuests. According to the original creators of WebQuests, as described on their website (WebQuest.org), a WebQuest is "an inquiry-oriented activity in which most or all of the information used by learners is drawn from the web." To complete the WebQuest projects in this book, navigate to the student resource center and choose the WebQuest for the lesson on which you are currently working. The subject of each WebQuest will be relevant to the material found in the lesson.

WebQuest Subject: Explore what Access databases are used for in industry.

Submit your final file(s) based on the guidelines provided by your instructor.

AC01-T02 Demonstrate Proficiency

Your employer, Stormy BBQ, bought out Grills R Us last year. You have discovered that Stormy BBQ's database tables still include the other company's obsolete merchandise, along with the new line of items. You need to remove the obsolete merchandise from the tables.

Stormy BBQ's signature line is staying on the books along with the new lines: Burner Grills and Fire Fly. The obsolete lines are Torchy Nites and Char-Cookery.

Open **AC01-T02-StormyBBQ** from the **AC2013 Lesson 01** folder and save it as `AC01-T02-StormyBBQ-[FirstInitialLastName]`. Update the company records using the Merchandise Form. Send the Merchandise Price report to a printer, save it as a new database object, or save it as a PDF or XPS file. Close the database and exit Access.

Submit your final file based on the guidelines provided by your instructor.

ACCESS 2013

Designing a Database and Creating Tables

LESSON OUTLINE

- Designing a Relational Database
- Normalizing Databases
- Linking Tables with Primary and Foreign Keys
- Creating Access Tables in a New Database
- Retrieving Data
- Concepts Review
- Reinforce Your Skills
- Apply Your Skills
- Extend Your Skills
- Transfer Your Skills

LEARNING OBJECTIVES

After studying this lesson, you will be able to:

- Plan, design, and create a relational database and associated tables
- Define and implement database normalization
- Define data relationships and primary and foreign keys
- Define and create an Entity Relationship Diagram
- Sort and filter records

Whether you are creating a new database to organize a soccer team or run a small business, it is essential to begin with careful planning. Successful projects often begin by examining existing business procedures and compiling a list of tasks to accomplish, designing an outline of how to accomplish those tasks, and making preparations to develop the final product. In short—analyze, design, and develop.

In this lesson, you will plan and design a database. You will gather information as needed to make a complete list of the required tables, records, and fields. You will define the data type for each field and assign ID fields so you can create relationships to link your tables. You will create several tables and enter records. Then, you will apply record sorts and filters.

CASE STUDY

Creating a Database

Winchester Web Design is a small website development company. The company specializes in websites for small businesses. The main deliverables are homepages (site navigation, overall website design, and cascading styles), secondary pages, blogs, and small business shopping carts.

Website designers must analyze a client's needs and desires before creating a website that includes the site homepage layout, navigation structure, and site styles. Once the homepage layout is determined, secondary pages can be developed. You have been asked to build a database for Winchester Web Design. As you begin your work, notice how the web design and development process has many similarities to designing a useful and efficient database: analyze, design, and develop.

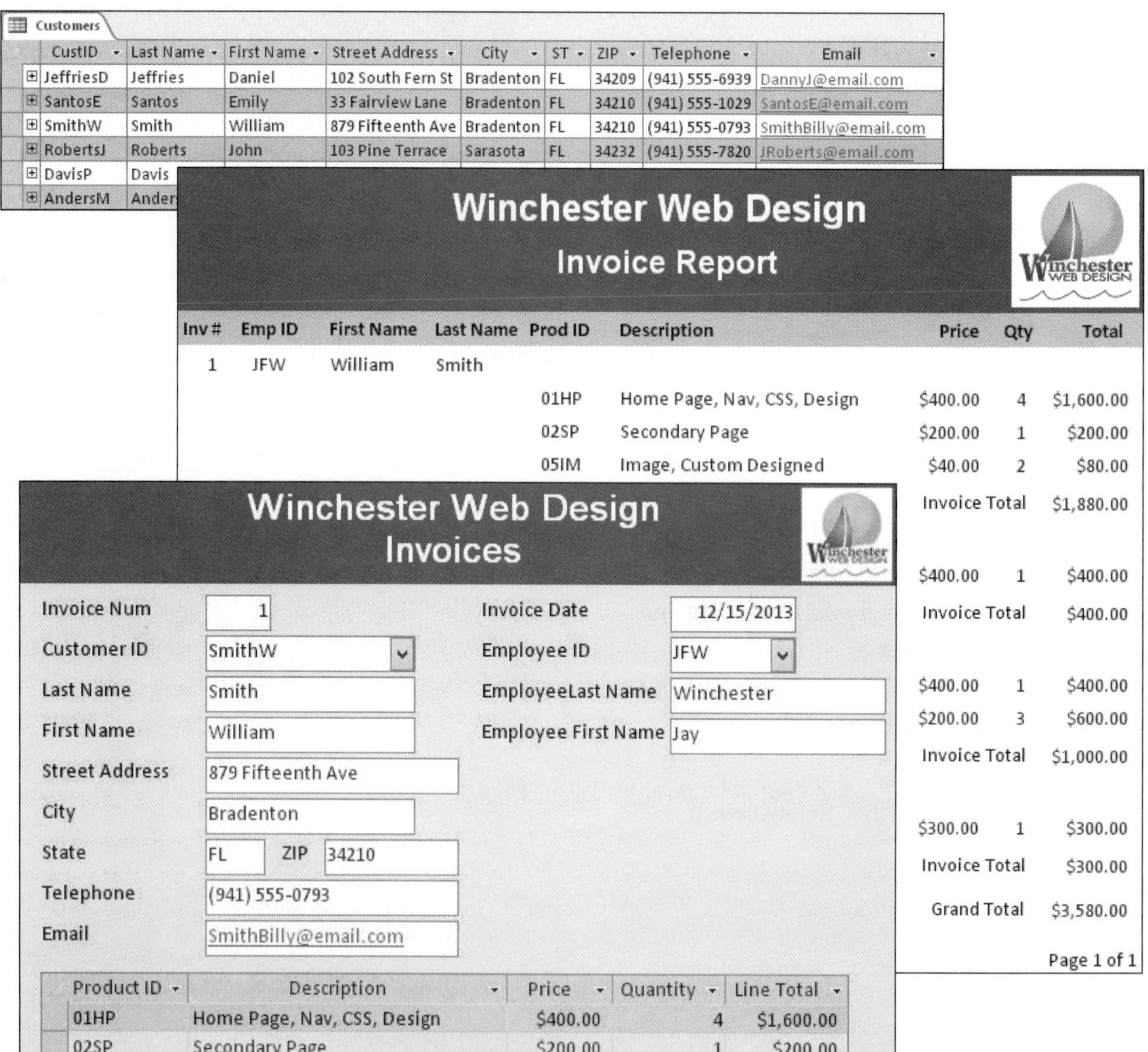

Customers

CustID	Last Name	First Name	Street Address	City	ST	ZIP	Telephone	Email
JeffriesD	Jeffries	Daniel	102 South Fern St	Bradenton	FL	34209	(941) 555-6939	DannyJ@email.com
SantosE	Santos	Emily	33 Fairview Lane	Bradenton	FL	34210	(941) 555-1029	SantosE@email.com
SmithW	Smith	William	879 Fifteenth Ave	Bradenton	FL	34210	(941) 555-0793	SmithBilly@email.com
RobertsJ	Roberts	John	103 Pine Terrace	Sarasota	FL	34232	(941) 555-7820	JRoberts@email.com
DavisP	Davis							
AndersM	Ander							

Winchester Web Design
Invoice Report

Inv #	Emp ID	First Name	Last Name	Prod ID	Description	Price	Qty	Total
1	JFW	William	Smith					
				01HP	Home Page, Nav, CSS, Design	$400.00	4	$1,600.00
				02SP	Secondary Page	$200.00	1	$200.00
				05IM	Image, Custom Designed	$40.00	2	$80.00
						Invoice Total		$1,880.00
						$400.00	1	$400.00
						Invoice Total		$400.00
						$400.00	1	$400.00
						$200.00	3	$600.00
						Invoice Total		$1,000.00
						$300.00	1	$300.00
						Invoice Total		$300.00
						Grand Total		$3,580.00

Page 1 of 1

Winchester Web Design
Invoices

Invoice Num	1	Invoice Date	12/15/2013
Customer ID	SmithW	Employee ID	JFW
Last Name	Smith	EmployeeLast Name	Winchester
First Name	William	Employee First Name	Jay
Street Address	879 Fifteenth Ave		
City	Bradenton		
State	FL ZIP 34210		
Telephone	(941) 555-0793		
Email	SmithBilly@email.com		

Product ID	Description	Price	Quantity	Line Total
01HP	Home Page, Nav, CSS, Design	$400.00	4	$1,600.00
02SP	Secondary Page	$200.00	1	$200.00

The Winchester Web Design database will contain tables from which forms, reports, and queries will be created.

Designing a Relational Database

Video Library http://labyrinthelab.com/videos Video Number: AC13-V0201

Early database programs stored data in one large, flat file similar to a spreadsheet. If a company sold merchandise and the same product was sold many times, these databases required a person to enter and store the same product description and product price for each transaction. Such repetitive data entry is time consuming and requires voluminous storage space.

Flat files also increase the chance of typos and are prone to inconsistent data. For example, just think of how many ways one might enter William into various tables: Will, Bill, Willy, Billy, or William. If you searched for all sales records for *William Smith*, you probably would not find the listing for *Bill Smith*.

Invoice

InvNum	InvDate	EmpID	CustID	First Name	Last Name	ProdID	ProdDescription	Qty	Price	InvTotal
1	12/15/2013	JMM	SmithW	William	Smith	HP	Home Page	1	$400.00	$400.00
1	12/15/2013	JFW	SmithW	William	Smith	SC	Shopping Cart	2	$400.00	$800.00
1	12/15/2013	JFW	SmithW	William	Smith	BL	Blog	1	$300.00	$300.00
2	1/7/2014	MJW	SantosE	Emily	Santos	HP	Home Page	1	$400.00	$400.00

Flat file databases repeat data for each record. *Smith* is physically entered and stored three times in this table; the description and price are manually entered for each record.

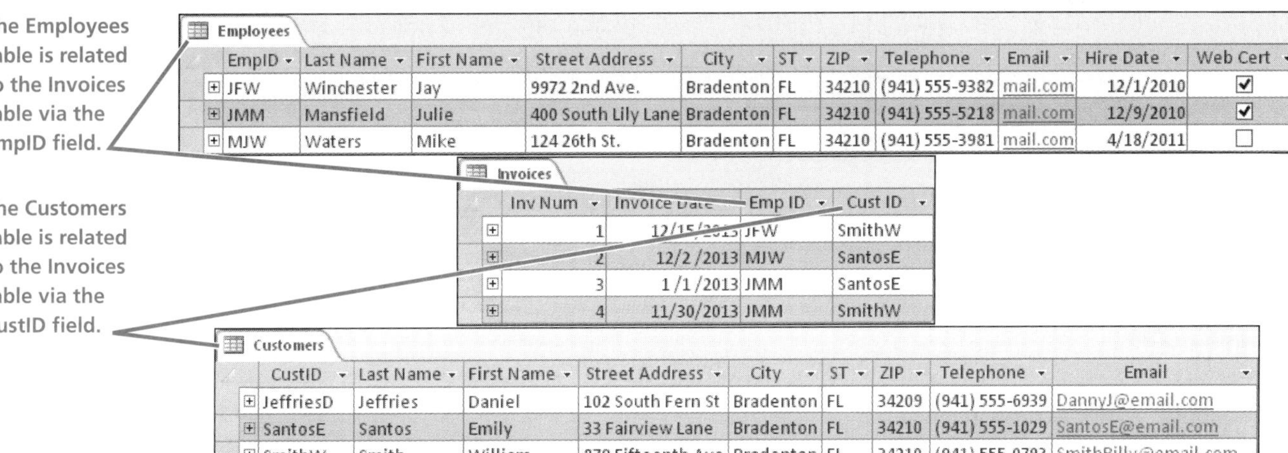

Employees

EmpID	Last Name	First Name	Street Address	City	ST	ZIP	Telephone	Email	Hire Date	Web Cert
JFW	Winchester	Jay	9972 2nd Ave.	Bradenton	FL	34210	(941) 555-9382	mail.com	12/1/2010	☑
JMM	Mansfield	Julie	400 South Lily Lane	Bradenton	FL	34210	(941) 555-5218	mail.com	12/9/2010	☑
MJW	Waters	Mike	124 26th St.	Bradenton	FL	34210	(941) 555-3981	mail.com	4/18/2011	☐

Invoices

Inv Num	Invoice Date	Emp ID	Cust ID
1	12/15/2013	JFW	SmithW
2	12/2/2013	MJW	SantosE
3	1/1/2013	JMM	SantosE
4	11/30/2013	JMM	SmithW

Customers

CustID	Last Name	First Name	Street Address	City	ST	ZIP	Telephone	Email
JeffriesD	Jeffries	Daniel	102 South Fern St	Bradenton	FL	34209	(941) 555-6939	DannyJ@email.com
SantosE	Santos	Emily	33 Fairview Lane	Bradenton	FL	34210	(941) 555-1029	SantosE@email.com
SmithW	Smith	William	879 Fifteenth Ave	Bradenton	FL	34210	(941) 555-0793	SmithBilly@email.com

Well-designed relational databases separate data into linked tables to reduce storage space, data repetition, and potential errors.

What Is a Relational Database?

A relational database contains two or more tables that are linked (related) to each other by unique and identifying key fields, such as ProductID or Invoice Number. For instance, if you are adding a record to the Invoice table, you could select the ProductID from the linked Products table and also display the product description and product price. The product information is only stored once in the Products table, but it is available to all the tables, queries, forms, and reports that are linked in the database.

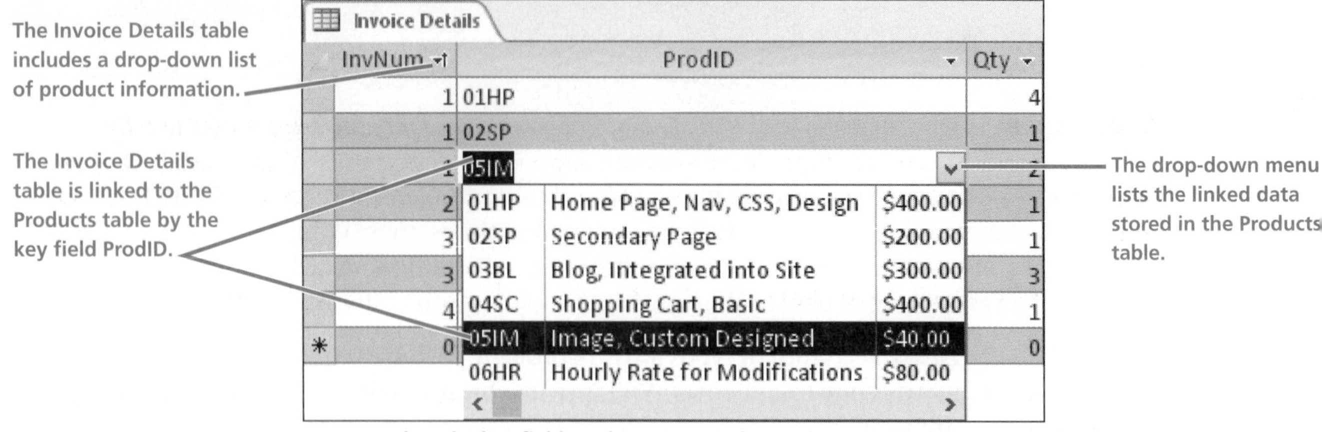

You can select the key field ProdID to access the Product Description and Product Price from the Products table, without storing those two fields in the Invoice Details table.

Gathering Data

Before you create a database, you must analyze the needs of the business and the requirements of the database. You will need sample copies of employee records, customer records, product or service records, and any other pertinent documents or forms. You will need copies of every existing report, ranging from individual invoices to yearly sales summaries. You will also need a sketch, or mockup, of the complete layout for any new forms and reports that the business desires to add.

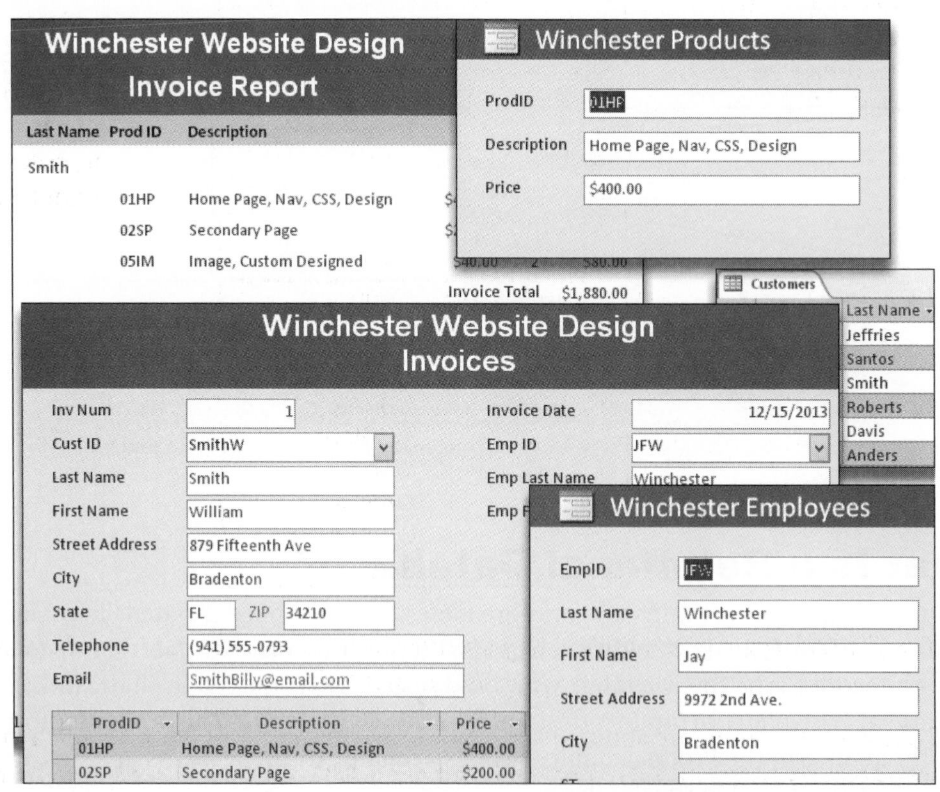

Samples of forms and reports collected at the start of a project. There may be handwritten forms as well.

This data gathering process must take place before you begin to design the objects in a database

DEVELOP YOUR SKILLS AC02-D01

Collect Information for a New Database

In this exercise, you will use Microsoft Excel to create a list of the reports and forms needed to fully analyze the needs of your database. Of course, as a student, you will not have real documents; this is a brainstorming exercise. With this in mind, you will create a worksheet that represents the typical design process.

1. Start **Microsoft Excel 2013** and click **Blank workbook** in the Backstage view.
   If you do not have Excel 2013, you can use an older version of Excel.
2. Follow these steps to create a list of Winchester Web Design reports, records, forms, and relevant documents:

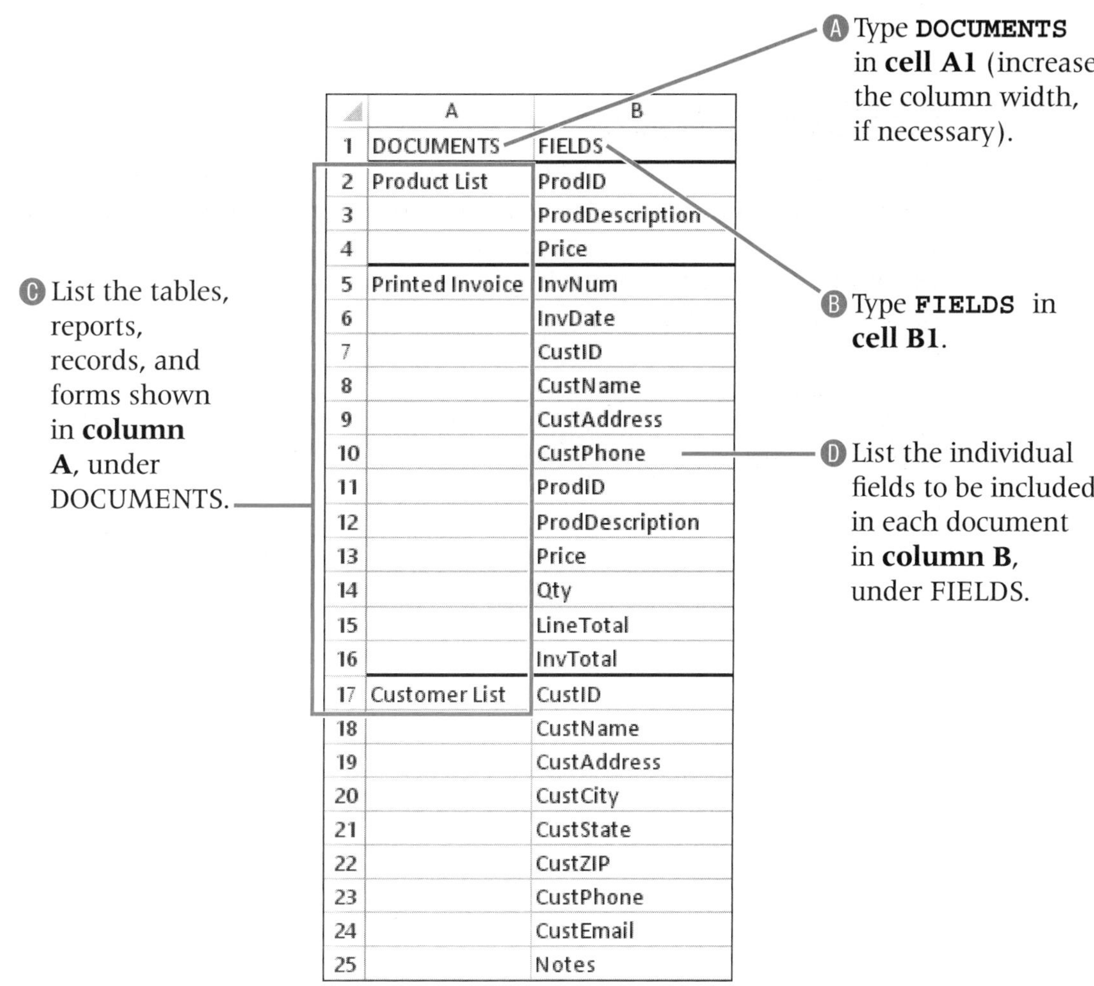

A Type DOCUMENTS in cell A1 (increase the column width, if necessary).
B Type FIELDS in cell B1.
C List the tables, reports, records, and forms shown in column A, under DOCUMENTS.
D List the individual fields to be included in each document in column B, under FIELDS.

	A	B
1	DOCUMENTS	FIELDS
2	Product List	ProdID
3		ProdDescription
4		Price
5	Printed Invoice	InvNum
6		InvDate
7		CustID
8		CustName
9		CustAddress
10		CustPhone
11		ProdID
12		ProdDescription
13		Price
14		Qty
15		LineTotal
16		InvTotal
17	Customer List	CustID
18		CustName
19		CustAddress
20		CustCity
21		CustState
22		CustZIP
23		CustPhone
24		CustEmail
25		Notes

This figure shows only part of the data gathering process. Some fields may be included on more than one document, such as ProdID, ProdDescription, and Price.

3. Following the template above, after the last field in the Customer List, add a table named **Employees** that contains **Name** and **Address**, **Telephone**, **Email**, and **Hire Date** fields, and a **Yes/No Web Certification** field.

4. Click **Save** , navigate to your **AC2013 Lesson 02** folder, and save the workbook as **`AC02-D01-WinWebDesign-[FirstInitialLastName]`**.

   Replace the bracketed text with your first initial and last name. For example, if your name is Bethany Smith, your filename would look like this: AC02-D01-WinWebDesign-BSmith.

5. Keep the workbook open for the next exercise.

   Unless directed otherwise, always keep your working file open at the end of each exercise.

Importance of Good Database Design

Video Library http://labyrinthelab.com/videos Video Number: AC13-V0202

There are a few basic principles to guide you through the database design process. Follow the steps outlined here to create a database that will perform efficiently.

PRINCIPLES FOR GOOD DATABASE DESIGN	
Objective	**Description**
Separate Tables	Organize and separate data fields into tables with specific subjects (e.g., person, place, or product) so you can easily locate records and reduce redundant data and inconsistencies. Example: A small business may have an Employees table, a Products table, and an Invoices table.
Assign Keys	Set a unique key field for each main table to link to data in other tables. This is done so data are only entered and stored one time, saving time and disk space, and reducing data entry errors. Example: If the ProductID key field is entered into the Invoices table, the ProductDescription and ProductPrice can be linked from the Products table and displayed in an invoice.
Atomize Fields	Break fields into the smallest single values, called atomization. Example: Instead of a Name field that contains the value of Jay Winchester, create two fields—FirstName (Jay) and LastName (Winchester). This allows you to sort/search by LastName and, if desired, print a report without including FirstName.

Normalizing Databases

Video Library http://labyrinthelab.com/videos Video Number: AC13-V0203

Organizing tables and fields into their smallest distinct parts, and then efficiently linking the data together through the relationships of key fields, is called normalization. Normalization eliminates data duplication, decreases data entry errors and inconsistencies, reduces file size, and streamlines the search for necessary information.

As you add table fields, be aware that Access has reserved words, which have special meanings and cannot be used as field names. Examples of reserved words are *Name* and *Date*. If you need to use such fields, name them FirstName, LastName and BirthDate or HireDate, which are more descriptive.

When assigning field names, it is common practice to avoid using spaces, which you have no doubt noticed already. This is especially helpful when performing calculations on a field. For instance, a field named Hours Worked, almost looks like two fields (one named Hours and one named Worked). Consequently, most professionals would use the field name HoursWorked or Hours_Worked. Space can be easily added for readability when designing your forms and reports.

As you work through the activities in this lesson, you will begin to shape the relationships among database objects toward normalization.

DEVELOP YOUR SKILLS AC02-D02

Separate Data into Tables and Assign Key Fields

In this exercise, you will divide your gathered document data into tables, each of which describes a single category. You will break down each field into its smallest components, then name each field and assign them to the most appropriate table. Finally, you will add a unique identifying key field to each table.

1. In the **WinWebDesign** workbook, click the **New Sheet** button.
2. Follow these steps to create a list of database tables and the fields that each table will contain:

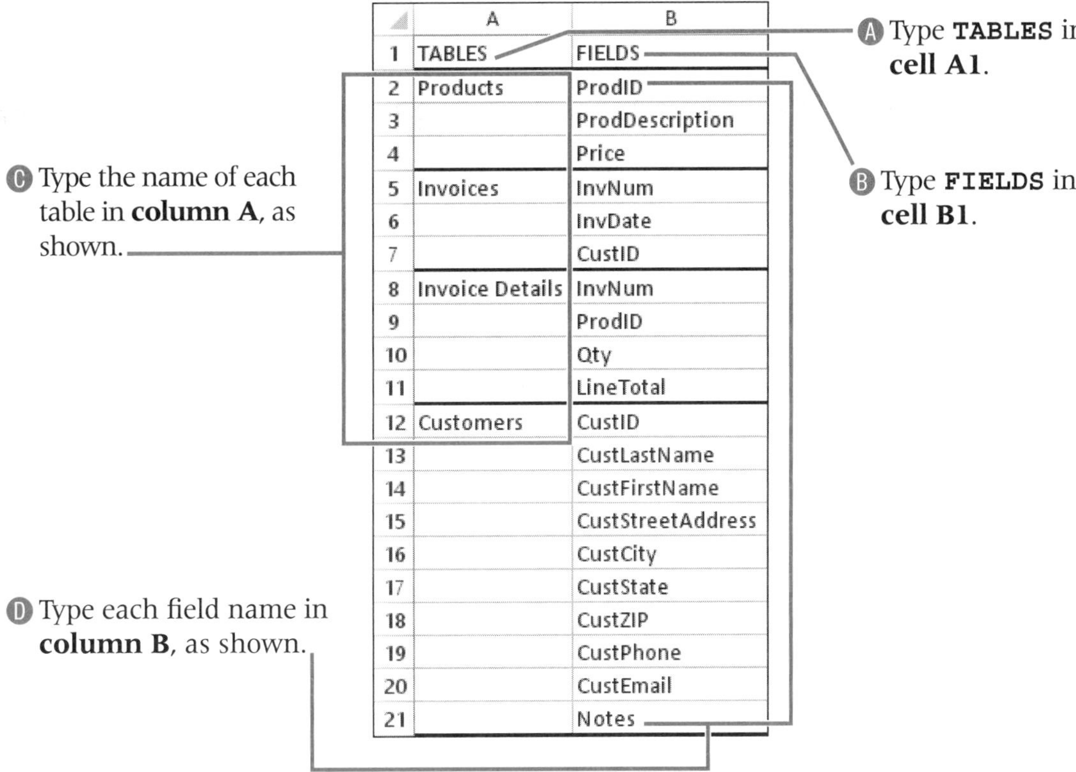

This figure shows only part of the normalization and data assigning process. With the exception of key ID fields, no field is listed more than once.

Access 2013

3. Enter the following fields for the **Employees** table:

- EmpID
- EmpLastName
- EmpFirstName
- EmpAddr
- EmpCity
- EmpST
- EmpZIP
- EmpPhone
- EmpEmail
- EmpHireDate
- EmpWebCert

4. **Save** the workbook.

Planning Related Tables

Video Library http://labyrinthelab.com/videos Video Number: AC13-V0204

In most cases, determining the tables required for a database and identifying the data or fields each table should contain is relatively simple. After analyzing the business reports and forms fo Winchester Web Design, you have determined that you will need an Employees table and a Customers table, in addition to a Products and an Invoices table. You have also identified which fields are required for each table. At this point you should examine each table and confirm that any unassociated data has been moved into a different but appropriate table.

Now you will link the tables with key ID fields so you don't have to enter the same names and products over and over. By establishing relationships between database tables, you prevent repeated data and redundant fields (except those key identifying fields that establish relationships between tables).

Linking Tables with Primary and Foreign Keys

Almost every database table should have a primary key field with a unique ID that will not be the same for any two database records. Your social security number and a student ID are examples of unique primary keys.

Primary Keys

Not everyone has a spouse or an email address, so some fields may remain null or empty. However, if a table contains a primary key, then a value must be entered for that key field every time a new record is added. Without a value, that record cannot be linked to any other table in the database. All taxpayers have a social security number; all students have a student ID.

Each time you create a new table in Datasheet View, Access automatically creates an ID field an marks it as the primary key field. When you manually create a table in Design View and do not assign a primary key field, Access asks if you want to create one before you save the table. By default, this primary key is the first field listed in a table and is assigned the AutoNumber data type. AutoNumber values start at 1 and are automatically increased by 1 for each subsequent record. You can also rename this field, change its data type, remove the primary key designation from the field, or assign the key to another field. The primary key field must contain data; the field cannot be empty.

Foreign Keys

As you review your Excel workbook, notice that most key fields (ProdID, EmpID, and CustID) are used in more than one table. In the Customers table, the CustID field is its unique primary key. However, individual customers will also need to be displayed in the Invoice table to show their purchases. A foreign key is a field in a secondary table that corresponds and links to the primary key field in the main table, where the specific information for a particular item is stored. The foreign key must be the same data type as the primary key, except in the case of AutoNumber. If the primary key is set to AutoNumber then the foreign key should be set to a Number data type with its Field Size property set to Long Integer.

Here, the CustID field in the Invoices table is a foreign key that links to the primary key in the Customers table to obtain the customer name, address, and customer contact information stored in the main table.

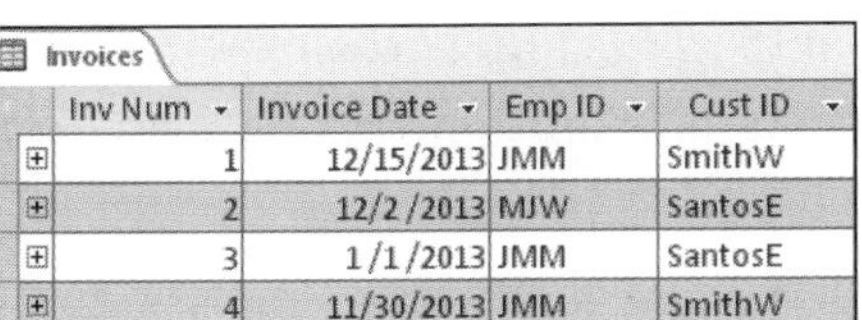

Invoices

Inv Num	Invoice Date	Emp ID	Cust ID
1	12/15/2013	JMM	SmithW
2	12/2/2013	MJW	SantosE
3	1/1/2013	JMM	SantosE
4	11/30/2013	JMM	SmithW

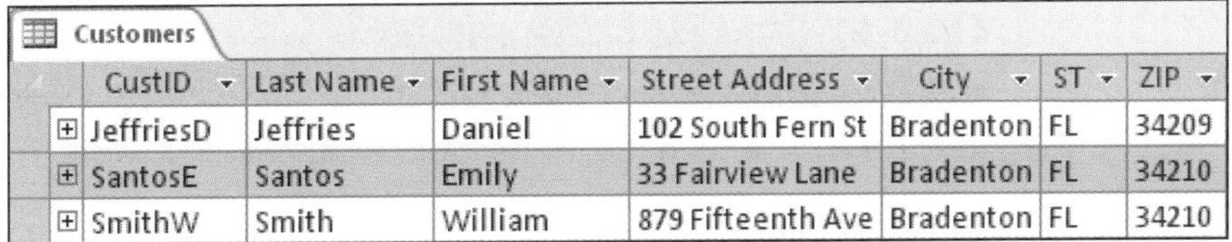

Customers

CustID	Last Name	First Name	Street Address	City	ST	ZIP
JeffriesD	Jeffries	Daniel	102 South Fern St	Bradenton	FL	34209
SantosE	Santos	Emily	33 Fairview Lane	Bradenton	FL	34210
SmithW	Smith	William	879 Fifteenth Ave	Bradenton	FL	34210

If the primary key is a number, then the foreign key must also be a number; if the primary key is text, then the foreign key must also be text.

DEVELOP YOUR SKILLS AC02-D03

Assign Key Types to Key Fields

In this exercise, you will assign primary and foreign keys in the Winchester Web Design workbook.

1. Follow these steps to label the keys as primary or foreign:

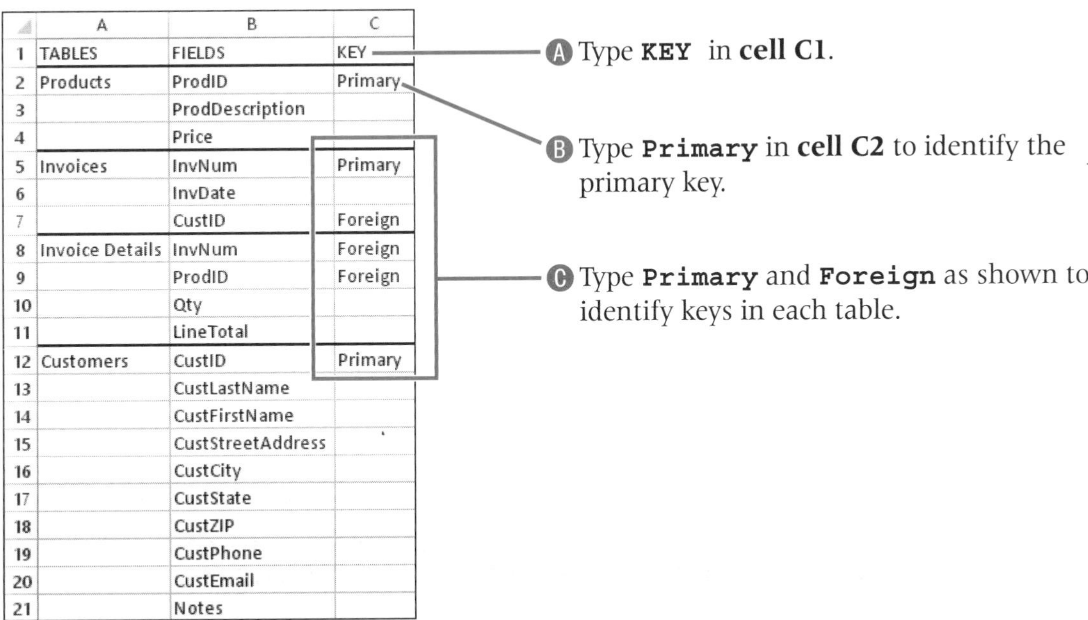

	A	B	C
1	TABLES	FIELDS	KEY
2	Products	ProdID	Primary
3		ProdDescription	
4		Price	
5	Invoices	InvNum	Primary
6		InvDate	
7		CustID	Foreign
8	Invoice Details	InvNum	Foreign
9		ProdID	Foreign
10		Qty	
11		LineTotal	
12	Customers	CustID	Primary
13		CustLastName	
14		CustFirstName	
15		CustStreetAddress	
16		CustCity	
17		CustState	
18		CustZIP	
19		CustPhone	
20		CustEmail	
21		Notes	

A Type KEY in cell C1.
B Type Primary in cell C2 to identify the primary key.
C Type Primary and Foreign as shown to identify keys in each table.

Access 2013

2. Assign the primary key designation to the **EmpID** field in the **Employees** table.
3. **Save** the workbook.

Identifying Relationship Types

Video Library http://labyrinthelab.com/videos Video Number: AC13-V0205

Individuals and teams within organizations establish relationships to effectively interact and cooperate with other teams. The same is true of tables within an Access database—relationships must exist. Relationships in databases connect data in one table to data stored in other tables. Access supports three different types of relationships:

- One-to-one
- One-to-many
- Many-to-many

One-to-One Relationships

A one-to-one relationship means that each record in Table A can have only one matching record in Table B, and each record in Table B can have only one matching record in Table A. This is the least frequently used relationship. A one-to-one relationship requires both of the related fields to be primary keys. This relationship is generally used for storing information that applies only to one small portion of the main table, such as to isolate part of the table for security purposes. A good example of this is a main Customers table linked to a CustPassword table.

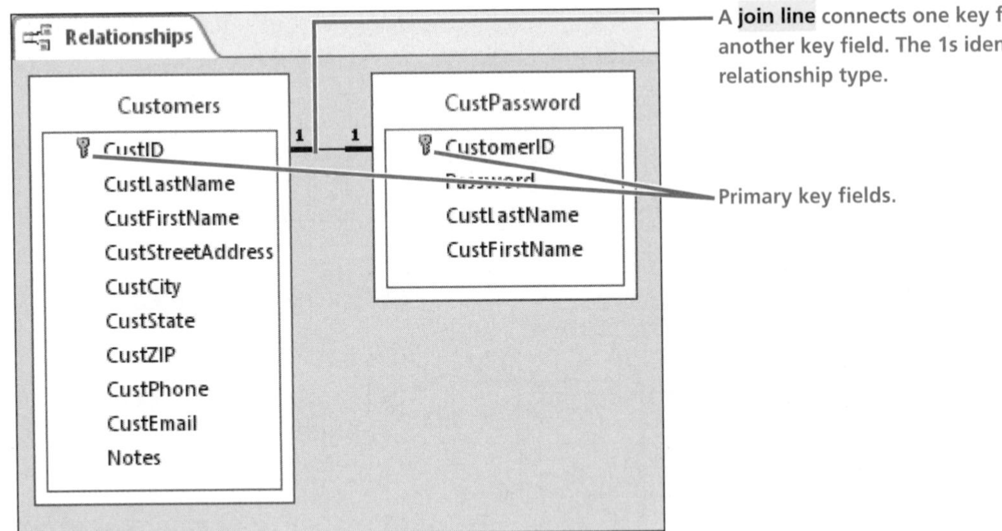

In this one-to-one relationship, each employee customer is only linked to one password.

One-to-Many Relationships

A one-to-many relationship means that each record in Table A can have multiple matching records in Table B, but a record in Table B can have only one matching record in Table A. For instance, one employee will have many sales, and a product will be sold many times. This is the most common type of relationship.

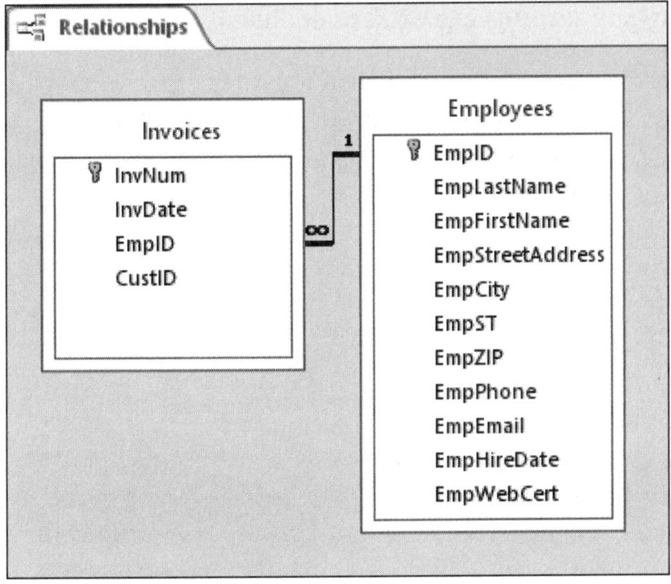

One employee may have many sales or invoices. The 1 on the join line for EmpID indicates *one* employee; the infinity (∞) symbol indicates *many* sales.

Many-to-Many Relationships

A many-to-many relationship occurs when two tables each have many matching records in the other table, but they do not share key fields, so they use a third *junction table* to tie other tables and complete the relationship. The junction table generally has a one-to-many relationship to each table. An example is a vendors table and a products table, where one vendor provides many different products and one product is available from many vendors.

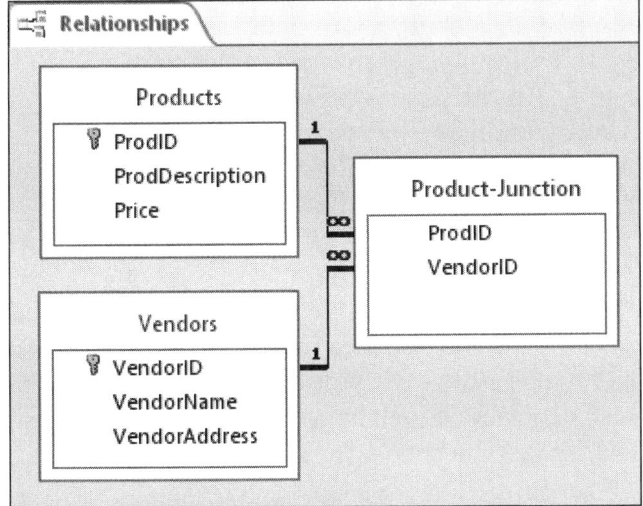

In this many-to-many relationship, items in the Products and Vendors tables each have a one-to-many relationship with the Product-Junction table. As a result, the business could buy the same products from multiple suppliers.

Access 2013

Developing an Entity Relationship Diagram

An Entity Relationship Diagram (ERD) helps to model and display relationships between entities, specifically the relationship between tables and fields, as established by key fields. There are a variety of tools that can be used to develop this diagram, ranging from Microsoft's Visio to the open source and free MySQLTM Workbench. And there are different techniques that may be used to display this relationship diagram. Microsoft Access's Relationships tool provides an excellent way to both set and view these relationships.

FROM THE RIBBON

Database Tools→ Relationships

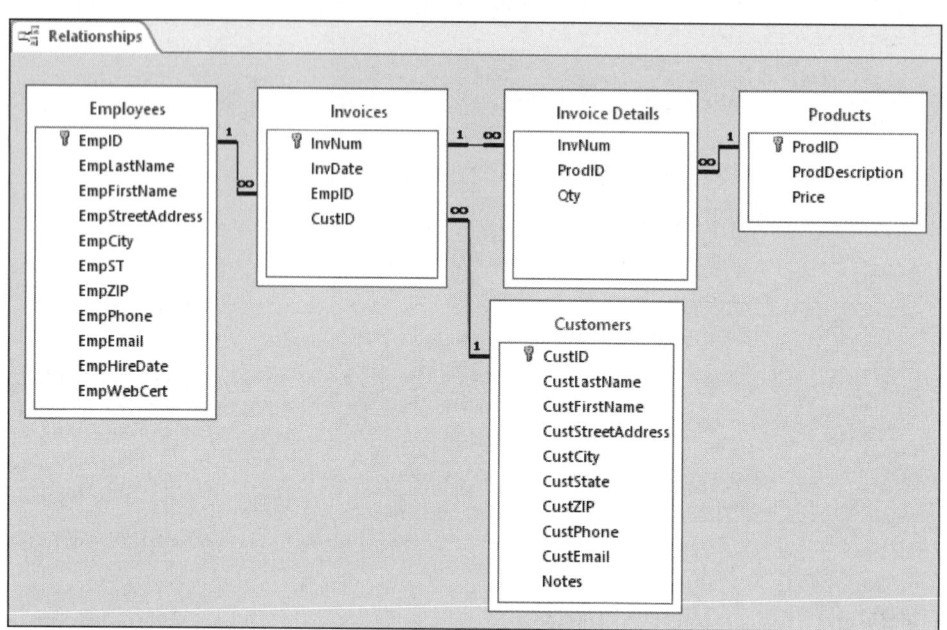

A relationship diagram generated by Microsoft Access displays each table, each field, and how the tables are linked by their key fields.

Defining Data Types

Video Library http://labyrinthelab.com/videos Video Number: AC13-V0206

If you have ever filled out an online form, you might have seen instant formatting of some fields. When typing in currency values, the dollar sign and decimal point may appear automatically, and when entering a date, the slashes between month, day, and year spontaneously appear. This can be accomplished by assigning a data type to the field. A data type sets the characteristics of a particular field, identifying the type of values it may hold, such as alphanumeric text, or numbers, or dates, yes/no values, or even a hyperlink.

Identifying Field Data Types

You have identified and named your fields and assigned them to a table. You also made sure you did not assign any field to more than one table—with the exception of a foreign key. Now you will assign each field a data type. As you define each field in a new table datasheet, Access displays a drop-down list from which you can choose the type of data you plan to enter in the field.

By defining the type of data each field will contain, you can reduce both the time and the amount of formatting you must apply as you enter the data. Defining a data type also reduces the potential for errors. For example, if you set a field's data type to a number, a user will not be able to enter values such as the letter l for the number 1 (one) or the letter O for the number 0 (zero). Defining data types can also decrease the storage space needed. A description of data types available in Access 2013 databases is shown in the following table.

ACCESS DATA TYPES

Data Type	Description
Short Text	Default data type that contains up to 255 characters (any combination of alphabetic and numeric characters, such as names, addresses, and phone numbers); text fields may contain numbers but are not used in calculations
Long Text	Text entries that contain between 1 and 63,999 characters
Number	Numeric data to be used in mathematical calculations
Date & Time	Fields that hold date and time values
Currency	Numeric values representing dollars and cents or fields in which you want to prevent rounding off during calculations
AutoNumber	A field for which Access automatically assigns a unique identifying number to records as they are added to a table; cannot be modified; cannot be reused in a table, so deleted records result in gaps
Yes/No	Single-character entries in a Yes/No checkbox format used to enter data that can be only one of two possible values (true/false, yes/no, or on/off) Use the Yes/No data type for a checkbox that indicates whether an employee has web certification or a college degree
OLE Object	Embedded or linked objects (e.g., Excel spreadsheets, Word documents, images, audio, video, etc.) with a storage limit of 1 gigabyte
Hyperlink	Links to web pages or other files when clicked
Attachment	Data type that identifies a file, such as a document or an image, that will be included in the database as an attachment
Calculated	Field created by doing math on values in other fields within the table
Lookup Wizard	Field that displays a drop-down list of values from another table or from a list of values you type; a common lookup field is a drop-down list of State abbreviations

DEVELOP YOUR SKILLS AC02-D04

Define Data Types

In this exercise, you will assign data types and sizes to the fields in your Winchester Web Design workbook.

1. In your workbook, enter the data type of each field in **column D** as shown. Then, specify field sizes in **column E** (on the right).

	A	B	C	D	E
1	TABLES	FIELDS	KEY	DATA TYPE	SIZE
2	Products	ProdID	Primary	Short Text	4
3		ProdDescription		Short Text	25
4		Price		Currency	10
5	Invoices	InvNum	Primary	AutoNumber	6
6		InvDate		Date	8
7		CustID	Foreign	Lookup>Customers	15
8	Invoice Details	InvNum	Foreign	Integer	6
9		ProdID	Foreign	Lookup>Products	4
10		Qty		Decimal	auto
11		LineTotal		Calculated (Price*Qty)	10
12	Customers	CustID	Primary	Short Text	15
13		CustLastName		Short Text	25
14		CustFirstName		Short Text	25
15		CustStreetAddress		Short Text	25
16		CustCity		Short Text	25
17		CustState		Lookup>States	2
18		CustZIP		Short Text	5
19		CustPhone		Short Text	15
20		CustEmail		Hyperlink	40
21		Notes		Long Text	

The Notes field is a Long Text memo/comment field and has no entered size limit.

2. Assign the **Short Text** data type to these fields in the **Employees** table: EmpID, EmpLastName, EmpFirstName, EmpAddr, EmpCity, EmpST, EmpZIP, and EmpPhone.
3. Assign the **Hyperlink** data type to EmpEmail.
4. Assign the **Date & Time** data type to EmpHireDate.
5. Assign the **Yes/No** data type to EmpWebCert.

When in Datasheet View, tap [Spacebar] to check or uncheck a checkbox.

6. Assign the same field sizes you assigned to similar fields in the Customers table.
7. Save the workbook.

Creating Access Tables in a New Database

Video Library http://labyrinthelab.com/videos Video Number: AC13-V0207

Now that you have analyzed the needs of your new database and designed the structure for the tables, fields, and primary keys, you are now ready to create your database in Microsoft Access.

Creating a New Database

An Access database serves as a container that holds all the tools, data, and various database objects that help users enter and organize data and obtain meaningful information from that data. As a result, you must name and save the database when you create it. After you create a new database, Access automatically creates and opens an empty table, named Table1, in Datasheet View. When a table is created in Datasheet View, the first field, by default, is the AutoNumber data type.

DEVELOP YOUR SKILLS AC02-D05

Create a New Table in Datasheet View

In this exercise, you will create a new blank database and add an Invoices table in Datasheet View.

1. Start **Access 2013**.
2. Follow these steps to create and name the new database:

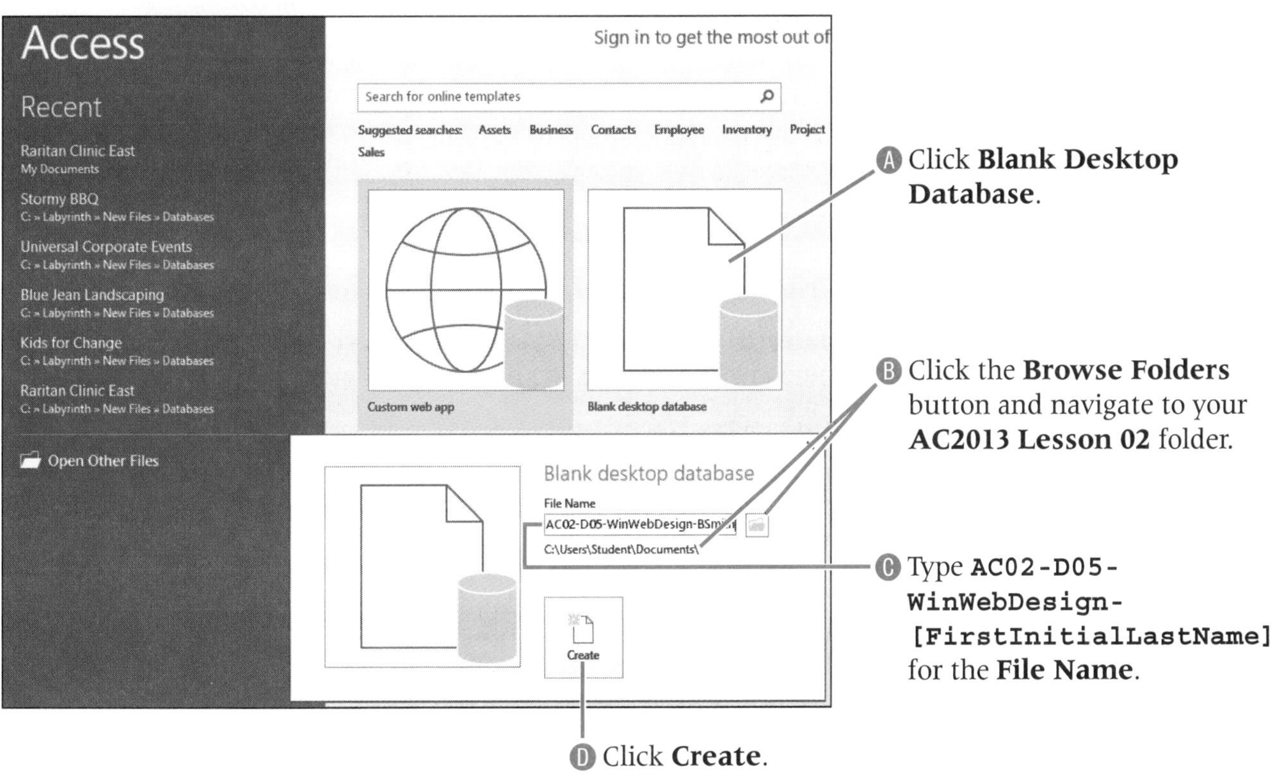

In step c, remember to replace the bracketed text with your first initial and last name.

Access creates the new database, shows the database name in the application title bar, and creates a new table named Table1 in the Access window.

3. Follow these steps to add field names and set data type:

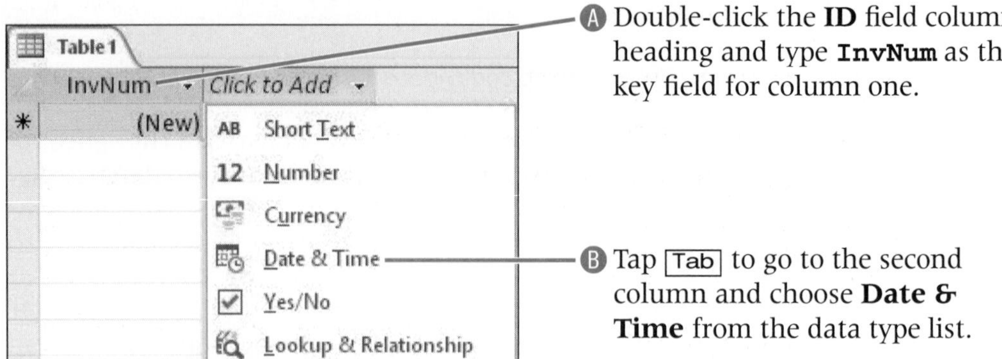

Table1
InvNum
Click to Add
(New)
AB Short Text
12 Number
Currency
Date & Time
Yes/No
Lookup & Relationship
A Double-click the **ID** field column heading and type **InvNum** as the key field for column one.
B Tap [Tab] to go to the second column and choose **Date & Time** from the data type list.

Once the data type is selected, the heading Click to Add a new field is automatically named Field1.

4. Type **InvDate** as the new name for **Field1** in the second column and tap [Tab] to complete the name and move to a new field in the third column.
5. Choose the data type **Short Text** for the third field and change the field name to **EmpID**.
6. Tap [Tab], choose **Short Text** for the fourth field and change the field name to **CustID**.
   Full field names/column headings may not appear if the columns are narrower than the field name. Drag the right edge of the column heading to adjust column size.
7. Follow these steps to enter data in your new table:

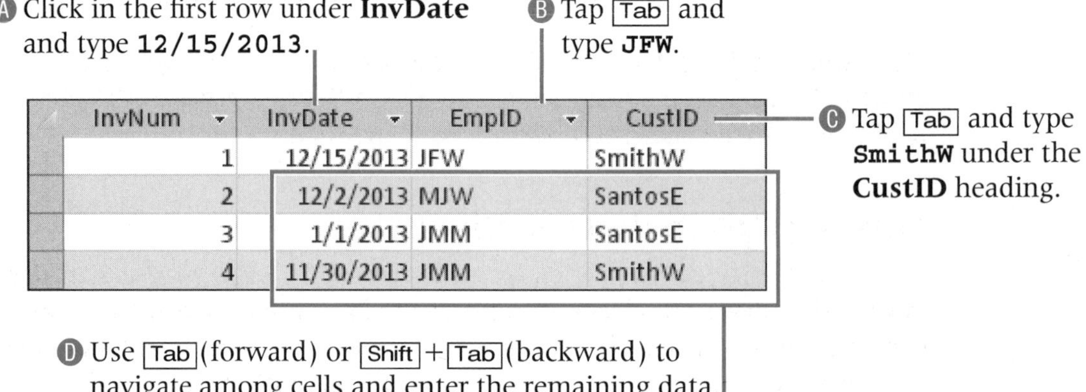

A Click in the first row under **InvDate** and type **12/15/2013**.
B Tap [Tab] and type **JFW**.
InvNum
InvDate
EmpID
CustID
1
12/15/2013
JFW
SmithW
2
12/2/2013
MJW
SantosE
3
1/1/2013
JMM
SantosE
4
11/30/2013
JMM
SmithW
C Tap [Tab] and type **SmithW** under the **CustID** heading.
D Use [Tab] (forward) or [Shift]+[Tab] (backward) to navigate among cells and enter the remaining data.

NOTE

When you create a table in Datasheet View, Access sets the first field as the Primary Key with an AutoNumber data type. Because InvNum uses the AutoNumber data type, Access fills in consecutive numbers automatically.

8. Follow these steps to save the table using a new table name:

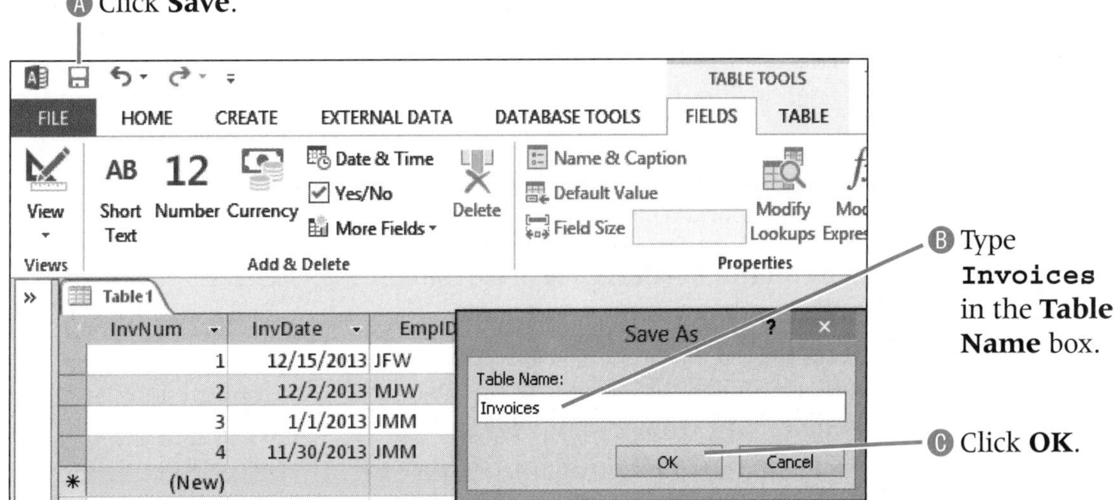

The name in the object tab changes from **Table1** *to* **Invoices**.

9. Click **Close** [×] to close the table. Leave the database open.

Creating Tables in Design View

Video Library http://labyrinthelab.com/videos Video Number: AC13-V0208

Many people believe that it's easier to create a new table in Design View because it offers a straightforward layout and provides intuitive options for entering field descriptions, setting field properties, and easily setting or removing primary keys.

Entering Optional Descriptions

In Design View, descriptions may be added to each field in a table to help identify special information about a field. For example, in the Customers table, the customer ID consists of the customer last name plus the customer first initial. So you might enter the following description for the CustID field: ID = Last name and customer first initial.

Setting Field Properties

Once you assign a data type, you can modify the field's properties further. As you define each field in a database table, Access sets properties for the field that control the number of characters the field can contain as well as the format of the data and the type of characters that are valid for the field. You can accept Access default properties or modify the properties. Properties available depend on the data type selected for the field.

Requiring Data in Key Fields

The field identified as the primary key field must contain data—it cannot be empty. When Access creates the primary key field, by default it sets the key field to automatically number the records. This ensures that each record has a unique number. Businesses often create their own coding system to identify customers and accounts, and use this identifying code for the key field.

If a column in the table is too long or too short for the data it contains, you can adjust its width. Access provides some useful tools for changing column width.

- **Drag a column border:** Dragging a column border enables you to make the column on the left of the border wider or narrower.
- **Double-click a column heading border:** Double-clicking the right border of a column changes the width of the column on the left to fit the longest data entry in the column or column heading, whichever is wider.
- **Right-click a field heading and choose Field Width:** Selecting the Field Width command in the context menu opens the Column Width dialog box so you can type the desired column width, reset the standard column width, or select Best Fit to automatically size the field width to the longest entry.

DEVELOP YOUR SKILLS AC02-D06

Create a New Table in Design View

In this exercise, you will create a new table using Table Design View. Then, you will adjust the width of the columns in the table.

1. Choose **Create→Table Design.**
   Access opens an empty table in Design View.
2. Follow these steps to create the first table field, which will be the primary key:

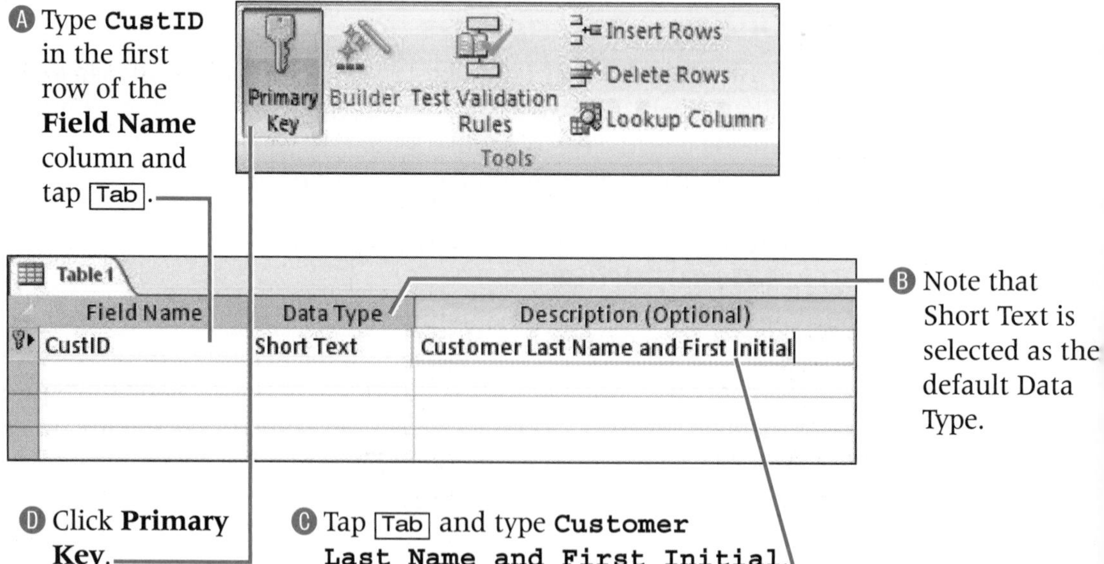

3. Tap Tab and repeat **step 2** to add the additional fields and field information shown here.

Table1

	Field Name	Data Type	Description (Optional)
🔑	CustID	Short Text	Customer Last Name and First Initial
	CustLastName	Short Text	
	CustFirstName	Short Text	
	CustStreetAddress	Short Text	
	CustCity	Short Text	
	CustState	Short Text	2 character state abbreviation
	CustZIP	Short Text	5 digit ZIP code
	CustPhone	Short Text	Area code and number
	CustEmail	Hyperlink	
	Notes	Long Text	Special comments

4. Click the CustLastName field and enter the values shown:

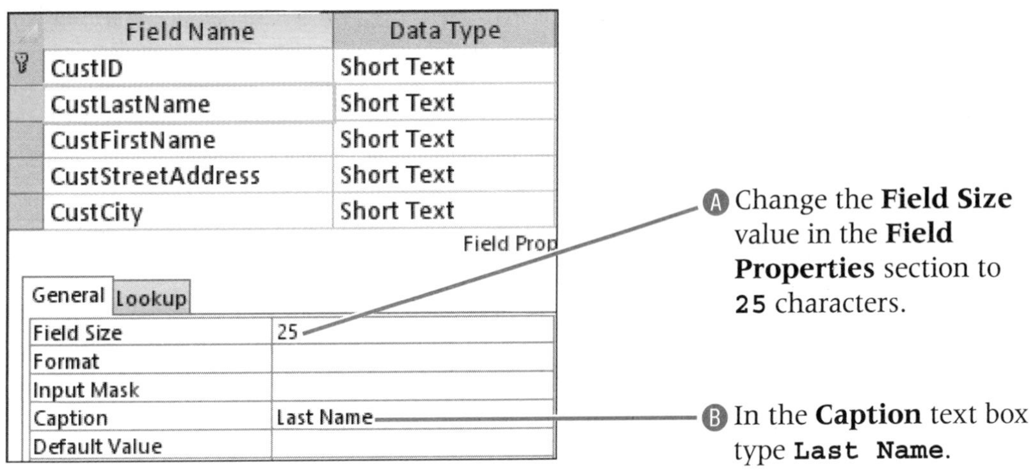

Ⓐ Change the **Field Size** value in the **Field Properties** section to **25** characters.

Ⓑ In the **Caption** text box type **Last Name**.

5. Repeat the procedure shown in **step 4** to change the caption properties of the following fields:

Field	Size	Caption
CustLastName	25	Last Name
CustFirstName	25	First Name
CustStreetAddress	25	Street Address
CustCity	15	City
CustState	2	ST
CustZIP	5	ZIP Code
CustPhone	15	Telephone
CustEmail		Email

6. **Save** the table as **Customers**.

If you forget to save, Access will prompt you to save when you close the table.

7. Click the **View** drop-down arrow and choose **Datasheet View**.
8. Enter these records:

Customers

CustID	Last Name	First Name	Street Address	City	ST	ZIP	Telephone	Email
AndersM	Anders	Mark	205 Montana St	Bradenton	FL	34211	(941) 555-2309	AndersM@email.com
DavisP	Davis	Peter	65 Terracotta Wa	Sarasota	FL	34228	(941) 555-1792	DavisAngie@email.com
JeffriesD	Jeffries	Daniel	102 South Fern St	Bradenton	FL	34209	(941) 555-6939	DannyJ@email.com

Notice that the street address for DavisP is slightly cut off (the "y" in "Way" is difficult to make out). You will adjust column width next.

Change the Column Width

9. Follow these steps to change the width of two columns:

Ⓐ Double-click the column header between **Street Address** and **City** to auto size it.

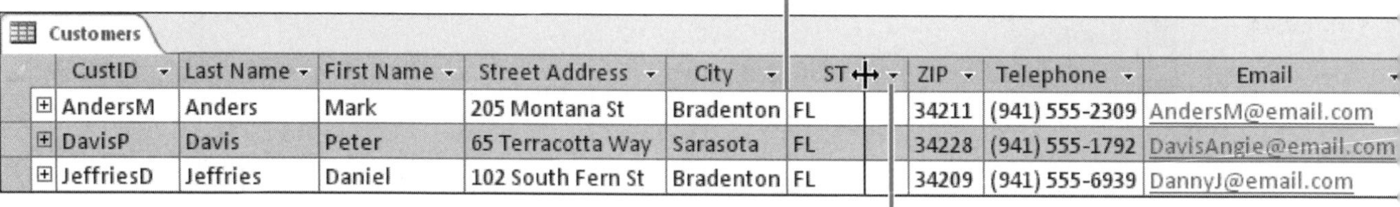

Customers

CustID	Last Name	First Name	Street Address	City	ST	ZIP	Telephone	Email
AndersM	Anders	Mark	205 Montana St	Bradenton	FL	34211	(941) 555-2309	AndersM@email.com
DavisP	Davis	Peter	65 Terracotta Way	Sarasota	FL	34228	(941) 555-1792	DavisAngie@email.com
JeffriesD	Jeffries	Daniel	102 South Fern St	Bradenton	FL	34209	(941) 555-6939	DannyJ@email.com

Ⓑ Click between the **ST** and **ZIP** header. The mouse pointer changes into a double-headed arrow. Drag the **ST** column header to the left to manually resize it.

10. Close the **Access** table and database. **Save** and close the **Excel** workbook.

Retrieving Data

Video Library http://labyrinthelab.com/videos Video Number: AC13-V0209

Whether you're processing an order, announcing statistics, or updating records, the primary purpose of any database is to be able to locate and retrieve data quickly and efficiently. Access provides three main tools and features for helping to locate and retrieve data.

- Sorting features
- Filtering tools
- Find and Replace commands

Sorting Records

Access automatically sorts records according to the primary key field identified when a table is created and fields are set up. You can also automatically sort tables by an AutoNumber as you enter records. The database sort feature enables you to rearrange table records based on data found in other table columns as well. Two main sort orders are available in Access.

- **Sort Ascending:** Arranges data in alphabetical order from A to Z, in numeric order from lowest to highest, or in chronological order from first to last.
- **Sort Descending:** Arranges data in reverse alphabetical order from Z to A, in numeric order from highest to lowest, or in reverse chronological order from last to first.

Sorting Records Using Tables and Forms

Regardless of whether you are working with a table or a form, the primary procedures for sorting records are the same.

Because the Winchester Web Design company is a small business with only a few employees, customers, and products, in the remainder of this lesson we will use the Raritan Clinic East database to get a better feel for the power of databases.

For the rest of this exercise, you will work with a Raritan Clinic East database.

DEVELOP YOUR SKILLS AC02-D07

Sort Records in a Table

In this exercise, you will sort records in the Raritan Clinic East database.

1. Open **AC02-D07-RCE** from the **AC2013 Lesson 02** folder and save it as **`AC02-D07-RCE-[FirstInitialLastName]`**.
2. Double-click the **Patients** table in the Navigation Pane to open it in Datasheet View.
3. Follow these steps to sort records alphabetically by last name:

Ⓑ Choose **Home→Sort & Filter→Ascending.**

Ⓐ Position the insertion point and click any record in the **Last Name** field.

Patient ID	Last Name	First Name	Street Address	City	ST	Zip	Phone	Doctor
0027	Ford	Barry	Persimmon Rd.	Tampa	FL	33213	(941) 555-0027	602
1416	Cook	Dale	Ash Lane	Tampa	FL	33599	(941) 555-1416	155
3565	Bush	Julie	Cypress Bend	Sarasota	FL	34032	(941) 555-3565	725
6136	Craft	Jason	Red Oak Lane	Sarasota	FL	34037	(941) 555-6136	223
6521	Bey	Mary	Camelia Row	Tampa	FL	33422	(619) 555-6521	710
7682	Brent	Barry	Fir Boulevard	Tampa	FL	33686	(619) 555-7682	114
8080	Cook	Ashlee	Asbury Lane	Sarasota	FL	34042	(619) 555-8080	209
8189	Hardy	Brenda	Oak Street	Tampa	FL	33120	(941) 555-8189	724
8617	Floyd	Marjorie	Pine Ave.	Tampa	FL	33188	(941) 555-8617	318
9728	Frost	Sheryl	Maple Street	Ruskin	FL	33574	(941) 555-9728	142
9982	Frost	Mary	Sassafrass Circle	Palmetto	FL	34332	(619) 555-9982	223

4. Follow these steps to set a descending sort order and then remove the sort:

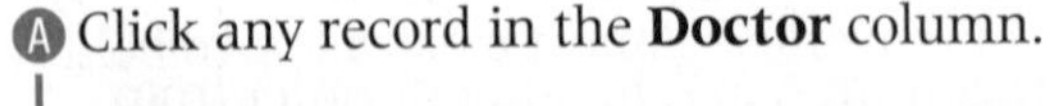

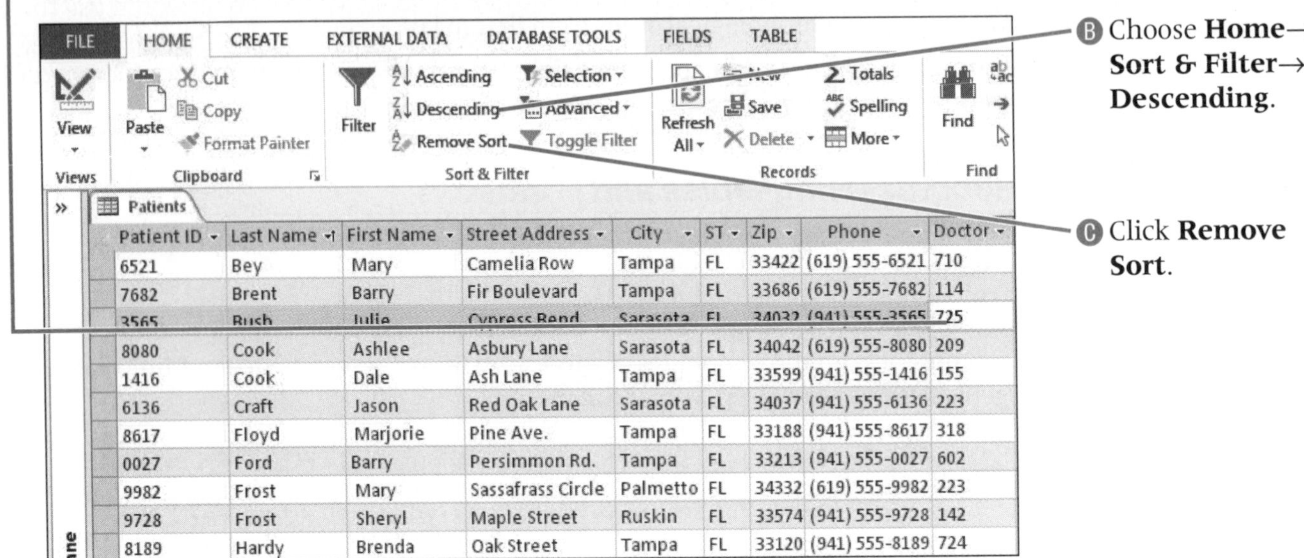

Records are rearranged in Patient ID order again—the default sort order.

Sorting Records Using Multiple Fields

Video Library http://labyrinthelab.com/videos Video Number: AC13-V0210

Data can be sorted in more than one table field at the same time. This can be useful, say, when more than one person in a family visits the same medical clinic. When this happens, selecting the first name field as a second sort field within a last name sort is appropriate. The last name field is the primary sort field and the first name field is the secondary sort field. The secondary sort field is only considered when multiple records contain the same data in the primary sort field.

How Multiple Column Sorts Work

Access sorts data in multiple fields from left to right. Consequently, the left column must be the one you want sorted first (primary sort field). Access then considers the second column (secondary sort field) only when it finds identical values in the primary sort field. You can perform more complex sorts on multiple fields using the Advanced Filter/Sort options, or sort multiple columns by rearranging them in the datasheet so that they appear side by side.

QUICK REFERENCE	SORTING RECORDS
Task	**Procedure**
Sort ascending	Click in the desired field and choose Home→Sort & Filter→Ascending.
Sort descending	Click in the desired field and choose Home→Sort & Filter→Descending.
Clear sorts	Choose Home→Sort & Filter→Remove Sort.
Sort in multiple fields	Arrange the desired fields with the primary field left of the secondary field then select both field column headings and click the desired sort button.

DEVELOP YOUR SKILLS AC02-D08

Sort Records Using Multiple Fields

In this exercise, you will sort data in a table based on the values found in two columns.

1. Follow these steps to sort table records based on the values in multiple fields:

Ⓐ Click the **Last Name** column heading and drag the mouse to select the **First Name** column heading. Notice the downward pointing arrow as you drag the mouse.

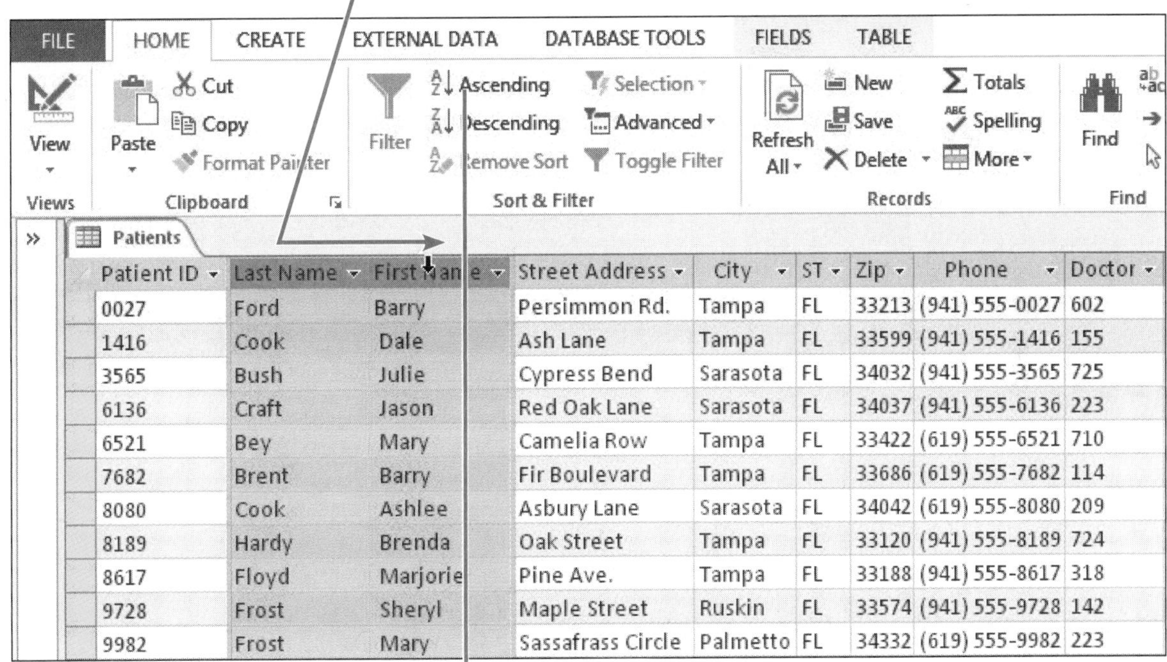

Patient ID	Last Name	First Name	Street Address	City	ST	Zip	Phone	Doctor
0027	Ford	Barry	Persimmon Rd.	Tampa	FL	33213	(941) 555-0027	602
1416	Cook	Dale	Ash Lane	Tampa	FL	33599	(941) 555-1416	155
3565	Bush	Julie	Cypress Bend	Sarasota	FL	34032	(941) 555-3565	725
6136	Craft	Jason	Red Oak Lane	Sarasota	FL	34037	(941) 555-6136	223
6521	Bey	Mary	Camelia Row	Tampa	FL	33422	(619) 555-6521	710
7682	Brent	Barry	Fir Boulevard	Tampa	FL	33686	(619) 555-7682	114
8080	Cook	Ashlee	Asbury Lane	Sarasota	FL	34042	(619) 555-8080	209
8189	Hardy	Brenda	Oak Street	Tampa	FL	33120	(941) 555-8189	724
8617	Floyd	Marjorie	Pine Ave.	Tampa	FL	33188	(941) 555-8617	318
9728	Frost	Sheryl	Maple Street	Ruskin	FL	33574	(941) 555-9728	142
9982	Frost	Mary	Sassafrass Circle	Palmetto	FL	34332	(619) 555-9982	223

Ⓑ Choose **Home→Sort & Filter→Ascending**.

Access 2013

2. Review the record sort results to see the effect of sorting on two columns.

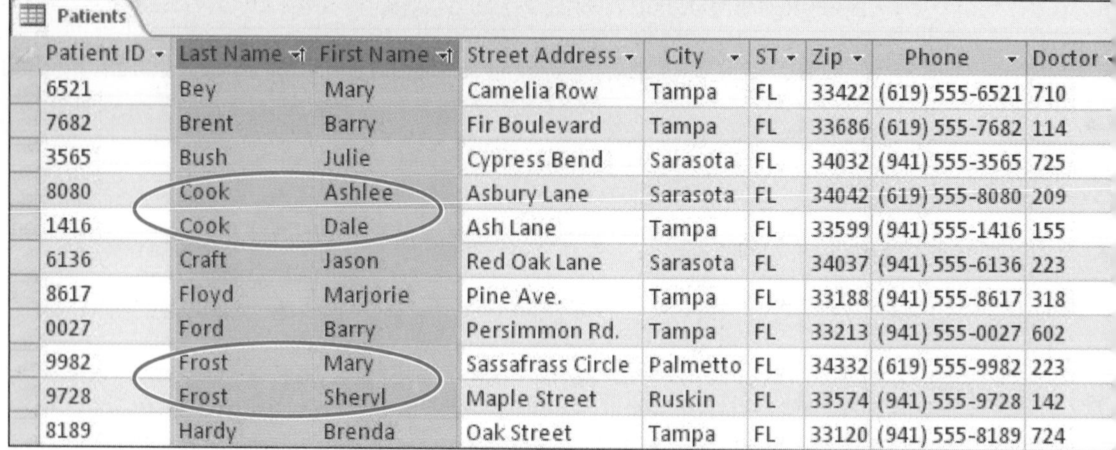

Patients

Patient ID	Last Name	First Name	Street Address	City	ST	Zip	Phone	Doctor
6521	Bey	Mary	Camelia Row	Tampa	FL	33422	(619) 555-6521	710
7682	Brent	Barry	Fir Boulevard	Tampa	FL	33686	(619) 555-7682	114
3565	Bush	Julie	Cypress Bend	Sarasota	FL	34032	(941) 555-3565	725
8080	Cook	Ashlee	Asbury Lane	Sarasota	FL	34042	(619) 555-8080	209
1416	Cook	Dale	Ash Lane	Tampa	FL	33599	(941) 555-1416	155
6136	Craft	Jason	Red Oak Lane	Sarasota	FL	34037	(941) 555-6136	223
8617	Floyd	Marjorie	Pine Ave.	Tampa	FL	33188	(941) 555-8617	318
0027	Ford	Barry	Persimmon Rd.	Tampa	FL	33213	(941) 555-0027	602
9982	Frost	Mary	Sassafrass Circle	Palmetto	FL	34332	(619) 555-9982	223
9728	Frost	Sheryl	Maple Street	Ruskin	FL	33574	(941) 555-9728	142
8189	Hardy	Brenda	Oak Street	Tampa	FL	33120	(941) 555-8189	724

There are two patients named Cook and two named Frost. The patients with the same last names are also sorted alphabetically by first name.

3. Choose **Home→Sort & Filter→Remove Sort**. Click any value in the **Street Address** column to deselect both name columns.

4. Follow these steps to sort on the same two columns and obtain different results:

Ⓐ Click the **First Name** column heading to select the column; then click and drag the column. left so that it appears to the left of the **Last Name** column. Click any other field to clear the selected column.

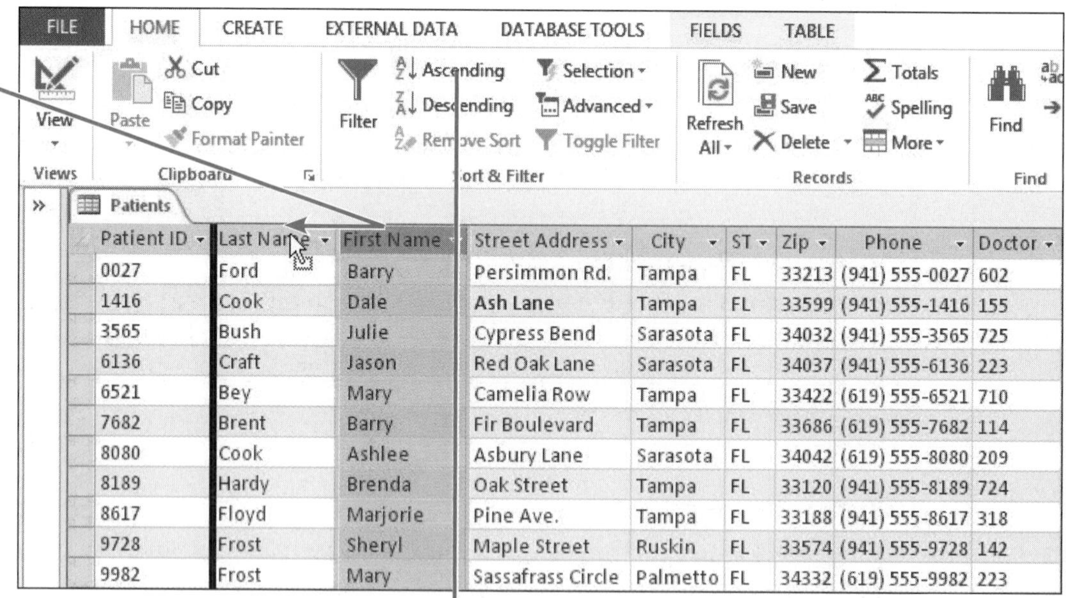

Patient ID	Last Name	First Name	Street Address	City	ST	Zip	Phone	Doctor
0027	Ford	Barry	Persimmon Rd.	Tampa	FL	33213	(941) 555-0027	602
1416	Cook	Dale	Ash Lane	Tampa	FL	33599	(941) 555-1416	155
3565	Bush	Julie	Cypress Bend	Sarasota	FL	34032	(941) 555-3565	725
6136	Craft	Jason	Red Oak Lane	Sarasota	FL	34037	(941) 555-6136	223
6521	Bey	Mary	Camelia Row	Tampa	FL	33422	(619) 555-6521	710
7682	Brent	Barry	Fir Boulevard	Tampa	FL	33686	(619) 555-7682	114
8080	Cook	Ashlee	Asbury Lane	Sarasota	FL	34042	(619) 555-8080	209
8189	Hardy	Brenda	Oak Street	Tampa	FL	33120	(941) 555-8189	724
8617	Floyd	Marjorie	Pine Ave.	Tampa	FL	33188	(941) 555-8617	318
9728	Frost	Sheryl	Maple Street	Ruskin	FL	33574	(941) 555-9728	142
9982	Frost	Mary	Sassafrass Circle	Palmetto	FL	34332	(619) 555-9982	223

Ⓑ Select both name columns and choose **Home→Sort & Filter→Ascending**.

The records appear in alphabetical order by first name—the Barrys are together and the Marys are together.

5. Click **Close** [×] to close the Patients table.

   Because you have changed the sort order a couple of times and then cleared the sorts, Access recognizes that you have changed the layout of the table and prompts you to save. If you click Yes, *the changes will become part of the table design. You want to discard the changes.*

6. Choose **No** in response to the prompt to save changes.

Filtering Records

Video Library http://labyrinthelab.com/videos Video Number: AC13-V0211

So far, you have sorted all the records contained in a table. When you work with large volumes of table data, there will be times when you want to locate a group of records that contain specific values in specific fields. Filtering enables you to select and work with a subset of records contained in a table.

Using the Filter Tools

The Filter tool lets you identify a value in a table field and tell Access to select only those records in the datasheet that contain the same value in the selected field. This process applies a filter to the table that hides (filters out) records whose active field contains data that does not match. For example, if you work with a database that contains thousands of records for consumers across the country, you could apply a filter to identify people who live in a specific state.

Access provides two types of methods for filtering records: Filter by Selection and Filter by Form.

- Filter by Selection: Selects records based on the value contained in the active field in the table.
- Filter by Form: Selects records based on values or conditions (criteria) you type into form fields. Access searches only the fields you specify.

Filtering Records by Selection

There are two basic ways to filter by selection. You can tell Access to select all records containing data that matches the value or selected text in the active field of the selected record. Or you can select all records containing any value *other than* the one selected. Access searches only the selected field to find matches.

Removing a Filter

If you close the table after you have applied a filter, Access prompts you to save changes to the table. You will often want to save changes, especially in cases where you widen or hide columns. However, filtering data in a table is typically a temporary view while you work with the data, so you do not want to save a filtered table. To remove a filter, choose Home, and in the Sort & Filter section, click the Advanced menu drop-down, then choose Clear All Filters.

Using the Toggle Filter Tool

The Toggle Filter tool in the Sort & Filter section of the Ribbon serves two purposes:

- After you apply a filter, clicking the Toggle Filter button removes the filter and displays all records.
- After removing a filter, clicking the Toggle Filter button reapplies the last filter applied.

In addition, when you point to the Toggle Filter button, a ToolTip displays to let you know what action you are performing. For example, when you point to the Toggle Filter button after applying a filter, the ToolTip displays *Remove Filter*. When you point to the Toggle Filter button after removing a filter, the ToolTip displays *Apply Filter*.

DEVELOP YOUR SKILLS AC02-D09

Filter Records by Selection

Two records in the Raritan Clinic East Doctors table contain an invalid zip code. In this exercise, you will filter table records, correct the zip code, and then remove the filter.

1. Open the **Raritan Clinic East Doctors** table.
2. Follow these steps to set a filter:

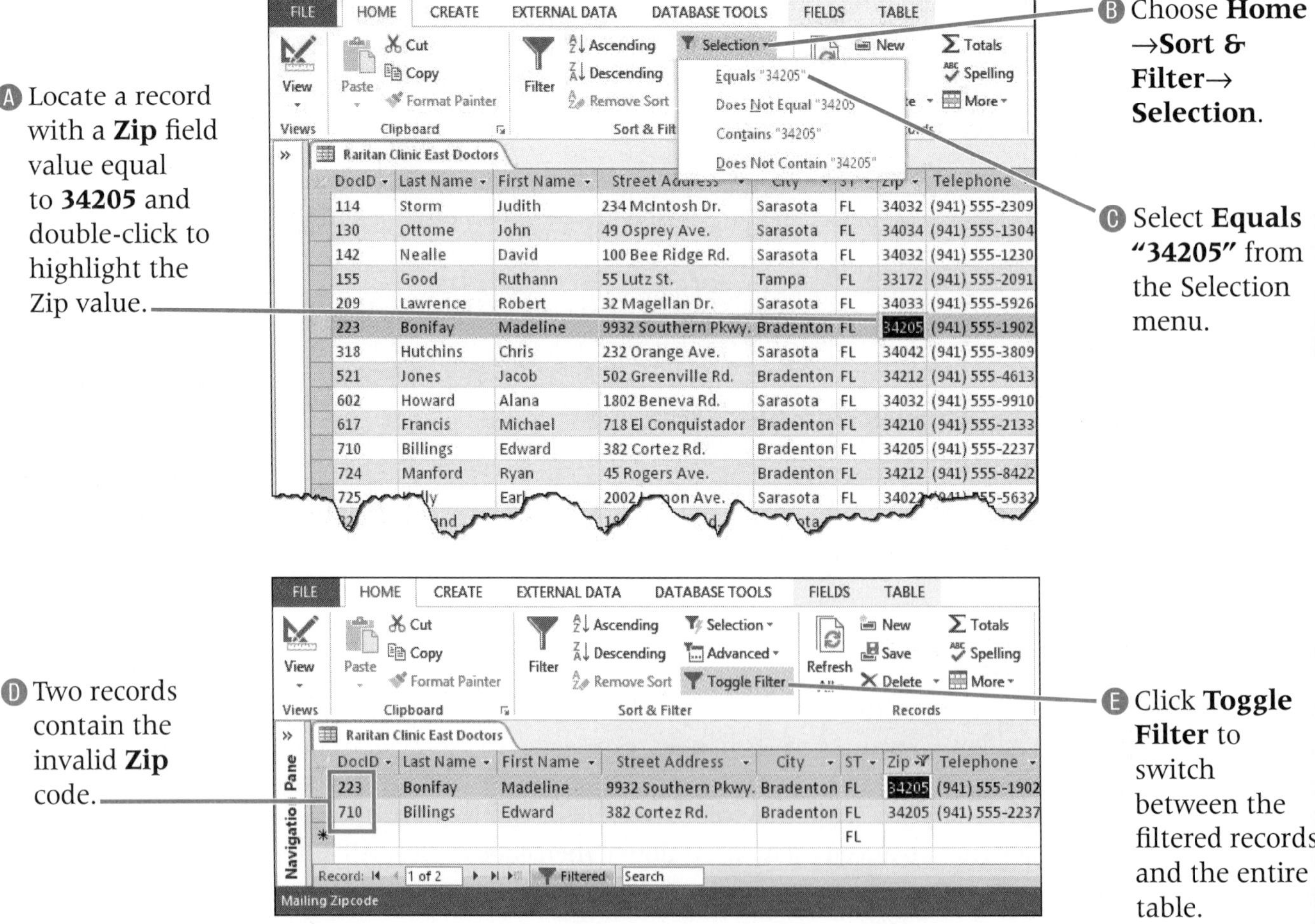

A Locate a record with a Zip field value equal to 34205 and double-click to highlight the Zip value.
B Choose Home→Sort & Filter→Selection.
C Select Equals "34205" from the Selection menu.
D Two records contain the invalid Zip code.
E Click Toggle Filter to switch between the filtered records and the entire table.

Access applies the filter immediately and displays two records that contain the value. The navigation bar indicates that the results are filtered.

3. Click the **Zip** field for each of the errant records and type **34207**.
4. Choose **Home→Sort & Filter→Advanced→Clear All Filters** to remove the filter and display all table records.

Filtering Records by Form

Video Library http://labyrinthelab.com/videos Video Number: AC13-V0212

Filter by Form allows you to select records based on values in multiple fields without rearranging the layout of table fields. When you filter by form, Access remembers the sort criteria. As a result, it is important to clear all filters after you apply this filter.

Identifying Comparison Operators

When you use the Filter by Form feature, you will often apply comparison operators so Access can locate the exact records or the range of records that contain the data you want to find.

COMPARISON INDICATORS AND SYMBOLS

Comparison Symbol	Description
=	*Equal*: Records in the table must contain a value that equals the value you set for the field.
<	*Less than*: Records in the table must contain a value less than the value you set for the field.
>	*Greater than*: Records in the table must contain a value greater than the value you set for the field.
<>	*Unequal*: Records in the table must contain a value different from the value you set for the field.
<=	*Less than or equal*: Records in the table must contain a value less than or equal to the value you set for the field.
>=	*Greater than or equal*: Records in the table must contain a value greater than or equal to the value you set for the field.

The format of the Filter by Form entry palette depends on whether you are filtering from a table or from a form. If you are filtering from a table, a datasheet palette opens. If you are filtering from a form, a blank form opens.

Using Wildcards

Database users often want to locate records that contain data in a specific field which may contain additional text or data. To accommodate this, Access accepts the use of wildcards, such as the asterisk (*), which can be used to represent multiple characters, or the question mark (?), where each question mark represents a single character.

USING WILDCARDS TO LOCATE DATA	
Example	**Description**
Will*	Finds all records with the search string text *will* at the beginning of the field value regardless of how many other characters follow it. This search string will find Will, Willy, and William.
*ill	Finds all records with the search string text *ill* at the end of the field value regardless of how many characters precede it. This search string will find Will, Bill, and Jill, but not Willy or William.
ill	Finds all records with the search string text *ill* anywhere in the field value, whether or not other characters appear before or after the search text. This search string will find Bill, Jill, Will, Willy, and William.
Will?	Finds all records with the search string text *will* at the beginning of the field value and with only one character after. This search string will find Willy but not Willie.
Will??	Finds all records with the search string text *will* at the beginning of the field value followed by exactly two additional characters. This search string will find Willie but not Willy or William.

DEVELOP YOUR SKILLS AC02-D10

Filter Records by Form

In this exercise, you will use a table to filter records by form.

1. If necessary, open the **Raritan Clinic East Doctors** table in Datasheet View.
2. Follow these steps to open the Filter by Form tool:

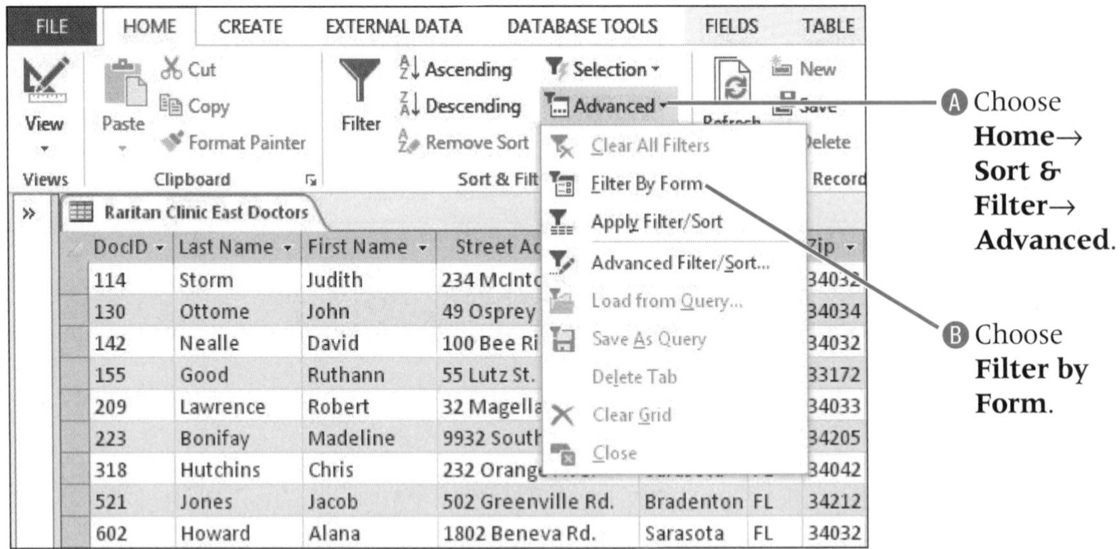

A blank record opens.

3. Follow these steps to filter and select records in which the City value is Sarasota:

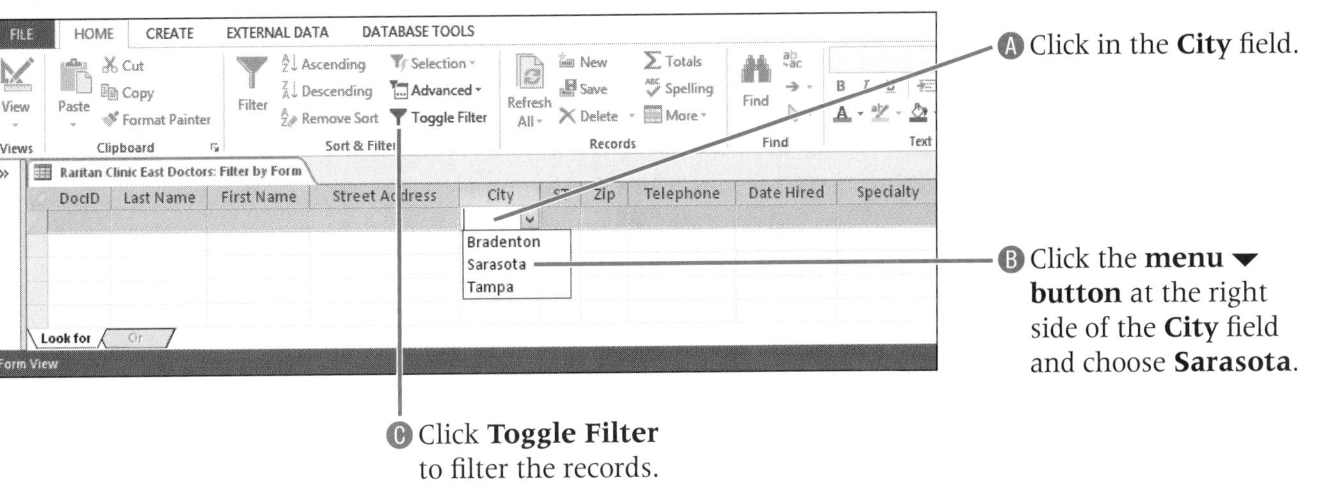

Ⓐ Click in the **City** field.
Ⓑ Click the **menu ▼ button** at the right side of the **City** field and choose **Sarasota**.
Ⓒ Click **Toggle Filter** to filter the records.

Access finds the records that meet the criteria and places a filter icon beside the field name.

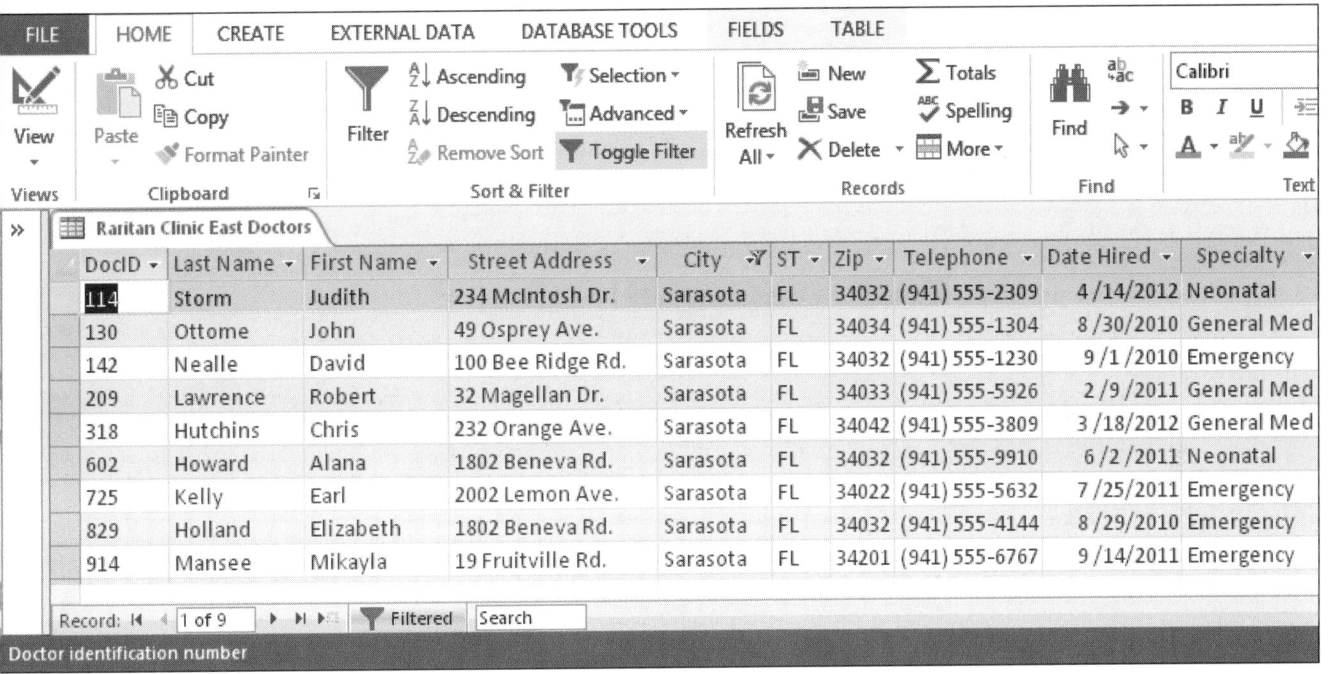

DocID	Last Name	First Name	Street Address	City	ST	Zip	Telephone	Date Hired	Specialty
114	Storm	Judith	234 McIntosh Dr.	Sarasota	FL	34032	(941) 555-2309	4/14/2012	Neonatal
130	Ottome	John	49 Osprey Ave.	Sarasota	FL	34034	(941) 555-1304	8/30/2010	General Med
142	Nealle	David	100 Bee Ridge Rd.	Sarasota	FL	34032	(941) 555-1230	9/1/2010	Emergency
209	Lawrence	Robert	32 Magellan Dr.	Sarasota	FL	34033	(941) 555-5926	2/9/2011	General Med
318	Hutchins	Chris	232 Orange Ave.	Sarasota	FL	34042	(941) 555-3809	3/18/2012	General Med
602	Howard	Alana	1802 Beneva Rd.	Sarasota	FL	34032	(941) 555-9910	6/2/2011	Neonatal
725	Kelly	Earl	2002 Lemon Ave.	Sarasota	FL	34022	(941) 555-5632	7/25/2011	Emergency
829	Holland	Elizabeth	1802 Beneva Rd.	Sarasota	FL	34032	(941) 555-4144	8/29/2010	Emergency
914	Mansee	Mikayla	19 Fruitville Rd.	Sarasota	FL	34201	(941) 555-6767	9/14/2011	Emergency

Only records with the City field value of Sarasota are displayed. Notice the Filter icon in the City heading to indicate that it is a filtered field.

4. Review the results then choose **Home→Sort & Filter→Advanced→Clear All Filters**.

Toggling the filter off does not remove the filter from the table; it just toggles between showing all the records and the filtered records. To remove a filter, choose Clear All Filters from the Advanced menu.

5. Click **Close** [×] to close the table. Choose **No** when prompted to save.

Update Records with Find and Replace

Access' Find and Replace tool improves the efficiency of maintaining a database that constantly changes. Using this tool, you can easily locate, delete, and edit records.

When you have specific edits to make to individual records, finding the records and making the edits works well. There are also times when you need to update the data in one field for multiple records with the identical replacement data. For example, if the area code for a city changed, multiple records would need to be updated with the same value. The Replace command allows you to update these records by replacing existing data with new data. Use the Replace command to:

- **Replace:** Replace text for each occurrence of the search text, one at a time.
- **Replace All:** Replace all occurrences of the search text with the new text, all at the same time.

Use Replace All with caution to avoid unexpected results. For example, if you wanted to replace the area code 813 with 941, Replace All would also change the phone number 555-6813 to 555-6941.

FROM THE KEYBOARD

Ctrl+F to open the Find command page of Find and Replace

Ctrl+H to open the Find and Replace dialog box

The Find and Replace dialog box is probably already familiar to you. However, because data stored in a database is somewhat different from the text stored in other files, you will find some fields that are unique to the Access application.

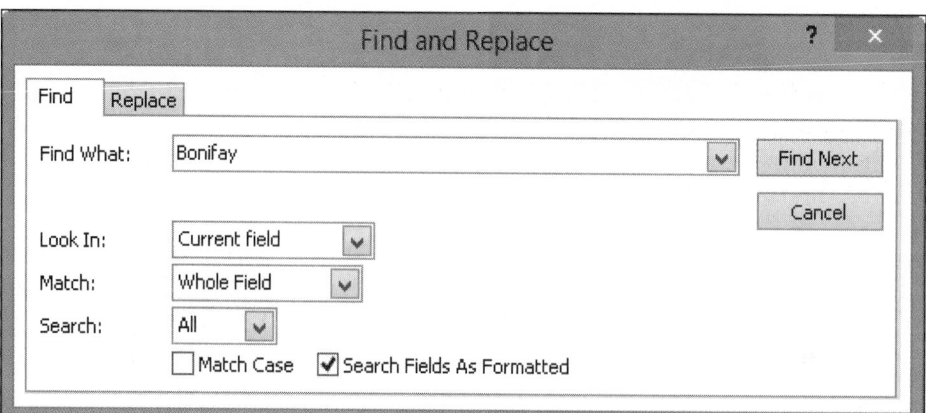

FIND AND REPLACE COMMANDS	
Feature	**Description**
Find What	Enter the text, numbers, dates, and other values to locate.
Replace With	Finds a value and replaces it with a value you specify.
Look In	Search only in the active field or in the entire document.
Match	Search for only data matching the whole field, any part of the field, or at the start of the field.
Search	Search up or down from the active cursor (to the end of the table or to the beginning of the table) or the whole table.
Match Case	Matches the exact capitalization pattern you type.
Search Fields As Formatted	Search for data as it is displayed in the datasheet rather than as you type it. If you uncheck the box, you would find March 5, 2013, even if it is formatted in the datasheet as 3/5/2013.

DEVELOP YOUR SKILLS AC02-D11

Update Records Using Find and Replace

After a long career, Dr. Bonifay (DocID 223) is retiring. In this exercise, you will use Find and Replace to transfer her patients to Dr. Lawrence (DocID 209).

1. Open the **Patients** table.
2. Click the **Doctor** column heading to select the field to search.
   You must select the field to search first.
3. Choose **Home→Find→**Replace
4. Follow these steps to locate and replace text with new values:

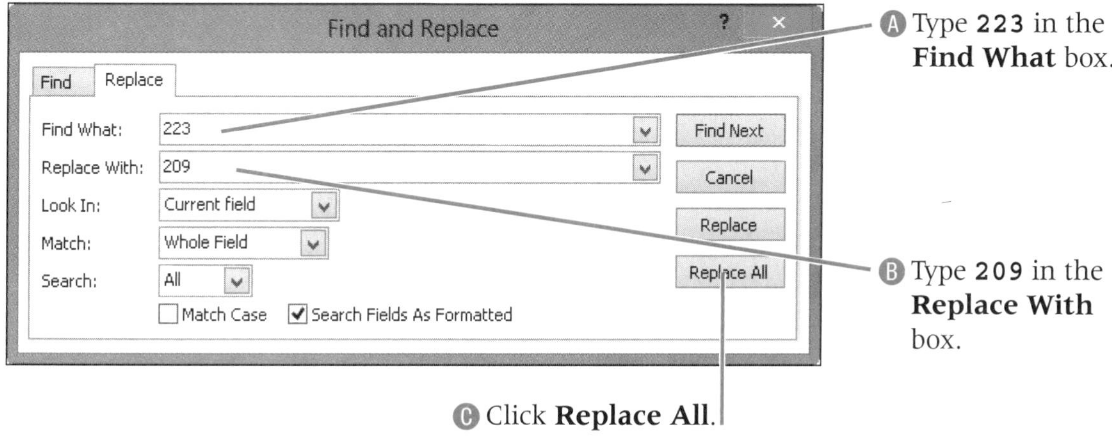

Access 2013

Access' warning states that you will not be able to undo this action.

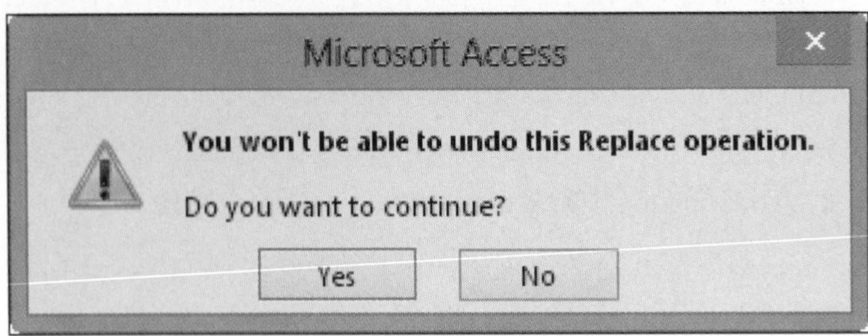

5. Choose **Yes** to replace all the values.
6. Click **Cancel** to close the Find and Replace dialog box then scroll to confirm that the 223 doctors values have indeed changed to 209.
7. Close the table, saving if prompted.
8. Press [Alt]+[F4] to exit **Access**.

Concepts Review

To check your knowledge of the key concepts introduced in this lesson, complete the Concepts Review quiz by choosing the appropriate access option below.

If you are...	Then access the quiz by...
Using the Labyrinth Video Library	Going to http://labyrinthelab.com/videos
Using eLab	Logging in, choosing Content, and navigating to the Concepts Review quiz for this lesson
Not using the Labyrinth Video Library or eLab	Going to the student resource center for this book

Reinforce Your Skills

REINFORCE YOUR SKILLS AC02-R01

Design a New Database

Kids for Change is a non-profit organization that helps young adults organize social/community service. They recently received an influx of funds to invest in computerizing the organization. In this exercise, you will gather and organize the information to determine the tables and fields needed for the new Kids for Change database.

Design a Database

1. Think about what pieces of information should be included in the database. Consider the kinds of forms and reports they might want to generate.
2. Start **Excel** and add the following headings for the columns in the first row:
   - Column A: `Table`
   - Column B: `Field`
   - Column C: `Key`
   - Column D: `Table`
   - Column E: `Field`
   - Column F: `Key`
3. Type a list of data that should be included in the database. Resize the columns as necessary.

Normalize the Database

4. As you examine the data, break down each piece of information into its basic parts.
5. Divide the data into tables based on the following categories: `Activities`, `Staff`, `Sites`, `Volunteers`, and `Children`. List the table names in **columns A and D**.
6. With the exception of key fields used to link tables, make sure no field appears in more than one table. List the corresponding fields for each table in **columns B and E**.

Relate Tables with Keys

7. Enter a key ID field for each table to show the relationships that should exist between tables. Indicate which fields are primary or foreign keys in **column C**.
8. Save the Excel spreadsheet to your **AC2013 Lesson 02** folder as `AC02-R01-K4C-[FirstInitialLastName]`.
9. Submit your final file based on the guidelines provided by your instructor.

   To view examples of how your file or files should look at the end of this exercise, go to the student resource center.

REINFORCE YOUR SKILLS AC02-R02

Create a New Database and Add Tables

In this exercise, you will create a new database and add tables.

Before You Begin: You must complete Reinforce Your Skills AC02-R01 before beginning this exercise. If necessary, open your AC02-R01-K4C-[FirstInitialLastName] file in Excel.

Create a Database and a Table in Datasheet View

1. Start **Access**. Start a **Blank Desktop Database**, saving it as **`AC02-R02-K4C-[FirstInitialLastName]`** in your **AC2013 Lesson 02** folder.

   The new database opens and a new empty table named Table1 is open in Datasheet View.

2. Double-click **ID** in the first field heading of Table1 and type **`StaffID`**.

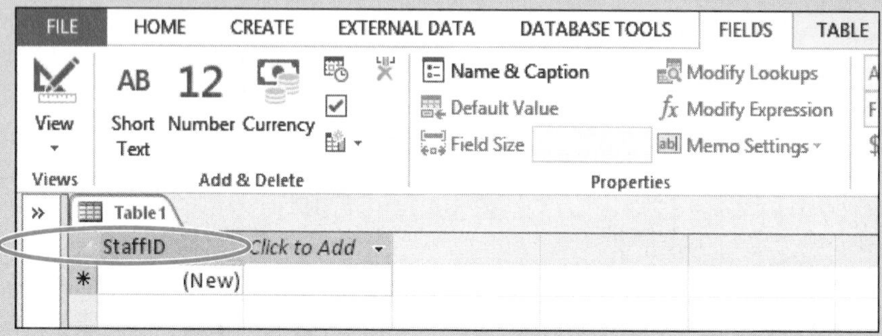

3. Press Tab, keep the default data type **Short Text** in the next field and change the **Field1** heading to **`StaffLastName`**.

4. Press Tab and repeat the above steps to enter the remaining fields from the Staff table you created in your **AC02-R01-K4C** spreadsheet. (Possible field names that you might choose are shown below in step 6.)

   All the remaining fields in this table are the Short Text data type.

Remember to tap Tab after each field entry.

5. **Save** the table as **`Staff`**.

6. Add the following records to the Staff table:

Staff

StaffID	StaffLastName	StaffFirstName	StaffAddress	StaffCity	StaffST	StaffZIP	StaffPhone	StaffAvail
1	Bryant	Matthew	12 E. MacIntosh	Sarasota	FL	34022	941-555-7523	Thursday
2	Earle	Kevin	77 Kingfisher	Sarasota	FL	34024	941-555-1368	Monday
3	Jacoby	Jane	4323 NW 63rd	Venice	FL	34222	941-555-5050	Tuesday
4	Pauly	Gerry	891 Waylon Lane	Bradenton	FL	34205	941-555-1988	Sunday

Because StaffID is an AutoNumber data type, Access fills in consecutive numbers automatically. The StaffPhone field has not been formatted, so you must add the hyphens.

7. If necessary, double-click the line between the column headings to automatically resize the columns to display all the data.

8. Save and close the **Staff** table.

Create a Table in Design View

9. Choose **Create→Table Design**.
10. Enter `ChildID` in the first row of the Field Name column.
11. Tap [Tab] and leave the Data Type for ChildID as **Short Text**.
12. Tap [Tab] and in the Description field, type `ID = Last Name and First Initial`.
13. Click Primary Key to designate **ChildID** as the primary key field.
14. Enter the remaining fields, data types, and descriptions shown, choosing the **Date/Time** data type for **ChildBirthday**.

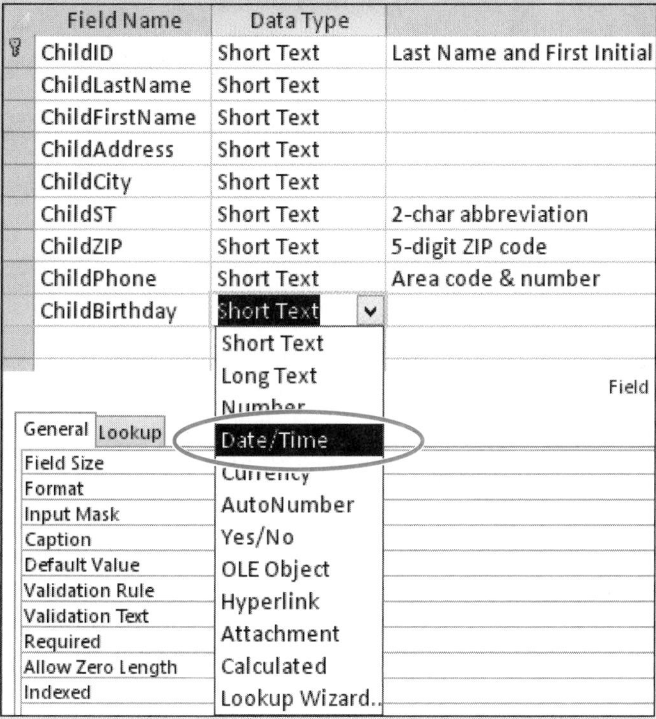

15. Click **Save** and name the table `Children`.
16. Open the **Children** table in Datasheet View.
17. Enter these field values.

ChildID	ChildLastName	ChildFirstName	ChildAddress	ChildCity	ChildST	ChildZIP	ChildPhone	ChildBirthday
CregerK	Creger	Kurt	503 Hillview	Sarasota	FL	34022	941-555-0245	10/12/2001
JonesP	Jones	Paul	892 Southern Pkwy	Sarasota	FL	34024	941-555-8929	09/03/1998
LangfordJ	Langford	James	43 Wisteria Way	Bradenton	FL	34209	941-555-1098	08/13/2000
PrestonW	Preston	Willy	162 Hamlet Lane	Sarasota	FL	34021	941-555-9372	03/11/2003

The ChildPhone and ChildBirthday fields have not been formatted, so you must add the hyphens and slashes.

18. Click **Close** [×] to close the **Children** table. Exit both **Excel** and **Access**.
19. Submit your final file based on the guidelines provided by your instructor.
To view examples of how your file or files should look at the end of this exercise, go to the student resource center.

REINFORCE YOUR SKILLS AC02-R03

Create New Tables and Enter Data

The staff director of Kids for Change would like you to add two new tables to the database, one that stores various community activities and one that stores parent volunteers. In this exercise, you will collect and organize the data needed for the lists, break down the data to its basic fields, and divide the fields into related tables. Then, you will create the tables.

Design and Normalize Database Tables

1. Start **Excel**. In a new blank worksheet, type a list of information to be included in a new **Volunteers** and a new **Activities** table. Break each piece of information into its smallest parts.
2. Type the **`Volunteers`** and **`Activities`** table names in **column A**.
3. Enter fields for each of the tables in **column B**. With the exception of key fields used to link tables, make sure no field appears in more than one table.

Relate Tables with Keys

4. Enter a key ID field for each table to show the relationships that should exist between tables. Indicate which fields are primary or foreign keys in **column C**.
5. Save the spreadsheet to your **AC2013 Lesson 02** folder as **`AC02-R03-K4C-Excel-[FirstInitialLastName]`**.

	A	B	C
1	**Table**	**Field**	**Key**
2	Volunteers	Vol ID	Primary
3		Vol Last name	
4		Vol First Name	
5		Vol Address	
6		Vol City	
7		Vol ST	
8		Vol ZIP	
9		Vol Phone	
10		Vol Avail	Foreign
11	Activities	Act ID	Primary
12		Act Name	
13		Act Day	Foreign
14		Act Time	
15		Act Address	
16		Act City	
17		Act Contact	

Your Excel worksheet should look similar to the figure above, though you may have different names.

Create a Table in Datasheet View

6. Start **Access**. Open **AC02-R03-K4C** from your **AC2013 Lesson 02** folder and save it as `AC02-R03-K4C-[FirstInitialLastName]`.
7. Choose **Create→Tables→Table** to create a new table in Datasheet View.
8. Double-click **ID** in the first field heading and type **`VolID`**.

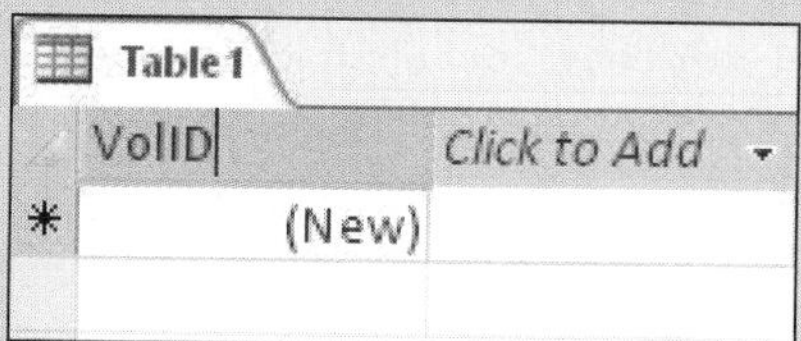

9. Press Tab, choose the **Short Text** data type, and change the **Field1** heading to **`VolLastName`**.
10. Press Tab and repeat enter the remaining fields from the **Volunteers** table that you entered in **Excel**.
11. Save the table as **`Volunteers`**.
12. Add these records to the Volunteers table.

VolID	VolLastName	VolFirstName	VolStreet	VolCity	VolST	VolZIP	VolPhone
1	Jones	Stan	892 Southern Pkwy.	Sarasota	FL	34024	941-555-8929
2	Langford	Kerry	43 Wisteria Way	Bradenton	FL	34209	941-555-1098
3	Creger	Cindy	503 Hillview	Sarasota	FL	34022	941-555-0245

The VolPhone field has not been formatted, so you must add the hyphens.

13. Close the **Volunteers** table.

Create a Table in Design View

14. Choose **Create→Tables→Table Design** to create a new table in Design View.
15. Enter **`ActivityID`** in the first row of the **Field Name** column.
16. Tap Tab and leave the Data Type as **Short Text**.
17. Tap Tab. In the **Description** field, type **`Activity Initials + Activity Day`**.
18. Set **ActID** as the primary key.

19. Enter the remaining **Short Text** fields from your **Excel** worksheet.

Field Name	Data Type	
ActID	Short Text	Activity Initials + Activity Day
ActName	Short Text	Name of Activity
ActLocation	Short Text	Where activity takes place
ActAddress	Short Text	Street Address
ActCity	Short Text	
ActDay	Short Text	Day of Week
ActTime	Date/Time	

20. Choose **Date/Time** from the drop-down menu for **ActTime**.
21. Save the table as **`Activities`**.
22. Open the table in **Datasheet View** and enter these records.

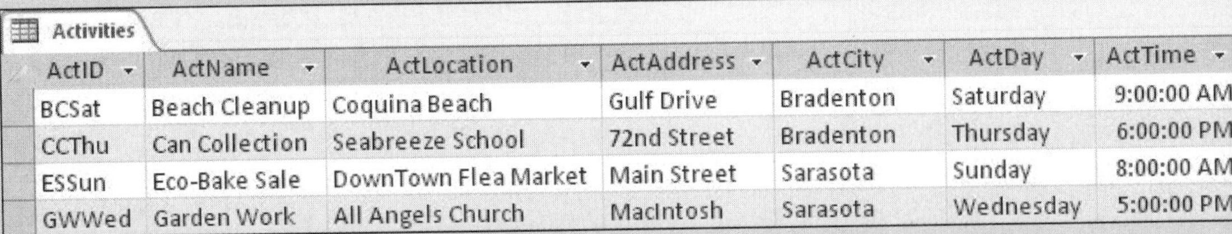

ActID	ActName	ActLocation	ActAddress	ActCity	ActDay	ActTime
BCSat	Beach Cleanup	Coquina Beach	Gulf Drive	Bradenton	Saturday	9:00:00 AM
CCThu	Can Collection	Seabreeze School	72nd Street	Bradenton	Thursday	6:00:00 PM
ESSun	Eco-Bake Sale	DownTown Flea Market	Main Street	Sarasota	Sunday	8:00:00 AM
GWWed	Garden Work	All Angels Church	MacIntosh	Sarasota	Wednesday	5:00:00 PM

23. Close the table, saving changes if prompted. Then, exit **Excel** and **Access**.
24. Submit your final file based on the guidelines provided by your instructor.

Apply Your Skills

APPLY YOUR SKILLS AC02-A01

Plan and Design a Database

Universal Corporate Events is a corporate meeting and event planning service. They have hired you to build a new database to automate the company. In this exercise, you will create a new database and add a table that organizes the types of events that Universal Corporate Events plans.

Design and Normalize a Database

1. In **Excel**, create a list of all fields and information that you want to include in the database, such as event types, locations, a calendar or schedule, menu plans, and other relevant subjects.
2. Divide the data into four tables: **Staff**, **Events**, **Scheduling**, and **Menus**.
3. Determine the common key ID fields you will use to relate the tables to each other.
4. Assign a data type to each field.
5. Save the spreadsheet to your **AC2013 Lesson 02** folder as **AC02-A01-UniversalCorp-[FirstInitialLastName]**.
6. Exit **Excel**.
7. Submit your final file based on the guidelines provided by your instructor.

   To view examples of how your file or files should look at the end of this exercise, go to the student resource center.

APPLY YOUR SKILLS AC02-A02

Add Tables to a New Database

Now that you have collected and organized the data fields, you can create the database for Universal Corporate Events. In this exercise, you will create the new database, add an EventStaff table in Datasheet View, and then add a Menus table in Design View.

Before You Begin: You must complete Apply Your Skills AC02-A01 before beginning this exercise. If necessary, open yourAC02-A01-UniversalCorp-[FirstInitialLastName] file in Excel.

Create a Database and a Table in Datasheet View

1. Start **Access**. Open a **Blank Desktop Database** and save it as **AC02-A02-UniversalCorp-[FirstInitialLastName]** in your **AC2013 Lesson 02** folder.
2. Referring to your **AC02-A01-UniversalCorp** Excel workbook, enter the **Staff** table field names.
3. Save the table as **EventStaff**.

4. Enter these records in the **EventStaff** table.

EventStaff

StaffID	StaffLastName	StaffFirstName	StaffAddress	StaffCity	StaffST	StaffZIP	StaffPhone	StaffDay
1	Parker	Wesley	894 Second Ave	Ellenton	FL	34213	941-555-3009	Monday
2	Swenson	Tommy	10 Beacon Place	Palmetto	FL	34091	941-555-0915	Tuesday
3	Faulkner	Karen	458 Western Run	Bradenton	FL	34207	941-555-9723	Saturday
4	Trilman	Peter	72 Davison Way	Sarasota	FL	34222	941-555-1396	Wednesday
5	Dauntin	Rahim	442 Beneva Rd	Sarasota	FL	34901	941-555-9992	Tuesday
6	Blare	Trina	2921 Fruitville	Sarasota	FL	33218	941-555-4263	Monday

5. Close the **EventStaff** table, saving if prompted.

Create a Table in Design View

6. Choose **Create→Tables→Table Design**.
7. Enter the fields and data types for the Menus table from your **AC02-A01-UniversalCorp** workbook.
8. Designate **MenuCode** as the primary key field.
9. Save the table as **`Menus`**.
10. Open the table in **Datasheet View** and enter this data.

Menus

MenuCode	MenuPlan	Chg/PP
BRKBUF	Buffet Breakfast	17.00
DESSRT	Dessert Selections	14.00
DINBUF	Dinner-Buffet	45.00
LUNSIT	Luncheon w/Servers	34.00

11. Close the **Menus** table, saving it if prompted. Then, Exit **Excel** and **Access**.
12. Submit your final file based on the guidelines provided by your instructor.

    To view examples of how your file or files should look at the end of this exercise, go to the student resource center.

APPLY YOUR SKILLS AC02-A03

Create a New Database and Add Related Tables

Every university and school has a giant database that stores data for students, faculty, classes, grades, and so forth. In this exercise, you will identify fields needed to store student data for such a database and group these fields into appropriate tables.

Design and Normalize a Database

1. Start **Excel**. In a new workbook, list the reports commonly generated by schools and universities, such as course schedules, grades, prerequisites, degree requirements, student aid, etc.
2. List data fields that would be required to generate the reports.
3. Determine the common key ID fields that can be used to relate the tables to each other.
4. Assign a data type to each field.

Create a Database and a Table in Datasheet View

5. Start **Access**. Create a new database named **A02-A03-SunStateU-[FirstInitialLastName]** and save it to your **AC2013 Lesson 02** folder.

   Access creates the new database, and opens a new table in Datasheet View.

6. In the new table, enter these fields and data types for university classes.

Field	Data Type
Department	Short Text
Class Number	Short Text
Section Number	Short Text
Building	Short Text
Room Number	Short Text
Start Time	Date/Time
End Time	Date/Time
Credit Hours	Number

7. Set **Department** as the primary key field.
8. Brainstorm and add at least four new records to the table.
9. Save the table as **Classes**.
10. Create a table in **Design View** containing these fields and data types, adding your own descriptions.

Field Name	Data Type	Description
ProfID	Short Text	
ProfLastName	Short Text	
ProfFirstName	Short Text	
ProfDept	Short Text	
ProfRank	Short Text	

11. Set **ProfID** as the primary key.
12. Save the table as **Professors**.
13. Close the **Classes** and **Professors** tables. Then, exit **Excel** and **Access**.
14. Submit your final file based on the guidelines provided by your instructor.

Extend Your Skills

In the course of working through the Extend Your Skills exercises, you will think critically as you use the skills taught in the lesson to complete the assigned projects. To evaluate your mastery and completion of the exercises, your instructor may use a rubric, with which more points are allotted according to performance characteristics. (The more you do, the more you earn!) Ask your instructor how your work will be evaluated.

AC02-E01 That's the Way I See It

Winchester Website Design is exploring expanding the number of items they currently recycle (cans, bottles, Styrofoam, paper, old electronics). To determine if there are additional ways to recycle, the company president has asked you to do some research. Go online and locate information about recycling in your state (recycling locations, contact persons, etc.). Plan the fields to include in a recycling information database. In Excel, create a spreadsheet that organizes your data into tables, along with key fields and data types. Save the spreadsheet as **`AC02-E01-ExcelRecycle-[FirstInitialLastName]`** in your **AC2013 Lesson 02** folder.

In Access, create a new database named **`A02-E01-Recycling-[FirstInitialLastName]`** Create a table that includes fields for recycling locations throughout the state and a contact name for the person in charge of the recycling facility. Enter data for at least three sites/companies. Finally, add a record containing your school as a site/company and your name as the contact.

You will be evaluated based on the inclusion of all elements, your ability to follow directions, your ability to apply newly learned skills to a real-world situation, your creativity, and your accuracy in creating objects and/or entering data. Submit your final files based on the guidelines provided by your instructor.

AC02-E02 Be Your Own Boss

You are the owner of Blue Jean Landscaping and have decided to sponsor the Sarasota Service Guild, a nonprofit organization created to raise money to help adults with disabilities. The guild has successfully raised more than $60,000 annually through sponsoring an historic home tour. They would like a database that will enable them to track memberships, donations from businesses, ticket sales, etc. You can help them plan their database by identifying fields, such as donor names and tour schedules, and tables, such as Members and Tour Home Addresses. Using Excel, identify sample tables that need to be included in the database and the fields that you would place in each table, assign primary and foreign keys to relate the tables, and select data types for each field. Save the Excel spreadsheet as **`AC02-E02-BJLandscaping-[FirstInitialLastName]`** in your **AC2013 Lesson 02** folder. Once you have designed the database in Excel, start Access and create a new database named **`AC02-E02-BJLandscaping-[FirstInitialLastName]`**. Add the tables that you included in your Excel spreadsheet.

You will be evaluated based on the inclusion of all elements, your ability to follow directions, your ability to apply newly learned skills to a real-world situation, your creativity, and your accuracy in creating objects and/or entering data. Submit your final files based on the guidelines provided by your instructor.

Transfer Your Skills

In the course of working through the Transfer Your Skills exercises, you will use critical-thinking and creativity skills to complete the assigned projects using skills taught in the lesson. To evaluate your mastery and completion of the exercises, your instructor may use a rubric, with which more points are allotted according to performance characteristics. (The more you do, the more you earn!) Ask your instructor how your work will be evaluated.

AC02-T01 Use the Web as a Learning Tool

Throughout this book, you will be provided with an opportunity to use the Internet as a learning tool by completing WebQuests. According to the original creators of WebQuests, as described on their website (WebQuest.org), a WebQuest is "an inquiry-oriented activity in which most or all of the information used by learners is drawn from the web." To complete the WebQuest projects in this book, navigate to the student resource center and choose the WebQuest for the lesson on which you are currently working. The subject of each WebQuest will be relevant to the material found in the lesson.

WebQuest Subject: Design elements of a high-quality Access database.

Submit your final file(s) based on the guidelines provided by your instructor.

AC02-T02 Demonstrate Proficiency

Stormy BBQ wants to modernize its business. They have hired you to design and create a database for their BBQ restaurant. Using Excel, plan the new database. Then, in Access, create three tables: one for staff/employees, one for the menu, and one for customer information. Brainstorm and add at least six records to each table (make it up). Relate the menu and customer tables using a customer favorite ID.

Save the database to your **AC2013 Lesson 02** folder as `AC02-T02-StormyBBQ-[FirstInitialLastName]`. Submit your final file based on the guidelines provided by your instructor.

ACCESS 2013

3 Working with Forms

LESSON OUTLINE

Exploring Form Design
Creating Forms
Modifying Form Controls
Modifying Form Layout
Printing Forms
Using Help
Concepts Review
Reinforce Your Skills
Apply Your Skills
Extend Your Skills
Transfer Your Skills

LEARNING OBJECTIVES

After studying this lesson, you will be able to:

- Identify form design elements
- Create and print forms
- Modify form controls and layout
- Create a multiple item form and a split form
- Use Microsoft Access Help

Forms are part of our everyday lives. If you have ever entered your personal information on a college application, filled out a loan application, or purchased an item from an online retailer, you have used a form. You also use forms to sign up for Facebook, Flickr, and Gmail accounts. A form ideally provides an attractive and easy-to-use interface, which allows a user to enter one record at a time into a table.

In this lesson, you will create an Access form from scratch based upon an existing table. You will use the Form tools to modify the font, color, and size of the text, text boxes, and other objects on the form. Then you will create forms using the different methods provided in Access.

CASE STUDY

Designing Forms at Winchester Web Design

As the information technology (IT) director at Winchester Web Design, you are responsible for designing and formatting the forms and reports in the company database to make them more attractive, consistent, and user-friendly. Part of your job is to customize forms so that they better identify the company. To accomplish this, you plan to create a consistent color scheme and add the corporate name and logo to all the company's forms.

Drafts of some of the sample forms that you plan to create are shown below.

Exploring Form Design

Video Library http://labyrinthelab.com/videos Video Number: AC13-V0301

A form is a database object used to enter, edit, or view the data for an individual record. Focusing on one record at a time allows you to design a layout that is more convenient and attractive than the row and column arrangement of a table in Datasheet View.

Examining Form Views

Both Form Design View and Layout View provide tools for designing and modifying new forms. You cannot edit or enter data in either view.

When you open an existing form in Design View, Access displays a palette that contains the text and the fields used on the form. By default, the palette background contains dots that you can use to align fields neatly. A Field List showing all the fields in all the database tables can be opened while in Design View so you can drag and position fields on the form.

Layout View displays actual sample data values in the form fields as you are editing. This makes it easier to adjust the placement and size of controls so data displays correctly and attractively.

DEVELOP YOUR SKILLS AC03-D01

Display Form Views

In this exercise, you will open an existing form in Design View, in Layout View, and in Form View. You will examine controls on the form and explore the available tools in each view.

1. Open **AC03-D01-WinWebDesign** from the **AC2013 Lesson 03** folder and save it as `AC03-D01-WinWebDesign-[FirstInitialLastName]`.

   Replace the bracketed text with your first initial and last name. For example, if your name is Bethany Smith, your filename would look like this: AC03-D01-WinWebDesign-BSmith.

2. If a Security Warning appears, click **Enable Content**.

3. Right-click the **Employees Form** in the Navigation Pane and choose **Design View**.

Access 2013

4. Follow these steps to view the Form Design tools:

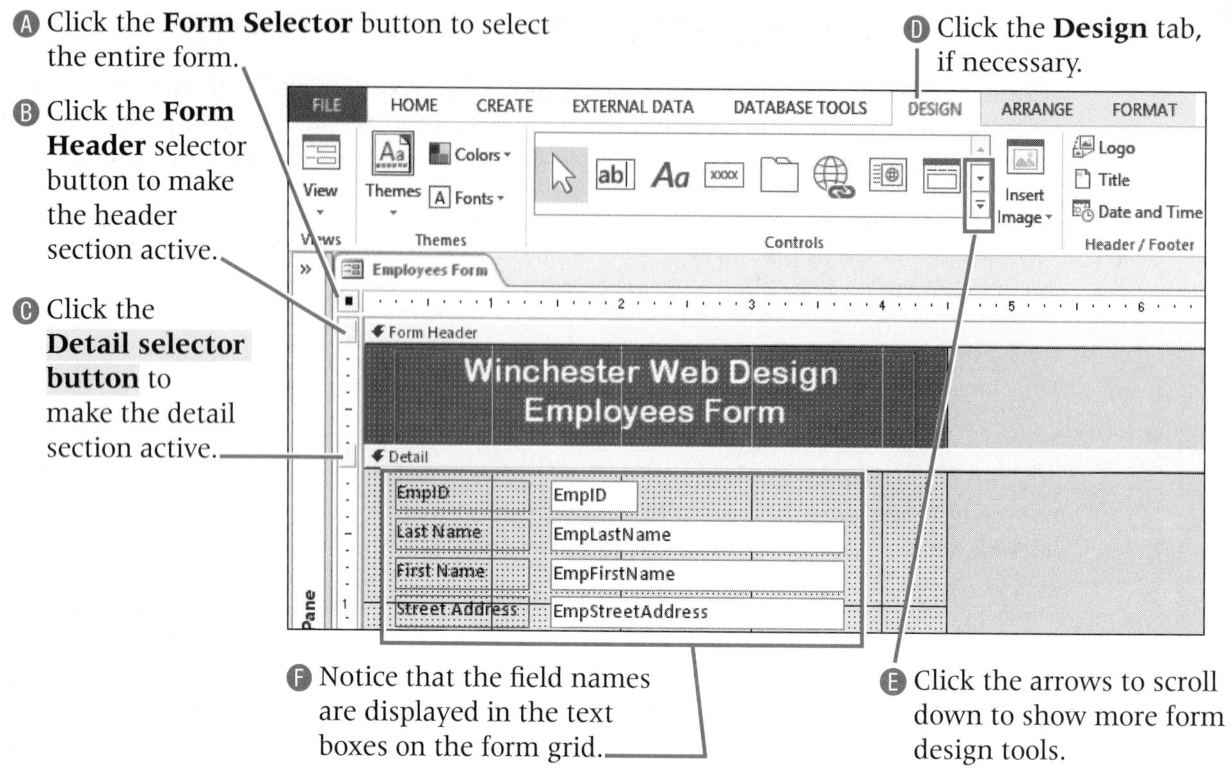

5. Follow these steps to open the form in Layout View:

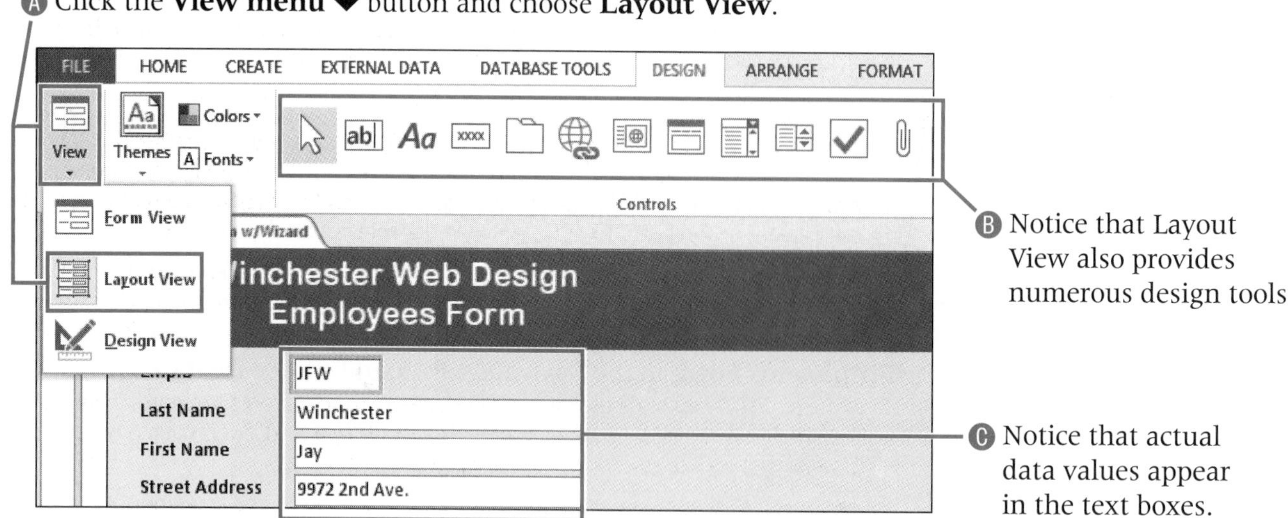

From this point forward, instructions for switching views will simply direct you to switch to the appropriate view. For example, "Switch to Design View" or "Switch to Layout View."

6. Choose **Views→View→Form View**.
7. Keep the **Employees Form** open for the next exercise.
   Unless directed otherwise, keep Access and any databases or database objects being used open at the end of each exercise.

The Property Sheet

Video Library http://labyrinthelab.com/videos Video Number: AC13-V0302

In Design View, Access provides a Property Sheet that contains attributes that control the appearance of different components of a form, each of its sections, and all controls on it. You can adjust colors, fonts, sizes, and other features on a form through the Property Sheet.

As you work on a form in Design View, it is important to know the key elements associated with form design. Each form in an Access database organizes data by sections and contains controls to display data and other items on the form.

BASIC FORM ELEMENTS

Element	Description
Sections	The main parts of a form, such as the Form Header, Form Footer, Detail, Page Header, and Page Footer. Section bars separate form sections.
Form Header	The top section with constant information, such as a title. It may also contain a logo, decorative line, or color scheme.
Form Footer	The bottom section that appears on the last page (or the first page of a one-page form). It might contain a summary or grand total. Unlike report footers, form footers are seldom used.
Page Header	The section that contains text and fields that repeat at the top of every *printed* page of an individual record displayed in the form, such as page number and perhaps the date. Page headers are not frequently used on forms.
Page Footer	The section contains text and fields that repeat at the bottom of every *printed* page of an individual record displayed in the form, such as page number and date. Unlike reports, page footers are seldom used in forms.
Detail section	The main section of a form that contains the text boxes that display data from database tables. Content values vary from record to record.
Controls	Items that display data, text, checkboxes, lines, images, and buttons.
Label	The part of a control that contains a caption identifying the data displayed in a text box or checkbox. By default, the label is either the field name or caption from the source table. For example, the caption *Last Name* (with a space) is a good label for the *LastName* field (no space). Label text cannot be edited in Form View.
Text Box	The control that displays the actual data from a table. The record source for a text box is a corresponding field in an underlying table. For example, *Smith* might be the data displayed in the *LastName* text box. Data can only be entered into a text box in Form View.
Bound control	A control that ties, or binds, form data to table data so the data appears on the form (i.e., the *LastName* text box is bound to the *LastName* field in the source table). Bound controls normally appear in the Detail section.
Unbound control	An item that is independent of any table data. Unbound controls can be text, shapes, and images, and may appear in any form section.
Calculated control	A control that is tied to a calculated field or expression built in a query (i.e., *Total=[Price]*[Quantity]* where *Total* is a text box and *Price* and *Quantity* are bound controls). Calculated controls normally appear in the Detail or Form Footer section of the form.

DEVELOP YOUR SKILLS AC03-D02

Examine Form Elements

In this exercise, you will open the Property Sheet for a form in Design View. You will select different sections and controls on the form and examine their properties.

1. Open the **Employees Form** in **Design View**.
2. If the Properties Sheet is not displayed, choose **Design→Tools→Property Sheet**.

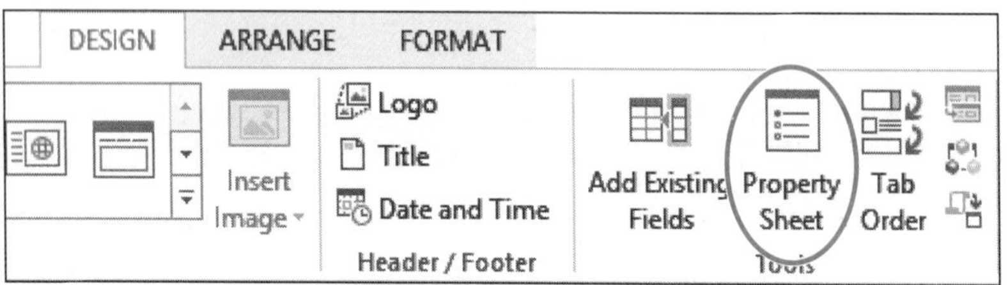

3. Follow these steps to examine the properties of the form:

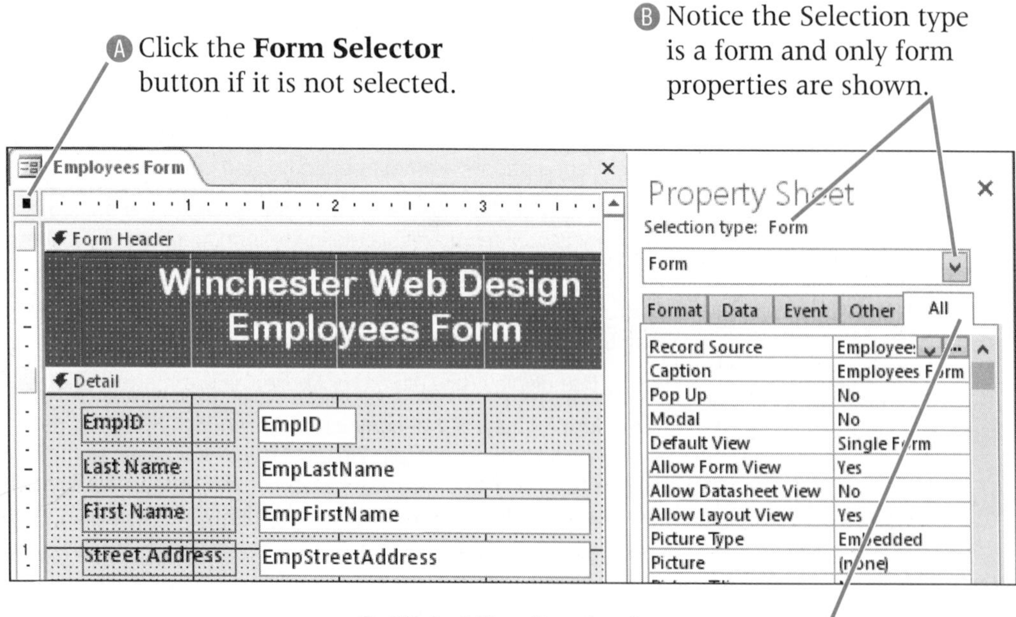

4. Click the **Last Name** label on the form grid.

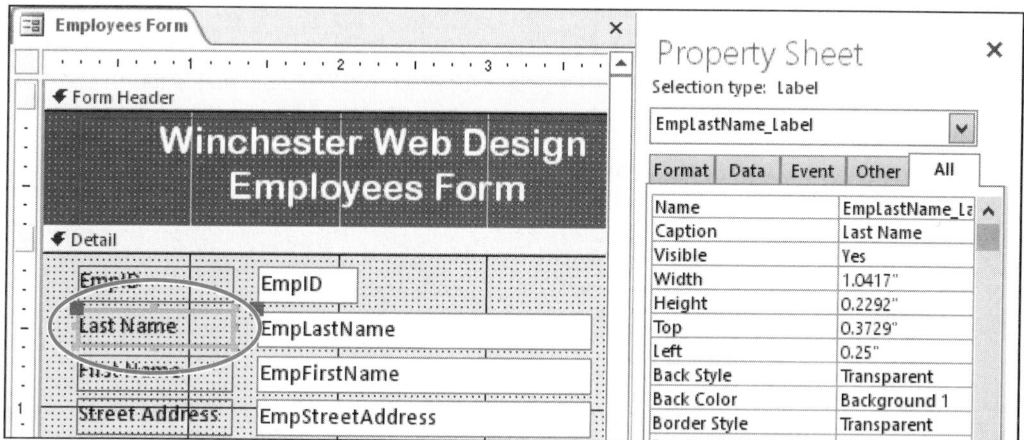

The Property Sheet now lists information about the selected control.

5. **Close** ☒ the Employees form.

Creating Forms

Video Library http://labyrinthelab.com/videos Video Number: AC13-V0303

Access provides a number of ways to create forms. A quick and simple form can be created by clicking the record source name in the Navigation Pane and choosing Create→Form. Access then generates a basic form, which contains all the fields from the record source listed in order and in a uniform layout. For those who prefer a more hands-on approach, you can create a form in Design View, Layout View, or with the help of a Form Wizard.

FROM THE RIBBON
Create→Forms→Form to create a simple form

Another way to create a form is to right-click an existing form in the Navigation Pane and then use the Copy and Paste commands. To rename an existing form, right-click on the form in the Navigation Pane, select Rename, and then type the new name.

Identifying a Record Source

Every form in an Access database obtains its data from the primary source—one or more tables. The field property that contains and displays the fields and data in a form is called the record source. Normally a form contains fields from one table or one query. However, when a relationship exists between two database tables, you can access fields in the related tables. An example is an Invoice form that displays data from the Invoice, Products, Customers, and Employees tables.

QUICK REFERENCE | **CREATING FORMS**

Task	Procedure
Create a simple form	■ Select the table for which you want to create a form. ■ Choose Create→Forms→Form.
Create a form using the Form Wizard	■ Select the table for which you want to create the form. ■ Choose Create→Forms→Form Wizard.
Create a form in Layout View	■ Select the table for which you want to create the form. ■ Choose Create→Forms→Blank Form.
Create a form in Design View	■ Select the table for which you want to create a form. ■ Choose Create→Forms→Form Design.
Create a form from an existing form	■ Right-click an existing form in the Navigation Pane and choose Copy. ■ Use Paste to create another instance of the form; rename it as desired.
Create a multiple item form	■ Choose Create→Forms→More Forms→Multiple Items.
Create a split form	■ Select the table for which you want to create the form. ■ Choose Create→Forms→More Forms→Split Form.

DEVELOP YOUR SKILLS AC03-D03

Create a Simple Form

In this exercise, you will use the quickest and easiest method to create a simple form using the Employee Spouses table.

1. Select the **Employee Spouses** table in the Navigation Pane.
2. Choose **Create→Forms→Form.**
   Access creates a simple, basic form and opens it in Layout View.

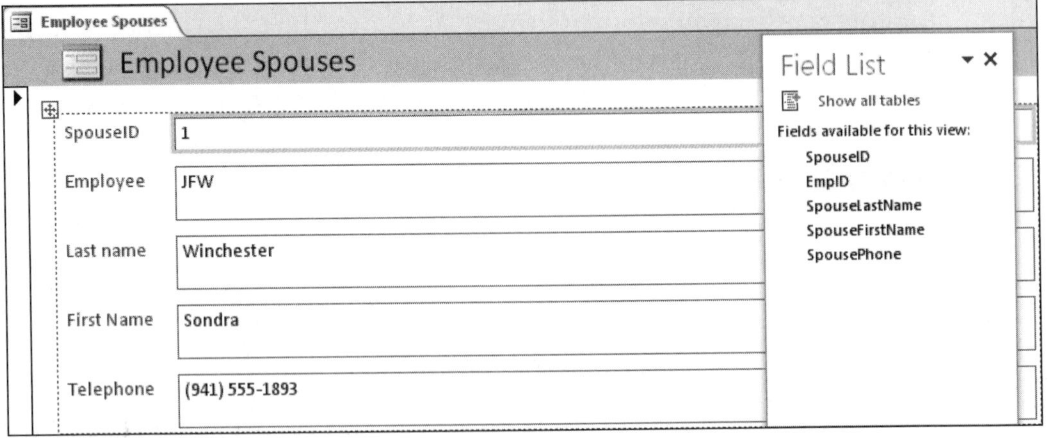

   Depending on your last Access session, the Field List may or may not show.
3. **Save** the new form as `SpousesSimpleForm`.
4. Close the form.
   You will modify form layouts later in this lesson.

Using the Form Wizard

Video Library http://labyrinthelab.com/videos Video Number: AC13-V0304

When you use the Form Wizard to create a form, the wizard walks you through the process of selecting the table or query that contains the specific fields and data you want to include on the form. Then Access places all the fields that you select from the source table or query onto the form.

Although you have complete freedom in field selection and placement when you create a form in Design View, many people prefer the ease of using the Form Wizard to initially select and place all the fields, and later use Form Design View to modify the layout and elements on the form. Regardless of which procedure you prefer, the techniques for building and designing the form—working with controls, setting properties, adding pictures, and so forth—are the same.

DEVELOP YOUR SKILLS AC03-D04

Create a Form Using the Form Wizard

In this exercise, you will create a form with the Form Wizard that displays all the fields from the Customers table.

1. Follow these steps to open the Form Wizard and add table fields:

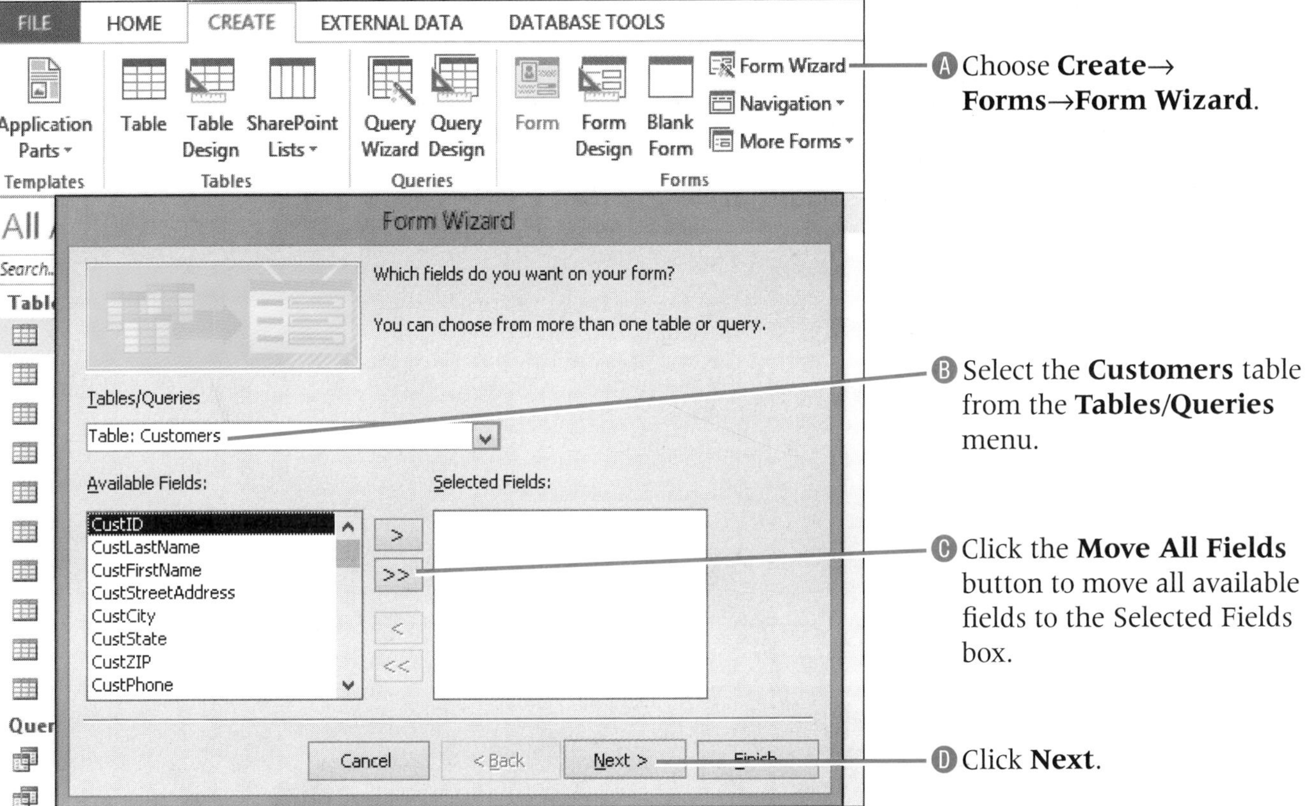

Ⓐ Choose **Create→Forms→Form Wizard**.

Ⓑ Select the **Customers** table from the **Tables/Queries** menu.

Ⓒ Click the **Move All Fields** button to move all available fields to the Selected Fields box.

Ⓓ Click **Next**.

Access 2013

2. Leave the **Columnar** option selected and click **Next**.

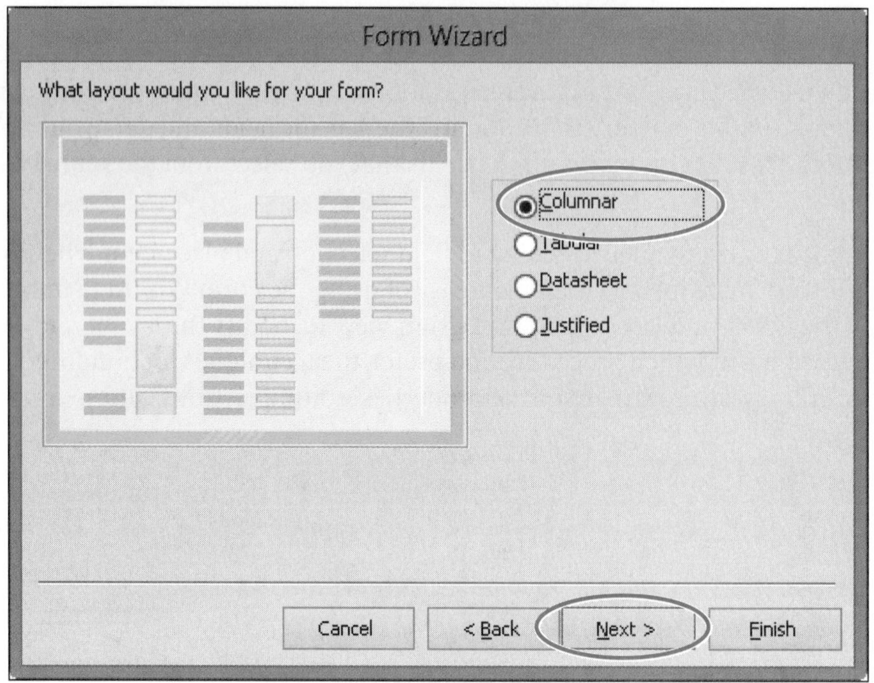

3. Follow these steps to name the form and open it in Form View:

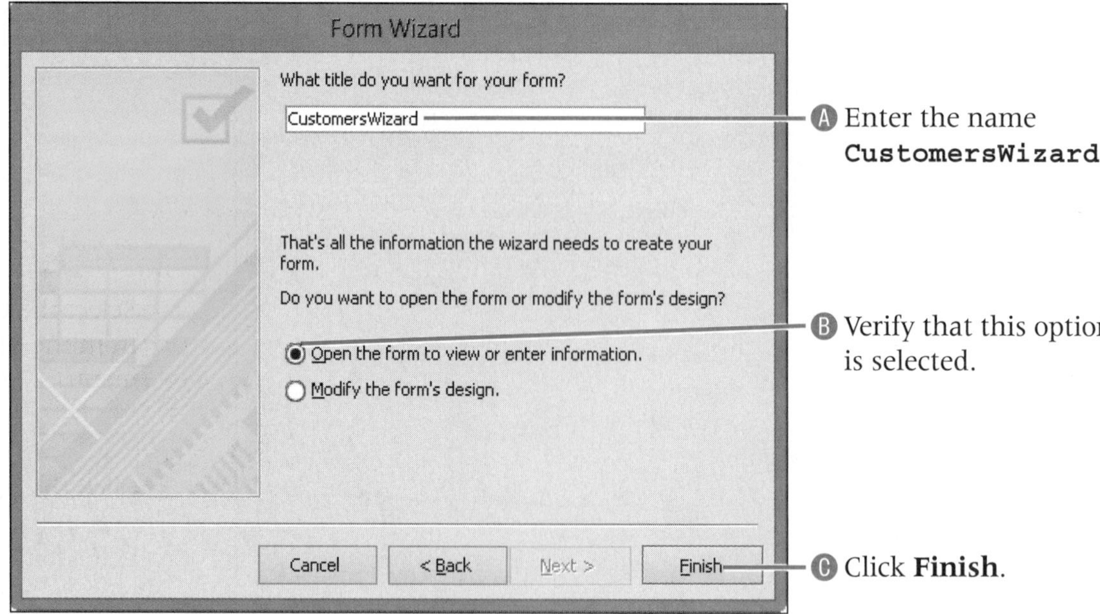

The form opens in Form View.

Customers	
CustomersWizard	
CustID	AndersM
Last Name	Anders
First Name	Mark
Street Address	205 Montana St
City	Bradenton
ST	FL
ZIP	34211
Telephone	(941) 555-2309
Email	AndersM@email.com
Notes	

4. **Close** [×] the CustomersWizard form.

Working with Form Controls

Video Library http://labyrinthelab.com/videos Video Number: AC13-V0305

Access provides three basic types of controls that you can add to forms: bound controls, unbound controls, and calculated controls. Bound controls tie form data to the source table data so that the data appears on the form. Unbound controls are independent of table data. Unbound controls can be text, shapes, and images, and may appear in any form section. A calculated control uses data from other fields to perform a calculation (i.e., Total=[Price]*[Quantity] where Total is a text box for the calculated control, and Price and Quantity are bound controls linked to fields in a table). Calculated controls normally appear in the Detail or Form Footer section of the form.

Adding Bound Controls to Forms

If you create a blank form, you will have to add all the controls to the form yourself—building the form from scratch. If you want to customize an existing form, you may also need to add controls to the form. These controls might be extra fields required to display additional data or they might be descriptive text and graphics. The fields used with bound controls appear in the Field List pane that opens when you create a new form and display it in Design View. To add a field to the form, you click it in the Field List panel, drag it onto the palette, and position it where you want it on the form.

Moving and Sizing Controls

When you create a form using the Form Design, Blank Form, or Form Wizard commands, you can easily move and resize text boxes and labels. Sizing controls in Access is similar to sizing drawn objects in other programs. You select the control and Access displays handles on the corners and sides of the control. You can drag the handle to resize the control. Because each bound control contains two parts by default—the label and the text box—you can size each part separately. You can also resize an object by selecting it, then resetting the Width and Height properties for the field in the Property Sheet.

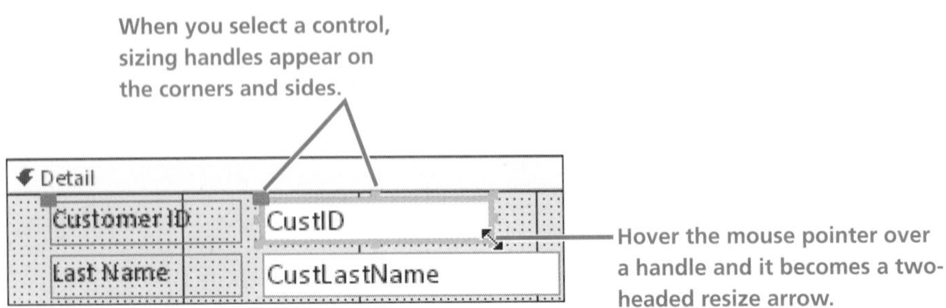
When you select a control, sizing handles appear on the corners and sides.
Detail
Customer ID
CustID
Last Name
CustLastName
Hover the mouse pointer over a handle and it becomes a two-headed resize arrow.

It is a bit trickier to move and resize text boxes and labels if you create a simple form by choosing the Form command, instead of using the Form Design, Blank Form, or Form Wizard commands. Quick forms tie all the automatically inserted text boxes and corresponding labels into one group. You can move the entire group but not the individual controls. In order to move or resize an individual control you must ungroup these controls using the Remove Layout command.

Moving and positioning controls on a form is similar to resizing a control. The main difference is that the mouse pointer appears as a white select arrow on a black move arrow when it is positioned to move a control. This permits you to move both the text box and its associated label together.

FROM THE KEYBOARD

 to move selected controls

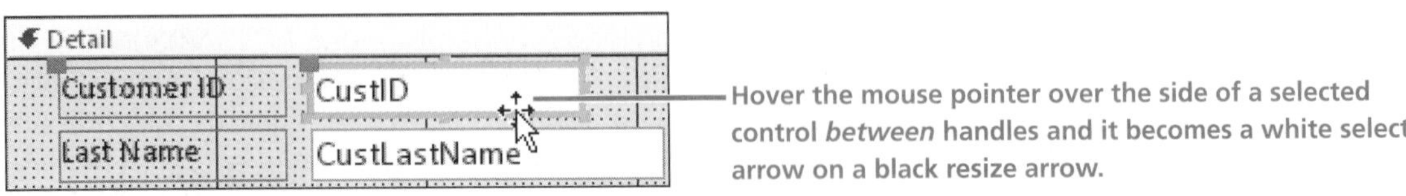
Detail
Customer ID
CustID
Last Name
CustLastName
Hover the mouse pointer over the side of a selected control *between* handles and it becomes a white select arrow on a black resize arrow.

Selected controls are identified by the thick, usually orange border and the handles on their sides and corners. You may have noticed that the top-left handle is larger than other handles on the selected control and is usually gray. This larger handle enables you to separate the label from the text box, moving each part of the control individually to position it where you want it.

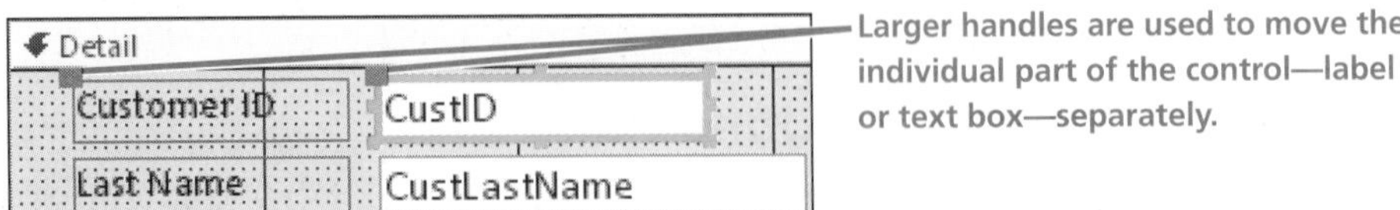
Larger handles are used to move the individual part of the control—label or text box—separately.
Detail
Customer ID
CustID
Last Name
CustLastName

When you create a form in Design View, Access opens an empty form palette and the Field List pane. Design View enables you to drag fields from the Field List onto the form, modify existing fields, arrange fields, and build the form manually. If you click the Show All Tables option at the top of the Field List, Access displays a list of related tables at the bottom of the list of fields.

FROM THE RIBBON

Design→Tools→Add Existing Fields to toggle the Field List pane open and closed

Although you have more control in Design View, it can be far more time consuming than using the Form Wizard.

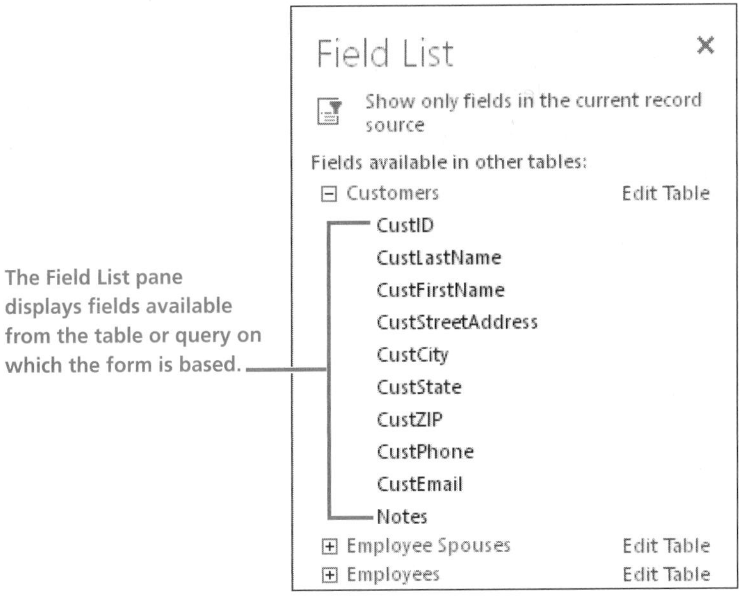

DEVELOP YOUR SKILLS AC03-D05

Create a Form Using Form Design

In this exercise, you will create a form in Design View for the Customers table. Then you will move and size the controls on the form.

1. Choose **Create→Forms→Form Design**.

   Access opens a new form in Design View.

2. Follow these steps to open the Field List pane and select the Customers table:

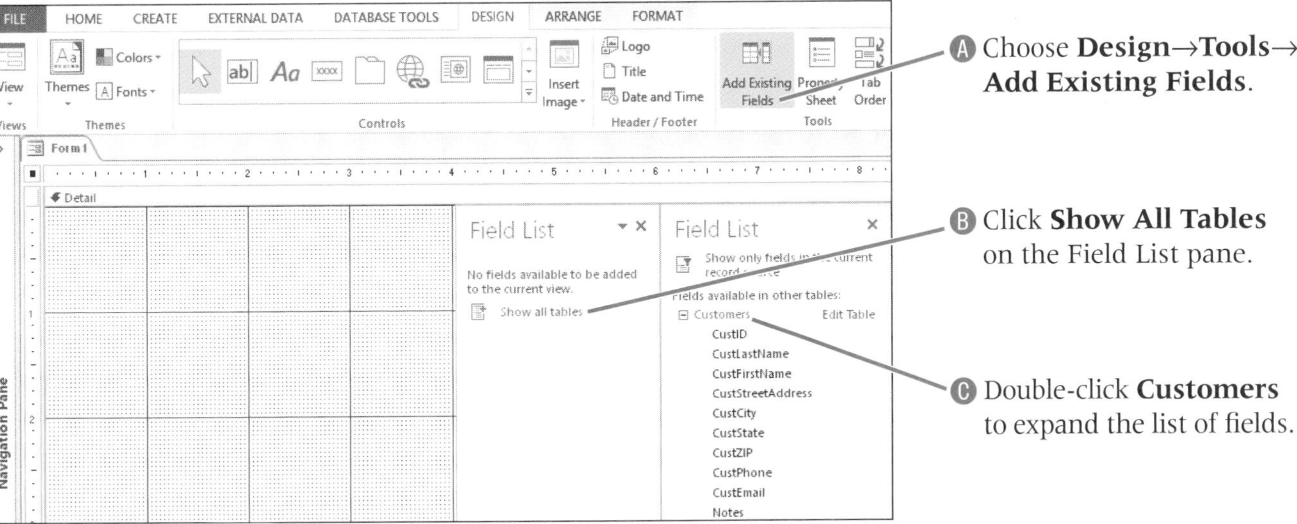

Access 2013

3. Follow these steps to add a field to the blank form:

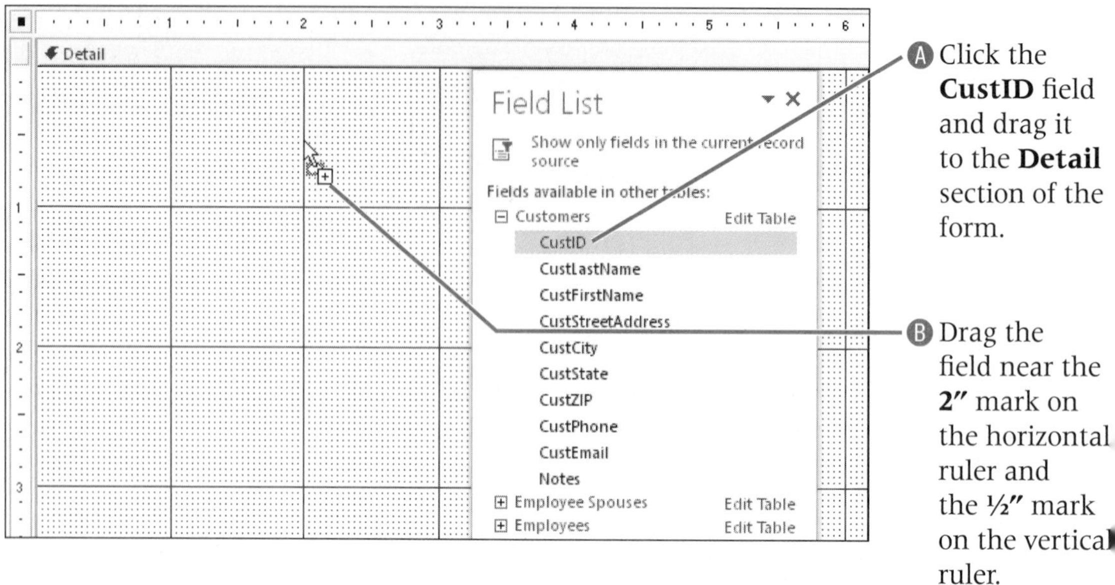

A plus symbol or crosshair appears just below the mouse pointer indicating it is copying the field. Each field you drag to the form grid includes a label control.

4. Repeat the procedures outlined in **step 3** to add the remaining fields as shown here and close the **Field List** pane.

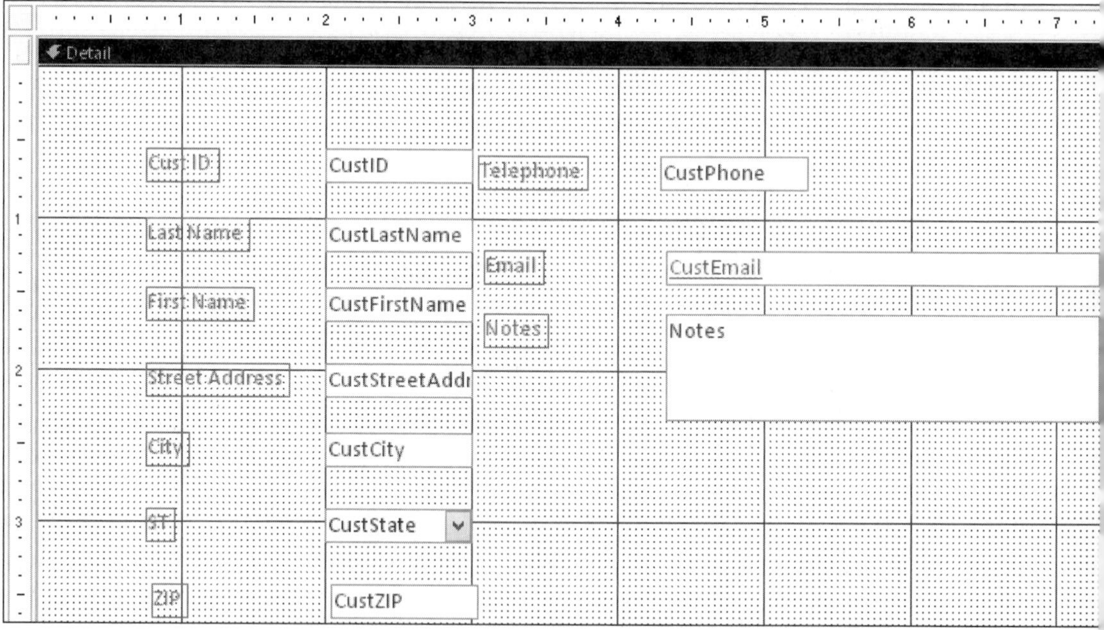

Don't worry about the alignment at this point. Next, you will move and arrange the Cust ID label and CustID text box to a location that makes them distinctively stand out on the form.

5. Follow these steps to move the label control separately from the text box control:

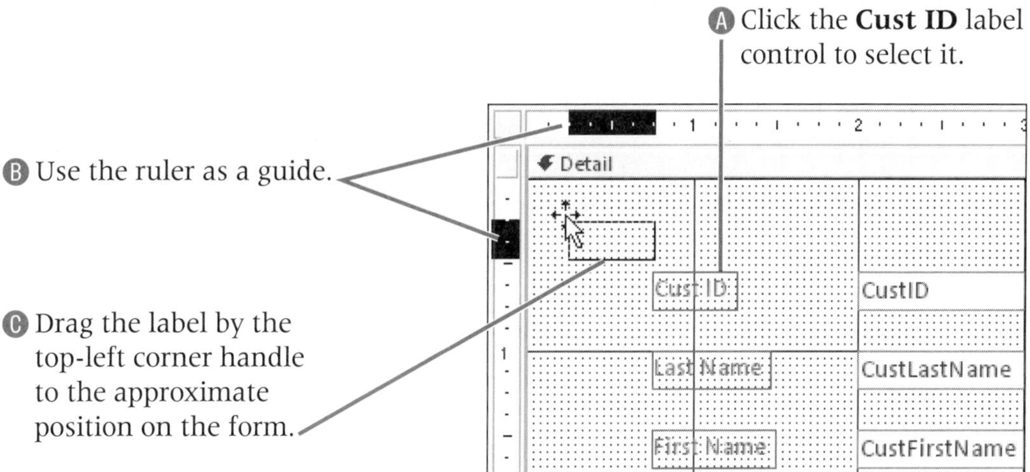

6. Repeat the procedures outlined in **step 5** to move the **CustID** text box under the **Cust ID** label.

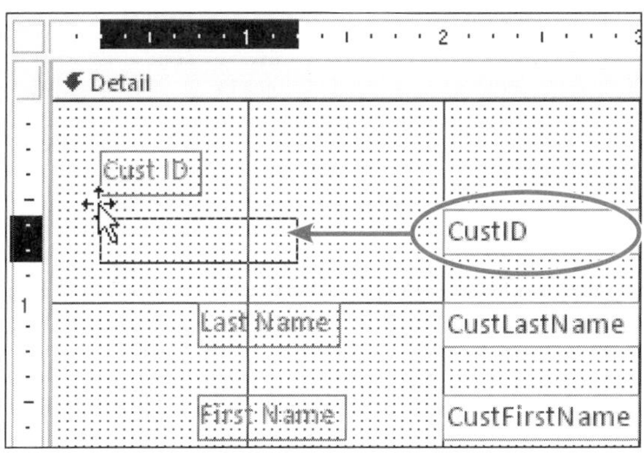

7. Hold the Ctrl key down while you click the **Telephone**, **Email**, and **Notes** labels to select all three objects; then tap → several times to move the labels and associated text boxes to the right.

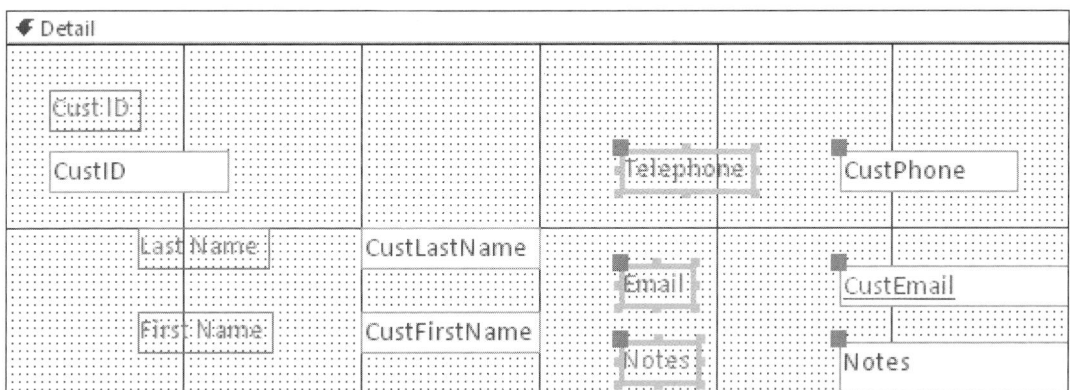

Access 2013

8. Follow these steps to size the CustID text box for its contents:

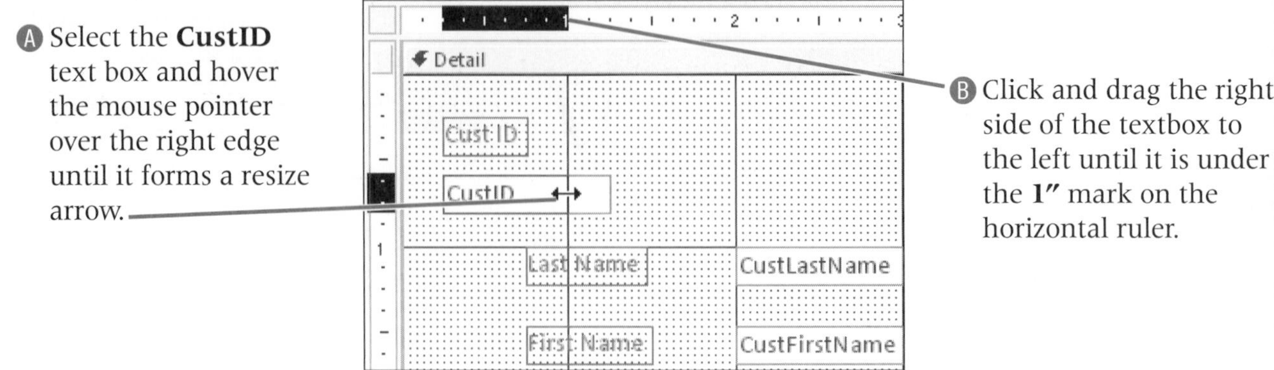

Ⓐ Select the **CustID** text box and hover the mouse pointer over the right edge until it forms a resize arrow.
Ⓑ Click and drag the right side of the textbox to the left until it is under the **1″** mark on the horizontal ruler.
Detail
Cust ID
CustID
Last Name
CustLastName
First Name
CustFirstName

9. Save the form as `CustomersDesign`.
10. Click the **View menu ▾** button to open the form in **Form View**.

If you don't see the View button, right-click the form's tab and choose Form View.

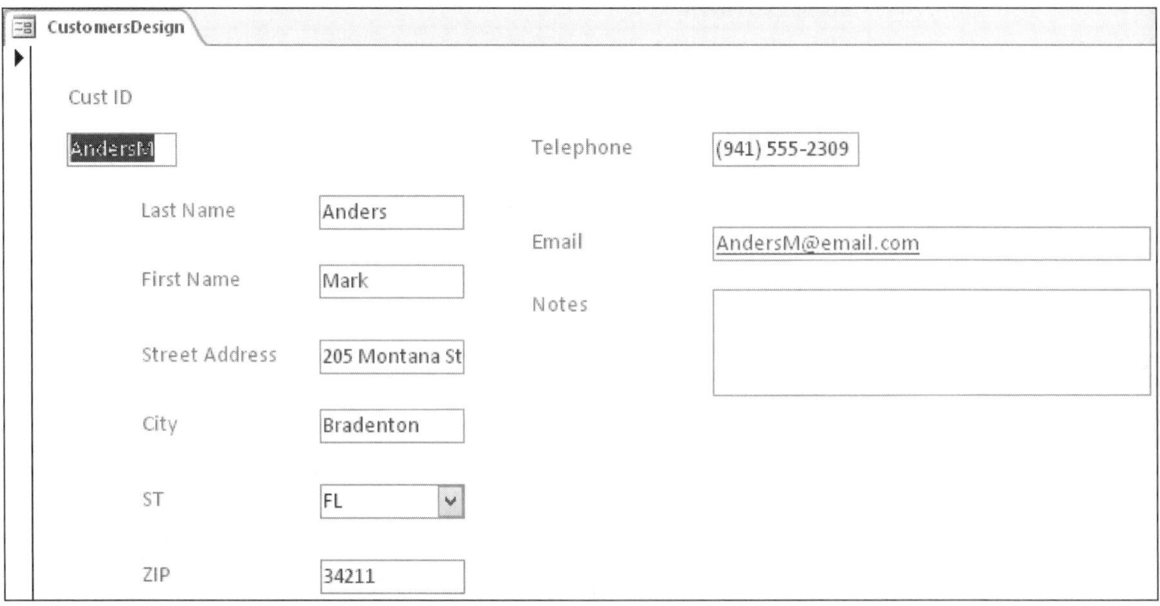

11. Leave the **CustomersDesign** form open.

Deleting Controls

Video Library http://labyrinthelab.com/videos Video Number: AC13-V0306

Some controls on a form stand by themselves without the need for a label. You can delete unnecessary labels to allow better arrangement and format on forms and also remove controls completely. Because each bound control contains two parts, removing labels and controls depends on the part of the control selected.

QUICK REFERENCE	DELETING CONTROLS AND LABELS
Task	**Procedure**
Delete an entire control (text box and label)	Select the text box part of the control then press [Delete].
Delete label only	Select the label part of the control then press [Delete].

DEVELOP YOUR SKILLS AC03-D06

Delete Labels and Edit Label Text

In this exercise, you will delete a label control and edit the text in another label on your CustomersDesign form.

1. Open the **CustomersDesign** form in **Design View**.
2. Follow these steps to delete a label:

Ⓐ Click the **Notes** label to select it.

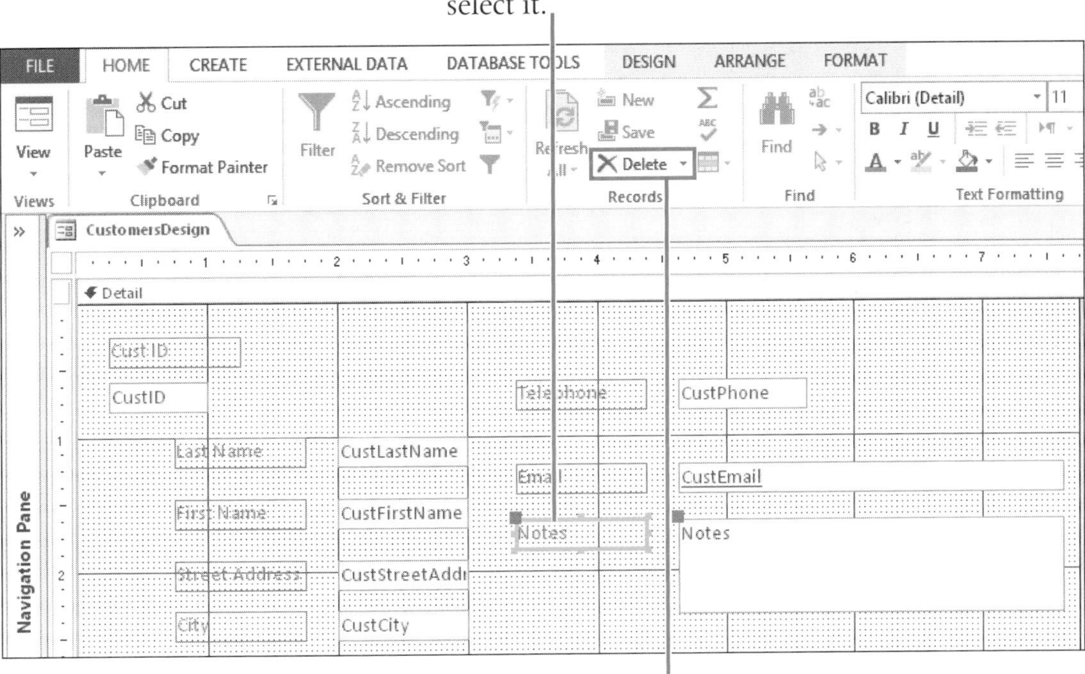

Ⓑ Choose **Home→ Records→ Delete**.

If you accidentally delete the wrong control, click Undo on the Quick Access toolbar to reverse the action and then try again.

Access removes just the label and leaves the text box.

Access 2013

Edit Control Labels

3. Click the **ST** label, highlight the text, and type `State`.

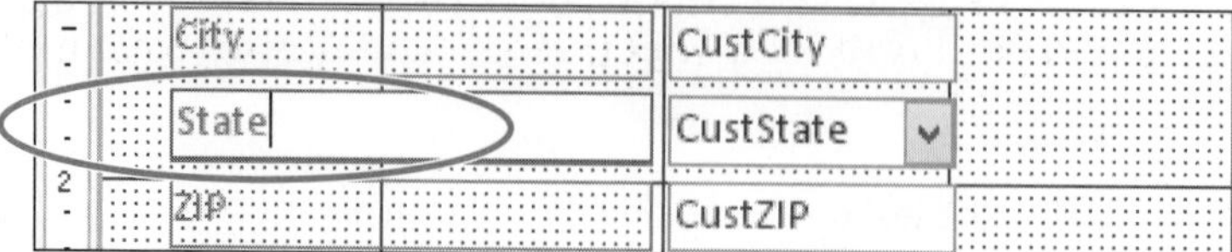

4. Repeat the procedures from **step 3** to change the **Cust ID** label to `Customer ID`, and the **ZIP** label to `ZIP Code`.
5. Switch to **Form View**.

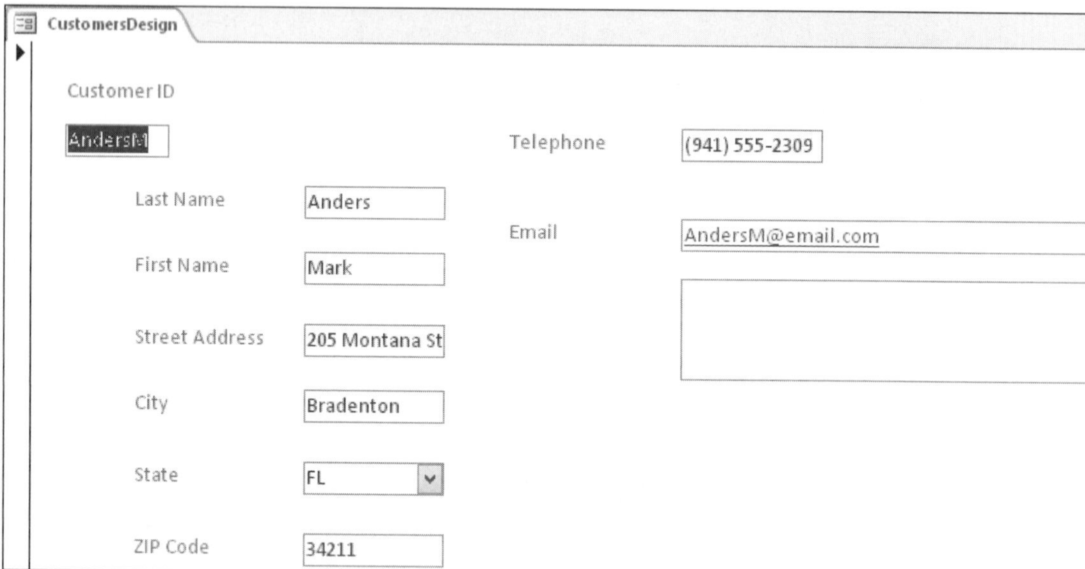

6. Save and close the **CustomersDesign** form.

Arranging Controls

Video Library http://labyrinthelab.com/videos Video Number: AC13-V0307

Now that you have positioned form controls where you want them to appear, you can arrange the controls more precisely and evenly to provide a more attractive, functional, and easy-to-read form. Tools for aligning, grouping, and distributing controls appear on the Arrange tab of the Ribbon.

Selecting Multiple Controls

Selecting, moving, positioning, and aligning each form control individually can be tedious and time-consuming. By selecting multiple controls and then moving or sizing them, you reduce the amount of time needed to position and format them. You may also select multiple controls in order to group them on a form.

QUICK REFERENCE	SELECTING MULTIPLE CONTROLS
Task	**Procedure**
Select controls individually	■ Click the first control on the form. ■ Press and hold [Shift] and click each additional control.
Select controls in a horizontal or vertical line	■ Click the vertical ruler to the left of the desired controls to select them all. ■ Click the horizontal ruler above the desired controls to select them all.
Select controls in one general area	■ Click above or to the left of the top left control and drag the pointer down and to the right to select the desired controls (aka *lassoing*.)

Aligning Controls

As you move and position controls on forms, it is sometimes challenging to position them so that they align properly. Access alignment tools help with aligning multiple controls.

FROM THE KEYBOARD

[Ctrl]+[←][↑][→] and [↓] to *nudge* a control into place

QUICK REFERENCE	ALIGNING SELECTED CONTROLS
Task	**Procedure**
Align controls using the Ribbon	■ Select multiple controls. ■ Choose Arrange→Sizing & Ordering→Align and click the desired alignment.
Align controls using the shortcut menu	■ Select multiple controls. ■ Right-click one of the selected controls and click Align. ■ Choose the desired alignment.

Anchoring Controls

You can also anchor controls—tie them to a section or to other controls so that moving or sizing a section adjusts the size and position of the anchored controls as well. Access provides nine different anchor positions that range from top left to bottom right. Although you anchor controls in Design View and Layout View, the results of the anchor display only in Layout View and Form View.

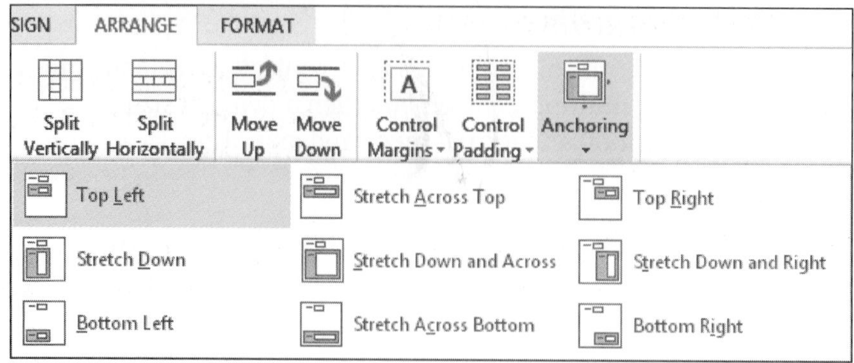

Access offers several different Anchor positions.

DEVELOP YOUR SKILLS AC03-D07

Arrange, Size, Group, and Anchor Form Controls

In this exercise, you will select multiple controls and arrange, resize, align, group, and anchor controls on the CustomersDesign form.

1. Open the **CustomersDesign** form in **Design View**.
2. Follow these steps to select and resize a group of form controls:

Ⓐ Click the **Customer ID** label.

Ⓑ Press and hold Ctrl and click each of the other labels.

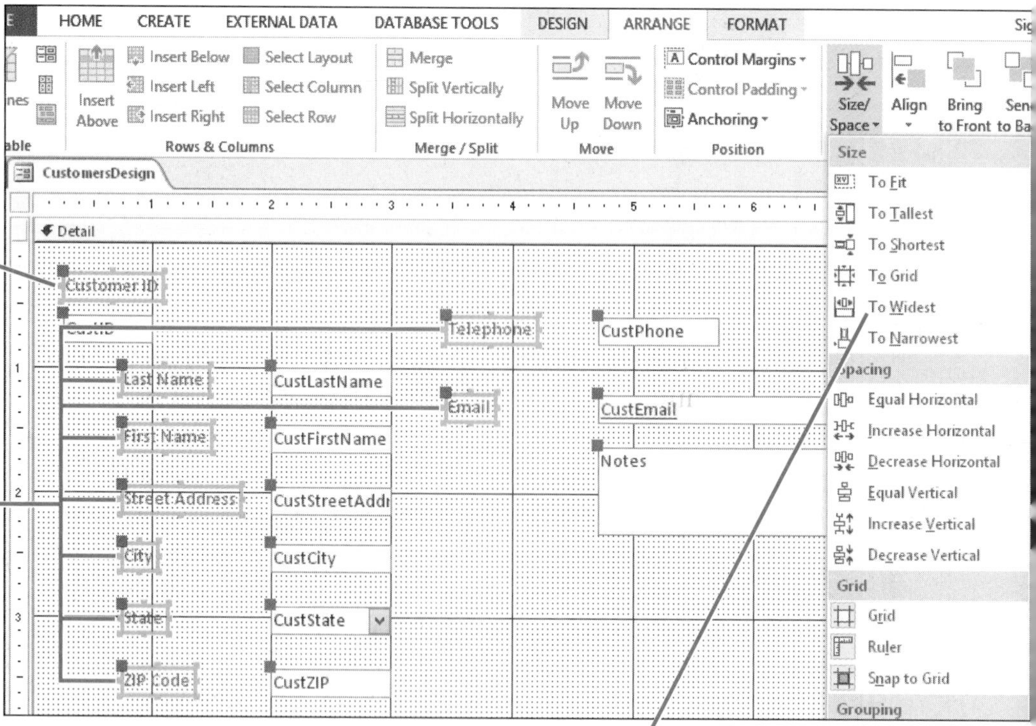

Ⓒ Choose **Arrange→Sizing & Ordering→Size/Space→To Widest**.

Don't worry if your form spacing isn't exactly as shown. You can move the controls to match the figures more precisely, if desired.

3. Click an unoccupied area of the form grid to deselect all controls.

4. Follow these steps to select and align controls:

Ⓐ Click the **Last Name** label.

Ⓑ Press and hold Ctrl and click the **CustLastName** text box, **Telephone** label, and **CustPhone** text box.

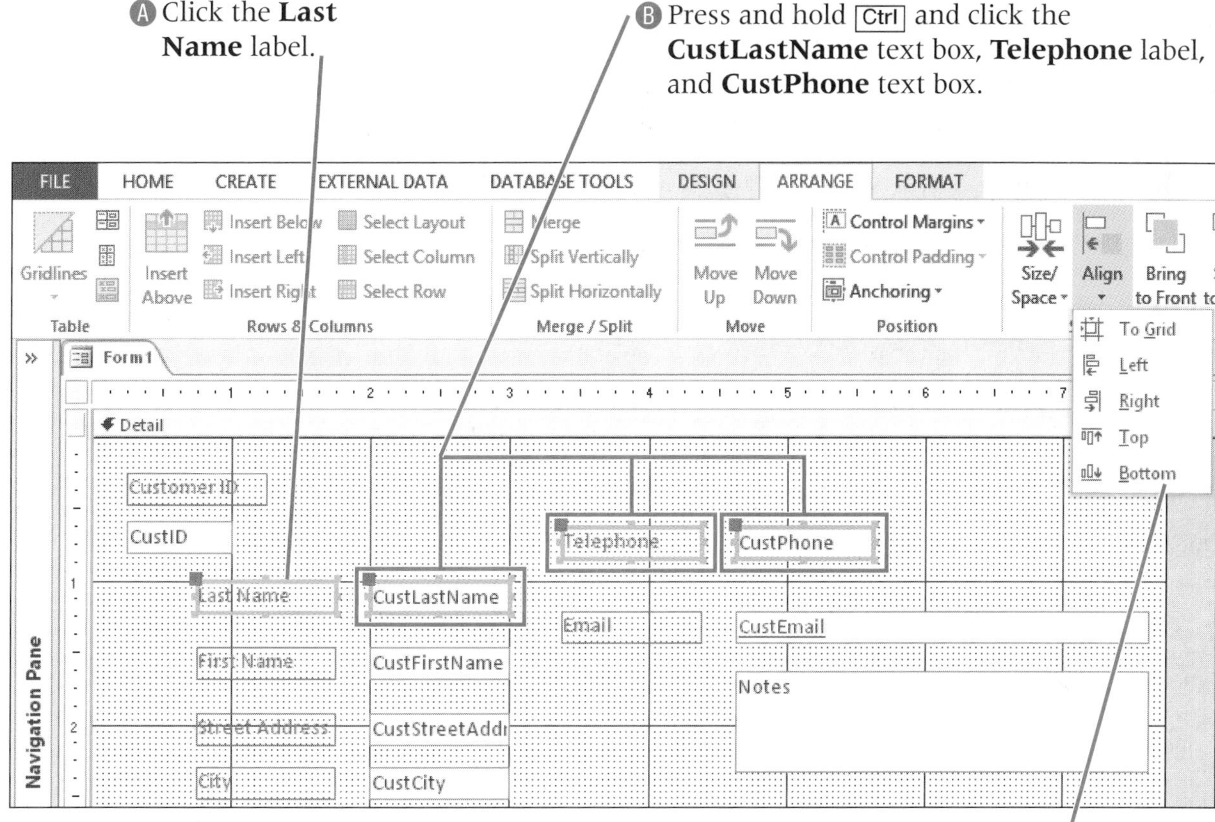

Ⓒ Choose **Arrange→Sizing & Ordering→Align→Bottom** to align the controls.

If the wrong control is selected, click a neutral area of the form and try again.

5. Select the **Email** label, **CustEmail** text box, and **Notes** text box, and tap ↓ until the **Email** controls are in line with the **FirstName** controls.

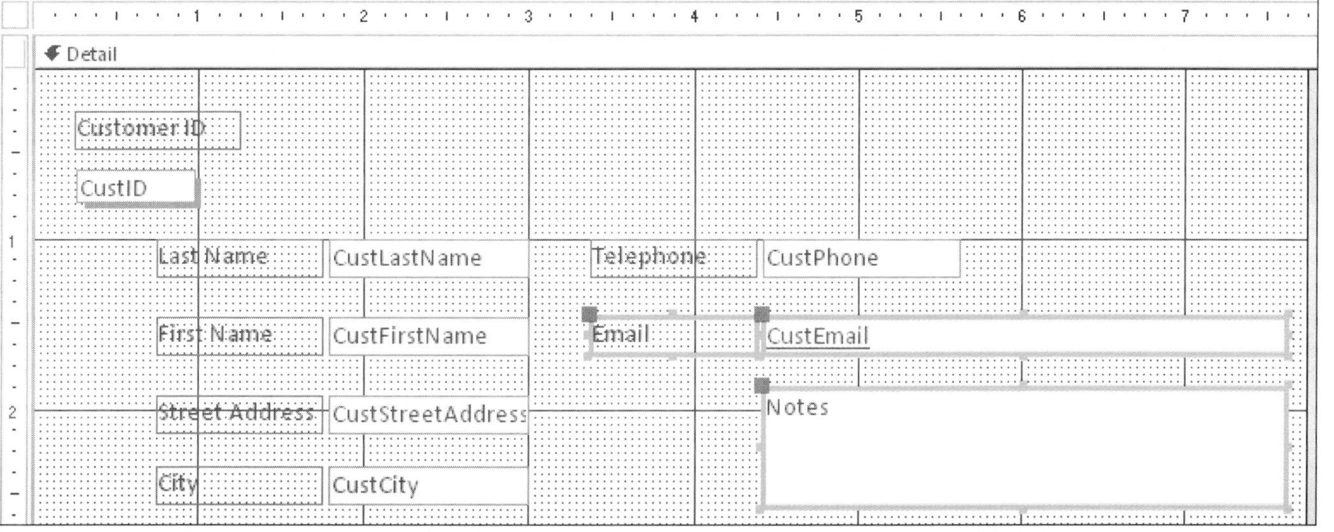

6. Click the vertical ruler to the left of the First Name controls and choose **Arrange→ Sizing & Ordering→Align→Top** .
7. Follow these steps to align a group of controls:

Ⓐ Click the horizontal ruler above these labels to select them: **LastName**, **FirstName**, **Street Address**, **City**, **State**, and **ZIP Code**.

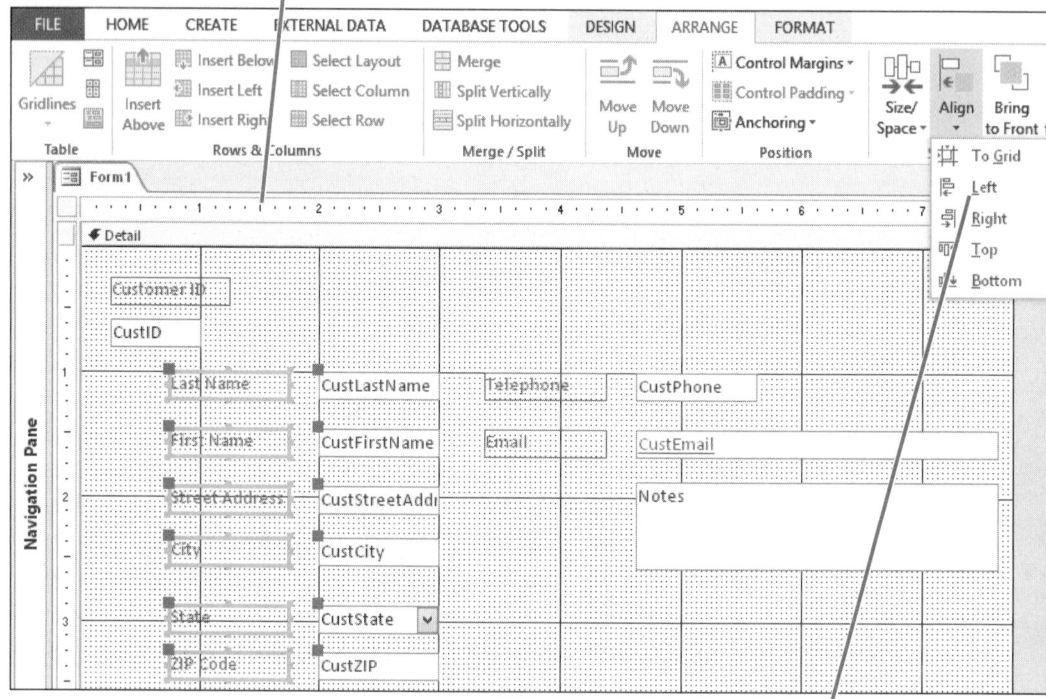

Ⓑ Choose **Arrange→Sizing & Ordering→Align→Left**.

If you select more objects than you intended, press and hold Shift as you click the undesired controls to deselect them without deselecting the desired controls.

8. Follow **step 7** to align the associated text boxes to the left.
9. Align the **Telephone** and **Email** labels to the left.

10. Align the **CustPhone**, **CustEmail**, and **Notes** text boxes to the left.

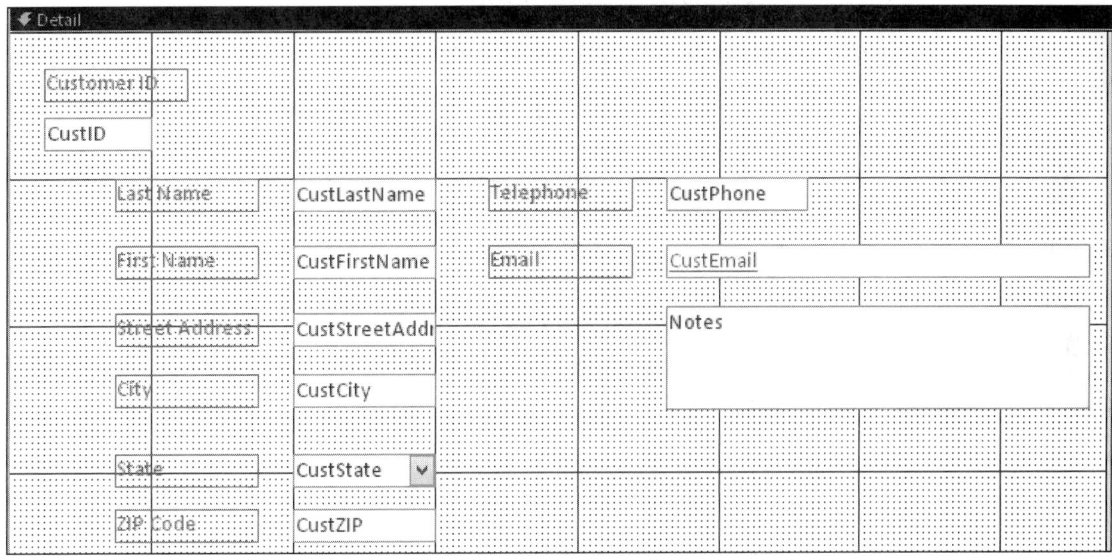

Size Multiple Controls

11. Follow these steps to size multiple text boxes at the same time:

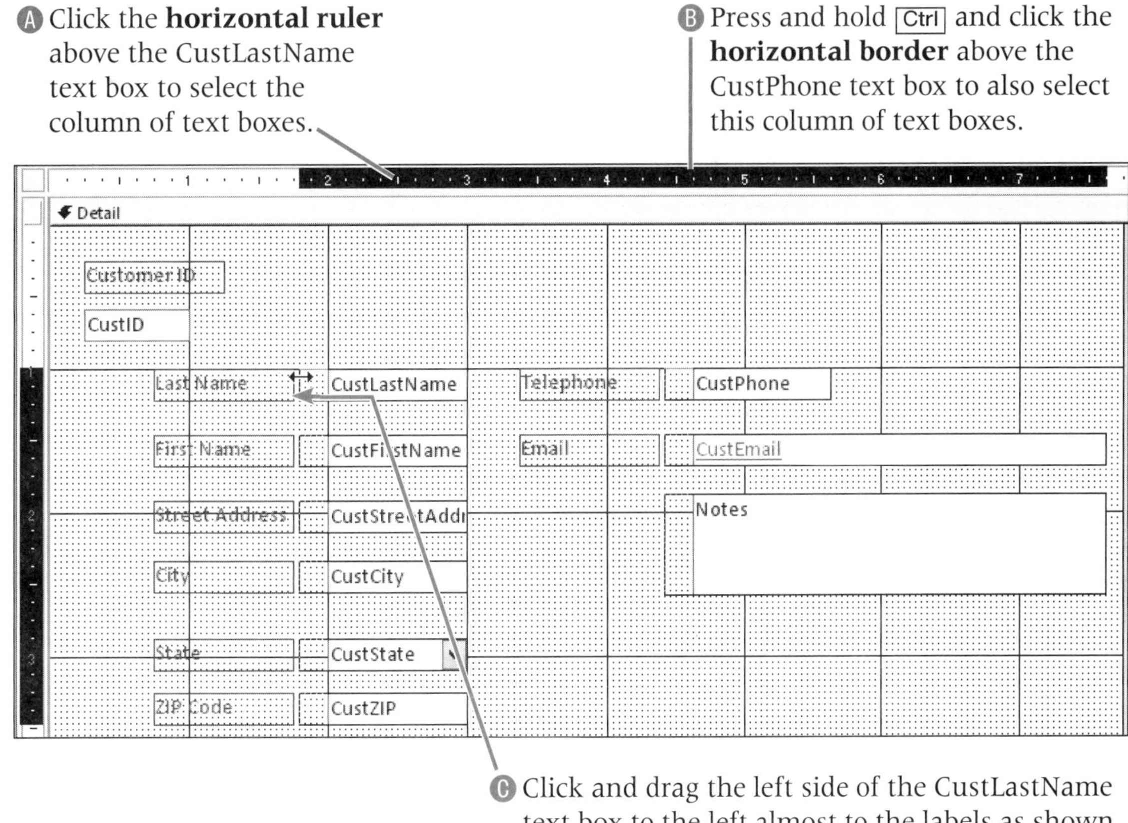

When you have multiple controls selected, you only have to drag the edge of one of them to resize them all.

Access 2013

Group Controls

12. Select the following controls using the technique you prefer: **Telephone** and **Email** labels, and **CustPhone** and **CustEmail** text boxes.
13. Choose **Arrange→Sizing & Ordering→Size/Space→Group**.
    Now whenever you click one of the grouped controls, you select them all.

Anchor Controls

14. Select the **Notes** text box.
15. Choose **Arrange→Position→Anchoring** .
16. Choose **Stretch Across Bottom** .
17. Switch to **Form View** to display the form as users will see it.

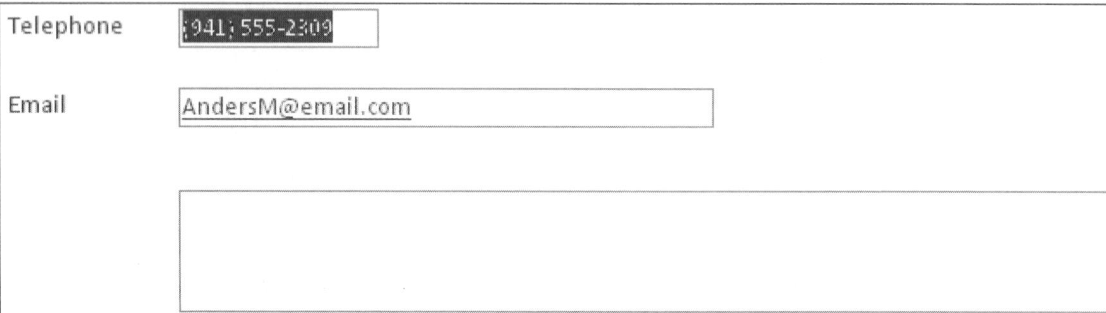

In Form View, the Notes text box is stretched and anchored across the bottom-right of the form.

18. Save the form.

Applying Themes to Forms

Video Library http://labyrinthelab.com/videos Video Number: AC13-V0308

Themes are designs that were developed by a group of professional design specialists and are similar to templates in Word and PowerPoint. When you apply a Theme to a database object, it applies the Theme to *every* object in the database. Themes contain colors, fonts, and control settings that enhance the form. You can use Themes to quickly and efficiently format all form sections and form controls. Rest the mouse pointer over a Theme icon to identify the Theme name in a ScreenTip.

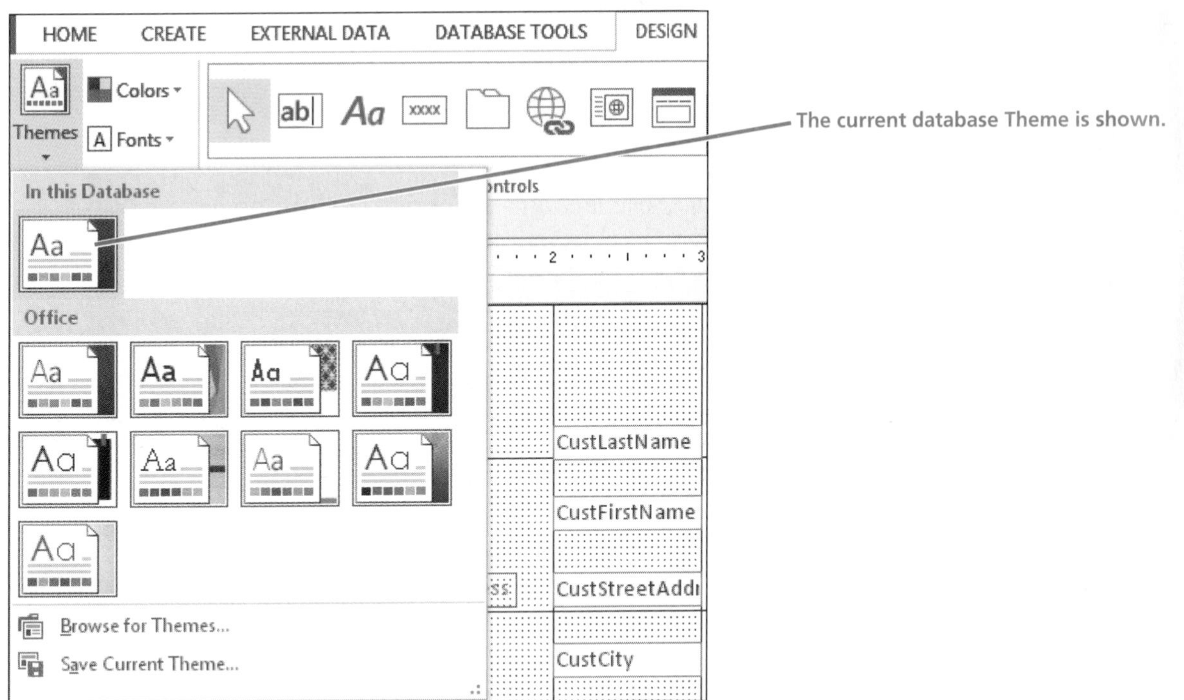

QUICK REFERENCE	APPLYING THEMES TO A FORM
Task	**Procedure**
Apply Themes to a form	■ Open the desired form in Design View. ■ Choose Design→Themes→Themes and select a Theme design.

Access 2013

DEVELOP YOUR SKILLS AC03-D08

Apply a Theme to a Form

In this exercise, you will apply Themes to the CustomersDesign form.

1. Display the **CustomersDesign** form in Design View.
2. Follow these steps to apply a new Theme to the form:

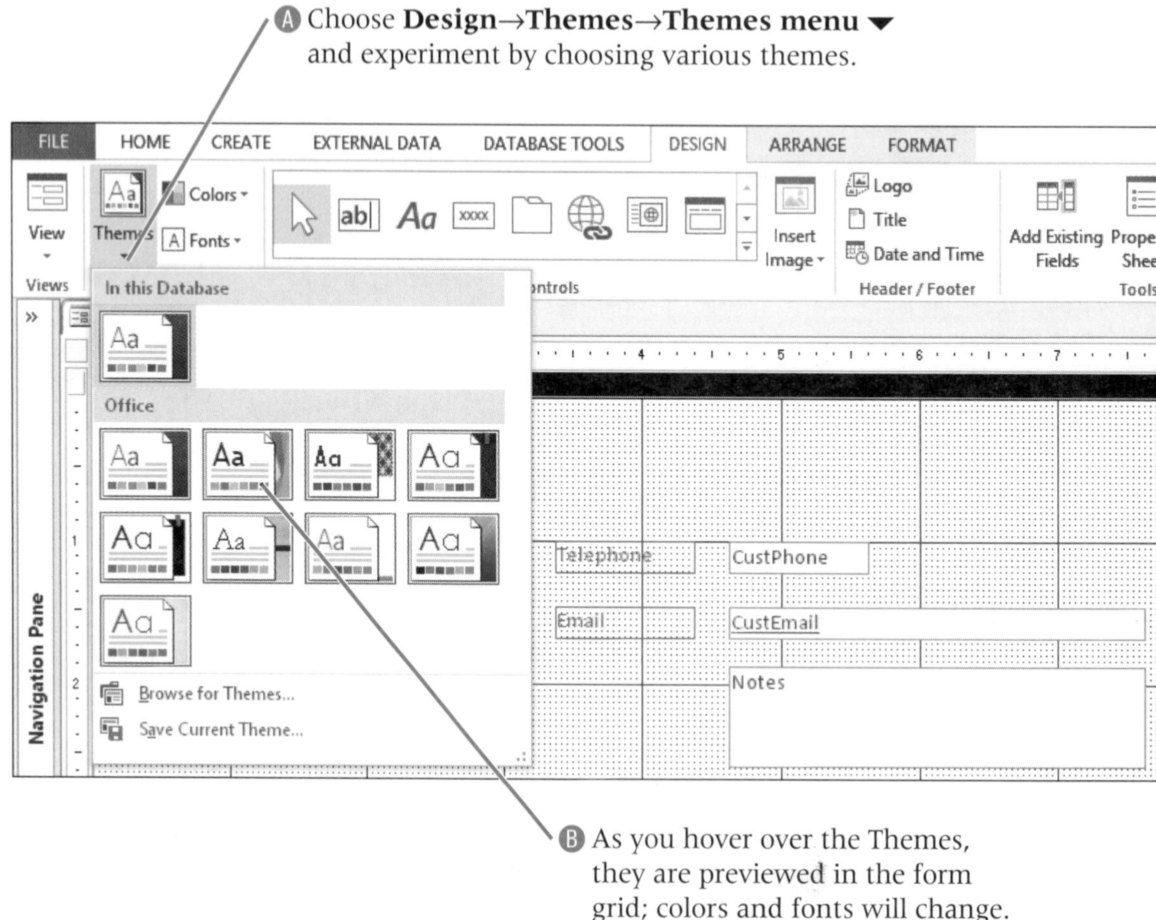

Themes are arranged alphabetically and may vary depending on screen size and resolution.

3. Repeat the procedures in **step 2** to return to the Office default Theme. Do not save the form

Modifying Form Controls

Video Library http://labyrinthelab.com/videos Video Number: AC13-V0309

As you design and work with forms, there will be times when you want to edit the appearance of controls or remove them from the form. Access offers tools that enable you to change the properties of form labels, change the format of the text box data to display as currency, for example, and to format the font and background color of controls.

Editing Labels

Label controls identify the values contained in the associated text boxes. As a result, they need to be as descriptive as possible and yet also be concise. You have already learned how to set field captions to change the column headings when field names contain text that runs together. When you add field controls to forms, you can edit the label text directly in the label control box.

Using Design Font Tools

Tools for formatting controls appear on the Design tab when Form Design and Layout views are active. Using these tools, you can change the font format, design, size, color, and alignment as well as the fill color of the control box.

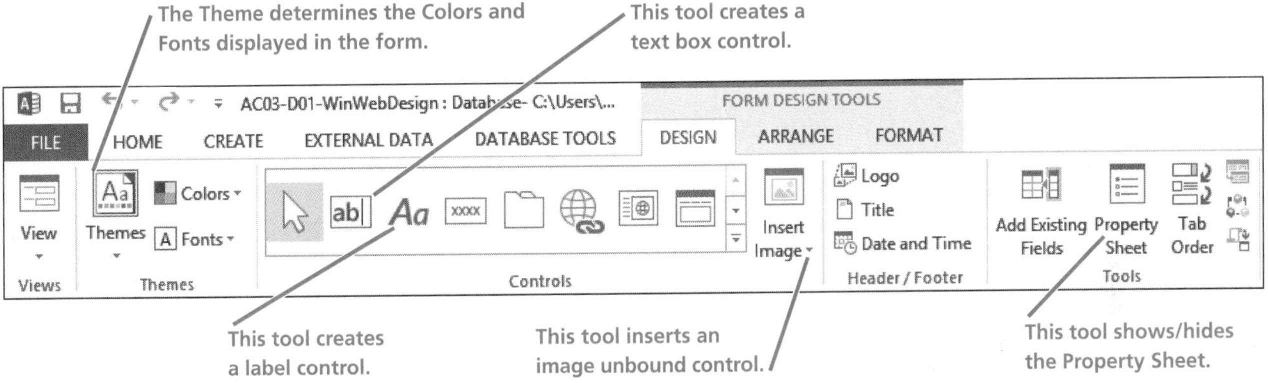

Using the Property Sheet

The Property Sheet provides a full range of formatting properties for form controls, such as, font name, size, and color, field alignment, background colors, numeric field formats (general number, currency, etc.), and many others. The properties displayed vary depending on the type of control selected and whether the label or the text box part of a control is selected.

FROM THE KEYBOARD

F4 to open/close the Property Sheet

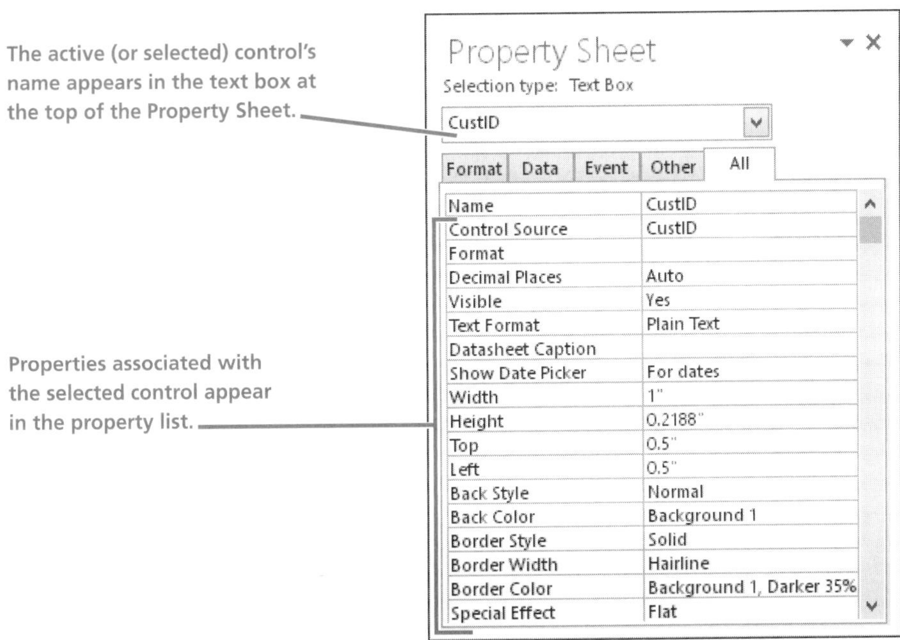

Access 2013

DEVELOP YOUR SKILLS AC03-D09

Use the Property Sheet to Format a Form Control

In this exercise, you will use the Property Sheet to apply a special effect to a control on the CustomersDesign form.

1. Display the **CustomersDesign** form in **Design View**.
2. Follow these steps to add a special effect to a form control:

Ⓐ Click the **CustID** text box to select it.

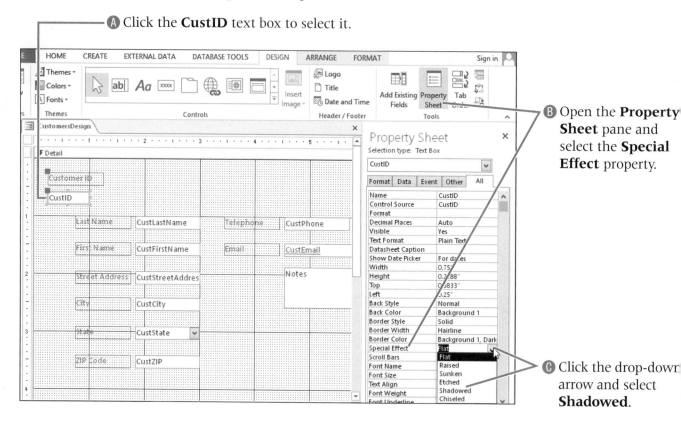

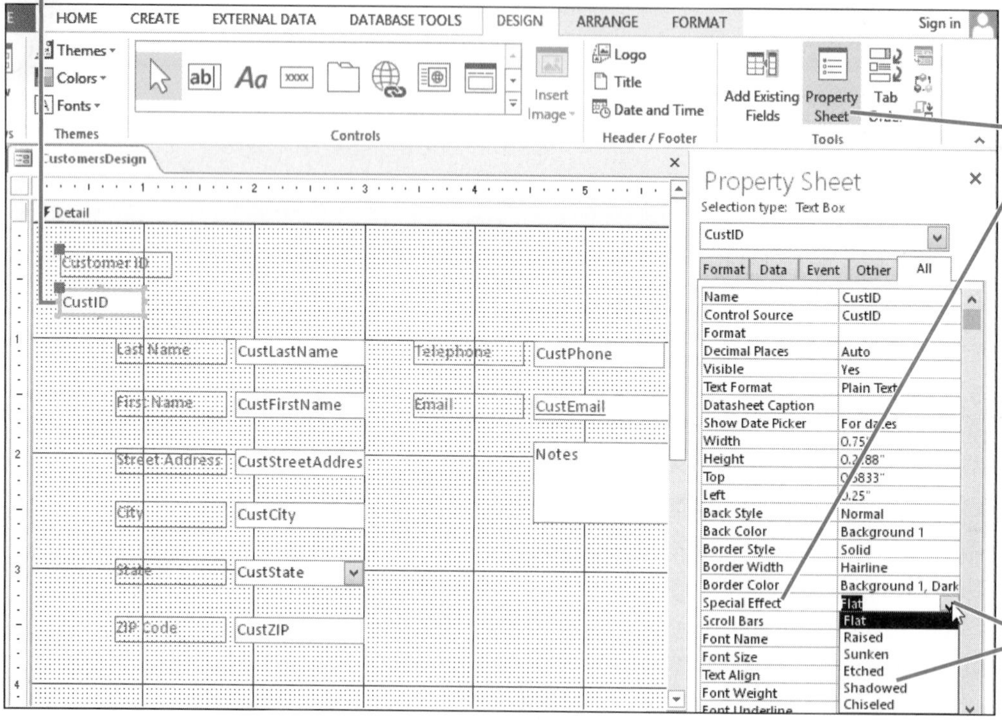

Ⓑ Open the **Property Sheet** pane and select the **Special Effect** property.

Ⓒ Click the drop-down arrow and select **Shadowed**.

Don't worry if your form spacing isn't exactly as shown here. You can move the controls to match the figures more precisely, if desired.

3. Save the form.

Using the Fill Color Palette

Video Library http://labyrinthelab.com/videos Video Number: AC13-V0310

Whether you are formatting text color or adding a background fill color, the techniques for using the color palette are the same. Access identifies the color names in three parts: Color Name, Color Type, Percent Light or Dark. So if you are formatting text or fill and the instructions say Dark Red, Accent 4, 20% Darker, you will be able to locate the appropriate color.

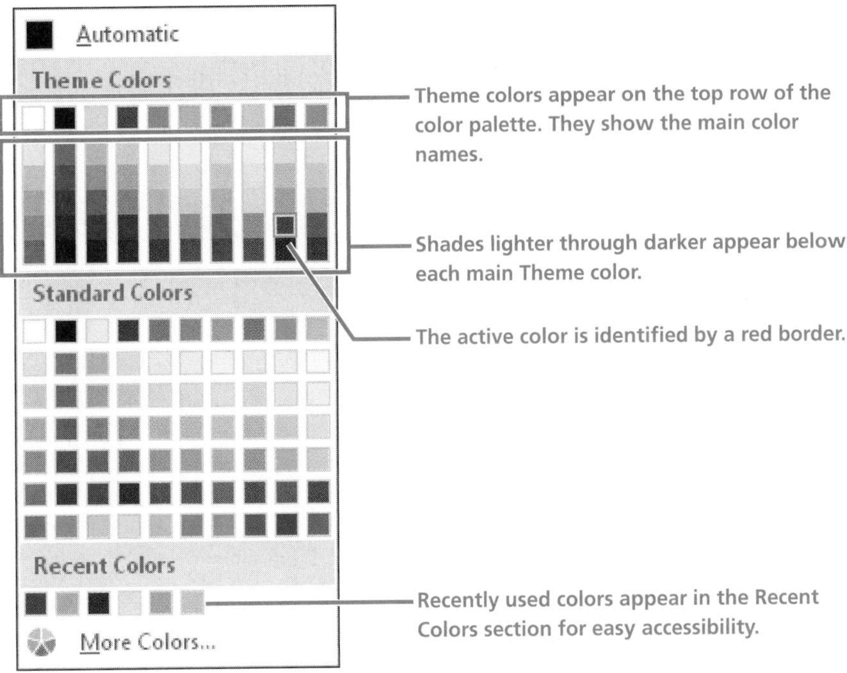
Automatic
Theme Colors
Standard Colors
Recent Colors
More Colors...
Theme colors appear on the top row of the color palette. They show the main color names.
Shades lighter through darker appear below each main Theme color.
The active color is identified by a red border.
Recently used colors appear in the Recent Colors section for easy accessibility.

DEVELOP YOUR SKILLS AC03-D10

Apply Formatting to Controls

In this exercise, you will format labels, set formatting, and use properties to format controls on the CustomersDesign form.

1. Open the **CustomersDesign** form in **Design View**.
2. Follow these steps to format label text:

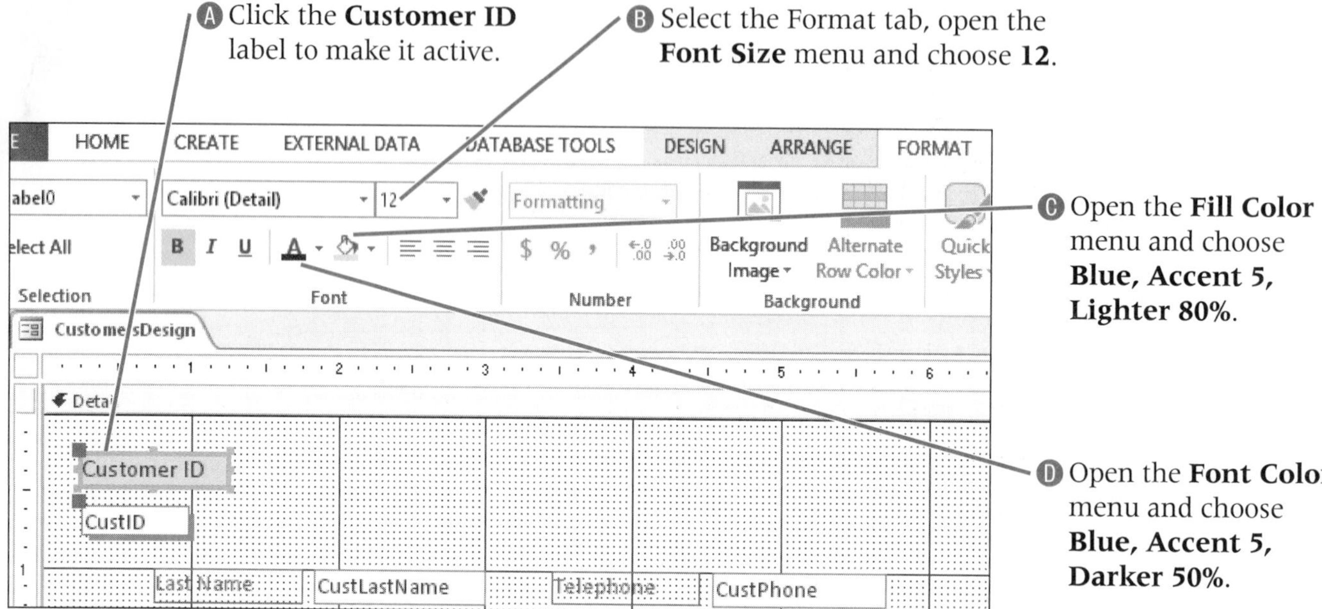

Ⓐ Click the **Customer ID** label to make it active.
Ⓑ Select the Format tab, open the **Font Size** menu and choose **12**.
Ⓒ Open the **Fill Color** menu and choose **Blue, Accent 5, Lighter 80%**.
Ⓓ Open the **Font Color** menu and choose **Blue, Accent 5, Darker 50%**.
HOME
CREATE
EXTERNAL DATA
DATABASE TOOLS
DESIGN
ARRANGE
FORMAT
Calibri (Detail)
12
Formatting
Background Image
Alternate Row Color
Quick Styles
Selection
Font
Number
Background
CustomersDesign
Detail
Customer ID
CustID
Last Name
CustLastName
Telephone
CustPhone

WARNING

If you chose a different Theme, your color selections will be different. Choose good contrasting colors from your palette.

Use the Property Sheet

3. Click the **Notes** text box to make it active.
4. If necessary, choose **Design→Tools→Property Sheet** to open the Property Sheet.
5. Follow these steps to set the Fore Color property for the Notes field:

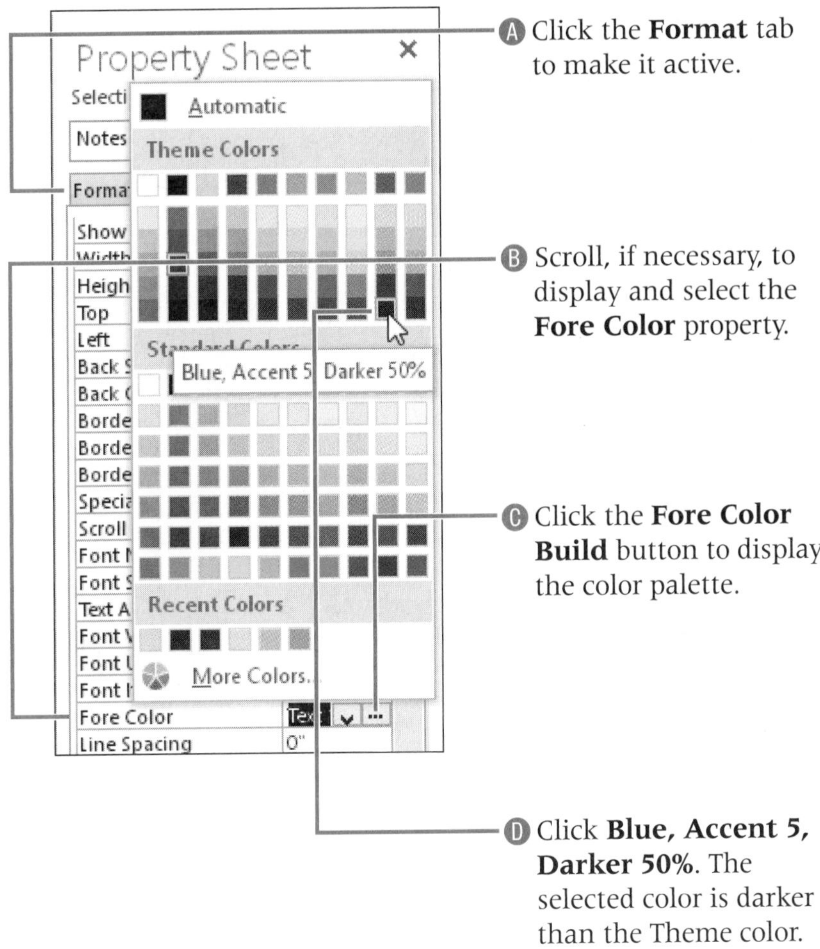

Ⓐ Click the **Format** tab to make it active.

Ⓑ Scroll, if necessary, to display and select the **Fore Color** property.

Ⓒ Click the **Fore Color Build** button to display the color palette.

Ⓓ Click **Blue, Accent 5, Darker 50%**. The selected color is darker than the Theme color.

Use Format Painter

6. Click the **Customer ID** label to make it active.
7. Choose **Format→Font** and double-click **Format Painter** to copy the formats applied to the **Customer ID** label.

   If you only single-click the Format Painter then it will only work one time and you will have to single-click it again to apply the formatting to the next object.

   Access picks up the format of the label, and the mouse pointer changes to a paint brush so you can "paint" the format onto other labels.
8. Click each of the other labels on the form, one at a time, to apply the format to them.
9. Press Esc to drop the paint brush.
10. Adjust the size of each label to show all the text.

11. Switch to **Form View**.

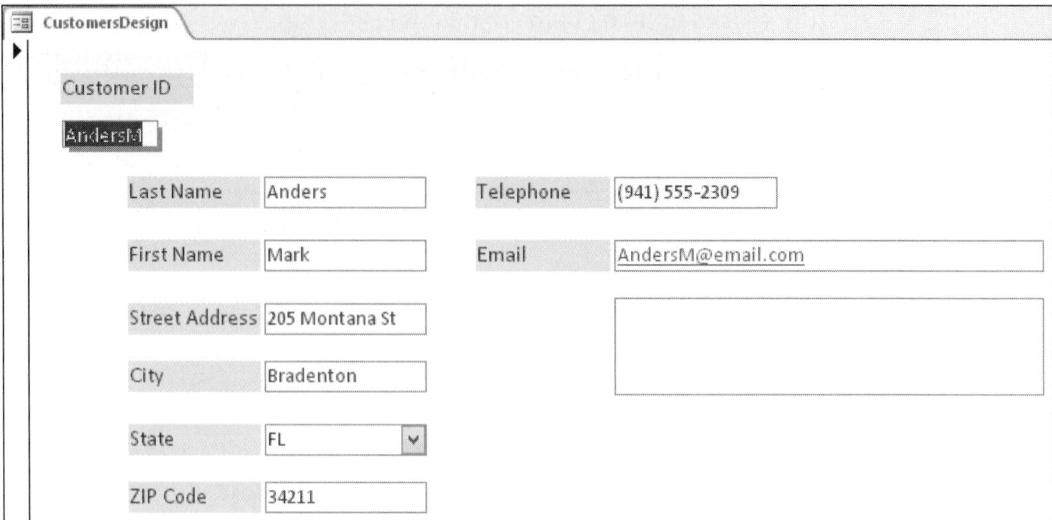

Don't worry if your form spacing isn't exactly as shown here. You can move the controls to match the figures more precisely, if desired.

12. Save and close the form.

Modifying Form Layout

Video Library http://labyrinthelab.com/videos Video Number: AC13-V0311

So far, you have added, edited, arranged, and formatted controls on a new form and saved the form. These changes had no effect on the form's layout and design. For example, the form palette is still white and the Detail section is the only section displayed. Formatting a form, as distinguished from formatting controls, involves such additional tasks as:

- Displaying and editing Form Header and Form Footer sections.
- Formatting section backgrounds.
- Adding design elements to sections.

Displaying Form Header and Form Footer

Controls such as page number, page title, logos, and lines that you choose to place in the header or footer sections of the form repeat on form pages just as they do on a Word document. By default, Access hides the Form Header and Form Footer sections of a new form until you are ready to display them. To display the Form Header and Footer, right-click the Detail section bar and choose Form Header/Footer. Then, select the control that you want to add to the sections on the Design tab.

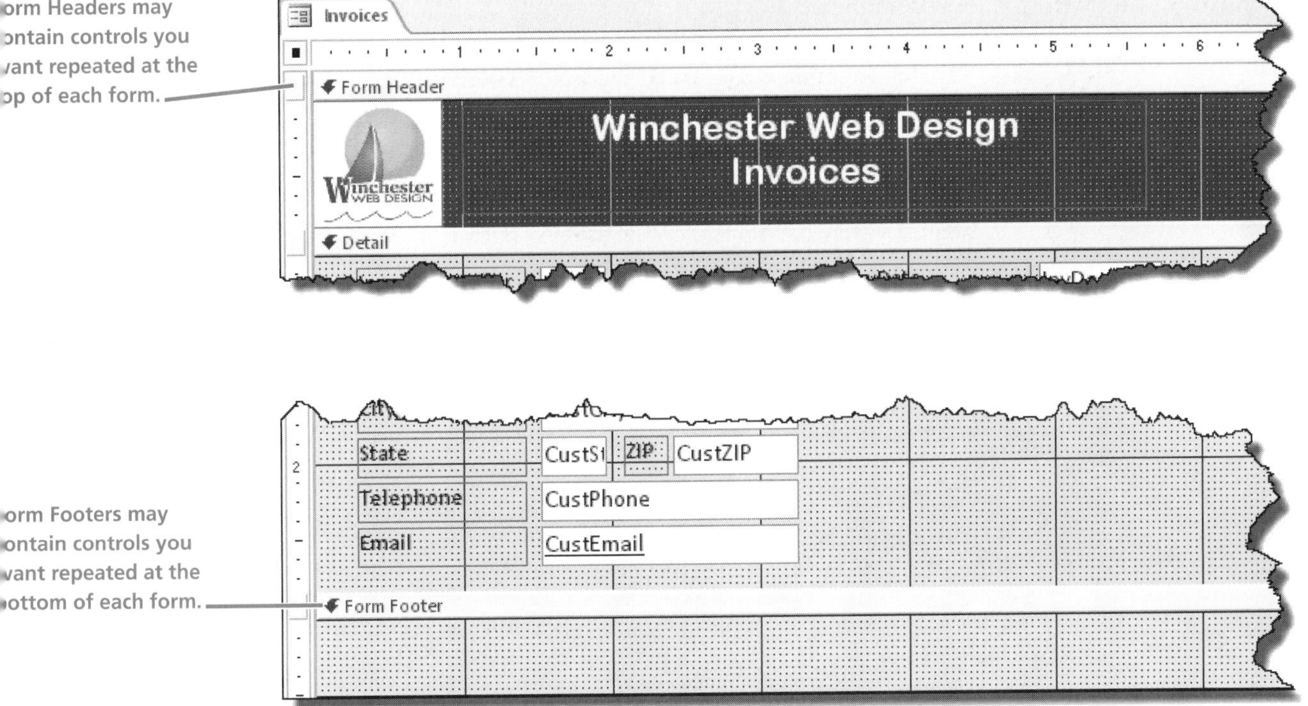

Sizing Form Sections

To resize form sections, drag the bottom of the section up or down, or drag the bar for the section that appears below the section you want to resize. For example, to make the Form Header section larger, drag the Detail section bar down. To make the Form Header section smaller, drag the Detail section bar up.

The mouse pointer appears as a two-headed arrow with a bar ✛ when positioned appropriately for sizing a section.

DEVELOP YOUR SKILLS AC03-D11

Display and Format a Form Header

In this exercise, you will display the Form Header and Footer sections and format the header background on the CustomersDesign form.

1. Open the **CustomersDesign** form in **Design View**.
2. Right-click the **Detail** section bar and choose **Form Header/Footer** to display the Form Header and Form Footer sections.

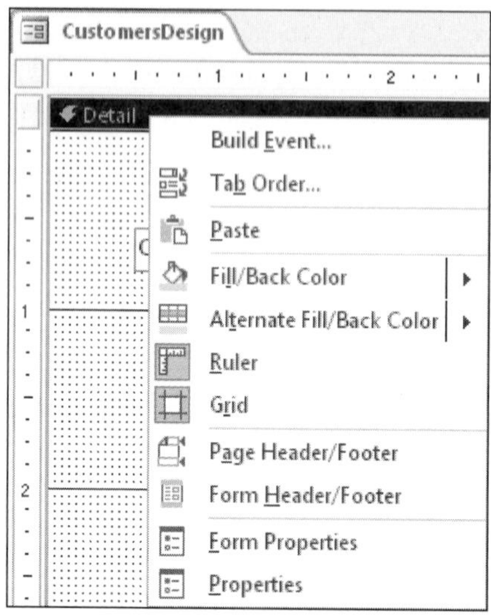

3. Follow these steps to make the Form Header section larger to accommodate a title and logo:

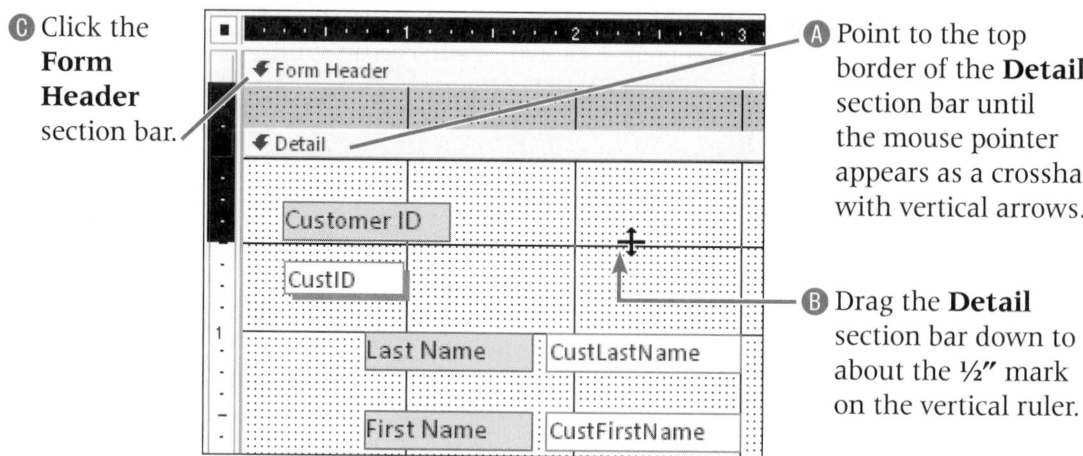

4. Choose **Format→Font→Fill Color** menu, and then choose **Blue, Accent 5, 60% lighter**.
5. Save the changes to the form.

Adding Unbound Controls to a Form

Video Library http://labyrinthelab.com/videos Video Number: AC13-V0312

Design elements (drawn shapes, logos, graphics, and titles) improve the appearance of a form. Because these elements do not require access to data in database tables, they are considered unbound controls and are not bound to data. Tools for adding unbound controls appear on the Design tab of Ribbon. You can point to a control and use the ToolTip to identify the control.

Titles and logos can be added to a form in more than one way. To add a title, you can drag a Label control to the Form Header section and then type in the caption. To add a logo, you can use the Image tool and drag the image where you want it, or click Logo on the Ribbon and Access will place the logo on the left-hand side of the Page Header section. If the Page Header section is not open and you use the Title or Logo tool, Access opens the Page Header section for you.

To add a subtitle to a form that already has a title, click at the end of the title, tap Ctrl + Enter, and add the subtitle text under the existing title.

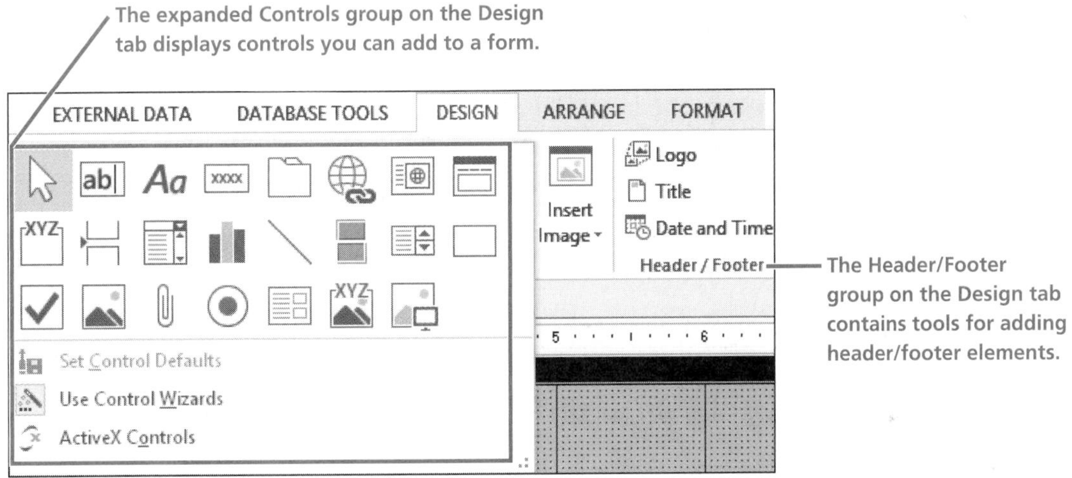

When you use most of the unbound controls to add design elements to a database object, the mouse pointer becomes a plus symbol called a *crosshair*. Sometimes the character, or symbol, on the control icon appears with the mouse pointer crosshair to identify the control you are adding to the form.

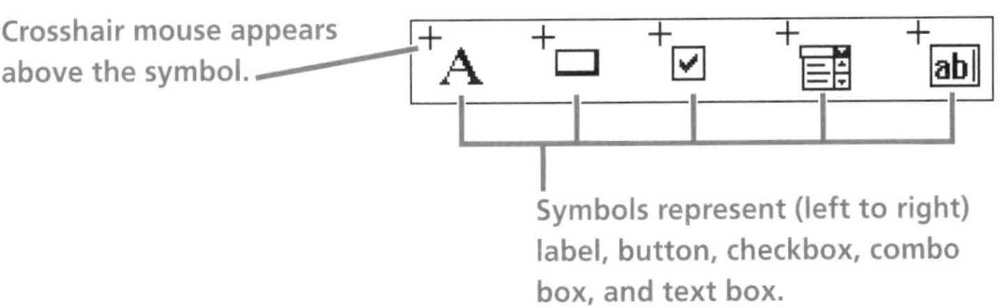

Crosshair mouse appears above the symbol.
Symbols represent (left to right) label, button, checkbox, combo box, and text box.

DEVELOP YOUR SKILLS AC03-D12

Add Unbound Controls to Forms

In this exercise, you will add a title and image to the Form Header section of the CustomersDesign form using unbound controls.

Add a Title

1. Display the **CustomersDesign** form in **Design View**.
2. Choose **Design→Header/Footer→Title**.
   Access adds the title section to the Form Header section and selects the CustomersDesign text so you can edit it.
3. Type **`Winchester Customers`** and press [Enter].
   When you add a title control, Access automatically places an empty Auto-Logo object immediately to the left of the title control. You will not be using the Auto-Logo on this form.
4. Follow these steps to delete the Auto-Logo and size the new title:

Ⓐ Click the **faint dotted border** of the logo control shown here to the left of the title and tap [Delete].

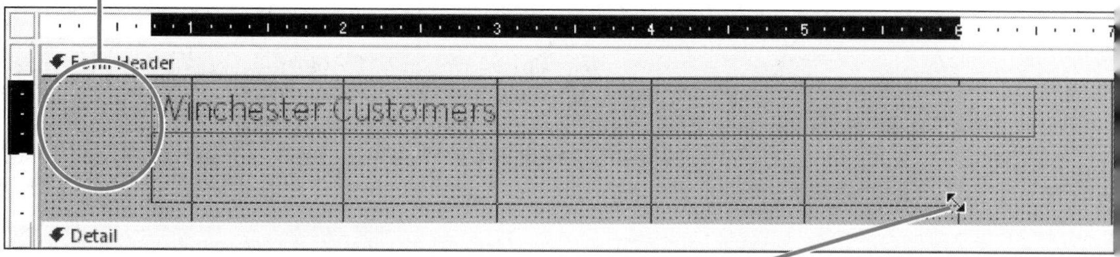

Ⓑ Drag the **lower-right corner handle** of the title control to the position shown.

5. Press [F4] to display the Property Sheet and set the following properties for the label control to format the label text:

Property	Setting
Back Color	Blue, Accent 5, Darker 50%
Border Color	Blue, Accent 5, Lighter 80%
Special Effect	Raised
Font Name	Lucida Calligraphy
Font Size	30
Text Align	Center
Fore Color	Blue, Accent 5, Lighter 80%

6. Adjust the size of the title, if necessary, by dragging the borders of the control.
7. Center the title using the left, right, up, and down arrows.

Add an Image

8. Click an unoccupied area of the form and choose **Design→Controls→Insert Image** and click **Browse**.
9. Navigate to the **AC2013 Lesson 03** folder, select **WWD-Logo.bmp**, and click **OK**.
   If you do not see WWD-Logo.bmp, click the file type arrow and select All Files.
10. Click to the left of the title and drag the mouse down and to the right.

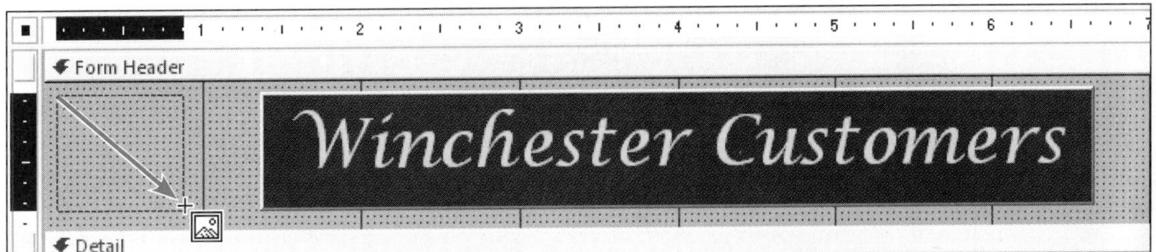

11. Select the new image and the title.
12. Choose **Arrange→Sizing & Ordering→Align→Top**.
13. Choose **Design→Views→View→Form View**.

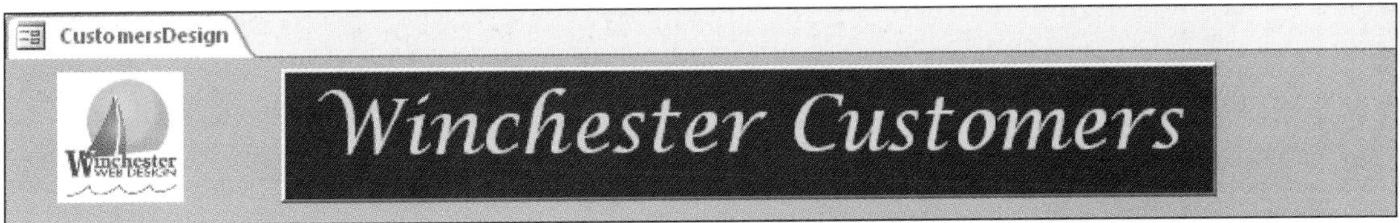

14. Save the changes to the form.

Access 2013

Setting Additional Form Properties

Video Library http://labyrinthelab.com/videos Video Number: AC13-V0313

You have already used the Property Sheet to format controls and sections on the form. Now that you have the visual elements of the form set, you can focus on the functional elements of the form. Additional form properties include those form items that affect the whole form, such as the record selector bar, scroll bars, and navigation buttons.

Choosing Items to Show on Forms

The navigation buttons at the bottom of most form windows are important to display different form records. Scroll bars can be useful when the form and data extend beyond the monitor boundaries. When the form is sized to display the complete form, there is no need for scroll bars; they can be removed from view. However, just because the entire form appears onscreen on one computer does not necessarily mean the entire form will appear onscreen on every computer. Allowances must be made for individual screen size and resolution.

The record selector bar can also be useful. However, many businesses find that their employees inadvertently click the record selector bar and delete records when they really want to delete data in a form field. As a result, many businesses remove the record selector bar from their forms to prevent accidental data loss.

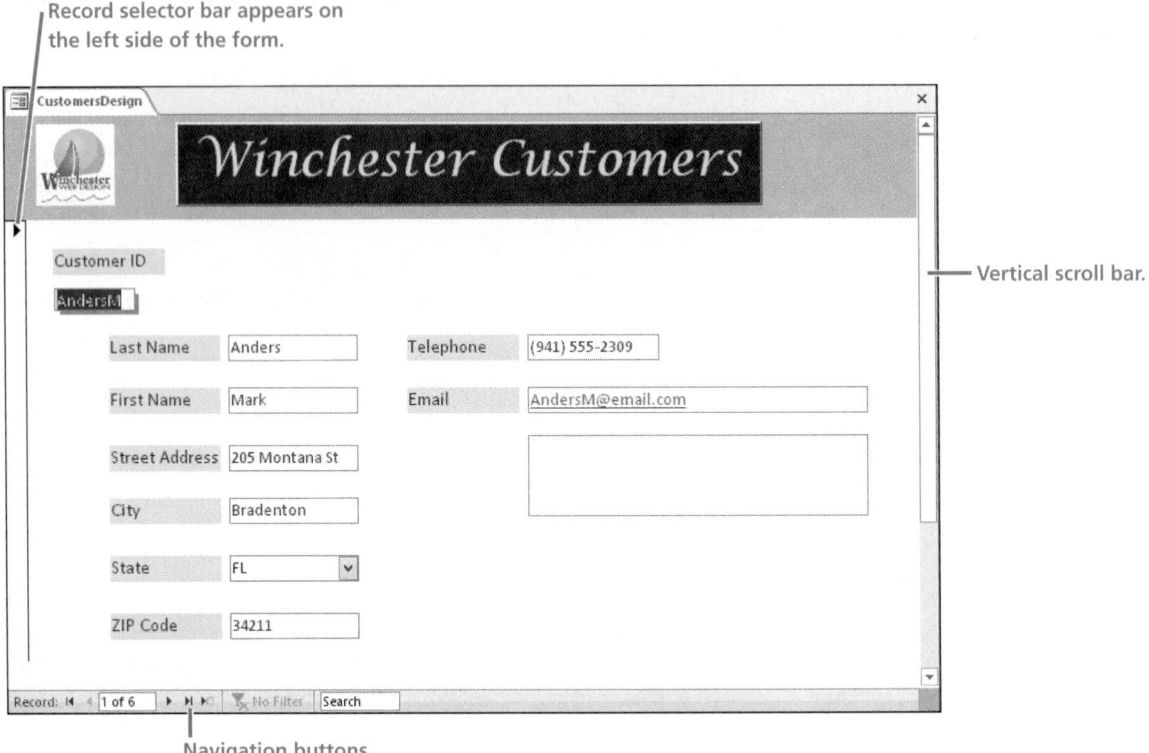

Displaying the Form Property Sheet

Properties displayed in the Property Sheet vary, depending on the item that is selected or active on the form. To access properties that affect the whole form, no other controls or sections on the form can be selected, other than the Form Selector button. You can click a blank area of the form outside of the entire form grid/palette to display Form properties or select Form from the Property Sheet Selection Type list, or right-click the Form Selector button and choose Properties. The Property Sheet is available in both Design and Layout Views.

FROM THE KEYBOARD

[Shift]+[Spacebar] to select an entire form when no record selector bar is displayed

The Property Sheet contains numerous properties, some familiar—such as caption—and some unfamiliar—such as Allow PivotTable View. To learn more about properties, use Access Help.

DEVELOP YOUR SKILLS AC03-D13

Set Form Properties

In this exercise, you will use the Property Sheet to set properties for the CustomersDesign form to remove the record selector bar and scroll bars, and to ensure that you will be able to use navigation buttons, the Close button, and Min and Max buttons.

1. Display the **CustomersDesign** form in **Design View**.
2. Press F4 to display the Property Sheet.
3. Follow these steps to set Form properties:

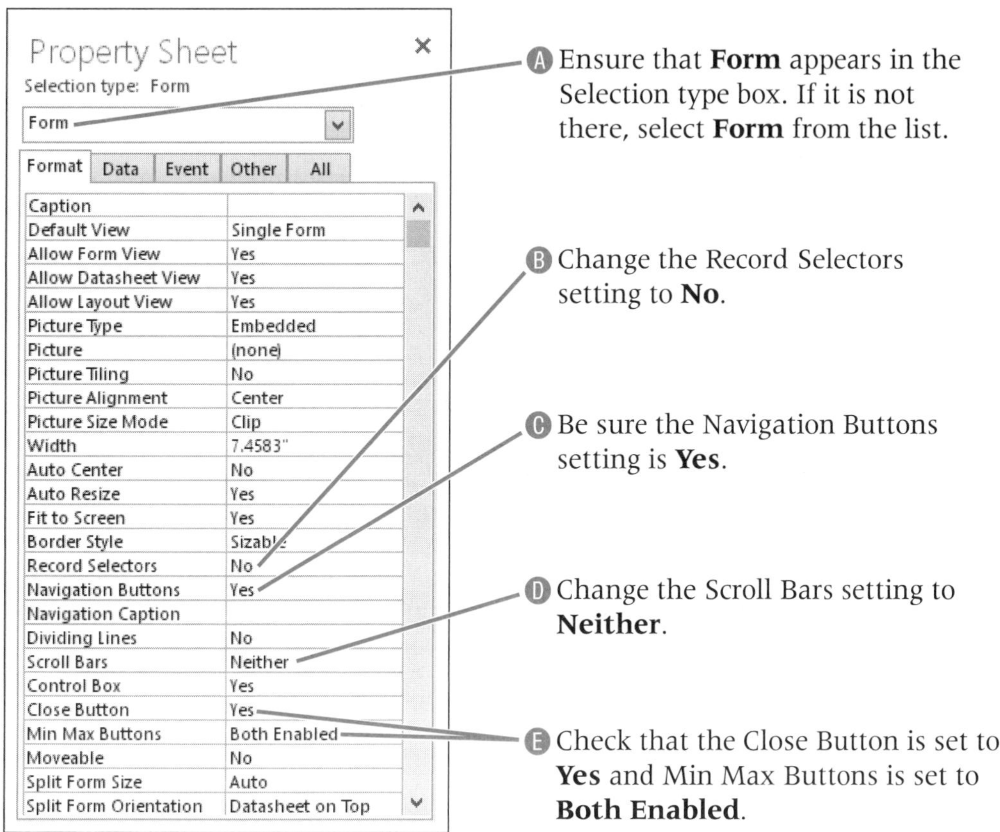

Ⓐ Ensure that **Form** appears in the Selection type box. If it is not there, select **Form** from the list.

Ⓑ Change the Record Selectors setting to **No**.

Ⓒ Be sure the Navigation Buttons setting is **Yes**.

Ⓓ Change the Scroll Bars setting to **Neither**.

Ⓔ Check that the Close Button is set to **Yes** and Min Max Buttons is set to **Both Enabled**.

Access 2013

4. Save changes and switch to **Form View** to display the form.

Setting a Form Tab Order

Video Library http://labyrinthelab.com/videos Video Number: AC13-V0314

Regardless of the arrangement of bound and unbound controls, when you use a form to enter records, Access moves from one field to the next each time you press Tab or Enter. Access moves among form fields in the order in which the fields appear in the table datasheet or query grid on which you base the form. When you design custom forms, how you position controls may be significantly different from the order in which they appear in a table datasheet. As a result, tapping Tab sometimes makes it appear as if Access is randomly hopping from control to control.

You can control the order in which Access moves by changing the tab order. This enables you to view data on the form and access each field in the order it appears onscreen. If you rearrange the field order or insert a new field in between two existing fields you often will alter the traditional tab order of top-down, left-right. If that is the case, you should reset the tab order. In addition, you may want to modify the tab order to skip fields containing data that should not be changed, move onscreen to fields in the order in which fields appear on a printed form, or move to fields in a more logical order.

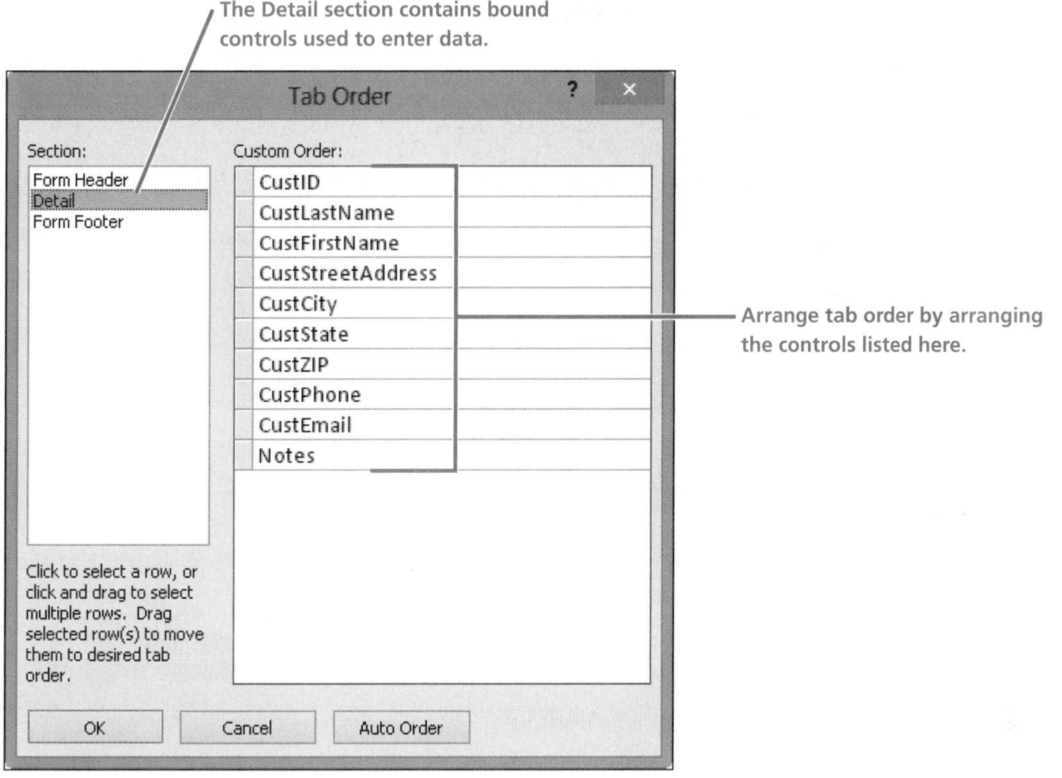

The Tab Order dialog box contains the setting to control tab order.

DEVELOP YOUR SKILLS AC03-D14

Set Tab Order

In this exercise, you will set the tab order for the CustomersDesign form.

1. Display the **CustomersDesign** form in **Form View** and press [Tab] to advance through all fields on the form.
2. Switch to **Design View**.
3. Choose **Design→Tools→Tab Order**.

Access 2013

4. Follow these steps to change the tab order:

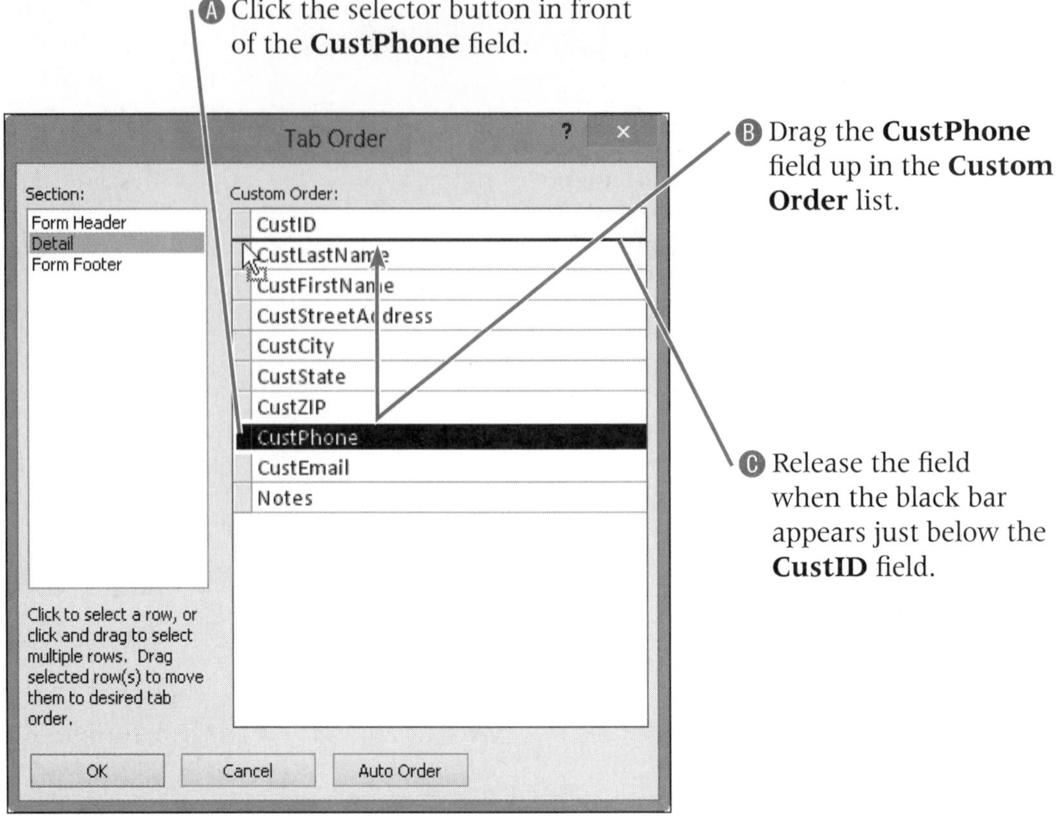

5. Click **OK**.

Test the Tab Order

6. Switch to **Form View** and press [Tab] to move through all fields.

   Access moves from field to field, starting in CustID, then moving to Telephone, stopping at each field, and finishing in the Notes field.

7. Save and close the form.

Creating Multiple Items Forms

Video Library http://labyrinthelab.com/videos Video Number: AC13-V0315

Custom designing a form and creating simple forms are good ways to format forms when you want to display or print each record individually. Sometimes, however, you will want to print multiple items in a table using a layout that is more appropriate for printing and distributing than a table datasheet. The Multiple Items form is used for those occasions.

When you create a Multiple Items form, Access creates a form that resembles a datasheet because data appears in rows and columns. However, you can customize a Multiple Items form. For example, you can adjust the size of text boxes, add graphic elements to the form, and enhance the form with color.

DEVELOP YOUR SKILLS AC03-D15

Create a Multiple Items Form

In this exercise, you will create a new form for the Customers table.

1. Follow these steps to create a Multiple Items form for the Customers table:

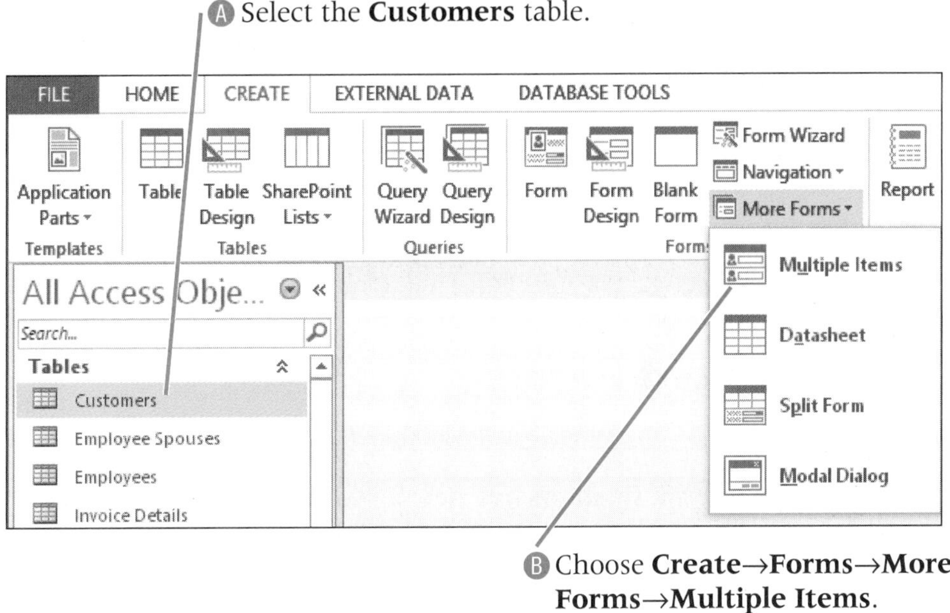

Access creates a new multiple item form and displays it in Layout View.

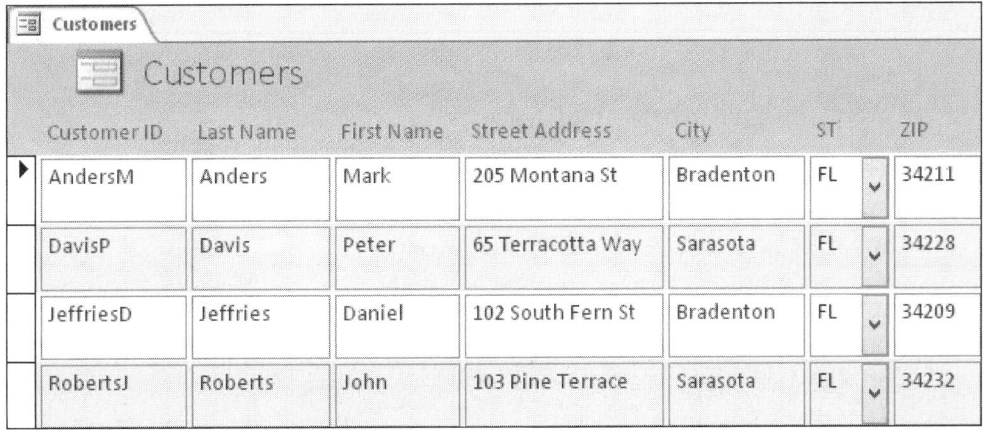

Customer ID	Last Name	First Name	Street Address	City	ST	ZIP
AndersM	Anders	Mark	205 Montana St	Bradenton	FL	34211
DavisP	Davis	Peter	65 Terracotta Way	Sarasota	FL	34228
JeffriesD	Jeffries	Daniel	102 South Fern St	Bradenton	FL	34209
RobertsJ	Roberts	John	103 Pine Terrace	Sarasota	FL	34232

2. Drag the **right border** of each column heading to resize the data fields.
3. Select the graphic to the left of the **Form Header** section and press Delete.

4. Switch back to **Form View**.

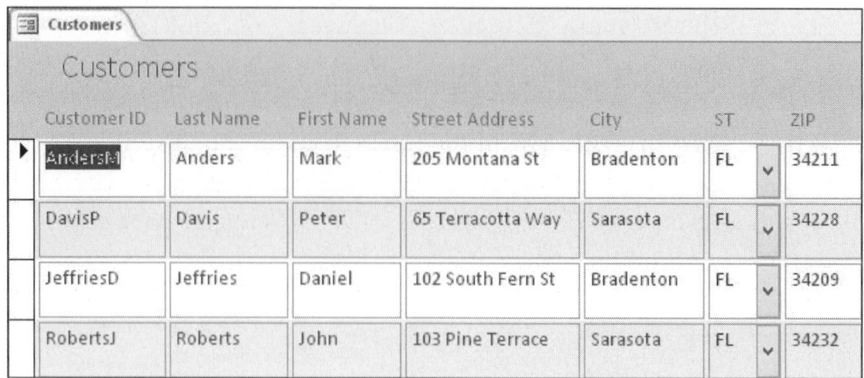

5. Close the form, saving it as `CustomersMultiItem`.

Creating Split Forms

Video Library http://labyrinthelab.com/videos Video Number: AC13-V0316

A split form simultaneously shows two views of your table data: Layout/Form View and Datasheet View. The views are synchronized so that a selected record in one view is also selected in the other view.

DEVELOP YOUR SKILLS AC03-D16

Create a Split Form

In this exercise, you will examine the Split Form feature using the Customers table.

1. Select the **Customers** table.
2. Choose **Create→Forms→More Forms→Split Form**.
   Access opens the new split form in Form Layout View on the top and Datasheet View on the bottom.

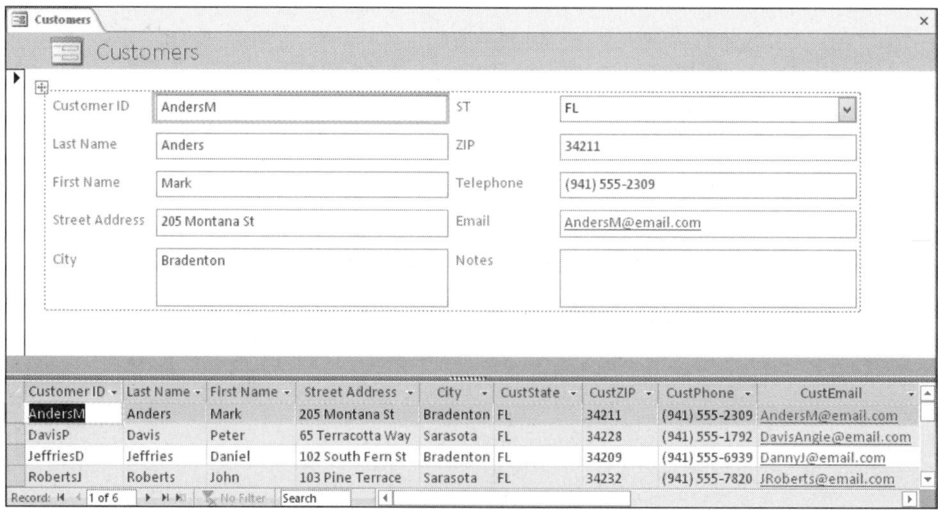

3. Save the form as `CustomersSplitForm` and close it.

Printing Forms

Video Library http://labyrinthelab.com/videos Video Number: AC13-V0317

Procedures for printing forms are basically the same procedures you would use to print in other programs, such as Word, Excel, and PowerPoint. As with each different program, print options in Access vary with different objects. For example, you can print individual forms—one for each record—or print forms so that they print continuously, one after another, on standard sheets of paper.

FROM THE RIBBON

File→Print→Print Preview to open Print Preview

File→Print→Print to open the Print dialog box

FROM THE KEYBOARD

ctrl + P to print

Printing All Record Forms

The default setting in Access for printing forms is to print as many individual records that can fit on one page. The easiest way to determine how forms will look when you print them is to view them in Print Preview before printing.

The Quick Print command sends all records directly to the printer without opening the Print dialog box. When dealing with large files, this option should be used with caution.

Printing Selected Record Forms

When you want to print selected records, you would first select the record and then display it in Print Preview. When you click the Print button on the Ribbon in Print Preview, the Print dialog box opens so that you can choose to print all records, print specific record numbers, or print the selected records.

QUICK REFERENCE	PRINTING RECORD FORMS
Task	**Procedure**
Open Print Preview	■ Choose File→Print→Print Preview.
Print all records	■ Choose File→Print→Quick Print.
Print specific records	■ Choose File→Print→Print and set the print options for the records to print, or press Ctrl+P and set the print options for the records to print.

DEVELOP YOUR SKILLS AC03-D17

Print Form Information

In this exercise, you will print the third record of the CustomersDesign form.

1. Display the **CustomersDesign** form in Form View.
2. Choose **File→Print→Print** to open the **Print** dialog box.

3. Follow these steps to print only record/page 3:

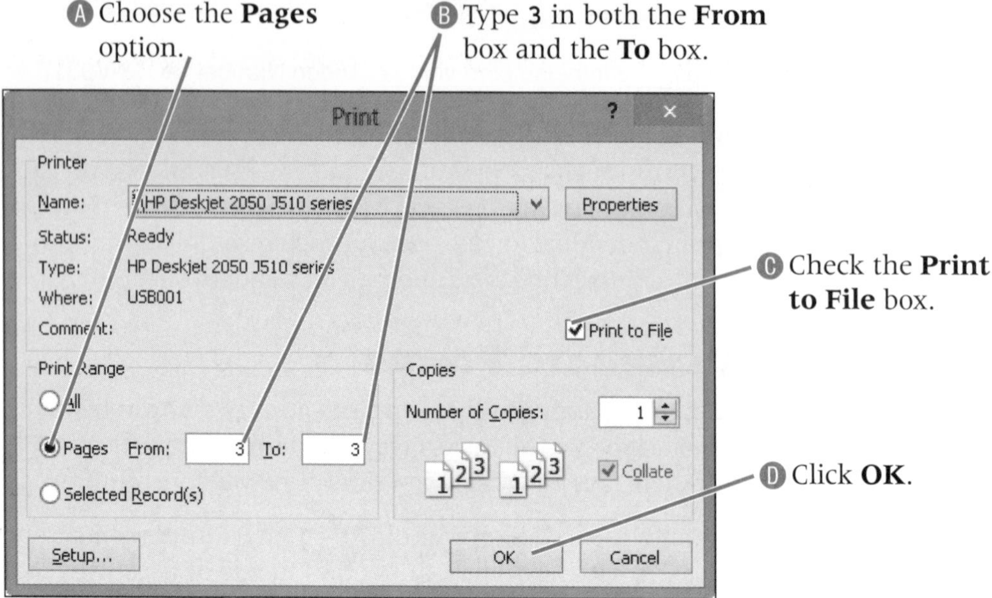

Access prints the third form record to your file.

4. Type CustomersDesign-[FirstInitialLastName] in the Print to File dialog box and click OK.
5. Close the form and save if prompted.

Using Help

Video Library http://labyrinthelab.com/videos Video Number: AC13-V0318

As you begin using Help in Access 2013, you will soon realize that the Help system is a massive database file comprised of numerous records, each of which is related to an Access feature. If you use the search tools available on most Web sites, you can also quickly and efficiently locate help for any Access feature.

FROM THE KEYBOARD
[F1] to launch Help

DEVELOP YOUR SKILLS AC03-D18

Use Help in Access 2013

In this exercise, you will use the Help tool to learn more about creating controls in Access.

1. Click the **Help** [?] button on the title bar.
2. Follow these steps to search for help on creating controls:

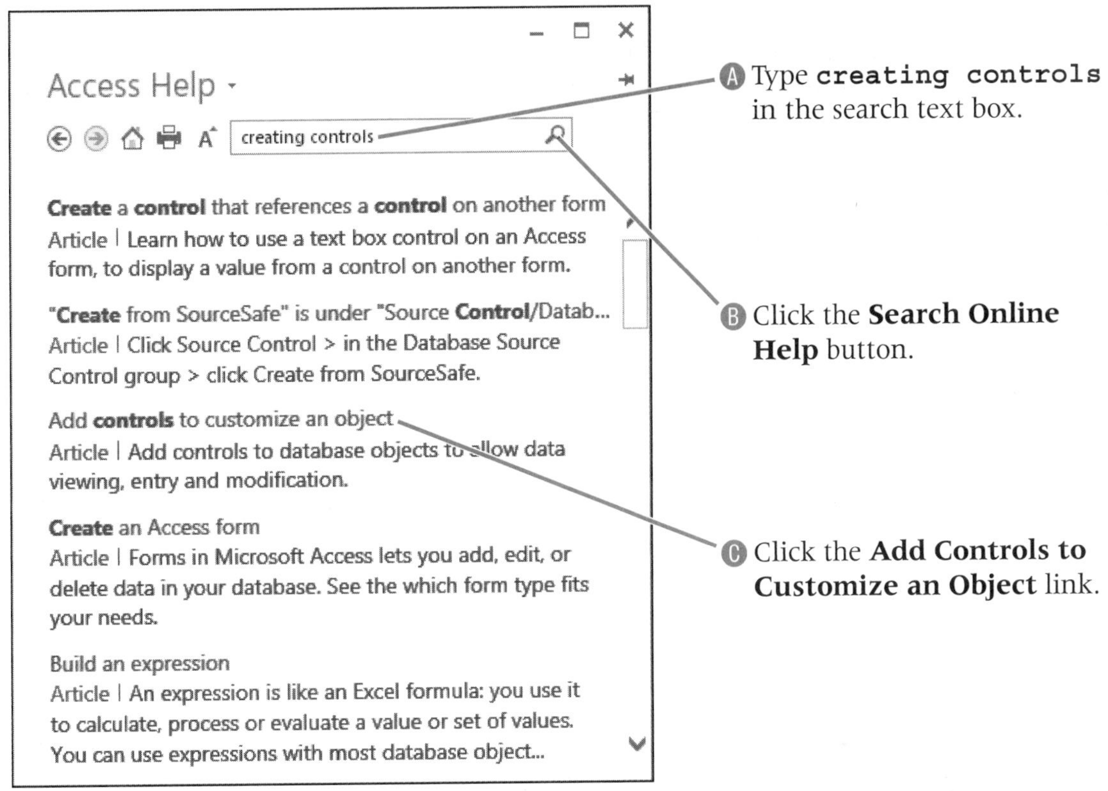

The topics listed in the Help window are constantly updated. As such, the topics listed when you do your search may differ from those shown here.

3. Review the article.

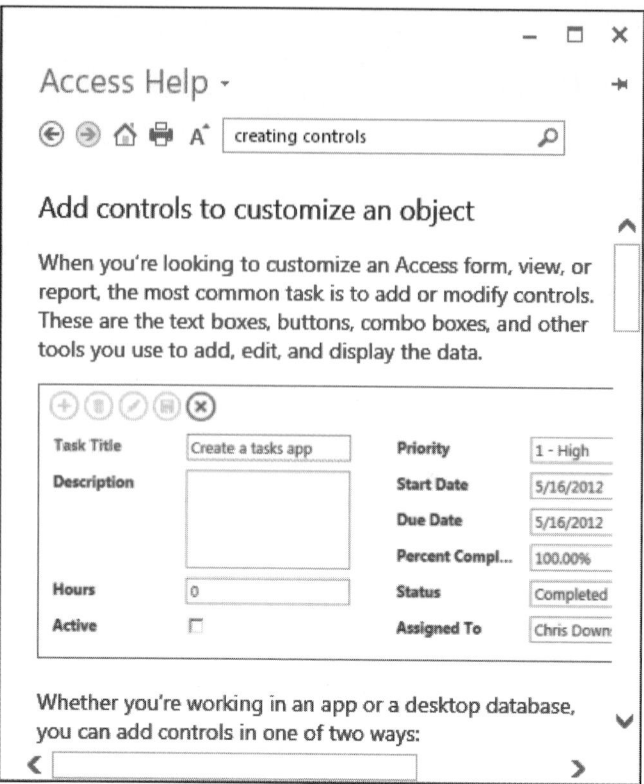

4. Close the article; exit **Access**.
   Closing the article also closes the Access Help dialog box.

Concepts Review

To check your knowledge of the key concepts introduced in this lesson, complete the Concepts Review quiz by choosing the appropriate access option below.

If you are...	Then access the quiz by...
Using the Labyrinth Video Library	Going to http://labyrinthelab.com/videos
Using eLab	Logging in, choosing Content, and navigating to the Concepts Review quiz for this lesson
Not using the Labyrinth Video Library or eLab	Going to the student resource center for this book

Reinforce Your Skills

REINFORCE YOUR SKILLS AC03-R01

Create a Form Using the Form Wizard and Customize It

Kids for Change has hired you to create a new form and customize it with a new design. In this exercise, you will use the Form Wizard to create a form, add an image, and set several formatting properties.

Create a Form Using the Form Wizard

1. Start **Access**. Open **AC03-R01-K4C** from the **AC2013 Lesson 03** folder and save it as `AC03-R01-K4C-[FirstInitialLastName]`.
2. If a Security Warning appears, click **Enable Content**.

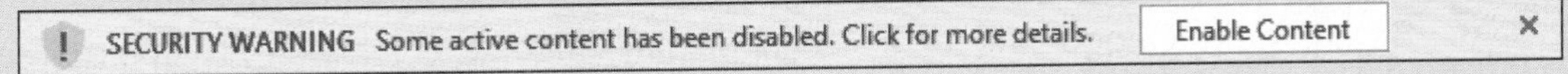

3. Click the **Children** table in the Navigation Pane.
4. Choose **Create→Forms→Form Wizard**.
5. Choose **Table: Children** from the Tables/Queries list.
6. Click **Move All** [>>] to add all fields to the Selected Fields box; click **Next**.
7. Keep the **Columnar** default layout selected; click **Next**.
8. Name the form `Kids for Change Children Volunteers` and click **Finish**.
   The form opens in Form View.

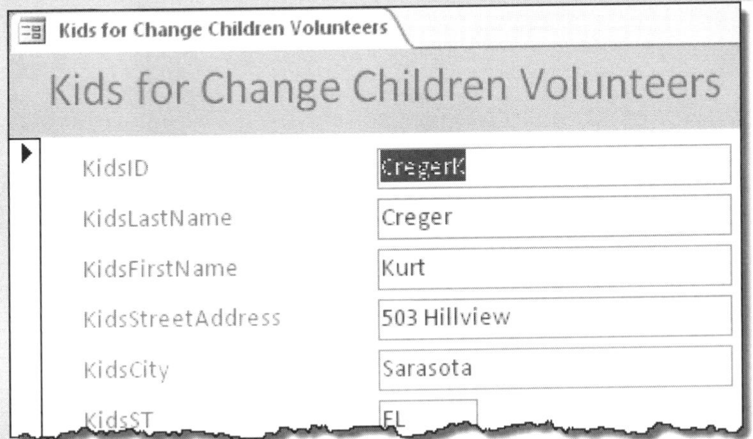

Edit Label Text

9. Choose **Home→Views→View menu ▾→Design View**.
10. Double-click the **Title** label to select it.

11. Click in front of the word **Children**, press Shift, and tap Enter to bump the last two words down under the name of the organization.

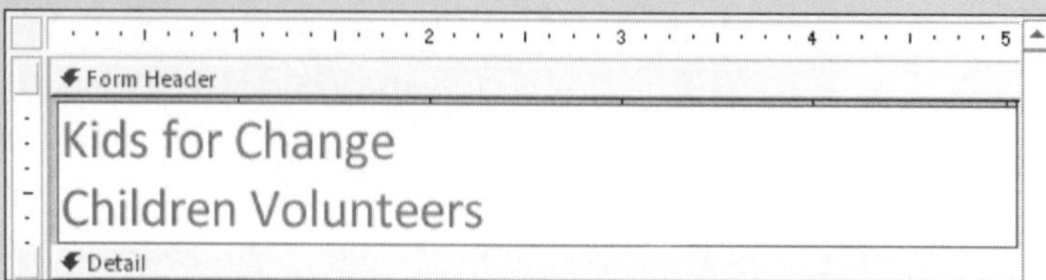

12. Click outside of the title control to make the **Insert Image** command available for the next step.

Add and Adjust an Image (Control)

13. Choose **Design→Controls→Insert Image** and click **Browse**.
14. Navigate to your **AC2013 Lesson 03** folder, select **K4C-logo.bmp**, and click **OK**.

If the K4C-logo.bmp file does not display, choose All Files (*.*) from the File type drop-down in the Browse dialog box.

15. Click to the right of the title and drag the mouse down and to the right.

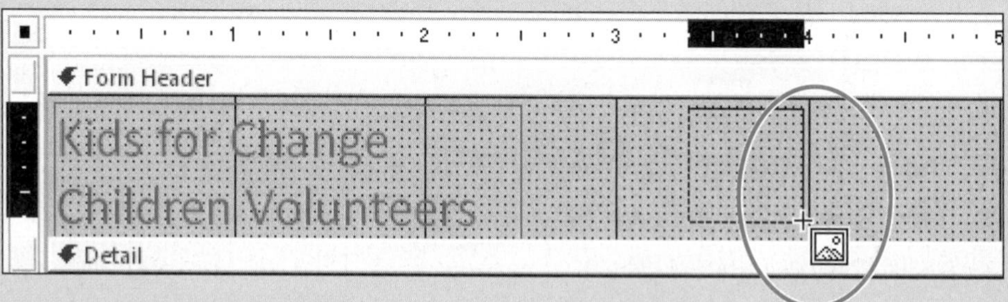

16. Release the mouse to insert the image.

Use the Property Sheet to Format Objects

17. Click the **All** tab on the Property Sheet, and set these properties for the new image.

Property	New Value
Name	`K4C-Logo`
Width	.7
Height	.7
Border Style	Solid
Border Width	1 pt
Border Color	Green, Accent 6, Darker 25%

18. Select and then set the following properties for the **Title** control.

Property	New Value
Name	`K4C-Title`
Width	3
Height	.7
Font Name	Arial
Font Size	18
Text Align	Center
Font Weight	Semi-bold
Fore Color	Green, Accent 6, Darker 50%

Modify a Form Layout

19. Click the vertical ruler to the left of the title and image to select the two controls.
20. Choose **Arrange→Sizing & Ordering→Align→Top**.

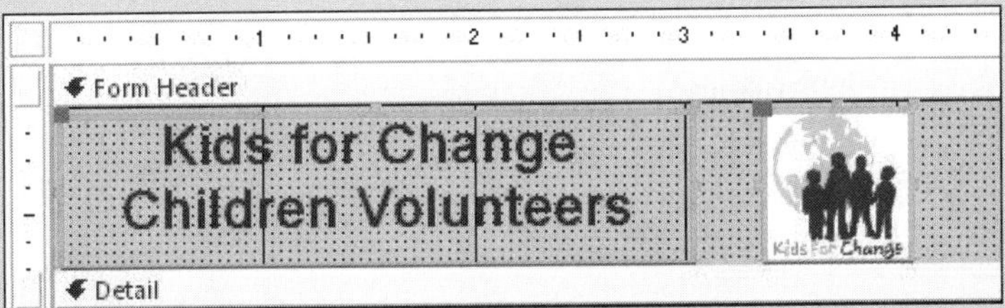

21. Click the **Form Header** section bar and change the Back Color property to **Green, Accent 6, Lighter 80%**.
22. Using any method, select all labels in the Detail section and change these properties. *Be sure not to include the title in your selection.*

Property	New Value
Width	1.5
Height	.25
Back Color	Green, Accent 6, Lighter 80%
Special Effect	Raised
Font Name	Arial
Font Weight	Semi-bold
Fore Color	Green, Accent 6, Darker 50%

23. Select all text boxes in the Detail section and change these properties.

Property	New Value
Height	.25
Special Effect	Sunken
Font Name	Arial
Font Weight	Semi-bold
Fore Color	Green, Accent 6, Darker 50%

24. Switch to **Form View**.

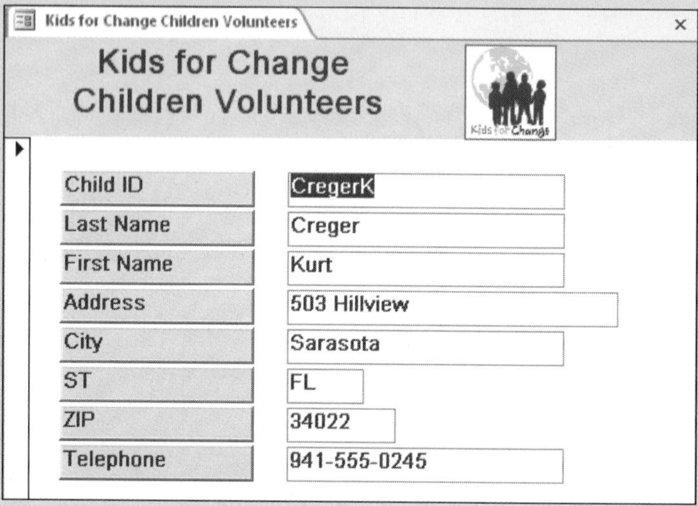

25. Save and close the form. Exit **Access**.

26. Submit your final file based on the guidelines provided by your instructor.

To view examples of how your file or files should look at the end of this exercise, go to the student resource center.

REINFORCE YOUR SKILLS AC03-R02

Create a Multiple Item Form and Apply a Theme

Kids for Change has hired you to redesign their database forms and apply a consistent and attractive Theme to both new and existing forms. In this exercise, you will create a multiple item form for entering and managing staff information. Then you will apply a Theme to the new form and print it for the next staff meeting.

Create a Multiple Item Form

1. Start **Access**. Open **AC03-R02-K4C** from the **AC2013 Lesson 03** folder and save it as `AC03-R02-K4C-[FirstInitialLastName]`.
2. If a Security Warning appears, click **Enable Content**.

3. Select the **Staff** table in the Navigation Pane and choose **Create→Forms→More Forms→Multiple Items**.

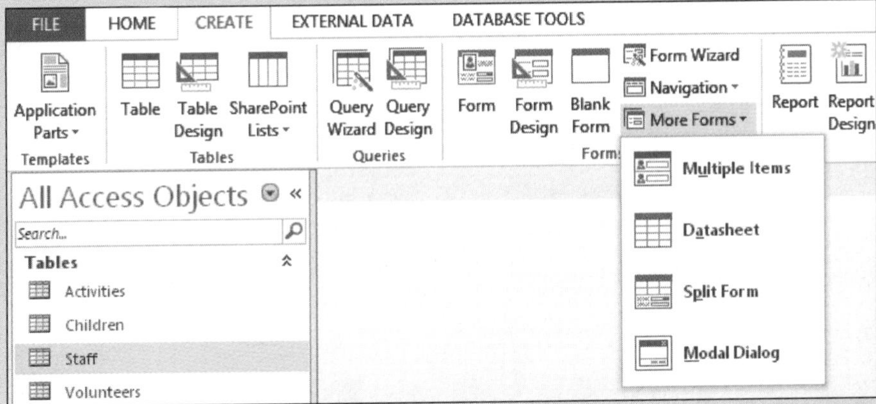

A new multiple item form displaying the staff information opens in Layout View.

4. Drag up the lower edge of the **Staff ID** text box to better fit the height of the data.

5. Resize each column by clicking in a text box and dragging the right border to the left to better fit the width of the data.

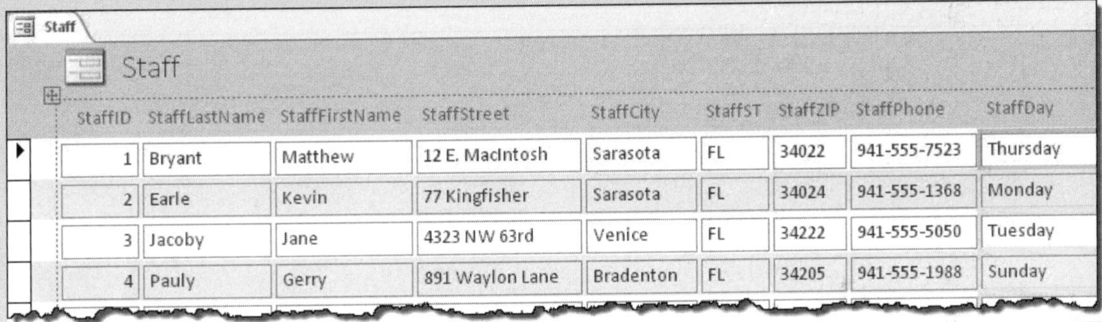

StaffID	StaffLastName	StaffFirstName	StaffStreet	StaffCity	StaffST	StaffZIP	StaffPhone	StaffDay
1	Bryant	Matthew	12 E. MacIntosh	Sarasota	FL	34022	941-555-7523	Thursday
2	Earle	Kevin	77 Kingfisher	Sarasota	FL	34024	941-555-1368	Monday
3	Jacoby	Jane	4323 NW 63rd	Venice	FL	34222	941-555-5050	Tuesday
4	Pauly	Gerry	891 Waylon Lane	Bradenton	FL	34205	941-555-1988	Sunday

If the Property Sheet is in the way, you may close it.

Apply a Theme to a Form

6. On the Design tab, choose any Theme from the Themes menu.

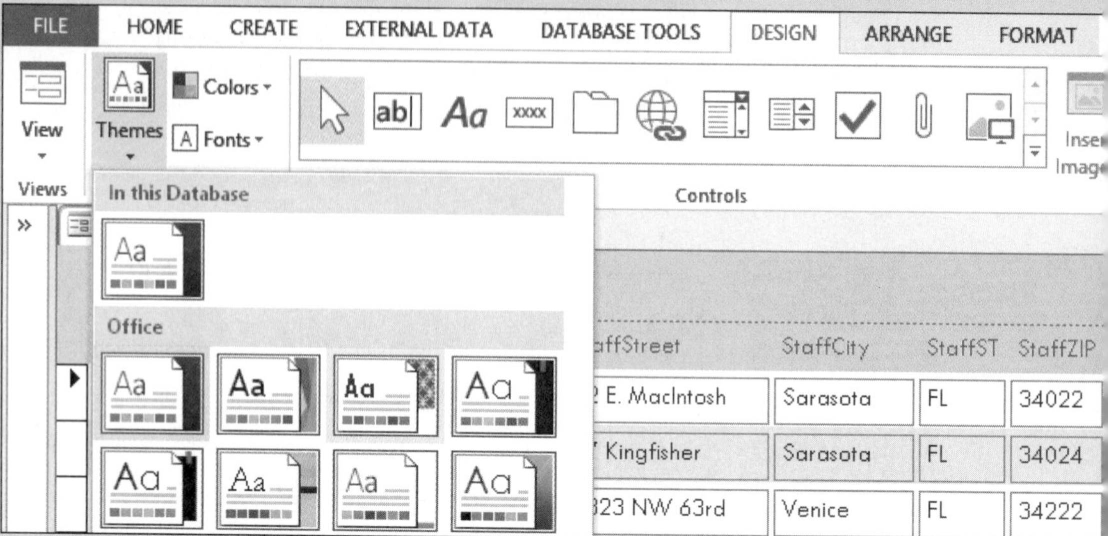

7. Resize the text boxes, as needed.
8. Switch to **Form View**.

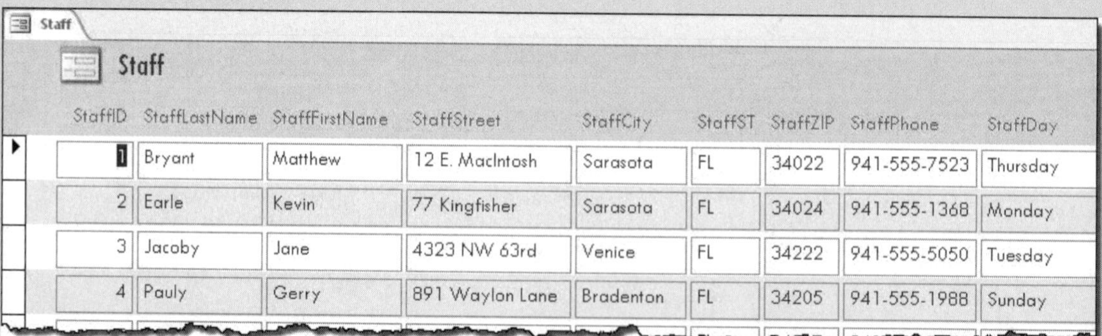

Print a Form Page

9. Choose **File→Print→Print**.
10. Choose the **Pages** option.
11. Type `1` in both the **From** box and the **To** box.
12. Check the **Print to File** box, and click **OK**.
13. Save the file as **`AC03-R02-K4CForm-[FirstInitialLastName]`** in your **AC2013 Lesson 03** folder.
14. Save the form as **`Staff-MultiItem`**, and then close all open objects and exit **Access**.
15. Submit your final files based on the guidelines provided by your instructor.
    To view examples of how your file or files should look at the end of this exercise, go to the student resource center.

REINFORCE YOUR SKILLS AC03-R03

Create a Form and Add a Title and an Image

Kids for Change, an organization that gets children involved in community activities, has hired you to help redesign their forms. In this exercise, you will create a form in Design View to facilitate management of the Activities table. Then you will add an image to the Form Header and print one page of the form. Finally, you will use Access Help to learn about the Image Gallery.

Create a Form in Design View

1. Start **Access**. Open **AC03-R03-K4C** from the **AC2013 Lesson 03** folder and save it as `AC03-R03-K4C-[FirstInitialLastName]`.
2. If a Security Warning appears, click **Enable Content**.

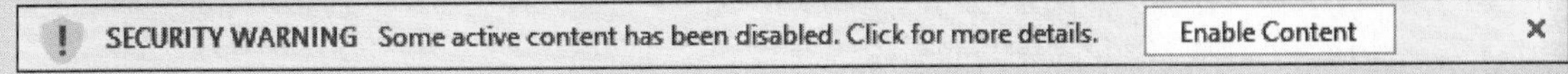

3. Choose **Create→Forms→Form Design**.
   A blank form design grid opens. The Property Sheet may also be open.
4. Choose **Design→Tools→Add Existing Fields**.
5. Click **Show All Tables** to display the available tables.
6. Double-click the **Activities** table to show the fields in the table.
7. Click and drag each field to the form design grid, then close the **Field List**.

Arrange Controls on a Form

8. Click in the **horizontal ruler** above the left column of labels to select the three controls (Activity ID, Activity, Location) and choose **Arrange→Sizing & Ordering→Align Left**.

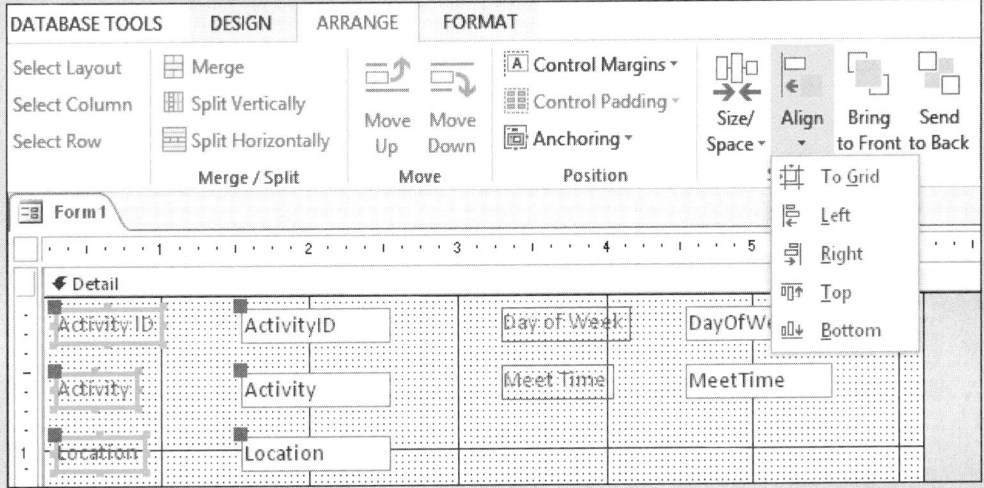

9. Left-align the three columns of the remaining controls (text boxes, labels, and text boxes).
10. Click the **vertical ruler** to the left of the top row of controls and choose **Arrange→Sizing & Ordering→Align Top**.
11. Top-align the second row of controls.

Modify Form Controls

12. Select all the label controls.
    Hint: Lasso the left column of labels, press [Shift] *and lasso the right column of labels.*
13. Choose **Design→Tools→Property Sheet** and click the **Format** tab.
14. Enter `1` in the **Width** property and `.25` in the **Height** property.
15. Select *all* the controls in the Detail section.
16. Make these settings.

Font Name	Arial Narrow
Font Size	14
Fore Color	Black (Text 1)

17. Select the **ActivityID** and **MeetTime** text boxes and type `.8` for the **Width** property.
18. Select the **Activity** and **Location** text boxes and type `1.8` for the **Width** property.
19. Select just the first column of labels and type `.1` for the **Left** property.
20. Select the first column of text boxes and type `1.2` for the **Left** property.
21. Type `3.1` for the **Left** property of the second column of labels, and type `4.2` for the **Left** property of the second column of text boxes.

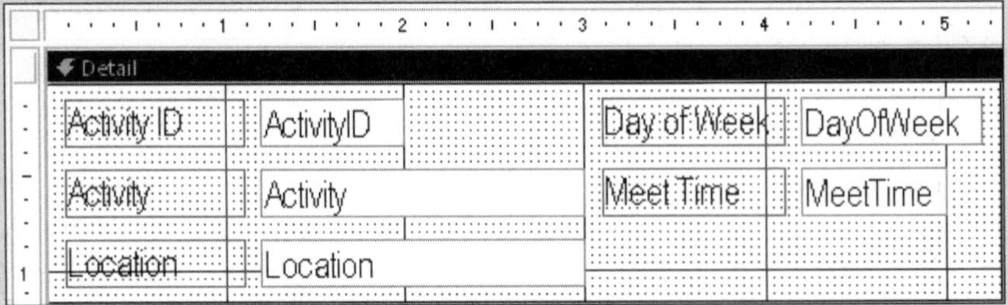

Modify Form Layout

22. Choose **Design→Header/Footer→Title**.
    Access opens the Form Header to accommodate the new title.
23. Type **`Kids for Change`** as the new **Title** label and tap [Enter].
24. Click the **Auto-Logo box** to the left of the new Title label and tap [Delete].
25. Click the Title control; press [Ctrl] and tap [C] to copy the title.

26. Press Ctrl and tap V to paste the copy below the title.

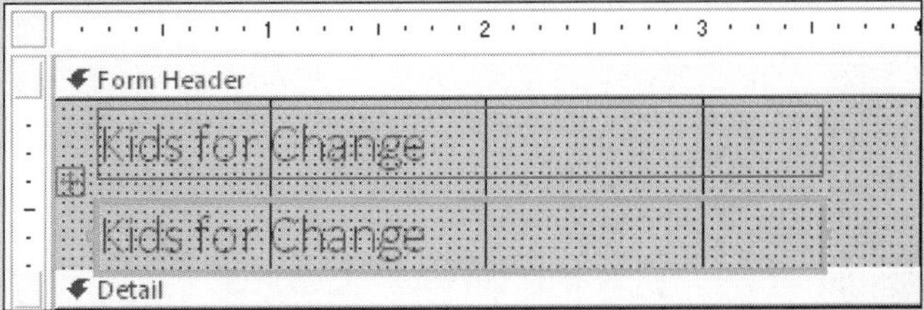

If Access does not automatically enlarge the Form Header section to accommodate the subtitle, you can resize the section manually.

Your form now includes a title and a subtitle in the Form Header section.

27. Highlight the existing text in the subtitle control; type `Activities` in the subtitle control, and tap Enter.

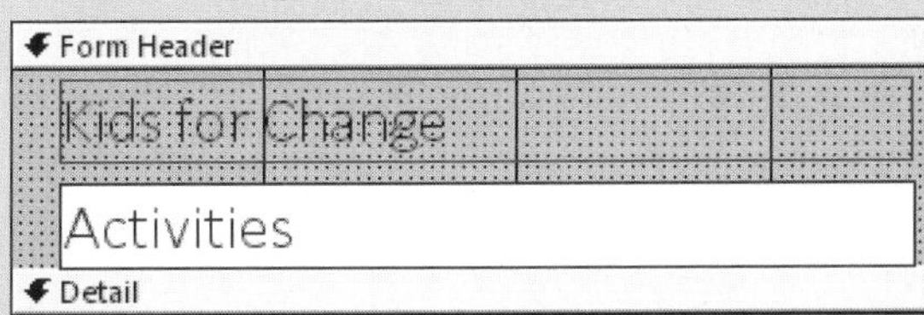

28. Save the form as `Activities Form`.

Apply a Theme and Add an Image

29. Choose **Design→Themes→Themes** and choose a Theme for the form.
30. Choose **Design→Controls→Insert Image** and click **Browse**.
31. Choose **All Files** (*.*) in the Browse dialog box and navigate to the **AC2013 Lesson 03** folder, select **K4C-logo.bmp**, and click **OK**.
32. Click to the right of the title, drag the mouse down and to the right, and release it to insert the image.

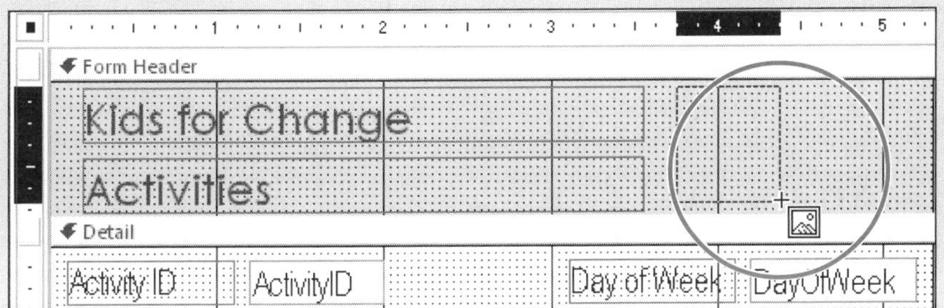

33. Change the **Width** and **Height** properties to `.7` for the image.

Access 2013

34. Switch to **Form View**.

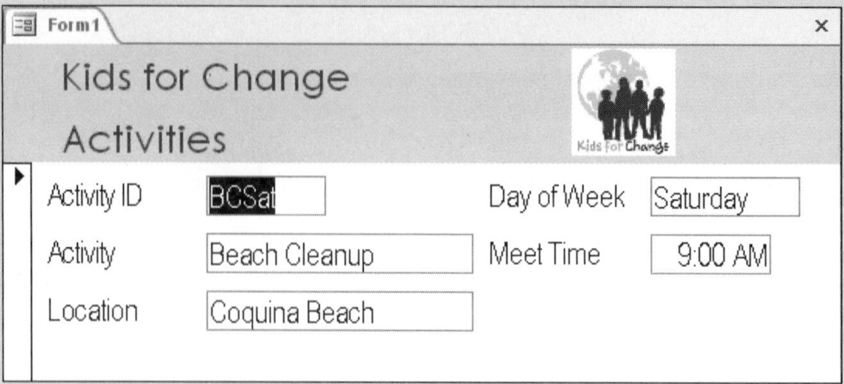

If some of your data values do not fit in the text boxes, you can switch to Layout View and resize the controls using the techniques you learned in this lesson.

Print a Form Page

35. Choose **File→Print→Print**.
36. Choose the **Pages** option.
37. Type `1` in both the **From** box and the **To** box.
38. Check the **Print to File** box, and click **OK**.
39. Save the file as `AC03-R03-K4CForm-[FirstInitialLastName]`, in your **AC2013 Lesson 03** folder.
40. Save and close the form.

Use Access Help

41. Click **Microsoft Access Help** [?].
42. Type `image gallery` in the Search box.
43. Find and read an article or video that teaches how to add images to the Image Gallery.
44. Exit **Access**. Submit your final files based on the guidelines provided by your instructor.

Apply Your Skills

APPLY YOUR SKILLS AC03-A01

Create a Form in Design View

Universal Corporate Events is a planner of corporate, professional, and high-end private events. UCE has been purchased by retired New York banker J. G. Buckley. As the head of in-house development for the newly-acquired company, you have been tasked with revamping the image of Universal Corp, including everything from reports to forms. In this exercise, you will create a new Personnel form in Design View.

Create a Form in Design View

1. Start **Access**. Open **AC03-A01-UniversalCorp** from the **AC2013 Lesson 03** folder and save it as `AC03-A01-UniversalCorp-[FirstInitialLastName]`.
2. If a Security Warning appears, click **Enable Content**.
3. Choose **Create→Forms→Form Design** and open the Field List.
4. Click **Show All Tables** in the Field List, and double-click the **Personnel** table.
5. Drag each field to the form design grid.
6. Select the left-most column of **labels**, and choose **Arrange→Sizing & Ordering→Align→Left**.
7. Neatly align the remaining controls.
8. Open the **Property Sheet** and resize all the Labels to `1` width.

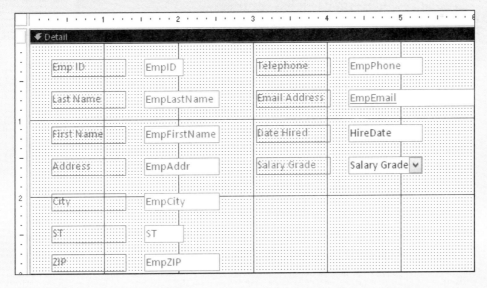

All the fields should be placed in the Detail section on the form grid.

Add a Logo and Apply a Theme

9. Display the **Form Header** section and choose **Design→Header/Footer→Title**.
10. Type **`Universal Corporate Events Ltd.`**, press Ctrl and tap Enter to move to the next line, and type **`Personnel`**.
11. Delete the **Auto_Logo** box to the left of the title then drag the left edge of the title to the right to make room for the logo.
12. Choose Insert Image, then navigate to the **AC2013 Lesson 03** folder and select **UCE-logo.bmp**.
13. Click to the left of the title, drag the mouse down and to the right, and release it to insert the image.

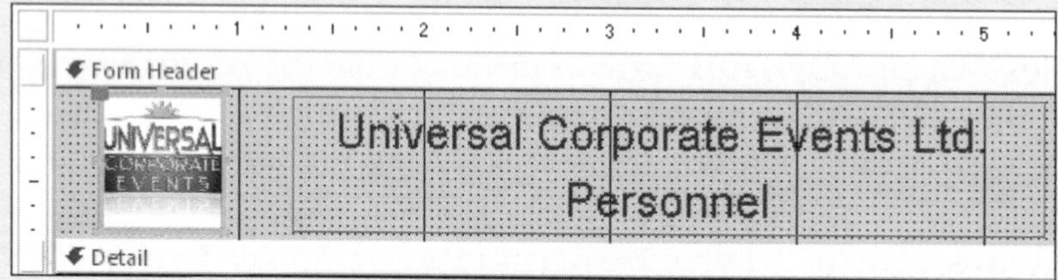

14. Open the **Property Sheet**, if necessary. Set the logo Width and Height to **`.7`** each.
15. Make the **Top** property **`.05`**.
16. Choose **Solid** for the Border Style property and **1 pt** for the Border Width.
17. Choose **Blue, Accent 5, Darker 50%** for the Border Color.
18. Make any desired cosmetic changes to the form, such as changing formatting properties of the labels and resizing text box controls.
19. Choose **Design→Tools→Tab Order** and change the tab order so the control passes from Emp ID to Telephone and then to Last Name.
20. Save the form as **`Personnel Mgmt`** and open it in **Form View**.

21. Close the **Personnel Mgmt** form and the database. Exit **Access**.
22. Submit your final file based on the guidelines provided by your instructor.
    To view examples of how your file or files should look at the end of this exercise, go to the student resource center.

APPLY YOUR SKILLS AC03-A02

Edit Labels, Format Controls, and Set Properties

J.G. Buckley's son, Hubert, new CEO of Universal Corporate Events, has asked you to revamp the image of Universal Corp. In this exercise, you will redesign a company form, editing the labels, formatting the controls, and setting its properties. Then, you will use Access Help to explore how to add a command button. You will finish by printing a sample page of the form for the CEO's approval.

Open a Form and Edit Label Text

1. Start **Access**. Open **AC03-A02-UniversalCorp** from the **AC2013 Lesson 03** folder and save it as **`AC03-A02-UniversalCorp-[FirstInitialLastName]`**.
2. If the Security Warning appears, click **Enable Content**.
3. Open the **Event Schedules** form in **Design View**.
4. Change the **Location** label to **Venue**.
5. Change the **Event ID** label to **Event Code**.

Modify Form Control Properties

6. If the Property Sheet is not shown, choose **Design→Tools→Property Sheet**.
7. Select the **Title** control (Universal Corporate Event) and set these properties.

Property	New Value
Caption	Universal Corporate Events Ltd.
Width	4.5
Height	.3
Left	.02
Font Name	Georgia
Fore Color	Blue, Accent 5, Darker 50%

8. Select the subtitle (Scheduling) and set these properties.

Property	New Value
Width	4.5
Height	.3
Left	.02
Font Weight	Light
Fore Color	Blue, Accent 5, Darker 50%

9. Select all the labels in the Detail section and change these properties.

Property	New Value
Width	1.3
Height	.3
Left	1
Special Effect	Raised
Font Name	Arial
Font Size	12
Font Weight	Semi-bold
Fore Color	Blue, Accent 5, Darker 50%

10. Select all the text boxes in the Detail section and change these properties.

Property	New Value
Height	.3
Left	2.75
Special Effect	Sunken
Font Name	Arial
Font Size	14

Modify Form Layout

11. Click the Form Header section bar and change the Back Color property to **White, Background 1**.
12. Click the Detail section bar and change the Back Color to **Blue, Accent 5, Lighter 80%**.
13. Open the form in **Form View**.

Print a Form Page

14. Check the **Print to File** box and print one page of the form (as a PDF file or a print file) to your **AC2013 Lesson 03** folder, naming the file **`AC03-A02-UCEForm-[FirstInitialLastName]`**.
15. Save and close the form.
16. Submit your final file based on the guidelines provided by your instructor.

Use Access Help

17. Click **Help** [?] and type **`command button`** in the Search Help box.
18. Find an article or video that instructs how to create a form command button.
19. As directed by your instructor, create and submit a write-up on what you found.
20. Close the database and exit **Access**.

    To view examples of how your file or files should look at the end of this exercise, go to the student resource center.

APPLY YOUR SKILLS AC03-A03

Create a Form, Work with Form Headers, and Add a Logo

In this exercise, you will create a new form for managing UCE's event venue information, add and format a form header and title, and add an original company logo.

Create a Form Using the Form Wizard

1. Start **Access**. Open **AC03-A03-UniversalCorp** from the **AC2013 Lesson 03** folder and save it as **`AC03-A03-UniversalCorp-[FirstInitialLastName]`**.
2. If a Security Warning appears, click **Enable Content**.
3. Use the Form Wizard to create a form that uses the **Venues** table as the record source. Include all the fields from the table, use the **Columnar** layout, and name the form **`Event Venues Form`**.

Access 2013

Add a Title and Logo (Controls) to a Form

4. Switch to **Design View**.
5. Select the default title, open the Property Sheet, and set these properties.

Property	New Value
Width	3.5
Top	.4
Left	.75
Font Name	Georgia
Text Align	Center
Fore Color	Blue, Accent 5, Darker 50%

Now you have room for a company name title and company logo.

6. Choose **Design→Header/Footer→Title**.
7. Delete the **Auto_Logo** control.
8. Click the new **Title** control and set the following properties:

Property	New Value
Caption	Universal Corporate Events
Width	3.5
Height	.35
Left	.75
Font Name	Georgia
Text Align	Center
Font Weight	Semi-bold
Fore Color	Blue, Accent 5, Darker 50%

9. Click the **Form Header** bar and choose **Design→Controls→Insert Image**.
10. Navigate to your **AC2013 Lesson 03** folder and select **UCE-logo.bmp**.
11. Click near the top-left corner of the **Form Header**, to the left of the title, and drag the mouse down and to the right.

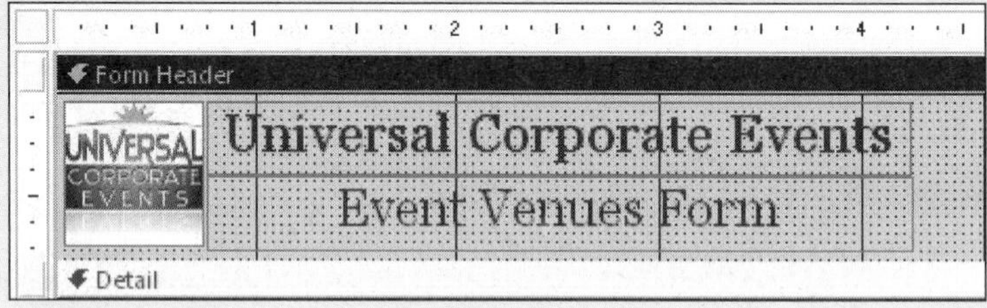

Modify Form Controls

12. Type **.7** as the **Width** and **Height** properties for the image.
13. Select all the labels in the Detail section and change these properties.

Property	New Value
Width	1.5
Height	.25
Left	.25
Special Effect	Raised
Font Name	Arial
Font Size	12
Font Weight	Semi-bold
Fore Color	Blue, Accent 5, Darker 50%

14. Select all the text boxes in the Detail section and change these properties.

Property	New Value
Height	.25
Left	2
Special Effect	Sunken
Font Name	Arial
Font Size	12

15. Press [Shift], deselect the **VenueWebSite** text box, and change the Fore Color property to **Black, Text 1** for all the other text box controls.

Modify Form Layout

16. Click the **Form Header** section bar and change the Back Color property to **White, Background 1**.

17. Click the **Detail** section bar and change the Back Color to **Blue, Accent 5, Lighter 80%**.

18. Switch to **Form View**.

Print a Form Page

19. Check the **Print to File** box and print one page of the form (as a PDF file or to a print file) to your **AC2013 Lesson 03** folder, naming the file **`AC03-A03-UCEForm-[FirstInitialLastName]`**.

20. Save and close the form. Close the database and exit **Access**.

21. Submit your final files based on the guidelines provided by your instructor.

Extend Your Skills

In the course of working through the Extend Your Skills exercises, you will think critically as you use the skills taught in the lesson to complete the assigned projects. To evaluate your mastery and completion of the exercises, your instructor may use a rubric, with which more points are allotted according to performance characteristics. (The more you do, the more you earn!) Ask your instructor how your work will be evaluated.

AC03-E01 That's the Way I See It

In this exercise, you will design and format a new form. In the **AC2013 Lesson 03** folder, open **AC03-E01-BJL** and save it as `AC03-E01-BJL-[FirstInitialLastName]`.

Use Access Help to learn about Navigation Forms; then create a navigation/switchboard form and save it as `AC03-E01-Navigation-[FirstInitialLastName]`. Use the Sales Invoices query as the source (include all the query fields on the form) for the form. Use the skills you learned in this lesson to customize the form and its controls, and add a title and image.

As directed, send one page of the form to a printer, save the form as a database object, or publish it as a PDF or an XPS file named `AC03-E01-NavigationForm-[FirstInitialLastName]`.

You will be evaluated based on the inclusion of all elements, your ability to follow directions, your ability to apply newly learned skills to a real-world situation, your creativity, and your accuracy in creating objects and/or entering data. Submit your final files based on the guidelines provided by your instructor.

AC03-E02 Be Your Own Boss

In this exercise, you will create and format a split form for Blue Jean Landscaping. You will use Access Help to learn how to change an existing form into a split form and then change a database form into a split form.

Open **AC03-E02-BJL** from the **AC2013 Lesson 03** folder and save it as `AC03-E02-BJL-[FirstInitialLastName]`. Search Access Help for information about creating split forms from existing forms, and then convert the Equipment Services form into a split form named `ESF-SplitForm`. Apply a Theme and resize the labels and text boxes to best fit the data. Brainstorm and enter ten new records. As directed, send one page of the form (that contains a new record) to a printer, save the form as a database object, or publish it as a PDF or an XPS file named `AC03-E02-SplitForm-[FirstInitialLastName]`.

You will be evaluated based on the inclusion of all elements, your ability to follow directions, your ability to apply newly learned skills to a real-world situation, your creativity, and your accuracy in creating objects and/or entering data. Submit your final files based on the guidelines provided by your instructor.

Transfer Your Skills

In the course of working through the Transfer Your Skills exercises, you will use critical-thinking and creativity skills to complete the assigned projects using skills taught in the lesson. To evaluate your mastery and completion of the exercises, your instructor may use a rubric, with which more points are allotted according to performance characteristics. (The more you do, the more you earn!) Ask your instructor how your work will be evaluated.

AC03-T01 Use the Web as a Learning Tool

Throughout this book, you will be provided with an opportunity to use the Internet as a learning tool by completing WebQuests. According to the original creators of WebQuests, as described on their website (WebQuest.org), a WebQuest is "an inquiry-oriented activity in which most or all of the information used by learners is drawn from the web." To complete the WebQuest projects in this book, navigate to the student resource center and choose the WebQuest for the lesson on which you are currently working. The subject of each WebQuest will be relevant to the material found in the lesson.

WebQuest Subject: Investigate designing and creating custom, original images for Access forms.

Submit your final file(s) based on the guidelines provided by your instructor.

AC03-T02 Demonstrate Proficiency

Stormy BBQ, a local BBQ restaurant featuring fresh locally grown vegetables and local farm raised pork and beef is opening a new restaurant on Main Street. The owner would like to change the look of their forms and reports to appeal to the downtown clientele.

Open **AC03-T02-StormyBBQ** from the **AC2013 Lesson 03** folder and save it as `AC03-T02-StormyBBQ-[FirstInitialLastName]`. Use the formatting tools and techniques you learned in this lesson to modify the Restaurant Form to reflect a more sophisticated, elegant look. Change the colors and styles of the form sections and the controls. Add the Stormy BBQ name to the title and a subtitle that describes the form. Select appropriate fonts. Be sure to add a Form Header to the Restaurant Form that maintains the same style as the Form Header in the Merchandise Form. Use Access Help to learn about background images and add the background image **SBQ-logo.bmp** to the Merchandise Form. Create a form using the Staff table as the record source, format it in the style you prefer, and save it as `Staff List`. Enter at least five more records using the Staff List form. Print one page from each form (Restaurant Form, Merchandise Form, and Staff List) and then save the database in your **AC2013 Lesson 03** folder.

Submit your final files based on the guidelines provided by your instructor.

Querying a Database

LESSON OUTLINE

LEARNING OBJECTIVES

After studying this lesson, you will be able to:

- Create, save, and run select queries
- Set query criteria and sort order
- Create and format a calculated field
- Use functions in query expressions
- Create special types of queries

One of the main goals of a database is to organize data so that information can be located and retrieved quickly. People in all types of businesses retrieve stored data and information daily, often at a moment's notice. When data is stored in tables in a relational database, you can search that information and extract records that meet specific criteria using a query, a database object used to locate records based on the conditions you set.

In this lesson, you will create select and crosstab queries and set query criteria. You will also create and format a calculated field, set a query sort order, and set multiple query conditions. Finally, you will create special queries designed to find unmatched records between tables and find duplicate entries in a database table.

CASE STUDY

Using Queries to Get Answers

As technology evolves, a smart business person will take advantage of the new opportunities that arise. An example of one such technology is *Quick Response* (QR) code. QR code is a square-shaped barcode that can be scanned by smartphones to quickly provide additional information about a product, open a website, send an email, or transfer contact information.

You have been asked to query the Winchester Web Design database and compile two separate customer lists. The lists will be used to notify all past clients of the QR code upgrade that can be added to their website contact forms. The first list will include only the first and last name of the clients and their email address. The second list will include the first and last name of the clients and their mailing addresses, sorted by ZIP code. Additionally, you have been asked to build queries that instantly calculate the total income from all the Winchester Web Design services, and from specific areas such as blogs or shopping carts.

Winchester Web Design Invoices

Inv Num	Inv Date	Description	Price	Qty	Line Total
1	3/15/2012	Home Page, Nav, CSS, Design	$400.00	1	$400.00
1	3/15/2012	Secondary Page	$200.00	3	$600.00
1	3/15/2012	Image, Custom Designed	$40.00	3	$120.00
2					
3					
3					
4					
5					
5					
6					
6					
6					
7					
7					
7					
7					
8					
8					
9					
9	7/20/2012	Image, Custo			
9	7/20/2012	Hourly Rate f			
10	7/30/2012	Secondary Pa			

Customer Mailing List

Last Name	First Name	Street Address	City	ST	ZIP
Blaser	Helen	600 Fowler	Sarasota	FL	33802
Mansur	Jo	985 Del Prado	Bradenton	FL	33850
Roberts	John	103 Pine Terrace	Tampa	FL	34022
Fleetwood	Candace	92 Highland St	Northport	FL	34023
Davis	Peter	65 Terracotta Way	Sarasota	FL	34024
Klein	Joyce				
Thibeaux	Pierre				
Hassan	Ahmed				
Jeffries	Daniel				
Santos	Emily				
Anders	Mark				
Abrams	John				
Winkler	Samuel				
Smith	William				

Customer Email List

Last Name	First Name	Email
Abrams	John	JPAbrams@email.com
Anders	Mark	AndersM@email.com
Blaser	Helen	BlasingHel@email.com
Davis	Peter	DavisAngie@email.com
Fleetwood	Candace	CandyWin@email.com
Hassan	Ahmed	HansAnge@email.com
Jeffries	Daniel	DannyJ@email.com
Klein	Joyce	KleinBrian@email.com
Mansur	Jo	Mansur@email.com

Creating Select Queries

Video Library http://labyrinthelab.com/videos Video Number: AC13-V0401

Some tables, such as a Customers table, may contain ten or more fields. Once you exceed seven or eight fields, it may be difficult to display the entire record on one line of a printout or screen. However, when you create a select query to display or select only certain fields, such as customer names and addresses, the resulting product will be small enough to attractively display each record on a single line. Consequently, the address list will be easier to look at in Datasheet View or on a printed report. You can create and save a query to use each time you need to print an updated list.

A select query allows you to select records based upon certain criteria that you set. A query asks a question, such as *What are the customer addresses?* Or, *How much money did the company make last month?* The answer to the question is a set of records. A select query is basically a database inquiry that selects only the requested records.

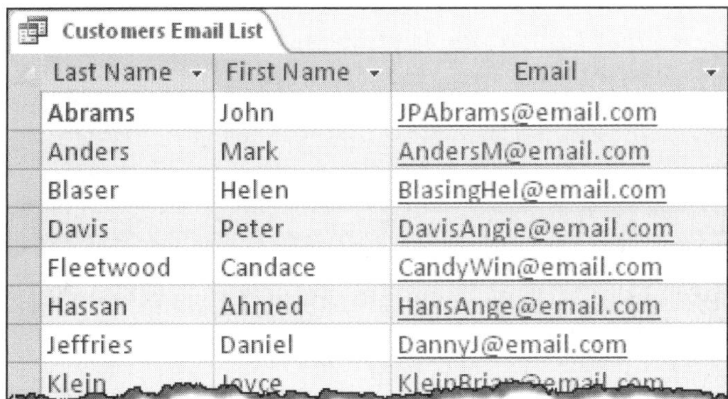
Customers Email List

Last Name	First Name	Email
Abrams	John	JPAbrams@email.com
Anders	Mark	AndersM@email.com
Blaser	Helen	BlasingHel@email.com
Davis	Peter	DavisAngie@email.com
Fleetwood	Candace	CandyWin@email.com
Hassan	Ahmed	HansAnge@email.com
Jeffries	Daniel	DannyJ@email.com
Klein	Joyce	[illegible]

A select query displays only the requested fields from the Customers table.

Reviewing Query Features

Some important points about queries to keep in mind:

- A query acts as a saved question you ask a database.
- A query is a subset of data from one or more tables.
- Data displayed in query results remain stored in the original table rather than in the query.
- When you edit data in query results, you are actually editing the data stored in the source table.
- Queries are dynamic objects that display up-to-date data stored in database tables.
- Queries can be used to create forms and reports, which may contain fields from multiple tables.

Query results datasheets enable you to filter or selectively organize data using the same techniques you may use to filter and organize table datasheets.

Identifying Tools for Creating Select Queries

The most common type of query is the select query. A select query retrieves data from one or more tables and displays the results in a datasheet. You can update records that appear in the query results datasheet, group records, and calculate sums, counts, averages, and other types of equations using query results.

Access provides two distinct tools for creating queries:

- Query Wizard
- Query Design

Buttons for creating queries are grouped in the Queries group on the Create tab. You will use both tools to create queries.

DEVELOP YOUR SKILLS AC04-D01

Create a Select Query Using the Query Wizard

In this exercise, you will create a select query using the Query Wizard to create a customer email list.

1. Open **AC04-D01-WinWebDesign** from the **AC2013 Lesson 04** folder and save it as **`AC04-D01-WinWebDesign-[FirstInitialLastName]`**.

   Replace the bracketed text with your first initial and last name. For example, if your name is Bethany Smith, your filename would look like this: AC04-D01-WinWebDesign-BSmith.

2. Follow these steps to activate the Query Wizard:

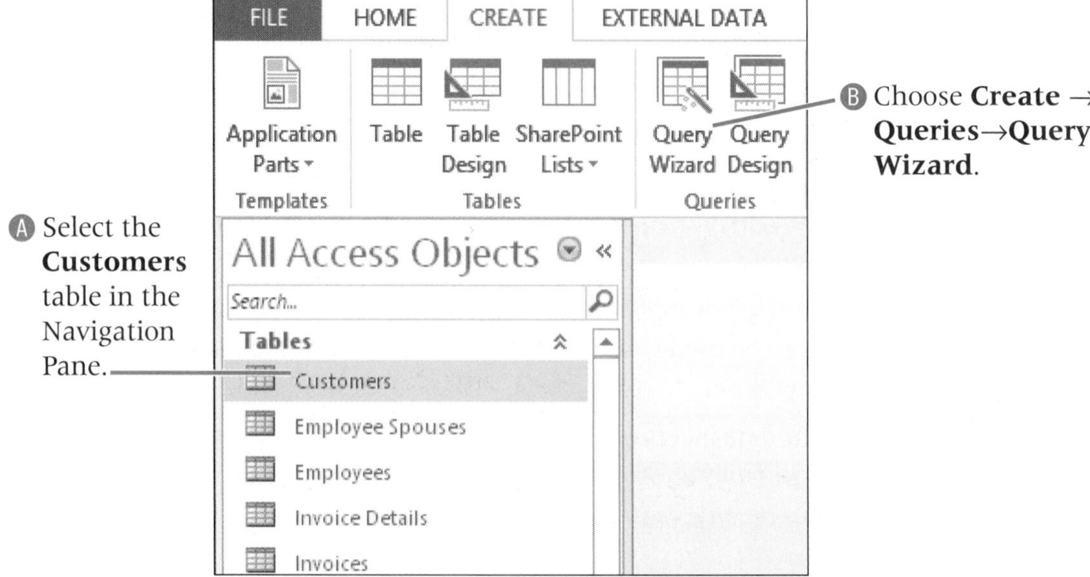

3. Follow these steps to select the query type:

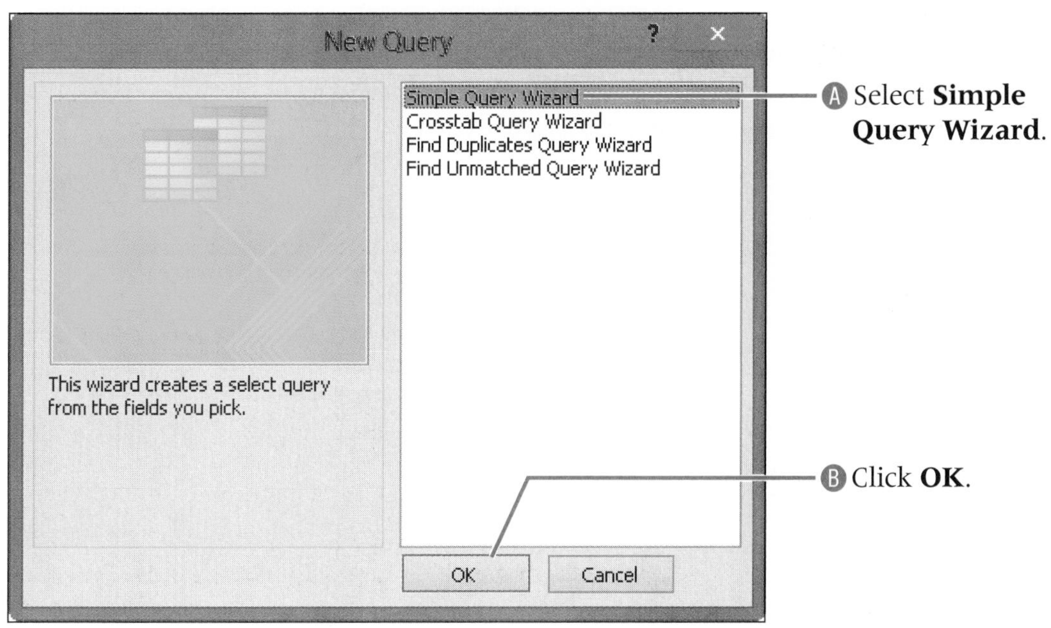
New Query
Simple Query Wizard
Crosstab Query Wizard
Find Duplicates Query Wizard
Find Unmatched Query Wizard
This wizard creates a select query from the fields you pick.
OK
Cancel
Ⓐ Select **Simple Query Wizard**.
Ⓑ Click **OK**.

4. Follow these steps to move selected fields to the query:

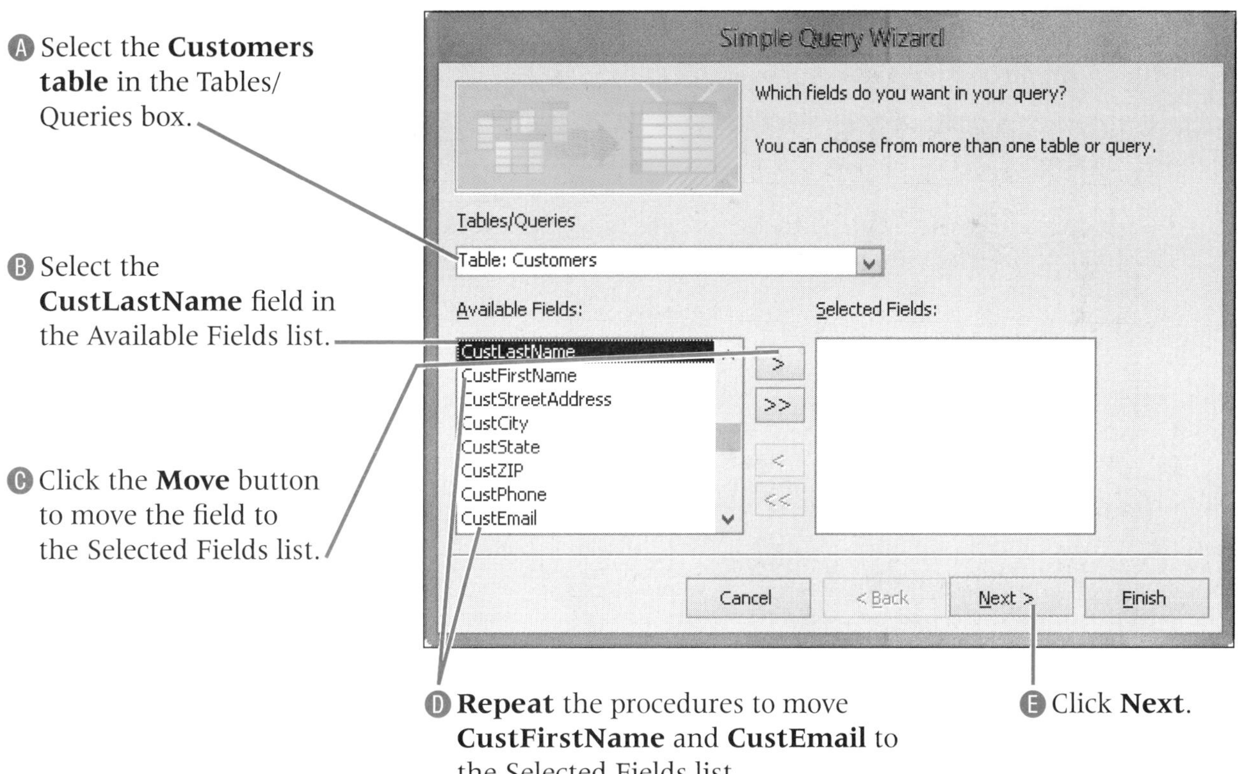
Simple Query Wizard
Which fields do you want in your query?
You can choose from more than one table or query.
Tables/Queries
Table: Customers
Available Fields:
Selected Fields:
CustLastName
CustFirstName
CustStreetAddress
CustCity
CustState
CustZIP
CustPhone
CustEmail
Cancel
< Back
Next >
Finish
Ⓐ Select the **Customers table** in the Tables/Queries box.
Ⓑ Select the **CustLastName** field in the Available Fields list.
Ⓒ Click the **Move** button to move the field to the Selected Fields list.
Ⓓ **Repeat** the procedures to move **CustFirstName** and **CustEmail** to the Selected Fields list.
Ⓔ Click **Next**.

If you add the wrong field by accident, double-click the name to move it back to the Available Fields list or select it and click Move Back.

Access 2013

5. Follow these steps to complete the query:

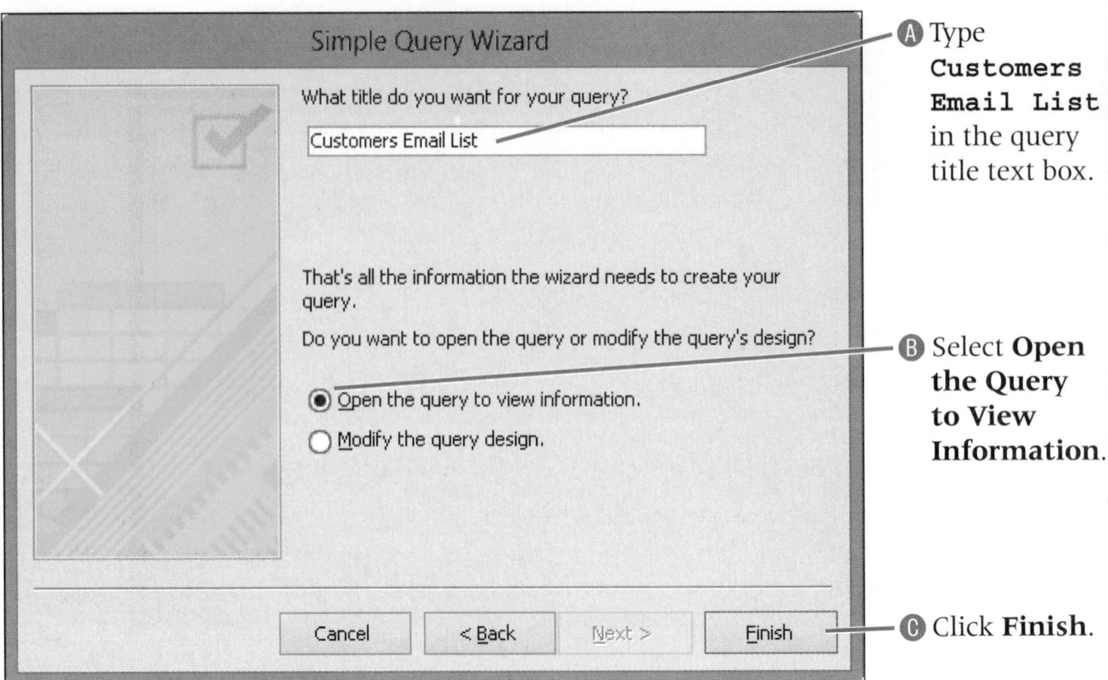

Customers Email List

Last Name	First Name	Email
Abrams	John	JPAbrams@email.com
Anders	Mark	AndersM@email.com
Blaser	Helen	BlasingHel@email.com
Davis	Peter	DavisAngie@email.com
Fleetwood	Candace	CandyWin@email.com
Hassan	Ahmed	HansAnge@email.com
Jeffries	Daniel	DannyJ@email.com
Klein	Joyce	KleinBrian@email.com
Mansur	Jo	Mansur@email.com
Roberts	Ilsa	IlsaRoberts@email.com
Roberts	John	JRoberts@email.com
Santos	Emily	SantosE@email.com
Smith	William	SmithBilly@email.com
Thibeaux	Pierre	PierreJT@email.com
Winkler	Samuel	SamWinkler45@email.com

The query results datasheet only includes the three selected fields from all the records.

6. Review the query results datasheet then **close** [×] the query.

   Unless directed otherwise, keep Access and any databases or database objects being used open at the end of each exercise.

Creating a Select Query Using Query Design

Video Library http://labyrinthelab.com/videos Video Number: AC13-V0402

The query you created in the previous exercise only displayed a few fields, but it reported every single record in the table. That may not be a problem for a small table, but when thousands of records and multiple tables are involved, it is often necessary to select only specific records by setting precise criteria. Using Query Design View, Access allows you to:

- Select fields from multiple tables.
- Set criteria to locate records based on data contained in one or more fields.
- Calculate totals.
- Show or hide fields containing criteria that are in the query results datasheet.

Identifying Features of the Query Design Grid

When in Query Design View, you are able to add fields from one or more tables into the display grid. You can place the fields in the order in which you want them to appear in the query results datasheet. In addition, the query design grid contains elements that enable you to set specific search criteria or sort the data.

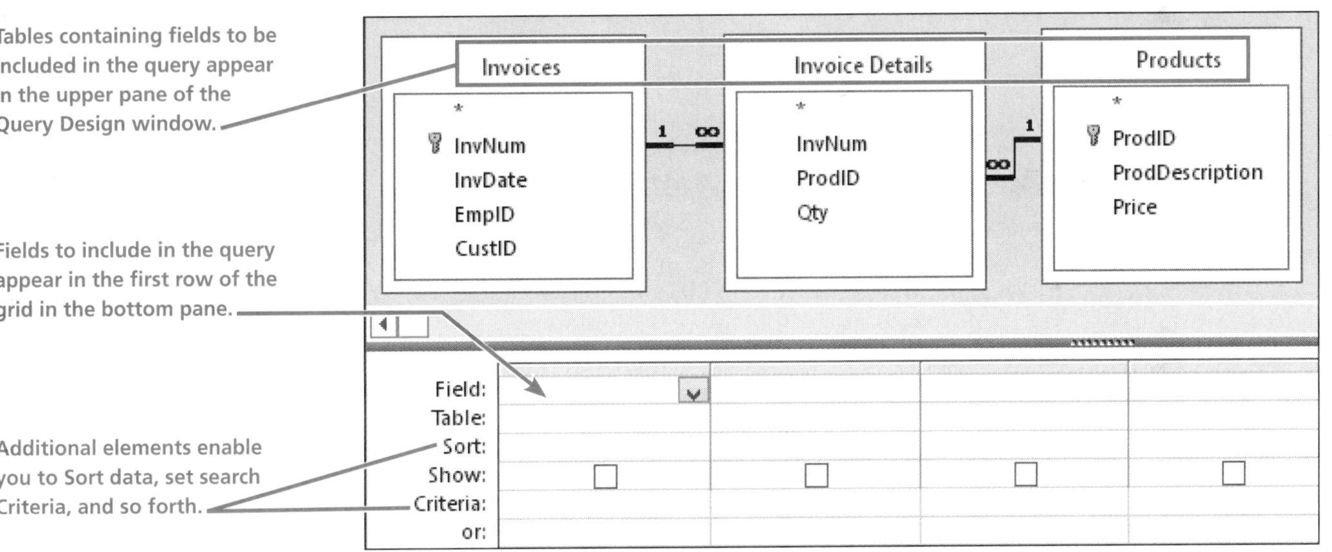
Tables containing fields to be included in the query appear in the upper pane of the Query Design window.
Fields to include in the query appear in the first row of the grid in the bottom pane.
Additional elements enable you to Sort data, set search Criteria, and so forth.
Invoices
*
InvNum
InvDate
EmpID
CustID
Invoice Details
*
InvNum
ProdID
Qty
Products
*
ProdID
ProdDescription
Price
1
1
Field:
Table:
Sort:
Show:
Criteria:
or:

The query design grid lets you add fields to a query.

Adding Fields to the Query Design Grid

Access offers a variety of techniques for adding fields to the query grid.

- Double-click a field name to add the field to the next available column of the query design grid.
- Drag a field to the next column in the grid.
- Click the Field row of a column in the query grid and select the field from the drop-down list.
- Double-click the asterisk (*) that appears at the top of the field list to add all fields to the grid.

Access 2013

NOTE

When you use the asterisk to add all table fields to the grid, Access only places the table name in the Field row followed by a .* (dot asterisk). But when you run the query, each field appears in a separate column of the query results datasheet.

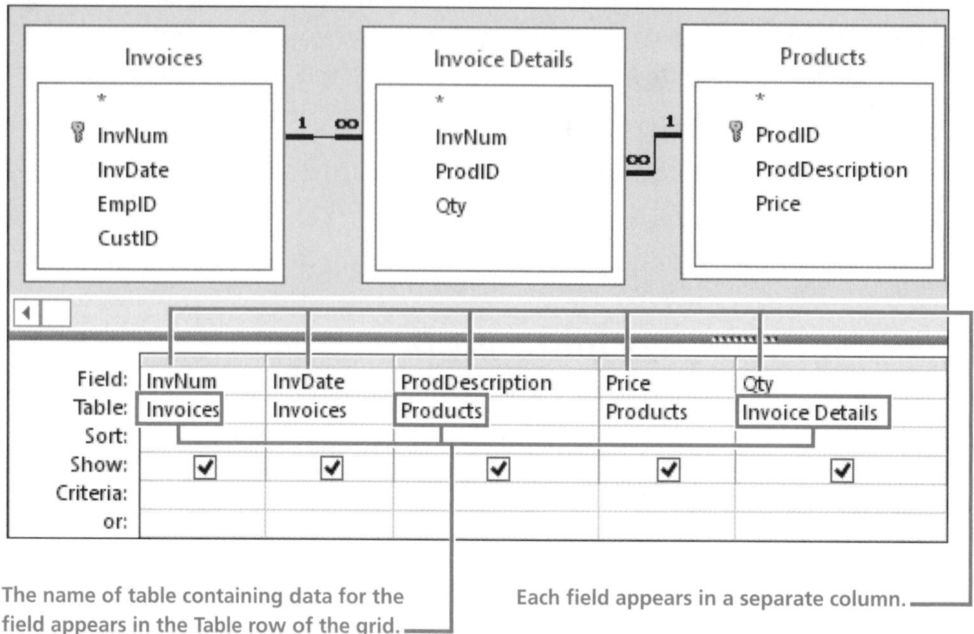
Invoices
*
InvNum
InvDate
EmpID
CustID
Invoice Details
*
InvNum
ProdID
Qty
Products
*
ProdID
ProdDescription
Price
Field: InvNum InvDate ProdDescription Price Qty
Table: Invoices Invoices Products Products Invoice Details
Sort:
Show:
Criteria:
or:
The name of table containing data for the field appears in the Table row of the grid.
Each field appears in a separate column.

Rearranging Fields in the Query Design Grid

You can rearrange query columns in Design View or Datasheet View by dragging and dropping them into position. Click the gray Column Heading selector that appears above the Field name in the query grid or datasheet to select the field column. Then, hover over the top of the selected column until the mouse pointer becomes a white arrow and drag the field column to a new position.

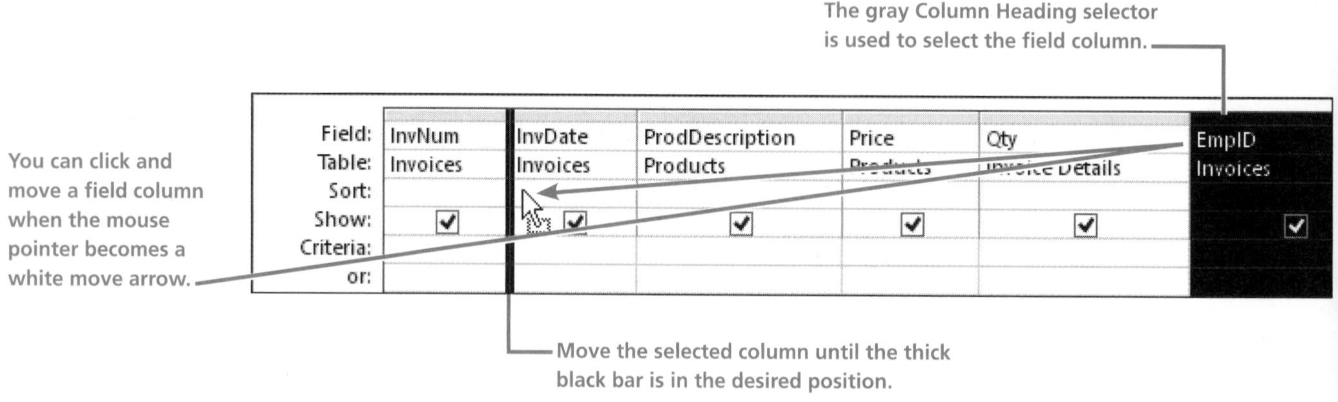
The gray Column Heading selector is used to select the field column.
You can click and move a field column when the mouse pointer becomes a white move arrow.
Field: InvNum InvDate ProdDescription Price Qty EmpID
Table: Invoices Invoices Products Invoices
Sort:
Show:
Criteria:
or:
Move the selected column until the thick black bar is in the desired position.

QUICK REFERENCE	USING QUERY DESIGN
Task	**Procedure**
Create a query using Query Design	Choose Create→Queries→Query Design.
Display query design from the query Datasheet View	Choose Home→Views→View to toggle between Design and Datasheet View; or, right-click the query tab and choose Design View.
Add fields to a query grid	Double-click a field name in the table field list; drag a field from the table field list to a query grid column; or, double-click the asterisk in the table field list to add all fields.
Add criteria to a query grid	Type the desired criteria into the Criteria row for the field that should contain the value. For instance, if you want all customers from Sarasota, type *Sarasota* in the Criteria row of the City field column.
Save a query	Click Save, name the query, and click OK; or close the query and name it when prompted.
Run a query	Double-click a query name in the Navigation Pane, or choose Design→Results→Run.

DEVELOP YOUR SKILLS AC04-D02

Create a Query Using Query Design

You have already created an email list for the Winchester Web Design customers and now need one for the company's employees. In this exercise, you will create a query to select fields from the Employees table in the Winchester Web Design database and then rearrange the columns in the query grid.

1. Choose **Create→Queries→Query Design** to display the Query Design Grid.

   Access displays a list of tables and existing queries in the database so you can choose the sources you want to include in the new query.

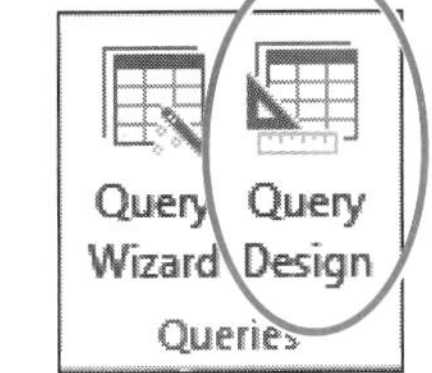

2. Follow these steps to add a table to the query:

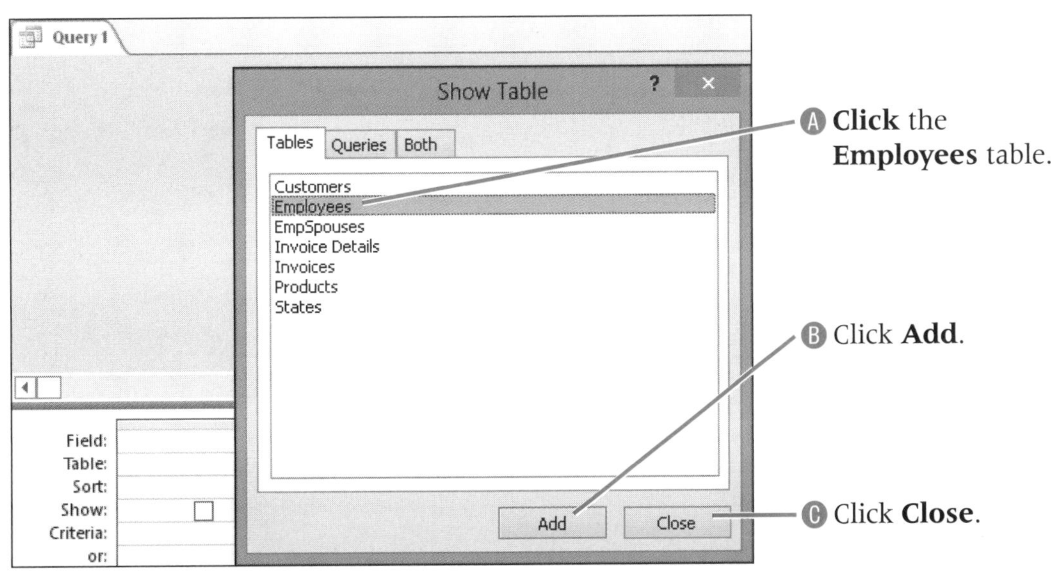

Access 2013

3. Follow these steps to add fields (in a different order than they are in the underlying table) to the query grid:

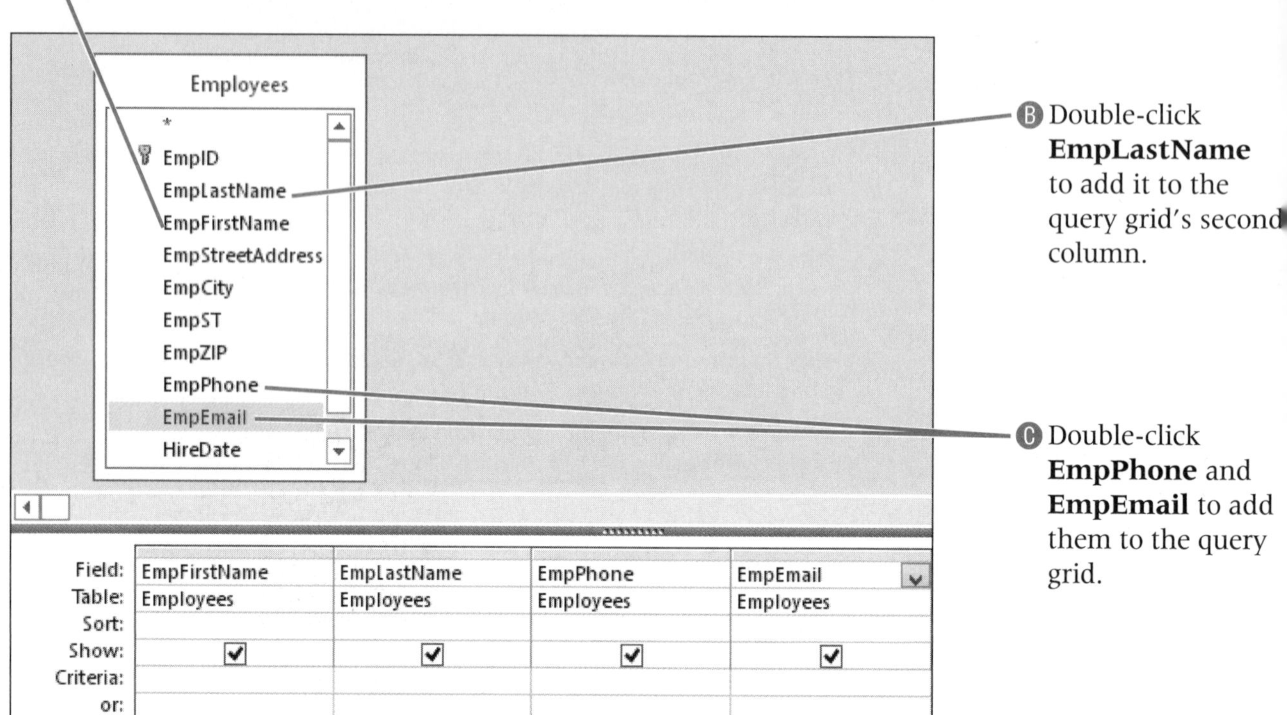

You can also click and drag fields to the query grid.

4. Follow these steps to save and then run the query:

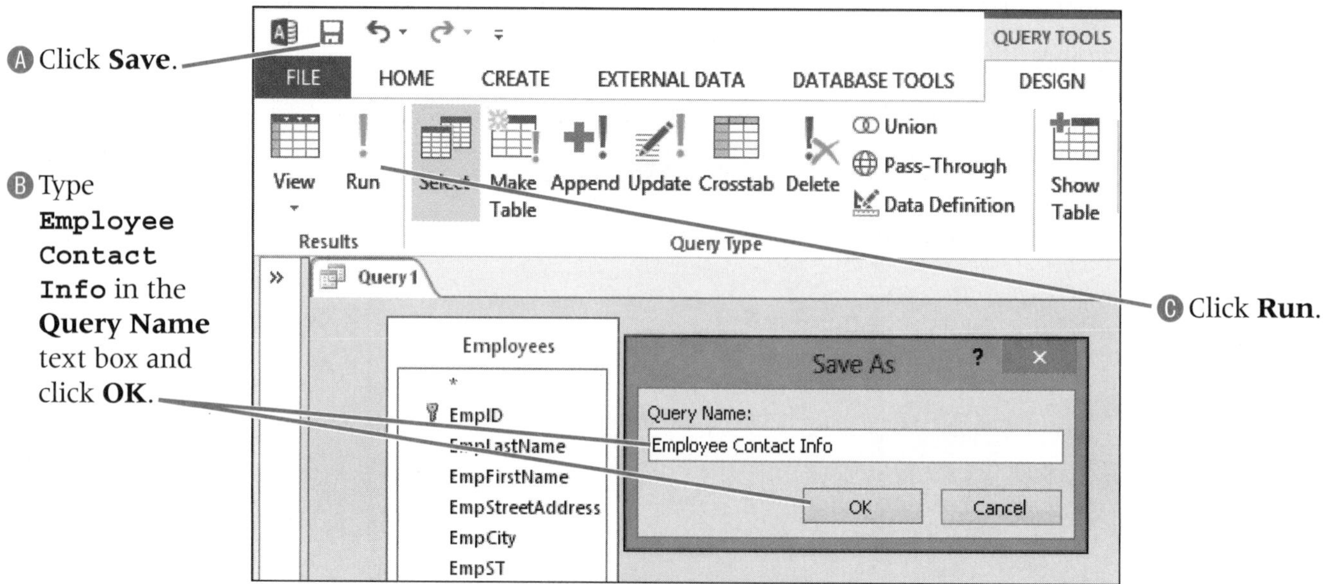

Access runs the query and displays four columns of data (First Name, Last Name, Telephone, and Email) for all Employee records.

First Name	Last Name	Telephone	Email
Jay	Winchester	(941) 555-9382	WinchesterJay@email.com
John	Kramer	(941) 555-3490	KramerJ@email.com
Julie	Mansfield	(941) 555-5218	JulieMansfield@email.com
Mike	Waters	(941) 555-3981	MikeWaters@email.com

5. Switch to **Design View**.
6. Follow these steps to rearrange fields in the query grid:

Ⓐ Hover the mouse pointer over the **Column Heading selector** for the EmpLastName column until the mouse pointer becomes a solid down-pointing arrow ⬇, and click to select the field.

Ⓑ Click the **Column Heading selector** for EmpLastName again and use the new white move arrow to drag the selected field column to the left of the EmpFirstName column.

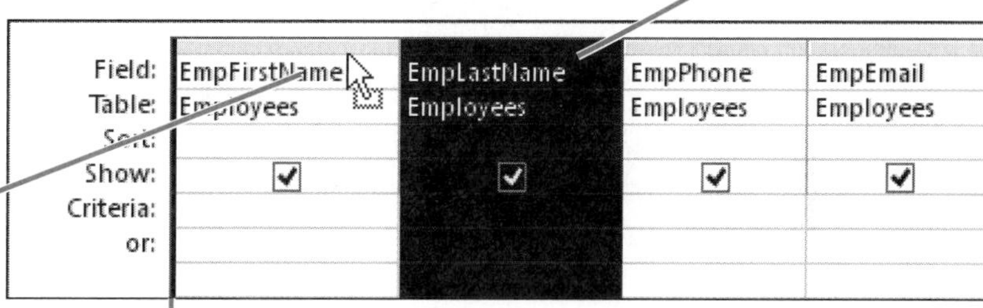

Ⓒ **Release** the **EmpLastName** field column when the thick black bar appears.

7. Choose **Design→Results→Run** to run the query again.

Last Name	First Name	Telephone	Email
Winchester	Jay	(941) 555-9382	WinchesterJay@email.com
Kramer	John	(941) 555-3490	KramerJ@email.com
Mansfield	Julie	(941) 555-5218	JulieMansfield@email.com
Waters	Mike	(941) 555-3981	MikeWaters@email.com

The Last Name field is now the first field displayed in the query.

8. Close the query, saving changes when prompted.

Designing a Query Using Multiple Tables

Video Library http://labyrinthelab.com/videos Video Number: AC13-V0403

Until now, the datasheets you have worked with have displayed data from only one table. There will be times when you need to view data contained in different tables within the same database. Queries allow you to do this.

Choosing Fields to Include in a Query

When you build a query, you select only those tables and fields that you want to display in the query results datasheet and leave out those fields that have no impact on the data you want to view or that are confidential. For example, if you were responsible for maintaining a list of FBI agents, would you want everyone with access to the database to know the addresses and phone numbers of all agents? By specifying only certain tables and fields in a database and displaying only the desired fields in a query, you can create a report or a form that only presents pertinent data.

Selecting a Field that Appears in Multiple Tables

When you work with table field lists, you may see multiple tables that contain the same ID field names. You may wonder which ID field to add to a query. The best practice is to identify the table for which the ID field is the *primary* key. This table will best allow you to retrieve other related data contained in that table.

Note that when you add fields from multiple tables, these tables must be related in order for the intended results to be displayed.

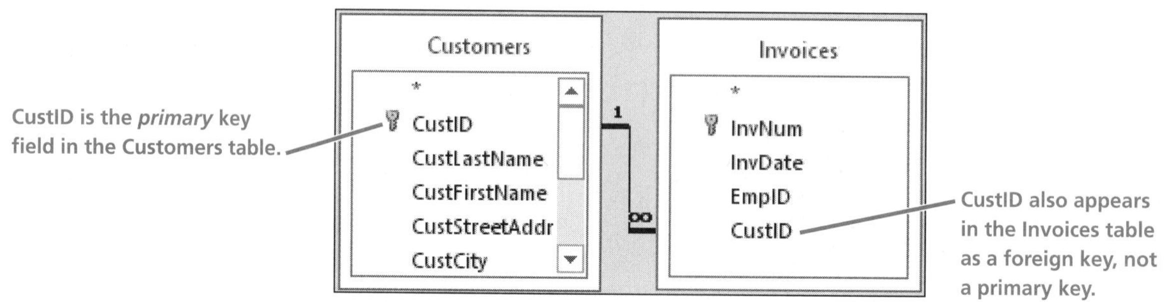

CustID is the *primary* key field in the Customers table.
Customers
*
CustID
CustLastName
CustFirstName
CustStreetAddr
CustCity
1
∞
Invoices
*
InvNum
InvDate
EmpID
CustID
CustID also appears in the Invoices table as a foreign key, not a primary key.

DEVELOP YOUR SKILLS AC04-D03

Create a Multi-Table Query

In this exercise, you will create a multi-table query to track the Winchester Web Design invoices by invoice number using Query Design View.

1. Choose **Create→Queries→Query Design** .
   An empty query grid and the Show Table dialog box open.
2. Double-click the following table names in the Show Table dialog box to add the table field lists to the upper pane of the query: **Invoices**, **Invoice Details**, and **Products**.
   If the Show Table dialog box does not appear, choose Design→Query Setup→Show Table.

3. Close the Show Table dialog box, then follow these steps to add fields to the query grid:

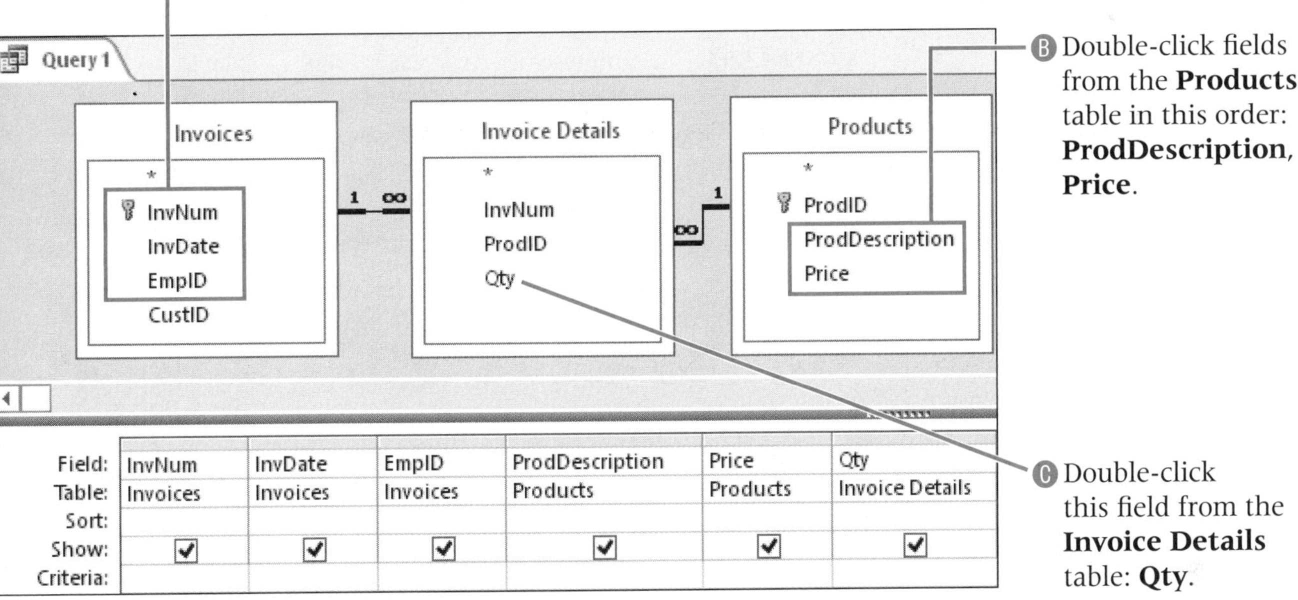

Your tables may be aligned differently, but the fields should appear in the query grid in the order shown.

If your tables do not line up neatly, click and drag the table title bar to the left or to the right as desired.

4. Click in the **Sort** row for the InvNum field in the query grid and choose **Ascending**.

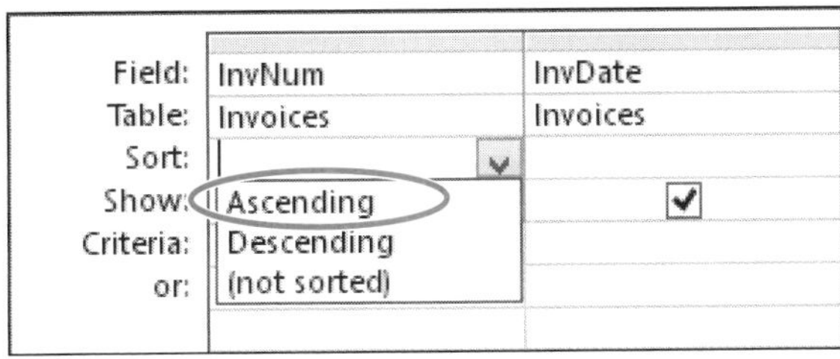

5. Save the query as `InvoicesList` and click **OK**.

6. Choose **Design→Results→Run** to display the query results.

InvoicesList

InvNum	Invoice Date	Emp ID	Description	Price	Qty
1	3/15/2012	JFW	Secondary Page	$200.00	6
1	3/15/2012	JFW	Image, Custom Designed	$40.00	11
1	3/15/2012	JFW	Home Page, Nav, CSS, Design	$400.00	1
2	4/2/2012	MJW	Image, Custom Designed	$40.00	14
2	4/2/2012	MJW	Home Page, Nav, CSS, Design	$400.00	1
2	4/2/2012	MJW	Secondary Page	$200.00	7
2	4/2/2012	MJW	Hourly Rate for Modifications	$80.00	5
3	5/11/2012	JMM	Image, Custom Designed	$40.00	6
3	5/11/2012	JMM	Secondary Page	$200.00	2
4	5/30/2012	JMM	Blog, Integrated into Site	$300.00	1
4	5/30/2012	JMM	Hourly Rate for Modifications	$80.00	2
4	5/30/2012	JMM	Image, Custom Designed	$40.00	2
5	6/19/2012	JFW	Image, Custom Designed	$40.00	9
5	6/19/2012	JFW	Secondary Page	$200.00	11
5	6/19/2012	JFW	Home Page, Nav, CSS, Design	$400.00	1
6	6/23/2012	MJW	Hourly Rate for Modifications	$80.00	3
6	6/23/2012	MJW	Blog, Integrated into Site	$300.00	1
6	6/23/2012	MJW	Home Page, Nav, CSS, Design	$400.00	1
6	6/23/2012	MJW	Secondary Page	$200.00	6
7	7/11/2012	JMM	Image, Custom Designed	$40.00	14

Setting Query Criteria

Video Library http://labyrinthelab.com/videos Video Number: AC13-V0404

As you begin working with large databases that contain thousands or even hundreds of thousands of records, you will experience the power behind queries that enables you to specify criteria, or conditions that data must meet. When you run the query, Access lists only those records containing data that meet the criteria. This is the feature used by sportscasters, live chat specialists working for an online retailer, and others who need data and questions answered right away.

Adding Criteria to a Query

You can filter and sort records while working in Table Design View, Form Design View, and to a limited degree in Report Design View. However, the best way to sort and filter data is through a query, because you can save each individual query with a meaningful name. Access uses standard comparison operators (<, >, =, >=, <=, <>) to set validation rules to help define a query's criteria. Setting query criteria limits the number of records displayed in query results to only those records with values in the selected field columns that meet the criteria. In addition, the following comparison and logical criteria can be used to limit data returned in queries.

Criteria Expression	Criteria Description and Sample
> 123	*Greater than*: For a numeric data field; returns records for all values greater than 123
< 100.45	*Less than*: For a currency data field; returns all values less than 100.45
>= Smith	*Greater than or equal*: For a text data field—all values from Smith through the end of the alphabet
<> 2	*Unequal*: For a numeric data field—all values unequal to 2. You could also use Not
Not Smith	For a text data field—all records for values except Smith
Not T*	For text data field—all values that don't start with the letter T
"London" Or "Hedge End"	For a text data field—orders shipped to London or Hedge End
In("Canada", "UK")	For a text data field—records containing the values Canada or UK in the criteria field
Between #1/1/2013# And #12/31/2013#	For date data field—dates from January 1, 2013 through December 31, 2013 (Access inserts the # signs after you type: Between 1/1/2013 and 12/31/2013)
Between Date( ) And DateAdd ("M", 3, Date( ))	For a date data field—values required between today's date and three months from today's date
Date()	For a date data field—values for today's date
< Date( ) – 30	For a date data field—values 30 days prior to the current date

Hiding Columns in the Query Results Datasheet

Suppose your company determines the price of a product by marking up the cost by 50%. So if your company bought a widget for $100, they would sell it for $150. As a salesperson, you need to show your customers the price of your products, but it would not be wise to disclose the amount of markup. Consequently, you include the Cost field in your query, but hide it when you run the query. This is easily accomplished by unchecking the Show checkbox for the Cost field in the query grid.

Access 2013

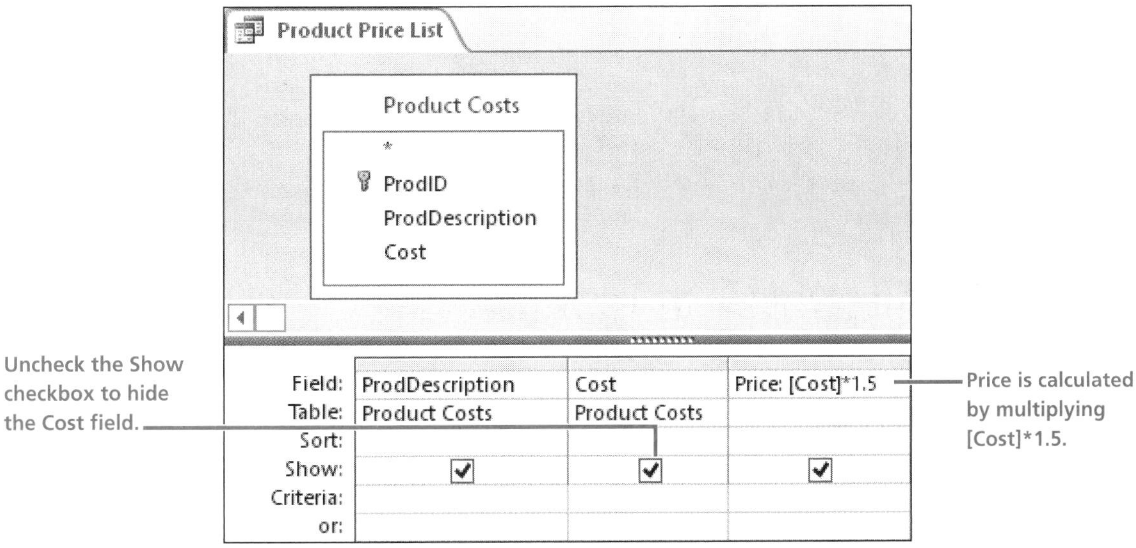

Building Queries with Criteria

When building a query you often add criteria to locate specific records in the database. Access recognizes any added or modified criteria as a change in the query design. As a result, when you close the query, Access prompts you to save it. Saving the query saves the criteria as part of the query. However, you may be just running what-if scenarios or you want to set different criteria each time you run the query. In those cases, you would choose *No* when Access prompts you to save the file.

DEVELOP YOUR SKILLS AC04-D04

Add Criteria and Run a Query

In this exercise, you will add criteria to the query grid and run the query.

1. Open the **InvoicesList** query, if necessary, and choose **Home→Views→View** .
2. Follow these steps to add criteria to the query grid:

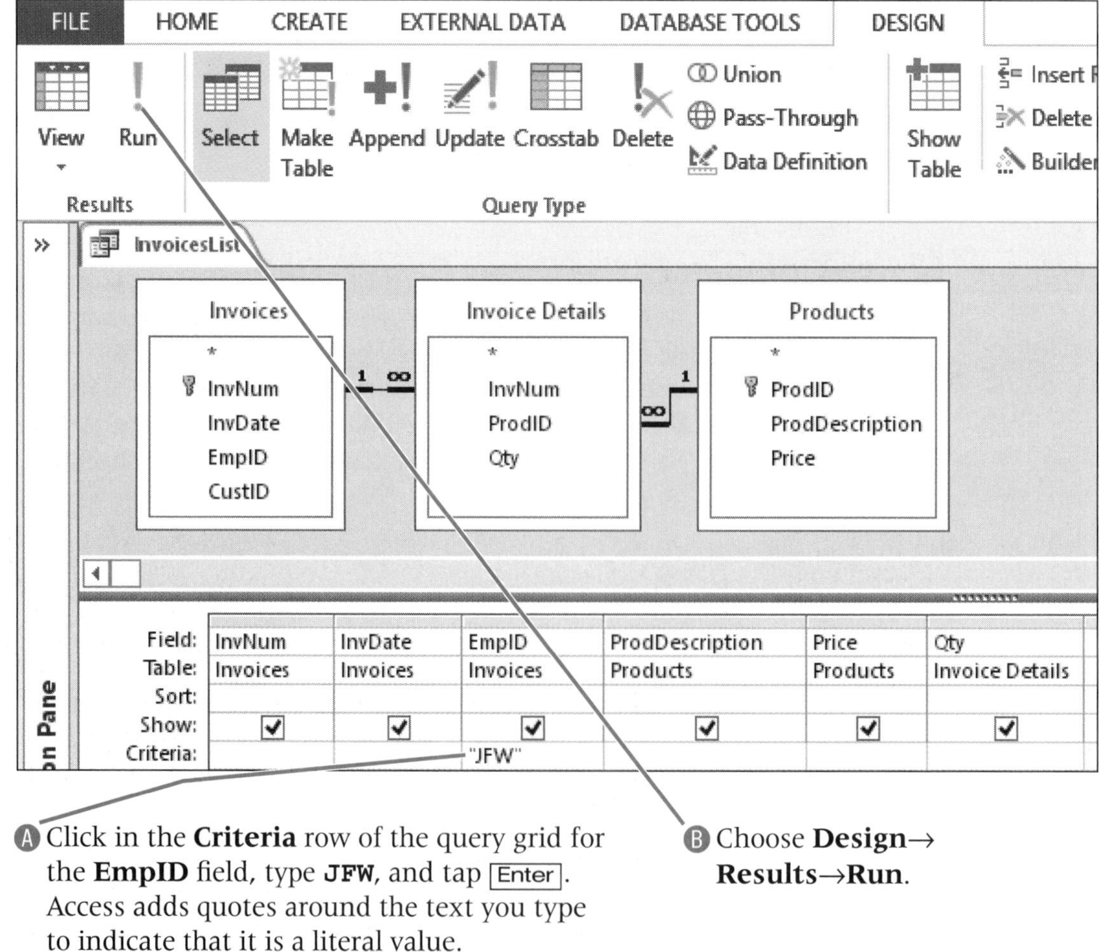

Access runs the query and only returns the invoices associated with EmpID JFW.

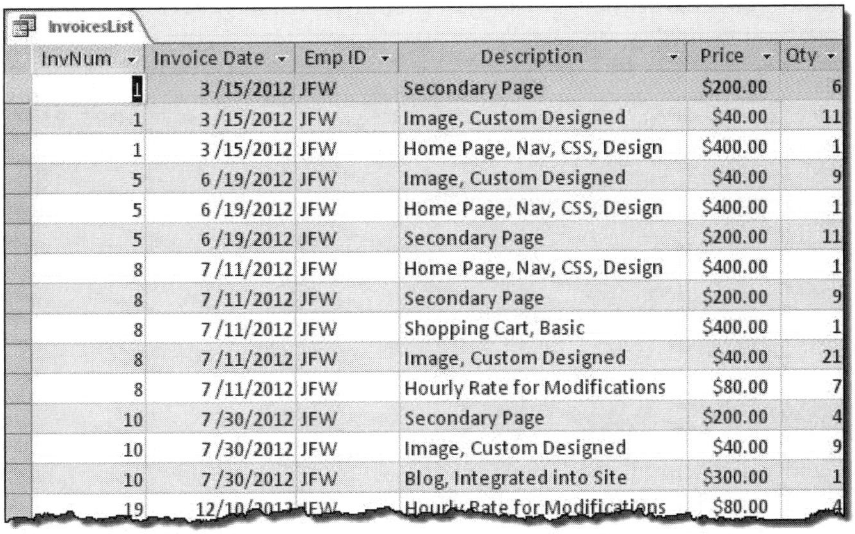

InvoicesList

InvNum	Invoice Date	Emp ID	Description	Price	Qty
1	3/15/2012	JFW	Secondary Page	$200.00	6
1	3/15/2012	JFW	Image, Custom Designed	$40.00	11
1	3/15/2012	JFW	Home Page, Nav, CSS, Design	$400.00	1
5	6/19/2012	JFW	Image, Custom Designed	$40.00	9
5	6/19/2012	JFW	Home Page, Nav, CSS, Design	$400.00	1
5	6/19/2012	JFW	Secondary Page	$200.00	11
8	7/11/2012	JFW	Home Page, Nav, CSS, Design	$400.00	1
8	7/11/2012	JFW	Secondary Page	$200.00	9
8	7/11/2012	JFW	Shopping Cart, Basic	$400.00	1
8	7/11/2012	JFW	Image, Custom Designed	$40.00	21
8	7/11/2012	JFW	Hourly Rate for Modifications	$80.00	7
10	7/30/2012	JFW	Secondary Page	$200.00	4
10	7/30/2012	JFW	Image, Custom Designed	$40.00	9
10	7/30/2012	JFW	Blog, Integrated into Site	$300.00	1
19	12/10/2012	JFW	Hourly Rate for Modifications	$80.00	4

3. Close the query. Choose **No** when prompted to save the changes.
   Saving changes to the query at this time would save the JFW criteria as part of the query. However, you plan to use the query for all employees in the future.

Using Wildcards

Video Library http://labyrinthelab.com/videos Video Number: AC13-V0405

The two most frequent wildcards with which you may be familiar are the asterisk (*) and the question mark (?). There are four additional wildcards. Each wildcard is described in the following table.

WILDCARD SYMBOLS

Symbol	Description of Use
An asterisk (*)	Substitutes for a group of characters that appear at the position of the asterisk **Example**: If you type `R*` in the last name column of a query grid, Access will locate all last names beginning with *R* regardless of how many characters make up the name. In this case, *Rogers, Rich,* and *Rodriquez* would all appear in the results datasheet.
A question mark (?)	Substitutes for a single character that might appear at the position of the question mark **Example**: If you type `m?s` in the criteria row for a column, Access will locate records containing values such as *mrs, ms, mbs.*
Open/close brackets [ ]	Matches text or individual characters placed within the brackets individually **Example:** If you type ca[rt], Access will find cat and car but not cab or cad.
Exclamation point (!)	Matches any character within the brackets *except* those characters that follow the ! **Example:** If you type ca[!rt], Access will find cab, cad, cam, etc., but not cat or car.
Hyphen (-)	Matches characters at the wildcard position that fall within a range of ascending values **Example:** If you type ca[a-r], Access finds cab, cad, cam, car, etc., but not cat or cay.
Number sign (#)	Locates any numeric digit at the position of the # **Example:** If you type #10, Access locates 010, 110, 210, etc.

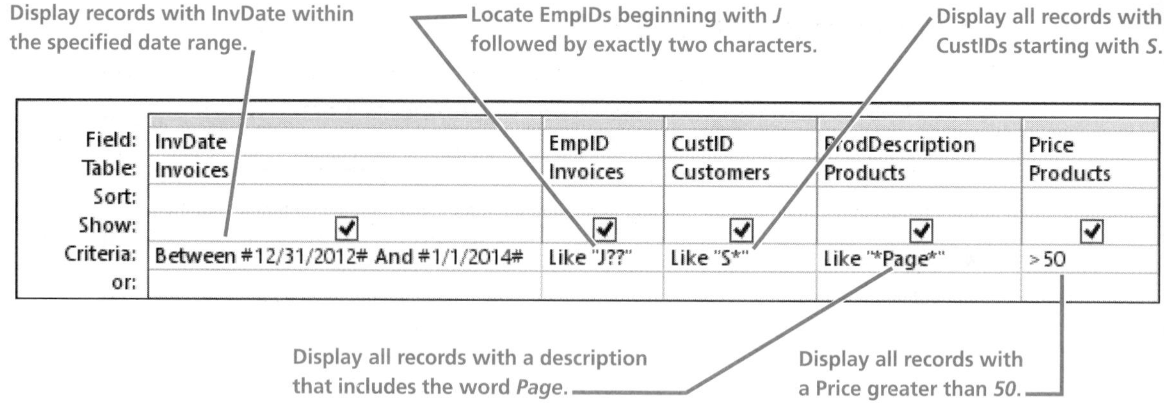
Display records with InvDate within the specified date range.
Locate EmpIDs beginning with *J* followed by exactly two characters.
Display all records with CustIDs starting with *S*.
Field: InvDate | EmpID | CustID | ProdDescription | Price
Table: Invoices | Invoices | Customers | Products | Products
Sort:
Show:
Criteria: Between #12/31/2012# And #1/1/2014# | Like "J??" | Like "S*" | Like "*Page*" | >50
or:
Display all records with a description that includes the word *Page*.
Display all records with a Price greater than *50*.

Setting AND and OR Criteria

In some cases, you may need to select records that meet multiple criteria. Access uses two basic criteria conditions that apply to setting multiple criteria for a query: AND and OR. The basic principles for determining whether to use AND criteria or OR criteria in queries are as follows.

AND AND _OR_ CRITERIA

Criterion Type	Description
AND operator	Use to select records that meet *all* criteria set in all query grid fields. **Example:** Set an AND criteria to locate employees who are from Sarasota *and* who are web-certified by using *Sarasota* in the City field and *Yes* in the Web Certification field on the query grid.
OR operator	Use to select records meeting *one* condition *or another* condition whether the criteria are set for the same field or different fields. **Example:** Set OR criteria to locate customers from *either* Sarasota *or* Bradenton.

Positioning Multiple Criteria in the Query Grid

In the query grid, the AND criteria all appear on the same Criteria row even when criteria are set for different fields. When you set OR criteria, the first criterion is entered on the Criteria row in the grid while other criteria appear on the Or row in the grid.

Example of an AND Criteria

Setting criteria for two different fields on the same Criteria row creates an AND condition. With this type of criterion, Access locates only those records for employees who live in Sarasota *and* are web certified.

Field:	EmpLastName	EmpFirstName	EmpCity	HireDate	WebCert
Table:	Employees	Employees	Employees	Employees	Employees
Sort:					
Show:	✓	✓	✓	✓	✓
Criteria:			"Sarasota"		Yes
or:					

The AND criteria are on the same row.

Example of an OR Criteria

Setting criteria on both the Criteria row and the Or row creates an OR condition. With this type of criterion, Access locates those records for employees who live in Sarasota *or* in Bradenton.

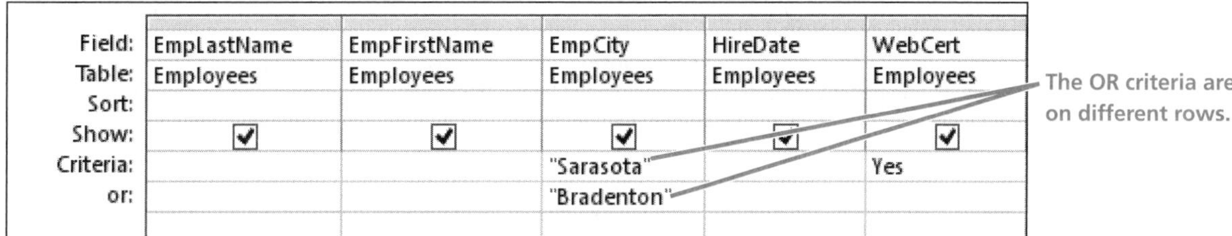

Setting OR criteria sometimes seems to operate backwards. In this example, you wanted to locate all records for employees from Sarasota *and* Bradenton, yet you use an OR condition. If you consider that there are no records that contain both Sarasota and Bradenton in the City field, it begins to make sense.

DEVELOP YOUR SKILLS AC04-D05

Use Wildcards and Multiple Criteria in Queries

In this exercise, you will use wildcards to locate variable data and set multiple criteria in a query to find out which customers have gotten blogs and which customers have added more than ten images at a time to their websites.

1. Right-click **Invoices Query** in the Navigation Pane and choose **Design View**.
2. Follow these steps to set multiple criteria in a query grid:

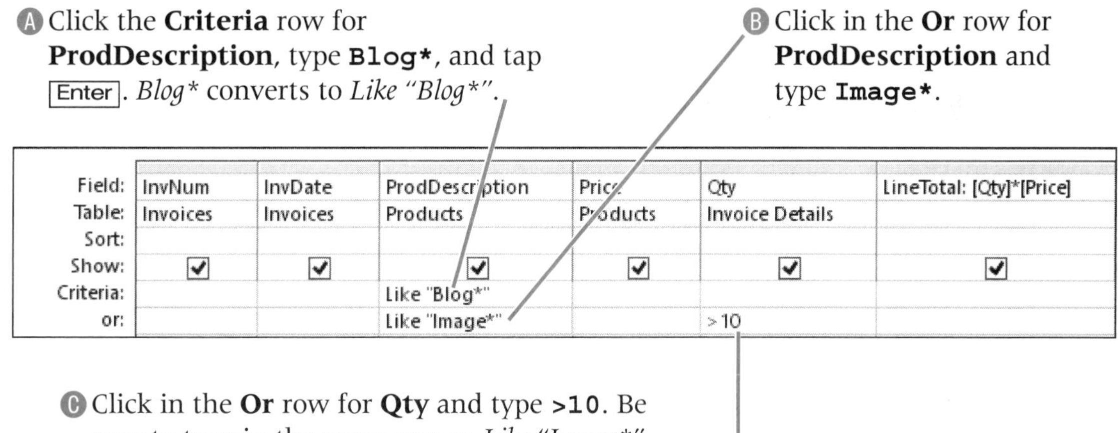

Ⓐ Click the **Criteria** row for **ProdDescription**, type **`Blog*`**, and tap [Enter]. *Blog** converts to *Like "Blog*"*.
Ⓑ Click in the **Or** row for **ProdDescription** and type **`Image*`**.
Field: InvNum | InvDate | ProdDescription | Price | Qty | LineTotal: [Qty]*[Price]
Table: Invoices | Invoices | Products | Products | Invoice Details
Sort:
Show: ✔ | ✔ | ✔ | ✔ | ✔ | ✔
Criteria: Like "Blog*"
or: Like "Image*" | >10
Ⓒ Click in the **Or** row for **Qty** and type **`>10`**. Be sure to type in the same row as *Like "Image*"*.

These criteria will select all records for Blogs and all records for Images with a Qty greater than 10.

3. Switch to **Datasheet View**.

Invoices Query

Inv Num	Inv Date	Description	Price	Qty	LineTotal
4	5/30/2012	Blog, Integrated into Site	$300.00	1	$300.00
6	6/23/2012	Blog, Integrated into Site	$300.00	1	$300.00
10	7/30/2012	Blog, Integrated into Site	$300.00	1	$300.00
15	10/30/2012	Blog, Integrated into Site	$300.00	1	$300.00
34	8/5/2013	Blog, Integrated into Site	$300.00	1	$300.00
13	9/3/2012	Blog, Integrated into Site	$300.00	1	$300.00
16	11/5/2012	Blog, Integrated into Site	$300.00	1	$300.00
24	2/7/2013	Blog, Integrated into Site	$300.00	1	$300.00
29	3/12/2013	Blog, Integrated into Site	$300.00	1	$300.00
1	3/15/2012	Image, Custom Designed	$40.00	11	$440.00
7	7/11/2012	Image, Custom Designed	$40.00	14	$560.00
20	1/5/2013	Image, Custom Designed	$40.00	14	$560.00
21	1/12/2013	Image, Custom Designed	$40.00	18	$720.00
2	4/2/2012	Image, Custom Designed	$40.00	14	$560.00
8	7/11/2012	Image, Custom Designed	$40.00	21	$840.00
17	11/20/2012	Image, Custom Designed	$40.00	12	$480.00
24	2/7/2013	Image, Custom Designed	$40.00	19	$760.00
26	2/12/2013	Image, Custom Designed	$40.00	14	$560.00

Access displays the records that meet the specified criteria: either a blog or a transaction with more than ten images.

4. Close the query. Choose **No** when prompted to save the changes.
   Saving changes at this point would store the temporary criteria with the query.

Entering Date Criteria

Video Library http://labyrinthelab.com/videos Video Number: AC13-V0406

You can set date criteria to determine age, hired date, invoice date, and so forth. Access acknowledges the same comparison criteria for performing date comparisons that it does for locating other types of data—regardless of the format used to enter dates.

SAMPLES OF DATE CRITERIA

Criterion	Locates
06/22/2013	Finds records containing a specific date
<22-Oct-2013	Finds records containing dates that occur before a specific date—regardless of how the date is typed
>01/01/13	Finds records containing dates that occur after a specific date
<=#06/01/13#	Finds records containing dates on or before a specific date; the # signs that appear before and after the date help Access identify the data between them as a date
Between 01/01/13 and 06/30/13	Finds records containing dates after the first date and before the second date

DEVELOP YOUR SKILLS AC04-D06

Use Date Criteria in Queries

Winchester Web Design needs to track all invoices issued in 2012. In this exercise, you will create a query to set criteria using date values for locating customers with invoices dated from Jan 1, 2012 through December 31, 2012.

1. Choose **Create→Queries→Query Design**.
2. Follow these steps to add table field lists to the query:

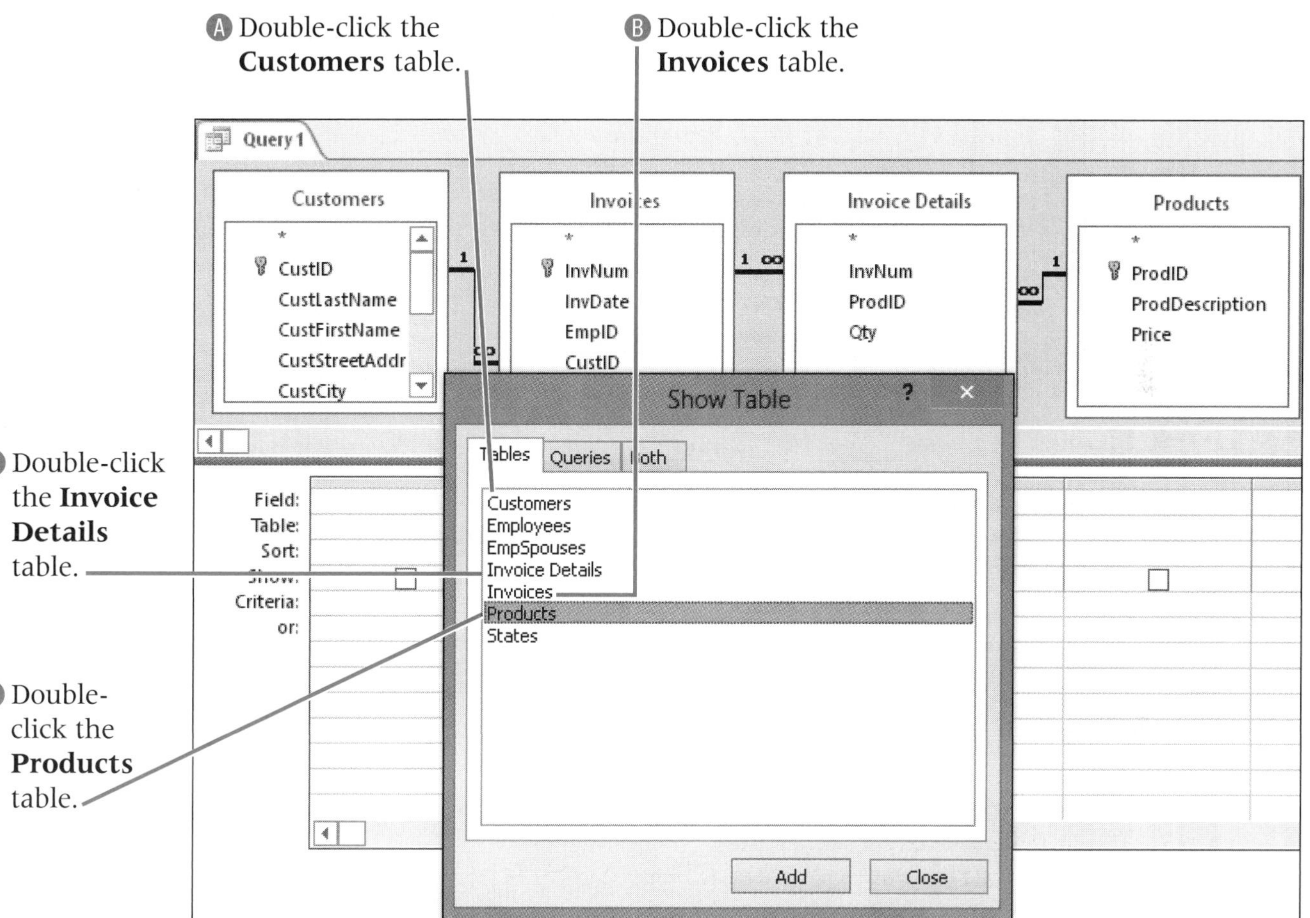

If the Show Table box does not appear, choose Design→Query Setup→Show Table.

3. Close the **Show Table** dialog box.

Access 2013

4. Follow these steps to add fields to the query grid:

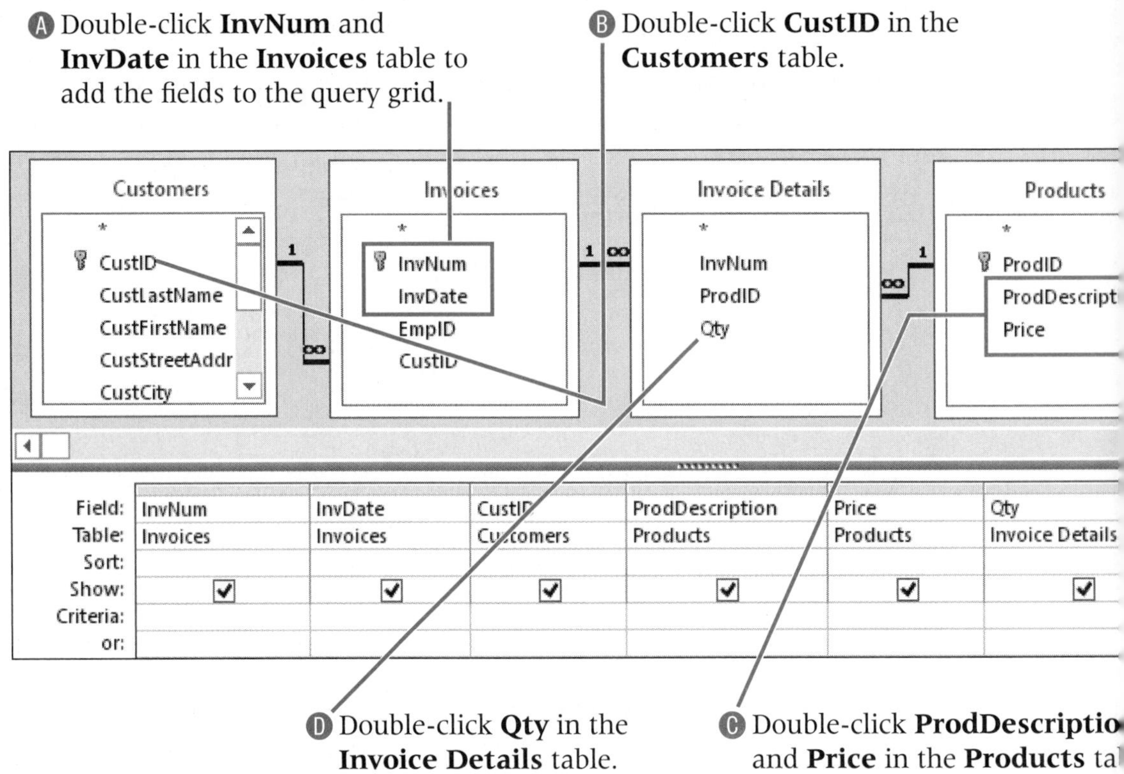

5. Type **`Between January 1, 2012 and December 31, 2012`** in the **Criteria** row for the **InvDate** field and tap [Enter].

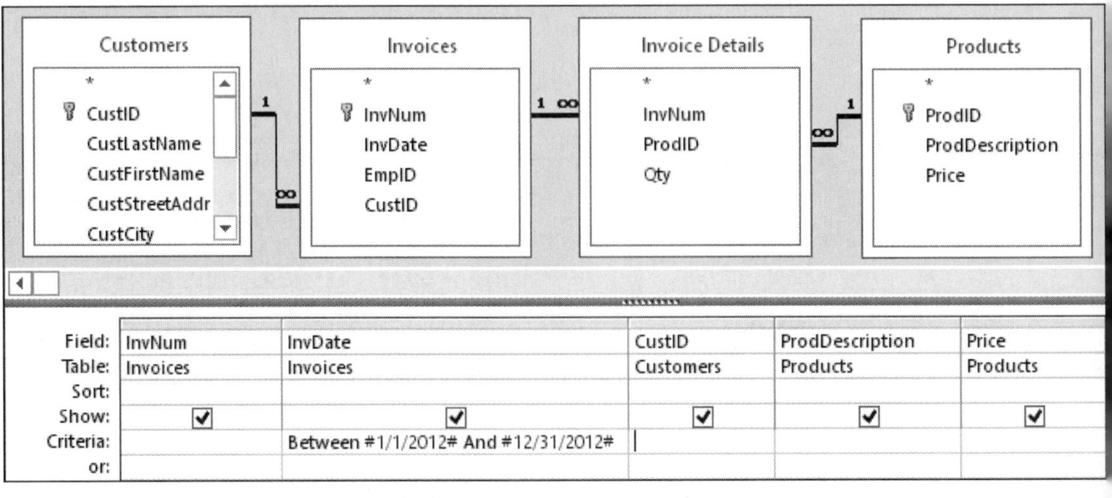

Regardless of how you type the dates, whether January 1, 2012, 01/01/12, or 1-1-2012, Access formats the date after you enter it so that it appears as #1/1/2012#.

6. Choose **Design→Results→Run.**

Query1

InvNum	Invoice Date	CustID	Description	Price	Qty
1	3/15/2012	SmithW	Home Page, Nav, CSS, Design	$400.00	1
1	3/15/2012	SmithW	Secondary Page	$200.00	6
1	3/15/2012	SmithW	Image, Custom Designed	$40.00	11
2	4/2/2012	SantosE	Home Page, Nav, CSS, Design	$400.00	1
2	4/2/2012	SantosE	Secondary Page	$200.00	7
2	4/2/2012	SantosE	Image, Custom Designed	$40.00	14
2	4/2/2012	SantosE	Hourly Rate for Modifications	$80.00	5
3	5/11/2012	SantosE	Secondary Page	$200.00	2
3	5/11/2012	SantosE	Image, Custom Designed	$40.00	6
4	5/30/2012	SmithW	Blog, Integrated into Site	$300.00	1
4	5/30/2012	SmithW	Hourly Rate for Modifications	$80.00	2
4	5/30/2012	SmithW	Image, Custom Designed	$40.00	2
5	6/19/2012	AndersM	Home Page, Nav, CSS, Design	$400.00	1
5	6/19/2012	AndersM	Secondary Page	$200.00	11
5	6/19/2012	AndersM	Image, Custom Designed	$40.00	9
6	6/23/2012	JeffriesD	Home Page, Nav, CSS, Design	$400.00	1
6	6/23/2012	JeffriesD	Secondary Page	$200.00	6
6	6/23/2012	JeffriesD	Blog, Integrated into Site	$300.00	1
6	6/23/2012	JeffriesD	Hourly Rate for Modifications	$80.00	3

Access locates the records for invoices from January 1, 2012 through December 31, 2012.

7. Save the query as **`Invoices2012`** then click **OK.**
8. Close the query.

Access 2013

Sorting a Query and Limiting Results

Video Library http://labyrinthelab.com/videos Video Number: AC13-V0407

The query grid contains a Sort row that you can use to sort data in ascending or descending order. Sorting queried data helps ensure consistency and makes locating data in the query results more efficient.

Setting a Query Sort Order

There may be times when you need to sort data based upon two fields. For instance, if there are duplicate last names, you have to do a secondary sort on first name. When two fields are set as sort fields, Access sorts the fields left to right as they appear in the query grid. The first sort field is identified as the *primary* sort field; the next sort field is the *secondary* sort field. Multiple sorted fields do not need to be side by side in the query grid.

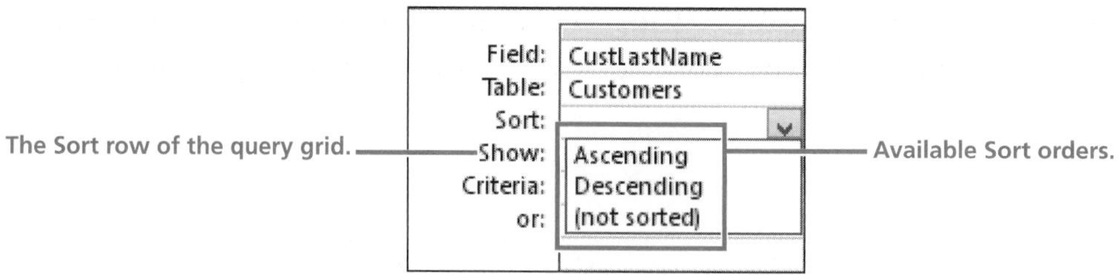

Limiting Number of Results Displayed

Running queries on large databases that contain hundreds of thousands of records often return such a large number of results that it can be challenging to find what you are looking for. So limiting the number of records displayed when you run a query can be beneficial, especially when these records are sorted.

For example, if you set up a query to sort in descending order and then limit the number of items displayed to ten, you would, in effect, have a list of the top ten items in the table being queried.

This query datasheet includes all the records in the database.

Notice the item totals are in random order.

InvoiceTotalQuery

Inv Num	Invoice Date	Description	Price	Qty	LineTotal
41	12/7/2013	Shopping Cart, Basic	$400.00	1	$400.00
41	12/7/2013	Secondary Page	$200.00	2	$400.00
41	12/7/2013	Image, Custom Designed	$40.00	6	$240.00
40	11/14/2013	Home Page, Nav, CSS, Design	$400.00	1	$400.00
40	11/14/2013	Secondary Page	$200.00	7	$1,400.00
40	11/14/2013	Image, Custom Designed	$40.00	3	$120.00
39	11/4/2013	Secondary Page	$200.00	3	$600.00
39					
38					
38					
37					
37					
36					
35					
35					
34					
34					
34					

InvoiceTotalQuery

Inv Num	Invoice Date	Description	Price	Qty	LineTotal
24	2/7/2013	Secondary Page	$200.00	13	$2,600.00
13	9/3/2012	Secondary Page	$200.00	12	$2,400.00
21	1/12/2013	Secondary Page	$200.00	12	$2,400.00
5	6/19/2012	Secondary Page	$200.00	11	$2,200.00
29	3/12/2013	Secondary Page	$200.00	9	$1,800.00
8	7/11/2012	Secondary Page	$200.00	9	$1,800.00
2	4/2/2012	Secondary Page	$200.00	7	$1,400.00
40	11/14/2013	Secondary Page	$200.00	7	$1,400.00
26	2/12/2013	Secondary Page	$200.00	6	$1,200.00

After sorting with the results limited, only the largest item totals are shown, and in descending order.

Depending on the content of your tables and specified criteria, this feature may not always return the *exact* number of records that you specify.

The Return feature on the Query Design tab enables you to set the number of records to be displayed, or returned, in the query results. The default setting for the Return feature is All.

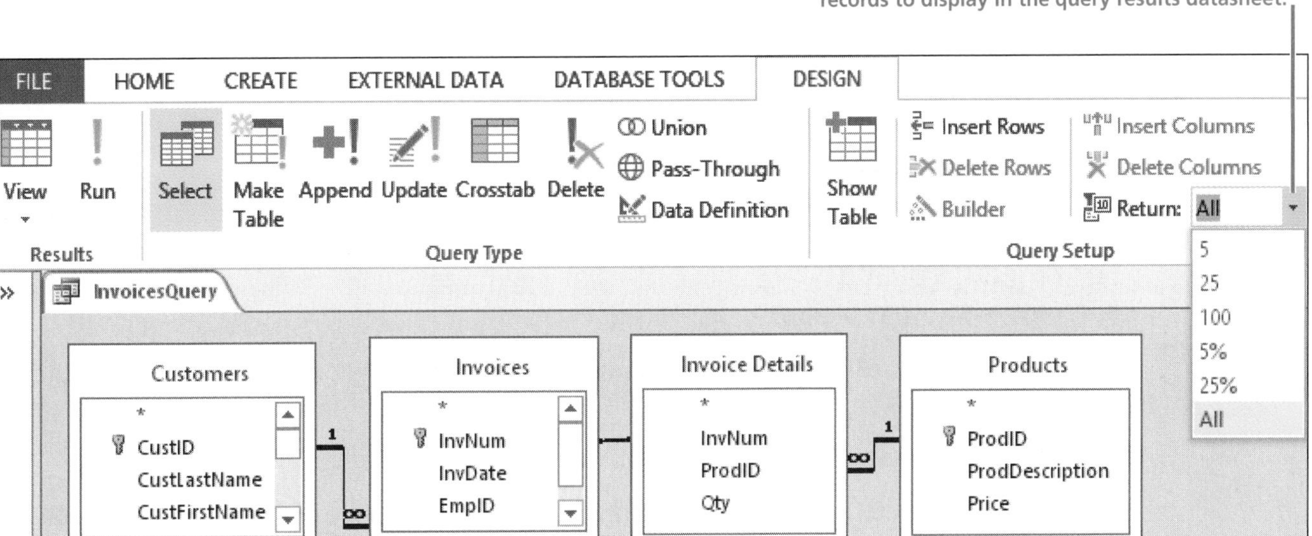

QUICK REFERENCE	SETTING A QUERY SORT ORDER
Task	**Procedure**
Set a sort order	■ Display the query in Query Design View. ■ Click the Sort row of the query grid for the desired sort field and select the appropriate field sort order.
Set sort orders for multiple fields	■ Display the query in Query Design View ■ Arrange the fields left to right in the order to sort. ■ Click the Sort row of the query grid for the desired sort field and select the appropriate field sort order. ■ Repeat steps for each additional field that you want to sort.
Limit the number of records returned	■ Display the query in Query Design View. ■ Choose Design→Query Setup→Return menu and select the number of records you want to view.

DEVELOP YOUR SKILLS AC04-D07

Set a Query Sort Order and Limit Records

The art department at Winchester Web Design wants to know which customers are using its services the most. In this exercise, you will create a query that sets a sort order in the query grid and limits the number of records in the query results to display the invoices with the most images from the art department.

Apply a Query Sort

1. Choose **Create→Queries→Query Design**.
2. Double-click the **Customers**, **Invoices**, **Invoice Details**, and **Products** tables in the Show Table dialog box.
3. Close the **Show Table box**.
4. Double-click **CustID** and **CustLastName** in the **Customers** table to add the fields to the query grid.
5. Double-click **InvDate** in the **Invoices** table to add it to the query grid.
6. Double-click **ProdDescription** in the **Products** table and **Qty** in the **Invoice Details** table.
7. Follow these steps to set criteria and a sort order:

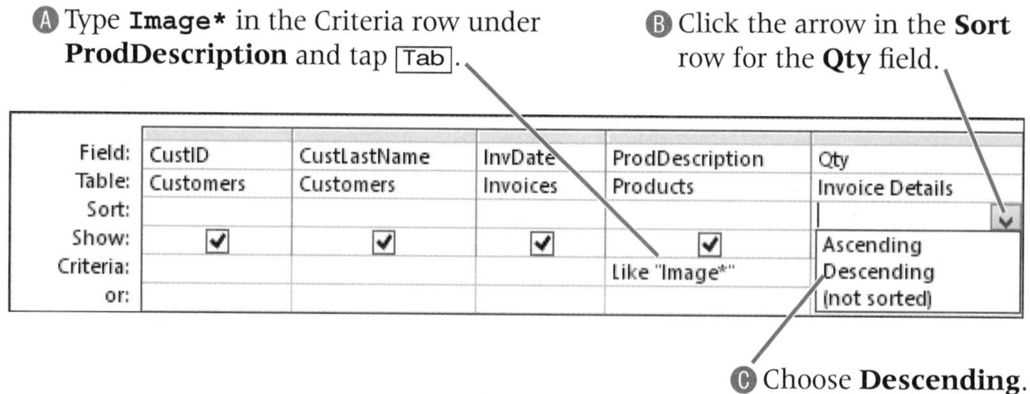

Limit the Number of Records to Display

8. Follow these steps to limit the number of records displayed in the results:

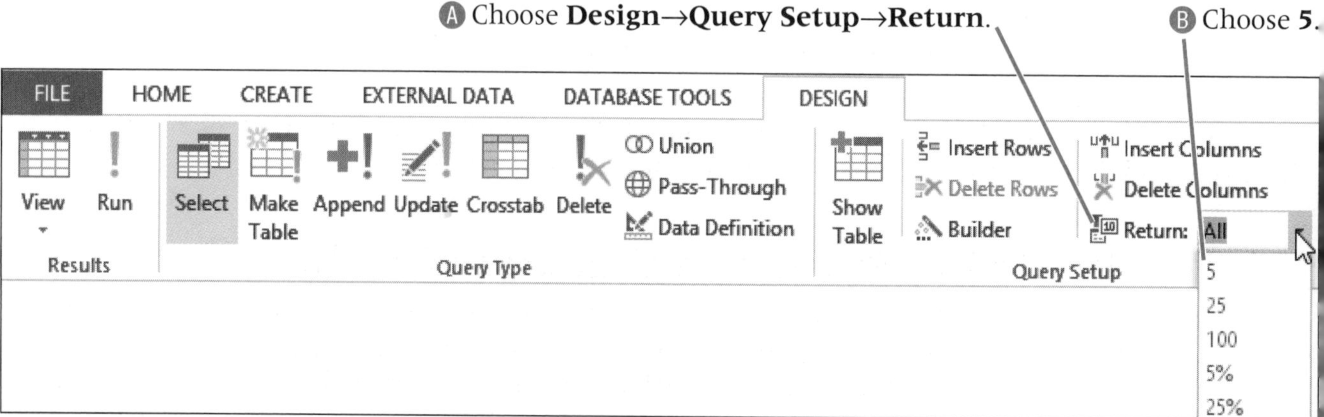

9. Choose **Design→Results→Run** [Run].

Access returns only the records with the largest quantities.

CustID	Last Name	Invoice Date	Description	Qty
DavisP	Davis	7/11/2012	Image, Custom Designed	21
ThibeauxP	Thibeaux	2/7/2013	Image, Custom Designed	19
JeffriesD	Jeffries	1/12/2013	Image, Custom Designed	18
SantosE	Santos	4/2/2012	Image, Custom Designed	15
RobertsJ	Roberts	7/11/2012	Image, Custom Designed	14
BlaserH	Blaser	2/23/2013	Image, Custom Designed	14
DavisP	Davis	2/12/2013	Image, Custom Designed	14

The number of records returned is not always the exact *number you have specified in Design View. The seven highest records are returned here because Access includes all records with a Qty value of 14.*

10. Close the query, saving it as `Most Images`.

Performing Calculations in Queries

Video Library http://labyrinthelab.com/videos Video Number: AC13-V0408

So far, the activities in this lesson have introduced the basics of creating, running, sorting, and selecting records based on criteria. As you developed the queries, you used fields already available in database tables. Access also contains features that enable you to use the query grid to create a *calculated field*, which contains no data in a table but uses data in other fields to obtain its value.

A calculated field:

- Creates a new field in the query that can be used in a form or report.
- Can be used to perform mathematical operations such as add, multiply, etc.
- Has a name and can be formatted with properties just like a regular field.
- Enables you to combine values in two text fields into one field, such as LastName and FirstInitial.
- Updates and recalculates each time you run the query.

Queries, forms, tables, and reports can contain calculated fields. It is helpful to identify calculated fields as Calculated data types as you design a database.

Identifying Parts of a Calculated Field

The structure of a calculated field includes a field name and expression elements that tell Access which fields, operators, and punctuation marks to use to create the field. Two examples of calculated fields in an Access query would be Wage: Hours * Rate and Total: Price * Quantity.

Each calculated field contains the following elements.

ELEMENTS OF CALCULATED FIELDS	
Element	**Description**
Calculated field name	■ The unique name you assign to the field, followed by a colon (:) to separate the field name from the expression
Field names from existing tables	■ The field containing the data used in the calculation. Access will add brackets [ ] around field names.
Arithmetic or comparison operators	■ +, -, *, /, ( ), ^, <, =,> to perform mathematical operations or compare values
Concatenation	■ Combining fields and expressions by using the ampersand (&) to join text values from multiple fields For example, FirstName&LastName ■ Required spaces appear within quotation marks (" ") For example, FirstName& " " &LastName

Price	Qty	ItemTotal: [Price]*[Qty]
Products	Invoice Details	
		Descending
✔	✔	✔

Existing field names.

Newly assigned field names must have a colon followed by the operands in brackets.

This is an example of elements that compose a simple query calculation.

Identifying Order of Calculations

Time for a little math. What is the answer to 6 + 6 / 2? Keep your answer in mind as you continue to read. As with Excel, Access calculates mathematical operations in a formula from left to right as it applies the order of calculations rules. The standard order for performing mathematical operations is often abbreviated *PEMDAS* (you may have learned the phrase *Please Excuse My Dear Aunt Sally*, a phrase often taught in middle schools to teach order of operations). The initials represent the order of mathematical operations Excel and Access use, as described in the following table.

ORDER OF MATHEMATICAL CALCULATIONS	
Calculation	**Description**
Parentheses ( )	Calculations enclosed in parentheses are performed first. In the calculation (6 + 6) / 2, the answer is 6 because what is in parentheses is always performed first. However, in the calculation 6 + 6 / 2 the answer is 9, because without the parentheses, multiplication and division occur before addition and subtraction.
Exponentials ^	Calculations "raised to the power of," such as squared or cubed, are performed next. Because superscripts are not on the keyboard, the caret (^) is used to represent exponentials. For example, 5^2 is 5 squared or 5^2 and equals 25.
Multiplication * **D**ivision /	Multiplication and division are equal in calculation order and are calculated left to right, after calculations on parentheses and exponentials.
Addition + **S**ubtraction -	Addition and subtraction are equal in calculation order and are calculated last, left to right across a formula after calculations on parentheses, exponentials, and multiplication and division.

Calculating Dates

In addition to performing simple calculations, Access provides alternative ways to use dates in calculated fields. You can use these expressions to calculate age, number of years in business, and so forth.

CALCULATED DATES IN EXPRESSIONS	
Sample Field	**Returns**
CurrentDate: =Date()	Displays the current date in the *mm/dd/yyyy* format, where *mm* is the month, *dd* is the day, and *yyyy* is the year. For example: 10/25/2013
CurrentDT: =Now()	Displays the current date and time, for example: 10/25/2013 1:02:41 PM
OrderProcessing: DateDiff("d", [OrderDate], [ShippedDate])	Displays the number of days (d) between the value in the OrderDate field and the ShippedDate field.
(Now()-[DOB])/365	Subtracts the value in the DOB (date of birth) field from the current date and divides the difference by 365 to display the calculated value in years.

Creating and Formatting a Calculated Field

Each calculated field stored in a query appears in a separate column in the query grid. You can type the calculated field expression directly into the Field row of the column. You can also create a calculated field by using the tools in Query Design View to access the expression builder.

Setting Calculated Field Properties

When you create tables in Access, you can set field properties, such as field size, format, caption, and default values. With the exception of small whole numbers, calculated fields almost always need to be formatted using field properties to indicate decimal places, commas, and currency formats. To assign field properties to calculated fields, you use the Query Property Sheet.

FROM THE RIBBON

Design→Show/Hide→Property Sheet to open the Property Sheet

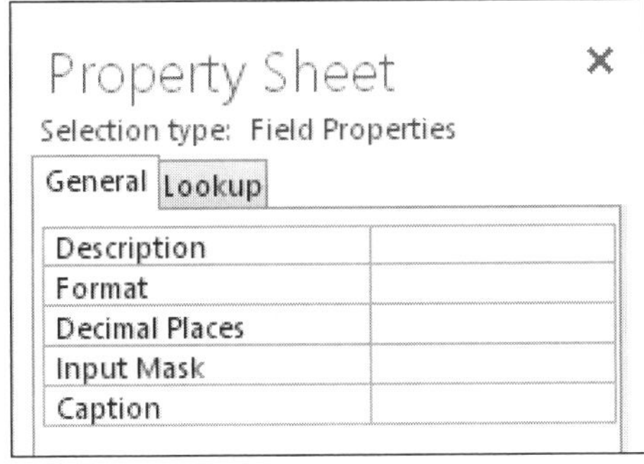

The Property Sheet for formatting query fields.

Access 2013

DEVELOP YOUR SKILLS AC04-D08

Create and Format a Calculated Field

In this exercise, you will add and format a calculated field for a query in the Winchester Web Design database.

1. Right-click the **InvoicesList** query in the Navigation Pane and choose **Design View**.
2. Follow these steps to create a calculated field:

Ⓐ **Type `LineTotal:Price * Qty`** in the top of the first blank column and tap Enter.

Ⓑ Notice that Access automatically adds brackets [ ] around existing fields.

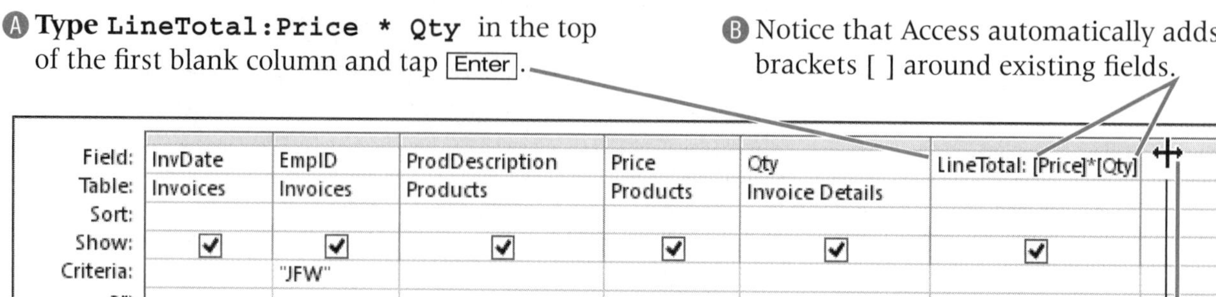

Field: InvDate | EmpID | ProdDescription | Price | Qty | LineTotal: [Price]*[Qty]
Table: Invoices | Invoices | Products | Products | Invoice Details
Sort:
Show:
Criteria: "JFW"
or:

Ⓒ Drag the column border to widen the query grid column so you can view the entire entry.

3. Right-click in the **LineTotal** column and choose **Properties** to open the Property Sheet, if necessary.
4. Follow these steps to format the field:

Ⓐ Select the **Format** property.

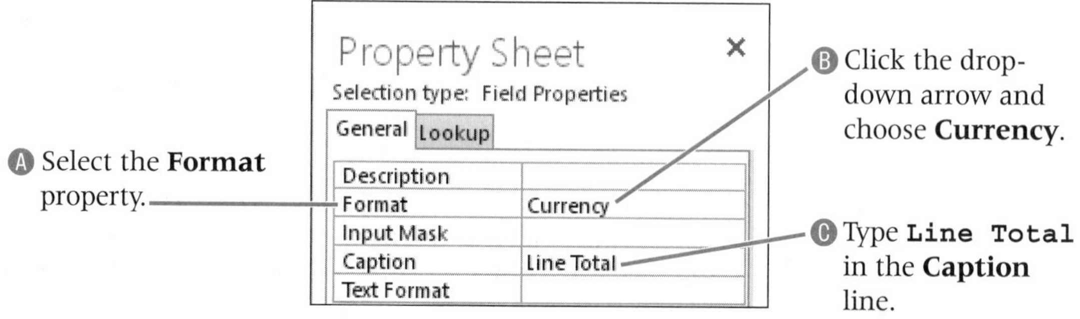

Ⓑ Click the drop-down arrow and choose **Currency**.

Ⓒ Type **`Line Total`** in the **Caption** line.

5. Run the query.

InvoicesList

InvNum	Invoice Date	Emp ID	Description	Price	Qty	Line Total
1	3/15/2012	JFW	Secondary Page	$200.00	6	$1,200.00
1	3/15/2012	JFW	Image, Custom Designed	$40.00	11	$440.00
1	3/15/2012	JFW	Home Page, Nav, CSS, Design	$400.00	1	$400.00
2	4/2/2012	MJW	Image, Custom Designed	$40.00	14	$560.00
2	4/2/2012	MJW	Home Page, Nav, CSS, Design	$400.00	1	$400.00
2	4/2/2012	MJW	Secondary Page	$200.00	7	$1,400.00
2	4/2/2012	MJW	Hourly Rate for Modifications	$80.00	5	$400.00
3	5/11/2012	JMM	Image, Custom Designed	$40.00	6	$240.00
3	5/11/2012	JMM	Secondary Page	$200.00	2	$400.00
4	5/30/2012	JMM	Blog, Integrated into Site	$300.00	1	$300.00
4	5/30/2012	JMM	Hourly Rate for Modifications	$80.00	2	$160.00
4	5/30/2012	JMM	Image, Custom Designed	$40.00	2	$80.00
5	6/19/2012	JFW	Image, Custom Designed	$40.00	9	$360.00
5	6/19/2012	JFW	Secondary Page	$200.00	11	$2,200.00
5	6/19/2012	JFW	Home Page, Nav, CSS, Design	$400.00	1	$400.00
6	6/23/2012	MJW	Hourly Rate for Modifications	$80.00	3	$240.00
6	6/23/2012	MJW	Blog, Integrated into Site	$300.00	1	$300.00
6	6/23/2012	MJW	Home Page, Nav, CSS, Design	$400.00	1	$400.00
6	6/23/2012	MJW	Secondary Page	$200.00	6	$1,200.00
7	7/11/2012	JMM	Image, Custom Designed	$40.00	14	$560.00

6. Save then close the query.

Using a Function in a Query Expression

Video Library http://labyrinthelab.com/videos Video Number: AC13-V0409

If you have worked with Microsoft Excel, you are most likely familiar with the types of functions that provide Excel with its calculating power. In Access, you have many of the same functions for performing specific calculations, such as finding the minimum, maximum, and average values, and counting and summing the entries in a datasheet. These are known as aggregate functions and are built into Access. You can use these functions in queries, forms, and reports to aid in database reporting.

Adding Functions to the Query Grid

When you want to add aggregate functions to total, average, or find minimum and maximum values you must first display the Total row on the query grid. From the Total row, you choose the function(s) you want to use for the specified field. You use a separate column for each additional function. For example, if you want to find the minimum, maximum, and average of the same field, you would add three new fields to the query grid—one for each function.

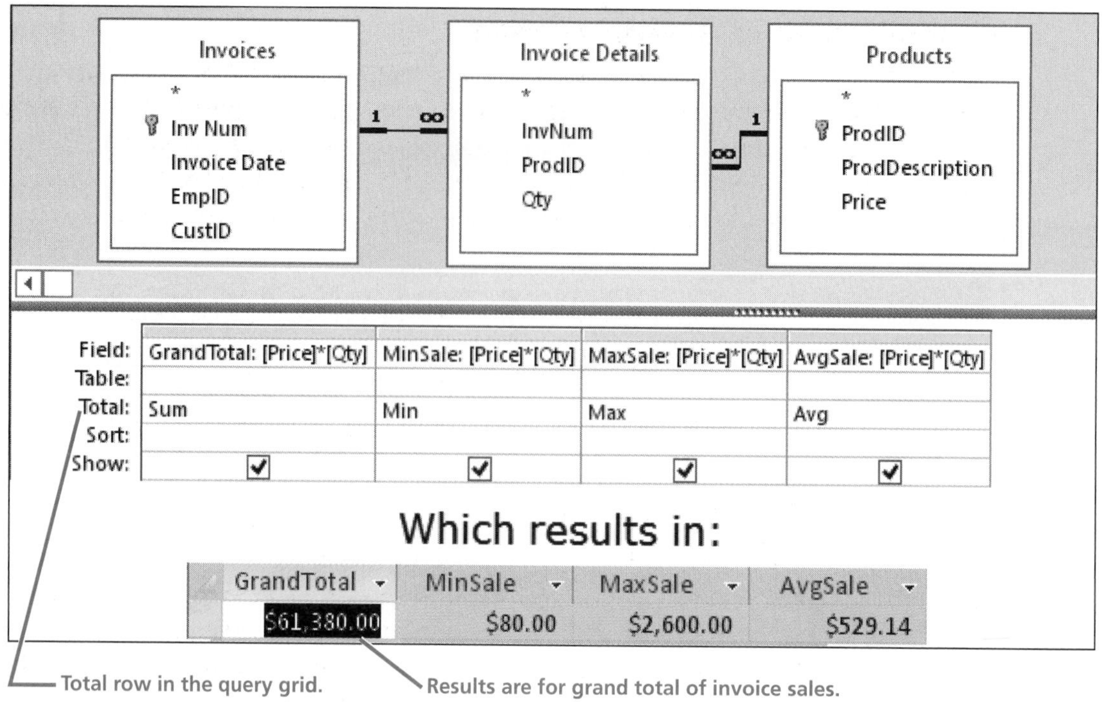

When you first display the Total row in the query grid, Access places the Group By command in the Total row of every occupied column. The Group By function allows you to calculate, among other things, the running total, minimum, maximum, and average for each group. This is handy if you need totals and averages for each employee, customer, or product.

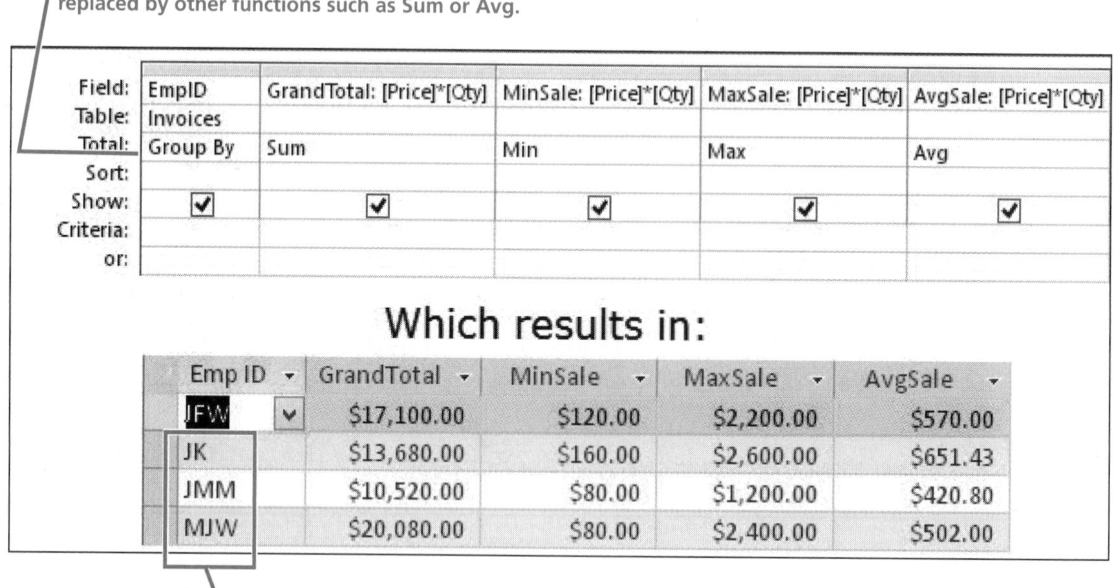

Creating Aliases in Query Fields

Aggregate functions are designed to summarize data. As a result, these values are not stored in database tables. Suppose you want to find the lowest price, highest price, and average price of the products in your inventory. Although all three columns are derived from the same Price field, you need a unique name for each calculated column. When the same expression or field is assigned to several different field names, each additional field name is referred to as an alias.

Price is the original field name.

Field:	MinPrice: Price	MaxPrice: Price	AvgPrice: Price
Table:	Products	Products	Products
Total:	Min	Max	Avg
Sort:			

MinPrice, MaxPrice, and AvgPrice are the calculated field name aliases.

Identifying Function Types

Simple aggregate functions allow you to count the number of entries in a field, locate the maximum or minimum values in a field, total the values of a group of records, and find the average value from a group of values. Access contains numerous additional functions that enable you to calculate the standard deviation and variance of values, and so forth. It is also important to know that Access limits or restricts the use of these functions to specific data field types. Some of the more commonly used aggregate functions are identified here.

AGGREGATE FUNCTION TYPES

Function	Description	Valid Field Data Types
Sum	Totals values in a field.	Number, Currency
Avg	Averages values in a field.	Number, Date/Time, Currency
Min	Identifies lowest value in a field.	Text, Number, Date/Time, Currency
Max	Identifies highest value in a field.	Text, Number, Date/Time, Currency
Count	Counts the number of values in a field, not counting blank values.	All types except multi-value lists
StDev	Calculates standard deviation of the values in a field.	Number, Currency
Var	Calculates variance of the values in a field.	Number, Currency
First	Locates the first record in the group on which you are performing calculations in chronological order without sorting.	All data types
Last	Locates the last record in the group on which you are performing calculations in chronological order without sorting.	All data types

DEVELOP YOUR SKILLS AC04-D09

Use Functions in Queries

In this exercise, you will create a query that uses functions to identify minimum, maximum, and average invoice amounts for customers of Winchester Web Design.

1. Choose **Create→Queries→Query Design**.
2. Double-click the **Employees, Invoices**, **Invoice Details**, and **Products** tables in the Show Table dialog box.
3. Close the **Show Table** dialog box.
4. Follow these steps to add the Group By field to the query:

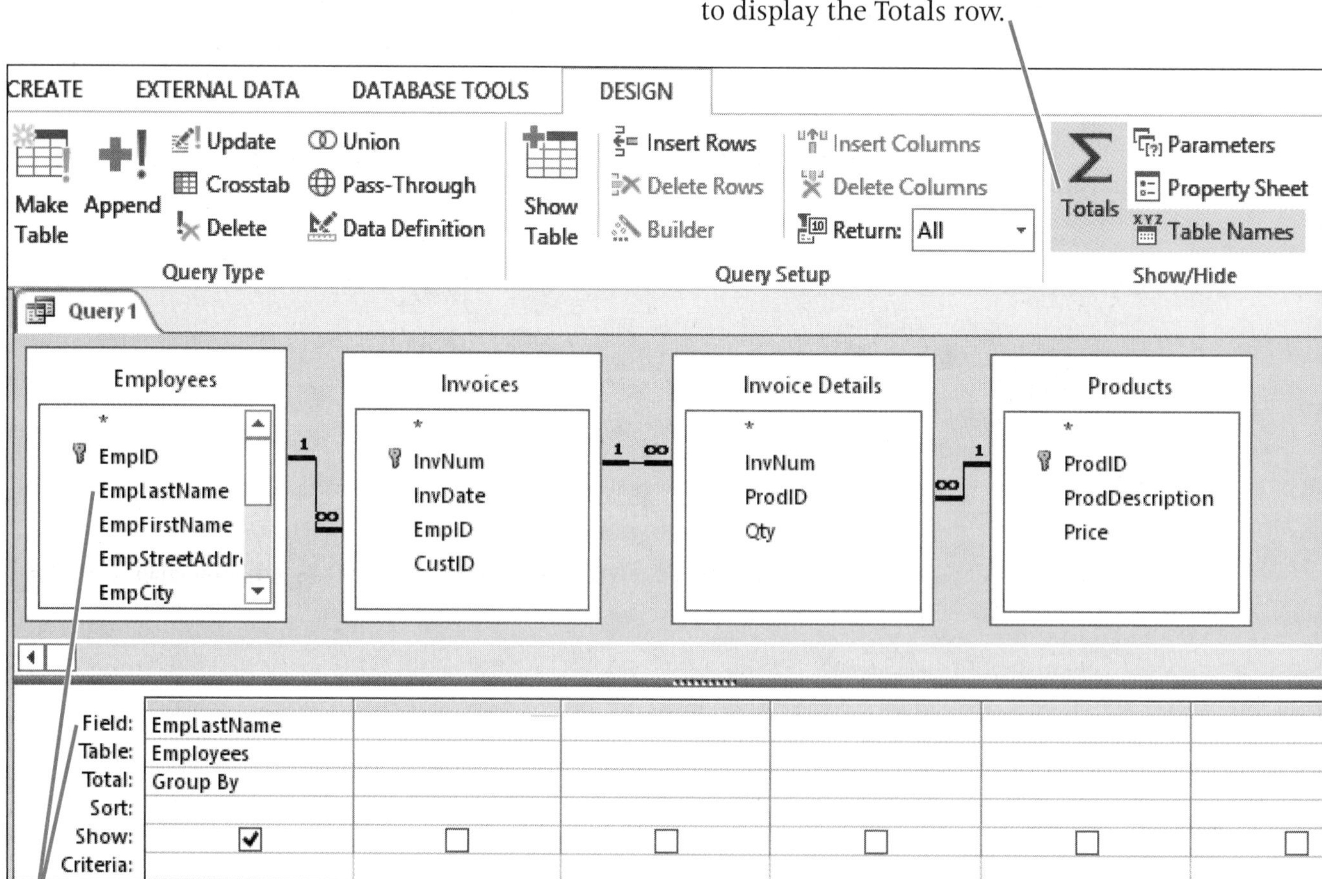

5. Follow these steps to add functions to the query:

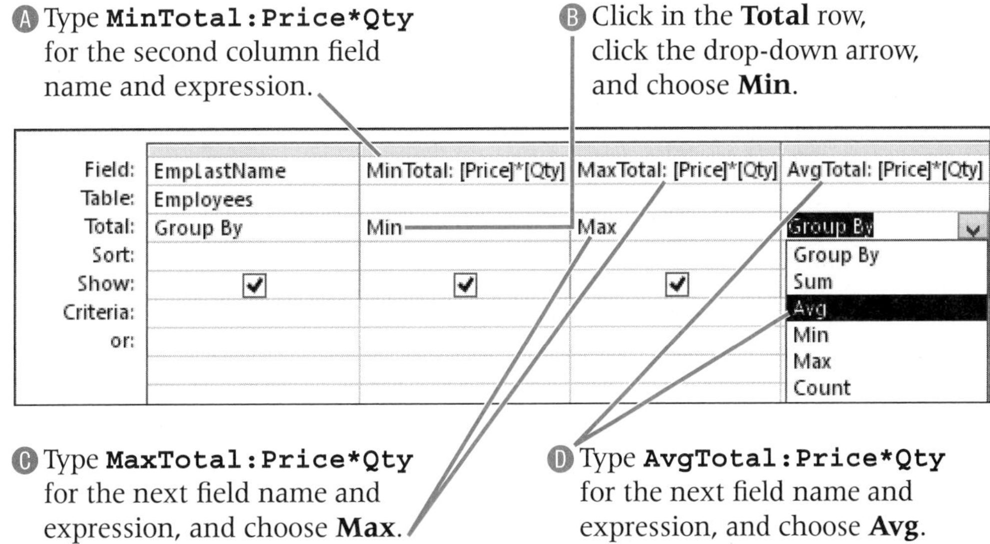

A Type **MinTotal:Price*Qty** for the second column field name and expression.
B Click in the **Total** row, click the drop-down arrow, and choose **Min**.
Field: EmplastName | MinTotal: [Price]*[Qty] | MaxTotal: [Price]*[Qty] | AvgTotal: [Price]*[Qty]
Table: Employees
Total: Group By | Min | Max | Group By
Sort:
Show:
Criteria:
or:
Group By
Sum
Avg
Min
Max
Count
C Type **MaxTotal:Price*Qty** for the next field name and expression, and choose **Max**.
D Type **AvgTotal:Price*Qty** for the next field name and expression, and choose **Avg**.

6. Choose **Design→Results→Run** [Run]. Adjust the datasheet column widths to display all data and field names.

Access displays the aggregate minimum, maximum, and average totals.

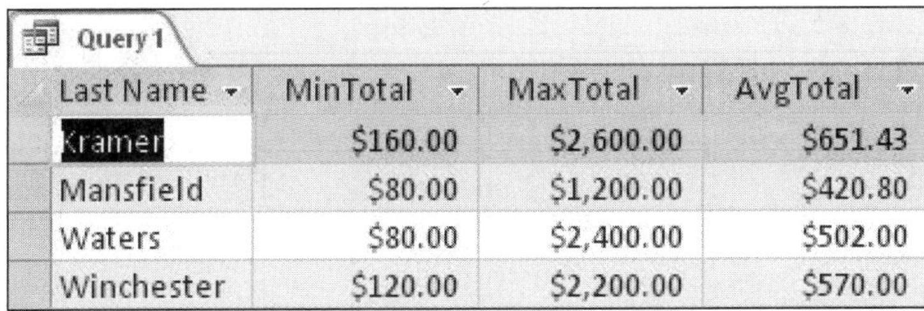

Query1

Last Name	MinTotal	MaxTotal	AvgTotal
Kramer	$160.00	$2,600.00	$651.43
Mansfield	$80.00	$1,200.00	$420.80
Waters	$80.00	$2,400.00	$502.00
Winchester	$120.00	$2,200.00	$570.00

Each Last Name is listed only one time. And, each calculated field column shows the column heading that identifies what the value represents.

7. Save the query as **InvoiceFunctions** and close it.

Creating Special Types of Queries

Video Library http://labyrinthelab.com/videos Video Number: AC13-V0410

The queries you have created so far are select queries where Access selects records according to the fields you add to the query grid and the criteria you set. Access also contains tools for creating special types of queries. In this lesson, you will explore three of these special queries:

- Crosstab query
- Find Unmatched query
- Find Duplicates query

Creating a Crosstab Query

Crosstab queries allow you to easily analyze data. A crosstab query lists the fields to be grouped on the left side of the datasheet. It arranges the fields to be summarized across the top so you can calculate sums, averages, counts, or totals by group and subgroup. For example, if you have a database that contains sales records for your employees, the description of each product they sell, and their total sales for each product, you could create a crosstab query to display the total sales by product for each employee. Such a grouping and summarization might appear as shown in the following illustrations.

Original Data

Employee	Product Description	Line Total
JFW	Secondary Page	$1,200.00
JFW	Image, Custom Designed	$440.00
JFW	Home Page, Nav, CSS, Design	$400.00
MJW	Image, Custom Designed	$560.00
MJW	Home Page, Nav, CSS, Design	$400.00
MJW	Secondary Page	$1,400.00
MJW	Hourly Rate for Modifications	$400.00
JMM	Image, Custom Designed	$240.00
JMM	Secondary Page	$400.00
JMM	Blog, Integrated into Site	$300.00
JMM	Hourly Rate for Modifications	$160.00
JMM	Image, Custom Designed	$80.00
JFW	Image, Custom Designed	$360.00
JFW	Secondary Page	$2,200.00
JFW	Home Page, Nav, CSS, Design	$400.00
MJW	Hourly Rate for Modifications	$240.00
MJW	Blog, Integrated into Site	$300.00

Original data format is arranged by record.

Reorganized by Crosstab Query							
Emp Name	**Tot Sales**	**Home Pg**	**2nd Page**	**Blogs**	**Carts**	**Images**	**Hourly**
Kramer	$13,680.00	$800.00	$7,600.00	$600.00		$2,520.00	$2,160.00
Mansfield	$10,520.00	$400.00	$4,800.00	$600.00	$1,200.00	$1,680.00	$1,840.00
Waters	$20,080.00	$1,600.00	$10,000.00	$1,200.00	$1,200.00	$2,080.00	$4,000.00
Winchester	$17,100.00	$2,000.00	$8,800.00	$300.00	$800.00	$3,040.00	$2,160.00

Using a crosstab query, you can display the data grouped by employee and product.

Using the Crosstab Query Wizard

As you work with crosstab queries, you will discover a vast difference between the query grid you have used to create select queries and the crosstab query palette. You can, of course, use the palette to manually construct a crosstab query. Until you become better acquainted with the queries, using the Crosstab Query Wizard is more helpful. Crosstab queries can use both tables and queries as the basis of the query.

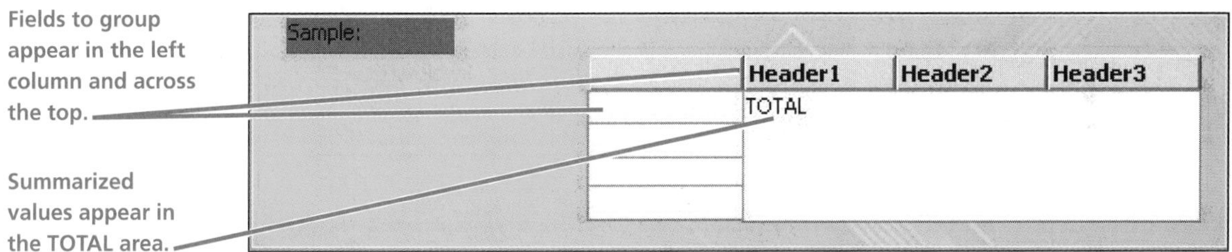

Fields to group appear in the left column and across the top.
Summarized values appear in the TOTAL area.
Sample:
Header1
Header2
Header3
TOTAL

The crosstab query palette organizes data so that it is easier to summarize.

QUICK REFERENCE	CREATING CROSSTAB, UNMATCHED, AND DUPLICATES QUERIES USING WIZARDS
Task	**Procedure**
Create a crosstab query	■ Choose Create→Queries→Query Wizard. ■ Double-click Crosstab Query Wizard. ■ Follow the prompts to select objects and fields for the query.
Create a find duplicates query	■ Choose Create→Queries→Query Wizard. ■ Double-click Find Duplicates Query Wizard. ■ Follow the prompts to select objects and fields for the query.
Create a find unmatched query	■ Choose Create→Queries→Query Wizard. ■ Double-click Find Unmatched Query Wizard. ■ Follow the prompts to select objects and fields for the query.

DEVELOP YOUR SKILLS AC04-D10

Create a Crosstab Query

In this exercise, you will create a crosstab query that lists each employee and their total invoice amount generated by product.

1. Choose **Create→Queries→Query Wizard** to open the New Query dialog box.
2. Double-click the **Crosstab Query Wizard** to launch the Crosstab Query Wizard.
3. Follow these steps to select the query to use for the crosstab query:

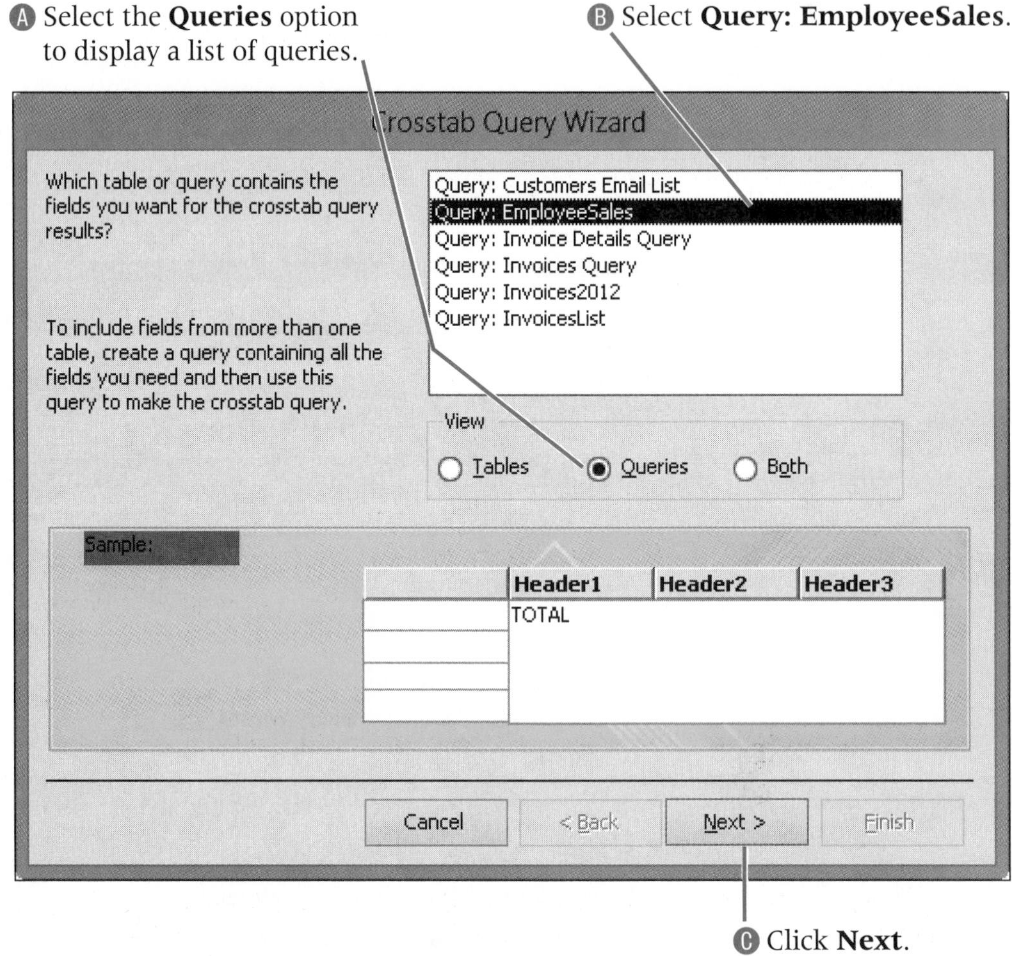

In the next wizard screen, Access asks what data you want to display down the left side of the query. In this query, you want the employee last name to appear down the left column.

4. Double-click **EmpLastName** in the Available Fields list to move it to the **Selected Fields** list.
5. Click **Next**, and then double-click **ProdDescription** as the field to appear in the column headings, and advance to the next wizard screen.

6. Select **LineTotal** in the Fields list and **Sum** in the Functions list to identify the field that contains values and the function you want to calculate.

Your crosstab query grid should look similar to the following illustration, with the EmpLastName fields as row headings, the ProdDescription as column headings, and the Sum function applied to the LineTotal field.

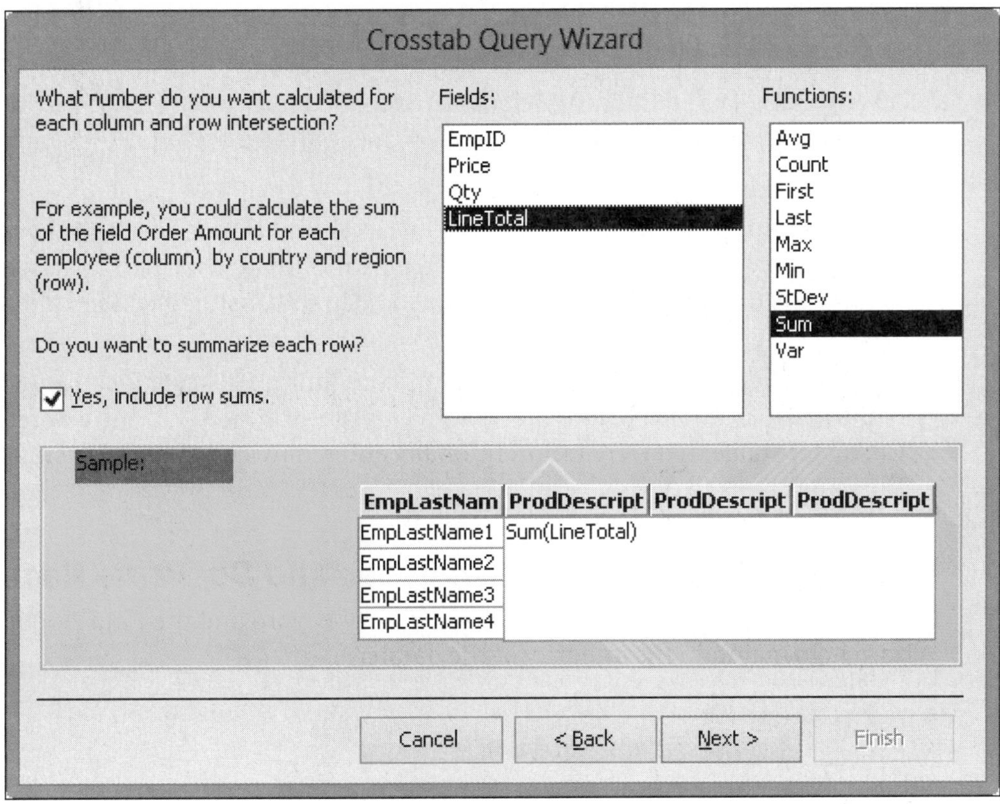

7. Click **Next** to display the final page of the Crosstab Query Wizard.
8. Name the query **`EmployeeCrosstab`** and click **Finish**.

Access runs and displays the query results, which show each employee and their total invoice amount generated by product. Adjust the columns as needed.

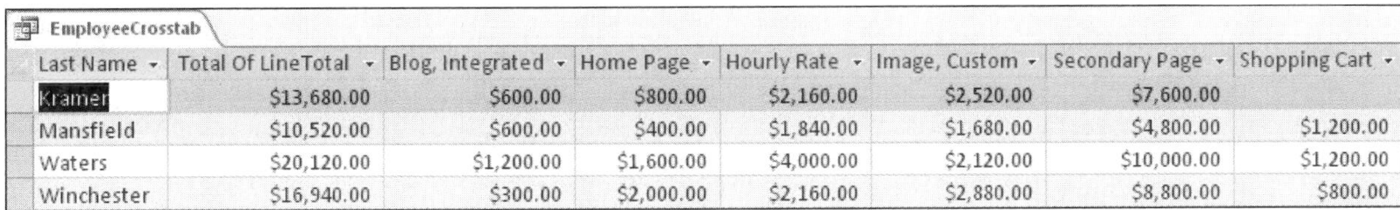
EmployeeCrosstab

Last Name	Total Of LineTotal	Blog, Integrated	Home Page	Hourly Rate	Image, Custom	Secondary Page	Shopping Cart
Kramer	$13,680.00	$600.00	$800.00	$2,160.00	$2,520.00	$7,600.00	
Mansfield	$10,520.00	$600.00	$400.00	$1,840.00	$1,680.00	$4,800.00	$1,200.00
Waters	$20,120.00	$1,200.00	$1,600.00	$4,000.00	$2,120.00	$10,000.00	$1,200.00
Winchester	$16,940.00	$300.00	$2,000.00	$2,160.00	$2,880.00	$8,800.00	$800.00

9. Save and close the query.

Creating Unmatched and Duplicates Queries

Video Library http://labyrinthelab.com/videos Video Number: AC13-V0411

Data contained in database tables often shares key fields so that you can include data from multiple tables in queries. As a result, it is important that records entered in one table have a matching record in the related table. For instance, you cannot have an invoice without a matching record in the products table.

Access contains two additional query wizards that enable you to create specialized queries for comparing such data—the Find Unmatched Query Wizard and the Find Duplicates Query Wizard.

- **Find Unmatched Query:** Locates records in one table that have no related records in another table. For example, you could create an Unmatched Query to ensure that each record in an Invoice table has a corresponding record in the Customers table or in the Products table.
- **Find Duplicates Query:** Locates records containing duplicate field values in a single table or query. For example, you could create a Duplicates Query to locate any records in the Customers table that were unintentionally entered twice, or to find customers from the same city.

Creating Queries to Find Unmatched and Duplicate Records

Creating and running the Find Unmatched Query Wizard and the Find Duplicates Query Wizard help maintain the integrity of the database.

DEVELOP YOUR SKILLS AC04-D11

Find Unmatched and Duplicate Records

In this exercise, you will create a query to locate customers in the Customers table who have no matching CustomerID in the Invoices table. You will then create a query to identify records with duplicate customer last names.

Create a Query to Find Unmatched Records

1. Choose **Create→Queries→Query Wizard** and double-click **Find Unmatched Query Wizard**.

   The Find Unmatched Query Wizard opens. From this screen, you select the table you want to check against another table.

2. Double-click **Table: Customers** to identify the table and automatically advance to the next screen.
3. Double-click **Table: Invoices** to identify the table to compare to the **Customers** table entries and automatically advance to the next screen.

   The next screen displays a list of fields in both selected tables. From the lists, you will identify the field in the Customers table that must have a matching record in the Invoices table.

4. Follow these steps to identify the fields that should match:

   The next screen asks you to identify the field(s) you want to view in the query results.

Ⓐ Ensure that the **CustID** field is selected in the Fields in 'Customers' list.

Ⓑ Ensure that the matching **CustID** is the selected field in the Fields in 'Invoices' list.

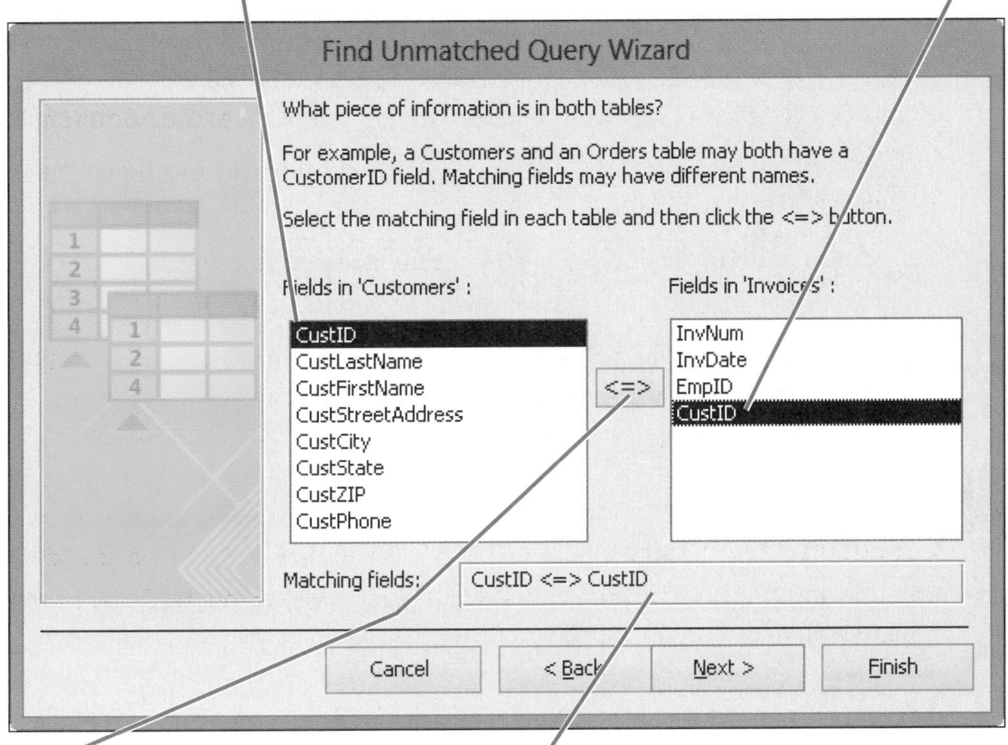

Ⓒ Click the **equate** button to indicate that these fields should match.

Ⓓ Note that the fields selected appear in the Matching Fields box and click **Next**.

5. Click **Move** [>] to add the following fields to the Selected Fields list: **CustLastName**, **CustFirstName**, **CustPhone**, and **CustEmail**.

6. Click **Next**, and then click **Finish** to accept the default query name Access assigns.

   Your query results should resemble the figure. You can use the results to find and delete the unmatched or contact those customers to offer your services.

Customers Without Matching Invoices

Last Name	First Name	Telephone	Email
Abrams	John	(941) 555-9902	JPAbrams@email.com
Fleetwood	Candace	(941) 555-9256	CandyWin@email.com
Winkler	Samuel	(941) 555-2054	SamWinkler45@email.com

7. Close the query.

Create a Query to Find Duplicate Records

8. Choose **Create→Queries→Query Wizard** and double-click **Find Duplicates Query Wizard**.
9. Double-click **Table: Customers** as the table you want to check for duplicates and to automatically advance to the next screen.
10. Select the **CustLastName** field, click **Move** [>] to move the field to the Duplicate-Value Fields box, and click **Next**.
11. Click **CustFirstName** and click **Move** [>] to move it to the Additional Query Fields box.
12. Click **CustPhone** and click **Move** [>] to move it to the Additional Query Fields box, and click **Next**.
13. Name the query `Customers with the Same Last Name` and click **Finish**.
    The query results show two customers with the last name Roberts.

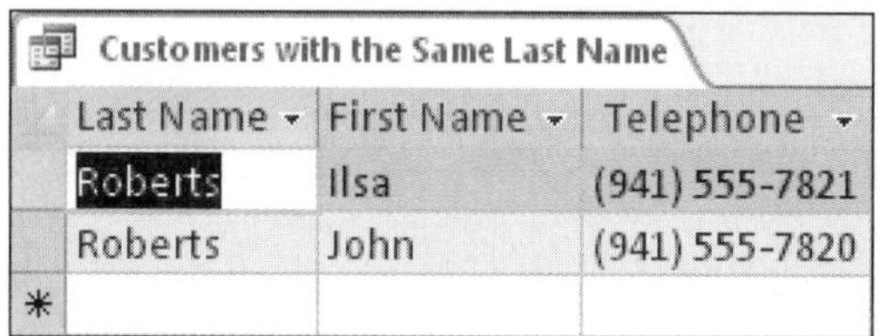

Customers with the Same Last Name

Last Name	First Name	Telephone
Roberts	Ilsa	(941) 555-7821
Roberts	John	(941) 555-7820

14. Save then close the query, close the database, and exit **Access**.

Viewing Structured Query Language (SQL)

Video Library http://labyrinthelab.com/videos Video Number: AC13-V0412

When you create queries, Access generates code that contains instructions for the query according to the criteria you set. For skilled users, viewing the coded instructions that Access creates may help identify reasons why a query might display inaccurate or unexpected results.

In Access, viewing the code is as simple as changing the query view to SQL View. SQL View for the Invoices Details Query is shown here.

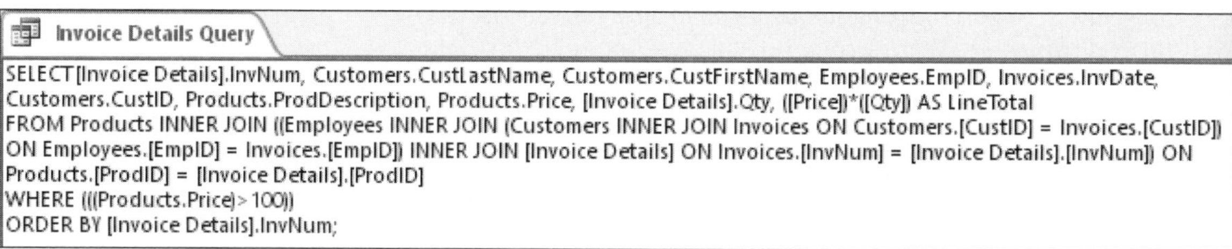

Invoice Details Query

```
SELECT [Invoice Details].InvNum, Customers.CustLastName, Customers.CustFirstName, Employees.EmpID, Invoices.InvDate,
Customers.CustID, Products.ProdDescription, Products.Price, [Invoice Details].Qty, ([Price])*([Qty]) AS LineTotal
FROM Products INNER JOIN ((Employees INNER JOIN (Customers INNER JOIN Invoices ON Customers.[CustID] = Invoices.[CustID])
ON Employees.[EmpID] = Invoices.[EmpID]) INNER JOIN [Invoice Details] ON Invoices.[InvNum] = [Invoice Details].[InvNum]) ON
Products.[ProdID] = [Invoice Details].[ProdID]
WHERE (((Products.Price)>100))
ORDER BY [Invoice Details].InvNum;
```

SQL CODE FOR QUERIES	
SQL command	**Purpose**
SELECT	Identify the fields to be selected or used in the query
FROM	Identify the tables that the query fields will come from
ORDER BY	Sort
WHERE	Find
GROUP BY	Arrange fields according to categories determined by key fields, such as EmpID
AS	Assign an alias or perform a calculation
AND	All fields in the query must match
OR	Only one field in the query must match
JOIN...ON	Combine tables that are linked by key fields

Concepts Review

To check your knowledge of the key concepts introduced in this lesson, complete the Concepts Review quiz by choosing the appropriate access option below.

If you are...	Then access the quiz by...
Using the Labyrinth Video Library	Going to http://labyrinthelab.com/videos
Using eLab	Logging in, choosing Content, and navigating to the Concepts Review quiz for this lesson
Not using the Labyrinth Video Library or eLab	Going to the student resource center for this book

Reinforce Your Skills

REINFORCE YOUR SKILLS AC04-R01

Create Queries and Use Criteria and Wildcards

Kids for Change is planning to fine-tune their database by adding queries that enable them to track activities as well as staff/volunteer availability. In this exercise, you will create various queries that will yield the desired information.

Create a Query Using the Query Wizard

1. Start **Access**. Open **AC04-R01-K4C** from the **AC2013 Lesson 04** folder and save it as `AC04-R01-K4C-[FirstInitialLastName]`.
2. Choose **Create→Queries→Query Wizard**.
3. Double-click **Simple Query Wizard**.
4. Select the **Activities** table from the Tables/Queries list.

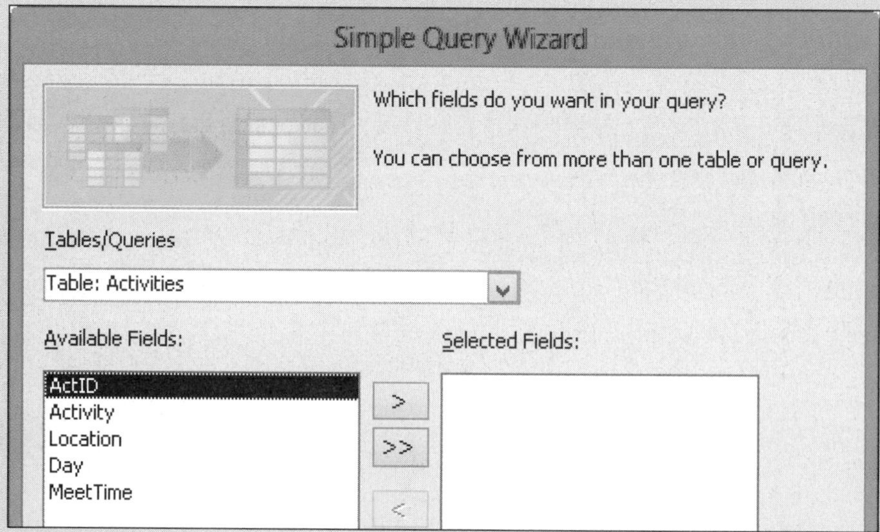

5. Click the **Activity** field in the Available Fields list then click **Move**.
6. Move the **Location**, **Day**, and **MeetTime** fields to the Selected Fields list.
7. Click **Next**.
8. Type `Activities List` in the query title text box.

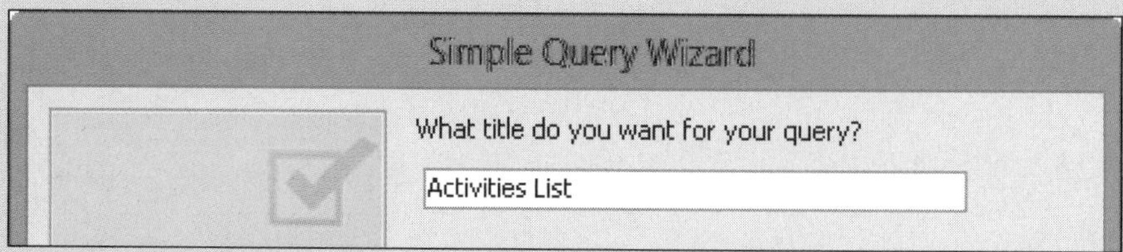

9. Click **Finish**. Then, close the query.

Activities List

Activity	Location	Day	Meet Time
Beach Cleanup	Coquina Beach	Saturday	9:00 AM
Can Collection	Seabreeze School	Thursday	6:00 PM
Car Wash	Sarasota Fairgrounds	Saturday	12:00 PM
Eco-Bake Sale	Downtown Flea Market	Sunday	8:00 AM
Eco-Tag Sale	River Village Market	Saturday	9:00 AM
Foodbank Collection	Community Center	Sunday	7:00 PM
Garden Work	All Angels Church	Wednesday	5:00 PM
Newspaper Collection	Seabreeze School	Monday	6:00 PM
Petition Signing	Hernando Mall	Sunday	2:00 PM
Recycling Drive	Seabreeze School	Tuesday	6:00 PM
Sign Waving	Cortez Rd. & Tamiami Tr.	Friday	5:00 PM

The query results datasheet includes just the four selected fields from all the records.

Create a Query in Design View

10. Choose **Create→Queries→Query Design**.
    Access displays a new query grid and a list of tables and existing queries contained in the database so that you can choose the sources you want to include in the new query.
11. Double-click the **Volunteers** table in the Show Table dialog box, then click **Close**.
    If the Show Table dialog box does not appear, choose Design→Query Setup→Show Table.
12. To add fields to the query grid, double-click **VolLastName**, **VolFirstName**, **VolPhone**, and **VolDay** (in that order).
13. Save the query as `Volunteer List`.
14. Click **Run** [! Run].
    Access runs the query and displays four columns of data (Last Name, First Name, Telephone, and Avail Day) for all the Volunteer records.

Volunteer List

Last Name	First Name	Telephone	Avail Day
Jones	Stan	941-555-8929	Tuesday
Langford	Kerry	941-555-1098	Thursday
Creger	Cindy	941-555-0245	Wednesday
Simpson	Lance	941-555-3431	Monday
Frith	Beverly	941-555-7489	Sunday

15. Switch to **Design View**.

16. To rearrange the field order, hover the mouse pointer over the top of the **VolDay** column until you see the black arrow. Click the column to select it.

Field:	VolLastName	VolFirstName	VolPhone	VolDay
Table:	Volunteers	Volunteers	Volunteers	Volunteers
Sort:				
Show:	☑	☑	☑	☑
Criteria:				

17. When the pointer becomes a white move arrow, click the selected column and drag it to the left of the **Last Name** field.

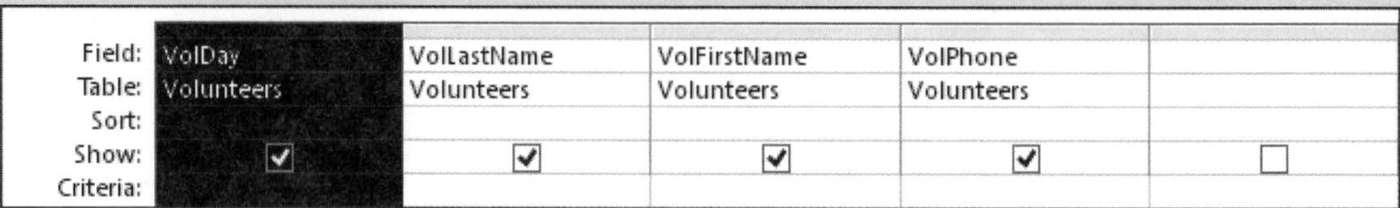

Field:	VolDay	VolLastName	VolFirstName	VolPhone	
Table:	Volunteers	Volunteers	Volunteers	Volunteers	
Sort:					
Show:	☑	☑	☑	☑	☐
Criteria:					

The VolDay field should now be the first field in the query grid.

18. Choose **Design→Results→Run**.
19. Close the query, saving the changes when prompted.

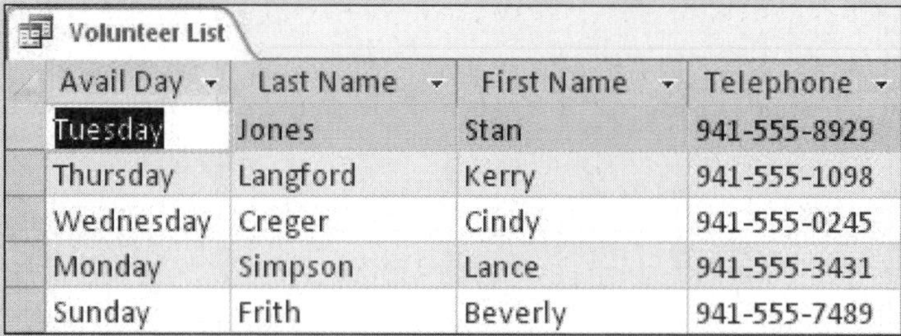

Volunteer List

Avail Day	Last Name	First Name	Telephone
Tuesday	Jones	Stan	941-555-8929
Thursday	Langford	Kerry	941-555-1098
Wednesday	Creger	Cindy	941-555-0245
Monday	Simpson	Lance	941-555-3431
Sunday	Frith	Beverly	941-555-7489

Create a Multi-Table Query

20. Choose **Create→Queries→Query Design**.
21. Double-click the following table names in the **Show Table** dialog box to add the table field lists to the top pane of the query: **Activities** and **Staff**.
22. Close the **Show Table** dialog box.
23. Double-click these fields from the **Activities** table in the order presented: **Activity, Day, MeetTime**.
24. Double-click these fields from the **Staff** table in the order presented: **StaffLastName, StaffFirstName, StaffPhone**.

25. Click in the **Sort** row for Activity, click the list arrow, and choose **Ascending**.

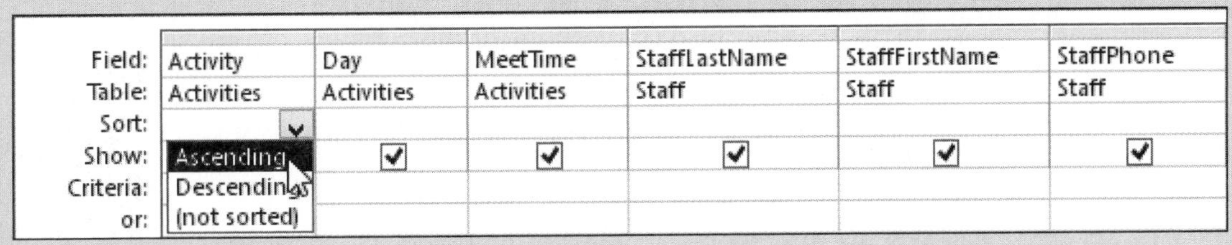

Field:	Activity	Day	MeetTime	StaffLastName	StaffFirstName	StaffPhone
Table:	Activities	Activities	Activities	Staff	Staff	Staff
Sort:						
Show:	Ascending	✓	✓	✓	✓	✓
Criteria:	Descending					
or:	(not sorted)					

26. Save the query as `Activity Staffing List`.
27. Choose **Design→Results→Run**. Then, close the query.

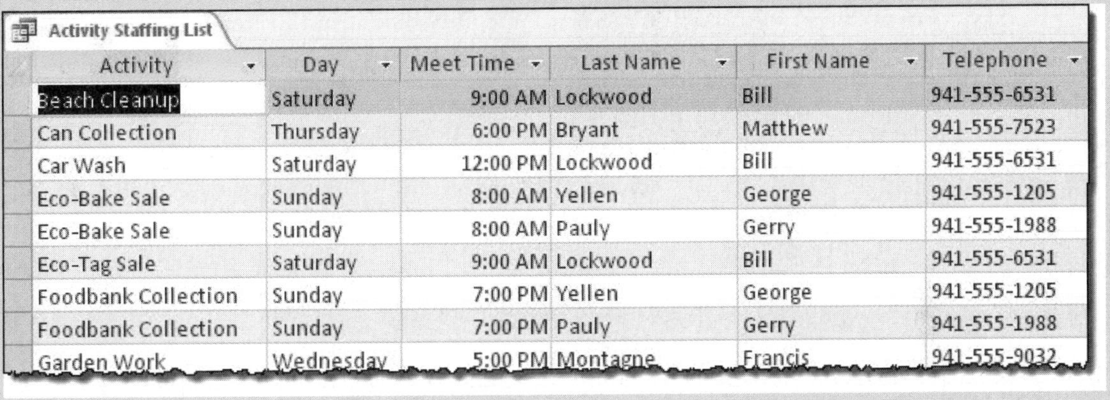

Activity Staffing List

Activity	Day	Meet Time	Last Name	First Name	Telephone
Beach Cleanup	Saturday	9:00 AM	Lockwood	Bill	941-555-6531
Can Collection	Thursday	6:00 PM	Bryant	Matthew	941-555-7523
Car Wash	Saturday	12:00 PM	Lockwood	Bill	941-555-6531
Eco-Bake Sale	Sunday	8:00 AM	Yellen	George	941-555-1205
Eco-Bake Sale	Sunday	8:00 AM	Pauly	Gerry	941-555-1988
Eco-Tag Sale	Saturday	9:00 AM	Lockwood	Bill	941-555-6531
Foodbank Collection	Sunday	7:00 PM	Yellen	George	941-555-1205
Foodbank Collection	Sunday	7:00 PM	Pauly	Gerry	941-555-1988
Garden Work	Wednesday	5:00 PM	Montagne	Francis	941-555-9032

Add Wildcard and AND/OR Criteria to a Query

28. Display the **Activities Staffing List** query in Design View.
29. Type `Saturday` in the Criteria row of the Day field.
30. Type `Sunday` in the Or row of the Day field, and tap [Tab].
31. Click **Run**.

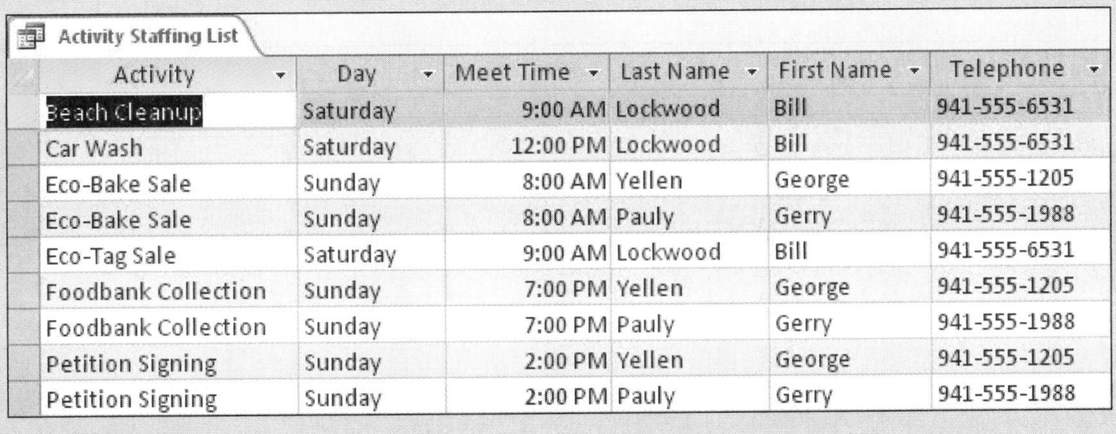

Activity Staffing List

Activity	Day	Meet Time	Last Name	First Name	Telephone
Beach Cleanup	Saturday	9:00 AM	Lockwood	Bill	941-555-6531
Car Wash	Saturday	12:00 PM	Lockwood	Bill	941-555-6531
Eco-Bake Sale	Sunday	8:00 AM	Yellen	George	941-555-1205
Eco-Bake Sale	Sunday	8:00 AM	Pauly	Gerry	941-555-1988
Eco-Tag Sale	Saturday	9:00 AM	Lockwood	Bill	941-555-6531
Foodbank Collection	Sunday	7:00 PM	Yellen	George	941-555-1205
Foodbank Collection	Sunday	7:00 PM	Pauly	Gerry	941-555-1988
Petition Signing	Sunday	2:00 PM	Yellen	George	941-555-1205
Petition Signing	Sunday	2:00 PM	Pauly	Gerry	941-555-1988

This is an OR condition: Activities for either Saturday or *Sunday are returned.*

32. Switch to **Design View**.
33. Delete **Sunday** from the Day Or row.

34. Type **12:00** in the Criteria row for the **MeetTime** field and tap [Tab].

35. Run the query.

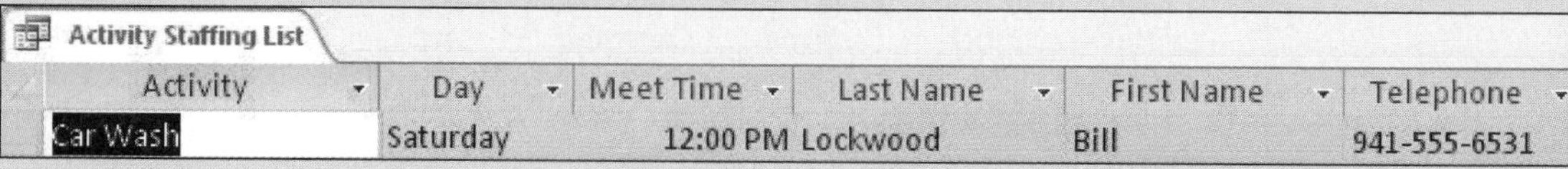

Activity Staffing List

Activity	Day	Meet Time	Last Name	First Name	Telephone
Car Wash	Saturday	12:00 PM	Lockwood	Bill	941-555-6531

This is an AND condition: only the activities on Saturday and *at 12:00 are returned.*

36. Switch to **Design View**.

37. Remove all criteria.

38. Type **S*** in the criteria row for the **Day** field and tap [Tab].
    Access changes the criteria to Like "S*":

39. Run the query.
    The results are the same as when you typed Saturday in the Criteria row and Sunday in the Or row.

40. Close the query. Choose **No** when prompted to save the changes.
    Saving changes to the query at this time would save the criteria as part of the query.

Add Date Criteria to a New Query

Now you will create a query that returns the records of the very youngest children so you can determine which children may need more supervision.

41. Choose **Create→Queries→Query Design**.

42. Add the **Children** table to the query work area; close the **Show Table** dialog box.

43. Add **ChildLastName**, **ChildFirstName**, and **BirthDate** to the query design grid.

44. Choose **Design→Results→Run**.

Query1

Last Name	First Name	BirthDate
Abbot	Sami	2/15/2005
Creger	Kurt	9/12/2003
Driver	Sally	7/22/2005
Finkel	Evelyn	2/26/2003
Frith	Hermy	10/14/2005
Georgia	Pete	6/6/2004
Jones	Paul	1/10/2005
Kendall	Olivia	4/21/2004
Langford	James	3/9/2003
Lockwood	Timmy	8/10/2005
Preston	Willy	12/4/2004
Riggs	Dina	11/2/2004
Shamik	Ravi	6/28/2003
Simpson	Belinda	7/17/2004

45. Switch to **Design View**.

46. Type >`January 1, 2005` in the **Criteria** row for the **BirthDate** field and tap [Enter].

    Regardless of how you type the dates (January 1, 2005 or 01/01/05 or 1-1-2005) Access formats the date after you enter it so that it appears as #1/1/2005# in the Criteria row.

47. Run the query.

Query1

Last Name	First Name	BirthDate
Jones	Paul	1/10/2005
Driver	Sally	7/22/2005
Lockwood	Timmy	8/10/2005
Abbot	Sami	2/15/2005
Frith	Hermy	10/14/2005

Your query returns only the records of children who were born after January 1, 2005.

48. Save the query as `Younger Children` and click **OK**.

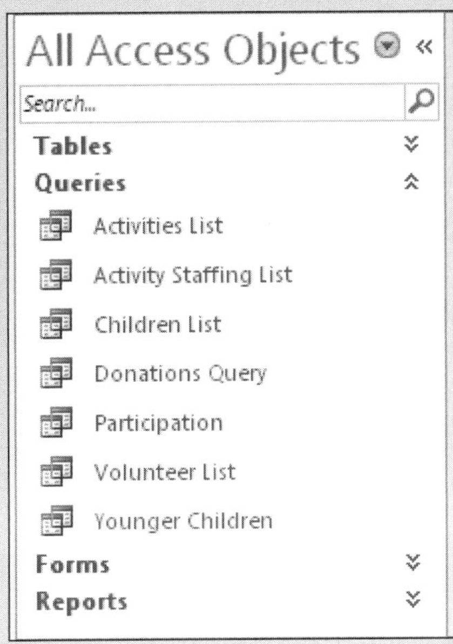

Your Queries Objects list now contains the names of the queries you created.

49. Save and close the query, then close the database; exit **Access**.

50. Submit your final file based on the guidelines provided by your instructor.

    To view examples of how your file or files should look at the end of this exercise, go to the student resource center.

REINFORCE YOUR SKILLS AC04-R02

Use Queries to Ensure Data Integrity

Kids for Change is planning to fine-tune their database by adding queries that will produce calculated results and also confirm and maintain data integrity. You are in charge of their IT department, and it is your responsibility to generate the desired query results.

Limit and Sort Query Results

1. Start **Access**. Open **AC04-R02-K4C** from the **AC2013 Lesson 04** folder and save it as `AC04-R02-K4C-[FirstInitialLastName]`.
2. Double-click the **Children List** query in the Navigation Pane to run it.

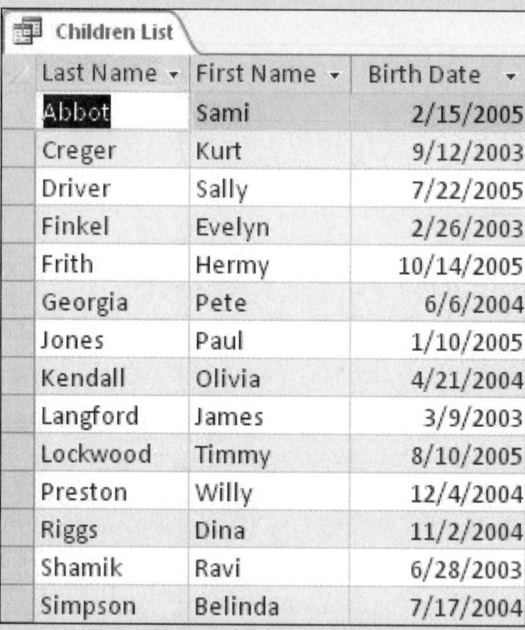

Children List
Last Name
First Name
Birth Date
Abbot Sami 2/15/2005
Creger Kurt 9/12/2003
Driver Sally 7/22/2005
Finkel Evelyn 2/26/2003
Frith Hermy 10/14/2005
Georgia Pete 6/6/2004
Jones Paul 1/10/2005
Kendall Olivia 4/21/2004
Langford James 3/9/2003
Lockwood Timmy 8/10/2005
Preston Willy 12/4/2004
Riggs Dina 11/2/2004
Shamik Ravi 6/28/2003
Simpson Belinda 7/17/2004

The query returns the records of all children in the table in alphabetical order by last name.

3. Switch to **Design View**.
4. Choose **Design→Query Setup→Return** and type `10` in the Return box.
   Access may add another zero to the 10 you enter. If Access displays 100 in the Return box, delete the last 0.
5. Click in the **Sort** row of the BirthDate field and choose **Descending**.

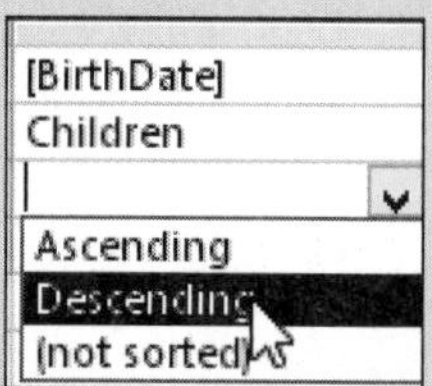

6. Click **Run**.

Children List

Last Name	First Name	Birth Date
Frith	Hermy	10/14/2005
Lockwood	Timmy	8/10/2005
Driver	Sally	7/22/2005
Abbot	Sami	2/15/2005
Jones	Paul	1/10/2005
Preston	Willy	12/4/2004
Riggs	Dina	11/2/2004
Simpson	Belinda	7/17/2004
Georgia	Pete	6/6/2004
Kendall	Olivia	4/21/2004

Your query should display the records of the ten youngest children.

7. Close the query without saving it.

Add a Calculated Field to a Query and Format the Field

As part of their community-give-back policy, Kids for Change puts 10 percent of all donations into a scholarship fund. Now you will add a field that calculates 10 percent of each donation.

8. Double-click the **Donations Query** in the Navigation Pane to run it.

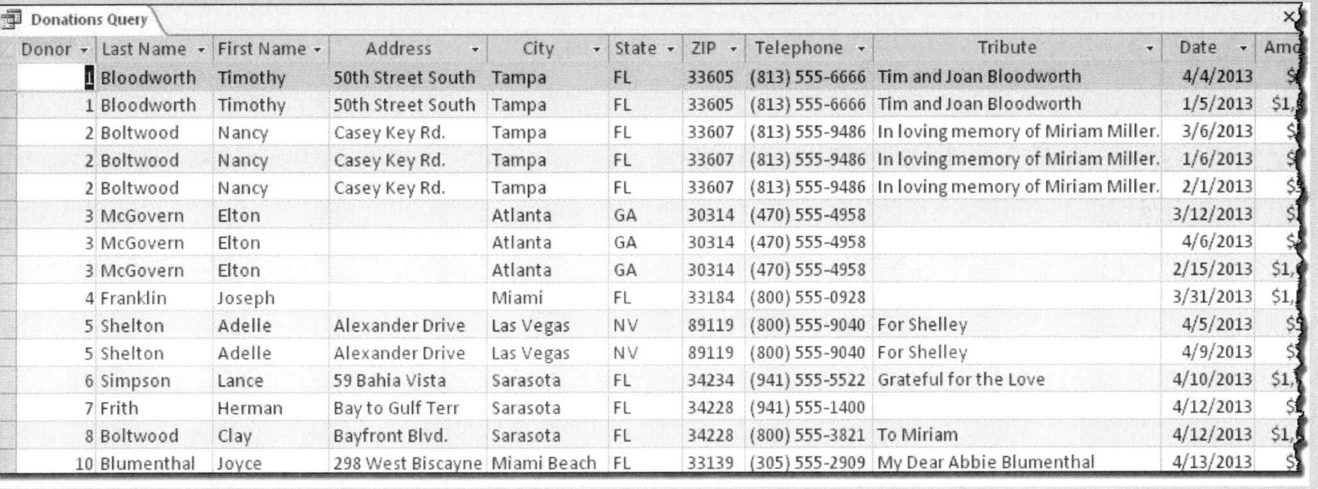
Donations Query

Donor	Last Name	First Name	Address	City	State	ZIP	Telephone	Tribute	Date	Amo
1	Bloodworth	Timothy	50th Street South	Tampa	FL	33605	(813) 555-6666	Tim and Joan Bloodworth	4/4/2013	$
1	Bloodworth	Timothy	50th Street South	Tampa	FL	33605	(813) 555-6666	Tim and Joan Bloodworth	1/5/2013	$1,
2	Boltwood	Nancy	Casey Key Rd.	Tampa	FL	33607	(813) 555-9486	In loving memory of Miriam Miller.	3/6/2013	$
2	Boltwood	Nancy	Casey Key Rd.	Tampa	FL	33607	(813) 555-9486	In loving memory of Miriam Miller.	1/6/2013	$
2	Boltwood	Nancy	Casey Key Rd.	Tampa	FL	33607	(813) 555-9486	In loving memory of Miriam Miller.	2/1/2013	$
3	McGovern	Elton		Atlanta	GA	30314	(470) 555-4958		3/12/2013	$
3	McGovern	Elton		Atlanta	GA	30314	(470) 555-4958		4/6/2013	$
3	McGovern	Elton		Atlanta	GA	30314	(470) 555-4958		2/15/2013	$1,
4	Franklin	Joseph		Miami	FL	33184	(800) 555-0928		3/31/2013	$1,
5	Shelton	Adelle	Alexander Drive	Las Vegas	NV	89119	(800) 555-9040	For Shelley	4/5/2013	$
5	Shelton	Adelle	Alexander Drive	Las Vegas	NV	89119	(800) 555-9040	For Shelley	4/9/2013	$
6	Simpson	Lance	59 Bahia Vista	Sarasota	FL	34234	(941) 555-5522	Grateful for the Love	4/10/2013	$1,
7	Frith	Herman	Bay to Gulf Terr	Sarasota	FL	34228	(941) 555-1400		4/12/2013	$
8	Boltwood	Clay	Bayfront Blvd.	Sarasota	FL	34228	(800) 555-3821	To Miriam	4/12/2013	$1,
10	Blumenthal	Joyce	298 West Biscayne	Miami Beach	FL	33139	(305) 555-2909	My Dear Abbie Blumenthal	4/13/2013	$

9. Switch to **Design View**.

10. Type **`ScholarFund:Amount*.1`** in the first empty query grid line and tap [↓].

11. If the Property Sheet is not shown, right-click in the **ScholarFund** column and choose **Properties**.

12. Click in the **Format** line, open the drop-down list, and choose **Currency**.

13. Type **`Scholar Fund`** in the **Caption** line.

Access 2013

14. Run the query.

City	State	ZIP	Telephone	Tribute	Date	Amount	Scholar Fund
Tampa	FL	33605	(813) 555-6666	Tim and Joan Bloodworth	4/4/2013	$500.00	$50.00
Tampa	FL	33605	(813) 555-6666	Tim and Joan Bloodworth	1/5/2013	$1,000.00	$100.00
Tampa	FL	33607	(813) 555-9486	In loving memory of Miriam Miller.	3/6/2013	$500.00	$50.00
Tampa	FL	33607	(813) 555-9486	In loving memory of Miriam Miller.	1/6/2013	$500.00	$50.00
Tampa	FL	33607	(813) 555-9486	In loving memory of Miriam Miller.	2/1/2013	$500.00	$50.00
Atlanta	GA	30314	(470) 555-4958		3/12/2013	$250.00	$25.00
Atlanta	GA	30314	(470) 555-4958		4/6/2013	$400.00	$40.00
Atlanta	GA	30314	(470) 555-4958		2/15/2013	$1,000.00	$100.00
Miami	FL	33184	(800) 555-0928		3/31/2013	$1,500.00	$150.00
Las Vegas	NV	89119	(800) 555-9040	For Shelley	4/5/2013	$500.00	$50.00
Las Vegas	NV	89119	(800) 555-9040	For Shelley	4/9/2013	$250.00	$25.00
Sarasota	FL	34234	(941) 555-5522	Grateful for the Love	4/10/2013	$1,000.00	$100.00
Sarasota	FL	34228	(941) 555-1400		4/12/2013	$500.00	$50.00
Sarasota	FL	34228	(800) 555-3821	To Miriam	4/12/2013	$1,000.00	$100.00
Miami Beach	FL	33139	(305) 555-2909	My Dear Abbie Blumenthal	4/13/2013	$750.00	$75.00

15. Save and close the query.

Create a Query Containing Functions

Now you will create a query that returns the total amount of donations received and the minimum, maximum, and average amount of donations.

16. Choose **Create→Queries→Query Design**.
17. Click the **Queries tab** in the Show Table dialog box to list the queries in the database.
18. Double-click **Donations Query** to add it to the query work area, and **close** the Show Table box.
19. Choose **Design→Show/Hide→Totals** to show the Total line in the query grid.
20. Type **`TotalDonations: Amount`** in the first line of the grid.
21. Click in the **Total** line and choose **Sum**.
22. Type **`MinDonation: Amount`** in the second Field line of the query grid.
23. Click in the **Total** line and choose **Min**.
24. Type **`MaxDonation: Amount`** in the third Field line of the query grid.
25. Click in the *Total* line and choose **Max**.
26. Type **`AvgDonation: Amount`** in the third Field line of the query grid.

27. Click in the **Total** line and choose **Avg**.

Field:	TotalDonations: Amount	MinDonation: Amount	MaxDonation: Amount	AvgDonation: Amount
Table:	Donations Query	Donations Query	Donations Query	Donations Query
Total:	Sum	Min	Max	Avg
Sort:				
Show:	✓	✓	✓	✓

28. Run the query.

    Access displays the aggregate total, minimum, maximum, and average donation amounts.

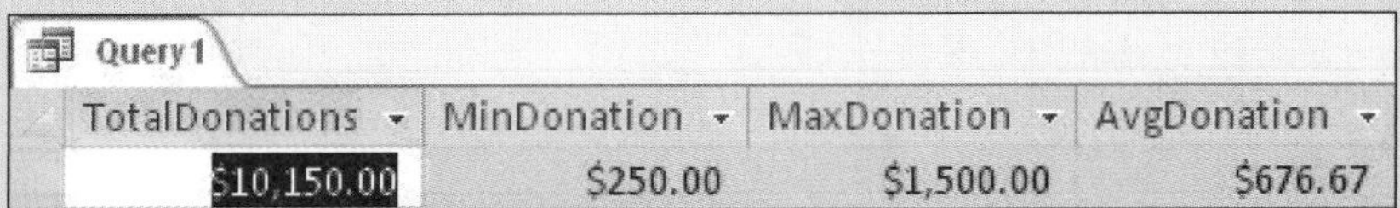

Query1

TotalDonations	MinDonation	MaxDonation	AvgDonation
$10,150.00	$250.00	$1,500.00	$676.67

29. Save the query as `Donation Functions` and then close it.

Create a Crosstab Query

30. Choose **Create→Queries→Query Wizard** to open the New Query dialog box.
31. Double-click **Crosstab Query Wizard**.
32. Select the **Queries** option button and choose **Query: Donations Query**.

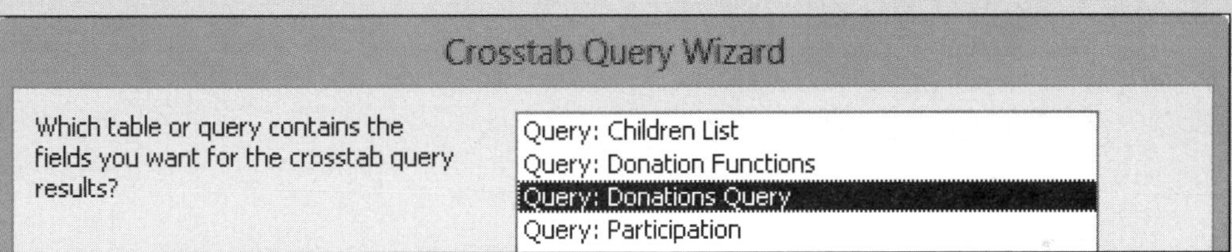

33. Click **Next** to display the next wizard screen.

    Access wants to know what data you want to display down the left side of the query. In this query, you want the employee last name to appear down the left column.

34. Double-click **DonorLName** in the Available Fields list to move it to the Selected Fields list.
35. Click **Next**, double-click **DonationDate** as the field to appear in the column headings, and advance to the next wizard screen.
36. Click **Month** as the interval by which you want to group your Date/Time column information and click **Next**.

37. Select **Amount** in the Fields list and **Sum** in the Functions list to identify the field that contains values and the function you want to calculate.

    Your crosstab query grid should show DonorLName fields as row headings, DonationDate as column headings, and Sum being applied to the Amount field.

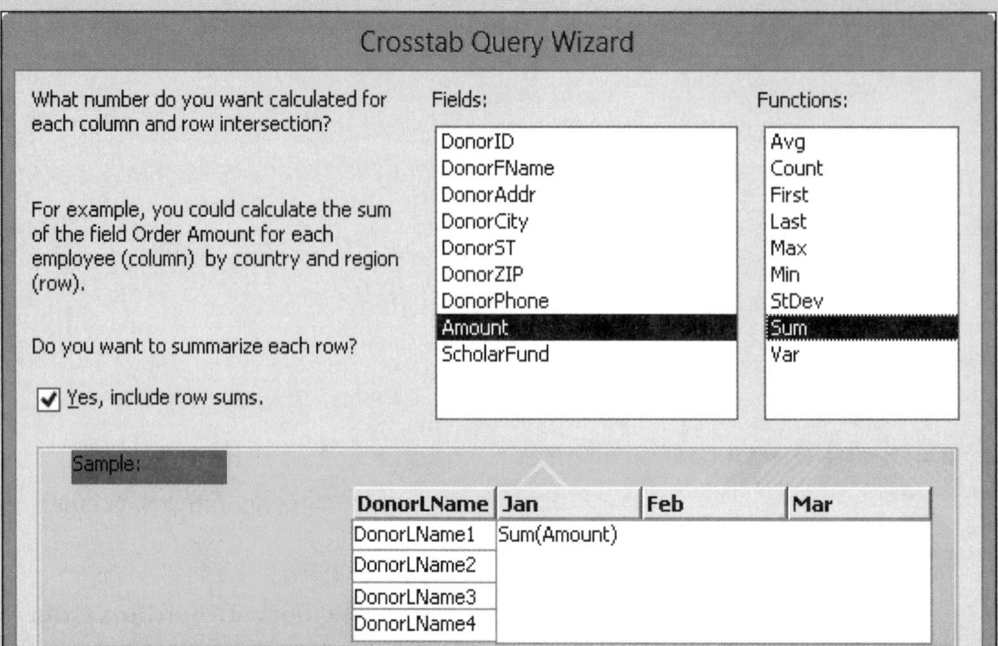

38. Click **Next** to display the final page of the Crosstab Query Wizard.
39. Name the query `DonationsCrosstab`, click the **Modify the Design** option button, and click **Finish**.

    Access displays the query in Design View.
40. Click in the **Total of Amount** column.
41. Open the Property Sheet, if necessary, and type `Donor Total` in the Caption property line.
42. Save, run, and then close the query.

DonationsCrosstab

Last Name	Donor Total	Jan	Feb	Mar	Apr
Bloodworth	$1,500.00	$1,000.00			$500.00
Blumenthal	$750.00				$750.00
Boltwood	$2,500.00	$500.00	$500.00	$500.00	$1,000.00
Franklin	$1,500.00			$1,500.00	
Frith	$500.00				$500.00
McGovern	$1,650.00		$1,000.00	$250.00	$400.00
Shelton	$750.00				$750.00
Simpson	$1,000.00				$1,000.00

Create an Unmatched Records and a Find Duplicate Records Query

43. Choose **Create→Queries→Query Wizard** and double-click **Find Unmatched Query Wizard**.

    Access opens the Find Unmatched Query Wizard. From this screen, you select the table you want to check against another table.

44. Double-click **Table: Activities** to identify the table and automatically advance to the next screen.

45. Double-click **Table: Volunteers** to identify the table to compare to the **Activities** table entries and automatically advance to the next screen.

    The next screen displays a list of fields in both selected tables. From the lists, you will identify the fields in the Activities and Volunteers tables to compare for matching values.

46. Click the **Day** field in the Fields in 'Activities' list.

47. Scroll down the Fields in 'Volunteers' list and click **VolDay**.

48. Click **Equate** <=> to locate any days without a matching volunteer record.

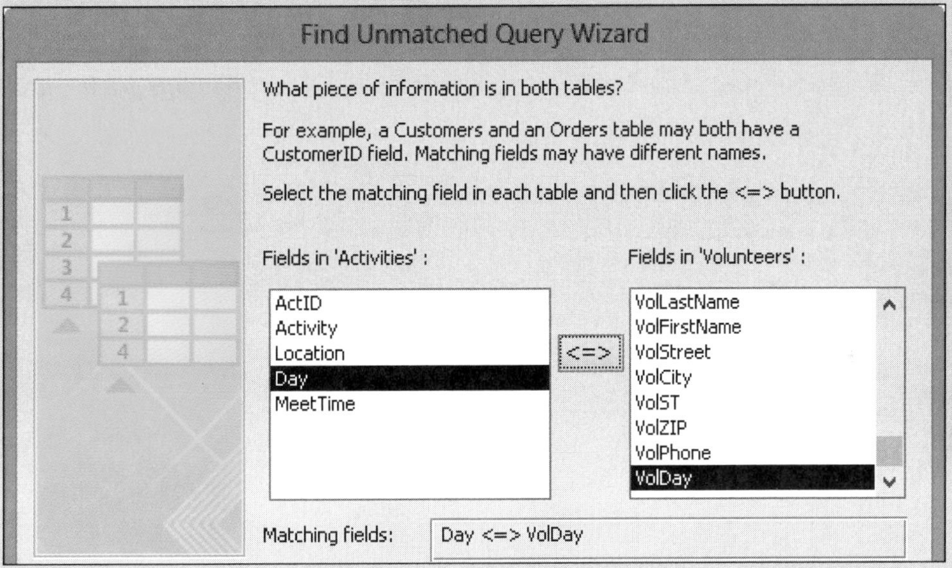

49. Click **Next** and **Move** > to move the following fields to the Selected Fields list: **Activity**, **Day**, and **MeetTime**.

50. Click **Next** and then click **Finish**.

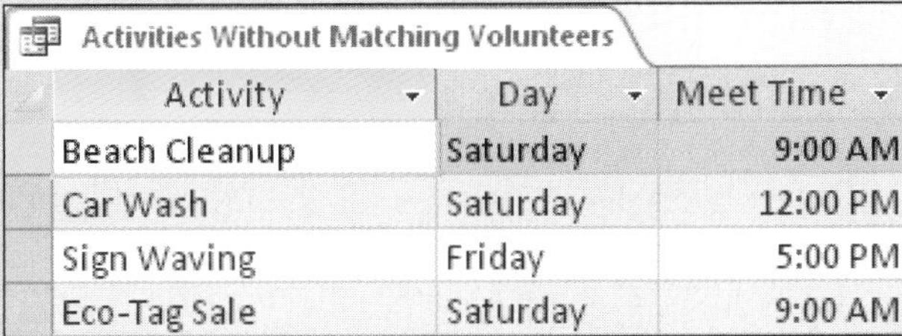

Activities Without Matching Volunteers

Activity	Day	Meet Time
Beach Cleanup	Saturday	9:00 AM
Car Wash	Saturday	12:00 PM
Sign Waving	Friday	5:00 PM
Eco-Tag Sale	Saturday	9:00 AM

You can use such results to find and delete unmatched activities from the schedule or to assign the unmatched activities to paid Staffers.

51. Close the query.
52. Choose **Create→Queries→Query Wizard** and double-click **Find Duplicates Query Wizard**.
53. Double-click **Table: Donors** as the table you want to check for duplicates and to automatically advance to the next screen.
54. Select the **DonorLName** field, click **Move** [>] to move the field to the Duplicate-Value Fields box, and click **Next**.
55. Move **DonorFName** to the Additional Query Fields box.
56. Move **DonorPhone** to the Additional Query Fields box, and click **Next**.
57. Type the name **`Donors with the Same Last Name`** for the query name, and click **Finish**.

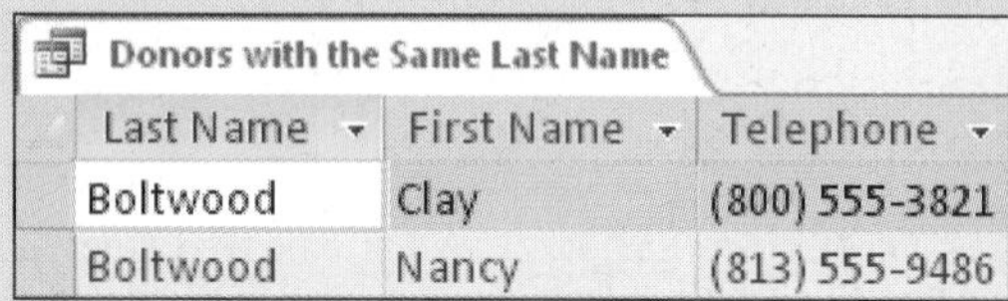

Donors with the Same Last Name

Last Name	First Name	Telephone
Boltwood	Clay	(800) 555-3821
Boltwood	Nancy	(813) 555-9486

The query results datasheet shows that there are two donors with the last name Boltwood.

View a Query in SQL View

58. Open the query in **SQL View**.

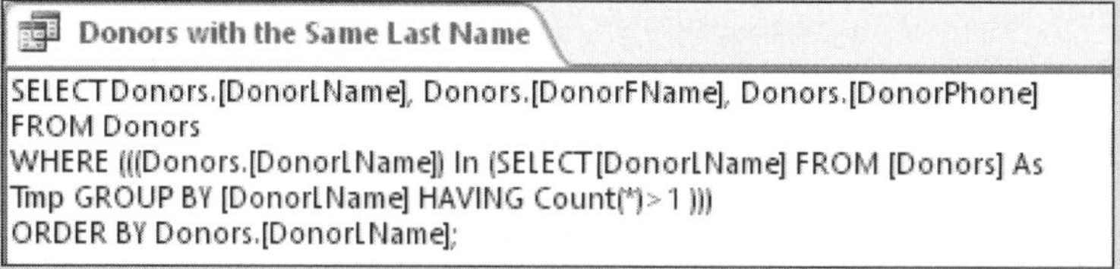

Donors with the Same Last Name
SELECT Donors.[DonorLName], Donors.[DonorFName], Donors.[DonorPhone]
FROM Donors
WHERE (((Donors.[DonorLName]) In (SELECT [DonorLName] FROM [Donors] As Tmp GROUP BY [DonorLName] HAVING Count(*)>1)))
ORDER BY Donors.[DonorLName];

59. Notice the SQL commands and reserved words are in uppercase lettering.

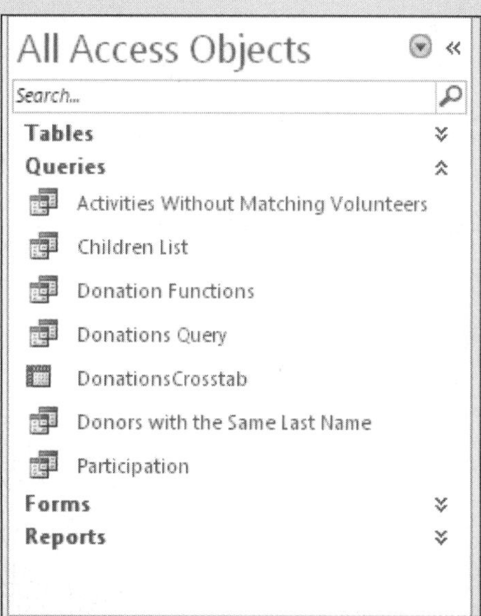

Your Queries Objects list now contains the names of the queries you created.

60. Save and close the query and the database, then exit **Access**.

61. Submit your final file based on the guidelines provided by your instructor.

    To view examples of how your file or files should look at the end of this exercise, go to the student resource center.

REINFORCE YOUR SKILLS AC04-R03

Create and Customize Queries

Kids for Change is planning to fine-tune their database by adding queries that will produce calculated and formatted results based on specific search criteria. In this exercise, you will use tables to create various queries.

Create a Query Using the Query Wizard

1. Start **Access**. Open **AC04-R03-K4C** from the **AC2013 Lesson 04** folder and save it as `AC04-R03-K4C-[FirstInitialLastName]`.
2. Choose **Create→Queries→Query Wizard**.
3. Double-click **Simple Query Wizard**.
4. Select the **Donors** table from the Tables/Queries list.
5. Click the **DonorLName** field in the Available Fields list and click the **Move** button.
6. Move the **DonorFName**, **DonorPhone**, and **DonorEmail** fields to the Selected Fields list.

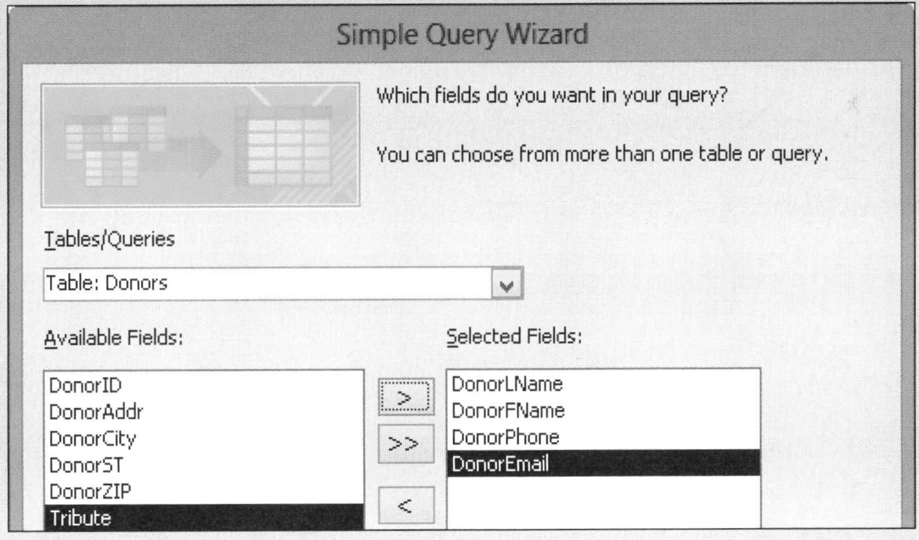

7. Click **Next**.

Access 2013

8. Type **Donor Contact List** in the query title box and click **Finish**.

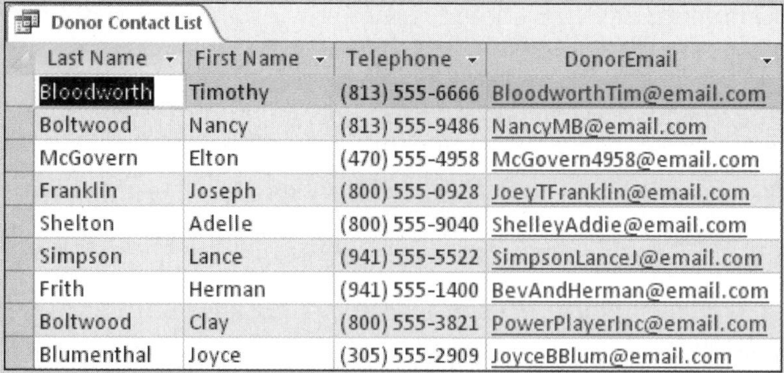

Donor Contact List

Last Name	First Name	Telephone	DonorEmail
Bloodworth	Timothy	(813) 555-6666	BloodworthTim@email.com
Boltwood	Nancy	(813) 555-9486	NancyMB@email.com
McGovern	Elton	(470) 555-4958	McGovern4958@email.com
Franklin	Joseph	(800) 555-0928	JoeyTFranklin@email.com
Shelton	Adelle	(800) 555-9040	ShelleyAddie@email.com
Simpson	Lance	(941) 555-5522	SimpsonLanceJ@email.com
Frith	Herman	(941) 555-1400	BevAndHerman@email.com
Boltwood	Clay	(800) 555-3821	PowerPlayerInc@email.com
Blumenthal	Joyce	(305) 555-2909	JoyceBBlum@email.com

The query results datasheet should include the four selected fields from every Donor record.

9. Review the query results datasheet then close the query.

Create a Query in Design View

10. Choose **Create→Queries→QueryDesign**.
11. Click the **Staff** table, click **Add**, then close the Show Table dialog box.
12. Double-click the **StaffLastName** field name to add it to the query grid.
13. Double-click **StaffFirstName**, **StaffStreet**, **StaffCity**, **StaffST**, and **StateZIP** to the query grid in the order shown.

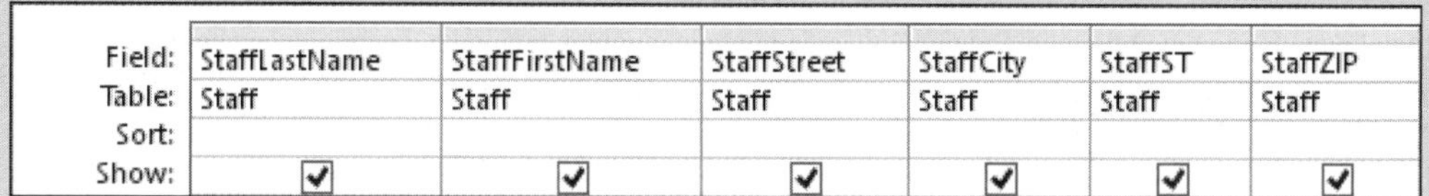

Field:	StaffLastName	StaffFirstName	StaffStreet	StaffCity	StaffST	StaffZIP
Table:	Staff	Staff	Staff	Staff	Staff	Staff
Sort:						
Show:	✓	✓	✓	✓	✓	✓

You can also click and drag fields to the query grid.

14. Click **Save**, name the query **Staff Mailing List**, and click **OK**.
15. Choose **Design→Results→Run**.

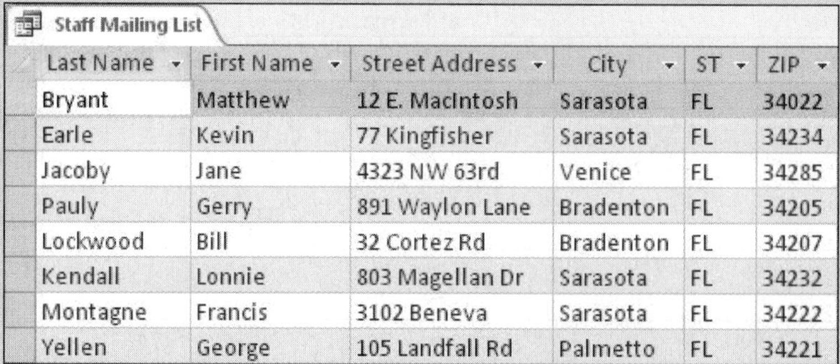

Staff Mailing List

Last Name	First Name	Street Address	City	ST	ZIP
Bryant	Matthew	12 E. MacIntosh	Sarasota	FL	34022
Earle	Kevin	77 Kingfisher	Sarasota	FL	34234
Jacoby	Jane	4323 NW 63rd	Venice	FL	34285
Pauly	Gerry	891 Waylon Lane	Bradenton	FL	34205
Lockwood	Bill	32 Cortez Rd	Bradenton	FL	34207
Kendall	Lonnie	803 Magellan Dr	Sarasota	FL	34232
Montagne	Francis	3102 Beneva	Sarasota	FL	34222
Yellen	George	105 Landfall Rd	Palmetto	FL	34221

Access runs the query and displays four columns of data for all Employee records. Resize the columns as desired by double-clicking the column heading borders.

16. Close the query, saving the changes if prompted.

Create a Multi-Table Query

17. Choose **Create→Queries→Query Design**.

    An empty query grid opens.

18. Double-click the following table names in the **Show Table** dialog box to add the table field lists to the upper pane of the query: **Activities**, **ActivityParticipation**, and **Children**.

19. Close the **Show Table** box.

20. In the Activities table, double-click **Activity** to move it to the query grid.

21. Double-click **Day** and **MeetTime**.

22. In the Children table, double-click **ChildLastName**, **ChildFirstName**, and **ChildPhone**.

Field:	Activity	Day	MeetTime	ChildLastName	ChildFirstName	ChildPhone
Table:	Activities	Activities	Activities	Children	Children	Children
Sort:						
Show:	☑	☑	☑	☑	☑	☑
Criteria:						

Your tables may be aligned differently, however the fields should appear in the query grid in the order shown in the figure above.

23. Save the query as `Participant List`.

24. Choose **Design→Results→Run**.

Participant List

Activity	Day	Meet Time	Last Name	First Name	Telephone
Beach Cleanup	Saturday	9:00 AM	Creger	Kurt	(941) 555-0245
Beach Cleanup	Saturday	9:00 AM	Driver	Sally	(941) 555-2272
Beach Cleanup	Saturday	9:00 AM	Finkel	Evelyn	(941) 555-2324
Beach Cleanup	Saturday	9:00 AM	Georgia	Pete	(941) 555-6121
Beach Cleanup	Saturday	9:00 AM	Kendall	Olivia	(941) 555-2356
Beach Cleanup	Saturday	9:00 AM	Langford	James	(941) 555-1098
Beach Cleanup	Saturday	9:00 AM	Preston	Willy	(941) 555-9372
Beach Cleanup	Saturday	9:00 AM	Riggs	Dina	(941) 555-2190
Beach Cleanup	Saturday	9:00 AM	Simpson	Belinda	(941) 555-0944
Can Collection	Thursday	6:00 PM	Abbot	Sami	(941) 555-2890
Can Collection	Thursday	6:00 PM	Creger	Kurt	(941) 555-0245
Can Collection	Thursday	6:00 PM	Frith	Hermy	(941) 555-7485
Can Collection	Thursday	6:00 PM	Lockwood	Timmy	(941) 555-6531
Car Wash	Saturday	12:00 PM	Abbot	Sami	(941) 555-2890

Add Criteria to a Query

Now you will add criteria to the Participant List query to list the children signed up for 9:00 AM Saturday activities.

25. Switch to **Design View**.
26. Type **Saturday** in the Criteria row of **Day**.
27. Type **9:00** in the Criteria row of **MeetTime**.

    This creates an AND condition. Only records with a Day value of Saturday AND *a MeetTime value of 9:00 will be returned.*

28. Run the query.

Activity	Day	Meet Time	Last Name	First Name	Telephone
Beach Cleanup	Saturday	9:00 AM	Creger	Kurt	(941) 555-0245
Beach Cleanup	Saturday	9:00 AM	Driver	Sally	(941) 555-2272
Beach Cleanup	Saturday	9:00 AM	Finkel	Evelyn	(941) 555-2324
Beach Cleanup	Saturday	9:00 AM	Georgia	Pete	(941) 555-6121
Beach Cleanup	Saturday	9:00 AM	Kendall	Olivia	(941) 555-2356
Beach Cleanup	Saturday	9:00 AM	Langford	James	(941) 555-1098
Beach Cleanup	Saturday	9:00 AM	Preston	Willy	(941) 555-9372
Beach Cleanup	Saturday	9:00 AM	Riggs	Dina	(941) 555-2190
Beach Cleanup	Saturday	9:00 AM	Simpson	Belinda	(941) 555-0944
Eco-Tag Sale	Saturday	9:00 AM	Frith	Hermy	(941) 555-7485
Eco-Tag Sale	Saturday	9:00 AM	Jones	Paul	(941) 555-8929
Eco-Tag Sale	Saturday	9:00 AM	Langford	James	(941) 555-1098
Eco-Tag Sale	Saturday	9:00 AM	Shamik	Ravi	(941) 555-1092

Access runs the query and returns the records with both Saturday and *9:00 AM.*

29. Save and close the query.

Use Wildcard Criteria

Now you will use a wildcard to select nearby donors so they can be invited to local activities.

30. Right-click **Donations Query** in the Navigation Pane and choose **Design View**.
31. Type **34*** in the Criteria row of DonorZIP and tap [Tab].

Field:	DonorLName	DonorFName	DonorAddr	DonorCity	DonorST	DonorZIP
Table:	Donors	Donors	Donors	Donors	Donors	Donors
Sort:						
Show:	✓	✓	✓	✓	✓	✓
Criteria:						Like "34*"
or:						

Access changes the 34 to* Like "34*".

32. Run the query.

Donor	Last Name	First Name	Address	City	State	ZIP
6	Simpson	Lance	59 Bahia Vista	Sarasota	FL	34234
7	Frith	Herman	Bay to Gulf Terr	Sarasota	FL	34228
8	Boltwood	Clay	Bayfront Blvd.	Sarasota	FL	34228

Add Date Criteria to a Query

33. Switch to **Design View**.

34. Remove the criteria from the **DonorZIP** field.

35. Type >`01/01/2013` in the Criteria row of the DonationDate field and tap [Tab].

36. Run the query.

Donor	Last Name	First Name	Address	City	State	ZIP	Telephone	Tribute	Date
3	McGovern	Elton		Atlanta	GA	30314	(470) 555-4958		3/12/2013
3	McGovern	Elton		Atlanta	GA	30314	(470) 555-4958		4/6/2013
10	Blumenthal	Joyce	298 West Biscayne	Miami Bea	FL	33139	(305) 555-2909	My Dear Abbie Blumenthal	4/13/2013
3	McGovern	Elton		Atlanta	GA	30314	(470) 555-4958		2/15/2013
4	Franklin	Joseph		Miami	FL	33184	(800) 555-0928		3/31/2013
5	Shelton	Adelle	Alexander Drive	Las Vegas	NV	89119	(800) 555-9040	For Shelley	4/5/2013
6	Simpson	Lance	59 Bahia Vista	Sarasota	FL	34234	(941) 555-5522	Grateful for the Love	4/10/2013
7	Frith	Herman	Bay to Gulf Terr	Sarasota	FL	34228	(941) 555-1400		4/12/2013
2	Boltwood	Nancy	Casey Key Rd.	Tampa	FL	33607	(813) 555-9486	In loving memory of Miriam Miller.	2/1/2013
5	Shelton	Adelle	Alexander Drive	Las Vegas	NV	89119	(800) 555-9040	For Shelley	4/9/2013
8	Boltwood	Clay	Bayfront Blvd.	Sarasota	FL	34228	(800) 555-3821	To Miriam	4/12/2013

Sort and Limit Query Results

37. Switch to **Design View**.

38. Click in the Sort row of the DonationDate field; click the list arrow, and choose **Descending**.

39. Choose **Design→Query Setup→Return**.

40. Click the list arrow and choose **5**.

41. Run the query.

Donor	Last Name	First Name	Address	City	State	ZIP	Telephone	Tribute	Date
10	Blumenthal	Joyce	298 West Biscayne	Miami Bea	FL	33139	(305) 555-2909	My Dear Abbie Blumenthal	4/13/2013
8	Boltwood	Clay	Bayfront Blvd.	Sarasota	FL	34228	(800) 555-3821	To Miriam	4/12/2013
7	Frith	Herman	Bay to Gulf Terr	Sarasota	FL	34228	(941) 555-1400		4/12/2013
6	Simpson	Lance	59 Bahia Vista	Sarasota	FL	34234	(941) 555-5522	Grateful for the Love	4/10/2013
5	Shelton	Adelle	Alexander Drive	Las Vegas	NV	89119	(800) 555-9040	For Shelley	4/9/2013

Access returns only the five most recent donor records.

Add a Calculated Field to a Query and Format the Field

42. Switch to **Design View**.
43. Choose **Design→Query Setup→Return** and choose **All**.
44. Type **`NetAmt:Amount-ScholarFund`** in the first empty **Field** row.
45. Open the **Property Sheet**.
46. Click in the **Format** line, open the drop-down list, and choose **Currency**.
47. Type **`Net Donation`** in the **Caption** line.
48. Run the query.

State	ZIP	Telephone	Tribute	Date	Amount	Scholar Fund	Net Donation
FL	33139	(305) 555-2909	My Dear Abbie Blumenthal	4/13/2013	$750.00	$75.00	$675.00
FL	34228	(800) 555-3821	To Miriam	4/12/2013	$1,000.00	$100.00	$900.00
FL	34228	(941) 555-1400		4/12/2013	$500.00	$50.00	$450.00
FL	34234	(941) 555-5522	Grateful for the Love	4/10/2013	$1,000.00	$100.00	$900.00
NV	89119	(800) 555-9040	For Shelley	4/9/2013	$250.00	$25.00	$225.00
GA	30314	(470) 555-4958		4/6/2013	$400.00	$40.00	$360.00
NV	89119	(800) 555-9040	For Shelley	4/5/2013	$500.00	$50.00	$450.00
FL	33184	(800) 555-0928		3/31/2013	$1,500.00	$150.00	$1,350.00
GA	30314	(470) 555-4958		3/12/2013	$250.00	$25.00	$225.00
GA	30314	(470) 555-4958		2/15/2013	$1,000.00	$100.00	$900.00
FL	33607	(813) 555-9486	In loving memory of Miriam Miller.	2/1/2013	$500.00	$50.00	$450.00

49. Save and close the query.

Create a Duplicate Records Query

50. Choose **Create→Queries→Query Wizard** and double-click **Find Duplicates Query Wizard**.
51. Double-click **Table: Children** as the table you want to check for duplicates.
52. Double-click **ChildLastName** to move it to the Duplicate-Value Fields box. Click **Next**.

53. In the next wizard screen, move **ChildFirstName**, **ChildStreetAddress**, **ChildCity**, **ChildST**, **ChildZIP**, and **ChildPhone** to the Additional Query Fields box.

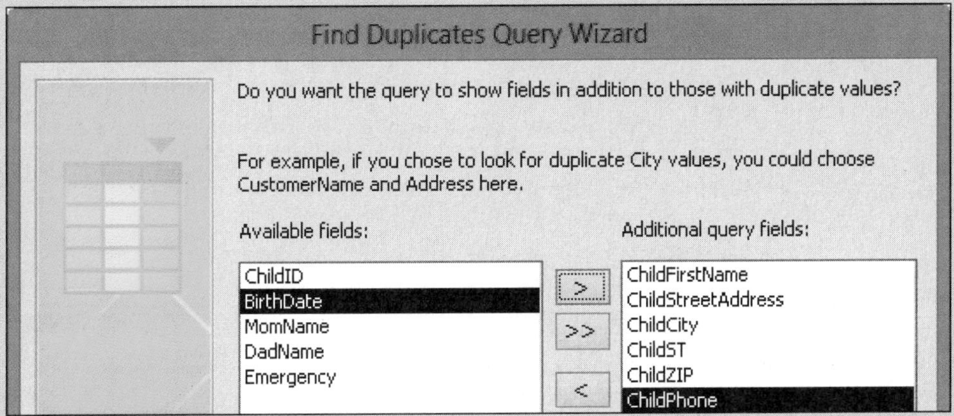

54. Click **Next**, type **`Children with the Same Last Name`** for the query name, and click **Finish**.

Children with the Same Last Name

Last Name	First Name	Address	City	ST	ZIP	Telephone
Driver	Joey	400 Spring Street	Bradenton	FL	34212	(941) 555-2272
Driver	Sally	400 Spring Street	Bradenton	FL	34212	(941) 555-2272
Riggs	Tina	121 Boston Rd.	Sarasota	FL	34234	(941) 555-2190
Riggs	Dina	121 Boston Rd.	Sarasota	FL	34234	(941) 555-2190

55. Close the query.

Create an Unmatched Record Query

56. Start the **Query Wizard** and double-click **Find Unmatched Query Wizard**.

57. Double-click **Table: Children** to identify the table that contains the values for which you are searching.

58. Double-click **Table: Volunteers** to identify the table to compare to the **Children** table entries.

59. Click **ChildLastName** in the Children list and **VolLastName** in the Volunteers list. Click **Equate**.

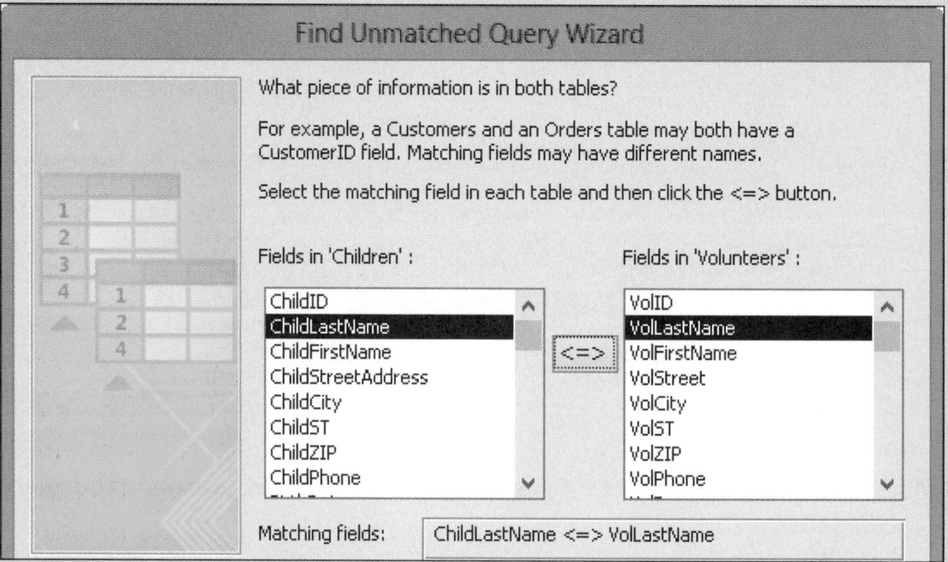

The Matching Fields box contains the selected fields to compare.

60. Click **Next**.

61. Move the following fields to the Selected Fields list: **ChildLastName**, **ChildFirstName**, **ChildPhone**, **MomName**, and **DadName**.

62. Click **Next** and then **Finish**.

Children Without Matching Volunteers

Last Name	First Name	Telephone	Mom's Name	Dad's Name
Preston	Willy	(941) 555-9372	Lisa	Bill
Driver	Sally	(941) 555-2272	Danielle	Joe
Shamik	Ravi	(941) 555-1092	Bhanu	Jaria
Riggs	Dina	(941) 555-2190	Tammy	David
Lockwood	Timmy	(941) 555-6531	Louise	Joseph
Kendall	Olivia	(941) 555-2356	Cathy	Frank
Finkel	Evelyn	(941) 555-2324	Suzanne	Morris
Georgia	Pete	(941) 555-6121	Alison	Richard
Abbot	Sami	(941) 555-2890	Melly	Fazai
Driver	Joey	(941) 555-2272	Danielle	Joe
Riggs	Tina	(941) 555-2190	Tammy	David

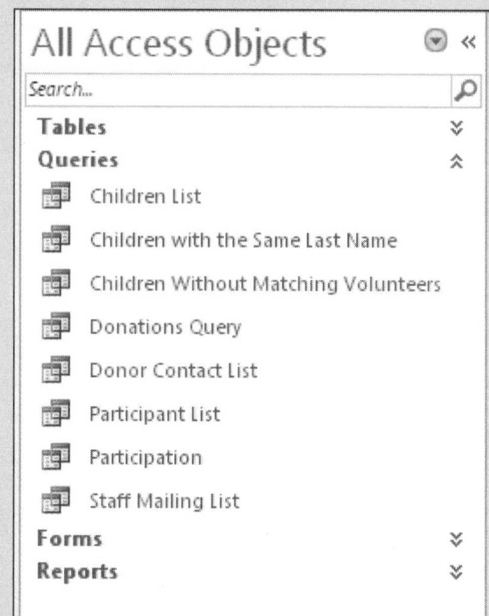

The Queries Objects list contains the names of the queries you created.

63. Close the query and the database, then exit **Access**.

64. Submit your final file based on the guidelines provided by your instructor.

Apply Your Skills

APPLY YOUR SKILLS AC04-A01

Create Queries Containing Criteria

Hubert Buckley, new CEO of Universal Corporate Events, has asked you to refine a number of queries to be more selective in data output. In this exercise, you will create queries; add criteria, wildcards, and AND/OR conditions to a query; and add date criteria to a query.

Create a Query Using the Query Wizard

1. Start **Access**. Open **AC04-A01-UCE** from the **AC2013 Lesson 04** folder and save it as `AC04-A01-UCE-[FirstInitialLastName]`.
2. Use the **Query Wizard** to create a simple select query from the **Personnel** table that includes the **PerLastName**, **PerFirstName**, **PerPhone**, and **PerEmail** fields.
3. Save the query as `Personnel Contact List` and then run it.

Query 1

Last Name	First Name	Telephone	Email Address
Wallace	Renee	(813) 555-2012	RJWallace@email.com
Dhana	Nazrene	(941) 555-6924	NazzJazz@email.com
Phattal	Rasha	(941) 555-6925	RashaP@email.com
Franks	Jade	(941) 555-9392	BobFranks@email.com
Montero	Jaime	(941) 555-2890	GourmetCiao@email.com
Winstead	Thomas	(941) 555-1921	TKWinstead@email.com
Buckley	Hubert	(813) 555-2000	BuckleyHJ@email.com
Buckley	J.G.	(813) 555-1000	BuckleyJG@email.com
Buckley	Connie	(813) 555-8811	BuckleyConnie@email.com
Goldstein	Marv	(941) 555-4603	MarvinGoldstein52@email.com

4. Close the query.

Create a Multi-Table Query in Design View

5. Create a query in **Design View** that uses the **Events**, **Schedules**, and **Menus** tables.
6. From the **Events** table, add **EventName** to the grid.
7. From the **Schedules** table, add **VenueID**, **ContactID**, **EventDate**, and **Guests**.
8. From the **Menus** table, add **MenuPlan** and **Chg/PP**.

9. Run the query.

Event Name	VenueID	Contact ID	Event Date	Guests	Menu Plan
Business Meeting	Meadow	LunaL	2/15/2014	50	Luncheon Sit Down
Holiday Party	Drake	CroftS	12/6/2013	150	Hors d'oeuvre
Holiday Party	Meadow	Miller	12/14/2013	100	Dinner Sit Down
Retirement Party	Meadow	Miller	1/15/2014	50	Dinner Buffet
Business Meeting	HyattS	LunaL	5/29/2014	80	Dinner Buffet
Course Training	Manate	Benson	6/8/2014	75	Dinner Sit Down
Holiday Party	Meadow	Miller	7/2/2014	25	Dessert Selections
Business Meeting	HyattS	LunaL	1/20/2014	55	Dinner Buffet
Business Seminar	HyattS	LunaL	1/30/2014	70	Dinner Sit Down
Business Seminar	Meadow	Miller	1/25/2014	45	Dinner Buffet
Group Retreat	Brooks	Benson	2/22/2014	50	Dinner Buffet
Group Retreat	Brooks	Benson	2/1/2014	40	Buffet Luncheon

10. Save the query as **`Event List`** and then close it.

Use Wildcards and AND/OR Criteria in a Query

UCE, Ltd. is planning a recruiting event in Sarasota and would like to contact employees from greater Sarasota (area code 941) to involve them in planning the event. You will modify a query to return the records of personnel who live in the Sarasota area.

11. Open the **Personnel Contact List** in Design View.
12. Type **`*941*`** in the Criteria row for **PerPhone**.
13. Run the query.

Last Name	First Name	Telephone	Email Address
Dhana	Nazrene	(941) 555-6924	NazzJazz@email.com
Phattal	Rasha	(941) 555-6925	RashaP@email.com
Franks	Jade	(941) 555-9392	BobFranks@email.com
Montero	Jaime	(941) 555-2890	GourmetCiao@email.com
Winstead	Thomas	(941) 555-1921	TKWinstead@email.com
Goldstein	Marv	(941) 555-4603	MarvinGoldstein52@email.com
Chauncy	Dina	(941) 555-3481	DinaWChauncy

*If the source table included records with the telephone numbers (813) 555-0***941*** and (800) 555-***941***7, they would also be included in the results based on the criteria *941*.*

14. Close the query, but do not save it.
15. Create a query in Design View from the **Venues** table that includes the **VenueName**, **VenueCity**, **VenuePhone**, and **VenueWebSite**.
16. In the **VenueCity**, type **`Sarasota`** in the Criteria row and **`Tampa`** in the Or row.

17. Click **Run**.

Query 1

VenueName	City	Phone	Website
Drake Country Club	Tampa	(813) 555-1700	DrakeCC@web.com
Hyatt Sarasota	Sarasota	(800) 555-1234	HyattSarasota@web.com
Sarasota Country Club	Sarasota	(800) 555-3366	SCC@web.com
Sarasota Yacht Club	Sarasota	(941) 555-7685	SYC@web.com
Tampa Bay Forum	Tampa	(800) 555-6500	TampaBayForum@web.com
Tampa Convention Ctr	Tampa	(813) 555-1100	TampaCenter@web.com
*			

18. Save the query as **`Tampa-Sarasota Venues`**. Close the query.

Add Date Criteria to a Query

19. Run the **Event List** query and examine the results.

20. Switch to **Design View**.

21. Type >**`June 1, 2013`** in the Criteria row of the **EventDate** field.

22. Click the **Sort** row and choose **Ascending** for the **EventDate** field.

23. Run the query.

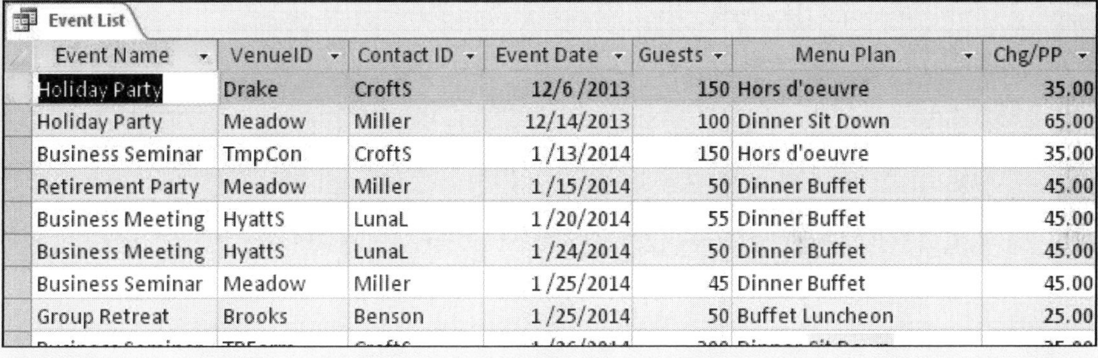

Event List

Event Name	VenueID	Contact ID	Event Date	Guests	Menu Plan	Chg/PP
Holiday Party	Drake	CroftS	12/6/2013	150	Hors d'oeuvre	35.00
Holiday Party	Meadow	Miller	12/14/2013	100	Dinner Sit Down	65.00
Business Seminar	TmpCon	CroftS	1/13/2014	150	Hors d'oeuvre	35.00
Retirement Party	Meadow	Miller	1/15/2014	50	Dinner Buffet	45.00
Business Meeting	HyattS	LunaL	1/20/2014	55	Dinner Buffet	45.00
Business Meeting	HyattS	LunaL	1/24/2014	50	Dinner Buffet	45.00
Business Seminar	Meadow	Miller	1/25/2014	45	Dinner Buffet	45.00
Group Retreat	Brooks	Benson	1/25/2014	50	Buffet Luncheon	25.00

Your results should include 31 records.

24. Close the query, clicking **No** when prompted to save it. Close the database and then exit **Access**.

25. Submit your finals file based on the guidelines provided by your instructor.

    To view examples of how your file or files should look at the end of this exercise, go to the student resource center.

APPLY YOUR SKILLS AC04-A02

Create Queries Using Comparison Criteria

Hubert Buckley has asked you to improve UCE data retrieval and formatting. In this exercise, you will sort and limit records returned in query results, add and format a calculated field, create a query that uses functions, create a crosstab query, and create a query that find records without matching fields between tables. You will also create a query that finds duplicate values within a table.

Limit and Sort Query Results

UCE wants to know which events and venues bring in the best revenue.

1. Start **Access**. Open **AC04-A02-UCE** from the **AC2013 Lesson 04** folder and save it as **`AC04-A02-UCE-[FirstInitialLastName]`**.
2. Run the **Event Revenue** query and examine the results.

Event Revenue

Event Name	VenueID	Contact ID	Event Date	Menu Plan	Guests	Chg/PP	Customer Total
Business Meeting	Meadow	LunaL	2/15/2014	Luncheon w/Servers	50	$34.00	$1,700.00
Holiday Party	Drake	CroftS	12/6/2013	Hors d'oeuvre	150	$20.00	$3,000.00
Holiday Party	Meadow	Miller	12/14/2013	Dinner-Sit Down	100	$65.00	$6,500.00
Retirement Party	Meadow	Miller	1/15/2014	Dinner-Buffet	50	$45.00	$2,250.00
Business Meeting	HyattS	LunaL	5/29/2014	Dinner-Buffet	80	$45.00	$3,600.00
Course Training	Manate	Benson	6/8/2014	Dinner-Sit Down	75	$65.00	$4,875.00
Holiday Party	Meadow	Miller	7/2/2014	Dessert Selections	25	$14.00	$350.00
Business Meeting	HyattS	LunaL	1/20/2014	Dinner-Buffet	55	$45.00	$2,475.00
Business Seminar	HyattS	LunaL	1/30/2014	Hors d'oeuvre-Deluxe	70	$35.00	$2,450.00
Business Seminar	Meadow	Miller	1/25/2014	Dinner-Buffet	45	$45.00	$2,025.00
Group Retreat	Brooks	Benson	2/22/2014	Dinner-Buffet	50	$45.00	$2,250.00
Group Retreat	Brooks	Benson	[illegible]	Buffet Luncheon	40	$25.00	$1,000.00

3. Switch to **Design View**. Then, choose **Descending** for the sort order of the **TotalRev** calculated field.
4. Choose **Design→Query Setup→Return**; choose **5** in the **Return** box.
5. Run the query.

Event Revenue

Event Name	VenueID	Contact ID	Event Date	Menu Plan	Guests	Chg/PP	Customer Total
Business Seminar	TBForm	CroftS	1/26/2014	Hors d'oeuvre-Deluxe	300	$35.00	$10,500.00
Holiday Party	Meadow	Miller	12/14/2013	Dinner-Sit Down	100	$65.00	$6,500.00
Business Meeting	HyattS	LunaL	2/20/2014	Dinner-Sit Down	75	$65.00	$4,875.00
Course Training	Manate	Benson	6/8/2014	Dinner-Sit Down	75	$65.00	$4,875.00
Business Seminar	HyattS	LunaL	3/14/2014	Dinner-Sit Down	65	$65.00	$4,225.00
Group Retreat	Brooks	Benson	4/12/2014	Dinner-Sit Down	65	$65.00	$4,225.00

The query returns the records of the five highest-grossing scheduled events, however six records are displayed due to the tie of $4,875.

6. Switch to **Design View** and change the Return value to **All**.

Add a Calculated Field to a Query and Format the Field

7. With the **Event Revenue** query in Design View, type **`Comm:TotalRev*.08`** in the first empty query grid line and tap [Enter].
8. Open the **Property Sheet**; choose **Currency** for the Format and type **`Commission`** for the **Caption**.
9. Run the query.

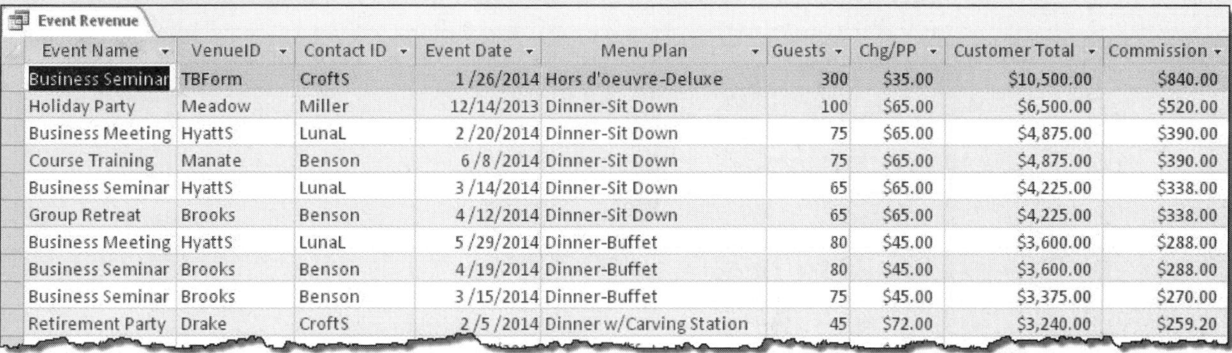

Event Revenue

Event Name	VenueID	Contact ID	Event Date	Menu Plan	Guests	Chg/PP	Customer Total	Commission
Business Seminar	TBForm	CroftS	1/26/2014	Hors d'oeuvre-Deluxe	300	$35.00	$10,500.00	$840.00
Holiday Party	Meadow	Miller	12/14/2013	Dinner-Sit Down	100	$65.00	$6,500.00	$520.00
Business Meeting	HyattS	LunaL	2/20/2014	Dinner-Sit Down	75	$65.00	$4,875.00	$390.00
Course Training	Manate	Benson	6/8/2014	Dinner-Sit Down	75	$65.00	$4,875.00	$390.00
Business Seminar	HyattS	LunaL	3/14/2014	Dinner-Sit Down	65	$65.00	$4,225.00	$338.00
Group Retreat	Brooks	Benson	4/12/2014	Dinner-Sit Down	65	$65.00	$4,225.00	$338.00
Business Meeting	HyattS	LunaL	5/29/2014	Dinner-Buffet	80	$45.00	$3,600.00	$288.00
Business Seminar	Brooks	Benson	4/19/2014	Dinner-Buffet	80	$45.00	$3,600.00	$288.00
Business Seminar	Brooks	Benson	3/15/2014	Dinner-Buffet	75	$45.00	$3,375.00	$270.00
Retirement Party	Drake	CroftS	2/5/2014	Dinner w/Carving Station	45	$72.00	$3,240.00	$259.20

10. Save and close the query.

Create a Query Containing Functions

11. Choose **Create→Queries→Query Design**, click the Queries tab, and add the **Event Revenue** query to the query work area.
12. Add the **ContactID** field to the grid.
13. Show the Total [Σ] line in the query grid.
14. Type **`MinEvent:TotalRev`** in the second Field line of the query grid, click in the **Total** line, and choose **Min**.
15. Type **`MaxEvent:TotalRev`** in the third Field line, click in the **Total** line, and choose **Max**.
16. Type **`AvgEvent:TotalRev`** in the third Field line, click in the **Total** line, and choose **Avg**.
17. Run the query.

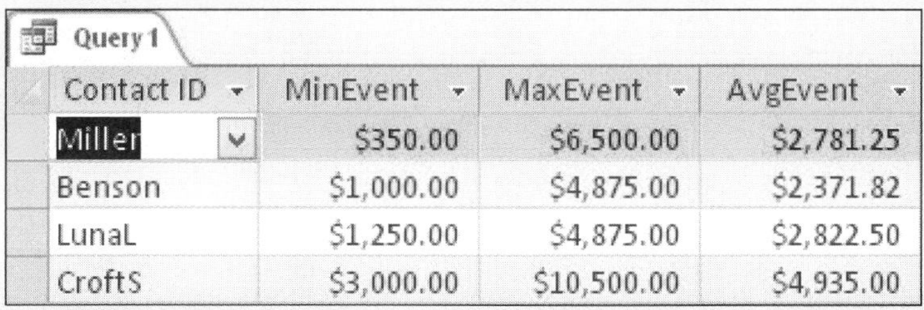

Query 1

Contact ID	MinEvent	MaxEvent	AvgEvent
Miller	$350.00	$6,500.00	$2,781.25
Benson	$1,000.00	$4,875.00	$2,371.82
LunaL	$1,250.00	$4,875.00	$2,822.50
CroftS	$3,000.00	$10,500.00	$4,935.00

Your query datasheet should show the minimum event revenue, maximum event revenue, and average event revenue for each venue contact person.

18. Save the query as **`Contact Functions`** and close it.

Create a Crosstab Query

19. Start the **Query Wizard** and double-click **Crosstab Query Wizard**.
20. Select the **Queries** option button and double-click **Query: Event Revenue**.
21. Choose **VenueID** as the field for the query results row headings and click **Next**.
22. Choose **ContactID** as the field to appear in the column headings and click **Next**.
23. Select **TotalRev** in the Fields list and **Sum** in the Functions list to identify the field that contains values and the function you want to calculate.

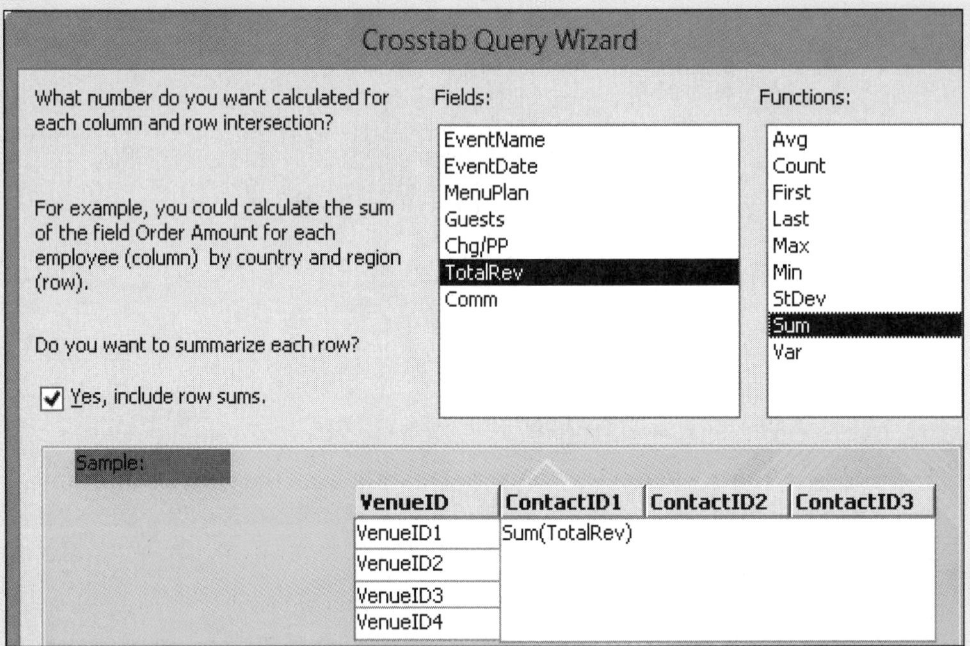

24. Click **Next**, name the query `Contact Revenue by Venue`, and click **Finish**.

Contact Revenue by Venue

Total Revenue	Total Of TotalRev	Gail	Harold	Lisa	Suzy
Brooks	$21,215.00		$21,215.00		
Drake	$6,240.00				$6,240.00
HyattS	$26,525.00			$26,525.00	
Manate	$4,875.00		$4,875.00		
Meadow	$12,825.00	$11,125.00		$1,700.00	
TBForm	$10,500.00				$10,500.00
TmpCon	$3,000.00				$3,000.00

25. Close the query, saving changes if prompted.

Create an Unmatched Records and a Find Duplicate Records Query

26. Start the **Query Wizard** and double-click **Find Unmatched Query Wizard**.
27. Choose **Venues** as the table with the field value for which you are seeking a match and **Schedules** as the table to compare values.
28. Verify that **VenueID** is selected in both lists; click **Equate**.
29. In the next wizard screen, move **VenueName**, **VenueStreet**, **VenueCity**, **VenueST**, **VenueZIP**, **VenuePhone**, and **VenueWebSite** to the Selected Fields list.
30. Name the query `Venues Without Events Scheduled` and click **Finish**.

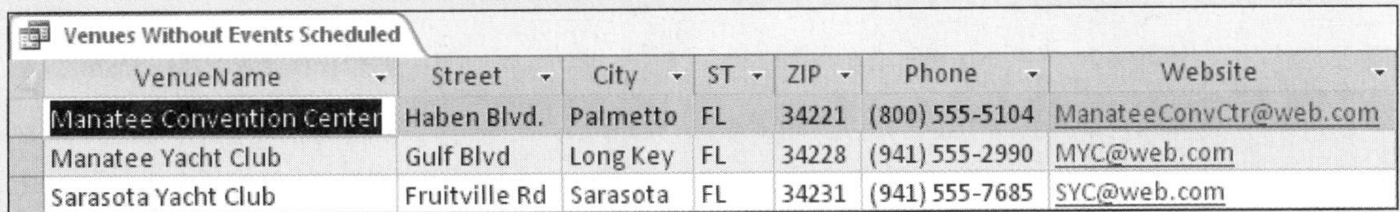

Venues Without Events Scheduled

VenueName	Street	City	ST	ZIP	Phone	Website
Manatee Convention Center	Haben Blvd.	Palmetto	FL	34221	(800) 555-5104	ManateeConvCtr@web.com
Manatee Yacht Club	Gulf Blvd	Long Key	FL	34228	(941) 555-2990	MYC@web.com
Sarasota Yacht Club	Fruitville Rd	Sarasota	FL	34231	(941) 555-7685	SYC@web.com

You can use such results to find and delete unscheduled venues or to call your venue contact and ask why no events have been scheduled at the location.

31. Close the query.
32. Start the **Query Wizard** and double-click **Find Duplicates Query Wizard**.
33. Choose **Query: Event List** as the query to search for duplicate values and **EventDate** as the Duplicate-Value Fields box. Click **Next**.
34. Include **VenueID**, **ContactID**, **MenuPlan**, and **Guests** in the query results.
35. Name the query `Find Double-Booked Dates`; click **Finish**.

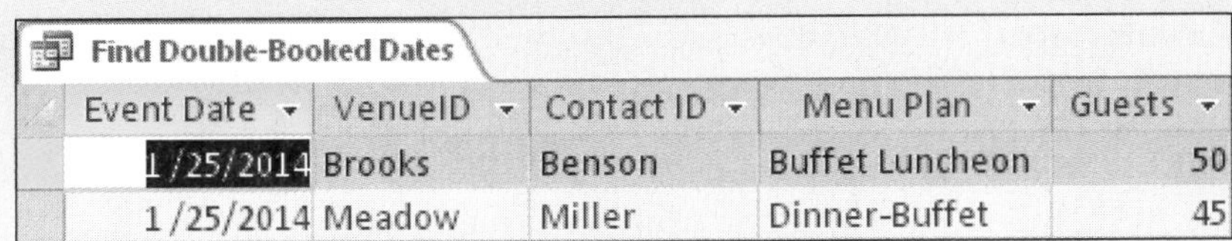

Find Double-Booked Dates

Event Date	VenueID	Contact ID	Menu Plan	Guests
1/25/2014	Brooks	Benson	Buffet Luncheon	50
1/25/2014	Meadow	Miller	Dinner-Buffet	45

The query results show two events scheduled for January 25, 2014. This kind of information can help you plan for extra personnel or scheduling conflicts.

View a Query in SQL View

36. Right-click the query name tab and choose **SQL View**.

Find Double-Booked Dates

```
SELECT [Event List].[EventDate], [Event List].[VenueID], [Event List].[ContactID], [Event List].[MenuPlan], [Event List].[Guests]
FROM [Event List]
WHERE ((([Event List].[EventDate]) In (SELECT [EventDate] FROM [Event List] As Tmp
GROUP BY [EventDate] HAVING Count(*)>1 )))
ORDER BY [Event List].[EventDate];
```

Commands/reserved words are uppercase and field names are preceded by the name of the table or query in which they are stored.

37. Close the query and the database, saving it if prompted. Exit **Access**.
38. Submit your final file based on the guidelines provided by your instructor.
To view examples of how your file or files should look at the end of this exercise, go to the student resource center.

APPLY YOUR SKILLS AC04-A03

Create Queries

In this exercise, you will create and modify a number of queries for more precise, targeted data selection for Universal Corporate Events.

Create Queries and Add Criteria

To begin, you will create a query to list contact information for the event venues that have an 800 telephone number so they can be reached by phone from anywhere at any time and at no charge to the caller.

1. Start **Access**. Open **AC04-A03-UCE** from the **AC2013 Lesson 04** folder and save it as `AC04-A03-UCE-[FirstInitialLastName]`.
2. Create a simple select query that uses the **Venues** table to generate a list of Venue names and their corresponding telephone numbers and websites.
3. Name the query `TollFreeVenues`.
4. In **Design View**, add criteria and wildcards to select only the venues that have an *800 phone number* by typing `*800*` in the Criteria row of the **VenuePhone** field.
5. Run the query to view the results; resize the columns, as necessary.

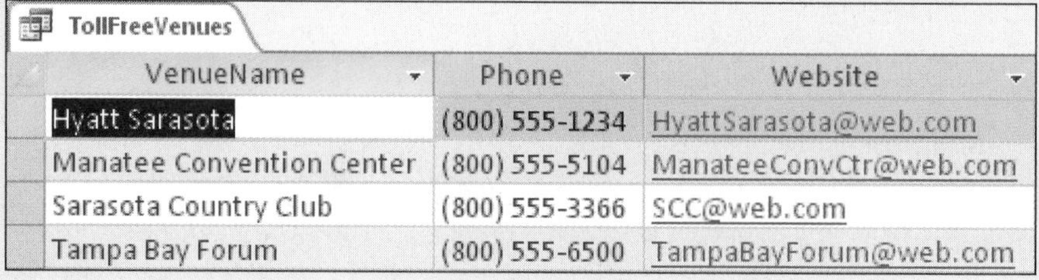

TollFreeVenues

VenueName	Phone	Website
Hyatt Sarasota	(800) 555-1234	HyattSarasota@web.com
Manatee Convention Center	(800) 555-5104	ManateeConvCtr@web.com
Sarasota Country Club	(800) 555-3366	SCC@web.com
Tampa Bay Forum	(800) 555-6500	TampaBayForum@web.com

6. Save and close the query.

Add Wildcard and Date Criteria to a Query and Sort the Query

Because June is the most popular month for weddings, UCE wants to pay special attention to weddings scheduled for June so they can hire extra part-time workers.

7. Create a new query that uses the **Event List** query as a record source.
8. Include all of the fields in Event List in the new query, leave the default Detail query option, name it **`June Weddings`**, and display it in Design View.
9. Add the wildcard criteria **`Wed*`** (for Weddings) to the EventName field.
10. Choose **Ascending** for the Sort order of EventDate, and type **`Between June 1, 2014 and June 30, 2014`** in the EventDate criteria row.
11. Run the query.
12. Close the query, saving it if prompted.

Limit the Number of Records in Query Results

Now you will sort the Location Scheduling query by the largest number of guests, and return the ten highest values so the company can focus extra personnel and resources to those events if the guests are scheduled for a full menu plan.

13. Display the **Location Scheduling** query in Design View.
14. Sort the query in **Descending** order by **Guests**, and type **`10`** as the number of records to be returned.

    If Access changes the 10 to 100, delete the extra zero (0).
15. Run the query. Then, save and close it.

Add and Format Calculated Fields to a Query

Now you will add a calculated field that subtracts the venue contact's commission from the total revenue to result in a net revenue amount.

16. Display the **Event Revenue** query in Design View.
17. Add a calculated field named **`NetRev`** that subtracts Comm from TotalRev; format the new field as **Currency**, and give it the Caption **`Net Revenue`**.
18. Add criteria to return only records with a **Total Revenue** greater than **5000**.

    Do not include a comma in the 5000 as you will get an error message.
19. Run the query.
20. Switch to **Design View**.
21. Delete the > **5000** criteria.
22. Save and close the query.

Access 2013

Create Special Queries

Now you will create a crosstab query that displays the full revenue generated from each venue broken down by month.

23. Open the **Query Wizard** and choose **Crosstab Query Wizard**.
24. Click the **Queries** option to list the queries, and select the **Event Revenue** query.
25. Choose **VenueID** for the Row Headings.
26. Choose **EventDate** for the Column Heading, and choose the **Month** interval.
27. Choose the **TotalRev** field and the **Sum** function.

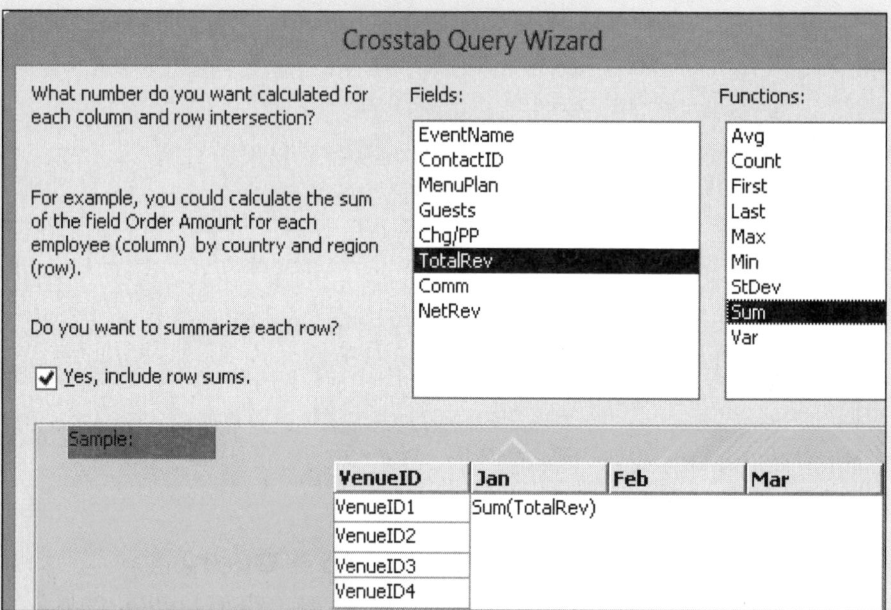

28. Name the query `Venue Revenue by Month` and open it to view the results. Save the query.

View Query SQL

29. Right-click the query name tab and choose **SQL View**.

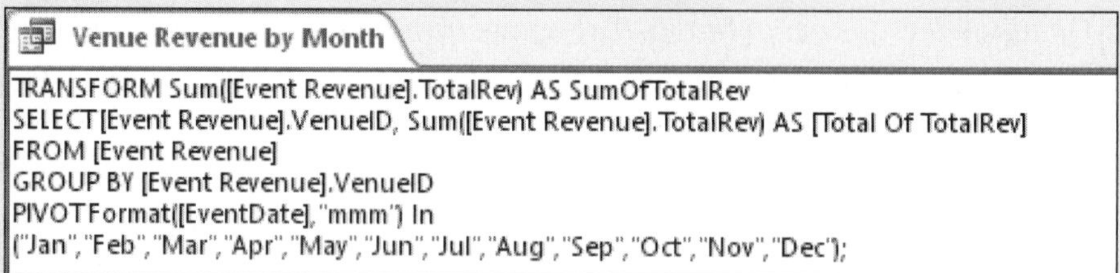

30. Examine the SQL, then close the query and exit **Access**.
31. Submit your final file based on the guidelines provided by your instructor.

Extend Your Skills

In the course of working through the Extend Your Skills exercises, you will think critically as you use the skills taught in the lesson to complete the assigned projects. To evaluate your mastery and completion of the exercises, your instructor may use a rubric, with which more points are allotted according to performance characteristics. (The more you do, the more you earn!) Ask your instructor how your work will be evaluated.

AC04-E01 That's the Way I See It

In this exercise, you will create several queries for either your own business or for Blue Jean Landscaping. Open **AC04-E01-BJL** from your **AC2013 Lesson 04** folder, and save the file as **`AC04-E01-BJL-[FirstInitialLastName]`**.

Using the skills you learned in this lesson, create queries to help your company better assess its needs in the areas of sales, recruitment, inventory, personnel, and any other aspects that you would find beneficial to managing a business. Use wildcards and other criteria—such as date ranges—to select records containing specified field values; sort query datasheet results; add at least one calculated field, format it, and give it a caption.

You will be evaluated based on the inclusion of all elements, your ability to follow directions, your ability to apply newly learned skills to a real-world situation, your creativity, and your accuracy in creating objects and/or entering data. Submit your final file based on the guidelines provided by your instructor.

AC04-E02 Be Your Own Boss

Blue Jean Landscaping wants to devise more targeted data retrieval. In this exercise, you will create several queries. Open **AC04-E02-BJL** from the **AC2013 Lesson 04** folder and save the file as **`AC04-E02-BJL-[FirstInitialLastName]`**. Create a query that will return a contact list for BJL's customers and sort it by last name. Create a mailing list sorted by ZIP code. Use wildcards to select records by area code. Add a calculated field to the Sales Invoices query that multiplies Cost by Qty Sold to produce a line total. Format the new field and assign it a caption; then limit the number of records returned to the largest five invoice totals, so those customers can be targeted for preferred customer offers.

You will be evaluated based on the inclusion of all elements, your ability to follow directions, your ability to apply newly learned skills to a real-world situation, your creativity, and your accuracy in creating objects and/or entering data. Submit your final file based on the guidelines provided by your instructor.

Transfer Your Skills

In the course of working through the Transfer Your Skills exercises, you will use critical-thinking and creativity skills to complete the assigned projects using skills taught in the lesson. To evaluate your mastery and completion of the exercises, your instructor may use a rubric, with which more points are allotted according to performance characteristics. (The more you do, the more you earn!) Ask your instructor how your work will be evaluated.

AC04-T01 Use the Web as a Learning Tool

Throughout this book, you will be provided with an opportunity to use the Internet as a learning tool by completing WebQuests. According to the original creators of WebQuests, as described on their website (WebQuest.org), a WebQuest is "an inquiry-oriented activity in which most or all of the information used by learners is drawn from the web." To complete the WebQuest projects in this book, navigate to the student resource center and choose the WebQuest for the lesson on which you are currently working. The subject of each WebQuest will be relevant to the material found in the lesson.

WebQuest Subject: Research the most effective ways to use queries for your business.

Submit your final file(s) based on the guidelines provided by your instructor.

AC04-T02 Demonstrate Proficiency

Business is booming for Stormy BBQ! They have opened a number of restaurants in Georgia and Florida, including their new flagship location in Key West. They would like to focus on what menu items sell best and use only the best vendors. They have hired you as lead tech to create a pilot program for the Key West store to track item receipts. The database includes a form written by a former employee, but no record source exists. Open **AC04-T02-StormyBBQ** from your **AC2013 Lesson 04** folder and save it as **`AC04-T02-StormyBBQ-[FirstInitialLastName]`**. Display the Daily Receipts form in Design View to see what fields are required for it. Use the DailyReceipts and MenuItems tables to create a query that will be the record source for the Daily Receipts form.

Examine the existing form in Design View to determine what fields you need in the query. Within the query, create a formatted, calculated field to generate gross profit. Name the new query **`Daily Receipts Query`**. (The form looks for Daily Receipts Query.) Stormy also wants a contact list for employees at each store that includes telephone numbers and email addresses, sorted by area code, and a mailing list for employees, as well, sorted by ZIP code. Use the skills you learned in this lesson to add the queries necessary to meet Stormy BBQ's needs.

Submit your final file based on the guidelines provided by your instructor.

ACCESS 2013

Using Reports to Display Information

LESSON OUTLINE

LEARNING OBJECTIVES

After studying this lesson, you will be able to:

- Design a report
- Create a report
- Modify a report
- Use report tools
- Print reports

Reports organize and summarize data into meaningful information for display. Although reports can summarize data from a single database table, they often present specific data from multiple tables or from queries based on multiple tables. Both forms and reports use many of the same tools and techniques to change layout and better organize and present information in a readable format. You may decide that you want to reposition fields, modify fonts, or add a title and images. You may also decide that you want to add calculated controls to generate subtotals and grand totals. In this lesson, you will create a report and modify the design and layout of a report. You will also format and align controls, create calculated and total controls, and print a report.

CASE STUDY

Turning Data into Information with Reports

Forms are great for entering data and displaying single records. Most businesses, however, want to filter and summarize data, as well as display specific data, such as running totals, in a readable format. Winchester Web Design needs a new report to summarize the sales for each employee and display sales totals. As their database manager, you have agreed to create a report to meet these needs. The draft of the report design is shown here.

Winchester Website Design
Invoice Details Report

Inv #	Emp ID	Inv Date	First Name	Last Name	Description	Price	Qty	Total
1	JFW	3/15/2012	William	Smith				
					Home Page, Nav, CSS, Design	$400.00	1	$400.00
					Secondary Page	$200.00	6	$1,200.00
					Image, Custom Designed	$40.00	11	$440.00
						Invoice Total		$2,040.00
2	MJW	4/2/2012	Emily	Santos				
					Home Page, Nav, CSS, Design	$400.00	1	$400.00
					Secondary Page	$200.00	7	$1,400.00
					Image, Custom Designed	$40.00	14	$560.00
					Hourly Rate for Modifications	$80.00	5	$400.00
						Invoice Total		$2,760.00
41	JMM	12/7/2013	Jo	Mansur				
					Secondary Page	$200.00	2	$400.00
					Shopping Cart, Basic	$400.00	1	$400.00
					Image, Custom Designed	$40.00	6	$240.00
						Invoice Total		$1,040.00
						Grand Total		$61,380.00

Sunday, December 30, 2012 Page 1 of 1

Designing Reports

Video Library http://labyrinthelab.com/videos Video Number: AC13-V0501

Access provides several ways for you to create a report. You can create a simple report based on a single record source. Or, you can create a new report using the Report Wizard, which permits you to select specific fields from multiple sources, set up grouping, add sort orders and totals, and choose a basic layout. Access also allows you to create a blank report from scratch in either Design View or Layout View, adding all the fields and controls yourself.

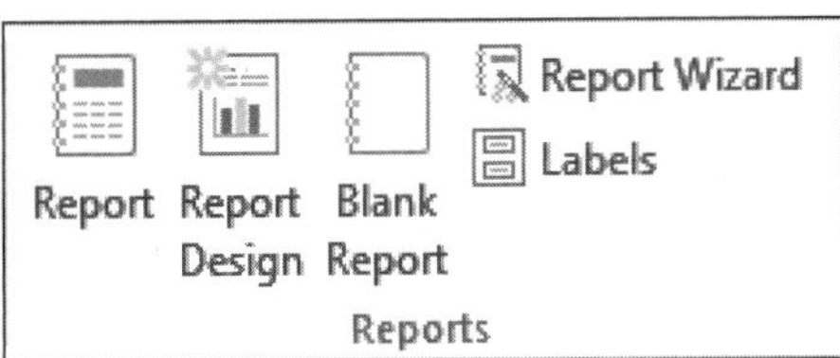

Report Essentials

Because reports are often presented in a readable format and end up as a printout, there are some basics that every report should include. Of course it should be well organized, look professional, and be visually appealing. Imagine finding a report on your desk without a date, without page numbers, or without a title that states what it is for. How might this affect the usability and readability of the data?

Most reports should have both a title and a subtitle. The title may simply be the company name. The subtitle should state specifically what the report is for, such as *Monthly Income* or *Product List*. Every report page requires a date and should include the page number; even if the report is only one page.

Once you have a good handle on the who, what, and when, you will be ready to create your first report.

Access 2013

DEVELOP YOUR SKILLS AC05-D01

Create a Quick Report

In this exercise, you will create a simple report.

1. Open **AC05-D01-WinWebDesign** from your **AC2013 Lesson 05** folder and save it as `AC05-D01-WinWebDesign-[FirstInitialLastName]`.

   Replace the bracketed text with your first initial and last name. For example, if your name is Bethany Smith, your filename would look like this: AC05-D01-WinWebDesign-BSmith.

2. Click the **Products** table in the Navigation Pane.

3. Choose **Create→Reports→Report**.

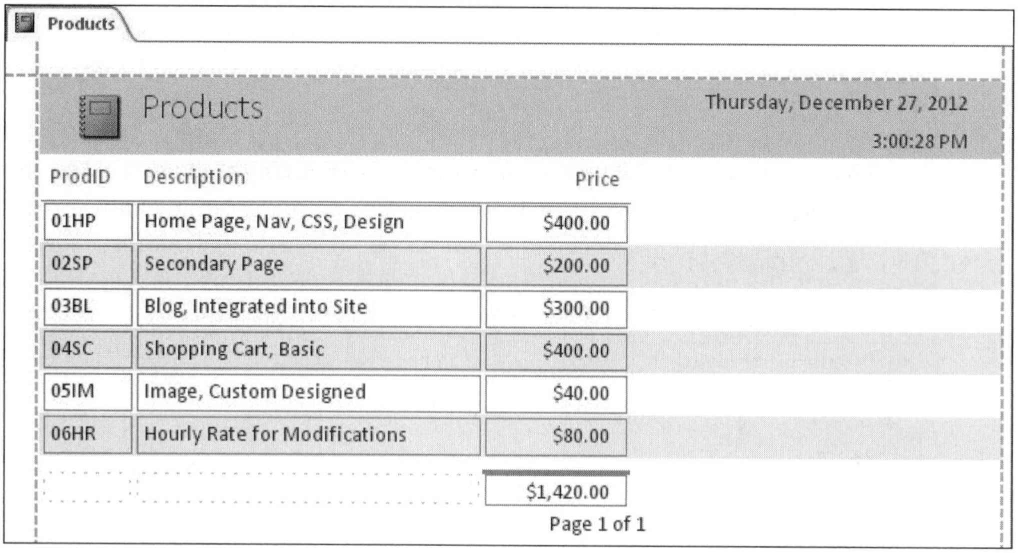

Products

Products — Thursday, December 27, 2012 3:00:28 PM

ProdID	Description	Price
01HP	Home Page, Nav, CSS, Design	$400.00
02SP	Secondary Page	$200.00
03BL	Blog, Integrated into Site	$300.00
04SC	Shopping Cart, Basic	$400.00
05IM	Image, Custom Designed	$40.00
06HR	Hourly Rate for Modifications	$80.00
		$1,420.00

Page 1 of 1

A simple report is displayed in Layout View. It may need additional formatting, but the basic layout is ready in just a few seconds.

4. Leave the **Products** report open.

Unless directed otherwise, keep Access and any databases or database objects being used open at the end of each exercise.

Identifying Report Design Tools

Video Library http://labyrinthelab.com/videos Video Number: AC13-V0502

If you have created and customized forms you will find that many of the same tools are available in Report Design View and Report Layout View.

Displaying Report Views

There are three views available for designing, creating, and editing reports: Report View, Layout View, and Design View. Working with these views is similar to working with views in Form design. Each view has its own distinct purpose.

REPORT VIEWS

View	Description	Procedure
Report View	Previews a report as it will print out. Displays when you open a report. Does not permit control modification or formatting.	Open a report or choose Home→Views→View→Report View.
Layout View	Previews a report layout with actual data displayed so you can format, resize, and position controls appropriately.	Right-click a report name in the Navigation Pane and choose Layout View.
Design View	Displays the design palette containing controls, labels, and other report design elements that you can add to a report.	Right-click a report name in the Navigation Pane and choose Design View.

DEVELOP YOUR SKILLS AC05-D02

Display Report Views

In this exercise, you will display a report in different views and examine the tools available and layout differences between the views.

1. If necessary, choose **Home→Views→View ▾ menu** and choose **Layout View** to display the **Products** report in Layout View.
2. Choose the **Design** tab.
3. Follow these steps to examine the tools and commands available in Layout View:

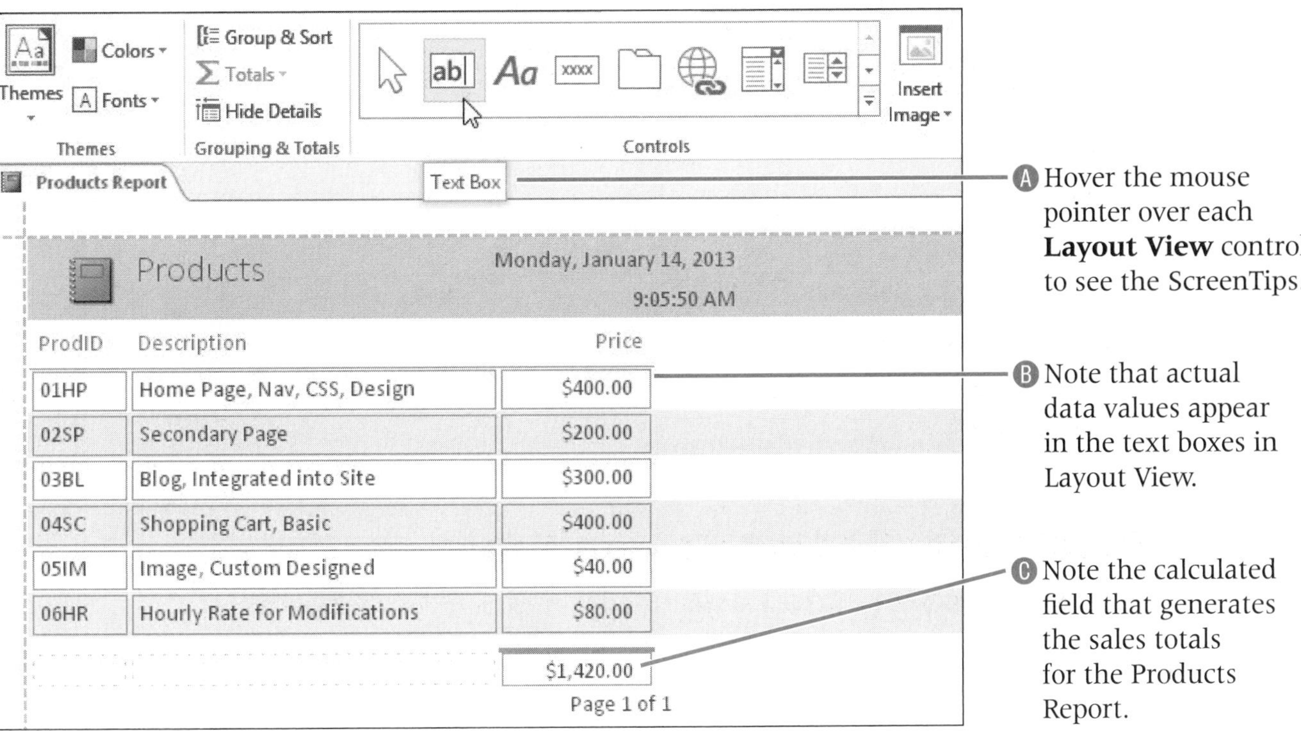

4. Choose **Home→Views→View ▾ menu** and choose **Design View**.

5. Follow these steps to examine the report in Design View:

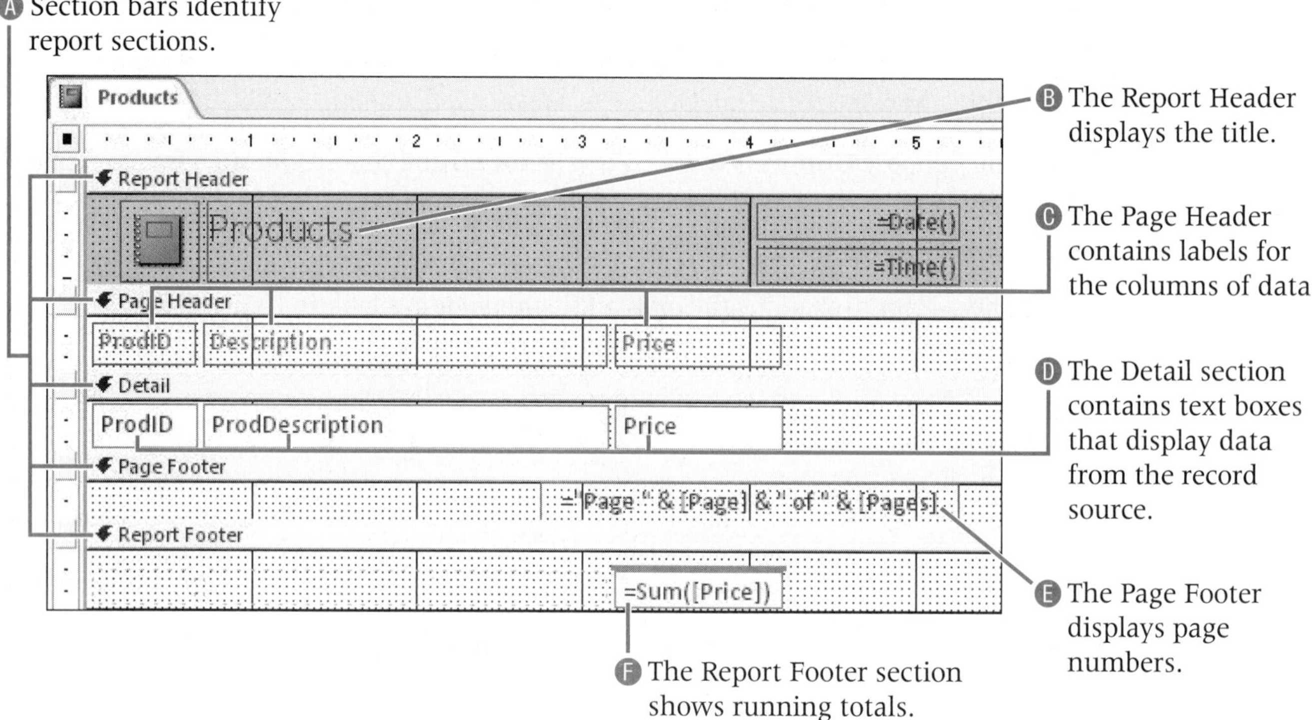

6. Choose **Design→Controls→Controls**.
The available controls are displayed.

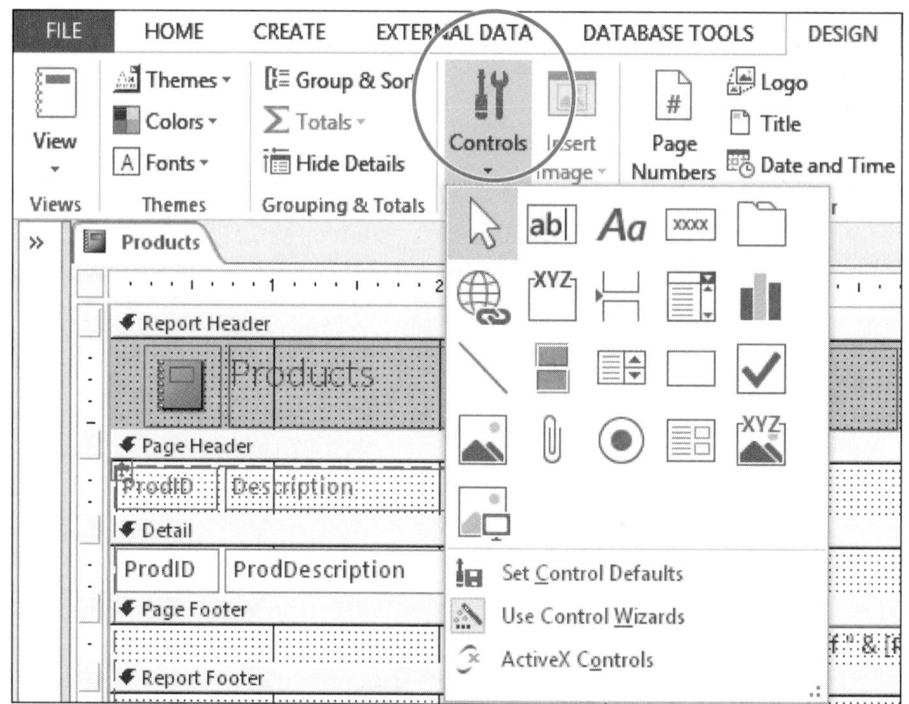

The Access report design tools.

7. Tap [Esc] to close the **Controls** menu.

8. Follow these steps to examine the properties of an unbound label control:

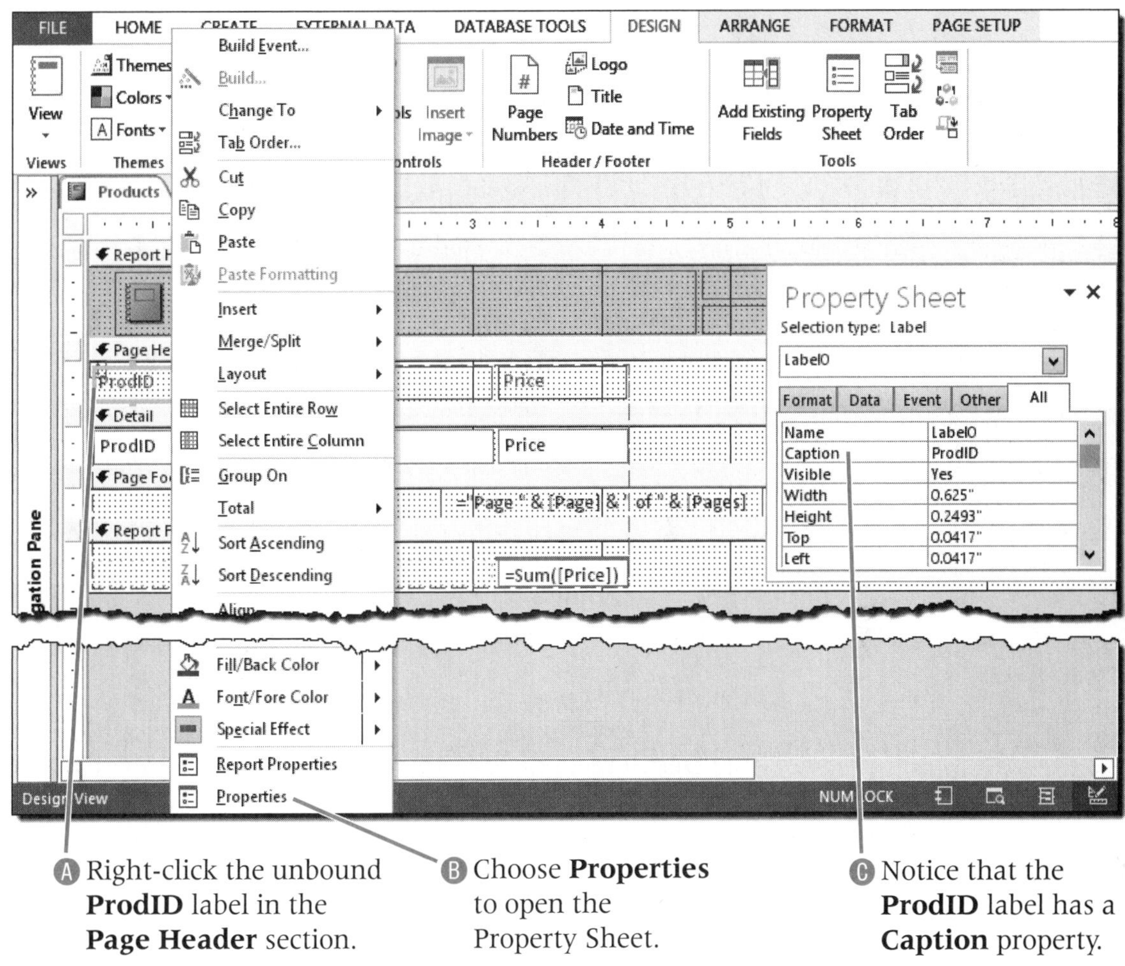

Ⓐ Right-click the unbound **ProdID** label in the **Page Header** section.

Ⓑ Choose **Properties** to open the Property Sheet.

Ⓒ Notice that the **ProdID** label has a **Caption** property.

Due to differences in screen settings, your property values may vary from those shown here.

Labels have a caption, or text, used to identify objects. Labels are unbound controls and do not have a Control Source property.

Access 2013

9. Follow these steps to examine the properties of a bound control:

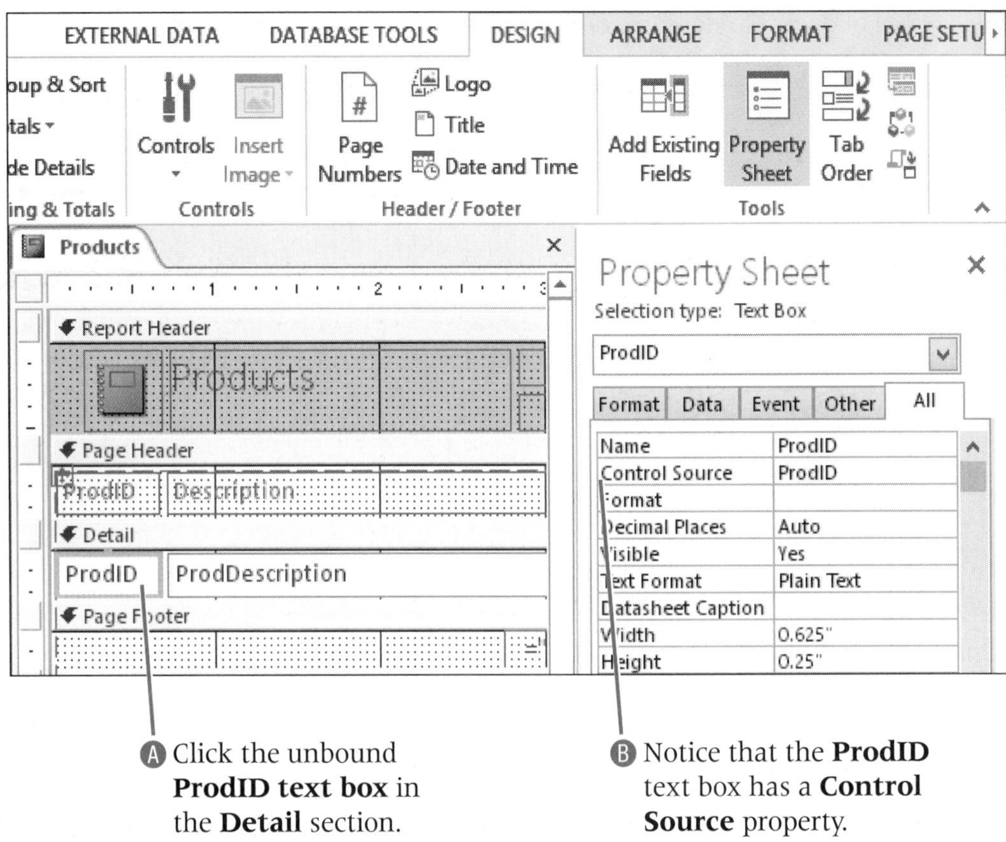

A Click the unbound **ProdID text box** in the **Detail** section.

B Notice that the **ProdID** text box has a **Control Source** property.

The ProdID text box does not have a Caption property. It is a bound control and has a Control Source property that binds or links it to the record source to display data from the ProdID field.

10. Switch to **Report View** to see how the report would look if it were printed.

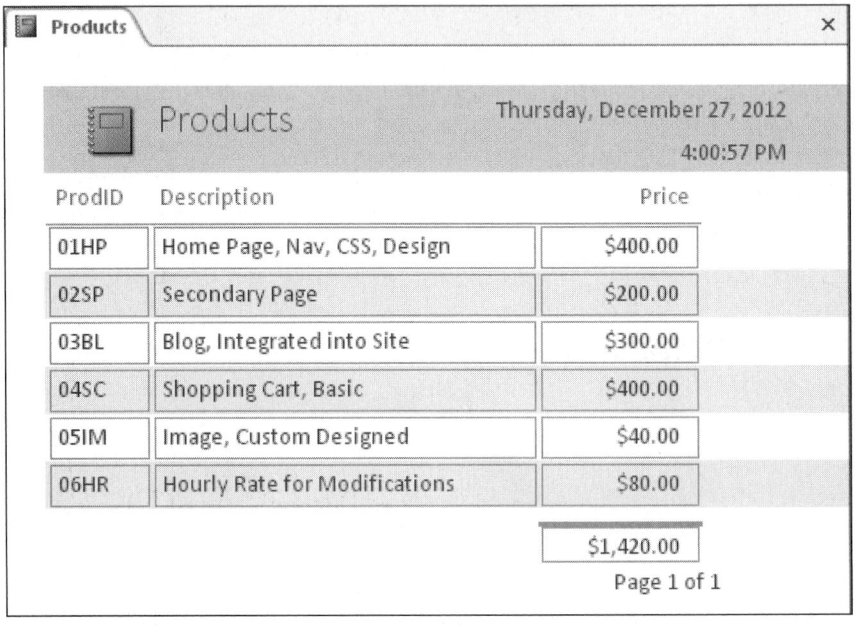

11. Save the report as `Products Report` and close it.

Creating Reports Based on Multiple Tables

Video Library http://labyrinthelab.com/videos Video Number: AC13-V0503

You can easily create a quick report based on a single table, but there are often times when you need to view data gathered from multiple tables. The Report Wizard allows you to do this.

Creating a Report Using the Report Wizard

You can create a report using the Report Wizard that uses one or more tables as the record source, or you can use a query based on multiple tables as the record source. You can create calculations in queries, whereas you cannot in tables. Therefore, it is usually easier to create the report from an existing query that already includes all the required tables, desired fields, and necessary calculations.

DEVELOP YOUR SKILLS AC05-D03

Create a Report Using the Report Wizard

In this exercise, you will create a detailed Invoice report using the Report Wizard.

1. Click the **Invoice Details Query Q1 2013** in the Navigation Pane to select it.
2. Choose **Create→Reports→Report Wizard**.
3. Double-click the **EmpID** field in the Available Fields box to move it to the Selected Fields box.
4. Double-click **InvNum**, **InvDate**, **CustLastName**, **ProdID**, **Price**, **Qty**, and **LineTotal**, in the order shown.

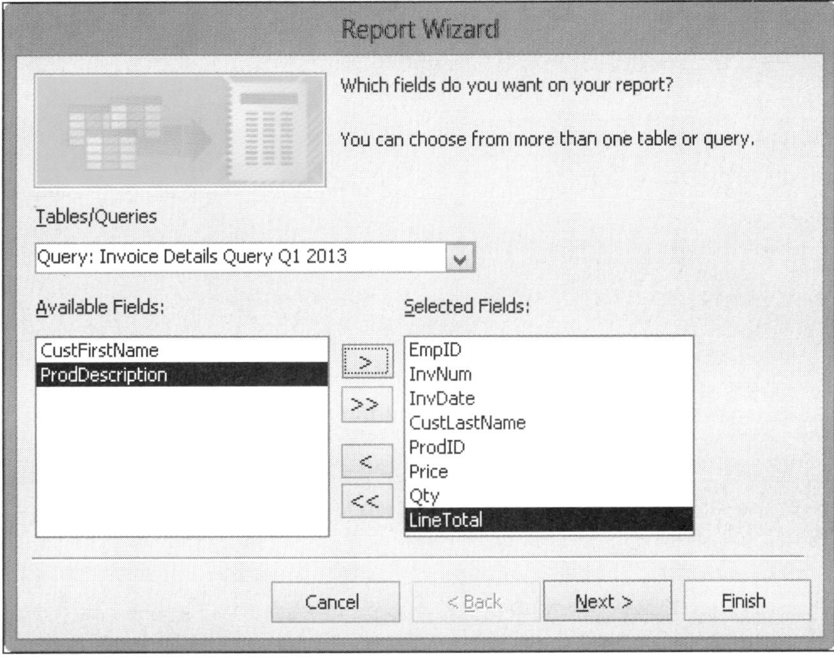

Do not select CustFirstName and ProdDescription. If you add every field to the report there will not be enough room to display all of the information. Be sure that EmpID is the first field in the row.

Access 2013

5. Click **Next**.

   The next wizard screen asks about grouping levels.

6. With **EmpID** selected, click **Move** [>] to set EmpID as the primary grouping level.
7. With **InvNum** selected, click **Move** [>] to set the secondary grouping level.

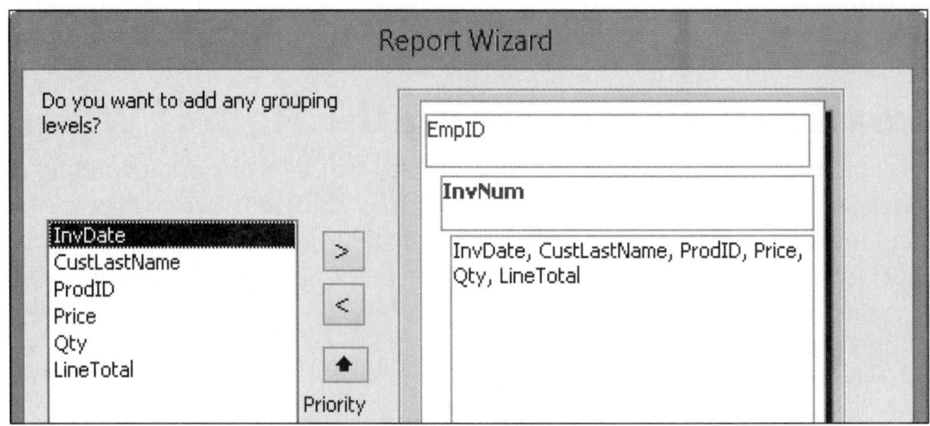

The grouping order should be set with EmpID at the first level and InvNum at the secondary level.

8. Click **Next**.
9. Follow these steps to set the Summary Options:

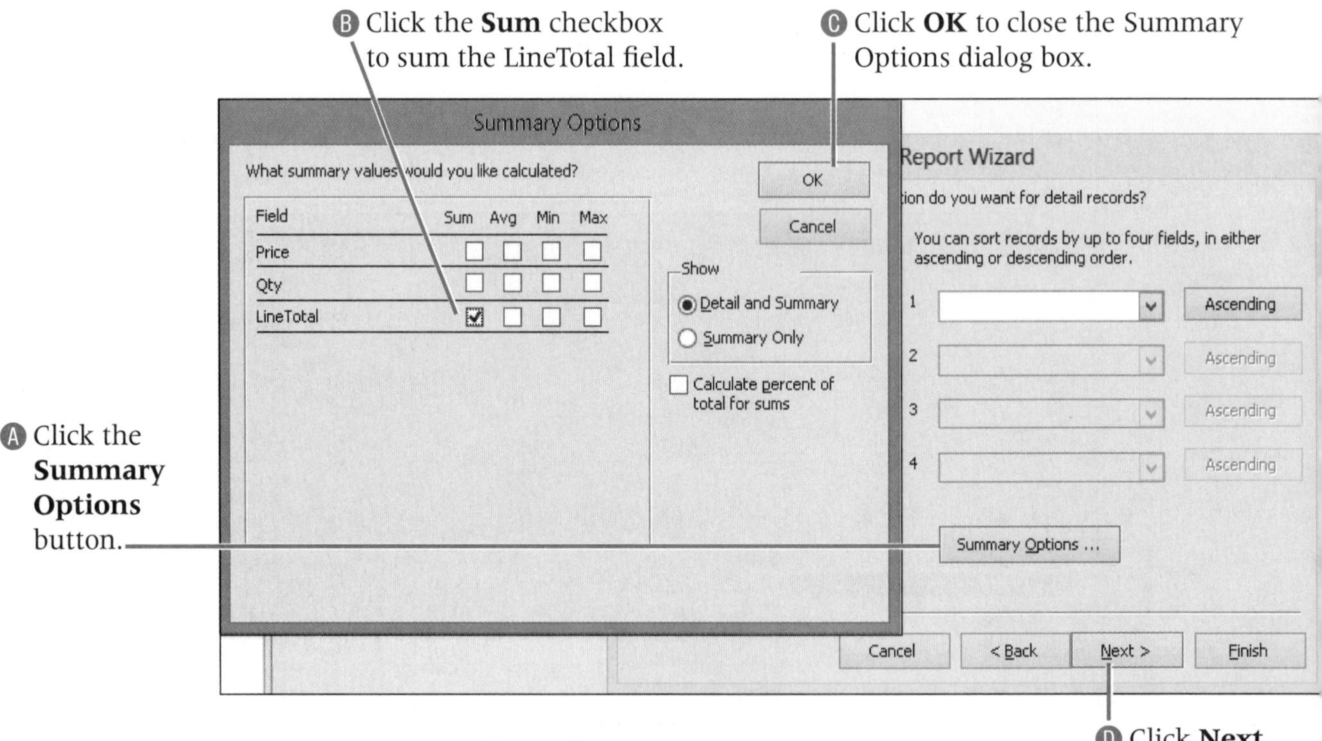

10. Choose the **Outline** layout.
11. Choose **Landscape** as the orientation for the report's layout.

12. Confirm that the **Adjust the Field Width So All Fields Fit on a Page** box is checked.

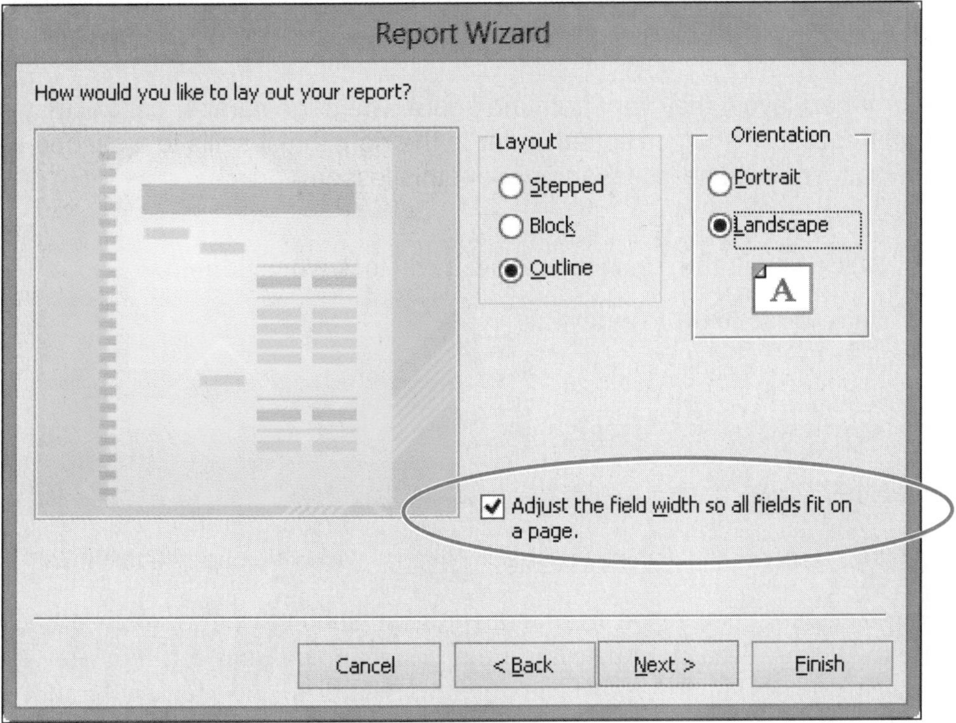

13. Click **Next**. Name the report `Invoice Details Report Q1 2013`.

14. Click **Finish**.

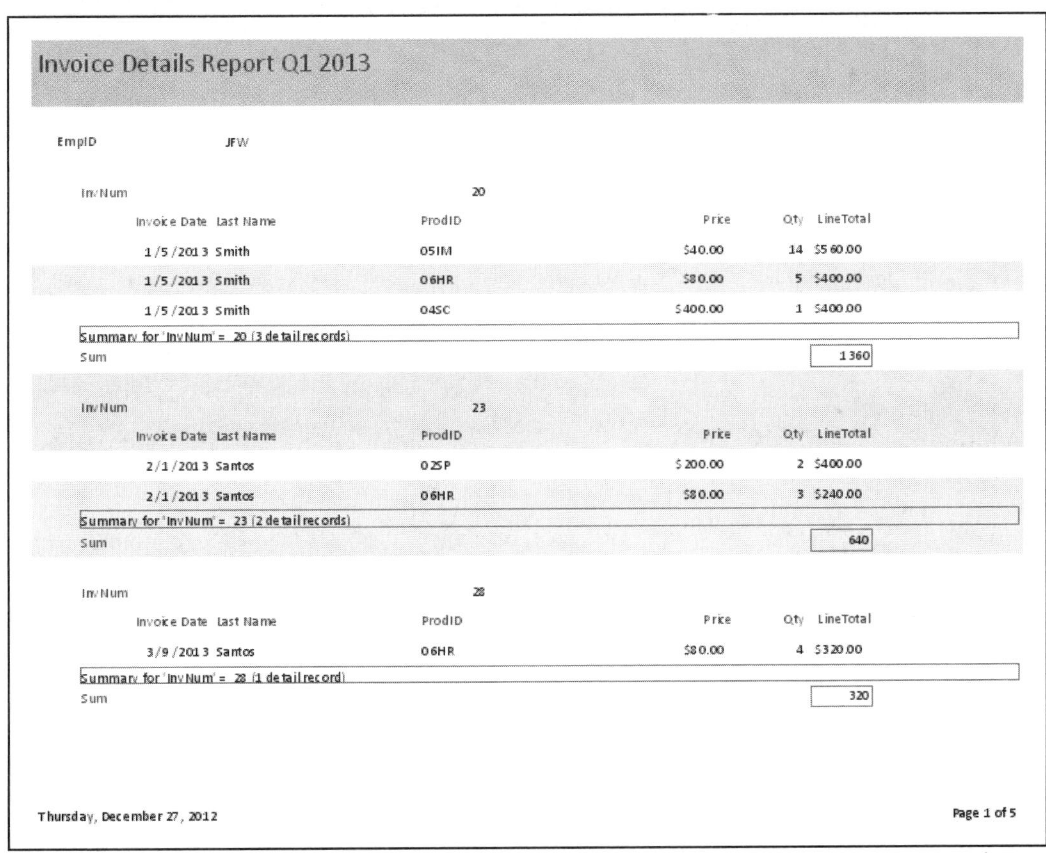

Access 2013

Your report displays in Print Preview, showing invoice totals and summary totals for each employee. The report needs formatting and layout work, which must be done in Design View. However, almost all of the controls and calculations are now in place.

Your report layout may vary from the figure. The page number control may be much wider than necessary and positioned so far to the right that it spills to a second page. You will learn how to resolve these issues throughout this lesson.

15. Page through the report to see how it will look when printed.
16. Click **Close Print Preview**.

Modifying a Report

Video Library http://labyrinthelab.com/videos Video Number: AC13-V0504

You can create a new report from scratch using Ribbon tools, but many professionals prefer to use the Report Wizard because it is much easier and far more efficient. However, when you finish using the Report Wizard you often find that fields may have to be added, deleted, resized, repositioned, and reformatted. You can correct these issues in Layout View or in Design View, if necessary. Design View has the same controls, functionality, and section layout that you have when you create a blank report.

REPORT SECTIONS

Section	Description
Sections	The major parts of the report—the Report Header, Report Footer, Detail, Page Header, Group Header, Group Footer, and Page Footer. Section bars divide report sections.
Report Header	Contains information that is only displayed on the first page, such as the title, subtitle, and possibly a logo.
Page Header	The section that contains controls that are repeated at the top of every printed page—mainly labels displaying column headings.
Group Header	Identifies a field (such as EmpID) by which report data is grouped, so a summary (such as a total of each employee's sales) can be displayed for the grouped field.
Detail	The section that contains the actual table data in the report.
Group Footer	Displays the summary for a grouped field, such as the total of each employee's sales, grouped by the EmpID.
Page Footer	Contains text and fields that are repeated at the bottom of every printed page, such as page number and date.
Report Footer	The bottom section that appears on the very last page of a report. It typically contains grand totals.

Working with Report Controls

If you create or modify a report in Design View, you can select the table that contains any new fields you want to add to the report and drag those fields to the appropriate sections. You can also add controls to create titles or subtitles, add graphics, and insert footer controls.

Access has three basic types of controls that you can add to reports.

- **Bound controls:** Controls that tie, or bind, the field value (data) displayed on a report to a field in a database table. Bound controls normally appear in the Detail section of a report.
- **Unbound controls:** Lines and other drawn objects, text for titles, graphics, etc., that can enhance a report's appearance or present additional text.
- **Calculated controls:** Controls that are tied to an expression, aggregate function, or calculated field constructed in a query or built directly on the report. These controls normally appear in the Detail or report Footer section.

REPORT CONTROLS

Control	Description
Controls	Items that display data, text, checkboxes, lines, and images.
Bound control	A control that ties data to be displayed to a field in a table. Bound controls normally appear in the Detail section (e.g., ProductID or ProdPrice).
Unbound control	An item that is independent of data and fields in a database table, such as text, lines, and images. Unbound controls may appear in any report section.
Calculated control	A control tied to a calculated field or an expression constructed in a query or in the report itself. Calculated controls normally appear in the Detail or Report Footer.
Control label	The part of a control that contains text that identifies the data in the associated text box. (e.g., Last Name).
Control text box	A control that displays the field value from an associated table (e.g., a textbox named LastName containing the value Smith).

Adding and Deleting Controls

Video Library http://labyrinthelab.com/videos Video Number: AC13-V0505

When you create a report with the Report Wizard you may want to add a company logo to the report header; or you may want to delete a field, such as the Summary for InvNum control that was added to the Invoice Details Report Q1 2013 that you just created. Fortunately, these controls can be added or deleted using the same techniques that you use in Form Design.

Adding Controls from the Ribbon

When you display a report in Design View, you can use the tools on the Ribbon to add bound and unbound controls to reports. A limited number of design tools are also available in Layout View, but it is often necessary to work in Design View to set and modify properties for controls.

QUICK REFERENCE	ADDING CONTROLS TO A REPORT
Task	**Procedure**
Drag bound controls	■ Display the report in Layout or Design View. ■ Choose Design→Tools→Add Existing Fields. ■ Expand the table containing the field you want to add. ■ Drag the field into position on the report.
Add unbound controls from a Ribbon	■ Display the report in Design View. ■ Choose Design→Controls and click the desired control. ■ Click or drag a control into the position and size you want.

Adding Controls from Field Lists

The Field List contains a list of all the tables that appear in the database. You can expand each table in the list to display all the fields the table contains.

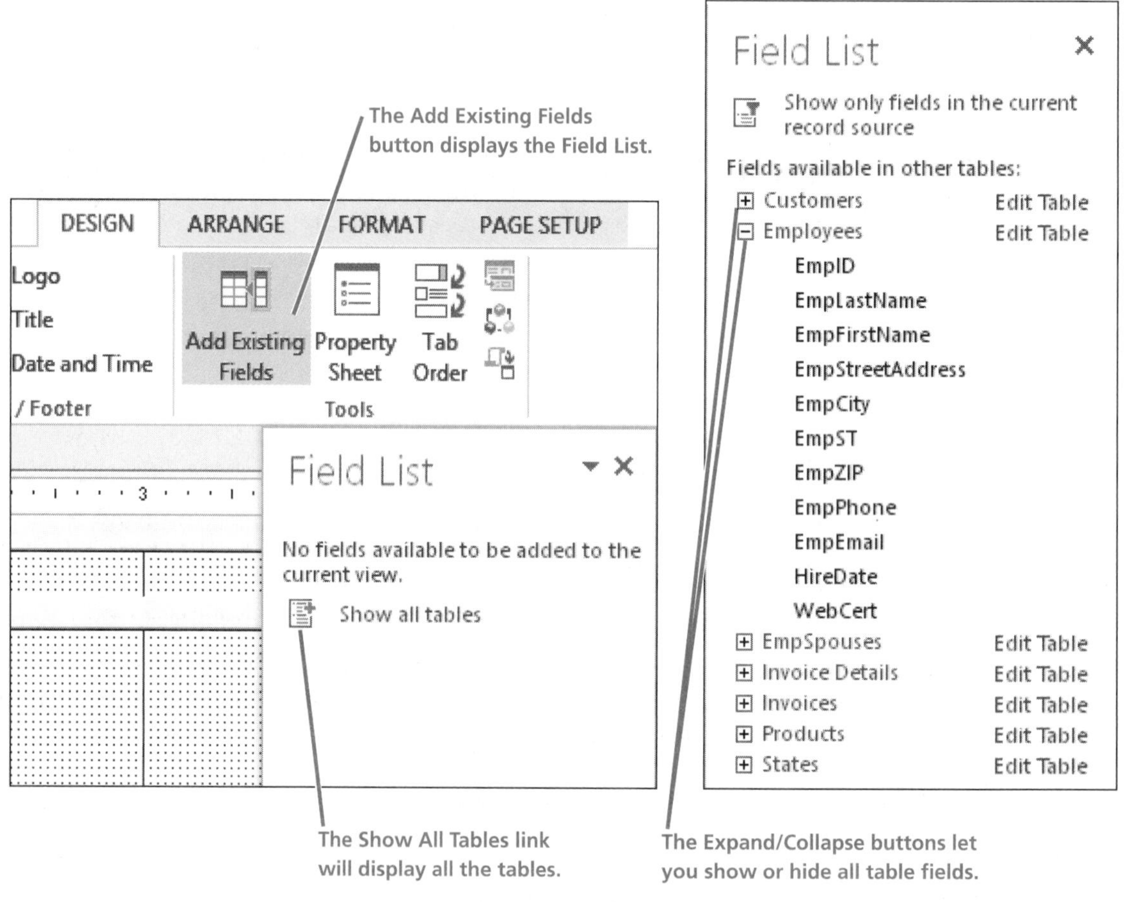

Dragging Controls from the Field List

To add bound controls from the available field list, click and drag the field name onto the appropriate report section. When you add a bound control from the Field List to the Detail section of the report page, Access places both the text box and label for the bound control on the report. Because most reports display the control label in the Page Header section, you will have to cut the label from the Detail section and paste it into the Page Header section.

DEVELOP YOUR SKILLS AC05-D04

Add, Delete, and Edit Controls on a Report

In this exercise, you will delete unneeded controls, add controls, and rearrange and resize controls to produce a more attractive, well-balanced report.

Delete a Report Control

1. Display the **Invoice Details Report Q1 2013** in Layout View.
2. Follow these steps to delete and rearrange report controls:

Ⓐ Click the first **Summary for 'InvNum'** control and tap [Delete].

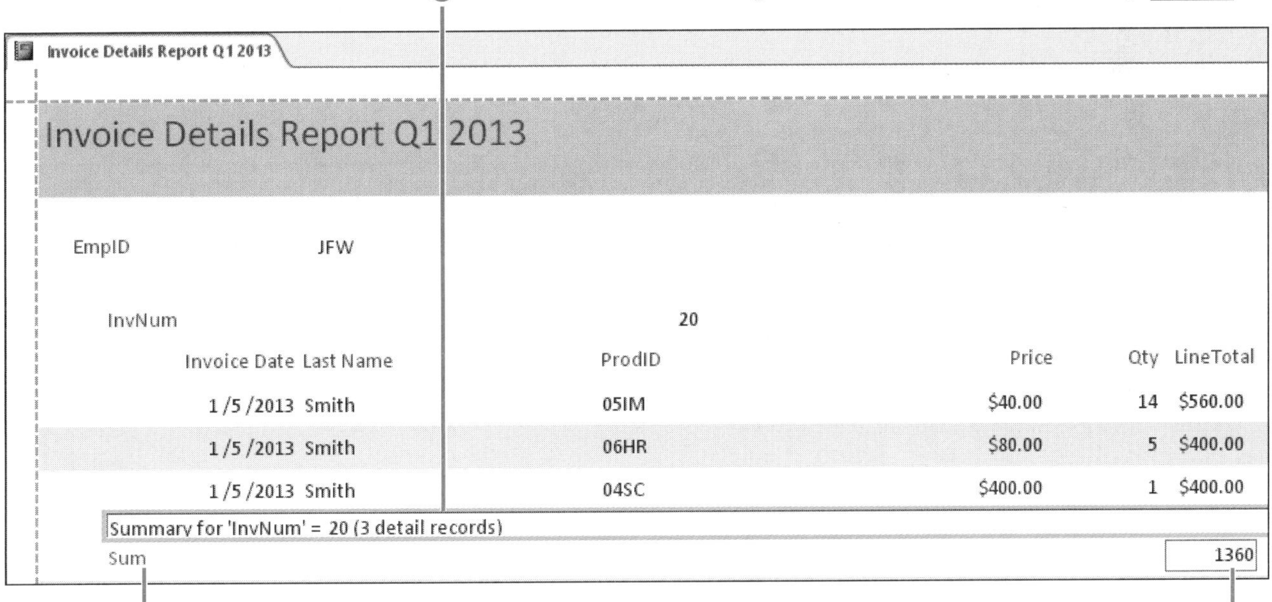

Ⓑ Select the **Sum** label and tap [→] to move the label so it is lined up under the **Qty** label.

Ⓒ With the **Sum** label still selected, press [Shift] and click the corresponding **Sum** text box. Tap [↑] three times to move both Sum controls up.

The right side of the page should look similar to this figure. More records appear on the page.

Price	Qty	LineTotal
$40.00	14	$560.00
$80.00	5	$400.00
$400.00	1	$400.00
	Sum	1360

3. Scroll down to the end of the first employee's records.

4. Follow the procedure outlined in **step 2** to delete the **Summary for 'EmpID'** control and move the **Sum** label.

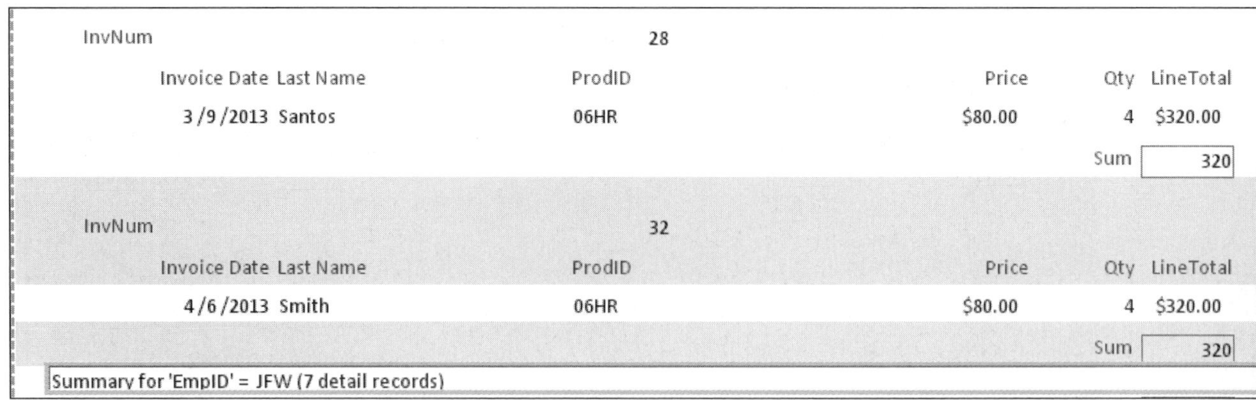

5. Click the **Price** label in the InvNumHeader section. Press Ctrl and click the **Price** text box in the Detail section.
6. If the Property Sheet is not shown, choose **Design→Tools→Property Sheet**.
7. Follow these steps to resize and align controls:

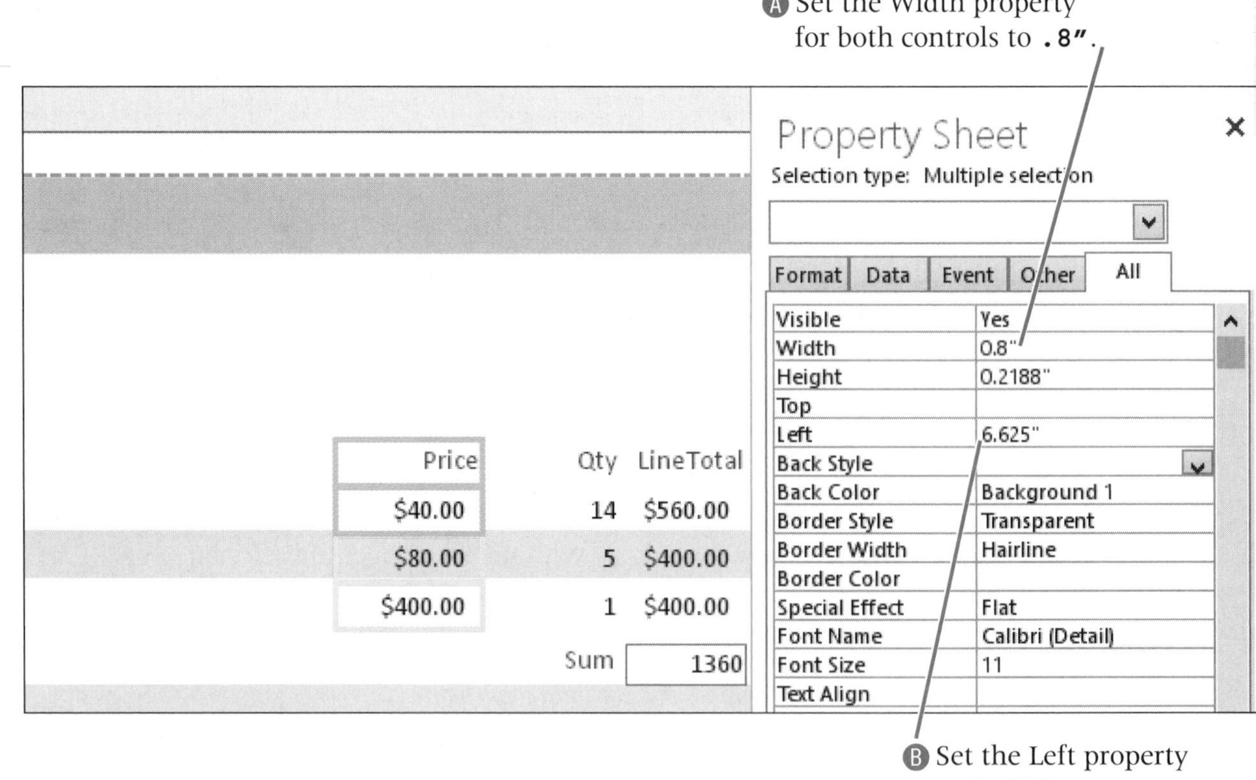

Add a Report Control

8. Switch to **Design View**.
9. Click the **="Page"** control in the Page Footer section to select it.
10. Type **2"** for **Width** property.
11. Click in the **Selection Type** drop-down list box at the top of the Property Sheet and choose **Report**.
12. Type **9"** for the **Width** property.

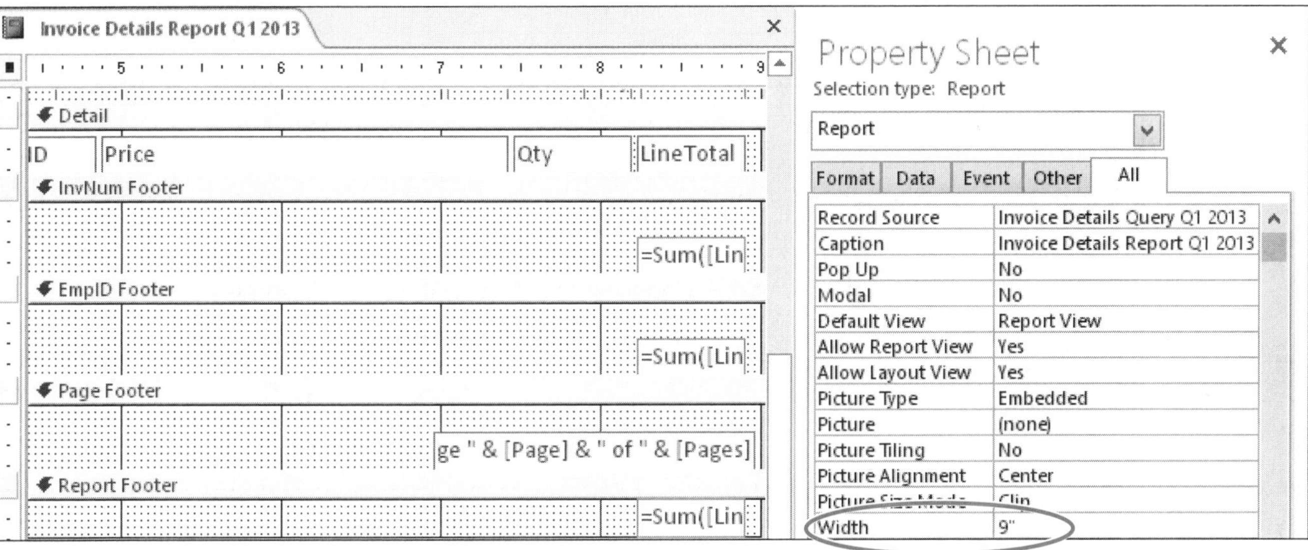

13. Choose **Design→Tools→Add Existing Fields** to open the Field List and click **Show All Tables**.
14. Double-click the **Products** table name in the Field List to show the table fields.

15. Follow these steps to add the ProdDescription controls to the report:

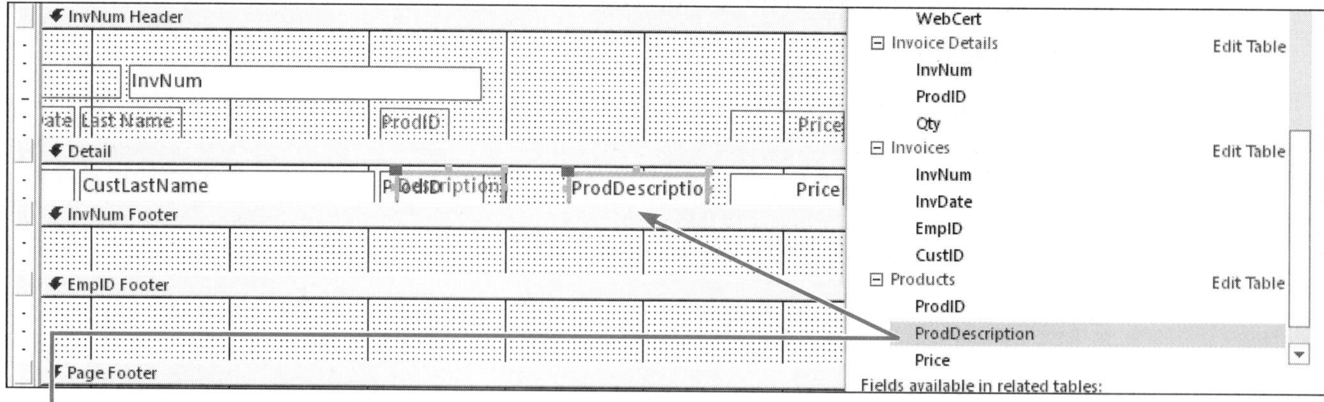

Ⓐ Drag **ProdDescription** from the Field List into the Detail section between **ProdID** and **Price**.

Ⓑ Right-click the Description label and choose **Cut**.

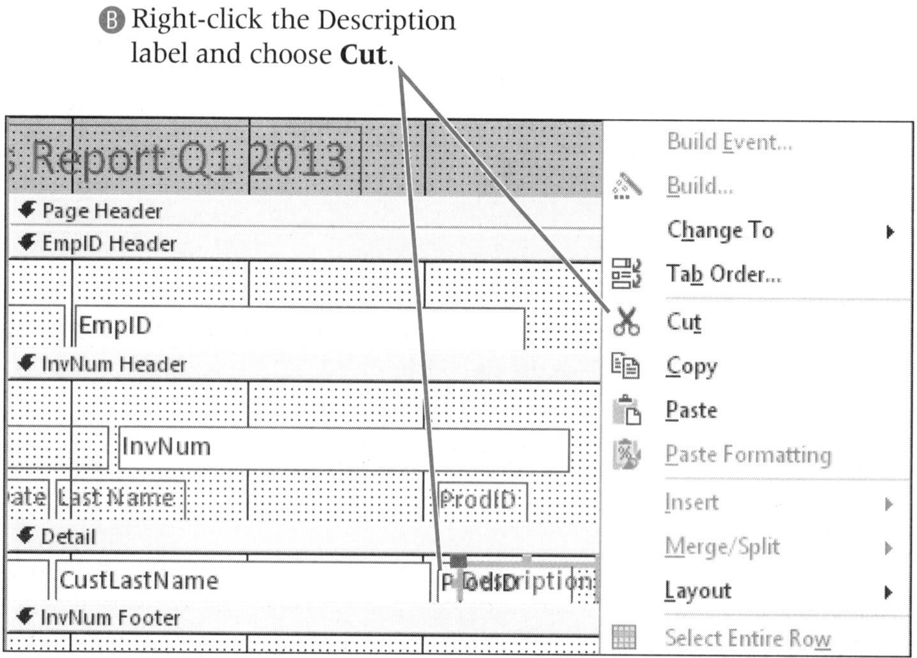

Ⓒ Right-click the InvNum Header section bar and choose **Paste**.

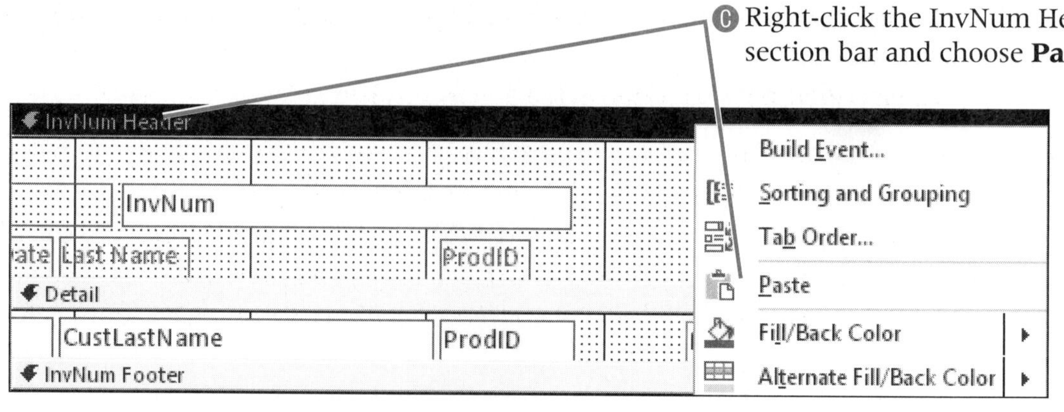

16. Drag the **Description** label in the Header section so that it is lined up above the ProdDescription text box in the Detail section.

17. Close the **Field List**.

18. Switch to **Layout View**.

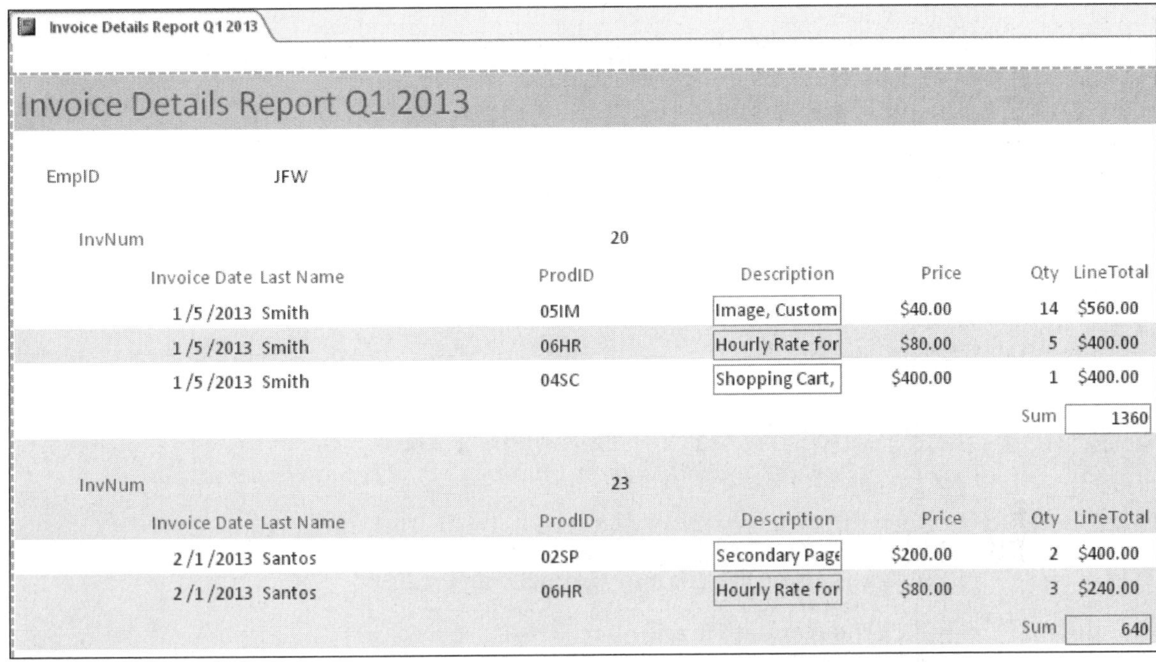

Invoice Details Report Q1 2013
Invoice Details Report Q1 2013
EmpID JFW
InvNum 20
Invoice Date Last Name ProdID Description Price Qty LineTotal
1/5/2013 Smith 05IM Image, Custom $40.00 14 $560.00
1/5/2013 Smith 06HR Hourly Rate for $80.00 5 $400.00
1/5/2013 Smith 04SC Shopping Cart, $400.00 1 $400.00
Sum 1360
InvNum 23
Invoice Date Last Name ProdID Description Price Qty LineTotal
2/1/2013 Santos 02SP Secondary Page $200.00 2 $400.00
2/1/2013 Santos 06HR Hourly Rate for $80.00 3 $240.00
Sum 640

At this point, your report begs for alignment and resizing. However, you still have controls to add, so you will wait until all items are on the report before making alignment and size adjustments.

Adding a Logo to the Report

Video Library http://labyrinthelab.com/videos Video Number: AC13-V0506

Adding a visual element or image is especially useful when creating forms and reports. A graphic that identifies the business, such as a corporate logo, can make forms and reports look more professional and visually appealing. Access provides two basic tools for adding graphics to a report or a form:

- **Image or Insert Image control:** Enables you to add and position a graphic on any report section
- **Logo control:** Places a logo in the Report Header section of a report

An inserted image is saved in the Image Gallery, which will make it easy to find it again later. Simply click Insert Image and the Image Gallery is displayed.

When you add a logo using the Logo control from the Ribbon, Access automatically adds a Title control. You can then type in your new report title. If you want to move the logo and title to separate locations, choose Arrange→Table→Remove Layout to detach and unlink the controls.

QUICK REFERENCE	ADDING A GRAPHIC TO A REPORT OR FORM
Task	**Procedure**
Add a logo to a report or form	■ Display the form or report in Design View. ■ Choose Design→Header/Footer→Logo.
Add a picture to a report or form:	■ Display the report or form in Design View. ■ Choose Design→Controls→Insert Image.

DEVELOP YOUR SKILLS AC05-D05

Add a Logo to the Page Header

In this exercise you will add a logo to your report's page header.

1. Display the **Invoice Details Report Q1 2013** in Design View.
2. Choose **Design→Header/Footer→**Logo. Navigate to and double-click **WWD-Logo.bmp** in the **AC2013 Lesson 05** folder.
   Access places the logo in the upper-left corner of the Report Header section.
3. Open the Property Sheet and type **4** for the **Left** property.
4. Type **.8** for the **Width** and **Height** properties.
5. Click the **Report Header** bar.

The new logo added to the report header.

6. Save the report.

Adding a Title or Subtitle to a Report

Video Library http://labyrinthelab.com/videos Video Number: AC13-V0507

FROM THE RIBBON
Design→Header/Footer→Title to add a title to a report

Titles identify the purpose of forms and reports and often contain only the name of the company. However, a more effective report also includes a subtitle that explains what the report is about, such as Invoice Summary or Customer Addresses. You can use Design View or Layout View to add a Label control containing the title or subtitle. If you create a report from scratch, you can use the Title tool to add a formatted title to the appropriate section of a form or report. You can then change the text and formatting using tools on the Ribbon and Property Sheet.

Using the Property Sheet

The Property Sheet contains property settings that control the way database objects look and function, such as font family, font size, font color, border style, and so on. You have probably used the Property Sheet to format data in tables and forms. Many of these same properties are available for controlling data display in reports.

DEVELOP YOUR SKILLS AC05-D06

Add a Report Title/Subtitle and Format Text

In this exercise, you will use Layout View to add a report title and subtitle. Then, you will format text using the Property Sheet and the Ribbon.

1. Display the **Invoice Details Report Q1 2013** in Design View.
2. If necessary, choose **Design→Tools→Property Sheet** to open the Property Sheet.
3. Select the **title** control (Invoice Details Report Q1 2013) in the Report Header and type `Winchester Web Design` as the *Caption* in the Property Sheet.
4. Click the **Report Header** section bar and type `.9` as the Height property to expand the section for a subtitle and logo.
5. Choose **Design→Controls→Label** Aa. Click and drag to draw a new label for the subtitle (under the report title).

Draw the new Label under the Title and release the mouse.

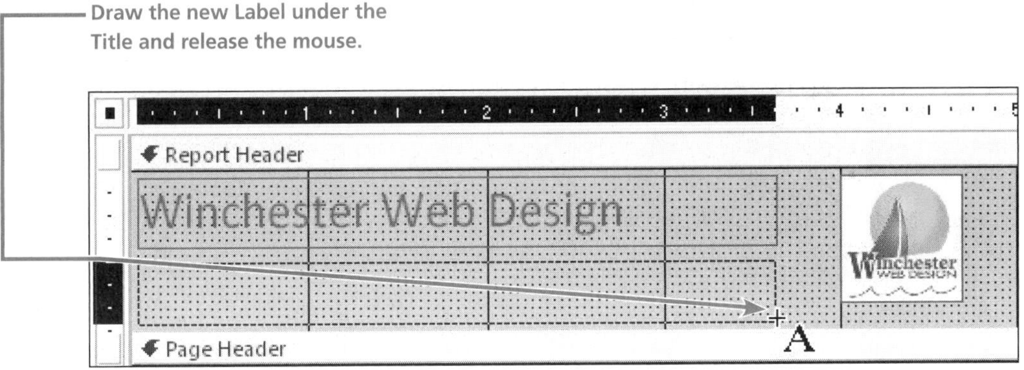

6. Type `Invoices for Q1 2013` as the subtitle; tap Enter.
7. Set the following properties for the new subtitle:

PROPERTY	SETTING
Width	3.5
Height	.35
Special Effect	Shadowed
Font Size	18
Text Align	Center
Font Weight	Bold

8. Select the **Winchester Web Design** title.

Access 2013

9. Set the following properties for the title:

PROPERTY	SETTING
Width	3.5
Font Size	22
Text Align	Center
Font Weight	Bold

10. Select the logo and type `.8` for both the **Width** and **Height** properties.

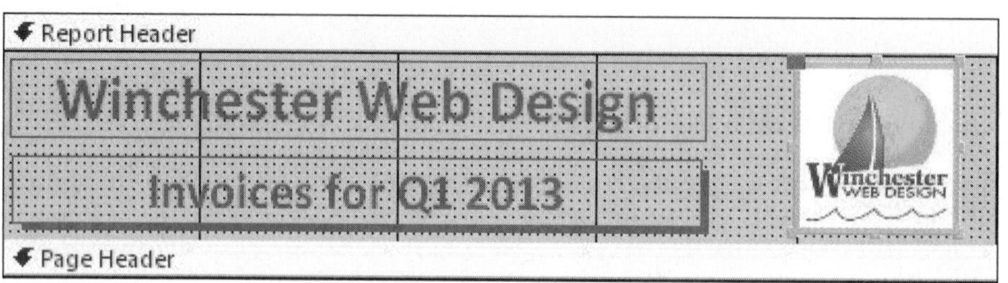

11. Save your changes.

Formatting Controls

Video Library http://labyrinthelab.com/videos Video Number: AC13-V0508

After using the Report Wizard to set up the basic report, you can format, align, size, and position the controls using the same procedures you use to format controls on forms.

Selecting Controls

Just as with forms, each report control contains two parts: the control label and the control text box. To select multiple controls at the same time, you have several options: Clicking each control individually, while pressing [Shift] or [Ctrl]; selecting all controls along a horizontal or vertical line by clicking on the horizontal or vertical rulers; or lassoing—or outlining—an area of the report to select all controls within the area.

Sizing Controls

It is important to ensure that the data values are fully displayed in a report, while at the same time taking care not to leave unsightly and unnecessary blank space between columns. To accomplish this, you must resize controls on the report. It is best to size controls in Layout View because you can see the actual field values for multiple records.

In Layout View, active—or selected—controls display a thicker border than inactive controls. Use these borders to size the control. As you drag the border to resize the active record, the controls for that field in all other records also resize.

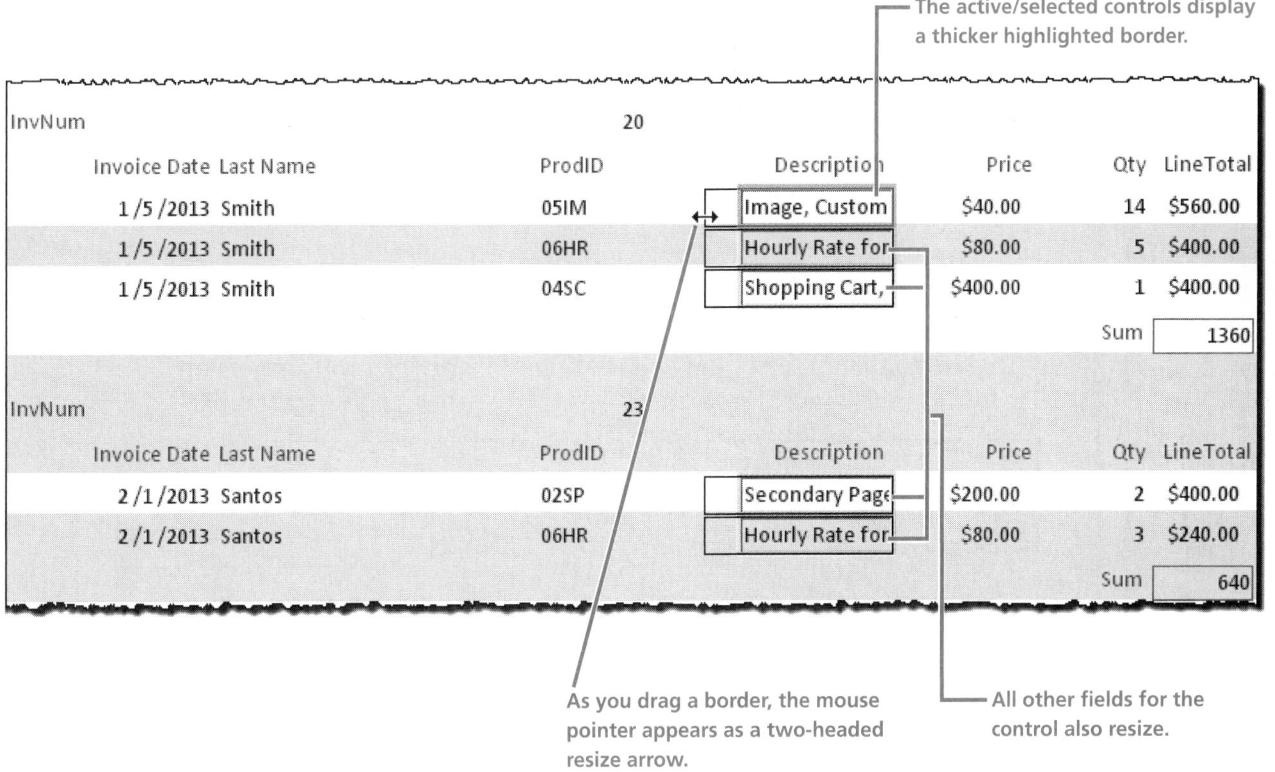

Identifying Mouse Shapes

The mouse pointer shape is important when working in Design View and Layout View.

REPORT MOUSE POINTERS	
Field Property	**Description**
✚	Section resize pointer
⟷	Resize a control
⇖	Select control to drag to desired location
✥	Select and move a control
⬇	Select a column
➡	Select a row

DEVELOP YOUR SKILLS AC05-D07

Size, Align, and Format Report Controls

In this exercise, you will use both Design View and Layout View to reposition and align controls. You will also size the controls to better accommodate the data values.

The Invoice Details Report Q1 2013 report should be opened in Design View.

1. Follow these steps to move the controls in the InvNum Header section:

Ⓐ Click the vertical ruler in front of the **InvNum** label to select the two InvNum controls in the InvNum Header.

Ⓑ Tap [↑] five times to nudge the selected controls up close to the section bar.

Ⓒ Click the vertical ruler in front of the **Invoice Date** label to select the lower row of controls in the InvNum Header. Tap [↑] five times to nudge the selected controls up.

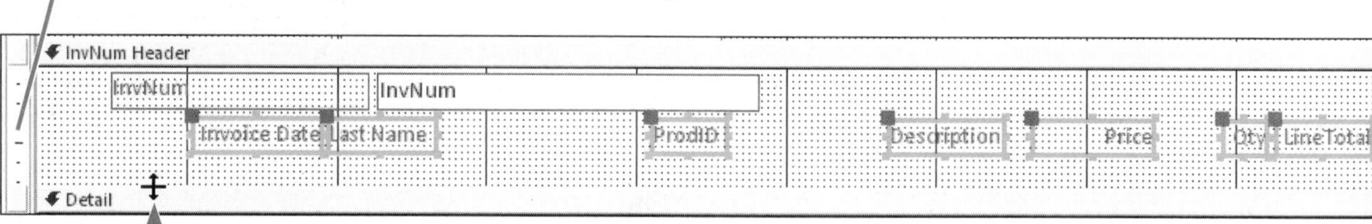

Ⓓ Hover the mouse pointer over the top of the **Detail** section bar until it becomes a Section Resize Pointer and drag the bar up to just under the lower row of controls.

2. If the Property Sheet is not open, choose **Design→Tools→Property Sheet**.

3. Follow these steps to move controls in a report section:

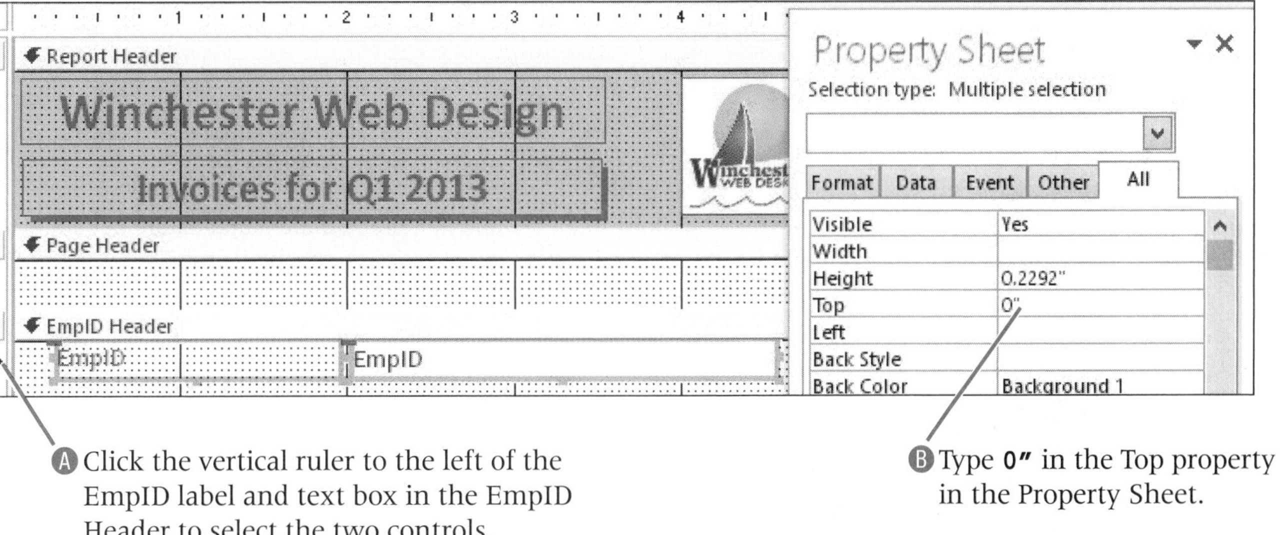

Ⓐ Click the vertical ruler to the left of the EmpID label and text box in the EmpID Header to select the two controls.

Ⓑ Type **0"** in the Top property in the Property Sheet.

4. Follow these steps to resize the EmpID Header section:

Ⓐ Click the **EmpID Header** section bar to select the section (*GroupHeader0*).

Ⓑ Type **.33** in the Height property to shorten the section and tap Enter.

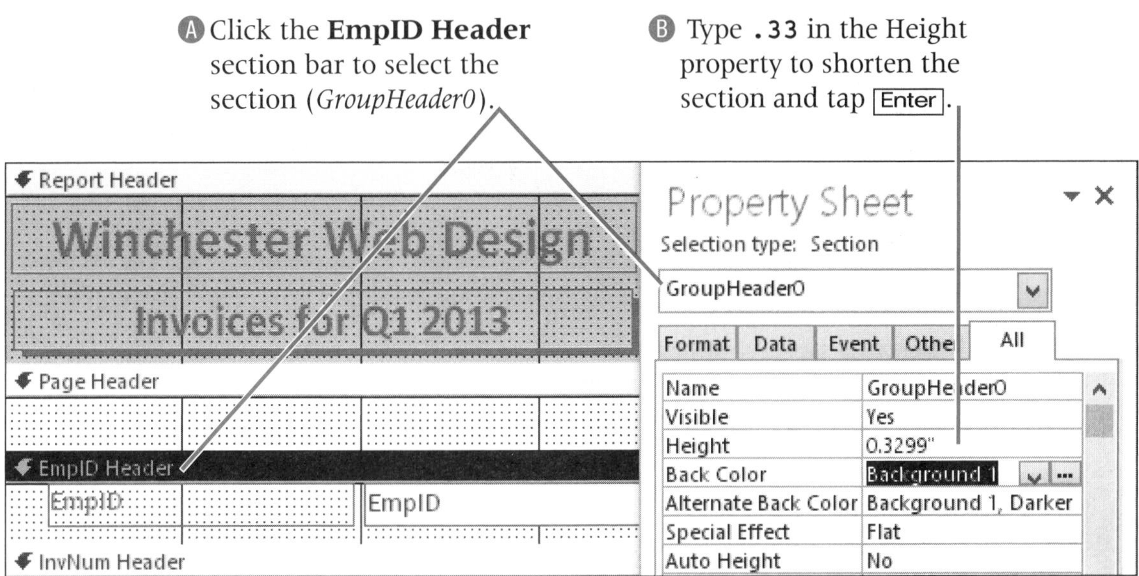

Access sometimes changes a precise property value that you type, so don't worry if your Height property differs slightly from the figure.

5. Switch to **Layout View**.

Access 2013

6. Follow these steps to size the controls:

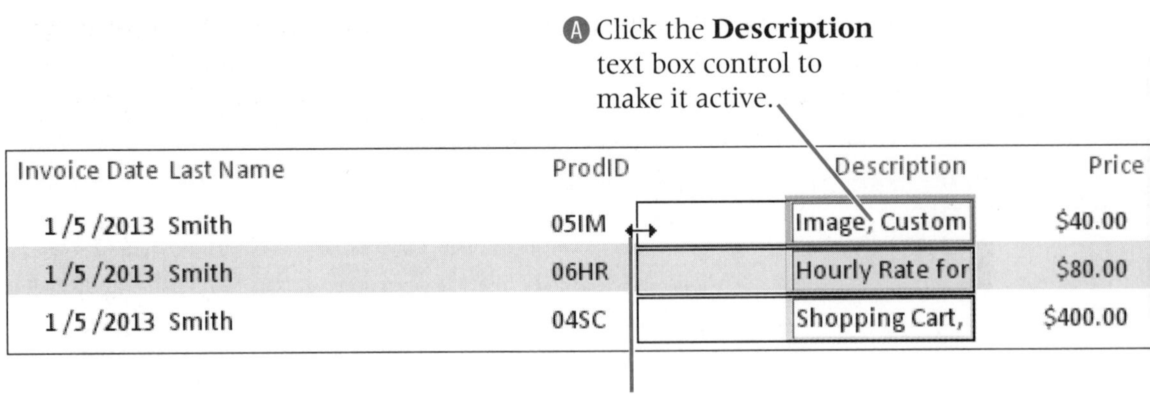

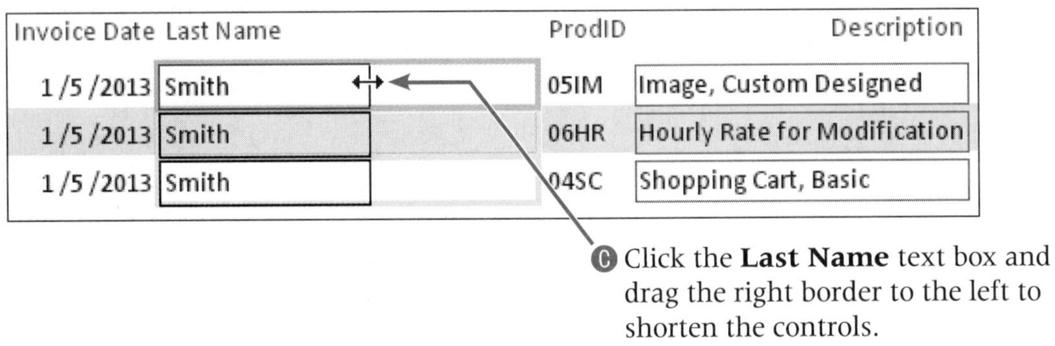

Leave the Last Name text boxes wide enough to display longer last names.

7. Select the **Last Name** label, press [Shift] and click a **Last Name** text box.

8. Tap [→] to nudge the selected controls to the right.

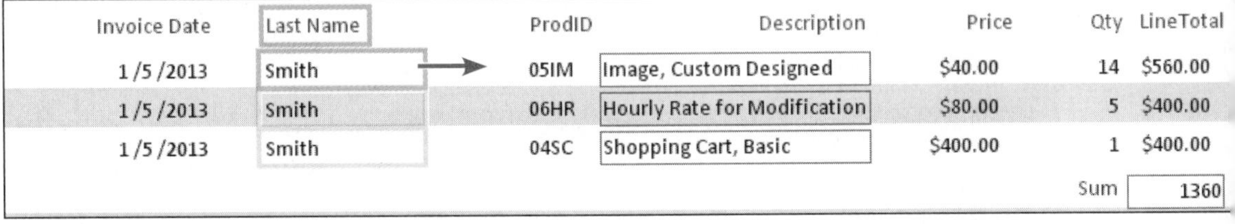

Sometimes while moving a group of controls in Layout View, the screen scrolls down to the end. If this occurs, scroll back up and continue moving the controls.

9. Select the **ProdID** labels and text boxes and nudge them to the left.

10. Select the **InvNum** text box and use the resizing arrow to make it narrower.

11. Follow these steps to align the InvNum text box and Description label:

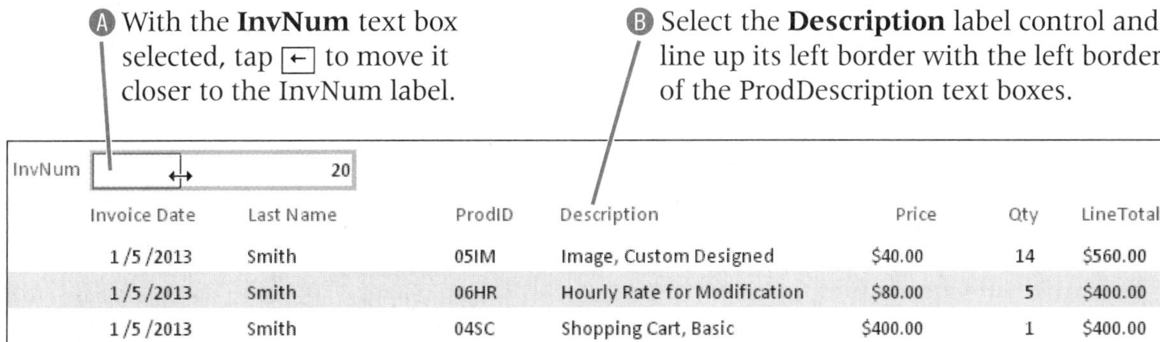

12. Scroll to the end of the report. Click the **Sum** calculated control for the InvNum group; press [Shift], click the **Sum** text box for the EmpID group and click the calculated control text box for the grand total at the end of the report.

13. Choose **Format→Number→**[ ]**→Currency**.

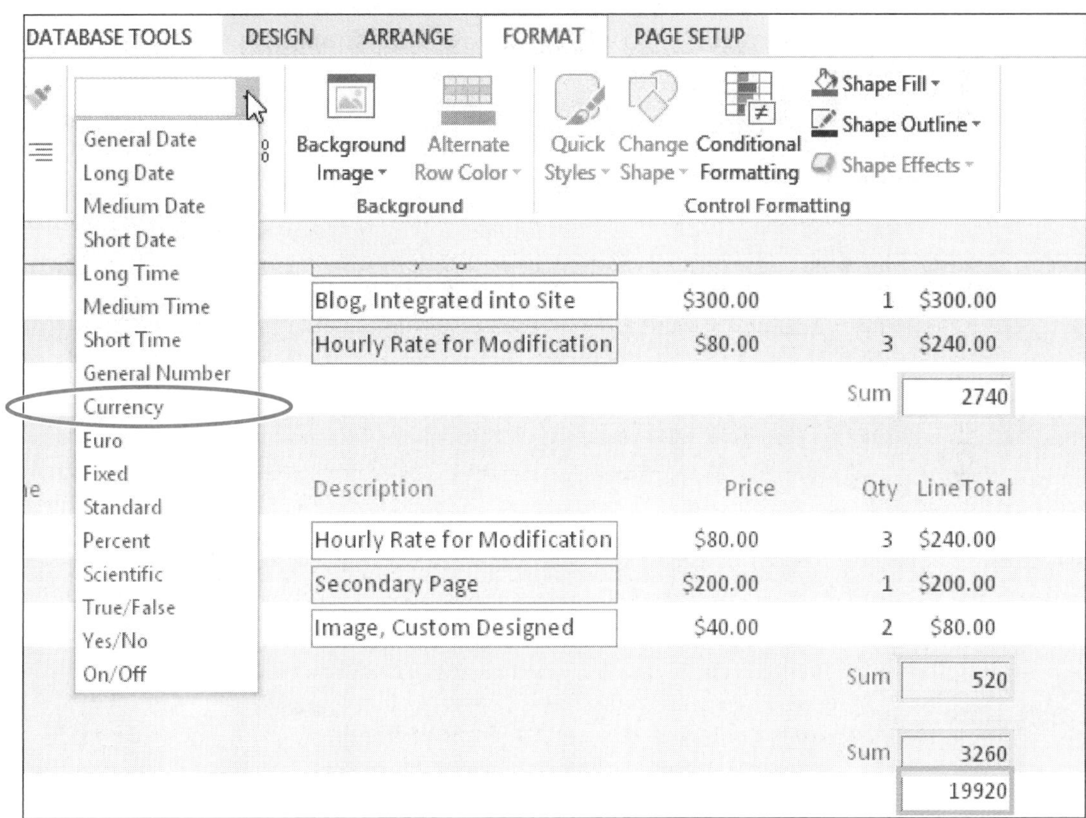

When you apply formatting, the fields may no longer fit in the text box. When a value is too large for the text box, it fills the box with the # symbol.

14. Follow these steps to resize the Currency controls:

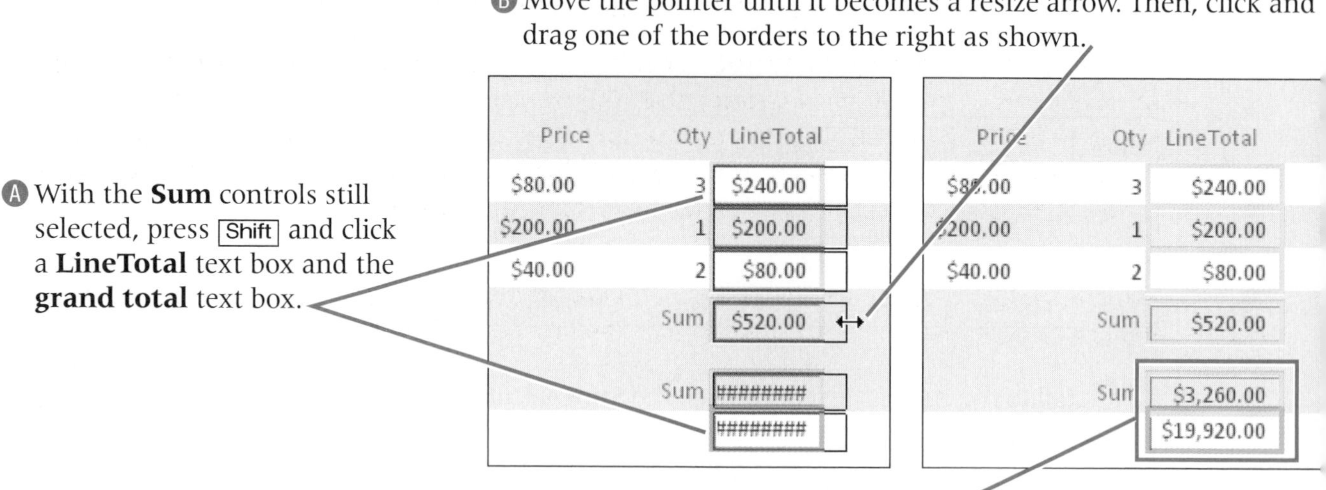

B Move the pointer until it becomes a resize arrow. Then, click and drag one of the borders to the right as shown.
A With the **Sum** controls still selected, press Shift and click a **LineTotal** text box and the **grand total** text box.
Price
Qty
LineTotal
$80.00
3
$240.00
$200.00
1
$200.00
$40.00
2
$80.00
Sum
$520.00
Sum
########
########
$3,260.00
$19,920.00
C The values display correctly.

15. Select the calculated controls. Choose **Transparent** for the Border Style property for the selected Sum controls.

16. Select the **Description** text box and set its Border Style property to **Transparent**.

17. Switch to **Print Preview**. Use the navigation buttons to page through the report.

Winchester Web Design

Invoices for Q1 2013

EmpID JFW

InvNum 20

Invoice Date	Last Name	ProdID	Description	Price	Qty	LineTotal
1/5/2013	Smith	05IM	Image, Custom Designed	$40.00	14	$560.00
1/5/2013	Smith	06HR	Hourly Rate for Modification	$80.00	5	$400.00
1/5/2013	Smith	04SC	Shopping Cart, Basic	$400.00	1	$400.00
					Sum	$1,360.00

InvNum 23

Invoice Date	Last Name	ProdID	Description	Price	Qty	LineTotal
2/1/2013	Santos	02SP	Secondary Page	$200.00	2	$400.00
2/1/2013	Santos	06HR	Hourly Rate for Modification	$80.00	3	$240.00
					Sum	$640.00

InvNum 28

Invoice Date	Last Name	ProdID	Description	Price	Qty	LineTotal
3/9/2013	Santos	06HR	Hourly Rate for Modification	$80.00	4	$320.00
					Sum	$320.00

InvNum 32

Invoice Date	Last Name	ProdID	Description	Price	Qty	LineTotal
4/6/2013	Smith	06HR	Hourly Rate for Modification	$80.00	4	$320.00
					Sum	$320.00
					Sum	$2,640.00

Tuesday, April 2, 2013 Page 1 of 4

18. Close **Print Preview**. Then, save and close the report.

Applying Themes

Video Library http://labyrinthelab.com/videos Video Number: AC13-V0509

Formatting a report using the Themes, or existing style schemes, available in Access can help make a report more readable and attractive. Themes contain design elements such as background color, font family and font size, and other properties to quickly format an entire report without the tedious formatting of each individual control. Because reports are designed for printing, the report Themes are much more subtle than for forms.

Caution should be used when applying Themes. Applying a Theme reformats all objects in the active database with the color scheme defined in the Theme.

QUICK REFERENCE	APPLYING THEMES TO FORMS AND REPORTS
Task	**Procedure**
Apply a Theme	■ Prepare the desired report or form. ■ Display the report or form in Design View or Layout View. ■ Choose Design→Themes→Themes. ■ Select the desired Theme.

DEVELOP YOUR SKILLS AC05-D08

Apply Themes to a Report

In this exercise, you will apply a Theme to the Invoice Details Report Q1 2013 report.

1. Open and display the **Invoice Details Report Q1 2013** report in Design View.
2. Choose **Design→Themes→Themes** and hover over each Theme's thumbnail to see how the report changes.
3. Choose your favorite **Theme** from the palette.

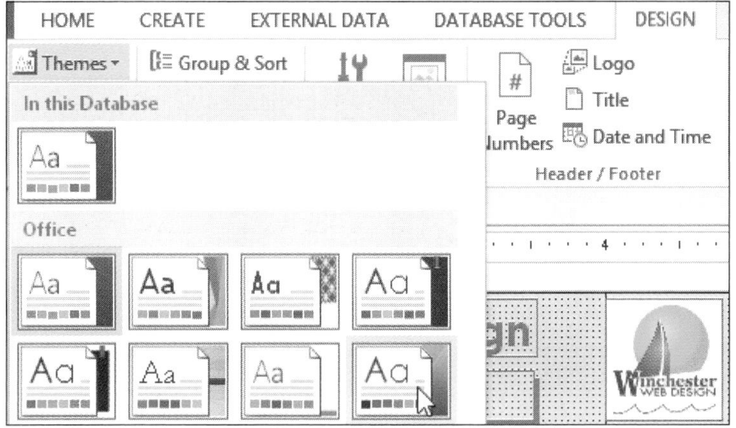

Depending on the Theme you select, you may see little or no difference until you display the report in Layout or Report View. You may also have to readjust control sizes because of font changes.

4. Save changes to the report.

Exploring Other Report Tools

Video Library http://labyrinthelab.com/videos Video Number: AC13-V0510

One important difference between customizing forms and reports is the general layout of the objects. Reports normally display control labels in the Report Header section to serve as column headings. Control text boxes appear in the Detail section. In addition, when you add group summary data in a report, Access displays Group sections that hold group titles, group field control labels, and group summary data.

Adding Report Sorting and Grouping Levels

A group is a collection of records that has at least one data element or key field in common. For example, if you group the data using the Employee ID field, you create a report that shows the total sales for each employee. If you want to display all vendors with offices in the same state, you could group by the State field. Or, you could group by the Vendor field to see all transactions with a particular vendor. A group consists of a Group Header, records, and a Group Footer. Grouping records enables you to separate records visually on a report and display introductory and summary data for each group. Access allows you to include totals by group level.

Most novices and professionals sort through queries and add grouping levels using the Report Wizard, which is far easier and more efficient. However, you can also sort and add grouping levels—with or without totals—in Design View.

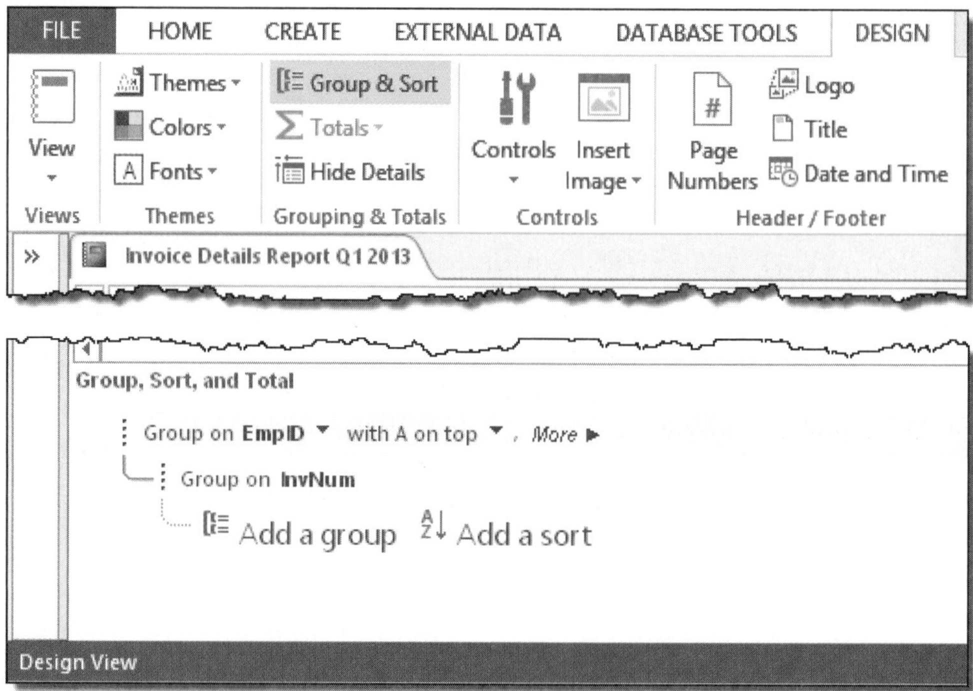

Records are grouped by each employee, then by invoice number.

Using the Group, Sort, and Total Pane

The Group, Sort, and Total pane allows you to add groups and sort settings or review them after you set them. You can also add groups using commands on the shortcut menus and then review them in the Group, Sort, and Total pane. You can set properties in the Group, Sort, and Total pane to display or hide group headers and footers. Additional properties enable you to tell Access how to group data, set a grouping interval, and set group properties for keeping items in a group together on a page.

FROM THE RIBBON

Design→Grouping & Totals→Group & Sort to add group/sort settings

Working with Group Sections

Manually setting a group and sort order on a report in Design View does not automatically place a control in the Group column heading. It simply sets the grouping and sorting order and creates a header section on the report to hold the controls. After manually setting the group, you must move the group field (i.e., the EmpID text box when you group by employees) from the Detail section to the Group Header section (i.e., the EmpID Header which is created when you group by EmpID). By placing the field text box control in the Group Header section, Access attractively arranges all entries by the group field you choose and the Group Header section prints only at the start of a new group value.

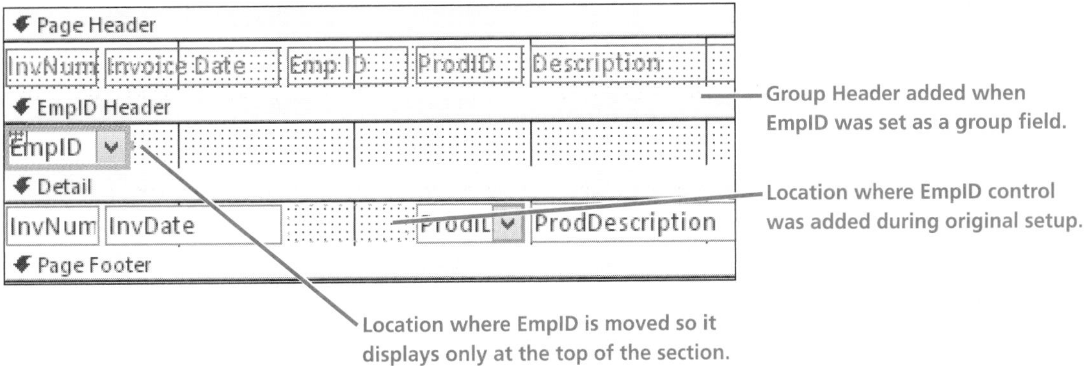

Creating Multi-Level Groupings

Access provides multi-level grouping for records on a report. If, for example, you want to print invoices that group items ordered by invoice for each employee, you would use two-level grouping. You can set multiple groups using the Sort, Group, and Total pane or you can right-click an empty area of the report design grid or a section bar and choose Sorting and Grouping from the shortcut menu.

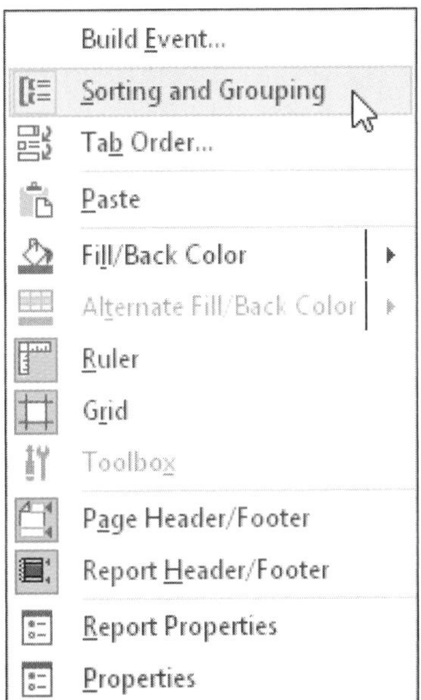

Access 2013

QUICK REFERENCE	ADDING SORT AND GROUP LEVELS
Task	**Procedure**
Display the Group pane using the Ribbon in Layout or Design View	■ Display the report in Design View. ■ Choose Design→Grouping & Totals→Group & Sort.
Add group level	■ Right-click the field on which you want to group data records. ■ Choose Group On Field Name.
Add sort order	■ Right-click the field on which you want to sort data or groups. ■ Choose Sort Ascending or Sort Descending.

The properties you see when you right-click a field name to group or sort by depends on the data type of the field.

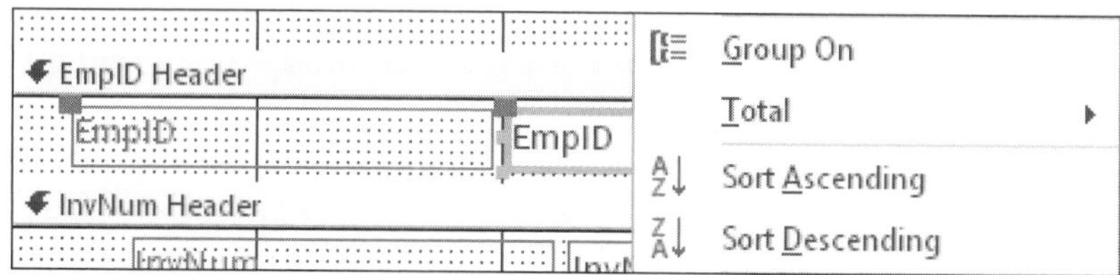

Sorting Group Control Levels

If a group control level, such as EmpID, is not sorted, it will not group properly. For example, assume Anderson was the salesperson for the first two invoices, and Williams was the salesperson for the third invoice, and Anderson was the salesperson for the fourth invoice. As soon as Access sees a different employee (Anderson changes to Williams) it will assume that it has arrived at a new group and will total the records for the preceding group—Anderson's first two sales, but it will not include Anderson's sales for the fourth invoice in the current group.

There are a couple ways to resolve this. The data could be presorted in the table or the query on which the report was based. Alternately, the data could be sorted by adding a Sort Level Control in the report.

DEVELOP YOUR SKILLS AC05-D09

Display the Group and Sort Pane

In this exercise, you will display the group and sort pane for the Invoice Details Report Q1 2013 report.

1. Display the **Invoice Details Report Q1 2013** in Design View.
2. Choose **Design→Grouping & Totals→Group & Sort** to open the Group, Sort, and Total pane.

3. Follow these steps to explore the Group, Sort, and Total pane.

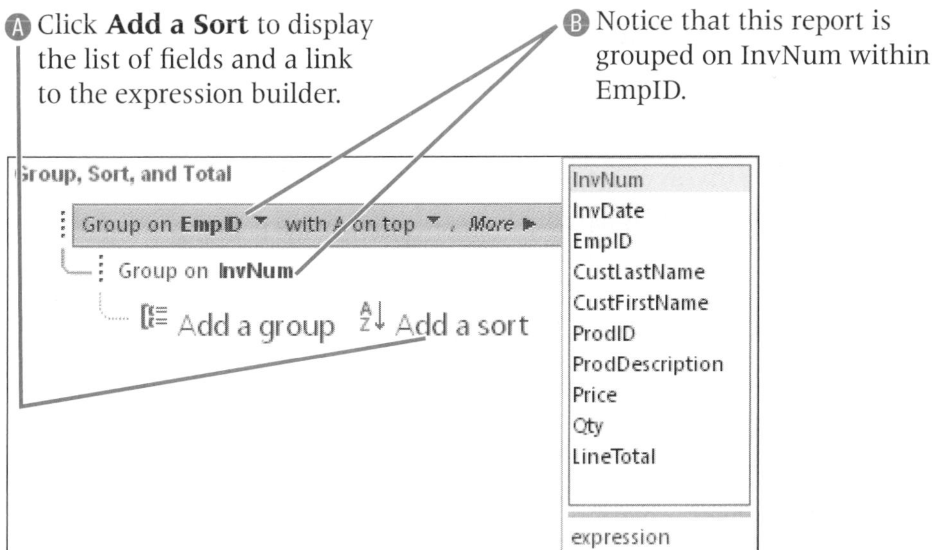

4. Tap Esc to exit without saving any changes. Close the **Group, Sort, and Total** pane.
5. Close the **Invoice Details Report Q1 2013** report. *Do not* save the file.

Adding Date and Time Data to a Report

Video Library http://labyrinthelab.com/videos Video Number: AC13-V0511

Keeping track of the most current report can be a challenge. Adding a date and/or time to the footer section of a report can help you track reports. When you add the date and time controls to an existing report, Access places the controls in the Report Header section by default. You can either move them or leave them in the Report Header.

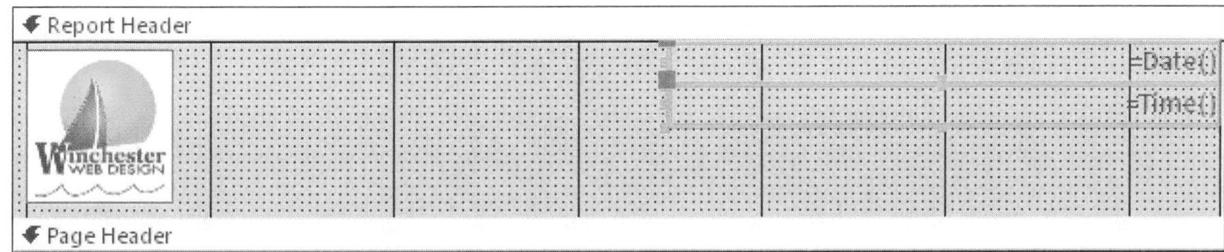

The Date and Time controls in the Report Header section.

QUICK REFERENCE	ADDING DATE AND TIME FIELDS TO A REPORT
Task	**Procedure**
Add a date field	■ Choose Design→Header/Footer→Date and Time. ■ Check the Include Date checkbox, select the format option, and click OK.
Add a time field	■ Choose Design→Header/Footer→Date and Time. ■ Check the Include Time checkbox, select the format option and click OK.

Access 2013

DEVELOP YOUR SKILLS AC05-D10

Add a Date Field to Page Header Section

In this exercise, you will delete the date from the Page Footer section and add the date to the Page Header section of your report.

1. Display the **Invoice Details Report Q1 2013** in Design View.
2. Follow these steps to delete the date from the Page Footer section:

Ⓐ Right-click the **=Now()** control in the Page Footer of the report.

Ⓑ Choose **Delete**.

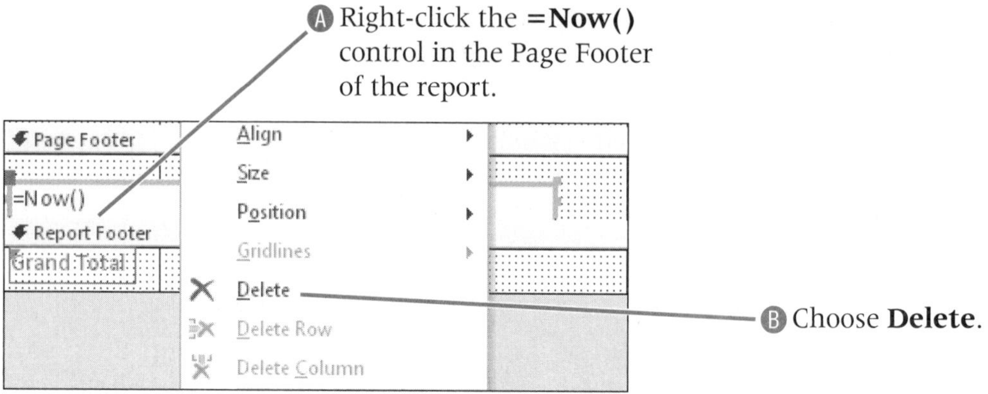

3. Follow these steps to add date and time controls to the Report Header:

Ⓐ Choose **Design→Header/ Footer→Date and Time**.

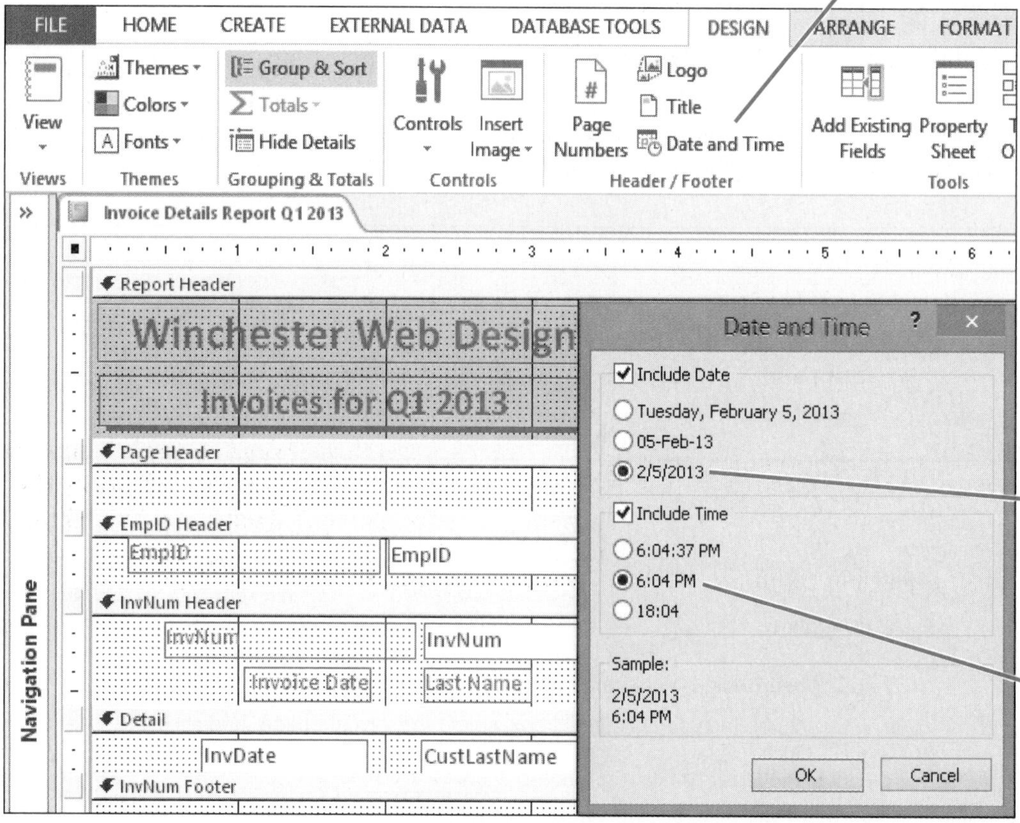

Ⓑ Choose the **mm/dd/yyyy** Date Format option.

Ⓒ Choose the middle Time Format option; click **OK**.

The date and time you see onscreen will vary from the figure.

4. Switch to **Report View** to see the new date and time controls.
5. Save your changes to the report.

Adding Page Breaks to a Report

Video Library http://labyrinthelab.com/videos Video Number: AC13-V0512

When you have a report with grouped data, such as EmpID, you may want to start a new page when the EmpID changes so each employee is shown on its own page or set of pages.

DEVELOP YOUR SKILLS AC05-D11

Add Page Break Controls to a Report

In this exercise, you will set page breaks to print each employee's summary records on a separate page or set of pages.

1. Display the **Invoice Details Report Q1 2013** in Design View.
2. Follow these steps to insert a page break after each EmpID group:

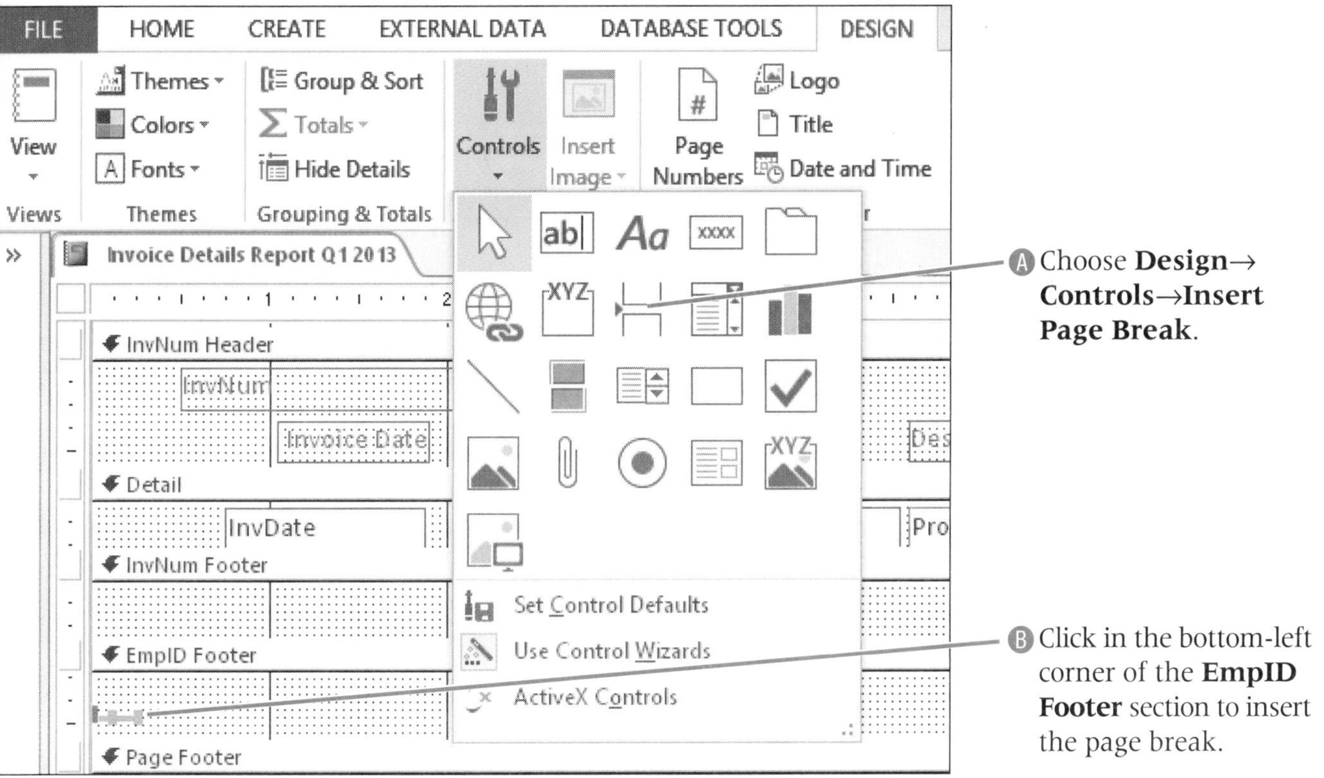

Ⓐ Choose **Design→Controls→Insert Page Break**.

Ⓑ Click in the bottom-left corner of the **EmpID Footer** section to insert the page break.

Access 2013

3. Switch to **Print Preview**.

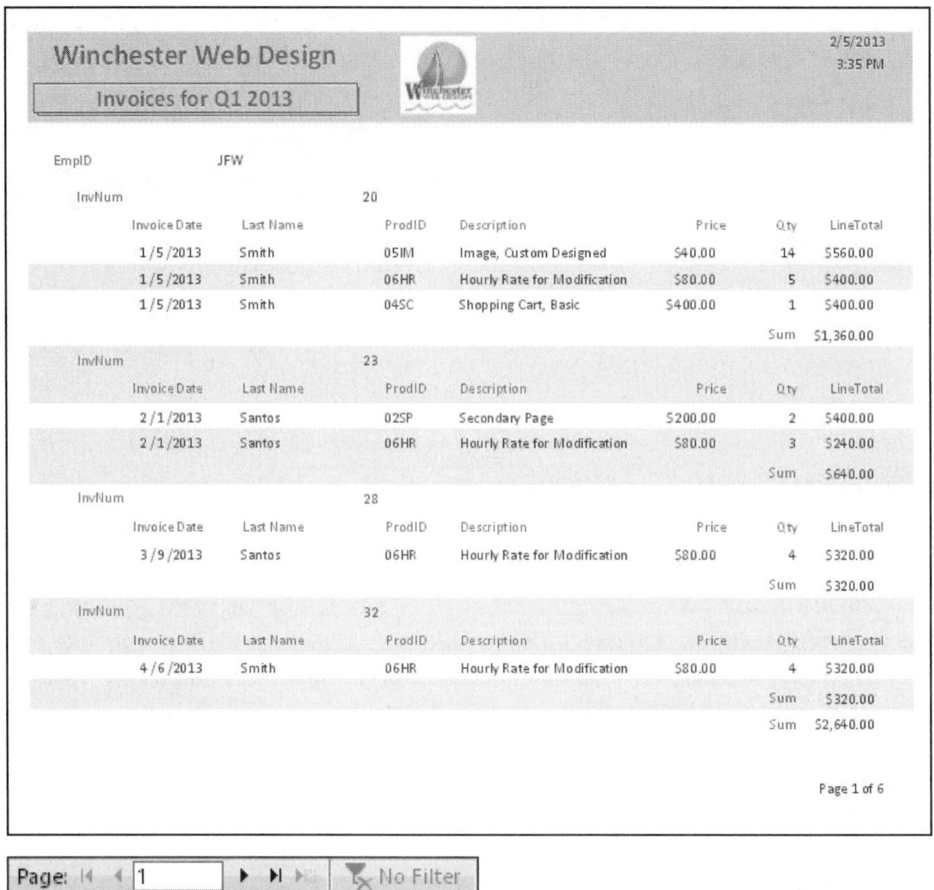

4. Click **Next Page** in the navigation bar to page through the report.
   No two employee's records appear on the same page. The grand total is shown on the last page.

If you want a report header to appear on every page, select all the report header controls, and cut and paste them into the page header section.

5. Save the report.

Printing Reports

Video Library http://labyrinthelab.com/videos Video Number: AC13-V0513

After you create and format a report, set grouping and sorting levels, and add summary controls, you are ready to print the report. Procedures for printing in Access are similar to those in other Microsoft applications (e.g., Word, Excel, and PowerPoint). For example, you can print individual pages, all pages, or a set range of pages. Print options in Access may vary slightly with different database objects.

Setting Report Print Layout

Commands on the Page Setup tab enable you to set up the basic page layout for a report. You can use these commands to change the paper size and orientation, to set margins and columns, or to print data only—leaving off the design elements and header controls.

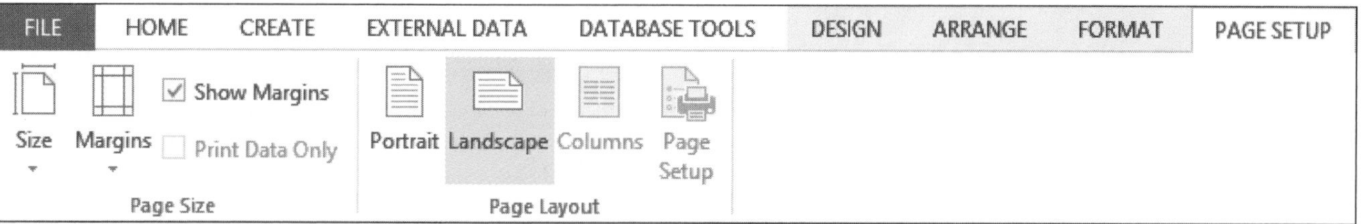

The Page Layout tools on the Page Setup tab.

Controlling Page Breaks

If you have used Word to create long documents, you know that controlling page breaks is important to prevent an individual line of a paragraph (often called an orphan) from appearing on a page by itself. The same is true for printing reports. You want to adjust settings so that a group header section stays with the first record in the report, or to prevent an individual record or line from appearing on a page by itself. Access offers tools to help you control what is contained in report sections and produce a better organized report.

Setting Page Breaks

Setting a page break for a report is different from setting a hard page break in a Word document or Excel worksheet. Because your report design contains controls for defining the report layout, it can be challenging to determine how many records will appear for each group—each employee will have a different number of sales. As a result, setting a page break is an uncertain way to try to control page printouts.

Setting Group Controls

Instead of setting page breaks for printing reports, Access lets you control how you want to keep groups together on report pages. Setting these controls prevents lone headers on report pages and enables you to keep each group on a single page. Setting these controls also reduces excessive pages.

QUICK REFERENCE	PRINTING REPORTS
Task	**Procedure**
Display Print Preview	■ Choose File→Print→Print Preview.
Print specific pages	■ Choose File→Print→Print to display the Print dialog box. ■ Select the Pages option and enter the page numbers you want to print.
Print all report pages	■ Choose File→Print→Print to display the Print dialog box. ■ Click OK.

Access 2013

DEVELOP YOUR SKILLS AC05-D12

Set Print Options

In this exercise, you will set up group controls for printing and view a report in Print Preview.

1. Display the **Invoice Details Report Q1 2013** in Design View.
2. Choose **Design→Grouping & Totals→** Group & Sort to open the Group, Sort, and Total pane.
3. Click **More**.

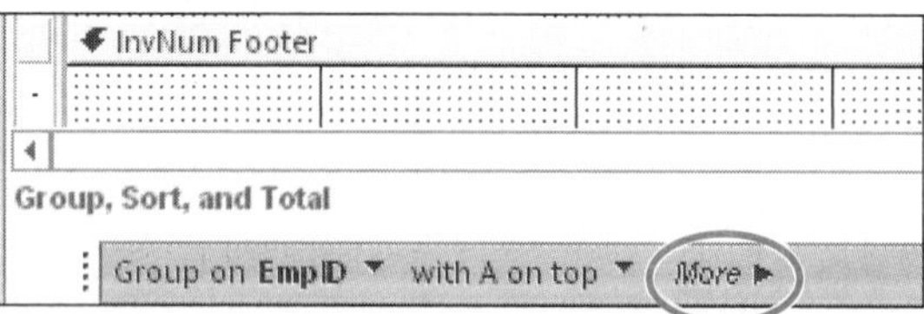

4. Follow these steps to set up group controls for printing:

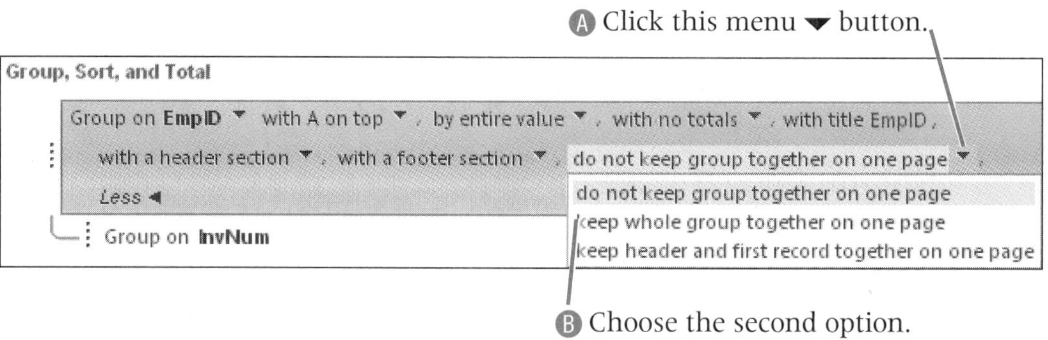

5. Switch to **Print Preview**.
   This option ensures that the headings will always be printed on the same page as the first detail section line (record).
6. Close **Print Preview**.
7. Save your report and close the database. Exit **Access**.

Concepts Review

To check your knowledge of the key concepts introduced in this lesson, complete the Concepts Review quiz by choosing the appropriate access option below.

If you are...	Then access the quiz by...
Using the Labyrinth Video Library	Going to http://labyrinthelab.com/videos
Using eLab	Logging in, choosing Content, and navigating to the Concepts Review quiz for this lesson
Not using the Labyrinth Video Library or eLab	Going to the student resource center for this book

Reinforce Your Skills

REINFORCE YOUR SKILLS AC05-R01

Create and Modify Reports

The president of Kids for Change wants a report that lists financial donations the organization has received since its inception, grouped by donor. He also wants to list the amount that K4C is depositing into its scholarship fund for local high school students. In this exercise, you will create a simple donations report and create a more customized report. Then, you will rearrange, resize, and format controls, and add a logo and title.

Create a Quick Report and Examine Report Views

1. Start **Access**. Open **AC05-R01-K4C** from your **AC2013 Lesson 05** folder and save it as **`AC05-R01-K4C-[FirstInitialLastName]`**.
2. Click the **Donations** table in the Navigation Pane.
3. Choose **Create→Reports→Report**.

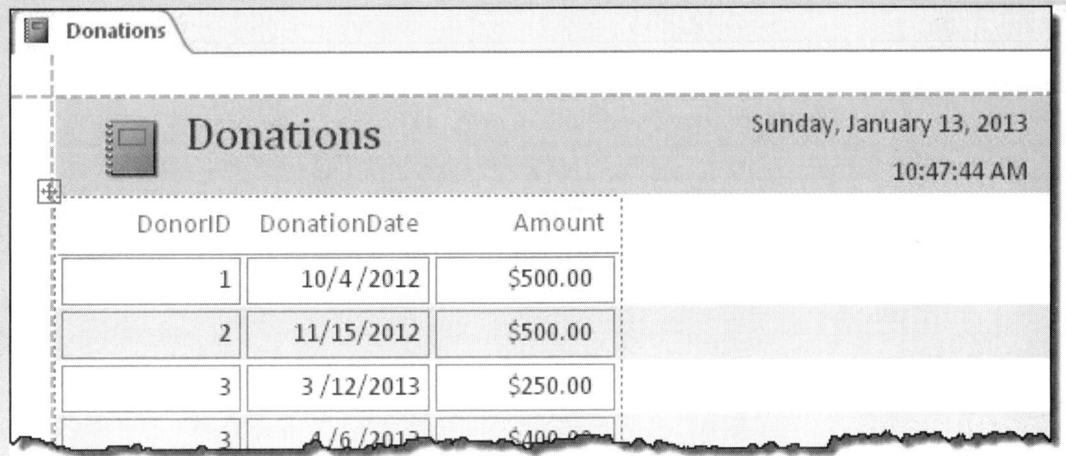

Access creates a report of all donations to K4C and displays it in Layout View. The report needs some formatting, but the basic layout is complete.

4. Hover the mouse pointer over the controls, tools, and features in **Layout View** to see the ScreenTip descriptions.
5. Choose **Home→Views→View menu ▼** and choose **Design View**.
6. Choose **Design→Controls→More** .
   You can see all the tools available in Design View.
7. Tap Esc.
8. Open the **Property Sheet**, if necessary.
9. Click the unbound **DonorID** label in the **Page Header** section.
   Notice that the DonorID label has a Caption property.

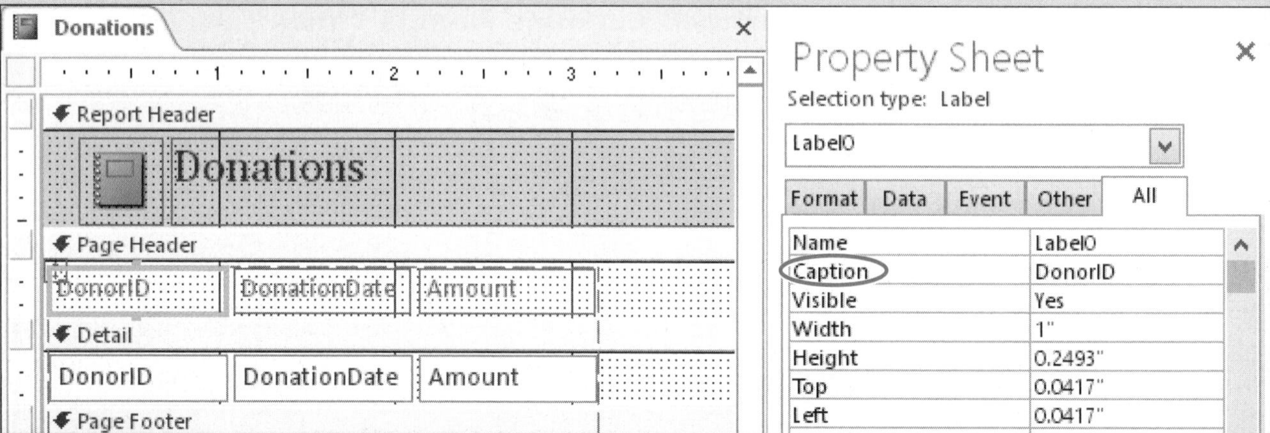

10. Click the bound **DonorID** text box in the **Detail** section.
    Notice that the DonorID text box has a Control Source property.

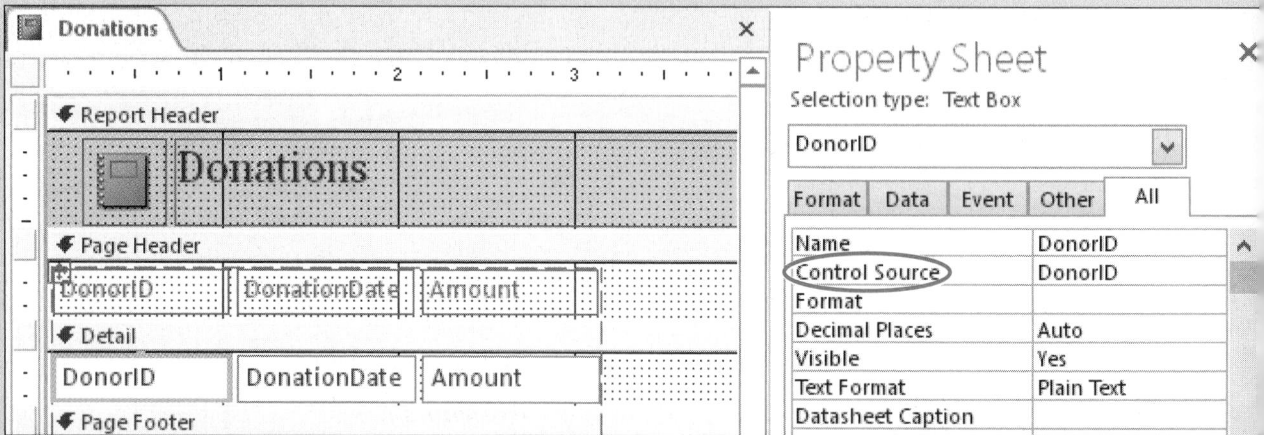

11. Switch to **Report View** and review its layout.
    Report View is similar to Layout View, but there are fewer tools and you cannot modify the formatting of the report or its controls.
12. Save the report as `Quick Donations List` and close it.

Create a Report Using the Report Wizard

Now you will create a donations report that is grouped by donor IDs and includes donation totals.

13. Click **Donations Query** in the Navigation Pane.
14. Choose **Create→Reports→Report Wizard**.
15. Double-click the **DonorID** field in the Available Fields box to move it to the Selected Fields box.
16. Double-click **DonorLName**, **DonorFName**, **DonationDate**, and **Amount** in the order shown.

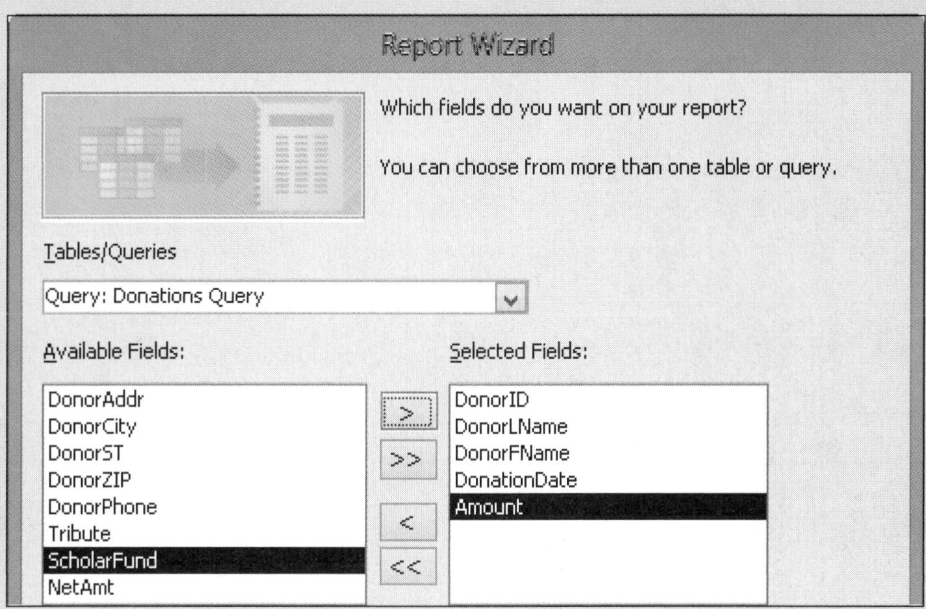

Many fields were not selected. If you select every field in a single report there won't be enough room to display all the information.

17. Click **Next**.

    The next wizard screen asks how you want to view the data.

18. Select **By Donations**.

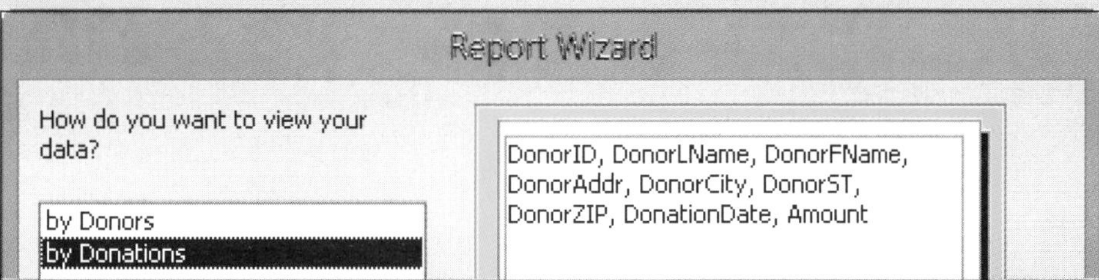

19. Click **Next**.

20. Select **DonorID** as the grouping field and click **Move** [>].

Be sure that your screen shows the grouping in the figure.

21. Click **Next**.
22. Click the **Summary Options** button and check the box for **Sum**. Leave the remaining options as they are.

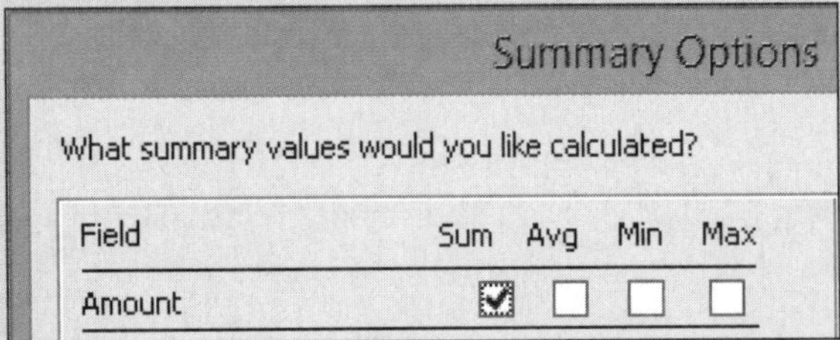

23. Click **OK** to close the Summary Options dialog box. Click **Next**.
24. Choose the **Block** Layout and **Landscape** Orientation.
25. Confirm that the **Adjust the Field Widths So All Fields Fit** box is checked.
26. Click **Next** and name the report `Donations Report 2013-2014`.
27. Click **Finish**.

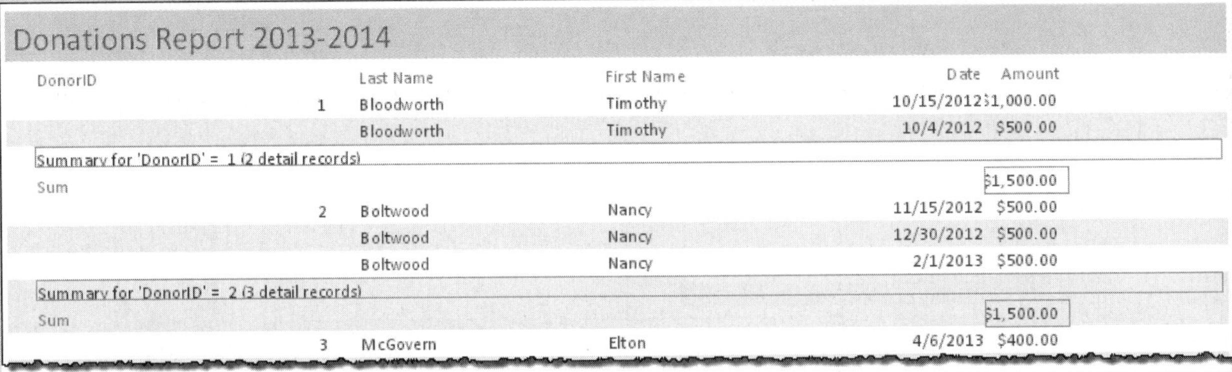

Donations Report 2013-2014

DonorID	Last Name	First Name	Date	Amount
1	Bloodworth	Timothy	10/15/2012	$1,000.00
	Bloodworth	Timothy	10/4/2012	$500.00
Summary for 'DonorID' = 1 (2 detail records)				
Sum				$1,500.00
2	Boltwood	Nancy	11/15/2012	$500.00
	Boltwood	Nancy	12/30/2012	$500.00
	Boltwood	Nancy	2/1/2013	$500.00
Summary for 'DonorID' = 2 (3 detail records)				
Sum				$1,500.00
3	McGovern	Elton	4/6/2013	$400.00

Your report displays in Print Preview, showing donation totals and summary totals for each donor. The report needs formatting and layout work, which must be done in Design View.

28. Navigate through the pages of the report. Then, click the Close Print Preview button but leave the report open.

The report is in Design View.

Add, Delete, and Edit Report Controls

29. In Design View, open the **Property Sheet**, if necessary.
30. Click the **DonorID** text box and type **.5** in the **Width** property line.
31. Click the **DonorLName** text box, press [Ctrl] and click the **DonorFName** text box to select both controls.
32. Type **1"** in the **Width** property to set the width for both controls.
33. Click the **Last Name** label, press [Ctrl], and click the **DonorLName** text box.
34. Type **1.5** for their **Left** Property.
35. Select the **First Name** label and the **DonorFName** text box and type **3** for their **Left** property.

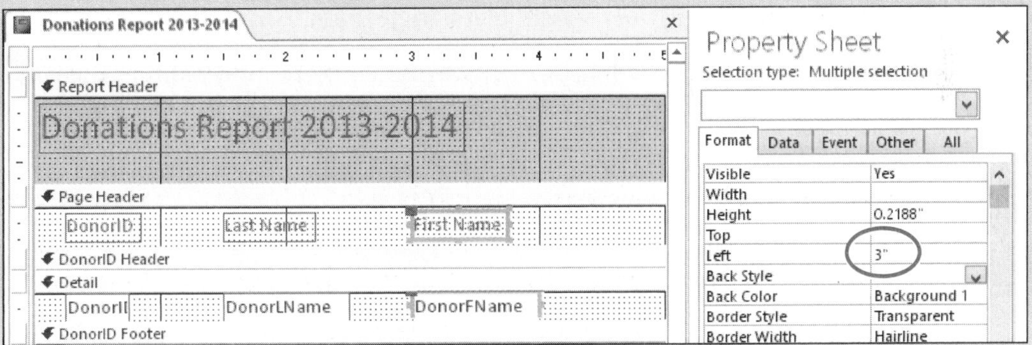

36. Scroll to the right of the report grid to see the other controls.
37. Click the **Date** label and type **5** for its **Left** property.
38. Click the **DonationDate** text box and type **4.5** for its **Left** property.
39. Click the **Amount** label and type **6.2** for its **Left** property.
40. Click the **Amount** text box, press [Ctrl], and click the two **=Sum(Amount)** controls.

Access 2013

41. Type **1** for their **Width** property and **6** for their **Left** property.

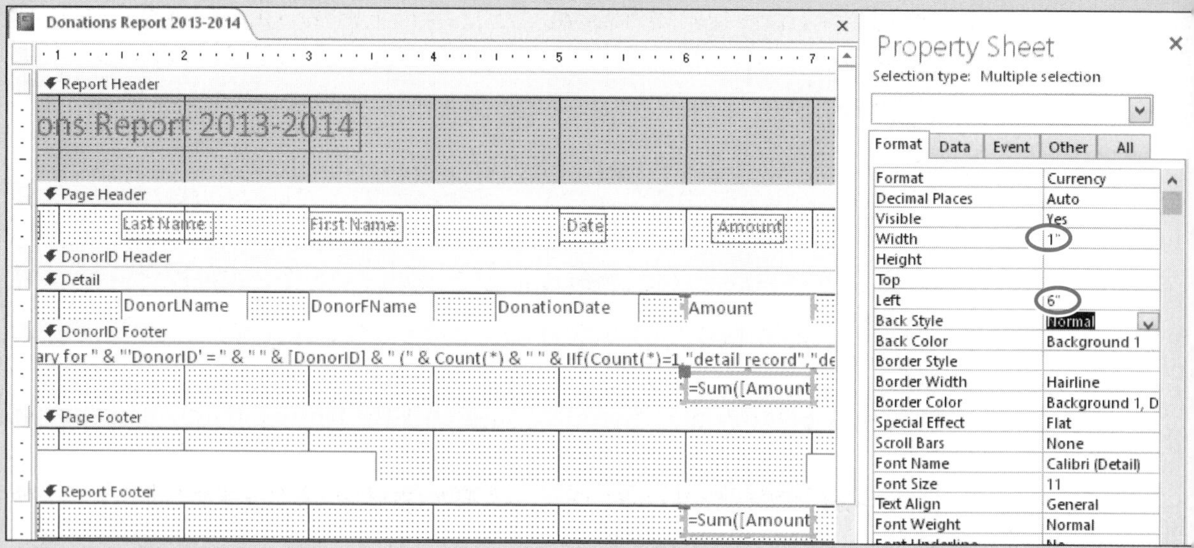

42. Choose **Design→Tools→Add Existing Fields** to open the **Field List**.
43. Drag **ScholarFund** from the Field List and drop it to the right of the **Amount** text box in the **Detail** section.

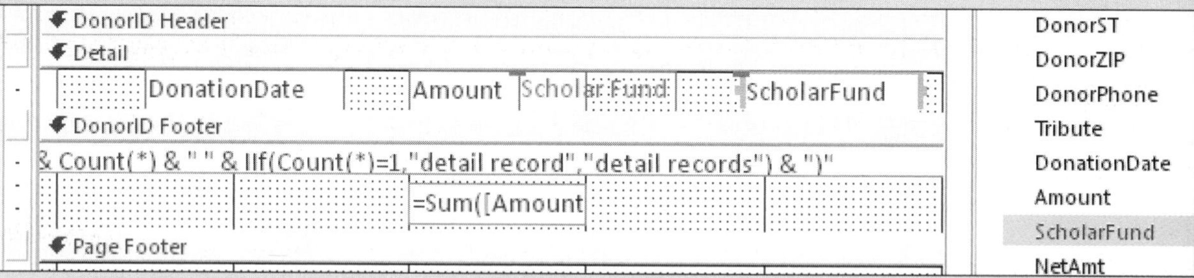

Access places a ScholarFund text box in the Detail section; the corresponding Scholar Fund label is partly on top of the Amount text box. If you recall, 10% of the donations are set aside for the scholarship fund.

44. Click the **Scholar Fund** label and tap Delete.
45. Choose **Design→Controls→Label** Aa.
46. Draw a label control in the **Page Header** section above the **ScholarFund** text box.
47. Type **Scholarship** into the new label.

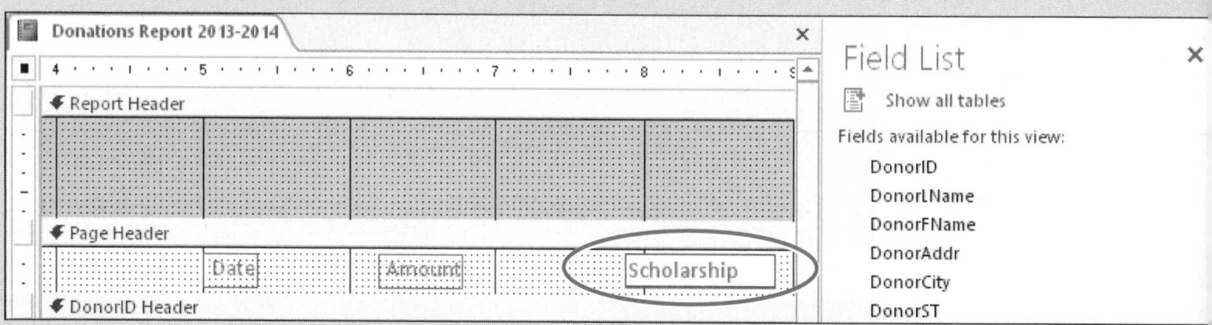

48. Close the Field List.

49. Click the **Summary for " & "'DonorID'...** control in the **DonorID Footer** section.

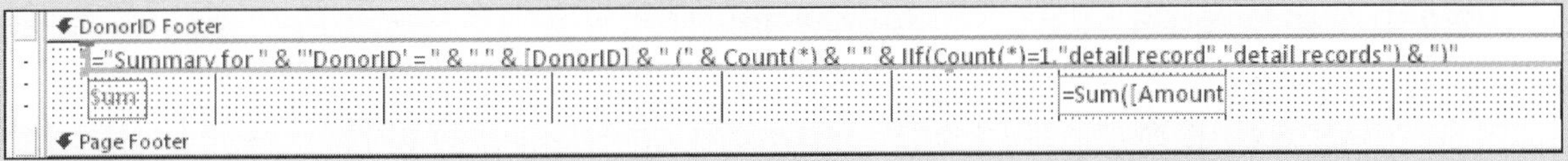

50. Tap [Delete].

51. Click the **Sum** label in the **DonorID Footer**. Click in the label and type `Donor ID Total`.

52. Select the title in the **Report Header** section, highlight the existing header text and type `Kids for Change`. Click an open area of the report grid to deselect all controls.

Add a Logo and a New Title to a Report

53. Drag the **Page Header** section bar down to about the .75" mark on the vertical ruler to make room for the logo and subtitle.

54. Choose **Design→Controls→Insert Image**.

55. Choose **Browse**, navigate to the **AC2013 Lesson 05** folder, choose All Files (*.*) from the file type drop-down list in the Insert Image dialog box, if necessary, and double-click **K4C-Logo.bmp**.

Once you have inserted an image, it is saved in the Image Gallery so you can find it quickly and easily.

56. Draw the logo as shown.

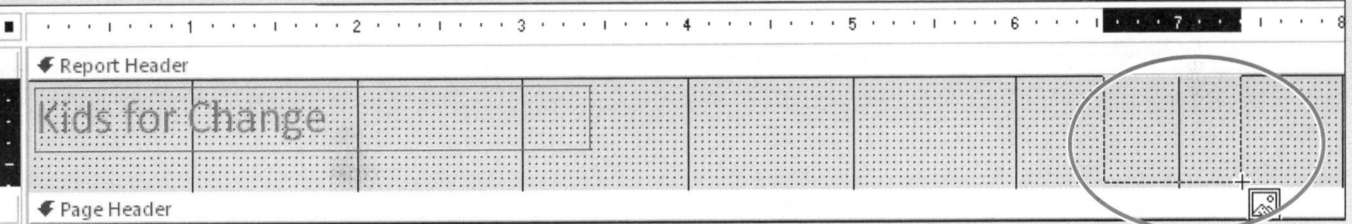

57. Choose **Design→Header/Footer→Title**.

The new title control sits in the Report Header section on top of the Kids for Change title.

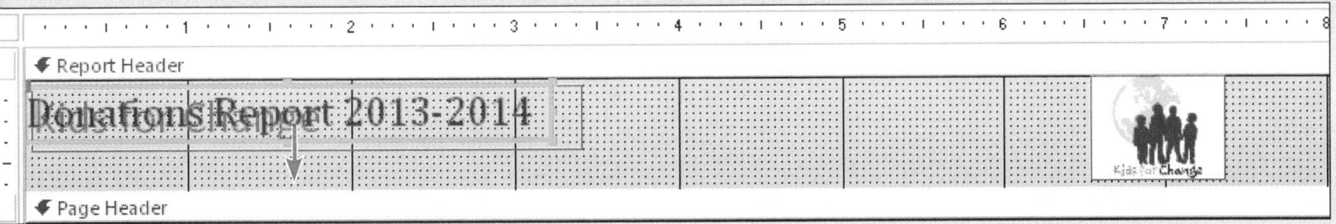

58. With the new title selected, tap [↓] until you can see the entire Kids for Change title.

59. Switch to **Report View**.

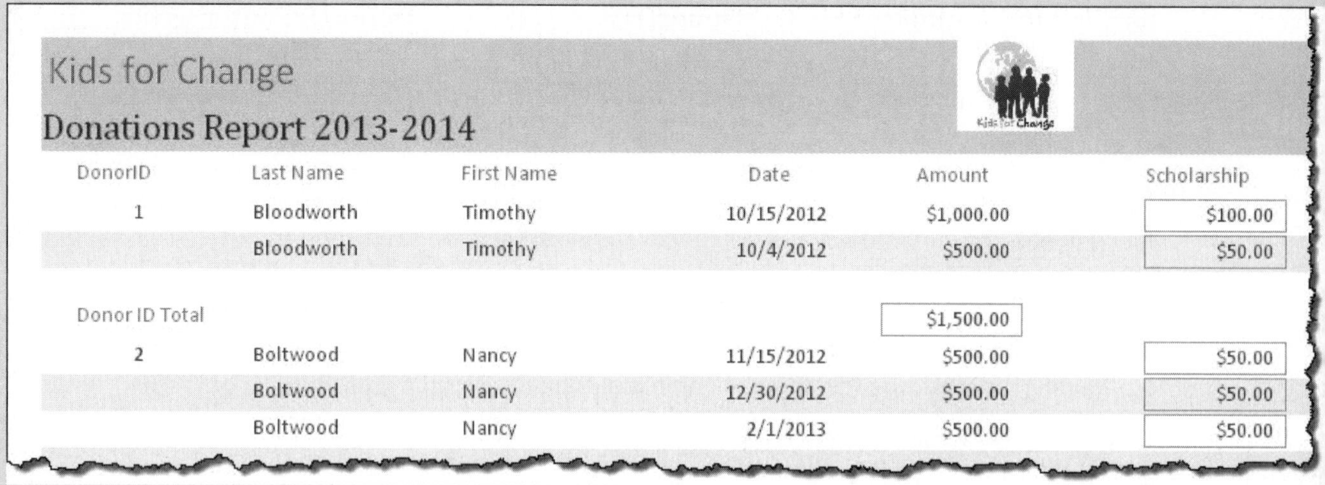

Kids for Change

Donations Report 2013-2014

DonorID	Last Name	First Name	Date	Amount	Scholarship
1	Bloodworth	Timothy	10/15/2012	$1,000.00	$100.00
	Bloodworth	Timothy	10/4/2012	$500.00	$50.00
Donor ID Total				$1,500.00	
2	Boltwood	Nancy	11/15/2012	$500.00	$50.00
	Boltwood	Nancy	12/30/2012	$500.00	$50.00
	Boltwood	Nancy	2/1/2013	$500.00	$50.00

60. Save and close **Donations Report 2013-2014**. Exit **Access**.

61. Submit your final file based on the guidelines provided by your instructor.

    To view examples of how your file or files should look at the end of the exercise, go to the student resource center.

REINFORCE YOUR SKILLS AC05-R02

Use Controls, Apply Themes, Sort and Print Reports

In this exercise, you will size, align, and format report controls, apply a Theme to a report, add the date to the page header, display the Sort and Group pane, add page break controls, and set print options.

Size, Align, and Format Report Controls

1. Start **Access**. Open **AC05-R02-K4C** from the **AC2013 Lesson 05** folder and save it as `AC05-R02-K4C-[FirstInitialLastName]`.
2. Double-click the **Donations Report 2013-2014**.

   The report has alignment problems, and the formatting of controls is inconsistent.
3. Switch to **Design View** and open the **Property Sheet**, if necessary.
4. Select the two title controls in the **Report Header** section and add these property values:

Property	Value
Width	4
Height	.4
Left	2
Text Align	Center
Font Name	Cambria (Header)
Fore Color	Blue, Accent 1, Darker 25%

5. Press Ctrl and click the **Donations Report** subtitle to deselect it.

6. With just the *Kids for Change* title selected, choose **22** for the **Font Size** property.
7. Click the **Kids for Change** logo.
8. Type `.8` for both the **Width** property and the **Height** property.
9. Type `.05` for the logo's **Top** property.
   Be sure to type .05 and not .5.
10. Click the **vertical ruler** to the left of the controls in the **Detail** section to select all the controls in the section.
11. Choose **Arrange→Sizing & Ordering→Size/Space→Equal Horizontal.**
    The Detail section controls are evenly spaced across the section.
12. Click the **Last Name** label, press [Shift], and click the **DonorLName** text box.
13. Choose **Arrange→Sizing & Ordering→Align→Left.**
    Access lines up the Last Name controls.
14. Follow the procedures in **steps 12–13** to left align the **First Name** controls.
15. Click the **Date** label in the Page header and drag it so it is centered above the **DonationDate** text box.
16. Select the **Donor ID Total** and **Grand Total** labels, and the **DonationDate** text box.
17. Choose **Arrange→Sizing & Ordering→Align→Right.**
18. Select the **ScholarFund** text box, press [Ctrl], and then click the two calculated field controls.
    You should have three selected controls.
19. Click **Border Style** in the Property Sheet and choose **Transparent.**

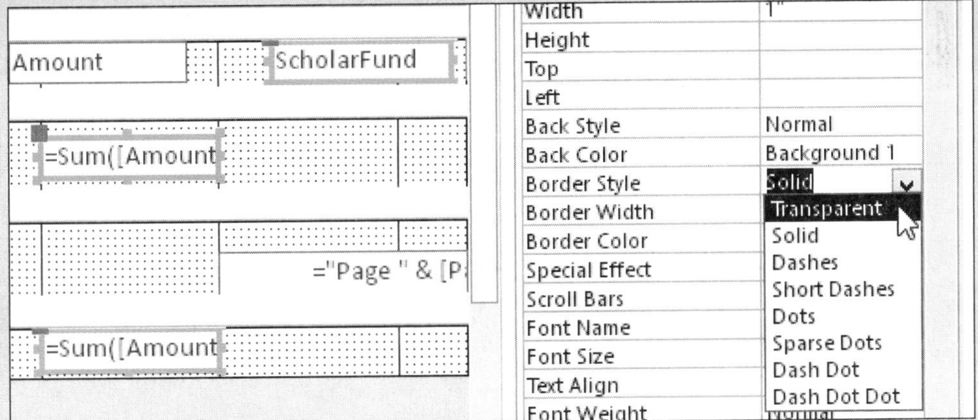

20. Right-align the **Amount** text box and the two **=Sum(Amount)** calculated fields.
21. Switch to **Print Preview.**
22. Save and close **Donations Report 2013-2014.**

Access 2013

Apply Themes to a Report

23. Display the **Quick Donations List** report in Design View.
24. Choose **Design→Themes→Themes** [Aa] and hover over each theme to see how the report style changes.
25. Select a **Theme** from the palette.
26. Save and close the report.

Add Date to the Page Header Section

Now you will add a date control to the Page Header section so when viewing the report on a computer, readers don't have to scroll to the very end of the report to check the date.

27. Open the **Donations Report 2013-2014** file in Design View.
28. Click the **=Now()** text box in the Page Footer section and tap [Delete].
29. Choose **Design→Header/Footer→Date and Time**.
30. Choose **mm/dd/yyyy**.
31. Uncheck the **Include Time** check box.
32. Click **OK**.

    The new date control is inserted on the right-hand side of the Page Header.

33. Click the new **=Date()** control and enter the following property values:

Property	Value
Width	1
Top	.875
Left	3.5
Text Align	Center

34. Switch to **Print Preview** to see the new date control centered under the titles.
35. Close **Print Preview** and save **Donations Report 2013-2014**.

Display the Group and Sort Pane

36. Display **Donations Report 2013-2014** in Design View.

    The report colors might have changed to the Theme you applied to the Quick Donations List.

37. Choose **Design→Grouping & Totals→Group & Sort** to open the Group, Sort, and Total pane.

    The report is grouped by DonorID.

38. Click **Add a Sort** to display the list of fields.
39. Tap [Esc] to exit without making any changes.
40. Close the **Group, Sort, and Total** pane.

Add Page Break Controls to a Report

You will now set page breaks so each donor's summary records on a separate page or separate set of pages.

41. Display the **Donations Report 2013-2014** in Design View.
42. Choose **Design→Controls→Insert Page Break** .
43. Click in the bottom-left corner of the **DonorID Footer** section. Then, click to add the page break.

An orange marker indicates a page break.

44. Switch to **Print Preview**. Click **Next Page** to see that no two donor's records appear on the same page.
    If you want the report header to appear on every page, you can select all the report header controls, cut them, and paste them into the page header section.
45. Close **Print Preview** and close the report *without* saving it.

Set Print Options

46. Display the **Donations Report 2013-2014** in Design View.
47. Choose **Design→Grouping & Totals→Group & Sort** Group & Sort to open the Group, Sort, and Total pane.
48. Click **More** in Group On DonorID.
49. Click the **menu** ▾ button for Do Not Keep Group Together on One Page, and choose **Keep Header and First Record Together on One Page**.

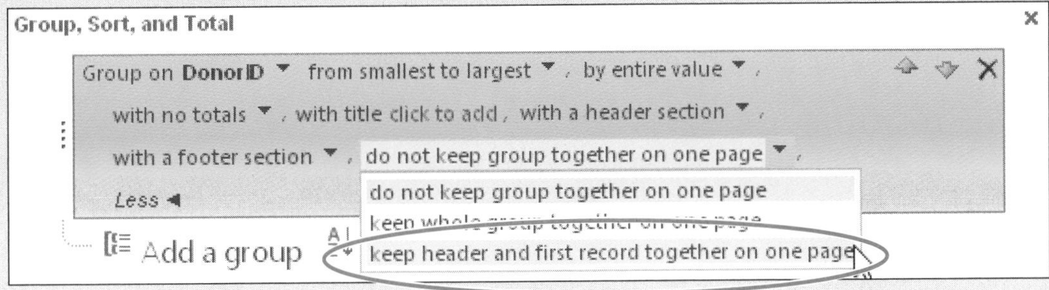

50. Switch to **Print Preview**.

Kids for Change

Donations Report 2013-2014

1/17/2013

DonorID	Last Name	First Name	Date	Amount	Scholarship
1	Bloodworth	Timothy	10/15/2012	$1,000.00	$100.00
	Bloodworth	Timothy	10/4/2012	$500.00	$50.00
			Donor ID Total	$1,500.00	
2	Boltwood	Nancy	11/15/2012	$500.00	$50.00
	Boltwood	Nancy	12/30/2012	$500.00	$50.00
	Boltwood	Nancy	2/1/2013	$500.00	$50.00
			Donor ID Total	$1,500.00	

51. Click the **Close Print Preview** button then close the **Group, Sort, and Total** pane.
52. Save and close the report. Exit **Access**.
53. Submit your final file based on the guidelines provided by your instructor.
    To view examples of how your file or files should look at the end of the exercise, go to the student resource center.

REINFORCE YOUR SKILLS AC05-R03

Create Reports, Modify Controls, Add a Title and Logo, and Print

Kids for Change (K4C) is rapidly expanding, adding new activities and staff members almost daily. To meet the organization's need to match staffers with the new activities, you will create two new reports for them.

Create a Quick Report and Display Different Report Views

First, you will create a simple report that lists all activities organized by K4C.

1. Start **Access**. Open **AC05-R03-K4C** from the **AC2013 Lesson 05** folder and save it as `AC05-R03-K4C-[FirstInitialLastName]`.
2. Click the **Activities** table in the Navigation Pane then choose **Create→Reports→Report**.

Activities

Activities

Sunday, January 13, 2013
4:06:05 PM

Activity ID	Activity	Location	Day	Meet Time	Act Lngth
BCSat	Beach Cleanup	Coquina Beach	Saturday	9:00 AM	3
CCThu	Can Collection	Seabreeze School	Thursday	6:00 PM	2
CWSat	Car Wash	Sarasota Fairgrounds	Saturday	12:00 PM	4
EBSun	Eco-Bake Sale	Downtown Flea Market	Sunday	8:00 AM	3
GWWed	Garden Work	All Angels Church	Wednesday	5:00 PM	2
NCMon	Newspaper Drive	Seabreeze School	Monday	6:00 PM	2
RDTue	Recycling Drive	Seabreeze School	Tuesday	6:00 PM	2
SWFri	Sign Waving	Cortez Rd. & Tamiami Tr.	Friday	5:00 PM	2

Access generates a report of K4C's activities in Layout View. Notice that the report extends beyond a standard 8.5" x 11" printed page (the vertical dotted line).

3. Click an **Activity** text box to select the Activity column of text boxes.
4. Hover the mouse pointer over the right border of the text box until it is a resize arrow. Click and drag its border to the left to resize the text boxes.

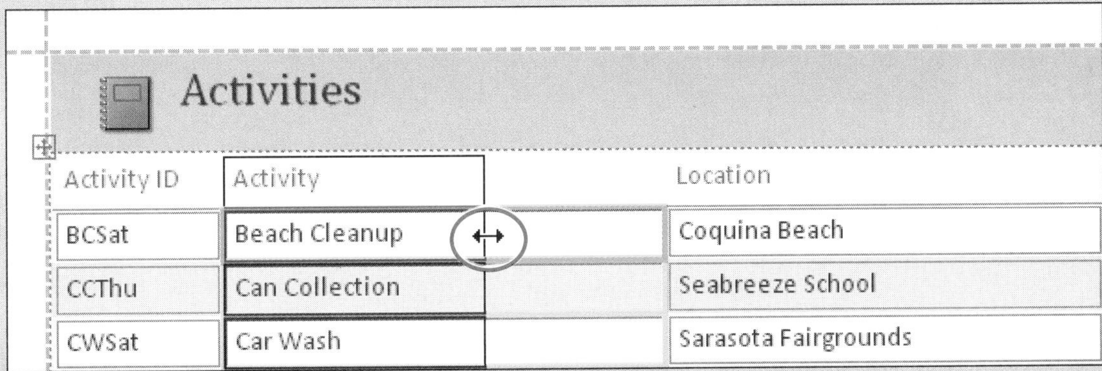

5. Resize the remaining text boxes, including the Date and Time controls.
6. Scroll to the bottom of the report and click the **Page** text box control to select it.
7. Switch to **Design View** and choose **Design→Tools→Property Sheet**.
8. Type `1"` for the Page control's **Width** property and type `6"` for the **Left** property.
9. Click in the upper-left corner of the report to select the entire report.
10. Type `7"` for the **Width** property.
11. Select the **=Count(*)** control in the **Report Footer** and type `.175` for the **Height** property.
12. Switch to **Print Preview**.
    The report fits a standard printed page.
13. Click the Close Print Preview button then open the **Property Sheet**, if necessary.
14. Click the unbound **Activity ID label** in the Page Header section.
    Notice that the Activity ID label has a Caption property.

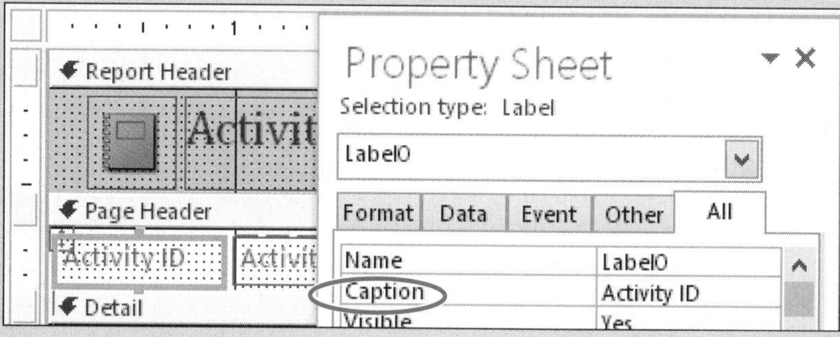

15. Click the bound **ActID** text box in the **Detail** section.
    Notice that the ActIDtext box has a Control Source property.

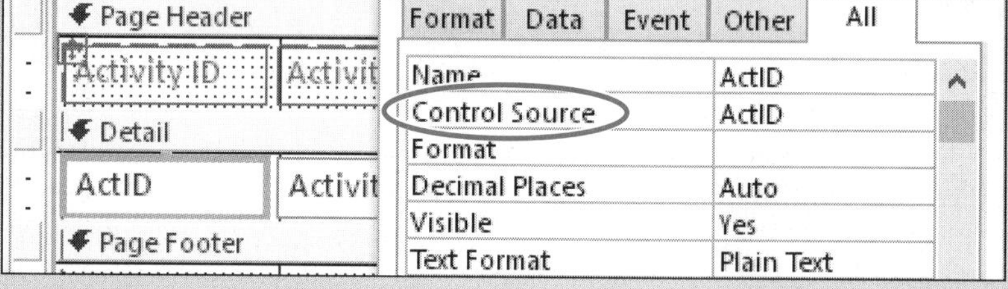

16. Save the report as `Activities Report` and close it.

Create a Report Using the Report Wizard

Now you will use the Report Wizard to create a staff availability report to match staffers with specific activities. The report will be grouped by activity.

17. Click the **Staff Schedule** query in the Navigation Pane then choose **Create→Reports→Report Wizard**.
18. Double-click the **Activity** field in the Available Fields box to move it to the Selected Fields box.

19. Double-click **Day**, **MeetTime**, **StaffLastName**, **StaffFirstName**, **StaffPhone**, and **Hours**, in the order shown.

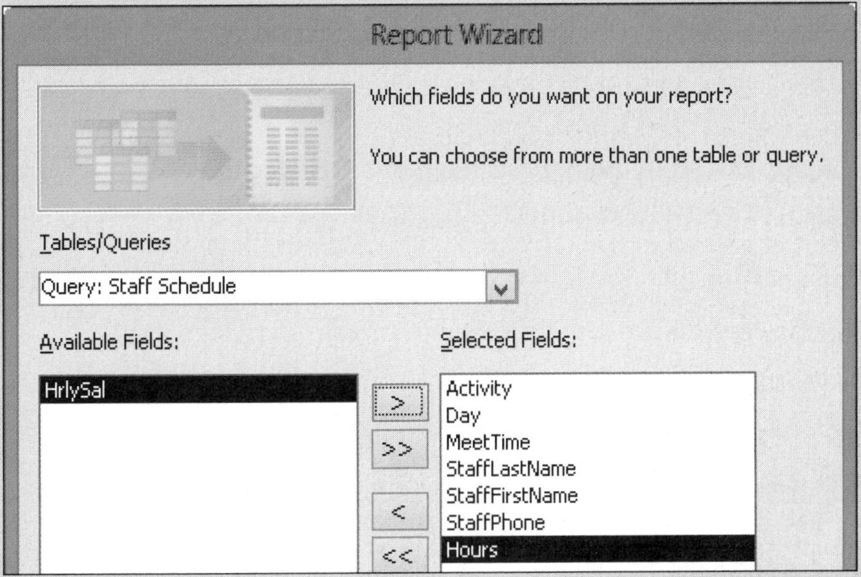

20. Click **Next**.

    The next screen asks if you want to add grouping.

21. Select **Activity** and click **Next**.

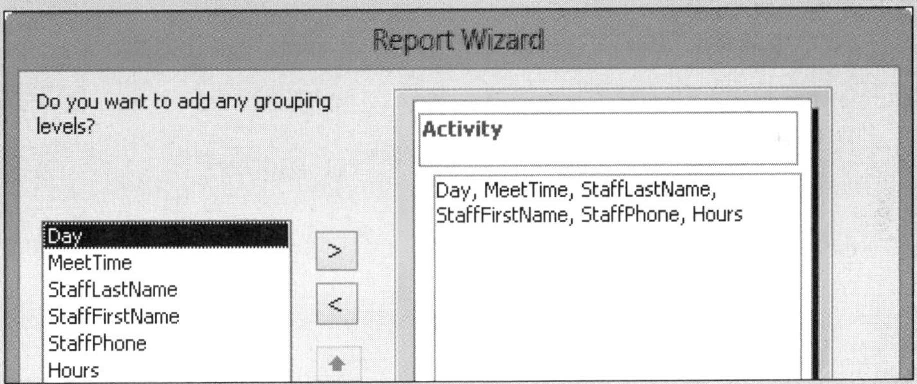

Activity appears in a header.

22. In the Sort Order and Summary Information screen, click **Next**.
23. Leave the default Layout options selected (**Stepped** and **Portrait**).

Access 2013

24. Confirm that the **Adjust the Field Widths so All Fields Fit** box is checked.
25. Click **Next** and name the report `Staff Availability Report`. Click **Finish**.

    Your report displays in Print Preview. It needs formatting and layout work, which will be done in Design View and Layout View. However, most of the controls are now in place.
26. Close **Print Preview**.

Size, Add, Delete, and Edit Report Controls

27. Display the **Staff Availability Report** in Layout View.
28. Open the **Property Sheet**, if necessary.
29. Click the **Activity** label, press [Ctrl], and click an **Activity** text box.
30. Type `1.2` for the **Width** property.
31. Click the **Day** label to select it, press [Ctrl], and click a **Day** textbox.
32. Type `.9` for the **Width** property and `1.5` for the **Left** property.
33. Select the **Meet Time** label and text boxes. Type `.75` for the **Width** property and `2.5` for the **Left** property.
34. Select the **Last Name** label and text boxes. Type `.8` for the **Width** property and `3.3` for the **Left** property.
35. Select the **First Name** label and text boxes. Type `.8` for the **Width** property and `4.2` for the **Left** property.
36. Select the **Telephone** label and text boxes. Type `1.1` for the **Width** property and `5.1` for the **Left** property.
37. Switch to **Design View**.
38. Choose **Design→Tools→Add Existing Fields**.
39. Drag **HrlySal** to the right of the **StaffPhone** text box in the Detail section.

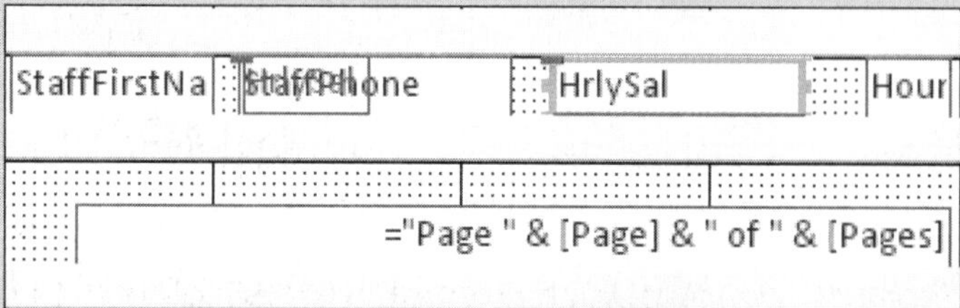

    Access includes a label control with the text box. You will add a new label in the Page Header section rather than using the default label.
40. Click the **Hrly Sal** label control and tap [Del].

If you delete the wrong control, tap [Ctrl]+[Z] to undo the last task.

41. Close the **Field List** and open the **Property Sheet**.

42. Select the **HrlySal** text box. Type `.55` for the **Width** property and `6.3` for the **Left** property.

43. Click the **Label** *Aa* button and drag a new label between the Telephone and Hrs labels in the Page Header section.

44. Type `Hrly Sal` in the new label and tap [Enter].

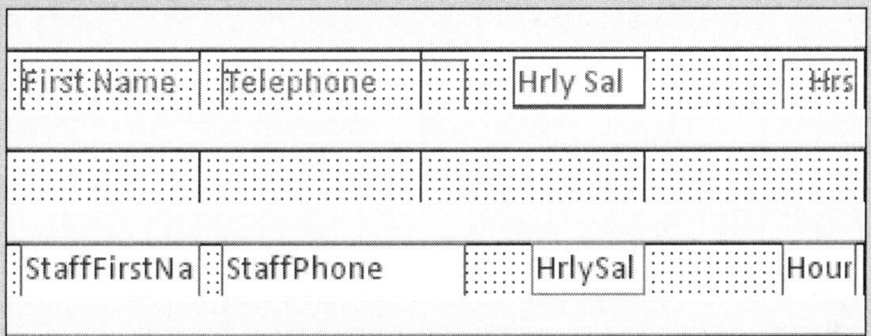

45. Type `.55` for the **Width** property and `6.3` for the **Left** property.

46. Select the **Hrs** label and the **Hours** text box. Type `.4` for the **Width** property and `7` for the **Left** property.

47. Choose Report from the Selection Type list at the top of the Property Sheet, and type `7.875"` for the report **Width** property.

48. Switch to **Print Preview**.

Staff Availability Report

Activity	Day	Meet Time	Last Name	First Name	Telephone	Hrly Sal	Hrs
Animal Shelter							
	Wednesday	5:00 PM	Kline	Victor	(941)555-6893	$18.50	10
	Friday	5:00 PM	Sanchez	Cokie	(941)555-0008	$23.50	4
	Monday	5:00 PM	Earle	Kevin	(941)555-1368	$18.00	9
	Tuesday	5:00 PM	Jacoby	Jane	(941)555-5050	$17.75	8
	Thursday	5:00 PM	Bryant	Matthew	(941)555-7523	$20.25	4
	Friday	5:00 PM	Kendall	Lonnie	(941)555-2356	$18.50	4
Beach Cleanup							

If an error message appears saying that the width is greater than the page width, make sure that you followed all the steps precisely. If the report does not display correctly, you may have to adjust the report width, depending on your settings.

49. Save the report and close **Print Preview**.

Add a New Title and a Logo to a Report

50. Display **Staff Availability Report** in Design View and, if necessary, open the **Property Sheet**.
51. Select the title control in the **Report Header**, type the caption `Kids for Change`, and tap [Enter].
52. Choose **Design→Header/Footer→Title** and tap [Enter].

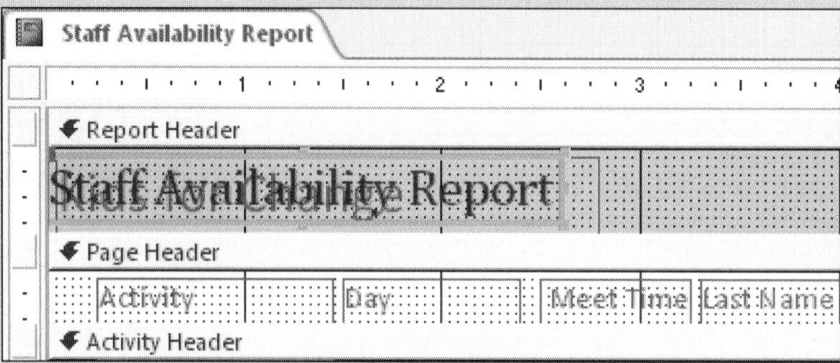

Access adds a new title control in the Page Header section on top of the Kids for Change title.

53. Type `.46"` for the **Top** property of the new title.
Access automatically resizes the Report Header section when you move the control.
54. Select the *Kids for Change* title and enter the following property values:

Property	New Value
Width	4
Left	2
Font Name	Georgia
Font Size	22
Text Align	Center
Fore Color	Blue, Accent 1, Darker 25%

55. Choose **Home→Clipboard→Format Painter**, and then click the *Staff Availability Report* subtitle to format the report, and type 20 for the Font Size property.
Your Report Header should look similar to this header.

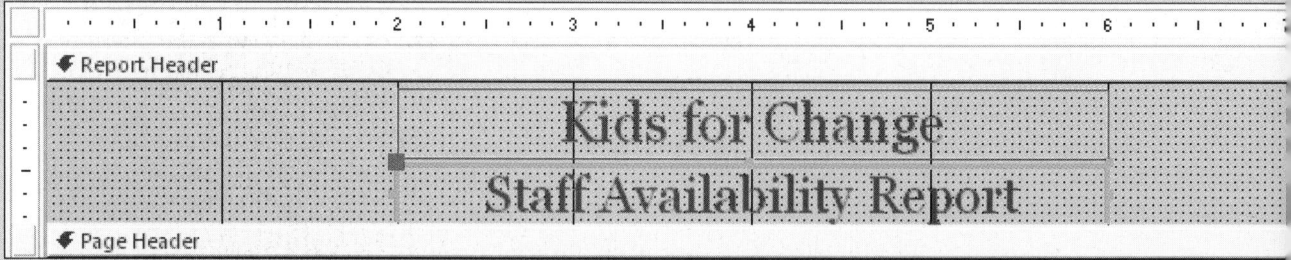

56. Choose **Design→Header/Footer→**[Logo].

57. Navigate to your **AC2013 Lesson 05** folder, select **K4C-Logo.bmp**, and click **OK**.
Access places the logo to the left of the title and subtitle in the Report Header.

58. Type `.8` for the **Width** and **Height** properties.

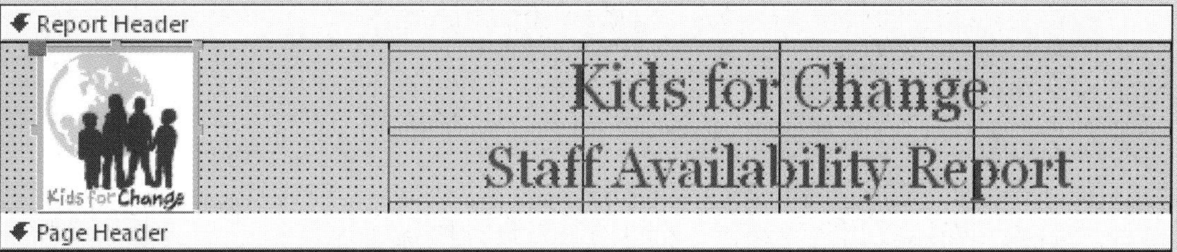

59. Save the **Staff Availability Report**.

Align and Format Report Controls

The Staff Availability Report is slightly too wide to fit on a standard printed page, so you will format and arrange the controls to make it fit.

60. Display the **Staff Availability Report** in **Design View**.

61. Click the **="Page"** control in the **Page Footer** to select it.

62. Type `1` for the **Width** property and `6.5` for the **Left** property.

63. Hover the mouse pointer over the right border of the report grid until it becomes a resize arrow and drag the report border left as shown.

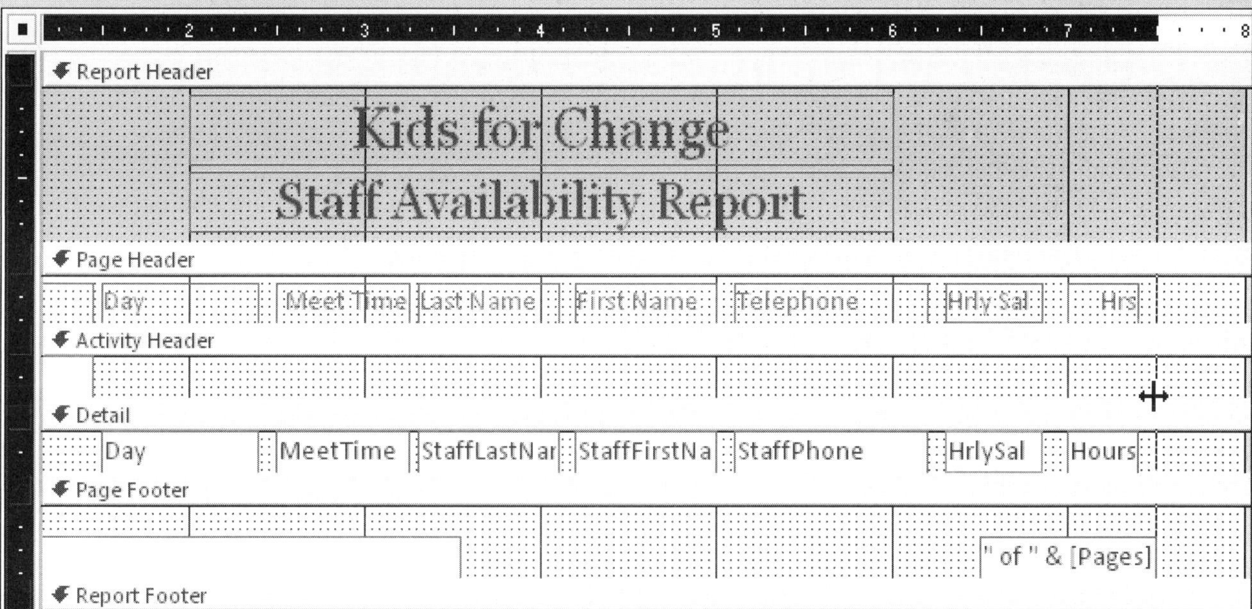

The report now fits on a standard sheet of paper.

64. Click the **HrlySal** text box and change the **Border Style** property to **Transparent**.

Access 2013

65. Switch to **Report View**.

Kids for Change
Staff Availability Report

Activity	Day	Meet Time	Last Name	First Name	Telephone	Hrly Sal	Hrs
Animal Shelter							
	Wednesday	5:00 PM	Kline	Victor	(941) 555-6893	$18.50	10
	Friday	5:00 PM	Sanchez	Cokie	(941) 555-0008	$23.50	4
	Monday	5:00 PM	Earle	Kevin	(941) 555-1368	$18.00	9
	Tuesday	5:00 PM	Jacoby	Jane	(941) 555-5050	$17.75	8
	Thursday	5:00 PM	Bryant	Matthew	(941) 555-7523	$20.25	4
	Friday	5:00 PM	Kendall	Lonnie	(941) 555-2356	$18.50	4
Beach Cleanup							

66. Save and close the **Staff Availability Report**.

Apply Themes to a Report

67. Display the **Activities Report** in Design View.
68. Choose **Design→Themes→Themes** and select a Theme for the report.
    You may have to readjust control sizes because of font changes.
69. Save and close the report.

Add Date to the Page Header Section

Now you will add a date control to the Page Header section so when viewing the report on a computer, readers do not have to scroll to the very end to check the date.

70. Display the **Staff Availability Report** in Design View.
71. Right-click the **=Now()** date text box in the Page Footer and choose **Delete**.
72. Choose **Design→Header/Footer→Date and Time**.
73. Choose the **mm/dd/yyyy** option, uncheck the **Include Time** checkbox, and click **OK**.
    Access places the new date control on the right-hand side of the Page Header section.
74. Click the new date control and tap [↑] repeatedly to move it to the top of the **Page Header** section.
75. Drag the left border to the right to the **6.5″ mark** on the horizontal ruler.

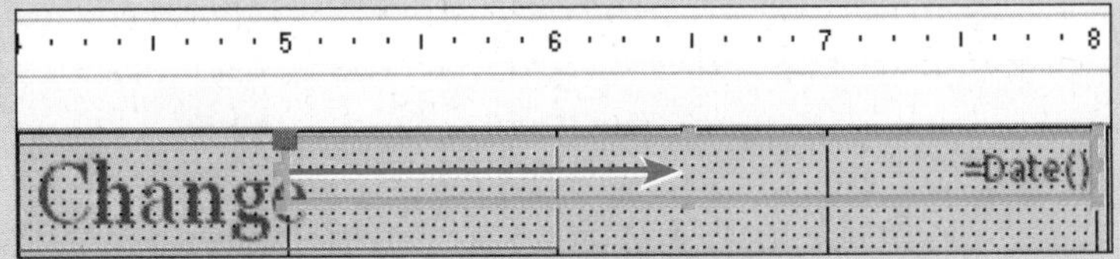

76. Save the report.

Display the Group and Sort Pane

77. Choose **Design→Grouping & Totals→Group & Sort**.
78. Click **Add a Sort** to display the list of fields.

    Notice that this report is grouped by Activity.

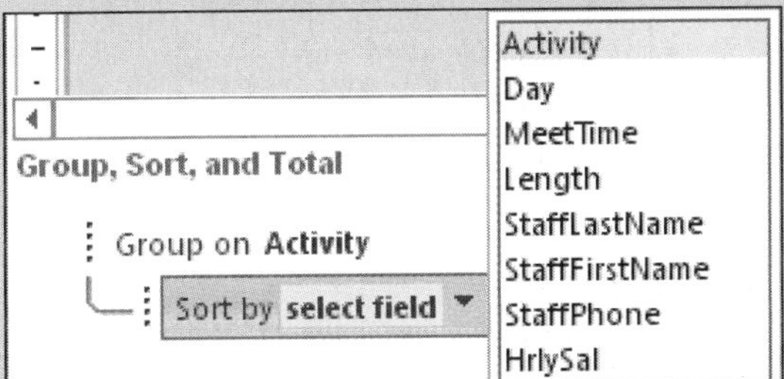

79. Tap [Esc] to exit without making any changes. Then, close the **Group, Sort, and Total** pane and the **Staff Availability Report**.

Add Page Break Controls to a Report

Now you will set page breaks so each donor's summary records on a separate page or separate set of pages.

80. Display the **Donations Report** in **Design View**.
81. Choose **Design→Controls→Insert Page Break** .
82. Click in the bottom-left corner of the **DonorID Footer** section and click to add the page break.

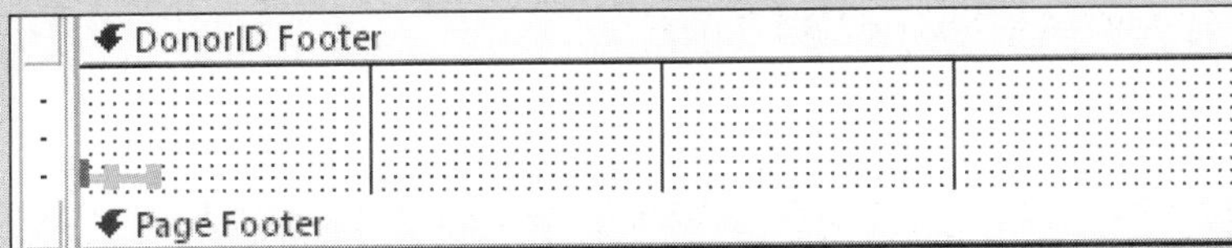

The orange marker indicates a page break.

83. Switch to **Print Preview** and click **Next Page** to view each page of the report. Each donor's records appear on a separate page.

    If you want the report header to appear on every page, select the report header controls, cut them, and paste them into the page header section.

84. Click the **Close Print Preview** button then close **Donations Report** *without saving* it.

Set Print Options

85. Display the **Donations Report** in **Design View**.
86. Choose **Design→Grouping & Totals→Group & Sort** [Group & Sort].
87. Click **More** in **Group on DonorID**.

Access 2013

88. Click the **menu ▾** button for Do Not Keep Group Together on One Page, and choose **Keep Header and First Record Together on One Page**.

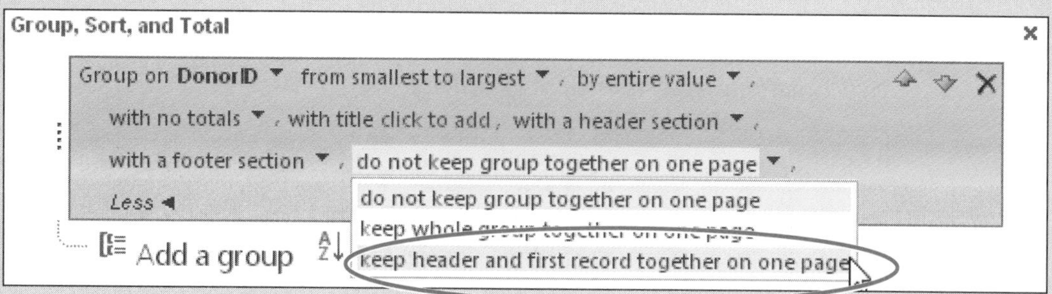

89. Save the report and display it in **Print Preview**.
90. Close your report. Close the database, and exit **Access**.
91. Submit your final file based on the guidelines provided by your instructor.

Apply Your Skills

APPLY YOUR SKILLS AC05-A01

Create and Modify Reports

Universal Corporate Events, Ltd. is ready to add several reports to its database. In this exercise, you will create two reports: the first is a simple report that lists contacts' telephone numbers; the second lists the event venues and their contact information (address, telephone number, and website), grouped by the contact person. Then you will add, delete, and edit the venue report controls, and add a logo and title.

Create a Quick Report and Examine Report Views

1. Start **Access**. Open **AC05-A01-UCE** from the **AC2013 Lesson 05** folder and save it as **`AC05-A01-UCE-[FirstInitialLastName]`**.
2. Click the **Contacts** table, and choose **Create→Reports→Report**.

   Access generates a quick report using the Contacts table and displays it in Layout View.
3. Hover the mouse pointer over each of the control tools on the Ribbon and features in Report **Layout View** to see the ScreenTip descriptions.
4. Switch to **Design View**.

   The Report Header section contains an auto-logo, a title, an auto-date control, and an auto-time control. The Detail section contains text box controls that display the data values.
5. Choose **Design→Controls→More** to see all the control tools available in Design View; then tap [Esc].
6. Select the unbound **ContactID** label in the Page Header section, open the **Property Sheet**, and notice that the label has a Caption property.
7. Select the bound **ContactID text box** in the Detail section and notice that it has a Control Source property.
8. Switch to **Report View**.
9. Save the report as **`Contacts List`** and close it.

Use the Report Wizard and Delete and Edit Report Controls

Now you will use the Report Wizard to create a list the event venues, their addresses, phone number, and website, grouped by the contact person.

10. Click the **Venues** table and start the Report Wizard.
11. Select all the fields *except* VenueID.
12. Leave **VenueContact** as the only grouping level.
13. Do not add a sort, leave the layout default values, and name the report **`Venues List`**. Click **Finish**.

    Access opens the report in Print Preview.

    Now you will delete the Page control from the Page Footer section in the Venues List and modify label captions to improve readability.

14. Close **Print Preview** and switch to **Design View**.
15. Select the **=Now()** control in the Page Footer and tap [Delete].

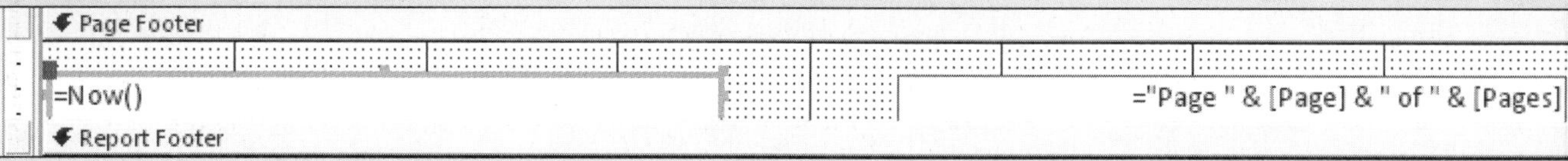

16. Change the caption of the **VenueContact** label in the Page Header to `Contact`.
17. Change the caption of the **VenueName** label in the Page Header to `Name of Venue`.
18. Save your changes.

Add a Logo and a New Title to a Report

19. If necessary, open the **Property Sheet**.
20. Choose **Design→Header/Footer→Logo**. Choose **UCE-Logo.bmp** from the **AC2013 Lesson 05** folder.

    Access adds the logo to the left side of the Page Header.
21. Type `.8` for the **Width** and **Height** properties.
22. Click the **Venues List** title control and enter the following property values:

Property	New Value
Caption	Universal Corporate Events, Ltd.
Width	4
Height	.4
Left	2
Font Name	Arial Narrow
Font Size	22
Text Align	Center
Fore Color	Blue, Accent 5, Darker 50%

23. Choose **Design→Header/Footer→Title**.
24. Use the **Format Painter** to paint the new title with the same format as the title.

25. Switch to **Report View**.

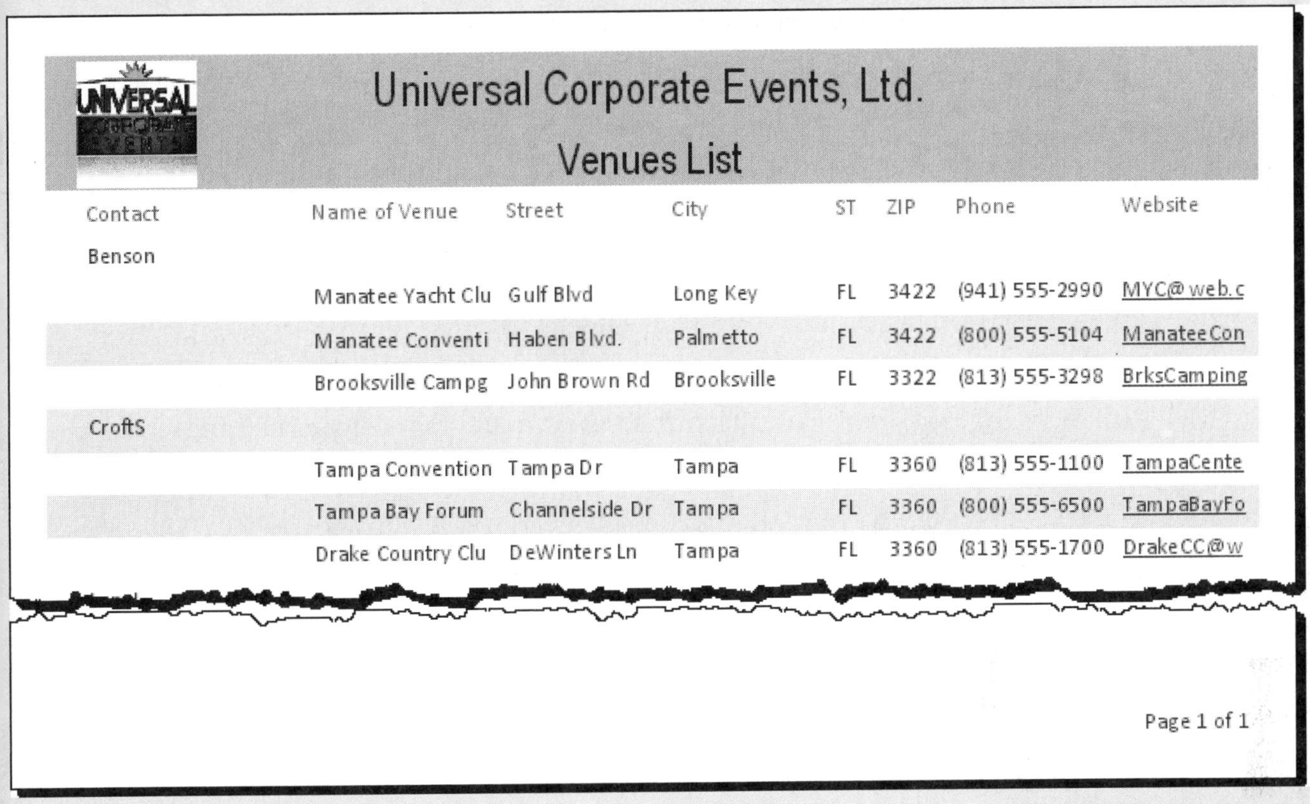

UNIVERSAL CORPORATE EVENTS

Universal Corporate Events, Ltd.

Venues List

Contact	Name of Venue	Street	City	ST	ZIP	Phone	Website
Benson							
	Manatee Yacht Clu	Gulf Blvd	Long Key	FL	3422	(941) 555-2990	MYC@web.c
	Manatee Conventi	Haben Blvd.	Palmetto	FL	3422	(800) 555-5104	ManateeCon
	Brooksville Campg	John Brown Rd	Brooksville	FL	3322	(813) 555-3298	BrksCamping
CroftS							
	Tampa Convention	Tampa Dr	Tampa	FL	3360	(813) 555-1100	TampaCente
	Tampa Bay Forum	Channelside Dr	Tampa	FL	3360	(800) 555-6500	TampaBayFo
	Drake Country Clu	DeWinters Ln	Tampa	FL	3360	(813) 555-1700	DrakeCC@w

Page 1 of 1

26. Save and close the report. Close the database and exit **Access**.

27. Submit your final file based on the guidelines provided by your instructor.

    To view examples of how your file or files should look at the end of the exercise, go to the student resource center.

APPLY YOUR SKILLS AC05-A02

Fine-Tune Reports

Universal Corporate Events, Ltd. CEO Hugh Buckley has sent back the first draft of the Contacts List and Venues List with a list of modifications he would like you to make. In this exercise, you will resize, align, and format controls on the Venues List, examine the sorting and grouping settings, and prepare it for printing. You will also apply a Theme to the Contacts List, and print the modified report.

Size, Align, and Format Report Controls and Apply a Theme

1. Start **Access**. Open **AC05-A02-UCE** from the **AC2013 Lesson 05** folder and save it as **`AC05-A02-UCE-[FirstInitialLastName]`**.

2. Display the **Venues List** report in **Layout View**.

   The report controls must be resized.

3. In either Layout View or Design View, modify the **Width** and **Left** properties of the labels and text boxes so that all the information displays.

4. Save and close the **Venues List** report.
5. Display the **Contacts List** report in **Design View**.
6. Apply a **Theme** to the report, and keep in mind that it will be applied to *every* object in the database.
7. Switch to **Layout View**. Resize the controls to display the full contents.
8. Save and close the **Contacts List**.

Add the Date to the Page Header and Display the Group, Sort, and Total Pane

9. Display the **Venues List** report in **Design View**.
10. Click Date and Time. Choose the **mm/dd/yyyy** format and do not include the time.
11. Move the new **Date** control to the top of the **Report Header**, and shorten its width so it doesn't overlay the title.
12. Switch to **Report View**.

UNIVERSAL CORPORATE EVENTS

Universal Corporate Events, Ltd. 1/14/2013

Venues List

Contact	Name of Venue	Street	City	ST	ZIP	Phone	Website
Benson							
	Manatee Yacht Club	Gulf Blvd	Long Key	FL	34228	(941) 555-2990	MYC@web.com
	Manatee Convention Center	Haben Blvd.	Palmetto	FL	34221	(800) 555-5104	NorthCC@web.com
	Brooksville Campgrounds	John Brown Rd	Brooksville	FL	33222	(813) 555-3298	BrksCamp@web.com
CroftS							
	Tampa Convention Ctr	Tampa Dr	Tampa	FL	33608	(813) 555-1100	TampaCtr@web.com
	Tampa Bay Forum	Channelside Dr	Tampa	FL	33602	(800) 555-6500	TBForum@web.com
	Drake Country Club	DeWinters Ln	Tampa	FL	33608	(813) 555-1700	DrakeCC@web.com
LunaL							
	Hyatt Sarasota	Tamiami Tr	Sarasota	FL	34236	(800) 555-1234	HyattSara@web.com
Miller							
	Sarasota Yacht Club	Fruitville Rd	Sarasota	FL	34231	(941) 555-7685	SYC@web.com
	Sarasota Country Club	Tamiami Tr	Sarasota	FL	34231	(800) 555-3366	SCC@web.com
	Meadows Clubhouse	Meadows Pkwy	Lakewood	FL	33505	(813) 555-5050	Meadows@web.com

Page 1 of 1

Your report should include the new date control in the Page Header section.

13. Switch to **Design View** and open the **Group, Sort, and Totals** pane.
    The report is sorted and grouped by Venue Contact.
14. Investigate the various settings, but make no changes.
15. Close the **Group, Sort, and Totals** pane. Then, close the **Venues List** report, but do not save it.

Add a Page Break Control and Set Print Options

16. Display the **Event Revenue Report** in **Design View**.
17. Click the **Page Break** control tool and click in the bottom-left corner of the **EventDate Footer** section to insert the page break.
18. Switch to **Print Preview** and page through the report.
    Each month's records are on a separate page.
19. Close the report *without saving* it.
20. Display the **Event Revenue Report** in **Design View**.
21. Open the **Group, Sort, and Totals** pane and click More ►.
22. Click the **menu** ▼ button for Do Not Keep Group Together on One Page and choose **Keep Header and First Record Together on One Page**.
23. Switch to **Print Preview**, and navigate to the second page.
    The second page of the report begins with the EventDate Header because you instructed Access to keep the group header together with the first detail record.

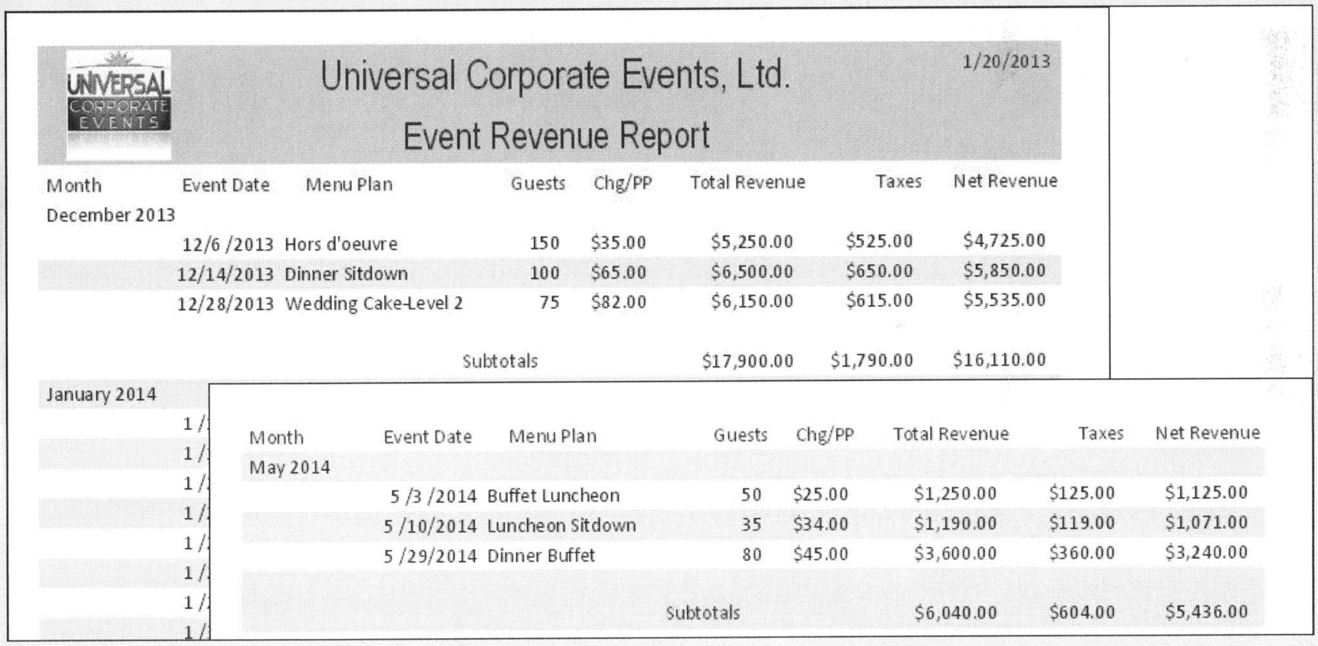

UNIVERSAL CORPORATE EVENTS

Universal Corporate Events, Ltd. 1/20/2013

Event Revenue Report

Month	Event Date	Menu Plan	Guests	Chg/PP	Total Revenue	Taxes	Net Revenue
December 2013							
	12/6 /2013	Hors d'oeuvre	150	$35.00	$5,250.00	$525.00	$4,725.00
	12/14/2013	Dinner Sitdown	100	$65.00	$6,500.00	$650.00	$5,850.00
	12/28/2013	Wedding Cake-Level 2	75	$82.00	$6,150.00	$615.00	$5,535.00
		Subtotals			$17,900.00	$1,790.00	$16,110.00
January 2014							
	1/						
	1/						
	1/						
	1/						
	1/						
	1/						
	1/						
	1/						

Month	Event Date	Menu Plan	Guests	Chg/PP	Total Revenue	Taxes	Net Revenue
May 2014							
	5 /3 /2014	Buffet Luncheon	50	$25.00	$1,250.00	$125.00	$1,125.00
	5 /10/2014	Luncheon Sitdown	35	$34.00	$1,190.00	$119.00	$1,071.00
	5 /29/2014	Dinner Buffet	80	$45.00	$3,600.00	$360.00	$3,240.00
		Subtotals			$6,040.00	$604.00	$5,436.00

24. Click the **Close Print Preview** button then close the **Group, Sort, and Total** pane.
25. Save and close the **Event Revenue Report**. Close the database and exit **Access**.
26. Submit your final file based on the guidelines provided by your instructor.
    To view examples of how your file or files should look at the end of the exercise, go to the student resource center.

APPLY YOUR SKILLS AC05-A03

Create Customized Reports

Universal Corporate Events, Ltd. is ready to add more reports to its database. In this exercise, you will create two reports: a quick, simple report using the Menus table as the record source and a report that lists Personnel contact information grouped by last name. Then, you will add, delete, and edit report controls, modify captions of several labels to make them more readable, and add a logo, title, and subtitle to the venue report.

Create Reports

1. Start **Access**. Open **AC05-A03-UCE** from the **AC2013 Lesson 05** folder and save it as **`AC05-A03-UCE-[FirstInitialLastName]`**.
2. Click the **Menus** table, and choose **Create→Reports→Report**.
   Access opens the new report in Layout View.
3. Save the report as **`Menus List`** and close it.
   Now you will use the Report Wizard to create a list of the company personnel, their addresses, phone numbers, and email addresses. The report will be grouped by last name.
4. Click the **Personnel** table and start the **Report Wizard**.
5. Include last and first name, address, city, state, ZIP, phone number, and email.
6. Group by last name.
7. Do not add a sort, and leave the layout default values. Name the report **`Personnel List`** and click **Finish**.
   Access opens the report in Print Preview.

Delete and Edit Report Controls; and Add a Logo and a New Title to a Report

8. Switch to **Design View**.
9. Select the **=Now()** control in the Page Footer and tap [Delete].
10. Delete the **="Page"** control in the Page Footer.
11. Change the caption of the **PerLastName** label in the Page Header to **`Last Name`**.
12. Save your changes.
13. Using either the **Logo** control or the **Insert Image** control, add **UCE-Logo.bmp** from the **AC2013 Lesson 05** folder to the Report Header.
14. Type **`.8`** for the Logo's **Width** and **Height** properties.

15. Click the **Personnel List** title control and enter the following property values:

Property	New Value
Caption	Universal Corporate Events, Ltd.
Width	4
Height	.4
Left	2
Font Name	Arial Narrow
Font Size	22
Text Align	Center
Fore Color	Blue, Accent 5, Darker 50%

16. Choose **Design→Header/Footer→Title**.
17. Enter the following property values for the new title:

Property	New Value
Width	4
Height	.4
Top	.5
Left	2
Font Name	Arial Narrow
Font Size	20
Text Align	Center
Fore Color	Blue, Accent 5, Darker 50%

18. Switch to **Report View** to determine what controls need realigning and resizing.
19. Save and close the report.

Size and Rearrange Report Controls and Apply a Theme

20. Display the **Personnel List** report in **Layout View**.
    Several report controls need resizing.
21. Click and drag the controls to space them out across the report.
22. Resize the controls to display their contents fully, but do not extend the report beyond the vertical dotted line.
23. Save the **Personnel List** Report.
24. Display the **Menus List** report in **Design View**.
25. Choose a *Theme* that you like for the report, keeping in mind that it will be applied to *every* object in the database.
26. Switch to **Layout View**, and resize controls to display the full contents, as necessary.
27. Save and close the **Menus List** report.

Add the Date to the Page Header and Display the Group, Sort, and Total Pane

28. Display the **Personnel List** report in **Design View**.
29. Click [Date and Time].
30. Choose the **Short Date** format (1/13/2013) and uncheck the **Include Time** box.
31. Move the new **Date** control to the top of the **Report Header**, and shorten it so it doesn't overlay the title.
32. Switch to **Report View** to see the new date control in the Report Header.
33. Save and close the **Personnel List** report.
34. Display the **Event Revenue Report** in **Design View**.
35. Open the **Group, Sort, and Totals** pane.
    The report is sorted and grouped by EventDate.
36. Investigate the various settings, but make no changes. Then close the **Group, Sort, and Totals** pane.

Set Print Options

37. Display **Event Revenue Report** in **Design View**.
38. Open the **Group, Sort, and Totals** pane. Choose to keep the header and first record together on one page.
39. View the results in **Print Preview**. Then, switch to **Design View**.
40. Now choose to keep the group together on one page.
41. View the results in **Print Preview** to see if there are any changes.
42. Click the **Close Print Preview** button then close the **Group, Sort, and Total** pane.
43. Save and close the report. Close the database and exit **Access**.
44. Submit your final file based on the guidelines provided by your instructor.

Extend Your Skills

In the course of working through the Extend Your Skills exercises, you will think critically as you use the skills taught in the lesson to complete the assigned projects. To evaluate your mastery and completion of the exercises, your instructor may use a rubric, with which more points are allotted according to performance characteristics. (The more you do, the more you earn!) Ask your instructor how your work will be evaluated.

AC05-E01 That's the Way I See It

In this exercise, you will create several reports for either your own business or for Blue Jean Landscaping. Open **AC05-E01-BJL** from your **AC2013 Lesson 05 folder** and save the file as `AC05-E01-BJL-[FirstInitialLastName]`.

Using the skills you learned in this lesson, create reports and lists to help your company track customers, sales, invoices, inventory, and any other aspects that you would find beneficial to managing your business. Include a title and a logo or other image in the Report Header. Remember that when you use the Logo control from the Ribbon, Access includes a Title control with the logo. You can use the auto-title or, if you want to edit the logo or title separately, choose Arrange→Table→Remove Layout to unlink the controls.

You will be evaluated based on the inclusion of all elements, your ability to follow directions, your ability to apply newly learned skills to a real-world situation, your creativity, and your accuracy in creating objects and/or entering data. Submit your final file based on the guidelines provided by your instructor.

AC05-E02 Be Your Own Boss

Blue Jean Landscaping wants to add several reports to the company database that will provide a listing of its equipment, services, and customer tables in an attractive and useful manner. In this exercise, you will create these reports. Open **AC05-E02-BJL** from the **AC2013 Lesson 05** folder and save the file as `AC05-E02-BJL-[FirstInitialLastName]`. Using the Store Inventory query as a record source, create a report using the Report Wizard that is grouped by manufacturer and includes item name, price, quantity in stock, and inventory amount, and a sum of the InvTot field. Use the default layout settings. Name the report `Store Inventory Report`. Use the skills you learned in this lesson to size, rearrange, and format the report controls. Add the **BJL-Logo** from your **AC2013 Lesson 05** folder, along with a title and subtitle using the existing Available Equipment as a guide. Then, create a report with the wizard using the Service Invoices Query that includes all the fields except InvNum. Group the results by InvDate, sum the LineTotal field, choose the Stepped and Landscape layout options, and name the report `Service Invoices Report`. Format the report controls and add the logo, title, and subtitle as directed above.

You will be evaluated based on the inclusion of all elements, your ability to follow directions, your ability to apply newly learned skills to a real-world situation, your creativity, and your accuracy in creating objects and/or entering data. Submit your final file based on the guidelines provided by your instructor.

Transfer Your Skills

In the course of working through the Transfer Your Skills exercises, you will use critical-thinking and creativity skills to complete the assigned projects using skills taught in the lesson. To evaluate your mastery and completion of the exercises, your instructor may use a rubric, with which more points are allotted according to performance characteristics. (The more you do, the more you earn!) Ask your instructor how your work will be evaluated.

AC05-T01 Use the Web as a Learning Tool

Throughout this book, you will be provided with an opportunity to use the Internet as a learning tool by completing WebQuests. According to the original creators of WebQuests, as described on their website (WebQuest.org), a WebQuest is "an inquiry-oriented activity in which most or all of the information used by learners is drawn from the web." To complete the WebQuest projects in this book, navigate to the student resource center and choose the WebQuest for the lesson on which you are currently working. The subject of each WebQuest will be relevant to the material found in the lesson.

WebQuest Subject: Using parameter values in reports.

Submit your final file(s) based on the guidelines provided by your instructor.

AC05-T02 Demonstrate Proficiency

Stormy BBQ wants a new, attractive, and exciting menu for their flagship Key West restaurant. The menu will have a tropical theme, include item names and prices, and use the new company logo, SBQ-Logo. You will also create a fun take-out menu for the store that will include their food as well as their off-the-shelf merchandise. Use the MenuItems and Merchandise tables for ideas on how to display what Stormy BBQ offers. Open **AC05-T02-StormyBBQ** from the **AC2013 Lesson 05** folder and save it as `AC05-T02-StormyBBQ-[FirstInitialLastName]`. Use the report design and formatting tools you learned in this lesson to create the two fun, tropical-themed menus described.

Submit your final file based on the guidelines provided by your instructor.

ACCESS 2013

Refining Table Design

LESSON OUTLINE

LEARNING OBJECTIVES

After studying this lesson, you will be able to:

- Create and modify relationships
- Format a table datasheet layout
- Modify table structure
- Set field properties
- Use the Lookup Wizard

By now you should have a good understanding of the basic features of a database. As you move forward, it's important to understand what makes Access a relational database management system and why well-designed databases perform better (reduce redundant data and create critical connections between the objects that help make them more efficient to use). In this lesson, you will manually set and modify table relationships and further examine how database objects relate. You will modify tables and field properties, and format font size and font color, background color, and other settings. You will also set field size values, default captions, default values, input masks, and validation rules. Finally, you will create lookup fields to speed data entry and ensure data accuracy.

CASE STUDY

Maintaining and Formatting Databases

You are tasked with maintaining the Winchester Web Design database. After reviewing the objects in the database, you decide to make some changes that will make the database more efficient and improve data entry. You will create a lookup field to streamline data entry. In the process you will add some formatting to make the tables more colorful. You also want to examine the relationships between tables to ensure that they define the database accurately.

Customers

CustID	Last Name	First Name	Business	Street Address	City
AbramsJ	Abrams	John	☑	1210 West Pier Way	Palmetto
AndersM	Anders	Mark	☐	205 Montana St	Bradenton
BlaserH	Bla				
DavisP	Da				
FleetwoodC	Fle				
HassanA	Ha				
JeffriesD	Jef				
KleinJ	Kle				
MansurJ	Ma				

Customers

CustID	Last Name	First Name	Business	Street Address	City
⊞ AbramsM	Abrams	Mark	☑	1210 West Pier Way	Palmetto
⊞ AndersM	Anders	Mark	☐	205 Montana St	Bradenton
⊞ BlaserH	Blaser	Helen	☑	600 Fowler	Tampa
⊞ DavisP	Davis	Peter	☐	65 Terracotta Way	Sarasota

Creating and Modifying Relationships

Video Library http://labyrinthelab.com/videos Video Number: AC13-V0601

As you build tables and other objects in a relational database, Access creates some of the relationships between tables based upon the field structure of each table. However, it's a good idea to examine and edit these relationships manually to cascade updated or deleted records—that is, to automatically update or delete all affected records as part of a single operation. Cascade options can be invaluable in cases where a store pulls a product off of its shelf, and therefore needs to remove that product from its merchandise list, order list, inventory list, and advertising list. And in most cases, you also must enforce referential integrity to ensure that relationships between records in related tables are valid. Finally, it may be wise to create and display those relationships in a report to add to the database documentation.

Relationship Types

Database relationships connect data in one table to data stored in other tables. Access supports three different types of relationships:

- A one-to-one relationship means that each record in Table A can have only one matching record in Table B, and each record in Table B can have only one matching record in Table A. This is the least common relationship. A good example is a main Customers table linked to a CustPassword table. One customer has one password.
- A one-to-many relationship means that each record in Table A can have multiple matching records in Table B, but a record in Table B can have only one matching record in Table A. This is the most common relationship. Here's an example: One employee will have many sales, and a product will be sold many times.
- A many-to-many relationship occurs when two tables may each have many matches in the other table, but they do not share key fields, so they use a third junction table to tie other tables to complete the relationship. The junction table has a one-to-many relationship to each table. An example is a vendors table and a products table, where one vendor provides many different products and one product is available from many vendors.

This lesson focuses on one-to-many relationships.

Adding, Deleting, and Modifying Relationships

There are times when a database designer must add, delete, or change a relationship. To modify tables after relationships have been set, you must temporarily delete existing relationships so Access is free to make the revisions without violating integrity rules. For example, if you want to convert an existing Short Text data type field, such as State, to a Lookup data type and attempt to change its data type, Access will display a warning message indicating that you must first delete its relationships to any other tables.

After you delete the relationship and change the field's data type, you may have to reestablish the relationship and edit those relationship properties.

Referential Integrity Requirements

Perhaps the most important database relationship protocol is referential integrity, which is a set of rules used to maintain the validity of the related data in a database. It ensures that you don't delete a record or change a primary key that is related to data in a foreign table. It also requires the data types of the related fields (both the primary and foreign keys) to be the same or compatible.

Referential integrity is a critical part of a relational database, so let's look at it from several different views, using real life examples.

- If the ProdID primary key in the Products table has a Number data type (i.e. Field Size property: Long Integer), then the ProdID foreign key in the Invoice Details table must also have the data type Number (i.e. Field Size property: Long Integer).
- You cannot have a listing in the Invoice Details table for a product that you don't sell. That is, you cannot have a foreign key (i.e. ProdID) in the Invoice Details table without a matching primary key (i.e. ProdID) in the Products table.
- You cannot delete the primary key (i.e. ProdID) from the Products table when there is a corresponding foreign key (i.e. ProdID) in the Invoice Details table.
- You cannot change the primary key value (i.e. 01HP) from the Products table when there is an existing and corresponding foreign key value (i.e. 01HP) in the Invoice Details table.

Relationship Cascade Options

Two additional relationship options are available so that you can control updates to related tables: Cascade Update and Cascade Delete. Each has a unique function for maintaining database relationships, and it's important to know what they control before using them.

RELATIONSHIP CASCADE OPTIONS

Cascade Option	Description
Cascade Update	Updates the value in the key field of a related table if you change the primary key value in the primary table. For example, if you change a ProdID in the Products table, the ProdID field value in the Invoice Details table updates for each invoice.
Cascade Delete	Deletes records in a related table any time you delete related records in the primary table. You might consider this option if you deleted an employee from the Employees table and want to also delete their spouse from the Spouses table. However, use this option with caution because it would not be wise to delete all 2012 invoice records for an employee just because that employee retired in 2013.

Referential Integrity in Microsoft Access

You can examine, create, and edit relationships between tables in the Relationships window. To create relationships manually, use the Edit Relationships dialog to identify the rules you want Access to check.

FROM THE RIBBON

Database Tools→Relationships→Relationships to view database relationships

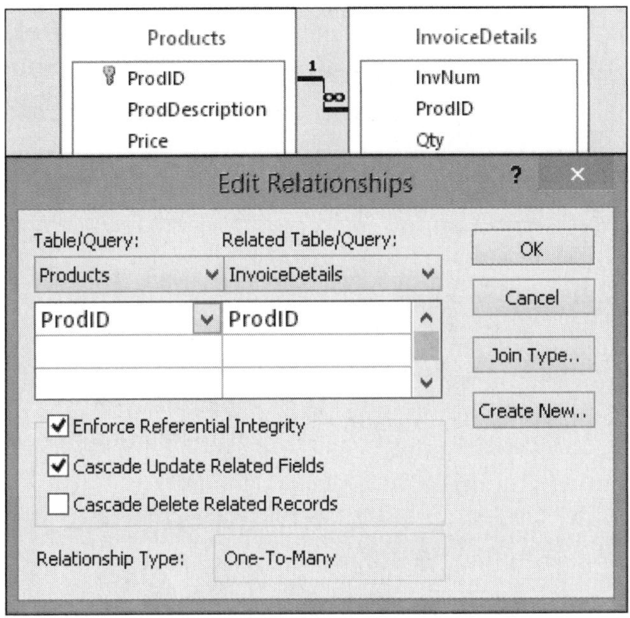

Notice the one-to-many (1 – ∞) relationship join line, which indicates that referential integrity has been enforced.

DEVELOP YOUR SKILLS AC06-D01

Create and Modify Relationships

In this exercise, you will open the Relationships window, add a table, and create a relationship between tables. You will also set referential integrity for the relationship.

1. Open **AC06-D01-WinWebDesign** from the **AC2013 Lesson 06** folder and save it as **`AC06-D01-WinWebDesign-[FirstInitialLastName]`**.

   Replace the bracketed text with your first initial and last name. For example, if your name is Bethany Smith, your filename would look like this: AC06-D01-WinWebDesign-BSmith. The first time you open a database on your system, a Security Warning may appear asking whether you want to make the file a Trusted Document. If it does, click Yes.

2. If an Information dialog box opens stating that the compact and repair operation has been cancelled, click **OK** to continue.

3. If a Security Warning bar displays, click **Enable Content**.

4. Choose **Database Tools→Relationships→Relationships**.

5. Follow these steps to add a table to the Relationships window:

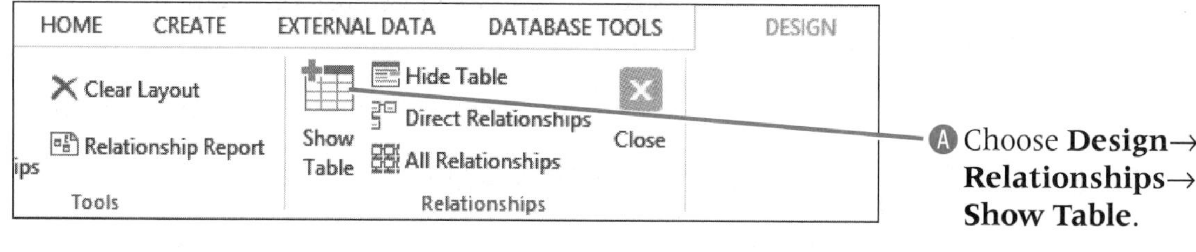

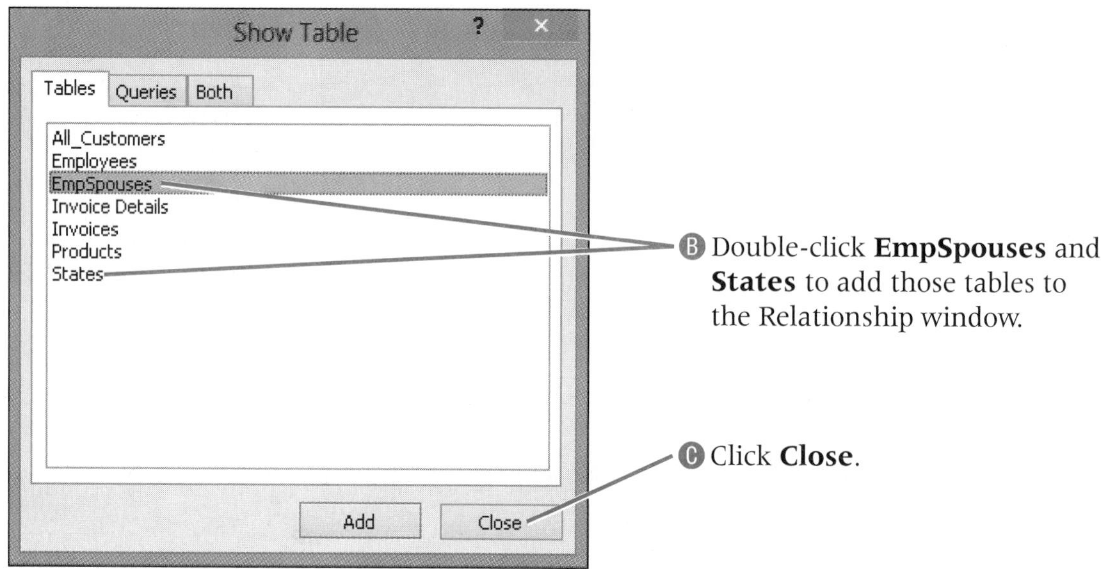

Typically all tables will be in the Relationships window, but sometimes a table is added later, like the EmpSpouses table.

6. Drag the title bar of each table to neatly line them up to see how they relate without relationship lines overlapping.

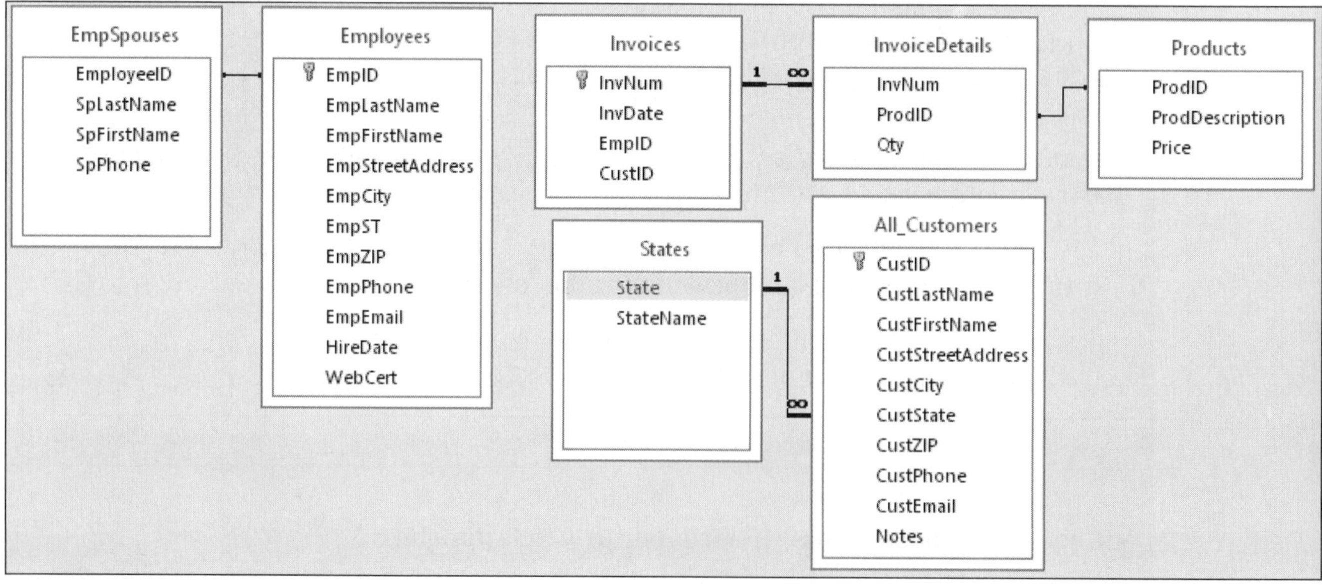

Manually Set Relationships

Now you will create a one-to-many relationship between the Invoices table and the Employees table so one employee may have many sales.

7. Follow these steps to create a relationship between the Invoices and Employees tables:

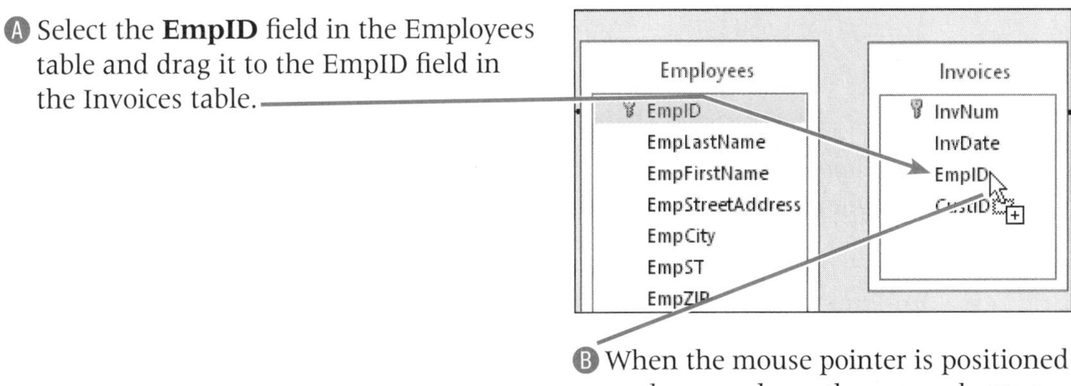

The Edit Relationships dialog box opens.

8. Click the checkbox next to **Enforce Referential Integrity**, and then click **Create**.

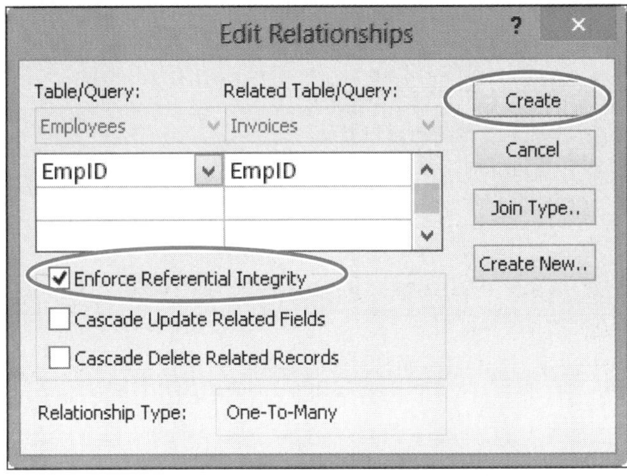

Access places characters at each end of the join line: the Employees table end displays a 1 and the Orders table end displays an infinity sign (∞).

9. Create a relationship between the **All_Customers** table and the **Invoices** table by dragging the **CustID** primary key to the **CustID** foreign key.

10. Save the changes and leave the **Relationships** window open.

Unless directed otherwise, keep Access and any databases or database objects being used open at the end of each exercise.

Access 2013

Editing Relationships

Video Library http://labyrinthelab.com/videos Video Number: AC13-V0602

Setting cascade options can have a ripple effect on records and data in a database. So, it's a good idea to back up a database before setting these options and then test the settings. That way you can restore the database from the backup if the setting results in data loss.

When to Review Relationships

Any time the structure of a table changes—whether it's through adding or removing fields, changing data types, or creating lookup fields—you should review and update the relationships among database tables.

DEVELOP YOUR SKILLS AC06-D02

Edit Relationships and Set Options

In this exercise, you will edit the relationship between the Invoices and Employees table so that if you change the Employee ID in the primary table (Employees), Access will update the Employee ID in the related foreign table (Invoices).

1. Right-click the join line between the **Invoices** table and the **Employees** table and choose **Edit Relationships**.

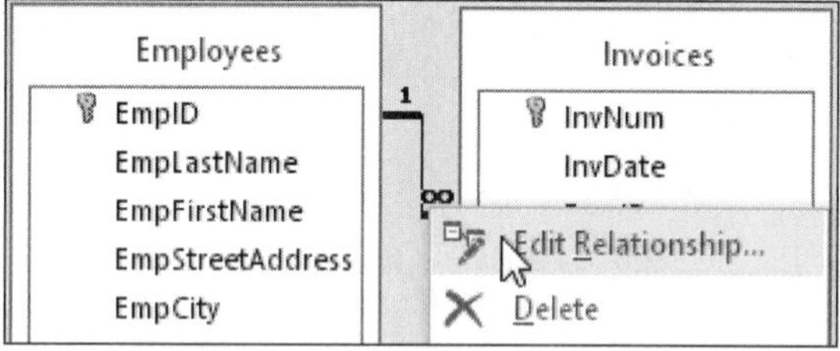

2. Check the **Cascade Update Related Fields** checkbox and click **OK**.

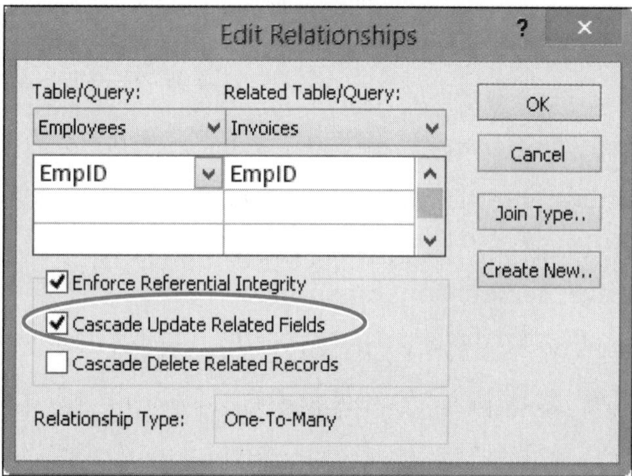

3. Save the changes to the relationship.

Documenting and Printing Relationships

After you have inspected the relationships, you may want to create a report to view a printable version of the relationships. You can also display the database objects that either use, or are used by, other objects in the database. This is done through the Object Dependencies panel.

FROM THE RIBBON

Database Tools→Relationships→Relationships→Relationship Report to print the relationships

DEVELOP YOUR SKILLS AC06-D03

Create a Relationship Report and View Dependencies

In this exercise, you will create a relationship report and examine object dependencies for the Employees table.

1. In the **Relationships** window, if necessary, drag the table title bars so that the join lines are clearly visible.
2. Choose **Design→Tools→Relationship Report**.
3. Save the report as **`AC06-D03-Relationships-[FirstInitialLastName]`**. Close the **Relationships** window.

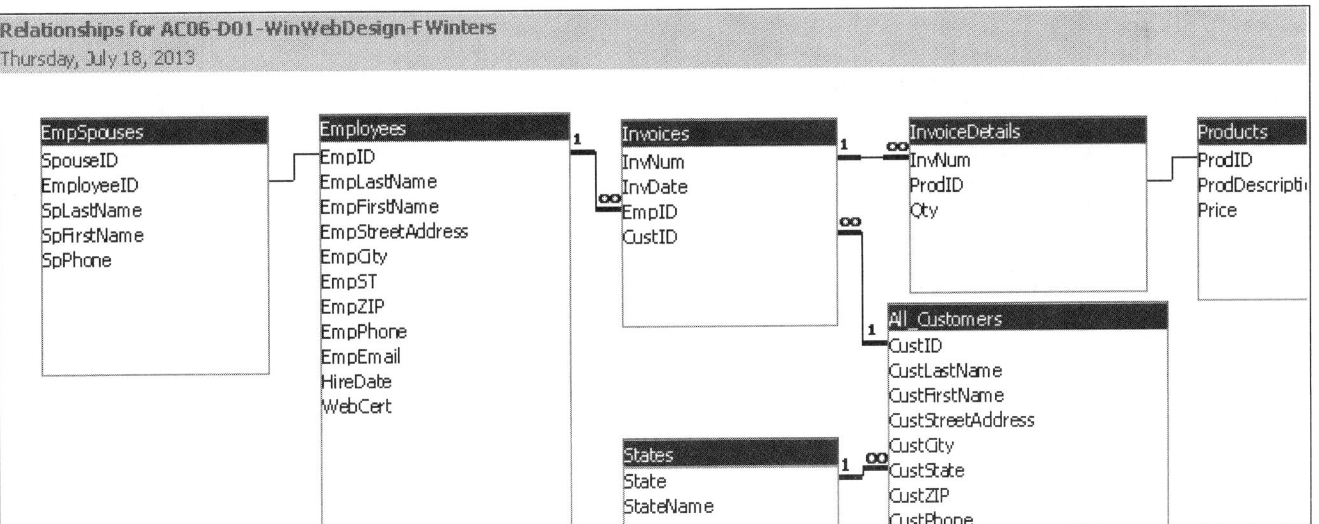

The new relationship report is added to the Report group in the Navigation Pane.

Display Object Dependencies

4. Close any open objects, and then click (but don't open) the **Employees** table in the Navigation Pane.
5. Choose **Database Tools→Relationships→Object Dependencies**.
6. Review the **Objects That Depend On Me** option in the Object Dependencies panel.
   Many objects—other tables, queries, forms, and reports—depend on the Employees table.
7. Choose the **Objects That I Depend On** option.

Access 2013

The Employees table has relationships with or depends on the EmpSpouses and Invoices tables.

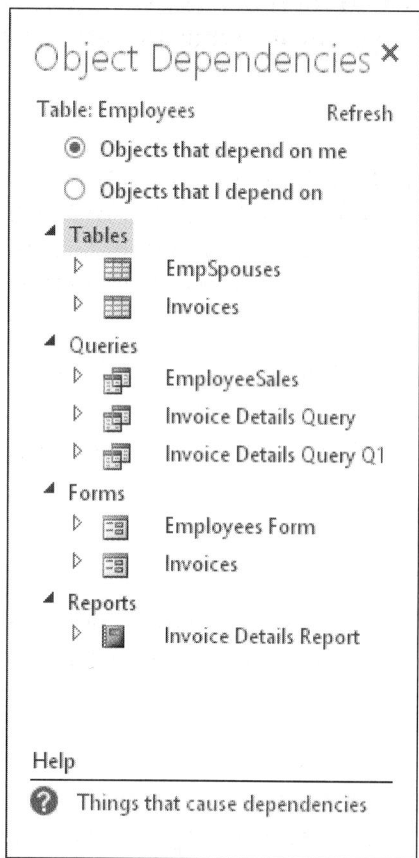

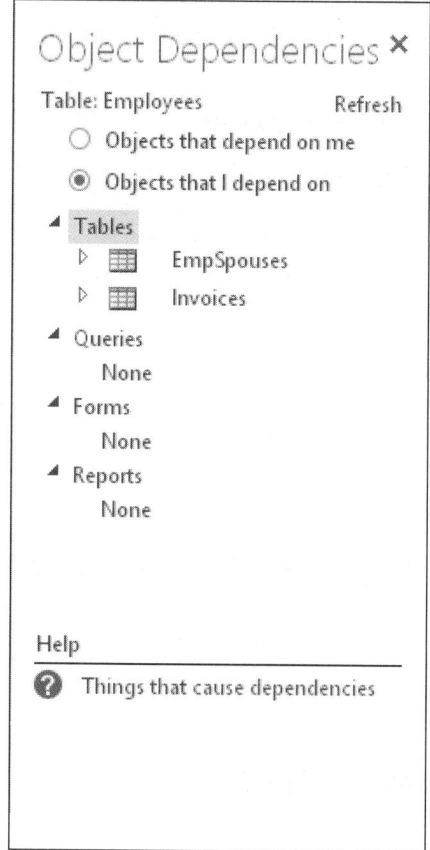

8. Close the **Object Dependencies** panel.

Modifying Table Structures

Video Library http://labyrinthelab.com/videos Video Number: AC13-V0603

Database integrity and data validity are important aspects of database maintenance. Access offers a number of features that enable you to modify table fields, control the data entered, and format the data to ensure consistent reporting. These features include, but are not limited to:

- Renaming tables, forms, and other database objects
- Adding and removing fields from tables
- Changing data types

Renaming Tables and Editing, Adding, and Deleting Table Fields

As you create tables, you define each field by setting the data type and entering the field name. Access works behind the scenes and sets default properties for the field that limit the number of characters in a field, as well as the format and data type of characters that are valid for the field.

You can accept the default properties Access sets or modify the properties. Properties available depend on the data type selected for the field. Care must be taken when adding, editing, or deleting fields because of the impact such actions might have on the table data.

Renaming Tables

When you save a table, give it a name that describes the data it contains. You can later change the name without affecting its data. However, note that table names are often included in other database objects that use the table's data. So, renaming a table can impact other database objects. If you rename a table, make sure that every form, query, or report that uses that table still works.

Traditionally, it was wise *to not* include spaces in table names because referencing the table in a query could be confusing. For instance—is *Invoice Details* two objects or one object? Fortunately, Access will enclose a table name like *Invoice Details* within square brackets ([ ]) when it uses it in an expression.

Adding Fields to Existing Tables

Periodically you will need to create new fields in existing database tables and then add data to these fields. You can add a field either in Datasheet View or in Table Design View, and then move it where you want it to be in the layout.

Deleting Fields

When you delete a field that contains data, Access displays a message warning you that deleting the field will remove all its data. If you delete a field in Design View and have not saved the table, you can recover the deleted field using the Undo command. If, however, you save the table after deleting the field, the data is lost and you have to add the field name to the Table Design and then re-enter all field data in the table to restore the data. After choosing to delete a field, Access displays a warning message. If you choose Yes, Access removes the field.

FROM THE KEYBOARD
Ctrl+Z to undo the last keystroke

Access 2013

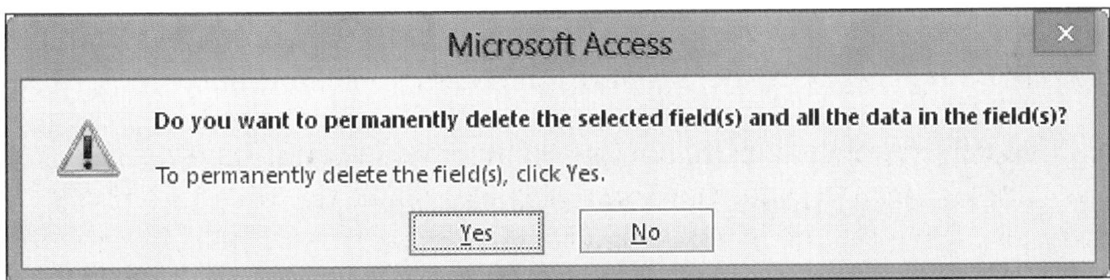

Take care when deleting a field from a table! If the field is used by other queries, forms, or reports, you will generate errors. It could take many hours of hard work to re-create the data that the field contained.

Editing Field Data Types

Many Access data types start with a different letter, which means you can type a letter and the data type that begins with that letter will display. For example, if you want to change the data type of a field from Short Text to Number, you click in the field's Data Type and type "N."

Any time you change the data type of a field that contains values that fail to conform to the new data type, Access deletes any nonconforming data. For example, if you change a field's data type from Short Text to a Number data type and someone had accidentally entered 1O (using capital O) instead of 10 (using zero) Access will warn you that you are about to delete data that did not conform. The great thing about this is that Access will only allow valid field data, which results in a much greater likelihood of accurate data.

Using the Yes/No Data Type

The Yes/No field data type sets the field so that only two entries are possible—Yes/No, True/False, or On/Off. When you set the Yes/No data type for a field, Access places a checkbox for the field in the datasheet and on forms where the data appears. Checking the checkbox indicates that the field will allow a value of Yes, True, On, etc.; clearing the checkbox indicates a value of No, False, or Off.

FROM THE KEYBOARD

[Spacebar] to check and uncheck a checkbox

Hire Date	Web Cert
12/1/2010	☑
1/7/2013	☐
12/9/2010	☑
4/18/2011	☐
	☐

Checkmarks identifying employees who are web certified.

DEVELOP YOUR SKILLS AC06-D04

Modify the Table Structure

In this exercise, you will rename a table, delete a table field, add a table field, and modify the data type of a field.

1. Right-click the **All_Customers** table in the Navigation Pane and choose **Rename**.
2. Type `Customers` and tap [Enter].
3. Right-click the **Customers** table and select **Design View**.

4. Follow these steps to delete the Notes field from the table:

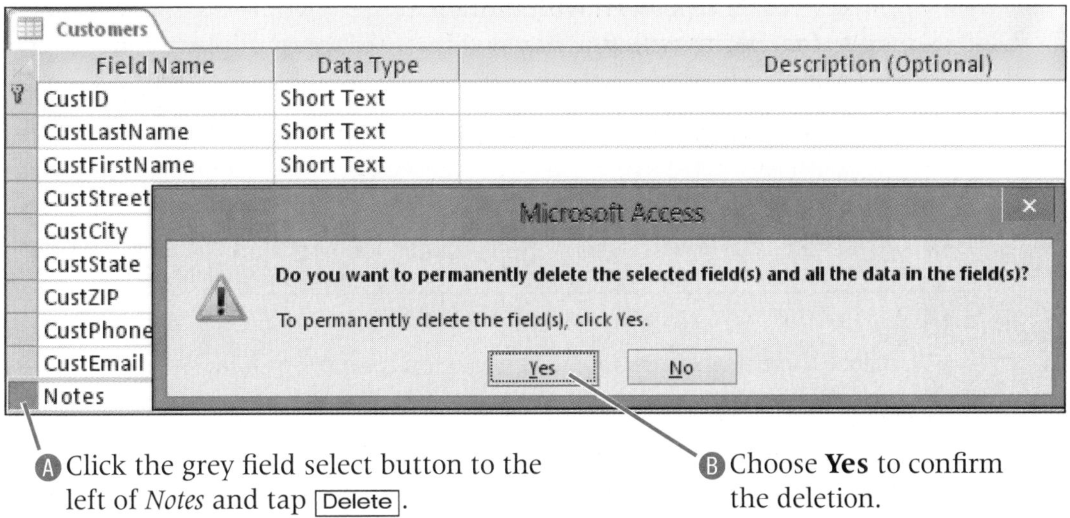

Access deletes the field.

Add New Fields

Now you will add a Yes/No field to the Customers table.

5. Right-click the **CustStreetAddress** field row button and select **Insert Rows**.

   A new row opens above the CustStreetAddress row.

6. Follow these steps to add a new Yes/No field:

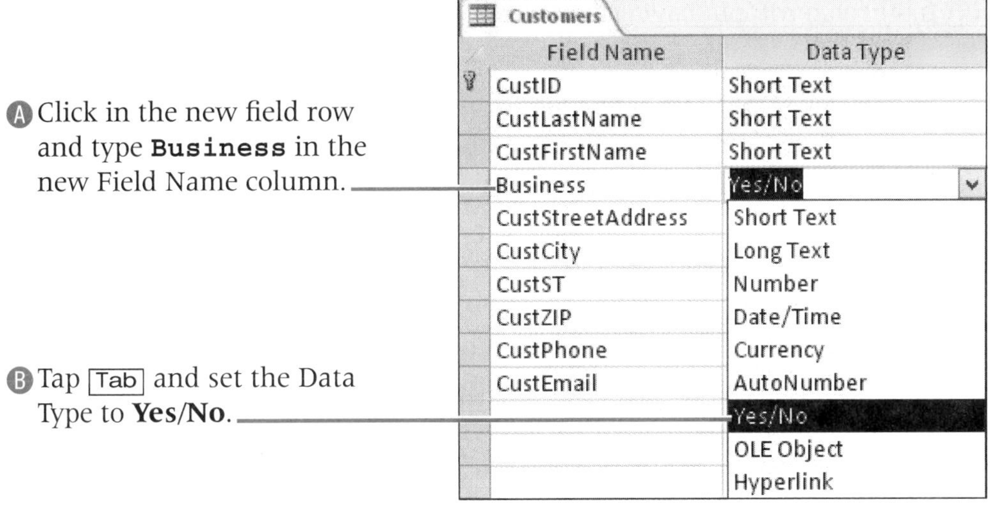

7. Save the table and switch back to **Datasheet View**.

8. Move to the new **Business** field column and check every other record by either clicking with the mouse or tapping the [Spacebar].

Customers

CustID	Last Name	First Name	Business	Street Address	City
AbramsJ	Abrams	John	☑	1210 West Pier Wa	Palmetto
AndersM	Anders	Mark	☐	205 Montana St	Bradenton
BlaserH	Blaser	Helen	☑	600 Fowler	Tampa
DavisP	Davis	Peter	☐	65 Terracotta Way	Sarasota
FleetwoodC	Fleetwood	Candace	☑	92 Highland St	Sarasota

9. Close the **Customers** table, saving changes if prompted.

Formatting a Table Datasheet Layout

Video Library http://labyrinthelab.com/videos Video Number: AC13-V0604

It's difficult to plan and prepare for all of the possibilities that may occur as a database is first developed. For instance, if field values are longer than anticipated Access will display only the portion of the data that fits within the column width, causing some of the data to be unseen. Or the opposite scenario may occur, where one or two fields were added, and you need to display all the fields on one screen, which means that you may have to modify the width of each column. Alternatively, you can maximize the Access window or close the Navigation Pane to provide more room without having to modify the width of each column.

Changing the Width of Columns

Access offers some useful techniques to adjust the width of each column in a datasheet to display all data in the column.

- **Drag a column border:** Drag a column border to make the column on the left of the border wider or narrower.
- **Double-click a column heading border:** Double-click the right border of a column to change the width of the column on the left to fit either the longest data entry in the column or column heading, whichever is wider.
- **Right-click a field heading and choose Field Width:** Select the Field Width command from the context menu to open the Column Width dialog box and type the width, reset the standard width, or select Best Fit to automatically size the field width to the longest entry.

Moving and Hiding Data Columns

There will be times when you want to reposition a column of data in a table layout—perhaps to display the email address before the telephone number. When you rearrange the columns in a datasheet, the table layout remains the same but the fields display in a different order in the datasheet. You may also want to hide some columns so you can better view other field columns. When you hide columns, Access temporarily removes them from display. The data, however, remains in the table—it is not deleted. If you want to view data in hidden columns at a later time, you unhide the column.

Saving a Table Layout

Changing the layout of a table datasheet has no real effect on table data or structure; however, when you make changes to a table datasheet, Access recognizes the differences between the structure of the table and its layout, and prompts you to save the changes to the layout when you close the table. If you abandon the changes, the next time you open the table datasheet, the column widths will return to their original size and any columns that were hidden will show. If you save the changes, the next time you open the table datasheet, Access recalls the layout and displays the formatting changes.

The shape and color of the mouse pointer are important when you are adjusting column width and repositioning columns in a table or datasheet layout. The mouse pointer changes shapes depending on the task being performed.

MOUSE POINTERS TO ADJUST TABLE LAYOUT	
Pointer Shape	**Description**
	Column width resizing—drag to manually adjust or double-click to auto adjust.
	Select column to move—click on column heading.
	Move selected column—drag to desired location.
	Move column—hover between column heading and top field.
	Select multiple fields in a column or row—drag left, right, up, and down.

DEVELOP YOUR SKILLS AC06-D05

Format a Table Datasheet Layout

In this exercise, you will adjust column width to allow for the best display of data in a datasheet, rearrange columns, and hide a column.

1. Display the **Customers** table in **Datasheet View**.
2. Follow these steps to change the width of the Street Address column:

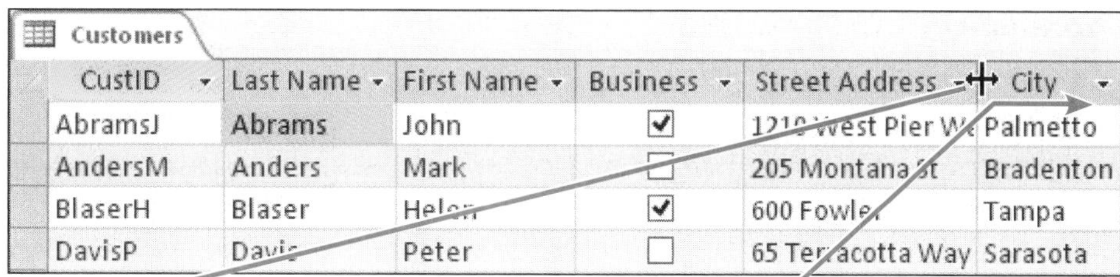

Ⓐ Hover the mouse pointer over the right border of the **Street Address** column heading until it becomes the resize pointer.

Ⓑ Double-click the border between the columns to widen the first column.

Access 2013

3. Follow these steps to resize two columns at the same time:

Ⓐ Point to the **CustID** column heading until the column selector pointer appears. Then click that heading and drag over the **Last Name** heading to select both columns.

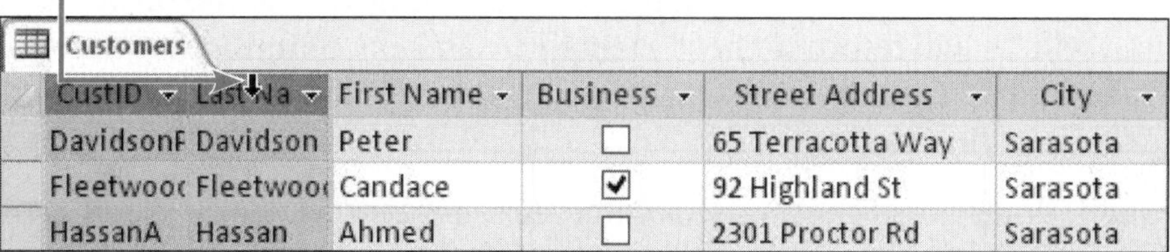

Customers

CustID	Last Name	First Name	Business	Street Address	City
DavidsonP	Davidson	Peter	☐	65 Terracotta Way	Sarasota
FleetwoodC	Fleetwood	Candace	☑	92 Highland St	Sarasota
HassanA	Hassan	Ahmed	☐	2301 Proctor Rd	Sarasota

Ⓑ Double-click the left border of the **Last Name** column once you see the column resize pointer.

4. Follow these steps to switch the First Name and Last Name columns:

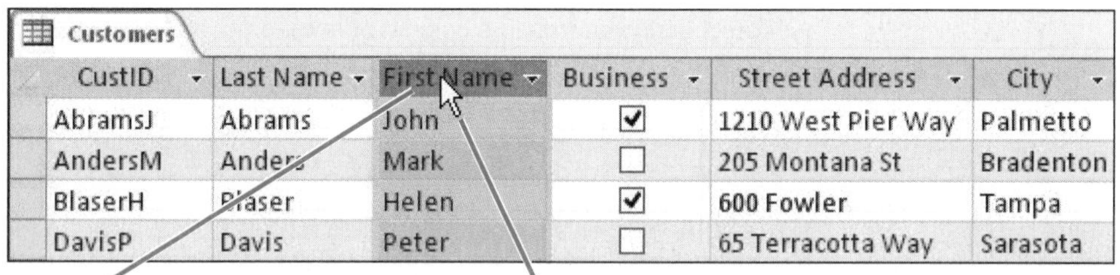

Ⓐ Click the **First Name** column heading to select the column.

Ⓑ Hover the mouse pointer over the **First Name** column heading until it becomes the move arrow.

Ⓒ Click and drag the **First Name** column to the left of the **Last Name** field.

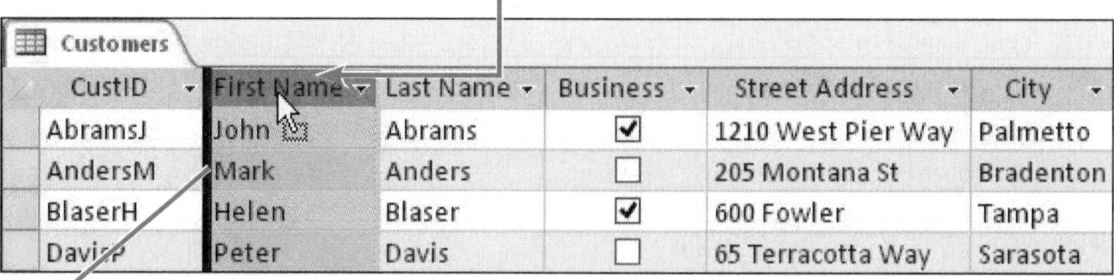

Ⓓ Notice as you drag, a black vertical bar indicates the active position of the column.

5. Follow these steps to simultaneously auto-adjust all columns in a table datasheet:

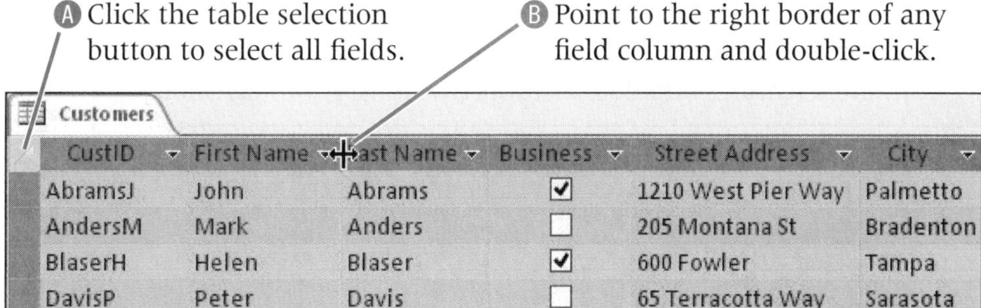

6. Follow these steps to hide the Telephone column:

7. Save and close the **Customers** table.

Enhancing a Datasheet

Video Library http://labyrinthelab.com/videos Video Number: AC13-V0605

Changing the datasheet layout enables you to make necessary adjustments, such as widening a data field so that a longer data value can be fully displayed. Enhancing the datasheet layout enables you to improve its readability. Some of the features you can apply to enhance a datasheet include:

- Gridlines
- Font, font size, and font color
- Background color

As you apply enhancements to the datasheet, Access formats all data and gridlines to match the format you choose.

Formatting the Datasheet Using the Ribbon

Two different Ribbon tabs contain tools for enhancing a datasheet:

- The Text Formatting group on the Home tab displays tools for enhancing the most commonly formatted features on a datasheet such as font, gridlines, color, fill, and alignment.

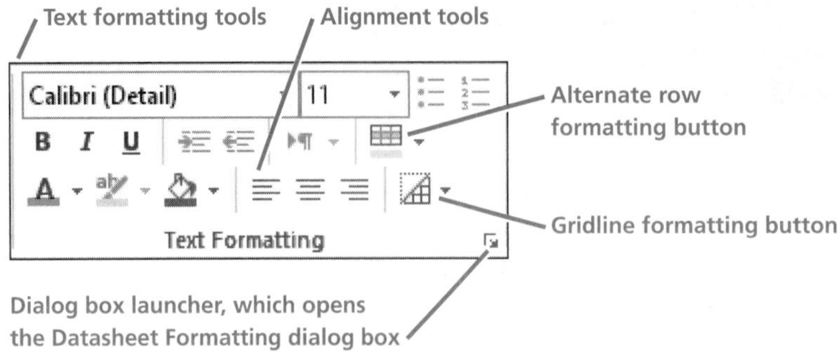

- The Table Tools→Fields tab contains tools for setting the data type and data format for numeric, currency, and date/time data.

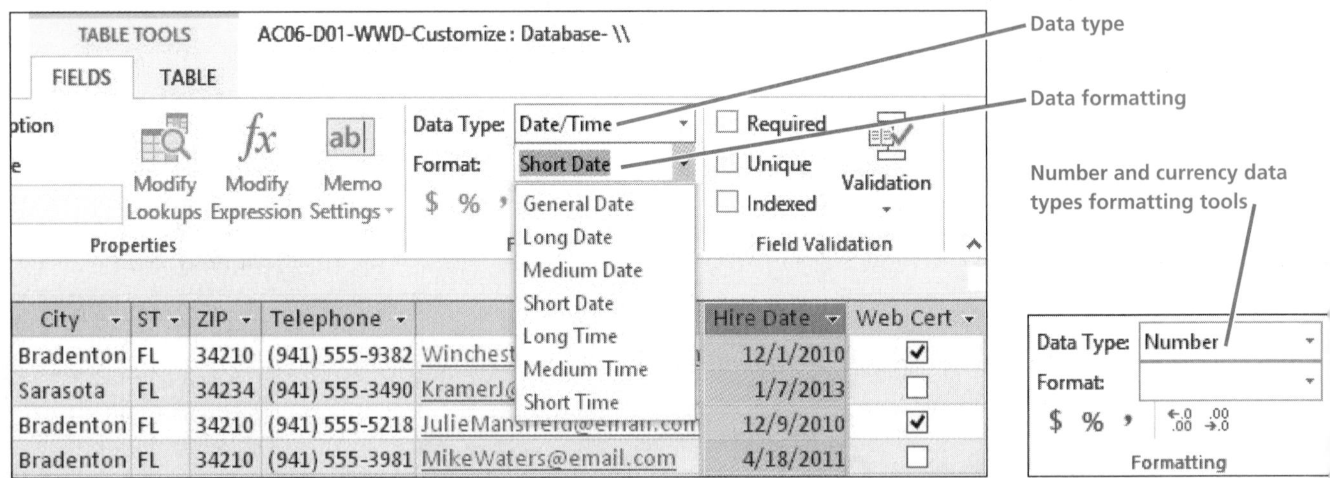

In addition to the Ribbon tools, the Datasheet Formatting dialog box contains tools that enable you to change the background color of table cells as well as the line style for the table.

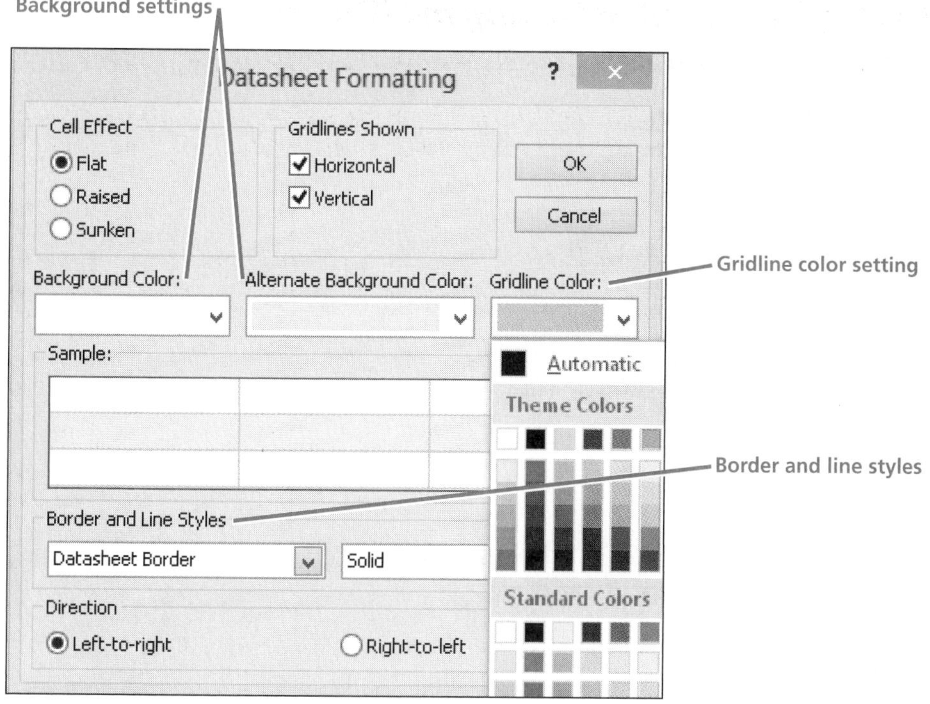

DEVELOP YOUR SKILLS AC06-D06

Enhance a Datasheet

In this exercise, you will use the Text Formatting tools to set datasheet enhancement options for the Customers table.

1. Open the **Customers** table in **Datasheet View**.
2. Choose **Home→Text Formatting→Alternate Row Color** to display the palette of colors.
3. Click the **Blue, Accent 1** color button on the top row.

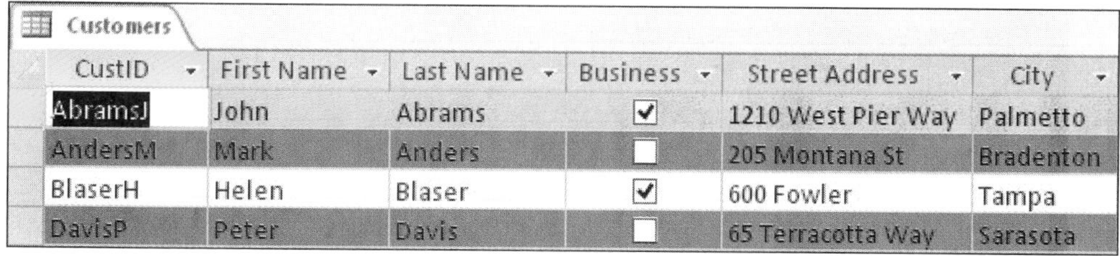

Customers
CustID
First Name
Last Name
Business
Street Address
City
AbramsJ
John
Abrams
1210 West Pier Way
Palmetto
AndersM
Mark
Anders
205 Montana St
Bradenton
BlaserH
Helen
Blaser
600 Fowler
Tampa
DavisP
Peter
Davis
65 Terracotta Way
Sarasota

Alternate rows in the datasheet are blue.

Format Datasheet Font

4. Choose **Home→Text Formatting→Font** and select **Arial**.

Access 2013

Format Gridlines

5. Choose **Home→Text Formatting→Gridlines** button and select **Gridlines: Horizontal**.

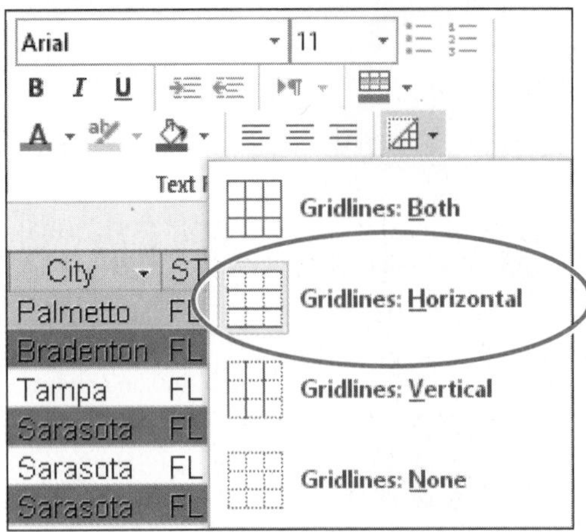

The datasheet will only display horizontal gridlines now.

6. Click the **Home→Text Formatting→dialog box launcher** to open the Datasheet Formatting dialog box.
7. Follow these steps to change the gridline color:

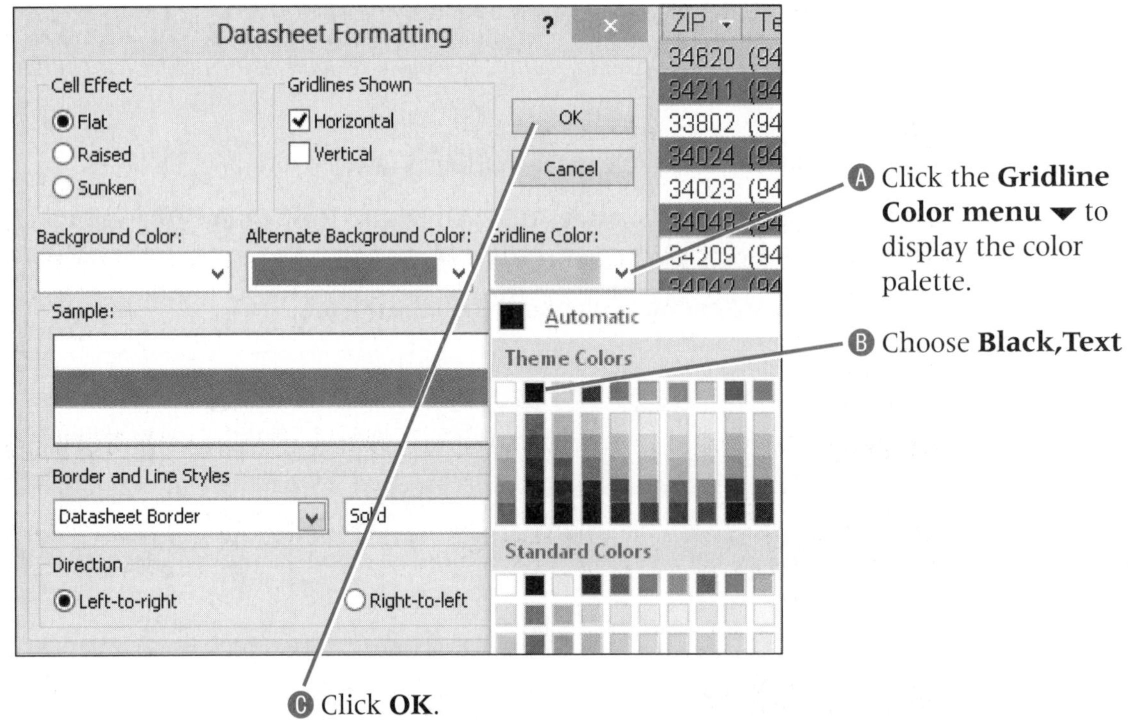

8. Close but *do not* save changes to the **Customers** table.

Setting Field Properties

Video Library http://labyrinthelab.com/videos Video Number: AC13-V0606

Field properties are settings that enable you to set and define the properties of each field. The Field Properties pane appears in the lower portion of the Table Design View or on the Fields tab in Datasheet View. The most frequently used properties are identified in the following table.

COMMON FIELD PROPERTIES	
Field Property	**Description**
Field Size	Sets a field length for the number of characters each field can hold.
Format	Sets a predefined display layout for fields, (i.e., currency or percent).
Input Mask	Identifies the format of values entered—with hyphens or without, alphabetic or numeric, uppercase or lowercase, etc.
Caption	Sets a column heading title to describe the data content better than the actual field name. Includes spaces where appropriate.
Default Value	Adds a default value for a specific field in each record, such as FL for state.
Validation Rule	Controls actual values entered into a field, such as less than 100 or greater than 01/01/2017.
Validation Text	Provides a tip that identifies valid data entries, such as "All dates must be after 01/01/2017."
Required	Sets the field as required to ensure a value is entered in the field.

Why Set Field Properties?

Different people add data to databases—and they often enter the data differently. For example, some people type parentheses around the area code when entering phone numbers into a database. Others may separate the area code from the number using a hyphen. Both formats are accurate, but displaying mismatched data can be distracting. Entering parentheses or hyphens can also be time consuming. Setting field properties to control how data appears helps maintain data consistency throughout a database.

Set Field Sizes, Captions, and Default Values

Maintaining database integrity, data validity, and data format are important considerations when building a database. You should make every effort to ensure that data is entered consistently, contains the required number of characters, and falls within valid data ranges.

Setting Field Size

Rather than using a default field size, you can set the Field Size property to limit the number of characters that can be entered into the field for each record. For example, you can limit data entry of state names to the two-character state abbreviation.

Sometimes, when you reduce an existing field size to limit data entry, Access displays a warning that data may be lost due to the reduced field size. In most cases, you are familiar with the data, so you can choose Yes to continue. For instance, truncating Florida to FL would not create invalid data. However, if you are uncertain you should choose No, check the data to ensure that it fits the new limit, and then set the field size.

Identifying Field Size for Number Fields

Number fields are identified by special formats in the Properties panel. In general, number fields should be set to define the largest value anticipated for the field. Setting the proper field size controls for number fields helps optimize database performance. The following table identifies each Number field format and describes the type of data each stores.

NUMBER FIELD FORMATS

Field Size Property	Description
Byte	Stores whole numbers between 0 and 255 using one byte and allows no fractions or decimal points; uses the minimum amount of memory, allowing for the fastest processing.
Integer	Stores whole numbers between –32,768 and 32,767 using 2 bytes rather than the standard 7 bytes normally used for high values.
Long Integer	Stores whole numbers between –2,147,483,648 and 2,147,483,647 using 4 bytes rather than the standard 14 bytes normally used for high values.
Single	Stores positive and negative numbers to exactly seven decimal places using 4 bytes.
Double	Stores positive and negative numbers to exactly 15 decimal places using 8 bytes.
Replication ID	Identifies replication of tables, records, and other objects in Access 2003 or earlier databases using 16 bytes.
Decimal	Stores positive and negative numbers to exactly 28 decimal places using 12 bytes.

Setting Text to Upper- or Lowercase Format

Text fields have unique field properties available for formatting data. Access provides a Format field that enables you to force a specific format to all characters in the field. The most common format characters are used to force uppercase (>) and lowercase (<). Using the Text Format property eliminates the need to spend valuable time entering multiple characters in the Input Mask property.

Setting Captions

As you may have noticed, many field names contain no spaces or include an underscore—such as LastName or Last_Name. The Caption field property enables you to type a more descriptive name for a field that is more suitable for display on forms, in datasheets, and on reports—such as Last Name.

Setting Default Field Values

Validation rules control the data you enter in table fields. Setting a default value for a field automatically enters the most common data value and can save time and help reduce the number of errors made during data entry.

For instance, all the employees at Winchester Web Design live in Florida. Consequently, it saves time and reduces inconsistency when the default value for the State field is set to FL. The default value appears whenever a new record is added. If you need to enter a different state, you simply type in the new state to replace the default value.

Making a Field Required

Whenever you create a primary key field, its properties are automatically set to be required and indexed, allowing no duplicates. A database index is a structure whose main function is to speed up database operations. An index that is set on key fields enables faster searches and retrieval of data.

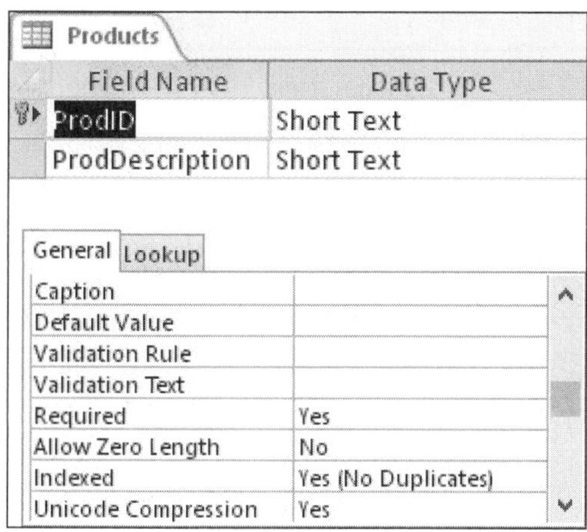

A key field must have a value; by default every other field does not require that a value be entered. There are times, however, when non-key fields must have values. For instance, you must include an employee last name and first name when entering a new record into your employees table. The Required field property helps to easily accomplish this.

DEVELOP YOUR SKILLS AC06-D07

Set Field Sizes, Captions, and Default Values

In this exercise, you will set field sizes, captions, and default values in the Customers table of the Winchester Web Design database.

1. Open the **Customers** table in **Design View**.
2. Select the **CustState** field.

3. Enter the information as shown to change the size, format, caption, and default value of the field.

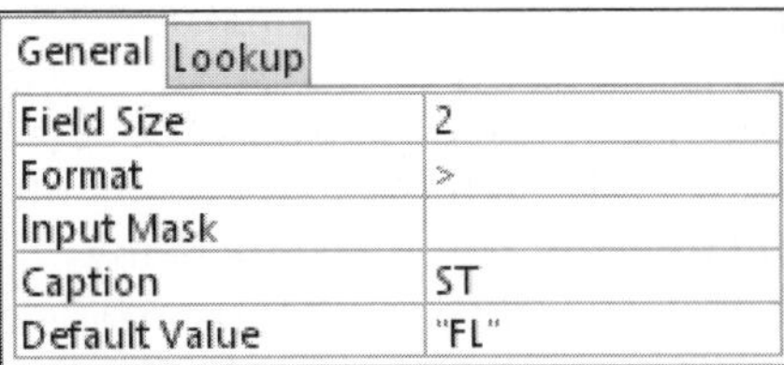

General	Lookup
Field Size	2
Format	>
Input Mask	
Caption	ST
Default Value	"FL"

Entering > for the Format property converts entries to uppercase. Access places quotation marks around the Default Value field property when you tap Enter *or save the table.*

Setting field sizes that are consistent with the data they hold helps the data display properly when it's included in forms and reports.

4. Select **CustLastName** in the Field Name list, and change the field size to **25** and the required property to **Yes**.
5. Select **CustPhone**, and change the field size to **15** and the required property to **Yes**.
6. Save the **Customers** table and click **Yes** when prompted to test the new rules.
7. Switch to **Datasheet View** and enter this data:

Field	Property
CustID	JonesK
CustLastName	Tab Tab and do not enter anything
CustState	**florida** (all lowercase) then tap Tab

You could only type in the first two letters of florida *and they would still be capitalized.*

8. Click **Save** and read the error message.

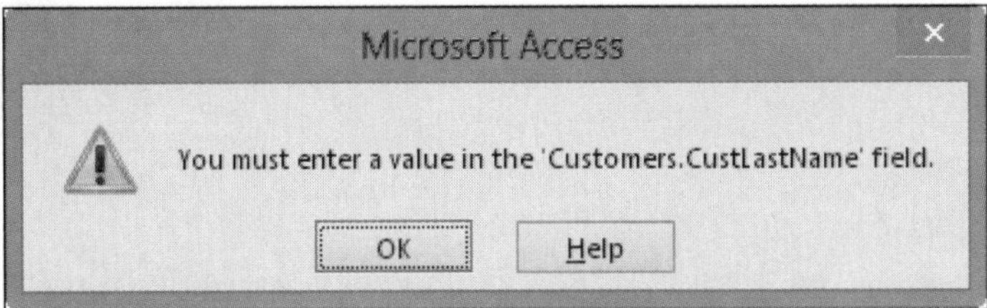

9. Click **OK**, then tap Esc to discard the changes.

Custom Text and Memo Field Formats

Video Library http://labyrinthelab.com/videos Video Number: AC13-V0607

Standard field formats in Access cannot meet the needs of every text or memo field contained in every database. That's why Access provides tools for creating custom formats. Custom formats for Text and Memo fields can contain two sections:

- **Section 1:** Contains a symbol and is followed by a semicolon when a second section is entered.
- **Section 2:** Contains the value of the alternate value when no value is entered. This alternate is a *null* value and is enclosed in quotation marks with no space between: "".

An example of a two-section format for a text field would look like this: @; "N/A"

The @ symbol tells Access to display the field data if a value is entered, and N/A tells Access to display N/A if no value is entered. The @ symbol displays all the characters that will fit the Field Size property, and if there are fewer characters than the Field Size value, Access pads the rest of the field with blank spaces.

Short Text and Long Text Field Unique Properties

Text and Memo fields are formatted to hold text characters (abc), symbols (#$%), and numbers (123) on which no mathematical calculations will be performed; such as FirstName, LastName, City, and also ZipCode, PhoneNumber, and SocSecNumber. Because of the broad scope of data that these data types can contain, Access provides several field properties for controlling and formatting data entry in the field.

SHORT TEXT AND LONG TEXT FIELD UNIQUE PROPERTIES

Property	Description
Allow Zero Length	Allows data entry of zero length in a field. Data is entered as open and close parentheses with no character or space between: (). The purpose of this entry is to show that there is no value to enter. For example, if you have a field in a Customers table that requires a land phone number and the customer has no land phone, you would enter () in the field.
Text Format	This property will set the text in a Long Text field as Plain Text or Rich Text. Rich text fields can be formatted with different fonts, font sizes, and colors.
Text Align	Positions the text on the left, center, or right side of the field box or column. The Distribute setting spreads out the text to fill the column or text box size.
Append Only	Adds a series of date-stamped comments to a single Long Text field, making it easy to create a history log of comments added to the fields. These comments are stored in a separate table and accessed through the Append Only Long Text field.

Entering Field Properties

Access provides three basic techniques for setting field properties:

- Type the value into the property box.
- Choose the value from the property list. (For example, click the drop-down menu button to select a valid entry from the list.)
- Click the Build button that appears at the right side of a field property to open the Wizard associated with that property. Then, choose the settings you want to apply. For example, click the Build button to open the Input Mask Wizard to format the display of text and field dates.

DEVELOP YOUR SKILLS AC06-D08

Set Additional Properties

In this exercise, you will set additional properties to require the entry of a customer's first name.

1. Display the **Customers** table in **Design View**.
2. Select the **CustFirstName** field and type **@** for the **Format** field property.
   Using the @ symbol will display all characters that fit within the field size and pad any remaining positions with spaces.
3. Choose **Yes** in the **Required** field property and **No** in the **Allow Zero Length** field property to prohibit a null value from being entered.
4. Save changes to the table, click **Yes** when advised that data integrity rules have changed.

Testing Control Settings

5. Switch to **Datasheet View**.
6. Click the **New Blank Record** button to add a new record and test the settings.
7. Type `SmithA` in the **CustID** field.
8. Type `Smith` in the **CustLastName** field, and click in the next available **CustID** field (the next record).
   Access tells you to enter the CustFirstName.
9. Click **OK**.
10. Type `Alexander` in the **CustFirstName** field, and click in the next available **CustID** field (the next record).
    Access tells you to enter the CustPhone.
11. Click **OK** and tap Esc to exit the record without saving it.
12. Close the **Customers** table.

Formatting Data Using Input Masks

Video Library http://labyrinthelab.com/videos Video Number: AC13-V0608

Consistency of data format is important for visual aesthetics; it also helps ensure accuracy in searches, queries, and sorts. You can control data formats using the field property input mask. Using input masks, you can set the characters you want displayed in fields, such as the parentheses in an area code, and Access requires the user to enter the data within that format.

The Input Mask Wizard

The Input Mask Wizard is a valuable tool for setting the most common formats used in databases. You can also set input masks to require a specific number of characters in a field or convert characters to capital or lowercase.

Setting input masks ensures that data format in tables is consistent. Because table data is consistent, data displayed in forms and reports is also consistent.

Telephone
941-55-52309
9415551792
941 555-6939
(941)555-7820
9415551029
9415550793

Telephone
(941) 555-2309
(941) 555-1792
(941) 555-6939
(941) 555-7820
(941) 555-1029
(941) 555-0793

Using input masks, unformatted data is automatically formatted.

A Build button appears at the right end of the Input Mask box when you click the box. It starts the Input Mask Wizard, which helps you build the mask.

Access 2013

Input Mask Symbols

When you use the Input Mask Wizard, Access places the necessary coding into the Field Properties pane. Access uses several symbols to control the appearance of data.

INPUT MASK SYMBOLS		
Symbol	**Description**	**Example**
0	Requires a numeric digit.	(000) 000-0000 requires the area code as part of the phone number.
9	Data is optional, but must be a digit.	(999) 000-0000 requires the seven-digit phone number with an optional three digit area code.
#	Restricts data to a digit, +, -, or space.	#99.99 permits + or – in the position of the #.
L	Requires a letter—an alphabetic character.	LL requires the entry of two alphabetic characters in the State field.
?	Restricts, but does not require, data to alphabetic characters.	L????L requires two characters, one on each end of the data, but permits four additional alphabetic characters between.
A	Requires an alphabetic or numeric character.	000-AAAA permits a phone number to be entered either as 555-1234 or 555-HOME.
a	Allows, but does not require, alphabetic or numeric characters.	(aaa) AAA-AAAA requires seven-character phone number but not the area code.
&	Requires any alphanumeric character or a space.	&&&& permits data entry such as a four-character ID such as 01HP, 1HP, or 1234.
C	Allows, but does not require, any character or space.	CCCC could contain 01HP, 1HP, HP, etc.
.,:;-/	Characters used to separate parts of numeric, date, time, and currency values.	#,###.## permits numeric data. 99/99/00 permits date data. 99:00:00 permits time date.
<	Converts characters to lowercase.	<aaa permits entry of three characters such as *ABC* and converts data to lowercase *abc*.
>	Converts characters to uppercase.	>aa permits entry of two characters such as *fl* and converts the data to *FL*.
!	Displays input mask characters from right to left.	!(#) 000-0000 would right-align the phone number so that if only seven numbers are entered, the area code is left blank. This affects fields defined with the Number data type.
\	Causes characters that follow the \ to display as literal characters.	(\A) would appear as (A).
"Literal Text"	Places text that appears between the quotation marks into the field value at the identified position.	"ID-"0000 places ID- before the numbers entered. A space may be enclosed in quotes to ensure it appears in the value.
Password	Creates a password entry text box. Any character typed in the text box is stored as a character but displays as an asterisk (*) as the password is entered.	When passWord1! is typed, Access shows **********.

Storing Input Mask Characters

Access provides two methods for storing the input mask with the table data—with or without the symbols. Storing the symbols with the data increases the size of the database file. Therefore, companies that store extremely large volumes of data often prefer storing the data without the input mask symbols.

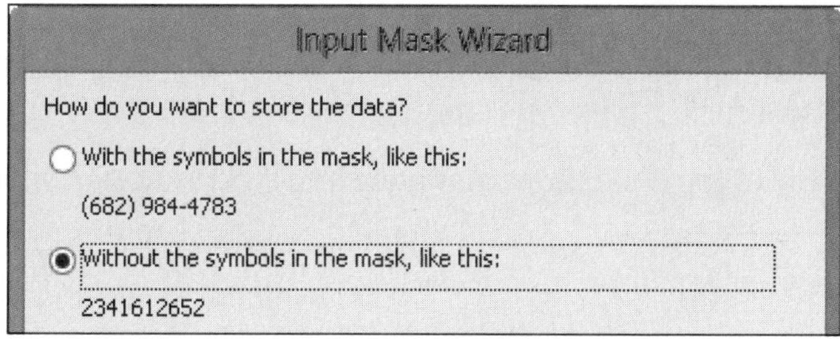

Two options for storing data formatted using input masks.

Using Smart Tags

As you work in Access, you will periodically see smart tags, such as the Paste Options smart tag, which you may have seen in Word and other Microsoft applications. Smart tags allow you to apply format changes you make to a field in one table to the same field anywhere else it occurs in the database. For example, if you modify the field format properties in a table, the Property Options smart tag lets you apply the same format changes to the field when it appears in other forms, queries, and reports. This helps ensure the consistency of data throughout the database.

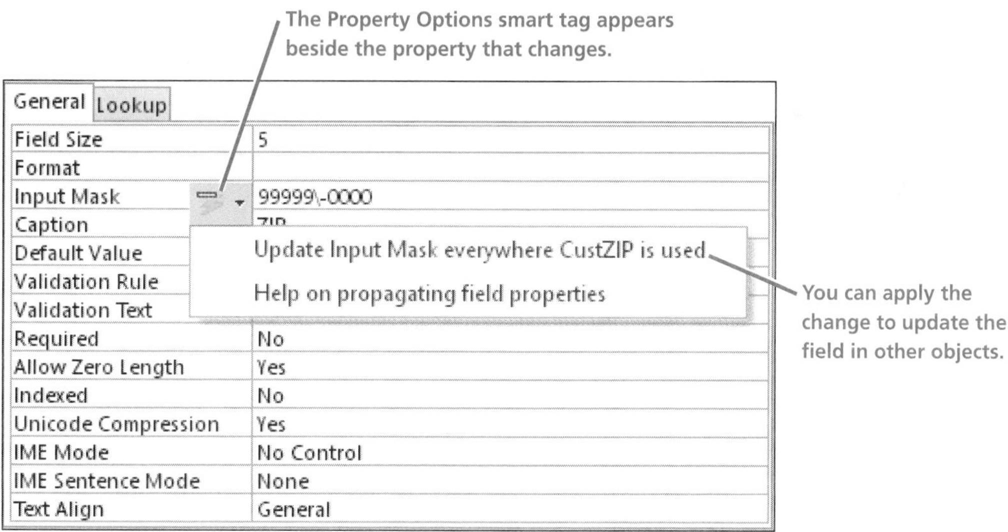

Access 2013

DEVELOP YOUR SKILLS AC06-D09

Set Input Mask Properties

In this exercise, you will set the primary key, change a field size, and apply a custom input mask to a field in the Products table. Then you will apply a standard telephone input mask to a field in the Employees table.

1. Open the **Products** table in **Design View**.
2. Select the **ProdID** field and click [Primary Key].
3. Click the **Input Mask** line in the Field Properties pane and type **"PROD-"00AA**.

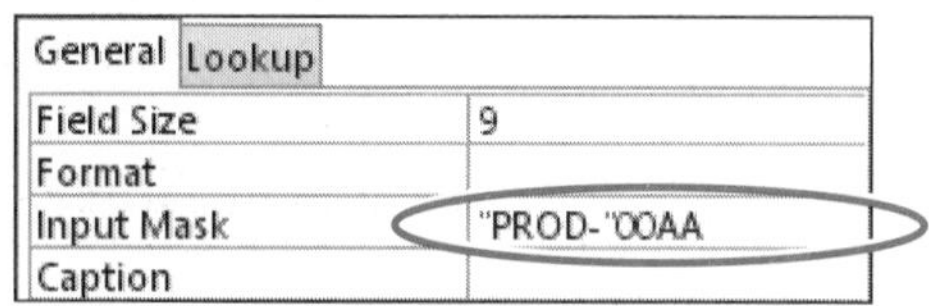

This input mask formats the ProdID field to automatically begin with PROD- followed by 2 numbers and then 2 letters.

4. Follow these steps to select Property Update options:

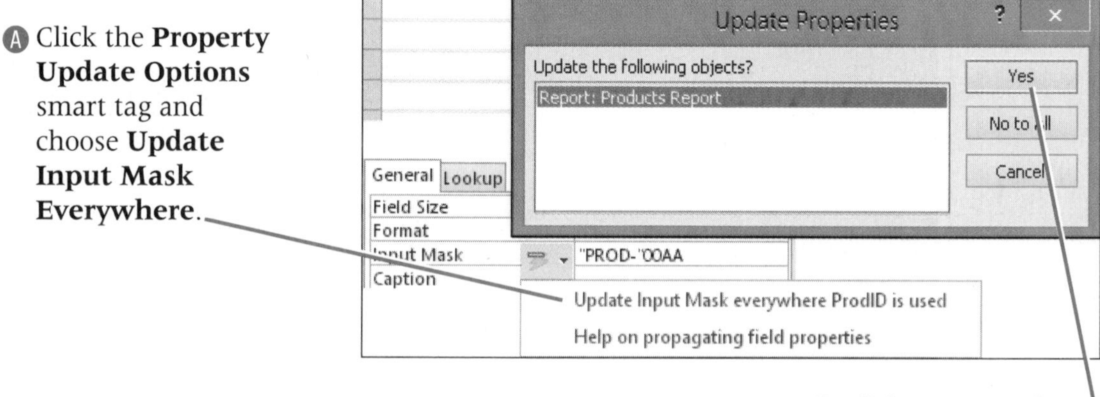

Access displays the Update Properties dialog box, which contains a list of all objects using the field. For this field, only one object is listed.

5. Save and close the **Products** table. Choose **Yes** if a warning message appears.

Use the Input Mask Wizard

Now you will apply a standard input mask format to a field.

6. Display the **Employees** table in **Design View**.
7. Follow these steps to format a field using the Input Mask Wizard:

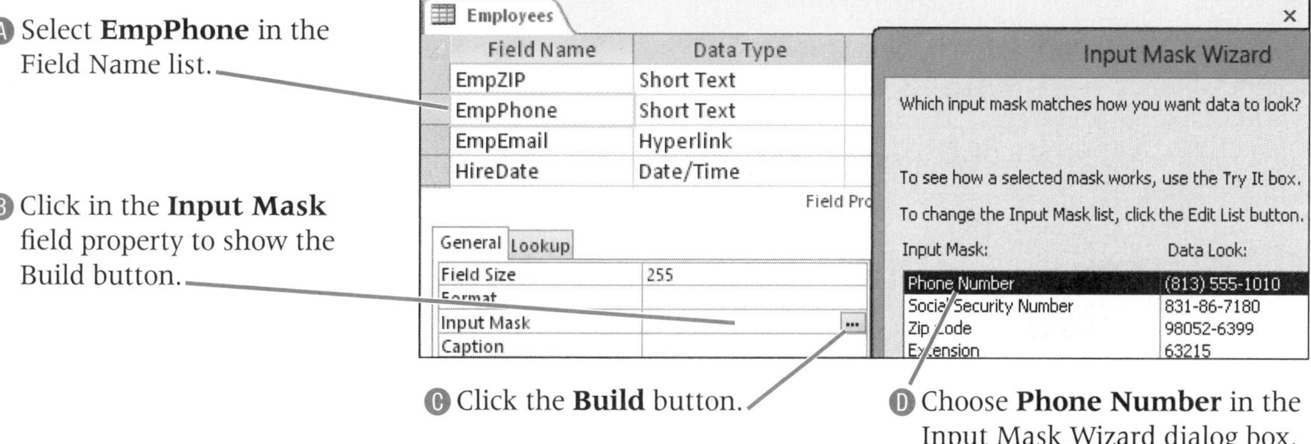

8. Click **Finish**.

Create Additional Settings

Next, you will assign properties for additional Employee table fields. Be sure to save when prompted. Use the Property Update Options smart tag to apply the changes to the field each time it appears and click Yes when advised that data may be lost.

When you start the Input Mask Wizard, you will have to save the table first if you have made any changes to it.

9. Change these field properties to set input masks and captions:

Field	Field Size	Input Mask	Caption
EmpLastName	25	>L<????????????????????????	Last Name
EmpFirstName	25	>L<????????????????????????	First Name
EmpStreetAddress	30		Street Address
EmpCity	15	>L<?????????????	City
EmpST	2	>LL	State
EmpZIP			ZIP
EmpPhone	14	Save the table and use Input Mask Wizard and choose Phone Number Format	Home Phone
EmpEmail			Email
HireDate			Hire Date
WebCert			Web Cert

10. Save your changes. Choose **Yes** when advised that some data may be lost.

11. Switch to **Datasheet View**.

    Column headings show the new Caption values and data is formatted consistently for the telephone numbers.

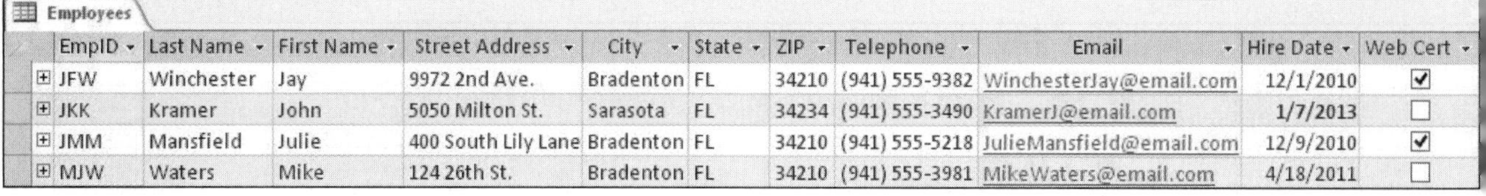

Employees

EmpID	Last Name	First Name	Street Address	City	State	ZIP	Telephone	Email	Hire Date	Web Cert
JFW	Winchester	Jay	9972 2nd Ave.	Bradenton	FL	34210	(941) 555-9382	WinchesterJay@email.com	12/1/2010	☑
JKK	Kramer	John	5050 Milton St.	Sarasota	FL	34234	(941) 555-3490	KramerJ@email.com	1/7/2013	☐
JMM	Mansfield	Julie	400 South Lily Lane	Bradenton	FL	34210	(941) 555-5218	JulieMansfield@email.com	12/9/2010	☑
MJW	Waters	Mike	124 26th St.	Bradenton	FL	34210	(941) 555-3981	MikeWaters@email.com	4/18/2011	☐

12. Close the **Employees** table.

Setting Validation Rules

Video Library http://labyrinthelab.com/videos Video Number: AC13-V0609

A validation rule is a field property that enables you to limit the values entered into the field in order to reduce inaccurate data entry. You could, for example, set a validation rule to limit the value typed into an HoursWorked field to 50 or fewer, or the value of Pay Rate to less than $60.

Setting Appropriate Data Types for Validation Rules

For validation rules to be effective, it is important that the field for which you are setting the rule be formatted appropriately for the data type that should be entered. For example, if you set a validation rule requiring a four-digit number, the data type for the field should be set to Number. If you are requiring dates that occur before a specific date, the data type for the field should be Date/Time.

Setting Validation Text Message for Rules

When you set a validation rule for a field, it is also a good idea to set validation text, which contains instructions or valid data values to help guide data entry. Access displays the text as a message each time an invalid value is entered in the field.

Setting Different Types of Validation Rules

Validation rules are used to examine data entered into tables and forms. You can set comparison rules. Samples of comparison rules you can set to determine if the value is within a valid range are shown in the following table.

VALIDATION RULES		
Comparison	**Validation Rule Example**	**Validation Text Example**
Greater than	>100	Enter a value greater than 100.
Less than	<100	Enter a value less than 100.
Equal to	=1 Or =2	Enter a value of 1 or 2.
Date after a date	>#1/1/2013#	Enter a date after Jan 1, 2013.
Greater than or equal to	>=100	Enter a value of 100 or more.
Less than or equal to	<=100	Enter a value of 100 or less.
Like	Like "ID-0000"	Enter a 4-digit value starting with ID-.
Between	Between 1 And 8	Enter a value from 1 to 8.

The same wildcards used to enter input masks are used in validation rules. For example, the question mark is substituted for each character that is required, such as in ID-????. The asterisk (*) can substitute for a group of characters that may vary, such as in ID-*.

DEVELOP YOUR SKILLS AC06-D10

Set Validation Rules

In this exercise, you will set validation rules for data entered into fields in the Products table.

1. If necessary, display the **Products** table in **Design View**.
2. Select the **Price** field and enter the Validation Rule and Validation Text shown.

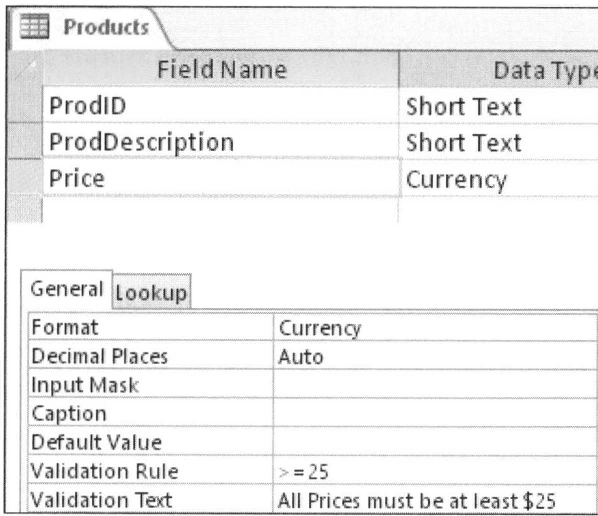

If you get an error message that the "expression is typed incorrectly, or it is too complex" it may be caused by a typo, invalid data that is already stored in the field, or because the data type is not consistent with the validation rule.

3. Save changes to the **Products** table. Choose **Yes** if advised that the process may take a long time.

Test the New Validation Rules

4. Switch to **Datasheet View**.
5. Follow these steps to test the validation rule you just set:

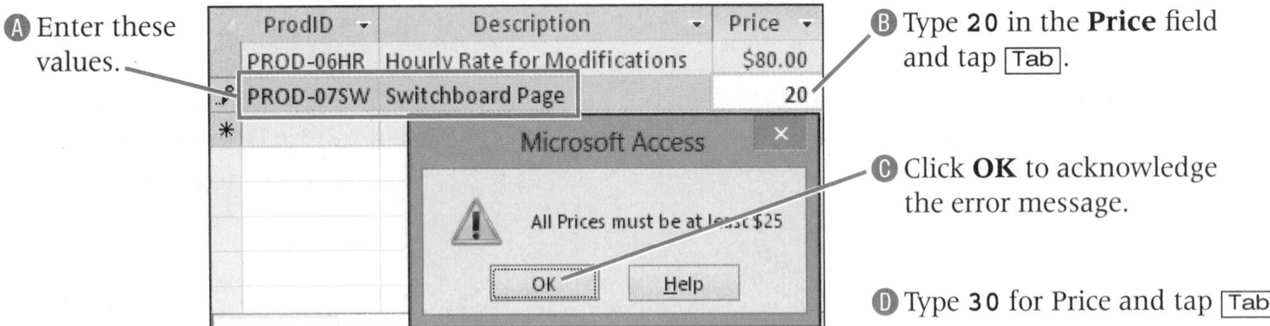

6. Save and close the **Products** table.

Setting Lookup Fields With the Lookup Wizard

Video Library http://labyrinthelab.com/videos Video Number: AC13-V0610

All tables in a relational database are related in some way to each other, as well as to other objects in the database. Data from one table is often used in another table. A lookup field enables you to select a field value in one table by looking up values from another table; or you could select from a list of values entered by the database designer. The list of valid entries appears in a drop-down menu in the table accessing the values.

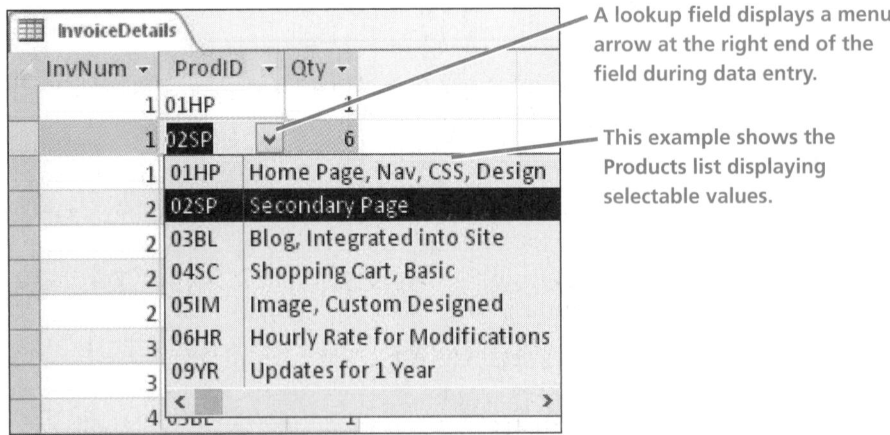

Using a lookup value also enables you to look up values from one field and return a value from a different field in the connected table. For example, you can look up a product number by typing the common product name.

Examining the Benefits of Lookup Tables

Adding a lookup field to a table serves three primary purposes:

- It reduces the time required to enter the data repeatedly.
- It reduces errors associated with data entry.
- It restricts data to valid entries.

For example, if you are processing time card data before issuing employee checks, setting a lookup field of valid employee IDs helps ensure that only valid employees receive checks. Lookup fields also help reduce the number of redundant fields contained in database tables.

Performing a Lookup

Access provides the following two ways to use the Lookup feature.

- **Lookup Wizard:** A data type that launches the Lookup Wizard, which walks you through the process of setting up a lookup field.

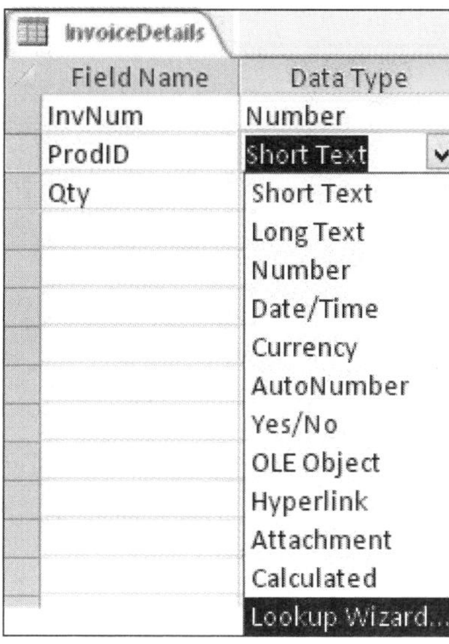

- **Lookup tab:** An option in the Design View Field Properties pane that sets the data source containing the values you want to display in the field.

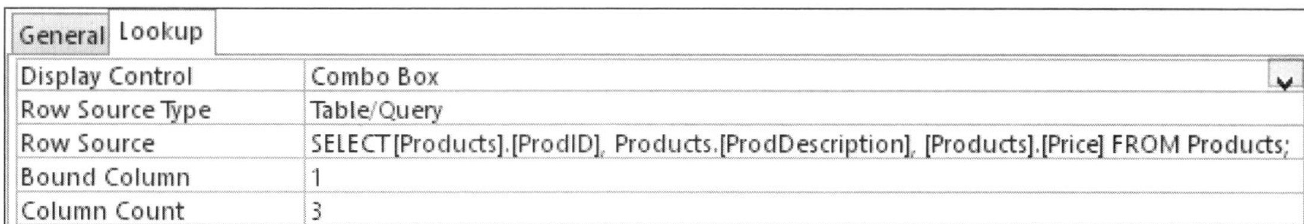

DEVELOP YOUR SKILLS AC06-D11

Set a Lookup Field Using a Wizard

In this exercise, you will delete the relationship between two tables and create a lookup field in the Products table that displays a list of valid products. You will then use the lookup field to enter data into the Invoice Details table.

The Products table must be closed. You cannot make relationship changes to an open table.

1. Choose **Database Tools→Relationships**.
2. Right-click the join line linking the **Products** and **InvoiceDetails** tables.

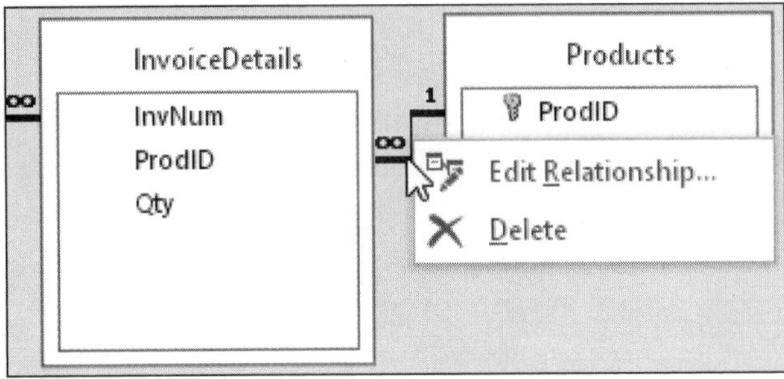

3. Choose **Delete** then click **Yes** to confirm.
4. Using the same procedure, delete the relationship between the **EmpID** fields in the **Employees** and **Invoices** tables, and between **EmpID** in the **Employees** table and **EmployeeID** in the **EmpSpouses** table.
5. Save and close the **Relationship** window.
6. Display the **InvoiceDetails** table in **Design View**.
7. Follow these steps to launch the Lookup Wizard:

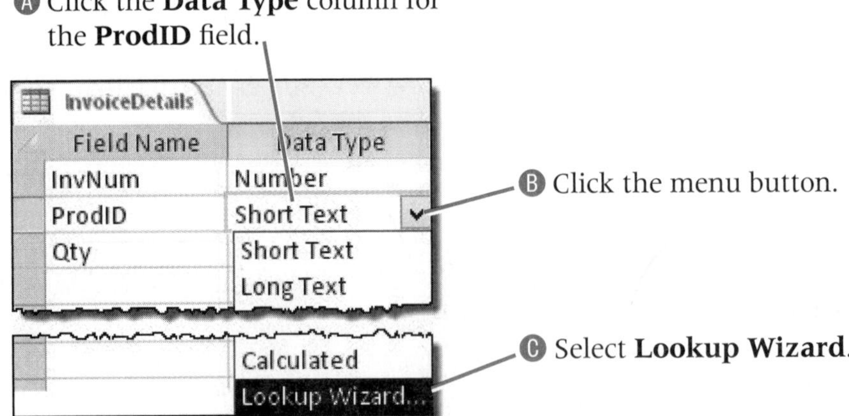

The Wizard asks you to identify the table containing the values to look up.

8. Choose **I Want the Lookup Column to Get the Values from Another Table or Query** and click **Next**.

9. Follow these steps to identify the table containing the values to look up:

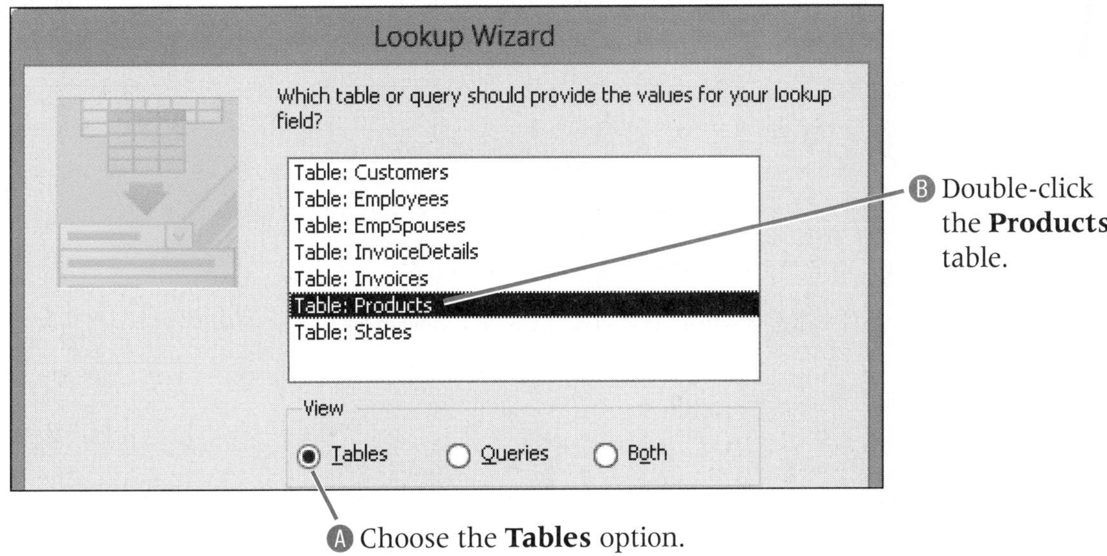

10. In the next wizard screen, click **Move All** [>>].

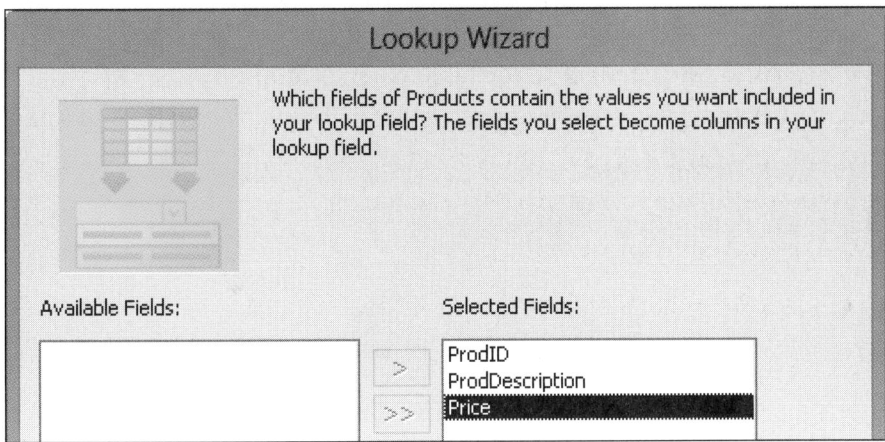

All the Available Fields have moved to the Selected Fields box.

11. Click **Next**.
12. Click the list arrow in the first sort field box, choose **ProdID**, and click **Next**.

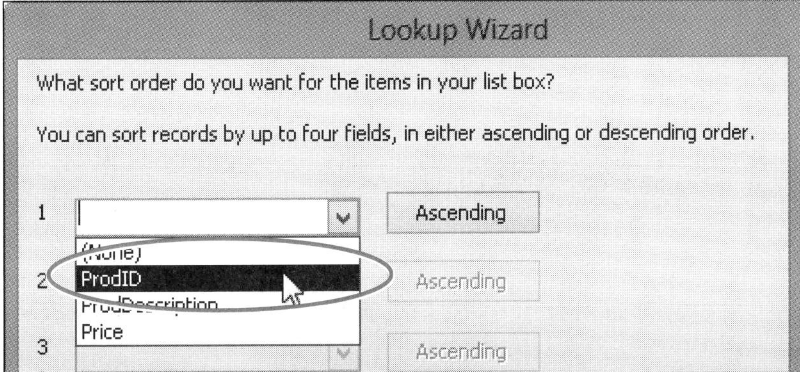

13. Uncheck the **Hide Key Column** checkbox and adjust column widths as needed.

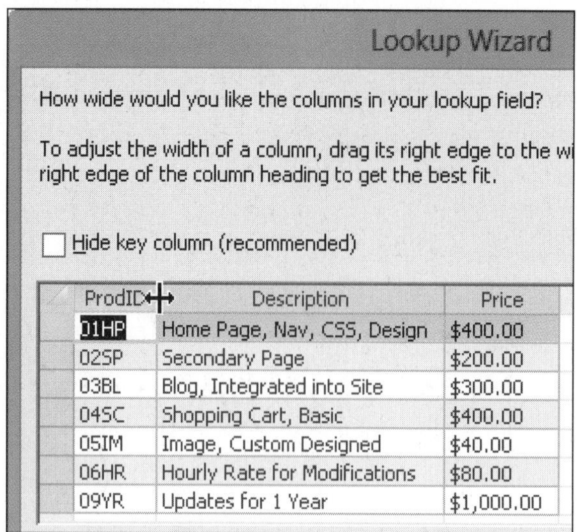

14. Click **Next**, choose **ProdD** as the value to display when you select the product, keep the default label, mark the **Enable Data Integrity** checkbox, choose the **Cascade Delete** option, and click **Finish**.

15. Choose **Yes** to save changes to the table when prompted.

    Creating lookup fields automatically creates a relationship between fields in both tables.

Test the Lookup Field

16. Choose **Design→Views→View**.

17. Follow these steps to review the lookup field format:

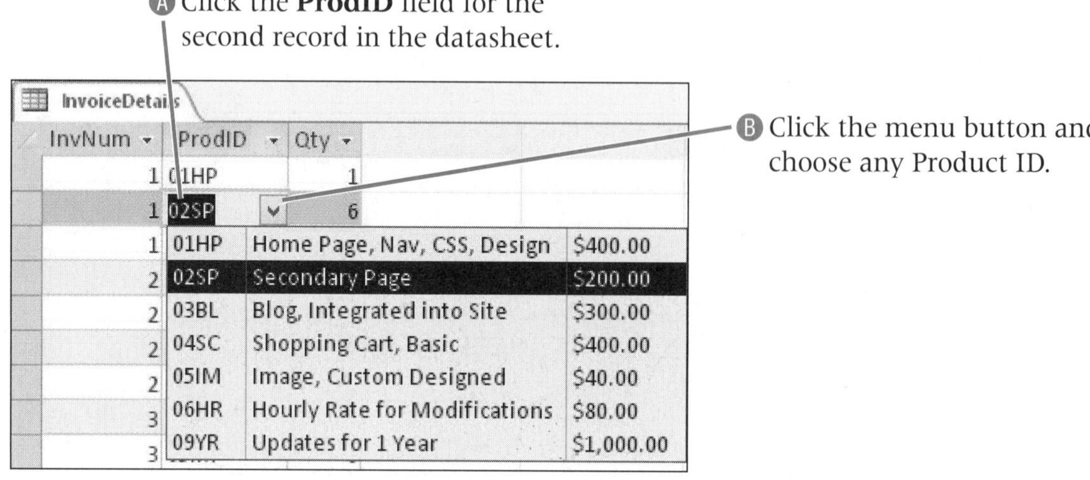

18. Close the **InvoiceDetails** table. Choose **Yes** if prompted to save the changes.

Creating Lookup Fields for Multiple Values

Video Library http://labyrinthelab.com/videos Video Number: AC13-V0611

You have already created a lookup field that enabled you to select a single item from a list. You can also set up lists that allow you to select multiple values to enter for each lookup field. If, for example, an inventory item is available from more than one supplier, you can set up the field to allow you to select all suppliers for an item. To create a selection list, simply check the Multiple Items option as you move through the Lookup Wizard screens.

DEVELOP YOUR SKILLS AC06-D12

Create Lookup Fields for Selecting Multiple Values

In this exercise, you will create a lookup field in the Invoices table that allows you to assign two or more employees to an inventory item.

1. Display the **Invoices** table in **Design View**.
2. Follow these steps to launch the Lookup Wizard:

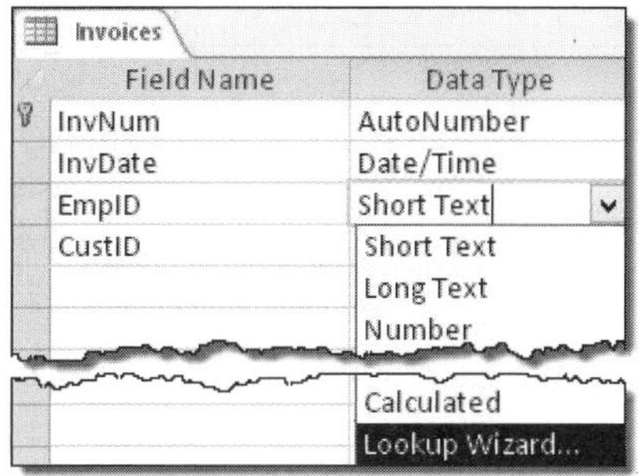

Ⓐ Click in the **Data Type** column of the **EmpID** field.

Ⓑ Click the menu button and select **Lookup Wizard**.

3. Select **I Want the Lookup Field to Get the Values from Another Table or Query** and click **Next**.

   If you choose the option "I will type the values in that I want," you can create your own list of items.
4. Double-click **Table: Employees** to select the **Employees** table and continue.
5. Move the **EmpID**, **EmpLastName**, and **EmpFirstName** fields from the Available Fields list to the **Selected Fields** list; click **Next**.

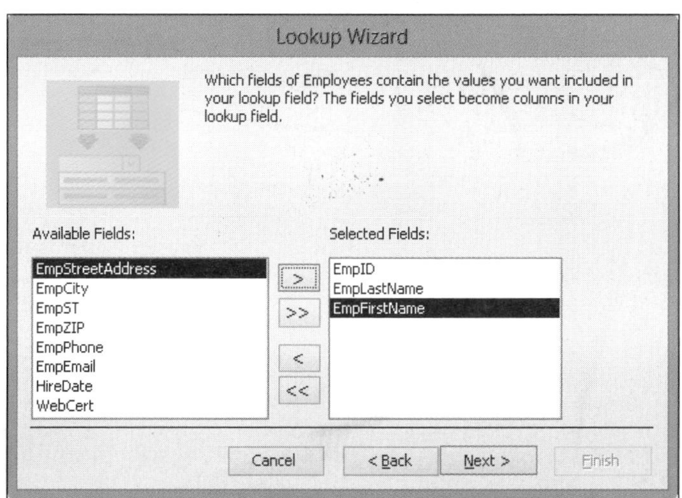

Access 2013

6. Select **EmpID** in the first sort order list, leave the sort order as **Ascending**, and click **Next**.
7. Click **Next** to accept the default settings for the columns.
8. Follow these steps to finalize the lookup field:

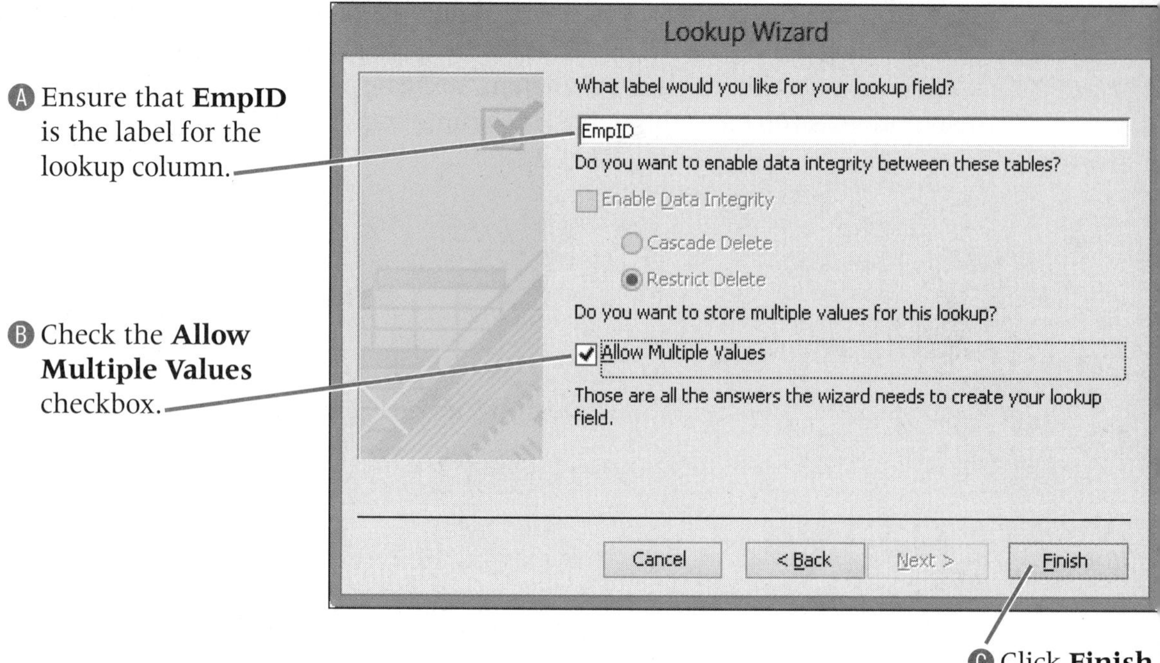

9. Choose **Yes** to store multiple values.

10. Choose **Yes** to save the changes to the table.
11. Click the **Lookup** tab in the Field Properties pane to view the lookup field settings.

General	Lookup
Display Control	Combo Box
Row Source Type	Table/Query
Row Source	SELECT [Employees].[EmpID], [Employees].[EmpLastName], [Employees].[EmpFirstName] FROM Employees ORDER BY [EmpID];
Bound Column	1
Column Count	3
Column Heads	No
Column Widths	0";1";1"
List Rows	16
List Width	2"

Test the Multiple Values Lookup Field

12. Switch to **Datasheet View**.
13. Follow these steps to select multiple employees for an invoice:

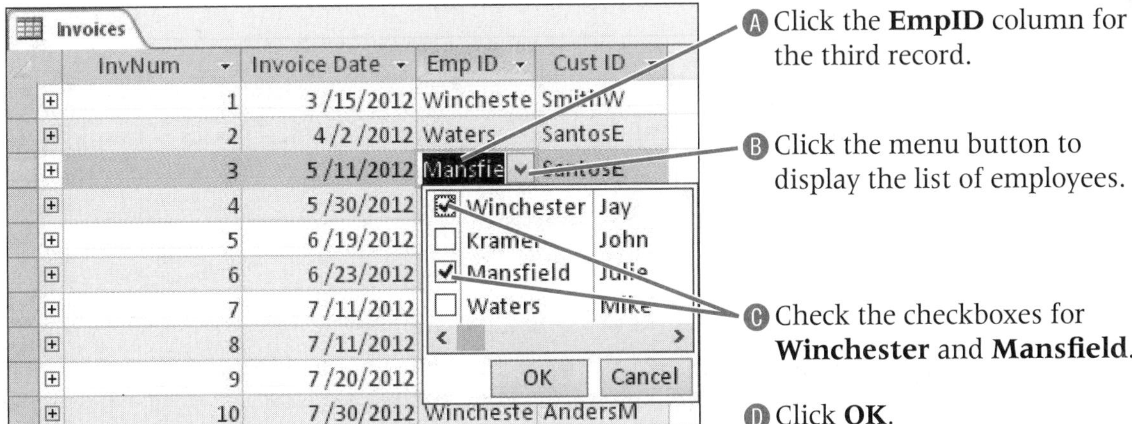

14. Double-click the right border of the **Emp ID** heading to view the multiple entries.

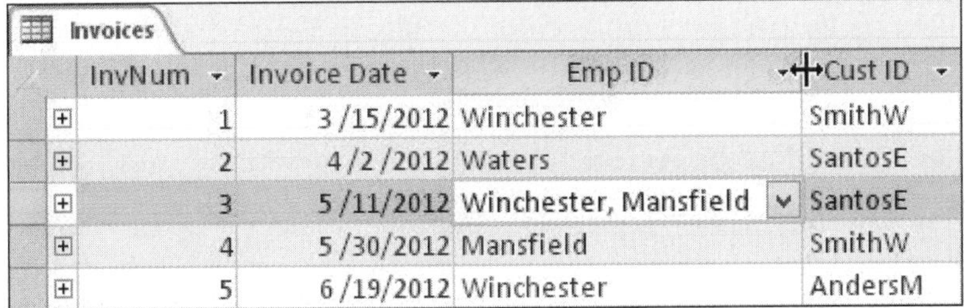

15. Close the **Invoices** table, saving changes if prompted.
16. Close the file and exit **Access**.

Access 2013

Concepts Review

To check your knowledge of the key concepts introduced in this lesson, complete the Concepts Review quiz by choosing the appropriate access option below.

If you are...	Then access the quiz by...
Using the Labyrinth Video Library	Going to http://labyrinthelab.com/videos
Using eLab	Logging in, choosing Content, and navigating to the Concepts Review quiz for this lesson
Not using the Labyrinth Video Library or eLab	Going to the student resource center for this book

Reinforce Your Skills

REINFORCE YOUR SKILLS AC06-R01

Create and Edit Relationships; Modify Table Structure and Appearance

John Kennerly, president of Kids for Change, an organization that encourages young people to participate in community-based projects, has asked you to modify the K4C database. In this exercise, you will create a relationship between tables, view the object dependencies in a table, and create a relationship report. You will rename a table and add a new field, delete and modify fields, and enhance the datasheet with color.

Create and Modify Table Relationships

1. Start **Access**. Open **AC06-R01-K4C** from your **AC2013 Lesson 06** folder and save it as `AC06-R01-K4C-[FirstInitialLastName]`.
2. Choose **Database Tools→Relationships→Relationships**.
3. Choose **Design→Relationships→Show Table**.
4. Double-click the **Volunteers** table; close the **Show Table** dialog box.
5. Drag down the lower edge of the **Volunteers** field list to show all fields.
6. Click the **ActID** field in the **Activities** table and drag it to the **ActID** field in the **Volunteers** table.
7. In the Edit Relationships dialog box, check the **Enforce Referential Integrity** checkbox.

   ☑ Enforce Referential Integrity

8. Click **Create**.
   The join has a 1 at the Activities table end and an infinity symbol at the Volunteers table end.
9. Click once to select but don't display the **Children** table in the Navigation Pane.
10. Choose **Database Tools→Relationships→Object Dependencies**.
11. Review the **Objects That Depend On Me** to see the tables, queries, and forms that depend on the Children table.
12. Choose the **Objects That I Depend On** option. There is only one other object that the Children table depends on.
13. Close the **Object Dependencies** panel.
14. Choose **Design→Tools→Relationship Report**.
    You will add more relationships as you progress through these exercises.
15. Close the report, saving it as `AC06-R01-Relationships-[FirstInitialLastName]`.
16. Close the **Relationships** window. Save the changes if prompted.

Modify the Table Structure

17. Right-click the **Staff** table and choose **Rename**.
18. Type `PaidStaff` and tap [Enter].
19. Display the **PaidStaff** table in **Design View**.
20. Right-click the row selector for the **StaffStreet** field and choose **Insert Rows**.

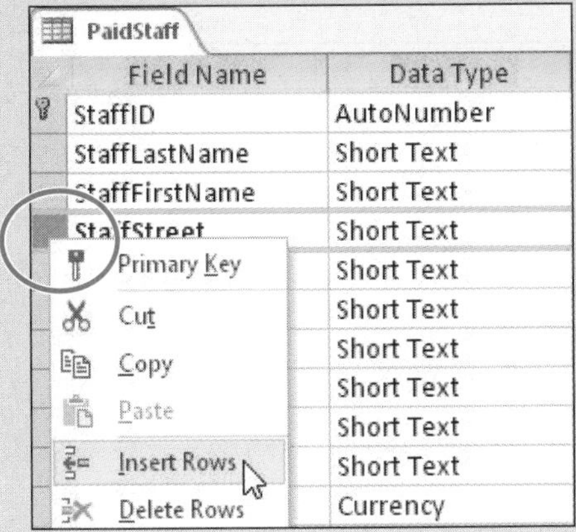

21. Click in the new **Field Name** line, type `Parent`, and tap [Tab].
22. Click the menu button for **Data Type** and choose **Yes/No** and tap [Tab].
23. Type `Parent of K4C child` as the Description.
24. Save the **PaidStaff** table and switch to **Datasheet View**.
25. Check the new **Yes/No boxes** for **Lockwood**, **Kendall**, and **Riggs**.

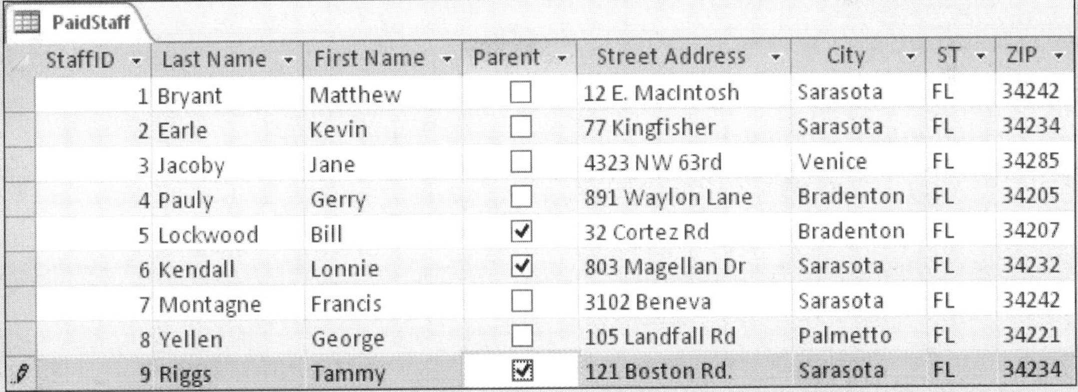

26. Close the **PaidStaff** table.
27. Open the **Donations** table in **Design View**.
28. Click the row selector for the **Acknowledgement** field and tap [Delete].
29. Choose **Yes** to confirm the deletion. Then save and close the **Donations** table.

Access 2013

Format a Table Datasheet Layout

30. Display the **Children** table in **Datasheet View**.
31. Hover the mouse pointer over the **First Name** column heading until it becomes the black select arrow.
32. Select the **First Name** column and point to the column heading until the pointer becomes the white move arrow. Drag the column to the left of the **Last Name** column.

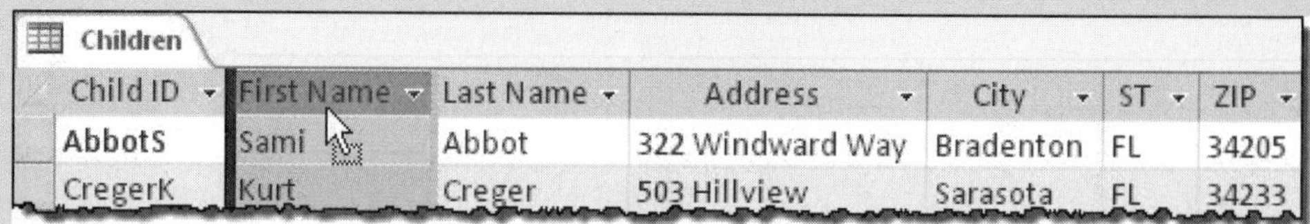

33. Hover the mouse pointer over the **Address** column heading until it becomes the black select arrow.
34. Click the **Address** column heading and drag the pointer to select the **Address**, **City**, **ST**, and **ZIP** columns.
35. Right-click the column heading of a selected column and choose **Hide Fields**.
    The children's address fields are hidden, but the data remains in the table.
36. Hover the mouse pointer over the right edge of the **Mother** column heading until it becomes the resize arrow; double-click to resize the column.
37. Resize the **Father** column.
38. Save the **Children** table.
39. Choose **Home→Text Formatting→Alternate Row Color menu ▾→Maroon 1**.
40. Choose **Home→Text Formatting→Gridlines menu ▾→Gridlines: Horizontal**.
41. Choose **Home→Text Formatting→dialog box launcher** to open the Datasheet Formatting dialog box.
42. Open the **Gridline Color** menu and choose **Dark Red** under Standard Colors.
43. Open the **Border Style** menu and select **Column Header Underline**.
44. Open the **Line Style** menu and select **Dots**. Click **OK**.
45. Click **Font Color** [A ▾] menu button and choose **Dark Blue** under Standard Colors.
46. Save and close the **Children** table. Then close the database and exit **Access**.
47. Submit your final file based on the guidelines provided by your instructor.
    To see examples of how your file or files should look at the end of this exercise, go to the student resource center.

REINFORCE YOUR SKILLS AC06-R02

Set Field Properties, Apply Input Masks, and Create Lookup Fields

As head of Tech Development for Kids for Change, you want to set some database field properties. In this exercise, you will set field size, convert values to uppercase, set captions and default values, make a field required, and create a custom format for an ID field. You will set a predefined telephone input mask, add a validation rule, and set a lookup field.

Set Table Field Properties

1. Start **Access**. Open **AC06-R02-K4C** from your **AC2013 Lesson 06** folder and save it as `AC06-R02-K4C-[FirstInitialLastName]`.
2. Display the **Volunteers** table in **Design View**.
3. Click in the **VolID** row and type `12` in the **Field Size** property in the Field Properties section of Table Design View.
4. Click in the **VolLastName** row and type `25` in the **Field Size** property.
5. Type `Last Name` in the **Caption** property.
6. Click in the **VolFirstName** row and type `25` in the **Field Size** property.
7. Type `First Name` in the **Caption** property.
8. Select the **VolStreet** and type `25` for the **Field Size** and `Street` for the **Caption**.
9. Select **VolCity** and type `25` for the **Field Size** and `City` for the **Caption**.
10. Select **VolST** and apply the settings as shown.

General | Lookup

Field Size	2
Format	>
Input Mask	
Caption	ST
Default Value	"FL"

The ">" as the Format property converts lowercase values to uppercase values.

11. Select **VolZIP**, and type `5` for the **Field Size** and `ZIP Code` for the **Caption**.
12. Select **VolPhone**, and type `15` for the **Field Size** and `Telephone` for the **Caption**.
13. Select **ActID**, and type `6` for the **Field Size** and `Act/Day` for the **Caption**.
14. With **ActID** still selected, click in the **Required** field property line, click the menu button, and choose **Yes**.
15. Click **Save**; click **Yes** in the warning box.

Access 2013

16. Switch to **Datasheet View** and enter these data values in the first empty row, tapping Tab after each field:

Field	Value
VolID	K4C-VOL-6198
Last Name	Graves
First Name	Matthew
Street	915 Beneva St.
City	Sarasota
ST	florida
ZIP	34232999999
Telephone	9415556198

Access only allows you to enter the first two characters in the State column and only allows you to type five characters in the ZIP code field.

17. Leave the **ActID** field (which follows the Telephone field) blank and tap Tab.
   An error message tells you that you must enter a value in the 'Volunteers.ActID' field.
18. Click **OK**, type `BCSat` in the **ActIDDay** field, and tap Tab.
19. Close the **Volunteers** table, saving it if prompted.

Set an Input Mask and Validation Rules

20. Display the **Activities** table in **Design View**.
21. With the **ActID** field selected, type `"K4C-">LLL<LL` in the Input Mask field property line.
   This input mask starts each ActID with the literal value K4C- followed by three uppercase (>) letters and two lowercase (<) letters, for example K4C-DWTue for dog walking on Tuesday.
22. Save the **Activities** table.
23. Switch to **Datasheet View**, scroll to the end of the table, and click in the first empty **Activity ID** field.
   Access automatically places the new prefix in the field.
24. Close the **Activities** table.
25. Display the **Volunteers** table in **Design View**.
26. Select the **VolPhone** field, click in the **Input Mask** field property line, and click the **Build** button.
   The Input Mask Wizard starts.
27. Choose the **Phone Number** mask and click **Finish**.
28. Save and close the **Volunteers** table.
29. Display the **Children** table in **Design View**.
30. Select the **BirthDate** field and type `>01/01/1996` in the **Validation Rule** field property line.

31. Type `Only children born after January 1, 1996 may enroll` in the **Validation Text** line.

32. Click **Save**; click **Yes** to acknowledge the warning.

33. Switch to **Datasheet View** and enter the record shown for Marty Casado, tapping [Tab] after each field.

The Input Mask will not allow you to enter the birth date since it is prior to 1/1/96.

34. Click **OK** then change the **Birth Date** value to `11/24/1996`.

35. Type `Sandy` for **Mother**, `Javier` for **Father**, and `9415551653` for **Emergency**; tap [Tab] to save the record.

36. Switch to **Design View**.

Set a Field As a Lookup Field

37. Select the **ChildST** field and click the **Lookup** tab in the Field Properties section.

38. Click in the **Display Control** line, click the menu button, and choose **Combo Box**.

39. Click in the **Row Source** line, click the menu button, and choose **States**.

40. Type 2 for **Column Count**.

41. Type `.3, 1.2` for **Column Widths**.

42. Type `1.5` for **List Width**.

43. Save the **Children** table and switch to **Datasheet View**.

General | Lookup

Display Control	Combo Box
Row Source Type	Table/Query
Row Source	States
Bound Column	1
Column Count	2
Column Heads	No
Column Widths	0.3";1.2"
List Rows	16
List Width	1.5"
Limit To List	No

44. Click in the **ST** field for **DriverJ** and open the combo box of lookup values, and choose **FL**.

45. Close the **Children** table, saving it if prompted. Close the database and exit **Access**.

46. Submit your final file based on the guidelines provided by your instructor.

To see examples of how your file or files should look at the end of this exercise, go to the student resource center.

REINFORCE YOUR SKILLS AC06-R03

Set Relationships, Format Datasheets, Set Field Properties, and Add a Lookup Field

The Kids for Change database is performing better, but you want to modify database tables to improve their appearance and facilitate data entry and validation. In this exercise, you will add a field to indicate whether a staffer has a Master's Degree, delete a table that K4C no longer uses, and rearrange fields. You will also hide a field for confidentially reasons, resize columns to better display data, create a custom input mask with data validation that requires certain categories of donations, and apply a predefined input mask using the Wizard.

Create and Edit Relationships; Examine Object Dependencies

1. Start **Access**. Open **AC06-R03-K4C** from your **AC2013 Lesson 06** folder and save it as `AC06-R03-K4C-[FirstInitialLastName]`.
2. Choose **Database Tools→Relationships→Relationships**.
3. Click the **DonorID** field in the **Donors** table and drag it to the **DonorID** field in the **Donations** table.

   The Edit Relationships dialog box opens.
4. Check the **Enforce Referential Integrity** checkbox and click **Create**.

   The join has a 1 at the Donors table end and an infinity symbol at the Donations table end.
5. Choose **Design→Tools→Relationship Report**.
6. Save the report as `AC06-R03-Relationships-[FirstInitialLastName]`.
7. Click [Close Print Preview] then close the report. Close the **Relationships window**.
8. Click the **Donors** table name in the Navigation Pane.
9. Choose **Database Tools→Relationships→Object Dependencies**.
10. Review the **Objects That Depend On Me**.

    Several tables, queries, and forms depend on the Donors table.
11. Choose the **Objects That I Depend On** option and review those objects.

    There is just one table that the Donors table depends on.
12. Close the **Object Dependencies** panel.

Modify the Table Structure

13. Display the **PaidStaff** table in **Design View**.
14. Right-click the row selector in front **ActID** and choose **Insert Rows**.
15. Type `Masters` for the new **Field Name** and tap [Tab].
16. Click the menu button for **Data Type**, choose **Yes/No**, and tap [Tab].

17. Type **`Masters Degree or higher`** as the **Description**.

StaffPhone	Short Text	
Masters	Yes/No	Masters Degree or higher

18. Save the **PaidStaff** table and switch to **Open/Datasheet View**.
19. Check the new **Masters** checkboxes for **Bryant**, **Lockwood**, and **Riggs**.
20. Switch to **Design View**.
21. Select the **2ndDay** field, a field that K4C has phased out, and tap [Delete].
22. Choose **Yes** to confirm the deletion.
23. Save the **PaidStaff** table.

Format a Table Datasheet Layout

24. Display the **PaidStaff** table in **Datasheet View**.
25. Hover the mouse pointer over the **Email** column heading until it becomes the black select arrow.
26. Click to select the **Email** column.
27. Point to the column heading until you see the white move arrow, and drag the column to the left of the **Masters** column.

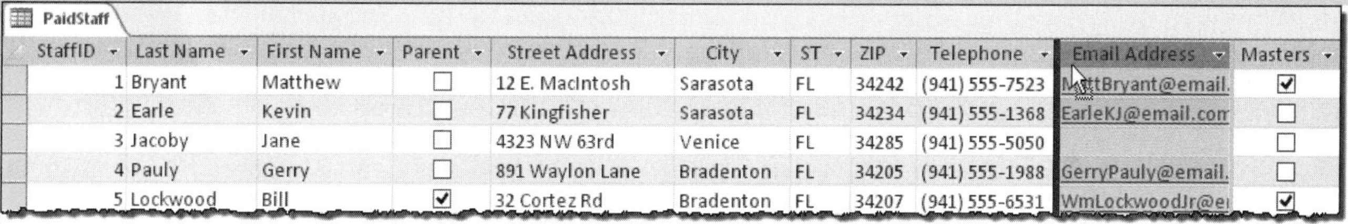

PaidStaff

StaffID	Last Name	First Name	Parent	Street Address	City	ST	ZIP	Telephone	Email Address	Masters
1	Bryant	Matthew	☐	12 E. MacIntosh	Sarasota	FL	34242	(941) 555-7523	MattBryant@email.	☑
2	Earle	Kevin	☐	77 Kingfisher	Sarasota	FL	34234	(941) 555-1368	EarleKJ@email.com	☐
3	Jacoby	Jane	☐	4323 NW 63rd	Venice	FL	34285	(941) 555-5050		☐
4	Pauly	Gerry	☐	891 Waylon Lane	Bradenton	FL	34205	(941) 555-1988	GerryPauly@email.	☐
5	Lockwood	Bill	☑	32 Cortez Rd	Bradenton	FL	34207	(941) 555-6531	WmLockwoodJr@e	☑

The Email column is now displayed after the Telephone column.

28. Point to the **Hrly Sal** column heading until you see the black select arrow.
29. Right-click the **Hrly Sal** column heading and choose **Hide Fields**.
    The hourly salary field is no longer displayed, but the data remains in the table.
30. Hover the mouse pointer over the right edge of the **Email** column heading.
31. When you see the resize arrow, double-click to resize the **Email** column.
32. Choose **Home→Text Formatting→Text Alternate Row Color menu ▾→ Light Blue2**.
33. Choose **Home→Text Formatting→Gridlines menu ▾→Gridlines: Horizontal**.
34. Choose **Home→Text Formatting→dialog box launcher** to open the Datasheet Formatting dialog box.

35. Open the **Gridline Color** menu and choose **Light Blue 5** under Standard Colors; click **OK**.

36. Click **Font Color** [A] and choose **Dark Blue** under Standard Colors.

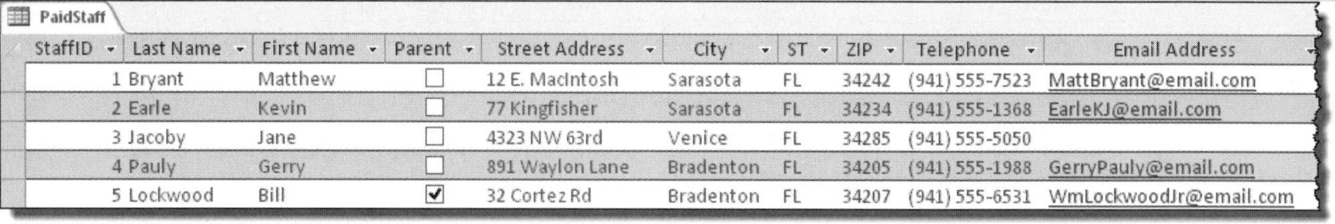

PaidStaff

StaffID	Last Name	First Name	Parent	Street Address	City	ST	ZIP	Telephone	Email Address
1	Bryant	Matthew	☐	12 E. MacIntosh	Sarasota	FL	34242	(941) 555-7523	MattBryant@email.com
2	Earle	Kevin	☐	77 Kingfisher	Sarasota	FL	34234	(941) 555-1368	EarleKJ@email.com
3	Jacoby	Jane	☐	4323 NW 63rd	Venice	FL	34285	(941) 555-5050	
4	Pauly	Gerry	☐	891 Waylon Lane	Bradenton	FL	34205	(941) 555-1988	GerryPauly@email.com
5	Lockwood	Bill	☑	32 Cortez Rd	Bradenton	FL	34207	(941) 555-6531	WmLockwoodJr@email.com

Your datasheet should resemble the figure with blue text, alternate rows and horizontal gridlines.

37. Save and close the **PaidStaff** table.

Set Field Properties

38. Display the **Donors** table in **Design View**.

39. Select the **DonorLName**, and type `25` for the **Field Size** and `Last Name` for the **Caption**.

40. With **DonorLName** still selected, click in the **Required** field property line, click the menu button, and choose **Yes**.

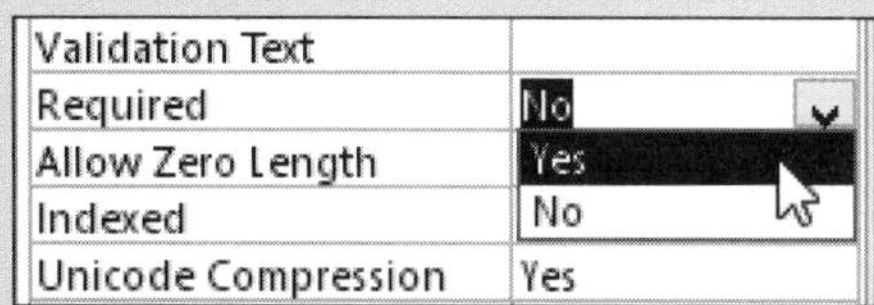

41. Choose **No** for the **DonorLName Allow Zero Length** property.

42. Select **DonorFName**, and type `25` for the **Field Size** and `First Name` for the **Caption**.

43. Select **DonorStreet**, and type `25` for the **Field Size** and `Street` for the **Caption**.

44. Select **DonorCity**, and type `25` for the **Field Size** and `City` for the **Caption**.

45. Select **DonorST**. Type **2** for the **Field Size**, type **>** for the **Format**, type `ST` for the **Caption**, and type `FL` for the **Default Value** field property.

    The ">" as the Format property converts lowercase values into uppercase values.

46. Select **DonorZIP**, and type `5` for the **Field Size** and `ZIP` for the **Caption**.

47. Select **DonorPhone**, and type `15` for the **Field Size** and `Telephone` for the **Caption**.

48. Select **DonorEmail** and type `Email Address` for the **Caption**.

49. Click **Save**; click **Yes** in the warning box.

50. Switch to **Datasheet View** and enter the highlighted record. Leave the *Acknowledgement* field at the end of the record blank and tap [Tab] after each field.

Donors

	DonorID	Last Name	First Name	Street	City	ST	ZIP	Telephone	Email Address
+	10	Blumenthal	Joyce	298 West Biscayne	Miami Beach	FL	33139	3055552909	JoyceBBlum@email.com
+	11	Kinsworth	Kendall	4040 Conquistador	Siesta Key	FL	34242	9415554040	
+	12	Castro	Lana	457 Palmer Drive	Bradenton	FL	34212	9415556626	MiguelLanaCastro@email.com

51. Save and close the **Donors** table.

Set Formats, Input Masks, and Allow Zero Length

52. Display the **Donations** table in **Design View**.

53. Select the **DonationType** field.

54. Type `>L<LL` for the **Input Mask** property.

    This input mask requires three letters: the first will be uppercase, the next two lowercase.

55. Type `Bus Or Pvt` for the **Validation Rule** property.

    This limits acceptable values to only those listed: Bus for Business or Pvt for Private.

56. Type `Must be Bus or Pvt` for the **Validation Text**.

General | Lookup

Property	Value
Field Size	8
Format	
Input Mask	>L<LL
Caption	
Default Value	
Validation Rule	"Bus" Or "Pvt"
Validation Text	Must be Bus or Pvt
Required	No

57. Save the table. Click **Yes** in the warning box.

58. Switch to **Datasheet View** and add this record to test the new input mask:

Field	Value
DonorID	2
DonationDate	04152013
Amount	1000
DonationType	Pmt

59. Tap [Tab] after entering the donation type.

    Because Pmt is not an allowable type, Access displays a warning with the validation text.

60. Click **OK**, then type `Pvt` in the **Type** field.

61. Save and close the **Donations** table.

62. Display the **Donors** table in **Design View**.

63. Select the **Acknowledgement** field.

    Financial donors can express thanks or share thoughts in memoriam in the Acknowledgement field.

64. Type `@; No Comments` in the **Format** field property to display **No Comments** if there is no data in the field.

65. Select the **DonorPhone** field, click the **Input Mask** field property line, and click the **Build** button. Save the table when prompted and click **Yes** in the warning box.

    The Input Mask Wizard starts.

66. Choose the **Phone Number** mask and click **Finish**.

67. Save the **Donors** table and switch to **Datasheet View**.

    All telephone numbers now have proper and consistent formatting.

68. Close the **Donors** table.

Set a Field As a Lookup Field

69. Display the **PaidStaff** table in **Design View**.

70. Select the **ActID** field and click the **Lookup** tab in the **Field Properties** section.

71. Click in the **Display Control** line, click the menu button, and choose **Combo Box**.

72. Click in the **Row Source** line, click the menu button, and choose **Activities**.

73. Leave the **Bound Column** value as 1.

74. Enter the values shown:

General | Lookup

Display Control	Combo Box
Row Source Type	Table/Query
Row Source	Activities
Bound Column	1
Column Count	2
Column Heads	No
Column Widths	0.5";1.5"
List Rows	16
List Width	2"

75. Save the **PaidStaff** table and switch to **Datasheet View**.

76. Right-click the **Email** column heading, then choose **Unhide Fields** and check the box for **HrlySal**.

    The hourly salary field reappears.

77. Test the new lookup field by adding this record:

Property	Value
Last Name	Francesco
First Name	Dominic
Parent	Yes
Street	26th Street
City	Sarasota
State	Florida
ZIP	34209
Telephone	9415558287

78. Tap [Tab] and type `E` in the **Activity** field.
   Access displays the first value that begins with the letter E: EBSun.
79. Tap [Tab] and type `27` in the **Hrly Sal** field and `DomFrancesco@email.com` in the **Email Address** field.
80. Save and close the **PaidStaff** table. Close any open objects and close the database; exit **Access**.
81. Submit your final file based on the guidelines provided by your instructor.

Apply Your Skills

APPLY YOUR SKILLS AC06-A01

Create and Edit Relationships; Modify Table Structure and Appearance

The CEO of Universal Corporate Events, Ltd. has asked you to make some changes to the UCE database. In this exercise, you will create a relationship between two tables, set referential integrity, and create a relationship report. Then you will examine the object dependencies for the Venues table, rename and add a Yes/No field to a table, and delete, modify, and rearrange fields. Finally, you will improve the appearance of the Menus table.

Add, Delete, Modify, and Print Table Relationships

1. Start **Access**. Open **AC06-A01-UCE** from your **AC2013 Lesson 06** folder and save it as `AC06-A01-UCE-[FirstInitialLastName]`.
2. Choose **Database Tools→Relationships→Relationships**.
3. Click the **VenueID** field in the **Venues** table and drag it to the **VenueID** field in the **Schedules** table, opening the **Edit Relationships** dialog box.
4. Check the **Enforce Referential Integrity** checkbox and click **Create**.
   The new join has a 1 at the Venues table end and an infinity symbol at the Schedules end.
5. Save changes to the **Relationships** window.
6. Choose **Design→Tools→Relationship Report** and save the report as `AC06-A01-Relationships-[FirstInitialLastName]`. Close the report and the **Relationships** window.
7. Click the **Venues** table name in the Navigation Pane.
8. Choose **Database Tools→Relationships→Object Dependencies**.
9. Review the **Objects That Depend On Me** and the **Objects That I Depend On**. Then close the **Object Dependencies** panel.

Modify a Table's Structure and Column Display

10. Right-click the **Contacts** table and choose **Rename**.
11. Type `VenueLiaisons` and tap [Enter].
12. Display the **Venues** table in **Design View**.
13. Select the **VenueWebSite** field and choose **Insert Rows**.
14. Click in the new **Field Name** line, type `Kitchen` and tap [Tab].
15. Click the **Data Type** menu button, choose **Yes/No**, and tap [Tab].
16. Type `Does Venue have a kitchen` as the Description.
17. Save the **Venues** table and switch to **Datasheet View**.

18. Check the new **Yes/No** boxes for **HyattS**, **ManYC**, and **SaraCC**, **SaraYC**, and **TmpCon**.
19. Close the **Venues** table.
20. Open the **Schedules** table in **Design View**.
21. Click the row selector for the **VenueName** field and tap [Delete].
22. Choose **Yes** to confirm.
23. Save and close the **Schedules** table.
24. Display the **Personnel** table in **Datasheet View**.
25. Click the **Date Hired** column heading and drag the column to the left of the **LastName** column.

    The Date Hired column is now between the ID and Last Name columns.
26. Right-click the **Date of Birth** column heading and choose **Hide Fields**.

    As you scroll through the records, you can see that some of the street addresses and email values are truncated and do not display fully in the column.
27. Double-click the right edge of the **Address** column heading to resize it to display all the contents.
28. Resize the **Email Address** column.
29. Save and close the **Personnel** table.

Change the Formatting of a Datasheet

30. Display the **Menus** table in **Datasheet View**.
31. Click the **Alternate Row Color menu ▼** and choose a light green.
32. Click the **Gridlines menu ▼** and choose **Gridlines: Horizontal**.
33. Choose **Home→Text Formatting→dialog box launcher**.
34. Open the **Gridline Color menu**, choose **Black, Text 1**, and click **OK**.
35. Click the **Font Name** menu button and choose **Arial**.
36. Click the **Font Size** menu button and choose **10**.
37. Click the **Font Color** menu button and choose **Black, Text 1**.
38. Save and close the **Menus** table. Close the database and exit **Access**.
39. Submit your final file based on the guidelines provided by your instructor.

    To see examples of how your file or files should look at the end of this exercise, go to the student resource center.

APPLY YOUR SKILLS AC06-A02

Set Field Properties, Apply Input Masks, and Create Lookup Fields

UCE has asked for your help again. In this exercise, you will modify field properties in the UCE database tables to more accurately describe and limit the data. You will set field sizes and captions, convert field values to uppercase, set a default value for easier data entry, and make a field required. You will also set a custom format for an ID field, apply a predefined input mask to a telephone field, add a validation rule so that no event with less than 35 guests can be entered, and you will finish by setting lookup fields.

Modify Table Field Properties

1. Start **Access**. Open **AC06-A02-UCE** from your **AC2013 Lesson 06** folder and save it as `AC06-A02-UCE-[FirstInitialLastName]`.
2. Display the **VenueLiaisons** table in **Design View**.
3. Type `12` in the **LiaisonID Field Size** property.
4. Type `25` in the **LiaisonLName Field Size** property.
5. Type `Last Name` for the **LiaisonLName Caption** property.
6. Type `25` for the **LiaisonFName Field Size** and `First Name` for the **Caption**.
7. Type `25` for the **LiaisonStreet Field Size** and `Street` for the **Caption**.
8. Type `25` for the **LiaisonCity Field Size** and `City` for the **Caption**.
9. Type `2` for the **LiaisonST Field Size**, type→for the **Format**, type `ST` for the **Caption** and `FL` for the **Default Value** field property.
10. Type `5` for the **LiaisonZIP Field Size** and `ZIP Code` for the **Caption**.
11. Type `15` for the **LiaisonPhone Field Size**, `Telephone` for the **Caption**, choose **Yes** in the **Required** property, and **No** in the **Allow Zero Length** property.
12. Type `Email Address` for the **LiaisonEmail Caption**.
13. Click **Save**; click **Yes** in the warning boxes.
14. Switch to **Datasheet View** and enter these data values, tapping [Tab] after each field:

Field	Value
LiaisonID	AntonV
Last Name	Anton
First Name	Vera
Street	44 West Florida St
City	Bradenton
State	fl
ZIP	34205999999

Access converts "fl" to "FL" and only accepts the first five characters of the ZIP code.

15. Leave the Telephone field blank and tap [Tab].

    An error message says you must enter a value in the telephone field.

16. Click **OK** then type `9415554248` in the **Telephone** field.

17. Type `VeraDrisana@email.com` in the **Email Address** field.

18. Save and close the **VenueLiaisons** table.

Create a Custom Field Format, Set an Input Mask and Validation Rules, and Set a Field As a Lookup Field

19. Display the **Personnel** table in **Design View**.

20. With the **PerID** field selected, type `10` in the **Field Size** field property, type `"UCE-"9999` for the **Input Mask**, and type `ID` for the **Caption**.

    Each PerID starts with the literal value UCE, followed by four numbers, such as UCE-1001.

21. Save the **Personnel** table.

22. Switch to **Datasheet View**. Scroll to the end of the table and click in the first empty **ID** field.

    Access automatically adds the prefix to the field.

23. Close the **Personnel** table.

24. Display the **VenueLiaisons** table in **Design View**.

25. Select the **LiaisonPhone** field, click in the **Input Mask** field property line, and click the **Build** button.

    The Input Mask Wizard starts.

26. Choose the **Phone Number** mask and click **Finish**.

27. Save the **VenueLiaisons** table and switch to **Datasheet View**.

    The Telephone field is now formatted.

28. Close the **VenueLiaisons** table.

29. Display the **Schedules** table in **Design View**.

30. Select the **Guests** field and type `>=35` in the **Validation Rule** field property line.

31. Type `At least 35 guests must be entered` in the **Validation Text** line.

32. Select the **EventID** field and click the **Lookup** tab in the **Field Properties** section.

33. Click in the **Display Control** line, click the menu button, and choose **Combo Box**.

34. Click in the **Row Source** line, click the menu button, and choose **Events**.

35. Enter the **Column Count**, **Column Widths**, and **List Width** values as shown.

36. Select the **Menu Code** field and click the **Lookup** tab in the **Field Properties** section.

General | Lookup

Display Control	Combo Box
Row Source Type	Table/Query
Row Source	Events
Bound Column	1
Column Count	2
Column Heads	No
Column Widths	0.6";1.5"
List Rows	16
List Width	2.1"

Access 2013

37. Click in the **Display Control** line, click the menu button, and choose **Combo Box**.

38. Click in the **Row Source** line, click the menu button, and choose **Menus**.

39. Type **2** for **Column Count**, type **0.6, 1.5** for **Column Widths**, and type **2.1** for **List Width**.

40. Click **Save**; click **Yes** in the warning box.

41. Switch to **Datasheet View**, scroll to the first available row, and enter these fields, tapping [Tab] after each entry:

Field	Value
Schedule ID	SEMBenson
Venue ID	ManCtr
Event ID	SEMNAR
Menu Code	DINBUF
Event Date	7/3/2014
Guests	30
Liaison	Miller

Access displays your validation text in a warning.

42. Click **OK**. Then change the **Guests** value to **40** and tap [Tab].

43. Close the **Schedules** table, saving it if prompted. Close the database and exit **Access**.

44. Submit your final file based on the guidelines provided by your instructor.

To see examples of how your file or files should look at the end of this exercise, go to the student resource center.

APPLY YOUR SKILLS AC06-A03

Set Relationships, Format Datasheets, Set Field Properties, and Add a Lookup Field

Universal Corporate Events, Ltd. CEO Buckley wants you to clean up the appearance of database tables and improve data readability and validation. In this exercise, you will add a new field to indicate salaried positions, delete a field UCE no longer uses, and rearrange fields. You will also hide cost per person in the Menus table, resize columns and set field sizes, and modify a field to convert data to uppercase. Finally, you will set captions, default values, and field requirements, create a custom input mask, and modify a field to look up values.

Create and Edit Relationships and Examine Object Dependencies

1. Start **Access**. Open **AC06-A03-UCE** from your **AC2013 Lesson 06** folder and save it as **AC06-A03-UCE-[FirstInitialLastName]**.

2. Choose **Database Tools→Relationships→Relationships**.

3. Click the **Grade** field in the **SalaryGrades** table and drag it to the **SalaryGrade** field in the **Personnel** table.

The Edit Relationships dialog box opens.

4. Check the **Enforce Referential Integrity** checkbox.
5. Click **Create**.

   The join has a 1 on the SalaryGrades end and an infinity symbol on the Personnel end.
6. Save changes to the **Relationships** window.
7. Choose **Design→Tools→Relationship Report** and save the report as `AC06-R03-Relationships-[FirstInitialLastName]`. Close the **Relationships** report and window.
8. Click the **Schedules** table name in the Navigation Pane.
9. Choose **Database Tools→Relationships→Object Dependencies**.
10. Review the **Objects That Depend On Me** and the **Objects That I Depend On**. Then close the **Object Dependencies** panel.

Modify Table Structure and Column Display

11. Display the **SalaryGrades** table in **Design View**.
12. Right-click the row selector in front of **Salary** and choose **Insert Rows**.
13. Type `Salaried` in the new **Field Name** line, choose **Yes/No** for **Data Type**, and type `Indicates salaried position` as the **Description**.
14. Save the **SalaryGrades** table and switch to **Datasheet View**.
15. Check the new **Yes/No** boxes for each record that has data in the salary field.
16. Close the **SalaryGrades** table.
17. Display the **Events** table in **Design View**.
18. Select the **MinGuests** field and tap Delete.
19. Choose **Yes** to confirm the deletion.
20. Save and close the **Events** table.
21. Display the **VenueLiaisons** table in **Datasheet View**.
22. Select the **Telephone** and **Email Address** columns.
23. Drag the columns to the left of the **Street Address** column.
24. Double-click the right edge of each column heading to resize them.
25. Save and close the **VenueLiaisons** table.
26. Display the **Menus** table in **Datasheet View**.
27. Right-click the **Cost/PP** column heading and choose **Hide Fields**. Then save and close the **Menus** table.

Change the Formatting of a Datasheet and Set Field Properties

28. Display the **Venues** table in **Datasheet View**.
29. Click the **Alternate Row Color menu ▾** and choose **Aqua Blue 1** under Standard Colors.

30. Click the **Gridlines menu ▼** and choose **Gridlines: Horizontal**.

31. Choose **Home→Text Formatting→dialog box launcher**.

32. Open the **Gridline Color menu** and choose **Aqua Blue 5** under Standard Colors.

33. Choose **Arial** for the **Font** type and **10** for the **Font Size**; click **OK**.

34. Save and close the **Venues** table.

Set Captions, Default Values, and Field Requirements

35. Display the **Personnel** table in **Design View**.

36. Select **PerLastName**, and type `25` for the **Field Size** and `Last Name` for the **Caption**. Choose **Yes** in the **Required** field property line.

37. Select **PerFirstName**, and type `25` for the **Field Size** and `First Name` for the **Caption**.

38. Select **PerAddr**, and type `25` for the **Field Size** and `Street` for the **Caption**.

39. Select **PerCity**, and type `25` for the **Field Size** and `City` for the **Caption**.

40. Select **PerST**. Type `2` for the **Field Size**, type→for the **Format**, type `ST` for the **Caption** and `FL` for the **Default Value** field property.

41. Select **PerZIP**, and type `5` for the **Field Size** and `ZIP Code` for the **Caption**.

42. Select **PerPhone**, and type `15` for the **Field Size** and `Telephone` for the **Caption**.

43. Select **SalaryGrade** and type `Salary Grade` for the **Caption**.

44. Click **Save**; click **Yes** in the warning box.

45. Switch to **Datasheet View**, and type `1017` in the first available **ID** field.

46. Tap [↓] to move to the next record without entering any data for the last name field.
    Access warns that you must enter a value in the last name field.

47. Click **OK** in the error message and tap [Esc] to exit the new record without saving and close the **Personnel** table.

Set Formats, Input Masks, Allow Zero Length, and Lookup Fields

48. Display the **Schedules** table in **Design View**.

49. With the **ScheduleID** field selected, type `>LLLL<??????` for the **Input Mask**.
    This mask forces four uppercase letters followed by from zero to six lowercase letters.

50. Save the **Schedules** table.

51. Switch to **Datasheet View** and type a series of lowercase letters in **Schedule ID**. Access converts the first four letters to uppercase.

52. Tap [Esc] to remove the data you just entered.

53. Press [Shift] and type in a series of uppercase letters in **ScheduleID** to see that Access converts all but the first four letters to lowercase.

54. Tap [Esc] to exit the record without saving it.

55. Close the **Schedules** table.

56. Display the **Venues** table in **Design View**.

57. Select the **VenueWebSite** field.

58. Type `@; No Website` in the **Format** field property to display *No Website* if there is no data in the VenueWebSite field.

59. Select the **VenueLiaison** field, and set the **Allow Zero Length** property to **No**.

60. Save the **Venues** table. Click **Yes** in the warning box.

61. Select the **VenuePhone** field, click in the **Input Mask** field property line, and click the **Build** button.

62. Choose the **Phone Number** mask and click **Finish**.

63. Select the **VenueST** field; click the **Lookup** tab, choose **Combo Box** for the **Display Control** field property, and choose **States** for the **Row Source** field property.

64. Type **2** for **Column Count**, `.3, 1.2` for **Column Widths**, and `1.5` for **List Width**.

65. Save the table. Switch to **Datasheet View** and test the new lookup field by entering the record shown, tapping Tab after each field.

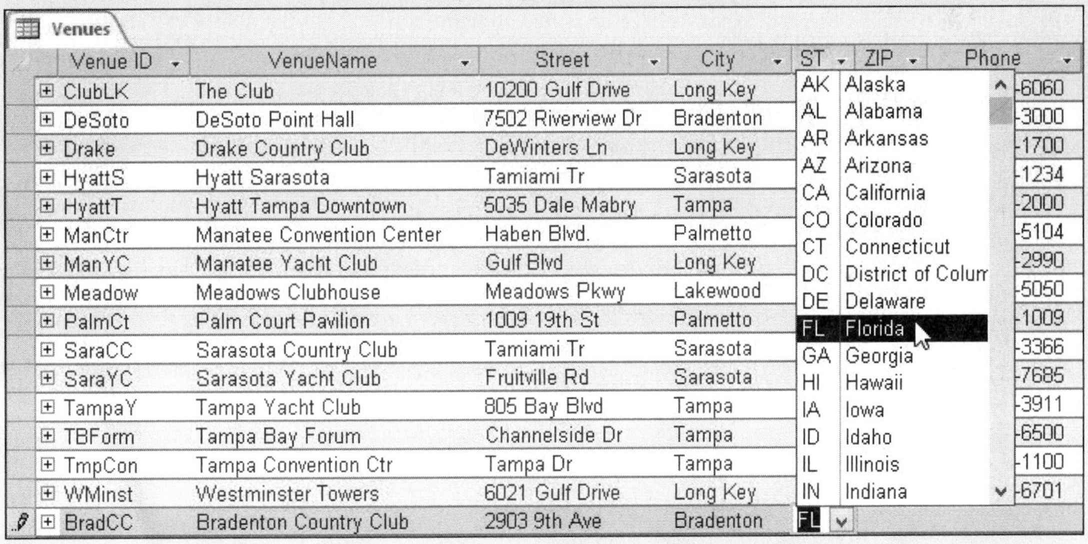

Venues

Venue ID	VenueName	Street	City	ST	ZIP	Phone
ClubLK	The Club	10200 Gulf Drive	Long Key			-6060
DeSoto	DeSoto Point Hall	7502 Riverview Dr	Bradenton			-3000
Drake	Drake Country Club	DeWinters Ln	Long Key			-1700
HyattS	Hyatt Sarasota	Tamiami Tr	Sarasota			-1234
HyattT	Hyatt Tampa Downtown	5035 Dale Mabry	Tampa			-2000
ManCtr	Manatee Convention Center	Haben Blvd.	Palmetto			-5104
ManYC	Manatee Yacht Club	Gulf Blvd	Long Key			-2990
Meadow	Meadows Clubhouse	Meadows Pkwy	Lakewood			-5050
PalmCt	Palm Court Pavilion	1009 19th St	Palmetto			-1009
SaraCC	Sarasota Country Club	Tamiami Tr	Sarasota			-3366
SaraYC	Sarasota Yacht Club	Fruitville Rd	Sarasota			-7685
TampaY	Tampa Yacht Club	805 Bay Blvd	Tampa			-3911
TBForm	Tampa Bay Forum	Channelside Dr	Tampa			-6500
TmpCon	Tampa Convention Ctr	Tampa Dr	Tampa			-1100
WMinst	Westminster Towers	6021 Gulf Drive	Long Key			-6701
BradCC	Bradenton Country Club	2903 9th Ave	Bradenton	FL		

AK	Alaska
AL	Alabama
AR	Arkansas
AZ	Arizona
CA	California
CO	Colorado
CT	Connecticut
DC	District of Colum
DE	Delaware
FL	Florida
GA	Georgia
HI	Hawaii
IA	Iowa
ID	Idaho
IL	Illinois
IN	Indiana

66. Finish the record by entering the following field values:

Field	Value
Zip	34205
Phone	9415550031
Kitchen	Yes
Website	BCC@web.com
Liaison	AntonV

67. Save and close the **Venues** table. Close any open objects and close the database; exit **Access**.

68. Submit your final file based on the guidelines provided by your instructor.

Extend Your Skills

In the course of working through the Extend Your Skills exercises, you will think critically as you use the skills taught in the lesson to complete the assigned projects. To evaluate your mastery and completion of the exercises, your instructor may use a rubric, with which more points are allotted according to performance characteristics. (The more you do, the more you earn!) Ask your instructor how your work will be evaluated.

AC06-E01 That's the Way I See It

In this exercise, you will edit relationships and modify tables. Use the database you used in AC05-E01, or open **AC06-E01-BJL** and save it to your **AC2013 Lesson 06** folder as **`AC06-E01-BJL-[FirstInitialLastName]`**.

Create a relationship between the MerchID fields in the StoreMerchandise and SalesInvoices tables, enforcing referential integrity, and create a report named **`AC06-E01-Relationships-[FirstInitialLastName]`**. (If using your own database, be sure all tables have the appropriate relationships created.)

Using the StoreMerchandise table in the BJL database (or a similar table in your database): apply color and formatting to improve readability; resize columns to view entire field contents; switch the order of the Manufacturer and the Item Name—or two similar fields; hide the Qty in Stock field; and apply the custom mask **`"BJL-"9999`** to MerchID. (Enclose BJL- in quotes.)

In the Customers table (or similar table): set captions and field sizes; make the last name required; make State a lookup field; apply an input mask to the phone number field; resize columns; and display **`No Email`** for customers with no email address on file.

You will be evaluated based on the inclusion of all elements, your ability to follow directions, your ability to apply newly learned skills to a real-world situation, your creativity, and your accuracy in creating objects and/or entering data. Submit your final file based on the guidelines provided by your instructor.

AC06-E02 Be Your Own Boss

As the owner of BJL, you want to improve how your database looks and behaves. Open **AC06-E02-BJL** and save it to your **AC2013 Lesson 06** folder as **`AC06-E02-BJL-[FirstInitialLastName]`**. Create a relationship between the CustID fields (Customers table) and the SalesInvoices and ServiceInvoices tables, enforcing referential integrity, and create a report named **`AC06-E02-Relationships-[FirstInintialLastName]`**.

In the Services table, add gridline and font formatting. Resize columns and move the Service Rep field to the left of Services. Hide the ServID field. Set the Required field property to Yes for all fields and set ServRep as a lookup field. In the ServiceReps table, set field sizes and captions. Apply the input mask **`"BJLRep-"9999`** to the RepID field and the phone number input mask to the RepPhone field. Set RepState as a lookup field (Bound Column=**`1`**, Column Count=**`2`**, Column Widths=**`.5, 1.5`** List Width=**`2`**) with a default value of **`FL`**. Resize columns as needed and add font and style formatting.

You will be evaluated based on the inclusion of all elements, your ability to follow directions, your ability to apply newly learned skills to a real-world situation, your creativity, and your accuracy in creating objects and/or entering data. Submit your final file based on the guidelines provided by your instructor.

Transfer Your Skills

In the course of working through the Transfer Your Skills exercises, you will use critical-thinking and creativity skills to complete the assigned projects using skills taught in the lesson. To evaluate your mastery and completion of the exercises, your instructor may use a rubric, with which more points are allotted according to performance characteristics. (The more you do, the more you earn!) Ask your instructor how your work will be evaluated.

AC06-T01 Use the Web as a Learning Tool

Throughout this book, you will be provided with an opportunity to use the Internet as a learning tool by completing WebQuests. According to the original creators of WebQuests, as described on their website (WebQuest.org), a WebQuest is "an inquiry-oriented activity in which most or all of the information used by learners is drawn from the web." To complete the WebQuest projects in this book, navigate to the student resource center and choose the WebQuest for the lesson on which you are currently working. The subject of each WebQuest will be relevant to the material found in the lesson.

WebQuest Subject: Cascade Update Related Fields and Cascade Delete Related Fields

Submit your final file(s) based on the guidelines provided by your instructor.

AC06-T02 Demonstrate Proficiency

Stormy BBQ is continuing to update its database to convey a tropical look and feel at its flagship location in Key West. Open **AC06-T02-SBQ** from the **AC2013 Lesson 06** folder and save it as **`AC06-T02-SBQ-[FirstInitialLastName]`**.

Apply the techniques you learned in this lesson to format and dress up the Staff table. Be sure to set appropriate field sizes and captions, set State as a lookup field, arrange fields in a functional order, resize columns as needed, and display the text **`No Email Available`** for staff without an email address. Open and format the Restaurants table using the same techniques and tools. Use your imagination or borrow ideas from the other objects in the database. Finally, create a relationship report named **`AC06-T02-Relationships-[FirstInitialLastName]`**. (Note: If you get an error message regarding no unique index, ensure the key fields in the two tables contain matching values.)

Submit your final file based on the guidelines provided by your instructor.

Customizing Input Forms

LESSON OUTLINE

LEARNING OBJECTIVES

After studying this lesson, you will be able to:

- Create a form that contains a subform
- Edit a data source
- Format a form and add a logo
- Add a calculated control and the current date to a form
- Set form properties to lock, add ScreenTips, and create pop-up forms

Forms provide an attractive and user-friendly interface for entering data. They are especially helpful for users who are unfamiliar with complex database structures. In this lesson, you will learn how to add a subform to a main form, which is a handy technique used to include data from a different source. You will also explore additional Access features to format forms, create calculated fields, replace data sources, add tips to form controls, and set control properties to protect and limit data entry.

CASE STUDY

Formatting Functional Forms

Winchester Web Design has seen sales increase over recent months and wants to simplify data entry. You must design advanced forms to calculate totals, while making data entry easier and less prone to errors. You will create an Invoice form that contains a subform for Invoice Details. This will allow users to use a drop-down menu to populate multiple form fields and perform calculations with just one click. The database relationships will be critical for setting up these forms.

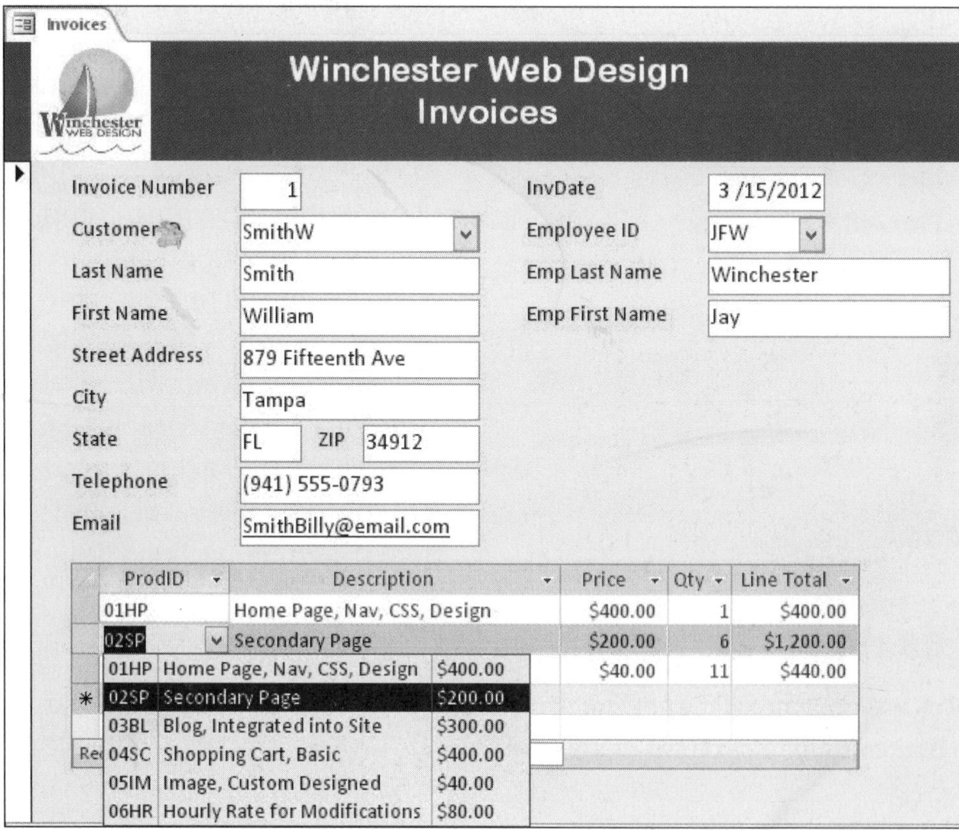

Identifying Complex Form Features

Video Library http://labyrinthelab.com/videos Video Number: AC13-V0701

Although many forms are designed to enter data into a single table, there are times when you may need forms that perform actions such as processing customer invoices, calculating totals, and locating data from multiple tables.

One of the best ways to accomplish this is through a subform, which is a secondary—or child—form placed on the main—or parent—form. Subforms work well when one-to-many relationships are set, allowing the user to view and enter complete data entries for multiple tables using one form. Subforms are simply subsets of data linked by master fields on the main form to child fields on the subform.

In addition to adding and aligning field controls and titles, Access contains additional features for formatting database forms that allow you to:

- Place a subform on a main form.
- Create calculated fields on forms, similar to those you can add to queries.
- Create pop-up forms that can display supplemental information.
- Create tips to assist in data entry.
- Disable form fields so that no one can edit the data.
- Hide screen elements.

Creating a Main Form with a Subform

Video Library http://labyrinthelab.com/videos Video Number: AC13-V0702

When relationships exist between tables in a database, Access is able to display related data when you open the table datasheet. These relationships are central to the creation of subforms.

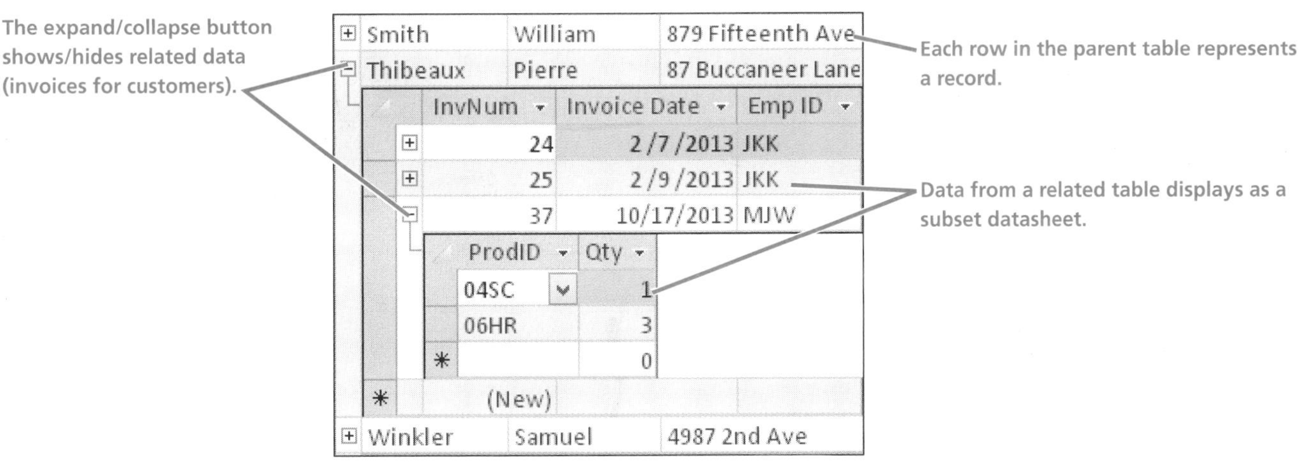

Removing the Layout

When you create a quick form, Access positions fields in a two-column layout; the first for the labels, and second for the text boxes. However, arranging individual form controls can be a challenge because Access links all of the label and text box controls. Consequently, if you drag one text box to shorten it, every other text box on the form is also shortened. And if you drag one text box to widen it, every other text box on the form is also widened.

FROM THE RIBBON
Create→Forms→Form to create a quick form

You can remove the linked layout so that you can move and size selected controls independently.

FROM THE RIBBON
Arrange→Table→Remove Layout to remove the linked layout of a quick form

Connecting Related Tables in Forms

Establishing relationships among database tables also enables Access to display table data on forms along with a subset of data from a related table. When relationships are established, Access creates the main form from data contained in the table or query on which you base the form and places related data in one or more subforms on the main form.

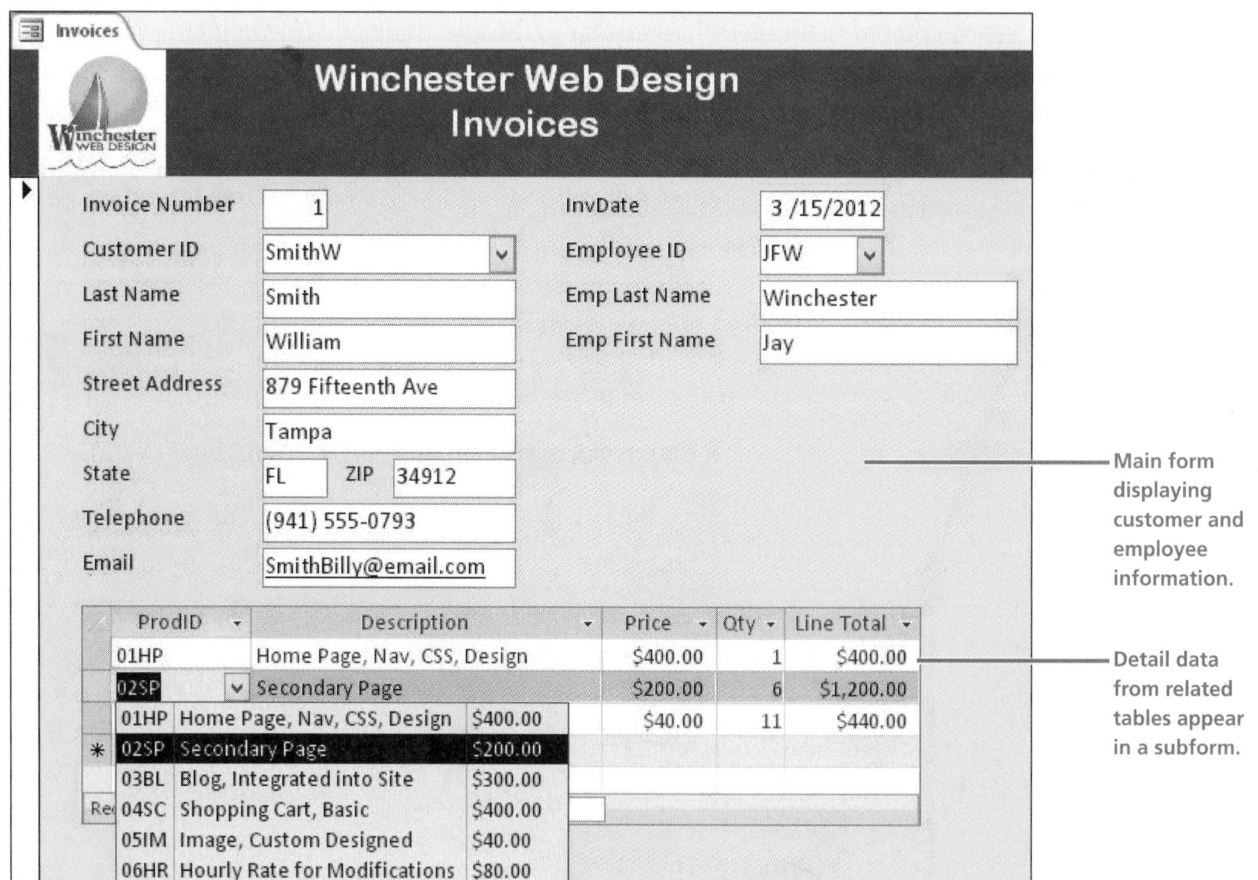

Creating a Form with a Subform

Creating a form with a subform makes data entry more efficient. If you have a lookup field in a main table and your relationships are properly established, you can quickly create a form and subform. The subform displays data from a related table created by the lookup field.

Using the Form Wizard

The Form Wizard allows you to select the related tables or queries containing fields to include on the form and then asks whether you want to create a form with a subform, or if you want to link the data from a subform to the main form.

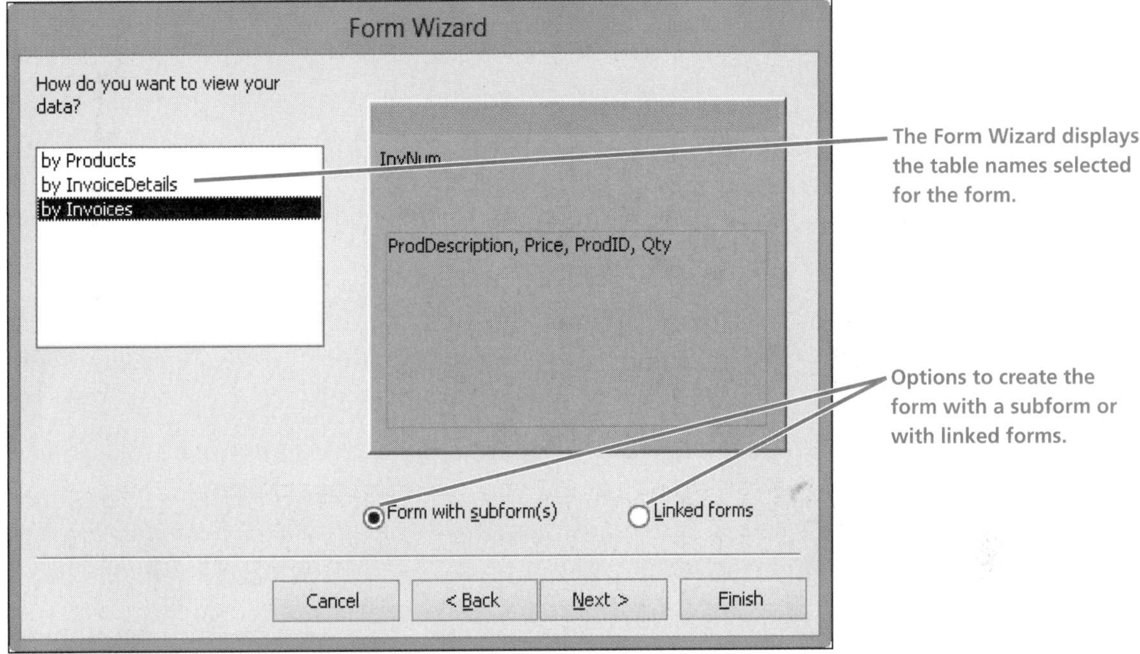

Using the Subform Control

FROM THE RIBBON

Design→Controls→Subform/Subreport to create a subform/subreport

To add a subform to an existing form, you can use the Subform control. This tool enables you to size the control to fit the area of the main form you want it to occupy. Access places an unbound control on the main form and starts the Subform Wizard. Alternately, you can close the Wizard and use the Property Sheet in Design View to set the Record Source from which you want Access to draw related records. The record source is the underlying table or query that contains the data for the text boxes or fields contained in a form, subform, or report. When you use the Subform control, its Source Object property is used to identify the record source of the subform.

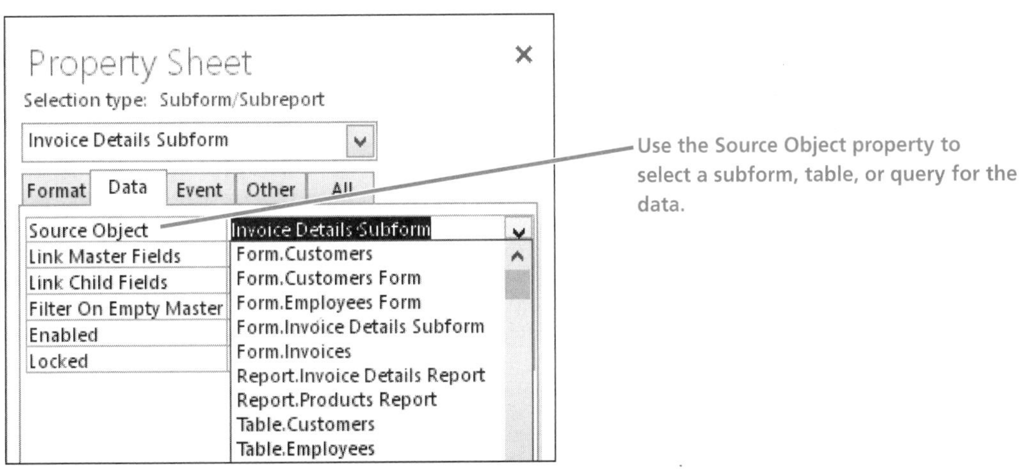

QUICK REFERENCE	CREATING A FORM CONTAINING A SUBFORM
Task	**Procedure**
Create a form with a subform using the wizard	■ Choose Create→Forms→Form Wizard and follow the wizard screens.
Add a subform to an existing form	■ Choose Design→Controls→Subform. ■ Draw, size, and position a subform control on the main form. ■ Follow the Subform Wizard screens.

DEVELOP YOUR SKILLS AC07-D01

Create a Form Containing a Subform

In this exercise, you will use the Form Wizard to create an invoice form that contains an invoice details subform.

1. Open **AC07-D01-WinWebDesign** from the **AC2013 Lesson 07** folder and save it as `AC07-D01-WinWebDesign-[FirstInitialLastName]`.

   Replace the bracketed text with your first initial and last name. For example, if your name is Bethany Smith, your filename would look like this: AC07-D01-WinWebDesign-BSmith.

2. Select the **Invoices** table in the Navigation Pane.
3. Choose **Create→Forms→Form Wizard**.
4. Follow these steps to select the initial fields from the Invoices table:

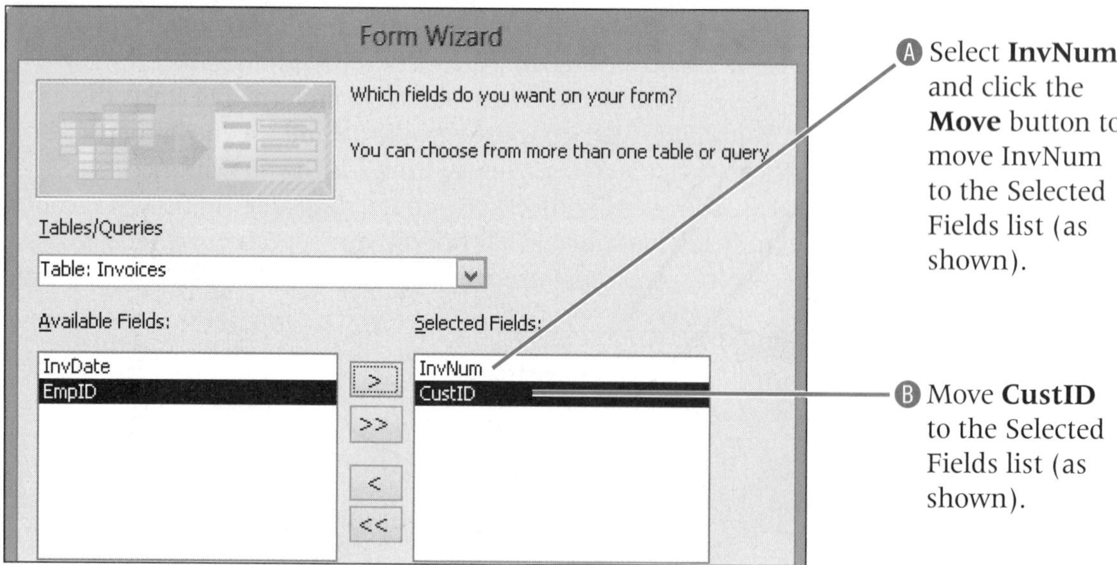

5. Move the following fields from their respective tables in the order shown.

Table	Fields
Customers	CustLastName
	CustFirstName
	CustStreetAddress
	CustCity
	CustState
	CustZIP
	CustPhone
	CustEmail
Invoices	InvoiceDate
Employees	EmpID
	EmpLastName
	EmpFirstName
InvoiceDetails	ProdID
Products	ProdDesription
	Price
InvoiceDetails	Qty

Be sure to move the fields in the order shown. Yes, you did access the InvoiceDetails tables twice. This process ensures that Access will place the fields on your form in the desired order, which will reduce the amount of post-creation editing.

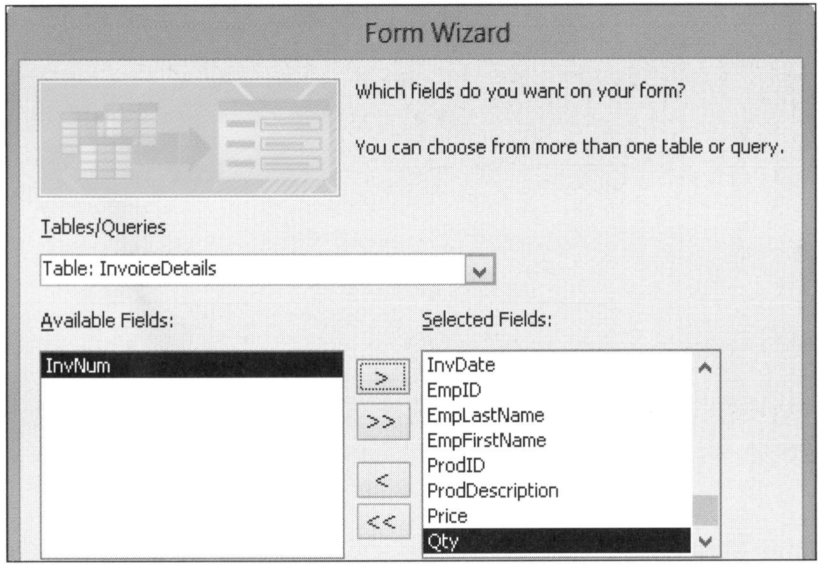

If you select ProdID from the Products table instead of the InvoiceDetails table, the subform will not allow you to use the ProdID drop-down menu later in the subform.

6. Click **Next** to review the arrangement of data as a form with a subform.

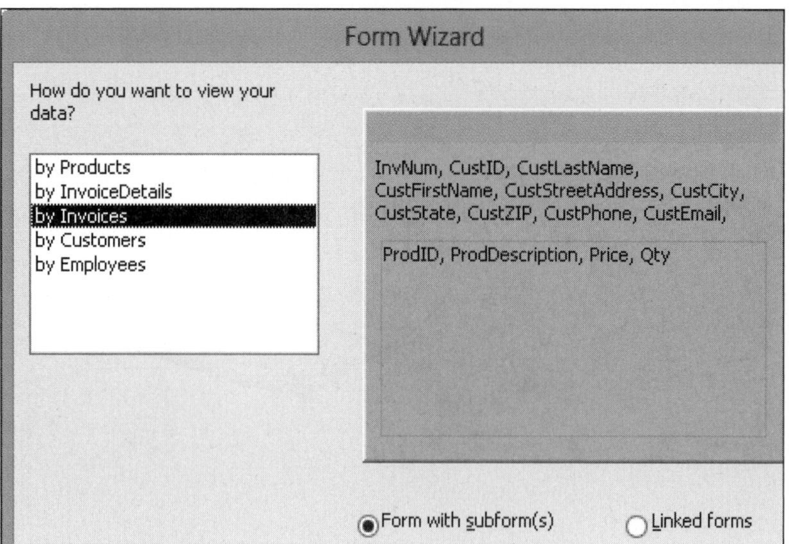

The subform will contain the ProdID, ProdDescription, Price, and Qty fields.

7. Click **Next** and leave the default Datasheet layout for your subform.

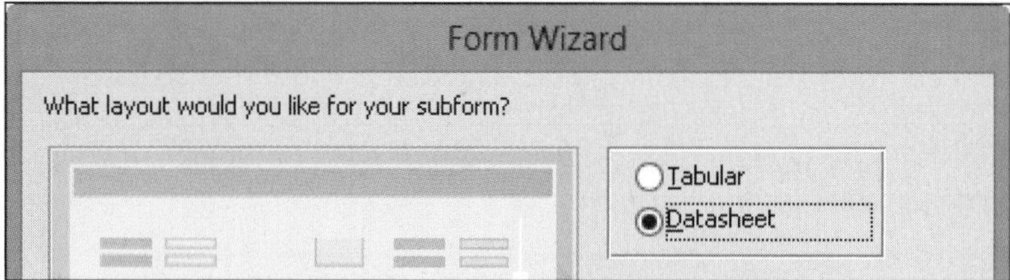

8. Click **Next**.
9. Name the form **`Customer Invoices`** and name the subform **`Customer InvoiceDetails Subform`**; click **Finish.**

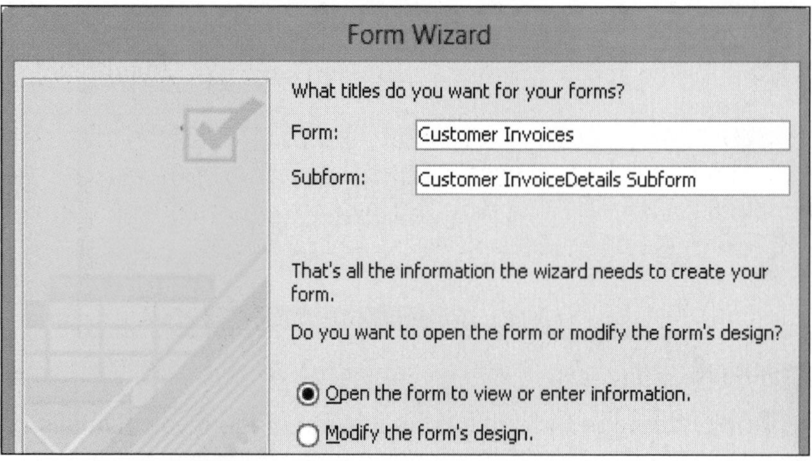

The new Invoices form displays in Form View.

10. Double-click the right border of each subform column heading to resize the fields in the subform.

ProdID	Description	Price	Qty
01HP	Home Page, Nav, CSS, Design	$400.00	1
02SP	Secondary Page	$200.00	6
05IM	Image, Custom Designed	$40.00	11
*			

11. Click in the first empty **ProdID** row, click the menu button, and choose **03BL Blog**.

The ProdIDs and corresponding Descriptions and Prices quickly populate three fields with one click of the mouse.

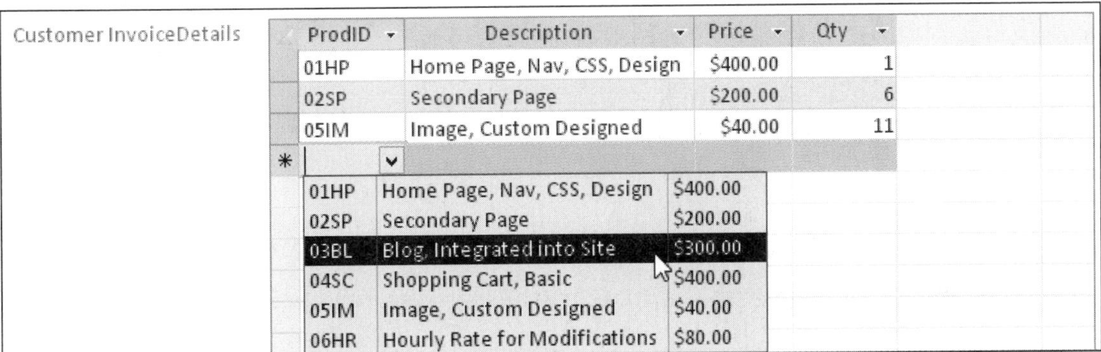

12. Type 1 in the **Qty** column and tap [Tab] to save the new item.
13. Close the form.

The Navigation Pane lists the Customer Invoices form and the Customer Invoice Details Subform.

Unless directed otherwise, keep Access and any databases or database objects being used open at the end of each exercise.

Identifying the Subform Data Source

Video Library http://labyrinthelab.com/videos Video Number: AC13-V0703

When you use the Form Wizard to create a form that has a subform, Access creates two separate forms and displays both in the Navigation Pane—the main form and the subform. Access identifies the subform by including the word *Subform* in its name. Each form has a separate record source—in this case, a table—from which it gets data.

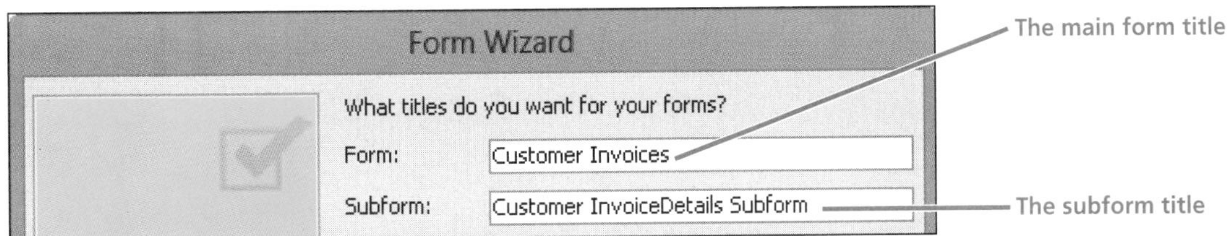

Analyzing the Customer InvoiceDetails Subform Record Source

Form properties display the record source for each form in an Access database. You can use the Property Sheet to set the record source for the main form and the subform and view the master and child fields (the primary and foreign keys) that are used to link the tables.

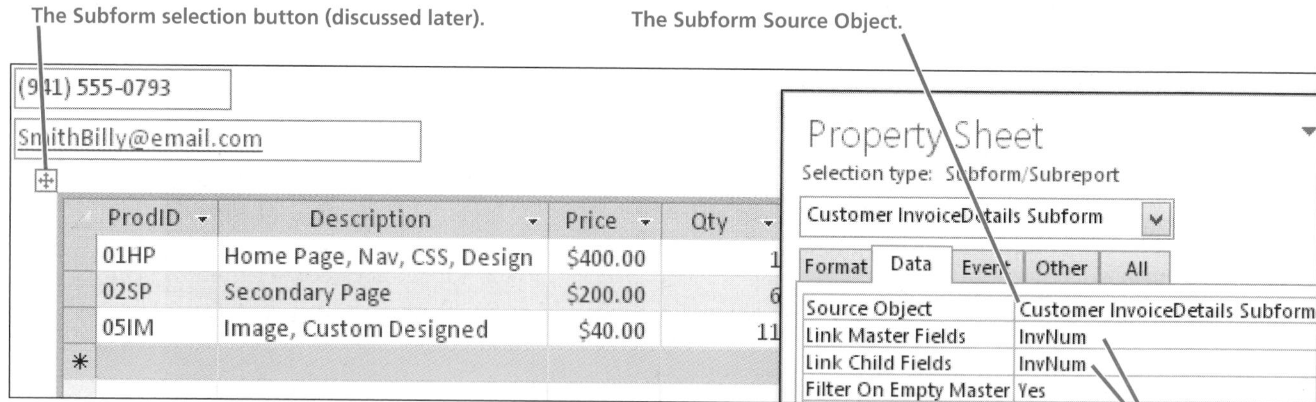

An Invoice form includes the invoice number, date, and any desired customer information. However, the Invoice Details table contains the specific sales data. As a result, you utilize a separate form with the InvoiceDetails table as its source.

Identifying Form Design Features

The major elements and controls found in the Form Design window are described in the following tables.

FORM DESIGN WINDOW: SECTIONS

Form Sections	Description
Sections	The major parts of the form, such as the Form Header, Form Footer, Detail, Page Header, and Page Footer.
Form Header	The top section of a form that contains constant data, such as a title, logo, or decorative line.
Form Footer	The bottom section of a form that appears on the last page (or the first page of a one-page form). It might contain a summary or grand total.
Page Header	The section of a form that contains text and fields that are repeated at the top of every *printed page* of an individual record displayed in the form, such as page number and date. Page headers are not frequently used on forms.
Page Footer	The section of a form that contains text and fields that are repeated at the bottom of every *printed page* of a record displayed in the form, such as page number and date. Unlike report footers, page footers are seldom used.
Detail section	The main section of the form, which contains text boxes that display the data.

FORM DESIGN WINDOW: CONTROLS	
Form Controls	**Description**
Controls	Items on a form that display data, text, checkboxes, lines, images, and buttons.
Bound control	A control that ties, or binds, form data to table data so that the data appears on the form (i.e., the *LastName* text box on a form is bound to the *LastName* field in the source table). Bound controls normally appear in the Detail section
Unbound control	An item on a form that is independent of any table data. Unbound controls can be text, shapes, and images.
Calculated control	A control that is tied to a calculated field or expression built in a query (i.e., *Total=[Price]*[Quantity]* where *Total* is a text box and *Price* and *Quantity* are bound). Calculated controls appear in the Detail or Form Footer section.
Control label	The part of a control that contains text identifying the data displayed in a text box or a checkbox. By default, the label is either the field name or caption from the source table. For example, the caption *Last Name* (with a space) is a good label for the *LastName* field (without a space).
Control text box	The control that displays the actual data from a table. For example, *Smith* might be the data displayed in the *LastName* text box.

Formatting the Form and Subform

Video Library http://labyrinthelab.com/videos Video Number: AC13-V0704

When you create a new form in Design View you can modify labels, resize text boxes, or change the form's style. When a form contains a subform, you can use the same techniques to modify the subform directly on the main form or open the subform separately and make changes to the form.

Tips for Working with Controls

Selecting, moving, positioning, and aligning form controls can be tedious and time-consuming. Fortunately, Access contains alignment and distribution options that enable you to accomplish these tasks more easily. Try these techniques when you have trouble positioning a control on a form. And don't forget that you can press Ctrl+Z or click Undo—to reverse actions, or restore controls deleted in error.

QUICK REFERENCE	ARRANGING, SIZING, AND DISTRIBUTING CONTROLS
Task	**Procedure**
Align controls	■ Select all controls you want to align. ■ Choose Arrange→Sizing & Ordering→Align and click Left, Right, Top, or Bottom.
Nudge controls into position	■ Select the control(s) you want to position. ■ Tap the arrow keys to nudge a control into place; or press and hold Ctrl and tap arrow keys to nudge in smaller increments.
Distribute controls equally	■ Select the controls to distribute. ■ Choose Arrange→Sizing & Ordering→Size/Space and click the desired spacing button.
Size controls equally	■ Select the controls you want to size. ■ Choose Arrange→Sizing & Ordering→Size/Space and click the desired control button.

Using the Subform Selection Button

You may already be familiar with the subform selection button; it is the same as a table's selection button that appears in the top-left corner of the table. The button allows you to select an entire table at once. With an entire table selected, you can move and position all table or field columns at the same time.

In Layout View you can select the subform by clicking on the two crossed double pointed arrows.

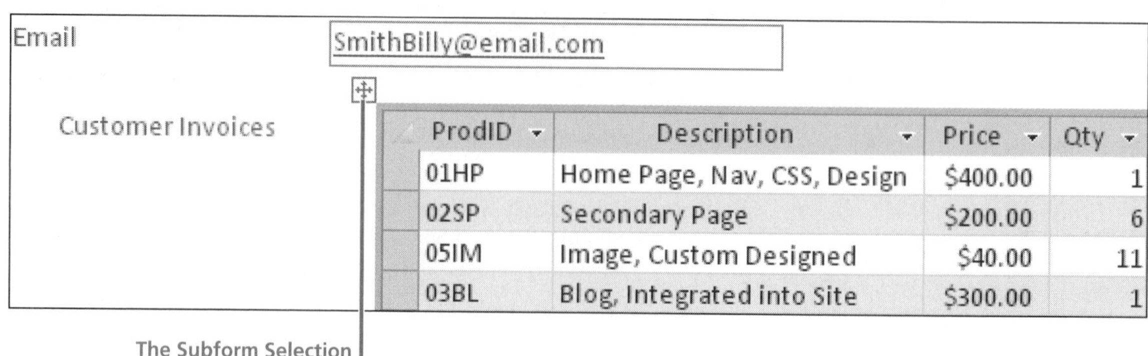

In Design View the subform selection button is the square in the top-left corner of the subform.

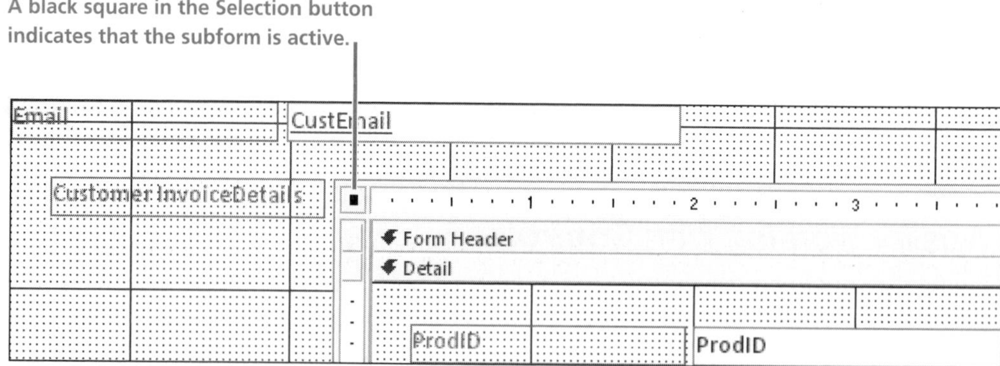

When you select the subform, the selection button is a gray square. Once a subform is selected, you can click inside it to edit it. Access indicates that the subform is active by placing a black square in the middle of the selection button. At this time the subform can be moved, formatted, or even deleted.

DEVELOP YOUR SKILLS AC07-D02

Format the Form and Subform

In this exercise, you will modify the Winchester Web Design Invoices form by deleting, moving, and sizing controls, and adding a graphic and title to the form.

1. Display the **Customer Invoices** form in **Design View**.
2. **Collapse** « the **Navigation Pane** and open the **Property Sheet**.
3. Select the **Customer Invoice Details label** of the subform and tap [Delete].

4. Click the subform.

   If you see the black square in the selection button, click outside of the subform to deselect it, then single-click the subform.

5. Click the move handle and drag the subform to the left to line it up with the first column of labels in the main form.

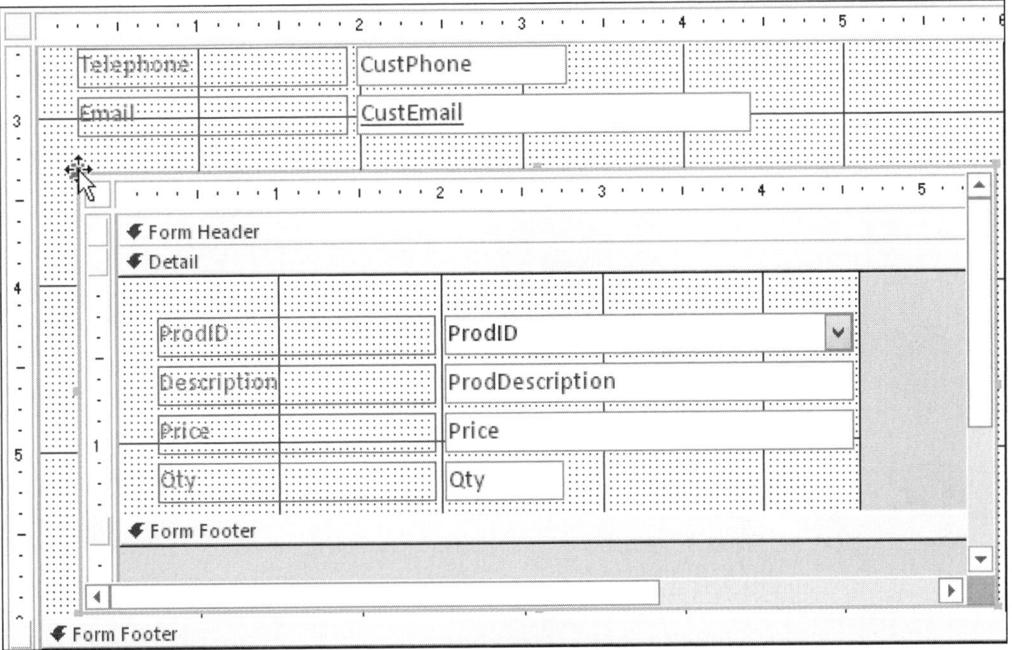

6. Click outside of the subform; then select all the labels on the main form.

You can select multiple boxes by *lassoing* them—just drag and encircle as much of the desired controls as possible without touching any other objects, or simply drag the mouse from above one control through the last control.

7. Type `1.5"` for the **Width** property and tap Tab.

   Now you will make a group of text boxes the same width using the Property Sheet.

8. Select the text boxes as shown:

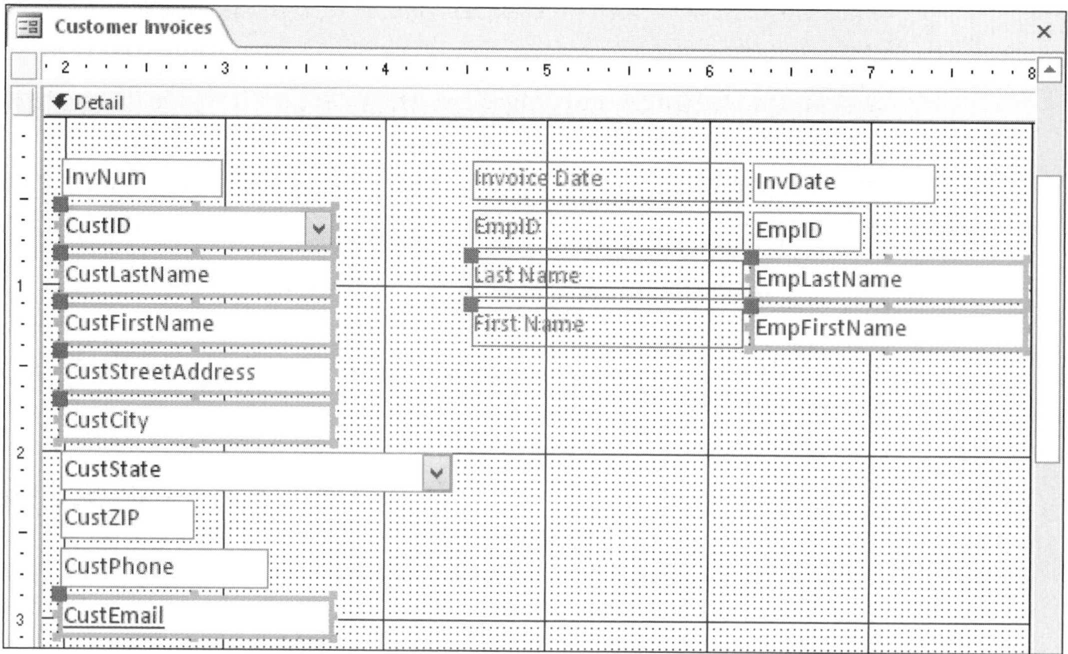

9. Type **1.7"** for the **Width** property and tap [Tab].

   And now you will make a group of controls the same width using the Ribbon.

10. Select the following controls: **InvNum**, **CustState**, **CustZIP**, and **EmpID**.

11. Choose **Arrange→Sizing & Ordering→Size/Space** and choose **To Narrowest**.

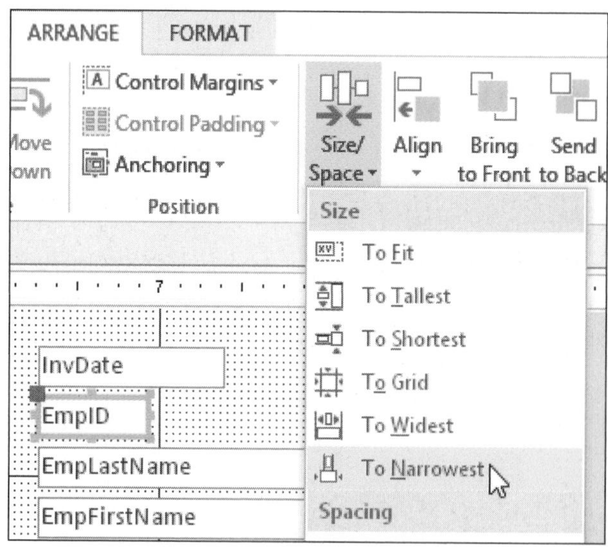

Line Up Form Controls Using the Property Sheet

Next you will set the Left property of the columns on the main form to space them neatly across the form grid.

12. Select the left column of text boxes (InvNum through CustEmail) and type **1.8"** for the **Left** property.

    If the text boxes overlay the labels after you set the Left property, make sure that the label width is 1.5 and the Left property is .25.

13. Select the second column of labels (Invoice Date, EmpID, Last Name, and First Name) and type **3.75** for the **Left** property.

14. Select the **InvDate**, **EmpID**, **EmpLastName**, and **EmpFirstName** text boxes and type **5.3** for the **Left** property.

    Next, you will move the CustZIP text box up next to the CustState text box.

15. Select the **CustZIP** text box, and drag it up to the right of the **CustST** text box under the CustCity text box.

    Just move the CustZIP text box, not the ZIP label.

16. Right-align the **CustZIP** text box with the **CustCity** text box.

17. Click the **ZIP** label.

18. Hover the mouse pointer over the right border until it is a double arrow ⟷, and click and drag the border to the left to make it smaller, as shown.

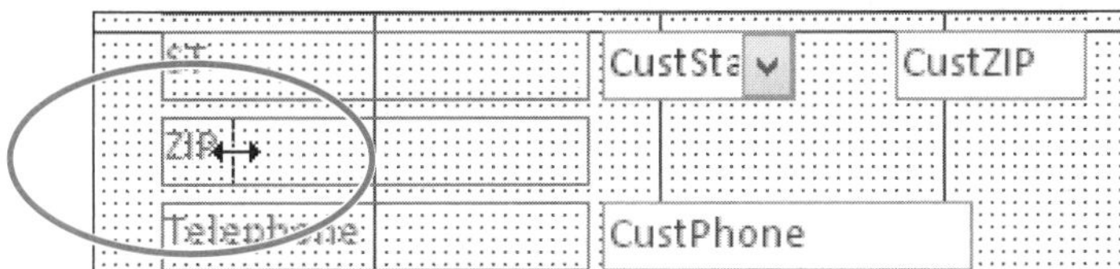

19. Drag the **ZIP** label between the **CustState** and **CustZIP** text boxes.

20. Select the **Telephone** and **Email** labels and text boxes, and the subform.

21. Tap [↑] as necessary to move the controls up to the other controls, as shown.

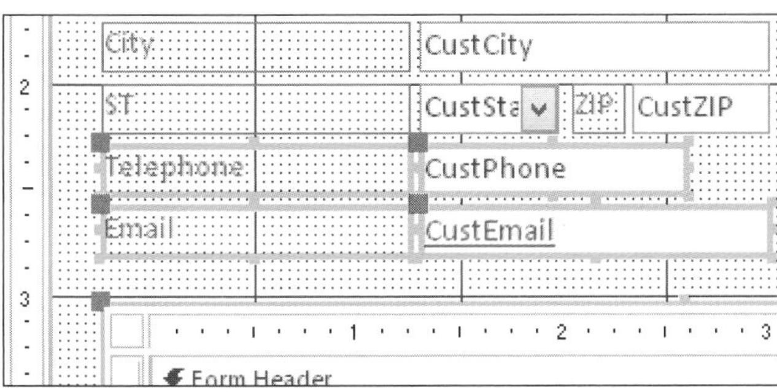

Access 2013

Reposition and Resize the Subform Controls

22. Switch to **Layout View** and select the subform.

23. Hover the mouse pointer over the right border until it is a double arrow ⟷; then click and drag the right border to the left to fit the contents.

24. Open the **Property Sheet** and click the **All** tab.

25. Follow these steps to view the subform's properties:

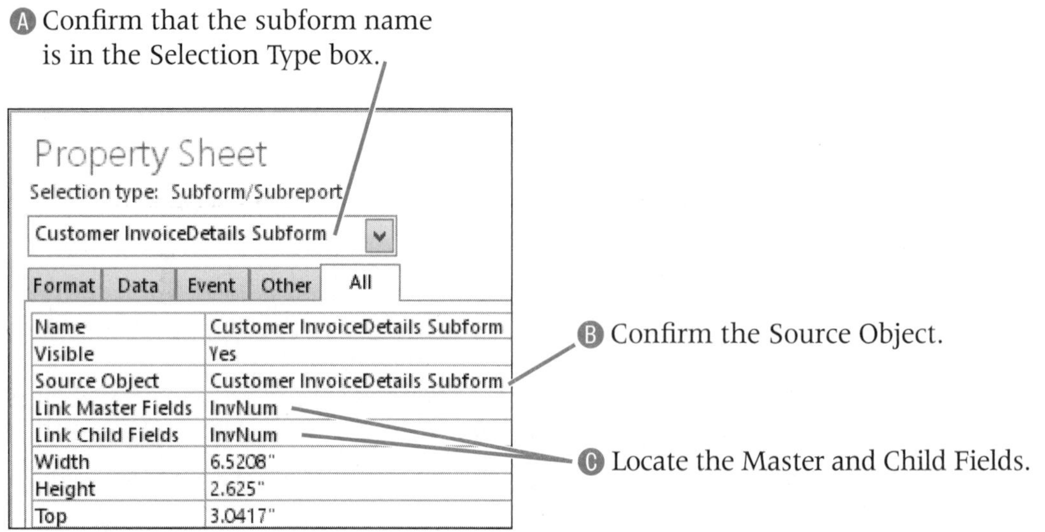

26. **Save** the Customer Invoices form.

Add a Title to the Form

27. Switch to **Design View**.

28. Select the **Customer Invoices** title in the **Form Header** section.

29. Choose **Format→Font→Font Color** and choose **White**.

30. Choose **Format→Font→Font Size** and choose 28.

31. Click **Center**.

32. Use the **Property Sheet** to set the properties as shown.

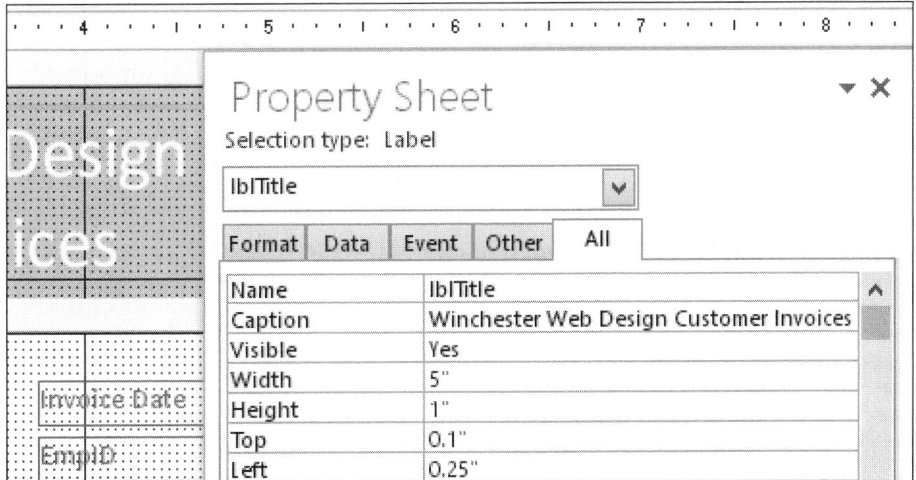

Add a Logo to the Form

33. Click the **Form Header** section bar.

34. Choose **Blue, Accent 5, Darker 25%** for the **Back Color** property.

35. Choose **Design→Controls→Insert Image**. Navigate to the **AC2013 Lesson 07** folder and double-click **WWD-Logo.bmp**.

36. Click and draw the image control in the **Form Header** section to the right of the title. Enter the properties as shown.

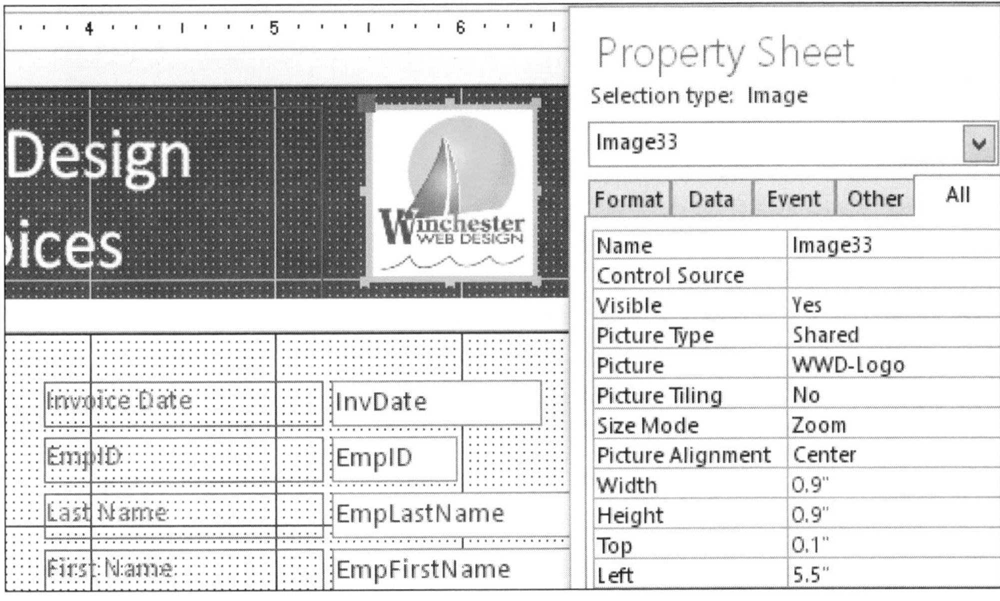

Your Form Header should include the image/logo to the right of the title.

37. Save and close the **Customer Invoices** form.

Adding Calculations to Forms

Video Library http://labyrinthelab.com/videos Video Number: AC13-V0705

There are several ways to add calculations to forms. You can build your form based on a query that already has a calculated field. You can use the Totals feature to automatically display totals in datasheet view, or you can type formulas directly into the control source property of a text box. Or you can also use the Expression Builder, which allows you to create formulas or expressions by selecting the desired fields and operands in the Expression Builder dialog box.

Applying Totals to Forms in Datasheet View

When you use the Form Wizard and choose the Datasheet layout, or if you display a table or query in Datasheet View, you can use the Totals feature to instruct Access to sum, count, average, or perform other aggregate functions for the items in a column. You can access the Totals feature from the Ribbon. A Totals row will appear at the bottom of the datasheet.

FROM THE RIBBON

Home→Records→Totals to calculate totals on a form

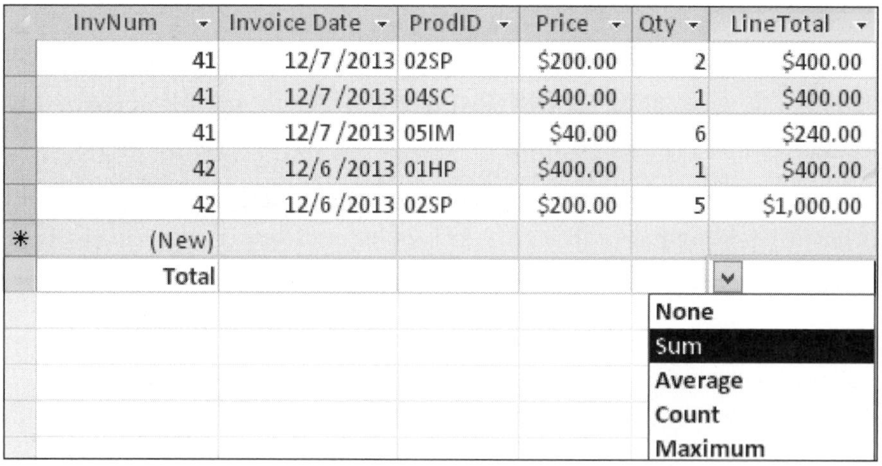

	InvNum	Invoice Date	ProdID	Price	Qty	LineTotal
	41	12/7 /2013	02SP	$200.00	2	$400.00
	41	12/7 /2013	04SC	$400.00	1	$400.00
	41	12/7 /2013	05IM	$40.00	6	$240.00
	42	12/6 /2013	01HP	$400.00	1	$400.00
	42	12/6 /2013	02SP	$200.00	5	$1,000.00
*	(New)					
	Total					

None
Sum
Average
Count
Maximum

DEVELOP YOUR SKILLS AC07-D03

Add Totals to a Form

In this exercise, you will create a form that uses the Totals feature to count the number of individual line items on customer invoices and total the amount of all invoices.

1. Expand the **Navigation Pane** and select the **Invoices Query**.
2. Choose **Create→Forms→Form Wizard**.
3. Click **Move All** [>>] to move all fields to the **Selected Fields** pane.

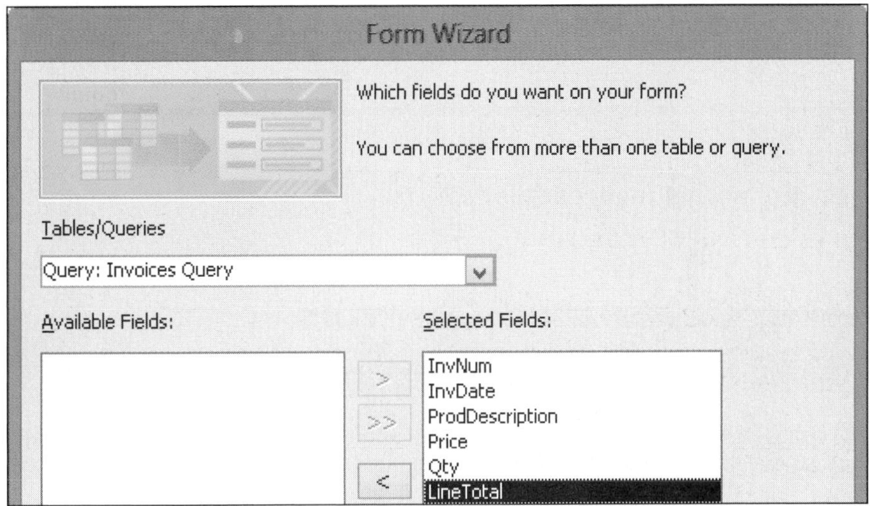

4. Click **Next**. In the next screen, choose the **Datasheet** layout.

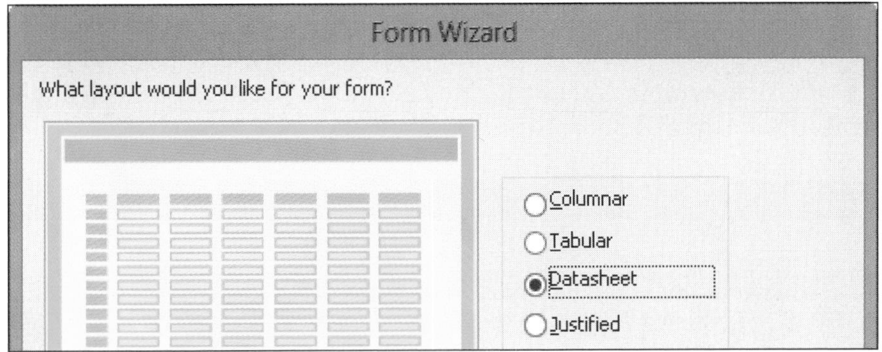

5. Click **Next**. Name the new form `Invoices Query Form` and click **Finish**.
   The new form is displayed in Datasheet View.
6. Choose **Home→Records→**[Σ Totals].
7. Click the **Qty** column on the Total row at the bottom of the datasheet. Choose **Count**. Access counts all the individual invoices.

8. Click the **LineTotal** column on the Total row at the bottom of the datasheet and choose **Sum** from the drop-down menu.

   Access sums the LineTotal items. The count of all the invoice items is 125 and the sum of all invoice line totals is $62,920.00.

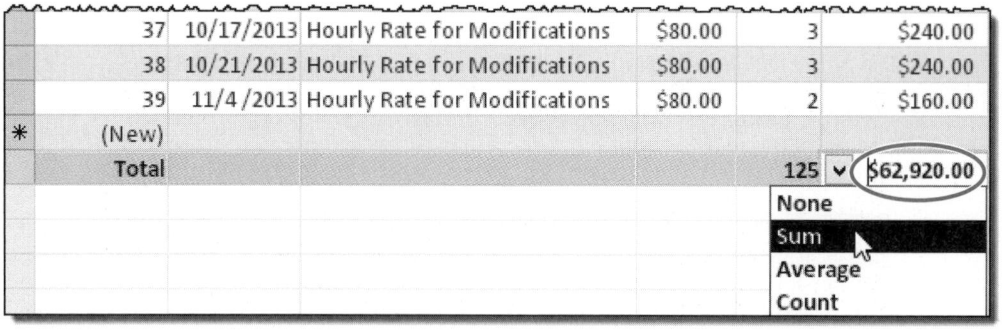

	37	10/17/2013	Hourly Rate for Modifications	$80.00	3	$240.00
	38	10/21/2013	Hourly Rate for Modifications	$80.00	3	$240.00
	39	11/4/2013	Hourly Rate for Modifications	$80.00	2	$160.00
*	(New)					
	Total				125	$62,920.00
					None	
					Sum	
					Average	
					Count	

9. Save and close the **Invoices Query Form**.

Creating Calculated Controls

Video Library http://labyrinthelab.com/videos Video Number: AC13-V0706

You *create* calculated fields in queries and you *add* calculated controls to forms and reports. When you work with a query, you give a name to the new calculated field, and then you enter an expression or formula using the existing table fields that will be used in the calculation. For example, you might enter into the field row of a query column LineTotal: Price * Qty to create a new calculated field name named LineTotal.

Form and report calculated controls are constructed by adding a new text box and entering a formula into its Control Source property. A calculated control's Control Source is associated with an expression or a formula, but not a table field name. For example, you might add a new text box, type LineTotal in its Name property, and then type =Price * Qty as its Control Source.

DEVELOP YOUR SKILLS AC07-D04

Add Calculated Controls to a Subform

In this exercise, you will add a calculated control to the Customer InvoiceDetails Subform.

1. Display the **Customer InvoiceDetails Subform** in **Design View**.
2. Hover the mouse pointer over the top of the **Form Footer** section bar until it is a vertical resize arrow.

3. Click and drag the **Form Footer** bar down, as shown.

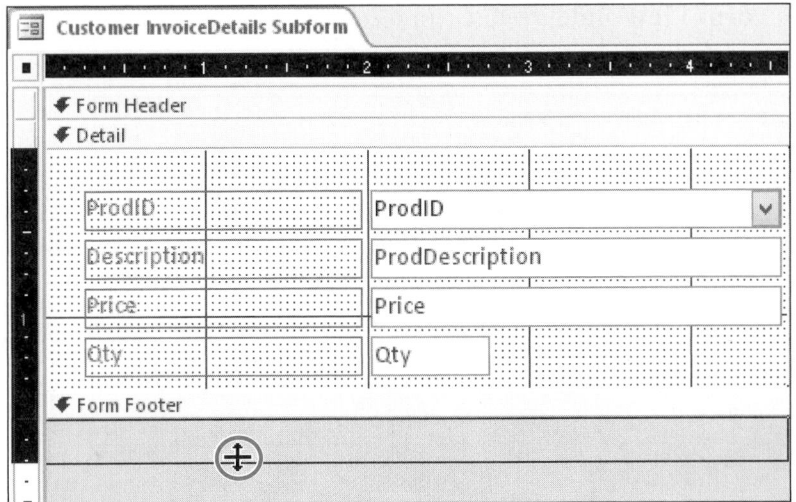

4. Choose **Design→Controls→Text Box** ab| and click in the **Detail** section just under the **Qty** text box.

   Instead of using the Text Box control tool, you could select the Qty label and text box, press Ctrl + C*, then press* Ctrl + V *to insert a copy of the controls under the Qty controls. Then you only have to change the label Caption property to* Line Total *and the text box Control Source property to* =Price*Qty. *The formatting would match the existing controls.*

5. Enter the property settings shown.

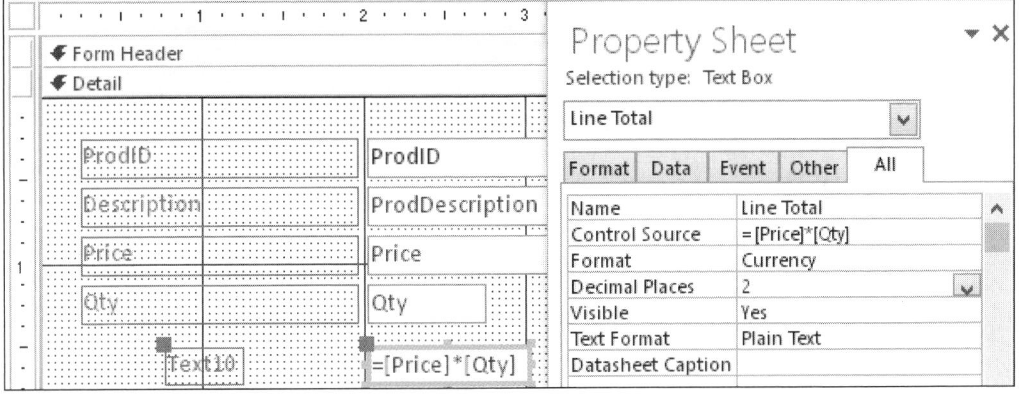

6. Select the new label and type `Line Total` for the Datasheet **Caption** property.
7. Select all the label controls.
8. Choose **Arrange→Sizing & Ordering→Align→Left**.
9. Type `1.7` for the **Width** property.
10. Select all the text box controls.
11. Type **2"** for the **Left** property.
12. Select all the controls in the **Detail** section of the form.

13. Choose **Arrange→Sizing & Ordering→Size/Space→Equal Vertical**.

14. Switch to **Form View** and navigate to a record that has a Qty value greater than 1 to verify that the control works.

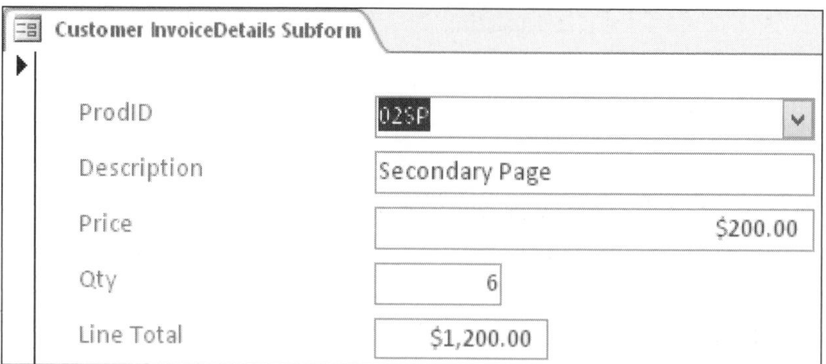

If the control does not work or generates a *#Name*? error message, it is probably because of a typo or spelling mistake.

15. Save the **Customer InvoiceDetails Subform**.

Totaling Calculated Subform Fields on a Form

Video Library http://labyrinthelab.com/videos Video Number: AC13-V0707

If you want to compute a running total of all the line totals in a subform, you would build an expression and use the Sum aggregate function. Other commonly used functions are Avg, Min, Max, Left, Right, and Round.

As an example for calculating running totals, the following steps allow you to display an Invoice Total of all the Line Totals on the subform of an invoice form.

- Add a text box to the Detail section on the subform to do a calculation for the Line Total for each item bought and enter the Control Source: =Price*Qty.
- In the Form Footer section of the subform, add a text box to calculate the total of all invoice items bought and enter the Control Source: =Sum(Price*Qty).
- Give the total of all invoice items text box in the subform Form Footer section a name, such as: txtInvoiceTotal. (The prefix *txt* is short for text box and is commonly used to identify text boxes that will be referenced later.)
- Add a text box to display the invoice total on the main form, and use the Expression Builder for the calculation: =[Customer InvoiceDetails Subform].[Form]![txtInvoiceTotal].

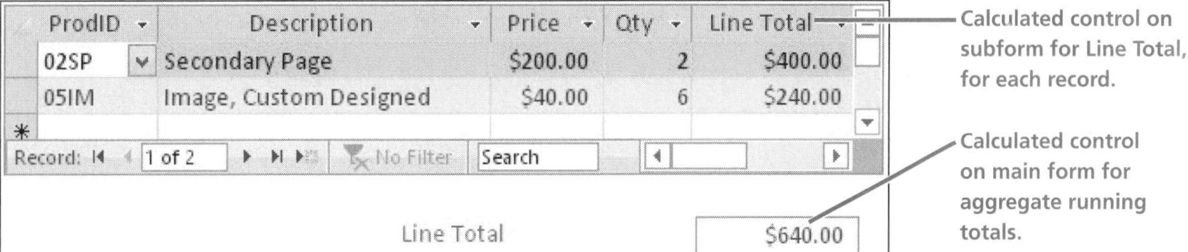

Using the Expression Builder

You can create a calculated control by typing control field names and operators (*, /, +, -, ^) directly into the text box's Control Source line in the Property Sheet. This works well when you refer to objects on the same form and have a simple formula, such as = Price * Qty. However, when you refer to objects on subforms, the Expression Builder dialog box is an easier way to build a formula.

To access the Expression Builder, click the ellipse that appears to the right of an object's Control Source.

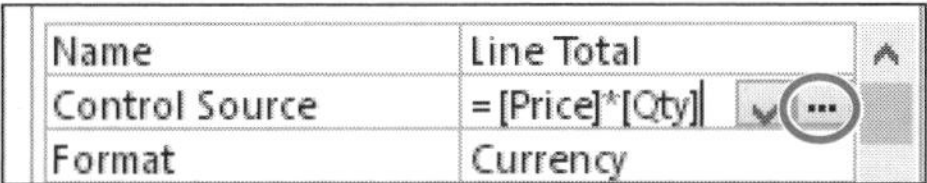

The Expression Builder dialog box enables you to double-click desired field names so you add them into formulas that have unwieldy expressions.

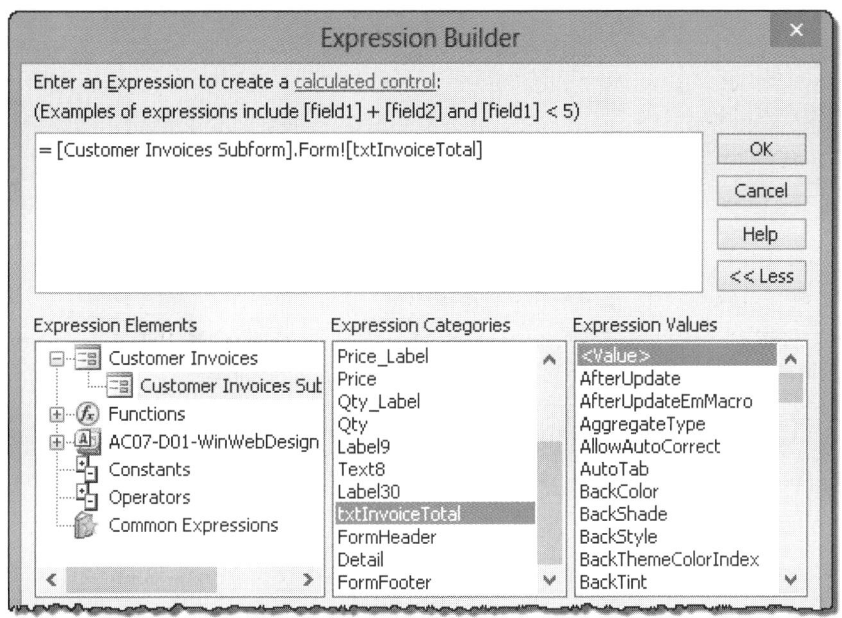

The Expression Builder dialog box contains tools for creating calculated controls.

DEVELOP YOUR SKILLS AC07-D05

Total a Calculated Subform Field on a Form

In this exercise, you will sum all the Line Totals on the Customer InvoiceDetails Subform and display the results on the Customer Invoices form.

1. Display the **Customer InvoiceDetails Subform** in **Design View**.
2. Hover the mouse pointer over the lower edge of the **Form Footer** section bar until it is a section resize pointer.
3. Click and drag the bottom of the **Form Footer** down to make room for a text box.

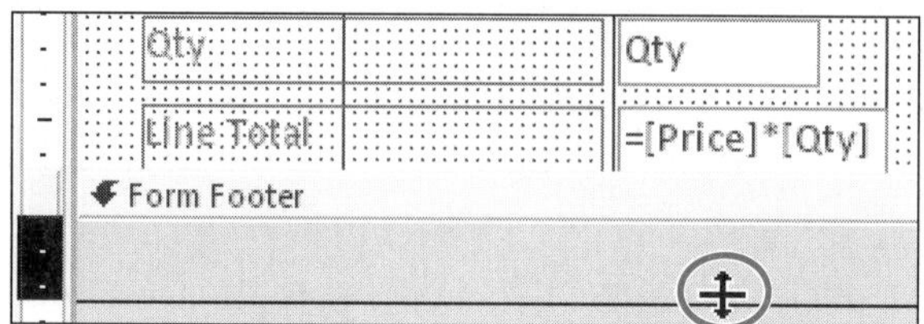

4. Choose **Design→Controls→Text Box** ab|.
5. Draw a text box in the **Form Footer** and line it up with the controls in the **Details** section.
6. Select the new text box and enter the following property values.

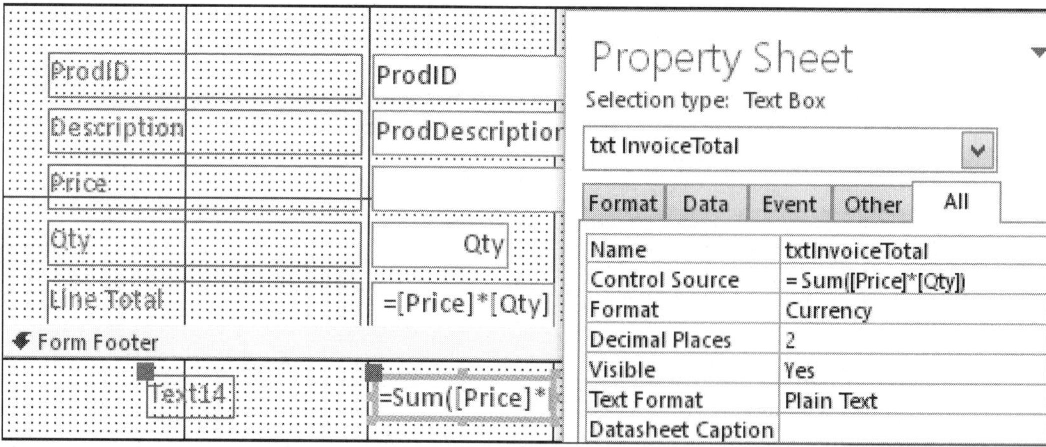

7. Delete the invoice total's associated label control, shown as *Text14* in the figure.
   The Form Footer section does not appear when you display the Customer Invoices form in Layout or Form View.
8. Save and close the **Customer InvoiceDetails Subform**.
9. Open the **Customer Invoices** form in **Layout View**.

10. Resize the right borders of the subform column headings.

ProdID	Description	Price	Qty	Line Total
01HP	Home Page, Nav, CSS, Design	$400.00	1	$400.00
02SP	Secondary Page	$200.00	6	$1,200.00
03BL	Blog, Integrated into Site	$300.00	1	$300.00
05IM	Image, Custom Designed	$40.00	11	$440.00

11. Follow these steps to resize the subform:

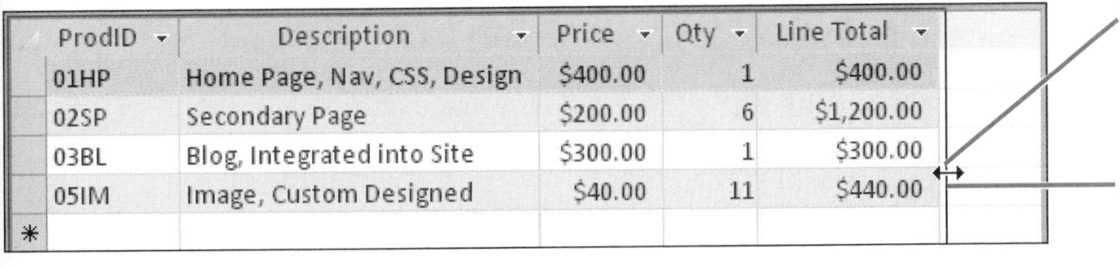

ProdID	Description	Price	Qty	Line Total
01HP	Home Page, Nav, CSS, Design	$400.00	1	$400.00
02SP	Secondary Page	$200.00	6	$1,200.00
03BL	Blog, Integrated into Site	$300.00	1	$300.00
05IM	Image, Custom Designed	$40.00	11	$440.00

Ⓐ Hover the mouse pointer over the right border of the subform until it is a double arrow.

Ⓑ Click and drag the edge of the subform as needed to fit the data.

12. Switch to **Design View**, saving if prompted.

13. Hover the mouse pointer over the top edge of the *main* form's **Form Footer** section bar until it turns into a resize pointer and drag down just enough to create a new text box control under the subform.

14. Choose **Design→Controls→Text Box** ab| and draw a text box in the **Detail** section of the main form, just below the subform.

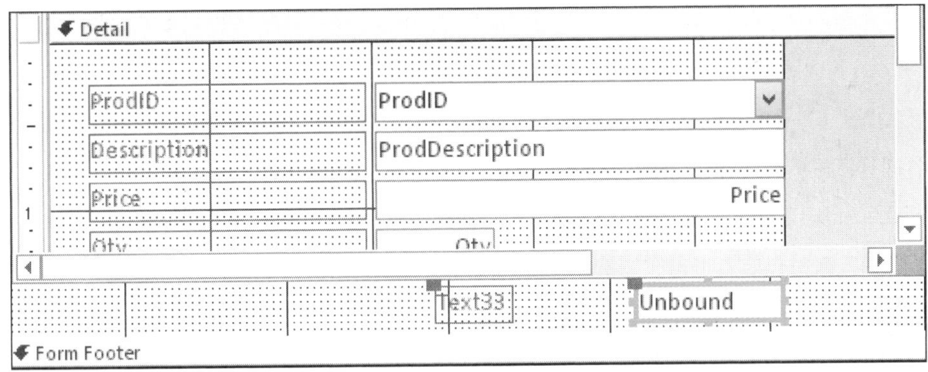

15. Select the new label and type `Invoice Total` for the **Caption** property; resize the label so that the entire caption is visible.

16. Select the new text box.

Access 2013

17. Follow these steps to use the Expression Builder to build an expression:

Ⓐ Choose the **Control Source** property and click the **Build** button.

Ⓑ Type **=** in the Expression pane.

Ⓒ Click the **Expand** button for *Customer Invoices* in the Expression Elements list.

Ⓓ Choose **Customer InvoiceDetails Subform**.

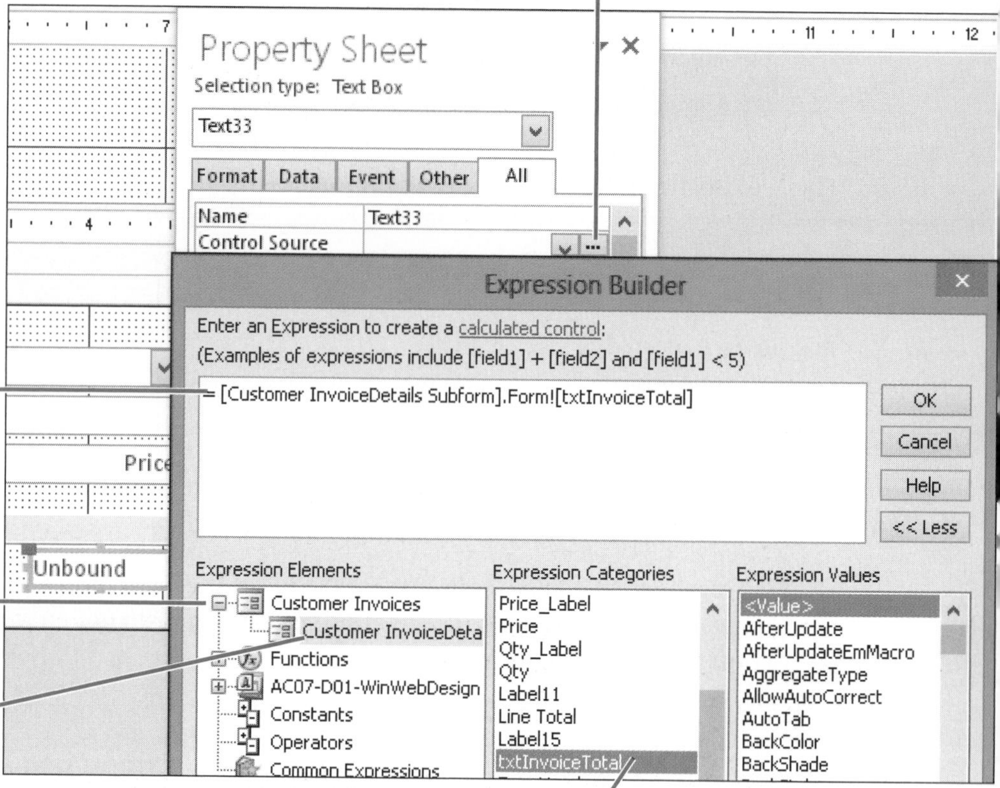

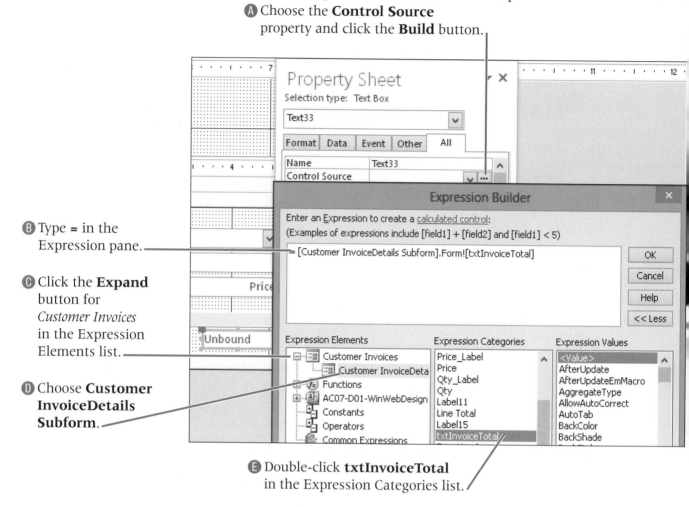

Ⓔ Double-click **txtInvoiceTotal** in the Expression Categories list.

18. Click **OK** to close the Expression Builder.
19. Enter the property values shown to format the Invoice Total text box.

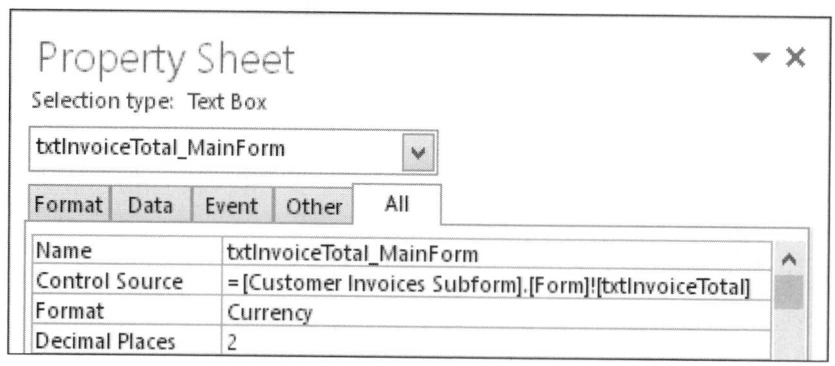

20. Switch to **Layout View**.

21. Line up the new text box and associated label under the subform **Line Total** column.

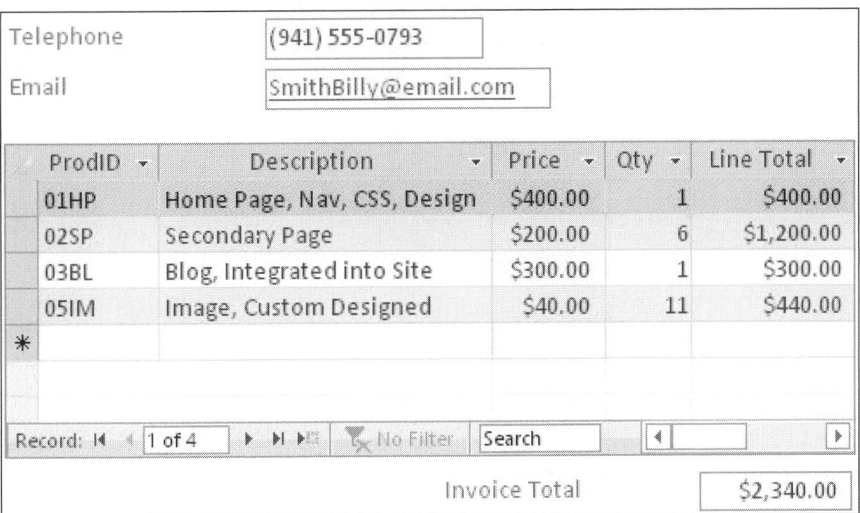

22. Use these troubleshooting tips to address any problems:
    - Formula not working: Do you have an even number of opening and closing parentheses?
    - Sometimes you must save the form/subform to update the new values.
    - The error message #Name? indicates a typo, spelling error, or an incorrect path entered in the Expression Builder.

Adding the Current Date to a Form

Video Library http://labyrinthelab.com/videos Video Number: AC13-V0708

Each time you open a form, Access updates the information on the form to reflect changes since the last time you viewed it. Because data contained in a database changes constantly, keeping track of the most current data is important. You can add a date and/or time to the Form Header or Form Footer section in a form to help you track data.

DEVELOP YOUR SKILLS AC07-D06

Add the Current Date to a Form

In this exercise, you will add the date to the Winchester Web Design Customer Invoices form, and then move it to the Form Footer section.

1. Display the **Customer Invoices** form in **Design View.**
2. Choose **Design→Header/Footer→Date and Time**.

3. Follow these steps to set date and time options:

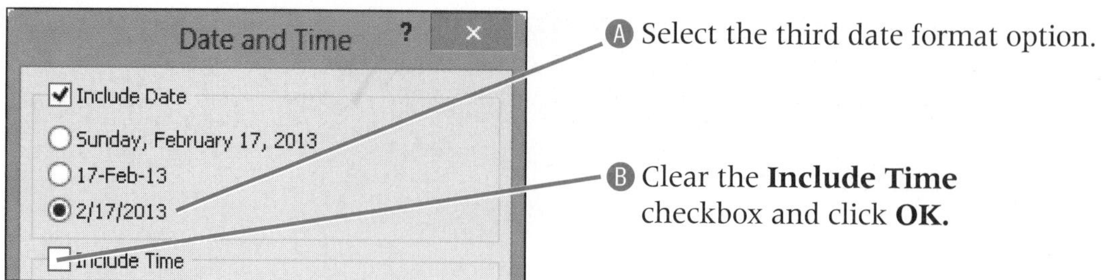

Ⓐ Select the third date format option.

Ⓑ Clear the **Include Time** checkbox and click **OK.**

Access places three controls in the Form Header section of the form: a logo placeholder, a title placeholder, and the Date control.

4. Follow these steps to drag the Date control to the Form Footer section:

Ⓐ Click the **Date** control in the top-right corner of the Form Header section.

Ⓑ Drag the control down through the Detail Section until you see the **Form Footer Section** bar.

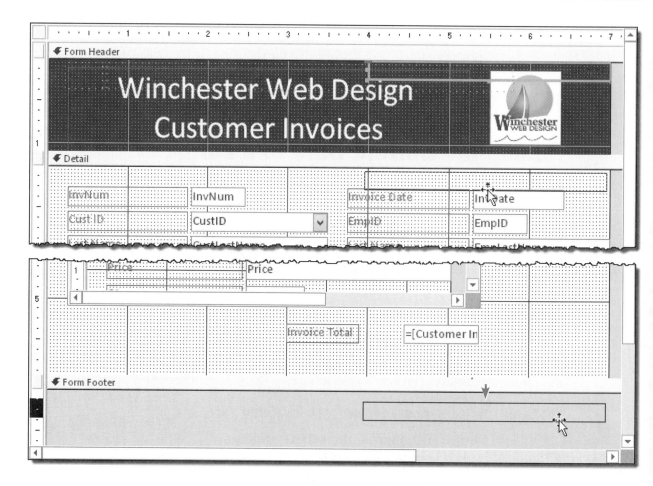

Ⓒ Drag the control just over the Form Footer section bar and release the mouse button to drop the control.

Access expands the Form Footer section to accommodate the date control.

5. Switch to **Form View**.

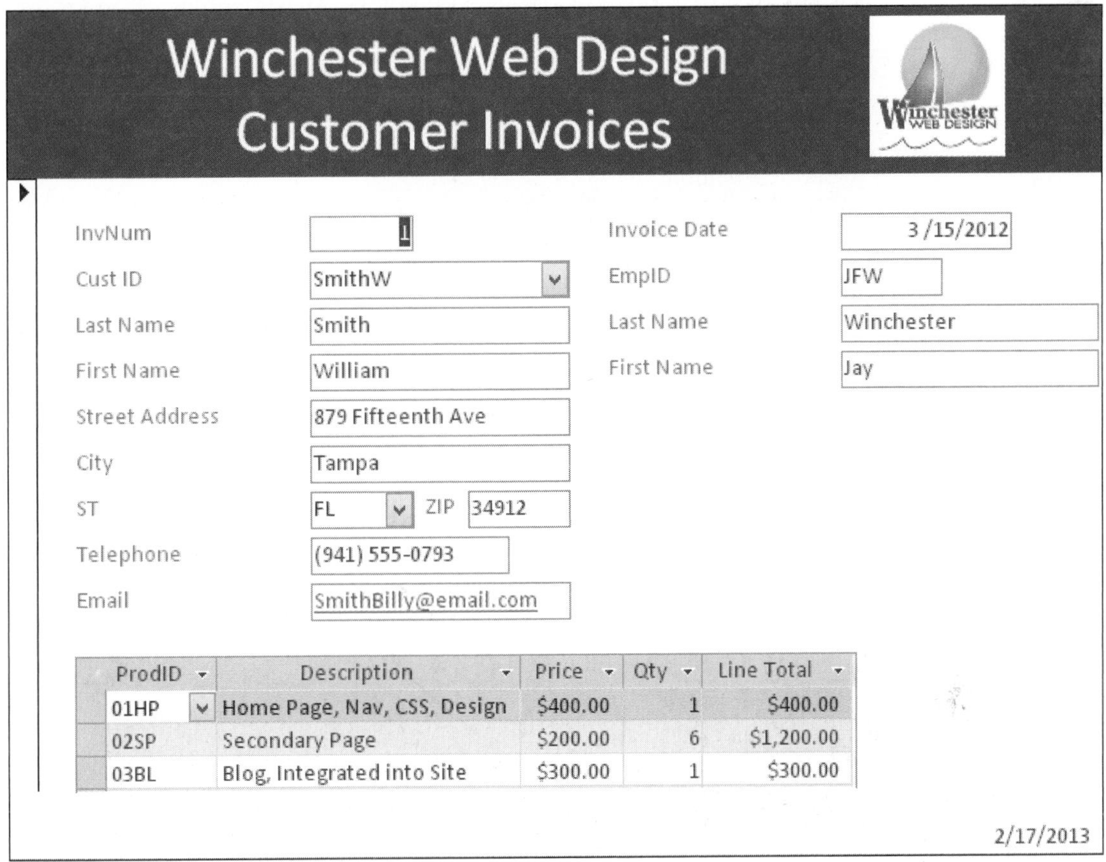

6. Save the **Customer Invoices** form.

Access 2013

Setting Properties to Assist and Control Data Entry

Video Library http://labyrinthelab.com/videos Video Number: AC13-V0709

You have already used many of the properties available in the Property Sheet and have also examined the different properties available for different types of controls. Some of these properties help you control or limit data entry, while others assist you with data entry. These properties are identified in this section.

Disabling Form Fields

In some circumstances, a form may include data that users do not enter and/or should not access. Many forms also contain settings that enter default values such as states or values such as cities that correspond to data contained in fields such as ZIP codes. To protect fields on a form from editing or to skip fields as you enter new data, you can *disable* the field in the Property Sheet. Disabled fields are unavailable for data entry. When a field is disabled, it appears grayed out and is not accessible to the user. During data entry, Access skips disabled fields and moves directly to the first field on a form that is enabled and accessible.

Customer ID	AbramsJ
Last Name	Abrams
First Name	John

A disabled form field appears grayed out and is unavailable.

Locking Form Fields

Another way to protect fields from being edited is by locking them. The advantage of locking a field is that it appears available on the form. The user can click in the field, but cannot change the data. Many people prefer locking to disabling because locked fields improve readability when a form is printed—whereas grayed disabled fields print faintly. To lock a field, set the Locked property to Yes.

ProdID	Description	Price	Qty	Line Total
01HP	Home Page, Nav, CSS, Design	$400.00	1	$400.00
02SP	Secondary Page	$200.00	6	$1,200.00
03BL	Blog, Integrated into Site	$300.00	1	$300.00

Locked form fields are available but do not allow edits.

QUICK REFERENCE DISABLING AND LOCKING FORM FIELDS

Task	Procedure
Disable a field	■ Display the form containing the control in Design View and display the Property Sheet. ■ Select the control to disable and set the Enabled property on the Data tab to No.
Lock a field	■ Display the form containing the control in Design View and display the Property Sheet. ■ Select the control to lock and set the Locked property on the Data tab to Yes.

DEVELOP YOUR SKILLS AC07-D07

Disable and Lock Form Fields

In this exercise, you will disable the InvNum field in the Customer Invoices form and the LineTotal field in the Customer InvoiceDetails Subform. In addition, you will lock the Price field in the subform so that it cannot be edited.

1. Display the **Customer Invoices** form in **Design View** and be sure the **Property Sheet** is open.
2. Click the **InvNum** text box on the main form and then click the **Data** tab on the Property Sheet.
3. Change the **Enabled** property to **No**.
4. Select the subform then disable the subform's **ProdID** text box.
5. Click the **Price** text box in the subform and set the Locked property to **Yes**.

Test the Property Settings

6. Switch to **Form View** and navigate to **record4**.
7. Follow these steps to explore the form:

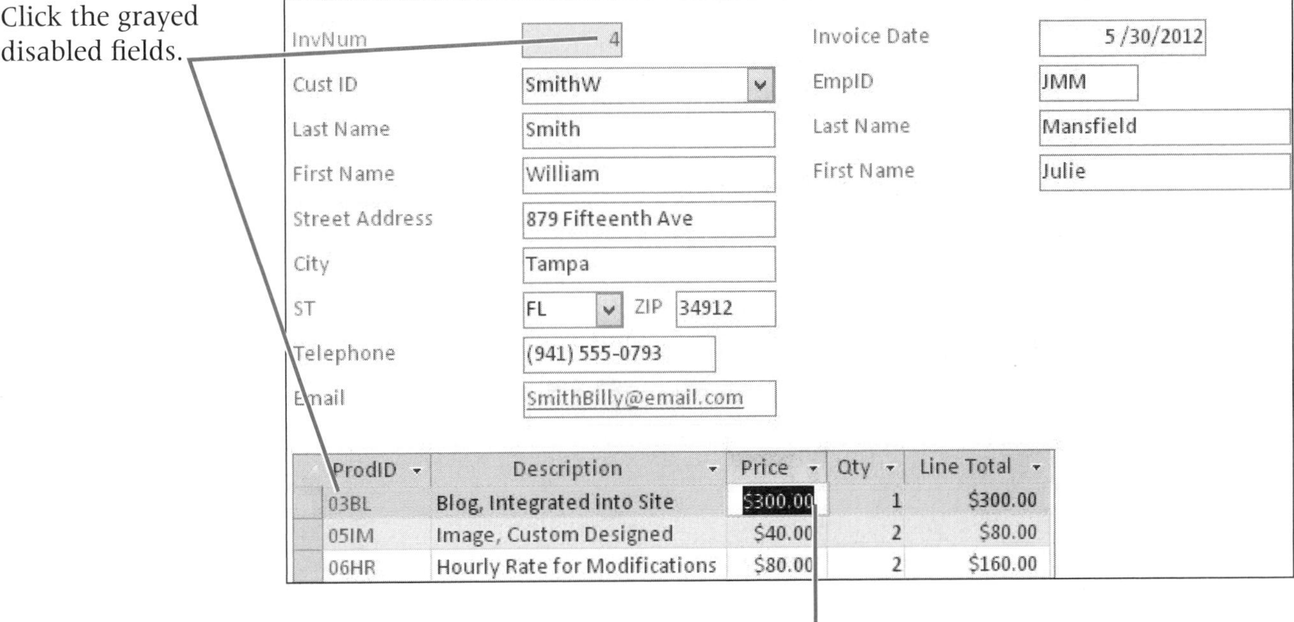

If you set the Locked property correctly, Access will not allow you to modify the data.

8. Save the **Customer Invoices** form.

Adding Tips to Controls

Video Library http://labyrinthelab.com/videos Video Number: AC13-V0710

When you create a database table and define each field, you have the opportunity to enter a description of the field in the Description column. Text you add to the Description field column of table Design View appears in the status bar when the field is active during data entry. These field descriptions also appear in the status bar when a table field appears on a form. Although forms identify most data with control labels, sometimes labels for specific fields such as State and ZIP are removed from a form when the controls are grouped together under a more general label such as Address. To help data entry personnel determine what data to type in a field, you can add additional tips to display onscreen by setting the ControlTip Text property for a control. ControlTip text appears as a ScreenTip when the user points to a field control. Setting ScreenTips helps to provide explanations for controls.

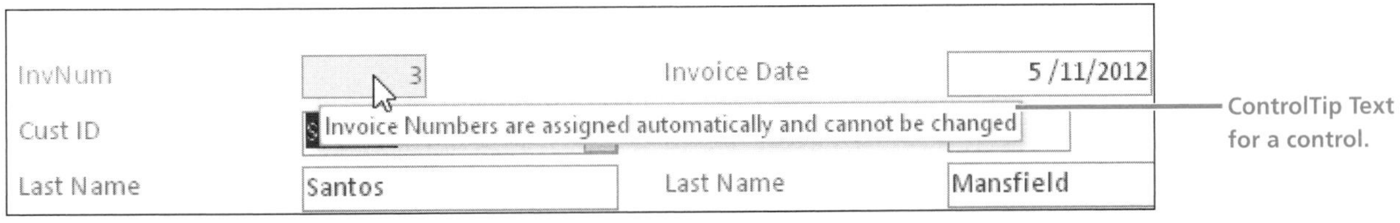

DEVELOP YOUR SKILLS AC07-D08

Create Control ScreenTips

In this exercise, you will create ScreenTips for the disabled and locked fields on the Customer Invoices form to explain why they are inaccessible.

1. Display the **Customer Invoices** form in **Design View**.
2. Click the **InvNum** text box and then click the **Other** tab on the **Property Sheet**.
3. Type **`Invoice Numbers are assigned automatically and cannot be changed`** into the **ControlTip Text** property line.
4. Enter the following text for the subform controls identified:

Control	ControlTip Text
ProdID Text Box	`Product IDs are assigned by supervisors and cannot be edited.`
Price Text Box	`Product prices cannot be changed.`

View the ScreenTips

5. Save the **Customer Invoices** form and switch to **Form View.**
6. Point to the **InvNum** field on the main form and review the ScreenTip.

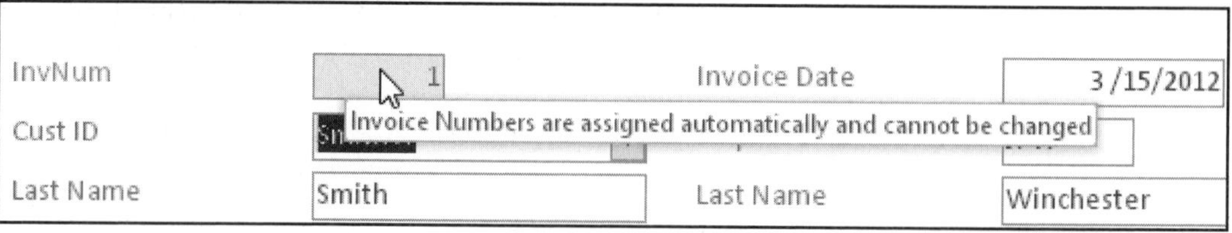

ScreenTips for fields on a subform do not display if the subform is in Datasheet View. Open the subform by itself and display it in Form View or Layout View to see the ScreenTips.

7. Save and close the **Customer Invoices** form.

Creating a Pop-Up Form

Video Library http://labyrinthelab.com/videos Video Number: AC13-V0711

Both forms and reports can be set to open in pop-up windows that stay on top of other open database objects. Pop-up forms can prompt a user for information or display a window containing supplemental data. Such forms or reports can help data entry personnel look up data entry values when they are processing orders or looking up the price of an item. You can apply different formats for pop-up forms you create in Access.

Modeless pop-up forms sit on top of other forms so you can continue to work.

POP-UP WINDOW MODES	
Mode	**Description**
Modal Pop Up	Displays a custom dialog box that prevents you from accessing other database objects until the dialog box is closed or its required actions are taken. *Example:* The Print dialog box is modal. If you choose to print a report and have the Print dialog box open, you cannot make changes to the report until you click OK or Cancel in the dialog box.
Modeless Pop Up	Creates a pop-up window that sits on top of other open windows in such a way that you can continue to work in the database while it is open. *Example:* When processing orders, you could set the Inventory List to open as a modeless pop-up form to ensure you have the correct inventory number.

DEVELOP YOUR SKILLS AC07-D09

Create a Pop-Up Form

In this exercise, you will create a new pop-up form using the Winchester Web Design Products table. You will also test the pop-up form.

1. Select the **Products** table and choose **Create→Forms→Form**.
2. Switch to **Design View**.
3. Choose **Form** in the **Selection Type** list box on the Property Sheet.
4. Click the **Other** tab and set the Pop Up property to **Yes**.

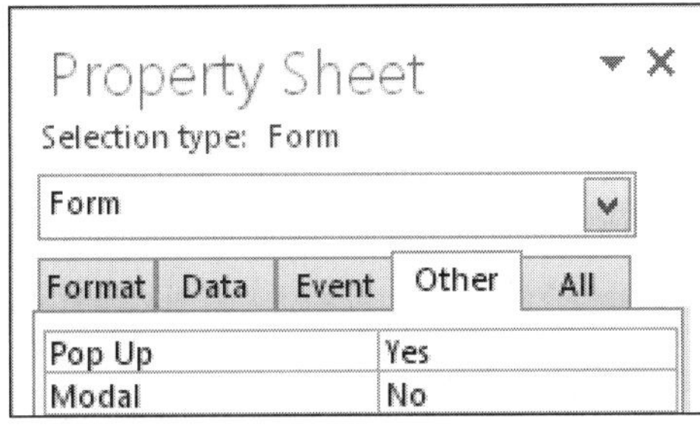

5. Click the **Format** tab and set the Default View property to **Datasheet**; then set the Allow Datasheet View to **Yes**.
6. **Save** the form as `Product List`.

Test the Property Setting

7. Display both the **Customer Invoices** form and the **Product List** form in **Form View**.
8. Hover the mouse pointer over the bottom-right corner of the pop-up **Product List**.
9. When the pointer appears as a **white resize pointer**, drag the corner of the form to size it to the data.
10. Click a field on the **Customer Invoices** form or the subform to see that the pop-up **Product List** remains available.

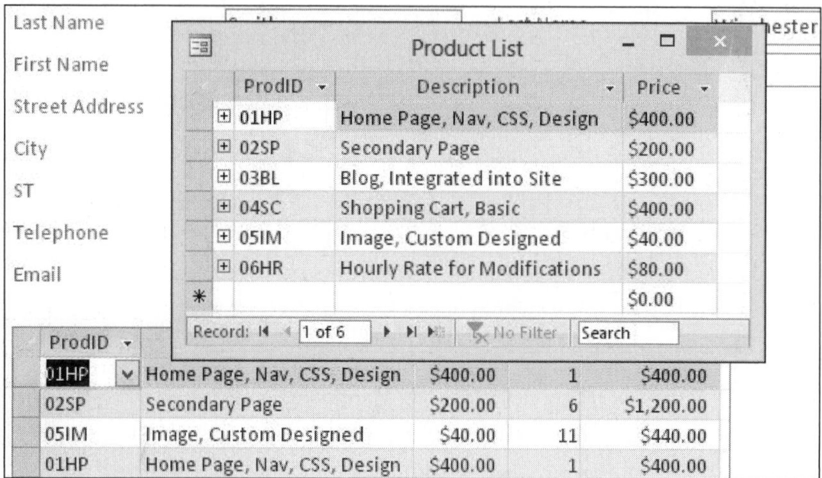

The pop-up form sits on top of the other form.

11. Close all open database objects. Close the database and exit **Access**.

Concepts Review

To check your knowledge of the key concepts introduced in this lesson, complete the Concepts Review quiz by choosing the appropriate access option below.

If you are...	Then access the quiz by...
Using the Labyrinth Video Library	Going to http://labyrinthelab.com/videos
Using eLab	Logging in, choosing Content, and navigating to the Concepts Review quiz for this lesson
Not using the Labyrinth Video Library or eLab	Going to the student resource center for this book

Reinforce Your Skills

REINFORCE YOUR SKILLS AC07-R01

Create and Format a Form with a Subform

In this exercise, you will create a new Donors form for Kids for Change. You will delete, move, and size controls, modify the title, and add a logo to the form. Then you will create a second form within the main form that uses the Totals row to count the number of individual donations and total the amount of donations.

Create a Form and Subform Using the Form Wizard

1. Start **Access**. Open **AC07-R01-K4C** from the **AC2013 Lesson 07** folder and save it as `AC07-R01-K4C-[FirstInitialLastName]`.
2. Select the **Donors** table in the Navigation Pane and choose **Create→Forms→Form Wizard**.
3. Select **DonorLName** and click the **Move** button to move it to the Selected Fields list.
4. Move these fields from the Donors and Donations tables to the Selected Fields list:

Table	Fields
Donors	DonorFName
	DonorStreet
	DonorCity
	DonorST
	DonorZIP
	DonorPhone
	DonorEmail
	Acknowledgement
Donations	DonorID
	DonationDate
	Amount
	DonationType

5. Click **Next** to see the viewing arrangement of data.
   Leave the default arrangement of Form with Subform(s).
6. Click **Next**. Leave the default Datasheet layout for your subform and click **Next**.
7. Name the form `Donors Form` and the subform `Donors Subform`. Keep the Open the Form to View or Enter Information option selected and click **Finish**.
   The new form displays in Form View.

8. Double-click the right border of each subform column heading to resize the fields in the subform for best fit.

The pointer becomes a resize arrow.

9. Save the **Donors Form**.

Format a Form

10. Switch to **Design View**.
11. Select the **Donors Subform label** to the left of the subform and tap [Delete].
12. Select the subform, press [Ctrl], and click the **DonorEmail** label to select both.
13. Choose **Arrange→Sizing & Ordering→Align→Left**.
14. Open the **Property Sheet**.
15. Select the **Acknowledgement** text box and type **2"** for the **Width** property on the Format tab.
16. Select the **DonorST** and **DonorZIP** text boxes, then type **.6"** for their **Width** property and tap [Tab].
17. Select the **DonorEmail** text box and type **2"** for the **Width** property.
18. Switch to **Layout View**.
19. Select the subform and hover the mouse pointer over the right border until it becomes a double arrow. Click and drag the right border to best fit the contents.

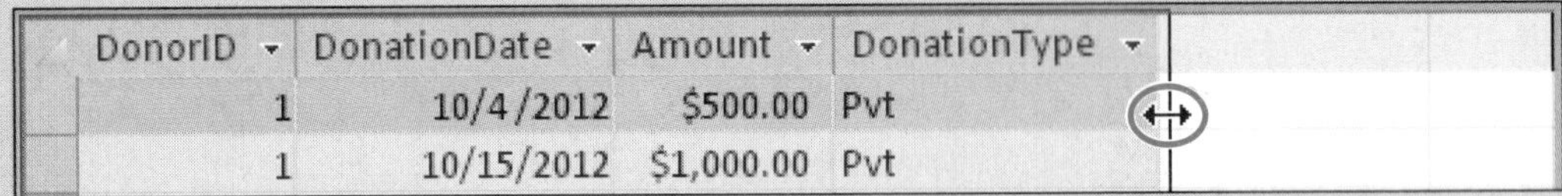

The pointer becomes a double arrow.

20. Type **2"** for the subform's **Height** property.
21. Select the **Donors Form title** in the **Form Header** section.

22. Enter the following **Property Sheet** values to format the selected control:

Property	New Value
Name	lblTitle
Caption	Kids for Change Donors Form
Width	4"
Left	1"
Font Name	Cambria (Header)
Font Size	20
Text Align	Center
Fore Color	Dark Blue, Text 2

23. Click between *Change* and *Donors* in the title, and press [Shift]+[Enter] to bump the words *Donors Form* to a second line.
24. Save your changes.
25. Choose **Design→Header/Footer→**[Logo] and double-click **K4C-Logo.bmp** in the **AC2013 Lesson 07** folder.

    Access adds the K4C logo control to the Form Header, along with an empty title control, which appears as a dotted rectangle.
26. Select the title control on the right side of the logo and tap [Delete].
27. Select the logo and set the following properties:

Property	Value
Width	.8
Height	.8
Left	5.5

28. Save and close the **Donors Form**.

Create a Totals Form Using the Form Wizard

29. Select the **Donations Query** in the Navigation Pane.
30. Choose **Create→Forms→Form Wizard**.
31. Move all fields *except* Acknowledgement, ScholarFund, and NetAmt to the Selected Fields pane.

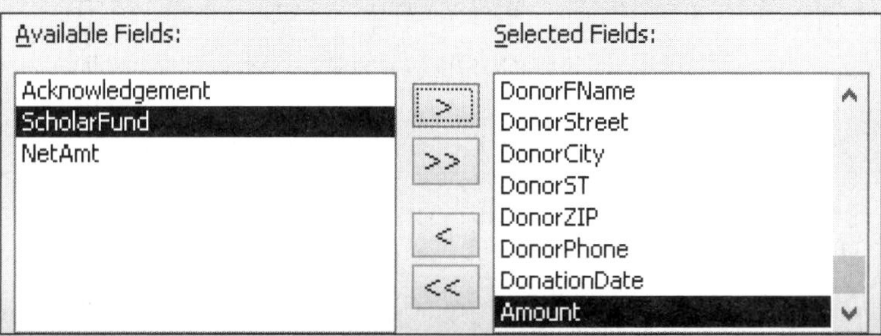

32. Click **Next**. In the next Wizard screen, choose the **By Donations** view (Single Form).
33. Click **Next**. Choose the **Datasheet** layout.
34. Click **Next**. Name the new form `Total Donations Form` and click **Finish**.
    The new form is displayed in Datasheet View.
35. Close the **Navigation Pane** and the **Field List**.
36. Double-click the right border of each column heading to resize the columns.
37. Choose **Home→Records→**Σ Totals.
38. Click the **Last Name** column on the Total row at the bottom of the datasheet and choose **Count** from the drop-down menu.
    Access counts all the individual donations.
39. Click the **Amount** column on the Total row at the bottom of the datasheet, open the drop-down menu, and choose **Sum**.
40. Click in another cell to see the sum.
    The form should display the count of donations to the organization and the total amount of their donations.
41. Save and close the **Total Donations Form**. Close the database and exit **Access**.
42. Submit your final file based on the guidelines provided by your instructor.
    To see examples of how your file or files should look at the end of this exercise, go to the student resource center.

REINFORCE YOUR SKILLS AC07-R02

Add to a Form, Set Form Properties, and Create a Pop-Up Form

Your new form is going over well, but team members have requested a few changes. In this exercise, you will build a calculated control on the main form that displays the total amount of donations from the subform. Then you will disable the subform's DonorID field, lock the Donor Total field on the main form, and create ScreenTips for the disabled and locked fields to explain why they are inaccessible. Finally, you create a pop-up form for donors' names.

Add Calculated Controls to a Form

1. Start **Access**. Open **AC07-R02-K4C** from the **AC2013 Lesson 07** folder and save it as `AC07-R02-K4C-[FirstInitialLastName]`.
2. Display the **Donors Form** in **Design View**; double-click the subform.
3. Hover the mouse pointer over the bottom-edge of the subform's **Form Footer** section bar until it becomes a vertical resize arrow.

4. Click and drag the subform's **Form Footer** bar down to make room for a new control.

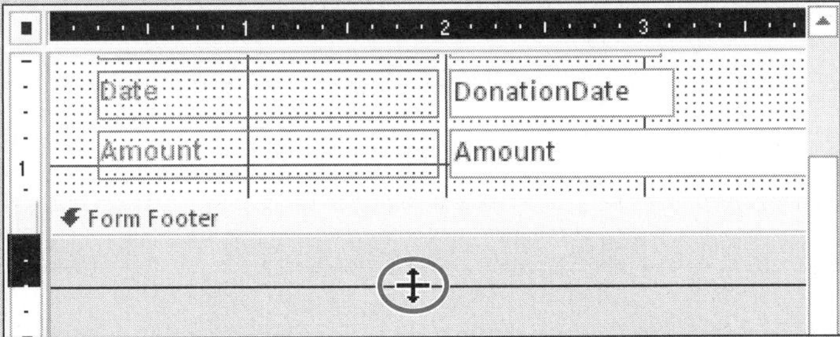

5. Choose **Design→Controls→Text Box** [ab|] and draw a text box control in the **Form Footer** of the subform, under the Amount text box.
6. Type **`txtTotalAmt`** for the **Name** property on the Property Sheet All tab.
7. Type **`=Sum(Amount)`** for the **Control Source** Property.
8. Choose **Currency** from the **Format** menu; choose **2** for the **Decimal Places** property.

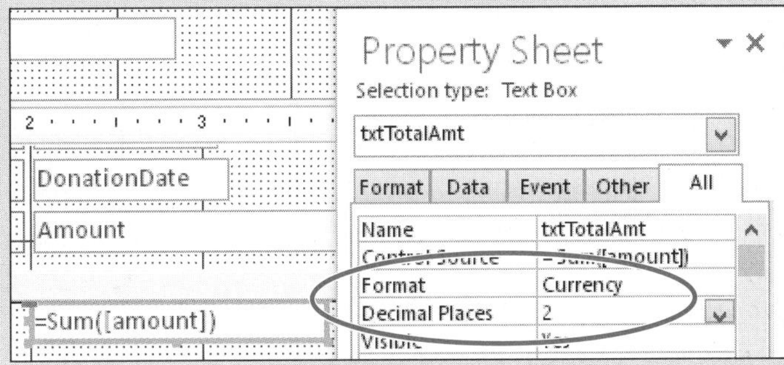

9. Click the label for the new calculated control and tap [Delete].
10. On the Property Sheet, click the **Selection Type** menu button and choose **Donors Subform**.
    If you cannot find the subform in the Selection Type *drop-down menu, click an empty area of the main form.*
11. Type **3"** for the **Width** property of the subform and **`1.5`** for the **Height** property.

Total a Calculated Subform Field on the Main Form

12. Choose **Design→Controls→Text Box** [ab|] and draw a text box control in the **Detail** section of the main form.

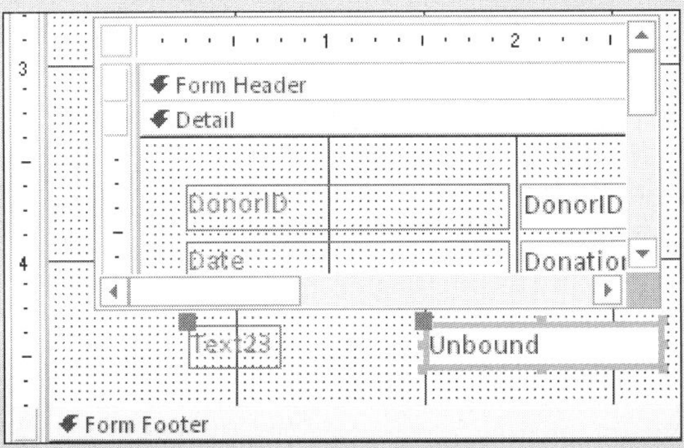

Access 2013

13. Select the associated label of the new control, and type `Donor Total` for the **Caption** property and `1.25` for the **Width** property.
14. With the label still selected, press Ctrl and click the subform.
15. Choose **Arrange→Sizing & Ordering→Align→Left** to left-align the label and subform.
16. Select the new text box and click the **Build** [...] button in the **Control Source** property.
17. Expand the **Donors Form** in the **Expression Elements** list and click **Donors Subform**.
18. Double-click **txtTotalAmt** in the **Expression Categories list**.

    When you double-click the field name it is added to the Expression pane.
19. Click **OK**.
20. Type `txtTotalAmt_Main` for the **Name** property.
21. Choose the **Currency Format** property and **2** for **Decimal Places**.
22. Switch to **Form View**.

Add the Current Date to a Form

23. Switch to **Design View**.
24. Choose **Design→Header/Footer→** Date and Time.
25. Select the shorter third date format option and clear the **Include Time** checkbox.
26. Click **OK**.

    Access places the date control and an empty auto-header in the Form Header.
27. Click the **Date** control in the **Form Header** section.

    Close the Property Sheet for easier viewing.
28. Drag the control through the **Detail Section** under the **Form Footer** section bar, as shown.

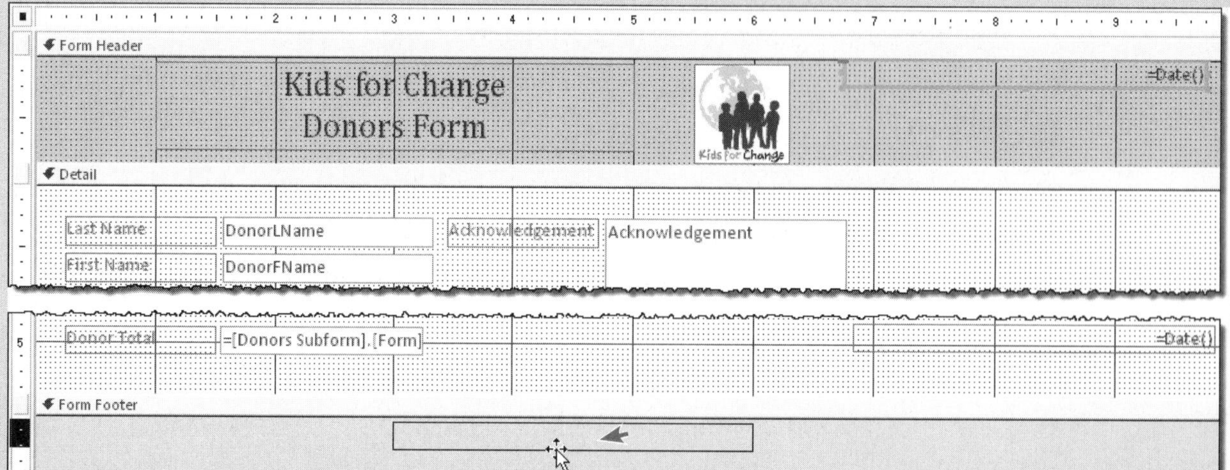

Access automatically expands the Form Footer section for the date control.

29. Scroll to the top of the form and select the empty auto-header control.
30. Tap Delete to delete the control.

31. Reopen the **Property Sheet**. Verify that *Form* is listed in the Selection Type box and type `7.75` for the **Width** property.
32. Select the new **Date** control in the Form Footer section.
33. Set the following properties:

Property	Value
Width	1.5
Top	0
Left	2.5
Text Align	Center

34. Drag up the **Form Footer** section just under the new **Date** control.
35. Switch to **Form View** to see the new date field.
36. Save the **Donors Form**.

Disable and Lock Form Fields and Create Control ScreenTips

37. Display the **Donors Form** in **Design View** and select the **Donations Subform**.
38. Click the **DonorID** text box and click the **Data** tab on the Property Sheet.
39. Change the **Enabled** property to **No**.
40. Click the **Other** tab on the Property Sheet.
41. Locate the **ControlTip Text** property and type: **`Donor IDs are set by the administrator and cannot be edited.`**
42. Select **Form** in the **Selection Type** list on the Property Sheet.
43. Click the **txtTotalAmt_Main** text box.
44. Click the **Data** tab on the Property Sheet and change the **Locked** property to **Yes**.
45. Click the **Other** tab on the Property Sheet.
46. Type: **`Donor Totals are calculated by the program and cannot be edited.`**
47. Save the **Donors Form** and switch to **Form View**.
48. Point to the **txtTotalAmt_Main** field on the subform.
    The disabled DonorID field is grayed out and the locked Total Amount displays a ScreenTip, but does not allow editing.

Create a Pop-Up Form

49. Select the **Donors** table and choose **Create→Forms→Form Wizard**.
50. Move the **DonorID**, **DonorLName**, and **DonorFName** to the Selected Fields list.
51. Choose the **Tabular** layout.
52. Enter `Donor Popup` as the name and choose the option to **Modify the Form's Design**.
    The form displays in Design View.

Access 2013

53. Delete the **Donor Popup title control**.
54. Select the three label controls in the Form Header and type `.1` for the **Top** property on the **Property Sheet Format** tab.
55. Click the **Form Header** section bar and type `.4` for the **Height** property.
56. Click the **Other** tab on the Property Sheet, choose **Form** from the Selection Type list, and set the **Pop-up** property to **Yes.**
57. Click the **Property Sheet Format** tab and set the **Default View** property to **Datasheet**.
58. Set the **Allow Datasheet View** property to **Yes.**
59. Save and close the **Donor Popup** form.
60. Open the **Donors Form** and then **Donor Popup** form from the Navigation Pane.
61. Close the forms and close the database. Exit **Access**.
62. Submit your final file based on the guidelines provided by your instructor.

    To see examples of how your file or files should look at the end of this exercise, go to the student resource center.

REINFORCE YOUR SKILLS AC07-R03

Create and Format a Form with a Subform and a Pop-Up Form

In this exercise, you will create an activity staffing form with a subform. You will edit controls, modify the title, and add the K4C logo. Then you will add a control to the main form that calculates payment per activity based on a staffer's wage. You will also add the current date to the new form and create a pop-up form for venue information.

Create a Form with a Subform Using the Form Wizard

1. Start **Access**. Open **AC07-R03-K4C** from the **AC2013 Lesson 07** folder and save it as `AC07-R03-K4C-[FirstInitialLastName]`.
2. Select the **Activities List** query in the Navigation Pane then choose **Create→Forms→Form Wizard**.
3. Move all the query fields to the Selected Fields list *except* VenueID.
4. Click **Next** to see the viewing arrangement of data.
5. Choose to view your data **By Activities**.
6. Click **Next**. Leave the default Datasheet layout and click **Next**.
7. Name the form `Activity Staffing` and the subform `Staffing Subform`; click **Finish**.

    The new form displays in Form View.
8. Switch to **Design View**.

Format the Form

9. Click the **Staffing Subform** label control to the left of the subform and tap [Delete].
10. Open the Property Sheet, if necessary. Change the **Caption** property for the **Venue Name** label to `Name of Venue`.
11. Type `Street Address` for the **Caption** of the **Street** label.
12. Type `Hours` for the **Hrs** label **Caption**.
13. Select the subform, and type `4.25"` for the **Width** property and type `1"` for the **Height**.
14. With the subform still selected, press [Ctrl] and click the **Hours** label.
15. Choose **Arrange→Sizing & Ordering→Align→Left**.
16. Switch to **Form View** and resize each column within the subform for fit.

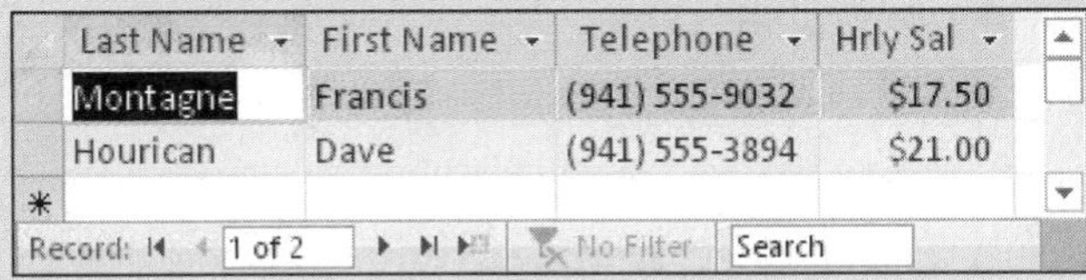

The Detail section of the form should resemble the figure shown.

17. Switch to **Design View** and select *Activity Staffing* in the Form Header.
18. Click in the title, in front of *Activity Staffing*.
19. Type `Kids for Change` and press [Shift] + [Enter] to move the existing text—*Activity Staffing*—to a second line.
20. Type `3"` for the **Width** property and `.5` for the **Left** property.
21. Choose **Center** for the **Text Align** property.
22. Choose **Dark Blue, Text 2** for the **Fore Color** property.
23. Choose **Design→Header/Footer→**[Logo] and double-click **K4C-Logo.bmp** in the **AC2013 Lesson 07** folder.
    Access adds the logo control and an empty title control to the Form Header.
24. Delete the title control on the right side of the logo.
25. Select the logo and set the following properties:

Property	Value
Width	.8
Height	.8
Left	4

26. Click the **Hrs** text box and type `.5` for the **Width** property.

Access 2013

27. Select all the label controls in the **Detail** Section. Choose **12** for the **Font Size** and **Dark Blue, Text 2** for the **Fore Color**.

28. Select all the text box controls in the **Detail** section. Choose **Arial** for the **Font Name** and **Black** for the **Fore Color**.

29. Switch to **Form View**.

Add a Calculated Control

30. Switch to **Design View**.

31. Select the **Hours** text box on the main form and type `txtHours` for the **Name** property on the Property Sheet All tab.

32. Select the **HrlySal** text box in the subform, and type `txtHrlySal` for the **Name** property.

33. Choose **Design→Controls→Text Box** [ab] and draw a text box control in the **Detail** section of the main form (under the right side of the subform).

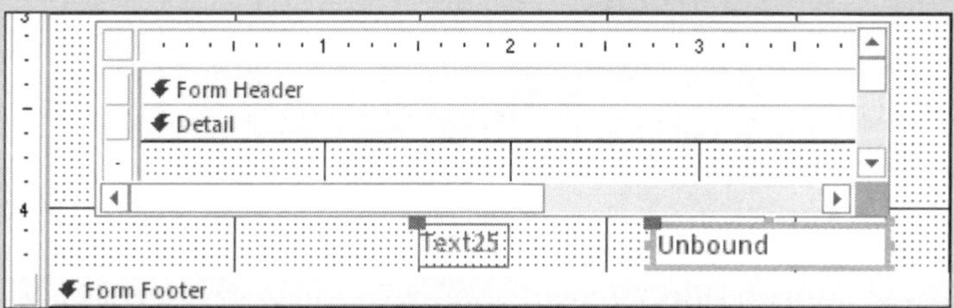

The new text box and associated label appear under the subform.

34. Select the label for the new control and type `Activity Cost` as the **Caption** property. Then type `1.5` for the **Width** and `1.75` for the **Left** property.

35. Select the new text box and click the **Build** [...] button in the **Control Source** property.

36. Type an equal (=) sign.
    All calculations must begin with an equal sign.

37. Select **Activity Staffing** in the **Expression Elements** list.

38. Double-click **txtHours** in the **Expression Categories** list.

39. Type * (asterisk) after the **Hours** field.

40. Expand the **Activity Staffing** form and click **Staffing Subform**.

41. Double-click **txtHrlySal** in the **Expression Categories** list.
    When you double-click the field name Access adds it to the Expression pane.

42. Click **OK**.

43. On the Property sheet, type `txtActivityCost` for the **Name** property. Then choose **Currency** for the **Format** of the new text box, **2** for **Decimal Places**, **Arial** for the **Font Name**, and **Black, Text 1** for the **Fore Color**.

44. Select the new label control and choose **12** for the **Font Size** and **Dark Blue, Text 2** for the **Fore Color**.

Add a Date Control

45. Choose **Design→Header/Footer→**[Date and Time].

46. Select the third date format option and clear the **Include Time** checkbox. Click **OK**.

Access places the date control and placeholders for a logo and a title in the Form Header.

47. Select any empty logo and title placeholders in the Form Header.

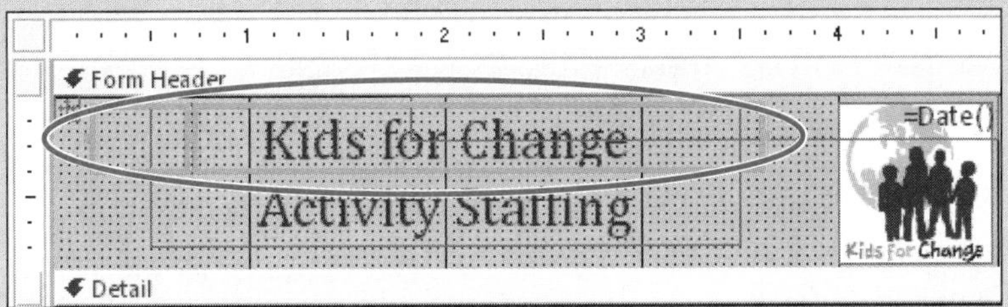

48. Tap [Delete].

49. Select the new **Date** control and drag it down just *under* the **Form Footer** section bar.

You can simply pull a control into the form's footer without resizing the Form Footer, and Access automatically resizes it to accommodate the control.

50. Set the following properties for the new Date control:

Property	Value
Width	1.5
Top	0
Left	1.5
Text Align	Center

51. Drag up the bottom-edge of the Form Footer section just under the new Date control.

52. Set the **Width** property of the main form to `4.8"` then switch to **Form View** to see your changes.

53. Save and close the **Activity Staffing** form.

Create a Pop-Up Form

54. Select the **Venues** table and choose **Create→Forms→Form Wizard**.

55. Move the **VenueID**, **VenueName**, and **VenuePhone** to the Selected Fields list; click **Next**.

56. Choose the **Tabular** layout and click **Next**.

57. Enter `VenuesPopUp` as the name and choose **Modify the Form's Design**.

The form displays in Design View.

58. Delete the **VenuesPopUp** title control.

59. Select the three label controls in the Form Header and type `.1` for the **Top** property.

60. Click the **Form Header section bar** and type **.4** for the **Height** property.
61. Click the **Other** tab on the **Property Sheet**, choose **Form** from the Selection Type list, and set the **Pop-up** property to **Yes.**
62. Click the **Property Sheet Format** tab and set the **Default View** property to **Datasheet** and set the **Allow Datasheet View** property to **Yes.**
63. Save the **Venues PopUp** form and display it in Datasheet View.
64. Adjust the width of each column heading.
65. Drag in the right and bottom edges of the form window for fit.
66. Display the **Activity Staffing** form in **Form View** and move the pop-up form so you can view the data, as needed.
67. Save and close the **Activity Staffing** form and the **Venues PopUp** form. Close the database and exit **Access**.
68. Submit your final file based on the guidelines provided by your instructor.

Apply Your Skills

APPLY YOUR SKILLS AC07-A01

Create and Format a Form with a Subform

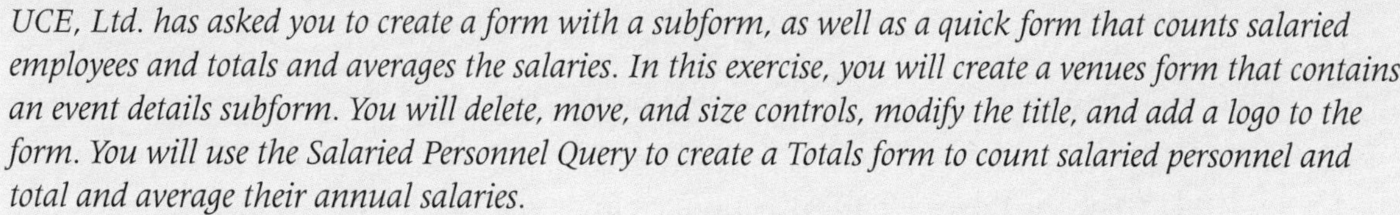

UCE, Ltd. has asked you to create a form with a subform, as well as a quick form that counts salaried employees and totals and averages the salaries. In this exercise, you will create a venues form that contains an event details subform. You will delete, move, and size controls, modify the title, and add a logo to the form. You will use the Salaried Personnel Query to create a Totals form to count salaried personnel and total and average their annual salaries.

Create and Format a Form and Subform

1. Start **Access**. Open **AC07-A01-UCE** from the **AC2013 Lesson 07** folder and save it as `AC07-A01-UCE-[FirstInitialLastName]`.
2. Select the **Venues** table and start the **Form Wizard**.
3. Move all the fields from the **Venues** table to the Selected Fields list *except* VenueLiaison.
4. Choose the **Schedules** table in the **Tables/Queries** list.
5. Move all the fields *except* VenueID to the Selected Fields list and click **Next**.
6. View the data **By Venues**.
7. Choose the **Datasheet** layout.
8. Name the main form `Venue Events` and the subform `Venue Events Subform`.
9. Choose **Modify the Form's Design**.

Format the Form and Subform

10. Select the **Venue Events Subform label** and tap [Delete].
11. Select the subform and the **Website label** and choose **Arrange→Sizing & Ordering→Align→Left**.
12. Select all the labels in the **Detail** section of the main form and type `1.5` for the **Width** property and `.25` for the **Height**; choose the **Raised Special Effect** property; choose **Arial** for **Font Name**, **12** for **Font Size**, and **Black, Text 1** for **Fore Color**.
13. Select all the text boxes in the **Detail** section of the main form, except the Kitchen checkbox, and type `.25` for the **Height**; choose **Sunken** for the **Special Effect** property; choose **Arial** for **Font Name**, **12** for **Font Size**, **Semi-Bold** for **Font Weight**, and a dark blue such as **Blue, Accent 5, Darker 50%** for **Fore Color**.
14. With the subform selected, type `6.5` for the **Width** property and type `2"` for the **Height**.
15. Click inside the title in the Form Header and place the insertion point in front of *Venue Events*.
16. Type `Universal Corporate Events, Ltd.` then press [Shift]+[Enter] to bump the *Venue Events* text to a new line, and tap [Enter].

17. With the title selected, enter these properties on the Property Sheet:

Property	Value
Width	4.5
Height	.7
Left	1"
Font Name	Cambria
Text Align	Center
Font Weight	Bold
Fore Color	Blue, Accent 5, Darker 50%

18. Click the **Form Header** section bar and type `.75` for the **Height** property and choose **White, Background 1** for the **Back Color**.
19. Click the **Detail** section bar and choose a lighter blue such as **Blue, Accent 5, Lighter 80%** for both the **Back Color** and the **Alternate Back Color**.
20. Choose **Design→Header/Footer→** Logo and double-click **UCE-Logo.bmp** from the **AC2013 Lesson 07** folder.
21. Select and delete the title placeholder to the right of the logo.
22. Select the new logo and type `.7` for the **Width** and **Height** properties.
23. Switch to **Form View** and navigate to the second record, which is for Brooksville Campgrounds.
24. Close the **Venue Events** form and **Venue Events Subform**, saving if prompted.

Create a Quick Totals Form

25. Select the **Salaried Personnel Query** in the Navigation Pane and start the **Form Wizard**.
26. Include all the fields, choose **Datasheet** layout, name the new form `Salaried Personnel Totals` and choose the option to **Modify the Form's Design**.
27. Select the **Salary** label and text box controls.
28. Press Ctrl+C, then Ctrl+V to copy and paste a duplicate salary field under the existing label and text box.
29. Type `Total Salaries` for the **Caption** property of the first **Salary** label.
30. Type `Average Salary` for the **Caption** property of the second **Salary** label.
31. Switch to **Datasheet View**.
32. Resize the widths of each column for fit.
33. Choose **Home→Records→** Σ Totals.
34. In the **Totals** row of the **Last Name** field, choose **Count** from the list.
35. In the **Totals** row of the *first* **Salary** field, choose **Sum** from the list.

36. In the **Totals** row of the *second* **Salary** field, choose **Average** from the list.

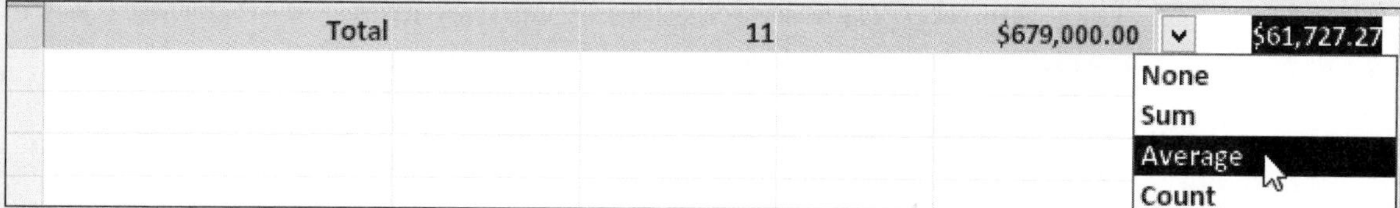

37. Save and close the **Salaried Personnel Totals** form and close the database. Exit **Access**.
38. Submit your final file based on the guidelines provided by your instructor.
    To see examples of how your file or files should look at the end of this exercise, go to the student resource center.

APPLY YOUR SKILLS AC07-A02

Add to a Form, Set Form Properties, and Create a Pop-Up Form

In this exercise, you will add calculated controls and the current date to a form and subform. You will also disable the Schedule ID field in the subform so it cannot be accessed, lock the Event Cost field on the main form so that it cannot be edited, and create ScreenTips for the disabled and locked fields. Finally, you will create a pop-up form for event information.

Add Calculated Controls to a Form

1. Start **Access**. Open **AC07-A02-UCE** from the **AC2013 Lesson 07** folder and save it as `AC07-A02-UCE-[FirstInitialLastName]`.
2. Display the **Event Costs** form in **Design View**.
3. Select the subform and type **6"** for the **Width** and **2"** for the **Height**.
4. Select both the **CostPP** label and text box controls on the subform.
5. Copy and paste the controls just under the existing controls.
   Access automatically adjusts the Detail section to accommodate the new controls.
6. Type `Line Total` for the **Name** property of the new label.
7. Select the new text box, type `txtLineTotal` for the **Name** property and `=Guests*CostPP` for the **Control Source** property.
   The Event Total text box is a copy of the CostPP text box and already formatted as Currency.
8. Choose **Design→Controls→Text Box** [ab] and draw a text box control in the **Form Footer** section of the subform
9. Delete the new label.
10. Select the new text box. Type `txtEventTotal` in the **Name** property and `=Sum(Guests*CostPP)` for the **Control Source** property. Then choose **Currency** for the **Format** and **2** for the **Decimal Places**.
11. Choose **Design→Controls→Text Box** [ab] and draw a text box control in the **Detail** section of the main form under the right side of the subform.
    Drag down the Form Footer section bar if you need room for the new text box and label.

Access 2013

12. Left align the label of the new control with the subform.
13. Select the **Event Name** label, choose **Home→Clipboard→Format Painter**, and click the new label to paste the same format on the new label.
14. Select the new label and type `Event Cost` for the **Caption** property.
    If the new caption does not fit in the label, drag the right border to display its contents.
15. Save the form.
16. Select the new text box and click the **Build** button in the **Control Source** property.
17. Expand the **Event Costs** form and select the **Event Costs Subform** in the Expression Elements list.
18. Double-click **txtEventTotal** in the Expression Categories list.
19. Click **OK**.
20. Type `txtGrandTotal` for the **Name** property of the new text box, choose **Currency** for the **Format**, and **2** for the **Decimal Places**.
21. Switch to **Form View**. Navigate to a record that includes subform details to view the calculated control.
    If you get an error in the new calculated field, make sure that you named each field correctly.

Add Current Date to a Form

22. Switch to **Design View** and choose **Design→Header/Footer→**Date and Time.
23. Select the third date format, clear the **Include Time** checkbox, and click **OK**.
    Access places the date control and placeholders for a logo and a title in the Form Header.
24. Delete any empty logo and title placeholders in the Form Header.
25. Select the **Date** control and drag it down just under the **Form Footer** section bar.
26. Set the following properties for the new Date control:

Property	Value
Width	1.5
Top	0
Left	2.5
Text Align	Center
Fore Color	Blue, Accent 5, Darker 50%

27. Click the **Form Footer** section bar and type `.25` for **Height** and choose a light blue such as **Blue, Accent 5, Lighter 80%** for the **Back Color** property.
28. Switch to **Form View** and navigate through the records.

Disable and Lock Form Fields and Create Control ScreenTip

29. Display **Event Costs** form in **Design View** and select the **EventCosts Subform**.
30. Click the **ScheduleID** text box and click the **Data** tab on the Property Sheet.
31. Change the **Enabled** property to **No**.

32. Click the **Other** tab on the **Property Sheet**.
33. Locate the **ControlTip Text** property and type: **`Schedule IDs cannot be edited.`**

    ControlTip text only displays when you open the subform separately from the main form.
34. Click the **txtGrandTotal** text box on the main form.
35. Click the **Data** tab on the Property Sheet and change the **Locked** property to **Yes**.
36. Click the **Other** tab on the **Property Sheet**.
37. Type this text: **`Event Cost is a calculated field and cannot be edited.`**
38. Save the **Event Costs** form, switch to **Form View**, and navigate to a record that includes subform details.
39. Try to type in the **txtGrandTotal** field on the main form.

    The disabled ScheduleID field is grayed out; the locked txtGrandTotal field cannot be edited and displays the ScreenTip indicating why it cannot be changed.
40. Close the **Event Costs** form.

Create a Pop-Up Form

41. Select the **Events** table and choose **Create→Forms→Form Wizard**.
42. Move the **EventID** and **EventName** to the Selected Fields list.
43. Choose the **Tabular** layout.
44. Enter **`EventsPopUp`** as the name and choose **Modify the Form's Design**.

    The form displays with a Form Header section containing a title (Events PopUp) and two column headers (Event ID and Event Name).
45. Select the title control (Events PopUp) in the Form Header section, and tap [Delete].
46. Select the label controls (Event ID and Event Name) in the Form Header and type **`.1`** for the **Top** property.
47. Click the **Form Header section bar** and type **`.4`** for the **Height** property.
48. Click the **Other** tab on the **Property Sheet**, choose **Form** from the Selection Type list, and set the **Pop-up** property to **Yes.**
49. Click the **Property Sheet Format** tab. Set the **Default View** property to **Datasheet** and the **Allow Datasheet View** property to **Yes.**
50. Save the **Events PopUp** form and display it in **Datasheet View**.
51. Double-click the right border of each column heading to adjust column width.
52. Drag in the right and bottom edges of the form window to best fit the data.
53. Display the **Venue Events** form in Form View and move the pop-up form so you can view the data, as needed.

    You can see what each Event ID on the Venue Events Subform means by looking on the Events PopUp form.

54. Save and close the forms and close the database. Exit **Access**.
55. Submit your final file based on the guidelines provided by your instructor.

    To see examples of how your file or files should look at the end of this exercise, go to the student resource center.

APPLY YOUR SKILLS AC07-A03

Create a Form and Subform, Add a Logo and Calculated Controls, and Create a Pop-Up Form

In this exercise, you will use the Form Wizard to create a venue revenue form that contains a revenue details subform. You will delete, move, and size controls, modify the title, and add a logo to the form. Then you will use the Event Revenue query to create a Totals form to count scheduled events and total each of the currency fields. You will add calculated controls, one of which is locked, add the current date to the venue revenue, *format it, and create a pop-up form that lists the menus offered by UCE.*

Create a Form and Subform

1. Start **Access**. Open **AC07-A03-UCE** from the **AC2013 Lesson 07** folder and save the file as `AC07-A03-UCE-[FirstInitialLastName]`.
2. Select the **Venues** table and start the **Form Wizard**.
3. Move these fields from the Venues table to the Selected Fields list: **VenueID**, **VenueName**, **VenueStreet**, **VenueCity**, **VenueST**, **VenueZIP**, **VenuePhone**.
4. Choose the **Event Revenue** query from the Tables/Queries list and move **EventDate, MenuPlan**, **Guests**, **ChgPP** and **TotalRev** to the Selected Fields list.
5. Click **Next** and choose to view the data **By Venues**.
6. Choose the **Datasheet** layout.
7. Name the main form `Venue Revenues` and the subform `Venue Revenues Subform`. Choose **Modify the Form's Design**.

Format the Form and Subform

8. Select the **Revenues Subform label** and tap [Delete].
9. Select the subform and the **Phone label** and choose **Arrange→Sizing & Ordering→Align→Left**.
10. Change the **Caption** of the **ST label** to `State` and the **Caption** of the **ZIP label** to `ZIP Code`.
11. Select all the labels in the **Detail** section of the main form and type `1.5` for the **Width** property and `.25` for the **Height**; choose the **Raised Special Effect** property; choose **Arial** for **Font Name**, **12** for **Font Size**, and **Black, Text 1** for **Fore Color**.
12. Select all the text boxes in the **Detail** section of the main form, and type `.25` for the **Height**; choose **Sunken** for the **Special Effect** property; choose **Arial** for **Font Name**, **12** for **Font Size**, **Semi-Bold** for **Font Weight**, and **Blue, Accent 5, Darker 50%** for **Fore Color**.

13. Click inside the Form Header title and place the insertion point before *Venue Revenues*.

14. Type **`Universal Corporate Events, Ltd.`** then press [Shift]+[Enter] to bump the *Venue Revenues* text to a new line; tap [Enter].

    Be sure to tap [Enter] so you can perform the next step.

15. Enter these properties for the title on the Property Sheet:

Property	Value
Width	4.5
Height	.7
Left	1"
Font Name	Cambria
Text Align	Center
Font Weight	Bold
Fore Color	Blue, Accent 5, Darker 50%

16. Click the **Form Header** section bar. Type **`.8`** for **Height** and choose **White, Background 1** for the **Back Color**.

17. Click the **Detail** section bar. Choose a light blue such as **Blue, Accent 5, Lighter 80%** for both the **Back Color** and the **Alternate Back Color**.

18. Choose **Design→Header/Footer→**[Logo] and double-click **UCE-Logo.bmp** in the **AC2013 Lesson 07** folder.

19. Delete the title placeholder to the right of the logo.

20. Select the new logo and type **`.7`** for the **Width** and **Height** properties.

21. Switch to **Form View** and resize each subform column, as needed.

22. Close the **Venue Revenues** form and **Venue Revenues Subform**, saving if prompted.

Create a Quick Totals Form

23. Select the **Event Revenue** query in the Navigation Pane and open the **Form Wizard**.

24. Include all the fields *except* LiaisonID, choose **Datasheet** layout, name the new form **`Event Revenue Totals`**, and open it.

25. Resize the widths of each column to fit the data.

26. Choose **Home→Records→**[Σ Totals].

27. In the Totals row of the **Menu Plan** field, choose **Count** from the drop-down menu.

28. In the Totals row of the **Tot Revenue** field, the **Taxes** field, and the **Net Revenue** field, choose **Sum** from the list. Resize columns, as necessary.

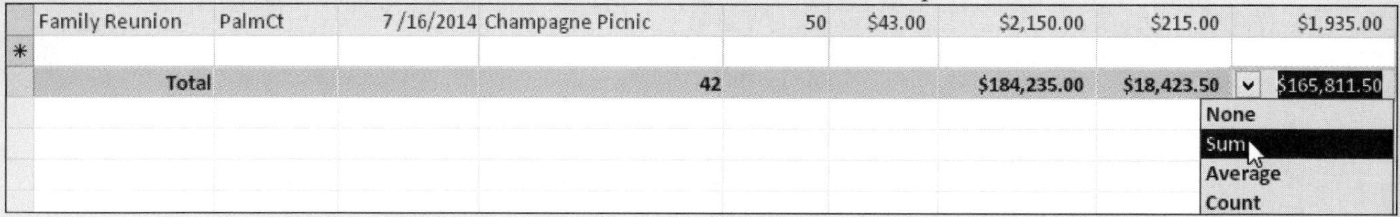

The form displays the count of records, using the Menu Plan field, and totals for the Tot Revenue, Taxes, and Tot Revenue fields.

29. Save and close the **Event Revenue Totals** form.

Add Calculated Controls to a Form

30. Display the **Venue Revenues** form in **Design View**.
31. Select the **TotalRev** text box in the subform and type `txtLineTotal` for the **Name** property in the Property Sheet.
32. Display the Form Footer in the subform.
33. Choose **Design→Controls→Text Box** [ab] and draw a text box in the Form Footer of the subform, under the TotalRev text box control.
34. Delete the label; then select the text box and type `txtEventTotal` for the **Name** property and type `=Sum(TotalRev)` for the **Control Source**.
35. Drag down the top of the Form Footer section bar in the **Main form** to make room for a new calculated text box control in the Detail section under the subform.
36. Draw a new text box under the right-hand side of the subform.
37. Select the new associated label and type `Venue Total` for the **Caption** property, type `.25` for the **Left** property, choose **Arial** for **Font Name**, choose **12** for **Font Size**, and choose **Black, Text 1** for **Fore Color**.
38. Save your changes to the **Venue Revenues** form.
39. Select the new text box, and click **Build** [...] in the **Control Source** line.
40. Expand **Venue Revenues** in the Expression Elements list and select the **Venue Revenues Subform**.
41. Double-click **txtEventTotal** in the Expression Categories list.

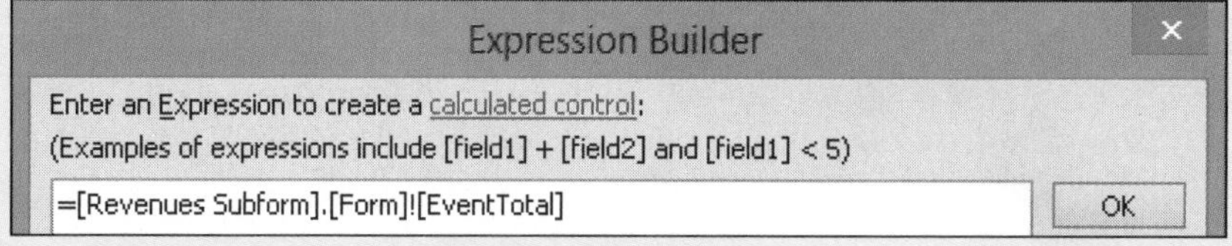

Access places the expression in the Expression pane.

42. Click **OK**.

43. With the calculated control still selected, choose **Currency** for the **Format**, choose **2** for **Decimal Places**, type `1.75` for the **Width**, type `.25` for the **Height**, type `4"` for the **Left** property, choose **Arial** for the **Font Name**, choose **Semi-Bold** for **Font Weight**, and choose a dark blue for the **Fore Color**.
44. Click the **Property Sheet Data** tab and choose **Yes** for the **Locked Property**.
45. Click the **Other** tab on the **Property Sheet** and type `This field is calculated by the program` for the **ControlTip Text** property.
46. Switch to **Form View**.

    If you see an error in the new field, check for errors in the Control Source property.
47. Save and close the **Venue Revenues** form.

Create a Pop-Up Form

48. Select the **Menus** table and choose **Create→Forms→Form Wizard**.
49. Move the **MenuCode**, **MenuPlan**, and **CostPP** to the Selected Fields list.
50. Choose the **Tabular** layout.
51. Enter `MenusPopUp` as the name and choose **Modify the Form's Design**.

    The form displays in Design View.
52. Delete the **MenusPopUp title control**.
53. Select the three label controls in the Form Header and type `.1` for their **Top** property.
54. Click the **Form Header** section bar and type `.4` for the **Height** property.
55. Click the **Other** tab on the **Property Sheet**, choose **Form** from the Selection Type list, and choose **Yes** for the **Pop-up** property.
56. Click the **Property Sheet Format** tab and choose **Datasheet** for the **Default View** property and choose **Yes** for the **Allow Datasheet View** property.
57. Save the **Menus PopUp** form and display it in **Datasheet View**.
58. Resize the columns and the pop-up form window to fit the data.
59. Display the **Venue Events** form in Form View and move the pop-up form so you can view the data, as needed.

    You can see what each Menu Code on the Venue Events Subform means using the Menus PopUp form.
60. Save and close the forms and close the database. Exit **Access**.
61. Submit your final file based on the guidelines provided by your instructor.

Extend Your Skills

In the course of working through the Extend Your Skills exercises, you will think critically as you use the skills taught in the lesson to complete the assigned projects. To evaluate your mastery and completion of the exercises, your instructor may use a rubric, with which more points are allotted according to performance characteristics. (The more you do, the more you earn!) Ask your instructor how your work will be evaluated.

AC07-E01 That's the Way I See It

In this exercise, you will add several forms to a database. Use the database you used in AC06-E01, or open **AC07-E01-BJL** and save it to your **AC2013 Lesson 07** folder as **`AC07-E01-BJL-[FirstInitialLastName]`**.

Use the Form Wizard to create a Blue Jean Landscaping Customer Sales form with a Cust Sales Details Subform that includes: SalesNum and SalesDate from the MerchSales table; CustLastName from the Customers table; ItemName, Manufacturer, and Price from the StoreMerchandise table; and QtySold from the MerchSalesDetails table.

In the subform, add calculated controls to multiply Price by QtySold to produce a line total. Add a control to the subform's Form Footer to sum the line totals. Finally, add a calculated control to the main form that displays the total of each sale and lock the control, adding a ScreenTip to indicate why it cannot be changed. Then create a pop-up form using the StoreMerchandise table to make data entry easier. Be sure to format and size all controls appropriately and include the company logo. Use formatting ideas from the SalesInvoices Form.

You will be evaluated based on the inclusion of all elements, your ability to follow directions, your ability to apply newly learned skills to a real-world situation, your creativity, and your accuracy in creating objects and/or entering data. Submit your final file based on the guidelines provided by your instructor.

AC07-E02 Be Your Own Boss

You want to add several forms to the Blue Jean Landscaping database to help track merchandise sales. Open **AC07-E02-BJL** and save it to your **AC2013 Lesson 07** folder as **`AC07-E02-BJL-[FirstInitialLastName]`**.

Use the Form Wizard to create a Merchandise Sales form with a Merch Sales Subform that includes: SalesNum and SalesDate from the MerchSales table; ItemName, Manufacturer, and Price from the StoreMerchandise table; and QtySold and InvNum from the MerchSalesDetails table.

In the subform, add calculated controls to multiply Price by QtySold to produce a line total. Add a control to the subform's Form Footer to sum the line totals. Finally, add a calculated control to the main form that displays the total of each sale and lock the control, adding a ScreenTip to indicate why it cannot be changed. Then create a pop-up form that displays RepID, RepLastName, and RepFirstName. Be sure to format and size all controls appropriately. Use formatting ideas from the SalesInvoices Form, including the company logo.

You will be evaluated based on the inclusion of all elements, your ability to follow directions, your ability to apply newly learned skills to a real-world situation, your creativity, and your accuracy in creating objects and/or entering data. Submit your final file based on the guidelines provided by your instructor.

Transfer Your Skills

In the course of working through the Transfer Your Skills exercises, you will use critical-thinking and creativity skills to complete the assigned projects using skills taught in the lesson. To evaluate your mastery and completion of the exercises, your instructor may use a rubric, with which more points are allotted according to performance characteristics. (The more you do, the more you earn!) Ask your instructor how your work will be evaluated.

AC07-T01 Use the Web as a Learning Tool

Throughout this book, you will be provided with an opportunity to use the Internet as a learning tool by completing WebQuests. According to the original creators of WebQuests, as described on their website (WebQuest.org), a WebQuest is "an inquiry-oriented activity in which most or all of the information used by learners is drawn from the web." To complete the WebQuest projects in this book, navigate to the student resource center choose the WebQuest for the lesson on which you are currently working. The subject of each WebQuest will be relevant to the material found in the lesson.

WebQuest Subject: Adding web browser controls to forms

Submit your final file(s) based on the guidelines provided by your instructor.

AC07-T02 Demonstrate Proficiency

Stormy BBQ is continuing to expand its database at its flagship location in Key West. Open **AC07-T02-SBQ** from the **AC2013 Lesson 07** folder and save it as `AC07-T02-SBQ-[FirstInitialLastName]`.

Create a new form named `MerchSales Form` with a subform that includes:

- SalesID and SalesDate from the MerchSales table
- SKU from the MerchSalesDetails table
- Manufacturer, ItemName, and ListPrice from the Merchandise table
- QtySold from the MerchSalesDetails table

In the subform, add calculated controls to multiply ListPrice by QtySold to produce a line total. Add a control to the subform's Form Footer to sum the line totals. Finally, add a calculated control to the main form that displays the total of each sale and lock the control, adding a ScreenTip to indicate why it cannot be changed. Then create a pop-up form using the Merchandise table that displays SKU, ItemName, and ListPrice. Be sure to format and size all controls. Use formatting ideas from the Restaurants Form, including the company logo.

Submit your final file based on the guidelines provided by your instructor.

ACCESS 2013

8 Creating Complex Queries

LESSON OUTLINE

LEARNING OBJECTIVES

After studying this lesson, you will be able to:

- Create a select query involving multiple tables
- Create a report based on multiple tables in a query
- Create and run parameter queries
- Create a calculated field in a query
- Create and run action queries

As the volume of data stored in database tables grows, so does the number of edits required to keep data for thousands of records up to date. Although relational databases reduce redundant data and increase efficiency, the accuracy and validity of a database is maintained through regular updates. In this lesson, you will explore queries designed to enhance the timeliness and accuracy of large relational databases. You will select and display desired fields in Datasheet View, calculate and summarize data, and use parameter queries that prompt you to enter values to generate or modify records. You will also use action queries to automate database tasks and specify criteria to display a subset of data to make updating, selecting, and deleting data more efficient.

CASE STUDY

Handling Growing Databases

You are responsible for analyzing the data retrieval processes for the growing Winchester Web Design database. You decide to develop queries to increase the efficiency of data entry and updates. You will create a parameter query to display information for only one customer, an append query to add records to the Products list, and a delete query to remove older invoices. You will also create additional queries to perform cleanup and automate database tasks.

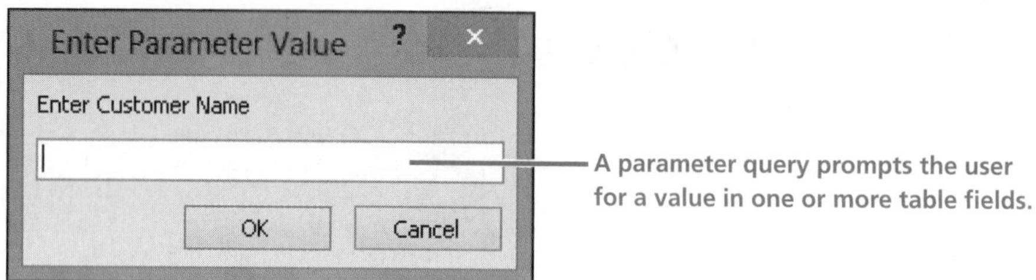

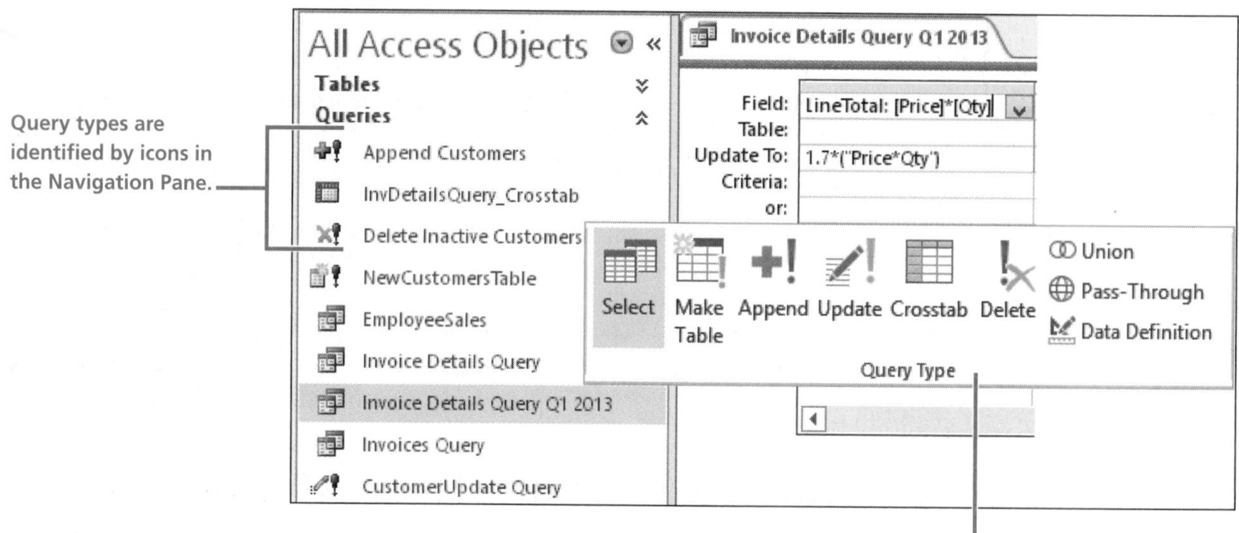

Identifying Advanced Query Features

Video Library http://labyrinthelab.com/videos Video Number: AC13-V0801

You may be familiar with simple queries such as the select query, crosstab query, unmatched query, and duplicates query. These queries are designed to quickly locate and display records that meet specific conditions and criteria.

Access also offers a variety of query types that are designed to address more advanced needs. Each query type, from the basic to the more advanced, is identified in the following table.

ACCESS QUERY TYPES

Query Type	Description
Select Query	Allows Access to retrieve desired fields from one or more tables that meet specific criteria conditions, and then sort, summarize, and calculate that data as needed.
Parameter Query	Prompts user to enter data that Access uses to filter records and return only a subset of records that match the value entered.
Crosstab Query	Displays row headings on the left side of the datasheet (i.e., *Customer ID*) and column headings across the top (i.e., *Products*), to sum, count, or average each column corresponding to the row field (i.e., total products purchased by customers).
Action Query	Performs one of four actions on a group of records: deletes records, updates records, appends records, or creates a new table.
SQL Query	Uses structured query language (SQL) to create a query. Very few developers program in the more difficult-to-use SQL, because any query designed with either the Wizard or in Design View is automatically converted to SQL when you choose SQL View.
Unmatched Query	Locates records in one table that have no match in another table. An unmatched query could ensure that each record in an *Invoices* table has a corresponding record in the *Customers* table.
Duplicates Query	Locates records containing duplicate field values in a single table or query. For example, a duplicates query could locate records in the *Customers* table that were entered more than once.

Querying Tables Containing No Relationships

When tables in a database have no established relationships, running queries on the tables can produce undesired results.

Cartesian Product Lists

A Cartesian product list displays all possible combinations from a database query which uses fields from two unrelated tables. Without relationships, Access has no idea how to relate the data contained in each table, so it presents every possible combination between the two tables in the query results datasheet, listing the same record many times. When the number of records in each table is large, these queries take a long time to run and provide quite meaningless results.

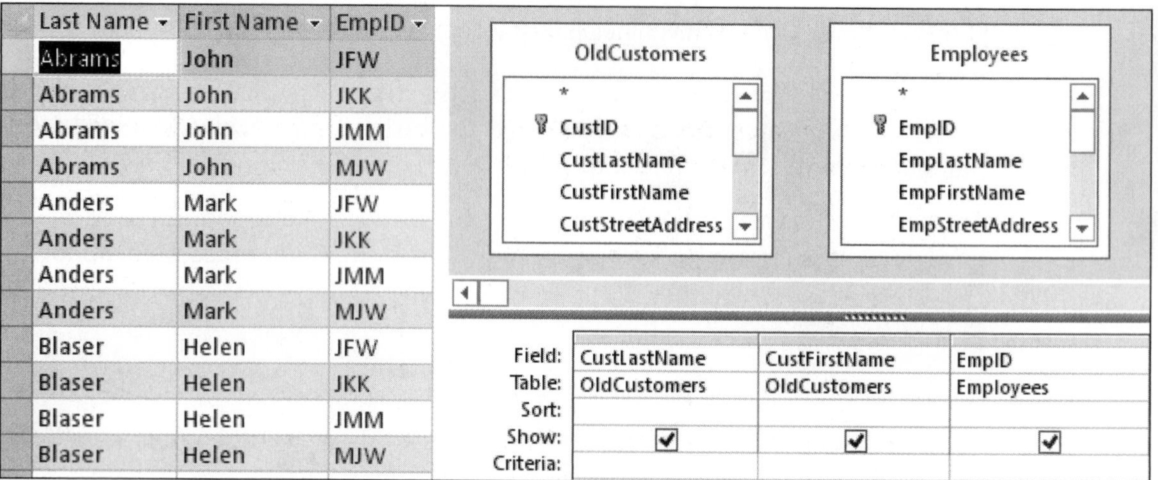

Cartesian product query results where every customer is listed with all four of the employees for a small company, greatly compounding the number of records displayed.

Avoiding Cartesian Products

To prevent meaningless and sometimes huge Cartesian product lists, you must establish proper relationships before creating a query. When you create a query from multiple tables make sure that a join line connects fields in different tables and that referential integrity has been established in the Relationship window.

Creating Select Queries

Video Library http://labyrinthelab.com/videos Video Number: AC13-V0802

Select queries, which can display selected fields from one or more database tables in a single datasheet, are the most common type of query. You can design a select query to retrieve records based on criteria, and then sort those records in the query results datasheet. You can group and summarize data using aggregate functions such as sum, count, min, max, and avg. In addition, you can create calculated fields using values contained in other fields.

One major advantage to running queries is that they are dynamic, meaning they display up-to-date data each time they are run. Select queries do not store data; they simply display the data. You can then edit the data or use the data to create reports. However, the data remains stored in the database tables—*not* in the query results datasheet.

DEVELOP YOUR SKILLS AC08-D01

Create a Select Query

In this exercise, you will create a select query that displays data from different tables in the Winchester Web Design database.

1. Open **AC08-D01-WinWebDesign** from the **AC2013 Lesson 08** folder and save it as **`AC08-D01-WinWebDesign-[FirstInitialLastName]`**.

   Replace the bracketed text with your first initial and last name. For example, if your name is Bethany Smith, your filename would look like this: AC08-D01-WinWebDesign-BSmith.

2. **Expand** the Navigation Pane, if it is collapsed, and review the table objects contained in the database.
3. Choose **Create→Queries→Query Design** to create a new query.
4. Double-click the following table names in the **Show Table** dialog box: **Customers, Invoices, InvoiceDetails,** and **Products**.
5. Close the **Show Table** dialog box. Arrange the table title bars as shown.

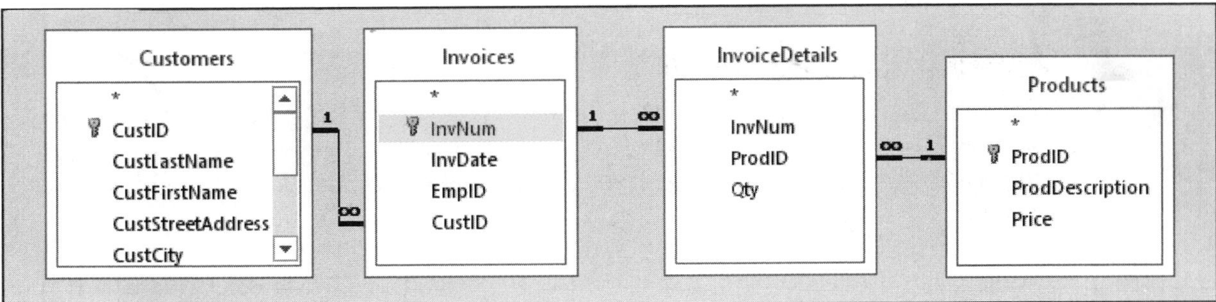

6. Double-click the **InvNum** and **InvDate** fields in the **Invoices** table to add them to the query grid.
7. Double-click each of the following fields to add them to the query grid:

Table	Fields
Customers	CustLastName
Products	ProdDescription, Price
Invoice Details	Qty

8. Click in the **Sort** row of **InvNum** and choose **Ascending**.
9. **Save** the query as **`Customer InvoiceDetails Query`**.

Access 2013

10. **Run** the query, returning 124 records.

InvNum	Invoice Date	Last Name	ID	Description	Price	Qty
1	3 /15/2012	Smith	SmithW	Image, Custom Designed	$40.00	11
1	3 /15/2012	Smith	SmithW	Secondary Page	$200.00	6
1	3 /15/2012	Smith	SmithW	Home Page, Nav, CSS, Design	$400.00	1
2	4 /2 /2012	Santos	SantosE	Home Page, Nav, CSS, Design	$400.00	1
2	4 /2 /2012	Santos	SantosE	Hourly Rate for Modifications	$80.00	5
2	4 /2 /2012	Santos	SantosE	Image, Custom Designed	$40.00	14
2	4 /2 /2012	Santos	SantosE	Secondary Page	$200.00	7
3	5 /11/2012	Santos	SantosE	Secondary Page	$200.00	2
3	5 /11/2012	Santos	SantosE	Image, Custom Designed	$40.00	6
4	5 /30/2012	Smith	SmithW	Blog, Integrated into Site	$300.00	1

Unless directed otherwise, keep Access and any database or database objects being used open at the end of each exercise.

Creating a Calculated Field in a Query

Video Library http://labyrinthelab.com/videos Video Number: AC13-V0803

Queries display fields contained in tables. You can also create a calculated field, which assigns a name to a new field and uses existing fields to perform mathematical or logical operations. Calculated fields can also be used to concatenate, or combine, fields, such as first and last names. For example:

Last Name	First Name	ID: [CustLastName]+Left([CustFirstName],1)
Smith	William	SmithW

Calculated fields generate up-to-date results each time you run the query. This can be quite valuable when the underlying data changes.

Identifying Features of a Calculated Field

A calculated field includes field name(s), operators, and punctuation marks that tell Access how to perform the calculation.

Calculated Field Terms

Calculated fields follow the same order of precedence used in all mathematical equations. Calculations contained in parentheses are performed first, and then multiplication and division, followed by addition and subtraction, in a left to right order. In Access, each calculated field is named and constructed as described in the following table.

BASIC CALCULATED FIELD TERMINOLOGY	
Term	**Description**
Calculated Field Name	Unique name assigned to a calculated field, which is followed by a colon to separate it from the rest of the expression.
Arithmetic Operators	Add (+), subtract (-), divide (/), multiply (*), and exponential (^).
Logical Operators	Equals (=), greater than (>), less than (<), greater than or equal to (>=), and so on; used to compare values.
Expression	The combination of field names and arithmetic and logical operators required to perform the calculation; basically an Access formula.
Field Names	Fields from database tables used in calculations, which Access encloses within square brackets ([]).

The following table provides a guide on how to create a calculated field.

QUICK REFERENCE	CREATING A CALCULATED FIELD
Task	**Procedure**
Create a calculated field in a query	■ Display query in Design View; add table field lists that contain the values you want to use in the expression. ■ Click Field row for first available column in the query grid. ■ Type calculated field expression in the cell using the following structure: New Calculated Field Name: [Field]Operand[Field].

DEVELOP YOUR SKILLS AC08-D02

Add Calculations to a Select Query

In this exercise, you will add a calculated field and a concatenated field to the Customer InvoiceDetails Query.

1. Display the **Customer InvoiceDetails Query** in **Design View**.
2. Click in the **Field row** of the first available column after the **Qty** column.
3. Type `LineTotal: Price * Qty` in the Field row and tap [Enter].
   Double-click the right border of the new field's column heading, if necessary, to see the entire calculation.
4. Click the new **LineTotal** field and open the **Property Sheet**.
5. Choose **Currency** for the **Format** property.
6. Click in the first available **Field row** after **LineTotal**.
7. Type `ID: [CustLastName]+Left([CustFirstName],1)` in the Field row and tap [Enter].
   This produces a resulting ID field that consists of the customer's last name followed by the first character of the customer's first name.

8. Select the new concatenated **ID** field and drag it to the left of ProdDescription in the query grid.

ID: [CustLastName]+Left([CustFirstName],1)	ProdDescription	Price	Qty	LineTotal: [Price]*[Qty]
	Products	Products	InvoiceDetails	
✓	✓	✓	✓	✓

The new ID now follows the CustLastName field.

9. Choose **Design→Results→Run** [Run].

Customer InvoiceDetails Query

InvNum	Invoice Date	Last Name	ID	Description	Price	Qty	LineTotal
1	3/15/2012	Smith	SmithW	Image, Custom Designed	$40.00	11	$440.00
1	3/15/2012	Smith	SmithW	Secondary Page	$200.00	6	$1,200.00
1	3/15/2012	Smith	SmithW	Home Page, Nav, CSS, Design	$400.00	1	$400.00
2	4/2/2012	Santos	SantosE	Home Page, Nav, CSS, Design	$400.00	1	$400.00
2	4/2/2012	Santos	SantosE	Hourly Rate for Modifications	$80.00	5	$400.00
2	4/2/2012	Santos	SantosE	Image, Custom Designed	$40.00	14	$560.00
2	4/2/2012	Santos	SantosE	Secondary Page	$200.00	7	$1,400.00
3	5/11/2012	Santos	SantosE	Secondary Page	$200.00	2	$400.00
3	5/11/2012	Santos	SantosE	Image, Custom Designed	$40.00	6	$240.00
4	5/30/2012	Smith	SmithW	Blog, Integrated into Site	$300.00	1	$300.00

The new concatenated ID field and the calculated LineTotal field.

10. Double-click the right border of each column heading to size the columns to display data.
11. **Save** the Customer InvoiceDetails Query.

Adding Totals to Datasheets

Video Library http://labyrinthelab.com/videos Video Number: AC13-V0804

Now that you have calculated the value of items in the Customer InvoiceDetails Query, it is possible to obtain a total count and value of all transactions. The Totals button appears on the Ribbon in the Records group of the Home tab.

FROM THE RIBBON
Home→Records→Totals to add a Total row in Datasheet View

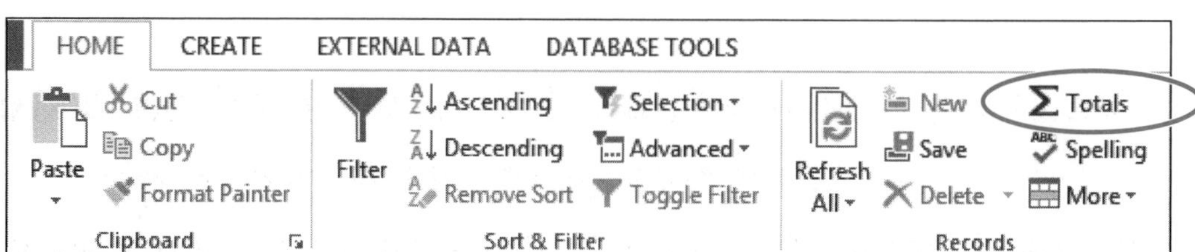

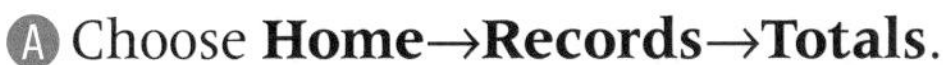

Add Total Row to the Query Datasheet

In this exercise, you will add a Total row to the Customer InvoiceDetails Query results datasheet.

1. Display the **Customer InvoiceDetails Query** in **Design View**.
2. **Run** the Customer InvoiceDetails Query.
3. Follow these steps to add the Total row to the query results datasheet:

Ⓐ Choose **Home→Records→Totals**.

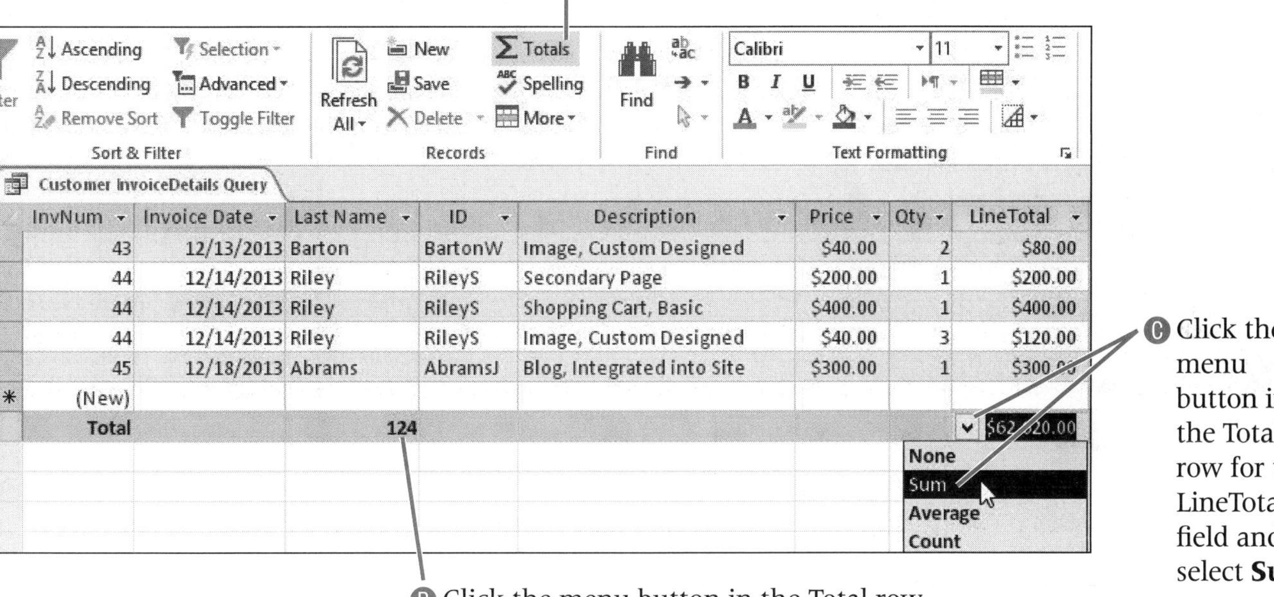

Ⓒ Click the menu button in the Total row for the LineTotal field and select **Sum**.

Ⓑ Click the menu button in the Total row for the Last Name field and select **Count**.

The Total row is added below the new row at the bottom of the datasheet. Access calculates the total value of all the LineTotal items and displays the results.

To remove totals from displaying each time you run the query, choose Home→Records→Totals again.

4. Save and close the **Customer InvoiceDetails Query**.

Creating a Multi-Table Report Based on a Query

Video Library http://labyrinthelab.com/videos Video Number: AC13-V0805

After you create a query that contains fields from multiple tables, you can use that query as the basis for creating a multi-table report. If the tables are joined in a relationship, creating a multi-table report is as easy as building a simple report.

DEVELOP YOUR SKILLS AC08-D04

Create a Report Using a Query

In this exercise, you will create a new multi-table report using the Customer InvoiceDetails Query as the source. Then you will format the report.

1. Choose **Create→Reports→Report Wizard**.
2. Follow these steps to create a report from a query using the Report Wizard:

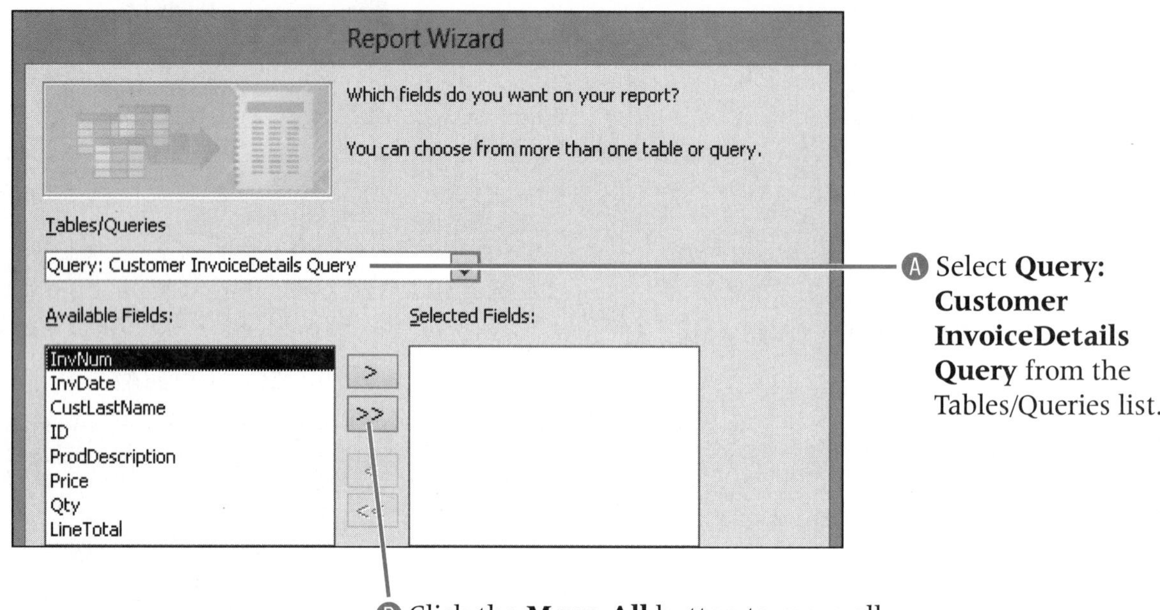

3. Click **Next**.

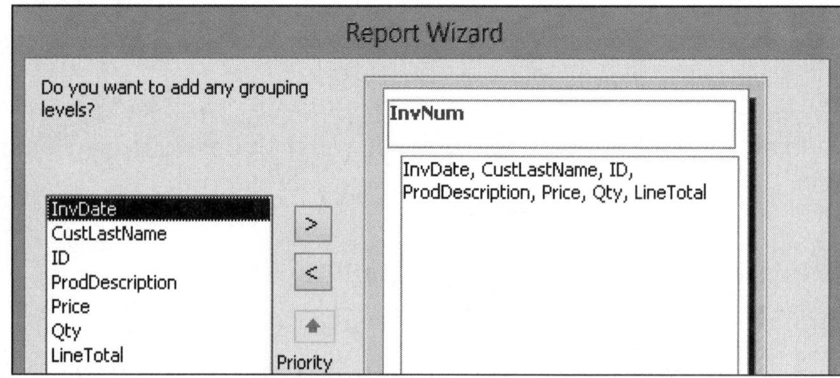

4. With the **InvNum** field selected, click **Move** [>].

   If Access sets the ProdID, or any other field as the grouping level, click the Move button to move the unsolicited field back to the left pane. Then select the InvNum field and move it over as the grouping level.

5. Click **Next**. On the next Wizard screen, click **Summary Options**.

6. In the Summary Options screen, click the checkbox to **Sum** the LineTotal.

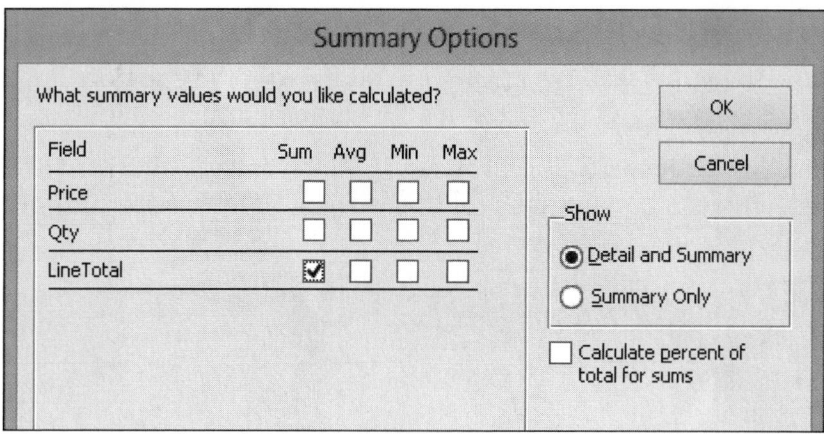

7. Click **OK** to close the Summary Options window. Click **Next**.

   Access asks you to select a layout for the report.

8. Choose the **Outline** layout and the **Landscape** orientation options; click **Next**.

9. Type `Customer Invoice Report` for the report title and click **Finish**.

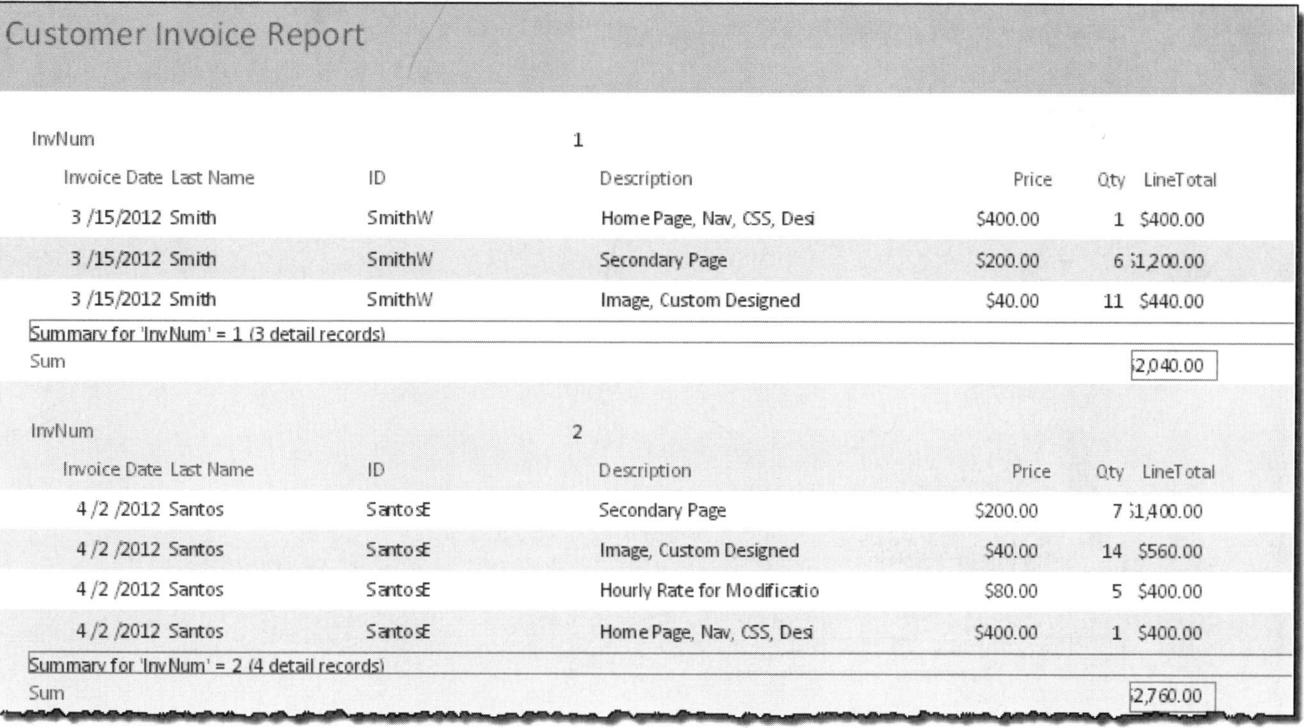

The report displays in Print Preview, showing invoice totals and summary totals for each transaction and a grouping level on the Customer Number field. Each order is identified, and the items ordered for each order are shown.

Format Report Controls

10. Click [Close Print Preview] and switch to **Design View**. Open the **Property Sheet**, if necessary.
11. Select the **InvNum** label. Type **`Invoice Number`** for the **Caption** property; type **`1.1"`** for the **Width** property, and type **`.25"`** for the **Left** property.
12. Set the following Property Sheet values to position and size the listed label and text box controls (if there is no value for a control listed in the table below, do not change that property):

Control	Width	Left
InvNum text box	.5	1.5
Invoice Date label	1	.25
InvDate text box	1	.25
CustLastName text box	1	
ID label		2.5
ID text box	1	2.5
Description label		3.6
ProdDescription text box	2.25	3.6
Price label		6.5
Price text box	1	6
Qty label		7.2
Qty text box		7
="Page " control (Page Footer)	1.5	4

Format Multiple Report Controls

13. Click the **Line Total label**, press [Ctrl], and click each **LineTotal** text box to select all four controls.

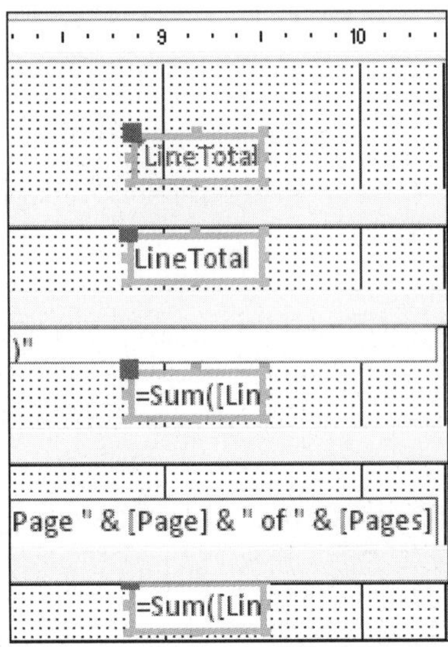

14. Type **`1"`** for the **Width** property and **`7.75"`** for the **Left** property.

Delete Report Controls

15. Select the **="Summary for "** control across the **InvNum Footer** section and tap [Delete].
16. Select the **=Now()** control on the left side of the **Page Footer** and tap [Delete].

Change Report Properties and Preview the Report

17. If necessary, choose **Report** in the **Selection Type** list box at the top of the Property Sheet and type **8.75** for the **Width** property of the report.

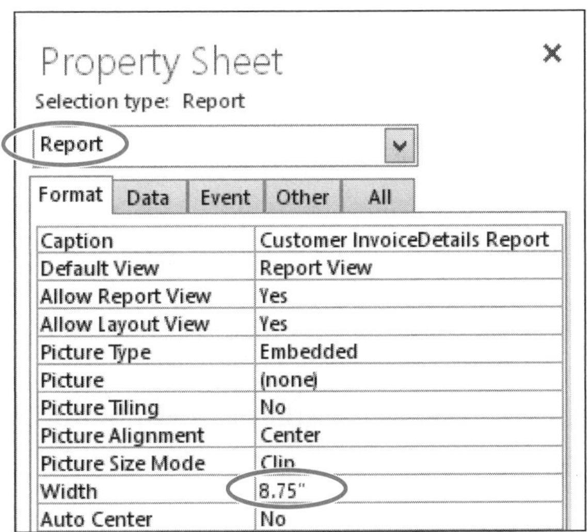

If the report width will not change to 8.75, verify that no controls extend beyond that point. You may have to resize and reposition the controls to solve the problem.

18. Switch to **Print Preview** to see your changes.

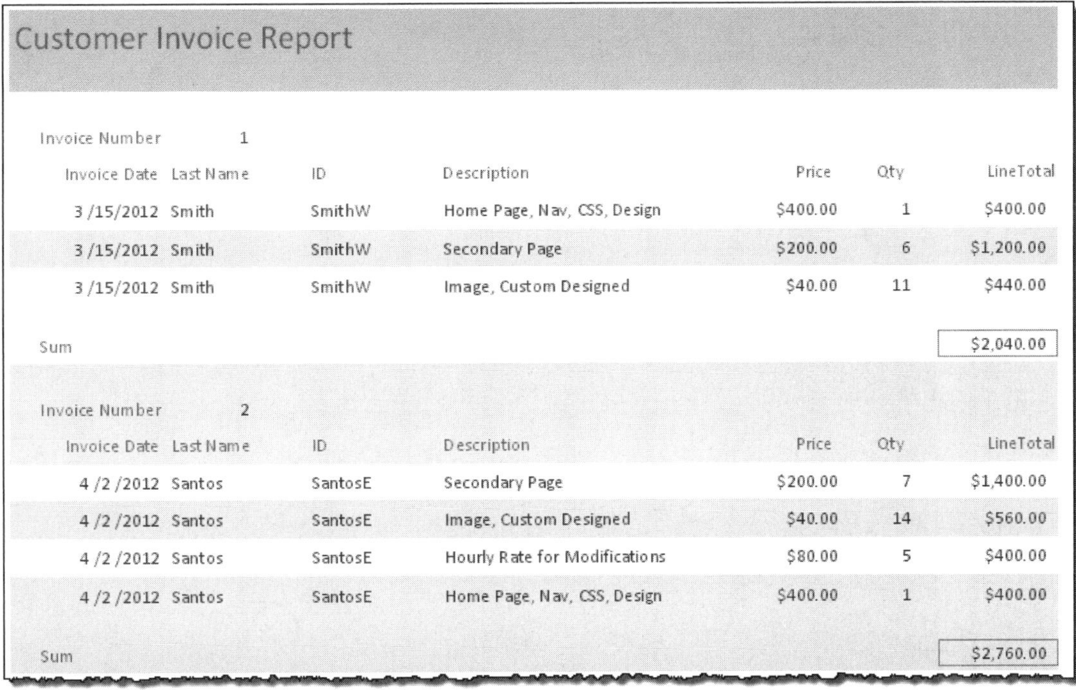

19. Save the **Customer Invoice Report**.

Creating and Running Parameter Queries

Video Library http://labyrinthelab.com/videos Video Number: AC13-V0806

In programming, a parameter is a value or type of variable that is used to pass input to a routine, or in Access, to a query. A parameter query is a select query that prompts the user to enter new criteria values each time they run the query; the query then generates results based on the value(s) entered. Parameter queries enable you to enter criteria to limit results without accessing Design View each time you want to run the query. This is especially useful when you create a query for users who are unfamiliar with query design.

Setting Up a Parameter Query

Parameter queries use the Criteria row of the query grid to create a criteria expression, or the text that you want to appear in the prompt. A prompt is the text that asks—or prompts—the user to enter a value. When you run a parameter query, you enter a value in the prompt box, and the query results datasheet displays only records containing the value entered.

In most cases, the parameter field appears in the query results datasheet. However, you can also use the field to limit query results without displaying the field in the results datasheet.

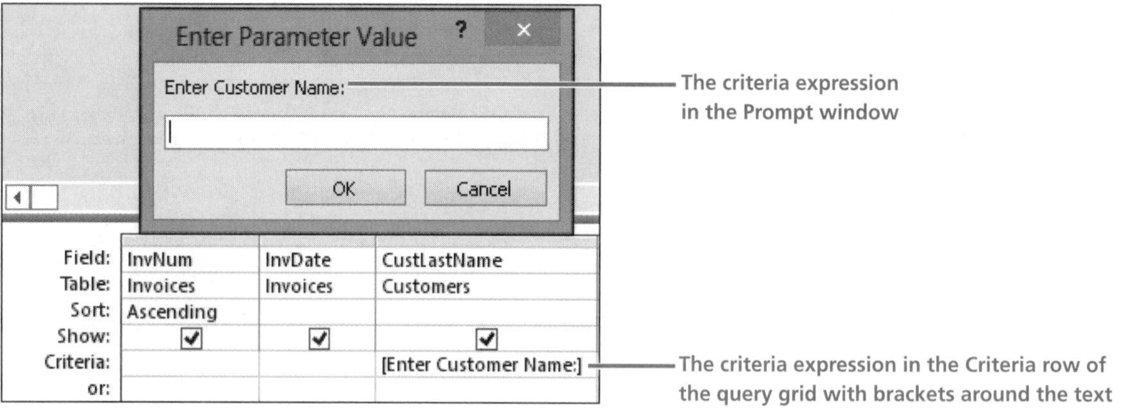

Sample query grid with criteria expression and prompt box

Formatting the Criteria Expression

Parameter criteria expressions must be enclosed in square brackets ([ ]). If you omit the brackets, Access places quotation marks around the text and searches for a value that matches the text rather than using the text as a user prompt.

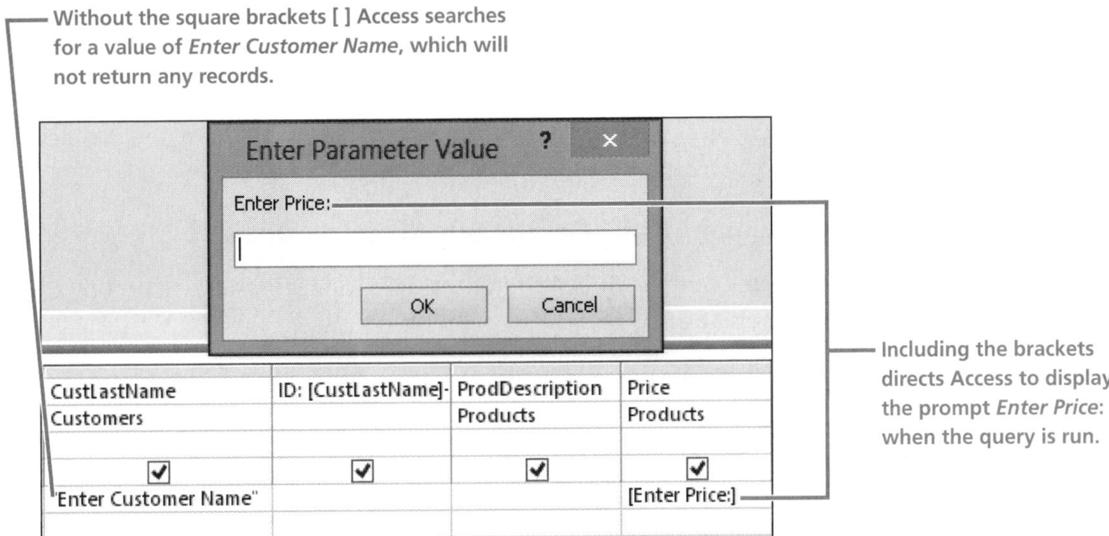
Without the square brackets [ ] Access searches for a value of *Enter Customer Name*, which will not return any records.
Enter Parameter Value
Enter Price:
OK
Cancel
CustLastName
Customers
"Enter Customer Name"
ID: [CustLastName]-
ProdDescription
Products
Price
Products
[Enter Price:]
Including the brackets directs Access to display the prompt *Enter Price*: when the query is run.

Creating Complex Parameter Prompts

Suppose you want the user to enter a product ID each time the query is run. Because the products may be handled by multiple employees, you may also want the view a specific product's sales by a particular employee. To create multiple prompts for this scenario, you would type [Enter ProdID] in the ProdID criteria row and [Enter EmpID] in the EmpID criteria row. You can also set prompts for multiple values in the same query column or include logical criteria such as greater than (>) and less than (<).

The following table shows common examples of parameter query criteria and the results they would create.

EXAMPLES OF PARAMETER QUERY CRITERIA FOR A SINGLE FIELD	
Parameter Criteria	**Result**
Between [What is the start date?] And [What is the end date?]	Prompts the user to enter the starting date. Then the user enters the end date, directing Access to display records that fall between the two dates entered.
<[What is the highest price you will pay?]	Displays the prompt shown within brackets. After the user enters a value, Access displays all records for values less than the one entered.

QUICK REFERENCE	CREATING A PARAMETER QUERY
Task	**Procedure**
Create a parameter query	■ Choose Create→Queries→Query Design. ■ Add required tables to the query, and then add the desired fields from the table field list(s) to the query grid. ■ Click the criteria row for the column for which users will enter a value and type the prompt text within square brackets in a format similar to `[Enter Date]`.

DEVELOP YOUR SKILLS AC08-D05

Create and Run a Parameter Query

In this exercise, you will create and run a parameter query that prompts the user for a customer's last name.

1. Click the **Customer InvoiceDetails Query**.
2. Press [Ctrl]+[C] to copy the query, then press [Ctrl]+[V] and name the copy **`Customer Invoice Parameter Query`**.
3. Display **Customer Invoice Parameter Query** in **Design View**.
4. Click the criteria row for the **CustLastName** column and type this text: **`[Enter Customer Name:]`**

Field:	InvNum	InvDate	CustLastName
Table:	Invoices	Invoices	Customers
Sort:	Ascending		
Show:	✔	✔	✔
Criteria:			[Enter Customer Name:]

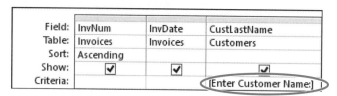

Be sure to include the square brackets.

Run and Test the Query

5. Choose **Design→Results→Run** [Run]. Type **`Abrams`** in the parameter box and press [Enter].

	InvNum	Invoice Date	Last Name	ID	Description	Price	Qty	LineTotal
	42	12/6/2013	Abrams	AbramsJ	Secondary Page	$200.00	5	$1,000.00
	42	12/6/2013	Abrams	AbramsJ	Home Page, Nav, CSS, Design	$400.00	1	$400.00
	45	12/18/2013	Abrams	AbramsJ	Blog, Integrated into Site	$300.00	1	$300.00
*	(New)							
	Total		3					$1,700.00

Access returns records that contain the value Abrams *in the customer last name field.*

6. Close the query, saving changes to the datasheet if prompted.

Creating and Running Action Queries

Video Library http://labyrinthelab.com/videos Video Number: AC13-V0807

An action query performs an action that modifies a database table or a group of records in a table. Action queries can modify, move, update, or delete groups of records with a single action. You can even use an action query to create a new table by adding various fields from other tables.

Each time you open an action query, Access *runs and generates the results*. So, if you create an update query designed to increase prices by 10 percent on all items in a table, Access will increase those prices every time you run the query. Because action queries do not open the table that they are updating, a user may run the query a second time, doubling the effect of the query.

Every time you open an action query, Access runs and generates results. It is good practice to delete action queries after running them to help maintain the validity of data in the database because these changes cannot easily be undone.

Identifying Action Query Types

There are four basic types of action queries available in Access. They are described in the following table.

ACTION QUERY TYPES

Action Query Type	Description
Make Table Query	A query that creates a new table from the selected data in one or more tables. For example, you may want to create a backup table to store 2012 records before you delete them from your main file.
Append Query	A query that adds a group of records from one or more sources to the end of one or more tables. For example, you could add a customer to a database the first time he or she places an order.
Update Query	A query that makes global changes to a group of records in one or more tables. For example, you can increase the prices of all products in a specific category or update phone numbers that change when the phone company adds a new area code.
Delete Query	A query that deletes a group of records from one or more tables. For example, you could create a delete query to remove records for a discontinued line of products.

Identifying Queries by Their Icons

Access identifies each type of query with a different icon. The following table displays the various icons and their query type.

QUERY TYPES AND THEIR ICONS

Icon	Query Type	Icon	Query Type
Select	Select query	Update	Update query
Make Table	Make Table query	Delete	Delete query
Append	Append query	Crosstab	Crosstab query

QUICK REFERENCE	CREATING AND RUNNING ACTION QUERIES
Task	**Procedure**
Create an append query	■ Create a new query in the source database and add all table fields to the query grid. ■ Choose Design→Query Type→Append; enter the name of the destination table. ■ Save and run the query.
Create an update query	■ Create a new query in the source database and add all table fields to the query grid. ■ Set criteria. ■ Choose Design→Query Type→Update. ■ Save and run the query.
Create a make table query	■ Create a new query in the source database and add all table fields to the query grid. ■ Set criteria if required. ■ Choose Design→Query Type→Make Table. ■ Save and run the query.
Create a delete query	■ Create a new query in the source database and add all table fields to the query grid. ■ Set criteria. ■ Choose Design→Query Type→Delete. ■ Save and run the query.

Enabling Content

Action queries require that content within a database be enabled. As a result, if you did not click the Enable Content button found at the top of the Access window when you first opened the database, Access will display an error message advising you to enable content before you can create or run action queries.

Creating a Make Table Query

A make table query is an action query that can create a new table based on data from multiple tables in a database. It's also a great way to place data produced from a calculated query field into a table.

If you rerun a make table query, Access will replace the existing table with a new one with new records that meet the query criteria. To retain your existing query-created table, rename and save it.

Moving Data to Tables and Databases

When you create a new table using a make table query, Access prompts you for a table name and even allows you to save the data in another database. An example of moving records to another database would be for archival purposes when they become obsolete, such as when a product is no longer available.

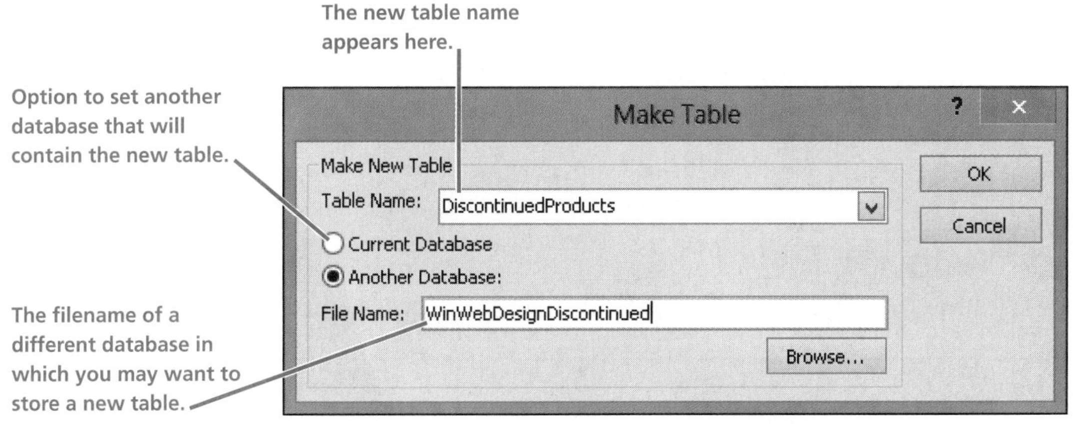

DEVELOP YOUR SKILLS AC08-D06

Create a Make Table Query

In this exercise, you will create a make table action query to save 2012 invoice records in a new table.

1. Run the **Invoices Query**.
2. Switch to **Design View**.
3. Type **`Between 1/1/2012 and 12/31/2012`** in the Criteria row for the **InvDate** field.

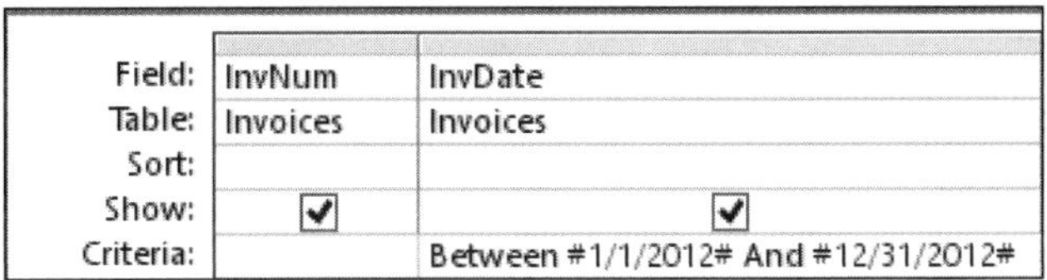

Field: InvNum | InvDate
Table: Invoices | Invoices
Sort:
Show:
Criteria: Between #1/1/2012# And #12/31/2012#

4. Follow these steps to create a make table query:

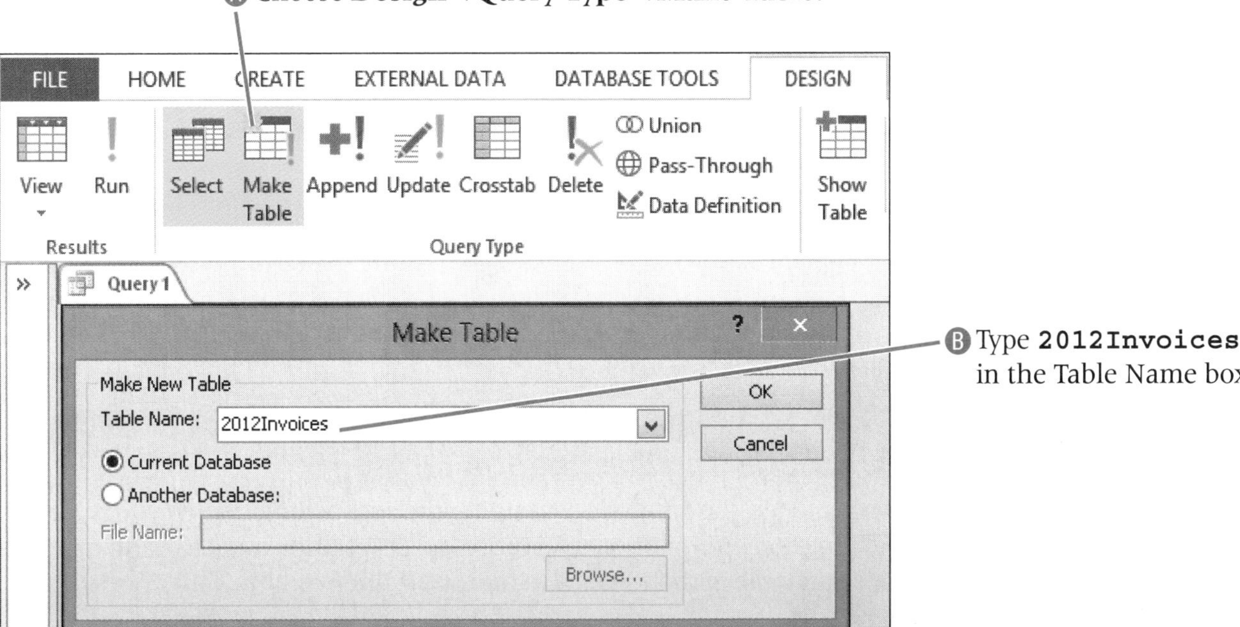

5. Click **OK**.
6. Run the query.

   Access displays an error message warning you that you are about to paste 61 records into a new table.
7. Choose **Yes** to continue.

   Access creates the table and displays it in the list of tables in the Navigation Pane.

Verify the Table

8. Display the **2012Invoices** table in **Datasheet View**.

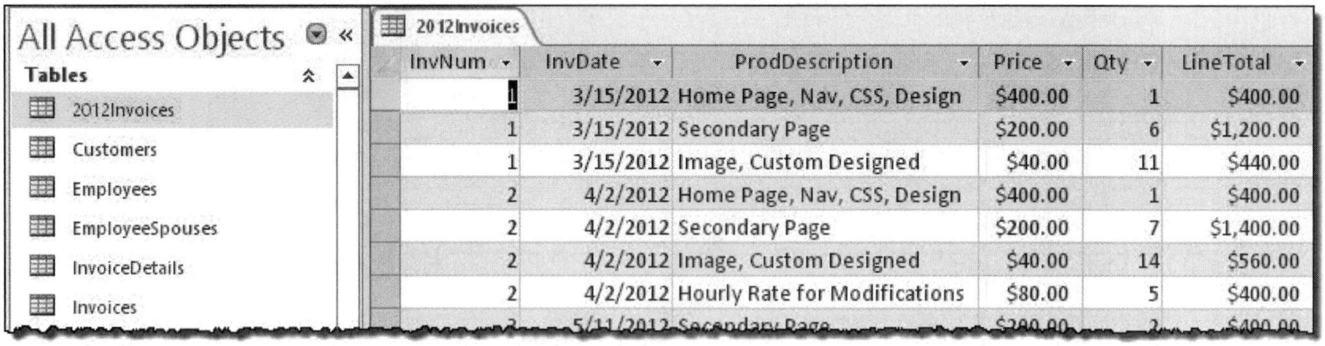

All Access Objects

Tables

- 2012Invoices
- Customers
- Employees
- EmployeeSpouses
- InvoiceDetails
- Invoices

2012Invoices

InvNum	InvDate	ProdDescription	Price	Qty	LineTotal
1	3/15/2012	Home Page, Nav, CSS, Design	$400.00	1	$400.00
1	3/15/2012	Secondary Page	$200.00	6	$1,200.00
1	3/15/2012	Image, Custom Designed	$40.00	11	$440.00
2	4/2/2012	Home Page, Nav, CSS, Design	$400.00	1	$400.00
2	4/2/2012	Secondary Page	$200.00	7	$1,400.00
2	4/2/2012	Image, Custom Designed	$40.00	14	$560.00
2	4/2/2012	Hourly Rate for Modifications	$80.00	5	$400.00

9. Close the **2012Invoices** table and the **Invoices Query**.

   Do not save the query. The 2012Invoices table has been successfully created, and you would not want to risk overwriting it.

Creating an Append Action Query

Video Library http://labyrinthelab.com/videos Video Number: AC13-V0808

An append query is an action query that adds a group of records from one or more tables to the end of one or more tables in the same or in another database. For example, if you want to offer a new set of products, you could use an append action query to add the new items to the existing products table. Or you might use an append action query to automatically add new customers to the customers table the first time a customer places an order.

Formatting the Source and Destination Tables

When you create an append action query, the table containing the records you want to add to another table is called the source table. The table receiving the records is the destination table. To successfully run an append action query, the structures—field names, data types, and field order—for both tables should be the same.

Identifying the Source and Destination Tables

Append queries are created in the database containing the source table. When you run the query, the Append dialog box prompts you to identify the destination database and table. Access identifies the destination table in the Append To row of the query grid.

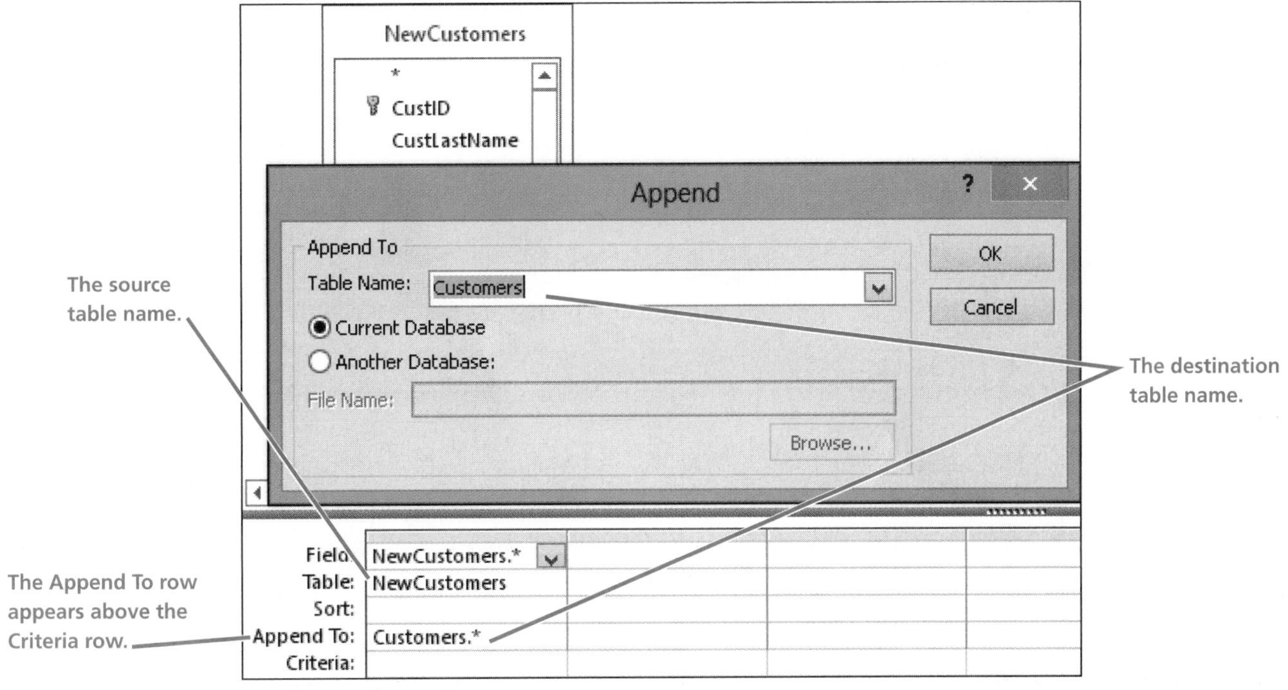

DEVELOP YOUR SKILLS AC08-D07

Create an Append Action Query

In this exercise, you will create an action query to append *records from the New Products table to the existing Products table.*

1. Open the **Products** table and notice that it contains six records.
2. Open the **NewProducts** table to see the records that will be appended to the **Products** table.
3. Close both tables.
4. Choose **Create→Queries→Query Design** to create a new query.
5. Add the **NewProducts** table to the query window. Close the **Show Table** dialog box.
6. Double-click the **asterisk (*)** in the **NewProducts** table to add all the fields to the query grid.

7. Follow these steps to change the query to an append query:

Ⓐ Choose **Design→Query Types→Append**.

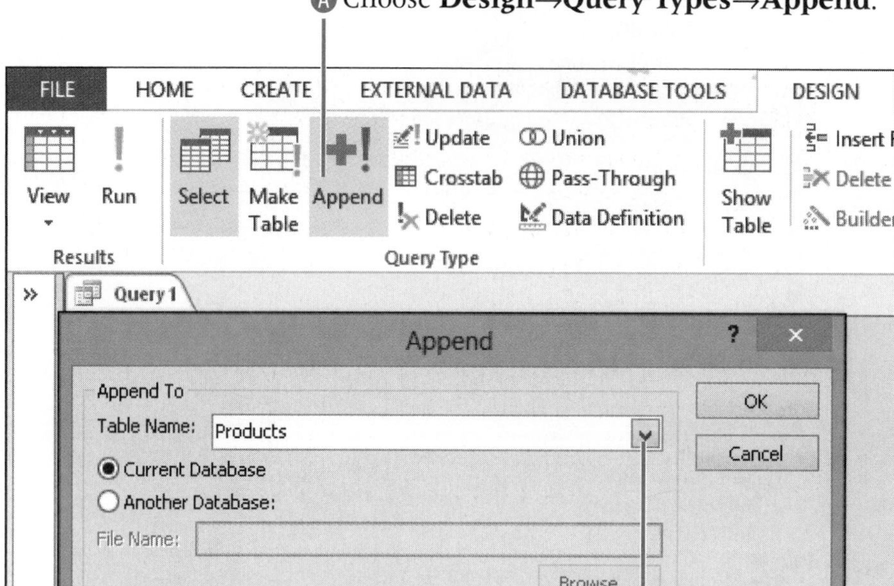

Ⓑ Click the **Table Name** menu button and choose **Products**.

8. Click **OK** to close the Append window.

   Access adds the Append To row to the query grid with the destination table name.

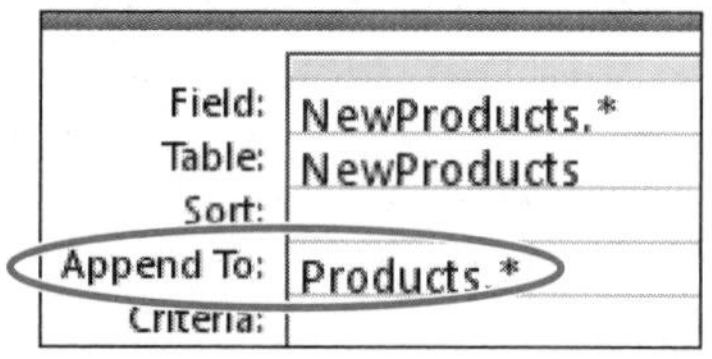

9. Choose **Design→Results→**Run.

   Access displays a warning that you are about to append five rows to another table.

10. Choose **Yes** to proceed.

Nothing *appears* to happen when you run the query. You can only see the changes after you open the destination table to which the records were appended. *Don't run the query again!* If you do, Access will add the same records to the destination table again.

11. Display the **Products** table in **Datasheet View** to verify that the new records were appended.

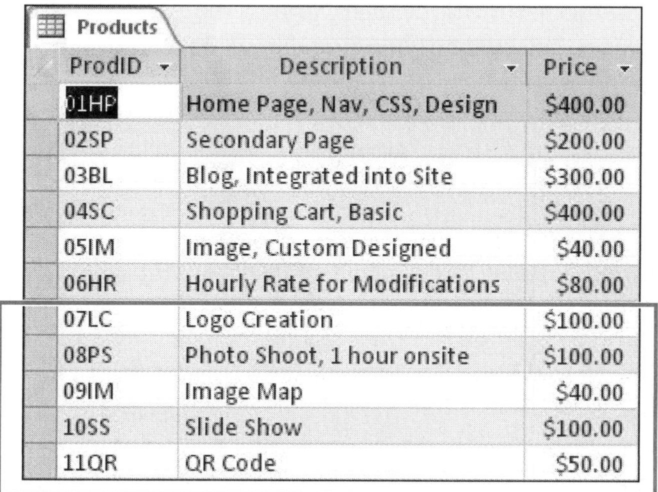

Products

ProdID	Description	Price
01HP	Home Page, Nav, CSS, Design	$400.00
02SP	Secondary Page	$200.00
03BL	Blog, Integrated into Site	$300.00
04SC	Shopping Cart, Basic	$400.00
05IM	Image, Custom Designed	$40.00
06HR	Hourly Rate for Modifications	$80.00
07LC	Logo Creation	$100.00
08PS	Photo Shoot, 1 hour onsite	$100.00
09IM	Image Map	$40.00
10SS	Slide Show	$100.00
11QR	QR Code	$50.00

The Products table now contains the new products.

12. Save the query as **Append Products**, and close it.

13. Close the **Products** table, but leave the database open.
    Remember: Do not run the query again.

Creating an Update Query

Video Library http://labyrinthelab.com/videos Video Number: AC13-V0809

An update query is an action query that makes global changes to a group of records in one or more tables. For example, you can use an update query to increase the prices for all products in a specific category or update the area code for phone numbers that change when the phone company adds a new one.

To ensure that corresponding fields in related tables are updated consistently, check the Cascade Update Related Fields checkbox in the Edit Relationships window.

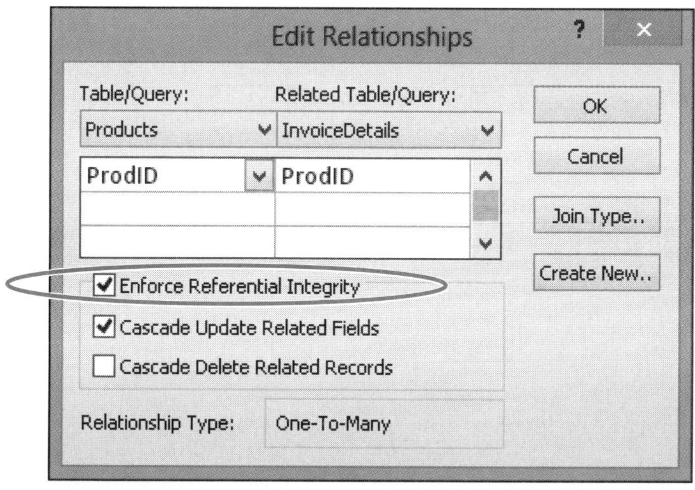

Identifying the Query Grid Update Row

Append, update, crosstab, and delete queries all add a query-specific row to the query grid. The update query places an Update To row in the query grid so that you tell Access how to update the desired field(s). In most cases, this will be changing one value to another by substitution, mathematical operation, formula, or comparison.

DEVELOP YOUR SKILLS AC08-D08

Create an Update Query

In this exercise, you will create an update action query that increases the prices of all items in the Products table by 10 percent.

1. Choose **Create→Queries→Query Design**, add the **Products** table to the query, and close the **Show Table** dialog box.
2. Double-click each field in the field list to add them to the query grid.
3. Follow these steps to create an update action query to increase prices by 10 percent:

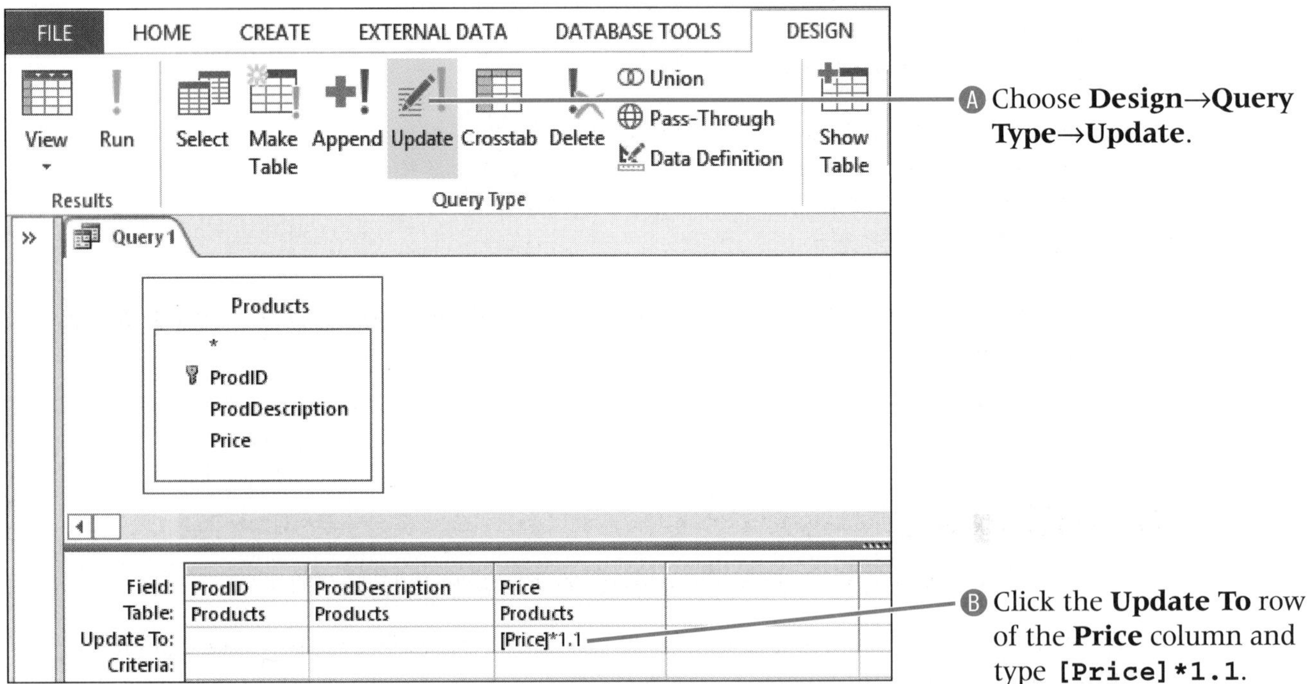

You must *type the brackets or select Price from the drop-down menu that appears when you type a P as you start to type Price.*

If you type "Price" without brackets, Access will not recognize it as a field, which means the query will base the calculation on something other than a value and wipe out all existing prices.

4. **Run** [Run] the query to update the values in the Products table.

   Access displays a warning message that you are about to update 11 row(s) and will not be able to reverse the action.

5. Choose **Yes** to run the query and then close the query, naming it `UpdatePricing Query`.

Don't run this query again, or you will increase prices by another 10 percent.

Verify the Data Update

6. Display the **Products** table in **Datasheet View**.

Products

ProdID	Description	Price
01HP	Home Page, Nav, CSS, Design	$440.00
02SP	Secondary Page	$220.00
03BL	Blog, Integrated into Site	$330.00
04SC	Shopping Cart, Basic	$440.00
05IM	Image, Custom Designed	$44.00
06HR	Hourly Rate for Modifications	$88.00
07LC	Logo Creation	$110.00
08PS	Photo Shoot, 1 hour onsite	$110.00
09IM	Image Map	$44.00
10SS	Slide Show	$110.00
11QR	QR Code	$55.00

The original price for a homepage with navigation and CSS design was $400. It is now $440—a 10 percent increase.

7. Close the **Products** table.

Creating a Delete Query

Video Library http://labyrinthelab.com/videos Video Number: AC13-V0810

A delete query is an action query that deletes a group of records from one or more tables. For example, you could create a delete query to remove records for a discontinued line of products or to delete records you have appended to another table to prevent inadvertently running an append query multiple times.

To ensure that corresponding records in related tables will all be deleted concurrently, check the Cascade Delete Related Records checkbox in the Edit Relationships window.

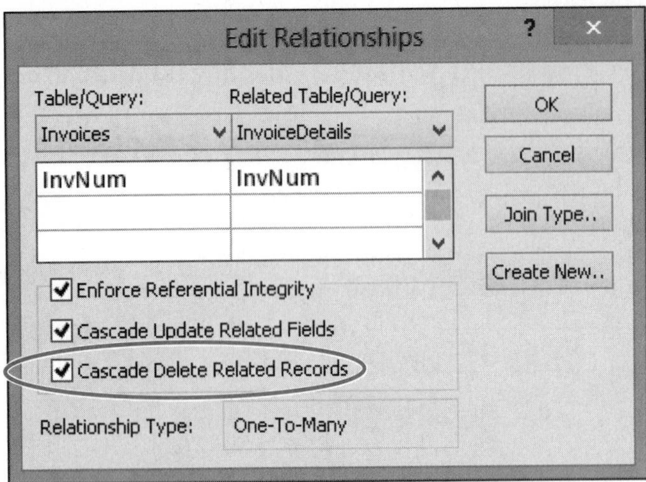

When you create a delete action query, Access replaces the Sort row of the query grid with the Delete row. You can set criteria for specific fields in a table to identify the conditions that must be met in order to delete records or set no criteria to remove all records from a table.

DEVELOP YOUR SKILLS AC08-D09

Create a Delete Query

Earlier you used a make table query to create a 2012Invoices table for older invoices. In this exercise, you will create a delete query to remove the 2012 invoices from the Invoices table.

1. Choose **Create→Queries→Query Design**.
2. Add the **Invoices** table to the query grid. Close the **Show Table** dialog box. Double-click the **InvDate** field to add it to the query grid.
3. Type `Between 1/1/2012 and 12/31/2012` in the **Criteria** row for the **InvDate** field.
4. Choose **Design→Query Type→** Delete to create a delete action query.
5. Save the query as `Delete 2012 Invoices`; run the query.
   Access warns that you are about to delete 19 records.
6. Choose **Yes** to remove all records meeting the 2012 criteria from the Invoices and InvoiceDetails tables.
   Because of cascading deletes in the relationship between the Invoices and InvoiceDetails tables, the 2012 records are deleted from both *tables.*

7. Open the **Invoices** table and the **InvoiceDetails** table to review the results.

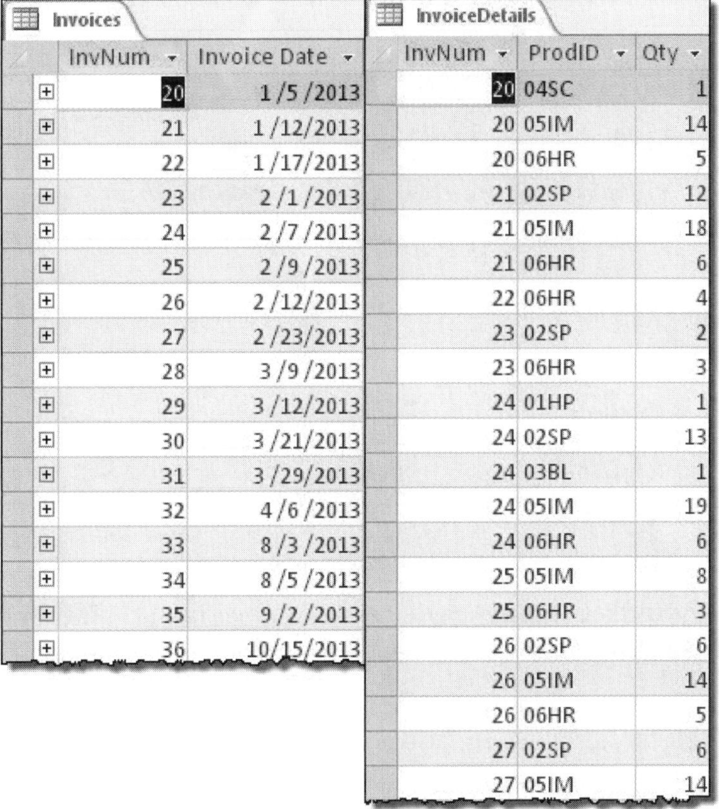

Invoices

InvNum	Invoice Date
20	1/5/2013
21	1/12/2013
22	1/17/2013
23	2/1/2013
24	2/7/2013
25	2/9/2013
26	2/12/2013
27	2/23/2013
28	3/9/2013
29	3/12/2013
30	3/21/2013
31	3/29/2013
32	4/6/2013
33	8/3/2013
34	8/5/2013
35	9/2/2013
36	10/15/2013

InvoiceDetails

InvNum	ProdID	Qty
20	04SC	1
20	05IM	14
20	06HR	5
21	02SP	12
21	05IM	18
21	06HR	6
22	06HR	4
23	02SP	2
23	06HR	3
24	01HP	1
24	02SP	13
24	03BL	1
24	05IM	19
24	06HR	6
25	05IM	8
25	06HR	3
26	02SP	6
26	05IM	14
26	06HR	5
27	02SP	6
27	05IM	14

All the invoices from 2012 have been deleted from the Invoices table and the corresponding records have also been removed from the InvoiceDetails table.

8. Close all open objects. Close the database and exit **Access**.

Concepts Review

To check your knowledge of the key concepts introduced in this lesson, complete the Concepts Review quiz by choosing the appropriate access option below.

If you are...	Then access the quiz by...
Using the Labyrinth Video Library	Going to http://labyrinthelab.com/videos
Using eLab	Logging in, choosing Content, and navigating to the Concepts Review quiz for this lesson
Not using the Labyrinth Video Library or eLab	Going to the student resource center for this book

Reinforce Your Skills

REINFORCE YOUR SKILLS AC08-R01

Create Queries with Calculations, a Report from a Query, and Parameter Queries

Kids for Change needs to refine the reports it generates. In this exercise, you will create a select query to calculate the cost of each activity based on staff salary and activity duration. You will also add a Totals row to generate the sum of staffed activities. Then, you will use a parameter query to return donor records by state.

Create a Select Query

1. Start **Access**. Open**AC08-R01-K4C** from the **AC2013 Lesson 08** folder and save it as `AC08-R01-K4C-[FirstInitialLastName]`.
2. Choose **Create→Queries→Query Design**.
3. Double-click the **PaidStaff** and **Activities** table names in the Show Table dialog box; then close the dialog box.
4. Double-click the **StaffLastName**, **StaffFirstName**, **StaffPhone**, and **HrlySal** fields in the **PaidStaff** table to add them to the query grid.
5. Add the **Activity** and **Hours** fields from the **Activities** table to the query grid.
6. Click in the Sort row of **StaffLastName** and choose **Ascending**.
7. **Save** the query as `ActivityCostQuery`.
8. Choose **Design→Results→Run**, returning 18 records.

Create Calculated and Concatenated Query Fields

9. Switch to **Design View**. Click in the **Field row** of the first available column after the **Hours** column.
10. Type `ActivityCost: HrlySal * Hours` in the Field row and tap Enter.
11. Double-click the right border of the column heading, if necessary, to see the entire calculation.
12. Right-click the new **ActivityCost** field and choose **Properties**.
13. Choose **Currency** for the **Format** property.
14. Click in the first available **Field row** after **ActivityCost**.
15. Type the following in the Field row then tap Enter: `ActStaffID: [StaffLastName] + Left([StaffFirstName],1)`

    The expression produces a concatenated ActStaffID field that consists of the staffer's last name and first initial.
16. Select the new concatenated **ID** field and drag it to the left of **StaffLastName** in the query grid.

    The new ActStaffID should now be the first field in the query grid.

17. Choose **Design→Results→Run** .

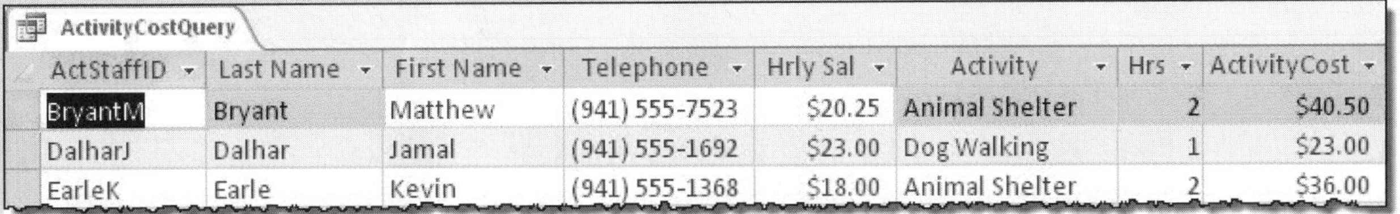

ActivityCostQuery

ActStaffID	Last Name	First Name	Telephone	Hrly Sal	Activity	Hrs	ActivityCost
BryantM	Bryant	Matthew	(941) 555-7523	$20.25	Animal Shelter	2	$40.50
DalharJ	Dalhar	Jamal	(941) 555-1692	$23.00	Dog Walking	1	$23.00
EarleK	Earle	Kevin	(941) 555-1368	$18.00	Animal Shelter	2	$36.00

The new concatenated ID field and the calculated ActivityCost field are displayed.

18. **Save** the ActivityCostQuery.

Add the Totals Row to a Query

19. Choose **Home→Records→Totals**.
20. Click the menu button in the Total row for the **Last Name** field and choose **Count**.
21. Click the menu button in the Total row for the **ActivityCost** field and choose **Sum**.

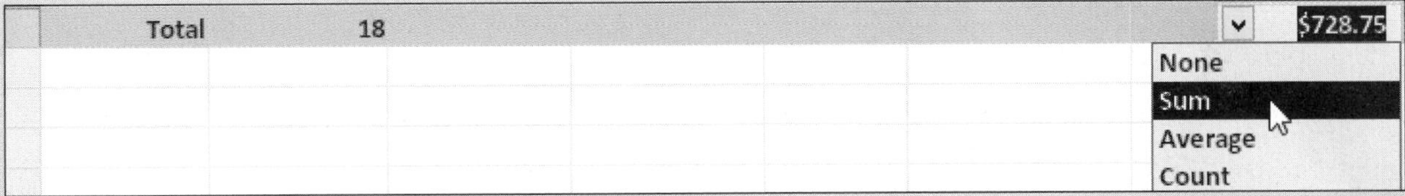

22. Save and close the **ActivityCostQuery**.

Create a Report Using a Query As Record Source

23. Choose **Create→Reports→Report Wizard** .
24. Choose **Query: ActivityCostQuery** from the **Tables/Queries** drop-down menu.
25. Add **StaffLastName**, **StaffFirstName**, **HrlySal**, **Activity**, **Hours**, and **ActivityCost** to the Selected Fields list; click **Next**.
26. Choose to group by **Activity**; click **Next**.
27. Click **Summary Options**.
28. Choose the **Sum** option for **ActivityCost**.

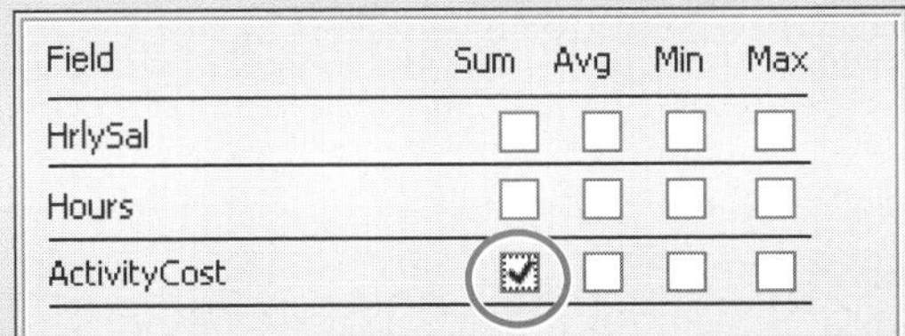

29. Click **OK** to close the window. Click **Next**.
30. Choose the **Outline** layout and click **Next** to keep the Portrait orientation.
31. Name the report `Activity Cost Report` and click **Finish**.
32. Click Close Print Preview. Then close the **Activity Cost Report**.

Modify a Query to Request a Parameter Value to Select Records

33. Right-click the **Donations Query** in the Navigation Pane and choose **Open**.
    All the donation records are returned.
34. Switch to **Design View**.
35. Type `[Enter State Abbr:]` in the **Criteria** row of the State field in the query grid, and tap [Enter].
    Be sure to include the square brackets.
36. Choose **Design→Results→Run** Run.
    A window opens displaying the criteria you entered.
37. Type `MA` (Massachusetts) for the State Abbr. and click **OK**.
38. Save and close the **Donations Query**. Close the database. Exit **Access**.
39. Submit your final file based on the guidelines provided by your instructor.
    To see examples of how your final file or files should look at the end of this exercise, go to the student resource center.

REINFORCE YOUR SKILLS AC08-R02

Create Action Queries

Kids for Change needs to fine-tune its database with several action queries. In this exercise, you will create a make table query that produces a table to store older donations, a query that appends new records to the Children table, an update query that reduces the duration of each activity by half, and a query that deletes old donations from the Donations table.

Create a Make Table Query

1. Start **Access**. Open **AC08-R02-K4C** from the **AC2013 Lesson 08** folder and save it as `AC08-R02-K4C-[FirstInitialLastName]`.
2. Right-click **Donations Query** in the Navigation Pane and choose **Copy**.
3. Right-click **Donations Query** again and choose **Paste**.
4. Name the new query `MakeTable2012` and click **OK**.
5. Right-click the **MakeTable2012**query in the Navigation Pane and choose **Open**.
   Every 2012 donation record copied from the existing query is displayed in the new query.
6. Switch to **Design View**.
7. Scroll to the right to the **DonationDate** field and type `Between 1/1/2012 and 12/31/2012` in the **Criteria** row.
8. Choose **Design→Query Type→Make Table**.
9. Type `2012Donations` as the **Table Name** and leave **Current Database** selected.
10. Click **OK**.
11. Save and run the query.
    Access warns that you are about to paste four records into a new table.

12. Choose **Yes** to continue.
    Access adds the table to the list of tables in the Navigation Pane.
13. Display the **2012Donations** table in **Datasheet View**.
14. Close the **MakeTable2012** query and the **2012Donations** table.

Create an Append Query

15. Open the **Children** table to view its records; close the table.
16. Choose **Create→Queries→Query Design** .
17. Add the **NewChildren** table to the query window. Close the Show Table dialog box.
18. Double-click the **asterisk (*)** in the NewChildren field list to add all the fields to the query grid.
19. Save the query as **`Append Children`**.
20. Choose **Design→Query Types→** Append.
21. Click the **Append To Table Name** menu button and choose **Children**.
22. Leave the Current Database option selected and click **OK**.
    Access adds the Append To row to the query grid and places the destination table name in the row.
23. Choose **Design→Results→Run** Run.
    Access warns that you are about to append 10 rows to another table.
24. Choose **Yes**.

You can only see the changes after you open the destination table to which the records were appended. *Do not run the query again!*

25. Close the **Append Children** query, saving changes if prompted.
26. Open the **Children** table in **Datasheet View** to verify that the records were appended.
    The Children table should contain 27 children.
27. Close the **Children** table.

Create an Update Query

28. Display the **Activities** table in **Datasheet View** to see the current Hrs values.
    Current activities are from two to four hours.
29. Close the **Activities** table.
30. Choose **Create→Queries→Query Design** .
31. Add the **Activities** table and close the **Show Table** dialog box.
32. Double-click the **Hours** field name in the **Activities** field list.
33. Choose **Design→Query Type→** Update.
    Access adds the Update row to the query grid.

34. Type **`[Hours] /2`** in the Update To row under **Hours** in the query grid.

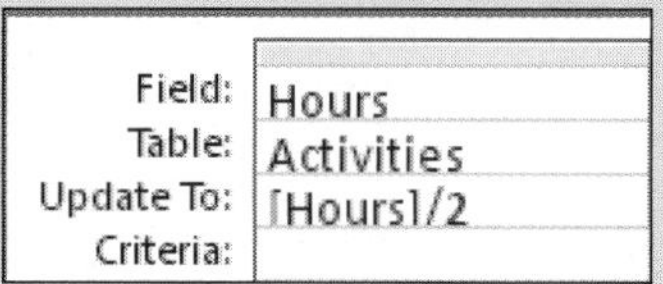

Field:	Hours
Table:	Activities
Update To:	[Hours]/2
Criteria:	

This calculation will divide the current activity Hours value in half. Be sure to include square brackets around the Hours field name.

35. Save the query as **`UpdateHours`**.
36. Choose **Design→Results→Run**.
    Access warns that you are about to update 25 rows.
37. Choose **Yes** to continue.

Do not run the query again.

38. Save and close the **Update Hours** query.
39. Display the **Activities** table in **Datasheet View** to see the new Hours values.
    Because of the change to the Hours values, the End Time values are no longer correct. Change the End Time values, as desired, to reflect the difference in Hours.
40. Close the **Activities** table.

Create a Delete Query

41. Choose **Create→Queries→Query Design**.
42. Add the **Donations** table to the query. Close the **Show Table** dialog box.
43. Double-click the **DonationDate** field to add it to the query grid.
44. Type **`Between 1/1/2012 and 12/31/2012`** in the **Criteria** row for the **DonationDate** field and tap Enter.
45. Choose **Design→Query Type→Delete**.
46. Save the query as **`Delete2012Donations`** and then run it.
    Access warns that you are about to delete four rows from the specified table.

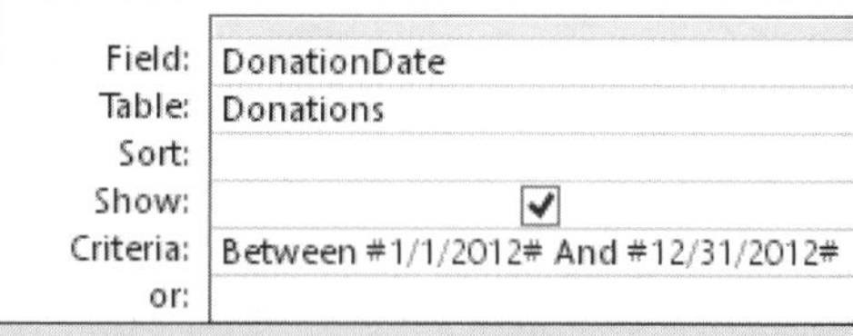

Field:	DonationDate
Table:	Donations
Sort:	
Show:	✓
Criteria:	Between #1/1/2012# And #12/31/2012#
or:	

47. Choose **Yes** to remove all donations records meeting the 2012 criteria from the **Donations** table.
48. Close the **Delete2012Donations** query.
49. Open the **Donations** table to review the results.
    The 2012 records are no longer in the Donations table.
50. Close all open objects and close the database. Exit **Access**.
51. Submit your final file based on the guidelines provided by your instructor.
    To see examples of how your final file or files should look at the end of this exercise, go to the student resource center.

REINFORCE YOUR SKILLS AC08-R03

Create a Select Query, Report from a Query, Query Calculations, and Action Queries

Kids for Change needs several new queries. In this exercise, you will create a select query that counts donations and calculate the sum of all donations. You will also create a report from a query and change an existing select query to a parameter query. You will then create a make table query to append new records to a table, and an update query to reflect pay increases.

Create a Select Query

1. Start **Access**. Open**AC08-R03-K4C** from the **AC2013 Lesson 08** folder and save it as `AC08-R03-K4C-[FirstInitialLastName]`.
2. Choose **Create→Queries→Query Design**.
3. Double-click the **Donors** and **Donations** tables in the **Show Table** dialog box; then close the dialog box.
4. Double-click the **DonationType** field in the **Donations** field list to add it to the query grid.
5. Choose **Ascending** from the drop-down menu in the **Sort** row.
6. Add the **DonorLName** and **DonorFName** fields from **Donors** to the query grid.
7. Add the **DonationDate** and **Amount** fields from **Donations** to the query grid.
8. Save the query as `DonorsType`.
9. Choose **Design→Results→Run**.
   The records are in alphabetical order by type, then name.

Create a Concatenated Query Field

10. Switch to **Design View**.
11. Click in the first available **Field row** after **Amount** and type the following, then tap Enter:
   `DonorType:[DonationType]+[DonorLName]+Left([DonorFName],1)`
   This expression will produce a new DonorType field that consists of donation type, donor's last name, and donor's first initial.
12. Choose **Design→Results→Run**.
   The new concatenated ID field is displayed.
13. Save the **DonorsType** query.

Add the Totals Row to a Query

14. Scroll down to the last few records in the datasheet.
15. Choose **Home→Records→Totals**.
16. Click the menu button in the Total row for the **Last Name** field and choose **Count**.

Access 2013

17. Click the menu button in the Total row for **Amount** and choose **Sum**.

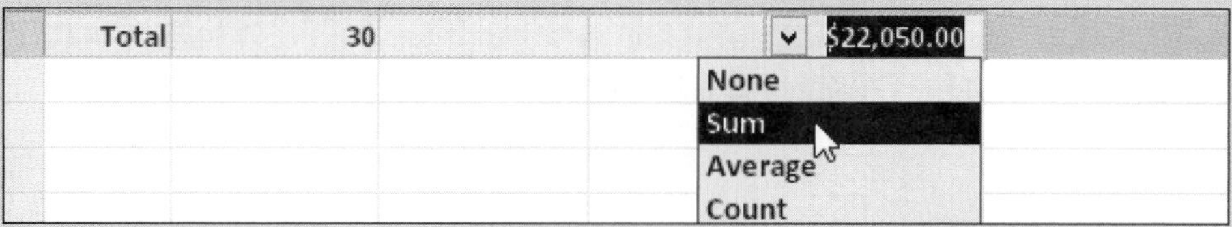

18. Save the **DonorsType** query.

Create a Report Using a Query As Record Source

19. Choose **Create→Reports→Report Wizard**.
20. Choose **Query: DonorsType** from the **Tables/Queries** drop-down menu.
21. Add all the fields to the Selected Fields list; click **Next**.
22. Group by **DonationDate**; click **Next**.
23. Click **Summary Options**.
24. Choose the **Sum** option for **Amount**.

25. Click **OK** to close the Summary Options window; click **Next**.
26. Choose the **Block** layout and **Portrait** orientation; click **Next**.
27. Name the report `DonorsType Report` and click **Finish**.
    The report opens in Print Preview.
28. Click Close Print Preview.
29. Switch to **Layout View**; resize and move the controls so all values are visible.
30. Switch to **Print Preview**.
31. Click Close Print Preview then save and close the **DonorsType Report**.

Modify a Query to Request a Parameter Value to Select Records

32. Right-click the **DonorsType** query in the Navigation Pane and choose **Design View**.
33. Type `[Enter Donor Type (Bus or Pvt):]` in the **Criteria** row of the **DonationType** field in the query grid and tap Enter.
    Be sure to include the brackets.
34. Save and close the **DonorsType** query.
35. Right-click the **DonorsType Report** in the Navigation Pane and choose **Print Preview**.
    An Enter Parameter Value dialog box opens displaying the criteria you entered.

36. Type **Bus** for the Donor Type, and click **OK**.

The Donors Type Report includes only records for donors with a Type of Bus *(or business).*

37. Save and close the **DonorsType Report**.

Create a Make Table Query

38. Run the **Children List** query to see the records of all 27 children.
39. Switch to **Design View**.
40. Scroll to the right to the **BirthDate** field and type **<1/1/2002** in the **Criteria** row.
41. Choose **Design→Query Type→** Make Table.
42. Type **OlderChildren** in the **Table Name** text box, leave the Current Database option chosen, and click **OK**.
43. Run the query.

Access warns that you are about to paste three records into a new table.

44. Choose **Yes** to continue.

Access creates the table and adds it to the Navigation Pane.

45. Display the **OlderChildren** table in **Datasheet View**.

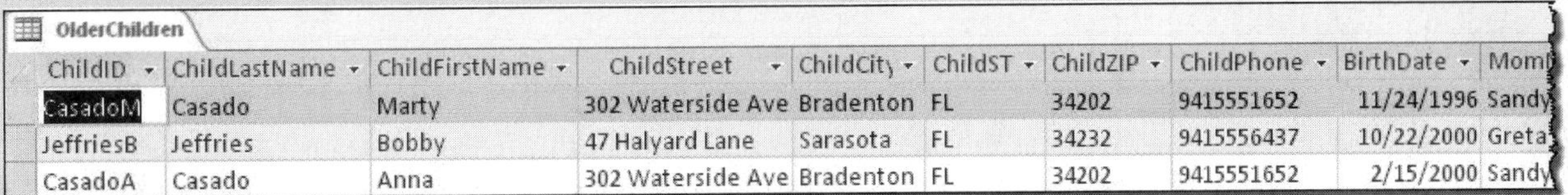
OlderChildren

ChildID	ChildLastName	ChildFirstName	ChildStreet	ChildCity	ChildST	ChildZIP	ChildPhone	BirthDate	Mom
CasadoM	Casado	Marty	302 Waterside Ave	Bradenton	FL	34202	9415551652	11/24/1996	Sandy
JeffriesB	Jeffries	Bobby	47 Halyard Lane	Sarasota	FL	34232	9415556437	10/22/2000	Greta
CasadoA	Casado	Anna	302 Waterside Ave	Bradenton	FL	34202	9415551652	2/15/2000	Sandy

The datasheet lists the three records for the children born before January 1, 2002.

46. Save the query as **OlderChildren Query**; then close the query and the **OlderChildren** table.

Create an Append Query

47. Display the **Volunteers** table in **Datasheet View** to see the records of all nine volunteers; then close the table.
48. Choose **Create→Queries→Query Design**.
49. Add the **NewVolunteers** table to the query window. Close the Show Table dialog box.
50. Double-click the **asterisk (*)** in the **NewVolunteers** field list to add all the fields to the query grid.
51. Save the query as **Append Volunteers**.
52. Choose **Design→Query Types→** Append.
53. Click the **Table Name** drop-down menu arrow and choose **Volunteers**.

54. Leave the Current Database option and click **OK**.

    Access adds the Append To row to the query grid and places the destination table name in the row.

55. Choose **Design→Results→Run**.

    Access warns that you are about to append six rows to another table.

56. Choose **Yes** to proceed.

You will only see the changes after you open the destination table to which the records were appended. *Do not run the query again!*

57. Close the **Append Volunteers** query, saving changes if prompted.

58. Display the **Volunteers** table in **Datasheet View** to see the appended records.

    The datasheet includes new volunteers 10 through 15.

59. Close the **Volunteers** table.

Create an Update Query

60. Display the **PaidStaff** table in **Datasheet View** to see the current HrlySal amounts.

61. Close the **PaidStaff** table.

62. Choose **Create→Queries→Query Design**.

63. Double-click the **PaidStaff** table in the Show Table dialog box. Close the dialog box.

64. Double-click the **HrlySal** field name in the field list to add it to the query grid.

65. Choose **Design→Query Type→** Update to change the query to an update action query.

66. Type `[HrlySal]*1.05` in the **Update To** row of the **HrlySal** field.

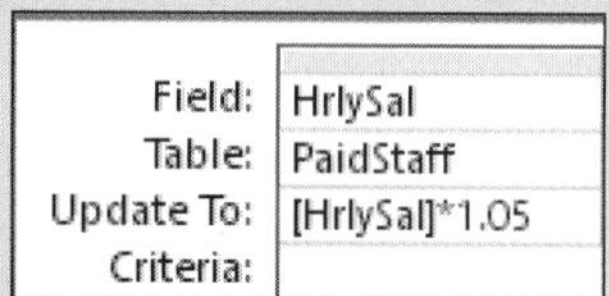

Include the brackets around the HrlySal field name.

67. Choose **Design→Results→Run**.

    Access warns that you are about to update 18 row(s).

68. Choose **Yes** to continue.

69. Close the query, naming it `UpdatePay`.

70. Display the **PaidStaff** table in Datasheet View.

    The HrlySal amounts for paid K4C staffers are increased by 5%.

Hrly Sal
$21.26
$18.90
$18.64
$17.33
$22.05
$19.43
$18.38

71. Save and close the **PaidStaff** table.

Create a Delete Query

72. Choose **Create→Queries→Query Design**.

73. Add the **Children** table to the query and close the Show Table dialog box.

74. Double-click the **BirthDate** field to add it to the query grid.
75. Choose **Design→Query Type→** Delete to create a delete action query.
76. Type `<1/1/2002` in the **Criteria** row for the **BirthDate** field and tap [Enter].

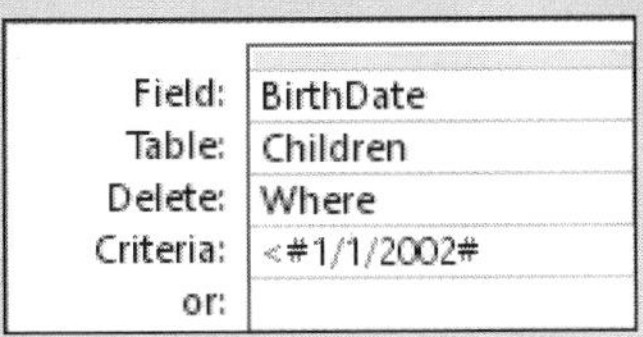

77. Save the query as `DeleteOlderKids` and then run it.
78. Choose **Yes** to remove the three Children records that meet the date criteria.
79. Close the **DeleteOlderKids** query.
80. Open the **Children** table to verify that the older children Marty Casado, Anna Casado, and Bobby Jeffries are no longer in the table.
    The records of these three older children are now stored in the OlderChildren table that you created when you ran the make table query earlier in this exercise.
81. Close all open objects then close the database. Exit **Access**.
82. Submit your final file based on the guidelines provided by your instructor.

Apply Your Skills

APPLY YOUR SKILLS AC08-A01

Create and Work with Queries

Universal Corporate Events, Ltd. is embarking on its second year under new leadership and wants to optimize data retrieval. In this exercise, you will use a select query to create a new concatenated ID field, add a Total row to count events and generate sums for revenue, taxes, and net revenue. Finally, you will create a parameter query that looks up personnel by city.

Create a Query with a Concatenated Field

1. Start **Access**. Open **AC08-A01-UCE** from the **AC2013 Lesson 08** folder and save it as `AC08-A01-UCE-[FirstInitialLastName]`.
2. Choose **Create→Queries→Query Design**.
3. Add the **Venues** and **VenueLiaisons** tables to the query. Close the Show Table dialog box.
4. Add the **LiaisonLName**, **LiaisonFName**, **LiaisonPhone**, and **LiaisonEmail** fields in the **VenueLiaisons** table to the query grid.
5. Add the **VenueName** field from the **Venues** table to the query grid.
6. Save the query as `VenueLiaisonID Query` and run it.
7. Switch to **Design View**.
8. Type `VenLiaID: [VenueID] + [LiaisonLName]` in the first available Field row after **VenueName** and tap Enter.
9. Select the new concatenated **VenLiaID** field and drag it to the left of **LiaisonLName** so that it is now the first field in the query grid.
10. Save and run the query.
    The query results datasheet shows a new VenLiaID field that concatenates the VenueID and Liaison Last Name so that event organizers know who to contact regarding each venue.
11. Close the **VenueLiaisonID Query**.

Add the Totals Row to a Query

12. Open the **Event Revenue** query and scroll down to the last few records.
13. Choose **Home→Records→Totals**.
14. Choose **Count** from the list of functions in the Total row for the **Liaison** field.
15. Choose **Sum** for the **TotRevenue**, **Taxes**, and **NetRevenue** fields.
    The Total row should display a Count of 42 for the number of staffed activities, Tot Revenue of $184,235.00, Taxes of $18,423.50, and Net Revenue of $165,811.50.
16. Save and close the **Event Revenue** query.

Modify a Query to Request a Parameter Value to Select Records

17. Choose **Create→Queries→Query Design**.
18. Add the **Personnel** table to the query and close the Show Table dialog box.
19. Add these fields to the query grid: **PerLastName**, **PerFirstName**, **PerAddr**, **PerCity**, **PerPhone**, and **PerEmail**.
20. Type `[Enter City:]` in the **Criteria** row of the **PerCity** field in the query grid.
    Be sure to include the brackets.
21. Run the query.
22. Type `Sarasota` in the **Enter Parameter Value** dialog box, and click **OK**.
    The query results displaying five Personnel records with a City value of Sarasota.
23. Save the query as `CitySelect Query`.
24. Close all open objects and close the database. Exit **Access**.
25. Submit your final file based on the guidelines provided by your instructor.
    To see examples of how your final file or files should look at the end of this exercise, go to the student resource center.

APPLY YOUR SKILLS AC08-A02

Create Action Queries

Universal Corporate Events, Ltd. needs several action queries in its database to handle specific situations. In this exercise, you will create a make table query to store older events, a query to append new records to the Schedules table, and an update query that changes personnel salary. Finally, you will create query to delete older events from the main Schedules table.

Access 2013

Create Make Table and Append Queries

1. Start **Access**. Open **AC08-A02-UCE** from the **AC2013 Lesson 08** folder and save it as `AC08-A02-UCE-[FirstInitialLastName]`.
2. Click the **Schedules Query** in the Navigation Pane and press Ctrl+C; then press Ctrl+V to create a copy of the Schedules Query.
3. Name the new query `MakeTable Old Events`.
4. Display the query in **Design View**.
5. In the Criteria row of the **EventDate** field, type `<01/01/2014`.
6. Choose **Design→Query Type→Make Table**.
7. Name the table `OlderEvents` and click **OK**.
8. Save and run the **MakeTable Old Events** query.
9. Choose **Yes** to paste the six rows and close the query.
10. Display the **OlderEvents** table in **Datasheet View**.
    The datasheet includes only records of events scheduled before 2014.

11. Close the **OlderEvents** table.
12. Open **AC08-A02-UCE-Append** from the **AC2013 Lesson 08** folder and save it as **`AC08-A02-UCE-Append-[FirstInitialLastName]`**.
13. Display the **NewSchedules** table in **Datasheet View** to see the new records; close the table.
14. Choose **Create→Queries→Query Design**.
15. Add the **NewSchedules** table to the query window. Close the Show Table dialog box.
16. Double-click the **asterisk (*)** in the **NewSchedules** field list to add all the fields to the query grid.
17. Save the query as **`Append Schedules`**.
18. Choose **Design→Query Types→Append**.
19. Choose the **Another Database** option and click **Browse**.
20. Navigate to your **AC2013 Lesson 08** folder and double-click **AC08-A02-UCE-[FirstInitialLastName]**.
21. Choose **Schedules** for the **Table Name**.
22. Click **OK**.
    Access adds the Append To row to the query grid and places the destination table name in the row.
23. Run the query, choosing **Yes** when warned that you are about to append 30 rows.
24. Close the **Append Schedules** query, saving changes if prompted.
25. Close **AC08-A02-UCE-Append-[FirstInitialLastName]**. Return to **AC08-A02-UCE-[FirstInitialLastName]**.
26. Display the **Schedules** table in **Datasheet View** to these the appended records.
    The main Schedules table should now contain 72 records.
27. Close the **Schedules** table.

Create Update and Delete Queries

28. Display the **SalaryGrades** table in **Datasheet View** to see the current salaries; then close the table.
29. Choose **Create→Queries→Query Design**.
30. Add the **SalaryGrades** table and close the **Show Table** dialog box.
31. Double-click the **SalaryAmt** field name to add it to the query grid.
32. Choose **Design→Query Type→Update**.
    Access adds the Update row to the query grid.
33. Type **`[SalaryAmt]*.9`** in the **Update To** row.
    This calculation will result in a 10% reduction—leaving all of the salaried personnel who have agreed to a 10% salary reduction for the next year with 90% of their former salary.
34. Save the query as **`Update Salaries`**.

35. Run the query clicking **Yes** when warned that you are about to update 21 rows.
36. Save and close the **Update Salaries** query.
37. Display the **SalaryGrades** table in **Datasheet View** to see the new values.

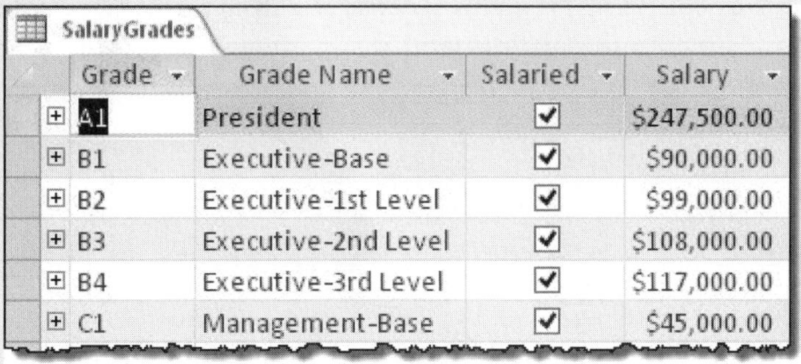
SalaryGrades

Grade	Grade Name	Salaried	Salary
A1	President	☑	$247,500.00
B1	Executive-Base	☑	$90,000.00
B2	Executive-1st Level	☑	$99,000.00
B3	Executive-2nd Level	☑	$108,000.00
B4	Executive-3rd Level	☑	$117,000.00
C1	Management-Base	☑	$45,000.00

38. Close the **SalaryGrades** table.
39. Choose **Create→Queries→Query Design**.
40. Add the **Schedules** table to the query and close the Show Table dialog box.
41. Double-click the **EventDate** field to add it to the query grid.
42. Type `<1/1/2014` in the **Criteria** row for **EventDate** and tap Enter.
43. Choose **Design→Query Type→Delete**.
44. Save the query as `Delete Old Events` and then run it, choosing **Yes** when Access warns that you are about to delete six rows from the specified table.
45. Close the **Delete Old Events** query.
46. Open the **Schedules** table.
47. Right-click the **Event Date** column heading and choose **Sort Oldest to Newest** to verify that only 2014 records are left in the table.
48. Save and close the **Schedules** table, and close the database. Exit **Access**.
49. Submit your final file based on the guidelines provided by your instructor.

    To see examples of how your final file or files should look at the end of this exercise, go to the student resource center.

APPLY YOUR SKILLS AC08-A03

Optimize Database Performance

Universal Corporate Events, Ltd must optimize database performance to fine-tune its operation. In this exercise, you will calculate weekly wages for hourly workers and assign new IDs based on job category, and then add a Totals row to count personnel and calculate wages. You will also create a report for a specific date range, and then create queries to: store hourly personnel records, append new records to another table, increase menu prices, and delete a closed venue.

Create Calculated and Concatenated Fields in a Query

1. Start **Access**. Open **AC08-A03-UCE** from the **AC2013 Lesson 08** folder and save it as `AC08-A03-UCE-[FirstInitialLastName]`.
2. Choose **Create→Queries→Query Design**.
3. Add the **Personnel** and **SalaryGrades** tables to the query window.
4. Add **PerLastName** and **PerFirstName** from the **Personnel** table.
5. Add **SalType**, **SalaryGradeName**, and **SalaryAmt** from the **SalaryGrades** table.
6. In the first available column after **SalaryAmt**, type `WrkWk: [HrlyWage]*40` in the Field row.
7. In the next column, type `SalaryID: [SalaryGrade]+[PerLastName]` in the Field row.
8. Save the query as `Personnel Wages` and run it.
9. Choose **Home→Records→Totals**.
10. In the **First Name** column, choose **Count** from the Total row list.
11. In the **WrkWk** columns, choose **Sum** from the Total row list.

	Blake	Serena	☐	Waitstaff-2nd Level		$240.00	E3Blake
	Tristan	Karen	☐	Waitstaff-2nd Level		$240.00	E3Tristan
	Adams	Chuck	☐	Bartender-Basic		$220.00	F1Adams
	Goldstein	Marv	☑	Event Organizer	$16,200.00		H1Goldstein
	Kenworthy	Sally Anne	☑	Event Organizer	$16,200.00		H1Kenworth
	Benson	Harold	☑	Event Organizer	$16,200.00		H1Benson
	Wright	Fran	☑	Event Organizer	$16,200.00		H1Wright
*			■				
	Total	20				1,720.00	

The datasheet displays the calculated 40-hour weekly wage for hourly workers, the concatenated ID comprised of each employee's salary grade and last name, the count of personnel, and the total of weekly wages for the hourly workers.

12. Save and close the **Personnel Wages** query.

Create a Report from a Parameter Query

13. Make a copy of the **Event Revenue** query and name it `Select Event Revenue`.
14. Open **Select Event Revenue** in **Design View**.
15. In the **EventDate** column in the query grid, type `Between [Enter Start Date] And [Enter End Date]` in the **Criteria** row.
16. Run the query.
17. Type `1/1/2014` for the **Enter Start Date** in the Enter Parameter Value box and click **OK**.
18. Type `6/30/2014` for the **Enter End Date** in the Enter Parameter Value box and click **OK**.
    The datasheet should return records from January through June 2014.
19. Save and close **Select Event Revenue**.
20. Start the Report Wizard, choose **Query: Select Event Revenue** and select all the fields except **LiaisonID**.
21. Group the report by **VenueID**; open the Summary Options box, and check the boxes to **Sum** TotalRev, TaxDue, and NetRev.
22. Choose the **Outline** layout and the **Landscape** orientation.
23. Name the report `Selected Events` and click **Finish**.
24. Type `6/1/2014` for **Enter Start Date** in the Enter Parameter Value box. Click **OK**.
25. Type `6/30/2014` for **Enter End Date** in the Enter Parameter Value box. Click **OK**.
    You may have to resize and move controls to better display the data.
26. Save and close the **Selected Events** report.

Create Make Table and Append Queries

27. Choose **Create→Queries→Query Design**, then add the **Personnel** and **SalaryGrades** tables to the query grid, and close the Show Table dialog box.
28. Add all the fields **(*)** from the **Personnel** table to the query grid.
29. Add the **SalType** field from the **SalaryGrade** table.
30. Clear the checkbox in the **Show** row of the **SalType** field.
31. Type `No` in the **Criteria** row of the **SalType** field.
    No *means that only records with an unchecked box (hourly employees) are selected.*
32. Choose **Design→Query Type→Make Table**.
33. Name the table `HourlyPersonnel` and click **OK**.
34. Save the query as `MakeTable Hourly` and run it.
35. Choose **Yes** to paste the eight rows.
36. Close the **MakeTable Hourly** query.
37. Display the **HourlyPersonnel** table in **Datasheet View**.
    The eight new records appear.

38. Close the **HourlyPersonnel** table.
39. Display the **NewMenus** table in Datasheet View to see the new records; close the table.
40. Choose **Create→Queries→Query Design**.
41. Add the **NewMenus** table to the query window and close the Show Table dialog box.
42. Double-click the **asterisk (*)** in the **NewMenus** field list to add all the fields to the query grid.
43. Save the query as **`Append Menus`**.
44. Choose **Design→Query Types→Append**.
45. Choose **Menus** for the **Table Name**.
46. Keep the **Current Database** option and click **OK**.
47. Run the query, choosing **Yes** to append seven rows.
48. Close the **Append Menus** query, saving changes if prompted.
49. Display the **Menus** table in **Datasheet View** to view the appended records.
    The Menus table now contains 26 records, including the new items added to their menu selection.
50. Close the **Menus** table.

Create Update and Delete Queries

51. Choose **Create→Queries→Query Design**.
52. Add the **Menus** table to the query window and close the Show Table dialog box.
53. Add the **ChgPP** field to the query grid.
54. Choose **Design→Query Type→Update**.
    Access places the Update To row in the query grid.
55. Type **`[ChgPP]*1.05`** in the Update To row of the ChgPP field.
56. Save the query as **`Update Prices`** and **run** it.
57. Choose **Yes** when Access warns to update the 26 rows.
58. Close the **Update Prices** query.
59. Display the **Menus** table in **Datasheet View** to see the 5 percent increase in menu prices.
60. Close the **Menus** table.
61. Choose **Create→Queries→Query Design**.
62. Add the **Schedules** table to the query grid and close the Show Table dialog box.
63. Add **VenueID** to the query grid.
64. Choose **Design→Query Type→Delete**.
    Access adds a Delete row to the query grid.
65. Type **`SaraYC`** in the **Criteria** row for VenueID.

66. Save the query as `Delete Venue` and then run it, choosing **Yes** to delete two rows from the specified table.

67. Close the **Delete Venue** query.

68. Open the **Schedules** table; right-click the **VenueID column heading** and choose **Sort Z to A** to verify that the **SarasotaYC** records are no longer in the table.

    The Sarasota Yachters' two scheduled events are no longer in the datasheet.

69. Save the **Schedules** table. Close all open objects and close the database. Exit **Access**.

70. Submit your final file based on the guidelines provided by your instructor.

Extend Your Skills

In the course of working through the Extend Your Skills exercises, you will think critically as you use the skills taught in the lesson to complete the assigned projects. To evaluate your mastery and completion of the exercises, your instructor may use a rubric, with which more points are allotted according to performance characteristics. (The more you do, the more you earn!) Ask your instructor how your work will be evaluated.

AC08-E01 That's the Way I See It

Blue Jean Landscaping needs to update the content of its database tables. Use the database you used in **AC07-E01**, or open **AC08-E01-BJL** and save your file to the **AC2013 Lesson 08** folder as **`AC08-E01-BJL-[FirstInitialLastName]`**.

First, concatenate CustIDfield and CustLastNamefield in the Customers table; name the field **`NewCustID`**. Add a calculated field to the Merch Sales Query that multiplies price by quantity sold. Add a Totals row and sum all sales. Next, create a report to request date range parameters using the Service Invoices Query as the record source with an InvDate date range of 10/15/2013–2/15/2014. Copy the Service Invoices Query and name it **`Service Invoices Query 2013`**. Select records with a 2013 InvoiceDate; name the new table **`ServiceInvoices2013`**. Finally, create an append query using **`NewMerchandise`** as the source and **`StoreMerchandise`** as the destination table for the new source table. Create an update query to increase prices in the StoreMerchandise table by 2% and a delete query to delete Service Invoices created in 2013.

You will be evaluated based on the inclusion of all elements, your ability to follow directions, your ability to apply newly learned skills to a real-world situation, your creativity, and your accuracy in creating objects and/or entering data. Submit your final file based on the guidelines provided by your instructor.

AC08-E02 Be Your Own Boss

Business has picked up at Blue Jean Landscaping and you must modify the database to ensure it is more efficient and can cope with unexpected situations. Open **AC08-E02-BJL** and save it to your **AC2013 Lesson 08** folder as **`AC08-E02-BJL-[FirstInitialLastName]`**.

First, in the MerchID field (StoreMerchandise table), concatenate the current ID and the Category field value. Count the number of items in the Store Inventory query to estimate whether you need a larger warehouse. Sum the Inventory Amt fields to find the total inventory value. Create a report that uses the Store Inventory query as the record source, and a parameter query to request a customer's last name to see their purchases. Copy the Merch Sales Query and name it **`Sales by Customer`**. Create a query to store 2013 sales records in a new table. Copy the Merch Sales Query and name it **`Merch Sales Query 2013`**. Modify the query to return records with a SalesDate from 2013. Name the new table **`MerchSales2013`**. Finally, create an append query to add all records in the NewCustomers to the Customers table, an update query to raise the AcreRate (Services table) by 5 percent, and a delete query to remove 2013 records from the MerchSales table.

You will be evaluated based on the inclusion of all elements, your ability to follow directions, your ability to apply newly learned skills to a real-world situation, your creativity, and your accuracy in creating objects and/or entering data. Submit your final file based on the guidelines provided by your instructor.

Transfer Your Skills

In the course of working through the Transfer Your Skills exercises, you will use critical-thinking and creativity skills to complete the assigned projects using skills taught in the lesson. To evaluate your mastery and completion of the exercises, your instructor may use a rubric, with which more points are allotted according to performance characteristics. (The more you do, the more you earn!) Ask your instructor how your work will be evaluated.

AC08-T01 Use the Web As a Learning Tool

Throughout this book, you will be provided with an opportunity to use the Internet as a learning tool by completing WebQuests. According to the original creators of WebQuests, as described on their website (WebQuest.org), a WebQuest is "an inquiry-oriented activity in which most or all of the information used by learners is drawn from the web." To complete the WebQuest projects in this book, navigate to the student resource center and choose the WebQuest for the lesson on which you are currently working. The subject of each WebQuest will be relevant to the material found in the lesson.

WebQuest Subject: Advanced Boolean expressions and their use in advanced queries

Submit your files based on the guidelines provided by your instructor.

AC08-T02 Demonstrate Proficiency

As owner of Stormy BBQ, you are in charge of refining the database at your Key West location, which first opened on November 15, 2013. Open **AC08-T02-SBQ** from the **AC2013 Lesson 08** folder and save it as **`AC08-T02-SBQ-[FirstInitialLastName]`**.

First, create a select query using the Staff table to return name and contact information for just those staffers who work at the Key West location (Store=5). Next, create a concatenated ID field in the MerchSales Query using the last five digits of the SKU and the Staffer Last Name fields to analyze staffer productivity, and sort the MerchSales Query by SKU to see which items were sold. Count the line items and total the opening day MerchSalesAmt fields. Use the Daily Receipts Query as the source for a report to print daily receipts. Sort the query by ItemID to analyze item sales. Copy the MerchSales Query to create two Parameter queries. Name one **`Sales by Sales ID`**, requesting SalesID; name the other **`Sales by SKU`**, requesting the SKU.

Tip: Use Merchandise Popup and MenuItems Popup to access SKU and ItemID.

Create a query to store 2013 merchandise sales records in a new table; then create a query to delete those records from the MerchSales table. Finally, create a query to add Cabinet City's products (see the NewMerchandise table in **AC08-T02-SBQ-Append** in your **AC2013 Lesson 08** folder) to the existing Merchandise table and create an update query to increase the menu item prices by 5%.

Submit your final file based on the guidelines provided by your instructor.

ACCESS 2013

9 Customizing Reports

LESSON OUTLINE

LEARNING OBJECTIVES

After studying this lesson, you will be able to:

- Import a report into a database
- Add a subreport to a main report
- Create a report from a subreport
- Create calculated controls on a subreport
- Set page breaks, customize controls, and analyze report performance

Database reports summarize the data contained in tables or displayed in query results and enable you to provide information in a page layout suitable for printing. Although forms and reports serve two different purposes within the context of a relational database, the techniques used to customize them are similar. By now, you have most likely created reports using both the Report Wizard and Design View and have customized elements of a report. In this lesson, you will import reports from other databases and use additional features to create custom reports.

CASE STUDY

Billing Customers

The company manager of Winchester Web Design, a small web page design company, wants you to improve its invoice report for customer billing. After reviewing invoices from several companies, the company manager has sketched out a design for the new invoice report layout. Your job is to create a sample of the new invoice report for company administrators.

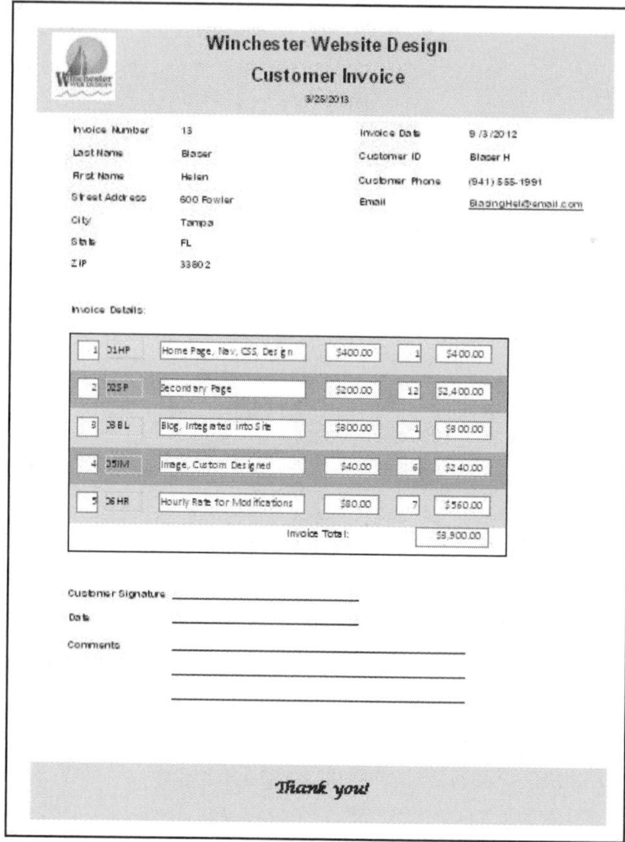

Winchester Website Design

Customer Invoice

3/25/2013

Invoice Number	13	Invoice Date	9/3/2012
Last Name	Blaser	Customer ID	Blaser H
First Name	Helen	Customer Phone	(941) 555-1991
Street Address	600 Fowler	Email	BlasingHel@email.com
City	Tampa		
State	FL		
ZIP	33802		

Invoice Details:

1	01HP	Home Page, Nav, CSS, Design	$400.00	1	$400.00
2	02SP	Secondary Page	$200.00	12	$2,400.00
3	03BL	Blog, Integrated into Site	$800.00	1	$800.00
4	05IM	Image, Custom Designed	$40.00	6	$240.00
5	06HR	Hourly Rate for Modifications	$80.00	7	$560.00
			Invoice Total:		$3,900.00

Customer Signature ________________

Date ________________

Comments ________________

Thank you!

Importing a Report into a Database

Video Library: http://labyrinthelab.com/videos Video Number: AC13-V0901

Access offers a variety of ways to create reports. In addition to using the Report Wizard or starting from scratch in Design View, you can also import reports from another database. Because most companies require some type of invoice to send with customer orders, locating a sample invoice report to import is not difficult.

Sometimes you have the report you want, but during design it may have become corrupted, either due to inadvertent changes to the report itself or changes to an underlying query. That's when backups are invaluable. If a report becomes corrupted, you can restore it by importing database objects from a backup copy of a database. The record source should already match and there should be no need to edit properties and field names.

Identifying Report Record Sources

Reports that you import retain two connections to their original database: the source database table or query name, shown in the Record Source property, and field names, which appear in report text boxes. As a result, when you import a report from another database, you often must establish new control sources to the destination database. You can accomplish this by:

- Editing the imported report's Record Source property to link to a table or query in the destination database.
- Editing, if necessary, the field names in the imported report's text boxes to match those shown in the new record source table or query.

Using Smart Tags

Many times, when Access identifies a conflict between an available data or control source and the one currently identified in the Record Source control, you will see smart tags attached to the fields affected. Smart tags indicate actions that may be taken if certain conditions are met or if a control has a problem. Clicking a smart tag will display a list of possible actions for that control, such as providing easy access to the correct Control Source property or Report Record Source property.

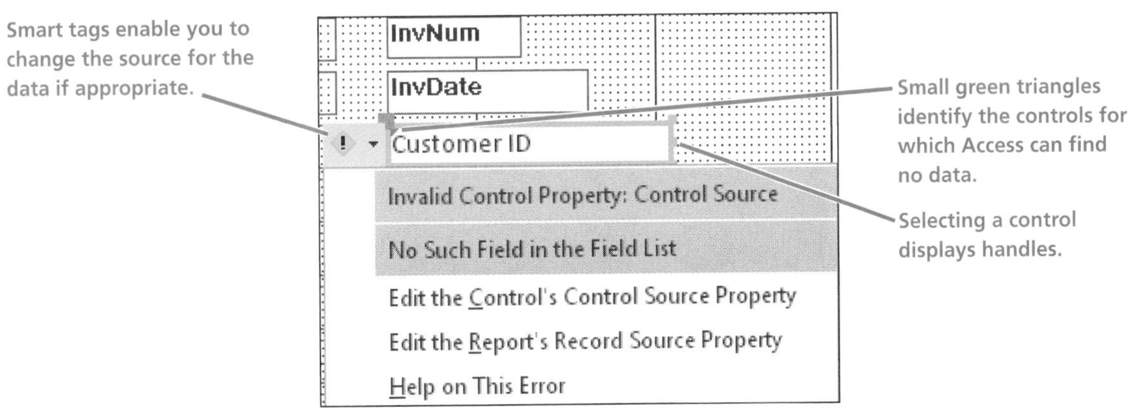

Access 2013

DEVELOP YOUR SKILLS AC09-D01

Import a Report and Edit the Record Source

In this exercise, you will import a report from a backup copy of a database. You will rename the report and view data from an existing table using the imported report.

1. Open **AC09-D01-WinWebDesign** from your **AC2013 Lesson 09** folder and save it as `AC09-D01-WinWebDesign-[FirstInitialLastName]`.

   Replace the bracketed text with your first initial and last name. For example, if your name is Bethany Smith, your filename would look like this: AC09-D01-WinWebDesign-BSmith.

2. Choose **External Data→Import & Link→**[Access].

   The Get External Data dialog box opens.

3. Click **Browse**, navigate to the **AC2013 Lesson 09** folder, and double-click **AC09-D01-WinWebDesign–Backup**.

   This database is a backup copy of the WinWebDesign database.

4. Choose **Import Tables, Queries, Forms, Reports, Macros, and Modules into the Current Database** and click **OK**.

   Access opens the Import Objects dialog box and displays object names contained in the backup database.

5. Follow these steps to select the report to import:

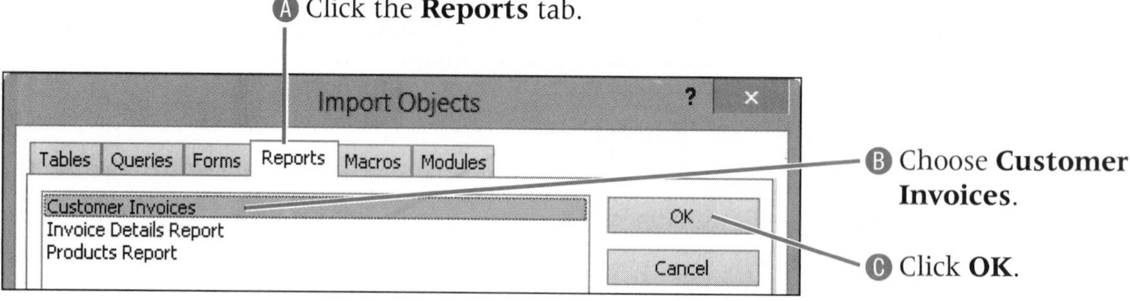

6. Leave the Save Import Steps checkbox unchecked and click **Close** in the Get External Data dialog box.

Rename and View the Report

7. From the Navigation Pane, right-click the imported **Customer Invoices** report and choose **Rename**.

8. Type `Customer Invoice Report` and tap [Enter].

9. Right-click **Customer Invoice Report** and choose **Print Preview**.

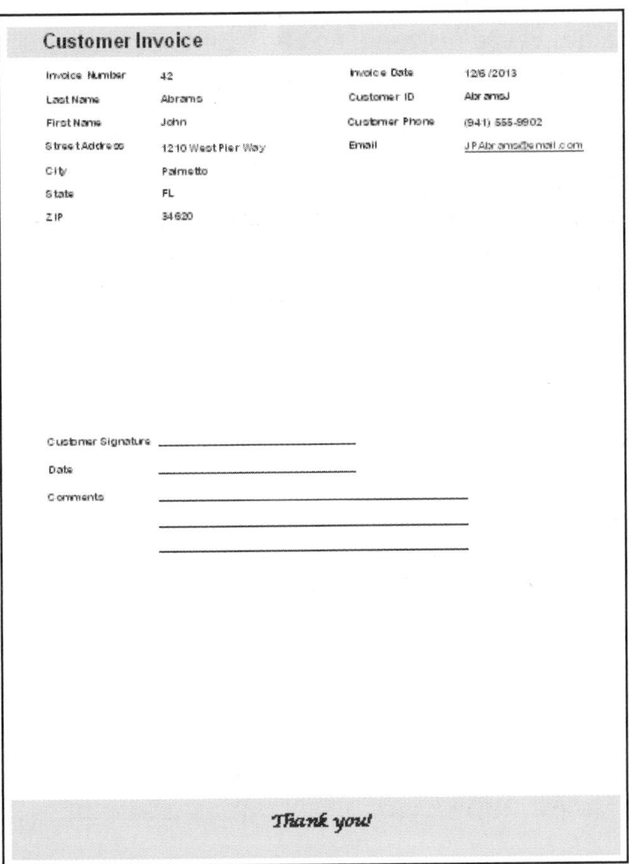

The empty area below the customer information is where you will insert the subform/subreport that includes the invoice detail lines.

10. Navigate through the pages.
11. Click Close Print Preview to close **Print Preview**.
    Unless directed otherwise, keep Access and any databases or database objects being used open at the end of each exercise.

Adding a Subreport to a Main Report

Video Library: http://labyrinthelab.com/videos Video Number: AC13-V0902

Subreports display subsets of data in reports and are derived from related database tables, similar to subforms on forms. However, a subreport can display table data by using a table, query, form, or another report as its source object. Because forms are frequently created before reports, and they may already display the desired data from multiple tables, using a subform to create a subreport streamlines report design and layout.

FROM THE RIBBON
Arrange→Table→Remove Layout to remove grouping

Creating a subreport from a quick form may present challenges. When you create a quick form from the Create tab on the Ribbon, Access ties—or groups—all controls in the Detail section as one object. Because of these ties, if you resize *one* text box in the Detail section, *all* text boxes are resized. If you want to modify or delete *individual* controls, you must first remove the ties, or grouping.

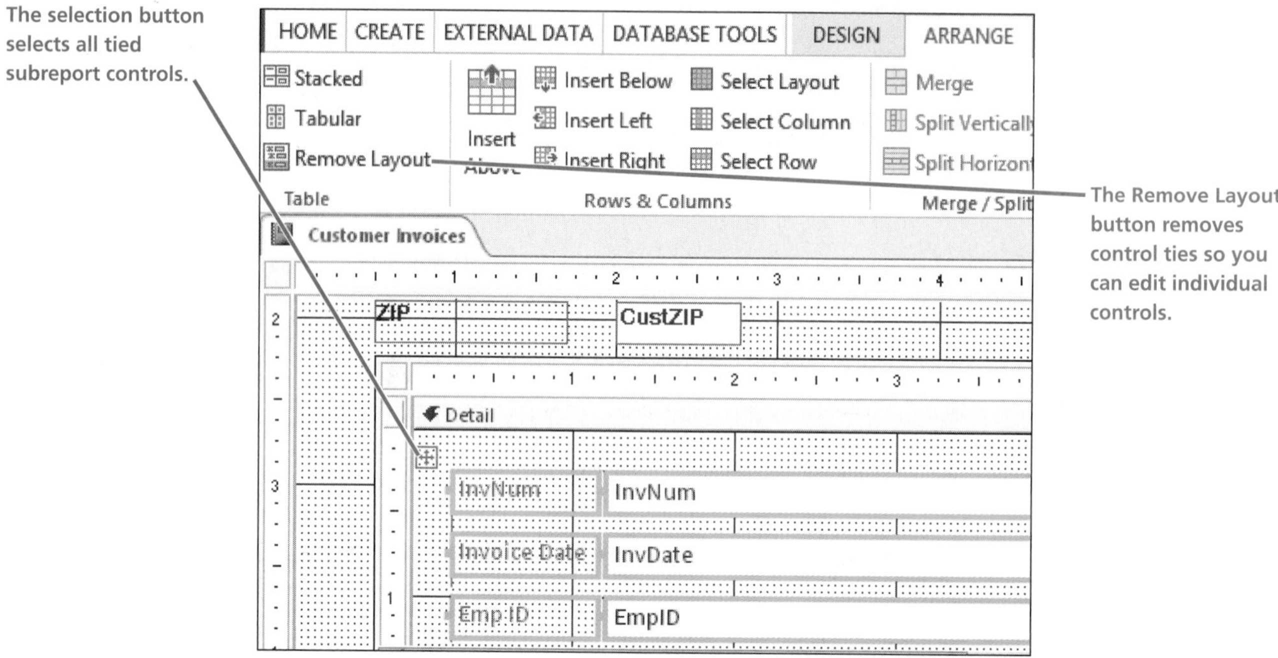

Examining Database Objects

Invoices normally display a list of all the items ordered or services performed, in addition to the customer name and address. There are several tables in the WinWebDesign database that contain the data required for the complete invoice—the Customers table, the Products table, and the Invoices and InvoiceDetails tables. Fields from all these tables appear in the Winchester Web Design Invoices Form—and the detail fields you want to add to the report appear in the InvoiceDetails subform. So if you use the existing InvoiceDetails subform for the subreport, creating the invoice report is easier and more efficient.

Winchester Web Design
Invoices

Invoice Number	1	InvDate	3 /15/2012
Customer ID	SmithW	Employee ID	JFW
Last Name	Smith	Emp Last Name	Winchester
First Name	William	Emp First Name	Jay
Street Address	879 Fifteenth Ave		
City	Tampa		
State	FL ZIP 34912		
Telephone	(941) 555-0793		
Email	SmithBilly@email.com		

ProdID	Description	Price	Qty	Line Total
01HP	Home Page, Nav, CSS, Design	$400.00	1	$400.00
02SP	Secondary Page	$200.00	6	$1,200.00
05IM	Image, Custom Designed	$40.00	11	$440.00

Record: 1 of 3 No Filter Search

The InvoiceDetails subform contains the data you want to include on the Customer Invoice Report.

Adding a Subreport

The procedures used to add a subreport to a report are basically the same as those used to add a subform to a form. You can create the subreport using the Report Wizard or add an unbound subreport control to the report. Then you identify the database object containing the fields you want to display as a subreport.

Access might warn you that the table, query, or form specified in the report does not exist in this database. This is more likely to occur with imported objects, but might be due to a typing error. You can fix this by modifying the Record Source property, importing the missing object, or correcting the typo.

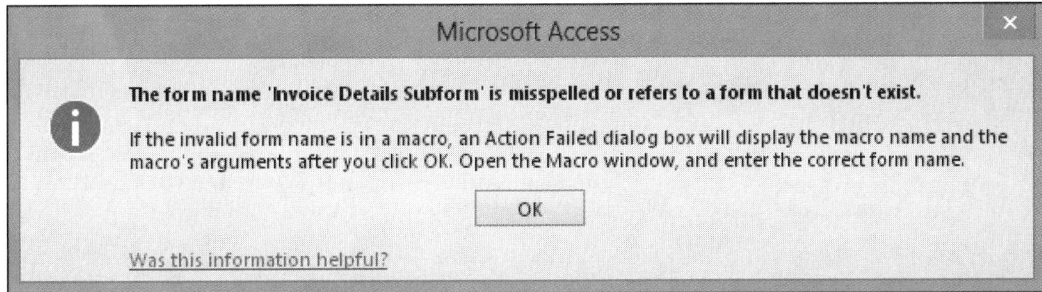

Error message warns that an object needed to run a report or form might be missing from the database.

To change the Record Source, click the smart tag list arrow and choose Edit the Report's Record Source Property.

DEVELOP YOUR SKILLS AC09-D02

Add a Subreport to a Report

In this exercise, you will add a subreport to the Customer Invoice Report. You will use the InvoiceDetails Subform as the source for the subreport.

1. Display the **Customer Invoice Report** in **Design View**.
2. Choose **Design→Controls→Subform/Subreport** .
3. Click and draw a subreport in the **Detail** section just below the **ZIP** label.
   Access opens the SubReport Wizard.

If the wizard doesn't launch, the Control Wizard was likely toggled off. Choose Design→ Controls and choose Use Control Wizards from the drop-down menu to toggle it back on.

4. Follow these steps to create the subreport control:

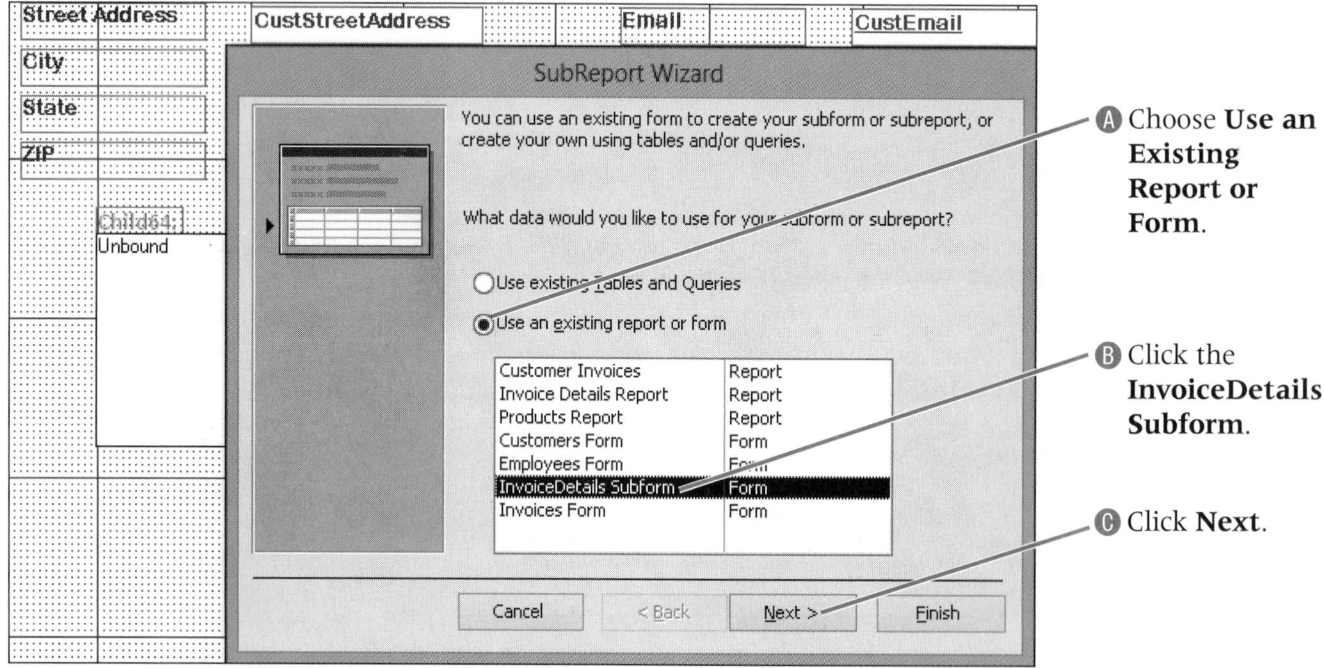

5. Click **Next** to accept the default links, keep the default name InvoiceDetails Subform, and click **Finish**.
6. Click the **Property Sheet Data** tab and ensure that **Form.InvoiceDetails Subform** is in the Source Object property box.

7. Click the **Property Sheet Format** tab and enter these property values:

Property	Value
Width	5.6"
Height	1.5"
Top	2.9"
Left	.5"
Border Color	Blue, Accent 5, Darker 50%

8. Select the subform label (**InvoiceDetails Subform**) and enter these property values:

Property	Value
Caption	Invoice Details:
Width	1.2"
Height	.25
Top	2.5
Left	.5
Font Name	Arial Rounded MT Bold
Font Size	10
Fore Color	Blue, Accent 5, Darker 50%

9. Click the **Report selector button** in the top-left corner of the report where the horizontal and vertical rulers meet to select the report.
10. Type `7.9"` for the **Width** property.
11. Switch to **Print Preview**.

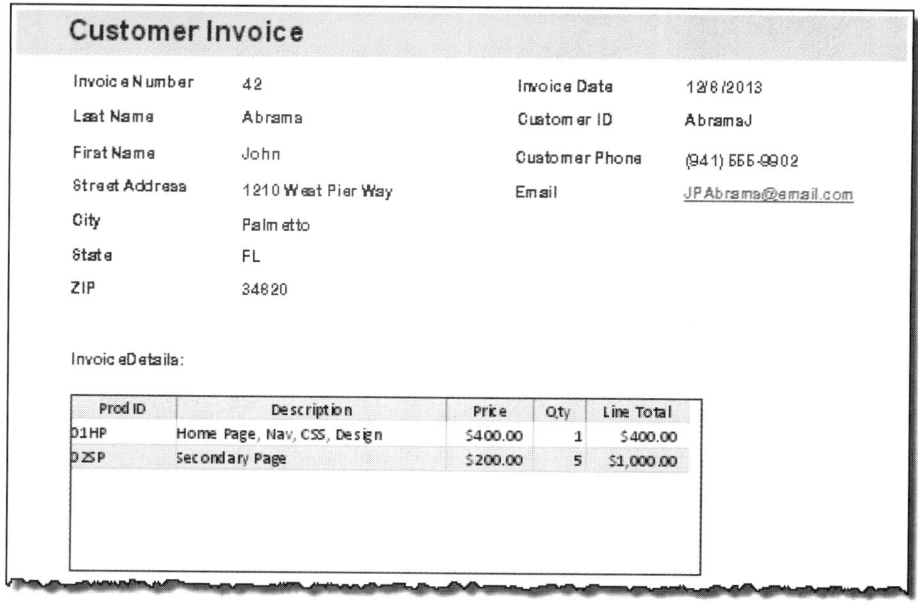

12. Click the navigation buttons at the bottom of the window to display several report invoices.
13. Click Close Print Preview.
14. **Save** the Customer Invoice Report.

Creating a Report from a Subreport

Video Library: http://labyrinthelab.com/videos Video Number: AC13-V0903

Using a subform as the record source for a subreport is convenient because the subform already includes all needed data. However, when a subreport uses a form as the record source, any changes made to the subreport layout are reflected in the source form. If you don't want the source form to be changed, you can save the subreport as a separate report in the database, change the main report's Record Source property to the new report object, and then edit the subreport.

Access allows you to save an existing form as a new form, and an existing report as a new report. When a subform is used as the record source for a subreport, you can open the subreport in a separate window and save it as a separate report.

QUICK REFERENCE	SAVING A SUBREPORT AS A REPORT
Task	**Procedure**
Open a subreport in a separate window	■ Right-click the subreport on the report in Design View. ■ Choose Subreport in New Window.
Save a subreport as a new report	■ Open the subreport in a new window. ■ Choose File→Save Object As. ■ Type the name of the new report, select Report from the Save Object As list, and click OK.

DEVELOP YOUR SKILLS AC09-D03

Create a New Report Using a Subreport

In this exercise, you will create and save a new report based on the subreport from the Customer Invoice Report and then edit the source object property in the Winchester Web Design Customer Invoice report to display the new report.

1. Display the **Customer Invoice Report** in **Design View**.
2. Right-click the subreport control and choose **Subreport in New Window**.

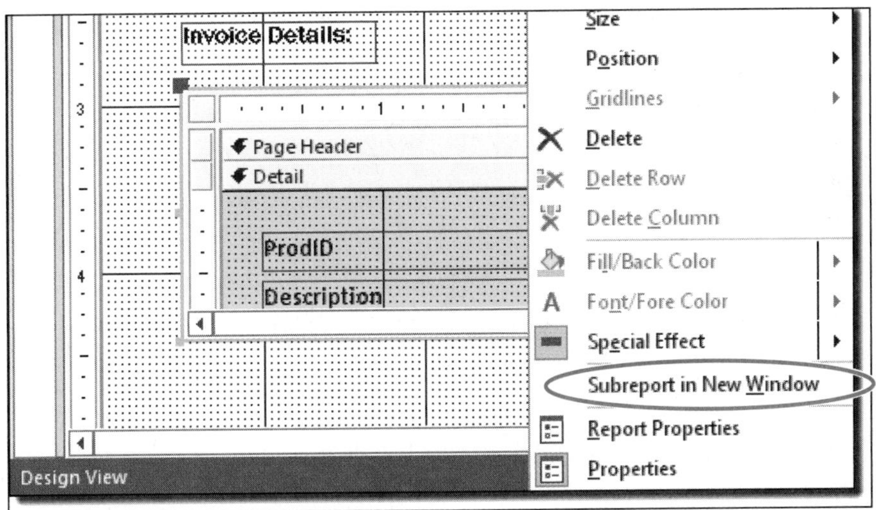

If you don't see the Subreport in New Window command, click an area of the main report and then right-click the subreport control again, or choose Design→Tools→Subreport in New Window.

Access opens the the InvoiceDetails Subform in a separate window.

3. Choose **File→Save As→Save Object As→**[Save As].
4. Follow these steps to save the form as a report:

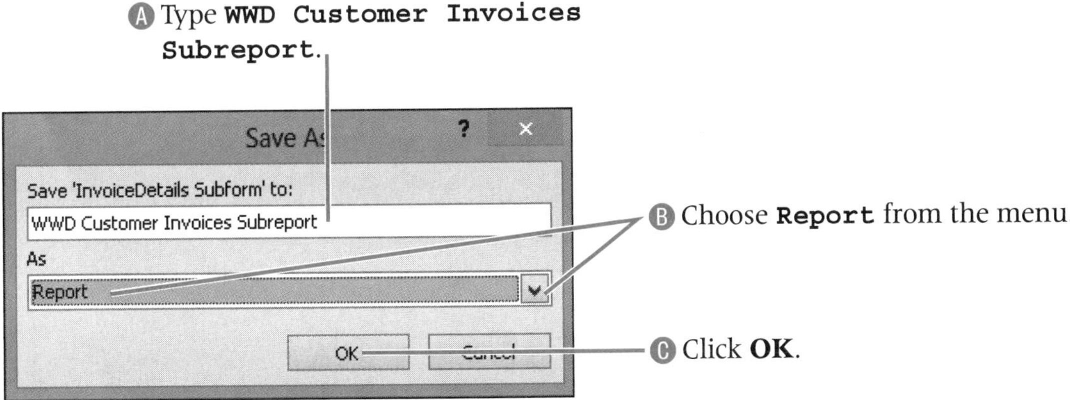

5. Close the **InvoiceDetails Subform**; display the **WWD Customer Invoices Subreport** in **Design View**.

Access 2013

6. Click the **All** tab on the Property Sheet and type **`Customer Invoices Subreport`** as the caption.
7. Choose **Design→Header/Footer→Title.**
   Access places a title and empty placeholder controls in the Report Header.
8. Type **`Winchester Web Design Invoice Details`** in the **Title control** and tap [Enter]
9. For the new **Title control**, enter these property values:

Property	Value
Width	3"
Height	.25"
Left	1"
Top	0"
Font Name	Arial
Font Size	12
Text Align	Center

10. Delete any empty placeholder controls in the Report Header section that were automatically inserted with the title, such as placeholders for a logo or date.

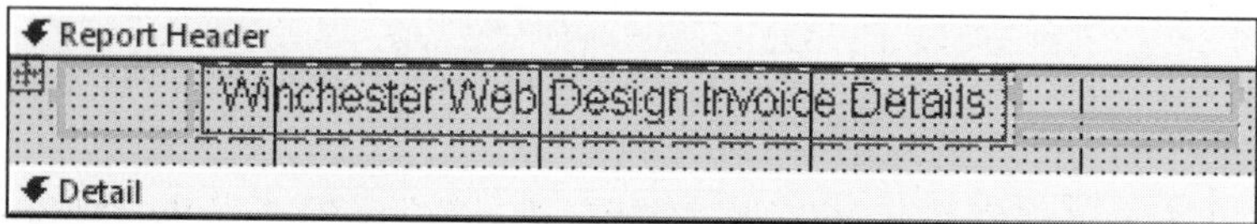

11. Click the **Report Header section bar** in the subreport and type **`.3"`** for the **Height**.
    Because the empty placeholders inserted with the Title control extend the width of the report, you will now reset the width of the subreport back to 5.6"
12. Click the **Report selector button** and type **`5.6"`** for the **Width** property.
13. Save and close the **WWD Customer Invoices Subreport**.
14. Return to the **Customer Invoice Report** in **Design View**.
15. Display the **Property Sheet** and then display the **Data** tab.
16. Select the subreport, click in the **Source Object** property line, and choose **Report.WWD Customer Invoices Subreport** from the drop-down menu.
17. Click the **Detail** section bar in the subreport.
18. Choose **Blue, Accent 5, Lighter 80%** for the **Back Color** property.
19. Choose **Blue Accent 5, Lighter 60%** for the **Alternate Back Color**.

20. Switch to **Print Preview** and review the report and subreport.

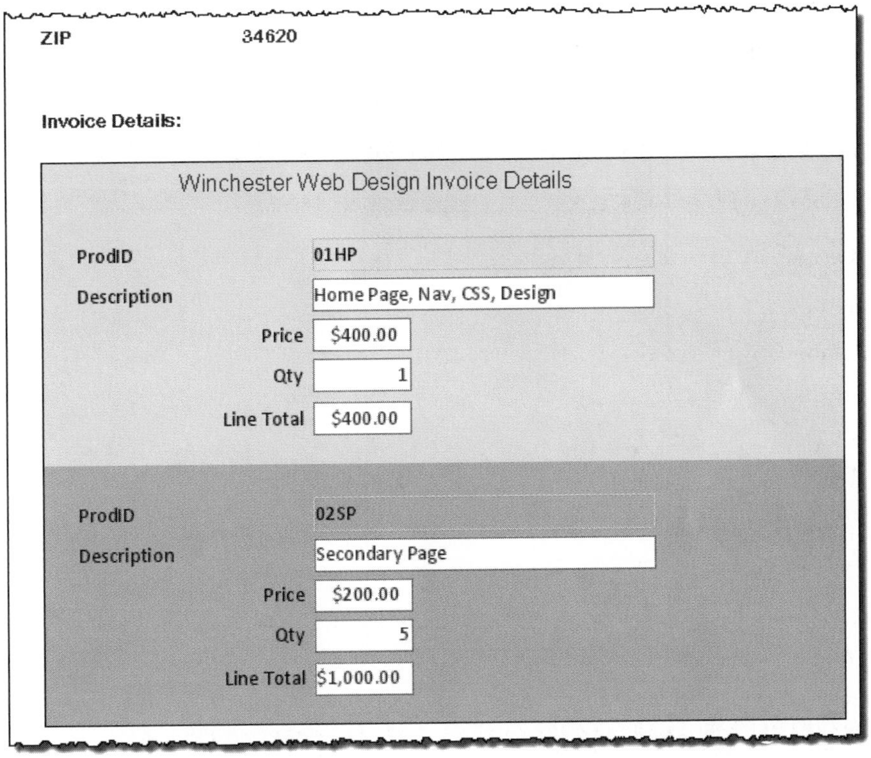

ZIP 34620

Invoice Details:

Winchester Web Design Invoice Details

ProdID	01HP
Description	Home Page, Nav, CSS, Design
Price	$400.00
Qty	1
Line Total	$400.00
ProdID	02SP
Description	Secondary Page
Price	$200.00
Qty	5
Line Total	$1,000.00

The new subreport will appear on the main report. Notice that because the subreport is not in Datasheet View, it appears differently on the page and takes up far more vertical space.

21. Navigate through the report.

    Because the new subreport is much longer than the subform, it throws off the page alignment. To fix this, you can set the source of the subform/subreport back to the InvoiceDetails Subform.

22. Close **Print Preview**; then save and close the **Customer Invoice Report**.

Numbering Items in a Report

Video Library: http://labyrinthelab.com/videos Video Number: AC13-V0904

As the number of records in a table grows, the length and number of records in a report or subreport also grows. You can number the records in a report to help track items listed. If a report is grouped, you can set the count to restart numbering at the beginning of each group.

Setting Properties to Number Items

By adding a text box to the Detail section and setting its Control Source property to `=1`, you can automatically number items in a report. In addition, you can set the Running Sum property to identify the portion of a report for which you want to count items. For example, suppose you have an invoice report that groups services by invoice number. You can set the Running Sum property to count the items in each group and then start counting again with the next group.

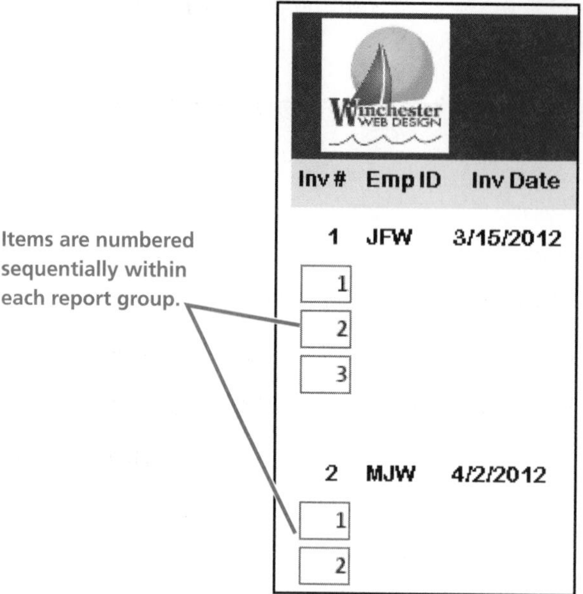

Numbering Subreports Separately

Access does not permit numbering items in a subreport control on a main report. However, because you saved the subreport as a separate report, you can add the numbering controls directly to the subreport by opening it in a separate window. Any edits you make when it is open as a separate item are reflected in the main report the next time you open it.

QUICK REFERENCE — NUMBERING REPORT ITEMS

Task	Procedure
Add a text box control to number report items	■ Display the report or subreport in Design View. ■ Choose Design→Controls→Text Box [ab]. ■ Click the position in the Detail section on the report or subreport to place the text box control. ■ On the Property Sheet Data tab, set the Control Source to =1 and the Running Sum to Over Group.

DEVELOP YOUR SKILLS AC09-D04

Number Items in a Report and Subreport

In this exercise, you will reposition controls in the Page Header of the WWD Customer Invoices Subreport and then add a text box control to count the number of line items.

1. Display the **WWD Customer Invoices Subreport** in **Design View**.
2. If the subreport does not show the Page Header and Page Footer section bars, right-click the **Detail** section bar and choose **Page Header/Footer**.
3. Click the **Page Header** section bar and change the **Height** to **.3"** on the Property Sheet.
4. Select the **ProdID** label in the **Detail** section and use Ctrl+X to cut the control.
5. Click in the **Page Header** section and use Ctrl+V to paste the label.
6. With the **ProdID** label still selected, type **.5"** for the **Width** and **.5"** for the **Left** property.
7. Add the following labels to the **Page Header** section; use the **Width** and **Left** property values shown.

Label	Width Property	Left Property
Description	2"	1.25"
Price	.75"	3.5"
Qty	.3"	4.5"
LineTotal	.75"	5"

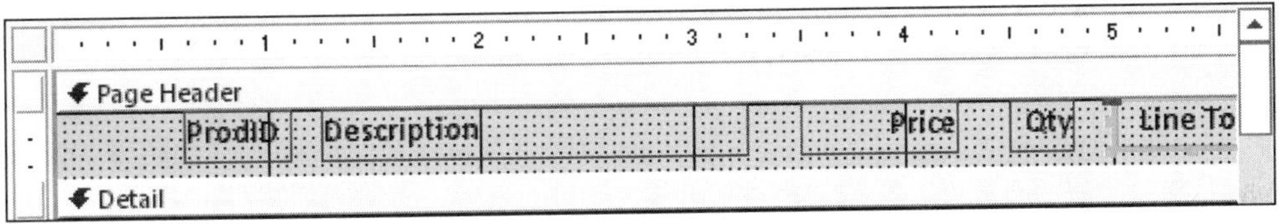

Move and Resize Report Text Box Controls

8. Set these property values for the text boxes in the **Detail** section.

Text Box Control	Width	Top	Left
ProdID	.5"	.1"	.5"
ProdDescription	2"	.1"	1.25"
Price	.75"	.1"	3.5"
Qty	.3"	.1"	4.5"
LineTotal	.75"	.1"	5"

9. Click the **Detail** section bar and type **.5"** for the **Height**.
10. Click the **Selection Type** menu button at the top of the Property Sheet and choose **Report**.
11. Type **6"** for the **Width** property.

Access 2013

12. Switch to **Report View**.

Winchester Web Design Invoice Details

ProdID	Description	Price	Qty	Line Total
01HP	Home Page, Nav, CSS, Design	$400.00	1	$400.00
01HP	Home Page, Nav, CSS, Design	$400.00	1	$400.00
01HP	Home Page, Nav, CSS, Design	$400.00	1	$400.00

There is room for a small field to the left of the Product ID field.

Add and Format a Text Box

13. Switch to **Design View** and choose **Design→Controls→Text Box** ab|.
14. Follow these steps to add the text box control to the **Detail** section:

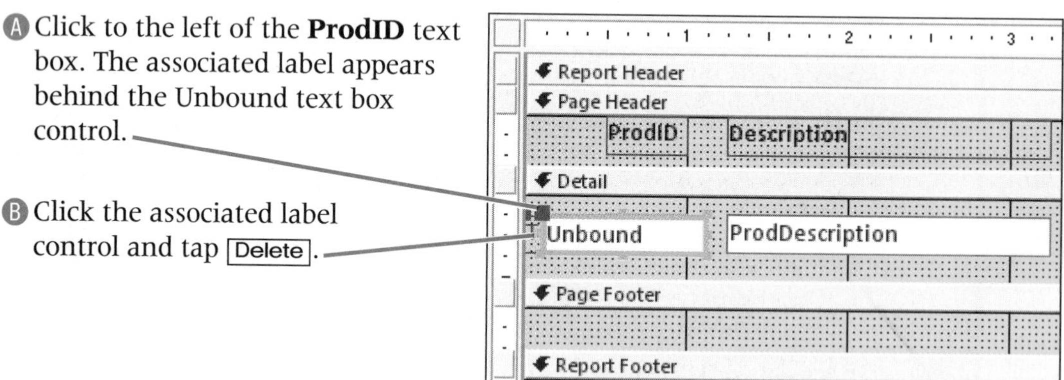

Ⓐ Click to the left of the **ProdID** text box. The associated label appears behind the Unbound text box control.
Ⓑ Click the associated label control and tap Delete.
Report Header
Page Header
ProdID
Description
Detail
Unbound
ProdDescription
Page Footer
Report Footer

15. Click the new text box control and set these property values:

Property	Value
Name	txtCount
Width	.3"
Top	.1"
Left	.1"

Set Control Properties to Sum

16. Follow these steps to set the data properties for the control:

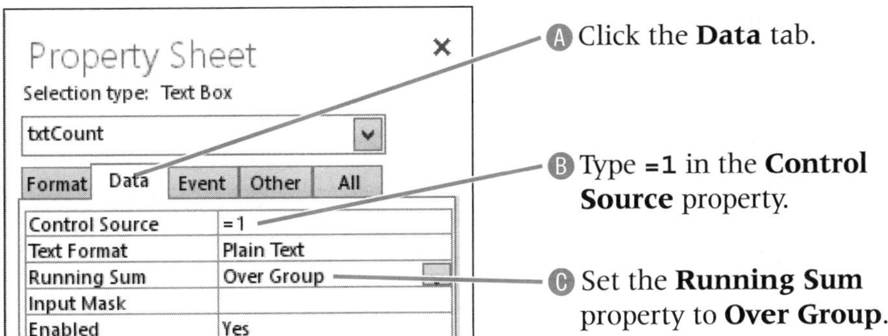

17. Switch to **Report View** and scroll to the end of the report.

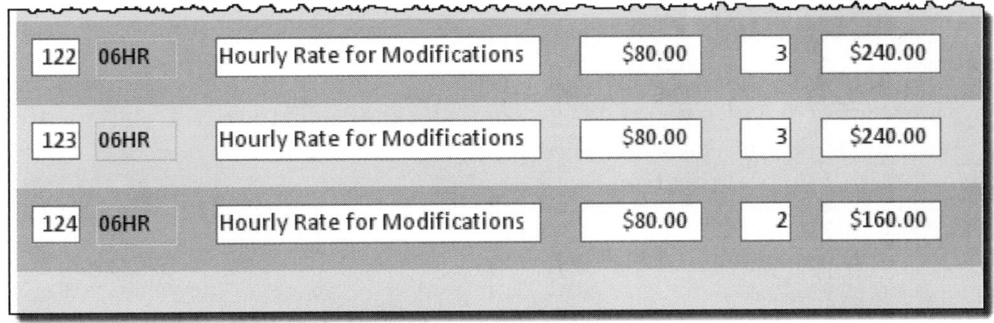

Access counts each line item in the report—from 1 to 124.

18. Save and close the **WWD Customer Invoices Subreport**.
19. Display the **Customer Invoice Report** in **Design View**.
20. Choose the **InvoiceDetails Subform** from the **Selection Type** list at the top of the Property Sheet.
21. Type `6"` for the **Width** property.
22. Switch to **Print Preview** and navigate through the report. Then display **page 2**.

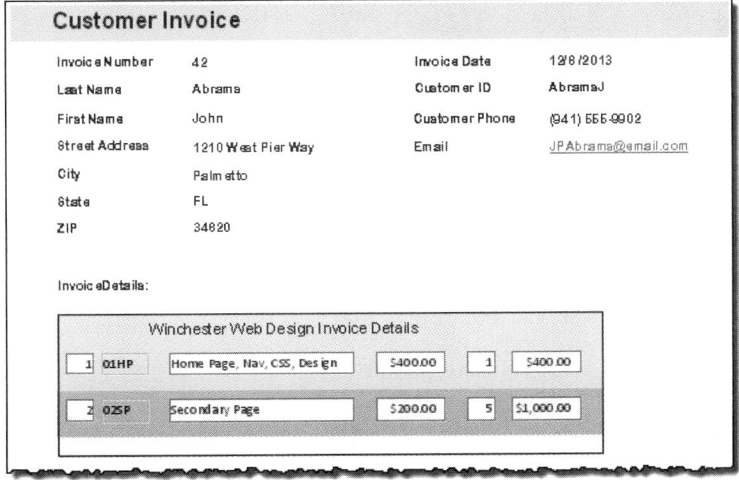

23. Close **Print Preview**.
24. Save and close the **Customer Invoice Report**.

Creating Calculated Controls on a Subreport

Video Library: http://labyrinthelab.com/videos Video Number: AC13-V0905

Reports summarize data contained in tables and queries to present useful, organized information. This typically means that calculated fields must be added to a report for subtotals, grand totals, and averages.

Positioning Calculated Controls

Calculated controls are built on reports by using the Control Source property of an unbound text box control to which you add the formula for the calculation. The placement of the calculated control determines how Access performs the calculation.

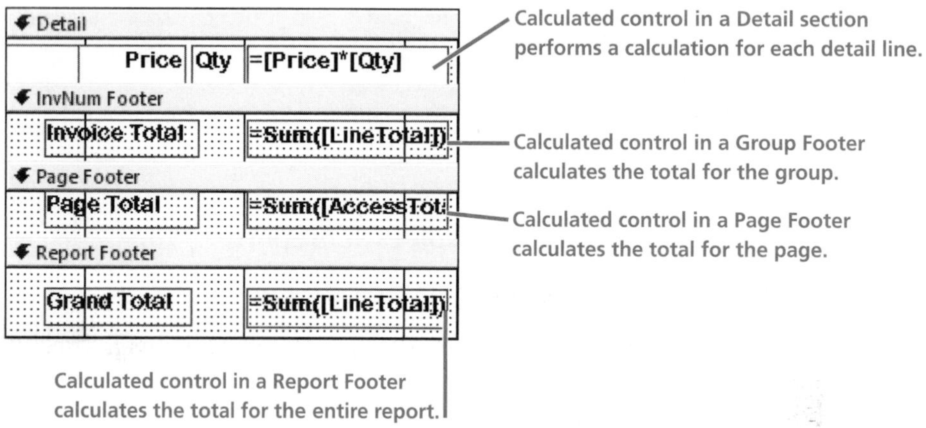

Detail
Price
Qty
=[Price]*[Qty]
InvNum Footer
Invoice Total
=Sum([LineTotal])
Page Footer
Page Total
=Sum([AccessTot
Report Footer
Grand Total
=Sum([LineTotal])
Calculated control in a Detail section performs a calculation for each detail line.
Calculated control in a Group Footer calculates the total for the group.
Calculated control in a Page Footer calculates the total for the page.
Calculated control in a Report Footer calculates the total for the entire report.

DEVELOP YOUR SKILLS AC09-D05

Create a Calculated Control

In this exercise, you will add a calculated control to the Report Footer section of the WWD Customer Invoices Subreport.

1. Display the **WWD Customer Invoices Subreport** in **Design View**.
2. Click the **Report Footer** section bar and type **.3"** for the **Height** property.
3. Choose **Design→Controls→Text Box** and draw a text box in the **Report Footer** section of the subreport under the **Line Total** text box.
4. Type **CustomerTotal** for the **Name** property.
5. Type **=Sum([Price]*[Qty])** for the **Control Source** property.

6. Enter the property values shown to format the CustomerTotal calculated field:

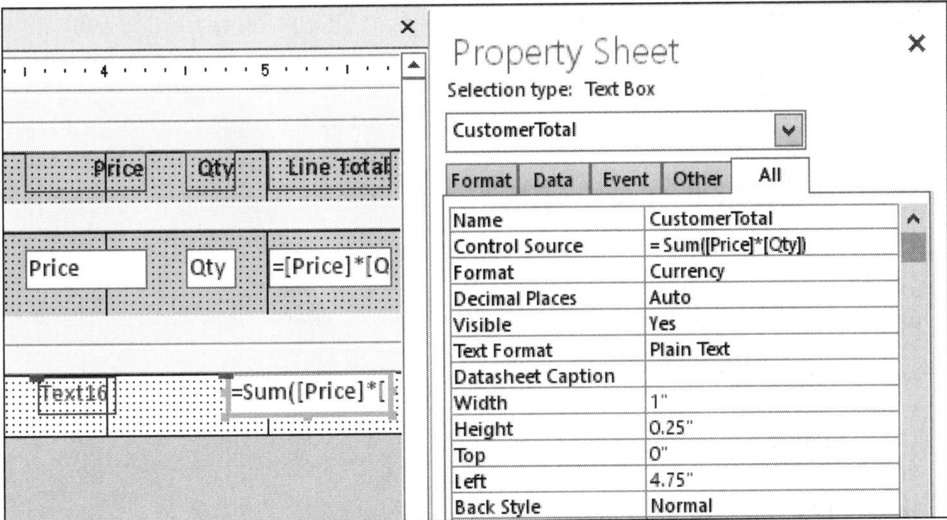

7. Select the associated label for the **CustomerTotal** text box and enter these property values:

Property	Value
Caption	Invoice Total
Width	1.2"
Height	.25"
Top	0"
Left	3"
Fore Color	Text 1

8. Save and close the **WWD Customer Invoices Subreport**.

9. Display the **Customer Invoice Report** in **Print Preview** and navigate through the report. Then display **page 2**.

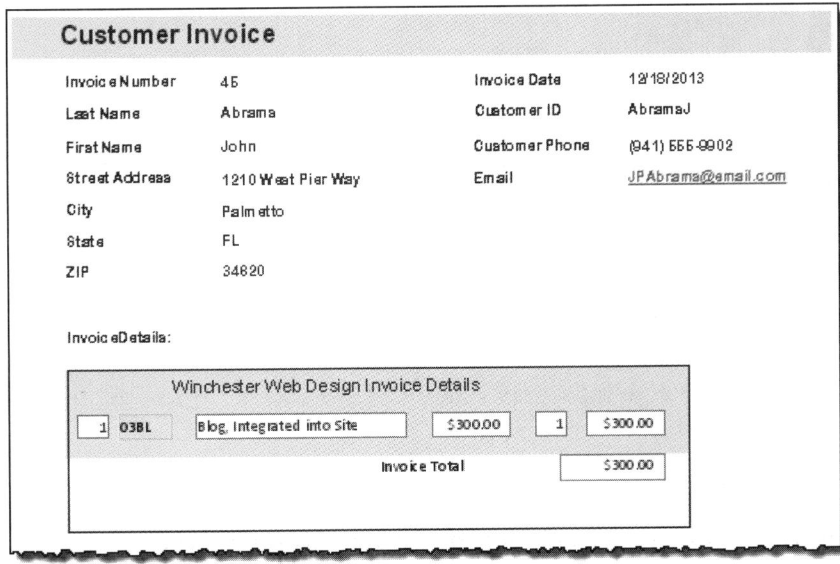

10. Save the **Customer Invoice Report**.

Growing a Subreport

Video Library: http://labyrinthelab.com/videos Video Number: AC13-V0906

When the number of records or amount of data displayed in a subreport varies, you can set the Can Grow property setting to allow the subreport space to expand so more data displays vertically. You can also change the orientation of the print layout to allow more horizontal space on each report page.

QUICK REFERENCE	SETTING MARGINS, ORIENTATION, AND CAN GROW/CAN SHRINK PROPERTIES
Task	**Procedure**
Set report margins	■ From Design/Layout View: Choose Page Layout→Page Size→Margins. ■ From Print Preview: Choose Print Preview→Page Size→Margins.
Set orientation	■ From Design/Layout View: Choose Page Layout→Page Layout and then choose Portrait or Landscape. ■ From Print Preview: Choose Print Preview→Page Layout and then choose Portrait or Landscape.
Set Can Grow property	■ Click the subreport control. ■ Display the Property Sheet, if necessary, and click the Format tab. ■ Set the Can Grow property to Yes.
Set Can Shrink property	■ Click the subreport control. ■ Display the Property Sheet and click the Format tab. ■ Set the Can Shrink property to Yes.

DEVELOP YOUR SKILLS AC09-D06

Set the Report Layout and Grow/Shrink Properties

In this exercise, you will adjust the margins of the Customer Invoice Report and set the Can Grow and Can Shrink properties to adjust the size of the subreport to fit the contents, which may vary in size.

1. Display the **Customer Invoice Report** in **Design View**.
2. Choose **Page Setup→Page Size→Margins** and choose **Narrow**.
3. Select the **InvoiceDetails Subreport** and click the **Format** tab on the Property Sheet to set the following properties:
   - Set the **Can Grow** property to **Yes**, if necessary.
   - Set the **Can Shrink** property to **Yes**.
4. Save the **Customer Invoice Report**.
5. Switch to **Print Preview** and navigate through the report.
   The subreport grows and shrinks to best fit the contents.

6. Display **page 2**.

Customer Invoice

InvoiceNumber	45	Invoice Date	12/18/2013
Last Name	Abrams	Customer ID	AbramsJ
First Name	John	Customer Phone	(941) 555-9902
Street Address	1210 West Pier Way	Email	JPAbrams@email.com
City	Palmetto		
State	FL		
ZIP	34820		

InvoiceDetails:

Winchester Web Design Invoice Details

1	03BL	Blog, Integrated into Site	$300.00	1	$300.00
			Invoice Total		$300.00

7. Close **Print Preview**.

Setting Page Breaks and Customizing Controls

Video Library: http://labyrinthelab.com/videos Video Number: AC13-V0907

As you view the Winchester Web Design Customer Invoice Report in Report View, you may notice that the number of invoice records displayed on each screen varies depending on the number of items ordered. To ensure that each customer invoice starts on a new page, you can add a page break control. By default, when you view a report in Print Preview, data for each customer/record automatically appear on a separate page; however, multiple records appear on the same page when the report is displayed in Report View.

To add a title or general company information to an invoice, place title controls in the Page Header section rather than the Report Header, which only prints on the first page.

Positioning the Page Break Control

To ensure that each invoice record prints on a separate sheet of paper, you can set page breaks. When you set page breaks, add the break at the end of the Detail section so Access knows to start a new page before printing the next page header.

QUICK REFERENCE	ADDING PAGE BREAK CONTROLS
Task	**Procedure**
Add a page break control	■ Drag the Page Footer section bar down to provide space at the bottom of the Detail section. ■ Click the bottom of the Detail section where you want the break. ■ Choose Design→Controls→Insert Page Break.

DEVELOP YOUR SKILLS AC09-D07

Add Logo, Title, Date, and Page Break Controls

In this exercise, you will modify the Winchester Web Design Customer Invoice Report. You will add a title, insert the company logo and current date, and set page breaks to print each invoice on a separate page.

1. Display the **Customer Invoice Report** in **Design View**.
2. Select the **Customer Invoice** title control in the **Page Header** section.
3. Follow these steps to edit the title:

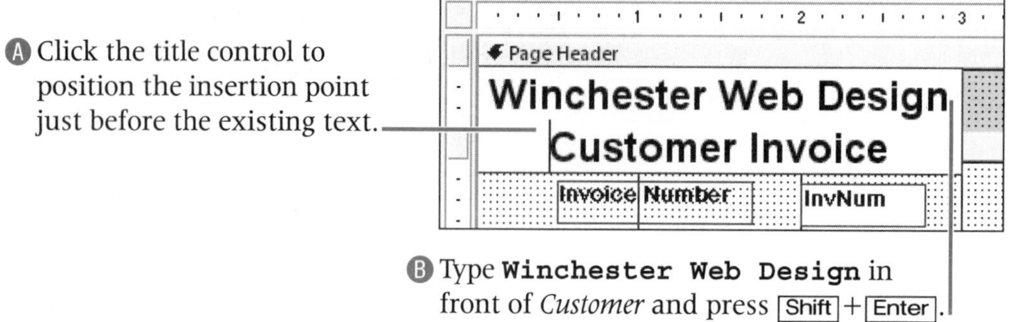

Ⓐ Click the title control to position the insertion point just before the existing text.

Ⓑ Type **Winchester Web Design** in front of *Customer* and press [Shift]+[Enter].

4. Tap [Enter]; type **4"** for the **Width** and **2"** for the **Left** property.

Add a Logo to the Page Header

5. Click the **Page Header** section bar, choose **Design→Controls→**[Insert Image], navigate to the **AC2013 Lesson 09** folder, and choose **WWD-Logo.bmp**.

   If you choose Design→Header/Footer→Logo instead, Access inserts the image in the Report Header section and placeholders for title, date, and time controls. The empty placeholders are normally deleted.

6. Draw the logo on the far left side of the **Page Header** section.

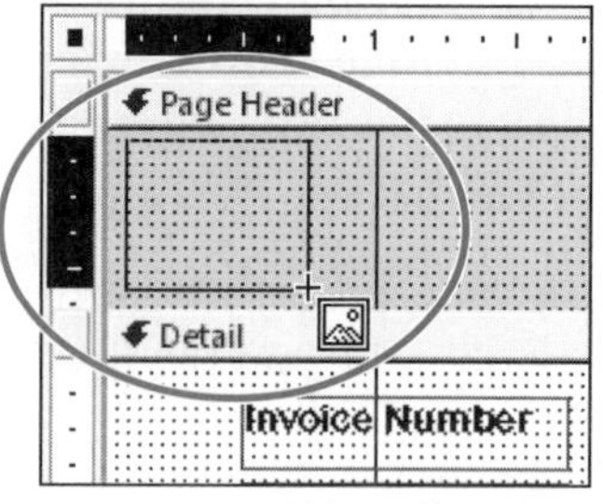

7. Type **.9"** for the **Width** and **Height** properties. Type **.05"** for the **Top** property and **.2"** for the **Left** property.

Add a Date Control to the Report

8. Choose **Design→Header/Footer→**[Date and Time] and choose the **MM/DD/YYYY** Date format; *do not* include the time.

   Access places the new date control in the Report Header section.

9. Select the date control and press [Ctrl]+[X] to cut the control from the **Report Header**.
10. Click the **Page Header** section bar and press [Ctrl]+[V] to paste the control into the Page Header.

11. Enter these property values for the **Date** control:
    - `2"` for the **Width** property
    - `.2"` for the **Height** property
    - `.75"` for the **Top** property
    - `3"` for the **Left** property
12. Choose **Center** for the **Text Align** property.
13. Right-click the **Report Header** section bar and choose **Report Header/Footer** .Click **Yes** to delete all controls in the section.
14. Switch to **Print Preview**.

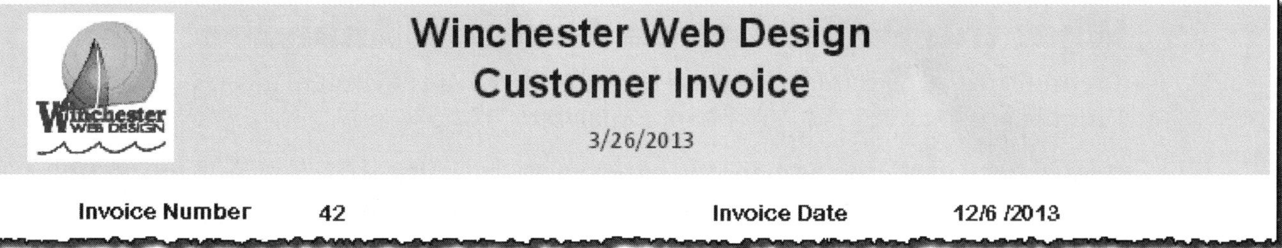

If every other page is blank, the report might be too wide or there might be a control placed beyond the margin. Remedy this by shortening or moving the errant control to the left and dragging the right edge of the report to the left.

Add a Page Break Control

15. Switch to **Design View** and scroll down to the bottom of the **Detail** section.
16. Follow these steps to position a page break:

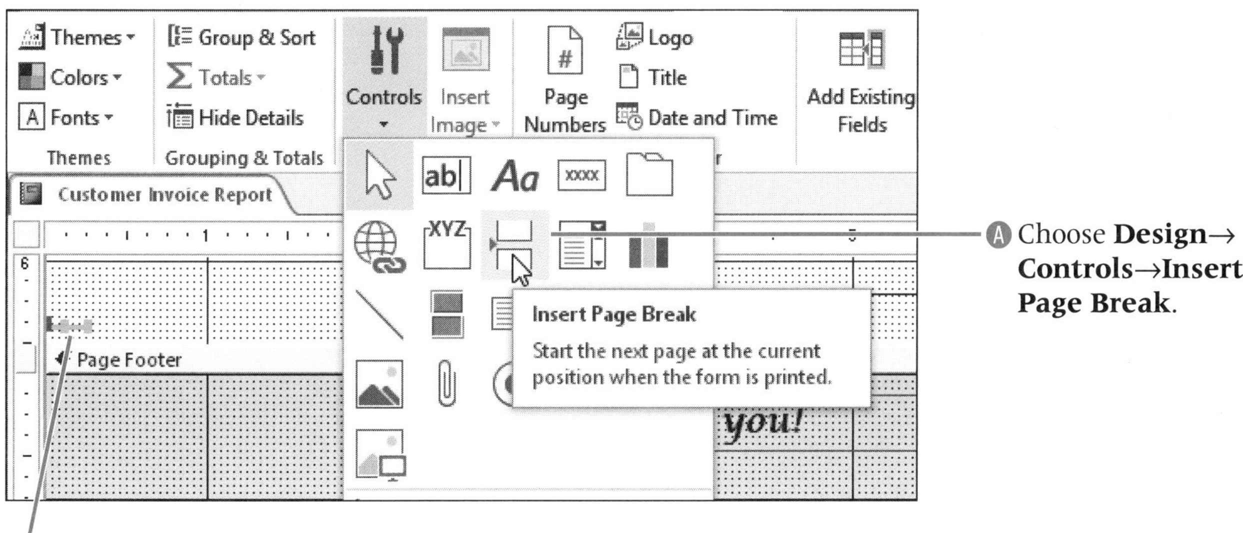

Ⓐ Choose **Design→Controls→Insert Page Break.**

Ⓑ Place the Page Break in the **Detail** section just above the Page Footer section bar.

17. Switch to **Print Preview** and page through the report.

    There are times when adding a page break to a report may cause an extra page to print for each record. So if the page break isn't needed, do not add it.

18. Save and close the **Customer Invoice Report**.

Analyzing Report Performance

Video Library: http://labyrinthelab.com/videos Video Number: AC13-V0908

Access tracks each database object and identifies how tables, queries, forms, and reports are related. Any changes you make by importing a report, editing the report structure, creating a subreport based on a form, and then saving the form as a report may have an impact on the performance of the database.

What the Performance Analyzer Analyzes

To ensure that all objects in a database work together in an efficient manner, you can run the Performance Analyzer. The Performance Analyzer:

- Analyzes database performance by reviewing each database object, identifying potential errors, and recommending modifications to maintain optimum efficiency in the database.
- Compares relationships between database tables and identifies data redundancy.
- Identifies items such as mismatched field definitions and displays a list of these instances so that you can consider modifications.
- Locates errors that could result in inaccurate data analysis and any disconnects between forms/subforms and reports/subreports.
- Identifies fields and property settings that can slow down the running of queries and the generation of reports.

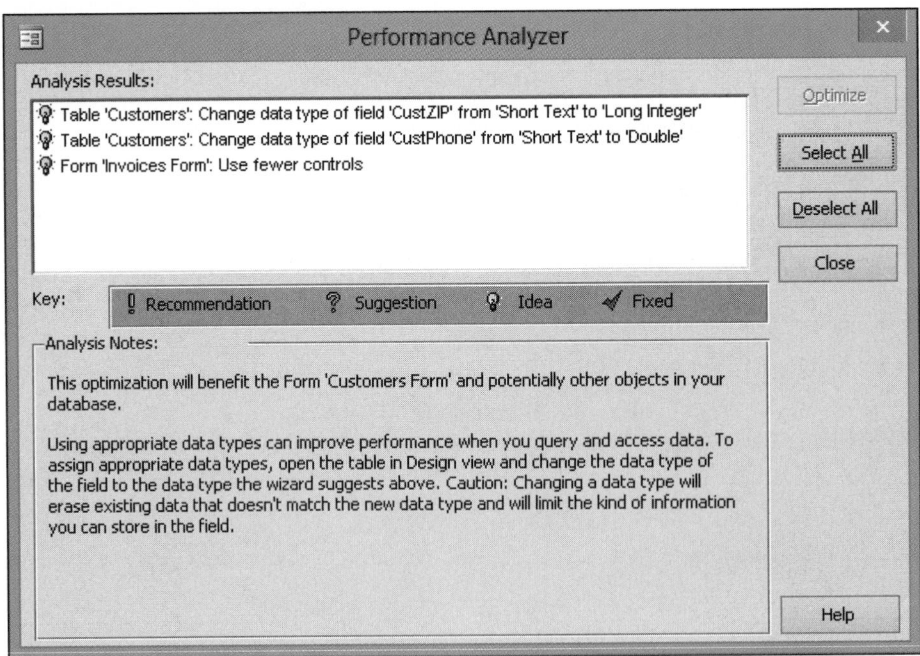

A sample Performance Analyzer report.

You can use the Performance Analyzer to analyze all objects in a database or selected objects. You can also instruct the analyzer to make corrections for you.

DEVELOP YOUR SKILLS AC09-D08

Analyze Report Performance

In this exercise, you will run the Performance Analyzer to analyze report performance in the Winchester Web Design database.

1. Choose **Database Tools→Analyze→** Analyze Performance to start the Performance Analyzer.
2. Follow these steps to run the Performance Analyzer on all database reports:

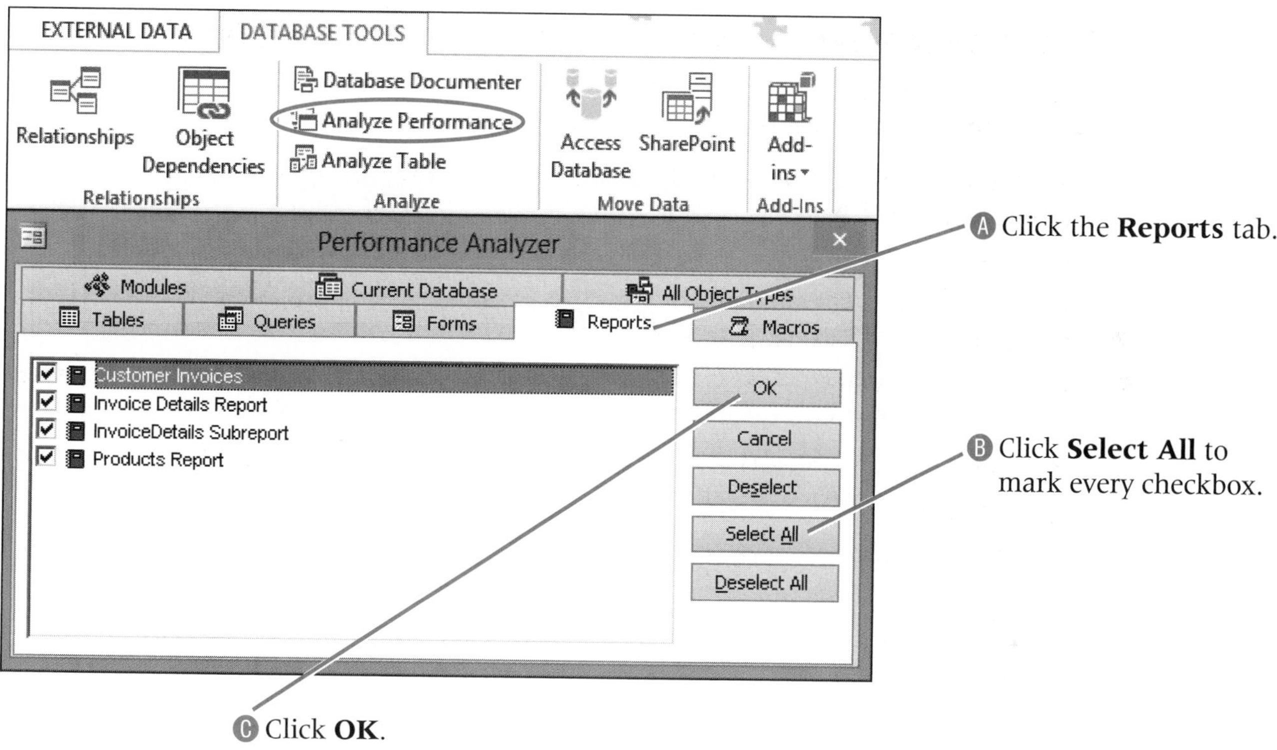

Access runs the Performance Analyzer and displays analysis results.

Access 2013

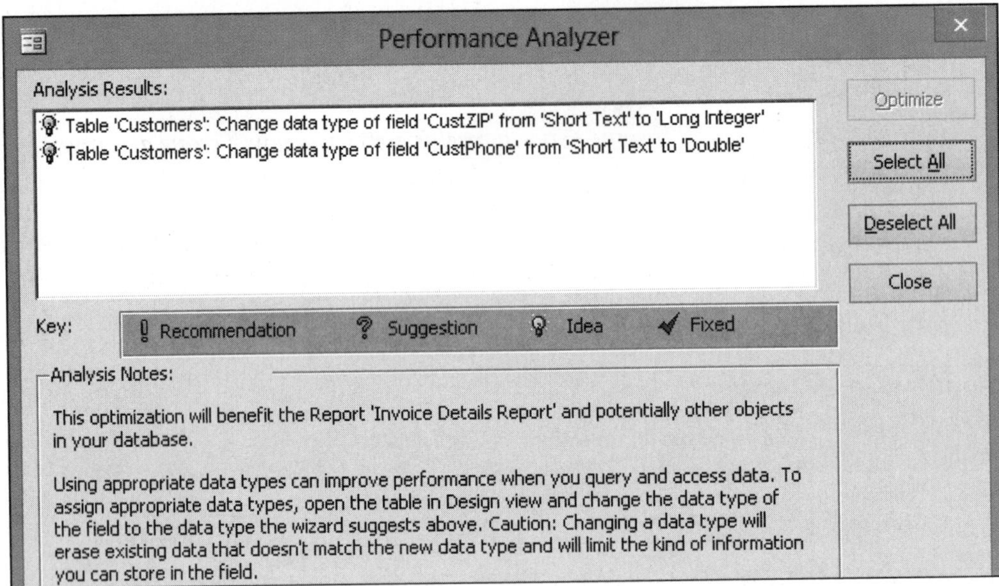

The analysis notes about each idea that appear in the bottom part of the Performance Analyzer dialog box indicate that the optimization will benefit the Invoice Details Report and potentially other objects in your database.

3. Close the **Performance Analyzer** dialog box and close the database. Exit **Access**.

Concepts Review

To check your knowledge of the key concepts introduced in this lesson, complete the Concepts Review quiz by choosing the appropriate access option below.

If you are...	Then access the quiz by...
Using the Labyrinth Video Library	Going to http://labyrinthelab.com/videos
Using eLab	Logging in, choosing Content, and navigating to the Concepts Review quiz for this lesson
Not using the Labyrinth Video Library or eLab	Going to the student resource center for this book

Reinforce Your Skills

REINFORCE YOUR SKILLS AC09-R01

Work with Reports and Subreports

Kids for Change needs a report that breaks down donors and their donations by month. In this exercise, you will import a report that includes space for a subreport that contains donor detail information. You will save the subreport as a new report and then add a report control that numbers the activities that have available volunteers.

Import a Report

1. Start **Access**. Open **AC09-R01-K4C** from your **AC2013 Lesson 09** folder and save it as `AC09-R01-K4C-[FirstInitialLastName]`.
2. Choose **External Data→Import & Link→**.
   The Get External Data dialog box opens.
3. Click **Browse**, navigate to the **AC2013 Lesson 09** folder, and double-click **AC09-R01-K4C–Backup**.
   This database is a backup copy of the K4C database.
4. Choose the **Import Tables, Queries, Forms, Reports, Macros, and Modules into the Current Database** option, and click **OK**.
   Access displays object names contained in the backup database.
5. Click the **Reports** tab and choose **Monthly Donations Report**.
6. Click **OK** and click **Close** in the Get External Data dialog box.
7. Display the newly-imported **Monthly Donations Report** in **Design View**.
   The Detail section contains no controls. This is where you will insert the subreport.

Add a Subreport

8. Choose **Design→Controls→Subform/Subreport** .
9. Draw a subreport control in the **Detail** section of the newly-imported **Monthly Donations Report**.
   The SubReport Wizard starts.
10. Choose **DonorDetail Subform** from the Use an Existing Report or Form list and click **Next**.
11. Scroll through the list and choose **Show DonorDetail Query for each record in Donations Query using DonationDate**.

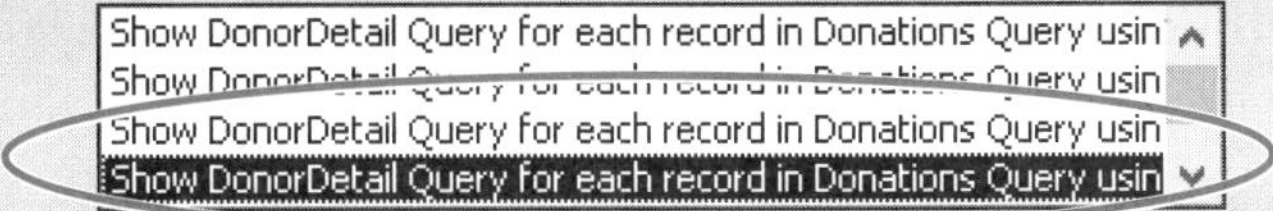

The Show items are too long to display completely in the list, but the highlighted one is shown in the box below the list.

12. Click **Next**, keep the default name, and click **Finish**.

13. Click the **DonorDetail Subform label** and tap [Delete].

    If you don't see the subform label, it might be hidden behind the subform. If necessary, click the Selection Type menu button at the top of the Property Sheet, choose DonorDetail Subform label, and tap [Delete].

14. Click the subreport control and enter these properties on the Property Sheet:

Property	Value
Width	6.5"
Height	.5"
Top	0"
Left	.5"
Border Style	Transparent

15. Click the **Detail section bar** and type `.5"` for the **Height**.

16. Save the **Monthly Donations Report** and switch to **Print Preview**.

    The report with subreport should include each detail line in subform layout.

Create a Report from a Subreport

17. Switch to **Design View**.

18. Right-click the left side of the subreport control and choose **Subreport in New Window**.

    Access opens the subreport (in this case, the DonorDetail Subform) in a separate window. If you don't see the Subreport in New Window choice on the shortcut menu, click an area of the main report then right-click the subreport control again.

19. Choose **File→Save As→Save Object As→**[Save As].

20. Type `K4C Donors Subreport` in the **Save...To** box and choose **Report** from the **As** menu.

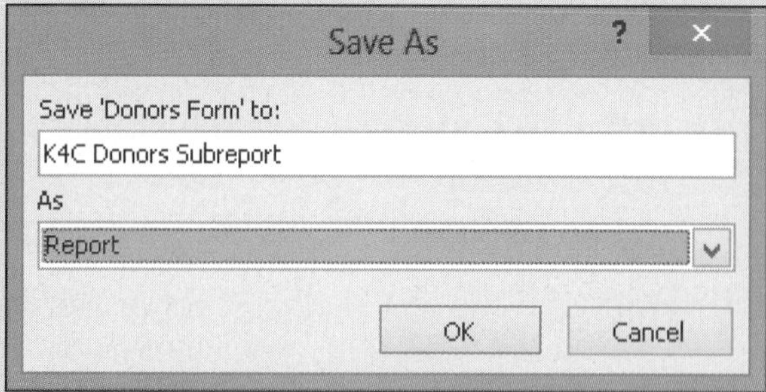

21. Click **OK** and close the **K4C Donors Subreport**.

    The DonorDetail Subform is saved as a separate report so that any changes made to it are not reflected in the original DonorDetail Subform.

22. Display the **Monthly Donations Report** in **Design View**.

23. Display the **Property Sheet** and then display the **Data** tab.

24. Select the subreport, click in the **Source Object** property line, and choose **Report.K4C Donors Subreport** from the drop-down menu.

25. Save and close the **Monthly Donations Report**.

Number Report Items

26. Display the **Volunteers Report** in **Design View**.

27. Choose **Design→Controls→Text Box** ab| and draw a new text box in the Detail section to the left of the ActID text box.

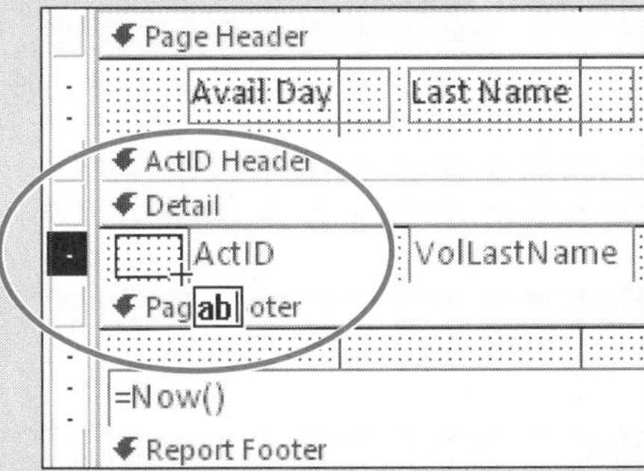

28. Delete the associated label control.

29. Click the new text box control and set these property values:

Property	Value
Name	txtCount
Control Source	=1
Width	.3"
Top	0"
Left	0"
Running Sum	Over All

30. Switch to **Report View**.

    Access numbers the detail lines consecutively for each activity having a volunteer.

31. Save and close the **Volunteers Report**. Close the database and exit **Access**.

32. Submit your final file based on the guidelines provided by your instructor.

    To see examples of how your file or files should look at the end of this exercise, go to the student resource center.

REINFORCE YOUR SKILLS AC09-R02

Add Fields and Controls, and Analyze Database Performance

Kids for Change wants to improve their Monthly Donations Report. In this exercise, you will add a field to calculate the total monthly donations for each donor. You will set the subreport to grow and shrink, depending on the contents, add custom controls and a page break to a report, and finally, run the performance analyzer on the database reports.

Add a Calculated Field to a Report

1. Start **Access**. Open **AC09-R02-K4C** from your **AC2013 Lesson 09** folder and save it as `AC09-R02-K4C-[FirstInitialLastName]`.
2. Display the **K4C Donors Subreport** in **Design View**.
3. Choose **Design→Controls→Text Box** and draw a new text box in the Page Footer section, under the Amount text box.
4. Select the associated label and tap Delete.
5. Click the new text box and enter these values on the Property Sheet:

Property	Value
Name	MonthTotal
Control Source	=Sum(Amount)
Format	Currency
Width	1.3"
Height	.2"
Top	0"
Left	5"
Font Name	Arial Rounded MT Bold
Text Align	Right

6. Save and close the **K4C Donors Subreport**.

Grow and Shrink a Subreport

7. Display the **Monthly Donations Report** in **Design View**.
8. Select the **K4C Donors Subreport**.
9. Choose **Yes** for the Can Grow property, if necessary; choose **Yes** for the Can Shrink property.
10. Save the **Monthly Donations Report**.

Add a Logo, Title, Date, and Page Break to a Report

11. Select the title control.
12. Click in the title control to position the insertion point just before the existing text. Type `Kids for Change` in front of *Monthly Donations Report*.
13. Press Shift+Enter to bump *Monthly Donations Report* to a second line.

14. Tap [Enter]; type `4"` for the **Width**, type `2"` for the **Left** property, and choose **Center** for **Text Align**.
15. Click the **Page Header** section bar.
16. Choose **Design→Header/Footer→**[Insert Image], navigate to the **AC2013 Lesson 09** folder; choose **All Files (*.*)**, and choose **K4C-Logo.bmp**.
17. Draw the logo on the far left side of the **Page Header** section.

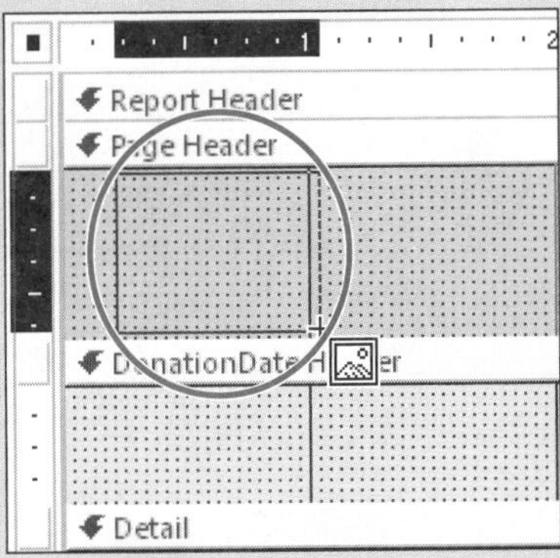

18. Type `.8"` for the **Width** and **Height** properties. Type `.1"` for the **Top** property and `.5"` for the **Left** property.

    Now you will add a Date control to the Page Header section and center it under the title.

19. Choose **Design→Header/Footer→**[Date and Time] and choose the **MM/DD/YYYY** format; *do not* include the time.

    By default, Access places the new date control at the far right side of the Report Header.

20. Select the date control and press [Ctrl]+[X]. Then click the **Page Header** section bar and press [Ctrl]+[V].
21. Delete all empty placeholder controls in the Report Header section. Drag up the **Page Header section bar** to meet the Report Header section bar.

    This report will not include a Report Header section because the titles are in the Page Header section so they will appear at the top of every report page.

22. Enter these property values for the Date control:

Property	Value
Width	2"
Height	.2"
Top	.75
Left	3"
Text Align	Center

23. Switch to **Print Preview**.

    The date will be centered in the Page Header section.

24. Close **Print Preview**.

25. In **Design View**, choose **Design→Controls→Insert Page Break** and click in the left side of the **DonationDate Footer** section.

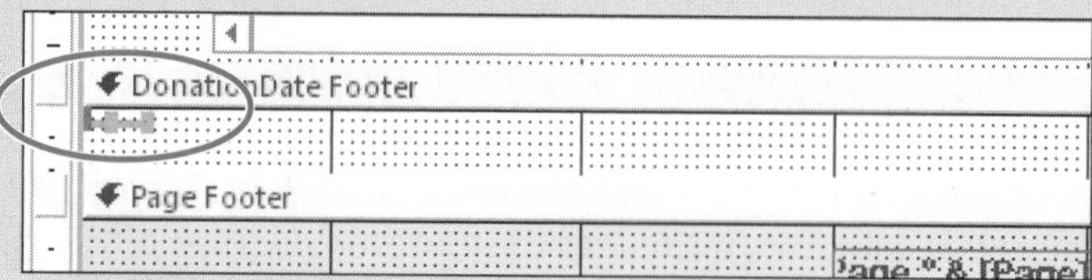
DonationDate Footer
Page Footer

Access places the page break control on the report.

26. Type `0"` for the **Top** property of the page break control.

27. Click the **DonationDate Footer section bar** and type `.001"` for the **Height**.
This will make the DonationDate Footer section as short as possible so that the page break doesn't push down the DonationDate header on the next page.

28. Switch to **Print Preview** and navigate to the **April** donations.
Each month's donations appear on a separate page.

29. Close **Print Preview**.

30. Save and close the **Monthly Donations Report**.

Analyze Report Performance

31. Choose **Database Tools→Analyze→** Analyze Performance.

32. Click the **Reports** tab, if necessary; click **Select All**, and click **OK**.
Access analyzes every report in the database and presents an analysis that shows relevant recommendations, suggestions, and ideas about data types, relationships, and design.

33. Click the third item in the list to see the recommendation that the analyzer has made.

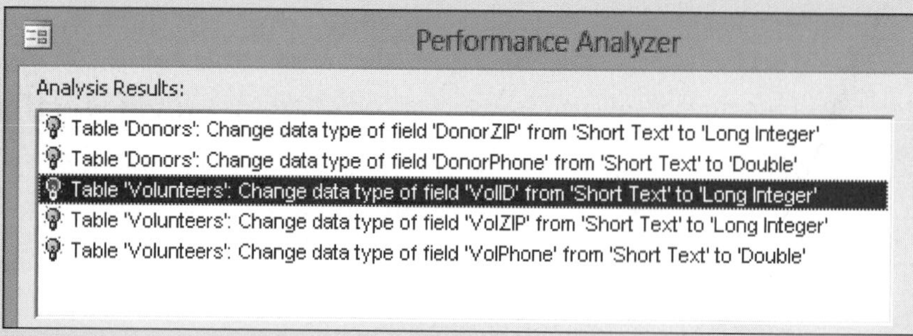
Performance Analyzer
Analysis Results:
Table 'Donors': Change data type of field 'DonorZIP' from 'Short Text' to 'Long Integer'
Table 'Donors': Change data type of field 'DonorPhone' from 'Short Text' to 'Double'
Table 'Volunteers': Change data type of field 'VolID' from 'Short Text' to 'Long Integer'
Table 'Volunteers': Change data type of field 'VolZIP' from 'Short Text' to 'Long Integer'
Table 'Volunteers': Change data type of field 'VolPhone' from 'Short Text' to 'Double'

The optimization will benefit the Volunteers Report and potentially other objects in your database. It suggests that you change the data type of the VolID field in the Volunteers table to Long Integer. No changes are needed because each current data type is valid.

34. Close the **Performance Analyzer** dialog box. Close the database and exit **Access**.

35. Submit your final file based on the guidelines provided by your instructor.
To see examples of how your file or files should look at the end of this exercise, go to the student resource center.

REINFORCE YOUR SKILLS AC09-R03

Work with Reports and Analyze Database Performance

Kids for Change needs a report that presents activity staffing assignments. In this exercise, you will import a report that includes room for a subform containing activity detail information and save the subreport as a separate report. You will add a count of donations per donor and modify a report. You will set a subreport to accommodate its data, add custom controls and a page break to a report, and analyze report performance.

Import a Report

1. Start **Access**. Open **AC09-R03-K4C** from your **AC2013 Lesson 09** folder and save it as `AC09-R03-K4C-[FirstInitialLastName]`.
2. Choose **External Data→Import & Link→**Access.
   The Get External Data dialog box opens.
3. Click **Browse**, navigate to the **AC2013 Lesson 09** folder, and double-click **AC09-R03-K4C-Backup**.
   This database is a backup copy of the K4C database.
4. Choose the **Import Tables, Queries, Forms, Reports, Macros, and Modules into the Current Database** option, and click **OK**.
   Access displays object names contained in the backup database.
5. Click the **Reports** tab and choose **Staff Report**.
6. Click **OK** and click **Close** in the Get External Data dialog box.
7. Display the newly-imported **Staff Report** in **Report View**.
   The empty space in the Detail section is where you will insert the subreport.

Add a Subreport

8. Switch to **Design View** and choose **Design→Controls→Subform/Subreport**.
9. Draw a subreport control under the existing controls in the **Detail** section.

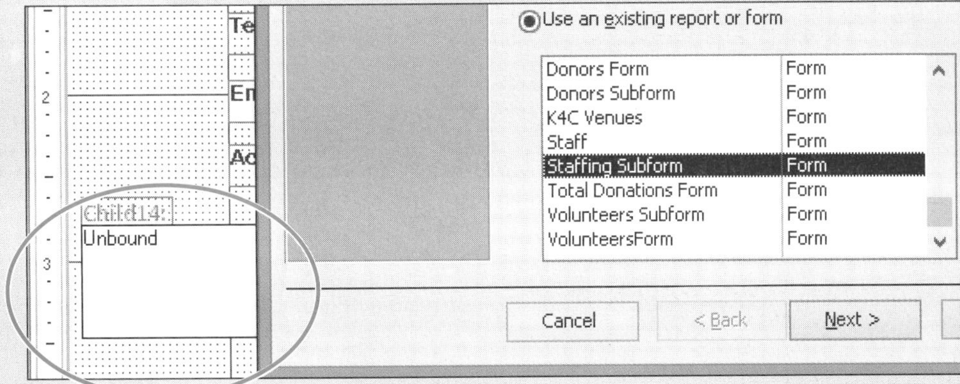

10. Scroll down the **Use an Existing Report or Form** list, choose **Staffing Subform**, and click **Next**.

Access 2013

11. Ensure that **Choose From a List** is the linking option.
12. Click **Next**, keep the default name, and click **Finish**.

    A small green triangle in the Report selector indicates a possible error. Click the triangle to view the Smart tag, which lists the error and possible solutions. In this case, the report is wider than a page. The next few steps will eliminate the error.

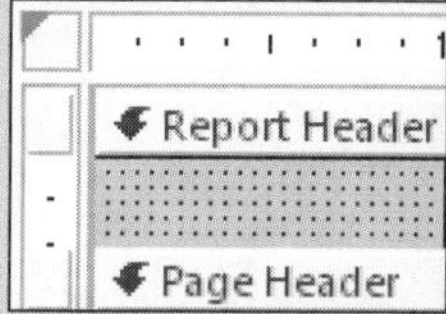

13. Click the **Staffing Subform label** and tap Delete.
14. Click the subreport and enter these properties on the Property Sheet:

Property	Value
Width	7.7"
Height	.5"
Top	3"
Left	0"
Border Style	Transparent

15. Click the **Report selector** and type `7.8"` for the **Width** property of the report.

    The green Smart tag indicator should be gone now.
16. Save the **Staff Report** and switch to **Print Preview**.

    The report should include the activity detail line under each staffer's information.

Create a Report from a Subreport

17. Close **Print Preview** and switch to **Design View**.
18. Right-click the subreport control and choose **Subreport in New Window**.

    The Staffing Subform subreport opens in a separate window. If you don't see the Subreport in New Window choice, click any area of the main report then right-click the subreport again.
19. Choose **File→Save As→Save Object As→**Save As.
20. Type `K4C Staffing Subreport` in the **Save...To** box, choose **Report** from the **As** drop-down menu, and click **OK**.
21. Close the subform.
22. Display the **K4C Staffing Subreport** in **Design View**. Then click the **Detail section bar** and type `.3"` for the **Height**.
23. Right-click the **Detail section bar** and choose **Report Header/Footer**.
24. Choose **Blue, Accent 1, Lighter 80%** for the **Back Color** of the Report Header section.
25. Choose **Design→Controls→Label** Aa to add the seven labels to the Report Header section.

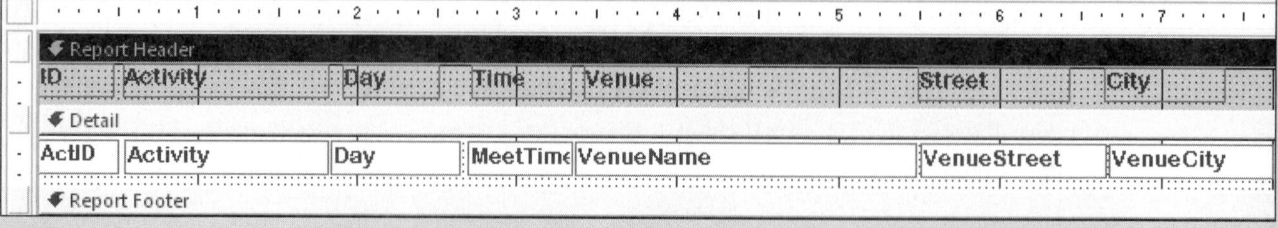

26. Select all the labels and enter these properties:

Property	Value
Height	.2"
Top	0"
Font Name	Arial Rounded MT Bold
Font Size	10
Fore Color	Blue, Accent 1, Darker 50%

27. Save and close the **K4C Staff Subreport**.
28. Display the **Staff Report** in **Design View**.
29. Select the subreport, type `Staffing Subreport` for the **Name** property, click in the **Source Object** line, and choose **Report.K4C Staffing Subreport**.
30. Save and close the **Staff Report**.

Number Report Items

31. Display the **Donations Report** in **Design View**.
32. Choose **Design→Controls→Text Box** [ab|] and draw a new text box in the Detail section to the left of the DonorID text box.

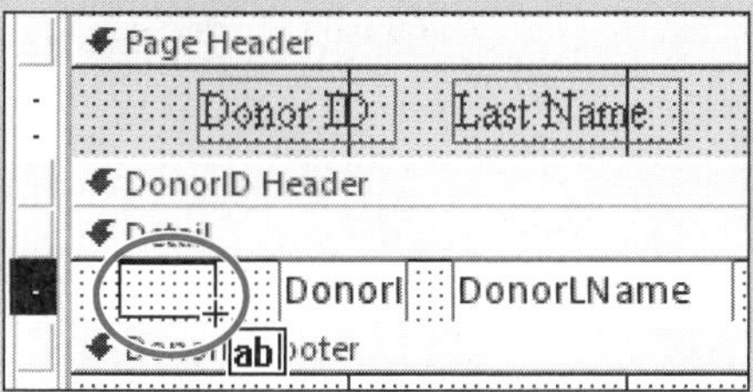

33. Delete the associated label control.
34. Click the new text box control and set these property values:

Property	Value
Name	txtCounter
Control Source	=1
Width	.3"
Top	0"
Left	.3"
Border Style	Transparent
Font Name	Arial
Font Weight	Semi-Bold
Running Sum	Over All

Access 2013

35. Switch to **Report View**.

    Access numbers the detail lines consecutively for each individual donation.

36. Save the **Donations Report**.

Add a Calculated Field to a Report and Change Page Layout

37. Switch to **Design View**, click the **Selection Type** menu button, and choose **Report**.
38. Drag the right edge of the report to the right to the **10" mark** on the horizontal ruler.
39. Choose **Design→Controls→Text Box** and draw a new text box in the Detail section, to the right of the Amount text box.
40. Select the associated label and tap [Delete].
41. Click the new text box and enter these values on the Property Sheet:

Property	Value
Name	ScholarFund
Control Source	=Amount*.1
Format	Currency
Width	.75"
Height	.25"
Top	0"
Left	7.9"
Border Style	Transparent

42. Choose **Design→Controls→Label** and draw a new label control above the ScholarFund text box.
43. Type `Scholar Fund` in the new label.
44. Click the **Amount** label, choose **Home→Clipboard→Format Painter** [icon], and click the new **Scholar Fund label** to paint the same formatting.
45. Select all labels in the **Page Header section**.

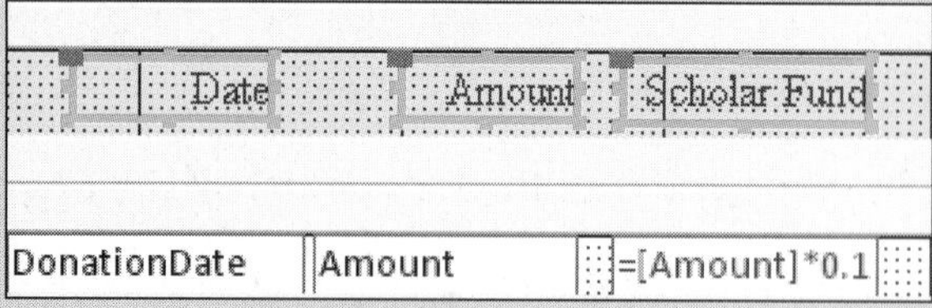

46. Choose **Arrange→Sizing & Ordering→Align→Top**.
47. Choose **Arrange→Sizing & Ordering→Size/Space→To Shortest**.

48. Add a text box to the right of the ScholarFund text box, delete the associated label, and enter these properties for the new NetDonation text box:

Property	Value
Name	NetDonation
Control Source	=Amount-ScholarFund
Format	Currency
Width	1"
Top	0"
Left	8.8"
Border Style	Transparent

49. Choose **Design→Controls→Label**. Draw a new label control above the ScholarFund text box named `Net Donation`.
50. Click the **Amount** label and paint its format on the new **Net Donation label**.
51. Align and size the **Net Donation label** to the other labels as above.
52. Choose **Page Setup→Page Size→Margins** →**Narrow**.
53. Choose **Page Setup→Page Layout→Landscape** .
54. Choose **Report** from the **Selection Type** list at the top of the Property Sheet and type `10"` for the **Width** property.

    The layout is wider and the Report Header should be centered on the report.
55. Select all the controls in the **Report Header section** and tap → until the left edge of the titles are at the **3" mark** on the horizontal ruler.
56. Switch to **Print Preview**.

    The report should include the Count running down the left side and the two new currency text fields and labels on the right.
57. Save and close the **Donations Report**.

    Now, you will modify the subreport in the Staff Report to grow and shrink depending on how many detail lines it contains.
58. Display the **Staff Report** in **Design View**.
59. Select the **K4C Staffing Subreport** and click the **Format** tab of the Property Sheet.
60. Choose **Yes** for the **Can Grow** property on the Property Sheet, if necessary; choose **Yes** for the **Can Shrink** property.
61. Save the **Staff Report** and leave it in **Design View**.

Add a Logo, Title, Date, and Page Break to a Report

62. Display the **Volunteers Report** in **Design View**.
63. Select all the controls in the Report Header section of the **Volunteers Report**.

64. Press Ctrl+C to copy the selected controls, click the **Page Header section bar** of the **Staff Report**, and press Ctrl+V to paste the controls.

65. Tap ↓ twice to move down the pasted controls slightly.

66. Close the **Volunteers Report**.

67. Select the logo and type `6.5"` for the **Left** property.

68. Select the two title controls and type `2"` for the **Left** property.

69. Select the **Date control** and type `3.5"` for the **Left** property.

70. Highlight the text in the **Volunteers subtitle**, type `Staff Report`, and tap Enter.

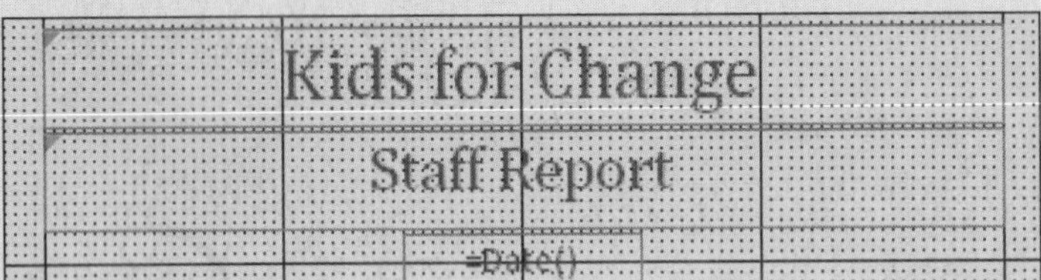

The Page Header with the new heading controls and Staff Report as the subtitle.

71. Switch to **Print Preview**.
    The report will be displayed with the new subtitle.

72. Switch to **Design View**. Choose **Design→Controls→Insert Page Break** and click in the bottom-left side of the Detail section of the main report.
    Access places the page break control on the report.

73. Switch to **Print Preview**.
    The report should display each staffer on a separate page.

74. Close **Print Preview**, and save and close the **Staff Report**.

Analyze Report Performance

75. Choose **Database Tools→Analyze→**Analyze Performance.

76. Click the **Reports** tab, click **Select All**, and click **OK**.
    Access provides more detail about how to optimize database performance with respect to each specific result. In the case above, the analyzer presents some "ideas" about changing field data types; however, each current data type is valid and acceptable.

77. Close the **Performance Analyzer** dialog box. Close the database and exit **Access**.

78. Submit your final file based on the guidelines provided by your instructor.

Apply Your Skills

APPLY YOUR SKILLS AC09-A01

Work with Reports and Subreports

In this exercise, you will help Universal Corporate Events, Ltd. create a report that breaks down revenue by venue, including numbered detail lines for each event. You will save the subreport as a separate report, and add a text box to count scheduled events at each venue.

Import a Report

1. Start **Access**. Open **AC09-A01-UCE** from your **AC2013 Lesson 09** folder and save it as `AC09-A01-UCE-[FirstInitialLastName]`.
2. Choose **External Data→Import & Link→**[Access].
   The Get External Data dialog box opens.
3. Click **Browse**, navigate to the **AC2013 Lesson 09** folder, and double-click **AC09-A01-UCE-Backup**.
   This database is a backup copy of an older UCE, Ltd. database.
4. Choose the **Import Tables, Queries, Forms, Reports, Macros, and Modules into the Current Database** option and click **OK**.
   Access displays object names contained in the backup database.
5. Click the **Reports** tab and choose **Venue Revenue Report**.
6. Click **OK** then close the **Get External Data** dialog box.
7. Display the newly imported **Venue Revenue Report** in **Design View**.
   The space in the VenueID Header section is where you will insert the subreport.

Add a Subreport

8. Draw a subreport control in the **VenueID Header** section under the other controls.
9. Choose **VenueRevenue Subform** and click **Next**.
10. Choose the **Show Statement Linking By VenueID**.
11. Click **Next**, keep the default name, and click **Finish**.
12. Delete the **VenueRevenue Subform label**.
13. Click the subreport control and enter these properties on the Property Sheet:

Property	Value
Width	7"
Height	1.5"
Top	1.3"
Left	.25"
Border Style	Transparent

14. Click the **VenueID Header section bar** and type `3"` for the **Height** property.

15. Save the **Venue Revenue Report** and switch to **Print Preview**.

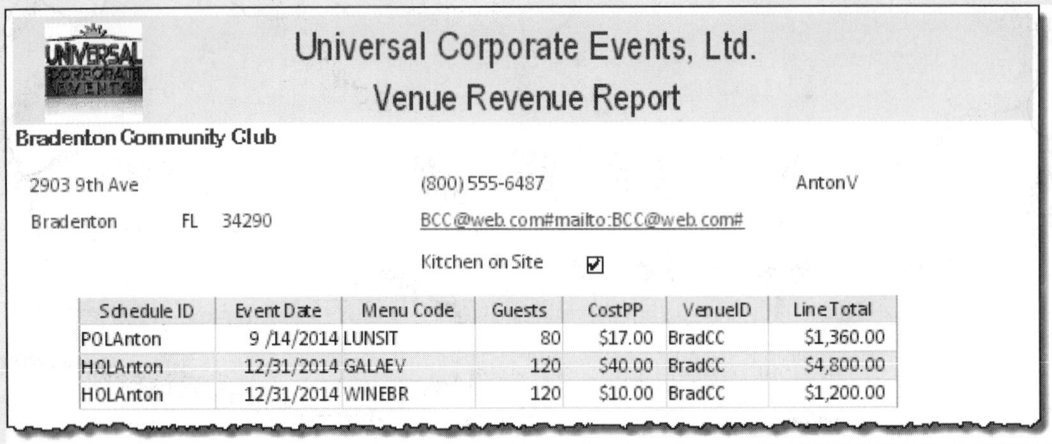

Universal Corporate Events, Ltd.

Venue Revenue Report

Bradenton Community Club

2903 9th Ave (800) 555-6487 AntonV

Bradenton FL 34290 BCC@web.com#mailto:BCC@web.com#

Kitchen on Site ☑

Schedule ID	Event Date	Menu Code	Guests	CostPP	VenueID	Line Total
POLAnton	9 /14/2014	LUNSIT	80	$17.00	BradCC	$1,360.00
HOLAnton	12/31/2014	GALAEV	120	$40.00	BradCC	$4,800.00
HOLAnton	12/31/2014	WINEBR	120	$10.00	BradCC	$1,200.00

Create a Report from a Subreport

16. Switch to **Design View**, right-click the left side of the subreport control, and choose **Subreport in New Window**.
    Access opens the subreport in a separate window.

17. Choose **File→Save As→Save Object As→Save As**.

18. Type `VenueRevenue SubReport` in the **Save...To** box, choose **Report** from the **As** menu, and click **OK**. Close the **VenueRevenue SubReport**.
    Access returns to the Venue Revenue Report in Design View.

19. With the subreport control selected, click in the **Source Object** line of the Property Sheet and choose **Report.VenueRevenue SubReport**.

20. Save the **Venue Revenue Report** then switch to **Print Preview**.
    The subreport will be displayed.

21. Close **Print Preview** and close the **Venue Revenue Report**.
    Next, you will resize the labels and move them from the Detail section into the Report Header section.

22. Display the **VenueRevenue SubReport** in **Design View** and drag the right edge of the report to the right a couple of inches.

23. Select all labels and text boxes, choose **Transparent** for the **Border Style** property, and choose **Text 1** (black) for the **Fore Color** property.

24. Reduce the size of each label to just fit its caption.

25. Click the **Report Header section bar** and type `.3"` for the **Height**.

26. Cut each label, in order, from the Detail section and paste them into the Report Header section, spacing them horizontally across the section.

27. Click and drag each text box within the Detail section to line up horizontally under each label, resizing them as necessary.

28. Right-align the **Line Total label**, the **Detail section calculated control**, and the **Report Footer section calculated control**.

29. Click the **Detail section bar** and type `.3"` for the **Height** property.

30. Switch to **Layout View** and resize and move the controls as shown.

VenueID	Schedule ID	Event Date	Menu Code	Guests	CostPP	Line Total
PalmCt	BRTLuna	10/12/2014	BARSNK	50	$7.50	$375.00
WMinst	HOLMiller	1/1/2015	CHFBRK	100	$16.00	$1,600.00
Meadow	HOLMiller	7/2/2014	DESSRT	25	$13.00	$325.00
ClubLK	HOLBreen	12/11/2014	DESSRT	50	$13.00	$650.00
WMinst	HOLMiller	1/1/2015	DESSRT	100	$13.00	$1,300.00

31. Save the subreport.

Number Report Items

32. Switch to **Design View**, and then type `6"` for the **Width** property of the subreport.

33. Select all report controls and tap [→] to nudge them just to the right edge of the subreport.

34. Draw a new text box in the Detail section to the left of the **VenueID** text box. Delete the associated label control.

35. Click the new text box control and set these property values:

Property	Value
Name	txtCount
Control Source	=1
Width	.2"
Top	0"
Left	0"
Border Style	Transparent
Running Sum	Over All

36. Save and close the **VenueRevenue SubReport**.

37. Display the **Venue Revenue Report** in **Print Preview**.
The detail lines for each venue are counted.

38. Save and close the reports. Then close the database and exit **Access**.

39. Submit your final file based on the guidelines provided by your instructor.
To see examples of how your file or files should look at the end of this exercise, go to the student resource center.

APPLY YOUR SKILLS AC09-A02

Add Fields and Controls, and Analyze Database Performance

Universal Corporate Events, Ltd. wants to refine their database reports and analyze report performance. In this exercise, you will add a field to calculate the total of all the venues' revenues; modify a subreport to ensure that all venue detail lines will display; add custom Report Header controls and a page break to another report, and run the analyze report performance.

Add a Calculated Field to a Report

1. Start **Access**. Open **AC09-A02-UCE** from your **AC2013 Lesson 09** folder and save it as `AC09-A02-UCE-[FirstInitialLastName]`.
2. Open the **Venue Revenue Report** in **Design View**.
3. Click the **Report Footer section bar** and type `.4"` for the **Height** property.
4. Draw a new text box in the **Report Footer** section, under the right end of the subreport.
5. Select the associated label and enter these values on the Property Sheet:

Property	Value
Caption	Grand Total for All Venues
Width	2"
Top	.1"
Left	2"
Font Weight	Semi-Bold
Fore Color	Blue, Accent 1, Darker 50%

6. Click the new text box and enter these property values:

Property	Value
Name	ActivityCost
Control Source	=Sum(Guests*ChgPP)
Format	Currency
Width	1.5"
Top	.1"
Left	5"
Border Style	Transparent
Font Weight	Semi-Bold
Fore Color	Blue, Accent 1, Darker 50%

7. Switch to **Print Preview** and navigate through the report.

   If you get an error message that says section width is greater than page width, click OK, display the report in Design View, and set the Width property of the report to 7.9".
8. Save the **Venue Revenue Report**.

Grow and Shrink a Subreport

9. Display the **Venue Revenue Report** in **Design View**.
10. Select the **VenueRevenue Subform** and click the **Format** tab on the Property Sheet.
11. Choose **Yes** for the **Can Grow** property, if necessary; choose **Yes** for the **Can Shrink** property.

    This ensures that all venue detail lines will be displayed.
12. Save the **Venue Revenue Report**.

Add a Logo, Title, Date, and Page Break to a Report

13. Open the **Event Revenue Report** in **Design View**. Delete the title control in the Report Header, click the **Report Header section bar**, and type `0"` for its **Height**.
14. Click the **Page Header section bar** and type `.85"` for its **Height** property
15. Choose **Blue, Accent 1, Lighter 80%** for the **Back Color** of the Page Header section.
16. Copy all the controls in the Report Header section of the **Venue Revenue Report**.
17. Paste the copied controls into the Page Header section **Event Revenue Report**; close the **Venue Revenue Report**.
18. Tap [↓] as necessary to move down the pasted controls in the Page Header.
19. Select the two title controls; type **4"** for the **Width** and **2"** for the **Left** property.
20. Select just the logo and type **.5"** for the **Left** property.
21. Select the **="Page " control** in the Page Footer section and choose **Right** for the Text Align property. Then, right-align the **="Page " control** with the **Total Revenue controls**.
22. Change the subtitle to `Event Revenue Report`, and tap [Enter].
23. Choose **Design→Controls→Insert Page Break** and click in the left side of the EventDate Footer under the Total for label.

    Access places the page break control on the report.
24. Switch to **Print Preview** and navigate to **January 2014**.

    Each month's donations appear on a separate page.
25. Save and close the **Event Revenue Report**.

Analyze Database Performance

26. Choose **Database Tools→Analyze→** Analyze Performance.
27. Choose the **Reports** tab, click **Select All**, and click **OK**.

    Access analyzes the reports and presents an analysis that returns several ideas.

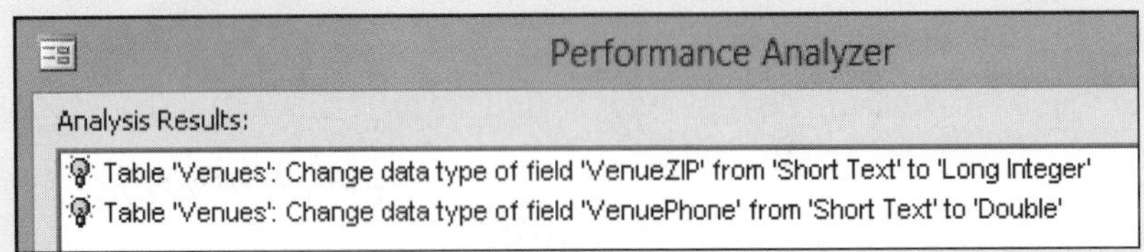

Performance Analyzer

Analysis Results:

Table 'Venues': Change data type of field 'VenueZIP' from 'Short Text' to 'Long Integer'

Table 'Venues': Change data type of field 'VenuePhone' from 'Short Text' to 'Double'

The analyzer presents "ideas" about changing field data types; but each current data type is valid and acceptable.

28. Close the **Performance Analyzer** dialog box. Then close the database and exit **Access**.
29. Submit your final file based on the guidelines provided by your instructor.

    To see examples of how your file or files should look at the end of this exercise, go to the student resource center.

APPLY YOUR SKILLS AC09-A03

Work with Reports and Analyze Database Performance

In this exercise, you will help Universal Corporate Events refine existing reports and analyze report performance. You will import a report and add a subreport that shows revenue from each venue liaison. You will create a separate report from the subreport, add a count of UCE's venues, and add a field to calculate revenue by liaison. You will then modify a subreport to grow or shrink, add Report Header controls and a page break, and analyze report performance.

Import a Report

1. Start **Access**. Open **AC09-A03-UCE** from your **AC2013 Lesson 09** folder and save it as **`AC09-A03-UCE-[FirstInitialLastName]`**.
2. Choose **External Data→Import & Link→** Access.

   The Get External Data dialog box opens.
3. Click **Browse**, navigate to the **AC2013 Lesson 09** folder, and double-click **AC09-A03-UCE-Backup**.
4. Choose the **Import Tables, Queries, Forms, Reports, Macros, and Modules into the Current Database** option, and click **OK**.

   Access displays object names contained in the backup database.
5. Click the **Reports** tab and choose **Liaison Revenue Report**.
6. Click **OK** then close the **Get External Data dialog box**.
7. Display the **Liaison Revenue Report** in **Design View** and open the Property Sheet.
8. Type `Liaison Revenue Report` for the **Caption** property.

Add a Subreport

9. Draw a subreport control in the **Detail** section.
10. Choose **VenueLiaison Subform** as the data source.
11. Choose the **Show VenueLiaison Query** option shown:

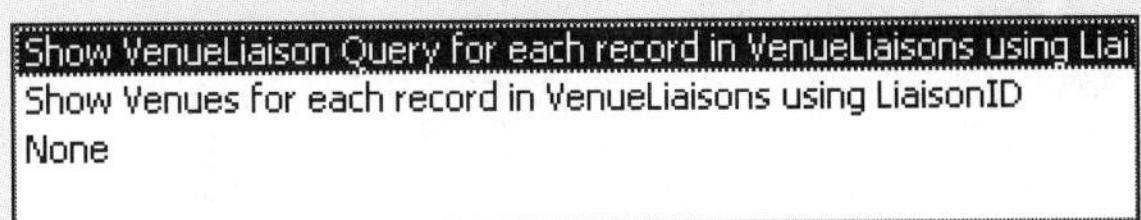
Show VenueLiaison Query for each record in VenueLiaisons using Liai
Show Venues for each record in VenueLiaisons using LiaisonID
None

12. Click **Next**, keep the default name, and click **Finish**.
13. Delete the **VenueLiaison Subform label**.
14. Click the subreport control and enter these properties on the Property Sheet:

Property	Value
Width	7.5"
Height	2"
Top	2"
Left	.1"
Border Style	Transparent

15. Click the **Detail section bar** and type **4"** for the **Height** property.
16. Save the **Liaison Revenue Report** and switch to **Print Preview**.
    The report should list each detail line in datasheet layout. If you get a page width error message, set the report's Width property to 7.9".
17. Close **Print Preview**.

Create a Report from a Subreport

18. Switch to **Design View**, right-click the left side of the subreport control, and choose **Subreport in New Window**.
    Access opens the subreport in a separate window.
19. Choose **File→Save As→Save Object As→Save As**.
20. Type **VenueLiaison SubReport** in the **Save...To** box, choose **Report** from the **As** menu, and click **OK**.
21. Close the subreport. Then, with the subreport control selected, click in the **Source Object** property line and choose **Report.VenueLiaison SubReport**.
22. Save the **Liaison Revenue Report** and switch to **Print Preview**.
23. Close **Print Preview** and close the **Liaison Revenue Report**.
24. Display the **VenueLiaison SubReport** in **Design View**.
25. Select all controls; choose **Transparent** for the **Border Style** and **Black, Text 1** for the **Fore Color**.

Access 2013

26. Resize and align the header controls with the detail controls.

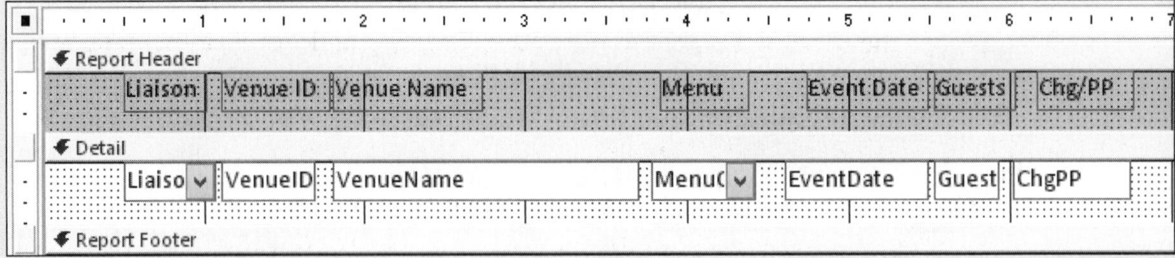

27. Save the **VenueLiaison SubReport**.

Number Report Items

28. Type `7.5"` for the **Width** property of the subreport.

    Report should appear in the Selection Type box at the top of the Property Sheet.

29. Draw a text box in the Detail section to the left of the **Liaison** text box. Delete the associated label control.

30. Click the new text box control and set these property values:

Property	Value
Name	txtCount
Control Source	=1
Width	.3"
Top	0"
Left	.1"
Border Style	Transparent
Fore Color	Text 1, Black
Running Sum	Over All

31. Save the subreport.

Add a Calculated Field to a Report

32. Draw a new text box in the Detail section to the right of the **Chg/PP** text box. Delete the associated label.

33. Click the new text box and enter these property values:

Property	Value
Name	NetAmt
Control Source	= Guests*ChgPP
Format	Currency
Width	.9"
Top	0"
Left	6.6"
Font Weight	Semi-Bold
Fore Color	Blue, Accent 1, Darker 50%

34. Draw a new label in the Report Header section to the right of the **Chg/PP label**.

35. Type `Net Amt` in the new label.

36. Use the **Format Painter** to paint the formatting of the other labels onto the new label.

37. Type `.6"` for the **Width** and `6.9"` for the **Left** property.

38. Save and close the subreport.

39. Display the **Liaison Revenue Report** in **Print Preview**.

    A field that multiplies the number of guests by the charge per person to produce a net amount is added to the subreport. If necessary, switch to Layout View to adjust the size and spacing of the controls for better display.

40. Close **Print Preview**.

Grow a Subreport

41. Switch to **Design View** and click to select the **VenueLiaison SubReport**.

42. Choose **Yes** for the **Can Grow** property, if necessary; choose **Yes** for **Can Shrink**.

    Setting the Can Grow and Can Shrink properties will ensure that all venue detail lines will be displayed, and that the spacing between the final venue total and the grand total will always be the same.

43. Save the **Liaison Revenue Report**.

Add a Logo, Title, Date, and Page Break to a Report

44. Display the **Venue Revenue Report** in **Design View** and copy all controls in the **Report Header** section. Close the report.

45. Display the **Liaison Revenue Report** in **Design View**, delete the existing title control, set the Report Header **Height** property to `0`, and paste the copied controls into the Page Header section.

46. Tap [↓] to align the pasted controls in the Page Header.

47. Select the two title controls and type `2"` for the **Left** property.

48. Select the logo and type `.5"` for the **Left** property.

49. Select the **Date control** and type `6.75"` for the **Left** property.

50. Change the subtitle to `Liaison Revenue Report`.

51. Click the **Page Header** section bar and choose **Blue, Accent 1, Lighter 80%** for the **Back Color** property.

52. Save the report and switch to **Print Preview**.

Universal Corporate Events, Ltd.
Liaison Revenue Report
04-Apr-13

53. Close **Print Preview**.

Access 2013

54. Choose **Design→Controls→Insert Page Break** and click in the bottom-left corner of the **Detail section** just below the subform.

    Access places the page break control on the report.

55. Switch to **Print Preview** and navigate through the pages.

    Each liaison's net amount should be displayed on a separate page.

If every other page is blank, the report might be too wide or there might be a control placed beyond the margin. To fix this, move the errant control to the left and drag the right edge of the report to the left.

56. Save and close the **Liaison Revenue Report**.

Analyze Database Performance

57. Choose **Database Tools→Analyze→** Analyze Performance.

58. Choose the **Reports** tab, click **Select All**, and click **OK**.

    Access analyzes the reports, presents an analysis, and suggests how to optimize performance.

59. Close the **Performance Analyzer** dialog box. Then close the database and exit **Access**.

60. Submit your final file based on the guidelines provided by your instructor.

Extend Your Skills

In the course of working through the Extend Your Skills exercises, you will think critically as you use the skills taught in the lesson to complete the assigned projects. To evaluate your mastery and completion of the exercises, your instructor may use a rubric, with which more points are allotted according to performance characteristics. (The more you do, the more you earn!) Ask your instructor how your work will be evaluated.

AC09-E01 That's the Way I See It

Blue Jean Landscaping needs to modify its database reports. Use the database you used in AC08-E01 or open **AC09-E01-BJL** from the **AC2013 Lesson 09** folder and save it as `AC09-E01-BJL-[FirstInitialLastName]`. Import the Customer Sales Report from **AC09-E01-BJL-Backup** in the **AC2013 Lesson 09** folder. (If using your own database, import a report from one of your backups or create a new backup.) Add the CustomerSales Subform to the Customer Sales Report; save the subform as a separate report, and number the lines within the subreport. (If using your own database, insert a related subform in your imported report.) Calculate each customer line total (Price*QtySold) in the Detail section of the subreport. Calculate each customer's total (=Sum(Price*QtySold)) in the Report Footer.

Add appropriate title/subtitles, date, and either the BJL logo or your own. Insert a page break to display each customer on a separate page and, finally, run the performance analyzer on the database reports.

You will be evaluated based on the inclusion of all elements, your ability to follow directions, your ability to apply newly learned skills to a real-world situation, your creativity, and your accuracy in creating objects and/or entering data. Submit your final file based on the guidelines provided by your instructor.

AC09-E02 Be Your Own Boss

In this exercise, you will modify reports for Blue Jean Landscaping. To begin, open **AC09-E02-BJL** from the **AC2013 Lesson 09** folder and save it as `AC09-E02-BJL-[FirstInitialLastName]`.

Import the Manufacturer Sales Report from the **AC09-E02-BJL-Backup** database (in **AC2013 Lesson 09**). Insert the ManufacturerSales Subform in the Manufacturer Sales Report and save the subform as a separate report. Number the line items in the subreport and main form. Calculate each line total (Price*QtySold) in the Detail section of the subreport.

Format titles, add the BJL-Logo and date, add a page break to display each manufacturer on a separate page, and analyze report performance.

You will be evaluated based on the inclusion of all elements, your ability to follow directions, your ability to apply newly learned skills to a real-world situation, your creativity, and your accuracy in creating objects and/or entering data. Submit your final file based on the guidelines provided by your instructor.

Transfer Your Skills

In the course of working through the Transfer Your Skills exercises, you will use critical-thinking and creativity skills to complete the assigned projects using skills taught in the lesson. To evaluate your mastery and completion of the exercises, your instructor may use a rubric, with which more points are allotted according to performance characteristics. (The more you do, the more you earn!) Ask your instructor how your work will be evaluated.

AC09-T01 Use the Web as a Learning Tool

Throughout this book, you will be provided with an opportunity to use the Internet as a learning tool by completing WebQuests. According to the original creators of WebQuests, as described on their website (WebQuest.org), a WebQuest is "an inquiry-oriented activity in which most or all of the information used by learners is drawn from the web." To complete the WebQuest projects in this book, navigate to the student resource center and choose the WebQuest for the lesson on which you are currently working. The subject of each WebQuest will be relevant to the material found in the lesson.

WebQuest Subject: Filtering data in reports

Submit your files based on the guidelines provided by your instructor.

AC09-T02 Demonstrate Proficiency

The Stormy BBQ Key West store and restaurant has been enjoying increased sales! You must make some changes to the database reports to produce more useful sales results. Open **AC09-T02-SBQ** from the **AC2013 Lesson 09** folder and save it as `AC09-T02-SBQ-[FirstInitialLastName]`.

Import the Merchandise Sales Report, which lists merchandise by SKU, from **AC09-T02-SBQ-Backup** in the **AC2013 Lesson 09** folder. Insert the MerchandiseSales Subform into the Detail section of the Merchandise Sales Report to add individual sale line items (Choose Show each record in Merchandise using SKU). Save the subform as a report. (Close the subform then open the subreport so the changes you make are not reflected in the subform). Number line items in the subreport and in the main report. Calculate each line total (ListPrice*QtySold) in the Detail section of the subreport. Copy the titles, logo, date, and formatting from the Merchandise Inventory Report into the Merchandise Sales Report, add a page break to display each SKU item on a separate page, and run the performance analyzer.

Submit your final file based on the guidelines provided by your instructor.

ACCESS 2013

Customizing the Database Interface and Startup Options

LESSON OUTLINE

LEARNING OBJECTIVES

After studying this lesson, you will be able to:

- Set Access options
- Split a database
- Explore switchboards and create a Navigation Form
- Set and modify startup options

Now that you have learned how to create customized forms and reports, you can focus on sharing your database with others. In this lesson, you will create a Navigation Form, which is an attractive, user-friendly interface to allow for quick and accurate data entry. You will also split a database so that the database tables and their data are protected, while allowing users to create and modify their own personal queries, forms, and reports, and set and modify various Access options.

CASE STUDY

Customizing – As You Like It

The Winchester Web Design database is almost complete. However, the owner is concerned about its ease of use and future maintenance. He would like to allow individuals to make their own customized queries and reports, while maintaining a standard company interface and ensuring data validity and database security.

A Navigation Form can display tabs across the top and along either side of a form to allow access to groups of objects and display them in the same work area, one item at a time.

Setting Access Options

Video Library http://labyrinthelab.com/videos Video Number: AC13-V1001

Each Microsoft Office application provides options to control the way the application performs. Access options can control the color of datasheets, set default fonts, create sections on the Navigation Pane, add a title to the application window, customize the Quick Access toolbar, set a default startup form, and so on. Some options control settings for the active database, while others control the default settings for all databases used on a particular machine.

Displaying Access Options

The Access Options dialog box groups features by type. It lists the categories in a panel on the left side and their associated options in the panel on the right side. Some options are used frequently while others are rarely used.

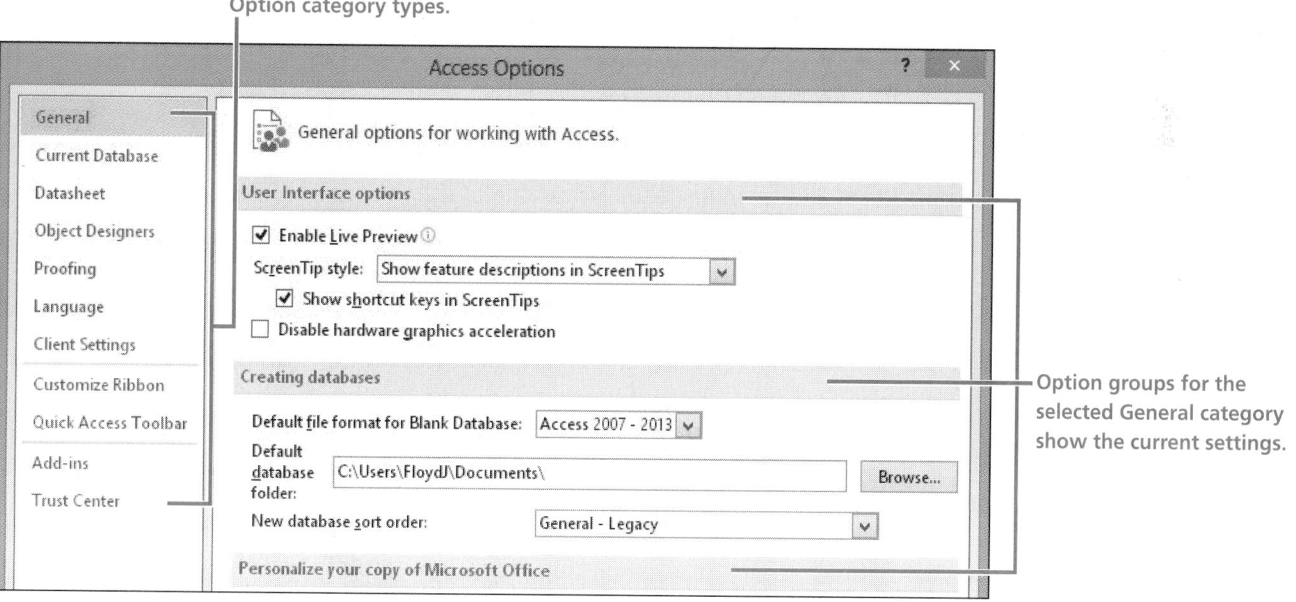

Access 2013

Exploring Datasheet Effects

Tools for setting default gridlines, cell effects, and font size and weight are found in the Datasheet category of the Access Options dialog box.

DEVELOP YOUR SKILLS AC10-D01

Display and Explore Access Options

In this exercise, you will display and explore options in the Access Options dialog box.

1. Open **AC10-D01-WinWebDesign** from your **AC2013 Lesson 10** folder and save it as `AC10-D01-WinWebDesign-[FirstInitialLastName]`.

   Replace the bracketed text with your first initial and last name. For example, if your name is Bethany Smith, your filename would look like this: AC10-D01-WinWebDesign-BSmith.

2. Choose **File→Options** and click the **Datasheet** category.

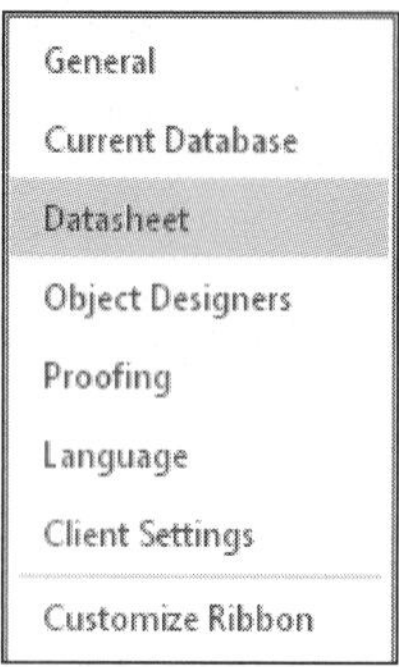

3. Review the options available in each category.
4. **Close** [×] the dialog box without changing any options.

   Unless otherwise directed, keep Access and any databases or database objects being used open at the end of each exercise.

Setting Personal Information

Video Library http://labyrinthelab.com/videos Video Number: AC13-V1002

The Access Options dialog box includes a General category that allows you to set the format in which databases are created, and also permits you to set personal information for your copy of Microsoft Office.

DEVELOP YOUR SKILLS AC10-D02

Set Personal Information

In this exercise, you will personalize your copy of Microsoft Office.

1. Choose **File→Options**.
2. In the **General** category, view and modify the personalized settings as desired.

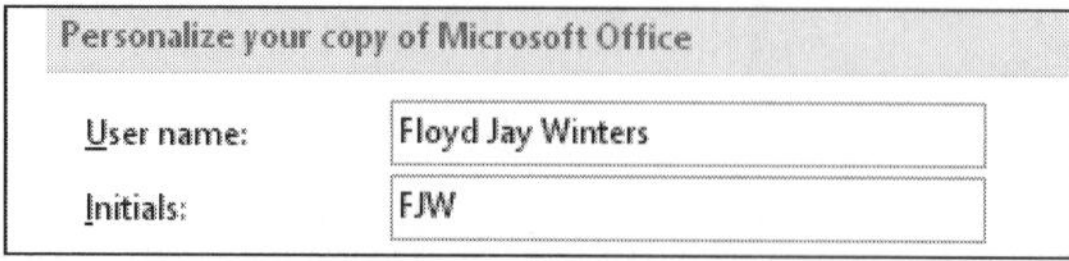

3. Click **OK** to save any changes and close the Access Options dialog box.

Customizing the Navigation Pane

Video Library http://labyrinthelab.com/videos Video Number: AC13-V1003

The Navigation Pane is your tool for selecting database objects and identifying objects associated with each object type. You use the Navigation Pane to display objects in different views. You can also customize the Navigation Pane to contain additional sections to make the pane even more useful.

Navigation Pane Categories and Groups

The Navigation Options dialog box shows two list boxes: one that identifies the categories of objects displayed on the Navigation Pane and one that shows the groups available for display on the pane.

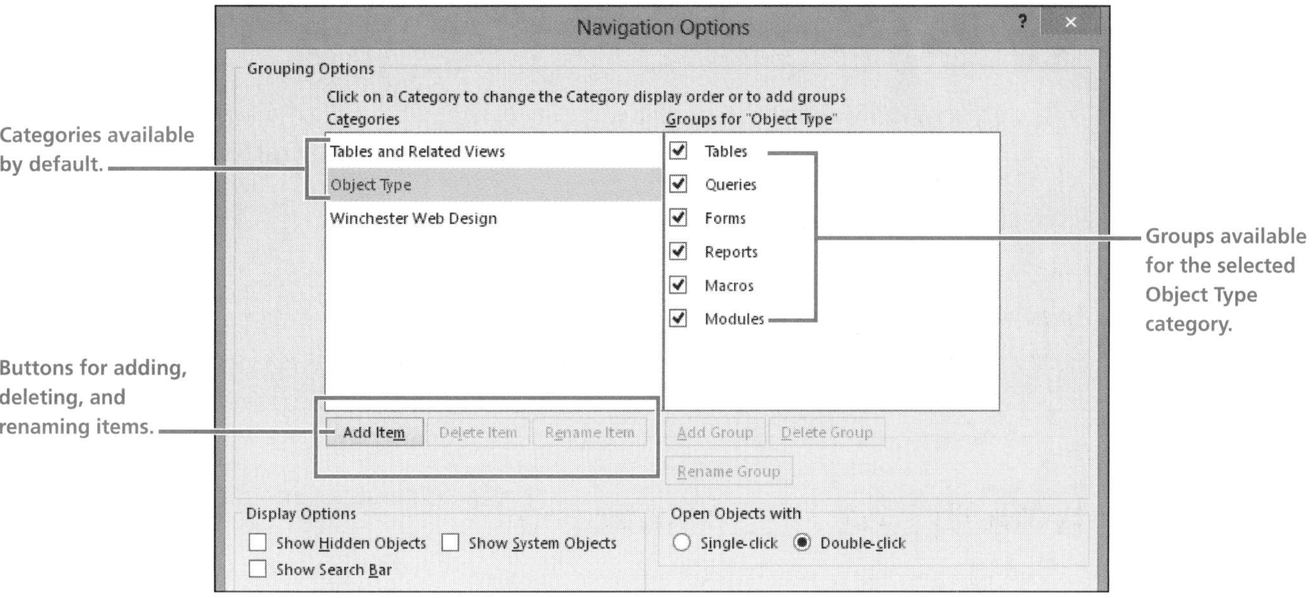

Working with Groups

Access prevents you from changing, deleting, or adding additional object type groups to the essential Tables and Related Views and Object Type categories. However, the Custom category allows you to rename, delete, and add groups to a category. When you add or rename groups in the Navigation Pane, you must reassign objects to the groups so Access knows where to place them.

Customizing the Navigation Pane controls settings for the active database only. You must customize the Navigation Pane for any other databases.

Access 2013

DEVELOP YOUR SKILLS AC10-D03

Customize the Navigation Pane

In this exercise, you will customize the Navigation Pane and assign objects to new Navigation Pane groups.

1. Choose **File→Options**, and follow these steps to customize the Navigation Pane:

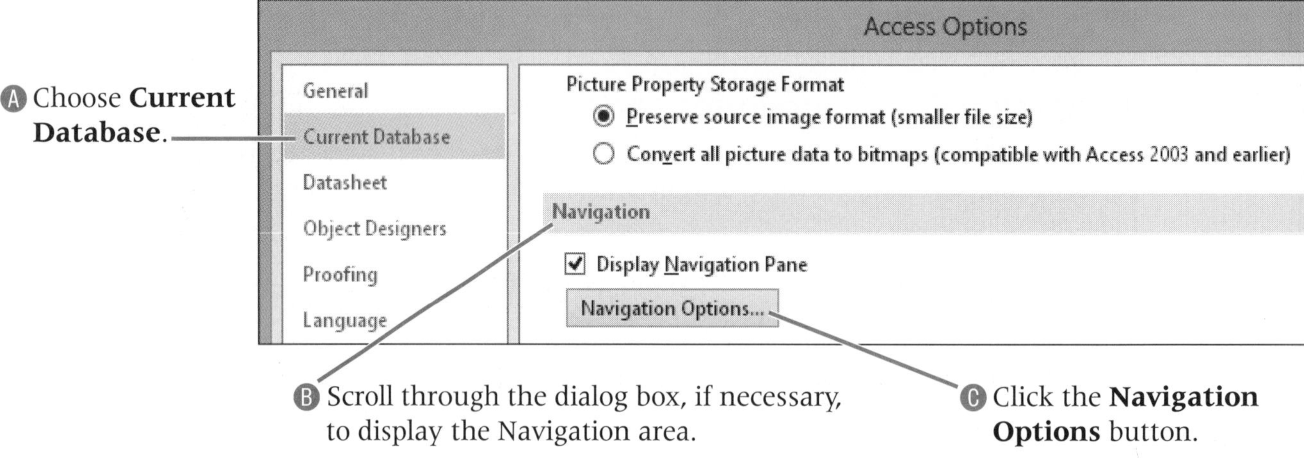

Access displays the Navigation Options dialog box.

2. Click **Add Item**.

A new item appears in the Categories list named Custom Category 1.

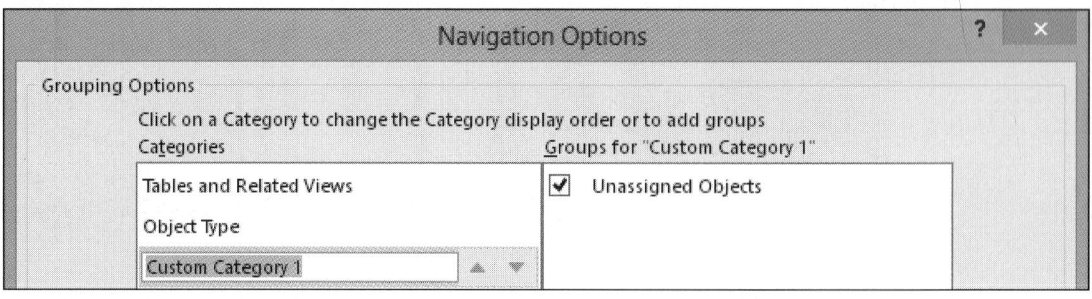

3. Type `Winchester Web Design` in the Custom Category 1 box and tap Enter.

4. Click **Add Group**.

A new item appears in the Groups list named Custom Group 1.

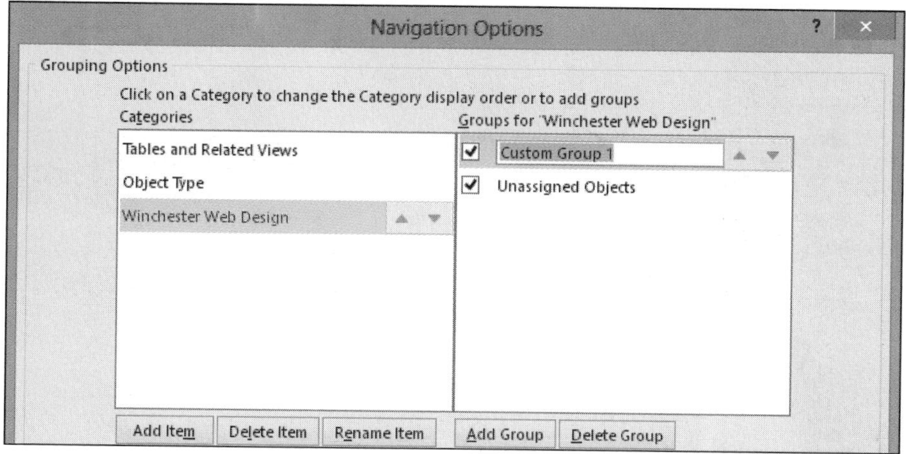

5. Type **`Customers`** in the Custom Group 1 box and tap [Enter].
6. Follow these steps to add a new group to the Groups list:

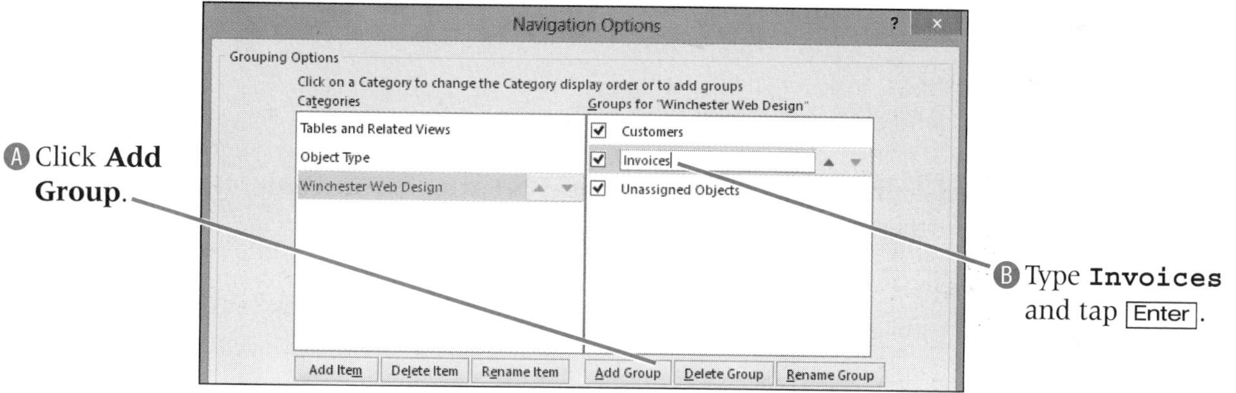

7. Click **OK** to close the Navigation Options dialog box. Click **OK** to close the Access Options dialog box.
8. Follow these steps to display the new Winchester Web Design category:

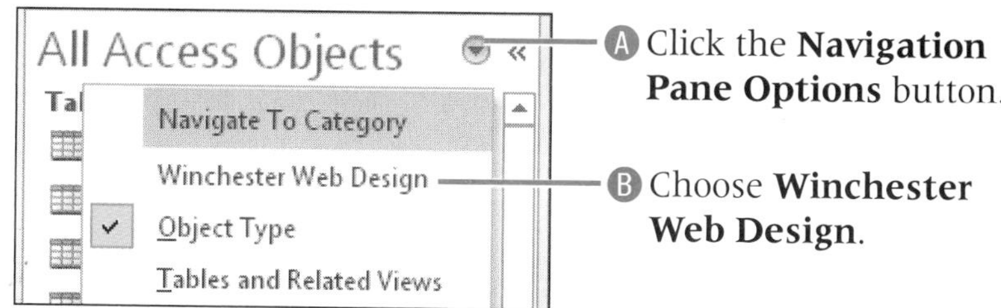

All objects for the Winchester Web Design category are in the Unassigned Objects group.

9. In the Unassigned Objects group on the Navigation Pane, right-click the **Customers** table object and choose **Add to Group→Customers**.

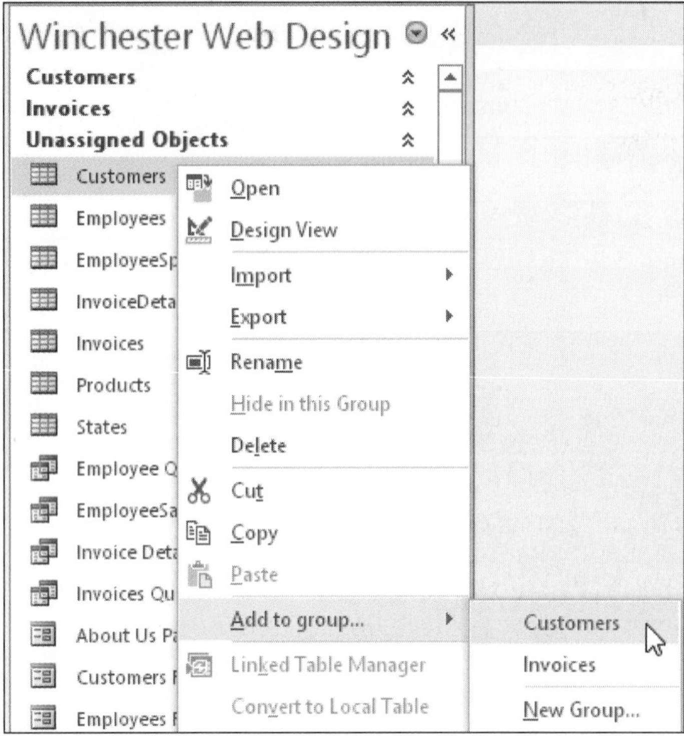

10. One at a time, right-click the **Customers Form**, the **Customer Invoice Report**, and **Customer Invoice Subreport** to add them to the Customers group.

11. Assign the following objects to the Invoice group:

Object	Type
InvoiceDetails	Table
Invoices	Table
Invoice Details Query	Query
Invoice Query	Query
Invoice Form	Form
Invoice Details Subform	Form
Invoice Details Report	Report

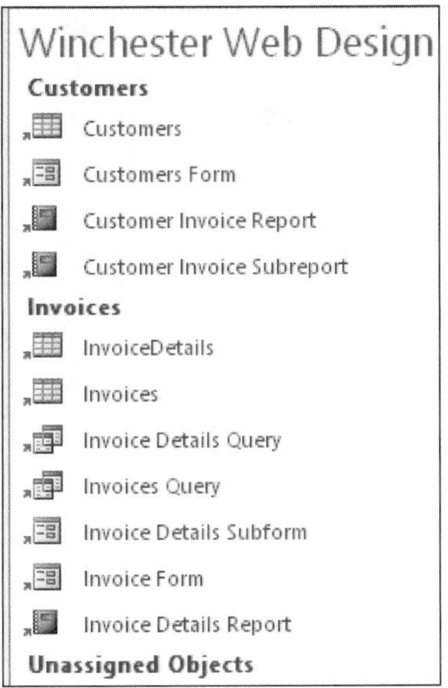

12. Click the **Navigation Pane Options** drop-down button and choose **Object Type**.
The Navigation Pane returns to the more traditional view, which groups objects by type (Tables, Queries, Forms, and Reports).

Setting Database Properties

Video Library http://labyrinthelab.com/videos Video Number: AC13-V1004

Database properties are similar to other object properties, except that they identify or describe an *entire* database, such as the database title and author, names of objects contained in the database, or the date and time it was created or last updated.

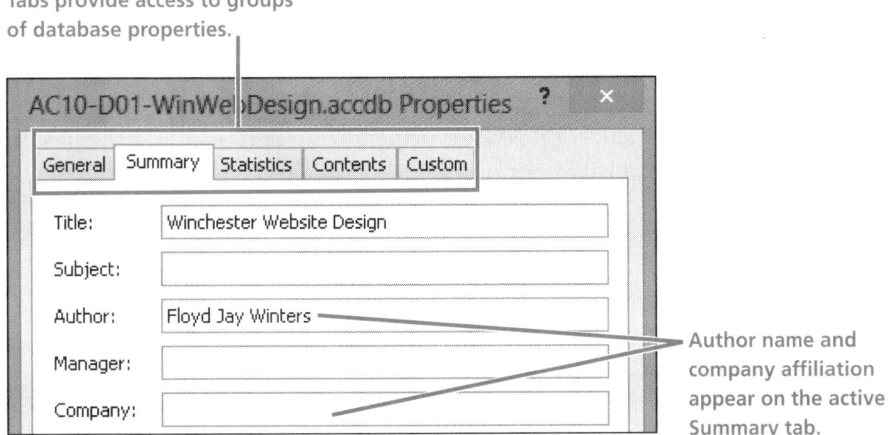

DEVELOP YOUR SKILLS AC10-D04

Set Database Properties

In this exercise, you will change database properties.

1. Choose **File→Info**, and follow these steps to set the database properties:

Ⓐ Click the **View and Edit Database Properties** link.

Ⓑ Click the **Summary** tab on the Properties dialog box.

Ⓒ Type your instructor's name in the **Manager** line.

Ⓓ Type your school's name in the **Company** line.

2. Click **OK**.

Setting Up Current Database Format

Video Library http://labyrinthelab.com/videos Video Number: AC13-V1005

Current database settings enable you to change the way Access displays and works with the *active* database. You can, for example, change the text Access displays in the title bar when the database is open, show or hide the Navigation Pane, enable views, or change the way Access displays open objects.

Changing Title Text in the Application Bar

Sometimes, the actual filename assigned to a database may be different from the text you want users to see when they open the database. You can change the text that appears in the title bar using the Current Database options window.

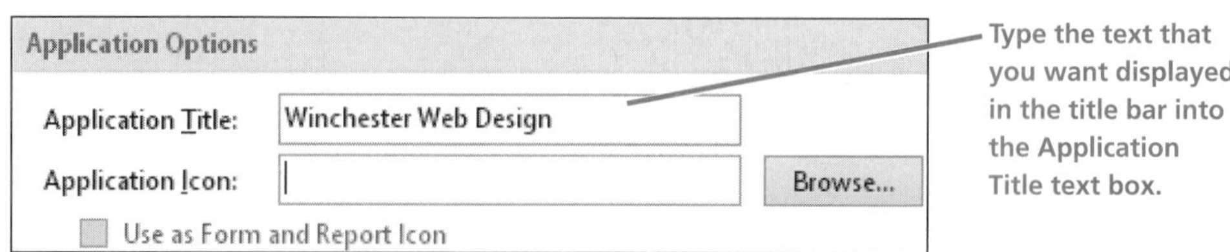

Type the text that you want displayed in the title bar into the Application Title text box.

Setting Object Window Format

Open database objects are set to format as tabs within the database work area. You have to click the tab of the object that you want to see in the work area.

> **FROM THE KEYBOARD**
> [Ctrl]+[F6] to navigate among open objects

Navigation Form | Invoices Query | Employee Report | Customers

CustID	Last Name	First Name	Street Address	City
AbramsJ	Abrams	John	1210 West Pier Wa	Palmetto
AndersM	Anders	Mark	205 Montana St	Bradenton
BlaserH	Blaser	Helen	600 Fowler	Tampa

Tabs for opened documents align at the top of the work area.

You can change the format so objects display as overlapping windows in the work area similar to what was used in previous versions of Access. You can also move and resize the objects for easier comparison of styles, layout, and contents.

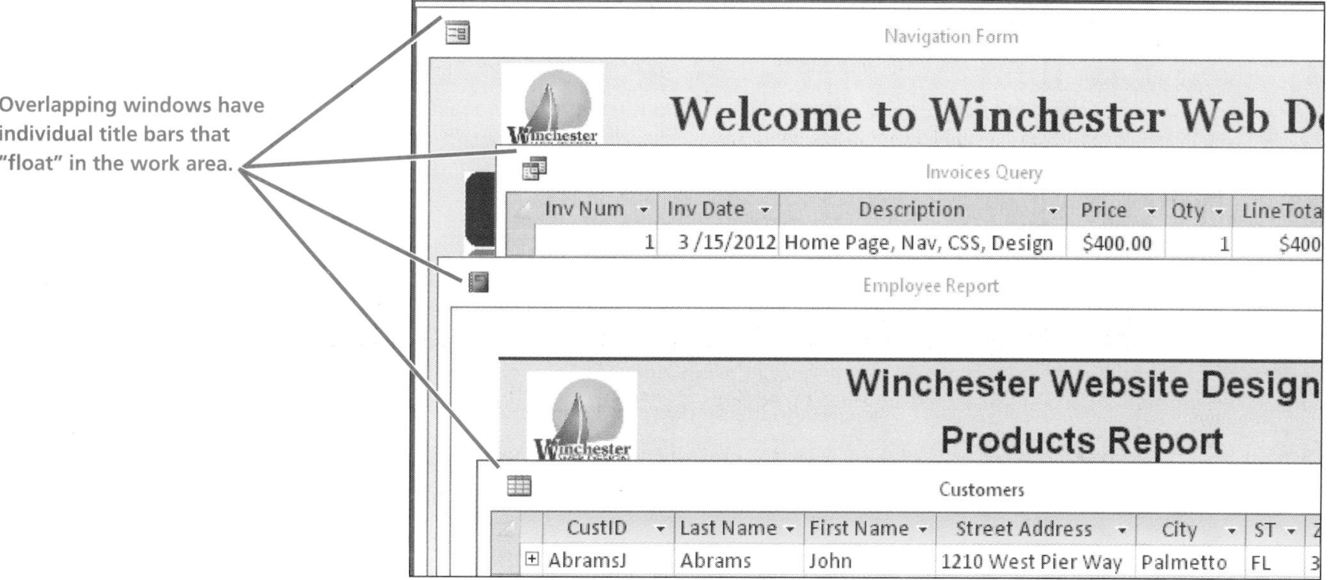

After changing the document window options, close and then reopen the database to view the new settings.

Access 2013

QUICK REFERENCE	SETTING ACCESS OPTIONS
Task	**Procedure**
Change the title in the Application bar	■ Choose File→Options→Current Database. ■ Click the Application Title text box and type the title text to appear at the top of your database window.
Set an Access background and theme	■ Choose File→Options→General category. ■ Under Personalize Your Copy of Microsoft Office, choose the desired background and theme.
Create a Navigation Pane group	■ Choose File→Options→Current Database. ■ In the Navigation section, click the Navigation Options drop-down menu button, choose Add Item, and add the name. ■ Choose Add Group and add the desired group name.
Assign objects to a new Navigation Pane group	■ Select the new or an existing item in the Navigation Pane option list. ■ Right-click the object to assign and choose Add to Group→Group Name. (Example: You would add the Employees form and report to the Employees group.)
Set object window format	■ Choose File→Options→Current Database. ■ Choose the option for the window display to apply under Document Window Options: Overlapping or Tabbed.
Set a default font size and weight	■ Choose File→Options→Datasheet. ■ Click the Size or Weight list button then choose the setting.
Set database default object properties	■ Choose File→Options→Object Designers category. ■ Click the tab containing the property to set, such as the default text field size or the query design font. ■ Change the property and click OK.
Enable error checking	■ Choose File→Options→Object Designers category. ■ Scroll to the bottom of the Access Options dialog box. ■ Select the desired error checking checkboxes. ■ Click the Error indicator color menu and choose a color.

DEVELOP YOUR SKILLS AC10-D05

Set Current Database Options

In this exercise, you will change settings for the current database, editing the title and changing the window options.

1. Choose **File→Options**, and follow these steps to change the application title text and window display:

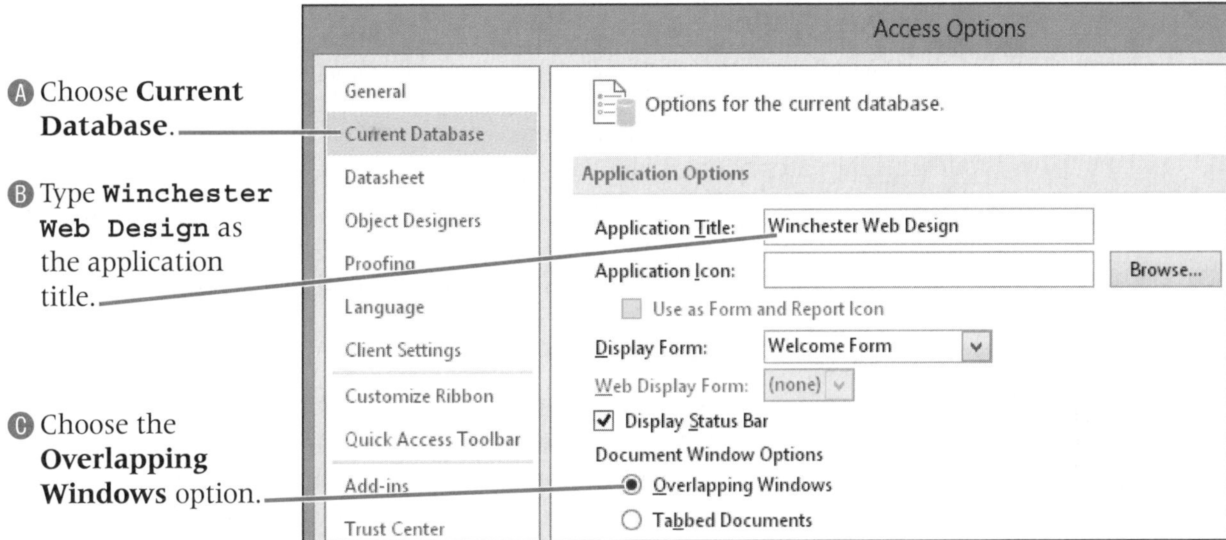

2. Explore other options available for the current database, and then click **OK**.
   You must close and then reopen the database for the settings to take effect.
3. Choose **OK** in the message dialog box; then close and reopen the database.
4. Display the **Customers** and **Products** tables in separate windows.
5. Drag down the title bar of the **Products** table window slightly to view the Customers table.

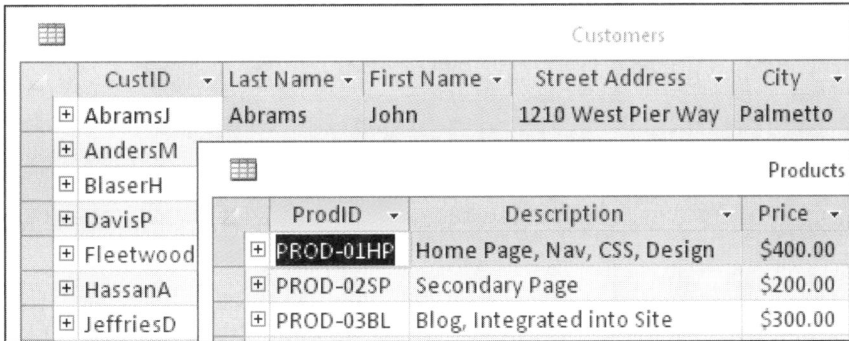

Move and resize the open objects so you can see both at the same time.

6. Choose **File→Options→Current Database**, reset the Document Window option for **Tabbed Documents**, and click **OK** in the message box.
7. Close both the **Customers** and **Products** tables; close the database.

Splitting a Database

Video Library http://labyrinthelab.com/videos Video Number: AC13-V1006

Sometimes users want to edit the design and layout of queries, forms, and reports or even develop their own objects to meet their particular needs. However, if the database is shared by other users, this may cause some potential problems.

Record Locking

Multiple users can simultaneously use an Access database to add, edit, and delete data. Whenever an Access database is opened, Access also creates a small temporary file by the same name, but with the extension .laccdb. This file manages record locking. The initial file extension character, *l*, stands for locked, which means whenever one user edits a record, that record is locked and no other user can edit it until the first user moves to another record. Record locking helps maintain consistent data and protects the integrity of record updates.

Reasons for Splitting Databases

Allowing users to create their own objects in a shared database can create confusion and increase the chance of data corruption or broken database relationships. To protect company data, many businesses prohibit users from creating and saving new objects. One alternate solution that protects table data while enabling users to create and customize objects to meet their personal needs is to split the database.

Using the Database Splitter

The database splitter converts a database into two files—one that contains the tables holding the data that support all other database objects and one that contains the database reports, forms, queries, and other objects that use the data. After splitting the database, multiple users in a networked environment can access the database at the same time. As a result, each user can access, design, and modify their own database objects, and update data from the database tables without interrupting other users or increasing the number of objects contained in the central database.

Split Database Terminology

Two terms are often associated with split databases:

- **Front-end** refers to the up-front portion of a split database with which users interact—the queries, forms, and reports that they use or may create and customize. Access places a blue arrow beside each table name in a split database to identify objects that users can view but not change.
- **Back-end** refers to the underlying database tables that support the front-end. These tables are protected so that users cannot modify their structure. Access adds *_be* to the end of the back-end portion of the database filename.

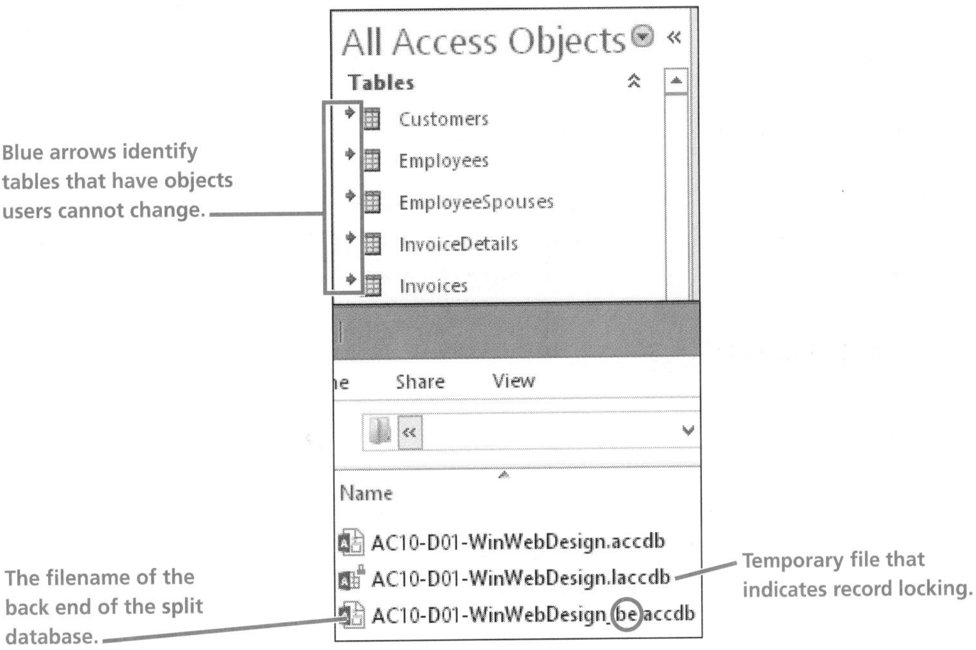
All Access Objects
Tables
Customers
Employees
EmployeeSpouses
InvoiceDetails
Invoices
Blue arrows identify tables that have objects users cannot change.
Share
View
Name
AC10-D01-WinWebDesign.accdb
AC10-D01-WinWebDesign.laccdb
AC10-D01-WinWebDesign_be.accdb
The filename of the back end of the split database.
Temporary file that indicates record locking.

When you split a database, Access links the front-end and back-end of the database so that users can work with controls on forms, queries, and reports.

Backing Up a Database Prior to Splitting

FROM THE RIBBON
File→Save As→Save Database As to copy a database

Access recommends that you back up a database before you split it to preserve the database in case an error occurs during the splitting process. One quick way to do this is to select and copy the database in Windows Explorer, and then paste a backup copy in the desired folder.

QUICK REFERENCE — SPLITTING A DATABASE

Task	Procedure
Split a database	■ Choose Database Tools→Move Data→Access Database. ■ Click the Split Database button. ■ Open the destination folder and click Split.

Access 2013

DEVELOP YOUR SKILLS AC10-D06

Split a Database

In this exercise, you will split the Winchester Web Design database.

1. Open **AC10-D01-WinWebDesign-[FirstInitialLastName]** but *do not* open any database objects.
2. Choose **File→Save As→Save Database As→Save As.**
3. Open your **AC2013 Lesson 10** folder and click **Save** to save a backup as `AC10-D06-WWD-Backup-[FirstInitialLastName]`.
   You back up the database so you have a copy in case errors occur when the database is split.

4. Close the new backup database then reopen **AC10-D01-WinWebDesign-[FirstInitialLastName]** without opening any objects.
5. Choose **Database Tools→Move Data→Access Database** .

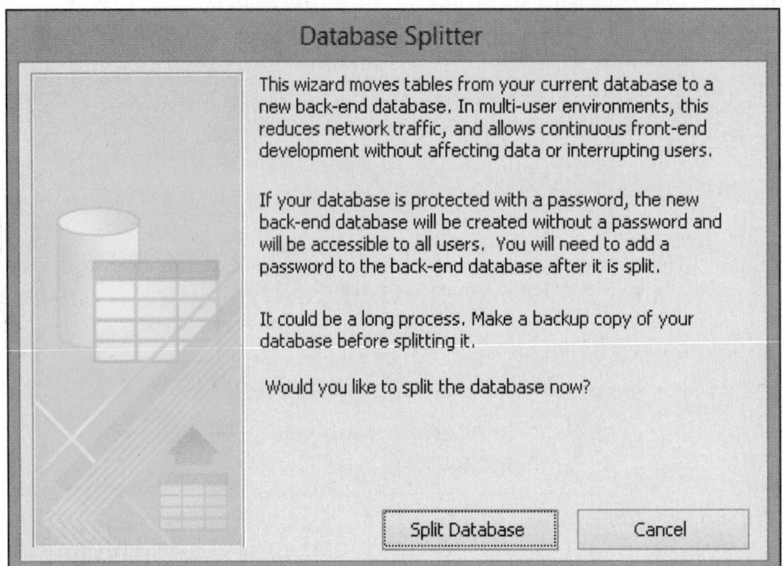

6. Review the information in the Database Splitter. Then, click **Split Database**.

   Access opens the Create Back-end Database dialog box and displays the same filename with _be *at the end to identify it as the back-end file.*
7. Navigate to your **AC2013 Lesson 10** folder and click **Split**.
8. Click **OK** in the message box.

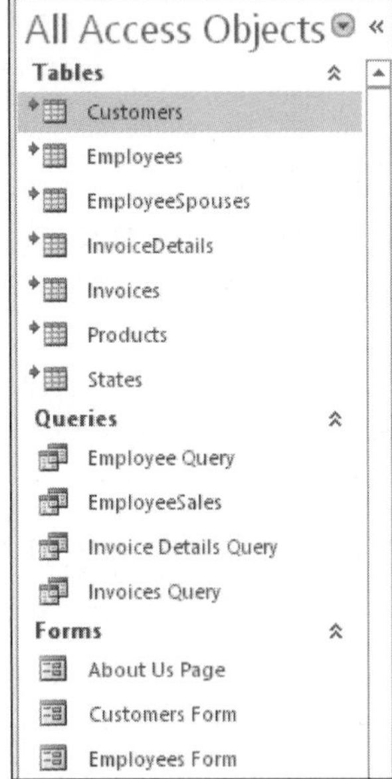

All the table names now have a blue arrow in front of them.

9. Right-click the **Customers** table in the Navigation Pane and choose **Design View**.

   Access warns the user that Customers is a linked table and can't be modified. It is linked to the back-end database. You can open the table in Design View, but you can't modify the structure or data types. You can, however, open the table in Datasheet View and add, change, and delete records. Any changes to data in the front-end database are reflected in the table in the back-end database.

10. Read the warning message, then click **No**.

11. Right-click the **Customers Form** in the Navigation Pane and choose **Design View**.

    The front-end form displays in Design View.

12. Select the **Notes label** and **Notes text box** and tap [Delete].

13. Save the form and close **AC10-D01-WinWebDesign-[FirstInitialLastName]**.

14. Navigate to your **AC2013 Lesson 10** folder. Rename the front-end database **`AC10-D01-WinWebDesign-Split-[FirstInitialLastName]`**, and open **AC10-D01-WinWebDesign-[FirstInitialLastName]_be**.

    The Winchester Web Design tables are the only objects in the back-end database.

15. Close the back-end database.

Customizing the Database Interface

Video Library http://labyrinthelab.com/videos Video Number: AC13-V1007

Access offers a number of options for customizing the user interface. Switchboards and Navigation Forms can be set to automatically open when a database is opened. They provide buttons and tabs to perform an array of functions from displaying forms and reports to printing, saving, and even closing the database and exiting Access.

Access 2013

Exploring a Database Switchboard

A switchboard is an easy-to-use interface that contains menus and buttons for opening database objects and performing common tasks such as adding records or printing reports. Switchboards were common in older versions of Access.

A sample switchboard form.

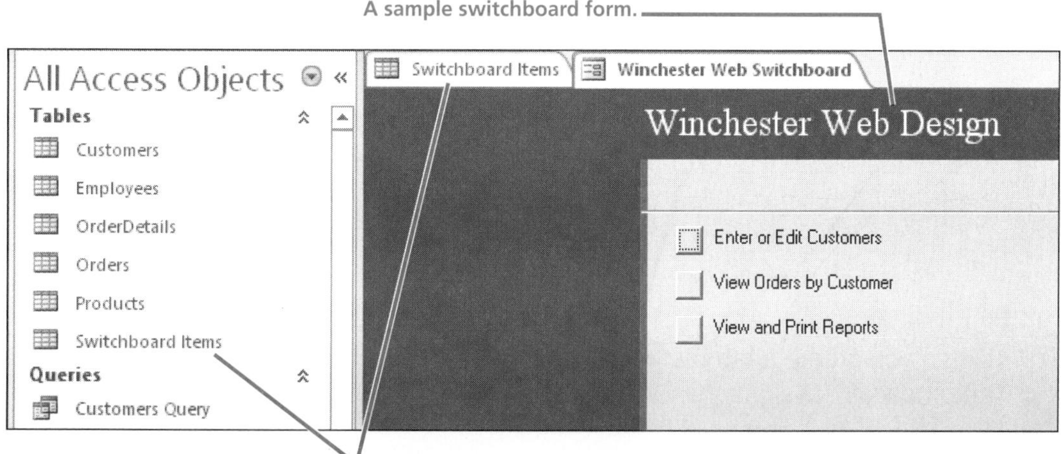

Underlying Switchboard Items table.

Adding Switchboard Manager to the Ribbon

To create a switchboard in Access 2013, the Switchboard Manager command button must be on the Ribbon. To add a command button to the Ribbon, right-click the Ribbon and choose Customize the Ribbon to open the Access Options dialog box. Then, from the All Commands menu, select the desired command.

FROM THE RIBBON

File→Options→
Customize Ribbon→
All Commands→
Switchboard
Manager→Add

The Switchboard Manager button might be on the Database Tools tab if you open a database created in a previous version of Access or one that already contains a database switchboard.

Creating a Navigation Form

An alternative to the older switchboard is a Navigation Form, or special interface that allows you to quickly access forms and reports in your database. Microsoft introduced Navigation Forms to accommodate online databases published to the web, because the Access Navigation Pane will not display in a browser.

Navigation Form Features

Navigation Forms usually have tabs across the top of the form to group common elements with sub-navigation links along the left side or directly below. The Navigation Form opens like a regular form in the Access window.

Tabs can group forms and reports by subject.

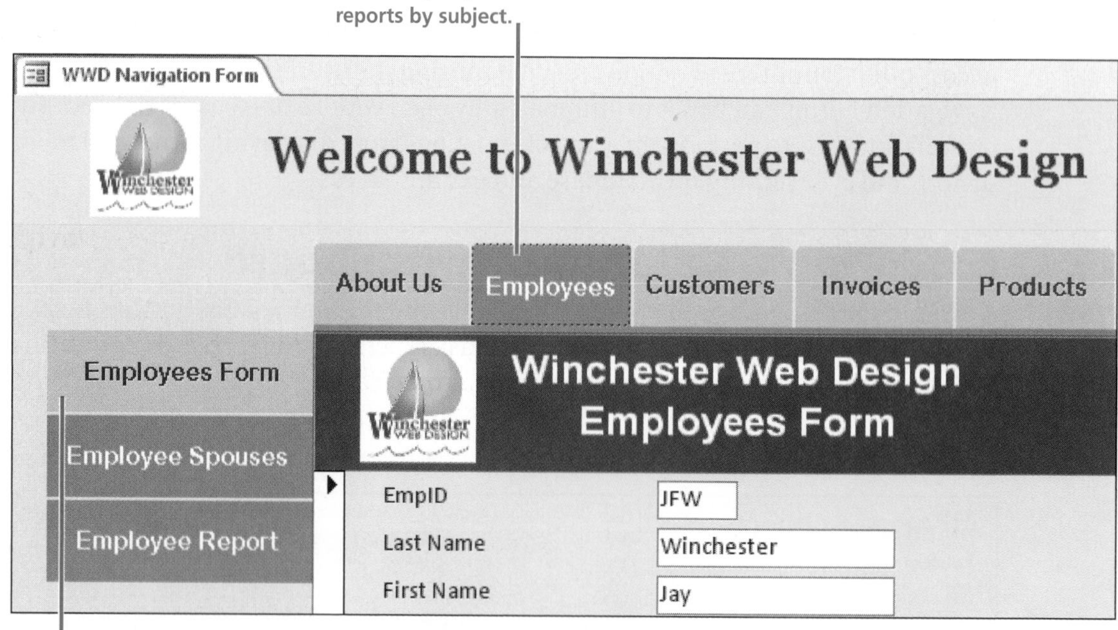

Individual objects can be accessed via controls listed on the side of an active tab.

When you create a tab that matches the name of a form or report in the database, Access automatically assigns the form or report to the tab in the Navigation Form.

Navigation Form Layouts

The Winchester Web Design database includes an Employees Form, an Employee Spouses Form, and an Employee Report that you can place on the same Employees tab on a Navigation Form. You can also add other forms and reports. Access offers six different Navigation Form layouts from which you can choose. You can also change fonts, colors, and themes for the Navigation Form.

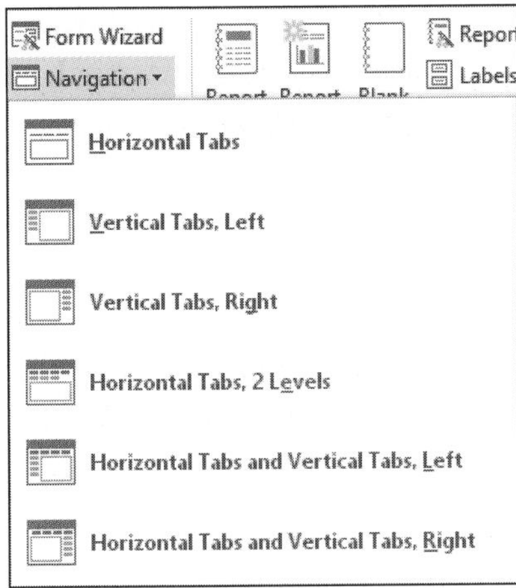

DEVELOP YOUR SKILLS AC10-D07

Create a Navigation Form

In this exercise, you will create a Navigation Form with tabs for the categories in the Winchester Web Design database. Then you will add sub-navigation links for forms and reports within each tab's category.

1. Rename the backup database **`AC10-D01-WinWebDesign-[FirstInitialLastName]`** then open it.
2. Follow these steps to create a new Navigation Form:

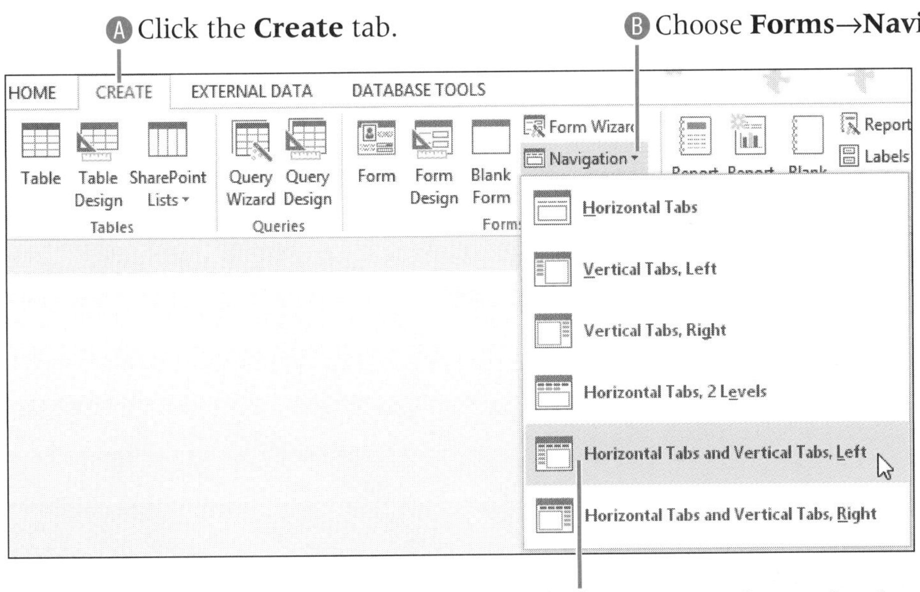

The new Navigation Form opens in Layout View, which is the recommended view for editing.

3. Follow these steps to review the new Navigation Form:

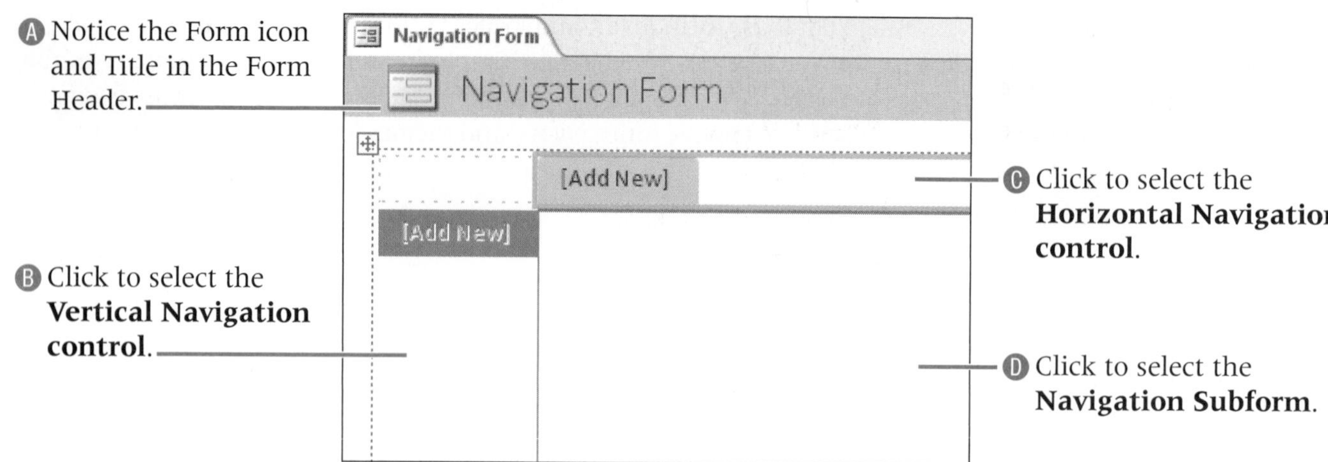

Ⓐ Notice the Form icon and Title in the Form Header.
Navigation Form
Navigation Form
[Add New]
[Add New]
Ⓑ Click to select the **Vertical Navigation control**.
Ⓒ Click to select the **Horizontal Navigation control**.
Ⓓ Click to select the **Navigation Subform**.

4. Double-click the **[Add New] tab** in the Horizontal Navigation control, type **`Employees`**, and tap Enter to display another [Add New] tab.

   You can point to the right border of a tab until the mouse appears as a two-headed pointer and drag the border to the left or right until the tab title is best displayed.

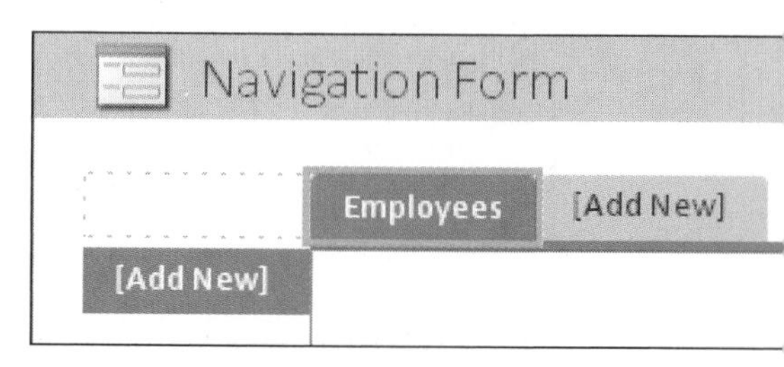

Navigation Form
Employees
[Add New]
[Add New]

5. Create additional tabs for **`Customers`**, **`Invoices`**, and **`Products`**.

Add Items to Tabs

6. Follow these steps to add an item to a tab:

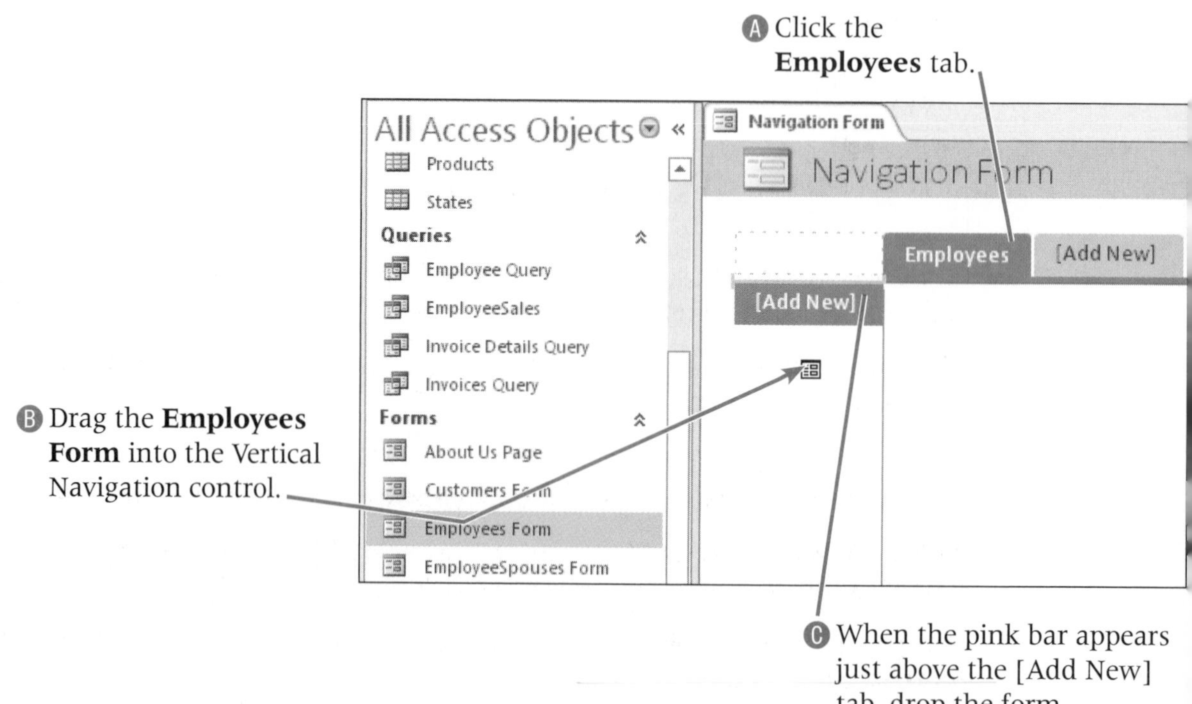

Ⓐ Click the **Employees** tab.
All Access Objects
Products
States
Queries
Employee Query
EmployeeSales
Invoice Details Query
Invoices Query
Forms
About Us Page
Customers Form
Employees Form
EmployeeSpouses Form
Navigation Form
Navigation Form
Employees
[Add New]
[Add New]
Ⓑ Drag the **Employees Form** into the Vertical Navigation control.
Ⓒ When the pink bar appears just above the [Add New] tab, drop the form.

7. Drag the forms and reports to the tab indicated:

Tab	Form or Report
Employees	EmployeeSpouses Form
Employees	Employee Report
Customers	Customers Form
Customers	Customer Invoice Report
Invoices	Invoice Form
Invoices	Invoice Details Report
Products	Products Form
Products	Products Report

8. Save the form as `WWD Navigation Form`. Switch to **Design View**.
9. Delete all the controls in the **Form Header** section.

Add a Title and Logo and Apply Formatting

10. Choose **Design→Controls→Label** and draw a title label in the Form Header section.
11. Type `Welcome to Winchester Web Design` as the label and tap [Enter].
12. Enter these properties for the new title label on the Property Sheet:

Property	Value
Width	5.5"
Height	.45"
Top	.1875"
Left	1.5"
Font Name	Georgia
Font Size	22
Text Align	Center
Font Weight	Semi-bold
Fore Color	Blue, Accent 1, Darker 50%

13. Click the **Form Header** section bar; type `.8"` for the **Height** and choose **Blue, Accent 1, Lighter 80%** for the **Back Color** property.
14. Choose **Design→Controls→Insert Image** [Insert Image], navigate to the **AC2013 Lesson 10** folder, and choose **WWD-Logo**.

    If the WWD-Logo is displayed in the Image Gallery, you can just click it.
15. Draw the new logo image in the **Form Header** section to the left of the title.
16. With the **WWD-Logo** selected, type `.7"` for the **Width** and **Height** properties, type `.05"` for the **Top** property and type `.5"` for the **Left** property.
17. Click the **Detail** section bar and type `Accent 1, Lighter 90%` for the **Back Color** and **Alternate Back Color** properties.

18. Select the left column of the navigation form (**NavigationControl5**) in the **Selection Type** list, and then choose **Transparent** for the **Back Style** property.

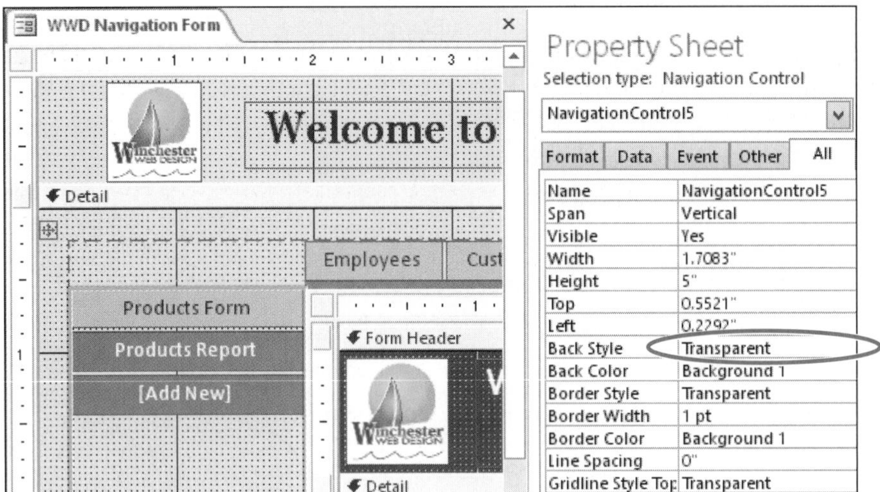

19. Select the top navigation control row (**NavigationControl0**) and choose **Transparent** for the **Back Style** property.

20. Switch to **Form View** and click the **Employees** tab.

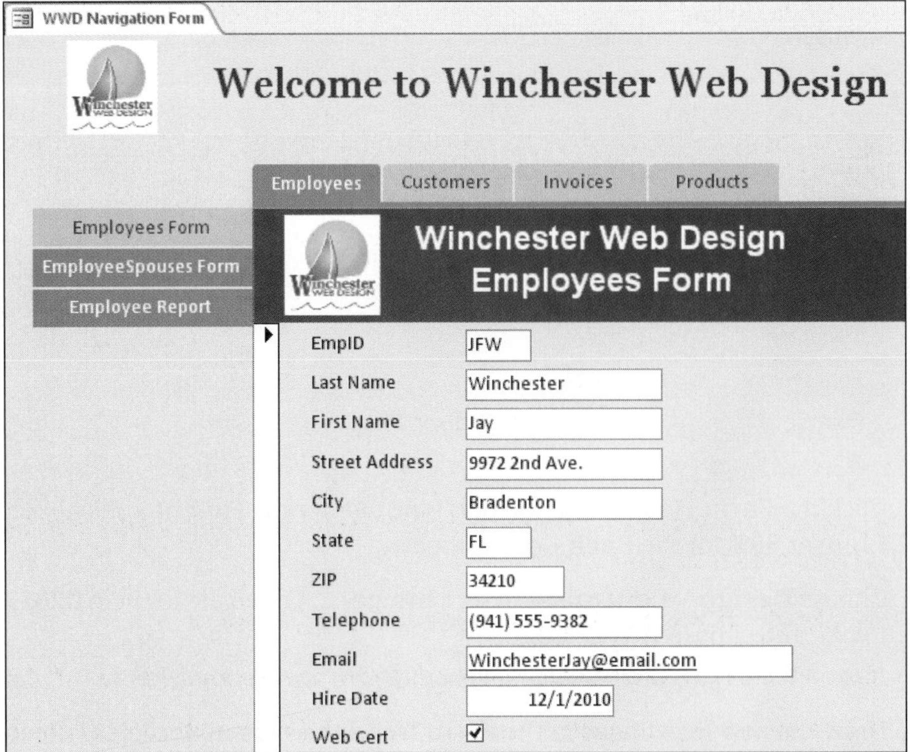

The form includes three objects listed for the Employees tab and the selected object displayed in the Navigation Subform.

21. Save the **WWD Navigation Form**.

Adding Custom Command Buttons

Video Library http://labyrinthelab.com/videos Video Number: AC13-V1008

Now that you have a Navigation Form that opens each of the forms and reports in the database, you can add command buttons that will perform functions using Design View. Then you can size and position the buttons, and add the text that will be displayed on each button.

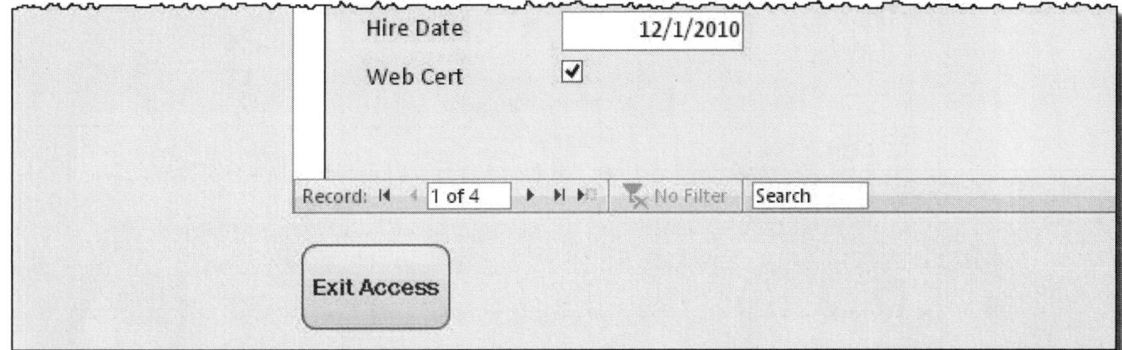

A button is added to the form to exit Access when work is completed.

When you use the Command Button control from the Ribbon to create an action command button on a form, the Command Button Wizard opens and walks you through the process. Placing command buttons in the Detail section will replicate the button for each entry in the form.

QUICK REFERENCE **CREATING ACTION BUTTONS ON FORMS**

Task	Procedure
Create an action command button on a database object	■ Choose Design→Controls→Button [xxxx] and draw a button in the appropriate position. ■ Follow the Command Button Wizard to set the button action then click Finish.

Access 2013

DEVELOP YOUR SKILLS AC10-D08

Add Command Buttons to a Switchboard

In this exercise, you will create a command button on the WWD Navigation Form. You will then add text and attach a command to the button.

1. Display the **WWD Navigation Form** in **Design View**.
2. Expand the **Form Footer** section by dragging the bottom of the form down.
3. Type `Accent 1, Lighter 90%` for the **Back Color** of the Form Footer section.

4. Choose **Design→Controls→Button** [xxxx] and draw a button in the Form Footer section.

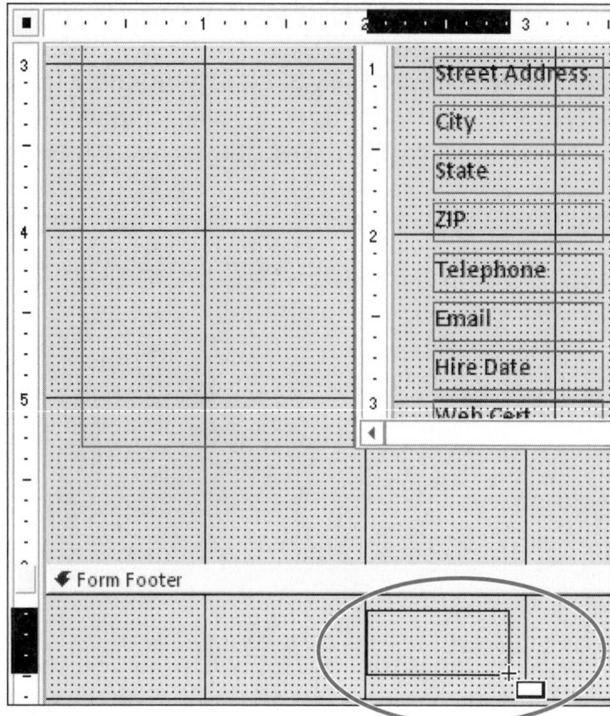

Access launches the Command Button Wizard after you draw the command button.

5. Follow these steps to complete the first button:

6. Click next and follow these steps to complete the button:

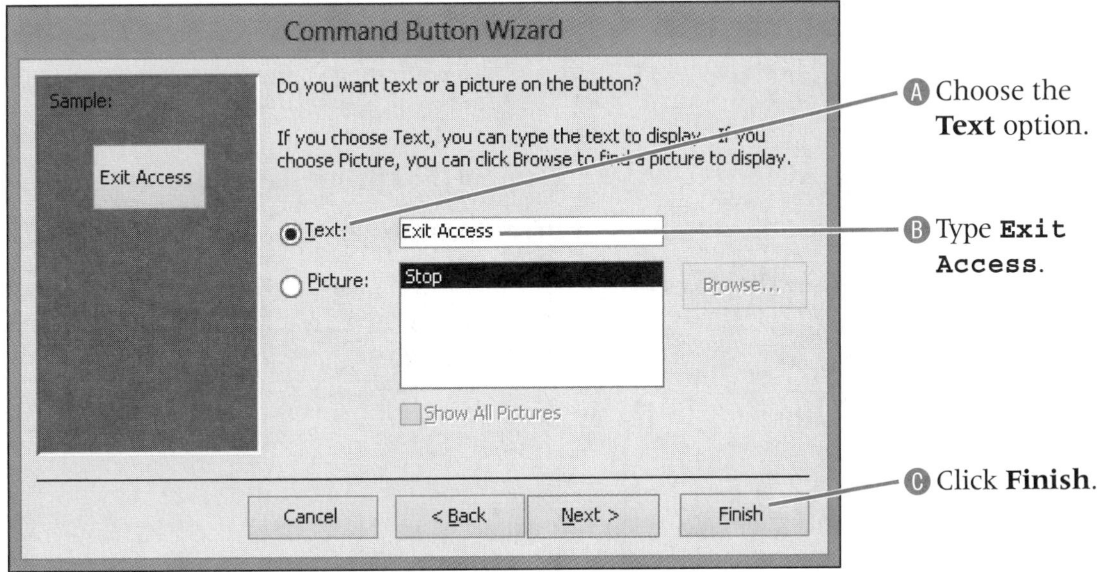

7. Save changes to the form and then switch to **Form View**.
8. Click the **Exit Access** command button on the form.
   The database and Access close.

Setting Startup Options to Open a Form

Video Library http://labyrinthelab.com/videos Video Number: AC13-V1009

Switchboards and Navigation Forms provide an interface between the user and the forms, queries, and reports contained in the database. In most cases, data entry personnel have no need to create objects or see the Navigation Pane.

As a result, many businesses set startup options that display either the most commonly used form, such as the Invoice Form, or the database interface so that it is the first thing a user sees when they open the database. Setting these startup options is also a way to protect the database from unauthorized access.

Overriding Startup Options

After you set startup options for a database, the Navigation Pane and many of the underlying objects and database tools may be hidden. To override the startup settings, press and hold the [Shift] key as you open the database in Access.

FROM THE KEYBOARD

Press [Shift] to override startup options

QUICK REFERENCE	SETTING A SWITCHBOARD AS A STARTUP FORM
Task	**Procedure**
Set a startup form	■ Choose File→Options→Current Database. ■ Click the Display Form list button, choose the form, and click OK.

Access 2013

DEVELOP YOUR SKILLS AC10-D09

Set a Startup Form

In this exercise, you will set the WWD Navigation form to open automatically each time you open the database.

1. Open **AC10-D01-WinWebDesign-[FirstInitialLastName]**.
2. Choose **File→Options→Current Database**.
3. Click the **Display Form** list button and choose **WWD Navigation Form**.

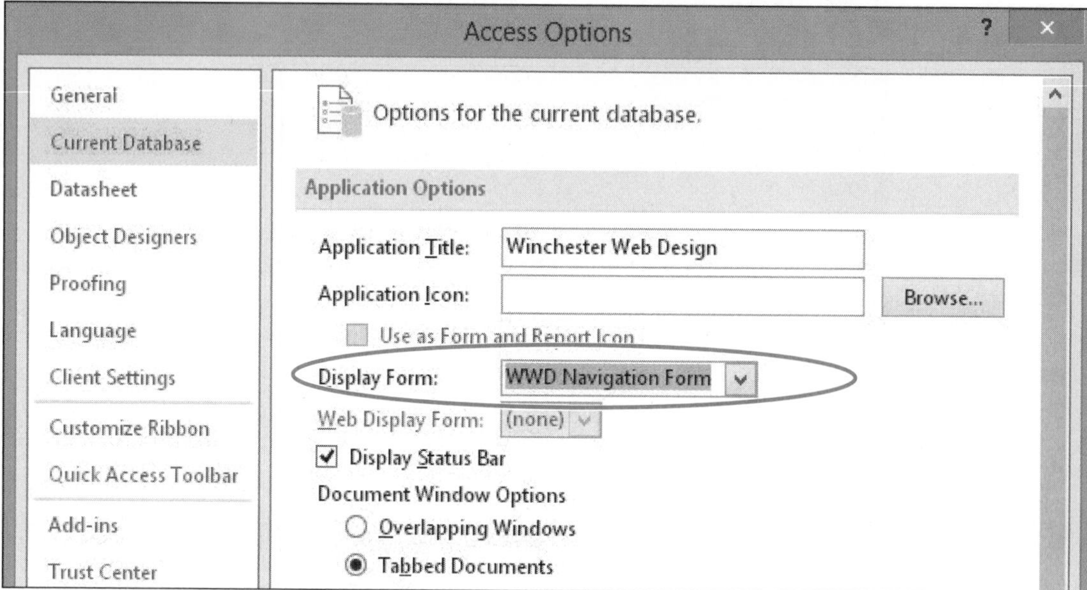

4. Click **OK** twice, once to close the Access Options dialog box and once to acknowledge the message box.
5. Close the database and open it again.
   Access opens the database and displays the WWD Navigation Form.
6. Click the **Exit Access** command button.

Concepts Review

To check your knowledge of the key concepts introduced in this lesson, complete the Concepts Review quiz by choosing the appropriate access option below.

If you are...	Then access the quiz by...
Using the Labyrinth Video Library	Going to http://labyrinthelab.com/videos
Using eLab	Logging in, choosing Content, and navigating to the Concepts Review quiz for this lesson
Not using the Labyrinth Video Library or eLab	Going to the student resource center for this book

Reinforce Your Skills

REINFORCE YOUR SKILLS AC10-R01

Set Options and Properties, and Split a Database

You have taken over all technological aspects for Kids for Change. In this exercise, you will personalize Windows with your name and initials, and modify navigation options. You will also display multiple objects in an overlapping format, and split the database to protect the table data from unauthorized users.

Set Access Options

1. Start **Access**. Open **AC10-R01-K4C** from your **AC2013 Lesson 10** folder and save it as `AC10-R01-K4C-[FirstInitialLastName]`.
2. Click **Enable Content**.
3. Choose **File→Options**. In the **General** category, modify the username and/or initials, if necessary.

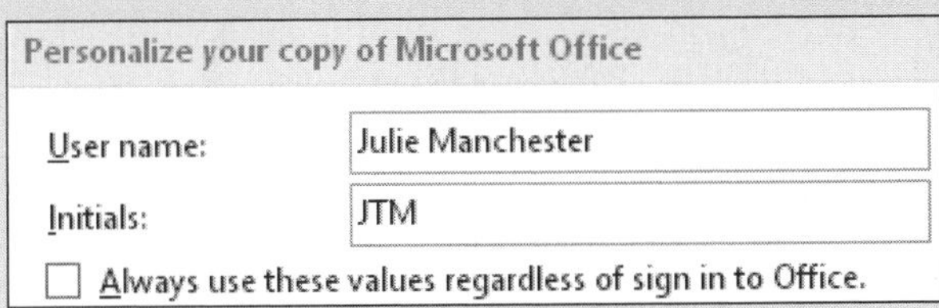

4. Choose **Current Database**. Scroll through the dialog box to display the Navigation area and click the **Navigation Options** button.
5. Click **Add Item**.
   A new item appears in the Categories list named Custom Category 1.
6. Type `Kids for Change` in the **Custom Category 1** box and tap [Enter].
7. Click **Add Group**.
   A new item appears in the Groups list named Custom Group 1.
8. Type `Activities`.

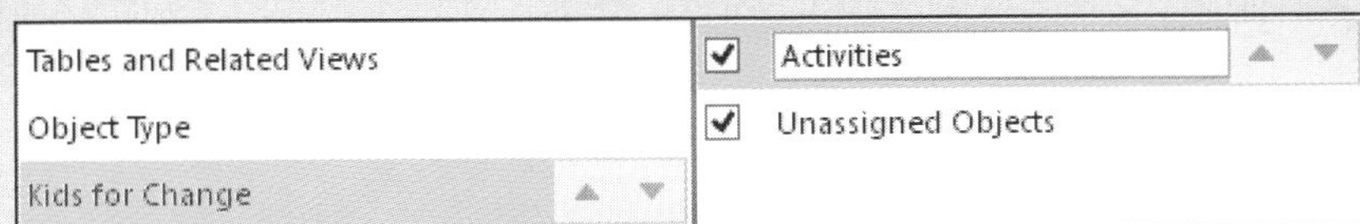

9. Add two more groups: `Children` and `Volunteers`.
10. Click **OK** twice, once to close the Navigation Options dialog box and once to close the Access Options dialog box.
11. Click the **Navigation Pane Options** button and choose **Kids for Change**.
    Access places all objects for the Kids for Change category into the Unassigned Objects group.

12. In the Unassigned Objects group on the Navigation Pane, right-click the **Activities table object** and choose **Add to Group→Activities**.
13. Right-click the **Activities List** query and add it to the **Activities Group**; then add the **Activities Form** and **Activity Costs Report**.

14. Assign the **Children** table, **Children List**, **Children Form**, and **Children Report** to the **Children Group**.
15. Assign the **Volunteers** table, **Volunteers Subform**, **VolunteersForm**, and **Volunteers Report** to the **Volunteers Group**.
16. Click the **Navigation Pane Options** drop-down button and choose **Object Type**.

    The Navigation Pane groups objects by type (Tables, Queries, Forms, and Reports).

Set Database Properties

17. Open the Access Options dialog box and choose **Current Database**.
18. Click the **Application Title** text box and type **`Kids for Change`**.
19. Choose the **Overlapping Windows** option and click **OK**.

    You must close and then reopen the database for the settings to take effect.

20. Choose **OK** in the message dialog box; then close and reopen the database.
21. Open the **Activities** and **Children** tables to display the objects in separate overlapping windows.

    You can move and resize the open objects so you can see both at the same time.

22. Choose **File→Options→Current Database** and reset the Document Window option for **Tabbed Documents**.
23. Close the database.

Split a Database

24. Open **AC10-R01-K4C-[FirstInitialLastName]** but *do not* open any database objects.
25. Choose **File→Save As→Save Database As→Save As**.
26. Open your **AC2013 Lesson 10** folder and click **Save** to save a backup copy as **`AC10-R01-K4C-Backup-[FirstInitialLastName]`**.
27. Close the new backup database and reopen **AC10-R01-K4C-[FirstInitialLastName]** without opening any objects.
28. Choose **Database Tools→Move Data→Access Database** .
29. Click the **Split Database** button.

    Access opens the Create Back-end Database dialog box and displays the same filename with _be *at the end to identify it as the back-end database.*

30. Navigate to your **AC2013 Lesson 10** folder and click **Split**.
31. Click **OK** in the message box.

    Table names now have a blue arrow in front of them.

32. Right-click the **Activities** table in the Navigation Pane and choose **Design View**.

    Access informs the user that Activities can't be modified because it is linked to the back-end database. You can still open the table in Design View, but you cannot modify the structure or data types. You can, however, open the table in Datasheet View and add, change, and delete records. Any changes to the data are reflected in the back-end database.

33. Click **No** in the message box.

34. Right-click the **VolunteersForm** in the Navigation Pane and choose **Design View**.

    The form displays in Design View.

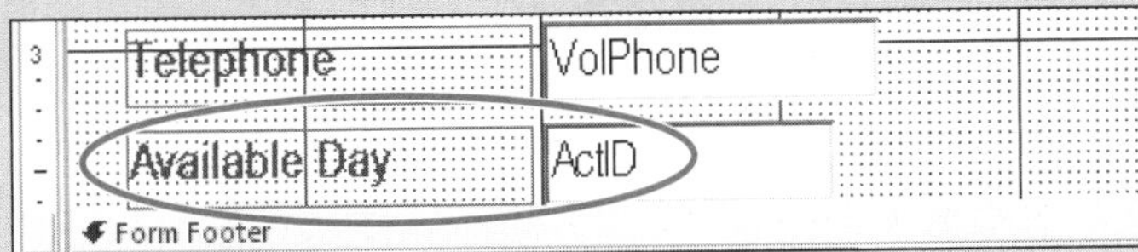

35. Select the **Available Day label** and the **ActID text box** at the bottom of the Detail section and tap [Delete]; save the form.

    Access permits you to make and save edits to the form in the front-end database.

36. Open **AC10-R01-K4C-[FirstInitialLastName]_be** from your **AC2013 Lesson 10** folder.

    The Kids for Change tables are the only objects in the back-end database.

37. Close all open databases. Exit **Access**.

38. Submit your final file based on the guidelines provided by your instructor.

    To see examples of how your file or files should look at the end of this exercise, go to the student resource center.

Access 2013

REINFORCE YOUR SKILLS AC10-R02

Create a Navigation Form and Set Startup Options

In this exercise, you will create a navigation form that displays when the Kids for Change database is opened. It will have links to open other forms and reports, and a command button that closes the database and exits Access.

Create a Navigation Form

1. Start **Access**. Open **AC10-R02-K4C** from your **AC2013 Lesson 10** folder and save it as `AC10-R02-K4C-[FirstInitialLastName]`.

2. Choose **Create→Forms→Navigation→Horizontal Tabs and Vertical Tabs, Left**

    The new navigation form opens in Layout View.

3. Double-click the **[Add New] tab** in the Horizontal Navigation control, type `Activities`, and tap [Enter].

4. Create tabs for `Children`, `Donors`, `PaidStaff`, and `Volunteers`.

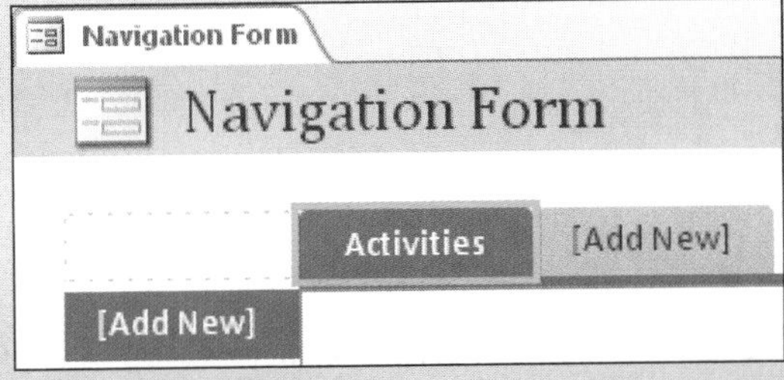

5. Click the **Activities** tab.
6. Drag the **Activities Form** from the Navigation Pane into the **Vertical Navigation link** area. When the pink bar appears just above the [Add New] tab, drop the form.

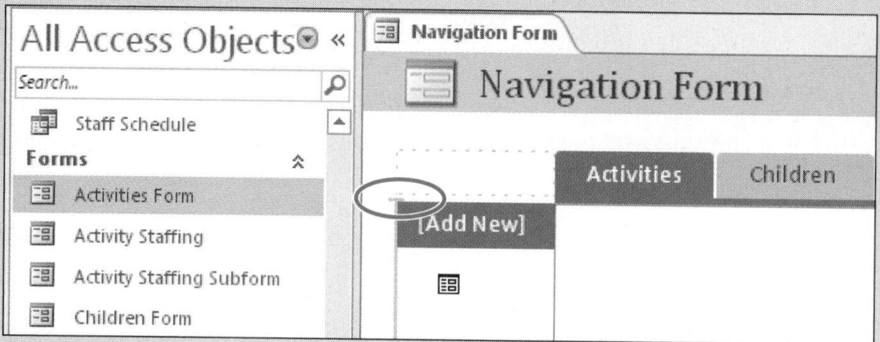

7. Add the following forms and reports to the tab indicated:

Tab	Form or Report
Activities	■ Activity Costs Report
Children	■ Children Form ■ Children Report
Donors	■ Donors Form ■ Donations Report ■ Monthly Donations Report
PaidStaff	■ Staff Form ■ Activity Staffing ■ Activity Costs Report
Volunteers	■ Volunteers Form ■ Volunteers Report

8. Save the form as `K4C Navigation Form`. Switch to **Design View**.
9. Delete all the controls in the **Form Header** section.
10. Choose **Design→Controls→Label** and draw a title label named `Kids for Change` in the **Form Header** section. Tap Enter.
11. Enter the following properties for the new title label on the Property Sheet:

Property	Value
Width	4"
Height	.4"
Top	.2"
Left	2"
Font Name	Cambria
Font Size	23
Text Align	Center
Fore Color	Blue, Accent 1, Darker 50%

12. Click the **Form Header** section bar; type `.8"` for the **Height** and choose **Dark Blue, Text 2, Lighter 80%** for the for the **Back Color** property.

13. Choose **Design→Controls→** Insert Image, navigate to the **AC2013 Lesson 10** folder, and choose **K4C-logo**.

    If the K4C-Logo is in the Image Gallery, you can click it there.

14. Draw the logo image in the **Form Header** section to the left of the title.

15. With the K4C-Logo selected, type `.7"` for the **Width** and **Height** properties, type `.05"` for the **Top** property and type `.5"` for the **Left** property.

16. Switch to **Form View** and click each tab to verify that the objects display in the navigation subform.

17. Save your changes to the **K4C Navigation Form**.

Add a Command Button

18. Switch to **Design View** and expand the **Form Footer** section by dragging the bottom of the form down.

19. Choose **Design→Controls→Button** xxxx and draw a button in the **Form Footer** section.

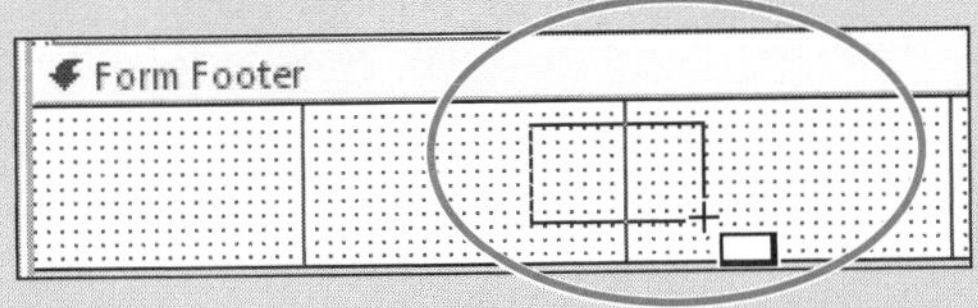

20. Choose **Application** and **Quit Application,** then click **Next**.

21. Choose the **Text** option, type `Exit Access`, and click **Next**.

22. Name the command button `cmdExitAccess` and click **Finish**.

23. Save your changes to the form.

24. Switch to **Form View**. Click the **Exit Access** command button.

    The database and Access both close.

Set Access Startup Options

25. Reopen **AC10-R02-K4C-[FirstInitialLastName]** and choose **File→Options→Current Database**.

26. Type `Kids for Change` for the application title.

27. Click the **Display Form** menu button and choose **K4C Navigation Form**.

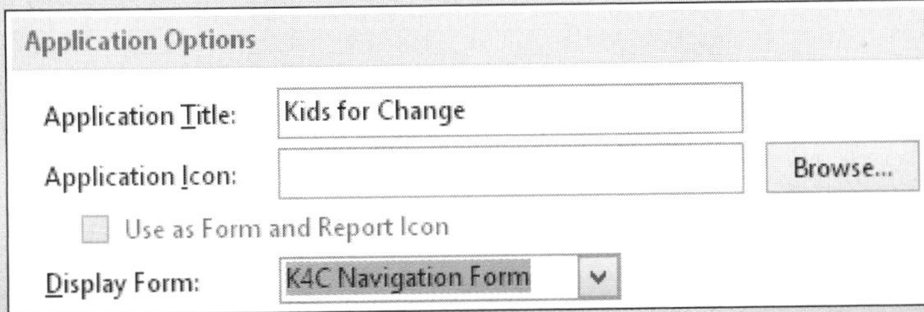

Access 2013

28. Click **OK** to close the Access Options dialog box and then click **OK** in the warning message box.
29. Close the database and open it again.
    Access opens the database and displays the K4C Navigation Form.
    The K4C Navigation Form automatically opens when the database is opened and includes Kids for Change in the Title bar and the Exit Access command button in the Form Footer.
30. Click the **Exit Access** command button to close the database and exit Access.
31. Submit your final file based on the guidelines provided by your instructor.
    To see examples of how your file or files should look at the end of this exercise, go to the student resource center.

REINFORCE YOUR SKILLS AC10-R03

Set Access Options, Split a Database, and Create a Navigation Form

In this exercise, you will personalize Microsoft Windows and modify the navigation options to group objects by category. You will open objects in overlapping format instead of tabs, back up a database, and then split the database. You will also create a navigation form that links to open donor and donation forms and reports, create a command button to close the database and exit Access, and instruct Access to open the navigation form when the database opens.

Set Personal Information

1. Start **Access**. Open **AC10-R03-K4C** from your **AC2013 Lesson 10** folder and save it as `AC10-R03-K4C-[FirstInitialLastName]`.
2. Choose **File→Options**. In the **General** category, modify the username and initials, if necessary.

Personalize your copy of Microsoft Office

User name:	Floyd Jay Winters
Initials:	FJW

Customize the Navigation Pane

3. Choose **Current Database**, scroll through the dialog box, and click **Navigation Options**.
4. Click **Add Item**.
   A new item appears in the Categories list named Custom Category 1.
5. Type `Kids for Change Finances` in the Custom Category 1 box and tap Enter.
6. Click **Add Group**.
   A new item appears in the Groups list named Custom Group 1.
7. Type `Donors`.
8. Click three more groups: `Donations`, `PaidStaff`, and `Venues`.
9. Click **OK** in both dialog boxes.

10. Click the **Navigation Pane Options** button and choose **Kids for Change Finances**.
Access places all objects for the Kids for Change Finances category into the Unassigned Objects group.

11. In the Unassigned Objects group on the Navigation Pane, right-click the **Donors table object** and choose **Add to Group→Donors**.

12. Assign these objects to the appropriate group:

Group	Objects	Group	Objects
Donors	■ Donor Contact List ■ Donors Query ■ Donor Popup ■ Donors Form ■ Donors Subform ■ Donors Report	Venues	■ Venues table ■ K4C Venues ■ Venues Form ■ Venues Report
Donations	■ Donations table ■ Donations Query ■ DonorDetail Subform ■ Total Donations Form ■ Donations Report ■ K4C Donors Subreport ■ Monthly Donations Report	PaidStaff	■ PaidStaff table ■ ActivityStaffing Query ■ Staff Mailing List ■ Staff Schedule ■ Activity Staffing form ■ Activity Staffing Subform ■ Staff Form ■ Activity Staffing Subreport ■ Staffing Report

The first two groups in the Navigation Pane should resemble the figure displayed.

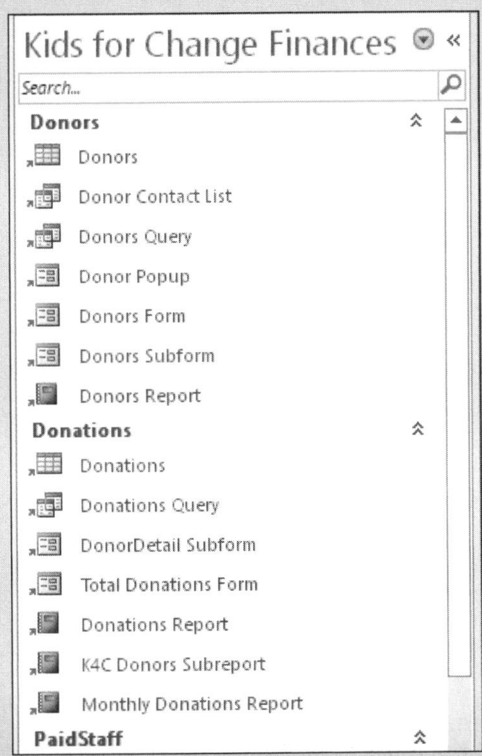

13. Click the **Navigation Pane Options** drop-down button and choose **Object Type**.

Access 2013

Set Database Properties

14. Open the **Access Options** dialog box and choose **Current Database**.
15. Click the **Application Title** text box and type **`Kids for Change Finances`**, choose the **Overlapping Windows** option, and click **OK**.

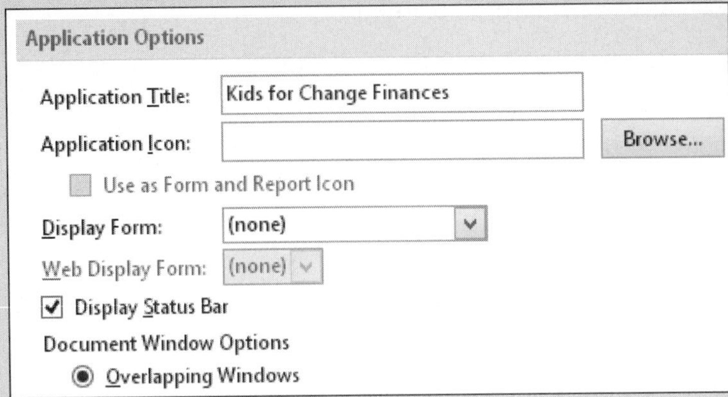

You must close and then reopen the database for the settings to take effect.

16. Choose **OK** in the message dialog box.
17. Close and then reopen the database.
18. Open the **Donors** and **Venues** tables to display the objects in separate windows.
    You can move and resize the open objects so you can see both at the same time.
19. Choose **File→Options→Current Database**, reset the Document Window option for **Tabbed Documents**, and close the database.

Split a Database

20. Open **AC10-R03-K4C-[FirstInitialLastName]** but *do not* open any database objects.
21. Choose **File→Save As→Save Database As→Save As**.
22. Open your **AC2013 Lesson 10** folder and then click **Save** to save a backup copy as **`AC10-R03-K4C-Backup-[FirstInitialLastName]`**.
23. Choose **Database Tools→Move Data→Access Database** .
24. Click **Split Database**.
    Access opens the Create Back-end Database dialog box and displays the same file name with _be *at the end to identify it as the back-end database.*
25. Navigate to your **AC2013 Lesson 10** folder and click **Split**.
26. Click **OK**.
    All the table names now have a blue arrow in front of them.
27. Right-click the **Donors** table in the Navigation Pane and choose **Design View**.
    The Donors table is linked to the back-end database and cannot be modified. You can, however, open the table in Datasheet View and add, change, and delete records. Any changes to the data are reflected in the table in the back-end database.
28. Click **No** in the message dialog box.

29. Right-click the **Donors Form** in the Navigation Pane and choose **Design View**.

30. Select the **Acknowledgement** label and text box and tap [Delete].

    Access permits you to make edits to the front-end form.

31. Close the **Donors Form**, saving when prompted.

32. Navigate to your **AC2013 Lesson 10** folder and open **AC10-R03-K4C-[FirstInitialLastName]-Backup_be**.

    The Kids for Change tables are the only objects in the back-end database.

33. Close all open databases, and reopen the un-split **AC10- R03-K4C-[FirstInitialLastName]**.

Create a Navigation Form

34. Choose **Create→Forms→Navigation→Horizontal Tabs and Vertical Tabs, Left**

    The new navigation form opens in Layout View.

35. Double-click the **[Add New] tab** in the Horizontal Navigation control, type **`Donors`**, and tap [Enter].

36. Double-click the **[Add New] tab** in the Horizontal Navigation control and create tabs for **`Donations`**, **`Staffing`**, and **`Venues`**.

37. Click the **Donors** tab and then drag and drop the **Donors Form** into the Vertical Navigation link area.

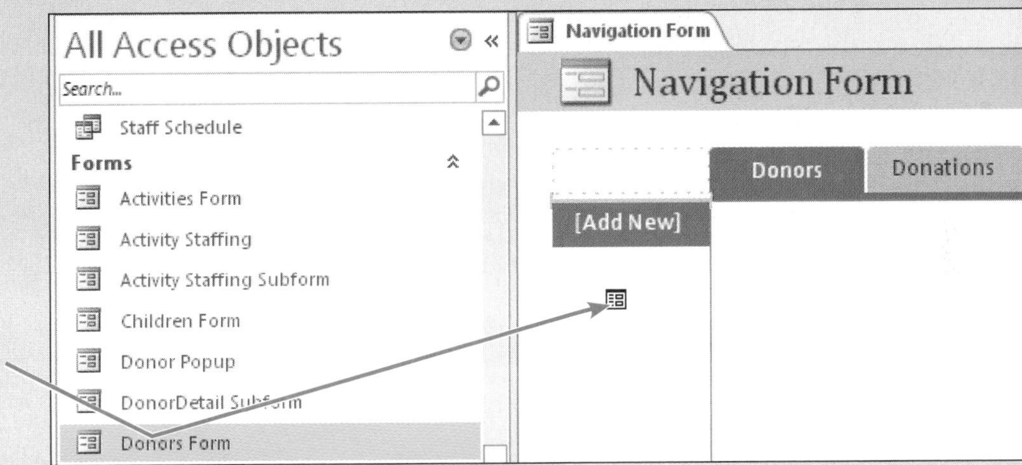

38. Add the following forms and reports:

Tab	Form or Report
Donors	■ Donors Report
Donations	■ Total Donations Form ■ Donations Report ■ Monthly Donations Report
Staffing	■ Staff Form ■ Staffing Report
Venues	■ Venues Form ■ Venues Report

39. Save the form as `K4C Finances Navigation Form`. Switch to **Design View**.

40. Delete all controls in the **Form Header** section.

41. Choose **Design→Controls→Label** and draw a title label named `Kids for Change Finances` in the **Form Header**. Tap [Enter].

42. Enter these properties for the new title label on the Property Sheet:

Property	Value
Width	4"
Height	.4"
Top	.2"
Left	2"
Font Name	Cambria
Font Size	23
Text Align	Center
Fore Color	Blue, Accent 1, Darker 50%

43. Click the **Form Header** section bar; type `.8"` for the **Height** and choose **Dark Blue, Text 2, Lighter 80%** for the **Back Color** property.

44. Choose **Design→Controls→Insert Image** [Insert Image] and choose **K4C-logo** from the Gallery or the **AC2013 Lesson 10** folder.

45. Draw the logo image in the **Form Header** section to the left of the title.

46. With the K4C-Logo selected, type `.7"` for the **Width** and **Height**, type `.05"` for the **Top** property and type `.5"` for the **Left** property.

47. Switch to **Form View** and verify that each object displays in the navigation subform.

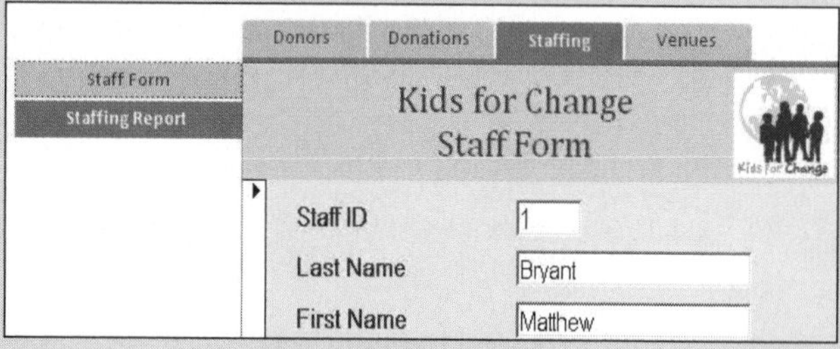

48. Save your changes to the **K4C Finances Navigation Form**.

Add a Command Button

49. Switch to **Design View** and expand the **Form Footer** section by dragging the bottom of the form down.

50. Choose **Design→Controls→Button** [xxxx] and draw a command button in the Form Footer section.

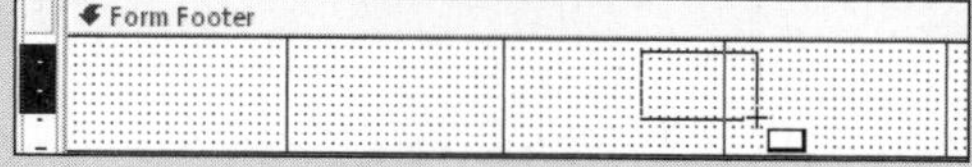

51. Choose the **Application** category and the **Quit Application** action, and click **Next**.

52. Choose the default **Stop** picture and click **Next**.

53. Name the command button `cmdQuit` and click **Finish**.

54. Save the **K4C Finances Navigation Form**.

55. Switch to **Form View** and click the **Quit App** command button.

    The database and Access both close.

Set Access Startup Options

56. Open **AC10-R03-K4C-[FirstInitialLastName]** and choose **File→Options→Current Database**.

57. Click the **Display Form** list button and choose **K4CFinances Navigation Form** as the Display Form.

58. Click **OK** to close the Access Options dialog box. Click **OK** in the message box.

59. Close the database and open it again.

    Access opens the database and displays the K4C Finances Navigation Form.

    The K4C Finances Navigation Form opens when the database is opened. The form includes Kids for Change Finances in the Title bar, and the Quit command button in the Form Footer.

60. Click the **Quit** command button to close the form and database and exit Access.

61. Submit your final file based on the guidelines provided by your instructor.

Apply Your Skills

APPLY YOUR SKILLS AC10-A01

Set Options and Properties, and Split a Database

As head of technology for Universal Corporate Events, Ltd., you have been tasked with fine-tuning its database. In this exercise, you will personalize Windows settings, modify the object navigation options, alter the way open objects appear on the screen, and split the database.

Set Access Options

1. Start **Access**. Open **AC10-A01-UCE** from your **AC2013 Lesson 10** folder and save it as `AC10-A01-UCE-[FirstInitialLastName]`.
2. Choose **File→Options**. In the **General** category, modify the personal settings, if necessary.
3. Choose **Current Database** and then open the **Navigation Options** dialog box.
4. Click **Add Item**, type **`Universal Corporate Events`**, and tap Enter.
5. Click **Add Group** and type **`Events`** in the **Custom Group 1** box in the Groups for "Universal Corporate Events" list.
6. Add two more groups: **`Menus`** and **`Venues`**.
7. Click **OK** to close the Navigation Options dialog box and then click **OK** to close the Access Options dialog box.
8. Click the **Navigation Pane Options** button and choose **Universal Corporate Events**.
   Access places all objects for Universal Corporate Events into the Unassigned Objects group.
9. In the Unassigned Objects group, right-click the **Events table object** and choose **Add to Group→Events**.
10. Assign these objects to their appropriate groups:

Group	Object
Events	■ Event Revenue ■ Event Pricing Entry ■ Event Schedules ■ EventCosts Subform ■ Events Form
Menus	■ Menus table ■ Menus Form ■ Event Menus Report

Group	Object
Venues	■ VenueLiaisons table ■ Venues table ■ Venue Events ■ Venue Events Subform ■ Venues Form ■ Venues Report

11. Click the **Navigation Pane Options** button and choose **Object Type**.
    The Navigation Pane groups objects by type (Tables, Queries, Forms, and Reports).

Set Database Properties

12. Open the **Access Options** dialog box and choose **Current Database**.
13. Click the **Application Title** text box and type `Universal Corporate Events`.
14. Choose the **Overlapping Windows** option and click **OK**.
15. Choose **OK** in the message dialog box; then close and reopen the database.
16. Open the **Personnel** and **Venues** tables in separate overlapping windows.

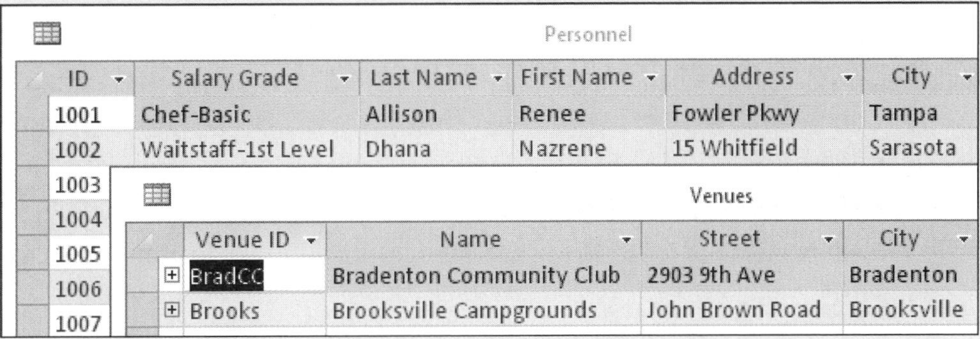

Split a Database

17. Close any open database objects. and choose **File→Save As→Save Database As**.
18. Save a backup copy of the database in your **AC2013 Lesson 10** folder as `AC10-A01-UCE-Backup-[FirstInitialLastName]` and close the database.
19. Open **AC10-A01-UCE-[FirstInitialLastName]**, choose **Database Tools→Move Data→Access Database**, and click **Split Database**.
20. Navigate to your **AC2013 Lesson 10** folder and click **Split**.
21. Click **OK** in the message box.
    All the table names now have a blue arrow in front of them.
22. Right-click the **Personnel** table in the Navigation Pane and choose **Design View**.
    Personnel is linked to the back-end database and can't be modified.
23. Click **No** in the message dialog box.
24. Right-click the **Personnel Form** in the Navigation Pane and choose **Design View**.
25. Select the **Salary Grade** label and text box then tap [Delete].
26. Close the **Personnel Form** without saving it.
27. Navigate to your **AC2013 Lesson 10** folder and open **AC10-A01-UCE-[FirstInitialLastName]_be**.
    Tables are the only objects in the back-end database.
28. Close all open databases then exit **Access**.
29. Submit your final file based on the guidelines provided by your instructor.
    To see examples of how your file or files should look at the end of this exercise, go to the student resource center.

APPLY YOUR SKILLS AC10-A02

Create a Navigation Form and Set Startup Options

The president of Universal Corporate Events, Ltd. wants a custom navigation form. In this exercise, you will create a navigation form with links that open associated forms and reports, and a command button that closes the database and exits Access. You will also modify the startup options so the new form displays each time someone opens the database.

Create a Navigation Form

1. Start **Access**. Open **AC10-A02-UCE** from your **AC2013 Lesson 10** folder and save it as `AC10-A02-UCE-[FirstInitialLastName]`.
2. Choose **Create→Forms→Navigation** and select **Horizontal Tabs and Vertical Tabs, Left**.

   The new navigation form opens in Layout View.
3. Double-click the **[Add New] tab** in the Horizontal Navigation control, type `Events`, and tap [Enter].
4. Create tabs for `Menus` and `Venues`.
5. Click the **Events** tab.
6. Drag the **Event Costs** form from the Navigation Pane and drop it into the **Vertical Navigation** link area.
7. Add these forms and reports to the tab indicated:

Tab	Form or Report
Events	■ Events Form ■ Event Pricing Entry ■ Event Schedules ■ Event Revenue Report
Menus	■ Menus Form ■ Event Menus Report
Venues	■ Venues Form ■ Venue Events Form ■ Venues Report

8. Save the form as `UCE Navigation Form`. Switch to **Design View** and delete all controls in the **Form Header** section.
9. Display the **Personnel Form** in **Design View**.
10. Copy the logo and title from the **Personnel Form** and paste them into the Form Header of the **UCE Navigation Form**. Then close the **Personnel Form**.
11. Click the **Form Header** section bar, type `.8"` for the **Height** property on the Property Sheet and choose **Blue, Accent 5, Lighter 80%** for the **Back Color** property.

12. Select the pasted title control, replace *Personnel Form* with `Navigation Form`, and tap [Enter].
13. Type `2"` for the **Left** property.
14. Select the logo and type `.5"` for the **Left** property.
15. Switch to **Form View** and verify that each object displays in the navigation subform.
16. Save your changes to the **UCE Navigation Form**.

Add a Command Button

17. Switch to **Design View**.
18. Expand the **Form Footer** section of the main form by dragging the bottom of the form down.
19. Draw a button in the **Form Footer** section to start the Command Button Wizard.
20. Choose **Application** and **Quit Application**, and click **Next**.
21. Choose the **Text** option and type `Exit Access`; click **Next**.
22. Name the command button `cmdExitAccess` and click **Finish**.
23. Save the form, switch to **Form View**, and click the new command button.
    The database and Access close.

Set Access Startup Options

24. Open **AC10-A02-UCE-[FirstInitialLastName]** and choose **File→Options→Current Database**.
25. Type `Universal Corporate Events` for the application title.
26. Click the **Display Form** list button and choose **UCE Navigation Form**.
27. Click **OK** twice, once to close the Access Options dialog box and once to acknowledge the message that you must close and reopen the database.
28. Close and then reopen the database.
    Access opens the database and displays the UCE Navigation Form.
    The UCE Navigation Form automatically opens in Form View when the database is opened. The form includes Universal Corporate Events in the title bar and the Exit Access command button in the Form Footer.
29. Click the **Exit Access** command button to close the database and exit Access.
30. Submit your final file based on the guidelines provided by your instructor.
    To see examples of how your file or files should look at the end of this exercise, go to the student resource center.

APPLY YOUR SKILLS AC10-A03

Set Access Options, Split a Database, and Create a Navigation Form

In this exercise, you will modify the Universal Corporate Events, Ltd. database's user interface.

Set Access Options

1. Start **Access**. Open **AC10-A03-UCE** from your **AC2013 Lesson 10** folder and save it as `AC10-A03-UCE-[FirstInitialLastName]`.
2. Choose **File→Options**. In the **General** category, modify your personal settings as necessary.
3. Choose **Current Database** and then open the **Navigation Options** dialog box.
4. Click **Add Item**, type `Universal Corporate Events Personnel and Venues`, and tap Enter.
5. Click **Add Group** and type `Personnel` in the **Custom Group 1** box in the Groups for "Universal Corporate Events Personnel and Venues" list.
6. Add two more groups: `Salary Info` and `Venues`.
7. Click **OK** twice.
8. Click the **Navigation Pane Options** button and choose **Universal Corporate Events Personnel and Venues**.
9. Right-click the **Personnel** table in the Navigation Pane and choose **Add to Group→Personnel**.
10. Assign these objects to the appropriate group:

Group	Objects
Personnel	■ Personnel Contact List ■ Personnel Form ■ Personnel Report
Salary Info	■ SalaryGrades ■ Salaried Personnel Query ■ Wage and Salary Form ■ Wage and Salary Report
Venues	■ VenueLiaisons table ■ Venues table ■ Venue Events Form ■ Venue Events Subform ■ Venues Form ■ Venues Report

11. Click the **Navigation Pane Options** drop-down button and choose **Object Type**.

Set Database Properties

12. Open the **Access Options** dialog box and choose **Current Database**.
13. Click the **Application Title** text box and type `Universal Corporate Events Personnel and Venues`.
14. Choose **Overlapping Windows** and click **OK**.
15. Choose **OK** in the message dialog box; then close and reopen the database.
16. Open the **Personnel** and **VenueLiaisons** tables to see them in separate windows.
    Move and resize the open objects so you can see both at the same time.
17. Choose **File→Options→Current Database** and reset the document window option for **Tabbed Documents**.
18. Click **OK** to acknowledge the message and close the database.

Split a Database

19. Open **AC10-A03-UCE-[FirstInitialLastName]**, but *do not* open any database objects.
20. Choose **File→Save As→Save Database As→Save As**.
21. Save a backup copy of the database to your **AC2013 Lesson 10** folder as `AC10-A03-UCE-Backup-[FirstInitialLastName]`.
22. Close the backup copy of the database and reopen **AC10-A03-UCE-[FirstInitialLastName]**, without opening any objects.
23. Choose **Database Tools→Move Data→Access Database** and click **Split Database**.
24. Navigate to your **AC2013 Lesson 10** folder and click **Split**.
25. Click **OK** in the message box.
26. Right-click the **Venues** table in the Navigation Pane and choose **Design View**.
    Venues is a linked table and can't be modified.
27. Click **No** in the message dialog box.
28. Right-click the **Venues Form** in the Navigation Pane and choose **Design View**.
    The form displays in Design View.
29. Select the **Liaison** label and **VenueLiaison** text box then tap [Delete].
    You can make edits to the front-end form.
30. Save the **Venues Form** and close the database, and then reopen **AC10-A03-UCE-Backup-[FirstInitialLastName]** to work with the un-split database.
31. Navigate to your **AC2013 Lesson 10** folder and open **AC10-A03-UCE-[FirstInitialLastName]_be**.
    Tables are the only objects in the back-end database.
32. Close **AC10-A03-UCE-[FirstInitialLastName]_be**.

Create a Navigation Form

33. Close any open objects, choose **Create→Forms→Navigation**, and select **Horizontal Tabs and Vertical Tabs, Left**.
    The new navigation form opens in Layout View.
34. Double-click **[Add New] tab** in the **Horizontal Navigation** control, type `Personnel`, and tap [Enter].
35. Create tabs for `Salary Info` and `Venues`.
36. Click the **Personnel** tab, and drag and drop the **Personnel Form** from the Navigation Pane into the **Vertical Navigation** link area.
37. Add these forms and reports to the tab indicated:

Tab	Form or Report
Personnel	■ Personnel Report
Salary Info	■ Wage and Salary Form ■ Wage and Salary Report
Venues	■ Venue Events Form ■ Venues Form ■ Venue Event Revenue ■ Venues Report

38. Save the form as `UCE Personnel/Venue Navigation Form` and then switch to **Design View**.
39. Delete all controls in the **Form Header** section.
40. Display the **Personnel Form** in **Design View**.
41. Copy the logo and title from the **Personnel Form** and paste them into the Form Header of the UCE Navigation Form.
42. Close the **Personnel Form**.
43. Click the **Form Header** section bar, type `.8"` for the **Height**, and choose **Blue, Accent 5, Lighter 80%** for the **Back Color** property.
44. Select the pasted title control, replace *Personnel Form* with `Personnel/Venue Navigation` and tap [Enter].
45. Type `2"` for the **Left** property.
46. Select the **logo** and type `.5"` for the **Left** property.
47. Switch to **Form View** and verify that each object displays in the navigation subform.
48. Save your changes to the **UCE Personnel/Venue Navigation Form**.

Add a Command Button

49. Switch to **Design View** and expand the **Form Footer** section.
50. Draw a button in the Form Footer section to start the Command Button Wizard.
51. Choose the **Application** category and the **Quit Application** action; click **Next**.
52. Choose the **Text** option and type **`Exit`**; click **Next**.
53. Name the command button **`cmdExit`** and click **Finish**.
54. Save the form and switch to **Form View**.
55. Click the **Exit** command button.
    The database and Access both close.

Set Access Startup Options

56. Reopen **AC10-A03-UCE-Backup-[FirstInitialLastName]** and choose **File→Options→Current Database**.
57. Click the **Display Form** list button. Choose **UCEPersonnel/Venue Navigation Form**.
58. Click **OK** twice.
59. Close and then reopen the database.
    Access opens the database and displays the UCE Personnel/Venue Navigation Form. The UCE Personnel/Venue Navigation Form automatically opens with Universal Corporate Events Personnel and Venues in the Title bar and the Exit command button in the Form Footer.
60. Click the **Exit** command button to close the form and database and exit Access.
61. Submit your final file based on the guidelines provided by your instructor.

Extend Your Skills

In the course of working through the Extend Your Skills exercises, you will think critically as you use the skills taught in the lesson to complete the assigned projects. To evaluate your mastery and completion of the exercises, your instructor may use a rubric, with which more points are allotted according to performance characteristics. (The more you do, the more you earn!) Ask your instructor how your work will be evaluated.

AC10-E01 That's the Way I See It

Blue Jean Landscaping needs to modify its database reports. Use the database you used in AC09-E01 or open **AC10-E01-BJL** from the **AC2013 Lesson 10** folder and save it as **`AC10-E01-BJL-[FirstInitialLastName]`**.

Personalize Windows with your name and initials. Modify the Navigation Pane options so you can more easily view related objects by creating a Blue Jean Landscaping Category and Customers and Manufacturers Groups; add the corresponding tables, queries, forms, and reports to the proper group. Modify the navigation options so objects in the work area overlap.

To protect your table data from unauthorized access, split the database. (Remember to make a backup copy first.) Create a navigation form in the un-split database with Customers and Manufacturers tabs, displaying forms and reports under their respective tabs, and add a command button to close the database and exit Access. Format your form consistently with the other forms in your database. Then, instruct Access to display the navigation form when the database is opened.

You will be evaluated based on the inclusion of all elements, your ability to follow directions, your ability to apply newly learned skills to a real-world situation, your creativity, and your accuracy in creating objects and/or entering data. Submit your final file based on the guidelines provided by your instructor.

AC10-E02 Be Your Own Boss

In this exercise, you will improve the user-database interface for Blue Jean Landscaping. Open **AC10-E02-BJL** from the **AC2013 Lesson 10** folder and save as **`AC10-E02-BJL-[FirstInitialLastName]`**.

Personalize Microsoft Windows with your name and initials. Modify the navigation options by creating a BJL Stock Category and Equipment, Services, and Store Merchandise Groups; add the corresponding Equipment, Services, and Store Merchandise tables, queries, forms, and reports to the appropriate. Display open objects in overlapping rather than tabbed format.

Split the database. Create a navigation form in the un-split database with Equipment, Services, and Store Merchandise tabs; display forms and reports under their respective tabs, and add a command button to close the database and exit Access. Format your navigation form to be consistent with the existing forms in the database. Finally, modify the startup options so that your navigation form displays when the database is opened.

You will be evaluated based on the inclusion of all elements, your ability to follow directions, your ability to apply newly learned skills to a real-world situation, your creativity, and your accuracy in creating objects and/or entering data. Submit your final file based on the guidelines provided by your instructor.

Transfer Your Skills

In the course of working through the Transfer Your Skills exercises, you will use critical-thinking and creativity skills to complete the assigned projects using skills taught in the lesson. To evaluate your mastery and completion of the exercises, your instructor may use a rubric, with which more points are allotted according to performance characteristics. (The more you do, the more you earn!) Ask your instructor how your work will be evaluated.

AC10-T01 Use the Web as a Learning Tool

Throughout this book, you will be provided with an opportunity to use the Internet as a learning tool by completing WebQuests. According to the original creators of WebQuests, as described on their website (WebQuest.org), a WebQuest is "an inquiry-oriented activity in which most or all of the information used by learners is drawn from the web." To complete the WebQuest projects in this book, navigate to the student resource center and choose the WebQuest for the lesson on which you are currently working. The subject of each WebQuest will be relevant to the material found in the lesson.

WebQuest Subject: Customizing and modifying the look of Microsoft Access command buttons.

Submit your final files based on the guidelines provided by your instructor.

AC10-T02 Demonstrate Proficiency

Business at the Stormy BBQ Key West store and restaurant continues to boom, and it is time to make some behind-the-scenes changes to improve the store's database interface for the new staff you plan to hire over the coming months. Open **AC10-T02-SBQ** from the **AC2013 Lesson 10** folder and save as `AC10-T02-SBQ-[FirstInitialLastName]`.

Apply the techniques you learned in this lesson to personalize Microsoft Windows with your name and initials. Then modify the navigation options by creating a Stormy BBQ Category and Merchandise, Restaurants, and Staff Groups; adding the corresponding tables, queries, forms, and reports to the appropriate Group. Set the database options to view overlapping objects in the Access work area.

To protect the Stormy BBQ table data from unauthorized access, split the database. Create a navigation form in the un-split database with Merchandise, Restaurants, and Staff tabs; drag forms and reports to display under their respective tabs, and add a command button that both closes the database and exits Access, while maintaining the look of the other forms in the database. Modify the startup options so the navigation form displays each time the database is opened.

Submit your final file based on the guidelines provided by your instructor.

ACCESS 2013

Importing and Exporting Data Using Word, Excel, and HTML

LESSON OUTLINE

LEARNING OBJECTIVES

After studying this lesson, you will be able to:

- Convert Access 2013 files to previous Access formats
- Attach files to database records
- Integrate Access data with Word and Excel
- Display Access data on the web

Data can be stored on all types of computer systems and in a large variety of formats. Maintaining files and other data so they are easy to share with others can be a challenge. Fortunately, Access tools make it relatively easy to import, export, and format files so you can share them with others. In this lesson, you will explore how to share Access data with other Microsoft Office programs, as well as how to format your data for other systems and for the web.

CASE STUDY

Capturing More Data

The Winchester Web Design database stores all data related to customers, employees, products, and invoices. Having all the data stored in one electronic file makes it very convenient for sharing data within the company. Sometimes, however, data must be exported so it can be used offsite by someone who may not have Access on their computer. You have been assigned the task to experiment with file formats to make both non-sensitive and sensitive data available to others.

Access Products report exported to Excel.

Access Products report exported to a Word document.

Winchester Website Design
Products Report

Product ID	Product Description	Price
01HP	Home Page, Nav, CSS, Design	$400.
02SP	Secondary Page	

	A	B	C
1	Product ID	Product Description	Price
2	01HP	Home Page, Nav, CSS, Design	$400.00
3	02SP	Secondary Page	$200.00
4	03BL	Blog, Integrated into Site	$300.00
			$400.00
			$40.00
			$80.00
			$100.00
			$100.00
			$40.00
			$100.00
			$50.00

Access Products report in HTML format.

Products

ProdID	Description	Price
01HP	Home Page, Nav, CSS, Design	$400.00
02SP	Secondary Page	$200.00
03BL	Blog, Integrated into Site	$300.00
04SC	Shopping Cart, Basic	$400.00
05IM	Image, Custom Designed	$40.00
06HR	Hourly Rate for Modifications	$80.00
07LC	Logo Creation	$100.00
08PS	Photo Shoot, 1 hour onsite	$100.00
09IM	Image Map	$40.00
10SS	Slide Show	$100.00
11QR	QR Code	$50.00

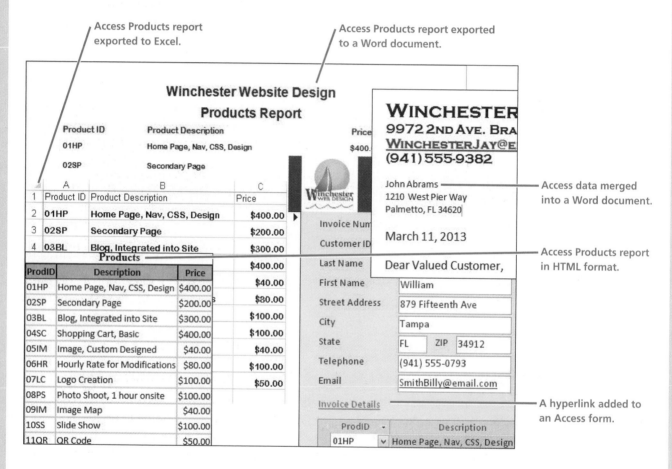

Access data merged into a Word document.

WINCHESTER
9972 2ND AVE. BRA
WINCHESTERJAY@E
(941) 555-9382

John Abrams
1210 West Pier Way
Palmetto, FL 34620

March 11, 2013

Dear Valued Customer,

A hyperlink added to an Access form.

Invoice Num
Customer ID
Last Name
First Name: William
Street Address: 879 Fifteenth Ave
City: Tampa
State: FL ZIP: 34912
Telephone: (941) 555-0793
Email: SmithBilly@email.com

Invoice Details

ProdID	Description
01HP	Home Page, Nav, CSS, Design

Converting Access 2013 Databases to Earlier Formats

Video Library: http://labyrinthelab.com/videos Video Number: AC13-V1101

> **FROM THE KEYBOARD**
> File→Save As→Save Database As→choose the database file type

Access 2013 databases carry a unique format that is incompatible with versions of Microsoft Access older than 2007. The obvious difference is the filename extension. Versions of Access prior to 2007 created files with an .mdb extension. Access 2007, 2010, and 2013 create files with an .accdb extension (for *Acc*ess *d*ata*b*ase). To share an Access 2013 database with users who have a version of Access prior to 2007, you must save the database in a format that the older version recognizes.

When you try to convert some newer databases to an earlier version of Access, you may get an error message.

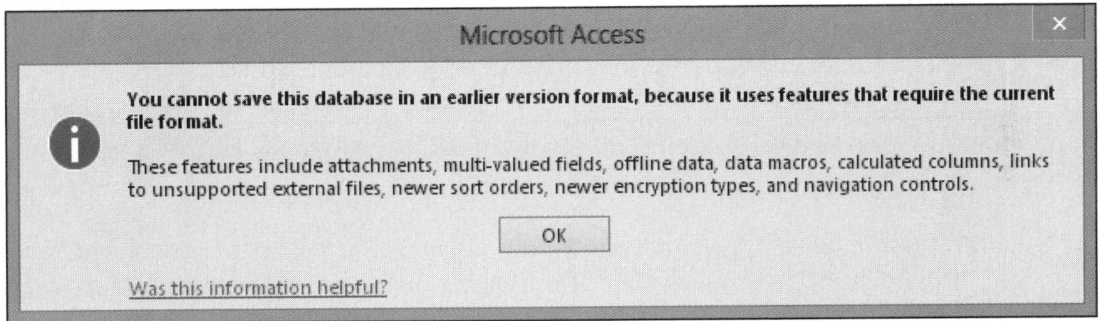

Older versions of Access do not support some of the newer features and formats available in Access 2013. Examples of some of the 2013 enhancements include the Long Text data type which has replaced the Memo field, the Attachment data type which has replaced the OLE object field, and the new 2013 Custom Web App and Web App Action Bar.

Identifying the Format of an Access Database

When you open a database, Access identifies the version of the file in the title bar. For example, when you open a database created in Access 2007, 2010, or 2013, the name of the database along with "Database (Access 2007–2013)" appears in the title bar. If you open a file created in or formatted for a previous version of Access, such as Access 2002–2003, Access places the words *Database (Access 2002–2003 file format)* in the title bar following the database name.

Database- C:\Users\FloydJ\Desktop\WWD.accdb (Access 2007 - 2013 file format) - Access

The Access 2007, 2010, and 2013 file format title bar.

Database- C:\Users\FloydJ\Desktop\WinWeb.mdb (Access 2002 - 2003 file format) - Access

The Access 2002–2003 file format title bar.

DEVELOP YOUR SKILLS AC11-D01

Save an Access 2013 Database in Access 2003 Format

In this exercise, you will save an Access 2013 database in the Access 2003 file format.

1. Open **AC11-D01-WWD2013** from your **AC2013 Lesson 11** folder and save it as **`AC11-D01-WWD2013-[FirstInitialLastName]`**.

   Replace the bracketed text with your first initial and last name. For example, if your name is Bethany Smith, your filename would look like this: AC11-D01-WWD2013-BSmith.

2. Enable content, if necessary.
3. Choose **File→Save As→Save Database As→Access 2002–2003 Database**.
4. Click the **Save As** button.

   The Save As dialog box opens.

5. Navigate to your **AC2013 Lesson 11** folder, type **`AC11-D01-WWD2003-[FirstInitialLastName].mdb`** for the filename, and click **OK**.

AC11-D01-WWD2003FWinters : Database- C:\Users\FloydJ\Desktop\AC11-D01-WWD2003-FWinters.mdb (Access 2002 - 2003 file format) - Access

   The filename and file format information display in the title bar, indicating that the database is now in Access 2002–2003 file format. The filename and path might be too long to show the file format, however. If you click the File tab, more of the path is visible.

6. **Close** [×] all open databases.

Attaching Files to Database Records

Video Library: http://labyrinthelab.com/videos Video Number: AC13-V1102

Older versions of Access used fields with the OLE Object data type to add images to records. For example, a company might want to include employee photos in the employee table. However, adding a single un-cropped, high-resolution image taken from one of today's smartphones or adding long and wordy comments to records with Long Text fields can significantly increase the size of the database.

Database size affects the speed and efficiency of the database. Attaching files to—rather than embedding the data—can significantly reduce the size of the database.

Using the Attachment Data Type

Access 2013 provides the Attachment data type to enable you to attach one or more pictures, spreadsheet files, documents, charts, and other file types to a specific field in the table. You can use an attachment field to store multiple files of varying file types without increasing the size of the actual database file.

Following are some basic guidelines that govern attaching files to table records.

Attachment Limitations and Notes

- Access 2007, 2010, and 2013 are the only versions of Access that allow you to attach files to database records.
- A maximum limit of two gigabytes of data can be attached to a database.
- The file size for individual attachments is limited to 256 megabytes.
- After assigning the Attachment data type to a field, you cannot change the data type.

Managing Attachments

Access identifies fields that contain attachments with a paperclip icon in the field name. A paperclip icon followed by a number identifies the number of attachments for each individual record. For instance, you might have a products database where you have a photo of the product from the front and a second photo of the product from the back. Or perhaps you want to store both a casual and a publicity dress photo for your employees.

Hire Date	Web Cert	📎
12/1/2010	☑	📎(2)
1/7/2013	☐	📎(0)
12/9/2010	☑	📎(1)

To add an attachment, double-click the paperclip icon for the record to which you want to attach the file. Access opens the Attachments dialog box. Click Add to browse to and select the image or file that you want to attach to the record.

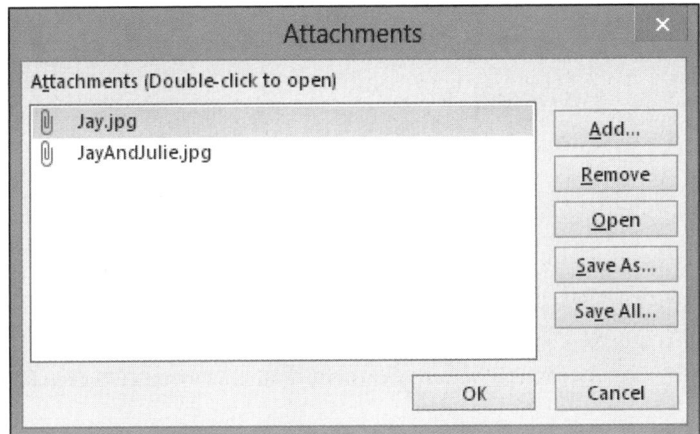

The Attachments dialog box.

QUICK REFERENCE	WORKING WITH ATTACHMENT FIELDS
Task	**Procedure**
Create an attachment field	■ Display the table in Design View. ■ Enter the new Field Name, such as ClientPhoto. ■ Choose Attachment from the Data Type list. ■ Save changes to the table.
Attach a file to a table record	■ Display the table in Datasheet View. ■ Double-click the paperclip icon for the record to which you want to attach a file. ■ Click Add and browse to the file you want to attach. ■ Double-click the filename to add it to the Attachment dialog box and click OK.
Open a record attachment	■ Double-click the paperclip icon for the record with the attachment. ■ Double-click the attachment filename.
Save a record attachment	■ Double-click the paperclip icon for the record with the attachment. ■ Click the attachment filename and then click Save As. ■ Save the item using standard save procedures and click OK.

DEVELOP YOUR SKILLS AC11-D02

Create an Attachment Field and Attach a File

In this exercise, you will add an Attachment field to the Winchester Web Design Employees table in Design View and attach two photos to a table record.

1. Open **AC11-D02-WinWebDesign** from the **AC2013 Lesson 11** folder and save it as `AC11-D02-WinWebDesign-[FirstInitialLastName]`.
2. Enable content and close any open objects, if necessary.
3. Display the **Employees** table in **Design View**.
4. Follow these steps to add a new field to the table:

Ⓐ Type **`EmpPhoto`** in the first available Field Name column.

Field Name	Data Type	Description (Optional)
EmpPhone	Short Text	
EmpEmail	Hyperlink	
HireDate	Date/Time	
WebCert	Yes/No	Web Certification
EmpPhoto	Attachment	Office ID Photo

Ⓑ Choose **Attachment** from the Data Type list.

Ⓒ Type **`Office ID Photo`** for the Description.

5. Save the changes to the table and then switch to **Datasheet View**.

6. Follow these steps to add an attachment to the first table record:

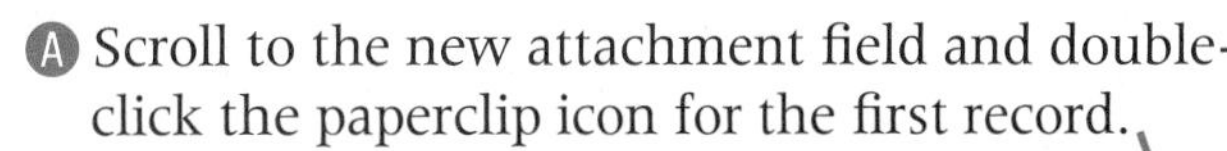

A Scroll to the new attachment field and double-click the paperclip icon for the first record.

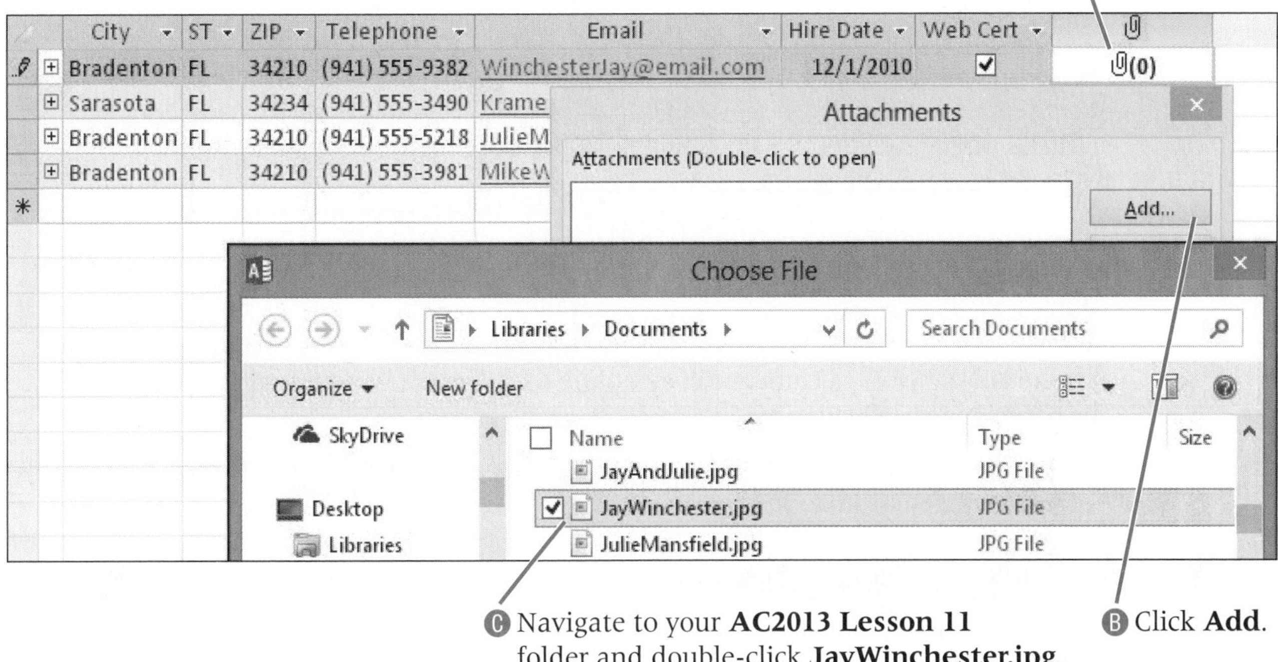

C Navigate to your **AC2013 Lesson 11** folder and double-click **JayWinchester.jpg**.

B Click **Add**.

Access adds the filename of the photo to the Attachments dialog box.

7. Click **OK**.
   Access places the number 1 in parentheses following the attachment icon for the first record.
8. Double-click the paperclip icon for **record 1** to open the Attachments dialog box.
9. Click **Add**, navigate to the **AC2013 Lesson 11** folder, and double-click **JayAndJulie.jpg**.
10. Click **OK** to close the Attachments dialog box.
    Now a 2 follows the paperclip icon for the first record.
11. Double-click the paperclip icon again, select **JayWinchester.jpg**, and click **Open**.
    The photo displays in your default program used to view images.
12. Close the **Attachments** dialog box. Save and close the **Employees** table.

Integrating Access with Word

Video Library: http://labyrinthelab.com/videos Video Number: AC13-V1103

There are several ways to share data between Access and Word. The easiest way is to copy an object in Access and then paste it as an unlinked object into Word. For instance, you can select all or part of an Access table or query, copy it, then open a Word or Excel document and paste the copied Access selection.

FROM THE RIBBON
Home→Clipboard→Copy to copy an Access object

A variation of this technique is to select the desired rows or the desired columns of an Access table or query and then export the data as a linked source to a Word document. A linked file allows source data to be placed into a destination file that is automatically updated when changes are made to the source file. For example, if you were to link an Access table to a Word document on Monday, and the Access data changed on Tuesday, those changes would be reflected in the Word document the next time the Word file was opened (as long as the Access file has not been deleted or moved).

Another process is called Mail Merge, which allows a business to merge selected data fields (such as names and addresses) with a Word document, producing personalized letters that can be mailed to thousands of potential customers. You can also publish Access data into a Word document for inclusion in a report.

There are additional Export tools on the External Data tab of the Ribbon that let you to connect to other Microsoft Office applications using various file formats. One of these formats is a text file, or a plain alphanumeric text file without any formatting or font information. A variation of a text file is a rich text file (RTF) which contains minimal formatting, such as color or bold. Both text files and rich text files are very small in size, relative to normal Word documents, and are compatible across virtually all hardware and software platforms.

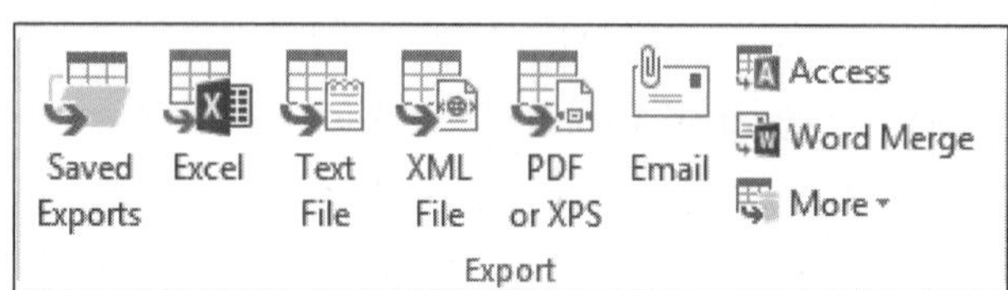

The Export tools on the External Data tab.

QUICK REFERENCE — EXPORTING ACCESS DATA TO WORD

Task	Procedure
Copy and paste data between Access and Word	■ Select all or part of the Access table or query to copy. ■ Press Ctrl+C or choose Home→Clipboard→Copy. ■ Open Word and press Ctrl+V or choose Home→Clipboard→Paste.
Export Access data to Word	■ Open the table, form, or query results datasheet to export. ■ Choose External Data→Export→More→Word.
Merge data with Word	■ Open the table or form containing the records to merge. ■ Choose External Data→Export→Word Merge. ■ Select the desired option (to use an existing merge document or create a new one). ■ Use Mail Merge on the Mailings tab to complete the merge.

Copying Data from Access to Word

Video Library: http://labyrinthelab.com/videos Video Number: AC13-V1104

You can use both copy-and-paste and drag-and-drop techniques to copy Access data into a Word document. However, it is important to note that pasted data is not linked, so editing data that has been inserted into Word has no effect on the data stored in Access, and vice versa. The data displayed in the Word document may be out of date.

DEVELOP YOUR SKILLS AC11-D03

Copy Data from Access to Word

In this exercise, you will copy data from an Access table into a new Word document using copy-and-paste and drag-and-drop techniques.

1. Display the **Products** table in **Datasheet View**.
2. Follow these steps to make a copy of all the records in the Products table:

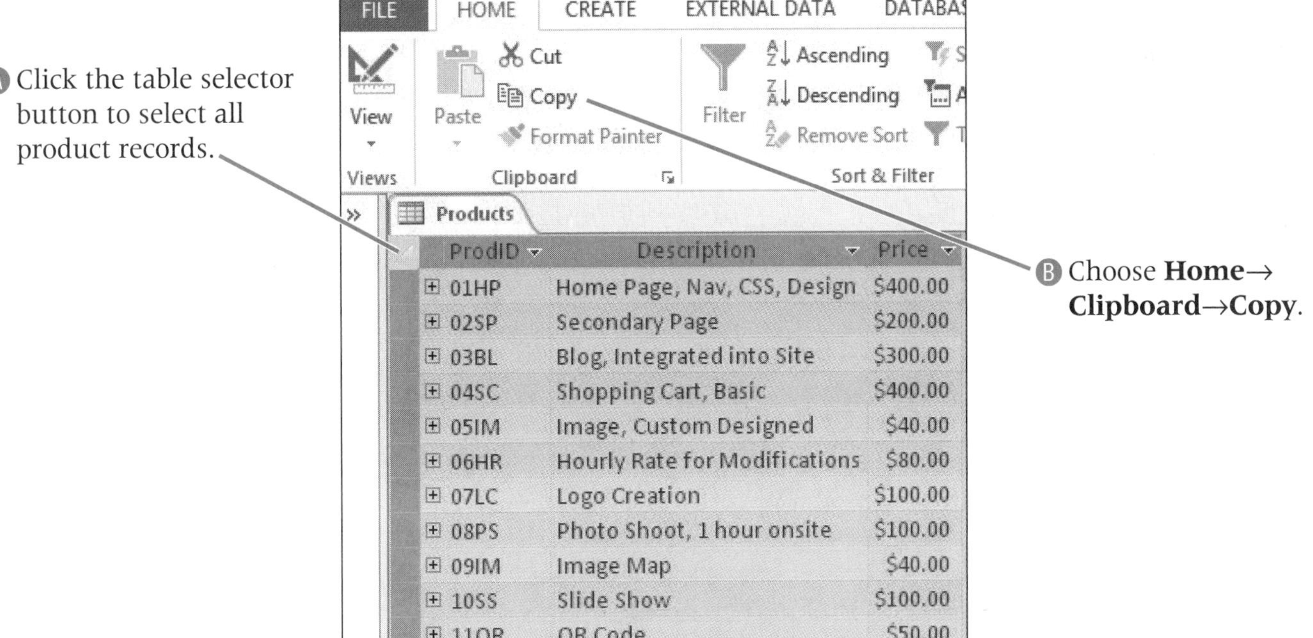

3. Start **Word**, navigate to your **AC2013 Lesson 11** folder, and double-click **AC11-D03-WWD-ProdLetter.docx**.

WINCHESTER WEB DESIGN
9972 2ND AVE. BRADENTON, FL 34210
WINCHESTERJAY@EMAIL.COM
(941) 555-9382

March 11, 2013

Dear Valued Customer,

We would like you to review our products and services and consider adding one of these product features to your current Web site:

If we can be of any assistance, please contact any of our employees at your convenience.

Thank you for allowing Winchester Web Design to serve you,

Jay Winchester
WinchesterJay@email.com
(941) 555-9382

The document, a letter to the company's customers, opens in Microsoft Word.

4. Position the insertion point under the line that reads *...and consider adding one of these product features to your current Web site.*
5. Choose **Home→Clipboard→**[Paste] and choose **Keep Source Formatting**.

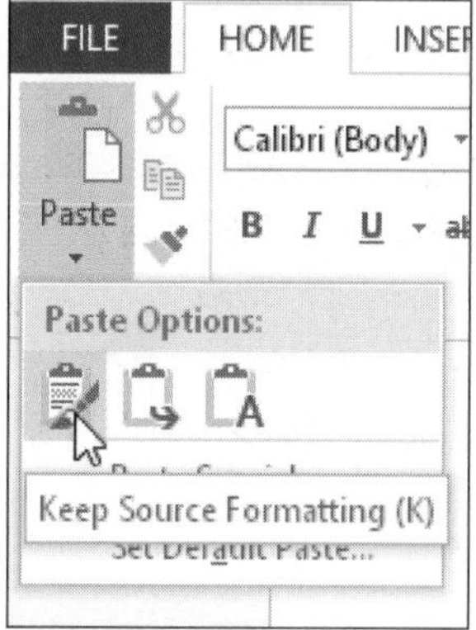

6. Close the **Products** table in Access.
7. Minimize all applications and then maximize **Word** and **Access**.
   If you are in the Metro View *of Windows 8 (tiles display), click the Desktop tile or type* desktop *and tap* [Enter] *to display the traditional Windows taskbar.*
8. Click the **Access title bar** and tap [Windows]+[←] to place the Access database on the left side of the screen.

9. Click the **Word title bar** and tap Windows + → to place the WWD Product Descriptions file on the right side of the screen.

   An alternative way to open both windows side by side onscreen is to right-click a blank area of the Windows task bar and choose Show Windows Side by Side.

10. Open the **Employee Contact Info** query.

11. Follow these steps to drag the Employee Contact Info query records into Word:

Ⓐ Click the table selector button.

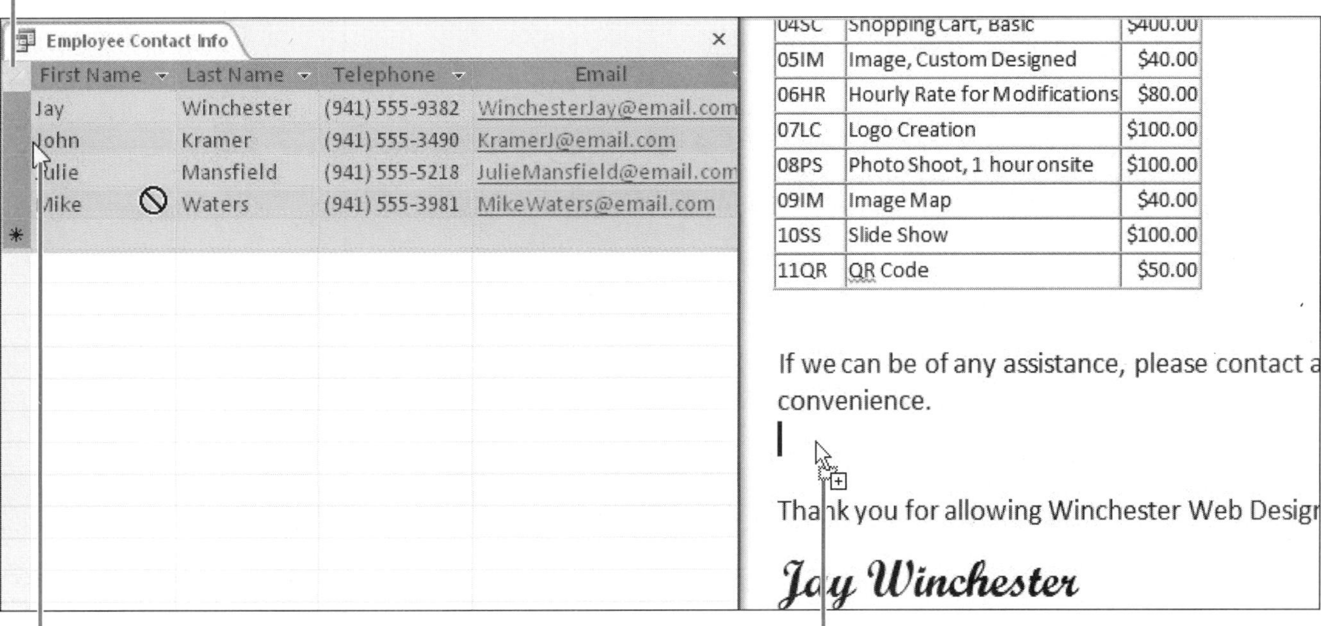

Ⓑ Hover the pointer over the left side of a field in the first column until the pointer becomes a white arrow.

Ⓒ Click and drag the records into the Word document and drop them at the insertion point.

The pointer becomes a black circle with a line through it ⊘ as you drag records over the Access work area. This pointer changes when you cross onto the Word document, becoming a white move arrow with a plus sign, indicating that you can copy the selection to that location.

The copy by dragging process can sometimes be very challenging. The pointer must be precisely positioned over the left side of a field in the first column. If you cannot get this step to work, then copy and paste the records into the Word document.

WINCHESTER WEB DESIGN
9972 2ND AVE. BRADENTON, FL 34210
WINCHESTERJAY@EMAIL.COM
(941) 555-9382

March 11, 2013

Dear Valued Customer,

We would like you to review our products and services and consider adding one of these product features to your current Web site:

Products		
ProdID	Description	Price
01HP	Home Page, Nav, CSS, Design	$400.00
02SP	Secondary Page	$200.00
03BL	Blog, Integrated into Site	$300.00
04SC	Shopping Cart, Basic	$400.00
05IM	Image, Custom Designed	$40.00
06HR	Hourly Rate for Modifications	$80.00
07LC	Logo Creation	$100.00
08PS	Photo Shoot, 1 hour onsite	$100.00
09IM	Image Map	$40.00
10SS	Slide Show	$100.00
11QR	QR Code	$50.00

If we can be of any assistance, please contact any of our employees at your convenience.

Employee Contact Info			
First Name	Last Name	Telephone	Email
Jay	Winchester	(941) 555-9382	WinchesterJay@email.com
John	Kramer	(941) 555-3490	KramerJ@email.com
Julie	Mansfield	(941) 555-5218	JulieMansfield@email.com
Mike	Waters	(941) 555-3981	MikeWaters@email.com

Thank you for allowing Winchester Web Design to serve you,

Jay Winchester
WinchesterJay@email.com
(941) 555-9382

The report with the pasted table and dragged query results. If the report extends to a second page, delete any unnecessary blank lines.

12. Close the **Employee Contact Info** query.
13. Save the Word document as **`AC11-D03-WWD-ProdLetter-[FirstInitialLastName].docx`** and then close it and exit **Word**. Maximize **Access**.

You can use these same techniques to drag Access table data into Excel and PowerPoint.

Publishing Data to Word

Video Library: http://labyrinthelab.com/videos Video Number: AC13-V1105

FROM THE RIBBON
External Data→Export→More to export Access data

The most commonly used tools for integrating Access data with other applications appear in the Export group on the External Data tab, and other tools appear on the More list. These tools enable you to send data from a database object to Word and other applications. When you export a database object to Word, Access formats it in rich text format, launches Word, and opens the data in a new document. A rich text file is relatively small in size, and is formatted so that it can be read by a wide variety of applications. You can then edit and save the document in Word without affecting the data in the database.

DEVELOP YOUR SKILLS AC11-D04

Send Access Data to Word

In this exercise, you will export a list of the Winchester Web Design employees to a Word document.

1. Open the **Employees** table.
2. Choose the **External Data→Export→More menu ▾** and choose **Word**.

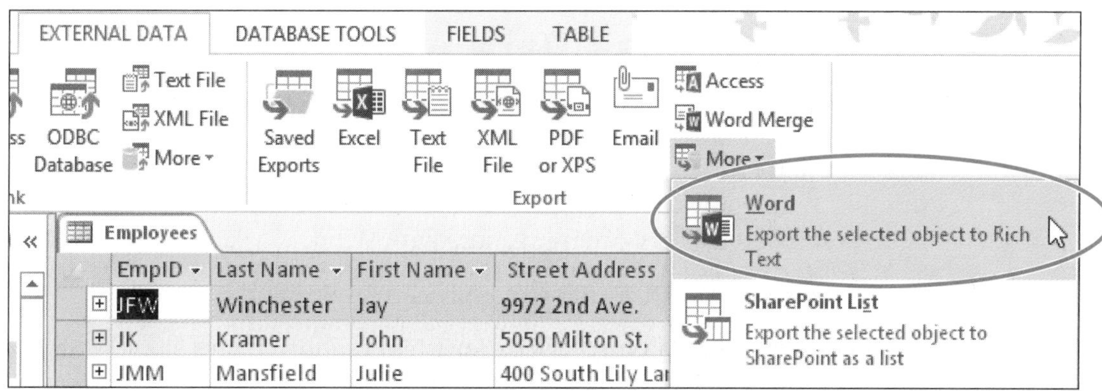

3. Follow these steps to export the table to Word as a small, cross-platform rich text file:

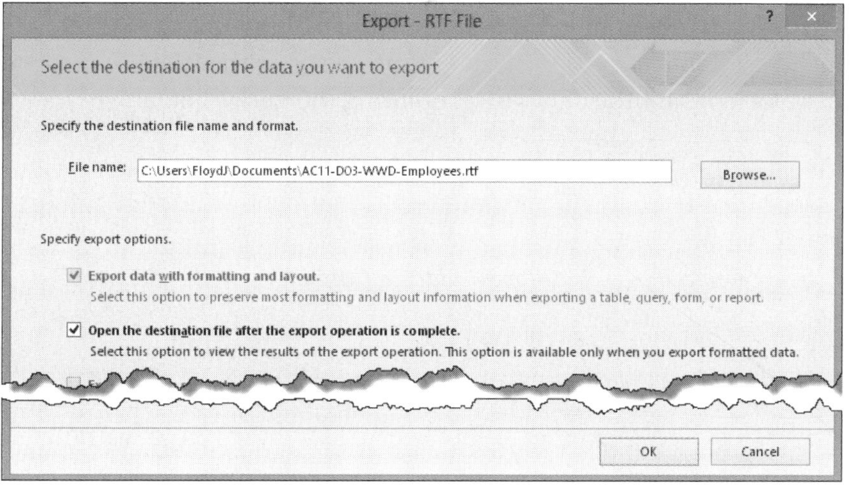

Ⓐ Click **Browse**, open the **AC2013 Lesson 11** folder, type **`AC11-D04-WWD-Emp-[FirstInitialLastName].rtf`**, and click **Save**.

Ⓑ Click in this checkbox.

Ⓒ Click **OK**.

Access exports the table and opens it in Word.

4. Close the **Export – RTF File** dialog box and switch to **Word**.
5. Choose **Page Layout→Page Setup→Margins**, and then choose **Narrow** to fit more of the data on the page.
6. Choose **Page Layout→Page Setup→Orientation**. Select **Landscape**.

Access 2013

7. Resize the columns to fit as much of the data on the page as possible.

EmpID	Last Name	First Name	Street Address	City	ST	ZIP	Telephone	Email	Hire Date	Web Cert	EmpPhot
JFW	Winchester	Jay	9972 2nd Ave.	Bradenton	FL	34210	(941) 555-9382	WinchesterJay@email.com	12/1/2010	Yes	1
JK	Kramer	John	5050 Milton St.	Sarasota	FL	34234	(941) 555-3490	KramerJ@email.com	1/7/2013	No	0
JMM	Mansfield	Julie	400 South Lily Lane	Bradenton	FL	34210	(941) 555-5218	JulieMansfield@email.com	12/9/2010	Yes	0
MJW	Waters	Mike	124 26th St.	Bradenton	FL	34210	(941) 555-3981	MikeWaters@email.com	4/18/2011	No	0

Access data exported to a Word document.

8. Close the **Word** file, saving changes if prompted.
9. Switch to **Access** and close the **Employees** table.

Merging Access Data with Word Documents

Video Library: http://labyrinthelab.com/videos Video Number: AC13-V1106

Access databases often contain valuable data that can be used in letters, mailings, and other documents. Retyping such data can be time-consuming and may result in inaccurate data entry. The Export tool is useful for merging data with Word.

When merging data with Word, Access gives you two options:

- **Link to an existing Word document:** This option creates a link to an existing document so Word can locate the database and pull the most up-to-date data into the merge document. The link between the Word document and the database includes a path that is used to locate the data each time you open the merge document. If the database file is moved to a different folder, Word will be unable to locate it and cannot complete the merge.
- **Create a new Word document:** This option creates a new Word document and merges it with the data linked to an Access database table. The next time you open the Word document, Word automatically looks for the database containing the merge data.

DEVELOP YOUR SKILLS AC11-D05

Merge Access Data with Word

In this exercise, you will export Access data containing customer addresses and link it to the Word customer letter.

1. Open the **Customers** table.
2. Choose **External Data→Export→** Word Merge.
   The Microsoft Word Mail Merge Wizard opens.
3. Choose the **Link Your Data to an Existing Microsoft Word Document** option and click **OK**.
   Access opens the Select Microsoft Word Document dialog box.
4. Navigate to your **AC2013 Lesson 11** folder, if necessary, and double-click **AC11-D03-WWD-ProdLetter-[FirstInitialLastName]**.
   Word opens your document along with the Mail Merge task pane.

5. Follow these steps to add fields to the merge document:

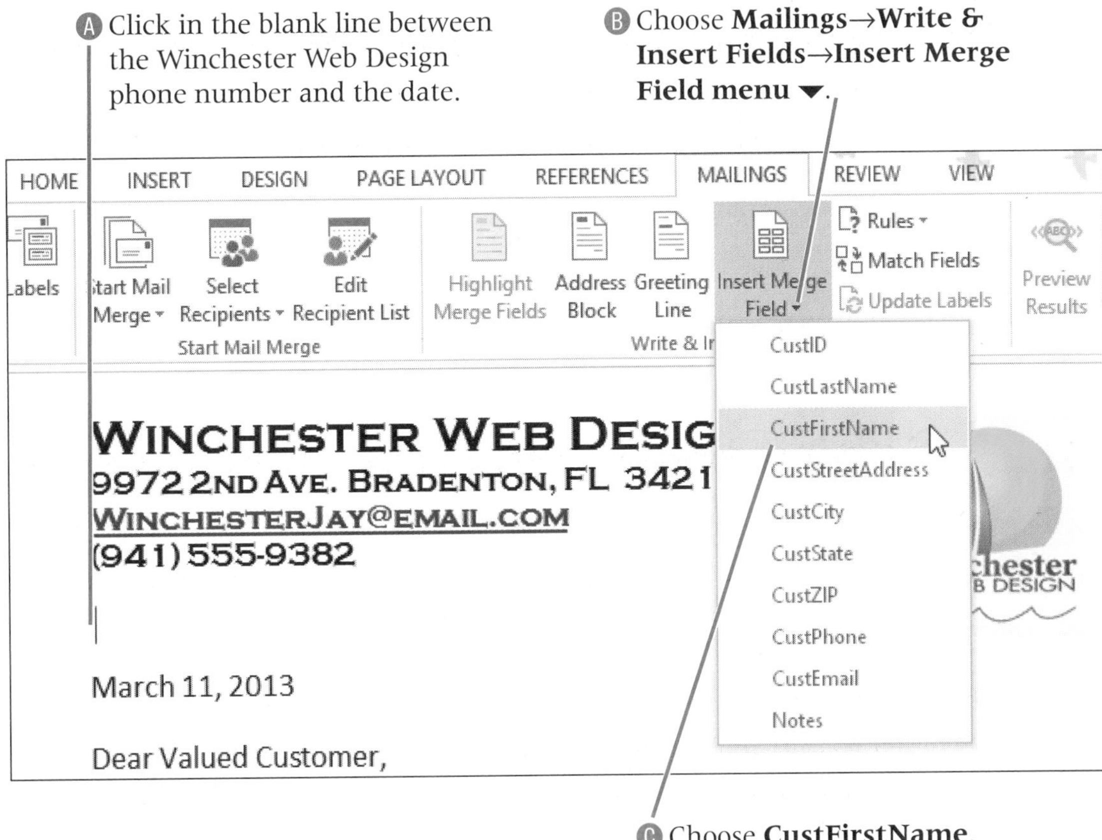

6. Tap [Spacebar] to insert a space after «CustFirstName».
7. Choose **Mailings→Write & Insert Fields→Insert Merge Field ▼→CustLastName**.
8. Tap [Enter] and choose **CustStreetAddress** from the **Insert Merge Field** list.
9. Tap [Enter] and choose **CustCity** from the **Insert Merge Field** list.
10. Type a comma, tap [Spacebar], and choose **CustState** from the **Insert Merge Field** list.
11. Tap [Spacebar] and choose **CustZIP** from the **Insert Merge Field** list.

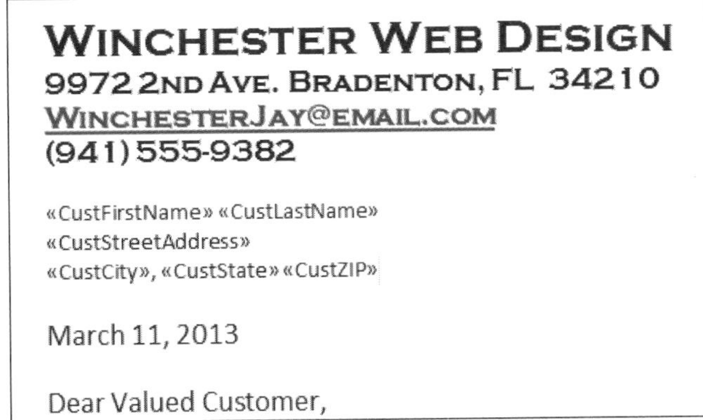

If the field names were FirstName, LastName, City, etc. instead of CustFirstName, CustLastName, CustCity, you could click the Address Block icon to insert the address fields in one step.

12. Choose **Mailings→Preview Results→Preview Results** [icon] to verify that the customer name and address display properly.

> **WINCHESTER WEB DESIGN**
> **9972 2ND AVE. BRADENTON, FL 34210**
> WINCHESTERJAY@EMAIL.COM
> **(941) 555-9382**
>
> John Abrams
> 1210 West Pier Way
> Palmetto, FL 34620
>
> March 11, 2013
>
> Dear Valued Customer,

13. Save and close the Word document; exit **Word**.
14. Switch to **Access** and close the **Customers** table.

Integrating Access with Excel

Video Library: http://labyrinthelab.com/videos Video Number: AC13-V1107

Many people consider the calculation capabilities in Excel more sophisticated than those available in Access. They also find the formulas easier to create in Excel than calculated fields in Access. As a result, Access data may be sent to Excel to perform calculations. The process of sending data to other files or applications is called exporting data. The process of retrieving data from other files or applications is called importing data.

Importing Data from Excel Files

When you import data from Excel, Access uses the Import Spreadsheet Wizard to guide the process. After you import the data, it becomes part of the database file. Because the data is imported and not linked, any changes you make to the Excel file after the import have no impact on the table data in Access.

Tools on the External Data tab can be used to import and to export data.

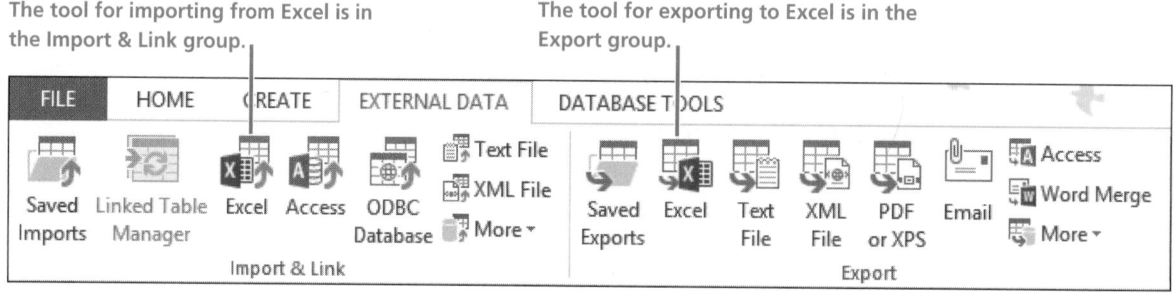

QUICK REFERENCE	IMPORTING AND EXPORTING EXCEL FILES
Task	**Procedure**
Import data into Access from Excel	■ Choose External Data→Import & Link→Excel. ■ Open the folder containing the file to import. ■ Double-click the file you want to import. ■ Follow the directions on the Import Spreadsheet Wizard.
Export Access data to Excel	■ Select or open the database object to export. ■ Choose External Data→Export→Excel. ■ Navigate to the folder into which you want to save the new Excel file and select appropriate options. ■ Click OK.

DEVELOP YOUR SKILLS AC11-D06

Import Excel Data into Access

In this exercise, you will import an Excel worksheet into your database.

1. Close all Access database objects and choose **External Data→Import & Link→Excel**.
   Access launches the Get External Data – Excel Spreadsheet dialog box.
2. Choose the **Import the Source Data into a New Table in the Current Database** option, click **Browse**, and navigate to the **AC2013 Lesson 11** folder.
3. Double-click the **AC11-D06-WebContacts.xlsx** filename to add this Excel file to the source filename.

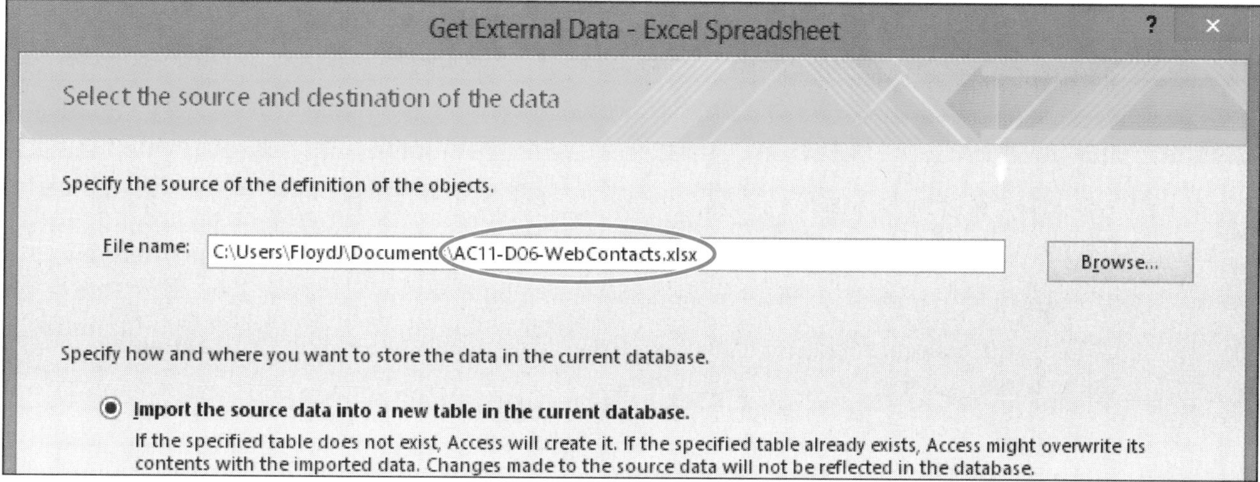

4. Click **OK** to launch the Import Spreadsheet Wizard.
5. Choose the **Show Worksheets** option and then click **Next**.

Access 2013

6. Check the **First Row Contains Column Headings** checkbox and click **Next**.

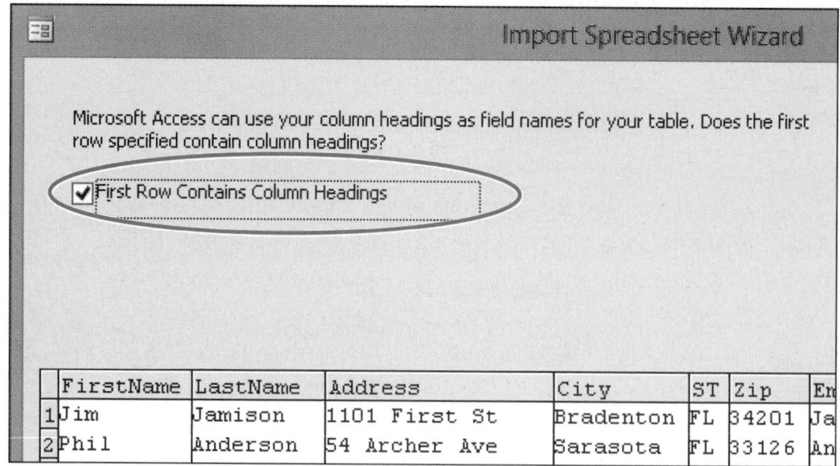

7. Click **Next** to import all the worksheet fields to the new table, without changes.
8. Click **Next** to let Access create a primary key.
9. Type `Web Contacts` for the Import to Table Name, and click **Finish**.
10. Close the **Get External Data** window.

View Imported Table Data

11. Open the new **Web Contacts** table.

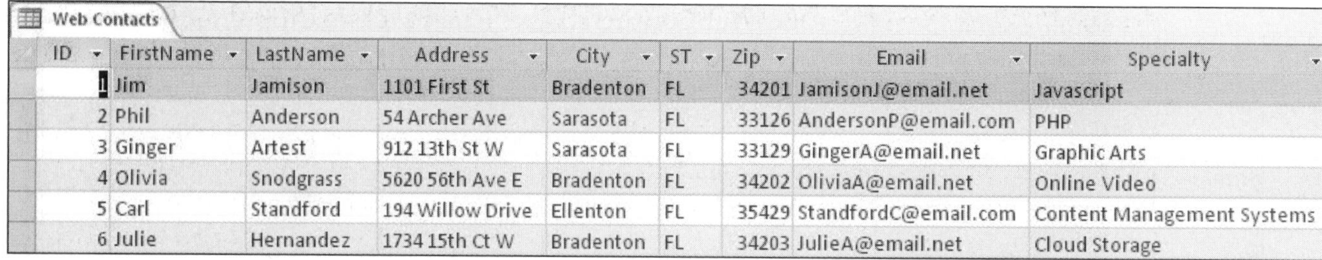

Web Contacts

ID	FirstName	LastName	Address	City	ST	Zip	Email	Specialty
1	Jim	Jamison	1101 First St	Bradenton	FL	34201	JamisonJ@email.net	Javascript
2	Phil	Anderson	54 Archer Ave	Sarasota	FL	33126	AndersonP@email.com	PHP
3	Ginger	Artest	912 13th St W	Sarasota	FL	33129	GingerA@email.net	Graphic Arts
4	Olivia	Snodgrass	5620 56th Ave E	Bradenton	FL	34202	OliviaA@email.net	Online Video
5	Carl	Standford	194 Willow Drive	Ellenton	FL	35429	StandfordC@email.com	Content Management Systems
6	Julie	Hernandez	1734 15th Ct W	Bradenton	FL	34203	JulieA@email.net	Cloud Storage

The data imported is not linked to the Excel spreadsheet. If you update the data in Excel, it will not be updated in the Access file. Once this data is imported, there is no longer a connection between the two files.

12. Adjust column widths, as needed; then save and close the **Web Contacts** table.
13. Close**AC11-D02-WinWebDesign-[FirstInitialLastName]**.

14. Open the **AC11-D06-WebContacts.xlsx** file in Excel and change the address field value for the first record from *1101 First St* to `999 Import St`.

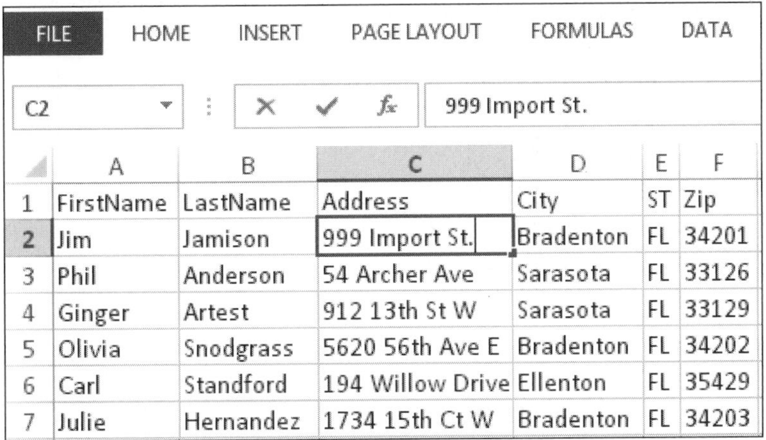

FILE HOME INSERT PAGE LAYOUT FORMULAS DATA

C2 | 999 Import St.

	A	B	C	D	E	F
1	FirstName	LastName	Address	City	ST	Zip
2	Jim	Jamison	999 Import St.	Bradenton	FL	34201
3	Phil	Anderson	54 Archer Ave	Sarasota	FL	33126
4	Ginger	Artest	912 13th St W	Sarasota	FL	33129
5	Olivia	Snodgrass	5620 56th Ave E	Bradenton	FL	34202
6	Carl	Standford	194 Willow Drive	Ellenton	FL	35429
7	Julie	Hernandez	1734 15th Ct W	Bradenton	FL	34203

15. Save and close the **AC11-D04-WebContacts.xlsx** file.

16. Open **AC11-D02-WinWebDesign-[FirstInitialLastName]**, close any open objects, and open the **Web Contacts** table.

    The address has not *been changed.*

17. Close the **Web Contacts** table.

Linking an Excel Worksheet to an Access Database

Video Library: http://labyrinthelab.com/videos Video Number: AC13-V1108

When you want the data in the Access database to reflect the most current data contained in an Excel spreadsheet, you can import and link the Excel spreadsheet to the Access database table. When you link a spreadsheet to a database, any change to the data in Excel, is reflected in Access when you open the linked table in Access. Access uses an Excel icon, with a small arrow to the left, to identify a table that is linked to a spreadsheet.

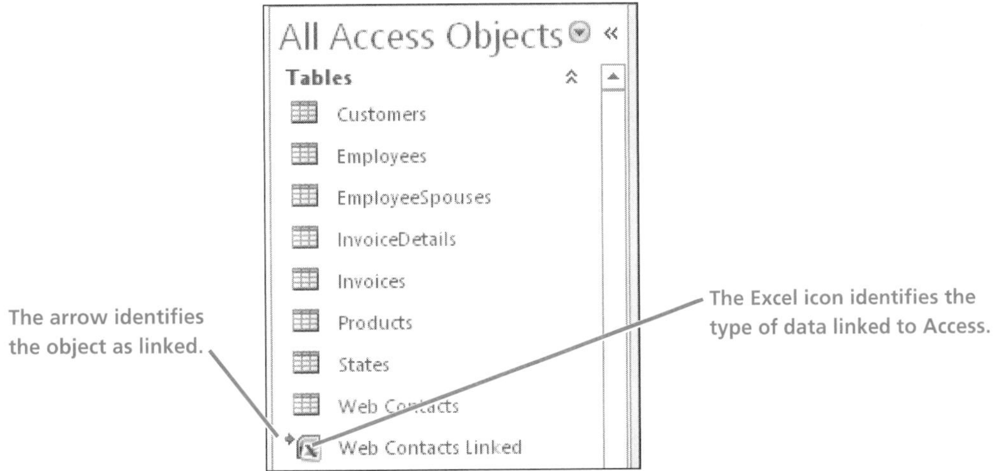

No edits can be made to linked spreadsheets from within the Access table. You must open the source Excel spreadsheet to make changes to the data or structure.

DEVELOP YOUR SKILLS AC11-D07

Link an Excel Spreadsheet to an Access Database

In this exercise, instead of merely importing, you will link the WebContacts.xlsx spreadsheet to the Winchester Web Design database.

1. Choose **External Data→Import & Link→** to open the Get External Data - Excel Spreadsheet dialog box.
2. Choose the **Link to the Data Source by Creating a Linked Table** option, click **Browse**, navigate to your **AC2013 Lesson 11** folder, and double-click **AC11-D06-WebContacts.xlsx**.

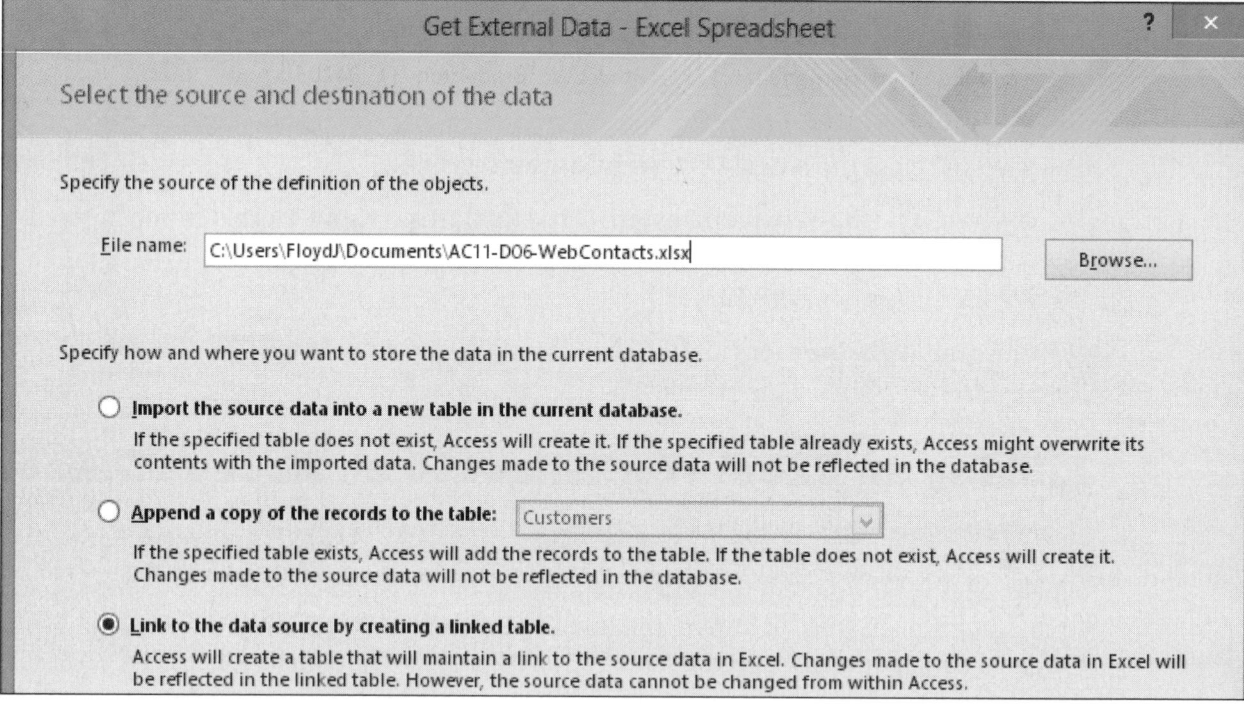

3. Click **OK** to launch the Link Spreadsheet Wizard.
4. Click **Next** to accept Sheet1.
5. Check the **First Row Contains Column Headings** checkbox and then click **Next**.
6. Type `Web Contacts Linked` in the Linked Table Name box and click **Finish**.
7. Click **OK** in the Link Spreadsheet Wizard message and locate the linked item as identified by the Excel icon and arrow in the Navigation Pane Tables group.

8. Open the **Web Contacts Linked** table in Access and try to edit the data.

   The object icon indicates that the table is linked. Access prevents data editing when the linked file is open in Access.

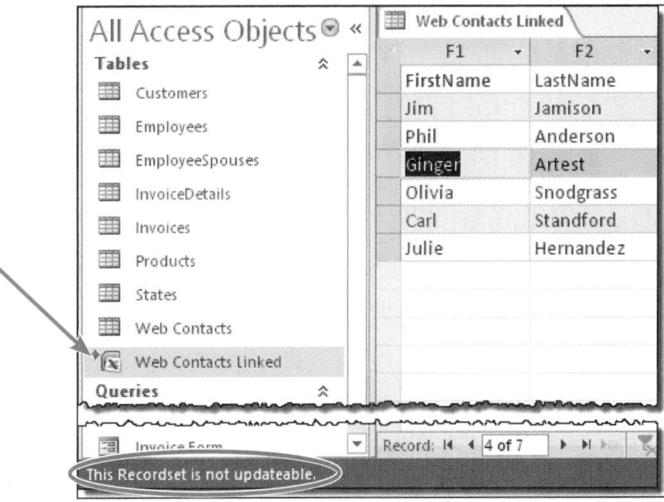

9. Close the **Web Contacts Linked** table.
10. Open the Excel **AC11-D06-WebContacts.xlsx** file and change the address field for the first record from *999 Import St* to `222 Link St`.
11. Save and close the **AC11-D06-WebContacts.xlsx** file.
12. Open the Access **Web Contacts Linked** table in Access and notice that the street address is now *222 Link St*.
13. Close the **Web Contacts Linked** table.

Fixing Broken Links

Video Library: http://labyrinthelab.com/videos Video Number: AC13-V1109

When you link an Excel spreadsheet to an Access database, Access identifies the drive and folder in which the Excel file was located at the time you created the link. Access searches for the Excel file each time you open the database. If the original Excel file was moved and the path is no longer valid, Access is unable to connect to the linked file. As a result, Access contains a feature called the Linked Table Manager that aids in locating and redirecting the database to the correct file so you can view the data.

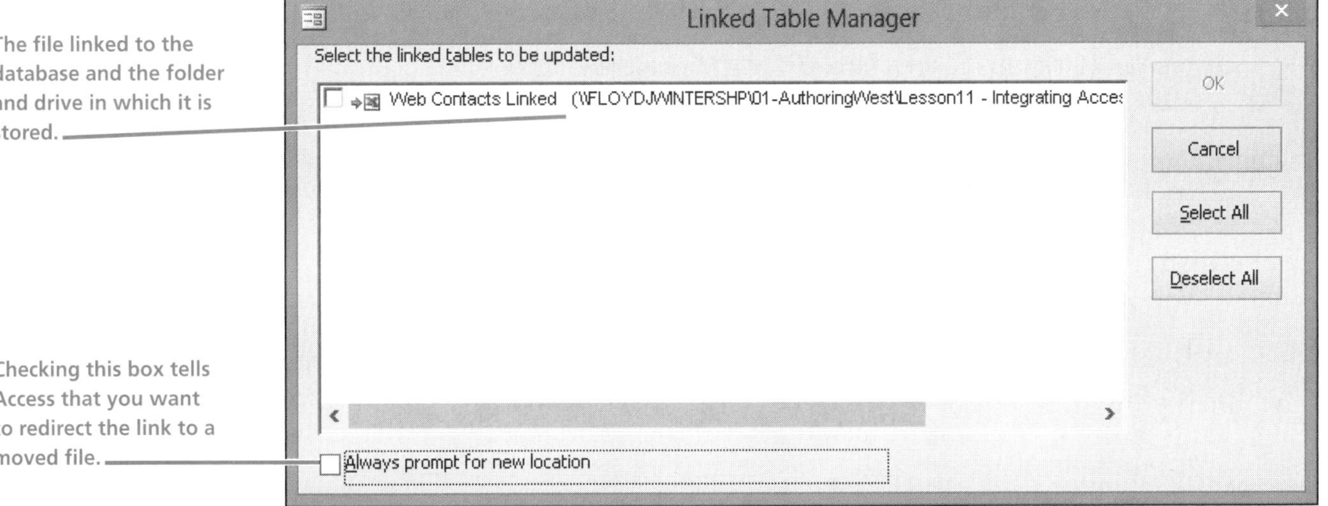

Access 2013

DEVELOP YOUR SKILLS AC11-D08

Use the Linked Table Manager

In this exercise, you will open the Linked Table Manager and update the linked table location.

1. Choose **External Data→Import & Link→[Linked Table Manager]**.
2. Follow these steps to review the information contained in the dialog box:

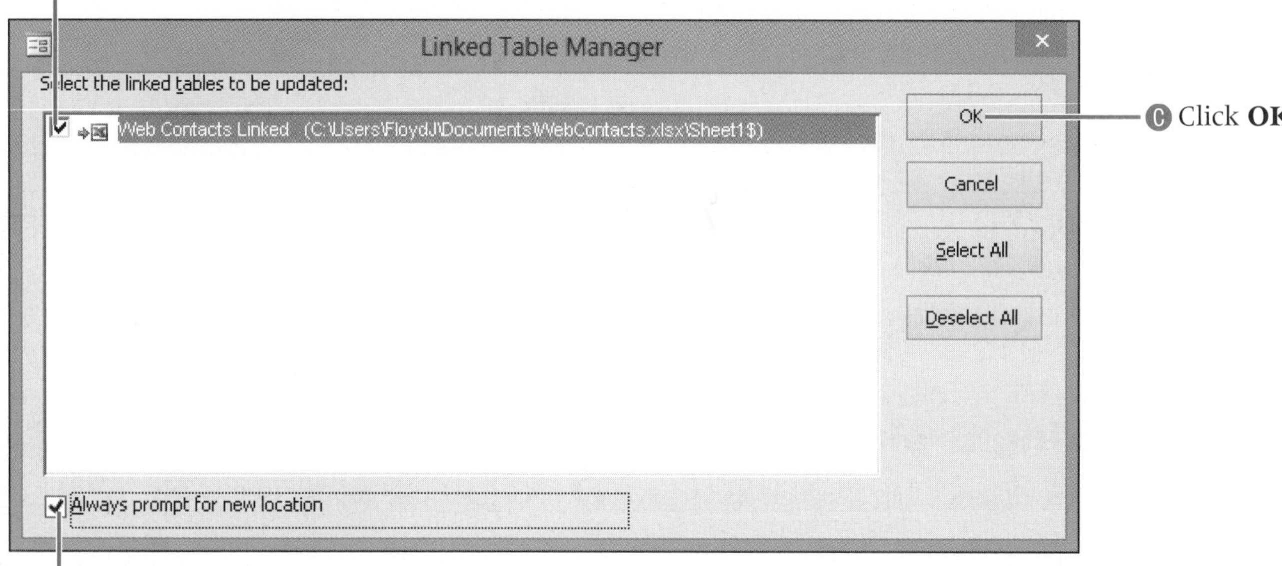

The Always Prompt for New Location option enables you to navigate to the folder containing the linked file, in the event that the file has been moved.

3. Locate the Excel file **AC11-D06-WebContacts.xlsx** and click **Open**.
4. Click **OK** to acknowledge that the linked tables were successfully refreshed.
5. Click **Close** in the Linked Table Manager dialog box.
6. Close the **AC11-D02-WinWebDesign-[FirstInitialLastName]** database.

Exporting Access Data to Excel

Video Library: http://labyrinthelab.com/videos Video Number: AC13-V1110

If you want to use the Excel calculations on Access data, you can export the data to create a new Excel file. Some fields, such as zip codes, which are defined as the Short Text data type, or a Yes/No data type, which displays values of True/False, may require additional formatting or manipulation in Excel, but overall the steps are similar to those used to export Access data to merge with Word.

DEVELOP YOUR SKILLS AC11-D09

Export Access Data to Excel

In this exercise, you will export data from an older Winchester Web Design Invoices table to create a new Excel workbook.

1. Open **AC11-D09-Invoices2011** from your **AC2013 Lesson 11** folder and save it as **`AC11-D09-Invoices2011-[FirstInitialLastName]`**.
2. Click **Enable Content**.
3. Click the **Invoices2011** table in the Navigation Pane to select it.
4. Choose **External Data→Export→Export to Excel Spreadsheet**.
5. Ensure that the file format is set to **Excel Workbook (*.xlsx)** and check the two checkboxes under **Specify Export Options**.

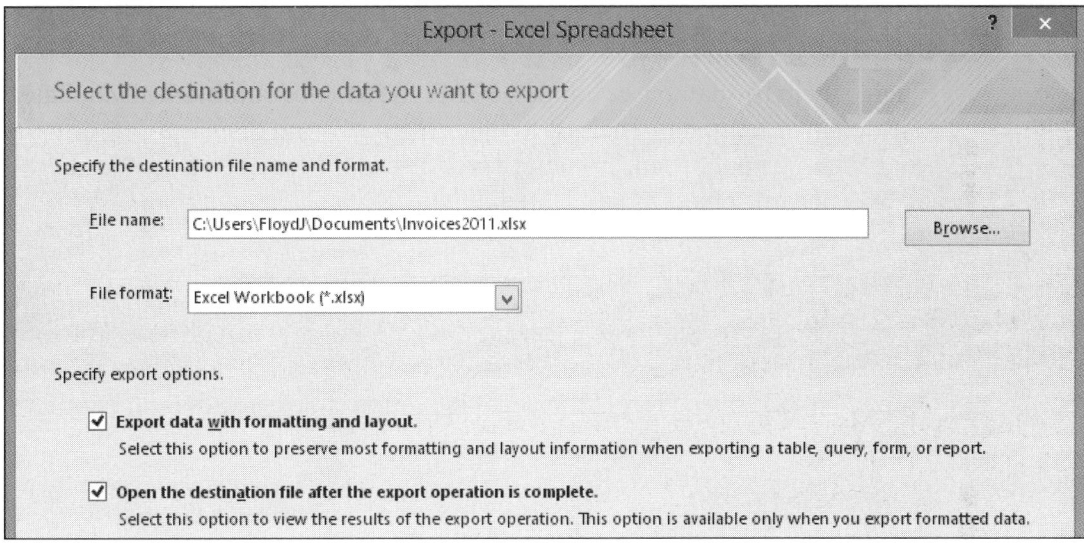

6. Click **Browse**, navigate to your **AC2013 Lesson 11** folder, and type **`AC11-D09-Invoices2011-[FirstInitialLastName].xlsx`** as the filename.
7. Click **Save** and then click **OK** in the Export – Excel Spreadsheet dialog box.
   Excel opens the new workbook containing the invoice data. Resize columns, if necessary.

	A	B	C	D	E	F	G
1	ID	InvDate	LastName	FirstName	Phone	Description	Amount
2	1	10-Sep-10	Walters	Sue	555-4578	Website for Pottery	$400.00
3	2	08-Oct-10	Williamson	Dan	555-9769	Mowing company site	$500.00
4	3	04-Nov-10	Roberts	Nancy	555-3421	Family Photo Website	$350.00
5	4	16-Nov-10	Hamilton	Becky	555-4673	Blog	$200.00
6	5	02-Dec-10	Sanchez	Javier	555-0879	Memorabilia site	$450.00
7	6	14-Dec-10	Smithers	Tim	555-8072	Add 1 page to existing site	$159.00

8. Close the workbook, saving if prompted. Exit **Excel** and switch back to **Access**.
   The Save Export Steps dialog box is displayed indicating that Invoices2011 was successfully exported.
9. Close the **Save Export Steps** dialog box, without saving the export steps, and close the database.

Displaying Access Data on the Web

Video Library: http://labyrinthelab.com/videos Video Number: AC13-V1111

In addition to sharing data from Access with other Microsoft Office applications, you can also save or import database objects from other applications and in other formats. And you can store Access data on the web in an HTML format universally available to anyone in the world. Additionally, there may be times when you want to add web page access to database objects.

Exporting Access Objects as Web Pages

Hypertext Markup Language (HTML), the code or language in which web pages are written, allows files to be formatted and viewed in any web browser, anywhere in the world. Access allows you to save each database object separately as an HTML file and display that data online.

Updating HTML Data

When data in the database changes, HTML files do not automatically update. Consequently, many companies update their HTML files regularly, and display a date and time to indicate when data was published. To create a web-based file for Access data, you use the External Data tab to export the object as an HTML file.

Saving HTML Formatted Objects

When you export a database object as an HTML file, you can preserve the formatting and layout of what you have already designed in Access. When you click OK, Access displays the HTML Output Options dialog box, which enables you to choose the default or other encoding to apply to the file.

QUICK REFERENCE	IMPORTING AND EXPORTING DATABASE OBJECTS AS HTML FILES
Task	**Procedure**
Export a database object in HTML format	■ Select the object to export. ■ Choose External Data→Export→More→HTML Document and follow the prompts.
View HTML data in a web browser	■ Launch your web browser. ■ Choose File→Open and locate the file to open. ■ Double-click the filename to open it in your default browser.
Import HTML data	■ Choose External Data→Import→More→HTML Document . ■ Browse and select the HTML file to open. ■ Select either the import, append, or link option.

DEVELOP YOUR SKILLS AC11-D10

Export a Table in HTML Format

In this exercise, you will export a table in HTML format and view it in a web browser.

1. Open **AC11-D02-WinWebDesign-[FirstInitialLastName]** and close any open objects.
2. Click the **Products** table in the Navigation Pane to select it (but don't open it).
3. Choose **External Data→Export→More→HTML Document** .
4. Click **Browse**, open your **AC2013 Lesson 11** folder, and click **Save**.
5. Check both boxes under **Specify Export Options**.

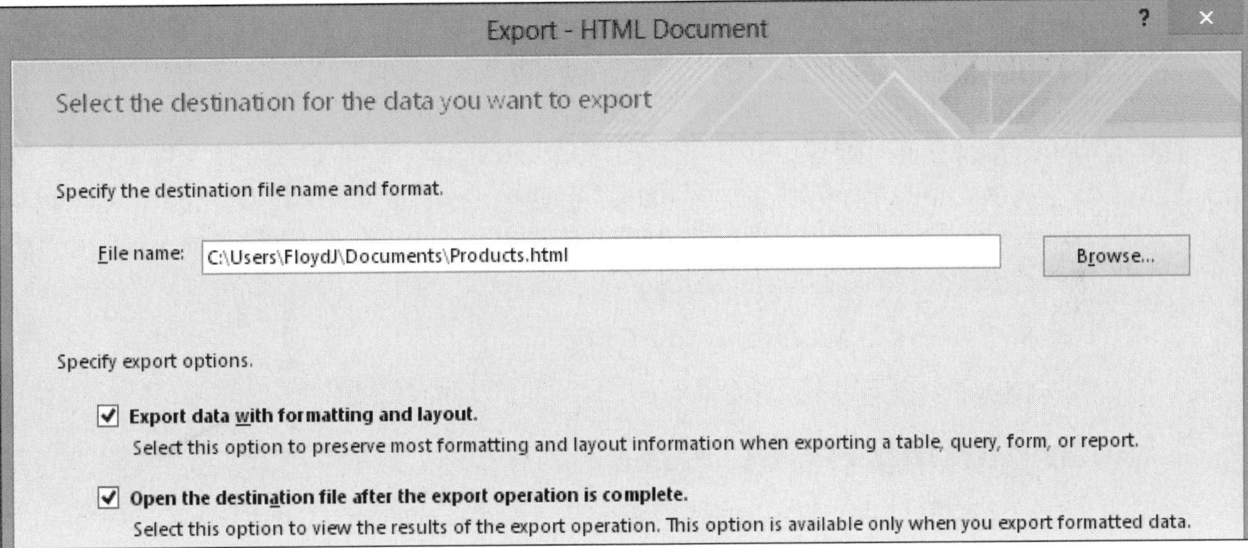

6. Click **OK**.

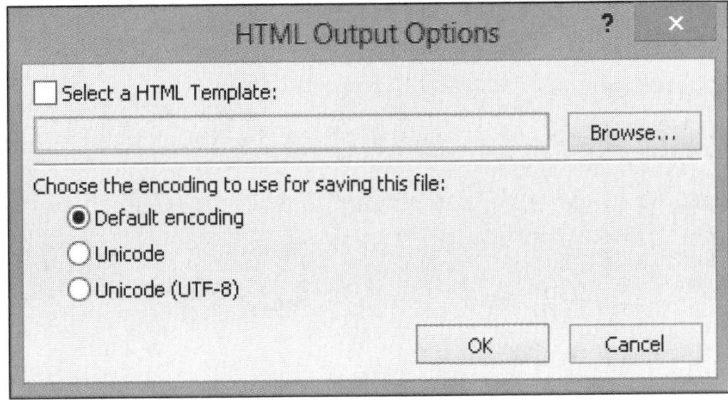

Access opens the HTML Output Options dialog box.

Access 2013

7. Click **OK** to create the file with the default encoding in the HTML Output Options dialog box.

Products		
ProdID	Description	Price
01HP	Home Page, Nav, CSS, Design	$400.00
02SP	Secondary Page	$200.00
03BL	Blog, Integrated into Site	$300.00
04SC	Shopping Cart, Basic	$400.00
05IM	Image, Custom Designed	$40.00
06HR	Hourly Rate for Modifications	$80.00
07LC	Logo Creation	$100.00
08PS	Photo Shoot, 1 hour onsite	$100.00
09IM	Image Map	$40.00
10SS	Slide Show	$100.00
11QR	QR Code	$50.00

Access creates the HTML file and opens it as a web page in your default web browser. You can now upload it to your website or to your network.

8. Close your web browser window.
9. Switch back to **Access** and close the dialog box.

Importing HTML Files

Video Library: http://labyrinthelab.com/videos Video Number: AC13-V1112

When data you want to use is in an HTML document, you can import the data to create a new table, append it to an existing table, or link the HTML file to the database. The steps for importing HTML data are similar to those used to import Excel and other types of data.

DEVELOP YOUR SKILLS AC11-D11

Import an HTML File as a Database Object

In this exercise, you will import a list of Web Resources contained in an HTML file into Access as a new table.

1. Close any open objects in the **Winchester Web Design** database.
2. Choose **External Data→Import& Link→More→HTML Document**.
3. Click **Browse** and navigate to the **AC2013 Lesson 11** folder.

4. Double-click **AC11-D11-WebResources.html** and select the **Import the Source Data into a New Table in the Current Database** option.

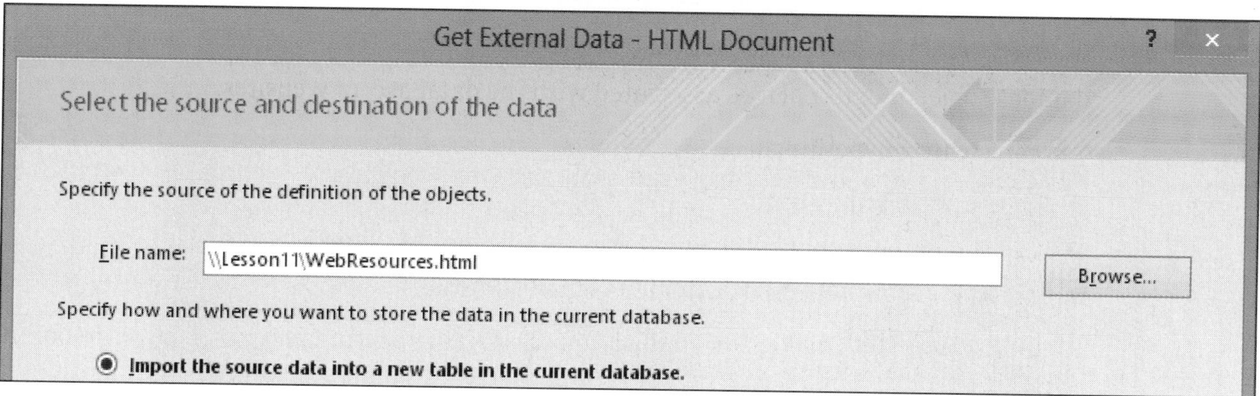

5. Click **OK** to launch the Import HTML Wizard.
6. Check the **First Row Contains Column Headings** checkbox and click **Next**.
7. Click **Next** again to keep the existing field names and data types and to import all the fields into the table.
8. Choose the **No Primary Key** option and click **Next**.

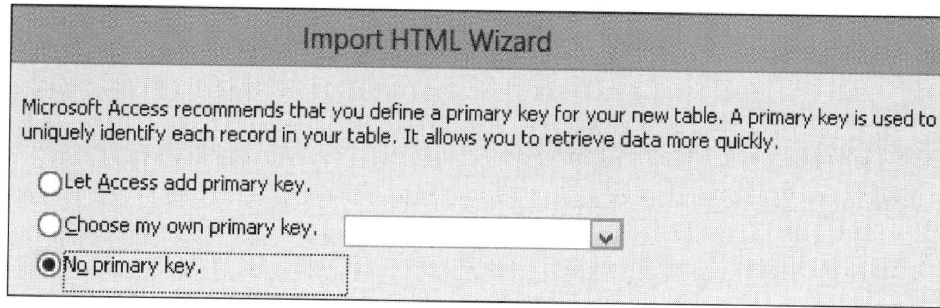

Because the HTML document is just a short list of website addresses, there is no need to set a primary key to uniquely identify each site.

9. Type `Resources` for the Import to Table name and click **Finish**.
10. Close the dialog box. Open the **Resources** table and resize the columns as necessary.

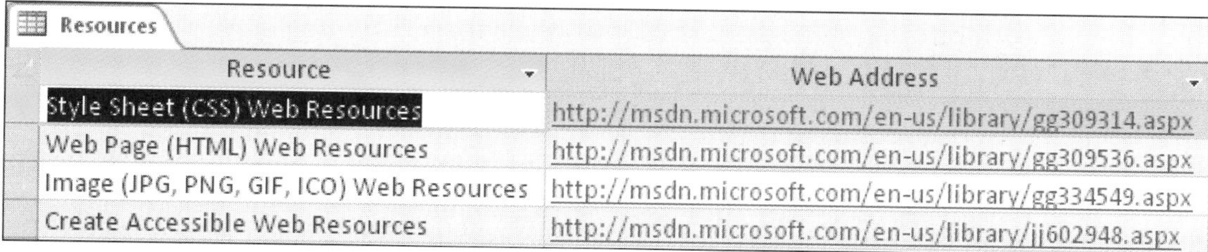

Resources

Resource	Web Address
Style Sheet (CSS) Web Resources	http://msdn.microsoft.com/en-us/library/gg309314.aspx
Web Page (HTML) Web Resources	http://msdn.microsoft.com/en-us/library/gg309536.aspx
Image (JPG, PNG, GIF, ICO) Web Resources	http://msdn.microsoft.com/en-us/library/gg334549.aspx
Create Accessible Web Resources	http://msdn.microsoft.com/en-us/library/jj602948.aspx

The imported Resources HTML table.

11. Review the data and then save and close the **Resources** table.

Adding Hyperlinks to Database Objects

Video Library: http://labyrinthelab.com/videos Video Number: AC13-V1113

Hyperlinks attached to database forms and reports are a convenient way to access other database objects, external files associated with the database, or websites.

You can create a hyperlink to:

- Open an external website.
- Launch another application and open a specific file.
- Add a new table field for a customer's email address.

The Insert Hyperlink dialog box enables you to select an existing file or web page, an object in the active database, or an email address. Although the hyperlink text generally identifies the action of the hyperlink, you can also add a ScreenTip to display more descriptive text when the user points to the hyperlink.

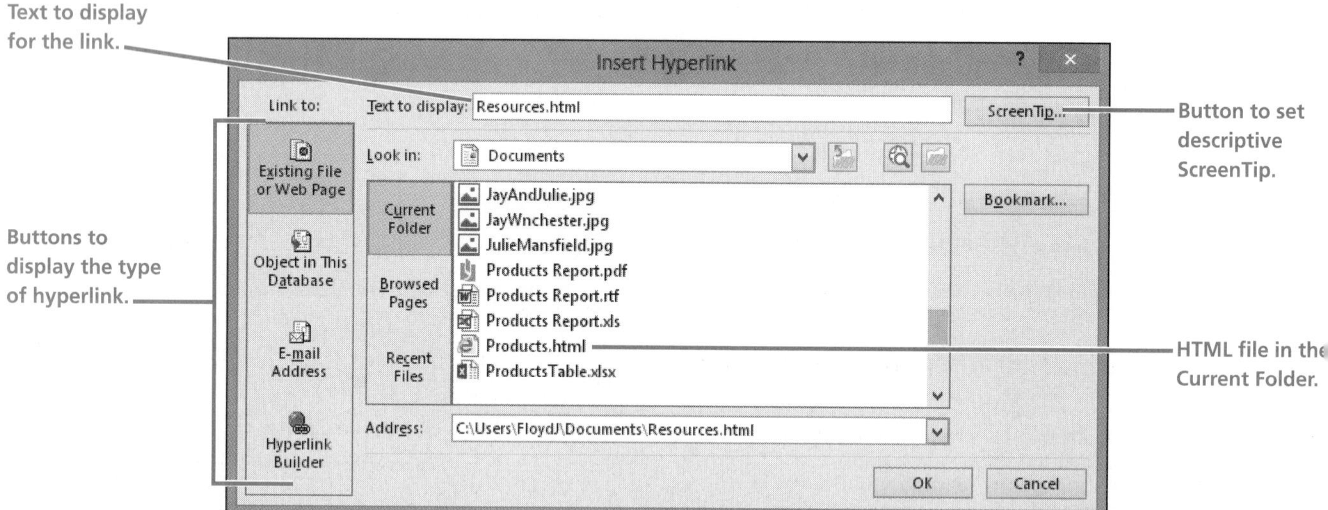

Using Hyperlinks

Typically hyperlinks are underlined and formatted a light blue text color. When you point to a hyperlink, the mouse pointer appears as a pointing hand. Clicking (rather than double-clicking) performs the action associated with the hyperlink.

Resource	Web Address
Style Sheet (CSS) Web Resources	http://msdn.microsoft.com/en-us/library/gg309314.aspx
Web Page (HTML) Web Resources	http://msdn.microsoft.com/en-us/library/gg309536.aspx
Image (JPG, PNG, GIF, ICO) Web Resources	http://msdn.microsoft.com/en-us/library/gg334549.aspx
Create Accessible Web Resources	http://msdn.microsoft.com/en-us/library/jj602948.aspx
Import Files as Web Resources	http://msdn.microsoft.com/en-us/library/gg327924.aspx

QUICK REFERENCE	ADDING, EDITING, AND REMOVING A HYPERLINK
Task	**Procedure**
Add a hyperlink to a form or report	■ Display the object in Design View. ■ Choose Design→Controls→Hyperlink. ■ Locate the file or website to which you want to link. ■ Add ScreenTip text, if desired, and click OK.
Edit hyperlink	■ Open the object containing the hyperlink in Design View. ■ Right-click the hyperlink control and choose Hyperlink→Edit Hyperlink. ■ Make the necessary edits and click OK.
Delete hyperlink	■ Right-click the hyperlink control and choose Delete; or, click the control to select the hyperlink and press [Delete].

DEVELOP YOUR SKILLS AC11-D12

Add a Hyperlink to a Database Form

In this exercise, you will add a hyperlink to the Winchester Web Design About Us Page form.

1. Display the **About Us Page** form in **Design View**.
2. Click the **Detail section bar**.
3. Choose **Design→Controls→Hyperlink** to open the Insert Hyperlink dialog box.
4. Follow these steps to add a hyperlink to the company web address:

Ⓐ Choose **Existing File or Web Page**.

Ⓑ Type **`Microsoft.com`** for the text to display.

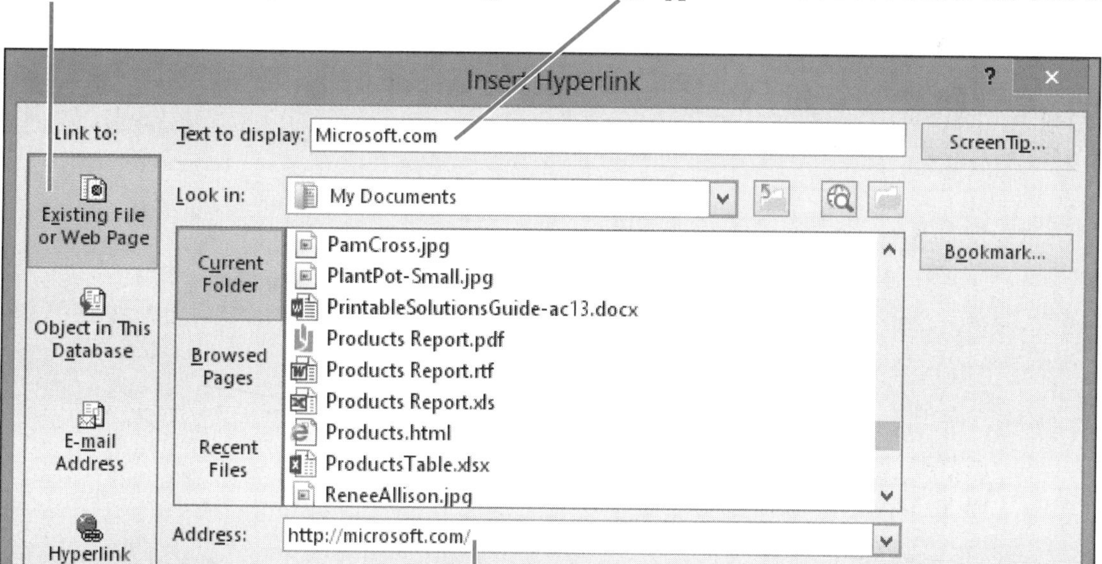

Ⓒ Type **`http://microsoft.com`** for the address.

D. Click OK

Access places the hyperlink control in the top-left corner of the Detail section.

5. Save your changes, switch to **Form View**, and click the hyperlink.
   The Microsoft website opens in your web browser.
6. Close your browser window. Close all database objects and exit **Access**.

Concepts Review

To check your knowledge of the key concepts introduced in this lesson, complete the Concepts Review quiz by choosing the appropriate access option below.

If you are...	Then access the quiz by...
Using the Labyrinth Video Library	Going to http://labyrinthelab.com/videos
Using eLab	Logging in, choosing Content, and navigating to the Concepts Review quiz for this lesson
Not using the Labyrinth Video Library or eLab	Going to the student resource center for this book

Reinforce Your Skills

REINFORCE YOUR SKILLS AC11-R01

Change the Format, Create Attachment Fields, and Integrate Access with Word

As Technology Director of Kids for Change, you are in charge of database maintenance. In this exercise, you will save a 2013 database in 2003 format so you can work on it at home. Then you will add an attachment field for staff photos, copy Access data to Word, and export a table to Word in rich text format.

Save an Access 2013 Database in the 2003 Format

1. Start **Access**. Open **AC11-R01-K4C2013** from your **AC2013 Lesson 11** folder, close any open objects, and save the database as `AC11-R01-K4C2013-[FirstInitialLastName]`.
2. Choose **File→Save As→Save Database As→Access 2002–2003 Database**, and then click the **Save As** button.
3. Navigate to your **AC2013 Lesson 11** folder, type `AC11-R01-K4C2003-[FirstInitialLastName].mdb` for the filename, and click **OK**.

   Access opens the new database file and identifies the file format in the title bar as Access 2002–2003 file format.
4. **Close** [×] all open databases.

Create an Attachment Field and Attach a File

5. Open **AC11-R01-K4C** from the **AC2013 Lesson 11** folder and save it as `AC11-R01-K4C-[FirstInitialLastName]`.
6. Enable content and close any open objects.
7. Display the **PaidStaff** table in **Design View**.
8. Scroll down and type `StaffPhoto` in the first available **Field Name** column.
9. Choose **Attachment** from the Data Type list.
10. Type `Staff ID Photo` for the Description.

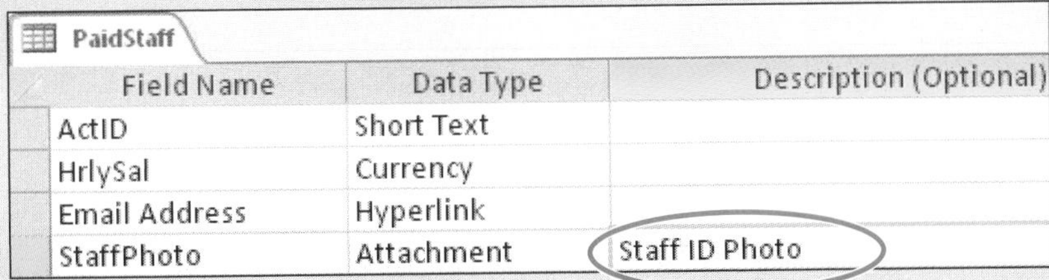

PaidStaff
Field Name
Data Type
Description (Optional)
ActID
Short Text
HrlySal
Currency
Email Address
Hyperlink
StaffPhoto
Attachment
Staff ID Photo

11. Save the **PaidStaff** table and switch to **Datasheet View**.
12. Scroll to the new attachment field and double-click the paperclip symbol for the first record (Matthew Bryant).

    The Attachments dialog box opens.

13. Click the **Add** button.
14. Navigate to your **AC2013 Lesson 11** folder and double-click **MathewBryant.jpg**.
    Access adds the filename of the photo to the Attachments dialog box.
15. Click **OK** to close the Attachments dialog box.
16. Double-click the paperclip icon again, select **MatthewBryant.jpg**, and click **Open**.
    The attached photo displays in your default program.
17. Close the **Attachments** dialog box and your photo viewer. Then save and close the **PaidStaff** table.

Copy Access Data to Word

18. Display the **K4CActivityList** table in **Datasheet View**.
19. Click the table selector button in the top-left corner of the table.
20. Choose **Home→Clipboard→**[Copy].
21. Start **Word**, navigate to your **AC2013 Lesson 11** folder, and double-click **AC11-R01-K4C-Welcome.docx**.
22. Position the insertion point under the line, *Below are just a few of the activities we are offering this year*.
23. Choose **Home→Clipboard→Paste menu ▾** and choose **Keep Source Formatting**.
24. Save the Word document as `AC11-R01-K4C-Welcome-[FirstInitialLastName].docx`. Leave the **Word** document open.
25. Close **K4CActivityList**. Minimize any open applications and then maximize **Word** and **Access**.
    If you are in the Metro View *of Windows 8 (tiles display), click the* Desktop tile *or type* desktop *and tap* [Enter] *to display the traditional Windows taskbar.*
26. Open the **Welcome Staffers** query.
27. Click the Access file title bar and tap [Windows]+[←] to move the Access database to the left side of the screen.
28. Click the Word document title bar and tap [Windows]+[→] to move the **AC11-R01-K4C-Welcome-[FirstInitialLastName]** to the right side of the screen.
    You can also position windows side by side by right-clicking a blank area of the Windows task bar and then selecting Show Windows Side by Side.
29. Click the table selector button to select all the staffer records.
30. Hover the pointer over the left side of a field in the first column until the pointer becomes a white arrow.

31. Click and drag the records to the **Word document**. Drop them at the insertion point.

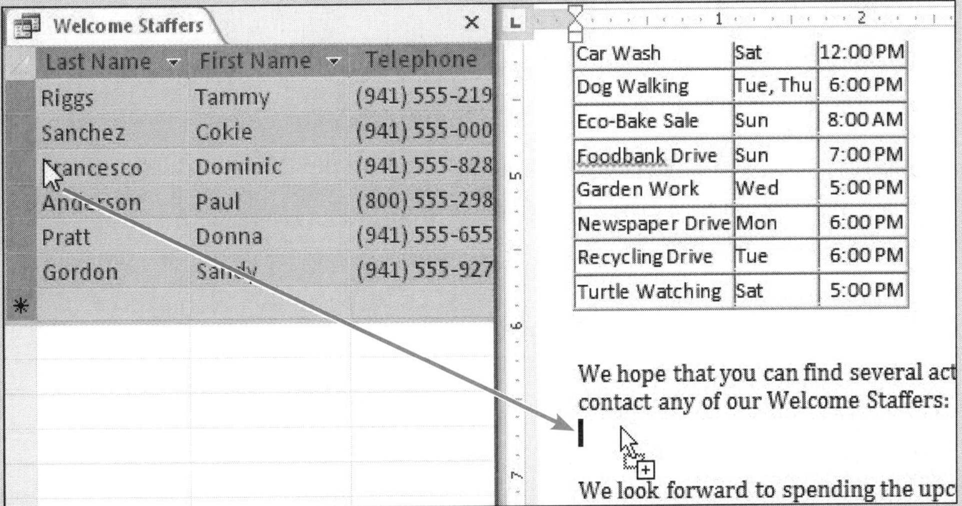

Position the mouse pointer exactly as shown, just to the right of the gray selector bar.

32. Close the **Welcome Staffers** query and maximize the **Word document**.
    When you copy and paste or drag data to a Word document, the name of the Access object is displayed as a title at the top of the object.
33. Save and close **AC11-R01-K4C-Welcome-[FirstInitialLastName].docx**.

Export Access Data to Word

34. Maximize the **AC11-R01-K4C-[FirstInitialLastName].accdb** database window.
35. Select the **Venues** table, but don't open it.
36. Choose **External Data→Export→More→Word** .
37. Navigate to your **AC2013 Lesson 11** folder, name the file `AC11-R01-K4C-Venues-[FirstInitialLastName].rtf`, and click **Save**.
38. Click the **Open the Destination File After the Export Operation Is Complete** checkbox.
39. Click **OK**.
    The document opens in Word. When you export data to a Word document, there is no title added as there is when you copy data into Word.
40. Close **AC11-R01-K4C-Venues-[FirstInitialLastName].rtf**, saving if prompted. Exit **Word**.
41. Close the **Export – RTF File dialog box**.

Merge Access Data into a Word Document

42. Open the **Volunteers** table.
43. Choose **External Data→Export→** Word Merge.

    The Microsoft Word Mail Merge Wizard opens.
44. Choose **Link Your Data to an Existing Microsoft Word Document** and click **OK**.
45. Navigate to your **AC2013 Lesson 11** folder, if necessary, and double-click **AC11-R01-K4C-Welcome-[FirstInitialLastName]**.
46. Position the pointer under the **K4C logo** and above the **Dear K4C Volunteer** greeting.
47. Choose **Mailings→Write & Insert Fields→Insert Merge Field menu ▼**.

    Access displays the list of field names from the Volunteers table.
48. Choose **VolFirstName** from list.

    Access pops the table field between chevrons on the document.

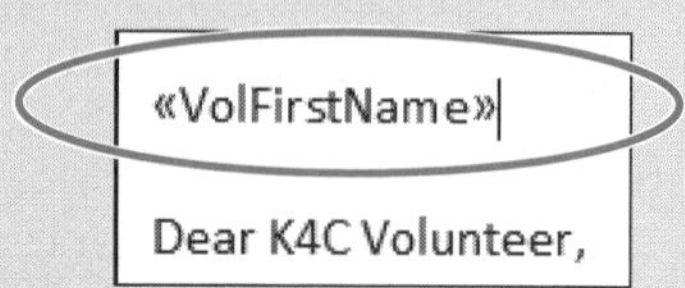

49. Tap Spacebar to insert a space after «VolFirstName».
50. Choose **Mailings→Write & Insert Fields** then choose **VolLastName**.
51. Tap Enter and choose **VolStreet**.
52. Tap Enter and choose **VolCity**.
53. Type a comma, tap Spacebar, and choose **VolST**.
54. Tap Spacebar and choose **VolZIP**.
55. Choose **Mailings→Preview Results→Preview Results** to verify that the customer name and address display properly.
56. Save and close **AC11-R01-K4C-Welcome-[FirstInitialLastName]**. Close **AC11-R01-K4C-[FirstInitialLastName]**. Exit **Word** and **Access**.
57. Submit your final file based on the guidelines provided by your instructor.

    To see examples of how your file or files should look at the end of this exercise, go to the student resource center.

Kids for Change

Stan Jones
892 Southern Pkwy.
Sarasota, FL 34024

Dear K4C Volunteer,

REINFORCE YOUR SKILLS AC11-R02

Integrate Access with Excel and the Web

Kids for Change would like to modify and share some of the data in its database. In this exercise, you will add a table that is linked to an Excel spreadsheet and export a table to Excel. Then, you will import an HTML file as a new database table, export a table to view on the web, and also add a hyperlink from the Activities Form to the Activity Costs Report.

Import Unlinked Excel Data into Access

1. Start **Access**. Open **AC11-R02-K4C** from your **AC2013 Lesson 11** folder, close any open objects, and save the database as `AC11-R02-K4C-[FirstInitialLastName]`.
2. Enable Content if necessary. Then close all open objects and choose **External Data→Import & Link→Excel**.

   Access launches the Get External Data – Excel Spreadsheet dialog box.
3. Choose **Import the Source Data into a New Table in the Current Database**, click **Browse**, navigate to the **AC2013 Lesson 11** folder, and double-click **AC11-R02-K4C-Contacts.xlsx**.
4. Click **OK** to launch the Import Spreadsheet Wizard.
5. Check the **First Row Contains Column Headings** and click **Next**.
6. Click **Next** to import all the worksheet fields to the new table, without changes.
7. Let Access add the primary key and click **Next**.
8. Type `Venue Contacts` for the Import to Table name and click **Finish**.
9. Close the **Get External Data** window without saving the import steps.
10. Open the new **Venue Contacts** table and resize the column as desired.

    The table should lists four fields and 19 records. The data is not linked to the source table in Excel. So, if you update the data in Excel, it will not be updated in the Access file.
11. Save and close the **Venue Contacts** table.

Link an Excel Spreadsheet to an Access Database

12. Choose **External Data→Import & Link→Excel**.

    Access launches the Get External Data – Excel Spreadsheet dialog box.
13. Choose the **Link to the Data Source by Creating a Linked Table** option, click **Browse**, and navigate to the **AC2013 Lesson 11** folder.
14. Double-click **AC11-R02-K4C-Contacts.xlsx** and click **OK**.
15. Check the **First Row Contains Column Headings** checkbox and click **Next**.
16. Type `Venue Contacts Linked` for the Import to Table name and click **Finish**.
17. Click **OK** in the message box.

    The imported table has a different icon than the other tables in the Navigation Pane. The icon has an arrow pointing toward the Excel icon instead of the Access table icon.
18. Double-click the **Venue Contacts Linked** table name in the Navigation Pane.

19. Close the **Venue Contacts Linked** table, saving it if prompted.
20. Open **AC11-R02-K4C-Contacts.xlsx** in Excel and change the contact for All Angels Church from *Kevin Gregory* to **`Dina McMullen`**.
21. Save and close **AC11-R02-K4C-Contacts.xlsx**; open the **Venue Contacts Linked** table.

    The name is also changed in the table.
22. Close the **Venue Contacts Linked** table.

Use the Linked Table Manager

23. Choose **External Data→Import & Link→** Linked Table Manager.
24. Click the checkbox beside the linked filename and review the linked file identified.
25. Check the **Always Prompt for New Location** checkbox.
26. Click **OK**.

    Access opens the Select New Location dialog box to enable you to navigate to the folder containing the linked file, in the event that the file has been moved.
27. Locate **AC11-R02-K4C-Contacts.xlsx** and click **Open**.
28. Click **OK** in the dialog box that informs you that all selected linked tables were successfully refreshed.
29. Click **Close** in the Linked Table Manager dialog box.

Export Access Data to Create a New Excel Workbook

30. Click **Donations Query** in the Navigation Pane.
31. Choose **External Data→Export→Excel** Excel.
32. Ensure that the file format is set to **Excel Workbook (*.xlsx)** and check the **Export Data with Formatting and Layout** and **Open the Destination File After the Export Operation Is Complete** checkboxes.
33. Click **Browse** and navigate to your student folder. Type **`AC11-R02-K4C-Donations-[FirstInitialLastName].xlsx`** for the filename and click **Save**.

    Excel opens and displays the new workbook containing the Donations Query data. Resize columns, as desired.
34. Switch to **Access** and close the **Export – Excel Spreadsheet** dialog box.
35. Close **AC11-R02-Donations-[FirstInitialLastName].xlsx**, saving if prompted, and exit **Excel**. Switch back to **Access**.

Export an Object in HTML Format

36. Single-click the **Activities Query** in the Navigation Pane.
37. Choose **External Data→Export→More→HTML Document**.
38. Click **Browse**, navigate to your **AC2013 Lesson 11** folder, and type **`AC11-R02-K4C-Activities-[FirstInitialLastName].html`** as the filename. Click **Save**.
39. Check the **Export Data with Formatting and Layout** and **Open the Destination File After the Export Operation Is Complete** checkboxes.

40. Click **OK** to create the file with the default encoding.

    Access creates the HTML file and opens it as web page in your default web browser. You can now upload it to your website or to your network.

41. Close your web browser window.
42. Switch back to **Access** and close the **Export – HTML Document** dialog box.

Import an HTML File as a Database Object

43. Close any open objects and choose **External Data→Import→More→HTML Document.**
44. Click **Browse** and navigate to the **AC2013 Lesson 11** folder.
45. Double-click **AC11-R02-K4C-Partners.html**, select **Import the Source Data into a New Table in the Current Database**, and click **OK**.
46. Check the **First Row Contains Column Headings** checkbox and click **Next**.
47. Click **Next** to accept the default options for field names and data types.
48. Choose the **No Primary Key** option and click **Next**.
49. Type `NonProfits` for the Import to Table name and click **Finish**.
50. Close the **Get External Data** dialog box. Open the **NonProfits** table and size the columns so you can view the data.
51. Review the data and then save and close the **NonProfits** table.

Add a Hyperlink to a Form

52. Display the **Activities Form** in **Design View** and click the **Detail section bar**.
53. Choose **Design→Controls→Hyperlink**.
54. Choose **Object in This Database**.
55. Expand **Reports** and click **Activity Costs Report**.

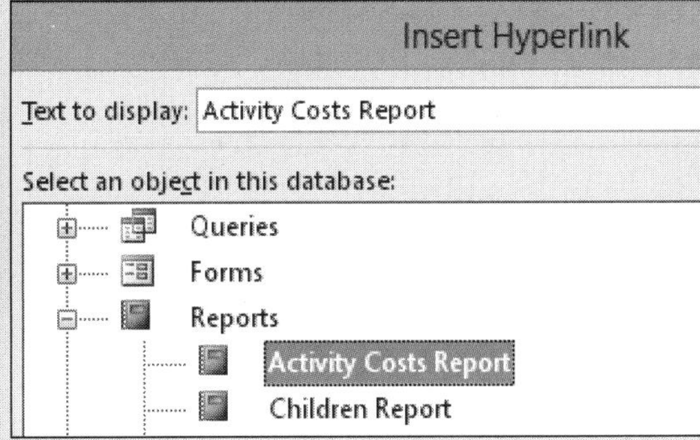

56. Click **OK**.

    Access places the hyperlink control in the top-left corner of the Detail section.

Access 2013

57. Drag the new hyperlink control to the right of the Telephone controls.

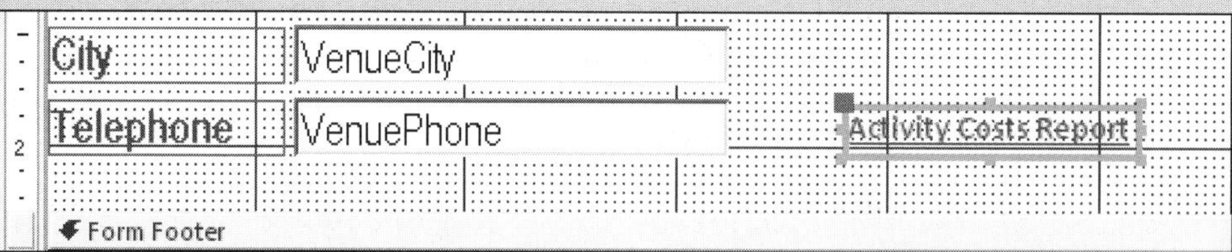

58. Save the changes to **Activities Form**, switch to **Form View**, and click the hyperlink.
    The Activity Costs Report opens when you click the new hyperlink.
59. Close all database objects and exit **Access**.
60. Submit your final file based on the guidelines provided by your instructor.
    To see examples of how your file or files should look at the end of this exercise, go to the student resource center.

REINFORCE YOUR SKILLS AC11-R03

Save Databases in Older Formats, Use Attachments, and Integrate and Export Access Data

You have a few more changes to make to the K4C database. In this exercise, you will save a database in an earlier format. You will also add an attachment field to a table, copy Access data to Word, export a table to Word, and merge data into a Word document. You will link a table to an Excel spreadsheet and export a table to Excel. Finally, you will import an HTML file as a table, export a table to the web, and add a hyperlink to a form.

Save an Access 2013 Database in the 2003 Format

1. Start **Access**. Open **AC11-R03-K4C2013** from your **AC2013 Lesson 11** folder and save it as `AC11-R03-K4C2013-[FirstInitialLastName]`.
2. Click **Enable Content**.
3. Choose **File→Save As→Save Database As→Access 2002–2003 Database**, and then click the **Save As** button.
4. Navigate to your **AC2013 Lesson 11** folder, type `AC11-R03-K4C2003-[FirstInitialLastName].mdb` for the filename, and click **Save**.
   Access identifies the file format in the title bar as Access 2002–2003 file format.
5. **Close** [×] all open databases.

Create an Attachment Field and Attach a File

6. Open **AC11-R03-K4C** from the **AC2013 Lesson 11** folder and save it as `AC11-R03-K4C-[FirstInitialLastName]`.
7. Enable content and close all open objects. Open the **Children** table in **Design View**.

8. Type `SelfPortrait` in the first available **Field Name**, choose **Attachment** as Data Type, and type `Child's self-portrait` for the Description.

Children

Field Name	Data Type	Description (Optional)
ChildST	Short Text	2-char abbreviation
ChildZIP	Short Text	5-digit ZIP code
ChildPhone	Short Text	Area code & number
BirthDate	Date/Time	
MomName	Short Text	
DadName	Short Text	
Emergency	Short Text	
SelfPortrait	Attachment	Child's self-portrait

9. Save the **Children** table and switch to **Datasheet View**.
10. Scroll to the new attachment field and double-click the paperclip icon for Sami Abbot.
    The Attachments dialog box opens.
11. Click **Add**, navigate to the **AC2013 Lesson 11** folder, and double-click **SamiAbbot.jpg**.
    Access adds the filename of the picture to the Attachments dialog box.
12. Click **OK** to close the Attachments dialog box.
13. Double-click the paperclip icon again, select **SamiAbbot.jpg**, and click **Open**.
    The picture displays in your default program.
14. Close your photo viewer and the **Attachment** dialog box; save and close the **Children** table.

Copy Access Data to Word

15. Display the **AppreciationDinner** table in **Datasheet View**.
16. Click the table selector button in the top-left corner of the table.
17. Choose **Home→Clipboard→**Copy.
18. Start **Word**, navigate to your **AC2013 Lesson 11** folder, and double-click **AC11-R03-K4C-Parents.docx**.
19. Position the insertion point under the line *...make your meal selection(s) on the form below and return it to us.*
20. Choose **Home→Clipboard→Paste menu ▼→Keep Source Formatting**.
    The letter now has the pasted table inserted. When you copy and paste or drag data to a Word document, the name of the Access object is displayed as a title at the top of the object.
21. Save the file as `AC11-R03-K4C-Parents-[FirstInitialLastName]` and exit **Word**.
22. Switch to **Access** and close the **AppreciationDinner** table.

Export Access Data to Word

23. Select the **Activities** table and choose **External Data→Export→More→Word**.
    The Export – RTF File dialog box opens.

24. Navigate to your **AC2013 Lesson 11** folder. Name the file **`AC11-R03-Activities-[FirstInitialLastName].html`** and click **Save**; check **Open the Destination File After the Export Operation is Complete**, and click **OK**
    The document opens in Word. When you export table data to Word, there no title is added.

25. Close **AC11-R03-Activities-[FirstInitialLastName]**, saving if prompted. Exit **Word**.

26. Switch back to **Access** and close the **Export – RTF File** dialog box.

Merge Access Data into a Word Document

27. Open the **Children** table. Choose **External Data→Export→** Word Merge.
    The Microsoft Word Mail Merge Wizard opens.

28. Choose **Link Your Data to an Existing Microsoft Word Document** and click **OK**.

29. Navigate to your **AC2013 Lesson 11** folder and open **AC11-R03-K4C-Parents-[FirstInitialLastName]**.

30. Position the pointer under the K4C logo and above the Dear K4C Parent, type **`Mr/Ms`**, and tap Spacebar.

31. Choose **Mailings→Write & Insert Fields** and choose **ChildLastName** from the list.

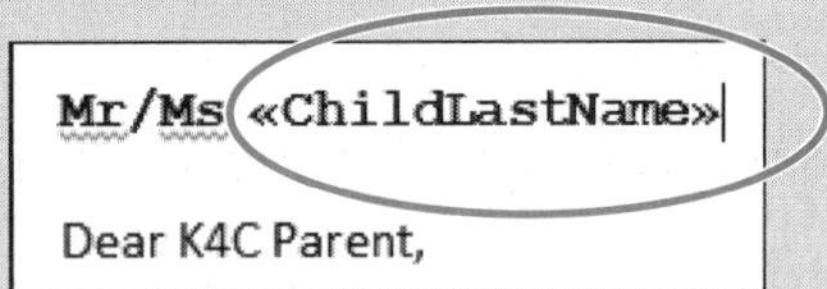

Access inserts the table field between chevrons on the document.

32. Tap Enter and choose **ChildStreet**; tap Enter and choose **ChildCity**.

33. Type a comma, tap Spacebar, and choose **ChildST**.

34. Tap Spacebar and choose **ChildZIP**.

35. Choose **Mailings→Preview Results→Preview Results**.

36. Save and close **AC11-R03-K4C-Parents-[FirstInitialLastName]**; exit **Word**. Close the **Children** table.

Import Linked Excel Data into Access

37. Choose **External Data→Import & Link→Excel**.
    Access launches the Get External Data – Excel Spreadsheet dialog box.

38. Choose **Link to the Data Source by Creating a Linked Table**, click **Browse**, and navigate to the **AC2013 Lesson 11** folder.

39. Double-click **AC11-R03-DonorEmp.xlsx** and click **OK**.

40. Check the **First Row Contains Column Headings** checkbox and click **Next**.

41. Type **DonorEmployers-Linked** for the Import to Table name and click **Finish**.
42. Click **OK** in the message box.
43. Close the **Get External Data** window.
    The imported table has a different icon than the other tables in the Navigation Pane
44. Double-click the new **DonorEmployers-Linked** table name in the Navigation Pane.
45. Close the **DonorEmployers-Linked** table, saving it if prompted.
46. Open **AC11-R03-DonorEmp.xlsx** in Excel and change the Donor Employer for Elton McGovern to **Peachtree Pediatric Clinic**.
47. Open the **DonorEmployers-Linked** table.
    The clinic name is also changed in the table.
48. Close **AC11-R03-DonorEmp.xlsx**. Exit **Excel**; close the **DonorEmployers-Linked** table.

Use the Linked Table Manager

49. Choose **External Data→Import & Link→** Linked Table Manager.
50. Click the checkboxes for **DonorEmployers-Linked** and **Always Prompt for New Location**. Click **OK**.
    The Select New Location dialog box enables you to navigate to the folder containing the linked file, in the event that the file has been moved.
51. Locate **AC11-R03-DonorEmp.xlsx** and click **Open**.
52. Click **OK**. Close the **Linked Table Manager** dialog box.

Export Access Data to Create a New Excel Workbook

53. Click **Staff Schedule** in the Queries group in the Navigation Pane.
54. Choose **External Data→Export→Export to Excel Spreadsheet** Excel.
55. Ensure that the file format is set to **Excel Workbook (*.xlsx)** and check the two checkboxes under **Specify Export Options**.
56. Click **Browse** and navigate to your **AC2013 Lesson 11** folder. Type **AC11-R03-Staff-[FirstInitialLastName].xlsx** for the filename and click **Save**, and then click **OK**.
    Excel opens and displays the new workbook containing the Staff Schedule data.
57. Close the workbook, saving if prompted, and exit **Excel**. Return to **Access**.
58. Close the **Get External Data** dialog box.

Export a Query Datasheet in HTML Format

59. Single-click the **Staff Schedule** query in the Navigation Pane to select it.
60. Choose **External Data→Export→More→HTML Document**.
61. Click **Browse**, open the **AC2013 Lesson 11** folder, type **AC11-R03-Staff-[FirstInitialLastName].html** for the filename, and click **Save**.
62. Check the **Export Data with Formatting and Layout** and **Open the Destination File After the Export Operation Is Complete** checkboxes.

63. Click **OK** to create the file with the default encoding.

    Access creates the HTML file and opens it as a web page in your default web browser. You can now upload it to your website or to your network.

64. Close your web browser window. Then switch back to **Access**, and close the **Export – HTML Document** dialog box and any open database objects.

Import an HTML File As a Database Object

65. Choose **External Data→Import& Link→More→HTML Document**.

66. Click **Browse** and navigate to the **AC2013 Lesson 11** folder. Double-click**AC11-R03-K4CFundraising.html**, select **Import the Source Data into a New Table in the Current Database**, and click **OK**.

67. Check the **First Row Contains Column Headings** checkbox and click **Next**.

68. Click **Next** again to accept the default options for field names and data types.

69. Choose the **No Primary Key** option and click **Next**.

70. Type `OtherFundraisingIdeas` for the Import to Table name and click **Finish**.

71. Close the **Get External Data** dialog box. Open the **OtherFundraisingIdeas** table and size the columns so you can view the data.

72. Review the data and then save and close the **OtherFundraisingIdeas** table.

Add a Hyperlink to a Form

73. Display the **Activity Staffing** form in **Design View**, click the **Detail** section bar and choose **Design→Controls→Hyperlink**.

74. Choose **Existing File or Web Page** type `Staff Schedule` for the Text to Display, navigate to your **AC2013 Lesson 11** folder, and choose **AC11-R03-Staff-[FirstInitialLastName].html**.

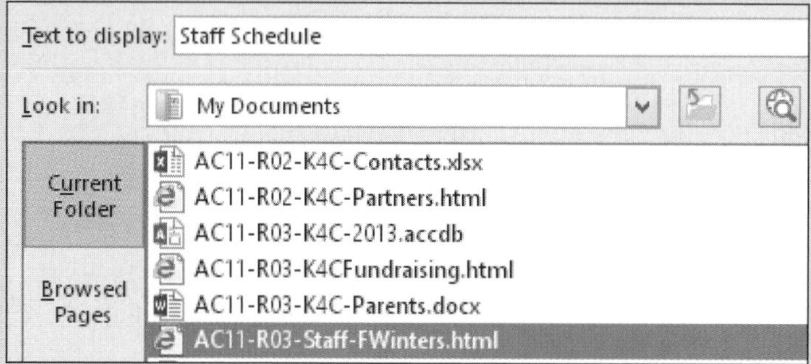

75. Click **OK**.

    Access places the hyperlink control in the top-left corner of the Detail section.

76. Save changes to **Activity Staffing**, switch to **Form View**, and click the new hyperlink.

    The Staff Schedule web page opens. If a warning appears stating that the location may be unsafe, click Yes to continue.

77. Close all database objects and exit **Access**. Close your web browser.

78. Submit your final files based on the guidelines provided by your instructor.

Apply Your Skills

APPLY YOUR SKILLS AC11-A01

Change the Database Format, Create Attachments, and Integrate Access with Word

Universal Corporate Events, Ltd. needs your help with a few tasks. In this exercise, you will change the database format so that the president can view it on his home computer. You will also add an attachment field to a table for employee photos. Finally, you will copy Access data into Word, export a table to Word, and merge Access data into a Word document.

Save a 2013 Database in an Older Format and Attach a File

1. Start **Access**. Open **AC11-A01-UCE2013** from your **AC2013 Lesson 11** folder and save it as `AC11-A01-UCE2013-[FirstInitialLastName]`.
2. Choose **File→Save As→Save Database As→Access 2002–2003 Database**, and click the **Save As** button.
3. Save the file in your **AC2013 Lesson 11** folder as `AC11-A01-UCE2003-[FirstInitialLastName].mdb`.
   The file format is shown in the title bar.
4. Close all open databases.
5. Open **AC11-A01-UCE** from the **AC2013 Lesson 11** folder, close any open objects, and save the database as `AC11-A01-UCE-[FirstInitialLastName]`.
6. Enable content and close all open objects.
7. Open the **Personnel** table in **Design View**. Type `PerPhoto` in the first available record for Field Name, choose the **Attachment** data type, and type `Personnel ID Photo` for the description.
8. Save the **Personnel** table and switch to **Datasheet View**.
9. In the attachment field, double-click the paperclip icon for Renee Allison.
10. Click **Add** in the Attachments dialog box.
11. Navigate to the **AC2013 Lesson 11** folder. Double-click **ReneeAllison.jpg**. Click **OK**.
12. Double-click the paperclip icon and click **Open** to open the photo attachment in your photo viewer.
13. Close your photo viewer and the **Attachments** dialog box, and save and close the **Personnel** table.

Copy and Export Access Data to Word

14. Start **Word**. Open **AC11-A01-UCE-Promotions.docx** from your **AC2013 Lesson 11** folder.
15. Run the **Event Organizers** query in Access.
16. Click the table selector button to select all the records in the query datasheet.

17. Point at the left side of a field in the first column until the pointer becomes a white arrow; then click and drag the query records to the Word document and drop them under the line that reads: "...contact one of our Event Organizers first!"
18. Close the **Event Organizers** query and maximize **AC11-A01-UCE-Promotions.docx**.
    The bottom portion of the letter includes the Event Organizers query. The name of the Access object is displayed as a title at the top of the object.
19. Save the file in your **AC2013 Lesson 11** folder as `AC11-A01-UCE-Promotions-[FirstInitialLastName]`, and close it.
20. Select the **Menus** table. Choose **External Data→Export→More→Word**.
21. Save the file in your **AC2013 Lesson 11** folder as `AC11-A01-Menus-[FirstInitialLastName].rtf`.
22. Check the **Open the Destination File After the Export Operation is Complete** checkbox and click **OK**.
23. Close **AC11-A01-Menus-[FirstInitialLastName].rtf**, saving if prompted. Exit **Word**.
24. Close the **Export – RTF File** dialog box.

Merge Access Data into a Word Document

25. Open the **BusinessOwners** table in **Datasheet View** and choose **External Data→Export→Word Merge**.
26. In the Mail Merge Wizard, choose the **Link Your Data to an Existing Microsoft Word Document** option and click **OK**.
27. Open **AC11-A01-UCE-Promotions-[FirstInitialLastName]** from within your **AC2013 Lesson 11** folder.
28. Position the pointer under the UCE website and above the date.
29. Choose **Mailings→Write & Insert Fields→Insert Merge Field menu ▼**.
    Access displays the field list from the BusinessOwners table.
30. Choose **First_Name** from list.
31. Tap [Spacebar] to insert a space after the «FirstName».
32. Choose **Mailings→Write & Insert Fields** then choose **Last_Name**.
33. Tap [Enter] and choose **Address**; tap [Enter] and choose **City**.
34. Type a comma, tap [Spacebar], and choose **ST**. Then tap [Spacebar] and choose **Zip**.

35. Choose **Mailings→Preview Results→Preview Results** .

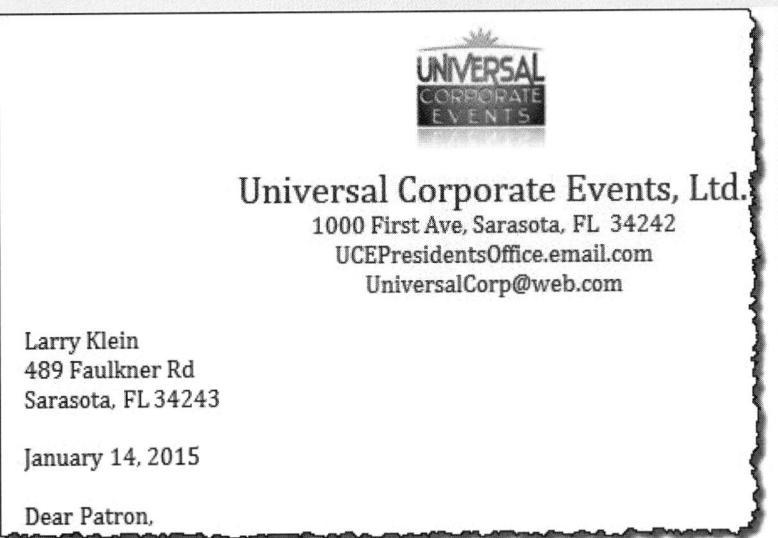
UNIVERSAL CORPORATE EVENTS

Universal Corporate Events, Ltd.
1000 First Ave, Sarasota, FL 34242
UCEPresidentsOffice.email.com
UniversalCorp@web.com

Larry Klein
489 Faulkner Rd
Sarasota, FL 34243

January 14, 2015

Dear Patron,

36. Save and close **AC11-A01-UCE-Promotions-[FirstInitialLastName]**.
37. Close the database. Exit **Word** and **Access**.
38. Submit your final file based on the guidelines provided by your instructor.
    To see examples of how your file or files should look at the end of this exercise, go to the student resource center.

APPLY YOUR SKILLS AC11-A02

Integrate, Display, and Hyperlink to Access Data

The president of UCE, Ltd. wants you to integrate some of the company's data with other programs and the web. In this exercise, you will add a table that links to an Excel spreadsheet and export a table to Excel. You will also import an HTML file as a table, export a table to make it available for viewing on the web, and add a hyperlink from the Venues Form to the Venue Revenue Report.

Import Linked Excel Data into Access and Use the Linked Table Manager

1. Start **Access**. Open **AC11-A02-UCE** from your **AC2013 Lesson 11** folder, close any open objects, and save the database as `AC11-A02-UCE-[FirstInitialLastName]`.
2. Enable content and close the **UCE Navigation Form**.
3. Without opening any objects, choose **External Data→Import & Link→Excel**.
4. Choose the **Link to the Data Source by Creating a Linked Table** option, choose **AC11-A02-UCE-Customers.xlsx** from your **AC2013 Lesson 11** folder, and click **OK**.
5. Check the **First Row Contains Column Headings** checkbox and click **Next**.
6. Click **Next**, type `BestCustomers-Linked` for the Import to Table name, and click **Finish**.

7. Click **OK** in the message box.
   The imported table has an arrow and Excel icon instead of the Access table icon.
8. Open the new **BestCustomers-Linked** table.
9. Close the table, saving it if prompted.
10. Open **AC11-A02-UCE-Customers.xlsx** in Excel and change the first name in the second record from *Fran* to `Francesca`.
11. Save and close **AC11-A02-UCE-Customers.xlsx** and exit **Excel**. Open the **BestCustomers-Linked** table.
    The first name is also changed to Francesca *in the table.*
12. Close the **BestCustomers-Linked** table.
13. Choose **External Data→Import & Link→**Linked Table Manager to verify that it is linked to the right location.
14. Mark the checkbox beside the linked filename, check the **Always Prompt for New Location** checkbox, and click **OK**.
15. Locate the **AC11-A02-UCE-Customers.xlsx** file and click **Open**.
16. Click **OK** in the dialog box and then close the **Linked Table Manager**.

Export Access Data to Create a New Excel Workbook

17. Select the **Menus** table in the Navigation Pane and choose **External Data→Export→Excel**.
18. Ensure that the file format is set to **Excel Workbook (*.xlsx)** and check the two checkboxes under **Specify Export Options**.
19. Save the file in your **AC2013 Lesson 11** folder as **`AC11-A02-UCE-Menus-[FirstInitialLastName].xlsx`**. Then, click **OK**.
    Excel opens and displays the workbook containing the Menus data.
20. Close **AC11-A02-UCE-Menus.xlsx**, saving if prompted, and exit **Excel**. Switch to **Access** and click **Close** after the file is successfully exported.

Export a Table in HTML Format

21. With the **Menus** table selected, choose **External Data→Export→More→HTML Document**.
22. Save the file in your **AC2013 Lesson 11** folder as **`AC11-A02-UCE-Menus-[FirstInitialLastName].html`**.
23. Check the boxes for **Export Data with Formatting and Layout** and **Open the Destination File After the Export Operation Is Complete**; click **OK**.
    Access creates the HTML file and opens it as a web page in your default web browser.
24. Close your web browser window. Switch back to **Access**, and close the **Export – HTML Document** dialog box.

Import an HTML File as a Database Object

25. Close any open objects.
26. Choose **External Data→Import & Link→More→HTML Document** .
27. From within your **AC2013 Lesson 11** folder, double-click **AC11-A02-UCE-Events.html** and select **Import the Source Data into a New Table in the Current Database**. Click **OK**.
28. Check the **First Row Contains Column Headings** checkbox and click **Next**.
29. Click **Next** again to accept the default field options.
30. Choose the **No Primary Key** option and click **Next**.
31. Type `AdditionalEvents` for the Import to Table name and click **Finish**.
32. Close the **Get External Data** dialog box. Open the **AdditionalEvents** table and size the columns as necessary.
33. Review the data and then save and close the **AdditionalEvents** table.

Add a Hyperlink to a Form

34. Display the **Venues Form** in **Design View**.
35. Click the **Detail section bar** and choose **Design→Controls→Hyperlink**.
36. Type `Open Venue Revenue Report` for the Text to Display.
37. Choose **Object in This Database** in the Insert Hyperlink dialog box.
38. Expand **Reports**, click **Venue Revenue Report**, and click **OK**.
    Access places the hyperlink control in the top-left corner of the Detail section.
39. Drag the hyperlink control to the right of the Venue ID in line with the VenuePhone text box.
40. Save changes to the **Venues Form**. Switch to **Form View**.

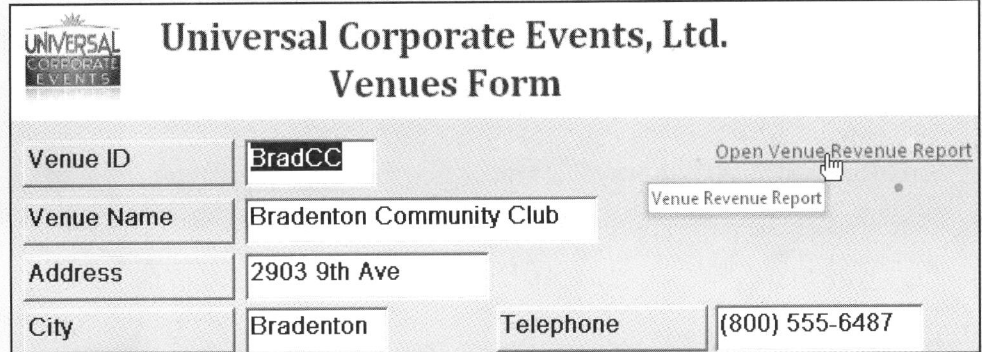

When you point to the hyperlink, a ScreenTip displays the hyperlink's destination.

Access 2013

41. Click the hyperlink and the **Venue Revenue Report** opens in **Report View**.
42. Close all open database objects then close the database. Exit **Access**.
43. Submit your final file based on the guidelines provided by your instructor.
    To see examples of how your file or files should look at the end of this exercise, go to the student resource center.

APPLY YOUR SKILLS AC11-A03

Change the File Format and Integrate and Export Data to Other Applications, Files, and the Web

The president of Universal Corporate Events, Ltd. needs your help integrating and exporting data. In this exercise, you will change the database format so that he can view data on his tablet. You will also add photos to a table of potential new clients. Then, you will integrate Access data with Word and Excel, import an HTML file as a new database object, export an Access object as a web page, and add a hyperlink to a form that opens a report.

Save a 2013 Database in an Older Format and Attach a File

1. Start **Access**. Open **AC11-A03-UCE-2013** from your **AC2013 Lesson 11** folder and save it as `AC11-A03-UCE-2013-[FirstInitialLastName]`. Enable content.
2. Choose **File→Save As→Save Database As→Access 2002–2003 Database**, and click the **Save As** button.
3. Save the file in your **AC2013 Lesson 11** folder as `AC11-A03-UCE-2003-[FirstInitialLastName].mdb`.
   The file format displays in the title bar.
4. Close all open databases.
5. Open **AC11-A03-UCE** from the **AC2013 Lesson 11** folder, close any open objects, and save the database as `AC11-A03-UCE-[FirstInitialLastName]`. Enable content and close any open objects.
6. Display the **BusinessOwners** table in **Design View**, type `BusPhoto` in the first available Field Name record, choose the **Attachment** data type, and type `Business Owner Photo` for the description.
7. Save the **BusinessOwners** table and switch to **Datasheet View**.
8. Double-click the paperclip symbol for the Bart Frost record.
9. Click **Add**, navigate to your **AC2013 Lesson 11** folder, and double-click **BartFrost.jpg**.

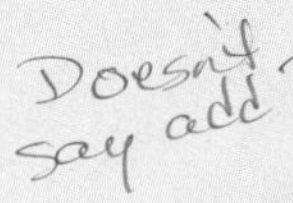

10. Close the **Attachments** dialog box.
11. Follow the previous steps to add a photo for **Pam Cross**.
12. Double-click the paperclip icon for **Bart Frost** and **Open** the new attachment.
13. Open the attachment for **Pam Cross** then close your photo viewer and the **Attachment** dialog box.
14. Save and close the **BusinessOwners** table.

Copy and Export Access Data to Word

15. Start **Word**. Open **AC11-A03-UCE-Customers.docx** from your **AC2013 Lesson 11** folder.
16. Open the **MenuList** table in Access.
17. Display the Access and Word window sides by side.
18. Select all records in the **MenuList** table.
19. Point at the left side of a field in the first column until the pointer becomes a white arrow; then click and drag the table records to the Word document under the line, *Our wide range of menu options can be customized to fit your specific needs.*
20. Close the **MenuList** table and maximize **Word**.
    The MenuList table is displayed in the document.
21. Save the file as `AC11-A03-UCE-Customers-[FirstInitialLastName]` and close it.
22. Close **Word** and maximize the **Access window**.
23. Select the **MenuList** table but don't open it.
24. Choose **External Data→Export→More→Word** . Save the file in your **AC2013 Lesson 11** folder as `AC11-A03-MenuList-[FirstInitialLastName]`.
25. Check the **Open the Destination File After the Export Operation is Complete** checkbox and click **OK**.
    The table displays with most of its Access formatting and layout, but does not include a title.
26. Close **AC11-A03-MenuList-[FirstInitialLastName]**, saving if prompted, and exit **Word**. Switch to **Access** and close the **Export – RTF File** dialog box.

Merge the Data into a Word Document

27. Open the **BestCustomers** table and choose **External Data→Export→** Word Merge.
28. Choose **Link Your Data to an Existing Microsoft Word Document** and click **OK**.
29. From your **AC2013 Lesson 11** folder, double-click **AC11-A03-UCE-Customers-[FirstInitialLastName]**.
30. Position the pointer under the UCE website and above the date.
31. Choose **Mailings→Write & Insert Fields→Insert Merge Field menu ▾**.
32. In the Select Microsoft Word Document dialog box, choose **Business** then tap [Enter].
    Access adds the field name, enclosed in chevrons, into the document at the insertion point.
33. Choose **Mailings→Write & Insert Fields** and choose **First_Name**.
34. Tap [Spacebar] to insert a space after the «FirstName».
35. Choose **Last_Name** from the **Insert Merge Field** list.
36. Tap [Enter] and choose **Address**. Tap [Enter] and choose **City**, type a comma, tap [Spacebar], and choose **ST**. Then tap [Spacebar] and choose **Zip**.

Access 2013

37. Choose **Mailings→Preview Results→Preview Results** .

Tampa Spirits
Walter James
2201 Dale Mabry
Tampa, FL 33608

38. Save and close **AC11-A03-UCE-Customers-[FirstInitialLastName]** and exit **Word**.

Import an Excel Spreadsheet and Use the Linked Table Manager

39. Close any open objects then choose **External Data→Import & Link→Excel**.
40. Choose **Link to the Data Source by Creating a Linked Table**, click **Browse**, navigate to the **AC2013 Lesson 11** folder, and double-click **AC11-A03-NewVenues.xlsx**. Click **OK**.
41. Check the **First Row Contains Column Headings** checkbox and click **Next**.
42. Type `NewVenues-Linked` for the Import to Table name and click **Finish**.
43. Click **OK** in the message box.
    The imported table appears in the Navigation Pane.
44. Open the new **NewVenues-Linked** table.
    The table includes records listing each venue's name and address information.
45. Close the **NewVenues-Linked** table, saving it if prompted.
46. To test the linked table, open **AC11-A03-NewVenues.xlsx** in Excel and change the First Name in the second record from *Billy* to `William`. Save and close **AC11-A03-NewVenues.xlsx** and exit **Excel**.
47. Open the **NewVenues-Linked** table.
    The first name is also changed to William *in the table.*
48. Close the **NewVenues-Linked** table.
49. Choose **External Data→Import & Link→** Linked Table Manager to verify that it is linked to the right location.
50. Mark the checkbox beside the **NewVenues-Linked**. Check the **Always Prompt for New Location** checkbox and click **OK**.
    Access allows you to navigate to the linked file, in the event that the file has been moved.
51. Locate the **AC11-A03-NewVenues.xlsx** file and click **Open**.
52. Click **OK**. Close the Linked Table Manager dialog box.

Export Access Data to Create a New Excel Workbook

53. Select the **BusinessOwners** table in the Navigation Pane.
54. Choose **External Data→Export→Export to Excel Spreadsheet** Excel.
55. Set the file format to **Excel Workbook (*.xlsx)** and check the two check boxes under **Specify Export Options**.
56. Save the file in your **AC2013 Lesson 11** folder as `AC11-A03-BusinessOwners.xlsx`.
57. Click **OK** in the Export – Excel Spreadsheet dialog box.
    Excel opens and displays the new workbook containing the BusinessOwners data.

58. Close the **AC11-A03-BusinessOwners.xlsx** workbook, saving if prompted. Exit **Excel**.

59. Switch back to **Access** and close the **Export – Excel Spreadsheet** box.

Export a Table in HTML Format

60. With the **BusinessOwners** table selected, choose **External Data→Export→More→HTML Document**.

61. Save the file in your **AC2013 Lesson 11** folder as `AC11-A03-BusinessOwners-[FirstInitialLastName].html`.

62. Place a checkmark in the two boxes under **Specify Export Options**. Click **OK**.
    Access creates and opens the HTML file as a web page.

63. Close the web browser. Switch to **Access** and close the **Export – HTML Document** dialog box.

Import an HTML File as a Database Object

64. Close any open objects then choose **External Data→Import & Link→More→HTML Document**.

65. Click **Browse** and navigate to the **AC2013 Lesson 11** folder. Double-click **AC11-A03-UCE-Events.html** and select the **Import the Source Data into a New Table in the Current Database** option.

66. Click **OK** to launch the Import HTML Wizard.

67. Check the **First Row Contains Column Headings** checkbox and click **Next**.

68. Click **Next** again to accept the default field options.

69. Choose the **No Primary Key** option and click **Next**.

70. Type `NewEvents` for the Import to Table name and click **Finish**.

71. Close the **Get External Data** dialog box. Open the **NewEvents** table.

72. Review the data in the imported HTML table. Save and close the **NewEvents** table.

Add a Hyperlink to a Form

73. Display the **Event Schedules** form in **Design View**.

74. Click the **Detail section bar** and choose **Design→Controls→Hyperlink**.

75. Type `Open Event Revenue Report` for the Text to Display.

76. Choose **Object in This Database** in the Insert Hyperlink dialog box.

77. Expand **Reports** and click **Event Revenue Report**; click **OK**.
    Access places the hyperlink control in the top-left corner of the Detail section.

78. Drag the new hyperlink control down to the right of the Guest controls.

79. Save the **Event Schedules** form, switch to **Form View**, and point to the hyperlink.
    A ScreenTip displays the name of the hyperlink's destination.

80. Click the hyperlink, and the **Event Revenue Report** opens in **Report View**.

81. Close all open database objects, and then close the database. Exit **Access**.

82. Submit your final file based on the guidelines provided by your instructor.

Extend Your Skills

In the course of working through the Extend Your Skills exercises, you will think critically as you use the skills taught in the lesson to complete the assigned projects. To evaluate your mastery and completion of the exercises, your instructor may use a rubric, with which more points are allotted according to performance characteristics. (The more you do, the more you earn!) Ask your instructor how your work will be evaluated.

AC11-E01 That's the Way I See It

Use your database from AC10-E01 or open **AC11-E01-BJL-2013** from the **AC2013 Lesson 11** folder and save it as `AC11-E01-BJL-2013-[FirstInitialLastName]`. Next, save it in 2003 format as `AC11-E01-BJL-2003-[FirstInitialLastName]`. If using your own database, save an early copy in 2003 format. Open your current database or **AC11-E01-BJL** and save it as `AC11-E01-BJL-[FirstInitialLastName]`. Add a Picture Attachment field to the StoreMerchandise table and attach **PlantPot-Small.jpg** to the Plant Pot-Sm record, or add an attachment field to one of your tables and attach a picture. Copy the Manufacturer Site Query table into **AC11-E01-BJL-CustLetter** and copy one of your tables into a Word document. Save as `AC11-E01-BJL-CustLetter-[FirstInitialLastName]`. Export the Store Inventory query to Word as a new RTF file named `AC11-E01-Inventory-[FirstInitialLastName]` (or export one of your tables or queries). Merge names and addresses from the Customers table into `AC11-E01-BJL-CustLetter-[FirstInitialLastName]` or create a new Word document. Import and link **AC11-E01-BJL-ServTechs.** Export the Store Inventory query to Excel and save as `AC11-E01-Inventory`. Or, adjust appropriately if using your own database. Export the Services table (or one of your own) in HTML format as `AC11-E01-Services-[FirstInitialLastName]`. Add a hyperlink to the Customers Form that opens the Customers Report (or adjust accordingly).

You will be evaluated based on the inclusion of all elements, your ability to follow directions, your ability to apply newly learned skills to a real-world situation, your creativity, and your accuracy in creating objects and/or entering data. Submit your final file based on the guidelines provided by your instructor.

AC11-E02 Be Your Own Boss

Open **AC11-E02-BJL-2013** from the **AC2013 Lesson 11** folder and save it as `AC11-E02-BJL-2013-[FirstInitialLastName]` and in 2003 format as `AC11-E02-BJL-2003-[FirstInitialLastName]`. Also, open and save **AC11-E02-BJL** as `AC11-E02-BJL-[FirstInitialLastName]`. Add an attachment field to the Customers table and attach David Harris' photo to his record. Copy the Large Equipment Query into **AC11-E02-BJL-PromoLetter** and save as `AC11-E02-BJL-PromoLetter-[FirstInitialLastName]`. Save the Equipment table as an RTF file named `AC11-E02-Equipment-[FirstInitialLastName]` and merge the Manufacturer Service Techs' names and addresses into **AC11-E02-BJL-PromoLetter**. Import and link **AC11-E02-BJL-NewMerchandise**. Export the ListPrice query to Excel and save as `AC11-E02-ListPrice-[FirstInitialLastName]`, import **AC11-E02-BJL-Mfrs** and name the table `NewManufacturers`; add a hyperlink to the MerchSales Form to open the Store Inventory Report.

You will be evaluated based on the inclusion of all elements, your ability to follow directions, your ability to apply newly learned skills to a real-world situation, your creativity, and your accuracy in creating objects and/or entering data. Submit your final file based on the guidelines provided by your instructor.

Transfer Your Skills

In the course of working through the Transfer Your Skills exercises, you will use critical-thinking and creativity skills to complete the assigned projects using skills taught in the lesson. To evaluate your mastery and completion of the exercises, your instructor may use a rubric, with which more points are allotted according to performance characteristics. (The more you do, the more you earn!) Ask your instructor how your work will be evaluated.

AC11-T01 Use the Web as a Learning Tool

Throughout this book, you will be provided with an opportunity to use the Internet as a learning tool by completing WebQuests. According to the original creators of WebQuests, as described on their website (WebQuest.org), a WebQuest is "an inquiry-oriented activity in which most or all of the information used by learners is drawn from the web." To complete the WebQuest projects in this book, navigate to the student resource center and choose the WebQuest for the lesson on which you are currently working. The subject of each WebQuest will be relevant to the material found in the lesson.

WebQuest Subject: Sending database objects as email attachments

Submit your files based on the guidelines provided by your instructor.

AC11-T02 Demonstrate Proficiency

The Stormy BBQ Key West store and restaurant have become one of the hottest spots for both tourists and locals. You are almost ready to for the database to go live. There are a few items that you want to export to different applications and a letter that you want to personalize and send to potential investors.

Open **AC11-T02-SBQ2013** from the **AC2013 Lesson 11** folder and save it as **`AC11-T02-SBQ2013-[FirstInitialLastName]`** as well as in 2003 format as **`AC11-T02-SBQ2003-[FirstInitialLastName].mdb`**. Open **AC11-T02-SBQ** and save it as **`AC11-T02-SBQ-[FirstInitialLastName]`**.

You want to add photographs to the Staff table. Start with Jean Thierry and Martine David. Then attach the photo of JeanEtMartine to Jean's and Martine's records.

Import the **AC11-T02-SBQ-Sponsors.xlsx** as a table named **`Sponsors`** and use it to merge the names and addresses into **AC11-T02-SBQ-Letter**. Copy the KeyWest Staff List query into the **`AC11-T02-SBQ-Letter`**. Export the Merchandise table to Excel as **`AC11-T02-SBQ-Merchandise-[FirstInitialLastName].xlsx`**.

Finally, Import **AC11-T02-SBQ-Vendors.html** as a new Access table named **`Vendors`**, export the Menu Items Form in HTML format as **`AC11-T02-SBQ-MenuItems-[FirstInitialLastName].html`**, and add a link on the Staff Form that opens Staff Report.

Submit your final file based on the guidelines provided by your instructor.

ACCESS 2013

Maintaining a Database

LESSON OUTLINE

LEARNING OBJECTIVES

After studying this lesson, you will be able to:

- Add command buttons to forms
- Manage database objects and create macros
- Backup, restore, analyze, compact, and repair a database
- Set database security using encryption and passwords
- Discuss Microsoft cloud computing

As you prepare your database for distribution, you will make your last design tweaks and confirm that it is optimized for speed and ease of use. And at this stage, security should be a main priority. It is important to protect a database from data loss and unauthorized access. In this lesson, you will customize Access 2013 settings and add easy-to-use command buttons to a form. You will create macros, explore database security features, set a database password, and then analyze, compact, and repair an Access database. You will also examine cloud computing and how to back up your data to SkyDrive.

CASE STUDY

Improving and Maintaining a Database

The prototype of the Winchester Web Design database is almost complete. After reviewing the database, the company's owner is pleased with the overall design. He now wants to add some command buttons and macros to improve navigation, and to ensure that the database runs as efficiently as possible.

A major concern is the security of the database and the data it contains. The owner would like to institute both security protocols and a regular backup policy. And finally, he is interested in exploring cloud computing and interfacing with mobile devices so he can work anywhere, anytime.

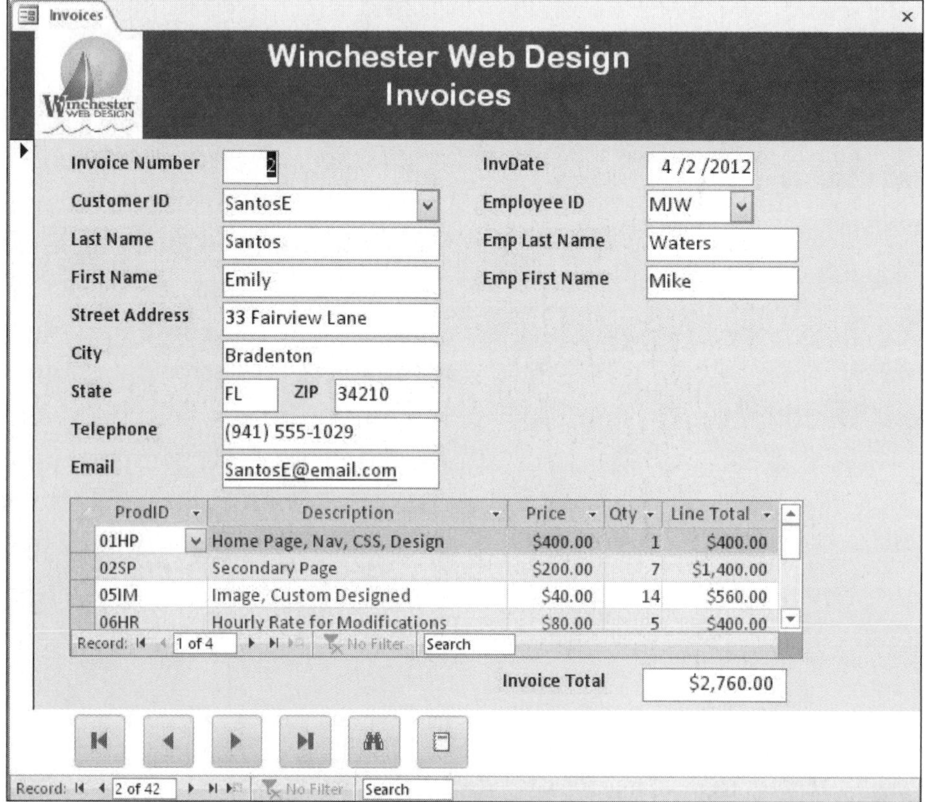

Using Command Buttons to Improve Navigation

Video Library: http://labyrinthelab.com/videos Video Number: AC13-V1201

In addition to adding labels, text boxes, images, and other controls to database forms, Access allows you to add command buttons that can be used for things such as record navigation and report operations. You can open a form, select the Button control from the Controls group on the Design tab, draw a button in the desired location on the form, and use the Command Button Wizard to add a custom button to find a record, go to the previous or next record, print a specific report, or even exit Access.

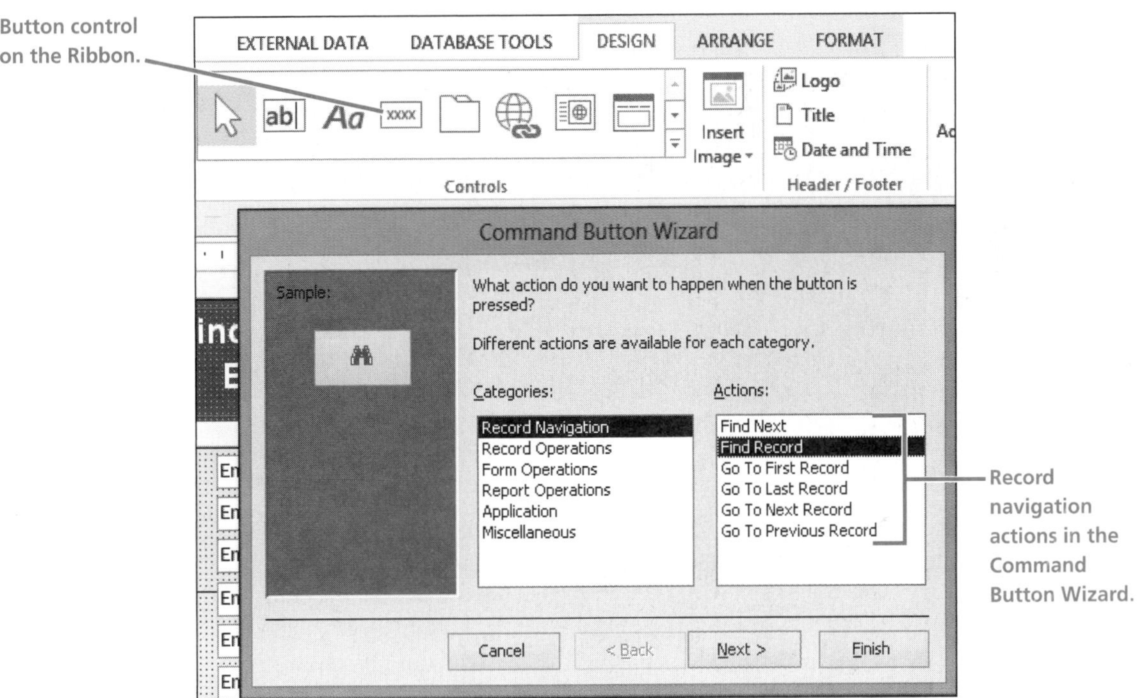

Access 2013

DEVELOP YOUR SKILLS AC12-D01

Add Command Buttons to a Form

In this exercise, you will add command buttons to the Form Footer section of the Invoice Form to make navigation easier and to quickly view an invoice report.

1. Open **AC12-D01-WinWebDesign** from the **AC2013 Lesson 12** folder, close any open objects, and save it as `AC12-D01-WinWebDesign-[FirstInitialLastName]`.

   Replace the bracketed text with your first initial and last name. For example, if your name is Bethany Smith, your filename would look like this: AC12-D01-WinWebDesign-BSmith.

2. Enable content, if necessary.
3. **Close** [×] the Winchester Web Design Navigation Form.

4. Open the **Invoice Form** in **Design View**.
5. Click the **Form Footer** section bar and type **.75"** for the **Height** property on the Property Sheet.

Tap [F4] to toggle the Property Sheet open and closed.

6. Choose **Design→Controls→Button** [xxxx].
7. Draw a button in the **Form Footer** under the left end of the subform.
   If the Command Button Wizard doesn't open, choose Design→Controls→Use Control Wizards.
8. Follow these steps to add a command button:

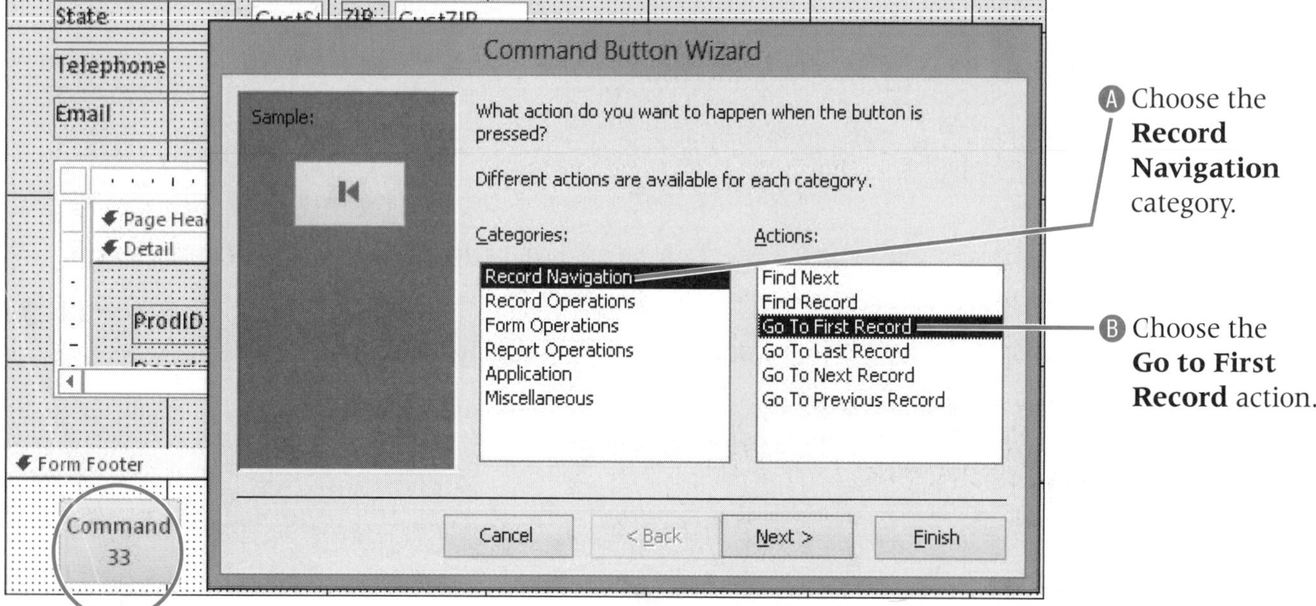

Your command button may show a different number (than 33).

9. Click **Next**, then click the **Picture** option, choose **Go To First**, and click **Next**.

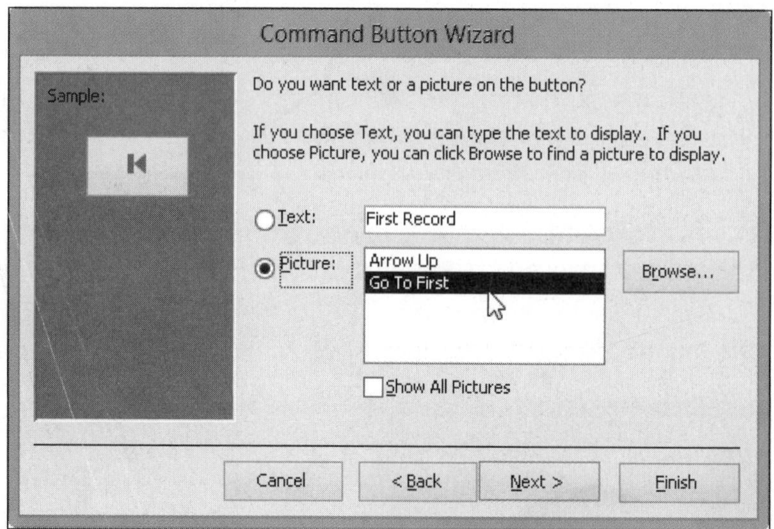

10. Enter **cmdFirst** for the Meaningful Name and click **Finish**.

The command button shows the Go To First picture in the Form Footer section and is programmed to go to the first record when in Form View.

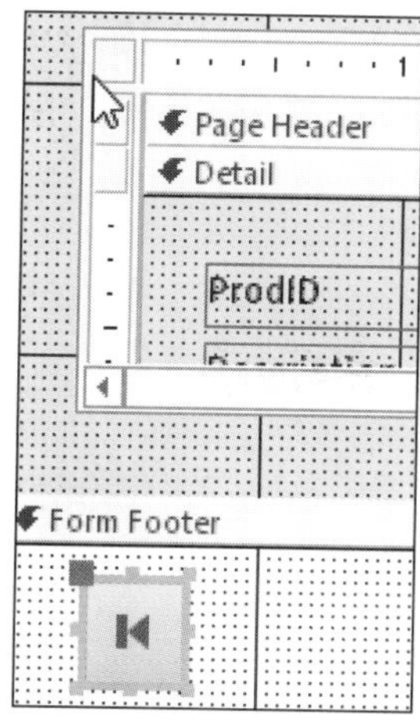

11. Repeat **steps 6–10** to add, in the order listed, command buttons for **Back** (Go To Previous Record: **cmdBack**), **Next** (Go To Next Record: **cmdNext**), **Last** (Go To Last Record: **cmdLast**), and **Find** (Find Record: **cmdFind**).

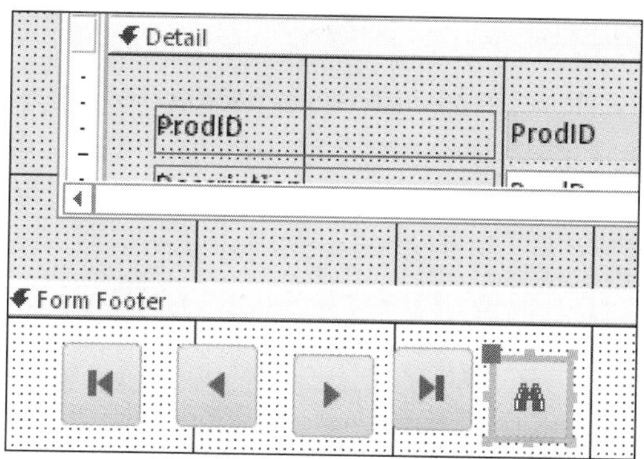

12. Draw a button to the right of the Find button. When the Command Button Wizard opens, choose **Report Operations** and **Preview Report**, and click **Next**.

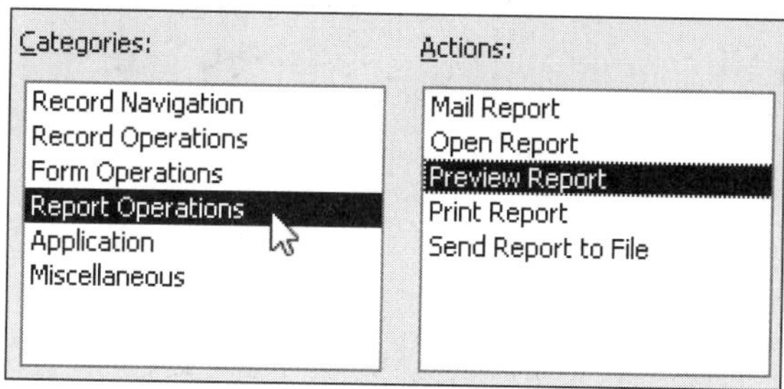

13. Select the **Invoice Details Report** as the Report to Preview and click **Next**.
14. Choose the **MS Access Report** picture, if necessary, then click **Next**.
15. Enter the name **cmdPreviewInvoices** and click **Finish**.
16. Select the new buttons and choose **Arrange→Sizing & Ordering→Align→Top**.

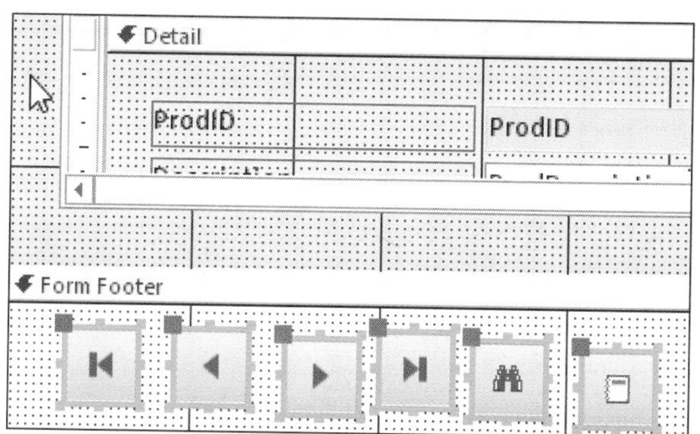

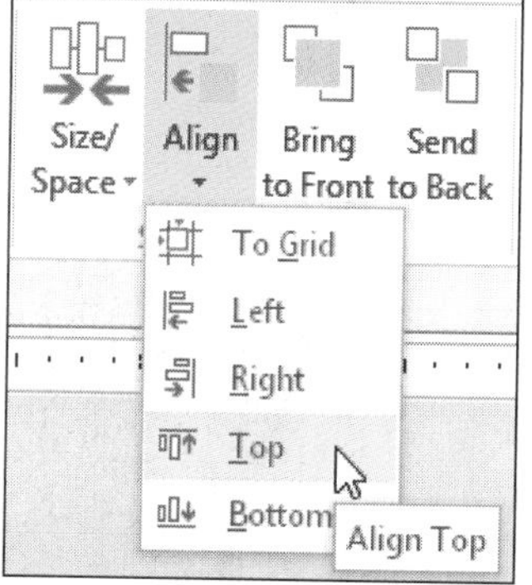

17. With the buttons still selected, choose **Arrange→Size & Ordering→Size/Space→ Equal Horizontal**.

Access 2013

18. Switch to **Form View** and test each button.
19. Close the **Invoice Details Report**. Save and close the **Invoice Form**.

Creating Macros to Improve Efficiency

Video Library: http://labyrinthelab.com/videos Video Number: AC13-V1202

A macro is an object that combines a series of steps into a single step so that a more detailed task can be automated. For example, if you regularly export your data to another database, instead of choosing External Data→Export→Text File and then entering the filename and selecting export options, you could create a macro to perform all the steps with one double-click of the mouse.

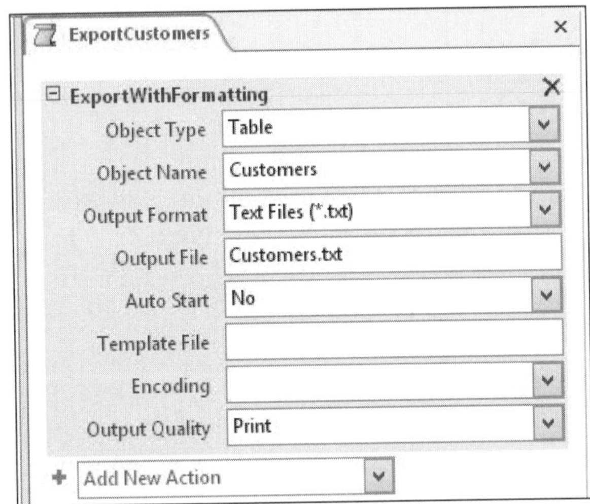

The ExportCustomers macro exports the Customers table to the default My Documents folder as a Text File. If needed, a specific file path could be entered for the Output File.

Customers.txt - Notepad

File Edit Format View Help

```
-------------------------------------------------------------------------------
|      CustID       |     Last Name      |     First Name     |     Street Address
-------------------------------------------------------------------------------
| AbramsJ           | Abrams             | John               | 1210 West Pier Way
-------------------------------------------------------------------------------
| AndersM           | Anders             | Mark               | 205 Montana St
-------------------------------------------------------------------------------
| BlaserH           | Blaser             | Helen              | 600 Fowler
-------------------------------------------------------------------------------
| DavisP            | Davis              | Peter              | 65 Terracotta Way
```

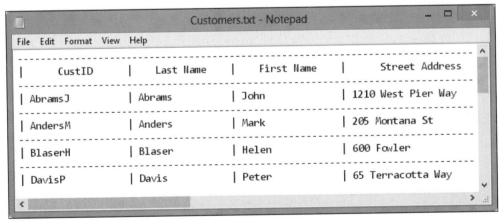

The Exported Text File.

Creating a macro starts from the same Ribbon path used to create other database objects: the Create tab. The next step is to select the action desired from the Add New Action drop-down menu.

FROM THE RIBBON
Create→Macros & Code→Macro to create a macro

DEVELOP YOUR SKILLS AC12-D02

Create a New Macro

In this exercise, you will create a macro that will display a message box to provide basic directions on when and where to back up the Winchester Web Design database.

1. Choose **Create→Macros & Code→**[Macro].
2. Choose **MessageBox** from the Add New Action drop-down menu.

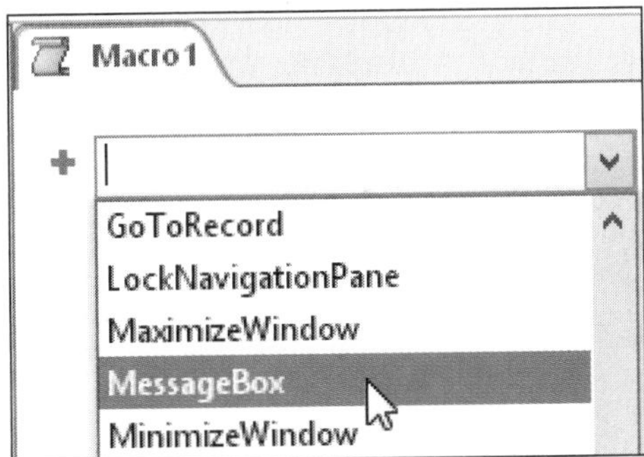

3. Enter the following into the **MessageBox** text boxes:

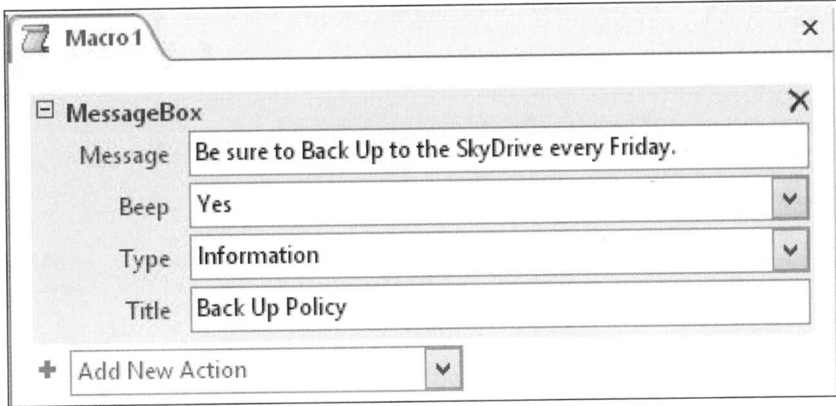

4. Save the macro as `Back Up Policy`.
5. Choose **Tools→Design→Run** [Run] to test the macro.

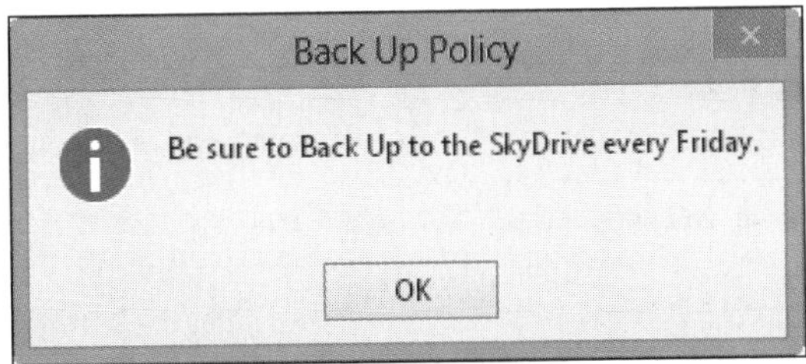

6. Click **OK** to close the message box.
7. Close the **Back Up Policy** macro.
   Back Up Policy is now listed in the Navigation Pane under the Macros group heading.

Access 2013

Using Macros to Display Adaptable Reports

Video Library: http://labyrinthelab.com/videos Video Number: AC13-V1203

Now that you have created a simple macro to display a reminder message, you can add a command button to a form that will run a macro to display a report.

DEVELOP YOUR SKILLS AC12-D03

Create a Macro to Display Adaptable Reports

In this exercise, you will create a macro button that will be placed on the Employees Form to display a report of all the sales for the specific employee selected.

1. Choose **Create→Macros & Code→**[Macro].
2. Choose **OpenReport** from the Add New Action drop-down menu.
3. Click the **Report Name menu ▼** and choose **Invoice Details Report**.

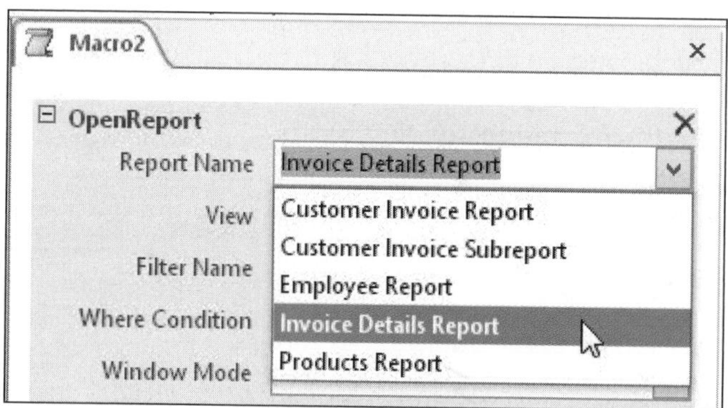

4. Enter the following into the OpenReport text boxes:

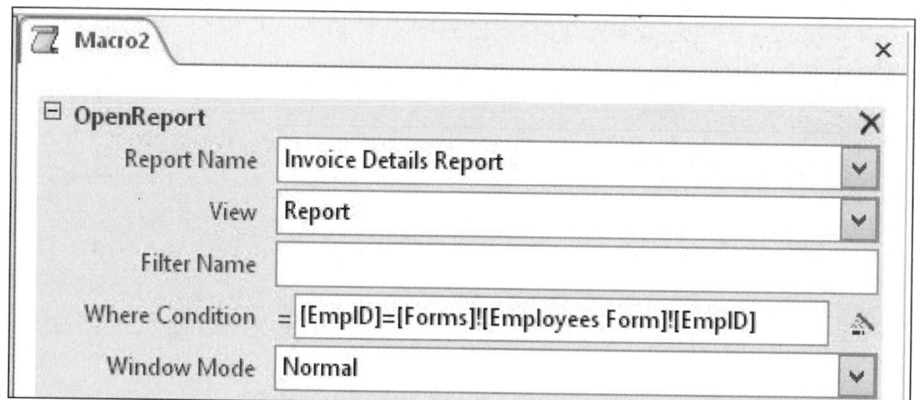

As you start to enter in the Where Condition text box, Access will suggest field names from a drop-down menu, allowing you to quickly and more accurately select from the list.

5. Save the macro as `Invoice Details Report by Employee`.
6. Display the **Employees Form** in **Design View**.

7. Choose **Design→Controls→Button** and draw a button in the top-right corner of the **Details section** of the Employees Form.

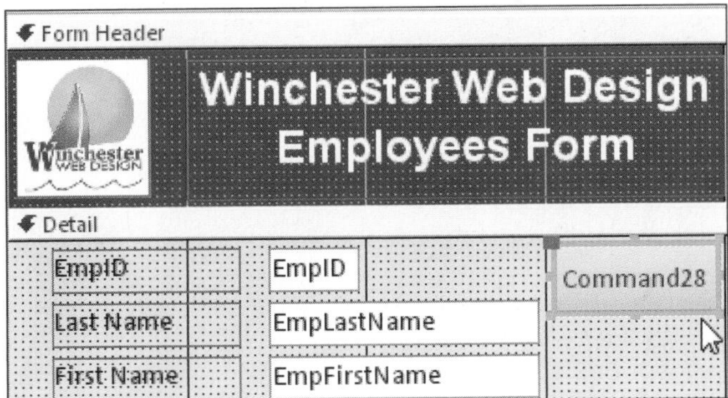

The Command Button Wizard starts.

8. Choose the **Miscellaneous** category and then choose the **Run Macro** action.

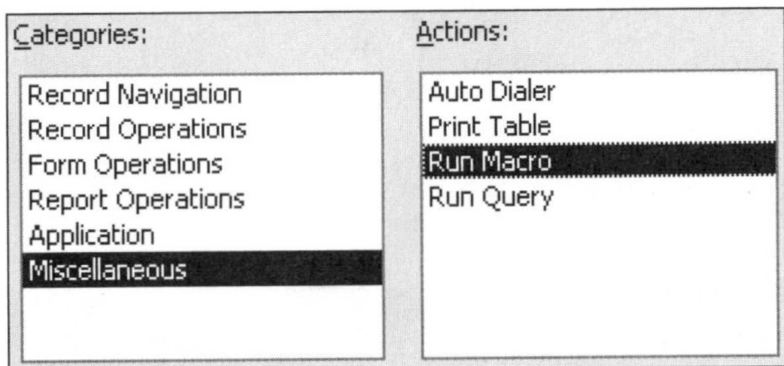

9. Click **Next** then choose **Invoice Details Report by Employee**.

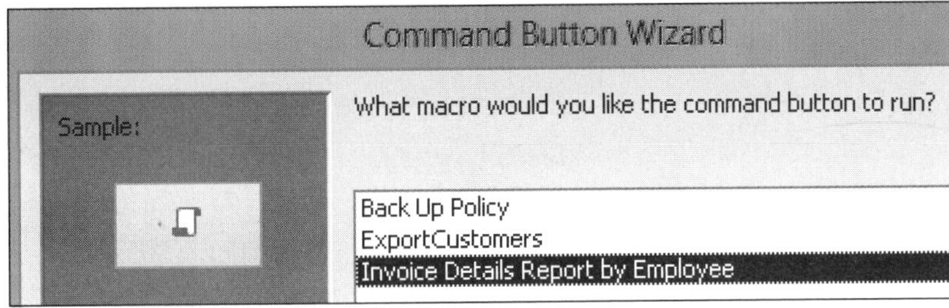

10. Click **Next**, accept the default macro picture, and click **Next** again.
11. Name the button `cmdRptByEmployees` and click **Finish**.

12. Switch to **Form View** and navigate to **Mike Waters** (EmpID MJW).

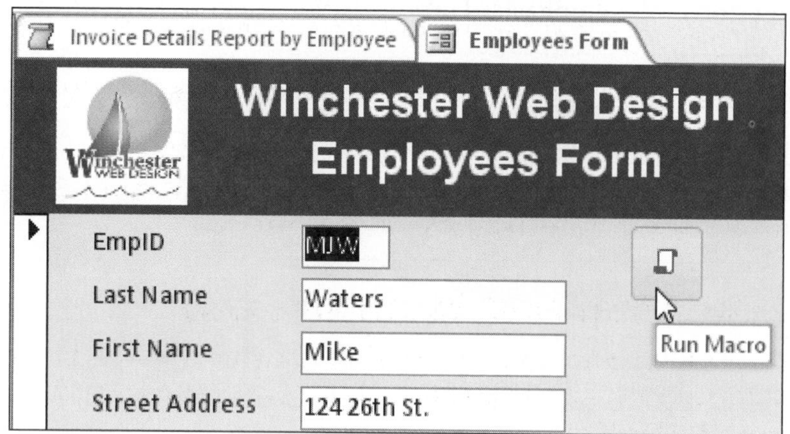

13. Click the new **Run Macro button** and to display only records for MJW.

Winchester Website Design

Invoice Details Report

Inv #	Emp ID	Inv Date	First Name	Last Name	Description	Price	Qty	Total
2	MJW	4/2/2012	Emily	Santos				
					Home Page, Nav, CSS, Design	$400.00	1	$400.00
					Secondary Page	$200.00	7	$1,400.00
					Image, Custom Designed	$40.00	14	$560.00
					Hourly Rate for Modifications	$80.00	5	$400.00
						Invoice Total		$2,760.00
6	MJW	6/23/2012	Daniel	Jeffries				
					Home Page, Nav, CSS, Design	$400.00	1	$400.00
					Secondary Page	$200.00	6	$1,200.00
					Blog, Integrated into Site	$300.00	1	$300.00
					Hourly Rate for Modifications	$80.00	3	$240.00
						Invoice Total		$2,140.00
9	MJW	7/20/2012	Peter	Davis				
					Secondary Page	$200.00	3	$600.00

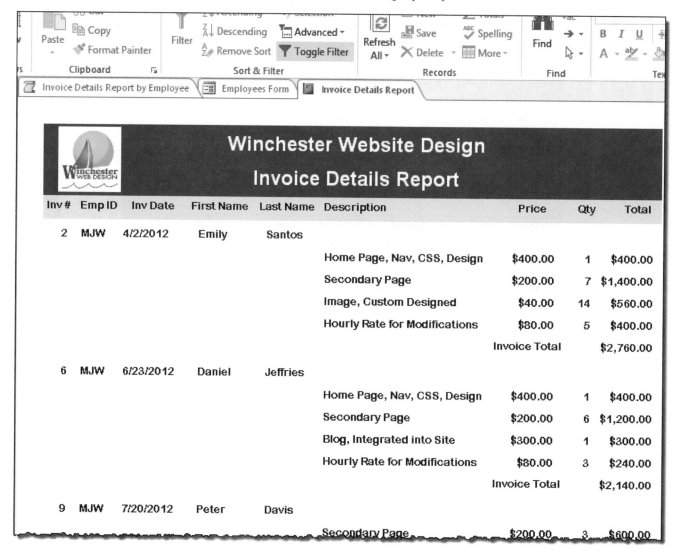

14. Save and close the form, the report, and the macro.

Managing Database Objects

Video Library: http://labyrinthelab.com/videos Video Number: AC13-V1204

Protecting databases and the quality of data they contain is vital to the reliability and performance of any database. At the same time, learning efficient ways to manage database objects helps to save a great deal of time as you build a database.

General Cleanup and Maintenance

The general cleanup and maintenance of a database can be accomplished in a number of ways. You can delete unneeded or duplicate database objects, rename database objects, and create new objects from existing objects.

Saving Database Objects As New Objects

You can use an existing file as a template for creating new files that may be similar in nature and format. For example, suppose you need to send each of your customers a letter that contains basically the same information. You can create the first letter, use the Save As command to save the original as a new file, and then edit the copy instead of having to retype all the information again.

Creating New Objects from Existing Objects

Often, databases contain separate objects that are similar in structure and in the data they hold. For example, the Employees table in the Winchester Web Design database contains fields similar to those found in the Customers table. When you build a database that contains similar objects, you can copy the original object, save it using a new name, and then modify the new object to fit its specific needs. Access provides two basic processes for copying objects:

FROM THE RIBBON
File→Save Object As to save an existing object as a new object

- The File→Save Object As command opens the Save As dialog box and identifies the name of the object being copied along with an object type.

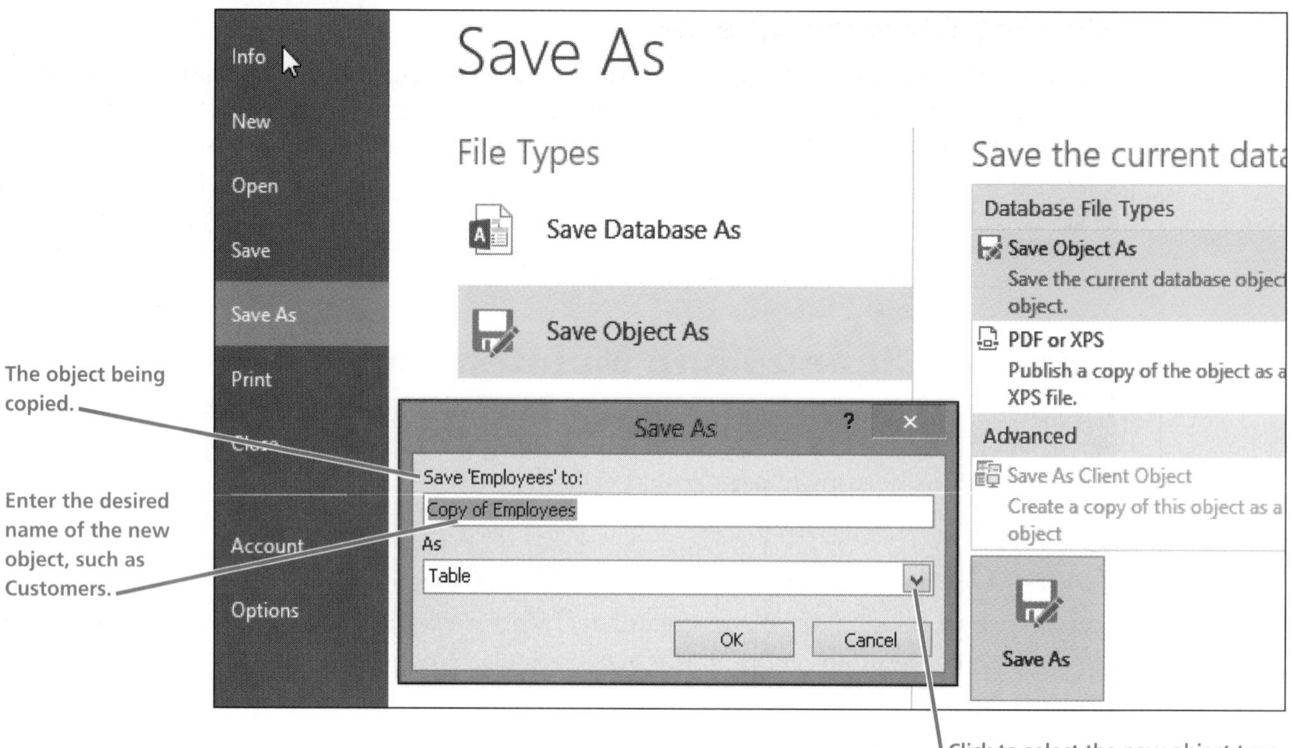

■ Right-click the object you want to copy and choose Copy. Then, right-click the object area in the Navigation Pane and choose Paste.

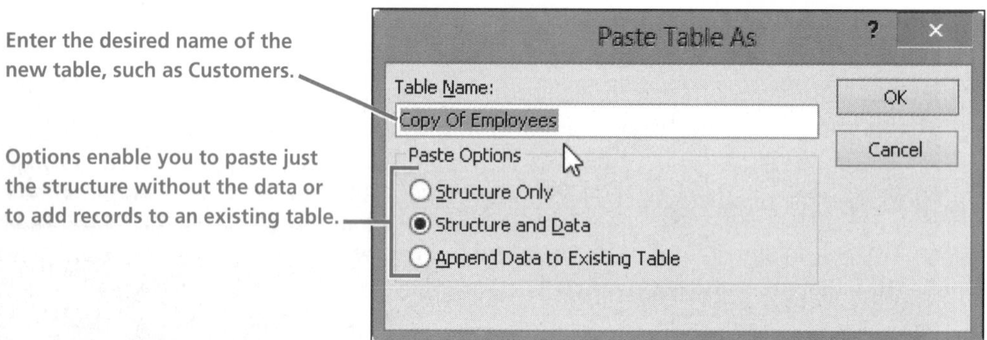

Renaming Database Objects

There are times when you create a table, query, form, or report and save it with the first name that comes to mind. Then after working with the object for a while, you might want a better name. To rename a database object, right-click the object and choose the Rename option. Access will automatically rename all the relationships and record sources that use the renamed object. For instance, if you update the Invoices table to Orders, the record source for the queries, forms, and reports that are based on the table will be updated to reflect the new name.

Deleting Database Objects

During the development of a database there are times when it is wise to create a temporary table, query, form, or report for testing purposes. Once the database is completed, you should remove these objects so they don't clutter the navigation pane or confuse users. To delete unwanted database objects, either right-click an object and choose the Delete option from the pop-up menu, or select the table, query, form, or report and simply tap the [Delete] key.

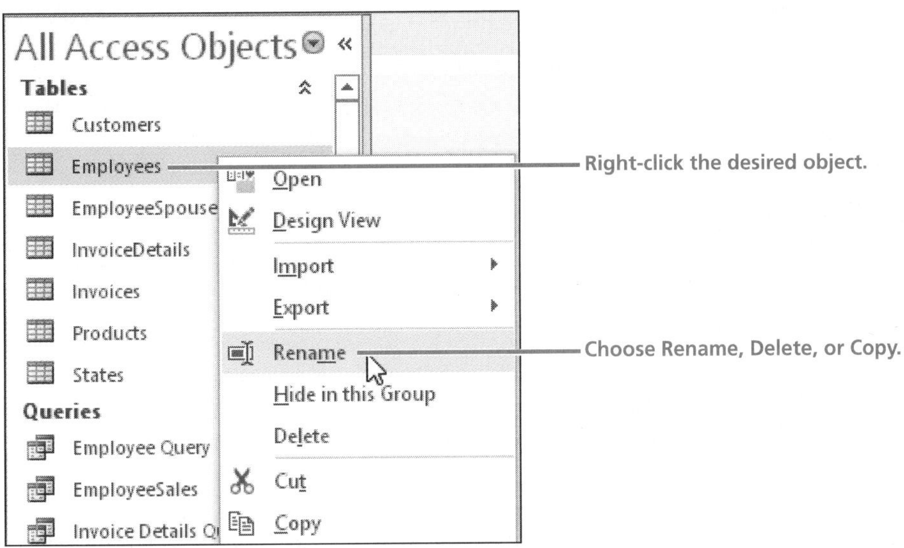

QUICK REFERENCE	COPYING DATABASE OBJECTS
Task	**Procedure**
Copy a database object	■ Choose File→Save Object As. ■ Type the desired name for the new object and click OK.
Copy a database table structure without data	■ In the Navigation Pane, right-click the table to copy. ■ Select Copy and then right-click the Navigation Pane. ■ Select Paste and type the desired name for the new object. ■ Select Structure Only in the Paste Options area of the dialog box and click OK.
Save a database object as a new object	■ In the Navigation Pane, select the object to use as a basis for the new object. ■ Choose File→Save Object As. ■ Type the desired name for the new object and click OK.

DEVELOP YOUR SKILLS AC12-D04

Rename, Delete, and Save an Object as a New Object

In this exercise, you will copy a report, rename a report, and delete a report. Then, you will save a table in the Winchester Web Design database as a new table and edit the field names for the new table.

1. Right-click the **Products Report** in the Navigation Pane and choose **Copy**.
2. Right-click again and choose **Paste**, keep *Copy Of Products Report* as the Report Name, and click **OK**.
3. Right-click *Copy Of Products Report*, choose **Rename** from the menu, and type **`Delete This Report Later`**.
4. Select the **Delete This Report Later** report in the Navigation Pane.
5. Tap [Delete] and click **Yes** to confirm the deletion.

6. Open the **Employees** table.
7. Choose **File→Save As→Save Object As→Save As**.
8. Type **`Business Contacts`** in the **Save 'Employees' To** text box and click **OK**.
9. Right-click the new **Business Contacts** table and choose **Design View**.

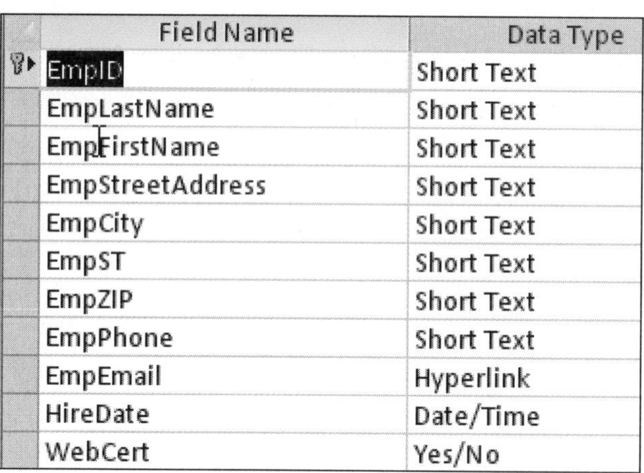

Field Name	Data Type
EmpID	Short Text
EmpLastName	Short Text
EmpFirstName	Short Text
EmpStreetAddress	Short Text
EmpCity	Short Text
EmpST	Short Text
EmpZIP	Short Text
EmpPhone	Short Text
EmpEmail	Hyperlink
HireDate	Date/Time
WebCert	Yes/No

10. Select and edit the **Business Contacts** field names, replacing each *Emp* prefix with a *Bus* prefix (so EmpID is BusID, and EmpLastName is BusLastName, and so on.).
11. Right-click the **HireDate** field. Choose **Delete Rows**. Delete the **WebCert** field, too.
12. Save changes to the **Business Contacts** table.
13. Switch to **Datasheet View** to confirm your changes, then close the **Business Contacts** table.

Backing Up a Database

Video Library: http://labyrinthelab.com/videos Video Number: AC13-V1205

Databases maintained by large companies often store thousands of records, which must be safeguarded. Most companies have a scheduled procedure to back up all files on their network, including the databases.

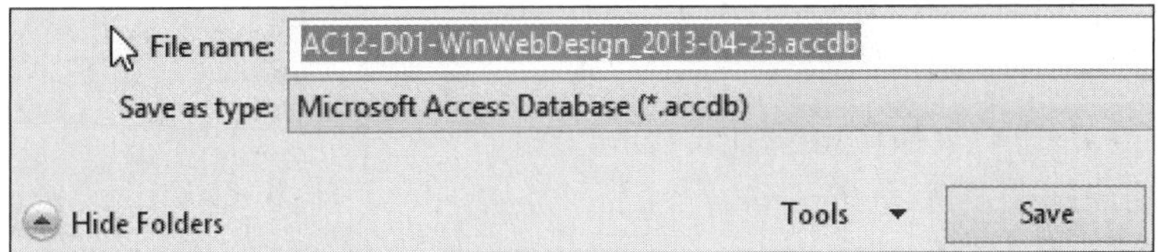

Save a backup copy of a database to prevent data loss.

When you back up a database using the built-in Access tools, Access automatically places the date of the backup in the filename so you can easily identify and retrieve each backup file. You choose the drive and folder in which you want to save the backup. To restore the database, simply open the backup.

QUICK REFERENCE — BACKING UP A DATABASE

Task	Procedure
Back up a database	■ Close all open database objects. ■ Choose File→Save As→Save Database As→Back Up Database. ■ Navigate to the folder in which you want to save the backup. ■ Choose Save.

DEVELOP YOUR SKILLS AC12-D05

Back Up a Database

In this exercise, you will back up your Winchester Web Design database.

1. Close any open objects in the Winchester Web Design database.
2. Choose **File→Save As→Save Database As→ Back Up Database** then click the **Save As** button.

   Access opens the Save As dialog box and adds the current date to the end of the filename.

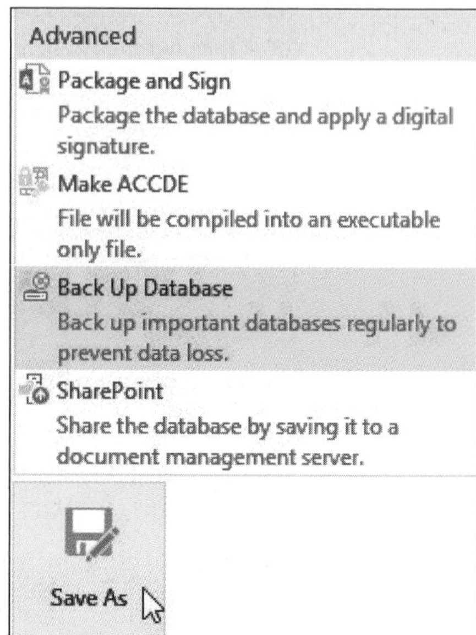

3. Save the file in your **AC2013 Lesson 12** folder.

   Access saves the backup file to the desired location; however, the database file in use is still the original Winchester Web Design database.
4. Close the database, navigate to your **AC2013 Lesson 12** folder, and open the backup database.

   A backup is only as current as the time the backup was created. It's important to have a policy that schedules and mandates a daily or weekly backup.
5. Close the backup database and reopen **AC12-D01-WinWebDesign-[FirstInitialLastName]**.

Analyzing and Documenting Databases

Video Library: http://labyrinthelab.com/videos Video Number: AC13-V1206

Each time you change the design or content of a database, the chance that the database will become corrupted increases. Access contains several tools that help you protect, document, analyze, and even repair databases. The main tools found in the Analyze group on the Database Tools tab are:

- **Performance Analyzer:** Analyzes the performance of a database to locate and identify potential trouble spots that affect how the database functions.
- **Database Documenter:** Documents objects in the database so that you can track changes to the design and relationships in the database; builds an Object Definition document that provides a detailed description of each database object.

Reviewing and Analyzing Performance

When you run the Performance Analyzer, Access reviews each selected object in the database, looks at all the relationships that exist, and identifies any problems that might affect database performance. Access often makes recommendations for improvements to optimize the efficiency of the database. In some cases, Access identifies tables where no primary key is set.

In other cases, Access will suggest a more efficient data type or that you use fewer controls on a form.

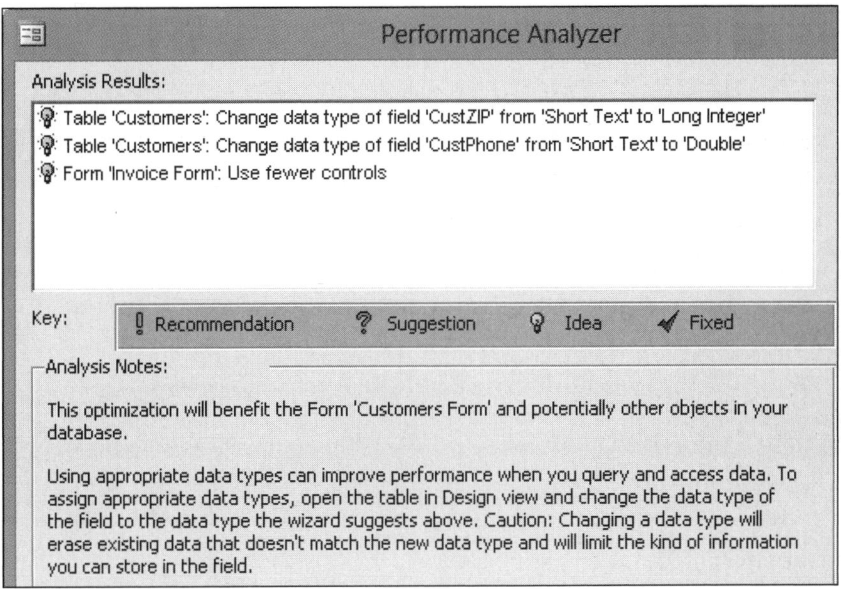

However, some changes recommended by the Performance Analyzer may not be necessary. For example, Access frequently recommends that phone numbers be formatted using the Number data type. Not only is this unnecessary, it may even cause problems for extensions that are commonly preceded by an X, such as X209. As you review the recommended changes, you will begin to identify those requiring your attention and those you can ignore.

Two options for analyzing database performance are available. The Analyze Performance tool enables you to choose those objects that you want to analyze. The Analyze Table tool analyzes a table using the Table Analyzer Wizard.

Documenting a Database

As you plan a new database you must analyze the needs of the business and the requirements of the database. In the process, you create a list of fields required; then organize and group those fields into the tables that will provide the data for forms, queries, and reports. The list identifies and defines each field and the tables and objects in which the fields are used within the database. When the database is finished, you may choose to document the database so that it can be efficiently updated and maintained in the future.

Documentation provides insight into the structure of the entire database as well as the structure of each object within the database. Maintaining a database can be very time-consuming. Without proper documentation to identify potential impacts of changing field properties, object structures, and so forth, you can potentially corrupt one database object that, in turn, wreaks havoc in the entire database. Each time you change the structure of any database object, remove an object from, or add an object to the database, you should run the Database Documenter to provide up-to-date documentation about the database. Such information will prove invaluable to database administration.

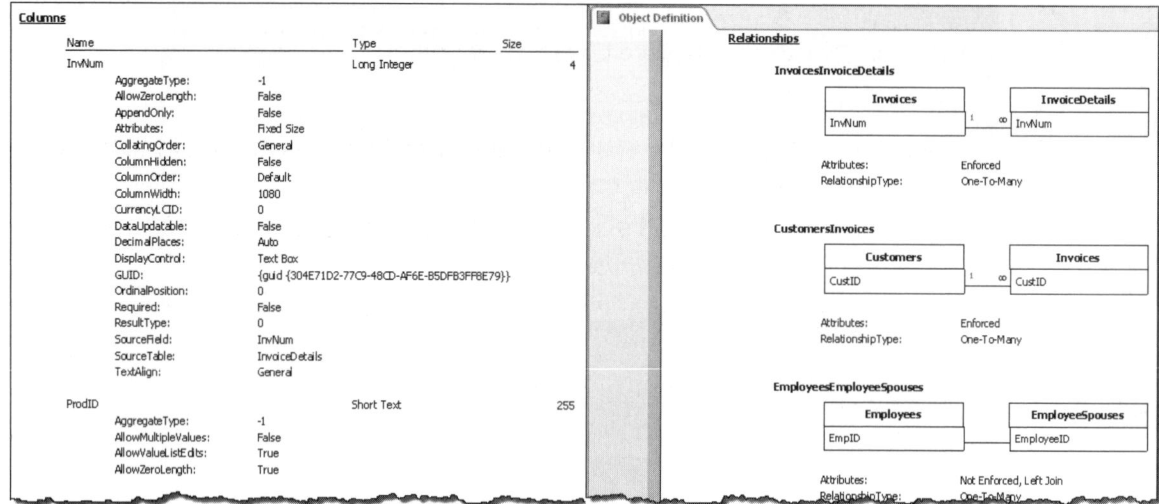

Reports produced by the Database Documenter can document the complete database, or document individual items or types of objects as they change.

QUICK REFERENCE — USING DATABASE ANALYZER AND DOCUMENTER TOOLS

Task	Procedure
Run Database Analyzer	Choose Database Tools→Analyze→Analyze Performance.
Run Database Documenter	Choose Database Tools→Analyze→Database Documenter.

DEVELOP YOUR SKILLS AC12-D06

Analyze and Document a Database

In this exercise, you will analyze and document your Winchester Web Design database.

1. Choose **Database Tools→Analyze→**Analyze Performance.

   The Performance Analyzer opens.

2. Click the **Tables** tab and click **Select All** to check all the tables listed.

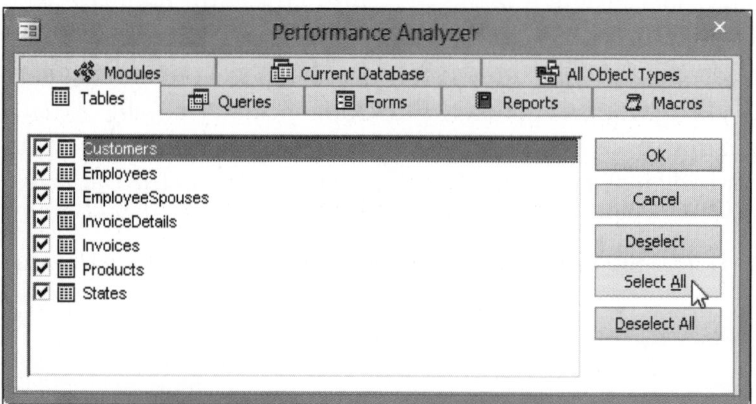

3. Click **OK** and view the suggestions under Analysis Notes.

   The data types have been set properly, so you can ignore the suggested ideas.

4. Click **Close**.

5. Choose **Database Tools→Analyze→**Database Documenter.

   The Documenter opens.

6. Click the **Tables** tab, check the **InvoiceDetails**, **Invoices**, and **Products** tables, and then click **OK**.

   Access produces a report that is about a dozen pages long documenting the tables, fields, and relationships of the selected tables.

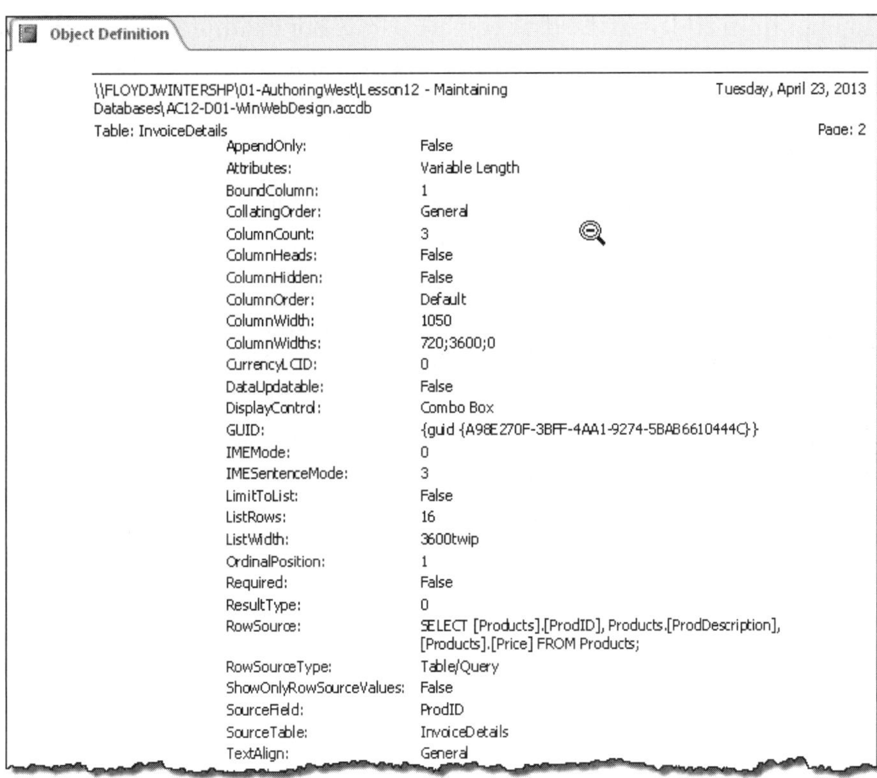

Object Definition

\\FLOYDJWINTERSHP\01-AuthoringWest\Lesson12 - Maintaining Databases\AC12-D01-WinWebDesign.accdb — Tuesday, April 23, 2013

Table: InvoiceDetails — Page: 2

AppendOnly:	False
Attributes:	Variable Length
BoundColumn:	1
CollatingOrder:	General
ColumnCount:	3
ColumnHeads:	False
ColumnHidden:	False
ColumnOrder:	Default
ColumnWidth:	1050
ColumnWidths:	720;3600;0
CurrencyLCID:	0
DataUpdatable:	False
DisplayControl:	Combo Box
GUID:	{guid {A98E270F-3BFF-4AA1-9274-5BAB6610444C}}
IMEMode:	0
IMESentenceMode:	3
LimitToList:	False
ListRows:	16
ListWidth:	3600twip
OrdinalPosition:	1
Required:	False
ResultType:	0
RowSource:	SELECT [Products].[ProdID], Products.[ProdDescription], [Products].[Price] FROM Products;
RowSourceType:	Table/Query
ShowOnlyRowSourceValues:	False
SourceField:	ProdID
SourceTable:	InvoiceDetails
TextAlign:	General

The second page of the report documenting tables in the Winchester Web Design database.

7. Scroll through the report and examine the documentation provided.

8. Choose **Data→Excel** to export the report to an Excel spreadsheet.

9. Check the **Open the Destination File After the Export Operation is Complete** box, if necessary.

10. Click **Browse** to navigate to your student folder, type **`AC12-D06-Objects-[FirstInitialLastName]`** for the filename, and then click **OK**.

11. Browse through the Excel spreadsheet, and close it when finished.

12. Close the **Export – Excel Spreadsheet Wizard**, without saving the export steps.

13. Click Close Print Preview.

Compacting and Repairing a Database

Video Library: http://labyrinthelab.com/videos Video Number: AC13-V1207

When you delete a record in Access, it is not really deleted—it is marked for deletion. The process of marking a record as deleted is quicker than completely deleting and reordering or rewriting all the records in a table. A similar process is used when you shorten the contents of a record—the space that was used for the longer data is not released.

As you work with databases, they can also become sluggish and the data stored in the databases can become fragmented—that is, parts of your database file become separated by incidental data that has been added to the disk you are using. For example: If you saved a ten megabyte database file to your hard drive and saved an Excel spreadsheet to the same hard drive shortly afterwards, it would be written next to the ten megabyte database file. Then, if a large group of new records were added to the database file they would have to be stored after the Excel file and not after the original database file, because the adjacent space is now occupied by the spreadsheet. As you add more records and save other files, both your files and storage drive become fragmented and less efficient.

Consequently, over time databases can become bulky and inefficient. This issue can be resolved by compacting—or compressing—your database to remove wasted and unused space left from deleted and edited records.

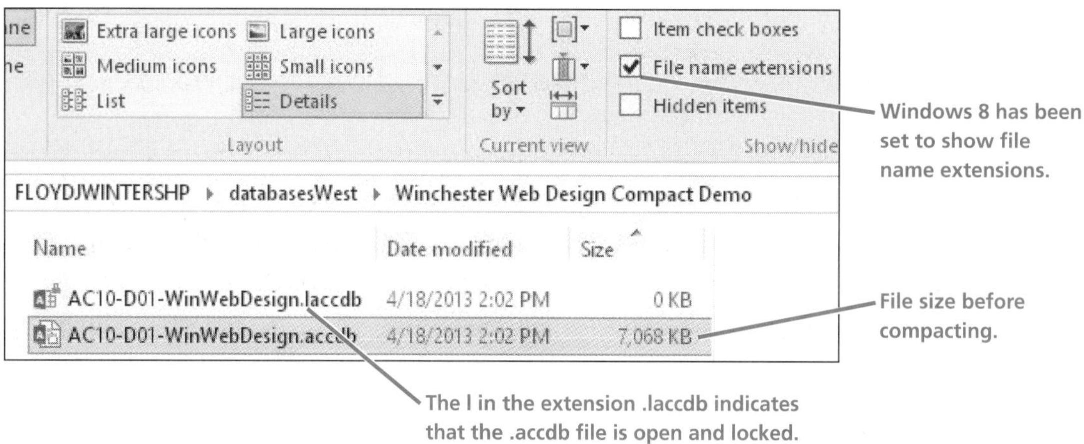

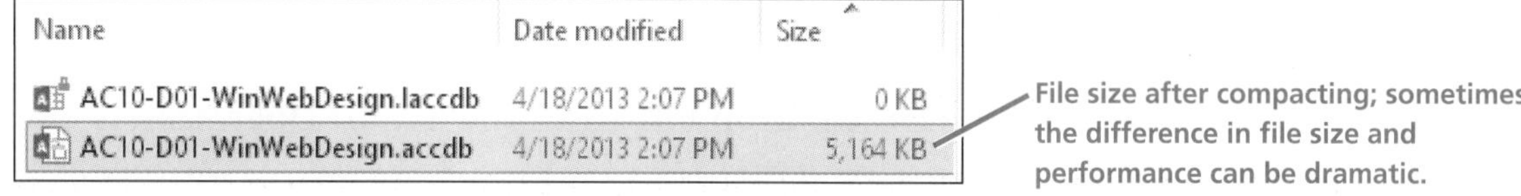

To ensure optimal performance, Access enables you to *compact* and *repair* databases as often as you want. Sometimes Access recognizes a problem when a database is opened and attempts to repair the file before you work with it. Even if there is no file corruption, the normal maintenance tasks of adding, deleting, and editing records, creating and running queries, and so forth, may reduce database performance. As a result, you may want to compact and repair the database manually on a regular basis, or set an option to automatically compact the database whenever you close Access.

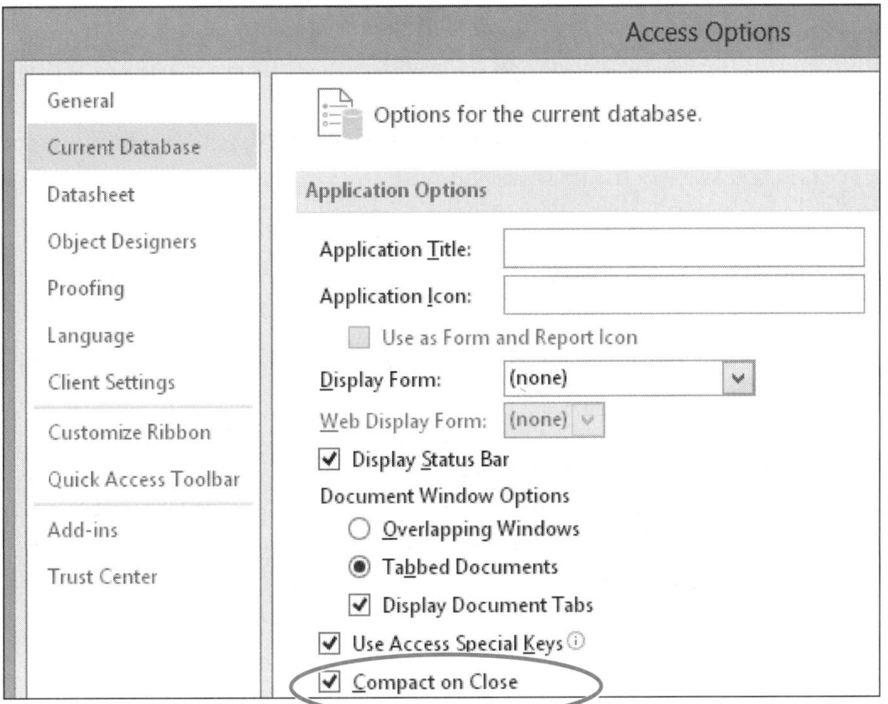

DEVELOP YOUR SKILLS AC12-D07

Compact and Repair a Database

In this exercise, you will compact and repair your Winchester Web Design database.

1. Close any open database objects.
2. Choose **Database Tools→Tools→Compact and Repair Database** .
   Access compacts and repairs the file. Because the database is relatively small, the compact and repair process takes only a moment. For larger databases, the process will take longer.
3. Close **AC12-D01-WinWebDesign-[FirstInitialLastName]** and exit **Access**.

Access 2013

Setting Database Security

Video Library: http://labyrinthelab.com/videos Video Number: AC13-V1208

Imagine that your doctor stores all your medical records in a large database that could be accessed by hospitals, clinics, and medical insurance companies who want to know more about the medications you take, conditions you might have, and doctor's visits. Databases, by nature, often hold confidential information. As a result, security is *imperative*. Companies that maintain large database files often restrict access to databases at the login or server level. Splitting a database can protect the data contained in databases, and Access offers tools that enable you to secure a database by assigning a password.

Opening a Database Exclusively

Most large business databases are designed to provide access to multiple users at the same time. As a result, the default setting for a database is as a shared file. Before you can set security for a database, you must first ensure that no one else is currently using the database. You do this by opening the file exclusively so that Access locks the database and prevents others from accessing it at that time.

Opening Database Commands

The Open dialog box contains numerous commands for opening databases, after a file has been selected. The following table identifies and describes when you should use each command on the Open drop-down menu.

COMMANDS FOR OPENING DATABASES	
Command	**Description**
Open	Provides full and typical access to the database, its objects and menus, so you can create and edit.
Open Read Only	Opens the database so that you can view and print data but does not allow design changes. However, you can save the database as a new file and edit the new file.
Open Exclusive	Opens the database and locks it to prevent other users in a shared environment from accessing the database.
Open Exclusive Read-Only	Opens the database and locks it so other users cannot access it and prevents edits to data and database objects.

DEVELOP YOUR SKILLS AC12-D08

Open a Database for Exclusive Use

In this exercise, you will open the Winchester Web Design database exclusively.

All databases should be closed.

1. Start **Access**. Choose **File→Open Other Files**, navigate to your **AC2013 Lesson 12** folder, and click **AC12-D01-WinWebDesign-[FirstInitialLastName]**.

   Do not *open the database.*

2. Follow these steps to open the database exclusively:

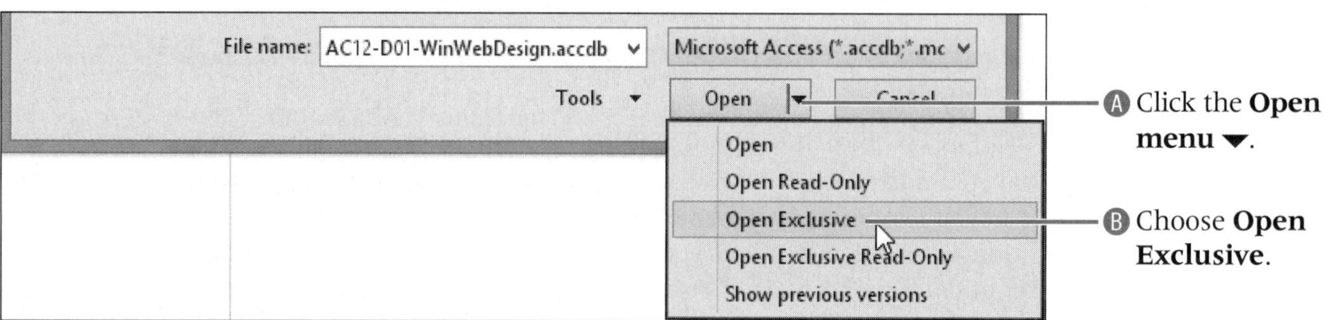

3. Enable content, if necessary.

   No one else will be able to use the database until you finish your settings and exit Access.

Encrypting a Database Using a Password

Video Library: http://labyrinthelab.com/videos Video Number: AC13-V1209

Regardless of whether a backup routine is in place, valuable time can be lost reconstructing data if unauthorized users damage the database. Database passwords are intended to protect the database just as the passwords you use to access bank accounts or email accounts protect your financial and personal information.

Limits of Passwords

Database passwords provide limited security for databases by preventing unauthorized users from opening the database. You can set a password for any database you have on your personal computer just as systems administrators set a password for shared databases on a network.

Access passwords are case sensitive, or capable of distinguishing between characters typed in uppercase and characters typed in lowercase.

Strong Passwords

Access passwords can use a combination of upper- and lowercase characters, symbols, and numbers. Access allows you to use any combination of characters in passwords *except* " \ [ ] : | <> + = ; , . ? and *. Strong passwords are at least eight characters long and contain at least one of each of the character types listed above. Passwords cannot start with a space.

Weak Password: webdesign

Strong Password: Hard2Cr@ck

Setting Up Databases for Assigning Passwords

To assign a database password, the database must initially be closed. The default access setting for databases that appear on a network is as a shared database, accessible to anyone who has access to its file location. To set a password, you must open the database *exclusively* using the Open Exclusive command in the Open dialog box. This ensures that no one else is currently using the database and that, once you open it, other users are prohibited from opening it until you close it. If the file is not opened exclusively, you will get a warning message.

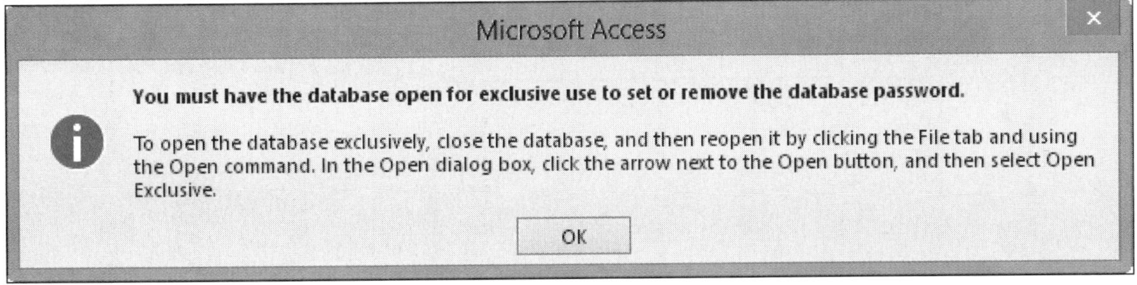

The Encrypt with Password command on the File menu is a toggle command. When a database has a password, the command button shows Decrypt Database.

QUICK REFERENCE	SETTING AND REMOVING A DATABASE PASSWORD
Task	**Procedure**
Set a password	■ Open the database in exclusive mode. ■ Choose File→Info→Encrypt with Password. ■ Type the password to assign in the Password text box. ■ Type the password again in the Verify text box. ■ Click OK.
Remove a password	■ Open the database in exclusive mode. ■ Choose File→Info→Decrypt Database. ■ Type the password in the Password box, and then click OK.

DEVELOP YOUR SKILLS AC12-D09

Set a Database Password

In this exercise, you will set a database password to protect the database.

Your Winchester Web Design database should be open in exclusive mode.

1. Choose **File→Info→Encrypt with Password**.

2. Type **`labyrinth`** in the Password text box and type **`labyrinth`** again in the Verify text box, then click **OK**.

Access displays asterisks (*) in the text boxes as you type.

3. Click **OK** to acknowledge that row level locking will be ignored.

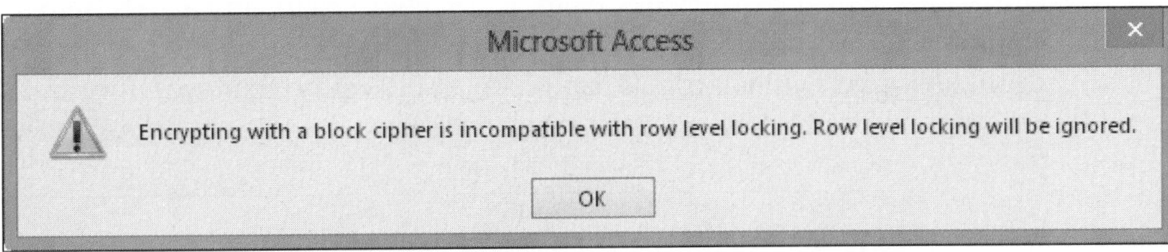

4. Close **AC12-D01-WinWebDesign-[FirstInitialLastName]** then open it again.

If you forget your password, you will not be able to open your database.

5. In the Password Required dialog box, type **`labyrinth`** in the Enter Database Password text box. Click **OK**.
   You must open the database exclusively again if you want to change or remove the password.
6. Close **AC12-D01-WinWebDesign-[FirstInitialLastName]** and exit **Access**.

Exploring Microsoft Cloud Storage

Video Library: http://labyrinthelab.com/videos Video Number: AC13-V1210

With high-speed broadband Internet connectivity and 4G mobile technology, online storage and mobile computing are becoming very common. And Microsoft is aggressively moving most of its applications onto the cloud.

Defining Cloud Storage

Cloud storage simply means online storage, which is saving, storing, or backing up your files remotely on a web server. A web server is a combination of hardware (computers and storage devices) and software used to store and deliver web content that can be accessed online. As an example, a web server is used to "host" or store and deliver the content for the Labyrinth website at http://www.lablearning.com. One of the benefits of cloud storage is that you can access your files online from numerous devices, at any time, and from almost any place. You can obtain free cloud storage from providers like Microsoft and Google, or pay for cloud storage from providers like Carbonite or Zip Cloud, or have cloud storage provided by your company. To use cloud storage, you must have a user account.

Microsoft's free SkyDrive provides cloud storage to anyone with a Microsoft account, which may be an older Hotmail.com, Live.com, or a new Outlook.com account. To sign up for or to log in to one of these accounts, you can go to http://hotmail.com, http://live.com, or http://outlook.com.

For many years Outlook has been the email, calendar, and contacts portion of the Microsoft Office suite, which also includes Word, Excel, PowerPoint, and Access. Today, a new, web-based Outlook interface provides email, an online contact list, an online calendar, and online storage called SkyDrive. Outlook.com is part of Microsoft's effort to move Office and the storage of files onto a cloud-based platform. You can go to SkyDrive by going to http://SkyDrive.com.

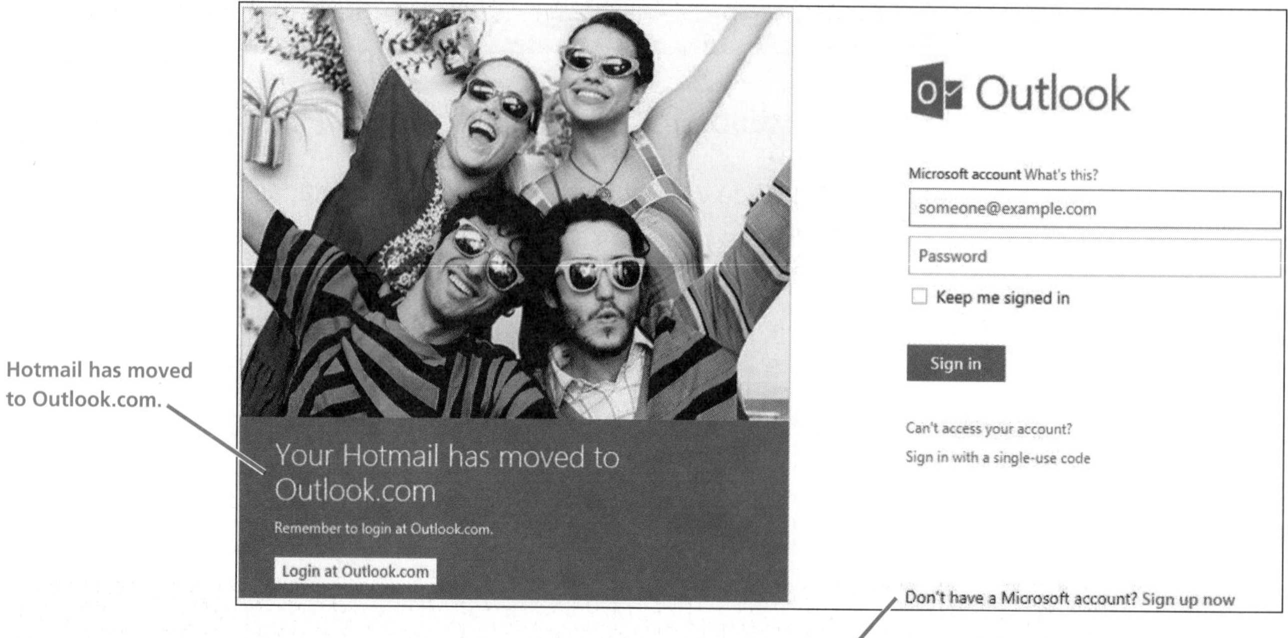

Another feature of cloud storage is file synchronization ("syncing"), or reliably updating files stored at different locations on different devices. In other words, you can create a document on your work PC and then later access and open that document on your laptop at home, on your tablet while traveling, or even on your Smartphone. You must be connected to the Internet in order to access and synchronize these online files. Saving to the SkyDrive leaves the local copy on the PC while at the same time synchronizing the copy stored on the SkyDrive. And if you remotely edit the document either on your tablet or laptop, the file will be synced back to the PC the next time that PC logs back into SkyDrive.

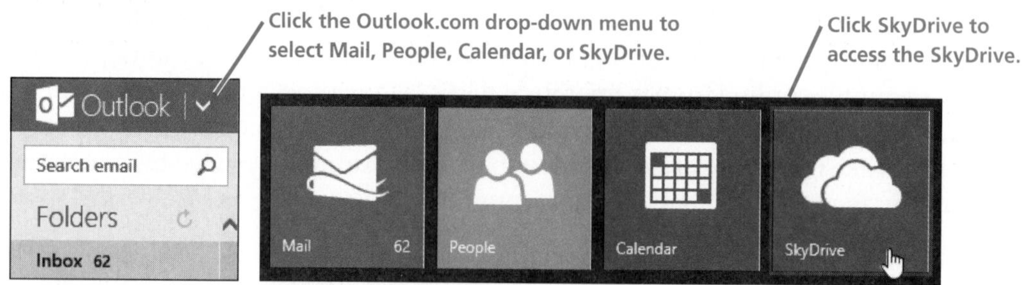

Outlook.com provides email, a contact list, a calendar, and online storage.

In addition to cloud storage, SkyDrive also allows you to use an online version of Microsoft Office from almost any device that uses a web browser (such as Internet Explorer, Firefox, Safari, or Chrome). You can open documents that have been created on the SkyDrive just like a web page. Many basic Office features are available online; some advanced features are not.

Files on your SkyDrive can be shared by sending a link to another person or by making that file public. You can create, edit, store, and share Word, PowerPoint, Excel, and OneNote files in a web browser. However, you cannot create an online Access database file while working on the SkyDrive.

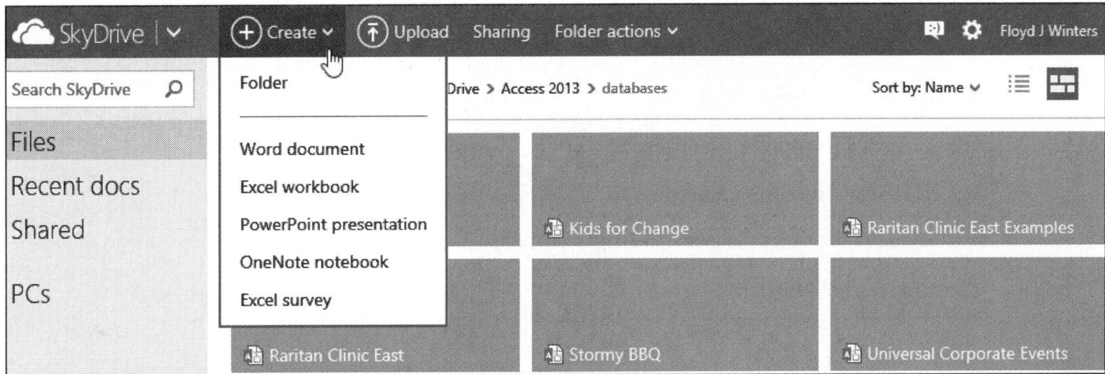

Access is not listed under the SkyDrive's Create menu.

Although you can't create an Access file via the SkyDrive's Create menu, you can back up, store, and share Access files on SkyDrive.

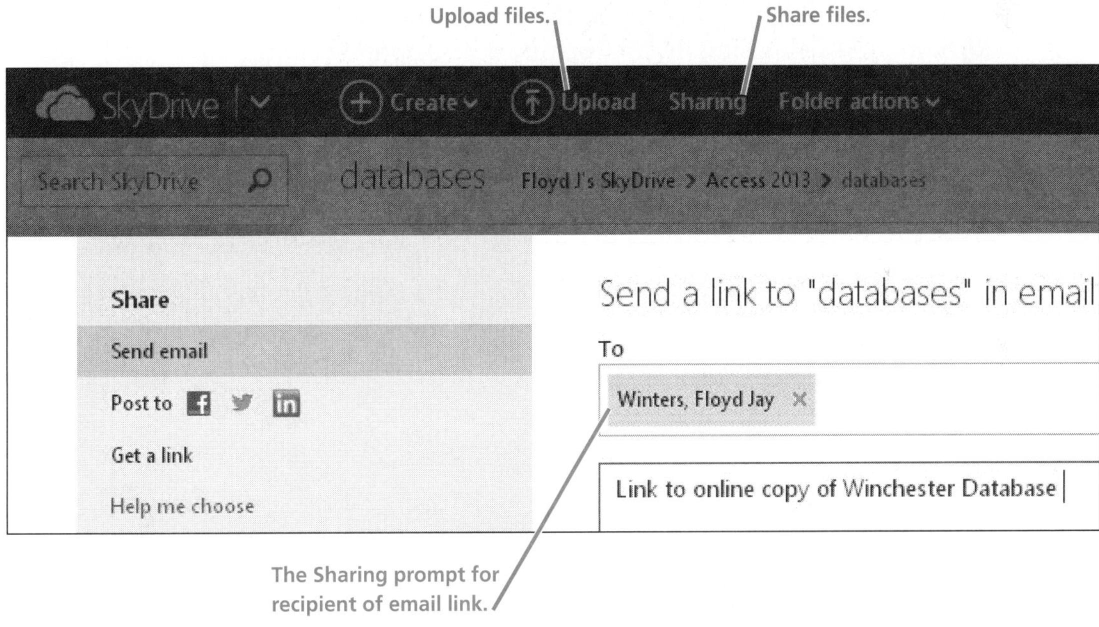

Access 2013

When you share Access files stored on the SkyDrive, an email with links is sent to the recipient. The recipient can conveniently click on the embedded email links and download the database files onto their local computer.

Floyd J has 6 files to share with you on SkyDrive. To view them, click the links below.

- Stormy BBQ.accdb
- Raritan Clinic East.accdb
- Universal Corporate Events.accdb
- Blue Jean Landscaping.accdb
- Raritan Clinic East Examples.accdb
- Kids for Change.accdb

Concepts Review

To check your knowledge of the key concepts introduced in this lesson, complete the Concepts Review quiz by choosing the appropriate access option below.

If you are...	Then access the quiz by...
Using the Labyrinth Video Library	Going to http://labyrinthelab.com/videos
Using eLab	Logging in, choosing Content, and navigating to the Concepts Review quiz for this lesson
Not using the Labyrinth Video Library or eLab	Going to the student resource center for this book

Reinforce Your Skills

REINFORCE YOUR SKILLS AC12-R01

Add Command Buttons, Create a Macro, and Manage Objects

In this exercise, you will wrap up some of the final tasks associated with the Kids for Change database. You will add command buttons to the Activities Form, create macros to increase efficiency, and do some cleanup tasks by copying, renaming, and deleting objects.

Add Command Buttons to a Form

1. Start **Access**. Open **AC12-R01-K4C** from the **AC2013 Lesson 12** folder, close any open objects, and save it as `AC12-R01-K4C-[FirstInitialLastName]`.
2. Enable content then close the **K4C Navigation Form**, if necessary.
3. Open the **Activities Form** in **Design View** and open the **Property Sheet**, if necessary.
4. Click the **Form Footer** section bar. Type `.75"` for the **Height** on the Property Sheet.
5. Choose **Design→Controls→Button** [xxxx] and draw a button in the **Form Footer** under the **Telephone** label.
   The Command Button Wizard opens.
6. Under **Record Navigation**, choose the **Go To First Record** action. Click **Next**.

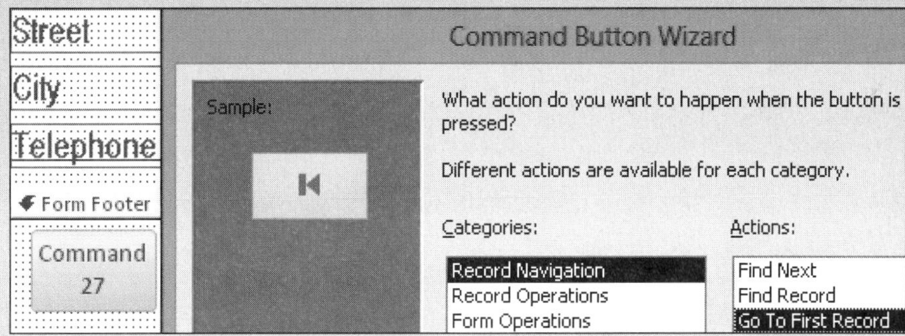

   The wizard displays a sample button picture for each action.
7. Click the **Picture** option, choose **Go To First**, and click **Next**.

8. Enter `cmdFirst` for the Meaningful Name and click **Finish**.
   The command button shows the Go to First image in the Form Footer section and is programmed to go to the first record when in Form View.

9. Add, in the order listed, command buttons for **Previous** (Go To Previous Record: `cmdPrevious`), **Next** (Go To Next Record: `cmdNext`), **Last** (Go To Last Record: `cmdLast`), and **Find** (Find Record: `cmdFind`).

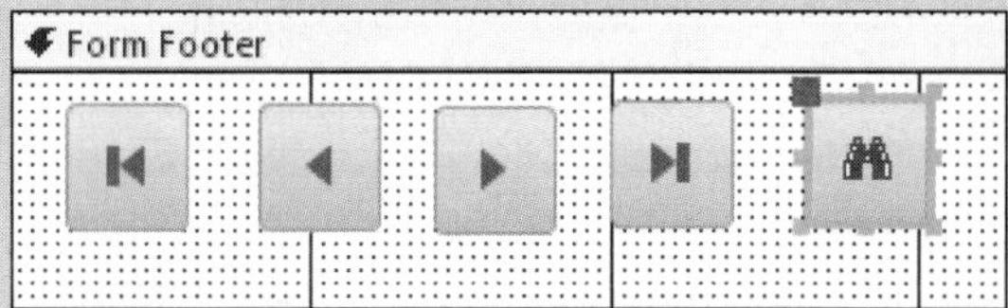

The command buttons should appear in the order shown.

10. Draw a button to the right of the Find button. When the Command Button Wizard opens, choose **Report Operations** and **Preview Report**. Click **Next**.

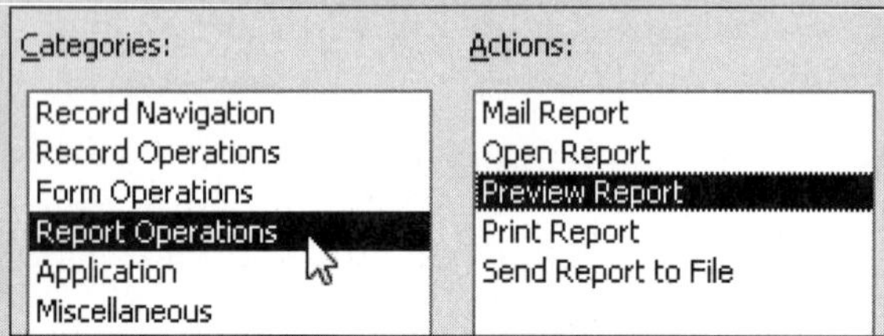

11. Select the **Activity Costs Report** as the Report to Preview and click **Next**.
12. Choose the **Preview** picture on the next screen, if necessary, and click **Next**.
13. Enter the name `cmdPreviewCosts` and click **Finish**.
14. Select the new command buttons and choose **Arrange→Sizing & Ordering→Align Top**.
    All of the command buttons are aligned to the top.
15. With all the buttons selected, choose **Arrange→Size & Ordering→Size/Space→Equal Horizontal**.
16. Switch to **Form View** and test each of the new buttons.
17. Close the **Activity Costs Report**; save and close the **Activities Form**.

Create a New Macro

18. Choose **Create→Macros & Code→**[Macro] to create a macro that displays a reminder message.
19. Choose **MessageBox** from the **Add New Action** drop-down menu.
20. Enter the following:

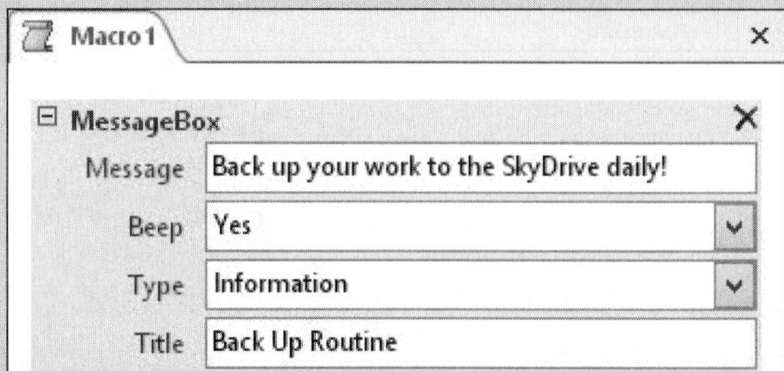

21. Save the macro as `Back Up Routine`.

22. Choose **Tools→Design→**[Run].
    The Back Up Routine Information message box opens.
23. Click **OK** to close the message box. Close the **Back Up Routine** macro.
    Back Up Routine is now listed under Macros in the Navigation Pane.

Create a Macro to Display Adaptable Reports

24. Choose **Create→Macros & Code→**[Macro].
25. Choose **OpenReport** from the **Add New Action** menu.
26. Choose **Volunteers Report** from the **Report Name** menu.
27. Choose **Report** for the view type.
28. Type `[ActID]=[Forms]![Activity Staffing]![ActID]` for the **Where Condition**.
29. Save the macro as `Available Volunteers` and close it.
30. Display the **Activity Staffing** form in **Design View**.
31. Choose **Design→Controls→Button** [xxxx] and draw the new button to the right of the Day and Meet Time controls.
32. Choose the **Miscellaneous** category and the **Run Macro** action.

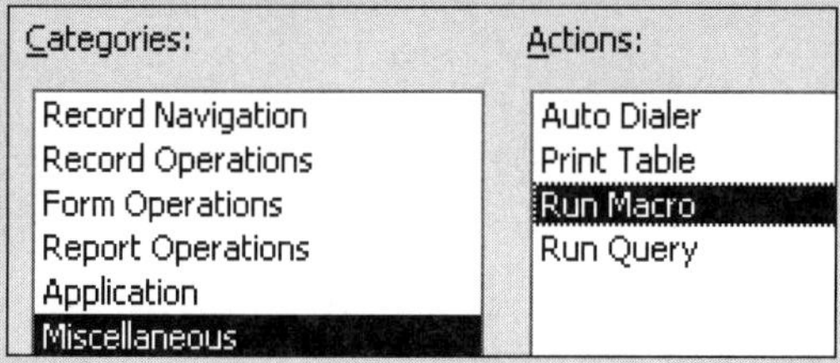

33. Click **Next** then choose **Available Volunteers**.
34. Click **Next**, accept the default macro picture, and click **Next** again.
35. Name the button `VolunteersMacro` and click **Finish**.
36. Switch to **Form View**.
37. Click the new **VolunteersMacro button**.
    The macro button displays the Volunteers Report record for the activity on the form.
    To display the Volunteers Report for another activity, close the report, navigate to the desired activity, and click the macro command button.
38. Close the **Volunteers Report**; save and close the **Activity Staffing** form.

Rename, Delete, and Save Object As a New Object

39. Right-click **Venues Report** in the Navigation Pane and choose **Copy**.
40. Right-click again and choose **Paste**. Type `Delete This Report` as the report name and click **OK**.

41. Select **Delete This Report** in the Navigation Pane.
42. Tap [Delete]; click **Yes** to confirm the deletion.
43. Open the **PaidStaff** table.
44. Choose **File→Save As→Save Object As→Save As**.
45. Type **`Professional Contacts`** in the **Save 'PaidStaff' To** text box and click **OK**.
46. Display the new **Professional Contacts** table in **Design View**.
47. Edit the field names in the **Professional Contacts** table, replacing each Staff prefix with a Prof prefix (so that StaffID is ProfID, etc.).
48. Right-click the **Parent** field and choose **Delete Rows**; confirm the deletion.
49. Delete the **Masters**, **ActID**, and **HrlySal** fields. Click **Yes** to permanently delete the fields and to delete the ActID indexes.
50. Rename **Email Address** as **`ProfEmail`**.

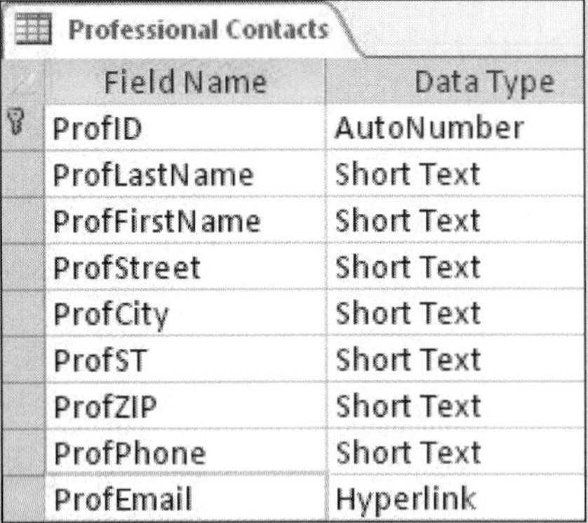

Professional Contacts

Field Name	Data Type
ProfID	AutoNumber
ProfLastName	Short Text
ProfFirstName	Short Text
ProfStreet	Short Text
ProfCity	Short Text
ProfST	Short Text
ProfZIP	Short Text
ProfPhone	Short Text
ProfEmail	Hyperlink

51. Save and close the **Professional Contacts** table, close the database, and exit **Access**.
52. Submit your final file based on the guidelines provided by your instructor.

    To see examples of how your file or files should look at the end of this exercise, go to the student resource center.

REINFORCE YOUR SKILLS AC12-R02

Perform Database Maintenance and Set a Password

In this exercise, you will perform some maintenance procedures on the Kids for Change database. You will also add a password to protect the data from unauthorized users.

Back Up a Database

1. Start **Access**. Open **AC12-R02-K4C** from the **AC2013 Lesson 12** folder, close any open objects, and save it as **`AC12-R02-K4C-[FirstInitialLastName]`**.
2. Enable content and close the **K4C Navigation Form**.
3. Choose **File→Save As→Save Database As→** [Back Up Database].
4. Click the **Save As** button.

5. Navigate to the **AC2013 Lesson 12** folder and click **Save**.
6. Return to the **AC2013 Lesson 12** folder and open the backup database to confirm that you can access it. Close the backup database.

Analyze and Document a Database

7. Choose **Database Tools→Analyze→** Analyze Performance.
8. Click the **Tables** tab and click **Select All** to check all the tables listed.
9. Click **OK** and view the Analysis Results.

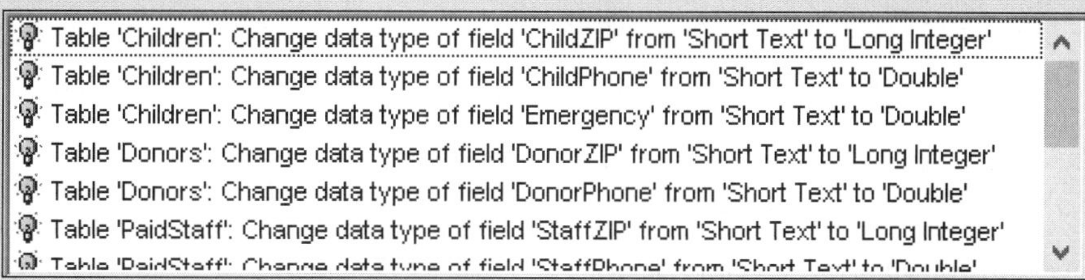
Table 'Children': Change data type of field 'ChildZIP' from 'Short Text' to 'Long Integer'
Table 'Children': Change data type of field 'ChildPhone' from 'Short Text' to 'Double'
Table 'Children': Change data type of field 'Emergency' from 'Short Text' to 'Double'
Table 'Donors': Change data type of field 'DonorZIP' from 'Short Text' to 'Long Integer'
Table 'Donors': Change data type of field 'DonorPhone' from 'Short Text' to 'Double'
Table 'PaidStaff': Change data type of field 'StaffZIP' from 'Short Text' to 'Long Integer'

Because the data types have already been set properly, you can ignore the suggested ideas.

10. Click **Close**.
11. Choose **Database Tools→Analyze→** Database Documenter.
12. Click the **Tables** tab, check the **Activities** and **PaidStaff** tables, and click **OK**.
The report documents the tables, fields, and relationships of the selected tables.
13. Choose **Data→More→Word** to export the report to a Word RTF.
14. Browse to your **AC2013 Lesson 12** folder, type `AC12-R02-Tables-[FirstInitialLastName].rtf` as the filename, check the **Open the Destination File After the Export Operation is Complete** box, and click **OK**.
Access creates and opens the Word document.
15. Page through the Word document. Then close it and exit **Word**.
16. Close the **Export – RTF File** dialog box without saving the export steps.
17. Click Close Print Preview.

Compact and Repair a Database

18. Close any open database objects.
19. Choose **File→Info→Compact & Repair Database**.
Access has compacted and repaired the file. The K4C Navigation Form might open, depending on your system.
20. Close **AC12-R02-K4C-[FirstInitialLastName]** and exit **Access**.

Access 2013

Open a Database for Exclusive Use

21. Start **Access**. Click **Open Other Files**, the last option under Access, click **Computer** under Open, navigate to the **AC2013 Lesson 12** folder, and click **AC12-R02-K4C-[FirstInitialLastName]** (*do not open it*).
22. Click the **Open menu ▾** and choose **Open Exclusive**.
23. Enable content, if necessary when the database opens.
    No one else will be able to use the database until you exit Access.

Set a Database Password

Because you opened the database exclusively, you can set a password to open the database.

24. Choose **File→Info→Encrypt with Password**.
25. Type **`labyrinth`** as the password. Verify the password by typing it again, then click **OK**.
26. Click **OK** to acknowledge the message about row-level locking.
27. Close **AC12-R02-K4C-[FirstInitialLastName]** then open it again.
    Access displays the Password Required dialog box.
28. Type **`labyrinth`** in the text box and click **OK**.
29. Close **AC12-R02-K4C-[FirstInitialLastName]** and exit **Access**.
30. Submit your final files based on the guidelines provided by your instructor.
    To see examples of how your file or files should look at the end of this exercise, go to the student resource center.

REINFORCE YOUR SKILLS AC12-R03

Improve and Maintain a Database

In this exercise, you will add command buttons, create macros, and perform a number of other tasks in order to improve the efficiency of and security for the Kids for Change database.

Add Command Buttons to a Form

1. Start **Access**. Open **AC12-R03-K4C** from the **AC2013 Lesson 12** folder, close any open objects, and save the database as **`AC12-R03-K4C-[FirstInitialLastName]`**.
2. Enable content and close the **K4C Navigation Form**, if necessary.
3. Open the **Venues Form** in **Design View**.
4. Click the **Form Footer** section bar and type **`.75"`** for the **Height** on the Property Sheet.
5. Choose **Design→Controls→Button** [xxxx] and draw a button in the **Form Footer** section under the Detail section labels.
    The Command Button Wizard starts.

6. In the **Record Navigation** category, choose **Go To First Record** and click **Next**.

   The wizard displays a sample button picture for the action.

7. Choose the **Go To First** Picture option and click **Next**.
8. Enter `cmdFirst` for the Meaningful Name and click **Finish**.

   The command button shows the Go To First image in the Form Footer section and is programmed to display the first record when in Form View.
9. Add, in the order listed, command buttons to Go To Previous Record: `cmdPrevious`, Go To Next Record: `cmdNext`, Go To Last Record: `cmdLast`, and Find Record: `cmdFind`.

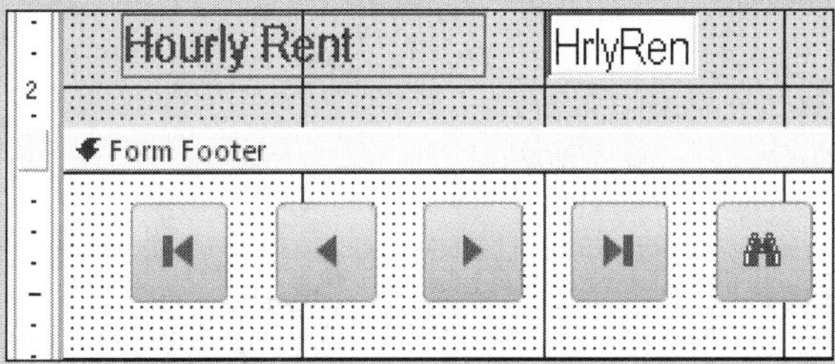

10. Draw a button to the right of the Find button. When the Command Button Wizard opens, choose **Report Operations** and **Preview Report**, and click **Next**.

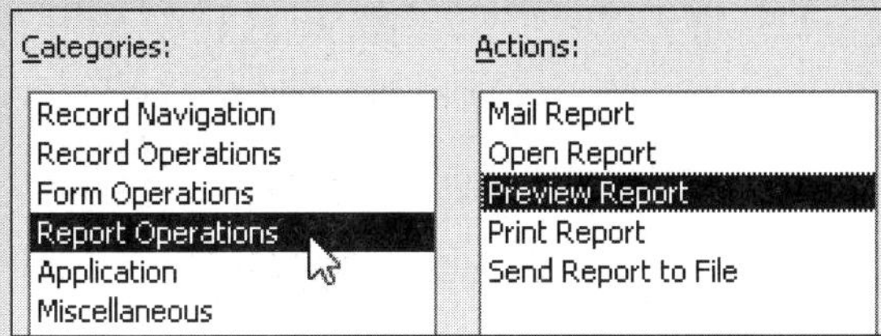

11. Select the **Venues Report** as the Report to Preview and click **Next**.
12. Choose the **Preview** picture, if necessary, and click **Next**.
13. Enter the name `cmdPreviewVenues` and click **Finish**.
14. Select all the buttons and choose **Arrange→Sizing & Ordering→Align→Top**.
15. With the buttons selected, choose **Arrange→Size & Ordering→Size/Space→Equal Horizontal**.

    The buttons will be aligned to the top and horizontally spaced equally.
16. Switch to **Form View** and test each of the new buttons.
17. Close the **Venues Report**; save and close the **Venues Form**.

Create a New Macro

18. Choose **Create→Macros & Code→**[Macro].
19. Choose **MessageBox** from the **Add New Action** menu.
20. Enter the following into the text boxes:

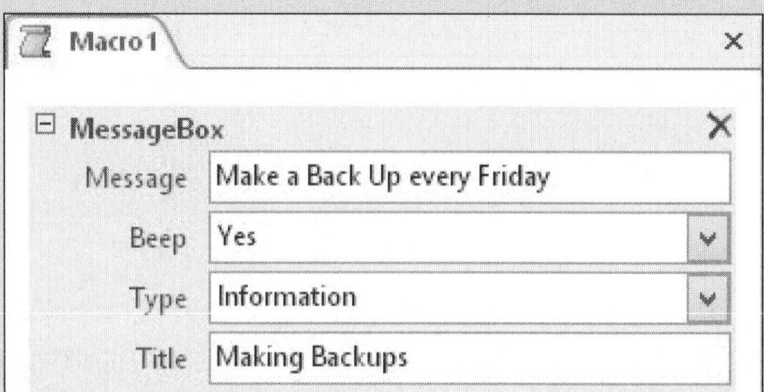

21. Save the macro as `Making Backups`.
22. Choose **Design→Tools→**[Run].
    The Making Backups information box opens.
23. Click **OK** to close the information box. Close the **Making Backups** macro.

Create a Macro to Display Adaptable Reports

24. Choose **Create→Macros & Code→**[Macro].
25. Choose **OpenReport** from the **Add New Action** menu.
26. Choose **Activity Costs Report** from the **Report Name** menu.
27. Choose **Print Preview** as the view type.
28. Type `Forms![Activities Form]![ActivityID]=[Activities]![ActID]` for the **Where Condition**.
29. Save the macro as `Staffing by Activity` then close it.
30. Display the **Activities Form** in **Design View**.
31. Choose **Design→Controls→Button** [xxxx] and draw a new button in the **Form Footer** in line with the other command buttons.
32. Choose the **Miscellaneous** category and choose **Run Macro**.
33. Click **Next** then choose **Staffing by Activity**.
34. Click **Next**, accept the default macro picture, and click **Next** again.
35. Name the button `cmdStaffingByActivity` and click **Finish**.

36. Switch to **Form View** and click the new **Run Macro button**.

Confirm that the report displays only records for the displayed activity.

If you want to display the Activity Costs Report for another activity, close the report, navigate to the desired activity in the form, and click the macro command button.

37. Close the **Activity Costs Report**; save and close the **Activities Form**.

Rename, Delete, and Save an Object as a New Object

38. Right-click the **Children Report** in the Navigation pane and choose **Copy**.
39. Right-click again and choose **Paste**. Type `Delete Report Later` for the **Report Name** in the Paste As dialog box and click **OK**.
40. Select the **Delete Report Later** report in the Navigation Pane.
41. Tap Delete and click **Yes** to confirm the deletion.
42. Open the **Children** table.
43. Choose **File→Save As→Save Object As** and click the **Save As** button.
44. Type `Sponsors` in the **Save 'Children' To** text box and click **OK**.
45. Display the new **Sponsors** table in **Design View**.
46. Edit the field names in the **Sponsors** table, replacing each *Child* prefix with a *Spon* prefix.
47. Delete the **BirthDate**, **MomName**, **DadName**, and **Emergency** fields. Click **Yes** to confirm the deletions.
48. Save and close the **Sponsors** table.

Access 2013

Back Up a Database

49. Choose **File→Save As→Save Database As→** Back Up Database and then click the **Save As** button.

    Access opens the Save As dialog box and adds the date to the end of the database filename.

50. Navigate to the **AC2013 Lesson 12** folder and click **Save**.
51. Return to the **AC2013 Lesson 12** folder and open the backup database. Close the backup database.

Analyze and Document a Database

52. Choose **Database Tools→Analyze→** Analyze Performance.
53. Click the **Reports** tab and click **Select All** to check all the reports listed.

54. Click **OK** and view the ideas presented.

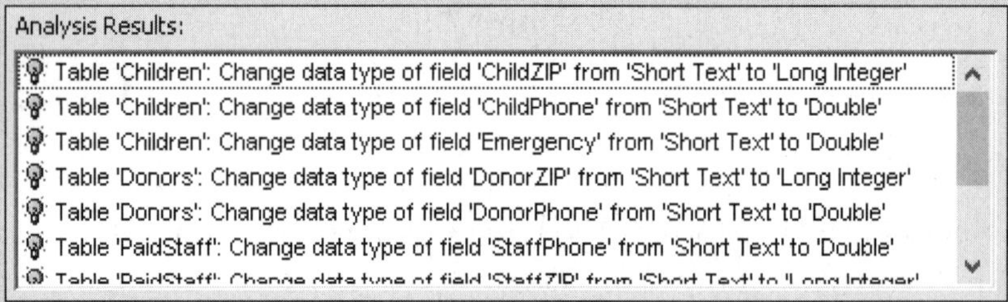
Analysis Results:
Table 'Children': Change data type of field 'ChildZIP' from 'Short Text' to 'Long Integer'
Table 'Children': Change data type of field 'ChildPhone' from 'Short Text' to 'Double'
Table 'Children': Change data type of field 'Emergency' from 'Short Text' to 'Double'
Table 'Donors': Change data type of field 'DonorZIP' from 'Short Text' to 'Long Integer'
Table 'Donors': Change data type of field 'DonorPhone' from 'Short Text' to 'Double'
Table 'PaidStaff': Change data type of field 'StaffPhone' from 'Short Text' to 'Double'

Because the data types have already been set properly, you can ignore the suggested ideas.

55. Click **Close**.
56. Choose **Database Tools→Analyze→** Database Documenter.
57. Click the **Macros** tab, click **Select All**, and click **OK**.
    Access creates a report documenting the properties, actions, and permissions of each macro. The report should include a page for each macro in the database.
58. Page through the report and examine the documentation provided.
59. Choose **Data→More→Word** to export the report to Word.
60. Browse to your **AC2013 Lesson 12** folder, type **`AC12-R03-Macros-[FirstInitialLastName].rtf`** as the filename, and click **Save**.
61. Check the **Open the Destination File After the Export Operation is Complete** box and click **OK**.
62. Close the RTF document and close **Word**.
63. Close the **Export – RTF File** dialog box without saving the export steps.
64. Click Close Print Preview.

Compact and Repair a Database

65. Close any open database objects then choose **Database Tools→Tools→Compact and Repair Database**.
    Access compacts and repairs the file.
66. Close **AC12-R03-K4C-[FirstInitialLastName]** and exit **Access**.

Open a Database for Exclusive Use

67. Start **Access**. Click **Open Other Files** under Access, click **Computer** under Open, navigate to the **AC2013 Lesson 12** folder, and click **AC12-R03-K4C-[FirstInitialLastName]** (*do not open it*).
68. Click the **Open menu ▾** and choose **Open Exclusive**. Enable content, if necessary.

Set a Database Password

69. Choose **File→Info→Encrypt with Password**.
70. Type `MyDataPWD` as the password. Verify the password and click **OK**.
71. Click **OK** to acknowledge the message.
72. Close **AC12-R03-K4C-[FirstInitialLastName]** then open it again.
    Remember: If you forget your password, you will not be able to open your database.
73. In the **Password Required** dialog box, type `MyDataPWD` and click **OK**.
74. Close **AC12-R03-K4C-[FirstInitialLastName]**, clicking **Yes** if a message appears warning that Access will empty the Clipboard. Exit **Access**.
75. Submit your final files based on the guidelines provided by your instructor.

Apply Your Skills

APPLY YOUR SKILLS AC12-A01

Add Command Buttons, Create a Macro, and Manage Objects

You have to perform maintenance on the Universal Corporate Events database. In this exercise, you will add command buttons to the Wage and Salary Form and create macros to increase efficiency. You will also clean up some of the database objects to ensure that the database runs smoothly.

Add Command Buttons to a Form

1. Start **Access**. Open **AC12-A01-UCE** from the **AC2013 Lesson 12** folder, close any open objects, and save the database as `AC12-A01-UCE-[FirstInitialLastName]`.
2. Enable content and close the **UCE Navigation Form**, if necessary.
3. Open the **Wage and Salary Form** in **Design View**.
4. Click the **Form Footer** section bar and type `.75"` for the **Height** property on the Property Sheet.
5. Draw a button in the **Form Footer** under the Detail section labels.
6. In the **Record Navigation** category, choose **Go To First Record** and click **Next**.
7. Click the **Picture** option, choose **Go To First**, and click **Next**.
8. Enter `cmdFirst` for the Meaningful Name and click **Finish**.
   The command button is programmed to go to the first record when in Form View.
9. Add, in the order listed, command buttons for Go To Previous Record: `cmdPrevious`, Go To Next Record: `cmdNext`, Go To Last Record: `cmdLast`, and Find Record: `cmdFind`.
10. Draw a button to the right of the Find button. In the Command Button Wizard, choose **Report Operations** and **Preview Report**, and click **Next**.
11. Select the **Wage and Salary Report** as the Report to Preview, and click **Next**.
12. Choose the **Preview** picture, if necessary, and click **Next**.
13. Enter the name `cmdPreviewReport` and click **Finish**.
14. Select all new command buttons and choose **Arrange→Sizing & Ordering→Align→Top**. Then choose **Arrange→Size & Ordering→Size/Space→Equal Horizontal**.
15. Switch to **Form View** and test the buttons.
16. Close the **Wage and Salary Report**.
17. Save and close the **Wage and Salary Form**.

Create Macros

18. To add a macro for a backup reminder, choose **Create→Macros & Code→**Macro.
19. Choose **MessageBox** from the **Add New Action** drop-down menu.
20. Use `Back up work to the SkyDrive on Friday` as the message, choose **Information** for the type, and use `Back Up Policy` for the title.
21. Save the macro as `Back Up Policy` then run it.
22. Click **OK** to close the information box then close the **Back Up Policy** macro.
23. Choose **Create→Macros & Code→**Macro to create a macro that will open the Event Revenue Report for just the event currently displayed on the form.
24. Choose **OpenReport** for the Add New Action.
25. Choose **Event Revenue Report** for the Report Name and **Report** for the **View**.
26. Type this text for the Where Condition: `[Forms]![Event Costs]![EventID]=[Event Revenue]![EventID]`
27. Save the macro as `Event Revenue by Name`, then close it.
28. Display the **Event Costs** form in **Design View**.
29. Draw a new button under the **Cost Details** label.
30. Choose the **Miscellaneous** category and then choose the **Run Macro** action.
31. Click **Next** and choose your new **Event Revenue by Name** macro.
32. Click **Next**, accept the default macro picture, and click **Next** again.
33. Name the button `cmdEventRevenue` and click **Finish**.
34. Switch to **Form View**. Go to the **Business Meeting** record/page in the main form.
35. Click the new **Run Macro** button. The report displays only Business Meeting records.
    If you want to display the Event Revenue Report for another event, close the report, navigate to the desired event, and click the macro command button again.
36. Close the **Event Revenue Report**; save and close the **Event Costs** form.

Rename, Delete, and Save an Object as a New Object

37. Right-click the **Personnel Report** in the Navigation Pane and choose **Copy**.
38. Right-click again. Choose **Paste**, keep *Copy Of Personnel Report* as the name, and click **OK**.
39. Right-click the *Copy Of Personnel Report*, choose **Rename**, and type `Delete This Report`.
40. Select **Delete This Report** in the Navigation Pane and tap [Delete]. Click **Yes** to confirm.
41. Open the **Menus** table.
42. Choose **File→Save As→Save Object As** and click the **Save As** button.
43. Type `Products` in the **Save 'Menus' To** text box and click **OK**.
44. Display the new **Products** table in **Design View**.

45. In the **Products** table, change *MenuCode* to `ProdCode`, *MenuPlan* to `ProdPlan`, *ChgPP* to `Cost`, and *CostPP* to `Price`.
46. Enter appropriate caption properties for each field.
47. If desired, save the table, switch to **Datasheet View,** and change the data values to reflect the new field names.
48. Save and close the **Products** table and close the database. Click **Yes** to empty the Clipboard and exit **Access**.
49. Submit your final file based on the guidelines provided by your instructor.

    To see examples of how your file or files should look at the end of this exercise, go to the student resource center.

APPLY YOUR SKILLS AC12-A02

Perform Database Maintenance and Set a Password

The UCE database requires regular tune-ups to run smoothly. In this exercise, you will perform some maintenance procedures to reduce wasted space, defragment objects, and improve efficiency. You will also add a password to protect data from unauthorized users.

Back Up a Database

1. Start **Access**. Open **AC12-A02-UCE** from the **AC2013 Lesson 12** folder, close any open objects, and save the database as `AC12-A02-UCE-[FirstInitialLastName]`.
2. Enable content and close the **UCE Navigation Form**, if necessary.
3. Choose **File→Save As→Save Database As→** Back Up Database. Then click the **Save As** button.

   The current date is added to the end of the database filename.
4. Save the file in the **AC2013 Lesson 12** folder.
5. Open the backup database to confirm that you can access it, then close the backup database.

Analyze, Document, Compact, and Repair a Database

6. Choose **Database Tools→Analyze→** Analyze Performance.
7. Click the **Tables** tab and click **Select All** to check all the tables listed.
8. Click **OK** to view the ideas presented then click **Close**.
9. Choose **Database Tools→Analyze→** Database Documenter.

   The Documenter opens.
10. Click the **Tables** tab, check the **Menus** and **Schedules** tables, and click **OK**.

    Access generates a report for the tables, fields, and relationships of the selected tables.
11. Page through the report and examine the documentation provided.
12. Choose **Data→More→Word** to export the documentation Word.

13. Browse to your **AC2013 Lesson 12** folder, use `AC12-A02-MenuSched-[FirstInitialLastName].rtf` as the filename, and click **Save**.
14. Check the **Open the Destination File After the Export Operation is Complete** box and click **OK**.
15. Exit **Word**. Close the **Export – RTF File** dialog box without saving the export steps, and close **Print Preview**. Close any open database objects.
16. Choose **Database Tools→Tools→Compact and Repair Database** .
17. Close **AC12-A02-UCE-[FirstInitialLastName]** and exit **Access**.

Open a Database for Exclusive Use and Set a Database Password

18. Start **Access**. Click **Open Other Files** under Access, click **Computer** under Open, navigate to the **AC2013 Lesson 12** folder, and click **AC12-A02-UCE-[FirstInitialLastName]** (*do not open it*).
19. Click the **Open menu ▾** and choose **Open Exclusive**.
20. Enable content, if necessary.
21. To set a password for the database, choose **File→Info→Encrypt with Password**.
22. Type `Labyrinth` as the password, verify the password, and click **OK**.
23. Click **OK** to acknowledge the encrypting message.
24. Close and reopen **AC12-A02-UCE-[FirstInitialLastName]**, entering the password when prompted.
25. Close **AC12-A02-UCE-[FirstInitialLastName]** and exit **Access**.
26. Submit your final file based on the guidelines provided by your instructor.

    To see examples of how your file or files should look at the end of this exercise, go to the student resource center.

Access 2013

APPLY YOUR SKILLS AC12-A03

Improve and Maintain a Database

To keep the UCE database on the right course, it must be regularly maintained. In this exercise, you will perform scheduled database maintenance tasks in order to improve performance and clean up and protect the UCE database.

Add Command Buttons to a Form

1. Start **Access**. Open **AC12-A03-UCE** from the **AC2013 Lesson 12** folder, close any open objects, and save the database as `AC12-A03-UCE-[FirstInitialLastName]`.
2. Enable content and close the **UCE Navigation Form**, if necessary.
3. Open the **Venues Form** in **Design View**.
4. Click the **Form Footer** section bar and type `.75"` for the **Height** property on the Property Sheet.

5. Draw a button in the **Form Footer** under the **VenueZIP** text box.
6. In the **Record Navigation** category, choose **Go To First Record** and click **Next**.
7. Click the **Picture** option, choose **Go To First** and click **Next**.
8. Enter `cmdFirst` for the Meaningful Name and click **Finish**.
9. Add, in the order listed, command buttons to Go To Previous Record: `cmdPrevious`, Go To Next Record: `cmdNext`, Go To Last Record: `cmdLast`, and Find Record: `cmdFind`.
10. Draw a button to the right of the Find button. In the Command Button Wizard, choose **Report Operations** and **Preview Report**, and click **Next**.
11. Select the **Venues Report** as the Report to Preview and click **Next**.
12. Choose the **Preview** picture, if necessary, and click **Next**.
13. Enter the name `cmdViewReport` and click **Finish**.
14. Select the command buttons and choose **Arrange→Sizing & Ordering→Align→Top**. Then, choose **Arrange→Size & Ordering→Size/Space→Equal Horizontal**.
15. Switch to **Form View** and test the buttons.

16. Close the **Venues Report**; save and close the **Venues Form**.

Create Macros

17. Choose **Create→Macros & Code→**Macro to create a macro for a reminder message.
18. Choose **MessageBox** from the **Add New Action** menu.
19. Type `Backup Database to the SkyDrive every Friday` for the message.
20. Choose **Information** as the type and use `Back Up Schedule` as the title.
21. Save the macro as `Back Up Schedule`, then run it.
22. Close the information box then close the **Back Up Schedule** macro.
23. Choose **Create→Macros & Code→**Macro to create a macro that will open the Venue Event Revenue report for just the venue currently displayed on the form.
24. Choose **OpenReport** from the **Add New Action** menu.
25. Choose **Venue Revenue Report** for report name and **Print Preview** for the view.
26. Type this as the **Where Condition**:

    `[Forms]![Venues Form]![VenueID]=[Venues]![VenueID]`

27. Save the macro as `Revenue by Venue`, then close it.
28. Display the **Venues Form** in **Design View**.

29. Draw a new button in the **Form Footer** in line with the other command buttons.
30. Choose the **Miscellaneous** category then choose the **Run Macro** action.
31. Click **Next** and choose **Revenue by Venue**.
32. Click **Next**, accept the default macro picture, and click **Next** again.
33. Name the button `cmdVenueRevenue` and click **Finish**.
34. Switch to **Form View** and click the new **Run Macro button**.

    Confirm that the report displays only records for the displayed venue.

    To display the Venue Event Revenue report for another venue, close the report, navigate to the desired venue, and click the macro command button, otherwise the report does not change to reflect the new venue.
35. Close the **Venue Event Revenue** report; save and close the **Venues Form**.

Rename, Delete, and Save an Object as a New Object

36. Right-click **Events Form** in the Navigation Pane and choose **Copy**.
37. Right-click again. Choose **Paste**, keep *Copy Of Events Form* as the Form Name, and click **OK**.
38. Right-click *Copy Of Events Form*, choose **Rename**, and type **`Delete Form Later`**.
39. Select the **Delete Form Later** form in the Navigation Pane and tap [Delete]. Click **Yes** to confirm the deletion.
40. Open the **Personnel** table.
41. Choose **File→Save As→Save Object As→Save As**.
42. Type **`Customers`** in the **Save 'Personnel' To** text box and click **OK**.
43. Display the new **Customers** table in **Design View**.
44. Edit the field names in the **Customers** table, replacing each *Per* prefix with a *Cust* prefix.
45. Delete the **SalaryGrade**, **DateofBirth**, and **HireDate** fields.
46. Save and close the **Customers** table.

Back Up, Analyze, and Document a Database

47. Choose **File→Save As→Save Database As→**[Back Up Database].
48. Click the **Save As** button, navigate to your **AC2013 Lesson 12** folder and click **Save**.
49. Open the backup database to confirm that you can access it in the event of a problem with your original database.
50. Close the backup database.
51. Choose **Database Tools→Analyze→**[Analyze Performance].
52. Click the **Reports** tab, click **Select All**, and click **OK**. View the suggestions, and close it when finished.

    The data types have already been set properly, so disregard the suggested ideas.
53. Choose **Database Tools→Analyze→**[Database Documenter].

54. Click the **Queries** tab, check the **Salaried Personnel Query** and **Wage and Salary Query** check boxes, and then click **OK**.

    Access generates a report of the query properties, SQL code, and columns, as displayed.

55. Choose **Data→More→Word** to export the documentation to Word.
56. Browse to your **AC2013 Lesson 12** folder, type `AC12-A03-SalaryQueries-[FirstInitialLastName].rtf` for the filename, check the **Open the Destination File After the Export Operation is Complete** box, and click **OK**.
57. Page through the Word document. Then close the file and exit **Word**.
58. Close the **Export – RTF File** without saving the export steps.
59. Click Close Print Preview.

Compact and Repair a Database

60. Close any open database objects.
61. Choose **Database Tools→Tools→Compact and Repair Database**.
62. Close **AC12-A03-UCE-[FirstInitialLastName]** and exit **Access**.

Open a Database for Exclusive Use and Set a Database Password

63. Start **Access**. Click **Open Other Files** under Access, click **Computer** under Open, and navigate to your **AC2013 Lesson 12** folder.
64. Click **AC12-A03-UCE-[FirstInitialLastName]** and then click the **Open menu ▼** button and choose **Open Exclusive**.
65. Choose **File→Info→Encrypt with Password**.
66. Type `MyDataPass` as the password, verify it, and click **OK**.
67. Click **OK** again.
68. Close and reopen **AC12-A03-UCE-[FirstInitialLastName]**, entering your password.
69. Close **AC12-A03-UCE-[FirstInitialLastName]** and exit **Access**.
70. Submit your final file based on the guidelines provided by your instructor.

Extend Your Skills

In the course of working through the Extend Your Skills exercises, you will think critically as you use the skills taught in the lesson to complete the assigned projects. To evaluate your mastery and completion of the exercises, your instructor may use a rubric, with which more points are allotted according to performance characteristics. (The more you do, the more you earn!) Ask your instructor how your work will be evaluated.

AC12-E01 That's the Way I See It

Use the database you used in AC11-E01 or open **AC12-E01-BJL** from the **AC2013 Lesson 12** folder and save it as `AC12-E01-BJL-[FirstInitialLastName]`. (If you are using your database, use similar forms, reports, and objects.)

Add First Record, Previous Record, Next Record, Last Record, and Find Record command buttons to the Merchandise Form. Then, add a command button that opens the Store Inventory Report (Report Operations, Preview Report). Create a macro that displays a useful message. Then, create a macro for the Manufacturer Form to display the Store Inventory Report. Where Condition: `[Forms]![Manufacturer Form]![Manufacturer]=[Store Inventory]![Manufacturer]`. Copy an existing table and save it as a new table, renaming fields appropriately and changing the captions and data values. Save a dated backup database. Run the Database Analyzer, run the Database Documenter on an object and export the report to Word. Run the Compact and Repair Tool. Then, set your database for Exclusive Use and set a password. Submit the password with your file.

You will be evaluated based on the inclusion of all elements, your ability to follow directions, your ability to apply newly learned skills to a real-world situation, your creativity, and your accuracy in creating objects and/or entering data. Submit your final file based on the guidelines provided by your instructor.

AC12-E02 Be Your Own Boss

Open **AC12-E02-BJL** from the **AC2013 Lesson 12** folder as `AC12-E02-BJL-[FirstInitialLastName]`. Add First Record, Previous Record, Next Record, Last Record, and Find Record navigation command buttons to the Customers Form. Add a command button that opens the Service Invoices Report (Report Operations, Preview Report). Create a macro to display a message. Then, create one for the Customers Form that displays the Customers Report for the displayed customer. Where Condition: `[Forms]![Customers Form]![CustID]=[Customers]![CustID]`

Copy the Customers table and save it as a Salesperson table, renaming the fields appropriately and changing the Captions and the data values. Save a dated backup database. Then, analyze the database, run the Database Documenter on the Manufacturers table and export the report to Word, and compact the database. Open the database exclusively and set a password.

You will be evaluated based on the inclusion of all elements, your ability to follow directions, your ability to apply newly learned skills to a real-world situation, your creativity, and your accuracy in creating objects and/or entering data. Submit your final file based on the guidelines provided by your instructor.

Transfer Your Skills

In the course of working through the Transfer Your Skills exercises, you will use critical-thinking and creativity skills to complete the assigned projects using skills taught in the lesson. To evaluate your mastery and completion of the exercises, your instructor may use a rubric, with which more points are allotted according to performance characteristics. (The more you do, the more you earn!) Ask your instructor how your work will be evaluated.

AC12-T01 Use the Web as a Learning Tool

Throughout this book, you will be provided with an opportunity to use the Internet as a learning tool by completing WebQuests. According to the original creators of WebQuests, as described on their website (WebQuest.org), a WebQuest is "an inquiry-oriented activity in which most or all of the information used by learners is drawn from the web." To complete the WebQuest projects in this book, navigate to the student resource center and choose the WebQuest for the lesson on which you are currently working. The subject of each WebQuest will be relevant to the material found in the lesson.

WebQuest Subject: SharePoint and Using Mobile Devices to Send and Receive Data

Submit your files based on the guidelines provided by your instructor.

AC12-T02 Demonstrate Proficiency

The Stormy BBQ database is set to go live in a few weeks. Open **AC12-T02-SBQ** from the **AC2013 Lesson 12** folder and save it as **`AC12-T02-SBQ-[FirstInitialLastName]`**.

Add First Record, Previous Record, Next Record, Last Record, and Find Record command buttons to the Form Footer section of each form (excluding the SBQ Navigation and subforms). Then, add a command button to the Staff Form that opens the Staff Report (Report Operations, Preview Report). Then, create a macro to display a back-up reminder or a notice of a policy change. Also create a macro for the Merchandise Form to display the Merchandise Sales Report for the item displayed on the form. Where Condition: **`[Forms]![Merchandise Form]![SKU]=[Merchandise]![SKU]`**

Add a new table that stores names, addresses, and contact information for your best customers by copying the Staff table and saving it as BestCustomers, renaming the fields appropriately and changing the captions. Switch to Datasheet View and enter new data. Save a dated backup copy of your database. Then, analyze the database, run the Database Documenter on the Restaurants table and save the report as an rtf document in Word, and run the Compact and Repair tool. Open the database for Exclusive Use and set a database password. Submit the password with your database file.

Submit your file based on the guidelines provided by your instructor.

Index

Index

Notes

Notes

Notes

Notes

Notes

Notes

Notes

Notes

Notes

Notes

Notes

Notes

Notes

Notes